WHO WAS WHO
IN
AMERICAN
POLITICS

WHO WAS WHO IN AMERICAN POLITICS

A BIOGRAPHICAL DICTIONARY
OF OVER 4,000 MEN AND WOMEN
WHO CONTRIBUTED TO THE UNITED STATES
POLITICAL SCENE FROM COLONIAL DAYS
UP TO AND INCLUDING THE IMMEDIATE PAST

By Dan and Inez Morris

HAWTHORN BOOKS, INC.

PUBLISHERS/*New York*

WHO WAS WHO IN AMERICAN POLITICS

Library of Congress Catalog Card Number: 76-39620.
ISBN: 0–8015–8624–0

1 2 3 4 5 6 7 8 9 10

ACKNOWLEDGMENTS

For their invaluable research advice and assistance, our sincere thanks to our good friend and colleague Alden Todd, author of *Finding Facts Fast,* to Bruce Hallett (Princeton '71), a young man newly embarked upon what appears to be a bright future as a journalist, and to Daniel M. Groden, who already is well on his way as assistant director of the Long Beach, New York, Public Library System.

REFERENCE SOURCES

Biographical Directory of the American Congress 1774-1961 and the annual congressional directories for the years since then; *Collier's Encylopedia; The Columbia Encyclopedia; Encyclopedia Americana; New York Times* and Associated Press obituaries; *Dictionary of American Biography* (Scribners, 1936); *Concise Dictionary of American Biography* (Scribners, 1964); *World Almanac; New York Times Almanac; The Negro Almanac* (Bellwether, 1971); *Who Was Who in America* (Marquis); *America, Its History and People* (McGraw-Hill, 1950); *Black Heroes in Our Nation's History* (Cowles, 1969); *American Parties and Elections* (The Century Company, 1927); *Encyclopedia of American History* (Harper & Row, 1970); *A History of the United States* (Dell, 1958); *Concise Dictionary of American History* (Scribners, 1962); *Founding the American Colonies 1583-1660* (Harper & Row, 1970); *America and Its Presidents* (Grosset & Dunlap, 1959); *The American Presidents* (Doubleday, 1969).

AUTHORS' NOTE

Who Was Who in American Politics is a biographical dictionary of past political figures, most of them dead, others of them still alive but (to the best of our knowledge) no longer active on the national political scene. Some of those whose biographies do not include time and/or place of death may or may not still be alive, those facts being absent because they escaped our best research efforts.

EDITOR'S NOTE

Dan Morris has long experience on newspapers and the electronic media and so has written many research-oriented obituaries, among them eulogies to Herbert Hoover, Dwight D. Eisenhower, and John F. Kennedy which were broadcast coast to coast. Inez Morris, a former house organ editor, long was active in the League of Women Voters and thus also was engaged in many research projects.

And so their approach to this, their twelfth book, was that of journalists who delve as deep as necessary into existing research, cull the known facts, and then feed those that are to be used into a typewriter to produce succinct, sharp, easy-to-read biographies of some 4,200 men and women who made their contributions, good or bad, to the American political scene from the days of the Founding Fathers until the immediate past.

The result is a work that students, scholars, and the politically and historically curious everywhere should find invaluable as a guide not by any means to all that can be learned about our nation's past political figures but rather as a point of departure, a taking-off point for those who would like to know more about America. This book is a place for researchers to begin.

WHO WAS WHO
IN
AMERICAN
POLITICS

AANDAHL, FRED GEORGE *(b April 9, 1897, Litchville, N.Dak.; d April 7, 1966, Litchville).* Agriculturist, North Dakota Republican. Litchville superintendent of schools (1922-1927), state senate (1931, 1939, 1941), governor (1945-1950), U.S. Representative (1951-1953), assistant U.S. secretary of the interior for water and power development (1953-1961).

ABBETT, LEON *(b Oct. 8, 1836, Philadelphia; d Dec. 4, 1894, Jersey City, N.J.).* Twice governor of New Jersey. Lawyer, Democrat; served four terms in the New Jersey State Assembly, twice as its speaker, then in 1875 was elected to the state senate and was its president in 1877. During his first term as governor (1884-1887), Abbett had enacted a law that forced corporations, particularly the railroads, to pay their fair share of taxes, thus making good a campaign pledge in which he said: "Our tax laws demand immediate and radical reform. They impose unequal burdens. The only true rule in taxation is equality." Unable by law to succeed himself, Abbett ran instead for the U.S. Senate but was defeated, mainly through the efforts of a vengeful railroad lobby. In 1889 he was elected to his second term (1890-1893) as governor by what was then an unprecedented majority.

ABBOTT, GRACE *(b 1878, Grand Rapids, Nebr.; d Chicago, Ill., 1939).* Social worker; administrator of the Child Labor Act, which was passed by Congress in 1916 and declared unconstitutional in 1918; director (1921-1934) of the Child Labor Division of the U.S. Children's Bureau. Author of *The Child and the State,* a two-volume work published in 1938.

ABBOTT, JOSEPH CARTER *(b July 15, 1825, Concord, N.H.; d Oct. 8, 1881, Wilmington, N.C.).* Journalist, North Carolina Republican leader and U.S. Senator, descendant of George Abbott of Andover who emigrated to New England about 1640, champion of Negro cause.

Admitted to the New Hampshire bar in 1852 but preferred journalism to law and was editor of the *Manchester American* from 1852 to 1857. Showed his first flair for politics in 1855 when he began moonlighting as New Hampshire adjutant general, a post he continued to hold into 1861, even while editor (1859-1861) of the *Boston Atlas and Bee,* New England's foremost Whig newspaper. Member of commission for adjustment of New Hampshire-Canadian border.

Fought on the side of the Union In the Civil War and was cited for gallantry in the capture of Fort Fisher, N.C. Honorably discharged (July 1865) with rank of brigadier general, Abbott settled in Wilmington, N.C., where he was for a time commandant but then became a GOP leader and was a delegate to the state constitutional convention (1868). In all three roles he stood on the side

1

of the Negro, thus antagonizing North Carolina whites. Upon the state's readmission to the Union, he was elected to the U.S. Senate with strong Negro support. Served from July 13, 1868, until March 3, 1871, failing to win GOP renomination. Through it all, editor of the *Wilmington Post,* a GOP weekly.

ABBOTT, LYMAN *(b Dec. 18, 1835, Roxbury, Mass.; d Oct. 22, 1922, New York City).* Reconstructionist, Congregational clergyman, editor, author, lawyer. Practiced law in New York City from 1853 until 1859 when he turned to the ministry. A foe of slavery, he did much to make clear, while pastor of a church in Terre Haute, ·Ind., the issues that led to the Civil War. Active in the reconstruction period that followed, Abbot resigned his pastorate to serve (1865-1869) as secretary of the American Freedman's Union Commission, comprised of laymen and New York City clerics to work with the government for reconstruction. Coincident with that service, he was the first pastor of the city's New England Congregational Church. Then followed until his death In 1922 a brilliant career as minister, author, editor, and internationalist. Abbott wrote or edited about fifty books and was a close associate of Henry Ward Beecher whom he succeeded both as editor of *The Christian Union,* later called the *Outlook,* and pastor of Brooklyn's Plymouth Congregational Church. Abbott was a strong supporter of Theodore Roosevelt and the Progressive party, greater U.S. influence abroad, and U.S. entry in World War I.

ABERNATHY, CHARLES LABAN *(b March 18, 1872, Rutherford College, N.C.: d Feb. 23, 1955, New Bern, N.C.).* Lawyer, North Carolina Democrat. Member state Democratic executive committee (1898-1900), Bryan-Stevenson presidential elector (1900), Parker-Davis presidential elector (1904), U.S. Representative (1922-1935).

ABERNATHY, GEORGE *(b Oct. 7, 1807, New York City; d May 2, 1877, Portland, Oregon).* Oregon's only provisional governor, merchant, churchman. Chosen to administer financial affairs of Methodist mission in Oregon, he sailed from New York City with a party of settlers via Cape Horn and arrived June 1, 1840. Provisional government was formed in 1843 with executive committee to run it but that system was short-lived and Abernathy in 1845 was elected provisional governor and reelected in 1847, serving until formation of territorial government in 1849.

ACHESON, ERNEST FRANCIS *(b Sept. 19, 1855, Washington, Pa.; d May 16, 1917, Washington, Pa.).* Lawyer, journalist, Pennsylvania Republican. National convention delegate (1884, 1896), president Pennsylvania Editorial Association (1893), U.S. Representative (1895-1909).

ACKER, EPHRAIM LEISTER *(b Jan. 11, 1827, Marlboro Township, Pa.; d May 12, 1903, Norristown, Pa.).* Teacher, journalist, lawyer, Pennsylvania Democrat. Montgomery County superintendent of schools (1854-1860), U.S. Representative (1871-1873), began study of law in 1877 and practiced until death.

ACKERMAN, ERNEST ROBINSON *(b June 17, 1863, New York City; d Oct. 18, 1931, Plainfield, N.J.).* Manufacturer, New Jersey Republican. McKinley-Hobart presidential elector (1896), state senate (1905-1911), president of senate (1911), national convention delegate (1908-1916), state board of education (1918-1920), U.S. Representative (1919 until death).

ACKLEN, JOSEPH HAYES *(b May 20, 1850, Nashville, Tenn.; d Sept. 28, 1938, Nashville).* Lawyer, sugar grower, wildlife writer, outdoorsman, Louisiana and Tennessee Democrat. In Louisiana: U.S. Representative (1878-1881). In Tennessee: chairman of Davidson County

Democratic executive committee (1886-1894), Nashville councilman (1900-1904), state game, fish and forestry warden (1903-1913), chief U.S. game warden (1913-1914), chairman of state constitutional convention central committee (1923-1927).

ADAIR, JACKSON LEROY *(b Feb. 23, 1887, Clayton, Ill.; d Jan. 19, 1956, Quincy, Ill.).* Lawyer, agriculturist, Illinois Democrat. Quincy city attorney (1914-1916), Adams County prosecutor (1916-1920, 1924-1928), state senate (1928-1932), U.S. Representative (1933-1937), U.S. district court judge for southern district of Illinois (1937 until death).

ADAIR, JOHN *(b Jan. 9, 1757, Chester County, S.C.; d May 19, 1840, Mercer County, Ky.).* Soldier, Indian fighter, Kentucky Democrat. Delegate to South Carolina convention that ratified U.S. Constitution before moving to Kentucky (1788) where in 1792 he was a delegate to the Kentucky constitutional convention. Member of state house of representatives (1793-1795, 1798, 1800-1803, 1817), speaker (1802-1803), U.S. land office register (1805), U.S. Senate to fill a vacancy (Nov. 1805-Nov. 1806), governor of Kentucky (1820-1824), U.S. Representative (1831-1833).

Adair interspersed his political life with his military life which began in the Revolutionary War when he was taken prisoner by the British. In Kentucky he gained fame as both an Indian fighter and as a champion of the common man only to fall into disfavor and near-indictment for listening too well to Aaron Burr, a political blunder that caused him to resign from the state legislature in 1803. But the War of 1812 restored the people's affection for him when he led 1,000 Kentucky riflemen in the battle of New Orleans.

Adair had little administrative or financial know-how and so, both as governor and head of the short-lived Relief party, he brought Kentucky close to bankruptcy. Adair County is named for him.

ADAIR, JOHN ALFRED McDOWELL *(b Dec. 22, 1864, Jay County, Ind.; d Oct. 5, 1938, Portland, Ind.).* Lawyer, banker, industrialist, Indiana Democrat. State house of representatives (1902-1903), U.S. Representative (1907-1917), unsuccessful candidate for governor (1916).

ADAMS, ABIGAIL *(b Nov. 11, 1744, Weymouth, Mass.; d Oct. 28, 1818, Quincy, Mass.).* Influential, politically aware wife of President John Adams and mother of President John Quincy Adams. Her gift as a letter writer has enriched the history of her times.

ADAMS, ALVA *(b May 14, 1850, Iowa County, Wis.; d Nov. 1, 1922).* Migrated to Colorado by wagon train in 1871, became successful businessman, banker, and active Democrat. Twice governor (1887-1889, 1897-1899), member of first state legislature (1876), and Democratic National Committee (1908). In Colorado he championed development of school and prison systems and tax reforms. Elected governor again in 1904, he was disqualified after serving one month because of unproven voting frauds.

ADAMS, ALVA BLANCHARD *(b Oct. 29, 1875, Del Norte, Colo.; d Dec. 1, 1941, Washington, D.C.).* Lawyer, Colorado Democrat. Pueblo County Attorney (1909-1911), Pueblo city attorney (1911-1915), national convention delegate (1916), delegate to all state party conventions (1899-1926), appointed to U.S. Senate to fill vacancy (1923-1924), elected to U.S. Senate (1933 until death).

ADAMS, ANDREW *(b Jan. 7, 1736, Stratford, Conn.; d Nov. 26, 1797, Litchfield, Conn.).* Connecticut lawyer. Litchfield County attorney (1772), state Council of Safety (1774-1776), colonel in Revolutionary Army, state house of representatives (1776-1781), speaker (1779-1780), member of Continental Congress (1777-1782), signer of Articles of Confederation (1778), chief justice of state supreme court (1793 until death).

ADAMS, BENJAMIN *(b Dec. 16, 1764, Mendon, Mass.; d March 28, 1837, Uxbridge, Mass.).* Lawyer, Massachusetts Federalist. State house of representatives (1809-1814), state senate (1814-1815, 1822-1825), U.S. Representative (1816-1821).

ADAMS (changed from Schwanbeck) **CHARLES** *(b Dec. 19, 1845, Pomerania, Germany; d Aug. 19, 1895, in Denver, Colo., hotel explosion).* Diplomat. Came to United States in teens, eventually settling in Colorado, first as an Indian fighter, then as an Indian agent and friend of the Indians, bringing about treaty between Utes and United States. Named minister to Bolivia (1880-1882) by President Hayes, he acted as arbitrator in its war with Chile at peace conferences.

ADAMS, CHARLES FRANCIS, SR. *(b Aug. 18, 1807, Boston; d Nov. 21, 1886, Boston).* Diplomat, lawyer, writer, historian. Began political career as a Democrat but, because of differences with party over slavery, successfully sought seat in Massachusetts legislature (1840-1845) as a Whig and caused state to take antislavery position. Vice presidential running mate of Martin Van Buren (1848) as candidates of Free-Soil party, which had been formed by men of seventeen states who could accept neither Zachary Taylor, the Whig candidate, nor Lewis Cass, the Democratic nominee, for the U.S. presidency. Taylor, whom the Free-Soilists considered the lesser of two evils, was elected by virtue of the votes won by Van Buren-Adams.

Upon evaporation of the Whig party, Adams was elected to Congress in 1858 as a candidate of the infant Republican party and two years later supported William Seward for the presidential nomination that nevertheless went to Abraham Lincoln. Elected to a second term in the House, Adams resigned in 1861 to become the Lincoln-appointed ambassador to the Court of St. James, arriving in England just as that country was announcing its support of the Confederacy in the Civil War. Nevertheless, thanks to diplomatic tact, Adams was able to exert some meaningful influence upon the British and remained in the post until May 1868, when he returned to America and abandoned public life.

Son of John Quincy Adams, father of Charles Francis Adams, Jr., and Henry Adams.

ADAMS, CHARLES FRANCIS, JR. *(b May 27, 1835, Boston; d March 20, 1915, Boston).* A man of extraordinary ability, he turned his talents to many things, writing expertly on all. As his father's companion on many political journeys, he became an astute political observer and commentator; thus came such articles as "The Reign of King Cotton," which was published by the *Atlantic Monthly* whose editor was then James Russell Lowell, and "An Episode in Municipal Government," which described the manipulations of New York's Tweed Ring. His Civil War service was marked by *A Cycle of Adams Letters, 1861-1865,* in which he told why he preferred remaining a colonel with the front-line Fifth Massachusetts Cavalry to becoming a rear-echelon general's aide: being with his Negro regiment was educationally more rewarding than his years at Harvard.

Out of his journalistic exposures of the frauds that accompanied much railroad financing of the day came both a book, *Chapters of Erie and Other Essays* (written with his brother, John), and formation of the Massachusetts Board of Railroad Commissioners, a regulatory agency that became a model for other states and which he served for ten years (1869-1879), seven as chairman; and out of that came not only *Railroads: Their Origin and Problems* and *Notes on Railroad Accidents*, but also chairmanship of the Union Pacific Railroad.

Still another area opened to him when, in 1874, he was invited to speak at the 250th anniversary of the town of Weymouth, Mass. That led to four decades of historical writing and membership in the Massachusetts Historical Society including twenty years as president. His works included biographies of his father and others, Civil War and New England histories.

Through it all, Adams repeatedly declined many chances to run for elective office (except for Quincy town moderator), including the governorship.

ADAMS, CHARLES HENRY *(b April 10, 1824, Coxsackie, N.Y.; d Dec. 15, 1902, New York City).* Lawyer, banker, manufacturer, New York Republican. First mayor of Cohoes (1870-1872), delegate to national convention (1872), state senate (1872-1873), U.S. Representative (1875-1877).

ADAMS, DUDLEY W. *(b Nov. 30, 1831, Winchendon, Mass.; d Feb. 13, 1897, Florida).* Leader in first, though unsuccessful, fight for federal railroad-freight legislation (1873-1874). Migrated to Iowa at twenty-one where he became a horticulturist and nationally known nurseryman, helping to organize the National Grange and becoming its leader in 1873. Although Congress refused to adopt rail legislation, Granger efforts helped bring about rail reforms in many states. Migrated to Florida in 1875 where he pioneered in the growth of citrus and other fruit trees.

ADAMS, GEORGE EVERETT *(b June 18, 1840, Keene, N.H.; d Oct. 5, 1917, Peterborough, N.H.).* Lawyer, Illinois Republican. State senate (1880-1883), U.S. Representative (1883-1891).

ADAMS, GEORGE MADISON *(b Dec. 20, 1837, Barbourville, Ky.; d April 6,* 1920, Winchester, Ky.). Lawyer, Kentucky Democrat. U.S. Representative (1867-1875), clerk of the House when his uncle, Green Adams, was chief clerk (1875-1881), register of Kentucky Land Office (1884-1887), Kentucky secretary of state (1887-1891), U.S. pension agent at Louisville (1894-1898).

ADAMS, GREEN *(b Aug. 20, 1812, Barbourville, Ky.; d Jan. 18, 1884, Philadelphia).* Lawyer, state house of representatives (1839), Clay-Frelinghuysen presidential elector (1844), Whig U.S. Representative (1847-1849), Kentucky circuit court judge (1851-1856), American party U.S. Representative (1859-1861), sixth auditor of U.S. Treasury Department (1861-1864), chief clerk of the U.S. House of Representatives (1875-1881). Uncle of George Madison Adams.

ADAMS, HENRY *(b Feb. 16, 1838, Boston; d March 27, 1918, Washington, D.C.).* Journalist, historian, self-styled "stable-companion of statesmen," and secretary to his father, Charles Francis Adams, Sr., both when latter was a congressman and ambassador to England. Actively opposed administration of President Grant and, as editor of the scholarly *North American Review*, provided a voice for dissent. Summed up his contempt for political skullduggery in his novel, *Democracy* (1880).

ADAMS, HENRY CULLEN *(b Nov. 28, 1850, Oneida County, N.Y.; d July 9, 1906, Chicago).* Taken to Wisconsin as a boy because of health and thus began lifelong interest in agriculture and betterment of the lot of both farmers and consumers. Served in state assembly (1883-1885) and as state dairy and food commissioner (1895-1902). As Republican U.S. Representative (1903-1906), sponsored and brought about the National Food and Drug Act, the Meat Inspection Law, and the Adams Act, which provided funds for agricultural research. Also successfully sponsored admission of New Mexico and Arizona as separate states.

ADAMS, HERBERT BAXTER *(b April 16, 1850, Shutesbury, Mass.; d July 30, 1901, Amherst, Mass.).* Professor who introduced studies of both political science and history to Johns Hopkins University. Man most responsible for formation of American Historical Association.

ADAMS, JAMES HOPKINS *(b March 15, 1812, Virginia; d July 13, 1861, South Carolina).* Democrat, governor of South Carolina (1854-1856), secessionist and advocate of states' rights whose advocacy of renewed African slave trade was too harsh even for South Carolina slave-owners to stomach.

ADAMS, JOHN *(b Oct. 30, 1735, Braintree [now Quincy], Mass.; d July 4, 1826, Quincy).* Lawyer, political science scholar, writer, diplomat, legislator, patriot, Massachusetts Federalist who was vice president under Washington (1789-1797), second president of the United States (1797-1801), father of John Quincy Adams, grandfather of Charles Francis Adams Sr., cousin of Samuel Adams, married (Oct. 25, 1764) to Abigail Smith Adams.

A man with a hot temper who was opposed as being too conservative by his vice president, liberal opposition party leader Thomas Jefferson (whom he defeated for the presidency by just three electoral votes), and yet was frequently at odds with Alexander Hamilton, powerful leader of his own party, who saw to it that he was not elected for a second term. In spite of opposition from Hamilton and many members of Congress, he was able to narrowly avert a war with France in 1798 but approved the Alien and Sedition Acts passed by Congress that same year in reaction to the war scare.

Adams was a leader (effectively using his pen as well as his legal talents) of the group of patriots who opposed British actions leading to the Revolutionary War; graduated Harvard College (1755); member of the general court, representing Boston (1768); member of the First Continental Congress (1774-1778); member of the drafting committee, a signer and eloquent supporter of the Declaration of Independence; served as a diplomat (1777-1788) in France, the Netherlands, and Great Britain, a difficult time because of his temperament, his suspicions of French motives, and the coldness with which the British treated him. However, in spite of the obstacles, he negotiated a treaty with the Dutch government that recognized his country's independence, twice negotiated much-needed loans from the Dutch, and, with Benjamin Franklin and John Jay, negotiated the Treaty of Paris (1783) that brought an end to the Revolutionary War.

After Jefferson's retirement from the presidency, Adams renewed his early friendship with his old political enemy. The two men carried on a friendly correspondence and both died on the same day, July 4, 1826.

ADAMS, JOHN *(b Aug. 26, 1778, Durham, N.Y.; d Sept. 25, 1854, Catskill, N.Y.).* Lawyer, New York Democrat. Greene County surrogate (1810), state assembly (1812-1813), U.S. Representative from March 4 to Dec. 26, 1815, when he was replaced by Erastus Root who had successfully contested his election; elected again to House eighteen years later (1833-1845), this time as a Jackson Democrat.

ADAMS, JOHN JOSEPH *(b Sept. 16, 1848, Douglas Town, New Brunswick, Canada; d Feb. 16, 1919, New York City).* Lawyer, New York Independent Democrat, U.S. Representative (1883-1887).

ADAMS, JOHN QUINCY *(b July 11, 1767, Braintree [now Quincy], Mass.; d Feb. 23, 1848, Washington, D.C.).* Sixth president, 1825-1829. Kept a famous and historically important diary; political writer whose early articles (signed with a pseudonym) were so well done they were thought to have come from his father's pen and attracted the interest of George Washington. His (outward) coldness and strongly independent nature made his political life difficult.

Son of diplomat and Federalist president John Adams and Abigail Adams, his youthful experiences and early European education equipped him well for his own diplomatic career (started at fourteen by serving as secretary to Francis Dana, minister to Russia). Graduated from Harvard University in 1788, he then studied law and (1790) opened his own office in Boston. Married Louisa Catherine Johnson (1797), daughter of the American consul at London, who bore him four children. The youngest, Charles Francis Adams Sr., became minister to Britain during the Civil War.

Minister to the Netherlands (1794), to Prussia (1797-1801, during his father's presidency), to Russia (1809-1814), a negotiator of the Treaty of Ghent (1814) which ended the War of 1812, and minister to England (1815-1817).

U.S. Senator from Massachusetts (1803-1808, when Massachusetts Federalists who had elected him forced him to resign after he crossed party lines and supported Jefferson's policies). Secretary of state under Monroe (1817-1825), a position for which he was uniquely well qualified. He rendered Monroe great assistance during preparation of the Monroe Doctrine and concluded at long last a treaty with Spain acquiring the territory of Florida.

In the four-way presidential election of 1824 (in which none of the candidates ran with a distinct party designation), Andrew Jackson received 99 electoral votes, John Quincy Adams 84, William H. Crawford 41, and Henry Clay 37. Since there was no clear majority for Jackson, the election was decided in the House. Clay withdrew from the contest and threw his support, and thereby the election, to Adams. When Clay was named secretary of state, Jackson made (unsubstantiated) claims that an improper deal had been made. Adams' plans for internal improvements with federal assistance for "the benefit of the people" were doomed to failure because he did not win the support of the people or of Congress and he had no party to back him up. Jackson easily took the presidency away from him in the election of 1828, receiving 178 electoral votes to Adams' 83.

The people of his home district in Massachusetts returned Adams to Washington by electing him to the U.S. House of Representatives where, as an able and respected elder statesman, he served from 1831 to 1848. Adams opposed slavery, and for eight years fought against and (1845) had the "gag" rule removed, a rule that had prevented presentation or discussion of petitions against slavery. Falling ill while at his desk in the House, he was carried to the Speaker's office where he died two days later.

ADAMS, ROBERT, JR.   *(b Feb. 26, 1849, Philadelphia; d June 1, 1906, Washington, D.C.).*   Lawyer-geologist who participated in exploration of what is now Yellowstone National Park. Pennsylvania Democrat. Minister to Brazil (1889-1890), U.S. Representative (1893 until death). As chairman of Foreign Affairs Committee, steered through House bills declaring Cuba independent (April 19, 1898) and declaration of war with Spain (April 25, 1898).

ADAMS, SAMUEL   *(b Sept. 27, 1722, Boston; d Oct. 2, 1803, Boston).*   Of the same family that gave the United States two presidents, this Adams was a poor administrator of his personal affairs but an astute politician. A signer of the Declaration of Independence, he served variously as delegate to First Continental Congress and Massachusetts constitutional convention, state senator, Boston tax collector, lieutenant governor, and governor (1794-1797). Also showed family flair for writing, contributing to journals of the day and penning many official papers, including reasons for opposing Stamp Act.

ADAMS, STEPHEN *(b Oct. 17, 1807, Pendleton District, S.C.; d May 11, 1857, Memphis, Tenn.).* Lawyer, Tennessee and Mississippi Democrat. In Tennessee: state senate (1833-1834). In Mississippi: circuit court judge (1837-1845, 1848), U.S. Representative (1845-1847), state house of representatives (1850), delegate to state constitutional convention (1851), U.S. Senate as a Union Democrat to complete term (1852-1857) of Jefferson Davis who had resigned.

ADAMS, WILLIAM LYSANDER *(b Feb. 5, 1821, Painesville, Ohio; d April 26, 1906, Hood River, Oreg.).* A founder of the Republican party in Oregon. Relative of the Adams family of Massachusetts, he had the same versatility and talent for the written word. Migrated (1848) from Ohio to Oregon where he was many things: doctor, farmer, Campbellite preacher, teacher, and collector of customs, but mainly a journalist and biting political satirist who wrote under the pseudonym Breakspear.

ADAMS, WILLIAM WIRT *(b March 22, 1819, Frankfort, Ky.; d May 1, 1888, Jackson, Miss.).* Member of Mississippi legislature (1858-1862). As member of a specially appointed commission (1861), got Louisiana to join Mississippi in seceding from the Union. Declined Jefferson Davis appointment as postmaster general in the Confederate cabinet to form and lead Wirt Adams' Regiment of Cavalry (First Mississippi Cavalry), which compiled outstanding Civil War record.

ADAMSON, WILLIAM CHARLES *(b Aug. 13, 1854, Bowdon, Ga.; d Jan. 3, 1929,* *New York City).* Lawyer, Georgia Democrat. Delegate to national convention (1892), Cleveland-Stevenson presidential elector (1892), U.S. Representative (1897-1917), U.S. Customs Court (1917-1928).

ADDAMS, JANE *(b Sept. 6, 1860, Cedarsville, Ill.; d May 21, 1935, Chicago).* Founder (1889), with Ellen Gates Starr, of Chicago's Hull House where her social work gained world renown. In 1915, with World War I raging in Europe, Miss Addams centered her interests on peace, which she saw as the main social need. A founder and president of the Women's International League for Peace and Freedom, her pacifism brought much wrath down upon her while also gaining her esteem as an outstanding woman of her time. Recognition also came with the awarding to her (1931) of the Nobel Peace Prize, also won that year by Nicholas Murray Butler.

ADDICKS, JOHN EDWARD SULLIVAN *(b Nov. 21, 1841, Philadelphia; d Aug. 7, 1919, New York City).* Multimillionaire grain, gas, and railroad promoter both in United States and abroad; unscrupulous dabbler in Philadelphia politics until his wheeling-dealing took him to Delaware where he played for higher stakes, seventeen times (1889-1906) seeking the office of U.S. senator and seventeen times failing. In the seventeen years he spent an estimated $3 million, formed a formidable Union Republican faction within the GOP, and earned for Delaware an unenviable reputation for political corruption. Died a pauper on the run from process servers.

ADDONIZIO, HUGH JOSEPH *(b Jan. 31, 1914, Newark, N.J.).* Clothing business, New Jersey Democrat. U.S. Representative (1949-1962), mayor of Newark (1962-1970), which was scene of two days of race rioting in 1967, convicted of conspiracy and extortion and sentenced to serve ten years in prison and pay a $25,000 fine (1970), unsuccessfully sought reelection as mayor while on trial.

ADEE, ALVEY AUGUSTUS (b Nov. 27, 1842, Astoria, Oreg.; d July 5, 1924, Washington, D.C.). Diplomat with a talent for analysis and succinct, to-the-point writing that he applied to treaties and countless other official papers during fifty-five years (1869 until death) in the State Department. Highest position was second assistant secretary but only because he refused anything more, preferring to remain out of the political and social limelight. However, he often served as acting secretary. First came to the attention of Washington in 1876 when New York's Boss Tweed escaped from jail and fled to Cuba. Then chargé d'affaires in U.S. embassy in Madrid, Adee convinced Spanish authorities that they should turn Tweed over to the United States. This they did, leading to the Adee-suggested Extradition Convention and Protocol of 1877.

ADKINS, CHARLES (b Feb. 7, 1863, Pickaway County, Ohio; d March 31, 1941, Decatur, Ill.). Agriculturist, Illinois Republican. Piatt County supervisor (1902-1906), state house of representatives (1907-1913), speaker (1911-1913), president of Illinois Live Stock Breeders' Association (1914-1915), state director of agriculture (1916-1920), U.S. Representative (1925-1933).

ADLER, FELIX (b Aug. 13, 1851, Alzey, Germany; d April 24, 1933, New York City). Social reformer extraordinaire, educator, religious leader. Brought to United States at six when his father, Samuel, became rabbi of New York City's Temple Emanu-El, he founded (1876) Society for Ethical Culture and weaned its growth on two continents. Then followed New York's first free kindergarten, Workingmen's Lyceum and School, out of which came the Ethical Culture School (1895), Manhattan Trade School for Girls, Child Study Association (1907), a nationwide district nursing program, housing and vice reforms, chairmanship of the National Child Labor Committee (1904-1921), and more.

Some of Adler's other credits include professor of political and social studies at Columbia University (1902-1933), Roosevelt Exchange Professor to Berlin (1908-1909), chairman of the first Universal Races Congress in London (1911), participation in the International Congress for Moral Education in Rome (1906), president of the Eastern Division of the American Philosophical Association (1928) and, at the very start of his remarkable career, professor of literature and Oriental languages at Cornell University (1874-1876).

AGGREY, JAMES EMMAN KWEGYIR (b Oct. 18, 1875, Anamabu, West African Gold Coast; d July 30, 1927, New York City). Educator, preacher. Though never active politically per se, he made imprint by espousing conviction that the black man and the white man are as important to each other as the white keys on a piano are to the black.

Son of Kodwo Kwegyir, a Fanti nation chieftain's spokesman, and Abna Andua, of a kingly clan, he was given a Methodist education in West Africa, taught school there for a time, then came to United States (1898) to continue his learning. Graduated (1902) from Livingston College, Salisbury, N.C., where he then became professor of literature and a country preacher, introducing several social programs to aid black people.

Always hungry for learning, years later Agrrey enrolled in Columbia University, receiving his master's degree in 1922 and passing preliminary exams for Ph.D. Named to Phelps-Stokes African Education Commission, he twice toured Africa, inspecting schools and suggesting improvements. Appointed vice principal of Gold Coast's Prince of Wales College (July 1924), Aggrey returned to United States (1927) to complete doctoral requirements but died of meningitis soon after arrival.

AGNEW, SPIRO THEODORE. See Calhoun, John Caldwell

AGNUS, FELIX *(b May 5, 1839, Lyons, France; d Oct. 31, 1925, Baltimore).* Came to U.S. (1860), rose from ranks to brigadier general in Union army. Became publisher (1883) of *Baltimore American* upon death of his father-in-law, Charles C. Fulton, and a power in Republican politics though never an office-seeker.

AIKEN, DAVID WYATT *(b March 17, 1828, Winnsboro, S.C.; d April 6, 1887, Cokesbury, S.C.).* Agricultural journalist, teacher, South Carolina Democrat. State legislature (1864-1868), organized politically potent state Grange (1872), Democratic National Convention delegate (1876); U.S. Representative (1877-1887), where he was a militant spokesman for the farmer. Father of Wyatt Aiken, cousin of William Aiken.

AIKEN, WILLIAM *(b Aug. 4, 1806, Charleston, S.C.; d Sept. 6, 1887, Flat Rock, N.C.).* Planter, South Carolina Democrat. State house of representatives (1838-1842), state senate (1842-1844), governor (1844-1846), U.S. Representative (1851-1857). Failed in 133 ballots to be elected speaker (1856) and refused renomination for a fourth term. Though steadfastly opposed to secession, he made heavy donations of supplies and cash loans to the Confederacy for which he was arrested (1865) by Union authorities. Released on parole, he was again elected to House (1867) but was denied a seat by well-organized Northern foes.

AIKEN, WYATT *(b Dec. 14, 1863, Macon, Ga.; d Feb. 6, 1923, Abbeville, S.C.).* South Carolina Democrat. U.S. Representative (1903-1917). Son of David W. Aiken.

AINSWORTH, FREDERICK CRAYTON *(b Sept. 11, 1852, Woodstock, Vt.; d June 5, 1934, Washington, D.C.).* Doctor, career army officer who exerted considerable influence on Congress and political opportunists through his iron-fisted, bureaucratic reign over the War Department's Record and Pension Division (1886-1912). He virtually made the records his private property, opening them only to favored legislators eager to help a constituent. Thus Ainsworth gained so much personal power that it was said that he had more influence upon Congress than anyone in government, including the president. Forced to retire by Secretary Henry L. Stimson who threatened him with court martial, Ainsworth did so (with the rank of major general) but remained in Washington, functioning much as a lobbyist, in support of military legislation, including the Military Defense Act of 1916 and such groups as the National Rifle Association.

AKERMAN, AMOS TAPPAN *(b Feb. 23, 1821, Portsmouth, N.H.; d Dec. 21, 1880, Cartersville, Ga.).* Moved to Georgia to teach school (1843), remaining for the rest of his life but switching to the practice of law. Served with Confederate forces in Civil War. As a member of the state constitutional convention (1868), he helped prevent carpetbaggers from seizing control of the proceedings. Appointed U.S. attorney general by President Grant, he opposed land-grab efforts of railroad magnates who retaliated by forcing his resignation at White House request (December 1871). An embarrassed Grant offered him a federal judgeship but he refused, returning to private practice in Cartersville.

ALCORN, JAMES LUSK *(b Nov. 4, 1816, near Golconda, Ill.; d Dec. 19, 1894, Coahoma County, Miss.).* Raised in Kentucky where, while studying law, served a year (1843) in the state legislature. Upon admission to the bar (1844) he began practice in Mississippi where he became an important political figure, something of a silver-tongued orator and what his foes construed to be a political opportunist.

A follower of Henry Clay, he was a Whig-elected state senator (1848-1856), a state representative (1846, 1856, and 1865), and a consistent foe of secession, opposing it at state conventions both in 1851, when he won, and 1861, when he lost. Undaunted by the loss, in a stirring convention speech said: "The die is cast. . . . the Rubicon is crossed, I enlist in the army that marches to Rome"; and he immediately enlisted. Cheering delegates lost no time in electing him a brigadier general in the Army of Mississippi. With the end of the war and the demise of the Whig party, he became a Republican in what was thought to be a bid for the black vote, and began playing checkers with high elective office. Elected governor, he served only from March 1870, until Nov. 30, 1871, having earlier that year, while occupying the executive mansion, also been elected to the U.S. Senate. There he stayed from Dec. 1, 1871 until 1877, but apparently only because he was defeated in an 1873 race for the governor's chair.

ALDRICH, JAMES FRANKLIN *(b April 6, 1853, Two Rivers, Wis.; d March 8, 1933, Chicago).* Manufacturer, Illinois Republican. Cook County Board of Commissioners (1886-1888), board president (1887), U.S. Representative (1893-1897), appointed consul general to Havana (1897) but never got there due to sinking of battleship *Maine* and outbreak of Spanish-American War. Son of William Aldrich.

ALDRICH, NELSON WILMARTH *(b Nov. 6, 1841, Foster, R.I.; d April 16, 1915, New York City).* Financier, Rhode Island Republican. U.S. Representative (1879-1881), resigning to fill a U.S. Senate seat vacated by death of Am-

brose E. Burnside. Reelected four times, serving until March 3, 1911. Chairman of National Monetary Commission (1908-1912). A protectionist and voice of big business, he was one of the Big Four (with Allison of Iowa, Platt of Connecticut, and Spooner of Wisconsin) whose main goal was to maintain the status quo. Father of Richard S. Aldrich.

ALDRICH, RICHARD STEERE *(b Feb. 29, 1884, Washington, D.C.; d Dec. 25, 1941, Providence, R.I.).* Lawyer, Rhode Island Republican. State house of representatives (1914-1916), state senate (1916-1918), U.S. Representative (1923-1933). Son of Nelson W. Aldrich.

ALDRICH, TRUMAN HEMINWAY *(b Oct. 17, 1848, Palmyra, N.Y.; d April 28, 1932, Birmingham, Ala.).* Mining executive, engineer, banker, Alabama Republican. He followed the same political route as his brother, William F. Aldrich, by successfully contesting the election of a Democrat incumbent (see Oscar W. Underwood) and thus winning a seat as a U.S. Representative (1896-1897); delegate to GOP National Convention (1904).

ALDRICH, WILLIAM *(b Jan. 19, 1820, Greenfield Center, N.Y.; d Dec. 3, 1885, Fond du Lac, Wis.).* Educator, manufacturer, merchant, wholesale grocer, and a man who got around geographically, too; Wisconsin and Illinois Republican officeholder after teaching school in Saratoga County, N.Y. and trying his hand at merchandising In Jackson, Mich. In Wisconsin: Manitowoc County superintendent of schools (1855-1856), chairman of county board of supervisors (1857-1858), state house of representatives (1859). In Illinois: chairman of Chicago City Council (1876), U.S. Representative (1877-1883). Father of James F. Aldrich.

ALDRICH, WILLIAM FARRINGTON *(b March 11, 1853, Palmyra, N.Y.; d Oct. 30, 1925, Birmingham, Ala.).* Mining ex-

ecutive, manufacturer, publisher of the
Birmingham Times, Alabama Republican. U.S. Representative (1896-1897,
1898-1899, 1900-1901) each time successfully contesting the election of the
incumbent Democrat (see Gaston A.
Robbins and Thomas S. Plowman), a
strategy also successfully employed by
his brother, Truman H. Aldrich. Delegate to GOP National Convention (1904).

ALESHIRE, ARTHUR WILLIAM *(b Feb.
15, 1900, Page County, Va.; d March 11,
1940, Springfield, Ohio).* Dairy farmer
who became grocer (1923) when accident confined him to wheelchair for
life. Democratic U.S. Representative
from Ohio (1937-1939).

ALEXANDER, ABRAHAM *(b 1717, Scotland; d April 23, 1786, N.C.).* Settled in
North Carolina (1745), presided over
meeting (May 31, 1775) at which Mecklenburg County declared itself independent of England, the first official
action in all the colonies toward independence.

ALEXANDER, DE ALVA STANWOOD
*(b July 17, 1846, Richmond, Maine; d
Jan. 30, 1925, Buffalo, N.Y.).* Journalist, lawyer, historian; seven times Republican U.S. Representative from Buffalo district (1897-1911), chairman of
Rivers and Harbors Committee. Historical works included *Political History of
New York* (4 volumes, published between 1906 and 1923) and *The History
and Procedures of the House of Representatives* (1916).

ALEXANDER, JOSHUA WILLIS *(b. Jan.
22, 1852, Cincinnati, Ohio; d Feb. 27,
1936, Gallatin, Mo.).* Lawyer, Missouri
Democrat. Daviess County public administrator (1877-1881), secretary and
then president of Gallatin Board of Education (1882-1901), state house of
representatives (1883-1887), speaker
(1887), mayor of Gallatin (1891-1892),
seventh judicial circuit judge (1901-
1907), U.S. Representative (1907-1919),

chairman of U.S. Commission to International Conference on Safety of Life
at Sea (London, Nov. 12, 1913-Jan. 20,
1914), President Wilson's Secretary of
Commerce (1919-1921), delegate to
state constitutional convention (1922).

ALEXANDER, MARK *(b Feb. 7, 1792,
Boydton, Va.; d Oct. 7, 1883, Scotland
Neck, N.C.).* Lawyer, Virginia States'
Rights Democrat. State house of delegates (1817-1819), U.S. Representative
(1819-1833), delegate to state constitutional convention (1829).

ALEXANDER, NATHANIEL *(b March
5, 1756, Mecklenburg County, N.C.; d
March 7, 1808, Salisbury, N.C.).* Revolutionary War surgeon (1778-1782),
member North Carolina House of Commons (1797), state senate (1801-1802),
U.S. Representative (1803-1805) resigning to become governor (1805-1807).

ALEXANDER, SYDENHAM BENONI *(b
Dec. 8, 1840, Mecklenburg County,
N.C.; d June 14, 1921, Charlotte, N.C.).*
Planter, railroad executive, North Caro-
lina Democrat. State senate (1879,
1883, 1885, 1887, 1901), U.S. Represen-
tative (1891-1895). Cousin of Adlai
Ewing Stevenson.

ALEXANDER, WILLIAM *(b 1726, New
York City; d Jan. 15, 1783, Basking
Ridge, N.J.).* Claimed to be the sixth
Earl of Stirling and so called himself,
and was called, Lord Stirling. Pre-Revolutionary New Jersey surveyor-general,
council member, and aide to his brother-
in-law, Governor Livingstone. Commanded New York City defenses in war,
fought at Long Island, Trenton, Brandywine, and Monmouth; one of Washington's most esteemed generals.

ALFORD, THOMAS DALE *(b Jan. 28,
1916, Pike County, Ark.).* Physician,
teacher at University of Arkansas School
of Medicine, Arkansas Democrat who
first became a U.S. Representative
(1959-1963) as a write-in candidate;

served on House Appropriations Committee.

ALGER, BRUCE REYNOLDS *(b June 12, 1918, Dallas, Tex.).* Real estate developer, Texas Republican. U.S. Representative (1955-1965), serving on the Ways and Means Committee.

ALGER, RUSSELL ALEXANDER *(b Feb. 27, 1836, Ohio's Western Reserve; d Jan. 24, 1907, Washington, D.C.).* Country school teacher in Ohio, moved to Michigan to practice law, became a wealthy lumberman and Republican politician there. Governor (1885-1887), favorite son nominee for president at GOP National Convention (1888). McKinley's secretary of war (March 1897-July 1899), resigning on presidential request because of charges of inefficiency, waste, and delivery of "embalmed beef" to troops in Spanish-American War. Appointed (1902) to U.S. Senate on death of James McMillan and served until his own death.

ALLAN, JOHN *(b Jan. 14, 1746, Edinburgh Castle, Scotland; d Feb. 7, 1805, Lubec Mills, Maine).* Family migrated, when he was three, to Nova Scotia where he served in Provincial Assembly from 1770 until forced to flee to Maine in 1776. His offense: "treason to the crown" for sympathizing with the American colonies. Appointed agent to the eastern Indians (1777) with rank of colonel by the Continental Congress, he was able throughout the Revolution to keep them from siding with the British.

ALLEN, AMOS LAWRENCE *(b March 17, 1837, Waterboro, Maine; d Feb. 20, 1911, Washington, D.C.).* Lawyer, Maine Republican. York County clerk of the courts (1870-1883), state house of representatives (1886-1887); delegate at large to GOP National Convention (1896), private secretary (1889-1891, 1895-1899) to U.S. House Speaker Thomas B. Reed of Maine. Elected U.S. Representative to complete term when

Reed resigned and was then reelected five times, thus serving from Nov. 6, 1899 until death.

ALLEN, ANDREW *(b June, 1740, Philadelphia; d March 7, 1825, London).* Of a prominent family, he held many important political positions in Pennsylvania up to and including being a delegate to the Continental Congress (1775-1776) where he showed decided Loyalist leanings. He opposed independence and was forced to flee to Trenton for British protection when war began. His property was confiscated and, though pardoned at war's end, was never able to recover it. He then went to live out his years in England on a pension from the crown.

ALLEN, ASA LEONARD *(b Jan. 5, 1891, Winn Parish, La.).* Teacher, lawyer, Louisiana Democrat. Winn Parish schools superintendent (1917-1922), Winnfield city attorney for several years before serving eight terms as a U.S. Representative (1937-1953).

ALLEN, CHARLES *(b Aug. 9, 1797, Worcester, Mass.; d Aug. 6, 1869, Worcester).* Lawyer, Massachusetts Whig and Free-Soiler. State house of representatives (1830, 1833, 1835, 1840), state senate (1836, 1837), member of northeastern boundary commission (1842), Common Pleas Court judge (1842-1845), delegate to Whig National Convention (1848), Free-Soil party U.S. Representative (1849-1853), delegate to state constitutional convention (1853), chief justice of Suffolk County Superior Court (1859-1867), delegate to Washington, D.C., peace convention (1861) that tried to head off Civil War. Grandson of Samuel Adams.

ALLEN, CHARLES HERBERT *(b April 15, 1848, Lowell, Mass.; d April 20, 1934, Lowell).* Manufacturer, banker, Massachusetts Republican. State house of representatives (1881-1882), state senate (1883), U.S. Representative

(1885-1889), unsuccessful gubernatorial candidate (1890), state prison commissioner (1897-1898), assistant secretary of navy (1898-1900), first civil governor of Puerto Rico (1900-1902).

ALLEN, CLARENCE EMIR *(b Sept. 8, 1852, Girard Township, Pa.; d July 9, 1932, Escondido, Calif.).* Teacher, lawyer, miner, Utah Republican. Territorial house of representatives (1888, 1890, 1894), Salt Lake County clerk (1890-1893), delegate to GOP National Conventions (1892, 1896), when Utah became a state was elected a U.S. Representative and served from Jan. 4, 1896, until March 3, 1897.

ALLEN, EDWARD PAYSON *(b Oct. 28, 1839, Sharon, Mich.; d Nov. 25, 1909, Ypsilanti, Mich.).* Lawyer, Michigan Republican. Washtenaw County attorney (1872), Ypsilanti alderman (1872-1874), state house of representatives (1876, 1878), speaker pro tem (1878), mayor of Ypsilanti (1880, 1899-1900), U.S. Indian agent for Michigan (1882-1885), U.S. Representative (1887-1891), member state agriculture board (1897-1903), and soldiers' home board (1903-1909).

ALLEN, ELISHA HUNT *(b Jan. 28, 1804, New Salem, Mass.; d Jan. 1, 1883, Washington, D.C.).* Lawyer, diplomat, Whig. Served in Maine House of Representatives (1836-1841) and as speaker (1838-1841), U.S. Representative (1841-1843), Maine House again (1846), Massachusetts House (1849).

Appointed consul to Honolulu in 1850, he was soon stolen away from the United States by the King of Hawaii with the offer of high position as the minister of finance. With that as the beginning, Allen remained in Hawaiian service for the rest of his life, serving as chief justice and regent, negotiating a reciprocity treaty with the U.S. and, the final diplomatic coup, living out his years as minister from the Kingdom of Hawaii to Washington until his death at a White House New Year's Day reception given the diplomatic corps by President Arthur.

ALLEN, ETHAN *(b Jan. 10, 1737, Litchfield, Conn.; d Feb. 12, 1789, Burlington, Vt.).* One of five brothers (Ira, Levi, Heman, Heber), all of whom were active in Vermont politics. Ethan, the most military minded, commanded the Green Mountain Boys, which was formed in 1770 to further the struggle of Vermont (at that time called the New Hampshire Grants) for independence from both New Hampshire and New York who each sought control.

Although Ethan captured Fort Ticonderoga (May 10, 1775), it has never been clear if his loyalties were mainly on the side of the Revolution or the creation of Vermont as a separate state. In September 1778 he unsuccessfully presented Vermont claims to the Continental Congress and, when placed in command of the Vermont militia, mainly made war on New York settlers. Ethan, Ira, and Levi negotiated unsuccessfully (1780-1783) with the British to recognize Vermont as an independent province with Redcoats to protect her borders— from whom is open to conjecture. This ploy is considered by many historians, though it has never been proved one way or the other, to have been meant only to force the Continental Congress to change its position.

ALLEN, HENRY JUSTIN *(b Sept. 11, 1868, Pittsfield, Pa., d Jan. 17, 1950, Wichita, Kans.).* Journalist, Kansas Republican. Spanish-American War correspondent (1898), member Washington press corps (1914-1916), American Red Cross communications director in France during World War I, governor of Kansas (1919-1923), Near East relief commissioner for Armenia, Turkey, Greece, and southeast Russia (1923-1924) under Herbert Hoover, publicity director for the GOP National Committee in Hoover's successful presidential campaign (1928) and therefore the man who must take responsibility for the "chicken in every pot" slogan; U.S. Senate to fill an unexpired term (1929-1930).

ALLEN, HENRY WATKINS *(b April 29, 1820, Prince Edward County, Va.; d April 22, 1866, Mexico City).* An outstanding Confederate officer, he was badly wounded at the battles of Shiloh and Baton Rouge and, unable to return to the field, was sent (1863) to the Trans-Mississippi Department as a brigadier general where he was elected Confederate governor of Louisiana virtually by acclamation.

Taking office on Jan. 25, 1864, he found people starving and the state in chaos. Swift, certain action was needed and Allen provided it. He set up state stores and factories, banned all luxuries, opened medical dispensaries, forced distilleries to manufacture alcohol only for medicinal use, imported iron ore from Texas and badly needed consumer commodities from Mexico. At war's end Louisiana was, for a Confederate state, in good shape. As for Allen, his health was rapidly failing, he was broke, and, expecting punishment by the Union, fled to Mexico (1865). But, even in exile, the people of Louisiana wanted him for governor and sought unsuccessfully to have him return.

ALLEN, IRA *(b May 1, 1751, Cornwall, Conn.; d Jan. 15, 1814, Philadelphia).* Youngest brother of Ethan Allen. Wrote preamble to Vermont constitution, member of Governor's Council and state's first treasurer, author of *Natural and Political History of Vermont*, which was published in 1798.

ALLEN, JAMES CAMERON *(b Jan. 29, 1922, Shelby, Ky.; d Jan. 30, 1912, Olney, Ill.).* Lawyer, Illinois Democrat with nine political lives, including one spent in Indiana where he was prosecuting attorney for the seventh judicial district (1846-1848). Then, in Illinois he was in the state house of representa-

tives (1850-1851); U.S. Representative (1853) and four months into his second term when the House decided (July 1855) he was not entitled to the seat. So he ran again to fill his own vacancy, won, and served six months (1856-1857), did not seek reelection and then became clerk of the house (1857-1859).

Next came an unsuccessful run for the governorship (1860), quickly followed by a successful campaign for a circuit court judgeship. But he sat only from April 1861 until 1863 when he resigned to run once again for Congress, winning and serving (1863-1865). Once more he tried for reelection and, when that failed, retired to private practice, emerging again as a circuit court candidate. This time he won not one set of robes but two with the coincidental creation of the Illinois Appellate Court and his appointment to sit in both courts simultaneously (1873-1879).

ALLEN, JOHN BEARD *(b May 18, 1845, Crawfordsville, Ind.; d Jan. 28, 1903, Seattle, Wash.).* Lawyer, Washington Republican. U.S. attorney for the Washington Territory (1875-1885), territorial delegate to U.S. Congress (1889). When Washington became a state he was elected to U.S. Senate (1889-1893), reelected but was disqualified (1893).

ALLEN, JOHN CLAYTON *(b Feb. 14, 1860, Hinesburg, Vt.; d Jan. 12, 1939, Monmouth, Ill.).* Merchant, banker, Nebraska and Illinois Republican. In Nebraska: McCook City Council (1887-1889). McCook mayor (1890), Nebraska secretary of state (1891-1895). In Illinois: state normal school board (1917-1927), U.S. Representative (1925-1933).

ALLEN, JOHN JOSEPH, JR. *(b Nov. 27, 1899, Oakland, Calif.).* Lawyer, California Republican. Oakland Board of Education (1923-1943), GOP county central committee (1936-1944), vice chairman of state commission on school districts (1946, 1947), U.S. Representative (1947-1959), undersecretary of commerce for transportation (1959-1961).

ALLEN, JOHN MILLS *(b July 8, 1846, Tishomingo County, Miss.; d Oct. 30, 1917, Toledo, Miss.).* Lawyer, Mississippi Democrat. U.S. Representative (1885-1901).

ALLEN, LEO ELWOOD *(b Oct. 5, 1898, Elizabeth, Ill.).* Teacher, lawyer, Illinois Republican who served fourteen terms as a U.S. Representative (1933-1961).

ALLEN, LEVI (see Allen, Ethan).

ALLEN, PHILIP *(b Sept. 1, 1785, Providence, R.I.; d Dec. 16, 1865, Providence).* A textile manufacturer who wove much political gain out of the phrase "law and order." Democratic governor of Rhode Island (1851-1853), U.S. Senator (1853-1859) where he was known as a Tariff Democrat.

Made his mark on Rhode Island politics in a struggle with Thomas W. Dorr for control of the Democratic party. Allen helped put down the so-called Dorr Rebellion by purchasing arms and forming the Rhode Island Carbineers, saying he was doing so to defend the state. The fight ended with Dorr in jail and Allen the undisputed boss. Or, as the *Providence Daily Journal* put it: "He holds the Democratic Party in his pocket. He owns it."

ALLEN, WILLIAM *(b Dec. 27, 1803, Edenton, N.C.; d July 11, 1879, Chillicothe, Ohio).* An orphan and poor, at sixteen he walked across the Alleghenies in the dead of winter to Ohio where a half-sister taught him to read and write. Became a lawyer and displayed a gift for oratory. Elected a U.S. Representative as a Democrat (1833-1835), winning by one vote and then marrying his opponent's daughter; served two terms in the U.S. Senate (1837-1849) where he was chairman of the Foreign Relations Committee, then retired from politics and devoted next twenty-five years to farming. Emerged to seek successfully and serve one term as governor (1874-1876). Name placed in nomination for U.S. presidency at Democratic National Convention (1876).

ALLEN, WILLIAM JOSHUA *(b June 9, 1829, Wilson County, Tenn.; d Jan. 26, 1901, Hot Springs, Ark.).* Illinois lawyer, state and U.S. district court judge, delegate to seven Democratic National Conventions (1864-1888). Active in move to have southern Illinois secede both from the state and the Union (1862), for which he spent several months in jail, going from there almost directly to the U.S. House of Representatives where he remained until 1865.

ALLEN, WILLIAM VINCENT *(b Jan. 28, 1847, Midway, Ohio; d Jan. 12, 1924, Los Angeles, Calif.).* A member of a strongly abolitionist family that maintained a way station on the underground railroad, he enlisted in the Union Army at the age of fifteen and served for the duration. Then studied law, practiced in Madison, Nebraska, and became a force in state politics. At first a member of the Farmers' Alliance, he became a Populist (1890); as a U.S. Senator (1893-1901), Allen was known as "the intellectual giant of Populism," once filibustering fifteen hours against repeal of the Sherman Silver Purchase Act.

ALLISON, JOHN *(b Aug. 5, 1812, Beaver, Pa.; d March 23, 1878, Washington, D.C.).* Manufacturer, Pennsylvania Whig and Republican. State house of representatives (1846, 1847, 1849), U.S. Representative (1851-1853, 1855-1857), GOP National Convention delegate (1856, 1860) gaining distinction at the former as the man who nominated Abraham Lincoln—for vice president. Register of the U.S. Treasury (1869 until death).

ALLISON, WILLIAM BOYD *(b March 2, 1829, Perry, Ohio; d Aug. 4, 1908, Dubuque, Iowa).* Served thirty-five years and five months (March 3, 1873, until death) as a U.S. Senator from Iowa. An unswerving Republican from almost the moment the party was formed, he was a delegate to the 1860 presidential convention that nominated Lincoln and a member of the House (1863-1871).

ALLSTON, ROBERT FRANCIS WITHERS *(b April 21, 1801, All Saints' Parish, S.C.; d April 7, 1864, All Saints' Parish).* West Point graduate, civil engineer, planter. Served almost continually in state government from 1823 until 1858, the last three years as governor, making lasting agricultural and public school reforms. Author of "Memoir of the Introduction and Planting of Rice in South Carolina" (1843) and "An Essay on Sea Coast Crops" (1854), which were read and followed by farmers throughout the South.

ALMON, EDWARD BERTON *(b April 18, 1860, Moulton, Ala.; d June 22, 1933, Washington, D.C.).* Lawyer, Alabama Democrat. State senate (1892-1894), Bryan-Sewall presidential elector (1896), eleventh judicial circuit judge (1898-1906), state house of representatives (1910-1915), speaker (1911), U.S. Representative (1915 until death).

ALMOND, JAMES LINDSAY, JR. *(b June 15, 1898, Charlottesville, Va.).* Lawyer, teacher, Virginia Democrat. Assistant commonwealth's attorney (1930-1933), hustings court judge (1933-1945), U.S. Representative (1946-1948), state attorney general (1948-1957), governor (1958-1962).

ALSTON, WILLIS *(b 1769, Littleton, N.C.; d April 10, 1837, Halifax, N.C.).* Farmer, North Carolina Democrat. State house of commons (1790-1792, 1820-1824), U.S. Representative (1799, 1815, 1825-1831).

ALTGELD, JOHN PETER *(b Dec. 30, 1847, Nieder Selters, Germany; d March* 12, 1902, Joliet, Ill.). Wealthy builder, lawyer, first post-Civil War Democratic governor of Illinois (1893-1897), champion of human rights and the common man whose battles against misapplication of the law highpointed his career.

A self-made, self-educated man, Altgeld was raised in Ohio from infancy, served briefly with Union forces, left home at twenty-one, worked at odd jobs while learning to teach, then was a school teacher while studying law. Elected prosecutor of Andrew County, Mo., served only briefly (1874), moving to Chicago in 1875. There he made his mark, his 1884 treatise, "Our Penal Machinery and its Victims," signaling his conviction that the cards were stacked against the underprivileged.

It was while a Cook County Superior Court judge (1886-1891) that an event occurred which was in later years to establish his place in history. For months Chicago had been a hotbed of labor unrest. Then a factory that had been shut by strike reopened with scab labor, and rock-throwing strikers had been dispersed by police. There were injuries but no fatalities. Nevertheless, a radical newspaper reported six strikers had been killed. Radical labor leaders called a protest meeting. Only a few hundred unionists attended and 200 police were there. Speakers called for armed uprising, police moved forward, someone hurled a dynamite bomb, police fired shots, the crowd scattered and fled in panic. The toll: Seven policemen dead and scores wounded on both sides. This was the Haymarket Square Riot of May 4, 1886.

There followed a roundup of radicals and eight subsequently were convicted on murder conspiracy charges; none was shown to be the bomb-thrower. Four were hanged (Nov. 11, 1887), another had committed suicide in jail, three were sent to prison terms, two of them for life. Meantime, throughout the country and the world there had been much criticism of the conduct of the trial and the severity of the sentences, and soon after Altgeld's inauguration as governor in 1893 there was laid on his desk a petition, signed by many prominent people, for pardon of the three.

Altgeld carefully reviewed the case, found that the jury had been packed and that the judge had been prejudiced. On June 26, 1893, he granted the pardons in a brief that has gained in stature over the years but at the time made him not only the victim of outraged public opinion and attempts to label him an anarchist, but also the focal point of GOP strategy to paint the Democratic party and revolutionists with the same brush.

A year later Altgeld provided his foes with further ammunition when he protested as unconstitutional the sending of federal troops into Chicago during another strike. Thus he lost his bid for a second gubernatorial term although not the esteem of his party. At the presidential convention (1896) that nominated William Jennings Bryan, it is said that the designation would have gone to Altgeld if not for his foreign birth.

ALVEY, RICHARD HENRY *(b March 6, 1826, St. Mary's Parish, Md.; d Sept. 14, 1906, Hagerstown, Md.).* Judge, Democrat, author of the "Alvey Resolution" (1861) calling for Maryland's secession from the Union. It failed adoption and he was held prisoner for a year.

AMBLER, JACOB A. *(b Feb. 18, 1829, Pittsburgh, Pa.; d Sept. 22, 1906, Canton, Ohio).* Lawyer, businessman, Ohio Republican. Judge of ninth judicial district (1859-1867), U.S. Representative (1869-1873), delegate to six GOP National Conventions (1876-1898).

AMES, ADELBERT *(b Oct. 31, 1835, Rockland, Maine; d April 12, 1933, Ormond, Fla.).* A brilliant Union officer in the Civil War, receiving the Congressional Medal of Honor and rising to the rank of brigadier general. Appointed Reconstructionist governor of Mississippi (1868) by President Grant, he was

elected to the U.S. Senate by a Republican legislature dominated by northerners, resigning four years later after becoming the regularly elected governor. His tenure (Jan. 4, 1874-March 29, 1876) was marked by disorder, riot, and political upheaval. When Democrats won control of the state legislature and threatened him with impeachment, Ames resigned and left Mississippi. Father of Butler Ames.

AMES, BUTLER *(b Aug. 22, 1871, Lowell, Mass.; d Nov. 6, 1954, Tewksbury, Mass.).* West Point graduate, manufacturer, Massachusetts Republican. Lowell Common Council (1896), state house of representatives (1897-1899) with time out (1898) for Spanish-American War combat duty and to serve as civil administrator of Puerto Rico's Arecibo district, U.S. Representative (1903-1913). Son of Adelbert Ames, grandson of Benjamin Franklin Butler.

AMES, FISHER *(b April 9, 1758, Dedham, Mass.; d July 4, 1808, Dedham).* Teacher, scholar, supporter of Alexander Hamilton, adversary of Thomas Jefferson, and conservative pamphleteer whose writings included: "We cannot live without society. The liberty of one depends not so much on the removal of all restraint upon him, as on the due restraint upon the liberty of others. Without such restraint, there can be no liberty."

As a Federalist Representative the first four U.S. Congresses (1789-1797), he gained much note as an orator with such phrases as those spoken (Jan. 27, 1794) in opposition to a trade war with Britain: "I hope we shall show, by our vote, that we deem it better policy to feed nations than to starve them, and that we shall never be so unwise as to put our good customers into a situation to be forced to make every exertion to do without us."

That speech, while causing Ames to be hung in effigy in Charleston, S.C., in the company of Benedict Arnold and the devil, also led to John Jay's mission and treaty with England. Ames retired from active political life at the "advancing age" of forty-seven to become the squire sage of Dedham.

AMES, OAKES *(b Jan. 10, 1804, Easton, Mass.; d May 8, 1873, North Easton)*. Wealthy manufacturer, GOP Representative from Massachusetts for five terms (1863-1873). While in the House became involved in construction of the first transcontinental railroad, engaging in questionable financial manipulations. Fearing legislative investigation, he made stock easily available (1868) to key congressmen. The scheme was exposed four years later by the *New York Sun* under the headline: "The King of Frauds: How the Crédit Mobilier Bought Its Way into Congress." The House launched an inquiry and Ames was censured for "seeking to procure congressional attention to the affairs of a corporation in which he was interested." Ames did not seek renomination, but defended his actions as the "same thing as going into the business community and interesting the leading businessmen by giving them shares." Father of Oliver Ames.

AMES, OLIVER *(b Feb. 4, 1831, North Easton, Mass.; d Oct. 22, 1895)*. Manufacturer, financier, philanthropist, patron of the arts, Massachusetts Republican. Son of Oakes Ames, made good his father's debts, put family manufacturing business back on its feet, then sought political office. State senator (1880-1882), lieutenant governor (1882-1886), governor (1886-1890). Introduced reforms of banks, public school systems, and state business procedures, then retired once again to private life.

AMHERST, JEFFERY *(b Jan. 29, 1717, Kent, England; d Aug. 3, 1797, Kent)*. A brilliant British military commander, he fought in Seven Years War, captur-

ing Cape Breton Island (1758) and Montreal (1760), the latter victory bringing Canada into the British Empire. Towns and counties were named for him in Virginia and New England and he was appointed sinecure governor of Virginia but never served. Died with rank of field marshal and the title Baron Amherst.

AMIDON, CHARLES FREMONT *(b Aug. 17, 1856, Chautauqua County, N.Y.; d Dec. 26, 1937, Tucson, Ariz.)*. Worked his way through college, graduating (1882) Phi Beta Kappa with medals in Latin, Greek, and oratory, and immediately going to Fargo, North Dakota, to establish a high school. Four years later he embarked on a law career. He served on commission (1893) to revise state laws, then was appointed (1896) U.S. District Court judge for the state and, though sitting in an isolated part of the country, gained a national reputation with many of his opinions setting legal precedent.

President Theodore Roosevelt, in a 1907 speech, hailed Amidon's declaration that interpretation of the Constitution should be elastic and that decisions must be guided by their effect on the nation. In 1911 the president went even further, stating in a letter to Amidon: "How I wish you were on the Supreme Court!"

Amidon opposed broad use of the injunction against labor unions and in 1931, three years after retirement from the bench, headed a Civil Liberties Union committee that swayed public opinion on the side of the Norris-LaGuardia Anti-Injunction Act, which was passed in 1932.

AMLIE, THOMAS RYUM *(b April 17, 1897, Griggs County, N.Dak.)*. Lawyer, North Dakota Republican-Progressive. U.S. Representative (1931-1933, 1935-1939), unsuccessful Progressive candidate for U.S. Senate nomination (1938), nominated by Roosevelt (1939) to Interstate Commerce Commission but asked that his name be withdrawn.

AMMONS, ELIAS MILTON *(b July 28, 1860, Macon County, N.C.; d May 20, 1925, Denver, Colo.).* A GOP legislator in Colorado, he quit party (1896) because of its espousal of the gold standard, helped found the Silver Republican party, and was elected (1898) to the state senate. Then he became a Democrat and was governor (1912-1915). Accused of favoring the mine owners in the bloody coal strike (1913-1914) that was marked by a pitched battle between strikers and state militia, a legislative move to force his resignation was defeated, 26 to 4.

ANDERSON, ALEXANDER OUTLAW *(b Nov. 10, 1794, Jefferson County, Tenn.; d May 23, 1869, Knoxville, Tenn.).* Lawyer, Tennessee and California Democrat, going west in the 1849 rush for gold. In Tennessee: appointed U.S. Land Office superintendent for Alabama (1836), Indian agent (1838), U.S. Senate to fill an unexpired term (1840-1841). In California: state senate (1850-1851), state supreme court judge (1851-1853). Son of Joseph Anderson.

ANDERSON, CHAPMAN LEVY *(b March 15, 1845, Macon, Miss.; d April 27, 1924, Kosciusko, Miss.).* Lawyer, Mississippi Democrat. Mayor of Kosciusko (1875), state house of representatives (1879-1880), U.S. Representative (1887-1891), U.S. attorney for Mississippi's northern district (1896-1897).

ANDERSON, GALUSHA *(b March 7, 1832, Clarendon, N.Y.; d July 20, 1918).* College president, clergyman, staunch abolitionist. Pastor of the Second Baptist Church of St. Louis, the largest Baptist church west of the Mississippi, from 1858 until after the Civil War—a period in which his strong, vocal stand against secession endangered his life. But Missouri, a border state, stayed in the Union.

ANDERSON, GEORGE WASHINGTON *(b May 22, 1832, Jefferson County, Tenn.; d Feb. 26, 1902, Rhea Springs, Tenn.).* Missouri lawyer. State house of representatives (1859-1860), Lincoln-Hamlin presidential elector (1860), Radical Republican U.S. Representative (1865-1869).

ANDERSON, JOHN ALEXANDER *(b June 26, 1834, Washington County, Pa.; d May 18, 1892, Liverpool, England).* College president, Presbyterian minister and, incongruously, entering the Union army in the Civil War as a chaplain and emerging as a sanitation expert. GOP Representative from Kansas (1879-1887), as an Independent (1887-1889), and again as a Republican (1889-1891), then was appointed U.S. consul general to Cairo, Egypt, by his old college roommate, President Benjamin Harrison. In Congress, Anderson was author of two-cent postage bill, fought to raise the Department of Agriculture to cabinet level, and helped bring about railroad land grant reforms, including the end of certain tax exemptions.

ANDERSON, JOHN ZUINGLIUS *(b March 22, 1904, Oakland, Calif.).* Farmer, fruit grower, California Republican. U.S. Representative (1939-1953), administrative assistant to President Eisenhower (1956-1961).

ANDERSON, JOSEPH *(b Nov. 5, 1757, White Marsh, Pa.; d April 17, 1837, Washington, D.C.).* Revolutionary War officer, lawyer, U.S. judge (1791) for the territory south of the Ohio River, delegate to Tennessee's first constitutional convention (1796), U.S. Senator from that state (1797-1815), first comptroller of the U.S. Treasury (1815-1836), Anderson County, Tenn., named for him. Father of Alexander Outlaw Anderson.

ANDERSON, MARY *(b 1872, Lidkoping, Sweden; d Jan. 29, 1964, Washington,*

D.C.). Labor expert who worked for "equal pay, equal opportunities" for women. Came to United States at age sixteen; starting as a dish washer and factory worker, she became president of her Boot and Shoe Workers' Union local, a founder and organizer for the National Women's Trade Union League, appointed chief of U.S. Department of Labor's Women's Bureau (1919-1944).

ANDERSON, RICHARD CLOUGH, JR. *(b Aug. 4, 1788, Louisville, Ky.; d July 24, 1826, Colombia, S.A.).* Lawyer, member Kentucky legislature (1815-1816 and again 1821-1822), U.S. Representative (1817-1821) when he championed independence of Spanish colonies in South America. When United States recognized the new republics, Anderson was named first minister plenipotentiary to Colombia (1823 until death) where he negotiated (Oct. 1824) the first U.S. treaty with a South American republic. Anderson died suddenly while enroute, as an envoy extraordinary, to the Panama Congress of Nations.

ANDERSON, SYDNEY *(b Sept. 18, 1881, Zumbrota, Minn.; d Oct. 8, 1948, Minneapolis).* Minnesota Republican. U.S. Representative (1911-1925), chairman of Joint Congressional Commission of Agricultural Inquiry (1921-1922), president of U. S. Wheat Council (1923-1924), president of Millers' National Federation (1924-1929).

ANDRESEN, AUGUST HERMAN *(b Oct. 11, 1890, Newark, Ill.; d Jan. 14, 1958, Bethesda, Md.).* Lawyer, Minnesota Republican. Served sixteen terms as a U.S. Representative (1925-1933, 1935 until death).

ANDREW, ABRAM PLATT, JR. *(b Feb. 12, 1873, LaPorte, Ind.; d June 3, 1936, Gloucester, Mass.).* Economist, Massachusetts Republican, director of the Mint (1909-1910), assistant secretary of

treasury (1910-1912), U.S. Representative (1921 until death), delegate to GOP National Conventions (1924, 1928).

ANDREW, JOHN ALBION *(b May 31, 1818, Windham, Maine; d Oct. 30, 1867, Boston).* Civil War governor (1861-1866) of Massachusetts whose lifelong dedication to the Negro cause drew him into politics. He was one of the founders (1848) of the Free-Soil Party ("Free Soil, Free Speech, Free Labor, Free Men"); raised defense funds for John Brown ("John Brown himself is right") and to support his family; chairman of state delegation to Republican National Convention that nominated Lincoln, and was sent to the state house on the same ticket that sent Lincoln to the White House.

One of his first acts as governor was to put the state militia on a war footing, thus enabling Massachusetts to be the first state to answer Lincoln's call for troops to defend Washington; then, after Emancipation, which he ardently advocated, organized one of the war's first all-Negro regiments ("I stand or fall, as a man and as a magistrate, with the rise and fall in history of the Fifty-fourth Massachusetts Regiment"). As the war neared its end, Andrew turned his efforts to winning full rights for the black man and reconstruction of the South without rancor or penalty.

ANDREWS, CHARLES OSCAR *(b March 7, 1877, Ponce de Leon, Fla.; d Sept. 18, 1946, Washington, D.C.).* Lawyer, Florida Democrat. Secretary of state senate (1905-1907, 1909-1911), assistant state attorney general (1912-1919), member state house of representatives (1927), state supreme court commissioner (1929-1932), U.S. Senate (1936 until death).

ANDREWS, SHERLOCK JAMES *(b Nov. 17, 1801, Wallingford, Conn.; d Feb. 11, 1880, Cleveland, Ohio).* As a Whig Representative from Ohio (1841-1843), he spoke out against slavery and for the rights of Negroes; member of the legal battery that in 1859 defended men who rescued a Negro from slave catchers. One of the men who developed Cleveland, he was first president of its city council and headed the library board.

ANDREWS, WILLIAM EZEKIEL *(b Dec. 17, 1854, Oskaloosa, Iowa; d Jan. 19, 1942, Washington, D.C.).* Ophaned at an early age, he worked as a farmhand in warm months, attended school in cold months, went on to college, entered the educational field, and became an active Nebraska Republican. Vice president of Hastings College (1889), president of State Teachers' Association (1890), secretary to governor (1893-1894), U.S. Representative (1895-1897, 1919-1923), U.S. Treasury Department auditor (1897-1915).

ANDREWS, WILLIAM HENRY *(b Jan. 14, 1846, Youngsville, Pa.; d Jan. 16, 1919, Carlsbad, N.Mex.).* Railroad builder, mine and oil field developer, Republican. In Pennsylvania: chairman of GOP state committee (1889-1891), state house of representatives (1889-1893), state senate (1895). Moved to New Mexico Territory (1900) where he continued his interest in politics, serving on the territorial council (1903-1904) and then being elected a delegate to the U.S. Congress (1905-1912).

ANFUSO, VICTOR L'EPISCOPO *(b March 10, 1905, Sicily, Italy; d Dec. 28, 1966, New York City).* Lawyer, New York Democrat who served with Office of Strategic Services (OSS) in Mediterranean Theater during World War II, becoming a special assistant to the Commissioner of Immigration. New York City magistrate (1954), U.S. Representative (1951-1953, 1955-1963), representing the people whose shoes he shined as a boy to help support his family. New York State Supreme Court justice (1963-1966).

ANGELL, HOMER DANIEL *(b Jan. 12, 1875, Wasco County, Oreg.).* Lawyer, Oregon Republican. State representative (1920, 1931, 1935), state senate (1937, 1938), U.S. Representative (1939-1955).

ANGELL, JAMES BURRILL *(b Jan. 7, 1829, Scituate, R.I.; d April 1, 1916, Ann Arbor, Mich.).* Editor of *Providence Journal* during Civil War, president of University of Vermont (1866-1871) and University of Michigan (1871-1909), ambassador to China (1880-1881) negotiating a treaty that limited Chinese migration to the U.S., member of Anglo-American Fisheries Commission (1887-1891) and Canadian-American Deep Waterways Commission (1896-1897), minister to Turkey (1897-1898). As an educator, Angell was a vigorous advocate of graduate schools in state universities and of coeducation.

ANKENY, LEVI *(b Aug. 1, 1844, St. Joseph, Mo.; d March 29, 1921, Walla Walla, Wash.).* Banker, Washington Republican. First mayor of Lewiston, Idaho, then moved to Walla Walla where he founded (1878) first of seven banks in Washington and Oregon, delegate to national convention (1900), member of GOP National Committee (1904-1908), U.S. Senate (1903-1909). Chairman of Pan American Exposition Commission.

ANSBERRY, TIMOTHY THOMAS *(b Dec. 24, 1871, Defiance, Ohio; d July 5, 1943, New York City).* Lawyer, Ohio Democrat. U.S. Representative (1907-1915), Wilson-Marshall presidential elector (1916), national convention delegate (1920, 1924).

ANTHONY, DANIEL READ, JR. *(b Aug. 22, 1870, Leavenworth, Kans.; d Aug. 4, 1931, Leavenworth).* Journalist, Kansas Republican. Mayor of Leavenworth (1903-1905), U.S. Representative (1907-1929).

ANTHONY, GEORGE TOBEY *(b June 9, 1824, Mayfield, N.Y.; d Aug. 5, 1896, Leavenworth, Kans.).* U.S. Collector of Internal Revenue (1868), Republican governor of Kansas (1877-1879).

ANTHONY, HENRY BOWEN *(b April 1, 1815, Coventry, R.I.; d Sept. 2, 1884, Providence, R.I.).* Editor and then publisher of the *Providence Journal* from 1838 until death, Whig governor (1849-1851), continuously a conservative Republican U.S. Senator from 1858 until death, in later years being called the father of the Senate.

ANTHONY, SUSAN BROWNELL *(b Feb. 15, 1820, Adams, Mass.; d March 13, 1906, Rochester, N.Y.)* Lifelong champion not only of women's rights but also of the right of Negroes to live as free and equal, seeing them as common cause. (Example: she insisted, though unsuccessfully, that the Fourteenth and Fifteenth Amendments give full rights of citizenship, including the vote, to Negro women as well as to Negro men.) Her life's work was a reflection of her Quaker upbringing; later, while a teacher and a temperance worker, it was Quaker friends who introduced her to both the antislavery and women's movements.

As an abolitionist, she represented the American Antislavery Society in New York (1856-1861), confronting and facing down many hostile mobs; at outset of Civil War she founded Women's National Loyal League to campaign for emancipation.

As the nation's leading suffragist, she won (1860) the right of New York State women to control their own wages and to be guardians of their own children; convinced women teachers that they should fight both for parity pay with men and the right to be heard at teachers' conventions; published (1868-1870) *The Revolution,* a New York City weekly whose logotype included the slogan: "The true republic—men, their rights and nothing more; women, their rights and nothing less"; formed first the National Woman Suffrage Association and then the National American Woman Suffrage Association, serving as its president from 1892 to 1900, to bring about adoption of a constitutional amendment giving voting rights to women.

The result: enactment of the Nineteenth Amendment in 1920, fourteen years after her death. But in her lifetime she did witness the arrival of woman suffrage in the states of Colorado, Wyoming, Idaho, and Utah, and, abroad, in Australia and New Zealand as the result of the broadening of her activities into the international arena, first with the formation (1888) of the International Council of Women and then (1904) the founding of the International Woman Suffrage Alliance in Berlin together with Carrie Chapman Catt.

Indefatigable almost to her dying day, she went wherever she was asked (and, even more, where she wasn't) to spread her message, defying the rigors of nineteenth-century travel, the hardships of the frontier, and, all too often, the jeers of hostile audiences—jeers that changed to cheers as the years went by and the hairs grew gray.

APPLEBY, THEODORE FRANK *(b Oct. 10, 1864, Old Bridge, N.J.; d Dec. 15, 1924, Baltimore, Md.).* Real estate broker, New Jersey Republican. Delegate to national convention (1896), mayor of Asbury Park (1908-1912), U.S. Representative (1921-1923).

APPLEGATE, JESSE *(b July 5, 1811, Ky.; d April 22, 1888, Umpqua Valley, Oreg.).* Writer, surveyor, cattleman, and a maverick in politics who preferred the pen to the soapbox. Led a 900-member wagon train (1843) from Missouri west across the Oregon Trail and into what is now the state of Oregon, later describing the journey in his *Day With the Cow Column in 1843,* which was published in 1934; opened (1845) a southern road into Oregon.

In the same year, Applegate was elected a member of the provisional government's legislative committee that established a politically unified administration which governed until Oregon became a territory (1849). Named (1857) a delegate to the state convention, he walked out in protest when his position went unheeded; became first a Whig and then a Republican, though Oregon was ruled by Democrats, and did much toward electing Lincoln and keeping Oregon on the side of the Union during the Civil War; played a key role in the construction of a rail link between Oregon and California, then refused nomination for a U.S. Senate seat on terms that would have made him beholden to railroad interests.

APPLETON, JOHN *(b Feb. 11, 1815, Beverly, Mass.; d Aug. 22, 1864, Portland, Me.).* Journalist, lawyer, diplomat, Maine Democrat. Chief clerk of Navy Department (1845-1848), minister to Bolivia (1848-1849), U.S. Representative (1851-1853), secretary of legation in London (1855), assistant secretary of state (1857-1860), minister to Russia (1860-1861).

APPLETON, JOHN *(b July 12, 1804, New Ipswich, N.H.; d Feb. 7, 1891, Bangor, Maine).* Associate justice of Maine Supreme Judicial Court (1852-1862); chief justice (1862-1883); responsible for many reforms in Maine's trial and court procedures.

APPLETON, NATHAN *(b Oct. 6, 1779, New Ipswich, N.H.; d July 14, 1861, Boston, Mass.).* Banker, textile manufacturer, Whig Representative from Massachusetts (1831-1833 and again, by appointment to fill a vacancy, four months in 1842); opened Waltham's first cotton mill; with Francis Cabot Lowell founded the textile city of Lowell; enlarged operations to Manchester, N.H., and Lawrence, Mass.; with associates introduced a new and lucrative principle to the American textile industry—power machinery and cheap female labor—and, as a congressman, fought for high tariffs to protect it.

ARCHER, BRANCH TANNER *(b 1790, Virginia; d Sept. 22, 1856, Texas).* Settled in Texas, member of commission with William H. Wharton and Stephen F. Austin sent to Washington in futile quest for recognition of the new Republic of Texas (1836) and aid in war with Mexico; supported Austin in unsuccessful effort to become first president of Texas; member of first Texas congress; secretary of war in cabinet of its second president, Mirabeau B. Lamar.

ARCHER, JOHN *(b May 5, 1741, Churchville, Md.; d Sept. 28, 1810, Churchville).* Physician, receiving first medical diploma issued on American continent upon graduation from the College of Philadelphia (1768); Maryland Democrat. Member of Revolutionary committee (1774-1776), delegate to first state constitutional convention (1776), state house of delegates (1777-1779), aide to General Anthony Wayne during war; presidential elector (1797-1801), U.S. Representative (1801-1807). Father of Stevenson Archer, Sr., grandfather of Stevenson Archer, Jr.

ARCHER, STEVENSON, SR. *(b Oct. 11, 1786, Churchville, Md.; d June 26, 1848, Churchville).* Lawyer, Maryland Democrat. State house of delegates (1809-1810), U.S. Representative (1811-1817, 1819-1821), appointed by President Madison to be U.S. judge and governor of Mississippi Territory (1817) but resigned after few months, chief justice of Maryland Court of Appeals (1844 until death). Son of John Archer.

ARCHER, STEVENSON, JR. *(b Feb. 28, 1827, Churchville, Md.; d Aug. 2, 1898, Bel Air, Md.).* Lawyer, Maryland Democrat. U.S. Representative (1867-1875).

ARCHER, WILLIAM SEGAR *(b March 5, 1789, Amelia County, Va.; d March 28, 1855, Amelia County).* Lawyer, Virginia Whig. U.S. Representative (1820-1835); U.S. Senate (1841-1847). As chairman of Senate Foreign Relations Committee he did much to bring about annexation of Texas. Relative of Branch Tanner Archer.

ARENTZ, SAMUEL SHAW *(b Jan. 8, 1879, Chicago, Ill.; d June 17, 1934, Reno, Nev.).* Mining engineer, rancher, Nevada Republican. U.S. Representative (1921-1923, 1925-1933), national convention delegate (1928, 1932).

ARMSTRONG, JOHN, SR. *(b Oct. 13, 1717, Ireland; d March 9, 1795, Carlisle, Pa.).* As a surveyor he laid out the town of Carlisle. British officer in Seven Years War, Yankee officer in Revolution, member of Continental Congress (1778-1780, 1787-1788).

ARMSTRONG, JOHN, JR. *(b Nov. 25, 1758, Carlisle, Pa.; d April 1, 1843, Red Hook, N.Y.).* Revolutionary officer who wrote "Newburgh Letters" protesting failure of troops to be paid; Pennsylvania secretary of state (1783-1787); U.S. Senator from New York (1800-1804); ambassador to France (1804-1810) including period when he doubled as minister to Spain (1806); secretary of war (1813-1814), forced to resign when British captured Washington.

ARMSTRONG, MOSES KIMBALL *(b Sept. 19, 1832, Milan, Ohio; d Jan. 11, 1906, Albert Lea, Minn.).* Surveyor, Dakota Territory Democrat. Went west as a young man, arriving in Minnesota Territory (1856) where he became Mower County surveyor assigned to survey U.S. lands and moving on to the Dakota Territory when Minnesota became thirty-second state (1858). Member of first territorial house of representatives (1861-1863), house speaker (1863), president of territorial council (1866-1867), secretary of Indian peace commission

(1867), member of territorial council again (1869), delegate to U.S. Congress (1871-1875). Established great meridian and standard lines for U.S. surveys in southern Dakota and the northern Red River Valley.

ARNOLD, ISAAC NEWTON *(b Nov. 30, 1815, Hartwick, N.Y.; d April 24, 1884, Chicago).* Lawyer, biographer-historian. Member Illinois House of Representatives (1842-1843); Democratic presidential elector for Polk (1844), delegate to Free-Soil convention (1848), Republican U.S. Representative (1861-1865), his hostility to slavery explaining his political shiftings. In Congress he saw passed (1862) his bill banning the use or ownership of slaves in any place subject to federal authority, and moved the amendment (1864) abolishing slavery in the United States. Literary works included *The History of Abraham Lincoln and the Overthrow of Slavery* (1866), *Life of Benedict Arnold* (1880), and he was nearing completion of *Life of Abraham Lincoln* when he died.

ARNOLD, JONATHAN *(b Dec. 3, 1741, Providence, R.I.; d Feb. 1, 1793, St. Johnsbury, Vt.).* Doctor-founder of the Revolutionary Army Hospital of Rhode Island and its surgeon (1776-1781); member of Rhode Island General Assembly (1776) that passed law, which he helped draft, repealing the oath of allegiance to England; delegate to Continental Congress (1782-1784), championed the Vermont cause in dispute with New Hampshire and New York, moved to Vermont in 1787 and founded the town in which he died. Father of Lemuel H. Arnold.

ARNOLD, LEMUEL HASTINGS *(b Jan. 29, 1792, St. Johnsbury, Vt.; d June 27, 1852, South Kingston, R.I.).* Lawyer, manufacturer. Member of Rhode Island House of Representatives (1826-1831), governor (1831-1832), member of executive council (1842-1843) during Dorr Rebellion (see Thomas W. Dorr), U.S.

Arnold, Marshall

Representative (1845-1847), being elected as a Liberation Whig. Son of Jonathan Arnold.

ARNOLD, MARSHALL *(b Oct. 21, 1845, Cook Settlement, Mo.; d June 12, 1913, Benton, Mo.).* Educator, lawyer, Missouri Democrat. State house of representatives (1877-1879), presidential elector (1880), U.S. Representative (1891-1895).

ARNOLD, PELEG *(b June 10, 1751, Providence, R.I.; d Feb. 13, 1820, Smithfield, R.I.).* Tavern keeper, lawyer, banker. Deputy to Rhode Island General Assembly (1777-1778, 1782-1783, 1817-1819), member of Continental Congress (1787-1789), assistant governor (1790), a founder of Providence Society for the Abolition of Slavery (1790), chief justice of state supreme court (1795-1809, 1810-1812).

ARNOLD, RICHARD DENNIS *(b Aug. 19, 1808, Savannah, Ga.; d July 10, 1876, in same room in which he was born).* A physician who was equally active in medicine and politics but confined the latter to the state and municipal arena. A founder (1846) and first secretary of the American Medical Association, he was the mayor who surrendered (1864) Savannah to General Sherman to prevent further bloodshed. Although he had been a secessionist, he then became a leader of Georgia's "peace party," going to Washington (1865) as head of a delegation seeking a provisional government for the state.

ARNOLD, SAMUEL GREENE *(b April 12, 1821, Providence, R.I.; d Feb. 14, 1880, Providence).* Historian, lawyer. Lieutenant governor of Rhode Island (1852, 1861, 1862), member of peace commission (Washington, D.C., 1861) that tried to avert Civil War, elected as a Republican to U.S. Senate to complete four-month term (Dec. 1, 1862-March 3, 1863) of incumbent who had resigned.

ARNOLD, THOMAS DICKENS *(b May 3, 1798, Spotsylvania County, Va.; d May 26, 1870, Jonesboro, Tenn.).* Lawyer, teacher, drummer boy in War of 1812, Tennessee Whig. U.S. Representative (1831-1833), surviving an assassination attempt on the Capitol steps and serving again (1841-1843), presidential elector (1840).

ARNOLD, WILLIAM WRIGHT *(b Oct. 4, 1877, Oblong, Ill.; d Nov. 23, 1957, Robinson, Ill.).* Lawyer, farmer, banker, Illinois Democrat. U.S. Representative (1923-1935), resigning to accept appointment to U.S. Board of Tax Appeals (1935-1950).

ARTHUR, CHESTER ALAN *(b Oct. 5, 1830—or 1829 according to family bible entry made public in 1972—Fairfield, Vt.; d Nov. 18, 1886, New York City).* Vice president (1881 until the death of President Garfield that same year), twenty-first president (1881-1885). Former New York Whig who helped organize his state's Republican party; lawyer; a handsome, six-foot, well-dressed machine politician who surprised many by becoming an honest, conscientious, and independent president.

Fifth child and oldest son of the seven children born to a Baptist clergyman, Arthur partially supported himself by teaching school while attending Union College at Schenectady, N.Y., from which he graduated in 1848. He continued teaching in order to support himself while he studied law. Admitted (1854) to the New York state bar. Staunchly antislavery, in 1855 he obtained a ruling that Negroes were to be treated the same as whites on New York City streetcars. He became a successful lawyer and opened his own New York City office in 1856. In 1859, Arthur married Ellen Lewis Herndon who bore him three children. (She died in 1880 and Arthur's sister, Mrs. John E. McElroy, served as mistress of the White House.)

Appointed by New York Governor Edwin D. Morgan to positions of engineer-in-chief, inspector-general, and quarter-master-general of the state. When Civil War broke out he was in charge of strengthening the defenses of the Port of New York and of equipping and maintaining the state's large number of army volunteers. In 1871, as a reward for his loyal support and in recognition of the important role he played in the Roscoe Conkling-bossed state machine, President Grant made Arthur Collector of the Port of New York. Since the Port with its large number of employees was one of the largest sources of political patronage in the country, when President Hayes took office, he zeroed in on Arthur as part of his move toward civil service reform and eventually (1878) he succeeded (in spite of Senator Conkling's intervention) in suspending him. Arthur was a delegate to the GOP National Convention (1880), where, in an attempt to restore party harmony, he was made presidential nominee Garfield's running mate. They were elected, and Arthur became President soon after (Sept. 19, 1881) when Garfield died from a gunshot wound inflicted by a mentally unbalanced assassin.

Although Arthur had subscribed to the spoils system in his New York State political career, as president he gave full support to the Civil Service Act passed in 1883, appointing able commissioners to administer it. In spite of embarrassment to the Republican party, he pressed for convictions in the scandalous star route cases in which kickbacks had been given for horse-drawn mail delivery contracts. He vetoed a "pork barrel" river and harbor appropriation bill, only to have Congress override his veto.

Arthur had lost favor with the Republican politicians who could have achieved his nomination at the 1884 convention. Although it has been assumed that he would have liked to succeed himself, papers have recently been discovered that indicate he spent much of his term in office with the secret knowledge that he was dying from a kidney ailment. He died in the year following his retirement.

ASH, MICHAEL WOOLSTON *(b March 5, 1789, Philadelphia, Pa.; d Dec. 14, 1858, Philadelphia).* Law partner of President Buchanan; U.S. Representative (1835-1837).

ASHBROOK, WILLIAM ALBERT *(b July 1, 1867, Johnstown, Ohio; d Jan. 1, 1940, Johnstown).* Newspaper publisher, banker, Ohio Democrat. Member state house of representatives (1904-1905), U.S. Representative (1907-1921, 1935 until death).

ASHE, JOHN *(b 1720, probably Grovely, N.C.; d October, 1781, Sampson County, N.C.).* Outspoken critic of British rule; speaker of North Carolina Assembly (1762-1765), led North Carolina opposition to Stamp Act; Whig member of the provincial congress and committees of correspondence and safety; foe of the Regulators, a vigilante-type antigovernment cabal that captured him (1771), tied him to a tree, and whipped him in vain effort to silence him; Revolutionary officer but a poor military tactician, losing the battle of Briar Creek (1778) which in turn led to the loss of Georgia to the British.

ASHE, JOHN BAPTISTA *(b 1748, Rocky Point, N.C.; d Nov. 27, 1802, Halifax, N.C.).* Committee chairman at North Carolina convention (1789) that ratified U.S. Constitution; field officer throughout Revolution, commanding North Carolina troops at Valley Forge; member of state house of commons (1784-1786) and speaker (1786), member of Continental Congress (1787), state senator (1789, 1795), Federalist member of First and Second U.S. Congresses (1789-1793), elected governor (1802) but died while waiting inauguration. Uncle of the younger John B. Ashe and of William S. Ashe.

ASHE, JOHN BAPTISTA *(b 1810, Rocky Point, N.C.; d Dec. 29, 1857, Galveston, Tex.)* Whig member of U.S. Congress from Tennessee (1843-1845), then migrated to Texas to practice law. Nephew of the elder John B. Ashe and brother of William S. Ashe.

ASHE, SAMUEL *(b 1725, Beaufort, N.C.; d Feb. 3, 1813, Rocky Point, N.C.).* Though for a time assistant attorney to the crown, became a staunch advocate of independence; chairman of North Carolina Council of Safety (1776) and one of twenty-four men who, in same year, drafted state constitution; senate speaker in first state legislature; presiding judge of first state supreme court; Jeffersonian governor (1795-1798) and an early advocate of states' rights. Grandfather of William S. Ashe.

ASHE, THOMAS SAMUEL *(b July 21, 1812, Graham, N.C.; d Feb. 4, 1887, Wadesboro, N.C.).* North Carolina lawyer but a Union man who later supported secession. Whig member of state house of commons (1842), solicitor (1847-1851), state senate (1854), Confederate house of representatives (1861-1864), U.S. Representative (1873-1877, first as a Conservative, then as a Democrat), member of judiciary committee that drew up articles of impeachment against Secretary of War William Worth Belknap and investigated Congressman James Gillespie Blaine; associate justice of North Carolina Supreme Court (1878 until death). Cousin of William S. Ashe.

ASHE, WILLIAM SHEPPERD *(b Aug. 12, 1813, Rocky Point, N.C.; d Sept. 14, 1862, Wilmington, N.C.).* North Carolina Democrat. President Wilmington & Weldon Railroad (1854 until death); presidential elector (1844) for James Polk; state senate (1846-1848, 1859-1861), U.S. Representative (1849-1855); national convention delegate (1860); Confederate Army transportation officer; killed riding hand car while rushing to

wounded soldier-son. Grandson of Samuel Ashe, nephew of North Carolina's John Baptista Ashe, brother of Tennessee's John Baptista Ashe, cousin of Thomas Samuel Ashe.

ASHLEY, JAMES MITCHELL *(b Nov. 14, 1824, near Pittsburgh, Pa.; d Sept. 16, 1896, Alma, Mich.).* Ran away from home at sixteen and educated self while working on Mississippi and Ohio river boats. Journalist, lawyer, railroad builder, one of country's earliest liberal Republicans.

Learned to hate slavery while accompanying father, a circuit-riding preacher in Virginia and Kentucky (later in life he was ordered out of Virginia for outspoken criticism) and witnessing treatment of slaves on river boats. At first a Democrat, the slavery issue drove him into the Free-Soil movement (1848) and then into the Republican Party (1854), helping to found the latter in Ohio where he had settled; delegate to GOP National Convention (1856) that nominated John C. Fremont; as U.S. Representative (1859-1869), was coauthor with Lot M. Morrill of Maine of bill (1862) to abolish slavery in District of Columbia; introduced (1863) antislavery amendment to Constitution, finally seeing it passed in 1865 (this he considered the greatest accomplishment of his life); instituted a move to have President Johnson impeached (1867); appointed territorial governor of Montana by President Grant, he served only about a year (1869-1870), then was removed for criticizing Grant's policies; delegate to Liberal Republican Convention (1872) and active supporter of Horace Greeley's presidential campaign; built Toledo, Ann Arbor & Northern Railroad and was its president (1877-1893).

ASHLEY, WILLIAM HENRY *(b 1778, Powhatan County, Va.; d March 26, 1838, near Boonville, Mo.).* As a fur trader, he blazed many new trails and did much to open the West. First lieutenant governor of Missouri (1820-1824),

Whig U.S. Representative (1831-1837) where he was a hard-line member of the Indian Affairs Committee.

ASHMORE, ROBERT THOMAS *(b Feb. 22, 1904, near Greenville, S.C.)*. Lawyer, South Carolina Democrat. Solicitor first of Greenville County Court (1930-1934), then South Carolina thirteenth judicial circuit (1936-1953), U.S. Representative (1953-1969), serving on the Administration and Judiciary committees.

ASHMUN, ELI PORTER *(b June 24, 1770, Blandford, Mass.; d May 10, 1819, Northampton, Mass.)*. Massachusetts State Senate (1808-1810, 113), member of governor's council (1816), U.S. Senate (1816-1818). Father of George Ashmun.

ASHMUN, GEORGE *(b Dec. 25, 1804, Blandford, Mass.; d July 16, 1870, Springfield, Mass.)*. Chairman of Republican National Convention (1860) that nominated Lincoln and, from then on, a close advisor of the Civil War president.

Member of Massachusetts House of Representatives (1833, 1835, 1836, 1838) and speaker (1841); state senator (1838-1839), Whig U.S. Representative (1845-1851), opposing war with Mexico and charging in a floor speech (July 27, 1846) that it "has been brought upon us by the men who are administering the offices of government [ed: Polk was president], in disregard of the principles of the Constitution and of their duties to the people of the country." When first shots of Civil War were fired, it was Ashmun who persuaded Stephen Douglas to call upon President Lincoln and pledge his support. Son of Eli P. Ashmun.

ASHURST, HENRY FOUNTAIN *(b Sept. 13, 1874, Winnemucca, Nev.; d May 31, 1962, Washington, D.C.)*. Lawyer, Arizona Democrat both as a territory and as a state. As a territory: territorial

house of representatives (1897, 1899), speaker (1899), territorial senate (1903), Coconino County prosecutor (1905-1908), chairman of constitutional convention (1911) that led to statehood. As a state: one of the first of two Arizonans (see Marcus A. Smith) to serve in the U.S. Senate, sent there by unanimous vote of the state assembly on March 27, 1912, and remained until Jan. 3, 1941; member of U.S. Immigration Appeals Board (1941-1943).

Born in a covered wagon enroute to the Arizona Territory, Ashurst went on to become one of the nation's most courtly of characters, starring in an arena, the U.S. Senate, where such traits are traditional. He was the embodiment of the traditional movie version of how a senator should look; in fact, in 1961 at the age of 86, he played the part in the film "Advise and Consent." But with Ashurst it was not a part. His everyday attire, no matter what the occasion, consisted of striped trousers, braided coat, winged collar, and corded spectacles; and when he rose to speak, the Senate chamber was soon packed with listeners hanging on his every word, if not on his inconsistencies.

That they did for two reasons: he knew by memory hundreds of quotations and he would weave them into his speeches with the skill of a Shakespearean actor, and he prided his ability to argue all sides of a question with equal eloquence, force, and conviction. In fact, he always kept on hand a supply of pamphlets explaining the need for and the virtue of being inconsistent. When one woman wrote to congratulate his stand on President Franklin D. Roosevelt's second term Supreme Court issue, he replied with a pamphlet and a one-line note: "Dear Madame: Which stand?"

Though a senator for twenty-seven years, many of them as chairman of the Judiciary Committee, Ashurst chose to pay more attention to purely Arizona issues than to national and international events, arguing that that was what the voters back home expected of him. In that he was consistent.

ASTOR, JOHN JACOB, III *(b June 10, 1822, New York City; d Feb. 22, 1890, New York City).* The first member of the several-generation capitalist family to delve into politics and that only briefly and ignobly, heading a committee of businessmen (1871) that supposedly investigated the doings of the Tweed Ring (see William Marcy Tweed) and then absolved it of all financial wrongdoings. Critics charged that this Astor was mainly concerned with protecting his real estate tax leniencies.

ASTOR, WILLIAM VINCENT *(b Nov. 15, 1891, New York City; d Feb. 3, 1959, New York City).* Son of John Jacob Astor IV, Vincent is considered to be the first member of the family ever to show a sincere and lasting interest in civic affairs—among other things, he shut down the Astors' vast slum holdings on the Lower East Side of New York. An early New Deal supporter of Franklin D. Roosevelt, he was active in the 1932 presidential campaign. Left half of his estimated $120 million estate to the Vincent Astor Foundation (1948) to "alleviate human misery."

ASWELL, JAMES BENJAMIN *(b Dec. 23, 1869, Vernon, La.; d March 16, 1931, Washington, D.C.).* Teacher, college president, Louisiana Democrat. As state superintendent of public education (1904-1908) he reorganized the public school system; ten terms as a U.S. Representative (1913 until death).

ATCHISON, DAVID RICE *(b Aug. 11, 1807, Frogtown, Ky.; d Jan. 26, 1886, Gower, Mo.).* A pro-slaver, he was considered while a U.S. Senator (1843-1855) to be Missouri's most powerful Democrat with the slave-owners of western Missouri providing his strongest support. In exchange, he promised to help establish territorial governments west of their holdings, advocating passage of the Kansas-Nebraska Bill (1853) and claiming credit for repeal of the Missouri Compromise.

Elected president pro tem of the Senate sixteen times, chairman of the Committee on Indian Affairs, supporter of land-grant legislation that would benefit Missouri railroads. Faded from politics after election defeat (1855) and became a leader of "Missouri border ruffians" in Kansas Territory raids (1855-1856). One biographer thus described him: "Although a Presbyterian, he indulged in intoxicants, in profanity, and in incitements to violence against the free-state settlers in Kansas." Yet both Atchison, Mo., and the city of Atchison, Kans., were named for him.

ATHERTON, CHARLES GORDON *(b July 4, 1804, Amherst, N.H.; d Nov. 15, 1853, Manchester, N.H.).* Lawyer, Jacksonian Democrat. Member New Hampshire House of Representatives (1830) and its speaker (1833-1835); U.S. Senate (1843-1849), chairman of its Finance Committee and member of Ways and Means Committee. A strict constructionist, he was a thorn in the side of abolitionists, contending that federal action on slavery would be an infringement on states' rights.

ATHERTON, JOSHUA *(b June 20, 1737, Harvard, Mass.; d April 3, 1809, Amherst, N.H.).* A tory lawyer at outset of Revolution, he was jailed from Aug. 21, 1777, to June 5, 1778, taking oath of allegiance to New Hampshire six months later. Delegate to state conventions (1784, 1788, 1792), at the second leading the opposition to adoption of the Federal Constitution because it did not prohibit slavery. Member state senate (1792-1793), state attorney general (1793-1797).

ATKINS, JOHN DeWITT CLINTON *(b June 4, 1825, Manly's Chapel, Tenn.; d June 2, 1908, Paris, Tenn.).* Farmer, Tennessee Democrat. U.S. Commissioner of Indian Affairs (1885-1888) to cap nearly a half-century in elective office both in the Confederacy and the Union. State house of representatives (1849-1851), state senate (1855-1857), presidential elector (1856 and again in 1884), U.S. Representative (1857-1859 and again, after the Civil War, 1873-1883), Confederate Provisional Congress (1861-1865).

ATKINSON, GEORGE WESLEY *(b June 29, 1845, Kanawha County, Va., [now W.Va.]; d April 4, 1925, Charleston, W.Va.).* Lawyer, journalist, lecturer, historian, West Virginia Republican. Charleston postmaster (1871-1877), U.S. marshal (1881-1885) gaining local fame for moonshine raids. U.S. Representative (1890-1891), governor (1897-1901), U.S. district attorney for southern district of West Virginia (1901-1905), associate judge of U.S. Court of Claims in Washington, D.C. (1905-1916).

ATKINSON, LOUIS EVANS *(b April 16, 1841, Delaware Township, Penn.; d Feb. 5, 1910, Mifflintown, Penn.).* Lawyer, Pennsylvania Republican. U.S. Representative (1883-1893).

ATKINSON, RICHARD MERRILL *(b Feb. 6, 1894, Nashville, Tenn.; d April 29, 1947, Nashville).* Lawyer, Tennessee Democrat. Smoky Mountain National Park commissioner (1931-1933), U.S. Representative (1937-1939).

ATKINSON, WILLIAM YATES *(b Nov. 11, 1854, Brunswick County, Va.; d Aug. 8, 1899, Newnan, Ga.).* Lawyer, two-term Democratic governor of Georgia (1894-1898), the first time becoming the first nonveteran in state to be so elected since the Civil War.

ATWATER, CALEB *(b Dec. 25, 1778, North Adams, Mass.; d March 13, 1867, Circleville, Ohio).* Lawyer, teacher, historian, author. During brief encounter with politics served (1821) in Ohio state legislature and then on Circleville

School Board (1824) where his innovations are credited with being the foundation of state's public education system; member of three-man presidential commission (1829) that negotiated treaties with Winnebago Indians in Wisconsin. Always more the scholar and the intellectual than the opportunist, he died a poor and publicly forgotten man.

ATWATER, JOHN WILBUR *(b Dec. 27, 1840, Rialto, N.C.; d July 4, 1910, Fearington, N.C.).* Joined North Carolina Farmers' Alliance (1887) and first president of Chatham County Alliance, elected Alliance Democrat state senator (1890) and again as a Populist (1892, 1896), Populist U.S. Representative (1899-1901).

ATWOOD, DAVID *(b Dec. 15, 1815, Bedford, N.H.; d Dec. 11, 1889, Madison, Wis.).* A newspaperman all his adult life, he founded the *Wisconsin State Journal* (1852) and so became an important factor in state politics while, however, never compromising his or the publication's journalistic integrity. Member of state assembly (1861); U.S. tax assessor in state's second congressional district (1862-1866), ousted when paper opposed President Andrew Johnson; mayor of Madison (1868-1869); Republican U.S. Representative (Feb. 1870-March 1871), completing term of deceased incumbent; delegate to GOP National Conventions in 1872 and 1876.

ATWOOD, HARRISON HENRY *(b Aug. 26, 1863, North Londonderry, Vt.; d Oct. 22, 1954, Boston, Mass.)* Architect, Massachusetts Republican. Delegate to two national conventions (1888 and 1892), U.S. Representative (1895-1897), state house of representatives (1887-1889, 1915, 1917, 1918, 1923, 1924, 1927, 1928).

AUCHINCLOSS, JAMES COATS *(b Jan. 19, 1885, New York City).* Stockbroker, New Jersey Republican who once was president of New York City's Better Business Bureau as well as being a deputy police commissioner there. Rumson, N.J., borough council (1930-1937), mayor (1938-1943), U.S. Representative (1943-1965).

AUF DER HEIDE, OSCAR LOUIS *(b Dec. 8, 1874, New York City; d March 29, 1945, West New York, N.J.).* Real estate broker, New Jersey Democrat. Member state assembly (1908-1911), mayor of West New York (1914-1917), Hudson County freeholder (1915-1924), U.S. Representative (1925-1935).

AUSTIN, ALBERT ELMER *(b Nov. 15, 1877, Medway, Mass.; d Jan. 26, 1942, Greenwich, Conn.).* Physician, teacher, banker. Connecticut Republican. Member state house of representatives (1917-1919, 1921-1923), U.S. Representative (1939-1941). Stepfather of Clare Boothe Luce.

AUSTIN, BENJAMIN, JR. *(b Nov. 18, 1752, Boston; d May 4, 1820, Boston).* A pamphleteer in the budding days of the new republic who signed himself Honestus and whose advocacy of reforms beneficial to the common man made him the prime enemy of Massachusetts' more moneyed class. His early position of objective opposition changed to stubborn intransigence in a long-lasting struggle. His 1786 articles, "Observations on the Pernicious Practice of the Law," were the beginning. In them Austin demanded, among other things, that the Commonwealth institute procedures somewhat akin to today's public defender system, thus doing away with much of the need of lawyers (whose abolishment he also advocated). Barristers responded with accusations that Austin was fomenting revolt and, in fact, blamed him for "Shay's Rebellion" of farmers that soon followed (see Daniel Shay). Then came a town meeting (1787) where Austin was elected a state senator and which John Quincy Adams later described as having

been packed with men, "who looked as if they had been collected from all the jails on the continent." Nevertheless, Austin was elected again in 1789 and served until 1794, a period in which he broadened his targets to include the federal administration and adopted the word "Democratic" to describe his following.

That following grew, matched every step of the way by Federalist opposition, to which Austin in his 1797 essay on "Constitutional Republicanism" gave this description: "Every attempt to restore the liberties of mankind, or to check the progress of arbitrary power is now styled Jacobinism." Brother of Jonathan L. Austin.

AUSTIN, JAMES TRECOTHICK *(b Jan. 10, 1784, Boston; d May 8, 1870, Boston).* Lawyer, writer, antiabolitionist who, to coin a phrase, considered slavery as American as apple pie. A factor in city and state politics, first as a Republican and then as a Whig, he held many offices including several terms as a state senator, Suffolk County attorney, town advocate, and attorney general. Probably best known for his speech likening the Alton, Ill., mob that four times wrecked the presses of journalist-abolitionist Elijah Parish Lovejoy to the Boston Tea Party patriots. Son of Jonathan L. Austin.

AUSTIN, JONATHAN LORING *(b Jan. 2, 1748, Boston; d May 10, 1826, Boston).* Revolutionary War messenger and emissary abroad; member of Massachusetts Senate (1801), house of representatives (1803-1806), state secretary (1806-1808), state treasurer (1811-1812). Brother of Benjamin Austin, Jr., but not nearly so controversial; father of James T. Austin.

AUSTIN, MOSES *(b Oct. 4, 1761, Durham, Conn.; d June 10, 1821).* Mine operator, merchant, manufacturer, banker in Virginia and Missouri, founder of Potosi, Mo. Wiped out by depression of 1819, obtained grant of Texas land from Spanish (January 1821) on which to establish a 300-family colony. Upon his death, son Stephen executed the plan.

AUSTIN, STEPHEN FULLER *(b Nov. 3, 1793, Wythe County, Va.; d Dec. 27, 1836, Tex.).* The man who founded Texas, beyond his father's (see Moses Austin) wildest dream. He managed a family lead mine in Missouri, was a director of the Bank of St. Louis, and member of the territorial legislature (1814-1820) when family was wiped out financially. Upon his father's death, began execution of father's Texas colonization plan, establishing (January 1822) an Anglo-American colony on the Gulf of Mexico between the Colorado and Brazos Rivers. When Mexico became independent of Spain, Stephen was sent to Mexico City to reaffirm his father's grant. He remained a year, returning with broad powers that until 1828 placed him in sole command of all official Texas functions, including the right to determine which settlers could remain and which must go. Thus, by 1825, his father's hoped-for 300 families were established in their new homes, including some with slaves, a situation that Stephen condoned, and land was set aside for, first, 900 families and then thousands to follow at a cost to each of $200 for a 4,428-acre tract.

Stephen's objective as expressed in a letter (1832) to a friend: "My ambition has been to succeed in redeeming Texas from its wilderness state by means of the plough alone, in spreading over it North American population, enterprise and intelligence; in doing this I hope to make the fortunes of thousands and my own amongst the rest."

A Texas convention (April 1833) delegated Austin to go to Mexico City to seek authority for the establishment of a separate Texas state government, a mission that landed him in jail on treason charges. Granted amnesty (July 1835) he returned to find Texas on the brink of armed revolt and, when the war came, was sent to Washington (December 1835) with William H. Wharton and Branch T. Archer to petition for aid and annexation. The mission failed and Austin returned to Texas in June 1836, was defeated for the presidency of the new Republic of Texas by Sam Houston in September, became secretary of state in October, and died in December.

AUSTIN, WARREN ROBINSON *(b Nov. 12, 1877, Highgate Center, Vt.; d Dec. 25, 1962, Burlington, Vt.).* Lawyer, statesman, Vermont Republican who climbed the political ladder from local affairs to United Nations Ambassador.

Politically, this was the route he followed: Franklin County state's attorney (1904-1906), U.S. commissioner (1907-1915), state GOP convention chairman (1908), mayor of St. Albans (1909), counsel for Vermont in boundary dispute with New Hampshire (1925-1937), delegate to three GOP National Conventions (1928, 1940, 1944), U.S. Senator (1931-1946).

Meantime he was showing a keen bent for international affairs, acquiring an early interest in his father's law office where he was counsel for an American cartel building canals, dams, and railroads in China, becoming a member (1917) of the U.S. Court for China.

Foreign policy and military affairs were his major specialties in the Senate and, as a participant in the Inter-American Conference on Problems of War and Peace (Mexico City, 1945), blueprinted a plan that became known as the Act of Chapultepec.

Austin was the acknowledged spokesman for the Republicans' internationalist bloc and so it was that, when the United Nations was founded, President Truman, a Democrat, appointed him to represent the United States, thus symbolizing this country's bipartisan support of the infant peace organization.

Austin, though the Senate's GOP whip at the time, readily accepted.

He was chairman of the committee that guided construction of UN headquarters in New York City, wrote the legislation and executive order establishing the Permanent U.S. Mission to the United Nations, and, in the Security Council, argued this country's position on such issues as the Berlin blockade, the war in Korea, and establishment of the Israeli republic.

AVERY, BENJAMIN PARKE *(b Nov. 11, 1828, New York City; d Nov. 8, 1875, Peking, China).* Journalist, diplomat. Sailed around Cape Horn (1849) to strike it rich in California gold fields, did not and established (1854) instead the *Hydraulic Press,* a Republican, anti-slavery weekly in North San Juan, a decidedly hostile community. His next stop (1860) was Marysville where, with Noah Brooks, he founded *The Appeal,* California's first daily newspaper outside of San Francisco, became state printer (1861-1863), then moved on to San Francisco where he was editor of *The Bulletin* for the next ten years. In 1874 President Grant appointed him minister to China, which was then on the verge of war with Japan; he helped negotiate an accord and remained the U.S. representative in Peking until his death.

AVERY, ISSAC WHEELER *(b May 2, 1837, St. Augustine, Fla.; d Sept. 8, 1897, Georgia).* Active politically in Georgia during Reconstruction but never sought nor held office other than as a delegate to Democratic National Convention (1872); author of the primarily political *History of the State of Georgia from 1850 to 1881;* editor in chief of the *Atlanta Constitution* for several years.

AVERY, WILLIAM WAIGSTILL *(b May 25, 1816, Burke County, N.C.; d July 3, 1864, Morganton, N.C.).* States' rights North Carolina legislator (1842, 1850,

1852, 1856, 1860) and political leader whose career was cut short by a Yankee bullet in a Civil War battle; chairman of state's delegation to Democratic National Convention (1860); a prime mover for secession when Lincoln won election; member of Confederate Provisional Congress. Two brothers also died in war.

AXTELL, SAMUEL BEACH *(b Oct. 14, 1819, Columbus, Ohio; d Aug. 6, 1891, Morristown, N.J.).* A lawyer who went west to find gold, instead found politics to his liking in: California where he was a member of the U.S. Congress (1867-1871), entering a Democrat and emerging a Republican; Utah Territory where he was sent by President Grant as governor (1874-1875); and New Mexico Territory, again as a Grant-appointed governor (1875-1878), becoming chief justice of the territory's supreme court (1882-1885) and then chairman of the Republican Territorial Committee. They added up to about twenty turbulent years, with miners fighting claim-jumpers in California, non-Mormons fighting Mormons in Utah, and cattlemen fighting each other, plus sundry bad men, in New Mexico. Example: during a criminal trial in Las Vegas, N. Mex., Axtell ordered everyone in the courtroom frisked; the search produced forty-two six-shooters. He died in New Jersey while on a peace-and-quiet-seeking vacation.

AYCOCK, CHARLES BRANTLEY *(b Nov. 1, 1859, Wayne County, N.C.; d April 4, 1912, Raleigh, N.C.).* Lawyer, North Carolina Democrat. The youngest of ten children, he had to struggle for an education, a fact that he did not forget when he occupied the statehouse (1901-1905) and quickly became known as the "education governor." He is credited with opening on the average of one schoolhouse a day, extending the school term to four months, raising the average $25 monthly salary of teachers to somewhere near a living wage, and generally improving curricula. While education had been one of two main planks in his campaign platform, on the other side of the coin was a white supremacy promise. And so, as governor, Aycock brought about enactment of a voter-literacy law, thus effectively depriving most Negroes of access to the ballot.

AYER, RICHARD SMALL *(b Oct. 9, 1829, Montville, Maine; d Dec. 14, 1896, Liberty, Maine).* Farmer, merchant. Settled in Virginia (1865), delegate to state constitutional convention (1867), Republican U.S. Representative (1870-1871). Returned to Maine and served in state house of representatives (1888).

AYERS, ROY ELMER *(b Nov. 9, 1882, Lewistown, Mont.; d May 23, 1955, Lewistown).* Lawyer, rancher, Montana Democrat. U.S. Representative (1933-1937), governor (1937-1941), delegate to two Democratic National Conventions (1920, 1940), all state conventions (1906-1940).

AYRES, STEVEN BECKWITH *(b Oct. 27, 1861, Fort Dodge, Iowa; d June 1, 1929, New York City).* Journalist, author, historian. Upstate New York Republican, downstate New York Democrat. Delegate to GOP state convention from Yates County (1884), Independent Democrat U.S. Representative from New York City (1911-1913).

AYRES, WILLIAM AUGUSTUS *(b April 19, 1867, Elizabethtown, Ill.; d Feb. 17, 1952, Washington, D.C.).* Lawyer, Kansas Democrat. U.S. Representative (1915-1921, 1923-1934), resigned to accept appointment to Federal Trade Commission (1934 until death).

B

☆ ☆ ☆

BABBITT, ELIJAH *(b July 29, 1795, Providence, R.I.; d Jan. 9, 1887, Erie, Pa.).* Pennsylvania lawyer. Erie County prosecutor (1833), deputy state attorney general (1834-1835), state house of representatives (1836-1837), state senate (1843-1846), U.S. Representative as a Unionist (1859-1861), as a Republican (1861-1863).

BABCOCK, JOSEPH WEEKS *(b March 6, 1850, Swanton, Vt.; d April 27, 1909, Washington, D.C.).* Lumberman, Wisconsin Republican. State assembly (1889-1893), U.S. Representative (1893-1907), chairman of GOP Congressional Campaign Committee (1894-1902) covering a period in which the majority on the Hill swung from Democratic to Republican.

BABCOCK, ORVILLE E. *(b Dec. 25, 1835, Franklin, Vt.; d June 2, 1884, Mosquito Inlet, Fla., by drowning).* West Point graduate, aide to General Ulysses S. Grant during Civil War, his private secretary when Grant became president. In the latter capacity he was involved with the infamous Whiskey Ring that was conceived in the time of President Andrew Johnson and grew to giant proportions under Grant. The conspiracy bilked the U.S. government out of millions of dollars in liquor taxes and resulted in the indictment of more than 350 distillers, revenue agents, and other government officials, including Colonel Babcock. He was tried for "conspiracy to defraud the revenue" (1876) and pronounced not guilty.

BABKA, JOHN JOSEPH *(b March 16, 1884, Cleveland, Ohio; d March 22, 1937, Cleveland).* Lawyer, Ohio Democrat. Special counsel to state attorney general (1911-1912), assistant Cuyahoga County prosecutor (1912-1919), U.S. Representative (1919-1921), national convention delegate (1920-1932).

BACHARACH, ISAAC *(b Jan. 5, 1870, Philadelphia; d Sept. 5, 1956, Atlantic City, N.J.).* Realty-insurance broker, New Jersey Republican. Atlantic City council (1905-1910), state assembly (1911), national convention delegate (1920), eleven terms as a U.S. Representative (1915-1937).

BACHE, BENJAMIN FRANKLIN *(b Aug. 12, 1769, Philadelphia, Pa.; d Sept. 10, 1798, Philadelphia).*
  The birth of the nation brought with it the birth of partisan politics and an era of partisan-political journalism and newspaper warfare that had the grandson of Benjamin Franklin as one of its fiercest participants. Franklin left him a printing house in Philadelphia and that was the beginning. There Bache, who quickly earned for himself the nickname Lightning Rod, Junior, published the *General Advertiser,* beginning in 1790, and about the only thing that he

36

did in the next eight years that did not invite robust retort and at least one beating was to change its name to *Aurora.*

Before he fell victim, at the age of twenty-nine, to a yellow fever epidemic that swept Philadelphia, Bache had become an ardent advocate of Jeffersonian Republicanism, accused President George Washington of overdrawing his salary, published the secret text of the Jay Treaty with England, been arrested under the Sedition Act for allegedly libeling President John Adams. Son of Richard Bache.

BACHE, RICHARD *(b 1737, Settle, England; d July 29, 1811, Philadelphia).* Merchant, Pennsylvania Whig. The husband of Benjamin Franklin's daughter, Sarah, and father of Benjamin Franklin Bache. During the Revolution served on Board of War, Committee on Non-Importation Agreements, and Committee of Correspondence; succeeded Franklin as postmaster general (1774-1782).

BACHMAN, NATHAN LYNN *(b Aug. 2, 1878, Chattanooga, Tenn.; d April 23, 1937, Washington, D.C.).* Lawyer, Tennessee Democrat. Chattanooga city attorney (1906-1908), Hamilton County Circuit Court judge (1912-1918), associate justice of state supreme court (1918-1924), U.S. Senate (1933 until death).

BACHMANN, CARL GEORGE *(b May 14, 1890, Wheeling, W. Va.).* Lawyer, banker, West Virginia Republican. Ohio County assistant prosecuting attorney (1917-1921), prosecuting attorney (1921-1925), GOP state conventions (1920-1940), national conventions (1936-1952), U.S. Representative (1925-1933), Wheeling city council (1939-1941), state liquor control commission (1941-1944), mayor (1947-1951).

BACON, AUGUSTUS OCTAVIUS *(b Oct. 20, 1839, Bryan County, Ga.; d Feb. 14, 1914, Washington, D.C.).* Lawyer, Confederate Army officer, Georgia Democrat. Seymour-Blair presidential elector (1868), state house of representatives (1871-1886), eight of the years as speaker, president of Democratic state convention (1880), delegate to national convention (1884), U.S. Senate (1894 until death) twice being chosen by the Georgia General Assembly and, upon enactment of the Seventeenth Amendment, becoming the first U.S. Senator to be elected by direct vote of the people.

As one of the Senate's great debaters and Foreign Relations Committee member (becoming chairman in 1913), Bacon led the successful fight against acquisition of the Philippine Islands ("the purpose of the United States is not permanently to retain the islands, but to give the people thereof their liberty") and took an active part in argument over such other issues as the Dingley and the Payne-Aldrich tariff bills. Upon his death, his colleagues honored him by conducting funeral services in the Senate chambers.

BACON, EZEKIEL *(b Sept. 1, 1776, Boston; d Oct. 18, 1870, Utica, N.Y.).* Lawyer, Massachusetts and New York Democrat. In Massachusetts: State house of representatives (1805-1806), U.S. Representative (1807-1813), chief justice of Common Pleas Court in state's western district (1811-1814), first comptroller of the U.S. Treasury (1814-1815). In New York: associate justice of Oneida County's Common Pleas Court (1818), state assembly (1819), delegate to state constitutional convention (1821). Son of John Bacon, father of William J. Bacon.

BACON, HENRY *(b March 14, 1846, Brooklyn, N.Y.; d March 25, 1915, Goshen, N.Y.).* Lawyer, New York Democrat. U.S. Representative (1886-1889, 1891-1893), national convention delegate (1892), Goshen corporation counsel (1909-1915).

BACON, JOHN *(b April 5, 1738, Canterbury, Conn.; d Oct. 25, 1820, Stockbridge, Mass.).* Clergyman, lawyer, Massachusetts Democrat. Studied theology at Princeton, became pastor of Boston's Old South Church (1771-1775), leaving by request because of differences with parishioners on meaning of word "patriotism," relocated in Stockbridge where he studied law and was admitted to the bar. Thus began thirty years of political and judicial service: delegate to state constitutional convention (1779, 1780), member of state house of representatives (1780, 1783, 1784, 1786, 1789-1791, 1793), state senate (1781-1782, 1794-1796, 1798, 1803-1806), senate president (1806), U.S. Representative (1801-1803), Jefferson-Clinton presidential elector (1804), associate judge of the Berkshire County Common Pleas Court (1779-1807) and its presiding judge (1807-1811), chief justice of state supreme court (1809).

In the year prior to Bacon's constitutional convention participation, the delegates had submitted to public referendum a document that included a clause that would exclude "Negroes, Indians and Molattoes" from voting. The constitution was rejected by the people with Bacon, displaying convictions similar to those that had led to his ouster from the Old South Church pulpit, vigorously arguing that the restrictive clause would justify people of color "in making the same opposition against us which we are making against Great Britain." As a result, the 1780 convention drafted a constitution that granted the right to vote to everyone and it was approved by the people. Father of Ezekiel Bacon.

BACON, LEONARD *(b Feb. 12, 1802, Detroit, Mich.; d Dec. 24, 1881, New Haven, Conn.).* Clergyman, church historian, editor, Connecticut Free-Soiler.

Bacon's world was theology, not politics, but in the latter he made a major contribution through his efforts to drive slavery from the land. It began when he was a schoolboy in Ohio and was part of a discussion group that included John Brown, then a student in a neighboring town, and continued through forty-one years in the pulpit of New Haven's First Church (1825-1866).

His written works included "On the Black Population of the United States" (1823), "Slavery Discussed in Occasional Essays" (1846), and editorials in the *Independent,* a Free-Soil newspaper of which he was a cofounder (1848) and senior editor.

Bacon's championship of the black man's cause brought stiff opposition from many sources, including extreme abolitionists whose tactics he abhorred. But he was well able to hit back, so much so that he became known throughout New England as the Fighting Parson. When the antislavery fight was won, Bacon wrote: "I make no complaint. All reproaches, all insults endured in a conflict with so gigantic a wickedness against God and man, are to be received and remembered not as injuries but as honors."

BACON, ROBERT LAW *(b July 23, 1884, Boston, Mass.; d Sept. 12, 1938, Lake Success, N.Y.).* Banker, New York Republican. Delegate to national convention (1920), eight terms as a U.S. Representative (1923 until death).

BACON, WILLIAM JOHNSON *(b Feb. 18, 1803, Williamstown, Mass.; d July 3, 1889, Utica, N.Y.).* Lawyer, New York Republican. Utica city attorney (1837), state assembly (1850), state supreme court judge in fifth district (1854-1870), U.S. Representative (1877-1879). Son of Ezekiel Bacon.

BADEAU, ADAM *(b Dec. 29, 1831, New York City; d March 19, 1895, Ridgewood, N.J.).* Author, diplomat, friend and aide of Ulysses S. Grant both in war and peace. U.S. consul general in London (1870-1881), consul general in Havana (1882-1884). Helped Grant write his memoirs; author of the three-volume *Military History of Ulysses S. Grant* (1868-1881) and *Grant in Peace* (1887) which did not hesitate to explore his presidential shortcomings.

BADGER, DeWITT CLINTON *(b Aug. 7, 1858, Madison County, Ohio; d May 20, 1926, Columbus, Ohio).* Teacher, lawyer, Ohio Democrat. Madison County prosecutor (1882-1885), Common Pleas Court judge (1893-1903), U.S. Representative (1903-1905), mayor of Columbus (1906-1908).

BADGER, GEORGE EDMUND *(b April 17, 1795, New Bern, N.C.; d May 11, 1866, Raleigh, N.C.).* One of North Carolina's great lawyers with a reputation as scholar, statesman, humorist, and orator; made the political transition from Federalist to Whig to the founding of the short-lived Constitutional Union party; also a man who knew the meaning of the word *compromise,* a fact that he evidenced throughout his career. State house of commons (1816), superior court judge (1820-1825), secretary of navy under two presidents—Harrison, who died a month after inauguration, and Tyler—in the short span of six months (March 5, 1841-Sept. 11, 1841), U.S. Senate (1846-1855) where among a great many other things he opposed the Wilmot Proviso banning slavery in the southwestern and California lands newly won from Mexico, yet upheld the proviso's constitutionality; went along with all of the Compromises of 1850 that were meant to resolve differences between South and North but insisted on the continuation of slavery in the District of Columbia; and turned thumbs down on the "squatter sovereignty" theory on the question of slavery, yet voted approval of the Kansas-Nebraska Act.

Nominated by President Fillmore (1853) to be an associate justice of the U.S. Supreme Court. His colleagues in the Senate refused confirmation, yet when he retired two years later the

same colleagues paid him an unusual tribute by unanimously adopting a resolution of regret. Delegate to state secession convention (1861) where he offered as an alternative a declaration of independence but accepted the will of the majority when secession carried.

BAER, GEORGE, JR. *(b 1763, Frederick, Md.; d April 3, 1834, Frederick).* Merchant, Maryland Federalist. State house of delegates (1794, 1808, 1809), U.S. Representative (1797-1801, 1815-1817), Frederick County Orphans' Court judge (1813), mayor of Frederick (1820).

BAGBY, ARTHUR PENDLETON *(b 1794, Louise County, Va.; d Sept. 21, 1858, Mobile, Ala., in a yellow fever epidemic).* Lawyer, Alabama National Republican turned Jackson Democrat. Backpacked from Virginia to Alabama (1818), state house of representatives (1821, 1822, 1824, 1834-1836), speaker (1822, 1836), state senate (1825), governor (1837-1841), U.S. Senate (1841-1848), minister to Russia (June 17, 1848-May 14, 1849), member of committee to codify Alabama state laws (1852).

BAILEY, CLEVELAND MONROE *(b July 15, 1886, Pleasants County, W.Va.; d July 13, 1965 Charleston, W.Va.).* Teacher, Associated Press editor (1923-1933), West Virginia Democrat. Clarksburg district supervisor of schools (1919-1922), Clarksburg councilman (1921-1923), Democratic National Convention delegate (1932), assistant state auditor (1933-1941), state budget director (1941-1944), state tax statistician (1947, 1948), U.S. Representative (1945-1947, 1949-1963) and a member of the Education and Labor Committee and a leader in efforts to legislate federal aid for public schools.

BAILEY, DAVID JACKSON *(b March 11, 1812, Lexington, Ga.; d June 14, 1897, Griffin, Ga.).* Lawyer, States' Rights Democrat. Elected to state legislature (1831) but not seated because he was under age, so he tried again and again, quite successfully: state house of representatives (1835, 1847), state senate (1838, 1849, 1850, 1855, 1856), secretary of the state senate (1839-1841), U.S. Representative (1851-1855), delegate to state secession convention (1861).

BAILEY, GAMALIEL *(b Dec. 3, 1807, Mount Holly, N.J.; d June 5, 1859, at sea).* Sailor, physician, journalist, adventurer, abolitionist, and one of the mightiest pens in the antislavery movement.

Stranded in Cincinnati, Bailey somehow attended the Lane Seminary missionary-student debate on colonization versus abolition which went on for nine days in 1834 and came away convinced that slavery was the greatest of all evils. In 1836 he became the editor and then the publisher of the *Cincinnati Philanthropist,* the West's first abolitionist journal, succeeding James G. Birney. Despite repeated mob attacks that three times left him with wrecked plant and presses, Bailey expanded it (1843) into a daily, *The Herald.* Then, answering a higher abolitionist call, he moved on to Washington, D.C., to edit the American Anti-Slavery Society's new weekly publication, *The National Era* (1847 until death).

Again Bailey faced angry mobs many times, in 1848 facing one down when for three days it besieged his plant. The *Era,* with its nationwide circulation, became required reading for virtually every member of the Senate and House. It often was quoted in debate and is credited with influencing many decisions.

Taken ill, Bailey died aboard ship while enroute to Europe to seek medical attention.

BAILEY, JOHN MOSHER *(b Aug. 24, 1838, Bethlehem, N.Y.; d Feb. 21, 1916, Albany, N.Y.).* Lawyer, New York Republican. Albany County assistant district attorney (1865-1867), collector of internal revenue, (1871-1874), Albany County district attorney (1874-1877), U.S. Representative (1878-1881), U.S. consul to Hamburg, Germany (1881-1885), delegate to GOP National Convention (1888), surveyor of customs in Albany (1889-1894).

BAILEY, JOSEPH *(b March 18, 1810, Pennsbury Township, Pa.; d Aug. 26, 1885, Bailey Station, Pa.).* Hatter, lawyer, Pennsylvania Democrat. State house of representatives (1840), state senate (1843, 1851-1853), state treasurer (1854), U.S. Representative (1861-1865), delegate to state constitutional convention (1872).

BAILEY, JOSEPH WELDON, SR. *(b Oct. 6, 1862, Copiah County, Miss.; d April 13, 1929, Sherman, Tex.).* Democrat noted as a constitutional lawyer and orator who opposed, with equal vigor: Woodrow Wilson, U.S. entry into World War I, women's suffrage, prohibition, and the Ku Klux Klan. In his later years the elder statesman of Texas politics.

In Mississippi: Cleveland-Hendricks presidential elector (1884). In Texas: Cleveland-Thurman elector (1888), five terms as a U.S. Representative (1891-1901), offered a seat on the U.S. Supreme Court bench by President Taft but declined (1909), U.S. Senate (1901-1913) resigning as a symbol of protest against the incoming president, Wilson, and resuming the practice of law with Washington as his base so that he could more effectively speak out against Wilson policies; returned to Texas after the war and unsuccessfully ran for governor (1920); led state fight against the Klan (1924).

Through many of all those years an intrastate battle that came to be known as the Bailey Controversy raged: the accusation, that Bailey used his office to promote the interests of an oil company doing business in Texas; the explanation, that while he may have been a friend of the company, its affairs were purely local and in no way involved either his seat in the Senate or the House.

BAILEY, JOSEPH WELDON, JR. *(b Dec. 15, 1892, Gainesville, Tex.; d July 17, 1943, in Gainesville military hospital).* Lawyer, Texas Democrat. Delegate to state party conventions (1922-1934), U.S. Representative (1933-1935), unsuccessful candidate for U.S. Senate (1934), Marine Corps captain (May 13, 1942, until death).

BAILEY, JOSIAH WILLIAM *(b Sept. 14, 1873, Warrenton, N.C.; d Dec. 15, 1946, Raleigh, N.C.).* Lawyer, North Carolina Democrat. State board of agriculture (1896-1900), Bryan-Kern presidential elector (1908), collector of internal revenue for North Carolina (1913-1921), state constitution commission (1915), U.S. Senate (1931 until death).

BAILEY, WILLIS JOSHUA *(b Oct. 12, 1854, Mount Carroll, Ill.; d May 19, 1932, Mission Hills, Kans.).* Farmer, stockman, banker, Kansas Republican who founded the town of Baileyville. State house of representatives (1888-1890), president of Republican State League (1893), state board of agriculture (1895-1899), U.S. Representative (1899-1901), governor (1903-1905).

BAIRD, JOSEPH EDWARD *(b Nov. 12, 1865, Perrysburg, Ohio; d June 14, 1942, Bowling Green, Ohio).* Land broker, Ohio Republican. Wood County clerk (1894-1900), mayor of Bowling Green (1902-1905), postmaster (1910-1914), secretary of state Public Utilities Commission (1921-1923), assistant secretary of state (1923-1929), U.S. Representative (1929-1931).

BAIRD, SAMUEL THOMAS *(b May 5, 1861, Oak Ridge, La.; d April 22, 1899, Washington, D.C.).* Lawyer, Louisiana Democrat. Sixth judicial district attorney (1884-1888), district judge (1888-1892),

state senate (1896), national convention (1896), U.S. Representative (1897 until death).

BAKER, CHARLES SIMEON *(b Feb. 18, 1839, Churchville, N.Y.; d April 21, 1902, Washington, D.C.).* Teacher, lawyer, New York Republican. State assembly (1879-1882), state senate (1884, 1885), U.S. Representative (1885-1891).

BAKER, EDWARD DICKINSON *(b Feb. 24, 1811, London, England; d Oct. 21, 1861, in Battle of Balls Bluff, Va.).* Lawyer, orator, citizen-soldier. Brought to United States as a boy, he began the practice of law in Springfield, Ill., where he became one of a group of outstandingly bright young attorneys, among them Abraham Lincoln and Stephen Douglas, to launch a career that spanned three states before it was cut short by war.

In Illinois: State house of representatives (1837), state senate (1840-1844), defeated Lincoln for the Whig congressional nomination (1844), was elected and served until Jan. 15, 1847, when he resigned to command an infantry regiment in the Mexican War. At war's end, Baker moved to Galena and three weeks later was again elected a U.S. Representative (1849-1851), this time as a Republican in a heavily Democratic district. In 1852 he moved to California, a silver-voiced Republican turned loose in a Democratic state. Nevertheless, he quickly was in demand both as a speaker and as a lawyer in the defense of unpopular causes.

Seven years later, in 1859, came an unusual honor: a delegation sent by a coalition of Republicans and Douglas Democrats from the new state of Oregon called upon him in San Francisco to ask him to run against Joseph Lane for the U.S. Senate. Baker accepted and won and so served from Oct. 2, 1860, until his death a year later. Very quickly he became a close adviser to Lincoln, then the president-elect, on a strategy for holding the Pacific states in the Union.

April 19, 1861, five days after the fall of Fort Sumter, Senator Baker was one of the principal speakers at a gigantic rally in New York City's Union Square. There he began to raise a regiment of volunteers, and it was as a major general of volunteers that Baker died with 920 of his men at Balls Bluff.

BAKER, HOWARD HENRY *(b Jan. 12, 1902, Somerset, Ky.; d Jan. 7, 1964, Knoxville, Tenn.).* Lawyer, banker, rail executive, Tennessee Republican. State representative (1929, 1930), attorney general of nineteenth judicial circuit (1934-1948), unsuccessful candidate for governor (1938) and U.S. Senate (1940), GOP National Conventions (1940, 1948, 1952, 1956), U.S. Representative (1951-1964), member of Ways and Means Committee.

BAKER, JAMES HEATON *(b May 6, 1829, Monroe, Ohio; d May 25, 1913, Blue Earth County, Minn.).* Journalist, historian, Republican. Ohio secretary of state (1855-1857), Minnesota secretary of state (1859-1861), U.S. commissioner of pensions (1871-1873), surveyor-general of Minnesota (1875-1879).

BAKER, JEHU *(b Nov. 4, 1822, Fayette County, Ky.; d March 1, 1903, Belleville, Ill.).* Journalist, scholar, lawyer, Illinois Republican who gained repute as a "radical" because of his forceful criticism of President Andrew Johnson whose impeachment he strongly advocated. Master in Chancery in St. Clair County (1861-1865), U.S. Representative (1865-1869, 1887-1889, and 1897-1899 as a Fusionist), minister to Venezuela (1878-1881, 1882-1885).

BAKER, JOHN HARRIS *(b Feb. 28, 1832, Parma Township, N.Y.; d Oct. 21, 1915, Goshen, Ind.).* Teacher, lawyer, Indiana Republican. U.S. Representative (1875-1881), national convention (1888), U.S. district court judge for Indiana (1892-1904).

BAKER, LUCIEN *(b June 8, 1846, Fulton County, Ohio; d June 21, 1907, Leavenworth, Kans.).* Lawyer, Kansas Republican. Leavenworth city attorney (1872-1874), state senate (1893-1895), U.S. Senate (1895-1901).

BAKER, NEWTON DIEHL *(b Dec. 3, 1871, Martinsburg, W.Va.; d Dec. 25, 1937, Shaker Heights, Ohio).* Lawyer, scholar, orator, Ohio Democrat. Secretary to U.S. postmaster general (1896-1897), Cleveland city solicitor (1901-1911), mayor of Cleveland (1912-1915); delegate to national convention (1912) where his successful floor fight against Ohio unit rule brought nineteen nominating votes into the Woodrow Wilson column; U.S. secretary of war under Wilson (1916-1921), years that spanned U.S. participation in World War I.

In municipal affairs, Baker gained renown as one of the nation's most enlightened mayors. He instituted many municipal reforms and programs, not the least among them the opening of three-cent dancehalls to give Cleveland's youth something to do at night other than roam the city streets.

As secretary of war, he went about his duties unruffled by criticism from all sides. Militarists called him a pacifist because of his membership in the League to Enforce Peace, pacifists wanted him impeached for giving in to the militarists, members of his own party thought he should be impeached for flouting legalities to get things done, members of the opposition wanted him impeached for moving too slowly. But Baker let the record speak for itself, ordering pursuit of Pancho Villa into Mexico (1916), increasing U.S. armed forces from 95,000 to 4 million, guiding the expenditure of $15 billion, backing General Pershing to the hilt.

The war over, he fought for the League of Nations and against U.S. isolationism, loomed as a dark horse nominee at the 1932 Democratic presidential convention, fought President Roosevelt on the constitutionality of the

Tennessee Valley Authority, and served on the Permanent Court of International Justice at The Hague.

BALDWIN, ABRAHAM *(b Nov. 2, 1754, North Guilford, Conn.; d March 4, 1807, Washington, D.C.).* Minister, lawyer, educator who taught at Yale before going south to Georgia where he helped institute a statewide educational system, became known as the father of the University of Georgia, and was one of the state's most astute political figures; nationally a Jeffersonian Democratic-Republican and a foe of helter-skelter legislative haste ("Take care, hold the wagon back; there is more danger of its running too fast than of its going too slow.").

Revolutionary Army chaplain (1777-1783), Georgia House of Representatives (1785), Continental Congress (1785, 1787-1789), U.S. constitutional convention delegate (1787) where he framed the compromise proviso that members of the U.S. House of Representatives be chosen by population of their states and that each state have two senators, member of the lower house in the first five U.S. Congresses (1789-1799), U.S. Senate (1799 until death), twice its president pro tem. Baldwin County, Ga., is named for him; half-brother of Henry Baldwin.

BALDWIN, HARRY STREETT *(b Aug. 21, 1894, Baldwin, Md.; d Oct. 19, 1952, Baltimore).* Farmer, Maryland Democrat. State house of delegates (1931), member of Baltimore County Board of Commissioners (1934-1942, 1950 until death), board president (1938-1942), U.S. Representative (1943-1947), unsuccessful gubernatorial candidate (1946).

BALDWIN, HENRY *(b Jan. 14, 1780, New Haven, Conn.; d April 21, 1844, Philadelphia, Pa.)* Lawyer, manufacturer, Pennsylvania Federalist. U.S. Representative (1817-1822), associate justice of U.S. Supreme Court (1830 until

death). Neither a liberal nor a constructionist, this half-brother of Abraham Baldwin dissented in seven cases in 1831 alone and many times more cast the deciding vote in his fourteen years as a jurist. A nonconformist in his personal life as well, he displayed many traits that some people considered odd, such as always carrying candy to pass out to children on the street.

BALDWIN, HENRY ALEXANDER *(b Jan. 12, 1871, Paliuli, Hawaii; d Oct. 8, 1946, Paia, Hawaii).* Sugar planter, banker, Territory of Hawaii Republican. Territorial senate (1913-1921, 1934-1937, the last session as president), delegate to U.S. Congress (1922-1923) to fill a vacancy. Hawaii House of Representatives (1933).

BALDWIN, HENRY PORTER *(b Feb. 22, 1814, Coventry, R.I.; d Dec. 31, 1892, Detroit, Mich.).* Merchant, banker, Michigan Republican. Delegate to state convention (1854) that resulted in formation of Michigan GOP, state senate (1861-1862), governor (1869-1873), delegate to national presidential convention (1876), U.S. Senate (1879-1881) to fill a vacancy.

BALDWIN, JOHN DENISON *(b Sept. 28, 1809, North Stonington, Conn.; d July 8, 1883, Worcester, Mass.).* Minister, journalist, Republican. Connecticut House of Representatives (1847-1852) when he was a newspaperman in Hartford; then, as a newspaperman in Worcester, delegate to national presidential convention (1860) where he proposed Hannibal Hamlin as Lincoln's vice presidential running mate, U.S. Representative (1863-1869).

BALDWIN, JOHN FINLEY, JR. *(b June 28, 1915, Oakland, Calif.; d Mar. 9, 1966, Washington, D.C.).* Lawyer, California Republican. U.S. Representative (1955-1966).

BALDWIN, JOSEPH CLARK *(b Jan. 11, 1897, New York City; d Oct. 27, 1957, New York City).* Journalist, New York Republican. New York City Board of Aldermen (1929-1934), state senate (1934-1936), state constitutional convention delegate (1938), New York City Council (1937-1941), U.S. Representative (1941-1947).

BALDWIN, ROGER SHERMAN *(b Jan. 4, 1793, New Haven, Conn.; d Feb. 19, 1863, New Haven).* Lawyer, abolitionist, Connecticut Whig, independent Republican. State senate (1837, 1838); with three other lawyers, among them John Quincy Adams, successfully defended slaves accused of mutiny and murder while being taken to Cuba from Africa aboard the *Amistad* (1839); state house of representatives (1840, 1841), governor (1844-1846), U.S. Senate (1847-1851) to fill a vacancy, Lincoln-Hamlin presidential elector (1860), delegate to National Peace Conference (1861) that sought alternative to civil war. Son of Simeon Baldwin.

BALDWIN, SIMEON *(b Dec. 14, 1761, Norwich, Conn.; d May 26, 1851, New Haven).* Educator, lawyer, Connecticut Federalist. New Haven city clerk (1789-1800), overlapping as clerk of U.S. district and circuit courts in Connecticut (1790-1803), U.S. Representative (1803-1805), associate judge of state superior court (1806-1808), judge of state supreme court of errors (1808-1818), Farmington Canal Commission chairman (1822-1830), New Haven mayor (1826). Father of Roger S. Baldwin, grandfather of Simeon E. Baldwin.

BALDWIN, SIMEON EBEN *(b Feb. 5, 1840, New Haven, Conn.; d Jan. 30, 1927, New Haven).* Lawyer, teacher, historian, author, humanitarian, highly independent Democrat who held far too many offices to list in full but all of them adding up to the undisputed title "The First Citizen of Connecticut."

Appointed to Yale Law School faculty (1869), an association that continued for 50 years, member of commission to revise state statutes (1875), a founder of the American Bar Association (1878) and its president (1890), member of commission to revise state tax system (1886) and thirty years later (1915-1917) its chairman, associate justice and then chief justice of state supreme court (1893-1910), president of American Social Science Association (1897), U.S. delegate to International Prison Congress (1900, 1905), vice president of Universal Congress of Lawyers and Jurists (1904), president of American Political Science Association (1910), governor of Connecticut (1910-1914).

And add to all of that, membership on the New Haven Common Council, the presidency of the city's YMCA, a director of New Haven Hospital, and the man who in 1911 sponsored state legislation to regulate the use of flying machines.

Through it all, Baldwin was known perhaps as much for his idiosyncrasies and his frugality. Legend has it, for example, that he accepted fifteen cents in payment for a worn high silk hat from a mission society while donating $1,500 to its treasury, and that he carried sandwiches with him when traveling by train as governor rather than expend state funds for dining car meals. Son of Roger S. Baldwin, grandson of Simeon Baldwin.

BALL, EDWARD *(b Nov. 6, 1811, Fairfax County, Va.; d Nov. 22, 1872, in railroad accident near Zanesville, Ohio).* Farmer, journalist, lawyer, Ohio Whig turned Republican. Muskingum County deputy sheriff (1837, 1838), sheriff (1839-1843), state house of representatives (1845-1849, 1868-1870), Whig U.S. Representative (1853-1857), delegate to GOP presidential convention (1860), Lincoln-Hamlin elector (1860), U.S. House of Representatives sergeant-at-arms (1861-1863).

BALL, JOSEPH HURST (*b Nov. 3, 1905, Crookston, Minn.*). Minneapolis-St. Paul newspaperman, writer, shipping executive, Minnesota Republican. U.S. Senate (1940-1942, 1943-1949).

BALL, LEWIS HEISLER (*b Sept. 21, 1861, Stanton, Del.; d Oct. 18, 1932, Faulkland, Del.*). Physician, Delaware Republican. State treasurer (1899-1901), U.S. Representative (1901-1903), U.S. Senate (1903-1905 to fill a vacancy and again 1919-1925).

BALL, THOMAS HENRY (*b Jan. 14, 1859, Huntsville, Tex.; d May 7, 1944, Houston, Tex.*). Lawyer, Texas Democrat. Mayor of Huntsville (1887-1893), chairman of Walker County Democratic executive committee (1884-1896), delegate to national presidential conventions (1892, 1924, 1928), U.S. Representative (1897-1903).

BALLARD, BLAND WILLIAMS (*b Oct. 16, 1759, near Fredericksburg, Va.; d Sept. 5, 1853, Shelby County, Ky.*). Early Kentucky pioneer who gained fame as Indian fighter. Served five terms in state legislature between 1795 and 1811.

BALLINGER, RICHARD ACHILLES (*b July 9, 1858, Boonesboro, Iowa; d June 6, 1922, Seattle, Wash.*). Lawyer. Jefferson County Superior Court judge in new state of Washington (1894), reform mayor of Seattle (1904-1906), General Land Office commissioner (1907-1908), U.S. secretary of interior (1909-1911), a Taft appointment that touched off national argument and congressional investigation of charges that Taft, through Ballinger, meant to scuttle President Theodore Roosevelt's conservation policies. Ballinger was exonerated, then resigned.

BALLOU, LATIMER WHIPPLE (*b March 1, 1818, Cumberland, R.I.; d May 9, 1900, Woonsocket, R.I.*). Printer, banker, active in Rhode Island political affairs that broadened into a major role

in the formation of the Republican party (1856), Lincoln-Hamlin presidential elector (1860), national presidential convention (1872), U.S. Representative (1875-1881).

BALTZ, WILLIAM NICOLAS (*b Feb. 5, 1860, Millstadt, Ill.; d Aug. 22, 1943, Millstadt*). Farmer, miller, banker, Illinois Democrat. Millstadt Board of Education (1892-1917), St. Clair County Board of Supervisors (1897-1913), its presiding officer (1908-1911), U.S. Representative (1913-1915).

BANCROFT, EDGAR ADDISON (*b Nov. 20, 1857, Galesburg, Ill.; d July 28, 1925, Karuizawa, Japan*). Lawyer, diplomat who was renowned for his oratory but who perhaps was best known for his part in a comprehensive study of the July 1919 Chicago race riot that resulted in the deaths of fifteen whites and twenty blacks. Bancroft was appointed chairman of a twelve-member biracial state Commission on Race Relations that delved deeply into the cause of the riot and in 1922 published its findings in a report entitled "The Negro in Chicago; a Study of Race Relations and a Race Riot."

The following year found Bancroft in Morocco and Algiers, invited there by the French to inspect its African colonies, and the next year, much to his surprise, he was offered the post of American ambassador to Japan. Bancroft accepted but died less than a year after arriving there. The Japanese gave him a funeral befitting a member of the Imperial Family and delivered his body to San Francisco in a battleship.

BANCROFT, GEORGE (*b Oct. 3, 1800, Worcester, Mass.; d Jan. 17, 1891, Washington, D.C.*). Educator, preacher, scholar, historian, author, diplomat, Massachusetts Democrat, friend of presidents and an exceedingly minor poet. His ten-volume *History of the United States from the Discovery of the Con-*

tinent which took forty years (1834-1874) to complete was the first major account of the birth of America ever published.

Far and away the ranking Democratic intellectual in overwhelmingly Whiggish New England and the master of a powerful pen, Bancroft soon became a national figure, writing in such periodicals as the *North American Review*. On the other hand, his oratory ranked with his poetry and so his few tries for elective office ended in failure. But his political influence and accomplishments were considerable.

Unsuccessful candidate for state general court (1834); Van Buren-appointed collector of the Port of Boston (1837-1844); delegate to national presidential convention (1844) where he had much to do with the nomination of James K. Polk while in the same year losing his own bid for the governorship; delivered official eulogy for Andrew Jackson before U.S. Congress (June, 1845); Polk-appointed U.S. secretary of the navy for eighteen months (1845-1846) during which time he established the U.S. Naval Academy at Annapolis and doubled as acting secretary of war (1845) when he signed the orders sending troops across the Texas border and the Pacific fleet into San Francisco and other California ports, thus triggering the Mexican War.

Ambassador to the Court of St. James (1846-1849), a post in which, happily, he could give more time to his writing and to the expression of his love and admiration for American democracy ("I can only say that my residence in Europe has but quickened and confirmed my love for the rule of the people" and "The world is growing weary of that most costly of all luxuries, hereditary kings") yet the British liked him and accepted him; during the Civil War, though a Democrat, supported Abraham Lincoln wholeheartedly, becoming one of his close confidantes; ghost writer of Andrew Johnson's first annual message to Congress (1865); delivered his "Memorial Address on the Life and Character of Abraham Lincoln" before Congress (Feb. 12, 1866); Johnson-appointed minister to Prussia (1867-1874), a period that was like an extended homecoming since Bancroft had studied in Germany as a youth and made many friends.

Then came years of "retirement" in Washington with his rose garden, his horseback riding, and his writing (in 1885, at the age of eighty-five, he wrote this to Oliver Wendell Holmes: "I am yet strong enough to rise in the night, light my own fire and candles, and labor with close application fully fourteen hours," to which Holmes replied: "You must be made of iron and vulcanized india rubber").

When Bancroft died in 1891, President Harrison ordered all flags on the White House and other public buildings flown at half-mast. This was done, not only in Washington but also in all the cities through which the funeral train passed, carrying Bancroft home to Worcester.

BANGS, FRANCIS NEHEMIAH *(b Feb. 23, 1828, New York City; d Nov. 30, 1885, Ocala, Fla.).* Lawyer, New York Republican but not a politician. As an attorney in a case involving a stock brokerage firm, triggered investigations of New York's Tweed Ring (1871) and, among other things, caused the unseating of three judges. President of the Bar Association of the City of New York (1882-1883).

BANISTER, JOHN *(b Dec. 26, 1734, Dinwiddie County, Va.; d Sept. 30, 1788, Dinwiddie County).* Lawyer, planter, officer in Revolutionary Army. Virginia assembly (1765, 1766-1774, 1775), state house of delegates (1776, 1777, 1781-1783), a framer and signer of the Articles of Confederation (1776), Continental Congress (1778-1779).

BANKHEAD, JOHN HOLLIS, SR. *(b Sept. 13, 1842, Moscow, Ala.; d March*

1, 1920, Washington, D.C.). Planter, Alabama Democrat. State house of representatives (1865-1867, 1880, 1881), state senate (1876, 1877), state prison warden (1881-1885), U.S. Representative (1887-1907), U.S. Senate (1907 until death). Father of John Hollis Bankhead, Jr., and William Brockman Bankhead.

BANKHEAD, JOHN HOLLIS, JR. *(b July 8, 1872, Lamar County, Ala.; d June 12, 1946, U.S. Naval Hospital, Bethesda, Md.).* Coal mine operator, lawyer, a New Deal Democrat except in matters that applied to the black man. State house of representatives (1904-1905), U.S. Senate (1931 until death). He and his brother, William, in the House were mainly responsible for passage of the Cotton Control Act to aid growers through subsidy (enacted in 1934, repealed in 1936).

BANKHEAD, WILLIAM BROCKMAN *(b April 12, 1874, Moscow, Ala.; d Sept. 14, 1940, U.S. Naval Hospital, Bethesda, Md.).* Lawyer through parental pressures, preferring to become an actor as his daughter, Tallulah, later became an actress; Alabama Democrat. In New York while trying to penetrate Broadway aided in Robert Van Wyck's mayoralty campaign (1897), soon after returning home to the career his father had chosen for him.

State house of representatives (1900, 1901), Huntsville city attorney (1898-1902), fourteenth judicial circuit solicitor (1910-1914), U.S. Representative (1917 until death). His House service included chairmanship of the Rules Committee, majority leader, and speaker, all key positions in which he was virtually always loyal to President Franklin D. Roosevelt although much more conservative at heart ("a New Dealer by adoption" it was said of him).

An eloquent speaker, Bankhead delivered the keynote address at the Democratic national presidential convention of 1940 where opponents of vice presidential nominee Henry A. Wallace gave him 329 first-and-only ballot votes. Son of John Hollis Bankhead, Sr., and brother of John Hollis Bankhead, Jr.

BANKS, JOHN *(b Oct. 17, 1793, Juniata County, Pa.; d April, 3, 1864, Reading, Pa.).* Lawyer, Pennsylvania Whig. U.S. Representative (1831-1836), Berks County judicial district judge (1836-1847), state treasurer (1847).

BANKS, LINN *(b Jan. 23, 1784, Madison County, Va.; d Jan. 13, 1842, by drowning, Madison County).* Lawyer, Virginia Democrat. State house of delegates (1812-1838, the last twenty years as speaker), U.S. Representative (1838-1841), his second term election being successfully contested by William Smith.

BANKS, NATHANIEL PRENTISS *(b Jan. 30, 1816, Waltham, Mass.; d Sept. 1, 1894, Waltham).* Machinist, actor, journalist, lawyer; a self-educated man whose many political labels were indicative of his fierce independence, particularly on the issues of slavery and equal rights; a man whose cotton-mill beginnings always stayed with him, earning him the life-long nickname, The Bobbin Boy of Massachusetts.

As a Democrat, member of state house of representatives (1849-1852, the last two years as speaker), president of 1853 state constitutional convention ("the ablest body that ever met in Massachusetts"), then came ten, noncontinuous, terms as a U.S. Representative as the candidate of five different parties: Coalition Democrat Congressman (1853-1855) opposing his party's position on the Kansas-Nebraska Bill which left the issue of slavery up to territorial settlers; American, also called the Know-Nothing, party Congressman (1855-1857), chosen House speaker in a bitter 133-ballot contest that earned for him the description "the very bone and sinew of Free-Soilism" and was considered the most meaningful setback of slavery in twenty-five years. In that session, Banks declined presidential nomination (1856) of the North American party; reelected to a third consecutive term, this time as a Republican, but served only from March 1857, until December when he resigned to run successfully for governor of Massachusetts as a Republican, defeating a solidly entrenched three-term incumbent by a large majority after stump-speaking the state, the first time a candidate ever had done so. Served one term (1858-1861), introducing educational and humanitarian reforms; Union Army general (1861-1865), winning congressional thanks and commendation for opening the Mississippi River to free navigation; again a member of Congress, this time as a Union Republican, to fill a vacancy (1865-1867); GOP member for next three terms (1867-1873), then was defeated when he supported coalition candidate Horace Greeley for the presidency over Ulysses S. Grant; liberal Republican member of state senate (1874); as a Democrat, back to Congress (1875-1877) and as a liberal Republican (1877-1879); U.S. marshall (1879-1888) and then back to Congress, again as an unhyphenated Republican, for the last time (1889-1891).

BANNEKER, BENJAMIN *(b Nov. 9, 1731, Ellicott's Mills, Md.; d Oct., 1806, Baltimore, Md.).* Self-taught mathematician and astronomer, man of peace, writer whose works are in the Library of Congress. Born of a free mother and a slave father who purchased his own freedom and thus the son was considered free. First Negro to receive a presidential appointment when asked by George Washington to help lay out (planning where streets and buildings would go) the territory that later became Washington, D.C. Wrote a plan for peace (1793) recommending U.S. government have a secretary of peace. He believed that if there were no uniforms there would be no armies.

BANNING, HENRY BLACKSTONE *(b Nov. 10, 1836, Bannings Mills, Ohio; d Dec. 10, 1881, Cincinnati).* Lawyer, Ohio Democrat. State house of representatives (1866, 1867), U.S. Representative (1873-1879).

BANNON, HENRY TOWNE *(b June 5, 1867, Portsmouth, Ohio; d Sept. 6, 1950, Portsmouth).* Lawyer, banker, writer, Ohio Republican. Scioto County prosecutor (1897-1902), U.S. Representative (1905-1909), delegate to five national presidential conventions (1924-1940).

BANTA, PARKE MONROE *(b Nov. 21, 1891, Berryman, Mo.; d May 12, 1970, Cape Girardeau, Mo.).* Lawyer, Missouri Republican. GOP state convention delegate (1916, 1920, 1922, 1924, 1926), Washington County prosecuting attorney (1917-1918), Arcadia Board of Trustees (1928-1929), Ironton-Arcadia school board (1932-1933), state social security administrator (1941-1945), U.S. Representative (1947-1949), general counsel of Department of Health, Education and Welfare in Washington, D.C. (1953-1961).

BARBER, NOYES *(b April 28, 1781, Groton, Conn.; d Jan. 3, 1844, Groton).* Merchant, Connecticut Democrat and Whig. State house of representatives (1818), seven terms as Democratic U.S. Representative (1821-1835), delegate to all Whig state conventions from 1836 until death.

BARBOUR, HENRY ELLSWORTH *(b March 8, 1877, Ogdensburg, N.Y.; d March 21, 1945, Fresno, Calif.).* Lawyer, California Republican. U.S. Representative (1919-1933).

BARBOUR, JAMES *(b June 10, 1775, Orange County, Va.; d June 7, 1842, Barboursville, Va.).* Lawyer, planter, an early advocate of states' rights but had little esteem for slavery. Virginia House of Delegates (1796-1812), speaker (1809-

1812); as governor of Virginia (1812-1814) he was a staunch advocate of educational reforms, including establishment of normal and industrial schools; Anti-Democrat and States' Rights member of U.S. Senate (1815-1825) where he was chairman of the Foreign Relations and Military Affairs committees and president pro tem; U.S. secretary of war under President John Quincy Adams (1825-1828), an assignment that turned many Virginians against him because of their differences with Adams on tariffs and other issues; Adams-appointed U.S. minister to England (1828-1829); chairman of Whig national presidential convention (1839) that nominated William Henry Harrison and John Tyler. Brother of Philip P. Barbour and cousin of John S. Barbour, Sr.

BARBOUR, JOHN STRODE, SR. *(b Aug. 8, 1790, Culpeper County, Va.; d Jan. 12, 1855, Culpeper County).* Lawyer, Virginia Democrat. State house of delegates (1813-1816, 1820-1823, 1833, 1834), States' Rights Democrat U.S. Representative (1823-1833), member of state constitutional conventions (1829, 1830), chairman of Democratic National Convention (1852) that nominated Franklin Pierce and William King. Cousin of James and Philip P. Barbour.

BARBOUR, JOHN STRODE, JR. *(b Dec. 29, 1820, Culpeper County, Va.; d May 14, 1892, Washington, D.C.).* Lawyer, Virginia Democrat. State house of delegates (1847-1851), appointed state representative on board of Orange & Alexandria Railroad (1849), became its president (1852-1882), U.S. Representative (1881-1887), chairman of Democratic state committee (1883-1890), revitalizing the party and regaining control of the state from Readjuster party of William Mahone; delegate-at-large to national presidential convention (1884, 1888), member of Democratic National Committee (1884-1892), U.S. Senate (1889 until death).

BARBOUR, PHILIP PENDLETON *(b May 25, 1783, Orange County, Va.; d Feb. 25, 1841, Washington, D.C.).* Lawyer, Virginia Democrat, associate justice of the U.S. Supreme Court and a strict states' rights constructionist.

State house of delegates (1813-1814), U.S. Representative (1814-1825, 1827-1830), its speaker (1821-1823), Virginia general court judge (1825-1827), president of state constitutional convention (1829), U.S. Circuit Court judge for Virginia's eastern district when President Andrew Jackson nominated him for the high court. That action was cheered by Barbour's Virginia constituents (Barbour, said the *Richmond Enquirer,* is "eminently fitted to adorn the Bench with his talents and enlighten it with his inflexible and uncompromising State Rights principles") but was roundly denounced by nationalists the country over. (Five years earlier, John Quincy Adams, whose cabinet once had included Barbour's brother, James, had expressed the fear that some day "some shallow-pated wildcat like Philip P. Barbour, fit for nothing but to tear the Union to rags and tatters," might be appointed.) However the appointment had no great influence upon the complexion of the court because of Barbour's death only four years after taking his seat. Cousin of John S. Barbour, Sr.

BARCHFELD, ANDREW JACKSON *(b May 18, 1863, Pittsburgh, Pa.; d Jan. 28, 1922, in Washington, D.C., Knickerbocker Theater disaster).* Physician, Pennsylvania Republican. Pittsburgh Common Council (1886, 1887), delegate to three state GOP conventions (1886, 1894, 1901), U.S. Representative (1905-1917), delegate to Brussels peace congress (1905), member of commission to Philippine Islands (1910) and Panama Canal commission (1912).

BARCLAY, CHARLES FREDERICK *(b May 9, 1844, Owego, N.Y.; d March 9, 1914, Washington, D.C.).* Teacher, lumber merchant, Pennsylvania Republican. Benjamin Harrison-Whitelaw Reid presidential elector (1892), national presidential convention delegate (1900), U.S. Representative (1907-1911).

BARD, DAVID *(b 1744, Adams County, Pa.; d March 12, 1815, Alexandria, Pa.).* Clergyman, U.S. Representative from Pennsylvania (1795-1799, 1803 until death).

BARDEN, GRAHAM ARTHUR *(b Sept. 25, 1896, Turkey Township, N.C.; d Jan. 29, 1967, New Bern, N.C.).* North Carolina teacher, lawyer, Democrat. Craven County judge (1920-1924), state house of representatives (1933), U.S. Representative thirteen terms (1935-1961).

Regarded as an ultraconservative and antiunion he supported Taft-Hartley legislation and other right-to-work proposals and in 1956 refused to continue as floor manager of a $1.5 billion aid-to-education bill when an Adam Clayton Powell amendment barring funds for segregated schools was added to it. While chairman of the House Education and Labor Committee he was forced by liberal members to hold regular meetings and to give them subcommittee assignments, but refused to put Powell on a subcommittee. The latter claimed it was because he was Negro, but Barden said it was for purely personal reasons. Powell later succeeded him as chairman.

At one time in his long career in Congress, Barden said he "never knew the Republic to be endangered by a bill that was not passed." He was cosponsor of such legislation as the Barden-LaFollette Act to aid in the rehabilitation of the handicapped and the George-Barden Act to provide training for home economics and agricultural teachers.

BARKER, JAMES WILLIAM *(b Dec. 5, 1815, White Plains, N.Y.; d June 26, 1869, Rahway, N.J.).* Merchant, insurance executive. A prime mover in the

founding of a secret society, "Order of the Star Spangled Banner," whose purpose was to keep foreign-born from holding political office and leader of its New York grand council (1853); unsuccessful candidate of the Know-Nothing party (1854) for the mayoralty of New York City.

BARKER, WHARTON *(b May 1, 1846, Philadelphia, Pa.; d April 9, 1921, Philadelphia).* Financier, adviser to prerevolutionary Russia on economic affairs, advocated U.S. cooperation in development of China's commercial resources, opposed third term for President Grant, supported James A. Garfield and Benjamin Harrison in their successful presidential campaigns; resigned Republican party (1896) and became Populist candidate for presidency in 1900.

BARKLEY, ALBEN WILLIAM *(b Nov. 24, 1877, Graves County, Ky.; d April 30, 1956, Lexington, Va.).* Kentucky Democrat, Lawyer, Vice President of the United States (1949-1953).

McCracken County prosecuting attorney (1905-1909), county judge (1909-1913), U.S. Representative (1913-1927), chairman of Democratic State Conventions (1919, 1924); delegate to all Democratic National Conventions (1920-1940), temporary chairman (1932, 1936), permanent chairman (1940); U.S. Senate (1927-1949), majority leader (1937-1947), minority leader (1947, 1948).

Although a political moderate with conservative leanings, Barkley supported the nomination of Franklin D. Roosevelt and, later, his New Deal and foreign policy programs; advocated repeal of Prohibition, and was chosen majority leader over Mississippi's Pat Harrison on the strength of FDR's "Dear Alben" letter of praise. He voted for Neutrality Act (1939) and lend-lease (1941), favored a reciprocal trade policy, headed the U.S. delegation to the Interparliamentary Union convening in Egypt (1947), sought U.S. recognition of Israel, opposed the Taft-Hartley labor act, supported the Marshall Plan and, in 1949, was present at the signing of the North Atlantic Treaty.

After serving as Harry Truman's affectionately nicknamed "Veep," he was returned to the Senate in 1955 and died while addressing 1,700 Washington and Lee University students at a mock political convention.

BARKSDALE, ETHELBERT *(b Jan. 4, 1824, Smyrna, Tenn.; d Feb. 17, 1893, Yazoo City, Miss.).* Journalist, farmer, Mississippi Democrat. Editor of official state journal (1854-1861, 1876-1883), member of Confederate Congress (1861-1865), delegate to four Democratic National Conventions (1860, 1868, 1872, 1880), Tilden-Hendricks presidential elector (1876) and president of state electoral college, chairman of state Democratic executive committee (1877-1879), U.S. Representative (1883-1887). Brother of William Barksdale.

BARKSDALE, WILLIAM *(b Aug. 21, 1821, Rutherford County, Tenn.; d July 2, 1863, Gettysburg, Pa.).* Lawyer, journalist, officer in Mexican and Civil wars, Mississippi Democrat. National presidential convention delegate (1852), States' Rights Democrat U.S. Representative (1853-1861) resigning when Mississippi voted to secede from Union; a brigadier general in Confederate forces, he was mortally wounded at the Peach Orchard in Battle of Gettysburg. In Congress, his major accomplishment was to run interference for Congressman Preston S. Brooks when he invaded chamber of the upper house to attack Senator Charles Sumner. Brother of Ethelbert Barksdale.

BARLOW, CHARLES AVERILL *(b March 17, 1858, Cleveland, Ohio; d Oct. 3, 1927, Bakersfield, Calif.).* Farmer, miner, California Democrat with Populist agrarian convictions. State assembly (1892-1893), chairman of state People's party convention (1896), Populist-Democrat U.S. Representative (1897-1899).

BARLOW, FRANCIS CHANNING *(b Oct. 19, 1834, Brooklyn, N.Y.; d Jan. 11, 1896, New York City).* Lawyer, New *York Tribune* editorial writer, several times wounded in Civil War in which he enlisted as a Union private (1861) and emerged as a major general (1865), then devoted the next eight years to politics and political reform, New York Republican.

New York secretary of state (1866-1867, 1870), U.S. marshal for New York's southern district (1869), state attorney general (1871-1873), then returned to the private practice of law. With those bases from which to work, Barlow ordered a halt of government-employee contributions to party campaign coffers, cracked down on "gifts" to anyone in his jurisdiction able to return the favor, and started the Tweed Ring prosecutions. He emerged from private practice (1876) long enough to participate in the investigation of presidential election irregularities in Florida (see Rutherford B. Hayes and Samuel J. Tilden).

BARLOW, JOEL *(b March 24, 1754, Redding, Conn.; d Dec. 24, 1812, Zarnowiec, Poland).* Teacher, merchant, banker, soldier, journalist, poet, author, one of the Hartford Wits of 1786-1787, and statesman—the last having its unwitting roots in 1788 when he sailed for Europe, remaining for seventeen years, most of that time in Paris where he became part of a close-knit American liberal literary clan, including Thomas Paine. There, as the result of his penned observations on the politics of the times, he was made an honorary citizen of France (1792).

His literary reputation, and news of the unusual honor, spread to the United States and in 1795 Barlow was offered his first diplomatic assignment as U.S. consul in Algiers where he negotiated treaties with Tripoli, Algiers, and Tunis and effected the release of American prisoners. Then it was back to Europe and his pen until 1805 when he succumbed to his wife's oft-repeated plea to "go home and be respectable."

In 1811, while residing in Washington, D.C., and at work on a history of America that Thomas Jefferson had suggested he write, President Madison named Barlow minister plenipotentiary to France with instructions to negotiate a commercial treaty with Napoleon. After a frustrating year of preliminaries, the French set up a rendezvous in Wilna, Poland, a long, arduous trip with winter closing in. Barlow arrived Nov. 18, 1812 and waited until Dec. 5 for Bonaparte to arrive. When he learned that Napoleon had met defeat in Russia and would not appear for the meeting, Barlow began the return trip to Paris, but exposure to the cold led to his death while enroute.

BARNARD, DANIEL DEWEY *(b July 16, 1797, Sheffield, Mass.; d April 24, 1861, Albany, N.Y.).* Lawyer, historian, writer, New York Whig. Monroe County prosecutor (1826), U.S. Representative (1827-1829, 1839-1845), state assembly (1838), minister to Prussia (1850-1853).

BARNES, GEORGE THOMAS *(b Aug. 14, 1833, Richmond County, Ga.; d Oct. 24, 1901, Augusta, Ga.).* Lawyer, Georgia Democrat. State house of representatives (1860-1865), Democratic National Committee (1876-1884), U.S. Representative (1885-1891).

BARNES, JAMES MARTIN *(b Jan. 9, 1899, Jacksonville, Ill.; d June 8, 1958, Washington, D.C.).* Lawyer, Illinois Democrat. Morgan County judge (1926-1934), U.S. Representative (1939-1943), administrative assistant to President Roosevelt (1943-1945).

BARNETT, IDA B. WELLS *(b 1864, in Mississippi; d 1931).* Black newspaperwoman, pamphleteer, lecturer, and civil rights worker. Campaigned against lynching and served as chairman of the Anti-Lynching Bureau of the National African Council, first president of the Negro Fellowship League, and Vice President of the Chicago Equal Rights League.

BARNEY, SAMUEL STEBBINS *(b Jan. 31, 1846, Hartford, Wis.; d Dec. 31, 1919, Milwaukee, Wis.).* Lawyer, educator, Wisconsin Republican. Washington County superintendent of schools (1876-1880), national presidential convention (1884), U.S. Representative (1895-1903), associate justice of the court of claims in Washington, D.C. (1904-1919).

BARNHART, HENRY A. *(b Sept. 11, 1858, Cass County, Ind.; d March 26, 1934, Rochester, Ind.).* Teacher, farmer, newspaper publisher, banker, telephone executive, lecturer, Indiana Democrat. U.S. Representative (1908-1919).

BARNUM, WILLIAM HENRY *(b Sept. 17, 1818, Boston Corner, N.Y.; d April 30, 1889, Lime Rock, Conn.).* Manufacturer, Connecticut Democrat. State house of representatives (1851, 1852), five terms as U.S. Representative (1867-1876), U.S. Senate to fill a vacancy (1876-1879), delegate to five national presidential conventions (1868-1888), chairman of Democratic National Committee (1876-1889).

BARNWELL, ROBERT *(b Dec. 21, 1761, Beaufort, S.C.; d Oct. 24, 1814, Beaufort).* South Carolina Federalist. Continental Congress (1788, 1789), state convention for the adoption of federal Constitution (1788), U.S. Representative (1791-1793), state house of representatives (1795-1797), its speaker (1795), state senate (1805-1806), its president (1805). Father of Robert W. Barnwell.

BARNWELL, ROBERT WOODWARD *(b Aug. 10, 1801, Beaufort, S.C.; d Nov. 24, 1882, Columbia, S.C.).* Educator, lawyer, South Carolina Democrat. State house of representatives (1826-1828), U.S. Representative (1829-1833), president of South Carolina College, which is now the University of South Carolina

(1835-1841), U.S. Senate to fill a vacancy (June-December, 1850), member of commission that called upon President Buchanan (1860) to discuss South Carolina secession, delegate to Southern Congress of seceding states (1861) where his deciding vote made Jefferson Davis president of the Confederacy, member of Confederate States Senate (1861-1865). Son of Robert Barnwell.

BARR, THOMAS JEFFERSON *(b 1812, New York City; d March 27, 1881, New York City).* Tavern keeper, New York Democrat. Assistant alderman (1849, 1850), alderman (1852, 1853), state senate (1854, 1855), U.S. Representative (1859-1861), New York City police commissioner (1870-1873).

BARRETT, FRANK A. *(b Nov. 10, 1892, Omaha, Nebr.; d May 30, 1962, Cheyenne, Wyo.).* Wyoming Republican, lawyer, rancher, and the only person in the state's history to serve as U.S. Representative, U.S. Senator, and governor.
   Niobrara County attorney (1923-1932), state senate (1933-1935); U.S. Representative (1943-1950), resigning to campaign for and serve as governor (1951-1953), leaving the State House to run for the U.S. Senate where he served until 1960; appointed general counsel to U.S. Department of Agriculture by President Eisenhower in 1959.

BARRETT, JOHN *(b Nov. 28, 1866, Grafton, Vt.; d Oct. 17, 1938, Bellows Falls, Vt.).* Foreign correspondent, diplomat and advocate of strong U.S. policies in the Orient ("American material interests in the Far East should be built up from Japan to Java. One of the greatest opportunities in the world is here.") and Latin America ("for peace, friendship and commerce"), Vermont Republican.
   U.S. minister to Siam (1894-1898), resigning to report on the Spanish-American War from Manila where he also became an adviser to Admiral George Dewey; U.S. delegate to the Second Annual Conference of American States in Mexico (1901), minister to Argentina (1904-1905), minister to Colombia (1905-1907), director general of the Pan American Union (1907-1920) which at the time of his appointment was called the International Bureau of the American Republics; returned to Vermont where he toyed with the idea of running for the U.S. Senate in 1924.

BARRETT, WILLIAM EMERSON *(b Dec. 29, 1858, Melrose, Mass.; d Feb. 12, 1906, Newton, Mass.).* Boston newspaper publisher, banker, Massachusetts Republican. State house of representatives (1887-1892), its speaker (1888-1892), U.S. Representative (1895-1899).

BARRINGER, DANIEL LAURENS *(b Oct. 1, 1788, Cabarrus County, N.C.; d. Oct. 16, 1852, Shelbyville, Tenn.).* Lawyer, North Carolina Democrat, Tennessee Whig. In North Carolina: state house of commons (1813, 1814, 1819-1822), U.S. Representative (1826-1835). In Tennessee: state house of representatives (1843-1845), Clay-Frelinghuysen elector (1844). Uncle of Daniel M. Barringer.

BARRINGER, DANIEL MOREAU *(b July 30, 1806, Cabarrus County, N.C.; d Sept. 1, 1873, White Sulphur Springs, Va.).* Lawyer, North Carolina Whig and a strong Union man who, however, was intensely loyal to the South even after secession. State house of commons (1829-1834, 1840, 1842, 1854), state constitutional convention (1835), U.S. Representative (1843-1849) where (1847-1849) he shared a desk with and became a close friend of Congressman Abraham Lincoln of Illinois; minister to Spain (1849-1853).
   During the next several years, though in failing health and therefore holding no public office, Barringer worked diligently to hold the nation together, among other things carrying on correspondence with such friends as Robert E. Lee of Virginia to enlist their

support; state delegate to abortive peace conference in Washington (1861), delegate to Union National Convention (1866), chairman of Democratic state committee (1872). Nephew of Daniel Laurens Barringer.

BARROWS, SAMUEL JUNE *(b May 26, 1845, New York City; d April 21, 1909, New York City).* Clergyman, journalist, and a humanitarian who was responsible for many of the nation's and his home state's prison reforms.

Private secretary to U.S. Secretary of State William H. Seward (1868); while a student at Harvard Divinity School worked as a summertime newspaper correspondent covering the Stanley and Custer Yellowstone and Black Hills expeditions (1873-1874); pastor of First Church in Dorcester, Mass. (1876-1880); editor of the *Christian Register,* a national Unitarian weekly (1880-1896), a position in which he could give full vent to his beliefs, thus ardently championing such unpopular causes as alcoholic abstinence, women's suffrage, and equal educational opportunities for the black man and the Indian; U.S. delegate to International Prison Congresses of 1895, 1900, 1905, and 1910 serving as president of the latter; U.S. Representative (1897-1899) as a Republican from Boston, in which position he fought against American entry into war with Spain and for civil service reform and a parole system in federal penitentiaries. As secretary of the New York Prison Association (1899 until death), Barrows wrote and won passage of the state's first probation law and finally saw enacted federal parole laws he had proposed while in Congress.

BARRY, JOHN STEWART *(b Jan. 29, 1802, Amherst N.H.; d Jan. 14, 1870, Constantine, Mich.).* Lawyer, business executive, Michigan Democrat. As governor (1842-1846) he restored financial stability to a state that was near bankruptcy. State law prohibited three consecutive terms, so the people in ap-

preciation returned him to the statehouse (1849-1851) after one term had intervened.

BARRY, WILLIAM BERNARD *(b July 21, 1902, County Mayo, Ireland; d Oct. 20, 1946, New York City).* Lawyer, New York Democrat. Queens County district attorney (1932, 1933), special U.S. Justice Department attorney (1933-1935), county executive committee (1930-1935), U.S. Representative (1935 until death).

BARRY, WILLIAM TAYLOR *(b Feb. 15, 1784, Lunenburg, Va.; d Aug. 30, 1835, Liverpool, England).* Lawyer, Kentucky Democrat. State house of representatives (1807, 1809, 1814), its speaker (1814), U.S. Representative to fill a vacancy (1810-1811), U.S. Senate (1814-1816), where, an orator of note in Kentucky, not once did he make a speech, then resigning to accept appointment as a state circuit court judge (1816-1817).

Then while in the state senate (1817-1821) and with Kentucky in the midst of a depression in which about 40 banks had failed, Barry became active in the hastily formed Relief party and, as its candidate for lieutenant governor, soundly trounced the antirelief candidate. In that office (1821-1825), he lobbied successfully for the issuance of worthless paper money and replevin and relief laws to aid the common man. Those laws were quickly ruled unconstitutional by the state's appeals court. In retaliation, the people in 1824 pressured the legislature to abolish the court, set up a new one, and appoint Barry both chief justice and secretary of state. Thus came into being two equally hostile factions, known as the Old Court and the New Court parties, and for the next two years Kentucky teetered on the brink of anarchy when the Old Court, gaining the upper hand, turned Barry out.

In 1828 he ran for governor, supporting presidential candidate Andrew Jackson against a Henry Clay supporter for control of Kentucky. Barry lost by about

700 votes but he won the state for Jackson in the presidential contest by an 8,000-vote majority. Jackson repaid the debt by appointing him postmaster general (1829-1835). In 1835 he resigned after almost continuous charges, innuendo, and investigation of his conduct in the Post Office Department. This time Jackson appointed Barry minister to Spain but he died while enroute to Madrid.

BARSTOW, WILLIAM AUGUSTUS (b Sept. 13, 1813, Connecticut; d Dec. 14, 1865, Madison, Wis.) Miller, banker, railroad executive, Wisconsin Democrat whose brief political career was clouded with charges of irregularities. As Wisconsin's secretary of state (1850-1852), he withstood allegations that he could be bought and was elected governor (1853-1855). Then, in a try for reelection, he was declared winner by 157 votes and was sworn to a second term (January 1856). But on the same day, his Republican opponent, Coles Bashford, who had accused Barstow of election frauds, also took the oath. So, pending the outcome of court litigation, Wisconsin had two pretenders to the state house until March 24, 1856, when the tribunal ruled in Bashford's favor.

BARTHOLDT, RICHARD (b Nov. 2, 1855, Schleiz, Germany; d March 19, 1932, St. Louis, Mo.) Journalist, Missouri Republican who served eleven terms in Congress after migrating to the United States at the age of twenty-two. First he settled in Brooklyn, N.Y., (1872) where he learned the printing trade, then switched to writing-reporting and moved to St. Louis (1877) where by the time he held his first public office he was editor-in-chief of the Tribune.
   City board of education (1888-1892), its president (1890-1892), U.S. Representative (1893-1915), state GOP convention chairman (1896), president of Interparliamentary Union (1903), Taft-appointed special envoy to German

emperor (1911) to present Germany with statue of Baron von Steuben.

BARTINE, HORACE FRANKLIN (b March 21, 1848, New York City; d Aug. 27, 1918, Winnemucca, Nev.) Farmer, manufacturer, lawyer, trade paper editor. Nevada Republican. Ormsby County district attorney (1880-1882), U.S. Representative (1889-1893), state tax examiner (1904-1907), railroad commissioner (1907 until death).

BARTLETT, BAILEY (b Jan. 29, 1750, Haverhill, Mass.; d Sept. 9, 1830, Haverhill). Merchant, Massachusetts Federalist. State house of representatives (1781-1784, 1789), constitutional convention delegate (1788), high sheriff of Essex County (1789-1811, 1812 until death), U.S. Representative to fill a vacancy (1797-1801), Essex County treasurer (1812).

BARTLETT, CHARLES LAFAYETTE (b Jan. 31, 1853, Monticello, Ga.; d April 21, 1938, Macon, Ga.). Lawyer, banker, Georgia Democrat. Solicitor general for Macon Judicial Court (1887-1881), state house of representatives (1882-1885), Macon city attorney (1887-1892), state senate (1888, 1889), superior court judge (1892-1894), ten terms as U.S. Representative (1895-1915), national presidential convention (1916).

BARTLETT, EDWARD LOUIS (b April 20, 1904, Seattle, Wash.; d Dec. 11, 1968, Cleveland, Ohio). Gold miner, newspaperman, Alaska Democrat. A self-made man who was taken to the territory by his parents at the age of one, became Alaska's most popular political figure, one of its staunchest advocates of statehood, known to everyone as Bob.
   Secretary to Alaska's delegate to Congress (1933, 1934), chairman of territorial Unemployment Compensation Commission (1937-1939); secretary of Alaska, a presidentially appointive post

equivalent to a state's lieutenant governor (1939-1944); member of Alaska War Council (1942-1944), delegate to U.S. Congress (1945-1959), U.S. Senate (1959 until death after heart surgery in a Cleveland hospital).

In Washington he was considered one of the most vigorous legislators ever, serving on many committees, introducing many bills, and battling indefatigably for what he considered right. Among his main causes besides statehood were development of America's maritime industry and noninvolvement in the Vietnam war, expressing opposition on the latter as early as 1964.

BARTLETT, GEORGE ARTHUR *(b Nov. 30, 1869, San Francisco, Calif.; d June 1, 1951, Reno, Nev.).* Lawyer, author, Nevada Democrat. Eureka County district attorney (1889, 1890), U.S. Representative (1907-1911), assistant U.S. district attorney (1915-1918), second judicial district judge (1918-1931).

BARTLETT, ICHABOD *(b July 24, 1786, Salisbury, N.H.; d Oct. 19, 1853, Portsmouth, N.H.).* Lawyer, New Hampshire Anti-Democrat. Clerk of state senate (1817, 1818), Rockingham County state solicitor (1819-1821), state house of representatives (1819-1821, 1830, 1838, 1851, 1852), its speaker (1821), U.S. Representative (1823-1829), unsuccessful gubernatorial candidate (1832), state constitutional convention delegate (1850).

BARTLETT, JOHN RUSSELL *(b Oct. 23, 1805, Providence, R.I.; d May 28, 1886, Providence).* Bookseller, historian, author, bibliographer. U.S. commissioner who ran boundary line between United States and Mexico (1850-1853). Rhode Island secretary of state (1855-1872) where one of his accomplishments was the classifying of a 200-year accumulation of official papers for binding into ninety-two volumes and twenty-eight portfolios.

BARTLETT, JOSIAH, SR. *(b Nov. 21, 1729, Amesbury, Mass.; d May 19, 1795, Kingston, N.H.).* Physician lawyer, New Hampshire Democratic-Republican and signer of Declaration of Independence. New Hampshire colonial legislature (1765-1775), Continental Congress (1775, 1776, 1778), chief justice of the court of common pleas (1779-1783), superior court justice (1784-1788), its chief justice (1788-1789), elected to U.S. Senate (1789) but declined to serve, his state's last president (1790-1792) and first governor (1792-1794), state constitutional convention delegate (1792), presidential elector (1792).

BARTLETT, JOSIAH, JR. *(b Aug. 29, 1768, Kingston, N.H.; d April 16, 1838, Stratham, N.H.).* New Hampshire physician. State senate (1809, 1810, 1824; its president in the last year), U.S Representative (1811-1813), John Quincy Adams presidential elector (1824).

BARTLETT, THOMAS, JR. *(b June 18, 1808, Sutton, Vt.; d Sept. 12, 1876, Lyndon, Vt.).* Lawyer, Vermont Democrat. Caledonia County state's attorney (1839-1842), state senate (1841, 1842), state house of representatives (1849, 1850, 1854, 1855), delegate to state constitutional conventions (1850-1857), U.S. Representative (1851-1853).

BARTLEY, MORDECAI *(b Dec. 16, 1783, Fayette County, Pa.; d Oct. 10, 1870, Mansfield, Ohio).* Farmer, frontier merchant, Ohio Whig turned Republican who, while in Congress, proposed that Ohio land grants be used to support public schools. State senate (1817-1818), land office register for the Virginia military district school lands (1818-1823), U.S. Representative (1823-1831), governor of Ohio (1844-1846) succeeding his son, Thomas, a Democrat who served only briefly in 1844 at the age of 32.

BARTON, BRUCE *(b Aug. 5, 1886, Robbins, Tenn.; d July 5, 1967, New York City).* Advertising executive who founded the firm of Batten, Barton, Durstine and Osborne (BBD&O), author and philosopher who, as a congressman (1937-1941), sought unsuccessfully, to "repeal one useless law a week," N.Y. Republican. Delegate to GOP state convention (1938), national convention (1940).

Son of a country preacher, Barton's first job after college was as a railroad construction job timekeeper. He soon moved on to newspaper and magazine writing and advertising. His books included two best sellers: *The Man Nobody Knows,* which was about the life of Christ, and *The Book Nobody Knows,* a résumé of the Bible.

BARTON, DAVID *(b Dec. 14, 1783, Greene County, N.C., which is now in Tennessee; d Sept. 28, 1837, Boonville, Mo.).* Missouri lawyer. Territorial attorney general (1813-1814), Howard County circuit judge (1815), its presiding judge (1816), territorial house of representatives (1818) and speaker at a special session in which he was a prime factor in drafting Missouri's statehood petition, president of territorial convention (1820) that produced a state constitution that, out of tribute to his contributions, became known as the Barton Constitution.

Barton received further honors for his contribution to statehood later that year when the state's first general assembly unanimously elected him Missouri's first U.S. Senator, a position to which four years later he was elected to a full term and so served from 1821 until 1831. Defeated in a third-term bid, Barton lived out his few remaining years in state service: state senate (1834), Cooper County circuit judge (1835 until death).

An ironic political footnote: At the same assembly that sent him to the Senate, Barton supported Thomas Hart Benton as Missouri's second senator. In Washington they became enemies and Barton went into political eclipse from which he never recovered.

BARUCH, BERNARD MANNES *(b Aug. 19, 1870, Camden, S.C.; d June 20, 1965, New York City).* Economist, financier, author, statesman, park-bench philosopher, adviser to Presidents Wilson, Harding, Coolidge, Hoover, Roosevelt, Truman, and Eisenhower. Son of a Confederate Army surgeon and a collegiate athlete, he made and lost a million dollars on Wall Street before he was thirty, made many millions more in the years that followed, giving most of them to charity; in all his decades of public service he never took a penny in payment nor sought elective office.

World War I: member Advisory Commission of the Council of National Defense, chairman of Commission on Raw Materials, Minerals and Metals; chairman of the Allied Purchasing Commission; chairman of the War Industries Board; member of American Commission to Negotiate Peace; only American representative on Reparations Commission, and Supreme Economic Council.

Between wars: member of President's Conference on Capital and Labor (1919), President's Agricultural Conference (1922), National Transportation Committee (1932), industrial mobilization advisor to Senate Committee on Military Affairs (1937), testified before Senate Special Committee on Unemployment and Relief (1938), chairman of Factfinding Commission on Synthetic Rubber (1942).

World War II: special advisor on war mobilization; drafted reports on both wartime and postwar planning for President Roosevelt. Postwar: U.S. representative on United Nations Atomic Energy Commission and author of proposals, known as Baruch Plan, for international control of atomic energy (1946).

BASHFORD, COLES *(b Jan. 24, 1816, Cold Spring, N.Y.; d April 25, 1878, Prescott, Ariz.).* Lawyer, New York Whig, Wisconsin Republican, Arizona Independent.

In New York: Wayne County district attorney (1847-1850), moving West when Wisconsin became a state. In Wisconsin: Helped organize Republican party, state senate (1853, 1855), ran for governor (1855), apparently lost to Democratic opponent William A. Barstow but his charges of voting frauds were upheld by the courts and he thus became the state's first Republican governor (1856-1858). After he left office it became known that he had accepted $50,000 in railroad bonds in exchange for a land grant and he departed the state. In Arizona: First territorial attorney general (1864-1866), president of first territorial council (1865), U.S. Representative (1867-1869), Arizona secretary of state (1869-1876).

BASS, CHARLOTTA A. *(b 1890, Little Compton, R.I.).* Negro woman who was vice presidential candidate (1952) on the Progressive party ticket that had Vincent Hallinan as its presidential candidate. (They polled 140,023 popular votes.) At one time a resident of Los Angeles where (1950) she ran unsuccessfully for Congress in the Fourteenth District on the Progressive party ticket and where she was editor and publisher of the *California Eagle.* A Republican until 1948, Mrs. Bass served (1940) as Western Regional Director for Wendell Wilkie's presidential campaign.

BASS, PERKINS *(b Oct. 6, 1912, East Walpole, Mass.).* Lawyer, banker, business executive, New Hampshire Republican. State representative (1939, 1941, 1947, 1951), state senate president (1949-1951), U.S. Representative (1955-1963) serving on the Public Works and Science and Aeronautics committees.

BASSETT, BURWELL *(b March 18, 1764, New Kent County, Va.; d Feb. 26, 1841, New Kent County).* Virginia Democrat who served nearly forty years in state or federal office. State house of delegates (1787-1789, 1819-1821), state senate (1793-1805), U.S. Representative (1805-1813, 1815-1819, 1821-1829).

BASSETT, RICHARD *(b April 2, 1745, Kent County, Md.; d Aug. 15, 1815, Cecil County, Md.).* Lawyer, Delaware Federalist and one of President John Adams' short-lived "midnight judges." State constitutional convention delegate (1776, 1792), state senate (1782), state house of representatives (1786), delegate to federal convention that framed U.S. Constitution (1787) and to state ratifying convention in same year, U.S. Senator (1789-1793) where it's said he was the first to vote to locate the capital on the Potomac, chief justice of the court of common pleas (1793-1799), Adams presidential elector (1797), governor of Delaware (1799-1801). Then came the midnight appointment to the U.S. Circuit Court bench: Late in the last night of his presidency (March 3, 1801), Adams made a host of judicial appointments, thus giving jobs to supporters, repaying favors, blocking patronage of the incoming administration, and making his successor, Thomas Jefferson, angry. Bassett got one of the posts, but not for long—the new Congress swiftly legislated the position out of existence.

BATCHELLER, GEORGE SHERMAN *(b July 25, 1837, Batchellerville, N.Y.; d July 2, 1908, Paris, France).* Lawyer, New York Republican who became first presiding justice of the International Tribunal for the administration of law in Egypt. State assembly at the age of twenty-one (1859, 1860, 1873, 1874, 1886, 1887), lieutenant colonel in Union Army during Civil War, Grant presidential elector (1868), Grant-appointed U.S. judge in the new International Tribunal where his fellow jurists chose him to preside (1876-1885), Harrison-appointed assistant secretary of the treasury (1889) and ambassador to Portugal (1891), returned to Tribunal (1898) at Egypt's request where he served until his death, becoming, however, Theodore Roosevelt-appointed member of its appellate division (1902).

BATE, WILLIAM BRIMAGE *(b Oct. 7, 1826, Sumner County, Tenn.; d March 9, 1905, Washington, D.C.).* A frontier boy who tried his hand at many things, among them working on riverboats, newspaper publishing, and shouldering a musket in the Mexican War, all while teaching himself the law; Tennessee secessionist Democrat.

State house of representatives (1849-1851), attorney general for the tri-county Nashville district (1854), Breckinridge-Lane presidential elector (1860), rose from private to major general in Confederate Army during Civil War, national presidential convention delegate (1868), Tilden-Hendricks presidential elector (1876), governor of Tennessee (1883-1887), U.S. Senator (1887 until death); funeral services were conducted in Senate chamber.

History, or perhaps legend, has it that Bate was offered the gubernatorial nomination while leading his troops in 1863 but refused, supposedly declaring that he'd rather be Tennessee's defender than Tennessee's governor. There are perhaps a dozen versions of his reply.

BATEMAN, EPHRAIM *(b July 9, 1780, Cedarville, N.J.; d Jan. 28, 1829, Cedarville).* Physician, New Jersey Democrat who elected himself to the U.S. Senate. State assembly (1808-1813, its speaker in the last year), U.S. Representative (1815-1823), president of state council (1826) where he cast the tie-breaking vote in favor of himself to fill a senatorial vacancy caused by the death of Joseph McIlvaine and thus delaying the career of his opponent, Theodore Frelinghuysen for three years.

Bateman served (1826-1829), then resigned two weeks before his death because of deteriorating health and the seat went to Frelinghuysen.

BATES, ARTHUR LABAN *(b June 6, 1859, Meadville, Pa.; d Aug. 26, 1934, Meadville).* Newspaper publisher, lawyer, banker, Pennsylvania Republican. Meadville city solicitor (1889-1896), U.S. Representative (1901-1913), delegate to International Peace Conference at Brussels (1905), at Rome (1911), state GOP convention delegate (1908), Hughes-Fairbanks presidential elector (1916), national presidential convention delegate (1924).

BATES, DANIEL MOORE *(b Jan. 28, 1821, Laurel, Del.; d March 28, 1879, Richmond, Va.).* Lawyer. Delaware secretary of state (1847-1851), U.S. district attorney for Delaware (1852-1861), delegate to Washington conference (1861) that sought to avert Civil War, state chancellor (1865-1873). Father of George H. Bates.

BATES, EDWARD *(b Sept. 4, 1793, Goochland County, Va.; d March 25, 1869, St. Louis, Mo.).* Missouri lawyer and Lincoln's opponent for presidential nomination. Territorial circuit prosecuting attorney (1818), member of state constitutional convention (1820) and state's attorney in same year, U.S. district attorney (1821-1826), a pro-Adams Anti-Democrat U.S. Representative (1827-1829), state senate (1830), president of River and Harbor Improvement Convention (1847) in Chicago where he made a speech that put him in the national limelight.

Offered cabinet post as secretary of war by President Fillmore (1850) but declined for personal reasons; St. Louis land court judge (1853-1856); presiding officer at Whig National Convention (1856); chosen the candidate of a coalition of border-state Free-Soilers, Whigs, and Republicans to seek the presidential nomination at GOP National

Convention (1860) but lost to Lincoln on the third ballot; attorney general in Lincoln's cabinet (1861-1864), resigning because of differences over admission of West Virginia to the Union and disapproval of what he considered to be misconduct of three fellow cabinet members (Chase, Seward and Stanton).

Back in Missouri once again, Bates fought a new state constitution drafted at a "radical" convention (1865) with every means at his command. His health broken, he lost the fight and took no further part in politics in his remaining four years. Brother of Frederick Bates.

BATES, FREDERICK *(b June 23, 1777, Goochland County, Va.; d Aug. 4, 1825, Bonhomme Township, Mo.).* Lawyer and merchant who, in the spirit of the times, did not hesitate to explore new horizons.

In Virginia: both postmaster and county court clerk, starting at the age of eighteen, while studying law. In Michigan: associate territorial judge (1805-1806). In Louisiana: Jefferson-appointed secretary of the territory (1806-1812) serving four times as acting governor. In Missouri: the state's second governor (1824 until death). Brother of Edward Bates.

BATES, GEORGE HANDY *(b Nov. 19, 1845, Dover, Del.; d Oct. 31, 1916, Philadelphia, Pa.).* Lawyer, Delaware Democrat. State deputy attorney general (1871-1874), delegate to three national presidential conventions (1880, 1884, 1888), state legislature (1882-1883), its speaker (1883), Cleveland-appointed special U.S. agent to check conditions in Samoa (1886), Harrison-appointed commissioner to Samoan treaty conference in Berlin with British and German representatives (1889). Son of Daniel Moore Bates.

BATES, GEORGE JOSEPH *(b Feb. 25, 1891, Salem, Mass.; d Nov. 1, 1949, in Washington, D.C., National Airport plane crash).* Massachusetts Republican. State house of representatives (1918-1924), mayor of Salem (1924-1937), seven times a U.S. Representative (1937 until death). Father of William H. Bates.

BATES, ISAAC CHAPMAN *(b Jan. 23, 1779, Granville, Mass.; d March 16, 1845, Washington, D.C.).* Lawyer, Massachusetts Whig. State house of representatives (1808, 1809), anti-Jackson U.S. Representative (1827-1835), Webster-Granger presidential elector (1836), Harrison-Tyler elector (1840), U.S. Senate (1841 until death).

BATES, JOSEPH BENGAL *(b Oct. 29, 1893, Republican, Ky.).* Kentucky Democrat, educator, lawyer. Raceland, Ky., high school superintendent (1917-1919), Greenup County clerk (1922-1938), U.S. Representative (1938-1953).

BATES, WILLIAM HENRY *(b April 26, 1917, Salem, Mass.; d June 22, 1969, Bethesda, Md.).* Massachusetts Republican who succeeded his father, George Joseph Bates, as U.S. Representative in 1950 and served until death. A former lieutenant commander and champion of a nuclear navy, he was the senior GOP member of the House Armed Services Committee and the second-ranking Republican on the Joint Congressional Committee on Atomic Energy.

BATTLE, BURRELL BUNN *(b July 24, 1838, Hinds County, Miss.; d Dec. 21, 1917, Little Rock, Ark.).* Considered one of Arkansas' outstanding jurists. State legislature (1871) where he was a leader in a vigorous but unsuccessful attempt to impeach Governor Powell Clayton; state supreme court justice for a quarter-century (1885-1911) where his conservatism (the established law was "the absolute master of his judicial work" and he brooked no bench-made law, a eulogist at his funeral said) was hailed by his progressive associates as "a sheet anchor of safety."

BATTLE, CULLEN ANDREWS *(b June 1, 1829, Powelton, Ga.; d April 8, 1905, Greensboro, N.C.).* Lawyer, editor, Alabama Democrat whose adamant unreconstructionism cost him at least one seat in Congress. Already an accomplished orator when he was admitted to the bar in 1852, he stumped the state throughout the 1850s ardently advancing his views on states' rights, slavery, and secession; in the presidential campaign of 1860 his stump-speaking for John Cabell Breckinridge spread into the north as far as Boston; much-cited Civil War field commander, being mustered out a major general; in 1868 he was elected a U.S. Representative but was denied a seat for refusing to take the "iron-clad oath of office." In 1870 he sought nomination for U.S. Senate but more pragmatic Democrats, fearing a repetition of 1868, scratched him from the race. He was a delegate to Alabama's constitutional convention in 1874. In 1880 he moved to New Bern, N.C., where he was editor of the *New Bern Journal* and, for a time, mayor.

BATTLE, WILLIAM HORN *(b Oct. 17, 1802, Edgecombe County, N.C.; d March 14, 1879, Chapel Hill, N.C.).* Lawyer, North Carolina Whig. State house of commons (1833-1834), delegate to national presidential convention (1839), superior court judge (1840-1843), associate justice of state supreme court (1852-1868). Twice he revised the state statutes, in the 1830s with two others and alone in the 1870s.

BAXTER, ELISHA *(b Sept. 1, 1827, Rutherford County, N.C.; d May 31, 1899, Batesville, Ark.).* Merchant, lawyer, farmer, Arkansas Whig-Republican who literally fought for and went to jail for his convictions.

In the state legislature (1854, 1858),

he vigorously opposed secession; when Civil War began he announced himself for the Union, a lone voice in a Confederate state, but declared he would not take up arms against his neighbors. He fled with his family to Missouri, was captured, tried for treason, and imprisoned. He escaped, organized and commanded the Fourth Arkansas Mounted Infantry. In 1864 he was part of a movement that formed a pro-union state government and was elected to its supreme court, serving only until he was elected to the U.S. Senate (where all attempts to have him seated failed).

The war over and Reconstruction begun, Baxter became a Third Circuit Court judge (1868-1871). With Arkansas torn by the mismanagement of a carpet-bag administration, he became the gubernatorial nominee of the GOP's "Minstrel" faction. The opposition "Brindletail" candidate was Joseph Brooks who also had the Democratic endorsement. The election campaign was bitter and after Baxter won by 2,919 votes and served (1872-1874), the struggle that became known as the Brooks-Baxter War continued. Brooks contested the election, the state supreme court supported Brooks, the state legislature supported Baxter. Brooks mounted an armed militia, marched on the capitol in Little Rock (April 1874), seized it, and pronounced himself governor. Baxter supporters took up arms and there were clashes up and down Main Street and along the banks of the Arkansas River. On May 13 there came a proclamation from President Grant, backed by federal troops, that Baxter was governor and everyone was to lay down their arms. Only then did Brooks give up.

Meanwhile, Baxter had lost the support of the Republicans but gained the backing of Democrats and it was the latter who provided the legislative votes to put through his reform program that included a new state constitution. The Democrats offered him their nomination if he would seek reelection, but Baxter declined and returned to the peace of his farm and his law office in Batesville.

BAXTER, PORTUS *(b Dec. 4, 1806, Browington, Vt.; d March 4, 1868, Washington, D.C.).* Vermont Whig-Republican. Whig presidential elector for Scott and Graham, Republican elector for Fremont and Dayton (1856), U.S. Representative (1861-1867).

BAYARD, JAMES ASHETON, SR. *(b July 28, 1767, Philadelphia, Pa.; d Aug. 6, 1815, Wilmington, Del.).* Delaware lawyer and one of the nation's leading Federalists. U.S. Representative (1797-1803), conducted impeachment proceedings (1798) against U.S. Senator William Blount; an emissary to Thomas Jefferson's camp, when the 1800 presidential contest with Aaron Burr resulted in deadlock, to help determine which, from the Federalist point of view, was the lesser of two evils; declined President Adams' offer to be minister to France (1801); U.S. Senate (1804-1813); a U.S. delegate to Ghent (1813-1814) where a peace treaty was negotiated with Britain to end the War of 1812; declined President Madison's appointment as ambassador to Russia (1815), returning to Ghent again in the same year, this time to negotiate a trade treaty with Britain. Ill health cut his participation in the mission short and he arrived home six days before his death. Father of James Asheton Bayard, Jr., and Richard Bayard.

BAYARD, JAMES ASHETON, JR. *(b Nov. 15, 1799, Wilmington, Del.; d June 13, 1880, Wilmington).* Delaware lawyer; unlike his staunchly Federalist father, a Democrat who took a fling at Republicanism. Coming into politics when the making of parties was having its birth pangs, he threw his lot in with the Democrats—a deed that did not sit at all well with his friends who were overwhelmingly Whig. Three times de-

feated (1828, 1832, 1834) in tries for the U.S. House of Representatives at general elections; in 1838 when he aspired to the U.S. Senate (offices which were at that time filled by state legislatures) the Whig state senate prevented it simply by refusing to meet in joint session with the Democratic house and so he settled for the appointive position of U.S. attorney (1838-1843), a bit of patronage over which the Whigs had no control. (He was somewhat avenged when, as a state constitutional convention delegate [1852-1853] he opposed and helped defeat the new document and Delaware thus went without a new constitution until 1882).

In 1851, Bayard had made it to the U.S. Senate on the sixteenth ballot and was reelected with somewhat less trouble in 1857 and 1863, during which period he became so disenchanted with some of his Democratic colleagues that he donned a Republican hat, still voting, however, with the Democrats on many GOP-proposed antislavery measures. And on Jan. 29, 1864, he resigned from the Senate rather than swear to the new oath of office that the Republicans had prescribed. However, when George R. Riddle who had succeeded him died, he readily agreed to fill the vacancy and from 1867 until 1869 completed his own term, then stepped aside so that his Democratic son, Thomas F. Bayard, Sr., could succeed him.

BAYARD, JOHN BUBENHEIM *(b Aug. 11, 1738, Bohemia Manor, Md.; d Jan. 7, 1807, New Brunswick, N.J.).* Federalist, Philadelphia merchant, patriot, and active foe of British rule. Pennsylvania General Assembly (1776-1779, 1784) and its speaker (1777-1778), Revolutionary Army colonel, Continental Congress (1785-1787), mayor of New Brunswick (1790). Uncle of James Asheton Bayard, Sr.

BAYARD, NICHOLAS *(b 1644, Alphen, Holland; d 1707, New York City).*

Brought to New York, then New Amsterdam, in 1647; nephew of Peter Stuyvesant and husband of Judith Varlith who was jailed as a witch in 1662 in Hartford, Conn. He held various positions in the Dutch province, was imprisoned for espousing religious freedom when the English took over but after four years made his peace with them and became variously city alderman, member of the governor's council, and mayor (1685-1687); driven from the last post by the forces of Jacob Leisler, hid out in Albany for five months, was captured, paraded through the streets of New York in chains, and jailed for a year. Arrival of a new governor from England resulted in Bayard's freedom and a death warrant for Leisler, following which still another governor accused Bayard of treason, stripped him of his property, sentenced him to death, and he went back into jail for another year. Then came still another governor, a direct appeal to Queen Anne, and reinstatement of property and honors. Through it all, Bayard remained a pillar of the Dutch church, serving as deacon and elder.

BAYARD, RICHARD HENRY *(b Sept. 23, 1796, Wilmington, Del.; d March 4, 1868, Philadelphia, Pa.).* Lawyer, Delaware Whig. Wilmington's first mayor (1832-1835), U.S. Senate (1836-1839, 1841-1845), chief justice of Delaware (1839-1841), chargé d'affaires to Belgium (1850-1853). Son of James Asheton Bayard, Sr.

BAYARD, THOMAS FRANCIS, SR. *(b Oct. 29, 1828, Wilmington, Del.; d Sept. 28, 1898, Dedham, Mass.).* Delaware Democrat, secretary of state in Cleveland cabinet (1885-1889), U.S. attorney in Delaware (1853, 1854), U.S. Senate (1869-1885) and president pro tem (1881), ambassador to Great Britain (1893-1897).

Son of James Asheton Bayard, Jr., he perhaps left more of a mark than did any of the Bayards who went to Washington. Internationally, he was consistently on the side of peace, conciliation, and arbitration in the settlement of international affairs; domestically, he was a staunch foe of class legislation of any kind including the expansion of federal power over the people. Twice supporters sought vainly (1880 and 1884) to win for him his party's presidential nomination.

BAYARD, THOMAS FRANCIS, JR. *(b June 4, 1868, Wilmington, Del.; d July 12, 1942, Wilmington).* Lawyer, Delaware and New York Democrat. New York City assistant corporation counsel (1891), chairman of Delaware Democratic state committee (1906-1916), Wilmington city solicitor (1917-1919), U.S. Senator from Delaware (1922-1929).

BAYLIES, FRANCIS *(b Oct. 16, 1784, Taunton, Mass.; d Oct. 28, 1852, Taunton).* Lawyer, author, pamphleteer. Bristol County register of probate (1812-1820), U.S. Representative (1821-1827), state representative (1827-1832, 1835), chargé d'affaires to Argentina (1832).

He was the only congressman from New England to vote against John Quincy Adams when the presidential election was thrown into the House in 1824, giving "moral unfitness" as his reason. President Jackson appointed him acting minister to Buenos Aires with power to negotiate a treaty and thus bring to an end a fishing war that had been raging between Falkland Islanders and New England fishermen since 1829, a conflict that had been marked by Jackson sending a ship of war there to protect U.S. fishing boats and to unseat the governor of the islands. Baylies arrived in Argentina in June and the government demanded reparations and an apology, but Baylies refused. Argentinians heaped indignities upon him and he returned home in September certain there would be war between the two countries; there was none but diplomatic relations were not renewed until 1844. Brother of William Baylies.

BAYLIES, WILLIAM *(b Sept. 15, 1776, Dighton, Mass.; d Sept. 27, 1865, Taunton, Mass.).* Massachusetts lawyer. State representative (1808, 1809, 1812, 1813, 1820, 1821), served three months in U.S. House of Representatives as a War Democrat in 1809, then his election was contested and he was replaced by Charles Turner, Jr.; elected and reelected again and served from 1813 until 1817; state senate (1825, 1826, 1830, 1831), and the U.S. House once more (1833-1835). Brother of Francis Baylies.

BAYLOR, ROBERT EMMETT BLEDSOE *(b May 10, 1793, Lincoln County, Ky.; d Jan. 6, 1874, Washington County, Tex.).* Preacher, teacher, lawyer, Indian fighter, Kentucky, Alabama, and Texas Democrat, cofounder of Baylor University. Kentucky representative (1819), Alabama house (1824), U.S. Representative (1829-1831); moved to Texas (1839) and became very much part of its life, both as a republic and as a state, until his death. Among his contributions he served as district judge, supreme court justice, and constitutional convention delegate who directly helped to frame its first state constitution.

BAYLY, THOMAS HENRY *(b Dec. 11, 1810, Accomac County, Va.; d June 23, 1856, in the same house in which he was born—"Mount Custis," the family plantation begun by his father [see next entry]).* Lawyer, planter, Virginia States' Rights Democrat. House of delegates (1835-1840), superior court judge (1842-1844), U.S. Representative (1844 until death).

BAYLY, THOMAS MONTEAGLE *(b March 26, 1775, Accomac County, Va.; d Jan. 7, 1834, Mount Custis, Va.).* Lawyer, farmer, Virginia Democrat.

House of Delegates (1798-1801, 1819, 1820, 1828-1831), state senate (1801-1809), U.S. Representative (1813-1815), delegate to state constitutional convention (1829, 1830). Father of Thomas Henry Bayly.

BAYNE, THOMAS McKEE *(b June 14, 1836, Bellevue, Pa.; d June 16, 1894, Washington, D.C.).* Lawyer, Pennsylvania Republican. Allegheny County district attorney (1870-1874), U.S. Representative (1877-1891).

BEAKES, SAMUEL WILLARD *(b Jan. 11, 1861, Burlingham, N.Y.; d Feb. 9, 1927, Washington, D.C.).* Lawyer, newspaper editor-publisher, Michigan Democrat. Mayor of Ann Arbor (1888-1890), city treasurer (1891-1893, 1903-1905), postmaster (1894-1898), city assessor 1906-1913), U.S. Representative (1913-1919), Democratic National Convention (1916), U.S. Veterans' Bureau aide (1919 until death).

BEALL, JAMES ANDREW "JACK" *(b Oct. 25, 1866, Ellis County, Tex.; d Feb. 12, 1929, Dallas).* Teacher, lawyer, banker, Texas Democrat. State house of representatives (1892-1895), state senate (1895-1899), U.S. Representative (1903-1915).

BEALL, JAMES GLENN *(b June 5, 1894, Frostburg, Md.; d Jan. 14, 1971, Frostburg).* Real estate and insurance business, bank director, Maryland Republican who served both in the U.S. House and U.S. Senate. Member of Allegany County Road Commission (1938, 1939), U.S. Representative (1943-1953), U.S. Senate (1953-1965) serving on the Armed Services, Commerce, and District of Columbia committees.

BEALL, SAMUEL WOOTTON *(b Sept. 26, 1807, Montgomery, Md.; d Sept. 25, 1868, Helena, Mont.).* One of the hearty breed of men who opened the West, and described by a biographer as "a curious compound of strength and instability." He first gave up the comforts of eastern living to become receiver for the sale of public lands and so set up a land office in what is now Green Bay, Wis., remaining there from 1827 until 1834 when he returned to the home of his wife, a niece of J. Fenimore Cooper, in Cooperstown, N.Y., and became part of a literary circle that included such notables as Washington Irving. In 1840 he returned to Wisconsin, became a staunch advocate of statehood and at the constitutional convention (1846) was chairman of a committee to organize a state government. He served as lieutenant-governor (1850-1852), then became an Indian agent and (1859) headed a party that both explored Pike's Peak and helped found the city of Denver. After the Civil War, in which he saw much combat as lieutenant-colonel of the Eighteenth Wisconsin Regiment, he pushed on to Montana where he was killed in a gun fight with a newspaper editor who had published critical stories about him.

BEAM, HARRY PETER (b Nov. 23, 1892, Peoria, Ill.). Lawyer, Illinois Democrat. Assistant corporation counsel in Chicago (1923-1927), U.S. Representative (1931-1942), municipal court judge (1942-1960).

BEAMAN, FERNANDO CORTEZ (b June 28, 1814, Chester, Vt.; d Sept. 27, 1882, Adrian, Mich.). Teacher, lawyer, Michigan Republican. Lenawee County prosecutor (1843-1850), delegate to convention (1854) that organized the Republican party "under the oaks" in Jackson, Mich.; delegate to first GOP national convention (1856), Fremont-Dayton presidential elector (1856), mayor of Adrian (1856), Lenawee County probate court judge (1857-1860, 1872-1878), U.S. Representative (1861-1871).

BEAMER, JOHN VALENTINE (b Nov. 17, 1896, Wabash County, Ind.). Farmer, businessman, Indiana Republican. State house of representatives (1949, 1950), U.S. Representative (1951-1959).

BEAN, BENNING MOULTON (b Jan. 9, 1782, Moultonboro, N.H.; d Feb. 6, 1866 Moultonboro). Teacher, farmer, New Hampshire Democrat. Moultonboro selectman (1811-1829, 1832-1838), justice of the peace (1816), state house of representatives (1815-1823, 1827), state senate (1824-1826, 1831, its president in 1832). U.S. Representative (1833-1837).

BEARDSLEY, SAMUEL (b. Feb. 6, 1790, Hoosick, N.Y.; d May 6, 1860, Utica, N.Y.). Teacher, lawyer, New York Democrat. Judge advocate in state militia during War of 1812, Rome town clerk (1817), Oneida County supervisor (1818-1820), state senate (1822), U.S. district attorney for northern New York (1823-1830), U.S. Representative (1831-1836, 1843-1844) were his speech (1834) on a currency controversy attracted national attention, state attorney general (1836-1838), associate state supreme court justice (1844-1846), chief justice (1847). An eloquent orator and champion of free speech, he was an adviser to presidents and governors and a leader of his party in New York.

BEATTY, JOHN (b Dec. 10, 1749, Neshaminy, Pa.; d May 30, 1826, Trenton, N.J.). Physician, banker, New Jersey state council (1781-1783), Continental Congress (1784-1785), delegate to state convention that adopted federal Constitution (1787), speaker of state general assembly (1789-1790), U.S. Representative (1793-1795), New Jersey secretary of state (1795-1805).

BEATTY, JOHN (b Dec. 16, 1828, Erie County, Ohio; d Dec. 21, 1914, Columbus, Ohio). Banker, author, Ohio Republican. Presidential elector for Lincoln-Hamlin (1860) and Blaine-Logan (1884), U.S. Representative (1868-1873).

BEAVER, JAMES ADDAMS *(b Oct. 21, 1837, Millerstown, Pa.; d Jan. 31, 1914).* Lawyer, manufacturer, Union soldier, Pennsylvania Republican. Ran unsuccessfully for governor (1882) but was later elected and served 1887-1891, improving roads, waterways, and flood control during his tenure. Superior court judge (1895 until death).

BECK, JAMES BURNIE *(b Feb. 13, 1822, Dumfriesshire, Scotland; d May 3, 1890, Washington, D.C.).* Lawyer, Kentucky Democrat. Democratic National Convention delegate (1860), U.S. Representative (1867-1875), member of commission that defined Maryland-Virginia boundary (1876), U.S. Senate (1877 until death).

BECK, JAMES MONTGOMERY *(b July 9, 1861, Philadelphia, Pa.; d April 12, 1936, Washington, D.C.).* Author, lawyer, Pennsylvania Democrat turned Republican and one of the leading conservatives of his time. As a Democrat, he served as assistant U.S. attorney for the eastern Pennsylvania district (1888-1892) and as U.S. attorney (1896-1900), then became a Republican. President McKinley welcomed this newcomer to the GOP ranks by appointing him assistant attorney general, a post that he filled from 1900 until 1903 when he switched to corporate law, numbering among his clients Standard Oil, the Mutual Life Insurance Co., the American Newspaper Publishers' Association, the Sugar Trust, and the American Anti-Boycott (labor) Association. Beck became a wealthy man.

He eloquently endorsed the Allied position early in World War I, his penned indictment of the enemy, *The Evidence in the Case,* became a widely read and quoted book, but when the United States entered the war he vehemently opposed President Wilson's policies and later jumped into the League of Nations fracas with both feet. He supported Warren G. Harding for the presidency, as a reward was named solici-

tor general and served from 1921 until 1925 when he quit because arguing before the Supreme Court on the side of the government on such litigation as the Second Child Labor case went against his grain.

But the lure of public life remained and he successfully ran for Congress in 1927, voting against such legislation as President Hoover's farm board program and the Smoot-Hartley tariff. He was thrice reelected congressman before declining to run in 1934 rather than continue to fight in vain against President Roosevelt's New Deal legislation. Beck then devoted his energies to the rightist affairs of the American Liberty League and appeared before the Supreme Court to argue against such constitutional issues as the Tennessee Valley Authority and the Securities and Exchange Commission.

BECK, JOSEPH DAVID *(b March 14, 1866, Vernon County, Wis.; d Nov. 8, 1936, Madison, Wis.).* Teacher, farmer, statistician, Wisconsin Republican who held many state appointive positions. U.S. Representative (1921-1929), unsuccessful candidate for GOP gubernatorial nomination (1928).

BECKER, FRANK JOHN *(b Aug. 27, 1899, Brooklyn, N.Y.).* Insurance broker, New York Republican. State assembly (1945-1953), U.S. Representative (1953-1965).

BECKHAM, JOHN CREPPS WICKLIFFE *(b Aug. 5, 1869, Wickland, Ky.; d Jan. 9, 1940, Louisville, Ky.).* Lawyer, Kentucky Democrat. State representative (1894-1898, its speaker in last year), lieutenant governor (1899), governor (1900-1907), national convention delegate five times (1904-1920), U.S. Senate (1915-1921).

BECKWORTH, LINDLEY GARY *(b June 30, 1913. South Bouie, Tex.).* Teacher lawyer, Texas Democrat. State representative (1936-1938), U.S. Representative (1939-1953, 1957-1967).

BEDE, JAMES ADAM (b Jan. 13, 1856, North Eaton Township, Ohio; d April 11, 1942, Duluth, Minn.). Newspaper reporter, editor, publisher, lecturer, lawyer, teacher, Minnesota Republican. U.S. Representative (1903-1909).

BEDFORD, GUNNING (b April 7, 1742, Philadelphia, Pa.; d Sept. 30, 1797, New Castle, Del.). Lawyer. Delaware general assembly (1784-1786), elected to Thirteenth Continental Congress but refused to serve, delegate to Delaware convention (1787) that ratified federal consitution, presidential elector (1789), governor of Delaware (1796 until death). (Not to be confused with Gunning Bedford, Jr. a cousin with a parallel career in Delaware life.)

BEDFORD, GUNNING, JR. (b 1747, Philadelphia, Pa.; d March 30, 1812, Wilmington, Del.). Lawyer, Delaware delegate to Continental Congress (1783-1785), state attorney general (1784-1789), delegate to federal Constitutional Convention (1787) and signer of the Constitution, delegate to state convention that ratified it (1787), state senate (1788), presidential elector (1789, 1793), U.S. judge (1789 until death). A gifted speaker, this Bedford played a leading but often losing role in the federal convention, championing the position of the small states, favoring a three-year presidential term, fighting against checks being placed upon the legislative branch and a strong central government, at one point delivering an impassioned speech that one critic described as the "most intemperate uttered in the Convention." (Not to be confused with his cousin Gunning Bedford.)

BEDINGER, GEORGE MICHAEL (b Dec. 10, 1756, Hanover, Pa.; d Dec. 7, 1843, Blue Lick Springs, Ky.). Revolutionary soldier, Indian fighter, frontiersman, Kentucky pioneer. Spent his early years on expeditions of exploration and adventure, but settled down in Boonesborough, to take up political affairs and farming. Member of Kentucky's first house of representatives (1792), state senate (1800, 1801), U.S. Representative (1803-1807). Uncle of Henry Bedinger.

BEDINGER, HENRY (b Feb. 3, 1812, Jefferson County, Va.; d Nov. 26, 1858, Shepherdstown, Va.). Lawyer, Virginia Democrat. U.S. Representative (1845-1849), minister to Denmark (1853-1858). Nephew of George Michael Bedinger.

BEE, THOMAS (b 1725, Charleston, SC.; d Feb. 18, 1812, Pendleton, SC.). Lawyer, planter. Member of commons house in province of South Carolina (1762-1764, 1765, 1772-1776), justice of the peace (1775), delegate to first and second provincial congresses (1775, 1776), member of state house of representatives (1776-1779, 1782) and its speaker (1777-1779), lieutenant governor (1779, 1780), Continental Congress (1780-1782), U.S. district judge (1790-1810).

BEEBE, GEORGE MONROE (b Oct. 28, 1836, New Vernon, N.Y.; d March 1, 1927, Ellenville, N.Y.). A lawyer-newspaperman with a wanderlust that took him from New York to Kansas to Missouri to Nevada and back to New York again, leaving a bit of an imprint upon them all. Member of Kansas territorial council (1858, 1859), secretary of the territory (1859), acting governor (1860, 1861). Then on to Missouri and Nevada and unsuccessful bids for office—and declination of presidential appointments—before returning to his native state. New York assemblyman (1872, 1873), Democratic state convention chairman (1873, 1874), U.S. Representative (1875-1879), delegate to national convention (1876, 1880, 1892), state court of claims (1883-1900).

BEECHER, CATHARINE ESTHER *(b Sept. 6, 1800, East Hampton, N.Y.; d May 12, 1878, Elmira, N.Y.).* An educator and staunch advocate of more liberal educational opportunities for women, her contribution to women's rights was more negative than affirmative in that she was one of the nation's foremost foes of women's suffrage. Sister of Henry Ward and Edward Beecher and Harriet Beecher Stowe, daughter of Lyman Beecher.

BEECHER, HENRY WARD *(b June 24, 1813, Litchfield, Conn.; d March 8, 1887, Brooklyn, N.Y.).* Clergyman-lecturer-author with a passion for freedom for all people, a brilliant orator with a flare for the theatrical and unorthodox. Like his father (see Lyman Beecher), he was a foe of slavery but by no means an extremist nor an abolitionist on the subject. He was pastor of Brooklyn's Plymouth Church from 1847 until death but never once, as he said, delivered a sermon nor spoke from a pulpit. Rather, he preferred to speak from "a platform" on public questions of the moment and for the many reforms he championed, often inviting other speakers to share the platform with him. He supported Fremont and Lincoln in their campaigns for the presidency (1856 and 1860), strongly endorsed the Civil War and, when it was over, backed the readmission of secessionist states without the yoke of military government. Brother of Catharine Beecher and Harriet Beecher Stowe.

BEECHER, LYMAN *(b Oct. 12, 1775, New Haven, Conn.; d Jan. 10, 1863, Brooklyn, N.Y.).* One of the best-known clergymen of his time and head of a large family (three wives and thirteen children) most of whom made positive contributions, directly or indirectly, to life, politics, and government in America (father of Catharine and Henry Ward Beecher and Harriet Beecher Stowe). One of his lesser theologic accomplishments was a series of anti-Catholic lectures (1831) in Boston that resulted in a raid upon a Charlestown, Mass., convent by an unruly mob.

BEECHER, PHILEMON *(b 1775, Litchfield, Conn.; d Nov. 30, 1839, Lancaster, Ohio).* Lawyer, Ohio Federalist. State representative (1803, 1805-1807, speaker in 1807), U.S. Representative (1817-1821, 1823-1829).

BEEDY, CARROLL LYNWOOD *(b Aug. 3, 1880, Philips, Maine; d Aug. 30, 1947, Washington, D.C.).* Lawyer, Maine Republican. Cumberland County prosecuting attorney (1917-1921), U.S. Representative (1921-1935).

BEER, GEORGE LOUIS *(b July 26, 1872, Staten Island, N.Y.; d March 15, 1920, New York, N.Y.).* Historian whose works did much to explain British pre-Revolution economic policy in the American colonies. World War I interrupted his then-British-based research efforts and he became a correspondent whose in-depth reports helped bring America into the conflict on the side of the Allies. President Wilson named him (1917) to an inquiry group assigned to study questions apt to arise when peace finally came. He was colonial-division chief of the American delegation to the Paris Peace Conference and had much to do with decisions on how Germany's former African colonies were to be administered.

BEERS, EDWARD McMATH *(b May 27, 1877, Nossville, Pa.; d April 21, 1932, Washington, D.C.).* Hotelman, farmer, banker, Pennsylvania Republican. Delegate to GOP state convention (1898), mayor of Mount Union (1910-1914), associate Huntington County judge (1914-1923), U.S. Representative (1923 until death).

BEGOLE, JOSIAH WILLIAMS *(b Jan. 20, 1815, Groveland, N.Y.; d June 5, 1896, Flint, Mich.).* Teacher, farmer, businessman, banker, Michigan Republican. State senate (1870, 1871), Flint city council (1872-1875), GOP National Convention (1872), U.S. Representative (1873-1875), governor (1883-1885).

BEHAN, WILLIAM JAMES *(b Sept. 25, 1840, New Orleans, La.; d May 4, 1928, New Orleans).* Wholesale grocer, sugar planter, Confederate soldier, Louisiana Democrat turned Republican in protest against sugar tariff reduction. His first major introduction to politics came after the Civil War when, as a fierce foe of carpetbag government, he helped to organize the Crescent City White League and in 1874 led its forces against federal troops in what became known as the Battle of the Customs House. He served one term as mayor of New Orleans (1882-1884) but, because of his war against backroom politicians, lost his bid for reelection; some said through fraud. State senate (1889-1891), delegate to many GOP national conventions from 1896 on, the party's candidate for governor in 1904.

BEIDLER, JACOB ATLEE *(b Nov. 2, 1852, Tredyffin Township, Pa.; d Sept. 13, 1912, Lake County, Ohio.).* Farmer, coal dealer, Ohio Republican. U.S. Representative (1901-1907).

BEIRNE, ANDREW *(b 1771, Dangan, Ireland; d March 16, 1845, Gainesville, Va.).* Merchant, farmer, Virginia Democrat. State house of delegates (1807, 1808), state constitutional convention (1829, 1830), state senate (1831-1836), Van Buren-Johnson presidential elector (1836), U.S. Representative (1837-1841).

BELCHER, HIRAM *(b Feb. 23, 1790, Hallowell, Maine; d May 6, 1857, Farmington, Me.).* Lawyer, Maine Whig. Farmington town clerk (1814-1819), state representative (1822, 1829, 1832), state senate (1838, 1839), U.S. Representative (1847-1849).

BELCHER, JONATHAN *(b Jan. 8, 1681/2, Cambridge, Mass.; d Aug. 31, 1757, Trenton, N.J.).* Merchant, colonial governor with a short temper and sharp tongue. Massachusetts Council (1718-1728), sent to England to argue against the high pay of the then-governor who died while Belcher was in England and the job of governing both Massachusetts and New Hampshire was given to him (1729-1741). He tried to walk a tightrope as a native son representing the crown but his biting temper was his downfall. Some colonists brought charges against him (there were rumors at the time that some signatures were forged) and he was finally removed by the crown. By 1746, however, he had returned to the good graces of the powers in London and he was chosen to be governor of New Jersey, a post that he held until death and in which he made one lasting contribution—the founding of the College of New Jersey (now Princeton University).

BELDEN, JAMES JEROME *(b Sept. 30, 1825, Fabius, N.Y.; d Jan. 1, 1904, Syracuse, N.Y.).* Banker, construction contractor (largely of public works), New York Republican. Mayor of Syracuse (1877, 1878), U.S. Representative (1887-1895, 1897-1899).

BELDEN, JOSIAH *(b May 4, 1815, Cromwell, Conn.; d April 23, 1892, New York City).* California Republican. Apprenticed out as a jeweler, he stuck to that work only until he was twenty-one and in 1836 joined the first wagon train from Missouri to the Pacific. He opened a small store in Santa Cruz, became a Mexican citizen, moved on to San Jose to run a store there and was the provisioner to many miners in the gold rush that came in 1849, himself succumbing to the lure of the fields only briefly. The next year San Jose was incorporated as a city and he was its first mayor and then a councilman. By then a wealthy man, Belden supported the Union party (1860-1861), helped finance the Sanitary Fund during the Civil War, and was a delegate to the 1876 GOP National Convention. In 1881, he left California for New York where he could guard his railroad interests from a seat in the window of the Union League Club.

BELFORD, JAMES BURNS *(b Sept. 28, 1837, Lewiston, Pa.; d Jan. 10, 1910, Denver, Colo.).* Lawyer, Indiana and Colorado Republican. In Indiana: Lincoln-Johnson presidential elector (1864), state representative (1867). In Colorado: associate supreme court justice (1870), U.S. Representative (1876, 1877, 1879-1885).

BELKNAP, WILLIAM WORTH *(b Sept. 22, 1829, Newburgh, N.Y.; d Oct. 13, 1890, Washington, D.C.).* An Iowa lawyer who served in the state legislature (1857-1858), and a Union officer who fought with Sherman. Belknap's star seemed very much on the rise when President Grant appointed him secretary of war in 1869. He held the cabinet post until 1876 and then came the fall —a unanimous House vote for impeachment because of "unquestioned evidence of malfeasance" in the alleged acceptance of $24,450 in exchange for a trading post franchise in Fort Sill. Belknap resigned before he could be tried and it later was said that it was his wife who took the bribe without his knowledge.

BELL, CHARLES HENRY *(b Nov. 18, 1823, Chester, N.H.; d Nov. 11, 1893, Exeter, N.H.).* Lawyer, historian, author, New Hampshire Republican. Rockingham County solicitor (1856-1866), state representative (1858-1860, 1872, 1873, house speaker in 1860), state senate (1863 and its president in 1864), served three months in the U.S. Senate (1879) until the state legislature could meet to fill a vacancy, governor (1881-1883), president of state constitutional convention (1889). President of New Hampshire Historical Society (1868-1887). Nephew of Samuel Bell.

BELL, CHARLES JASPER *(b Jan. 16, 1885, Lake City, Colo.).* Lawyer, Missouri Democrat. Kansas City City Council (1926-1930), Jackson County circuit court judge (1931-1934), U.S. Representative (1935-1949), member of Filipino Rehabilitation Commission (1945, 1946) and recipient of Philippine Republic's Distinguished Service Star.

BELL, CHARLES KEITH *(b April 18, 1853, Chattanooga, Tenn.; d April 21, 1913, Forth Worth, Tex.).* Lawyer, Texas Democrat. Hamilton County prosecuting attorney (1876), district attorney (1880-1882), national convention (1884), state senate (1884-1888), twenty-ninth judicial district judge (1888-1890), U.S. Representative (1893-1897), state attorney general (1901-1904).

BELL, HIRAM PARKS *(b Jan. 19, 1827, Jackson County, Ga.; d Aug. 17, 1907, Atlanta, Ga.).* Lawyer, Confederate soldier, Georgia Democrat. Delegate to secession convention (1861) where he opposed the secession ordinance, then served on state commission that sought Tennessee's cooperation in formation of a southern confederacy; state senate (1861, 1900, 1901), Second Confederate Congress (1864, 1865), Seymour-Blair presidential elector (1868), Democratic state executive committee (1868-1871), U.S. Representative (1873-1875, 1877-1879), national convention (1876), state representative (1898, 1899).

BELL, JOHN *(b Feb. 15, 1797, Mill Creek, Tenn.; d Sept. 10, 1869, Stewart County, Tenn.).* Lawyer, iron works operator, a southern statesman and national figure who was loyal to his own convictions and principles rather than to party or political leaders, a slave owner who believed the slavery issue should not be allowed to destroy the Union. Ran against Lincoln for the presidency.

A U.S. Representative fourteen years (1827-1841), he went to Congress as a Democrat and at first backed the policies of President Jackson; then became a Whig, heading the party in Tennessee. In 1834 he was chosen speaker, defeating his Jackson-supported fellow Tenneseean James K. Polk. For a few months in 1841 (March 5-Sept. 12), he was President Harrison's secretary of war but resigned when the latter died and Tyler, on becoming president, introduced a states' rights legislative program that Bell could not support. Returned to Washington six years later as a senator (1847-1859), taking a moderate position on most questions but opposing President Polk on the war with Mexico and the banning of slaves in territories (Wilmot Proviso) acquired during the war. Supported the 1850 Compromise provisions that he felt would strengthen the Union but opposed the Kansas-Nebraska Bill; refused to follow instructions of his state legislature to have slavery forced upon Kansas. Tried to unite conservative Whigs and moderate Republicans and became the presidential nominee of the new Constitutional Union party. Campaigning (1860) under the slogan "The Constitution of the country, the Union of the states and the enforcement of the laws," he won only three border states: Kentucky, Virginia and Tennessee.

After Lincoln's inaugural he fought against secession, vainly seeking a compromise between North and South; when Fort Sumter was fired upon, however, he reluctantly urged Tennessee to side with the South "at all hazards, at any cost and by arms." Then, a heartbroken man, he remained in exile in the Deep South throughout the war.

BELL, JOHN CALHOUN (b Dec. 11, 1851, Franklin County, Tenn.; d Aug. 12, 1933, Montrose, Colo.). Lawyer, Colorado Democrat. Saguache County attorney (1874-1876), Hinsdale County clerk (1878), Lake City mayor (1885), seventh judicial district judge (1889-1892), U.S. Representative (1893-1903), state court of appeals judge (1913-1915), state board of agriculture (1931-1933).

BELL, LUTHER VOSE (b Dec. 20, 1806, Francestown, N.H.; d Feb. 11, 1862, while on active duty at Budd's Ferry, Md.) Physician, writer, Union Army surgeon, Massachusetts Whig who, while superintendent of McLean Hospital for Insane (1836-1856), wrote a paper describing a form of insanity that thereafter has been known as Bell's Disease or Bell's Mania. State legislature (1835, 1836), executive councillor to the governor (1850), delegate to Whig National Convention (1852).

BELL, PETER HANSBROUGH (b March 11, 1810, Spotsylvania County, Va.; d March 8, 1898, Littleton, N.C.). Texas pioneer who fought in its war for independence and in the Mexican War as a Texas Ranger. Governor (1849-1853), U.S. Representative as a Democrat (1853-1857).

BELL, SAMUEL (b Feb. 9, 1770, Londonderry, N.H.; d Dec. 23, 1850, Chester, N.H.). Lawyer, banker, New Hampshire Democrat. State representative (1804-1807, its speaker 1805-1807), state senate president (1807-1809), state councillor (1809-1810), state supreme court judge (1816-1819), governor (1819-1823), U.S. Senate (1823-1835). Uncle of Charles Henry Bell.

BELL, THOMAS MONTGOMERY (b March 17, 1861, Nacoochee Valley, Ga.; d March 18, 1941, Gainesville, Ga.). Teacher, salesman, Georgia Democrat who served thirteen terms in Congress. Hall County superior court clerk (1898-1904), U.S. Representative (1905-1931).

BELLAMY, EDWARD (b March 26, 1850, Chicopee Falls, Mass.; d May 22, 1898, Chicopee Falls). Newspaper editor-publisher, pamphleteer, one of the most popular American authors of his time (his books selling in the millions), and an advocate of utopian socialism beginning "in the fall or winter of 1886 that I sat down to my desk with the definite purpose of trying to reason out a method of economic organization by which the republic might guarantee the livelihood and material welfare of its citizens." Tuberculosis cut short his career. His books include *Dr. Heidenhoff's Process* (1880), *Mrs. Ludington's Sister* (1884), *Looking Backward* (1888) and the latter's sequel, *Equality* (1897).

BELLAMY, JOHN DILLARD *(b March 24, 1854, Wilmington, N.C.; d Sept. 25, 1942, Wilmington).* Lawyer, writer, North Carolina Democrat. Wilmington city attorney (1892-1894), state senate (1900-1902), national convention delegate (1892, 1908, 1920), U.S. Representative (1899-1903).

BELLINGHAM, RICHARD *(b 1592, Boston, England; d Dec. 7, 1672, Boston, Mass.).* Lawyer, popular New England settler, Massachusetts deputy governor (1635, 1640, 1653, 1655-1665), governor (1641, 1654, 1665 until death), in 1641 defeating the incumbent, John Winthrop, by six votes. He irritated his fellow legislators by marrying Penelope Pelham without first publishing his intentions, performing the ceremony himself, and by refusing to leave office in order to stand trial for both "offenses." This so confused the magistrates that they dropped the charges.

BELMONT, ALVA ERTSKIN SMITH VANDERBILT *(b Jan. 17, 1853, Mobile, Ala.; d Jan. 26, 1933, Paris, France).* Social leader who, in her mid-fifties became actively involved in the fight for women's suffrage. Opened her palatial homes to suffrage meetings; lecturer; president National Woman's Party (1920-1933) but presided most of the time in absentia from a chateau she purchased in France.

BELMONT, AUGUST *(b Dec. 8, 1816, Alzei, Germany; d Nov. 24, 1890, New York City).* Banker, diplomat, sportsman, patron of the arts, New York Democrat. An employee in the financial house of Rothschild, he came to the U.S. during the 1837 panic, entered the banking business in New York City, numbering Rothschild as one of his accounts, flourished, became an American citizen, and cast his first vote in 1844. He was an antislavery supporter of Stephen A. Douglas, a delegate to the Democratic National Convention of 1860 and most of those that followed.

When Civil War came, he wrote: "I prefer to leave to my children, instead of the gilded prospects of New York merchant princes, the more enviable title of American citizen and as long as God spares my life I shall not falter in my efforts to procure them that heritage." He backed his words with deeds, raised and equipped New York's first German regiment, corresponded with friends abroad and visited London (1861) and Paris (1863) to gain support for the Union cause. Through it all, the only official position he held in his lifetime was that of minister to the Netherlands (1853-1857). At war's end he divided his interests equally between politics, art collecting, and thoroughbred horse racing. Father of Perry Belmont.

BELMONT, OLIVER HAZARD PERRY *(b Nov. 12, 1858, New York City; d June 10, 1908, Hempstead, N.Y.).* Banker, publisher, New York Democrat. National convention delegate (1900), U.S. Representative (1901-1903).

BELMONT, PERRY *(b Dec. 28, 1851, New York City; d May 25, 1947, Newport, R.I.).* Lawyer, diplomat, Spanish-American War and World War I officer, author, New York Democrat who did much to reform national and state campaign practices. U.S. Representative (1881-1888), minister to Spain (1888, 1889), national convention delegate (1892, 1896, 1904, 1912). In 1905 began a drive to better campaign publicity proceedings and saw his efforts enacted (1911) into law. Son of August Belmont.

BELTZHOOVER, FRANK ECKELS *(b Nov. 6, 1841, Silver Spring Township, Pa.; d June 2, 1923, Los Angeles, Calif.).* Lawyer, Pennsylvania Democrat, Cumberland County Democratic committee chairman (1868, 1873), district attorney (1874-1877), national convention delegate (1876), U.S. Representative (1879-1883, 1891-1895).

BENDER, GEORGE HARRISON *(b Sept. 29, 1896, Cleveland, Ohio; d June 18, 1961, Chagrin Falls, Ohio).* Insurance broker, editor-publisher of national Republican magazine, Ohio political leader. State senate (1920-1930), chairman Cuyahoga central committee (1936-1954), U.S. Representative (1939-1949), U.S. Senate to fill vacancy caused by death of Robert A. Taft (1954-1957), special assistant to secretary of interior (1957, 1958).

BENJAMIN, JOHN FORBES *(b Jan. 23, 1817, Cicero, N.Y.; d March 8, 1877, Washington, D.C.).* Lawyer, banker, Union officer, Missouri Democrat turned Republican. State representative (1850-1852), Buchanan-Breckinridge presidential elector (1856), GOP National Convention delegate (1864), a radical Republican U.S. Representative (1865-1871).

BENJAMIN, JUDAH PHILIP *(b Aug. 6, 1811, St. Croix, Virgin Islands; d May 8, 1884, Paris, France).* Lawyer of great renown on two continents, teacher, planter, writer, member of Confederate cabinet, Louisiana Whig turned Democrat who said no when offered appointment to the U.S. Supreme Court.

State constitutional convention delegate (1845), Taylor-Fillmore presidential elector (1848), U.S. Senate (1853-1856) entering as a Whig and switching parties in 1856, Confederate attor-

ney general (February 1861), becoming secretary of war (November 1861), secretary of state (March 1862) and one of Jefferson Davis' closest advisers until end of Civil War.

With Union forces overrunning the South, Benjamin escaped to England, became one of Britain's most-sought-after barristers, and wrote *A Treatise on the Law of Sale of Personal Property (1868),* a work that is still referred to today under the title *Benjamin on Sales.*

BENJAMIN, SAMUEL GREENE WHEELER *(b Feb. 13, 1837, Argos, Greece; d July 19, 1914, Burlington, Vt.).* Son of a missionary, an artist who specialized in seascapes, a teacher, author, and diplomat. America's first minister to Persia (1883-1885), he is still remembered there with high regard, and two of his literary works are still in use: *Persia and the Persians* (1886) and *The Story of Persia* (1887).

BENNET, HIRAM PITT *(b Sept. 2, 1826, Carthage, Maine; d Nov. 11, 1914, Denver, Colo.).* Lawyer, Nebraska and Colorado Republican. In Nebraska Territory: territorial council (1856), speaker of house of representatives (1858). In Colorado Territory and State: delegate to U.S. Congress (1861-1865), secretary of state (1867), Denver postmaster (1869-1874), member of first state senate (1876), state land agent (1888-1895).

BENNET, WILLIAM STILES *(b Nov. 9, 1870, Port Jervis, N.Y.; d Dec. 2, 1962, Central Valley, N.Y.).* Lawyer, New York Republican. State assembly (1901-1902), New York City municipal court justice (1903), U.S. Immigration Commission (1907-1910), GOP National Convention (1908, 1916, 1920, the last year its official parliamentarian), U.S. Representative (1905-1911, 1915-1917), received some votes for GOP vice presidential nominee (1936), state constitutional convention (1938).

BENNETT, CALEB PREW *(b Nov. 11, 1758, Kennett Township, Pa.; d May 9, 1836, Wilmington, Del.).* Enlisted in Revolutionary Army at fifteen, mustered out at twenty-three; ferry operator, innkeeper, treasurer of New Castle County, Del. (1807-1833). By then a Jackson Democrat, he ran for governor, was elected by fifty-four votes, and served from 1833 until death as Delaware's first Democrat to hold that office.

BENNETT, CHARLES GOODWIN *(b Dec. 11, 1863, Brooklyn, N.Y.; d May 25, 1914, Brooklyn).* Lawyer, New York Republican. U.S. Representative (1895-1899), secretary of U.S. Senate (1900-1913).

BENNETT, GRANVILLE GAYLORD *(b Oct. 9, 1833, Fayette County, Ohio; d June 28, 1910, Hot Springs, S.Dak.).* Lawyer, Iowa and Dakota Territory Republican. In Iowa: state representative (1865-1867), state senate (1867-1871). In Dakota: associate supreme court justice (1875-1878), delegate to U.S. Congress (1879-1881).

BENNETT, HENRY *(b Sept. 29, 1808, New Lisbon, N.Y.; d May 10, 1868, New Berlin, N.Y.).* Lawyer, New York Whig turned Republican. New Berlin town clerk (1846-1847), U.S. Representative (1849-1859).

BENNETT, JAMES GORDON *(b 1795, Keith, Scotland; d June 1, 1872, New York, N.Y.).* Newspaper reporter, editor, publisher, founder of the *New York Herald.* A powerful supporter of the Democratic party when he thought it was right, but supported Lincoln in his campaign for reelection in 1864. Throughout his lifetime, Bennett refused all offers of political and diplomatic posts.

BENNETT, JOHN BONIFAS *(b Jan. 10, 1904, Garden, Mich.; d Aug. 9, 1964, Chevy Chase, Md.).* Lawyer, Michigan Republican. Ontonagon County prose-

cuting attorney (1929-1934), deputy state commissioner of labor and industry (1935-1937), U.S. Representative (1943-1945, 1946 until death), serving on House Administration and Interstate and Foreign Commerce committees.

BENNETT, JOSEPH BENTLEY *(b April 21, 1859, Greenup County, Ky.; d Nov. 7, 1923, Greenup, Ky.).* Lawyer, teacher, merchant, Kentucky Republican. Greenup County judge (1894-1901), U.S. Representative (1905-1911).

BENNETT, MARION TINSLEY *(b June 6. 1914, Buffalo, Mo.).* Lawyer, Missouri Republican. Greene County GOP central committee (1938-1942), secretary to his father, Congressman Philip Allen Bennett (1941-1943), elected to his father's seat upon the latter's death and served from 1943 until 1949, commissioner of U.S. Court of Claims (1949-——).

BENNETT, PHILIP ALLEN *(b March 5, 1881, Dallas County, Mo.; d Dec. 7, 1942, Washington, D.C.).* Teacher, newspaper publisher, real estate and insurance broker, Missouri Republican. Eight years chairman of Dallas County GOP committee. National convention (1912), state senate (1921-1925), federal land bank appraiser (1923-1925), lieutenant governor (1925-1929), U.S. Representative (1941 until death). Father of Marion T. Bennett.

BENNETT, RISDEN TYLER *(b June 18, 1840, Wadesboro, N.C.; d July 21, 1913, Wadesboro).* Lawyer, Confederate soldier, North Carolina Democrat. Anson County solicitor (1866, 1867), state representative (1872-1874), state constitutional convention (1875), superior court judge (1880-1882), U.S. Representative (1883-1887).

BENNETT, THOMAS WARREN *(b Feb. 16, 1831, Union County, Ind.; d Feb. 2, 1893, Richmond, Ind.).* Lawyer, Union soldier, Indiana political figure with an

Idaho touch. Indiana State Senate (1858-1861, 1864-1867), mayor of Richmond (1869, 1870, 1877-1883, 1885-1887), appointed governor of Idaho Territory by President Grant (1871-1875), territorial delegate to U.S. Congress (1875-1876).

BENNING, HENRY LEWIS *(b April 2, 1814, Columbia County, Ga.; d July 10, 1875, Columbia, Ga.).* Lawyer, planter, Confederate soldier, Georgia Democrat. A firm advocate of slavery and secession, he thought a Southern Republic was the answer to strife of the times and favored Georgia's withdrawal from the Union as early as 1850. As a justice of the Georgia Supreme Court (1853-1859) he wrote a decision holding that a state supreme court is not bound by U.S. Supreme Court decisions in matters pertaining to the Constitution.

BENSON, CARVILLE DICKINSON *(b Aug. 24, 1872, Baltimore County, Md.; d Feb. 8, 1929, Baltimore).* Lawyer, Maryland Democrat. State representative (1904-1910, 1918, speaker in 1906), state senate (1912-1914), U.S. Representative (1918-1921), state insurance commissioner (1924 until death).

BENSON, EGBERT *(b June 21, 1746, New York City; d Aug. 24, 1833, Jamaica, N.Y.).* Lawyer, New York Federalist. Deputy to the provincial convention (1775), Council of Safety (1777-1778), New York's first attorney general (1777-1789), state assembly (1777-1781, 1788), associate state supreme court judge (1784-1801), Continental Congress (1784-1788), member of state constitutional convention (1788) that ratified federal Constitution, U.S. Representative (1789-1793 and five months in 1813), a founder and first president of the New York Historical Society (1804-1816).

BENSON, ELMER AUSTIN *(b Sept. 22, 1895, Appleton, Minn.).* Clothier, bank cashier, farmer, Minnesota Farmer-Laborite. State securities commissioner (1933), state commissioner of banks (1933-1935), U.S. Senate to fill an unexpired term (1936), governor (1937-1939).

BENSON, SAMUEL PAGE *(b Nov. 28, 1804, Winthrop, Maine; d Aug. 12, 1876, Yarmouth, Maine).* Lawyer, railroad builder. Maine state representative (1833-1841), state senate (1836, 1837), Maine secretary of state (1838-1841), chairman of Winthrop Board of Selectmen (1844-1848), U.S. Representative (1853-1857) entering a Whig, emerging a Republican.

BENT, CHARLES *(b Nov. 11, 1799, in what is now Charleston, W.Va.; d Jan. 19, 1847, Taos, N.Mex.).* Brother-in-law of Kit Carson, fur trapper-trader and member of expedition (1828-1832) that built one of the West's most famous trading posts, Bent's Fort, 80 miles from Taos. Appointed civil governor of New Mexico in 1846, he was killed in Mexican-Indian uprising the following year.

BENTLEY, ALVIN MORELL *(b Aug. 30, 1918, Portland, Maine; d April 10, 1969, Tucson, Ariz.).* Career diplomat, Michigan Republican who was seriously wounded when four Puerto Rican nationalists, shouting "freedom for our country," opened fire from the House visitors' gallery and shot five congressmen. As a member of the U.S. diplomatic corps (1942-1950), he saw service in Mexico, Colombia, Italy, and Hungary before resigning in disagreement over U.S. policy toward Communist countries. Delegate to Michigan GOP conventions (1950, 1951, 1952), U.S. Representative (1953-1961) being first elected in the Eisenhower landslide of 1952.

BENTON, LEMUEL *(b 1754, Granville County, N.C.; d May 18, 1818, Darlington, S.C.).* Planter, Revolutionary sol-

62..850..Who Was Who in Politics

dier, South Carolina colonial leader. State representative (1781-1784, 1787), Darlington County court justice (1785, 1791), Cheraw District escheator (1787), delegate to state convention (1788) that ratified federal Constitution, Cheraw District sheriff (1789, 1791), state constitutional convention (1790), U.S. Representative (1793-1799).

BENTON, MAECENAS EASON *(b Jan. 29, 1848, Obion County, Tenn.; d April 27, 1924, Springfield, Mo.).* Lawyer, Confederate soldier, Missouri Democrat. President of three state conventions (1890, 1896, 1898) and delegate to many others, Newton County prosecuting attorney (1878-1884), U.S. attorney (1885-1889), Democratic National Convention (1896), U.S. Representative (1897-1905), state constitutional conventions (1922, 1924).

BENTON, THOMAS HART *(b March 14, 1782, Harts Mill, N.C.; d April 10, 1858, Washington, D.C.).* Teacher, lawyer, editor, author, aide to General Andrew Jackson in War of 1812, Tennessee and Missouri Democrat, and the first man ever to serve thirty consecutive years in the U.S. Senate (Aug. 10, 1821-March 3, 1851). Served a term in the Tennessee senate (1809-1811) before migrating to the frontier town of St. Louis where he prospered as a lawyer and became prominent as editor of the *Missouri Inquirer.*

As a senator, he was a vigorous champion of all measures that would open up the West, including free public lands for settlers, which finally resulted, after his death, in enactment of the homestead laws. Opposed annexation of Texas (1844) fearing—rightly—that it would bring war with Mexico. But when war did come he supported the government position. On the debates over hard (gold) versus soft (silver) money he so strongly advocated the former that he became known as Old Bullion.

A middle-of-the-roader on slavery,

fearing the issue would destroy the Union, he favored neither its end nor its growth. However, the issue was his downfall when he voted for antislavery constitutions in California, Oregon, and New Mexico. He was defeated for reelection in 1850; two years later, as a Missouri Compromise Democrat, he was elected a U.S. Representative (1853-1855), only to be defeated once again for reelection because of his opposition to the Kansas-Nebraska Bill.

BENTON, WILLIAM *(b April 1, 1900, Minneapolis, Minn.; d March 18, 1973, New York City).* Diplomat, internationalist, advertising executive who founded Benton & Bowles, publisher of Encyclopaedia Britannica (1943-1945, 1947-1960), Connecticut Democrat active in the United Nations from its beginning. Assistant secretary of state (1945-1947), chairman of U.S. delegation to UNESCO conferences (1946, 1947), founding vice chairman of Committee for Economic Development (1942-1945), and a trustee (1947-1960). U.S. Senate to fill unexpired term of Raymond E. Baldwin (1949-1953).

BERGEN, JOHN TEUNIS *(b 1786, Brooklyn, N.Y.; d March 9, 1855, Batavia, N.Y.).* Merchant, manufacturer, publisher of *Long Island Patriot,* which later became the *Brooklyn Daily Eagle,* New York Democrat. Kings County sheriff (1821-1825, 1828-1831), U.S. Representative (1831-1833).

BERGER, VICTOR LUITPOLD "LOUIS" *(b Feb. 28, 1860, Nieder Rebbach, Austria-Hungary; d Aug. 7, 1929, Milwaukee, Wis.).* Teacher, editor, publisher, trade unionist, a founder of Socialist party who, as a Congressman from Wisconsin, became the first Socialist ever elected to Congress.

Delegate to People's party convention (1896), joined with Eugene V. Debs and Seymour Stedman to form the Social Democracy of America

(1897), then internal differences led the three to form the Social Democratic party, later known (1901) as the Socialist party, with Berger as its Wisconsin leader. A member of the Milwaukee charter convention (1907), he was elected an alderman at large (1910). He ran for Congress for the first time in that year, defeating the candidate of Robert M. La Follette, and as a U.S. Representative (1911-1913) advocated such then-radical proposals as old age pensions, child labor laws, farm relief, and an eight-hour workday. Defeated for reelection, but won again in 1918. The House refused to seat him because he had written articles in his newspaper opposing U.S. entry into World War I. Indicted and convicted of violating the Espionage Act, sentenced to twenty years, appealed, and won a reversal in the U.S. Supreme Court in 1921. The House twice more refused to seat him before finally relenting and he served from 1923 until 1929. Defeated for reelection in a campaign (1928) in which he backed Alfred E. Smith for the presidency. He died as the result of a streetcar accident.

BERKELEY, SIR WILLIAM (b 1606, Somersetshire, England; d July 9, 1677, London, England). Playwright, courtier, governor of Virginia Colony (1642-1677) where he fought Indians and the Dutch, opened mountain trails, modernized farming methods, and yet was very much a despot.

BERNARD, SIR FRANCIS (b July, 1712, England; d June 16, 1779, Aylesbury, England). Lawyer, governor of New Jersey (1758-1759) and of Massachusetts (1760-1769), thus was very much on the hot seat during the turbulent uprisings that resulted in such events as the Boston Tea Party and shots being fired at Lexington and Concord. Through it all he remained steadfast to the crown, so there was rejoicing when he sailed for home.

BERNHISEL, JOHN MILTON (b July 23, 1799, Tyrone Township, Pa.; d Sept. 28, 1881, Salt Lake City, Utah). Physician, Utah Whig. Territorial delegate to U.S. Congress (1851-1859, 1861-1863).

BERNSTEIN, HERMAN (b Sept. 21, 1876, Neustadt-Scherwindt, Russia; d Aug. 13, 1935, Sheffield, Mass.). Diplomat, journalist, poet, author, editor-publisher and founder of The Day, a Yiddish newspaper in New York; translator who first exposed the "Protocols of the Wise Men of Zion" as a fraud and won from Henry Ford, its chief American advocate, an apology to the Jewish people.

A foreign correspondent for such papers as the New York Herald and New York Times, Bernstein traveled the world, rubbed shoulders with the great, was a constant advocate of peace; as a translator he put into English works of such masters as Gorki and Chekhov; as an author and political observer he wrote such books as Herbert Hoover, the Man Who Brought America to the World; as a diplomat he was minister to Albania (1930-1933) and negotiated extradition and naturalization treaties.

Asked once to tell which accomplishment he cherished most, Bernstein replied: "My exposé of Russian tyranny, my presentation of some of the best Russian literature to the English-reading public, my interpretation of Jewish life and ideals to the non-Jewish world, the establishment of The Day which is recognized as the best Jewish daily in the world, and the documentary exposé of the forged 'Protocols of the Wise Men of Zion.'"

BERRIEN, JOHN MacPHERSON (b Aug. 23, 1781, Rocky Hill, N.J.; d Jan. 1, 1856, Savannah, Ga.). Lawyer, Georgia Democrat-Whig-American party Know-Nothing advocate, who resigned three times from the U.S. Senate in order to take other office or do other things in the strife over slavery and secession. Solicitor of Georgia's eastern judicial district (1809)), its judge (1810-1821), state senate (1822-1823), U.S. Senator (1825-1829; 1841-May 1845, November 1845-March 1847; November 1847-May 1852).

Attorney general in Jackson cabinet (1829-1831), Whig National Convention delegate (1844), state supreme court justice (1845), president of Know-Nothing party convention (1855).

BERRY, ALBERT SEATON *(b May 13, 1836, Fairfield, Ky.; d Jan. 6, 1908, Newport, Ky.).* Lawyer, Confederate soldier, Kentucky Democrat. Newport prosecuting attorney (1859), Newport mayor (1870-1876), state senate (1878, 1884), U.S. Representative (1893-1901), judge of seventeenth Kentucky judicial district (1905 until death).

BERRY, CAMPBELL POLSON *(b Nov. 7, 1834, Jackson County, Ala.; d Jan. 8, 1901, Wheatland, Calif.).* Farmer, merchant, California Democrat. Sutter County supervisor (1866, 1869), state assembly (1869, 1871, 1873, 1875 and its speaker 1877, 1878), U.S. Representative (1879-1883), U.S. subtreasurer at San Francisco (1894-1898).

BERRY, GEORGE LEONARD *(b Sept. 12, 1882, Lee Valley, Tenn.; d Dec. 4, 1948, Pressmen's Home, Tenn.).* Printing pressman, labor leader, farmer, banker, Tennessee Democrat. President of International Pressmen and Assistants Union of North America (1907 until death), named to U.S. Senate to fill vacancy (1937-1938).

BERRY, JAMES HENDERSON *(b May 15, 1841, Jackson County, Ala.; d Jan. 30, 1913, Bentonville, Ark.).* Lawyer, teacher, Confederate soldier, Arkansas Democrat. State representative (1866, 1872, its speaker in 1874), chairman of party's state convention (1876), circuit court judge (1878-1882); while governor (1882-1884) Arkansas enacted its first

labor laws and repudiated "carpetbag" bonds to finance the building of railroads; as U.S. Senator (1885-1907) was chairman of committee on public lands, a foe of lumber-interest abuses, and champion of a better deal for Indians.

BERRY, NATHANIEL SPRINGER *(b Sept. 1, 1796, Bath, Maine; d April 27, 1894, Bristol, N.H.).* Tannery operator, New Hampshire Democrat turned Republican who was one of the nation's fiercest abolitionists and a staunch advocate of emancipation. State legislature (1828, 1833, 1837, 1854), state senate (1835, 1836), associate common pleas court justice (1841), Grafton County probate judge (1856-1861), delegate to Democratic National Convention (1840) where he became dissatisfied with the party's position on slavery and consequently helped to organize first the Liberty and then the Free-Soil party and six times was an unsuccessful candidate for governor. By 1861 he had enlisted in the GOP ranks and this time ran successfully for the state's highest office, serving until 1863.

BETHUNE, MARY McLEOD *(b July 10, 1875, Mayesville, S.C.; d May 18, 1955, Daytona Beach, Fla.).* Teacher, daughter of former slaves. Founded (1904) the Daytona Normal and Industrial Institute for Negro Girls (now Bethune-Cookman College) serving as its president until 1942. Served (1930) on Herbert Hoover's White House Conference on Child Health and Protection, special adviser to President Roosevelt on minority affairs, director (1936-1944) of the Division of Negro Affairs of the National Youth Administration, consultant on interracial understanding at the San Francisco Conference of the United Nations. A vice president of the National Association for the Advancement of Colored People, she was awarded its Spingarn Medal (1935); also received the Francis A. Drexel and Thomas Jefferson awards and the Haitian Medal of Honor and Merit.

BETTON, SILAS *(b Aug. 26, 1768, Londonderry, N.H.; d Jan. 22, 1822, Salem, N.H.).* Lawyer, New Hampshire state representative (1797-1799, 1810, 1811), state senate (1801-1803), U.S. Representative (1803-1807), high sheriff of Rockingham County (1813-1818).

BEVERIDGE, ALBERT JEREMIAH *(b Oct. 6, 1862, Concord Township, Ohio; d April 27, 1927, Indianapolis, Ind.).* Lawyer, writer, Indiana Republican turned Progressive turned Republican. U.S. Senate as a Republican (1899-1911), unsuccessful Progressive candidate for governor (1912) and chairman of National Progressive Convention in same year, vainly again sought Senate seat as a Progressive in 1914 and as a Republican in 1922.

BEVERIDGE, JOHN LOURIE *(b July 6, 1824, Greenwich, N.Y.; d May 3, 1910, Hollywood, Calif.).* Teacher, lawyer, Union soldier, Illinois Republican. Cook County sheriff (1866), state senate (1871), U.S. Representative (1871), lieutenant governor (1872), governor (1873-1877), U.S. subtreasurer at Chicago (1877-1881).

BEVERLEY, ROBERT *(b 1673, Middlesex County, Va.; d 1722, Beverley Park, Va.).* Writer-historian whose biting wit and satirical writings cut short what promised to be a bright political career in colonial Virginia. Among his offices held: scrivener in the office of the provincial secretary, legislative committee clerk, clerk to the general court and to the general assembly, burgess. His best known work still referred to today is his *History and Present State of Virginia* (1705), a satire upon the life of a Southern planter.

BEWLEY, ANTHONY *(b May 22, 1804, Tennessee; d Sept. 13, 1860, Fort Worth, Tex.).* Methodist Episcopal minister in Missouri who preached so vehemently against slavery that his children did not dare attend school. He was sent to Texas as a missionary where an inflammatory letter, supposedly written to him, fell into the wrong hands and he was hanged by an anti-Negro mob.

BIBB, GEORGE MORTIMER *(b Oct. 30, 1776, Prince Edward County, Va.; d April 14, 1859, Washington, D.C.).* Lawyer, Kentucky Democrat. State representative (1806, 1810, 1817), state appeals court judge (1808 and its chief justice (1809-1810, 1827), U.S. Senate (1811-1814, 1829-1835) where in 1811 as one of the then-called War Hawks he was a leading advocate of war with England; Louisville chancery court chancellor (1835-1844), secretary of the treasury in Tyler cabinet (1844-1845).

BIBB, WILLIAM WYATT *(b Oct. 1, 1780, Prince Edward County, Va.; d July 9, 1820, Elmore County, Ala.).* Physician, Georgia and Alabama Democrat. In Georgia, he was state representative (1803-1805), U.S. Representative (1807-1813); U.S. Senate (1813-1816), resigning to accept presidential appointment as Alabama's first territorial governor and subsequent election to that office when Alabama became a state, serving as governor until his death. His brother, Thomas, then president of the state senate, succeeded him and served for a year.

BICKETT, THOMAS WALTER *(b Feb. 28, 1869, Monroe, N.C.; d Dec. 28, 1921).* Teacher, lawyer, North Carolina Democrat. State representative (1906), state convention (1907), attorney general (1908-1916) appearing five times before the U.S. Supreme Court; governor (1917-1921), in that time sending forty-eight measures to the legislature and seeing forty of them adopted, among them: tax reforms, higher pay for teachers, better roads and agricultural methods, increased aid for educational and charitable institutions, and improved conditions for blacks and tenant farmers, black or white.

BIDDLE, EDWARD *(b 1738, Philadelphia, Pa.; d Sept. 5, 1779, Chatsworth, Md.).* Lawyer, Revolutionary soldier. Pennsylvania Assembly (1767-1775, 1778, its speaker in 1774), provincial convention (1775), Continental Congress (1774-1776, 1778, 1779). Uncle of Richard Biddle.

BIDDLE, JOHN *(b March 2, 1792, Philadelphia, Pa.; d Aug. 25, 1859, White Sulphur Springs, Va.).* Farmer, railroad executive, War of 1812 soldier, Michigan Whig. Indian agent at Green Bay, Wis. (1821-1822), register of Detroit Land Office (1823-1827), mayor of Detroit (1827, 1828), delegate from Michigan Territory to U.S. Congress (1829-1831), president of state constitutional convention (1835), state representative and speaker of the house (1841).

BIDDLE, NICHOLAS *(b Jan. 8, 1786, Philadelphia, Pa.; d Feb. 27, 1844, Philadelphia).* Scholar, lawyer, poet, author, editor, financier who was president of the Second Bank of the United States during its unsuccessful effort to renew its national charter, briefly a Pennsylvania legislator.

A precocious child who entered the University of Pennsylvania at ten, completed all requirements by thirteen, was denied a diploma because of his age, went to Princeton (then the College of New Jersey) and graduated at fifteen, his class (1801) valedictorian. At eighteen he was secretary to the U.S. minister to Paris, at twenty-one he was secretary to James Monroe, the minister to London.

When Monroe became president, he appointed Biddle one of the five government directors of the Bank of the United States (1819); three years later Biddle was elected president of the bank and so served until 1836. Denied a renewed federal charter after a battle with President Jackson (a still controversial case), the institution continued as the United States Bank of

Pennsylvania with Biddle as its president until 1839.

Biddle, who had learned finance only because Monroe had asked him to, then returned to the life he loved: the world of letters. In his earlier years, he had been a member of a writers' group called the Tuesday Club; a contributor to *Port Folio*, the foremost literary magazine of the times; its editor (1812-1815); and author of the *History of the Expeditions of Captains Lewis and Clark*, which was published in 1814.

BIDDLE, RICHARD *(b March 25, 1796, Philadelphia, Pa.; d July 6, 1847, Pittsburgh, Pa.).* Scholar, writer, lawyer, Pennsylvania Whig. U.S. Representative (1837-1840), resigning so that he could spend more time practicing law and publishing works on American travel and discovery. Nephew of Edward Biddle.

BIDLACK, BENJAMIN ALDEN *(b Sept. 8, 1804, Paris, N.Y.; d Feb. 6, 1849, Bogota, Colombia).* Lawyer, newspaper editor, Pennsylvania Democrat, diplomat who made possible the Panama Canal. Luzerne County district attorney (1825), Pike County treasurer (1834), state representative (1835, 1836), U.S. Representative (1841-1845), minister to Colombia (1845 until death), negotiated the peace treaty of 1846 that also gave the United States the right to construct a canal or railroad across the Isthmus of Panama.

BIDWELL, BARNABAS *(b Aug. 23, 1763, Tyringham [now Monterey] Mass.; d July 27, 1833, Kingston, Canada).* Writer, teacher, lawyer, Massachusetts politician. State senate (1801-1804), state representative, U.S. Representative (1805-1807), the latter a post in which he was considered "cunning, supple, and sly"; state attorney general (1807-1810), and all the while the position that led to his downfall—Berkshire County treasurer from 1791 until a $10,000 shortage was discovered in his accounts in 1810. To avoid trial, he took his family to Canada where he lived out his years, earning for himself this epithet: "A profound jurist, a man of great culture and attainments outside the law as well as in it."

BIDWELL, JOHN *(b Aug. 5, 1819, Chautauqua County, N.Y.; d April 4, 1900, Chico, Calif.).* Teacher who traveled to California in first wagon train from Missouri (1841) to become cowboy, prospector said to have found the first gold in Feather River, a drafter of resolution of independence from Mexico (1846), rancher, farmer, and friend of the Indians. State senate (1849), California census supervisor (1850, 1860), Democratic National Convention delegate (1860), brigadier general in state militia (1863). Republican National Convention delegate (1864), Unionist U.S. Representative (1865-1867), unsuccessful Anti-Monopoly candidate for governor (1875) as Prohibitionist (1890), and Prohibitionist candidate for president (1892).

BIGELOW, ABIJAH *(b Dec. 5, 1775, Westminster, Mass.; d April 5, 1860, Worcester, Mass.).* Lawyer, Massachusetts Federalist. Leominster town clerk (1803-1809), state representative (1807-1809), U.S. Representative (1810-1815), Worcester County court clerk (1817-1833).

BIGELOW, HERBERT SEELY *(b Jan. 4, 1870, Elkhart, Ind.; d Nov. 11, 1951, Cincinnati, Ohio).* Clergyman, Ohio Democrat. President of state constitutional convention (1912), state representative (1913, 1914), Cincinnati City Council (1936, 1940, 1941), U.S. Representative (1937-1939).

BIGELOW, JOHN *(b Nov. 25, 1817, Bristol, [now Malden] N.Y.; d Dec. 19, 1911, New York City).* Author, a

founder and editor of the *New York Post* (1848-1861), diplomat, and a New York Free-Soil Democrat who was outspokenly opposed to slavery. Consul-general in Paris (1861-1865), minister to France (1865-1866), New York secretary of state (1875-1876), state constitutional convention (1893). One of foremost U.S. emissaries (some said because of his rapport with the foreign press), he is credited with keeping France from throwing its support to the Confederacy during the Civil War. As an author and biographer, one of his best-known works was the compilation of *The Complete Works of Benjamin Franklin.*

BIGGS, ASA *(b Feb. 4, 1811, Williamston, N.C.; d March 6, 1878, Norfolk, Va.).* Lawyer, North Carolina Democrat. State constitutional convention (1835), house of commons (1840, 1842), state senate (1844, 1845), U.S. Representative (1845-1847), a codifier of state laws (1851-1855), U.S. Senate (1855-1858) resigning to become U.S. district judge (1858-1861), secession convention delegate (1861), Confederate States judge (1861-1865).

BIGGS, BENJAMIN THOMAS *(b Oct. 1, 1821, New Castle County, Del.; d Dec. 25, 1893, Middletown, Del.).* Teacher, farmer, railroad executive, Delaware Democrat. State constitutional convention (1853), U.S. Representative (1869-1873), Democratic National Convention (1872), governor (1887-1891).

BIGLER, JOHN *(b Jan. 8, 1805, Carlisle, Pa.; d Nov. 29, 1871).* Newspaper editor, lawyer, California Democrat. Traveled to California behind an ox team (1849) in answer to the lure of gold. One of two brothers who at the same time were governors of states a continent apart (see William Bigler). State assembly speaker (1850, 1851), governor (1852-1856), minister to Chile (1857-1861), delegate to three Democratic National Conventions.

BIGLER, WILLIAM *(b Jan. 1, 1814, Shiremanstown, Pa.; d Aug. 9, 1880, Clearfield, Pa.).* Newspaper editor-publisher, lumberman, railroad executive, Pennsylvania Democrat. State senate (1841-1847 and its speaker twice), governor (1852-1855), U.S. Senate (1856-1861) where he fought vainly to hold the Union together, Democratic National Conventions (1864, 1868), Union National Convention (1866). Brother of John Bigler.

BILBO, THEODORE GILMORE *(b Oct. 13, 1877, Pearl River County, Miss.; d Aug. 21, 1947, New Orleans, La.).* Teacher, lawyer, Mississippi Democrat and a white supremacist who urged deportation of Negroes to Africa. State senate (1908-1912), lieutenant governor (1912-1916), the state's first two-term governor (1916-1920, 1928-1932), U.S. Senate (1935-1947). In 1946, the same year that he was reelected to another term, disclosures forced him to admit membership in the Ku Klux Klan. The Senate refused to readminister the oath of office but suspended investigation of fraud in office when he became ill.

BINDERUP, CHARLES GUSTAV *(b March 5, 1873, Horsens, Denmark; d Aug. 19, 1950, Minden, Neb.).* Farmer, merchant, Nebraska Democrat and organizer of the Constitutional Money League of America. U.S. Representative (1935-1939).

BINGHAM, GEORGE CALEB *(b March 20, 1811, Augusta County, Ga.; d July 7, 1879, Kansas City, Mo.).* Portrait painter with an avocation for state politics, Missouri Whig. State legislature (1848), state treasurer (1862-1865), attorney general (1875 until death).

BINGHAM, HARRY *(b March 30, 1821, Concord, Vt.; d Sept. 12, 1900).* Lawyer, New Hampshire Democratic leader who nevertheless had an abhorrence for machine politics and seventeen times between 1861 and 1891 was elected a state representative, each time serving as his party's legislative leader; also state senator (1883-1887), national convention delegate (1868, 1872, 1880, 1884, 1890), peace convention delegate (1866), state constitutional convention (1876).

BINGHAM, HENRY HARRISON *(b Dec. 4, 1841, Philadelphia, Pa.; d March 22, 1912, Philadelphia).* Lawyer, Union soldier who was awarded the Congressional Medal of Honor in 1893 for "distinguished gallantry" in the Battle of the Wilderness twenty-nine years earlier; Pennsylvania Republican who served seventeen consecutive terms in Congress. Philadelphia postmaster (1867-1872), delegate to seven GOP National Conventions between 1872 and 1900, U.S. Representative (1879 until death).

BINGHAM, HIRAM *(b Nov. 19, 1875, Honolulu, Hawaii; d June 6, 1956, Washington, D.C.).* Professor of history and politics at Harvard, Princeton, and Yale; South American explorer who discovered Inca ruins at Machu Picchu (1911), World War I aviator, banker, author, lecturer, Connecticut Republican. GOP National Convention delegate four times (1924-1936), Hughes-Fairbanks presidential elector (1916), lieutenant governor (1922-1924), elected governor in November 1924 to take office in 1925 but in December 1924 was elected U.S. Senator to fill a vacancy caused by death and so served in Washington rather than in Hartford until 1933; member President's Aviation Board (1925), Loyalty Review Board (1951-1953).

BINGHAM, JOHN ARMOR *(b Jan. 21, 1815, Mercer, Ohio; d July 2, 1885, Cadiz, Ohio).* Lawyer, diplomat, Union soldier, an orator of note and Ohio Republican who served as a judge advocate both in trial of Lincoln's assassins and impeachment of President Andrew Johnson. Tuscarawas County district attorney (1846-1849), U.S. Representative (1855-1863, 1865-1873), minister to Japan (1873-1885).

BINGHAM, KINSLEY SCOTT *(b Dec. 16, 1808, Camillus, N.Y.; d Oct. 5, 1861, Green Oak, Mich.).* Lawyer, farmer, Michigan Democrat turned Republican. As a Democrat: member of his state's first house of representatives (1837) and reelected four times, U.S. Representative (1847-1851). As a Republican: elected governor on Michigan's first Republican ticket (1854), reelected (1856) and served until 1859, doing much to set up educational institutions; U.S. Senate (1859 until death).

BINGHAM, ROBERT WORTH *(b Nov. 8, 1871, Orange County, N.C.; d Dec. 18, 1937, Baltimore, Md.).* Lawyer, publisher of *Louisville Journal* and *Louisville Times,* an ardent advocate of League of Nations and, later, the New Deal; diplomat, Kentucky Democrat.

Jefferson County attorney (1903-1907), appointive mayor of Louisville for several months in 1907 when all candidates for the office were disqualified by the courts, chancellor of Jefferson County circuit court (1911).

Bingham embarked upon his newspaper career in 1918 and, in addition to vigorously supporting the League and Franklin D. Roosevelt, led in the organization of the Burley Tobacco Growers Cooperative Association. In 1933, FDR pondered whether to name him secretary of state or ambassador to England and finally decided upon the latter, a position that Bingham filled until he died of Hodgkin's disease in Johns Hopkins Hospital.

BINGHAM, WILLIAM *(b March 8, 1752, Philadelphia, Pa.; d Feb. 7, 1804, Bath, England).* Banker, trader, operating owner of a fleet of privateers and consequently a man of great wealth with political influence both at home and abroad. British consul to Martinique (1770-1776), continental agent in the West Indies (1776-1780), Continental Congress representing Pennsylvania (1787, 1788), state house (1790, 1791), its speaker (1791), president of state senate (1794, 1795), U.S. Senate 1795-1801), moving to England upon expiration of his term.

BINNS, JOHN *(b Dec. 22, 1772, Dublin, Ireland; d June 16, 1860, Philadelphia, Pa.).* Publisher, author, and orator with a gift of what one biographer described as "typical Irish eloquence"; considered quite a radical for his time both in England and in America.

In London, he was a friend of William Godwin; in 1801 he moved to Northumberland, Pa., then the gathering place of free spirits with like social and political opinions, where he began a long career as publisher-provocateur. Among his publications were the *Northumberland Republican Argus* and the *Philadelphia Democratic Press,* one of whose prime targets was "the tyrant" Andrew Jackson, which led to his support of the pro-British John Quincy Adams in the presidential election of 1828. Politicians hated Binns and his golden tongue but the people loved him. Time and again they voted him a Philadelphia alderman and he served from 1822 until 1844.

BIRD, JOHN TAYLOR *(b Aug. 16, 1829, Bloomsbury, N.J.; d May 6, 1911, Trenton, N.J.).* Lawyer, New Jersey Democrat. Hunterdon County prosecutor of the pleas (1862-1867), U.S. Representative (1869-1873), state constitutional convention (1876), New Jersey vice chancellor (1882-1896), master in chancery (1900-1909).

BIRDSEYE, VICTORY *(b Dec. 25, 1782, Cornwall, Conn.; d Sept. 16, 1853, Pompey, N.Y.).* Lawyer, New York Whig. U.S. Representative (1815-1817, 1841-1843), Pompey Hill postmaster (1817-1838), Onondaga County district attorney (1818-1833), master of chancery (1818-1822), state constitutional convention (1821), state senate (1827), state assembly (1823, 1838-1840).

BIRNEY, JAMES (b June 7, 1817, Danville, Ky.; d May 8, 1888, Bay City, Mich.). Publisher of Bay City Chronicle, lawyer, diplomat, Michigan Republican. State senate (1859), lieutenant governor briefly in 1861, resigning to fill a vacancy on the eighteenth judicial circuit bench where he sat until 1866, state constitutional convention (1867), minister to the Netherlands (1876-1882). Son of James G. Birney.

BIRNEY, JAMES GILLESPIE (b Feb. 4, 1792, Danville, Ky.; d Nov. 25, 1857, Eagleswood, N.J.). Lawyer, counsel to Cherokee Nation, lecturer, author, Kentucky and Alabama legislator who, though for a time a slave owner himself (as part of his wife's dowry), was a vigorous foe of slavery, fighting both the Democrats and the Whigs on the issue and running twice for president (1840, 1844) on the Liberty party ticket.
Kentucky legislature (1816), Alabama General Assembly (1819) where his opposition to endorsement of the presidential candidacy of Andrew Jackson cost him reelection. Responsible for inclusion in the state constitution of an emancipation proviso and one that would bar the importing of slaves for sale. Both were later repealed. Organized Kentucky's branch of the Anti-Slavery Society; became executive secretary of the American society and relocated in New York. In the 1840 presidential election he polled 7,069 votes, in 1844, 62,300. The next year he fell from a horse, was partially paralyzed, and so ended his public career. Father of James Birney.

BISHOP, PHANUEL (b Sept. 3, 1739, Rehoboth, Mass.; d Jan. 6, 1812, Rehoboth). Innkeeper, Massachusetts Senate (1787-1791), state representative (1792, 1793, 1797, 1798), U.S. Representative (1799-1807).

BISHOP, ROSWELL PETER (b Jan. 6, 1843, Sidney, N.Y.; d March 4, 1920, Pacific Grove, Calif.). Teacher, lawyer, Union soldier, Michigan Republican who gave up politics to become a California fruit grower. Mason County prosecuting attorney (1876, 1878, 1884), state representative (1882, 1892), U.S. Representative (1895-1907).

BISSELL, WILLIAM HARRISON (b April 25, 1811, Hartwick, N.Y.; d March 18, 1860, Springfield, Ill.). Teacher, doctor, lawyer, Illinois Democrat turned Republican. State representative (1840-1842), St. Clair County prosecuting attorney (1844), U.S. Representative (1849-1855), governor (1857 until death).

BIXLER, HARRIS JACOB (b Sept. 16, 1870, New Buffalo, Pa.; d March 29, 1941, Johnsonburg, Pa.). Teacher, manufacturer, banker, farmer, Pennsylvania Republican. President of Johnsonburg city council (1900-1904), mayor (1908-1912), Elk County sheriff (1916-1920), chairman of GOP county committee (1916-1925), county treasurer (1920-1922), U.S. Representative (1921-1927).

BLACK, EDWARD JUNIUS (b Oct. 30, 1806, Beaufort, S.C.; d Sept. 1, 1846, Millettville, S.C.). Georgia lawyer. State representative (1829-1831); U.S. Representative as a States' Rights Whig (1839-1841), as a Democrat (1842-1845).

BLACK, FRANK SWETT (b March 8, 1853, York County, Maine; d March 22, 1913, Troy, N.Y.). Teacher, newspaper editor, lawyer with a gift for oratory, New York Republican. U.S. Representative (1895-1897) resigning to become governor (1897-1899).

BLACK, HUGO LAFAYETTE (b Feb. 27, 1886, Clay County, Ala.; d Sept. 25, 1971, in U.S. Naval Hospital, Bethesda,

Md.). The youngest in a farming family of eight children, he studied medicine for a year, switched to the law, began practice at twenty, enrolled in every organization in sight from the Ku Klux Klan to the Democratic party in order to get ahead both professionally and politically and went on, according to his *Washington Post* obituary, to be "recognized as one of the authentic giants in the history of the U.S. Supreme Court" where in a thirty-four-year tenure he was considered a judicial activist, yet strict constructionist, who believed that the Constitution and its Bill of Rights meant exactly what they said. As a result, he wrote more dissenting opinions that later became law than any justice before him. The obituary went on to say: "He shaped the course of American constitutional law as powerfully, perhaps, as any other single jurist of the 20th Century."

World War I field artillery officer, Birmingham police court judge for eighteen months, Jefferson County prosecutor for two years, Democratic National Convention delegate (1936), successful independent candidate for the U.S. Senate where he served ten years (1927-1937) and supported most of the New Deal program before resigning to become a Roosevelt-appointed associate Supreme Court justice where his tenure was the second-longest in history (Aug. 13, 1937, until eight days before death).

BLACK, JAMES *(b Sept. 23, 1823, Lewisburg, Pa.; d Dec. 16, 1893, Lancaster, Pa.).* Pennsylvania lawyer, a founder of the National Prohibition party and its first candidate (1872) for president, polling 5,608 votes. His first and last encounter with the demon rum came at the age of sixteen when, while a mule driver on the Pennsylvania and Union Canal, he tried to match drink for drink with older men on the job. (Not to be confused with James Black of Newport, Pa.)

BLACK, JAMES *(b March 6, 1793, Newport, Pa.; d June 21, 1872, New Bloomfield, Pa.).* Merchant, Pennsylvania Democrat. State representative (1830, 1831), U.S. Representative (1836-1837, 1843-1847), Perry County associate judge (1842, 1843). (Not to be confused with James Black of Lewisburg, Pa.)

BLACK, JAMES AUGUSTUS *(b 1793, near Abbeville, S.C.; d April 3, 1848, Washington, D.C.).* Iron miner, bank cashier, cotton dealer, War of 1812 soldier, South Carolina Democrat. U.S. Representative (1843 until death).

BLACK, JAMES CONQUEST CROSS *(b May 9, 1842, Stamping Ground, Ky.; d Oct. 1, 1928, Augusta, Ga.).* Lawyer, Confederate soldier, Georgia Democrat. State representative (1873-1877), Hancock-English presidential elector (1880), U.S. Representative (1893-1897).

BLACK, JEREMIAH SULLIVAN *(b Jan. 10, 1810, near Stony Creek, Pa.; d Aug. 19, 1883, York, Pa.).* Lawyer who was the nation's chief legal officer in the days immediately preceding the Civil War, Pennsylvania Democrat. Common pleas court judge (1842-1851), state supreme court justice (1851-1857), attorney general in Buchanan cabinet (1857-1860) and secretary of state in the four difficult months preceding Lincoln's inauguration March 3, 1861.

Eccentric, absentminded, often letting emotion take the place of prudence, Black was by no means the most popular man in Washington but he was effective. He uncovered widespread fraud in California land titles, combatted the slave trade, while applying the law equally in both South and North and held his own in a continuing debate with Stephen Douglas over squatter sovereignty, his position being that territorial legislatures did not have the right to violate the Fifth Amendment.

Secession posed his biggest problem. He advised President Buchanan that he was dutybound to protect federal property located in states that were seceding, but the president did not take his advice until it was too late and kicked him upstairs when Lewis Cass resigned as secretary of state. A month before leaving office, Buchanan nominated Black for the Supreme Court but a combination of Republicans, Southern sympathizers, and Douglas Democrats voted him down.

BLACK, JOHN CHARLES (b Jan. 27, 1839, Lexington, Miss.; d Aug. 17, 1915, Chicago, Ill.). Lawyer, Union Army soldier, Illinois Democrat. U.S. commissioner of pensions (1885-1889), U.S. Representative (1893-1895), U.S. attorney for northern Illinois district (1895-1899), U.S. Civil Service Commission (1904-1913), its president nine of those years.

BLACK, LORING MILTON, JR. (b May 17, 1886, New York City; d May 21, 1956, Washington, D.C.). Lawyer, New York Democrat. State senate (1911, 1912, 1919, 1920), U.S. Representative (1923-1935).

BLACKBURN, JOSEPH CLAY STILES (b Oct. 1, 1838, Woodford County, Ky.; d Sept. 12, 1918, Washington, D.C.). Lawyer, planter, Confederate soldier, Kentucky Democrat, and orator of such sharp tongue that his debates often ended in fisticuffs. State representative (1871-1875), U.S. Representative (1875-1885), U.S. Senate (1885-1897, 1901-1907), national convention delegate (1896, 1900, 1904), governor of Panama Canal Zone (1907-1909).

BLACKBURN, LUKE PRYOR (b June 16, 1816, Fayette County, Ky.; d Sept. 14, 1887, Frankfort, Ky.). Physician, Confederate Army surgeon, Democrat who, though not a politician, realized a lifelong ambition and became governor of his native state, serving from 1879 until 1883, a period in which he

granted an unusually large number of pardons in order to relieve horrible prison conditions. His most valuable contribution, however, was in combating medical epidemics, particularly yellow fever. He opened a hospital in Natchez, Miss., advised Louisiana legislators, brought an epidemic under control on Long Island, traveled to Bermuda to do the same there, and visited hospitals in France, Germany, England, and Scotland.

BLACKBURN, WILLIAM JASPER (b July 24, 1820, Randolph County, Ark.; d Nov. 10, 1899, Little Rock, Ark.). Louisiana and Arkansas newspaper printer-editor-publisher, Louisiana Republican. State constitutional convention (1867), U.S. Representative (1868-1869) when Louisiana was readmitted to the Union, state senate (1874-1878).

BLACKMON, FRED LEONARD (b Sept. 15, 1873, Lime Branch, Ga.; d Feb. 8, 1921, Barstow, Fla.). Lawyer, Alabama Democrat. Anniston city attorney (1898-1902), state senate (1900-1910), fourth congressional district chairman (1906-1910), U.S. Representative (1911 until death).

BLACKNEY, WILLIAM WALLACE (b Aug. 28, 1876, Clio, Mich.; d Mar. 14, 1963). Lawyer teacher, Michigan Republican. Genesee County clerk (1905-1912), assistant prosecuting attorney (1913-1917), Flint School Board (1924-1934), GOP state central committee (1925-1930), U.S. Representative (1935-1937, 1939-1953).

BLACKWELL, ALICE STONE (b Sept. 14, 1857, East Orange, N.J.; d Mar. 15, 1950, Cambridge, Mass.). Woman suffragist, author, daughter of Henry Brown Blackwell and Lucy Stone. After graduating from college in 1881, she worked with her parents on the Woman's Journal; at their deaths continuing until 1917 as editor in chief.

BLACKWELL, ANTOINETTE LOUISA BROWN *(b May 20, 1825, Henrietta, N.Y.; d Nov. 1921, Elizabeth, N.J.).* Congregational, later a Unitarian, minister, she put to good use her ability as a speaker in her role as one of the group of pioneers in the women's suffrage movement and also espoused the causes of prohibition and the abolition of slavery. Married to Dr. Samuel C. Blackwell (brother of Elizabeth and Henry Brown Blackwell) who supported her activities; close friend and associate of Lucy Stone and Susan B. Anthony.

BLACKWELL, HENRY BROWN *(b May 4, 1825, Bristol, England; d Sept. 7, 1909, Dorchester, Mass.).* Book dealer, sugar refiner, real estate broker, editor, brother of Elizabeth Blackwell who was one of America's first woman doctors, and husband of Lucy Stone, one of the country's foremost suffragettes, and himself a lifelong champion of equal rights for women. He first spoke out in that vein in Cleveland (1853), met Lucy at a legislative hearing in Massachusetts in the same year, and on their wedding day (May 1, 1855) issued a joint statement of protest against the inequities of the marriage law. He urged Southern states (1867) to give voting rights to women and later became editor, without pay, of the American Woman Suffrage Association magazine *Woman's Journal*, remaining in that position until death.

BLAINE, JAMES GILLESPIE *(b Jan. 31, 1830, West Brownsville, Pa.; d Jan. 27, 1893, Washington, D.C.).* Teacher, editor of *Kennebec* (Maine) *Journal*, lawyer, Maine Republican who ran for president in 1884. State representative (1859-1862) and house speaker (1861, 1862), U.S. Representative (1863-1876) and House speaker (1869-1875), U.S. Senate (1876-1881), secretary of state to President Garfield (1881) and to President Harrison (1889-1892).

A Whig early in his career, Blaine

became a liberal supporter of Lincoln and helped give credence to the new party title: Republican. Always opposed to slavery, he favored voting rights for Negroes and as a newcomer to Congress was instrumental in passage of "universal suffrage" legislation. He gained many friends, among them Garfield, and many enemies in the Grant wing of the party, a factor that cost him the presidential nomination both in 1876 and 1880, when he was also hurt by hints of railroad graft.

Although one of the most astute political leaders of his time, Blaine's main strength was in the field of foreign affairs and as secretary of state he did much to improve relations with Latin America and was first president of the Pan-American Congress (1889).

BLAINE, JOHN JAMES *(b May 4, 1875, Wingville Township, Wis.; d April 18, 1934, Boscobel, Wis.).* Lawyer, orator, progressive Wisconsin Republican who opposed conservative policies of Coolidge and Hoover and supported for presidency La Follette (1924), Smith (1928), and Roosevelt (1932). Mayor of Boscobel (1901-1904, 1906-1907), Grant County supervisor (1901-1904), state senate (1909-1913), national convention delegate (1916, 1920, 1924), state attorney general (1919-1921), governor (1921-1927), U.S. Senate (1927-1933), director of Reconstruction Finance Corporation (1933 until death).

BLAIR, AUSTIN *(b Feb. 8, 1818, Caroline, N.Y.; d Aug. 6, 1894, Jackson, Mich.).* Lawyer, Michigan Whig–Free-Soiler–Republican who as a state legislator (1845-1849) advocated full voting rights for all citizens no matter what their racial origins, yet survived politically to become a "war governor" (1861-1865) who gave complete support to President Lincoln.

Free-Soil National Convention delegate (1848), Jackson County prosecuting attorney (1852), delegate to Jackson's "Under the Oaks" convention of

Whigs, Democrats, and Free-Soilers who gave birth to the Republican party, state senate (1855-1857), GOP National Convention that nominated Lincoln (1860), U.S. Representative (1867-1873).

BLAIR, FRANCIS PRESTON, SR. *(b April 12, 1791, Abingdon, Va.; d Oct. 18, 1876, Silver Spring, Md.).* Farmer who preferred politics to the soil, banker, newspaperman and Jacksonian Democrat who was summoned from his home in Kentucky to Washington by the president to establish the *Globe* (1830) whose masthead motto was: "The world is governed too much."

In this new position of power, Blair became a member of Jackson's kitchen cabinet, his vacation companion, and confidante, discussing policy at breakfast and hurrying to his office to write editorials that flashed the new administration line to sympathetic papers around the country. When Polk became president, the *Globe* got a new editor, but by that time Blair did not want for creature comforts.

He held political court at his estate outside Washington, became a Free-Soiler, helped organize the Republican party, campaigned for Lincoln, and showed his desire for peace and unity by secretly meeting with Jefferson Davis (1864) in hope of bringing the Civil War to an end. Father of Francis P., Jr. and Montgomery Blair.

BLAIR, FRANCIS PRESTON, JR. *(b Feb. 19, 1821, Lexington, Ky.; d July 8, 1875, St. Louis, Mo.).* Lawyer, publisher, Union soldier, a slave owner who opposed an extension of slavery, Missouri Free-Soiler turned Republican turned Democrat and was sent to Congress under the banner of each of them, thus very much showing his father's flair for politics.

Organized Free-Soil party in Missouri and supported Van Buren in 1848, state representative (1852-1856, 1870), U.S. Representative (1857-1859, 1860,

1861-1862, 1863-1864), GOP National Convention delegate (1860), unsuccessful Democratic candidate for vice president (1868), U.S. Senate to fill a vacancy (1871-1873), state insurance commissioner (1874).

BLAIR, HENRY WILLIAM *(b Dec. 6, 1834, Campton, N.H.; d March 14, 1920, Washington, D.C.).* Lawyer, Union soldier, New Hampshire Republican champion of public education who shocked the nation in 1881 by introducing a Senate bill that called for the appropriation of $120 million to pay for such education. He also advocated voting rights for women and proposed a cabinet-level Department of Labor.

Grafton County prosecuting attorney (1860), state representative (1866), state senate (1867, 1868), U.S. Representative (1875-1879, 1893-1895), U.S. Senate (1879-1891), appointed minister to China (1891) but he never served because the Chinese considered him persona non grata, apparently because they disapproved of his position on immigration.

BLAIR, JACOB BEESON *(b April 11, 1821, Parkersburg, Va.; d Feb. 12, 1901, Salt Lake City, Utah).* Lawyer, diplomat, Eastern Unionist who answered the call of the West. U.S. Representative from Virginia (1861-1863), from West Virginia (1863-1865), minister to Costa Rica (1868-1873), Wyoming associate supreme court justice (1876-1888), Salt Lake County, Utah, probate judge (1892-1895), Utah surveyor general (1897 until death).

BLAIR, JAMES *(b about 1790, Waxhaw settlement, S.C.; d April 1, 1834, Washington, D.C.).* Planter, South Carolina Democrat. U.S. Representative (1821-1822, 1829 until death).

BLAIR, JOHN *(b Sept. 13, 1790, Washington County, Tenn.; d July 9, 1863, Jonesboro, Tenn.).* Lawyer, Tennessee Democrat. State representative (1815-

1817, 1849, 1850), state senate (1817-1821), U.S. Representative (1823-1835).

BLAIR, MONTGOMERY *(b May 10, 1813, Franklin County, Ky.; d July 27, 1883, Silver Spring, Md.).* Lawyer who defended Dred Scott and obtained counsel for John Brown; Lincoln's postmaster general (1861-1864); newspaper publisher; Maryland Democrat-Republican-Democrat who strove to prove, unsuccessfully, that the slavery issue could be settled peacefully.

Delegate to Democratic National Conventions (1844, 1848, 1852); presided at state GOP convention (1860) and delegate to national convention; at Civil War's end he advocated compassion for the South and by 1868 had rejoined the Democratic party. To aid Samuel Tilden's bid for the presidency (1876), he launched the Washington Union and acted as Tilden's counsel before the Electoral Commission; in 1878 he was elected to the state legislature.

Before settling in Maryland, he lived in Missouri where he was mayor of St. Louis (1842-1843) and common pleas court judge (1845-1849). It was said to be his desire to argue cases before the U.S. Supreme Court in Washington, D.C., that caused him to migrate from Missouri to Maryland. Son of Francis Preston Blair, Sr.

BLAISDELL, DANIEL *(b Jan. 22, 1762, Amesbury, Mass.; d Jan. 10, 1833, Canaan, N.H.).* Farmer, lawyer, Revolutionary soldier, New Hampshire Federalist. State representative (1793, 1795, 1799, 1812, 1813, 1824, 1825), executive council (1803-1808), Canaan moderator (1808, 1809, 1812, 1822, 1824, 1826, 1830), U.S. Representative (1809-1811), Canaan selectman (1813, 1815, 1818), state senate (1814, 1815), chief justice of court of sessions (1822).

BLAKE, HARRISON GRAY OTIS *(b March 17, 1818, Newfane, Vt.; d April 16, 1876, Medina, Ohio).* Lawyer, merchant, banker, Union soldier, Ohio Re-

publican. State representative (1846, 1847), state senate president (1848, 1849), U.S. Representative (1859-1863), refused appointment as governor of Idaho Territory, delegate to Loyalist convention (1866).

BLAKE, JOHN, JR. *(b Dec. 5, 1762, Ulster County, N.Y.; d Jan. 13, 1826, Montgomery, N.Y.).* Revolutionary War militiaman. Ulster County deputy sheriff (1793-1797), state assembly (1798-1800, 1812, 1813, 1819), Orange County sheriff (1803-1805), U.S. Representative (1805-1809), common pleas judge (1815-1818), Montgomery town supervisor for fifteen terms.

BLAKELEY, WILLIAM A. *(b Nov. 17, 1898, Miami Station, Tex.).* Attorney, accountant, rancher, oilman, real estate dealer, Texas Democrat who served twice in the U.S. Senate yet his total time in office was less than a year. Appointed to fill vacancy when Price Daniel became governor and served from Jan. 15, 1957, to April 28, 1957; appointed to fill vacancy caused when Lyndon B. Johnson became vice president and served from Jan. 3, 1961, until June 14, 1961, but lost election to hold the seat until expiration of term.

BLANCHARD, JONATHAN *(b Sept. 18, 1738, Dunstable, N.H.; d July 16, 1788, Dunstable).* New Hampshire patriot. Member of Council of Twelve (1775), delegate to Fifth Provincial Congress (1775), member of first state house of representatives (1776), state attorney general (1777), Committee of Safety (1777, 1778), New Hampshire representative at price regulating convention in New Haven (1778), Continental Congress (1783), state's first probate judge (1784).

BLANCHARD, NEWTON CRAIN *(b Jan. 29, 1849, Rapides Parish, La.; d June 22, 1922, Shreveport, La.).* Lawyer, Louisiana Democrat who achieved prominence by resisting Reconstruction and physically trying to bar Negroes from the polls. Thus began forty years of political service.

Caddo Parish Democratic Committee chairman (1876), state constitutional convention (1879), president of convention in 1913, U.S. Representative (1881-1894) and chairman of Rivers and Harbors Committee that improved Mississippi levee system, U.S. Senate to fill vacancy created when Edward D. White was appointed to the U.S. Supreme Court (1894-1897), national conventions (1896, 1912), associate justice of state supreme court (1897-1903), governor (1904-1908).

During his administration, Louisiana placed more of the tax load upon business and industry, made many appointive positions elective, improved educational facilities, revamped charities, and set up a system of statewide primaries for all state and federal offices.

BLAND, OSCAR EDWARD *(b Nov. 21, 1877, Green County, Ind.; d Aug. 3, 1951, Washington, D.C.).* Teacher, lawyer, Indiana Republican. State senate (1907-1909), U.S. Representative (1917-1923), associate judge of the U.S. Court of Customs and Patent Appeals (1923-1949).

BLAND, RICHARD *(b May 6, 1710, Orange County, Va.; d Oct. 26, 1776, Williamsburg, Va.).* Historian, author, champion of public rights and foe ol colonial taxation, pre-Revolution statesman who saw weapons as the last resort and whom Jefferson described as "the most learned and logical man of those who took prominent lead in public affairs." Virginia House of Burgesses (1745-1775), Committee of Correspondence (1773), Continental Congress (1774-1775), Revolutionary conventions (1775, 1776). Uncle of Theodorick Bland.

BLAND, RICHARD PARKS *(b Aug. 19, 1835, Ohio County, Ky.; d June 15, 1899, Lebanon, Mo.).* Teacher, lawyer,

mine operator who began by working the fields of Colorado, Nevada, and California; Missouri Democrat who was called Silver Dick because of his advocacy of free silver coinage and who was a serious contender for the Democratic presidential nomination (1896), receiving 290 delegate votes, then withdrawing his name after leading on the first three ballots. U.S. Representative (1873-1895, 1897 until death). He led the fight for free silver as chairman of the Committee on Mines and Mining (1875-1877) and gained national renown when (1878) the Congress overrode President Hayes' veto of the Bland-Allison Act.

BLAND, SCHUYLER OTIS *(b May 4, 1872, Gloucester County, Va.; d Feb. 16, 1950, U.S. Naval Hospital, Bethesda, Md.).* Teacher, lawyer, Virginia Democrat who served seventeen terms as a U.S. Representative (1918 until death).

BLAND, THEODORICK *(b March 21, 1742, Cawsons, Va.; d June 1, 1790, New York City).* Physician, planter, Revolutionary soldier. Virginia delegate to Continental Congress (1780-1783), member of Virginia convention (1788) that adopted federal Constitution despite his negative vote, U.S. Representative in First Congress (1789 until death). Nephew of Richard Bland.

BLANTON, THOMAS LINDSAY *(b Oct. 25, 1872, Houston, Tex.; d Aug. 11, 1957, Albany, Tex.).* Lawyer, cattleman, Texas Democrat. Judge of forty-second judicial district (1908-1917), U.S. Representative (1917-1929, 1930-1937).

BLANKENBURG, RUDOLPH *(b Feb. 16, 1843, Barntrup, Germany; d April 12, 1918, Philadelphia, Pa.).* Immigrated to United States (1865) after reading *Uncle Tom's Cabin,* became a successful Philadelphia businessman-reformer with Quaker leanings. Although nationally a Republican, he was at constant loggerheads with his party; was elected mayor of Philadelphia by 5,000 votes as an independent and in his four-year term (1911-1915) became known as Old Dutch Cleanser. Made war on loan sharks, organized worldwide charities, created a charity pawn shop.

BLASDEL, HENRY GOODE *(b Jan. 20, 1825, Dearborn County, Ind.; d July 26, 1900).* Lawyer, merchant, ore mill operator who prospected the fields of California and the Utah Territory and, when Nevada became a state, became its first governor (1864-1871). Politically he was an old-line Whig who in 1860 became a Republican and in 1864 was a delegate to the national convention that nominated Lincoln for a second term.

BLATCH, HARRIOT EATON STANTON *(b Jan. 20, 1856, Seneca Falls, N.Y.; d Nov. 20, 1940, Greenwich, Conn.).* Daughter of abolitionist Henry Brewster Stanton and Elizabeth Cady Stanton in whose steps she followed as a radical social reformer; active in England (where she married William Henry Blatch and lived from 1882 to 1902); orator, writer. After her return from England to the United States, she was active in the Women's Trade Union League, effective in redirecting the fight for women's suffrage into the political field, instrumental in forming (New York, 1907) the Equality League of Self-Supporting Women and serving as its president. One of the leaders who (1910) organized the first women's suffrage parade down New York City's Fifth Avenue. A leading supporter of Robert M. La Follette in the 1924 presidential campaign; active in the Socialist party (and opposed to communism) from the time women were permitted to vote until her death; unsuccessful Socialist candidate for U.S. Senate (1926). Involved in war work during World War I. Her experiences and research she did for a book, *A Woman's Point of View, Some Roads to Peace* (1920), convinced her that worldwide

peace depended on women's suffrage and participation in the League of Nations.

BLEASE, COLEMAN LIVINGSTON *(b Oct. 8, 1868, Newberry County, S.C.; d Jan. 19, 1942, Columbia, S.C.).* Lawyer, South Carolina Democrat. State representative (1890-1894, 1899, 1900; speaker 1892-1894), mayor of Helena (1897), presidential elector for Bryan-Sewell (1896) and Bryan-Stevenson (1900), Newberry city attorney (1901, 1902), state senate (1905-1909, speaker 1906, 1907), mayor of Newberry (1910), governor (1911-1915), U.S. Senate (1925-1931).

BLEDSOE, ALBERT TAYLOR *(b Nov. 9, 1809, Kentucky; d Dec. 8, 1877, Alexandria, Va.).* West Point classmate (1830) of Jefferson Davis and Robert E. Lee, college professor, author, founding editor-publisher of the *Southern Review*, Confederate soldier. He was the Confederacy's assistant secretary of war (1861-1865) whose mission was to search British records for precedents that might apply to the issues separating North and South.

BLEECKER, HARMANUS *(b Oct. 9, 1779, Albany, N.Y.; d July 19, 1849, Albany).* Lawyer, diplomat, New York Federalist. U.S. Representative (1811-1813), state assembly (1814, 1815), minister to Netherlands (1837-1842).

BLENNERHASSETT, HARMAN *(b Oct. 8, 1765, Hampshire, England; d Feb. 2, 1831, Isle of Guernsey, England).* An Irish lawyer, educated in Dublin, he came to the United States in 1796 and settled on an island in the Ohio River where his mansion became a frontier rendezvous point for Aaron Burr and his followers. The Wood County, Va., militia raided the island and looted the mansion, but Blennerhassett had fled. Ultimately he was arrested but never brought to trial. He raised cotton in Mississippi and practiced law in Montreal before returning to England in 1822.

BLISS, AARON THOMAS *(b May 22, 1837, Peterboro, N.Y.; d Sept. 16, 1906, Milwaukee, Wis.).* Merchant, manufacturer, banker, gentleman farmer, Union soldier, Michigan Republican. State senate (1882), U.S. Representative (1889-1891), governor (1900-1904). A progressive, Bliss advocated educational and charitable programs and an end to railroad tax windfalls.

BLISS, ARCHIBALD MESEROLE *(b Jan. 25, 1838, Brooklyn, N.Y.; d March 19, 1923, Washington, D.C.).* Transportation executive, real estate broker, New York Republican-Liberal-Democrat. Brooklyn board of aldermen (1864-1867, its president in 1866), GOP National Convention delegate (1864, 1868), Liberal National Convention (1872), Democratic National Convention (1876, 1880, 1884, 1888), U.S. Representative (1875-1883, 1885-1889).

BLISS, CORNELIUS NEWTON *(b Jan. 26, 1833, Fall River, Mass.; d Oct. 9, 1911, New York City).* Merchant, textile manufacturer, New York Republican who shunned public office, rejecting the offer of vice presidential running mate to President McKinley in 1901; Theodore Roosevelt ran instead and, McKinley having died in September of the same year, became president. Chairman of GOP state committee (1887), GOP National Committee treasurer (1892-1904), McKinley's secretary of interior (1896-1898), resigning because he had had enough of political office.

BLISS, GEORGE *(b Jan. 1, 1813, Jericho, Vt.; d Oct. 24, 1868, Wooster, Ohio)* Lawyer, Ohio Democrat. Presiding judge of eighth judicial district (1850 until discontinued), U.S. Representative (1853-1855, 1863-1865), delegate to Union National Convention (1866). (Not to be confused with George Bliss of New York.)

BLISS, GEORGE *(b May 3, 1830, Springfield, Mass.; d Sept. 2, 1897, Wakefield, R.I.).* Lawyer; Union soldier who, acting for the Union League Club, organized three Negro regiments; New York Republican and skilled legal draftsman responsible for New York City's 1873 charter and its first Tenement House Act. U.S. attorney for southern district (1873-1877), special federal prosecutor (1882) in star route case (in which kickbacks had been given for horse-drawn mail delivery contracts) involving Senator Stephen W. Dorsey and others, represented Roman Catholic Church in aid-to-religious school debate at state constitutional convention (1884). (Not to be confused with George Bliss of Ohio.)

BLISS, PHILEMON *(b July 28, 1813, Canton, Conn.; d Aug. 25, 1889, St. Paul, Minn.).* Jurist, Missouri law school dean. Ohio foe of slavery who changed party labels from Federalist to Whig to Free-Soiler to Republican. Ohio's fourteenth judicial district presiding judge (1848-1851), U.S. Representative (1855-1859), Lincoln-appointed chief justice of the Dakota Territory (1861-1863), then relocated in Missouri where he became associate supreme court justice (1868-1872) and first dean of the state university's new law department (1872 until death).

BLITCH, IRIS FAIRCLOTH *(b April 25, 1912, Toombs County, Ga.).* Georgia Democrat. Elected twice to state senate (1946, 1952), state representative (1948), Democratic national committeewoman (1948-1956), chosen Woman of the Year in Agriculture (1957) by *Progressive Farmer*, U.S. Representative (1955-1963), serving on Public Works Committee.

BLODGETT, RUFUS *(b Oct. 9, 1834, Dorchester, N.H.; d Oct. 3, 1910, Long Branch, N.J.).* Railroad executive, banker, New Jersey Democrat. State assembly (1878, 1879), national convention delegate (1880, 1896), U.S. Senate (1887-1893), mayor of Long Branch (1893-1898).

BLOODWORTH, TIMOTHY *(b 1736, New Hanover County, N.C.; d Aug. 24, 1814, Wilmington, N.C.).* North Carolina teacher, jack of all trades, and gunsmith who made muskets and bayonets for the Continental Army. State house of commons (1778, 1779), Wilmington district treasurer (1781, 1782), commissioner of confiscated property (1783), Continental Congress (1786-1787), state senate (1788-1789), U.S. Representative in the First Congress (1790-1791), state representative (1793, 1794), U.S. Senate (1795-1801), Wilmington collector of customs (1802 until death). An anti-Federalist and a radical, so much so that one biographer described him as "a red Republican."

BLOOM, SOL *(b March 9, 1870, Pekin, Ill.; d March 7, 1949, Washington, D.C.).* Businessman, civic-minded New York Democrat who undertook many assignments besides serving thirteen terms as a U.S. Representative (1923 until death). Among his civic and quasi-governmental roles: director of U.S. George Washington Bicentennial Commission, director general of U.S. Constitutional Sesquicentennial Commission, chairman of Committee on Celebration of the 150th Anniversary of the U.S. Supreme Court.

BLOOMER, AMELIA JENKS *(b May 27, 1818, Homer, N.Y.; d Dec. 30, 1894, Council Bluffs, Iowa).* Editor, temperance advocate, and pioneer in women's rights, who worked with such leaders as Elizabeth Cady Stanton, founded the *Lily,* a successful women's magazine. Although an effective lecturer and active for the causes she espoused, Amelia Bloomer is best remembered for a revolutionary type of women's suit with full, gathered (bloomer) pants which she did not originate but which she wore at work and while lecturing.

BLOOMFIELD, JOSEPH *(b Oct. 5, 1753, Woodbridge, N.J.; d Oct. 3, 1823, Burlington, N.J.).* Lawyer, Revolutionary soldier, New Jersey Democrat-Republican. Admiralty court registrar (1779-1783), state attorney general (1783-1792), Washington-Adams presidential elector (1792), mayor of Burlington (1795-1800), governor (1801-1812) who signed gradual emancipation act and intervened for his friend Aaron Burr after the latter's duel with Alexander Hamilton in Weehawken, U.S. Representative (1817-1821).

BLOUNT, JAMES HENDERSON *(b Sept. 12, 1837, Jones County, Ga.; d March 8, 1903, Macon, Ga.).* Lawyer, planter, Confederate soldier, Georgia Democrat who, as commissioner to Hawaiian Islands (1893), recommended against their annexation. State constitutional convention delegate (1865), U.S. Representative (1873-1892).

BLOUNT, THOMAS *(b May 10, 1759, Craven [now Pitt] County, N.C.; d Feb. 7, 1812, Washington, D.C.).* Merchant, Revolutionary soldier who was captured at seventeen and held prisoner in England until end of war, North Carolina politician who was more interested in horse racing than affairs of state. State house of commons (1788), U.S. Representative (1793-1799, 1805-1809, 1811 until death). Brother of William Blount, half-brother of Willie Blount.

BLOUNT, WILLIAM *(b March 26, 1749, Bertie County, N.C.; d March 21, 1800, Knoxville, Tenn.).* Merchant, frontier land speculator, North Carolina and Tennessee politician who was expelled from the U.S. Senate but never lost the support of his constituency. North Carolina House of Commons (1780-1784, once its speaker), Continental Congress (1782, 1783, 1786, 1787), delegate to federal Constitutional Convention (1787), state senate (1788-1790), governor of the territory south of the Ohio River and superintendent of Indian affairs (1790-1796), chairman of convention that resulted in statehood for Tennessee (1796) and its first U.S. senator (Aug. 2, 1796, until expulsion July 8, 1797), president of Tennessee State Senate (1798 until death). His ouster from the U.S. Senate came as the result of his part in a plot to mount an attack by Indians and frontiersmen, in conjunction with a British armada, upon Spanish territory in West Florida. Brother of Thomas Blount, half-brother of Willie Blount, and father of William G. Blount.

BLOUNT, WILLIAM GRAINGER *(b 1784, near New Bern, N.C.; d May 21, 1827, Paris, Tenn.).* Lawyer, farmer, Tennessee Democrat. State representative (1811), Tennessee's secretary of state (1811-1815), U.S. Representative (1815-1819). Son of William Blount.

BLOUNT, WILLIE [pronounced Wiley] *(b April 18, 1768, North Carolina; d Sept. 10, 1835, Montgomery County, Tenn.).* Jurist, planter, Tennessee Democratic-Republican. State superior court judge (1796), state legislature (1808), governor (1809-1815), state constitutional convention (1834). Half-brother of Thomas and William Blount.

BLOW, HENRY TAYLOR *(b July 15, 1817, Southampton County, Va.; d Sept. 11, 1875, Saratoga, N.Y.).* Financier interested in lead mining, lead-product manufacturing, railroads, and banks; diplomat, Missouri Whig–Free-Soiler–Republican with a strong antipathy for slavery who resigned as minister to Venezuela (1861-1862) in order to run for Congress as a "charcoal" Republican on an emancipation platform. U.S. Representative (1863-1867), minister to Brazil (1869-1871), member of District of Columbia Board of Commissioners (1874-1875).

BLOXHAM, WILLIAM DUNNINGTON *(b July 9, 1835, Tallahassee, Fla.; d March 15, 1911, Tallahassee).* Lawyer, planter, Confederate soldier, conservative Florida Democrat who made his political mark after the Civil War largely through his opposition to his state's so-called radical Negro government. State representative (1861), lieutenant governor (1870-1872), Florida secretary of state (1876-1880), governor (1881-1885, 1897-1901).

BOATNER, CHARLES JAHLEAL *(b Jan. 23, 1849, Columbia, La.; d March 21, 1903, New Orleans).* Lawyer, Confederate soldier, Louisiana Democrat. State senate (1876-1878), U.S. Representative (1889-1895 and nine months in 1896-1897), unseated because of a contest over his election to a fourth term.

BOCKEE, ABRAHAM *(b Feb. 3, 1784, Shekomeko, N.Y.; d June 1, 1865, Shekomeko).* Lawyer, farmer, Jackson Democrat. New York State Assembly (1820), U.S. Representative (1829-1831, 1833-1837), state senate (1840-1844), court of errors judge (1843), first judge of the Dutchess County Court (1846).

BOCOCK, THOMAS STANHOPE *(b May 18, 1815, Buckingham Court House, Va.; d Aug. 5, 1891, Appomattox County, Va.).* Lawyer, Conservative Virginia Democrat. State house of delegates (1842-1844, 1869, 1870, 1877, 1878), Appomattox County prosecuting attorney (1845, 1846), U.S. Representative (1847-1861) and Naval Committee chairman for ten years, Confederate Congress (1861-1865), its speaker in 1862-1863), Democratic National Convention delegate (1868, 1876, 1880).

BOEHNE, JOHN WILLIAM, SR. *(b Oct. 28, 1856, Scott Township, Ind.; d Dec. 27, 1946, Evansville, Ind.).* Accountant, manufacturer, St. Louis Federal Reserve Bank Director, Indiana Democrat. Mayor of Evansville (1905-1908), Democratic National Convention delegate (1908),

U.S. Representative (1909-1913). Father of John W. Boehne, Jr.

BOEHNE, JOHN WILLIAM, JR. *(b March 2, 1895, Evansville, Ind.).* Manufacturer, tax counselor, Indiana Democrat. U.S. Representative (1931-1943). Son of John W. Boehne, Sr.

BOEN, HALDOR ERICKSON *(b Jan. 2, 1851, Sondre Aurdal, Norway; d July 23, 1912, Aurdal Township, Minn.).* Teacher, farmer, Minnesota People's party representative in U.S. Congress (1893-1895). Computed first tax levies (1872) in Ottertail County, justice of the peace (1875-1900), county commissioner (1880).

BOGGS, LILLBURN W. *(b Dec. 14, 1792, Lexington, Ky.; d March 14, 1860, Napa Valley, Calif.).* Bank teller, storekeeper, Indian trader, farmer, Missouri Democrat and early California settler. In Missouri: state senate (1826-1832, 1842-1846), lieutenant governor (1832-1836), governor (1836-1840) who called out the militia to drive Mormons from the state. In California: alcalde (chief administrative and judicial officer) of all territory north of the Sacramento River (1846-1850).

BOGGS, THOMAS HALE *(b Feb. 15, 1914, Long Beach, Miss.; missing and presumed dead after the Oct. 16, 1972, disappearance of an Alaskan bush plane).* Lawyer, Louisiana Democrat who went to Washington as a U.S. Representative in 1941, served until November 1943 when he took time out for World War II service in the Navy, returned to the House in 1947 for an unbroken tenure, was made Democratic Whip in 1962, and did not hesitate to go anywhere to lend a helpful hand to a party constituent in need of vote-getting support. Thus he was in Alaska, flying from one part of Congressman Nick Begich's rugged district to another when their plane vanished.

BOGY, LEWIS VITAL *(b April 9, 1813, Ste. Genevieve, Mo.; d Sept. 20, 1877, St. Louis, Mo.).* Merchant, lawyer, railroad founder, Missouri Democrat and a leader in rebirth of the party there after the Civil War (during which he was a sideline Southern sympathizer). St. Louis alderman (1838), state representative (1840, 1841, 1854, 1855), commissioner of Indian affairs (1867, 1868), city council president (1872), U.S. Senate (1873 until death).

BOHN, FRANK PROBASCO *(b July 14, 1866, Charlottesville, Ind.; d June 1, 1944, Newberry, Mich.).* Physician, banker, Michigan Republican. Newberry village president (1904-1919), state senate (1923-1926), U.S. Representative (1927-1933), state hospital commission (1935-1937).

BOIES, HORACE *(b Dec. 7, 1827, Erie County, N.Y.; d April 4, 1923).* Lawyer, landowner, New York Whig turned Republican who served one term (1857) in state assembly, migrated to Iowa and became Democratic governor (1889-1893) campaigning on the issue of wet versus dry and siding with the anti-prohibitionists. His ability to defeat the entrenched Republican power bloc gained him nationwide attention and he seemed destined for the Democratic presidential nomination (1896) until William Jennings Bryan delivered his cross-of-gold speech.

BOIES, REUBEN PATRICK *(b June 9, 1819 Blandford, Mass.; d April 10, 1907).* Teacher, lawyer, farmer, writer who migrated to Oregon in the 1850s to become one of the territory's and state's foremost jurists, having much to do with the writing of both the Oregon code and constitution, and sitting, usually as presiding judge, in high state courts until he was well past eighty. Farming was his avocation and he wrote many articles for agricultural journals and for many years was president of the state Grange.

BOIES, WILLIAM DAYTON *(b Jan. 3, 1857, Boone County, Ill.; d May 31, 1932, Sheldon, Iowa).* Lawyer, Iowa Republican. Judicial district court judge (1913-1918), U.S. Representative (1919-1929) where he was appointed, with others, to conduct impeachment proceedings against federal Judge George W. English of Illinois.

BOISSEVAIN, INEZ MILHOLLAND *(b Aug. 6, 1886, New York City; d Nov. 25, 1916, Los Angeles, Calif.).* Women's suffrage leader, daughter of newspaperman John E. Milholland. Attended Vassar College where she excelled as an athlete, shocked college officials with her views on socialism and feminism and launched the suffrage movement there. When refused permission to hold a meeting in the chapel, she held it in a graveyard at night. Received LL.B. degree at New York University Law School (1912) after being refused admission at Oxford, Cambridge, and Harvard because of her sex. An active member of the militant women's organizations of the times and an irritant to the police; hired a room overlooking New York's Fifth Avenue and shouted "Votes for Women" through a megaphone as startled members of a political parade marched by; took a prominent part (1912) in New York City "shirtwaist strike." Because the Republican party had pledged itself to support a women's suffrage amendment, she traveled through twelve states speaking on their behalf in the 1916 presidential campaign. She collapsed while addressing a Los Angeles audience and died shortly thereafter.

BOK, EDWARD WILLIAM *(b Oct. 9, 1863, Den Helder, the Netherlands; d Jan. 9, 1930, Lake Wales, Fla.).* A poor Dutch boy who came to the United States and became a journalist and author who in 1923 founded the American Peace Award, which gave $100,000 to proponents of "the best practicable plan by which the United States may cooperate with other nations to achieve and preserve the peace of the world." The twenty best ideas were published under the title *Ways to Peace.*

As the first male editor of the *Ladies Home Journal* (1889-1919), Bok instituted an editorial policy that, among other accomplishments, was responsible for the Food and Drugs Act (1906). A conservationist, notable among his causes were opposition to the encroachment of power plants on the nation's waterways and women's hats that were decorated with bird feathers. His autobiography, *The Americanization of Edward Bok,* won him a Pulitzer Prize (1921).

BOLAND, PATRICK JOSEPH *(b Jan. 6, 1880, Scranton, Pa.; d May 18, 1942, Scranton).* Construction contractor, Pennsylvania Democrat. Scranton city council (1905-1906), Lackawanna County commissioner (1915-1919), U.S. Representative (1931 until death).

BOLLES, STEPHEN *(b June 25, 1866, Springboro, Pa.; d July 8, 1941, Washington, D.C.).* Newspaper reporter, editor, publisher in Ohio, Pennsylvania, New York, and Wisconsin; a Republican, he served as a U.S. Representative from Wisconsin (1939 until death) and held many quasi-governmental positions throughout his career.

BOLTON, CHESTER CASTLE *(b Sept. 5, 1882, Cleveland, Ohio; d Jan. 3, 1939, Cleveland).* Cattle raiser, businessman, Ohio Republican. Lyndhurst village council (1918-1921), state senate (1923-1928, its president in 1927 and 1928), GOP National Convention (1928), U.S. Representative (1929-1937, 1939 until death), chairman of GOP Congressional Campaign Committee (1934-1936).

BOLTON, FRANCES PAYNE *(b March 29, 1885, Cleveland, Ohio).* Public health nurse, social service worker,

Ohio Republican who first went to Washington in 1940 to complete the unexpired term of her husband, Chester Castle Bolton, and remained until 1969, serving on the House Foreign Affairs Committee. Member of the Mackinac Conference (1943) that wrote the first foreign policy plank in the GOP platform, she was active in a long list of organizations that included the Women's Africa Committee and the African-American Institute, received honorary doctorate degrees from fifteen colleges and more than twenty-five awards for distinguished service. Grand-daughter of Henry B. Payne and mother of Oliver P. Bolton.

BOLTON, OLIVER PAYNE *(b Feb. 22, 1917, Cleveland, Ohio).* Lawyer, publisher of *Lake County News Herald* in Willoughby and the *Dover Daily Reporter,* Ohio Republican. U.S. Representative (1953-1957), state director of commerce (1957). Son of Chester and Frances Bolton, great-grandson of Henry B. Payne.

BONAPARTE, CHARLES JOSEPH *(b June 9, 1851, Baltimore, Md.; d June 28, 1921, on estate outside Baltimore).* A grand-nephew of Napoleon and a wealthy lawyer whose main interest lay in public causes and both civic and civil service reform, this Bonaparte attracted the attention of Theodore Roosevelt when the latter was U.S. Civil Service Commissioner and later became a member of his cabinet.

Politically an independent Republican who (1912) accompanied Roosevelt into the Progressive party, he was a founder of the Baltimore Reform League, the Maryland Civil Service League, and the National Municipal League. Governmentally, under President Roosevelt, he served on the Board of Indian Commissioners that investigated territorial abuses, as a prosecutor in postal fraud cases, and in the cabinet as secretary of the navy (1905-1906) and attorney general (1906-1909), instituting twenty

antitrust suits and winning eight of them, including one that called for the dissolution of the American Tobacco Co.

BOND, HUGH LENNOX *(b Dec. 16, 1828, Baltimore, Md.; d Oct. 24, 1893, Baltimore, Md.).* Lawyer, jurist from Maryland whose decision made Rutherford B. Hayes president of the United States. State criminal court judge (1860-1867), judge of fourth U.S. Circuit Court (1873 until death). Not only did Bond render the Hayes decision in the latter court, but in another case he broke the back of the Ku Klux Klan which for years had been conducting a reign of terror in nine South Carolina counties.

BOND, SHADRACK *(b Nov. 24, 1773, Frederick, Md.; d April 12, 1832, Kaskaskia, Ill.).* Farmer, Democrat who became the first governor of Illinois. Member of Indiana Territory legislature (1805-1808), delegate to U.S. Congress from Illinois Territory (1813, 1814), receiver of public moneys in Kaskaskia land office (1814-1818); governor (1818-1822), register of Kaskaskia land office (1823 until death).

BOND, WILLIAM KEY *(b Oct. 2, 1792, St. Marys County, Md.; d Feb. 16, 1864, Cincinnati, Ohio).* Lawyer, railroad developer, Ohio Whig. U.S. Representative (1835-1841), surveyor of the Port of Cincinnati (1849-1853).

BONÉ, HOMER TRUETT *(b Jan. 25, 1883, Franklin, Ind.).* Lawyer, Washington State Republican turned Democrat. Tacoma corporation counsel (1918-1932), state representative (1923, 1924), U.S. Senate (1933-1944), judge of the U.S. Circuit Court of Appeals for ninth judicial circuit (1944-1956).

BONHAM, MILLEDGE LUKE *(b Dec. 25, 1813, Edgefield District, S.C.; d Aug. 27, 1890, White Sulphur Springs, N.C.).* Lawyer, planter, insurance broker, Mexican War colonel, Indian fighter, Confederate general, South Carolina Democrat. State representative (1840-1844, 1865-1867), southern South Carolina circuit solicitor (1848-1857), U.S. Representative (1857-1860), Confederate Congress (1862), governor (1863, 1864), Democratic National Convention delegate (1868), state convention (1876), state railroad commissioner (1878 until death).

BONNER, HERBERT COVINGTON *(b May 16, 1891, Washington, N.C.; d Nov. 7, 1965, Washington, D.C.).* Salesman, farmer, North Carolina Democrat. U.S. Representative (1940 until death), first stepping up into the seat when Congressman Lindsay C. Warren resigned to become comptroller general. Until then Bonner had been Warren's secretary. Chairman of Merchant Marine and Fisheries Committee (1955-1965).

BONYNGE, ROBERT WILLIAM *(b Sept. 8, 1863, New York City; d Sept. 22, 1939, New York City).* Lawyer, Colorado Republican. State representative (1893, 1894), U.S. Representative (1904-1909), member of National Monetary Commission (1908-1912); returned to New York and became chief counsel of State Industrial Commission (1916-1918), U.S. agent before Mixed Claims Commission (1923) and Tripartite Claims Commission (1927).

BOODY, DAVID AUGUSTUS *(b Aug. 13, 1837, Jackson, Maine; d Jan. 20, 1930, Brooklyn, N.Y.).* Lawyer, banker, stockbroker, New York Democrat. National convention delegate (1884, 1892), state convention (1890), U.S. Representative for seven months in 1891 when he resigned to run for mayor of Brooklyn, which was not then part of New York City, won and served in 1892 and 1893; president of board of trustees of Brooklyn Public Library (1897 until death), Wilson-Marshall presidential elector (1912).

BOOHER, CHARLES FERRIS *(b Jan. 31, 1848, Livingston County, N.Y.; d Jan. 21, 1921, Savannah, Mo.).* Teacher, lawyer, real estate dealer, Missouri Democrat. Andrew County prosecuting attorney (1875-1877, 1883-1885), Hancock-English presidential elector (1880), mayor of Savannah (1886-1890), U.S. Representative (1889) to fill a vacancy and then in his own right (1907 until death).

BOON, RATLIFF *(b Jan. 18, 1781, Franklin County, N.C.; d Nov. 20, 1844, Louisiana, Mo.).* Gunsmith, Indiana Democrat-Republican. Warrick County's first treasurer (1813-1815), state representative (1816, 1817), state senate (1818), lieutenant governor (1819-1824) except for two months in 1822 when he was governor because of the resignation of Jonathan Jennings who had served from 1816 as the state's first chief executive; U.S. Representative (1825-1827, 1829-1839) moving to Missouri on completion of his last term.

BOONE, ANDREW RECHMOND *(b April 4, 1831, Davidson County, Tenn.; d Jan, 26, 1886, Mayfield, Ky.).* Lawyer, Kentucky Democrat. Graves County judge (1854-1861), state representative (1861), first judicial district circuit judge (1868-1874), U.S. Representative (1875-1879), chairman of state railroad commission (1882-1886).

BOONE, DANIEL *(b Nov. 2, 1734, Berks County, Pa.; d Sept. 26, 1820, at home of son, Nathan, outside St. Charles, Mo.).* Backwoods pioneer whose life has become legend beginning when his parents moved to North Carolina in 1750. Lesser known than his frontier deeds are his socio-political-judicial functions beginning when he negotiated a treaty with Indians (1775) for land that became known as Transylvania where he laid out a settlement known as Boonesborough; moved on to found Boone's Station in what later became Fayette County, Ky., and became sheriff and deputy surveyor through most of the 1780s, including membership in the Virginia Assembly (1787-1788); then, losing his land to speculators with political connections, moved on to Missouri's Femme Osage Valley where, given a Spanish land grant, he served as district magistrate (1800-1804).

BOOTH, JOHN WILKES *(b Aug. 26, 1838, on family farm outside Bel Air, Md.; d April 26, 1865, Bowling Green, Va.).* The man who shot President Abraham Lincoln on April 14, 1865, in Ford's Theater.

BOOTH, NEWTON *(b Dec. 25, 1825, Salem, Ind.; d July 14, 1892, Sacramento, Calif.).* Lawyer who went to California in the gold rush days, struck it rich as a provisioner for miners, turned to writing and lecturing, became interested in politics, and was a staunch Republican supporter of President Grant. State senate (1863), governor (1871-1874), U.S. Senate (1875-1881).

BOOTHMAN, MELVIN MORELLA *b Oct. 16, 1846, Williams County, Ohio; d March 5, 1904, Bryan, Ohio).* Lawyer, Union soldier, Ohio Republican. Williams County treasurer (1871-1875), U.S. Representative (1887-1891).

BORAH, WILLIAM EDGAR *(b June 29, 1865, Fairfield, Ill.; d Jan. 19, 1940, Washington, D.C.).* Idaho Republican whose dream of becoming a Shakespearean actor was nipped in the bud (he ran away from home to play Mark Antony with a traveling troupe) by an irate father, returned to the study and practice of law, found politics a fitting substitute for professional theatrics, and went on to become a U.S. senator, serving thirty-three years (1907 until death).

He moved to Boise in 1890 where he practiced law, ran unsuccessfully for city attorney (losing by three votes), became chairman (1892) of the GOP State Central Committee, then secretary to Governor William J. O'Connell, married his daughter Mary (called Mamie). A foe of the "monopolistic goldbugs" and a champion of silver, Borah bolted the GOP to back Bryan against McKinley for the Presidency (1896). He returned to the party, and was elected to the Senate (1907) and designated chairman of the Education and Labor Committee where he proceeded to disappoint the conservatives who thought him one of them by sponsoring measures calling for an eight-hour day, a children's bureau, a labor department, a probe of steel industry working conditions, and equal opportunity for all. Thus, the progressives numbered him in their ranks only to have him oppose conservation measures, the forest bureau, and control of water and power development. A Republican maverick who recognized neither party loyalty nor leadership and held himself accountable only to the people of Idaho who, in turn, regarded him as their favorite son.

A staunch supporter and leader of the Theodore Roosevelt faction in the Republican National Committee (1908-1912), he nevertheless refused to join Teddy's Progressive party and was a delegate to the 1912 GOP convention that nominated Taft and Sherman; a fierce nationalist, he voted for entry into World War I, then led the fight against the League of Nations; a strong foe of the Ku Klux Klan, yet he opposed civil rights for Negroes; as chairman of the Foreign Relations Committee he was known around the world as one of America's foremost statesmen, yet not once did he visit a foreign country.

So it went throughout his long tenure in the Senate. An orator who never forgot his Shakespearian aspirations, Borah became known in Washington as the Great Opposer.

BORCHERS, CHARLES MARTIN *(b Nov. 18, 1869, Fairfield County, Ohio; d Dec. 2, 1946, Decatur, Ill.).* Teacher, lawyer, Illinois Democrat. Mayor of Decatur (1909-1911, 1919-1923), U.S. Representative (1913-1915), unsuccessful candidate for governor (1924).

BORDEN, NATHANIEL BRIGGS *(b April 15, 1801, Fall River, Mass.; d April 10, 1865, Fall River).* Manufacturer, banker, railroad executive, Massachusetts Democrat-Whig. State representative (1821, 1834, 1851, 1864), U.S. Representative as a Van Buren Democrat (1835-1839) and as a Whig (1841-1843), state senate (1845-1848), mayor of Fall River (1856, 1857).

BOREMAN, ARTHUR INGRAM *(b July 24, 1823, Waynesburg, Pa.; d April 19, 1896, Parkersburg. W.Va.).* Lawyer, Virginia and West Virginia Republican and the latter state's first governor (1863-1869). A member of the Virginia House of Delegates (1855-1860) and a participant in the 1861 secession convention where he strongly but vainly favored remaining in the Union, Boreman presided over a splinter convention of delegates from northwestern counties that subsequently became the state of West Virginia. Unanimously chosen governor and twice reelected, he resigned to run for the U.S. Senate, won and served (1869-1875). Additionally, he twice served as a circuit court judge (1861 until becoming governor and 1888 until death).

BOREN, LYLE H. *(b May 11, 1909, Waxahachie, Tex.).* Farmer, author, merchant, Oklahoma Democrat who became railway representative in Washington, D.C., after completing five terms as U.S. Representative (1937-1947).

BOSONE, REVA ZILPHA BECK *(b ——, American Fork, Utah).* Teacher, lawyer, Utah Democrat. State representative (1933-1935, floor leader in latter year), Salt Lake City judge (1936-1948), chairman of Women's Army Corps Civilian Advisory Committee (ninth service command) during War World II,

official observer at founding United Nations Conference (1945), first director of Utah Board for Education on Alcoholism (1947, 1948), U.S. Representative (1949-1953), Democratic National Conventions (1952, 1956), counsel to Safety and Compensation Subcommittee of House Education and Labor Committee (1957-1960), Post Office Department judicial officer (1961-   ).

BOUDINOT, ELIAS *(b May 2, 1770, Philadelphia; d Oct. 24, 1821, Burlington, N.J.).* Lawyer, New Jersey patriot who presided over Continental Congress (1782, 1783) and signed peace treaty with England. Member of Committee of Safety (1775), commissary general of prisoners in Revolutionary Army (1776-1779), Continental Congress (1777, 1778, 1781-1783), U.S. Representative in first three Congresses (1789-1795), director of the Mint (1795-1805), first president of American Bible Society (1816).

BOULDIN, JAMES WOOD *(b 1792, Charlotte County, Va.; d March 30, 1854, Charlotte County).* Lawyer, Jacksonian Democrat of Virginia. U.S. Representative (1834-1839), filling the seat left vacant upon the death of his brother, Thomas T. Bouldin.

BOULDIN, THOMAS TYLER *(b 1781, Charlotte County, Va.; d Feb. 11, 1834, Washington, D.C., while addressing the House of Representatives).* Lawyer, Virginia Democrat. U.S. Representative (1829-1834). Brother of James W. Bouldin.

BOULIGNY, CHARLES JOSEPH DOMINIQUE *(b Aug. 22, 1773, New Orleans, La.; d March 6, 1833, New Orleans).* Ensign in his father's Spanish regiment and municipal council commissioner prior to the Louisiana Purchase (1803), then became a U.S. citizen and a lawyer. As a territory: territorial representative (1806), New Orleans justice of the peace (1807-1812). As a state: member of the committee on public defense during the British invasion (1814, 1815), U.S. Senator (1824-1829) to fill a vacancy. Uncle of John E. Bouligny.

BOULIGNY, JOHN EDWARD *(b Feb. 5, 1824, New Orleans, La.; d Feb. 20, 1864, Washington, D.C.).* Lawyer, Louisiana Democrat who was bitterly opposed to secession, he was elected a U.S. Representative as a candidate of the American (Know-Nothing) party and served from March 1859 until March 1861, the only Louisianan to keep his seat after the state seceded, remaining in the North during the war. Nephew of Charles J. D. Bouligny.

BOURN, BENJAMIN *(b Sept. 9, 1755, Bristol, R.I.; d Sept. 17, 1808, Bristol).* Lawyer, Rhode Island Federalist. U.S. Representative (1790-1796), resigning to become first U.S. District Judge for Rhode Island and then judge of the U.S. Circuit (Eastern) Court.

BOURNE, JONATHAN, JR. *(b Feb. 23, 1855, New Bedford, Mass.; d Sept. 1, 1940, Washington, D.C.).* Oregon lawyer, farmer, mine operator, business executive; Massachusetts mill operator; Alabama citrus grower; Washington, D.C. newspaperman; Oregon Republican. Oregon representative (1885, 1886, 1897), GOP National Conventions (1888, 1892), GOP National Committeeman (1888-1892), U.S. Senate (1907-1913).

BOURNE, SHEARJASHUB *(b June 14, 1746, Barnstable, Mass.; d March 11, 1806, Boston, Mass.).* Massachusetts lawyer. State representative (1782-1785, 1788-1790), member of convention that ratified the U.S. Constitution (1788), U.S. Representative (1791-1795), Suffolk County Common Pleas Court justice (1799 until death).

BOUTELL, HENRY SHERMAN *(b March 14, 1856, Boston; d March 11, 1916, San Remo, Italy).* Lawyer, law profes-

sor, diplomat, Illinois Republican. State representative (1884, 1885), U.S. Representative (1897-1911), GOP National Convention (1908), minister to both Portugal and Switzerland (1911-1913).

BOUTELLE, CHARLES ADDISON *(b Feb. 9, 1839, Damariscotta, Maine; d May 21, 1901, Waverley, Maine).* Shipmaster, editor-publisher of the *Bangor Whig and Courier,* Union Navy officer, Maine Republican. National convention (1876), U.S. Representative (1883-1901).

BOUTWELL, GEORGE SEWEL *(b Jan. 28, 1818, Brookline, Mass.; d Feb. 7, 1905, Groton, Mass.).* Teacher, merchant, lawyer, Massachusetts Democrat turned Republican. State representative (1842-1844, 1847-1850), bank commissioner (1849-1851), governor (1851, 1852), state constitutional convention (1853), secretary of state board of education (1855-1861), delegate to 1861 peace convention that failed to avert Civil War, War Department military commission (1862), first commissioner of internal revenue (1862, 1863), U.S. Representative (1863-1869), one of managers appointed (1868) to conduct President Andrew Johnson impeachment proceedings, secretary of the treasury in Grant cabinet (1869-1873), U.S. Senate (1873-1877) when President Hayes appointed him commissioner to codify and edit the Statutes at Large, French and American claims commission counsel (1880), counsel for Haiti (1885), for Hawaii (1886), for Chile (1893, 1894), president of Anti-Imperialist League (1898-1905).

BOWDOIN, JAMES, JR. *(b Aug. 7, 1726, Boston, Mass.; d Nov. 6, 1790, Boston).* Merchant, land owner, Revolutionary patriot and governor of Massachusetts whose poor health caused him to decline such honors as a seat in the Continental Congress and prevented him from going further in politics. Member Massachusetts general court (1753-1788), including three terms in the lower house and membership on the Governor's Council for sixteen years; provincial congress (1775-1777); president of state constitutional convention and chairman of subcommittee (1779) that drafted constitution, assigning to John Adams the task of writing most of it; governor (1785-1787) during which occurred Shay's Rebellion which he dealt with firmly and effectively. Father of James Bowdoin III.

BOWDOIN, JAMES, III *(b Sept. 22, 1752, Boston, Mass.; d Oct. 11, 1811, Buzzard's Bay, Mass.).* Merchant, diplomat, philanthropist who made large gifts to Bowdoin College (named for his father), Massachusetts Jeffersonian Republican. Member general court (1786-1790), state senate (1794, 1801), delegate to federal Constitution ratification convention (1788), Governor's Council (1796), minister to Spain (1804-1808) conducting new but unsuccessful negotiations concerning Florida.

BOWEN, THOMAS MEAD *(b Oct. 26, 1835, near what is now Burlington, Iowa; d Dec. 30, 1906, Pueblo, Colo.).* Lawyer, miner, Union soldier, Arkansas and Colorado Republican. In Arkansas: GOP National Convention (1864), president of state constitutional convention (1866), state supreme court justice (1867-1871), presidentially appointed governor of Idaho Territory (1871). In Colorado: fourth judicial district judge (1876-1880), state representative (1882), U.S. Senate (1883-1889).

BOWERS, EATON JACKSON *(b June 17, 1865, Canton, Miss.; d Oct. 26, 1939, New Orleans, La.).* Lawyer, newspaper editor-publisher, Mississippi Democrat. State Democratic executive committee (1886-1900), presidential elector for Cleveland-Thurman (1888) and Cleveland-Stevenson (1892), state senate (1896), state representative (1900), Democratic National Convention dele-

gate (1900, 1916), U.S. Representative (1903-1911).

BOWERS, GEORGE MEADE *(b Sept. 13, 1863, Gerrardstown, W.Va.; d Dec. 7, 1925, Martinsburg, W.Va.).* Banker, West Virginia Democrat. State house of delegates (1883-1887), state census supervisor (1890), GOP National Convention (1892), commissioner of fisheries (1898-1913) , U.S. Representative (1916-1923).

BOWERS, WILLIAM WALLACE *(b Oct. 20, 1834, Whitestown, N.Y.; d May 2, 1917, San Diego, Calif.).* Wisconsin rancher, Union soldier, innkeeper, California Republican. State assembly (1873, 1874), San Diego collector of customs (1874-1879, 1902-1906), state senate (1887-1889), U.S. Representative (1891-1897).

BOWERSOCK, JUSTIN DeWITT *(b Sept. 19, 1842, Columbiana County, Ohio; d Oct. 27, 1922, Lawrence, Kans.).* Merchant, miller, manufacturer, banker, grain shipper, Kansas Republican. Mayor of Lawrence (1881-1885), state representative (1887), state senate (1895), U.S. Representative (1899-1907).

BOWIE, RICHARD JOHNS *(b June 23, 1807, Georgetown, D.C.; d March 12, 1888, Montgomery County, Md.).* Lawyer, farmer, Maryland Whig turned Republican and one of the state's outstanding jurists. State house of delegates (1835-1837), state senate (1837-1841), Whig National Convention delegate and presidential elector for Harrison-Tyler (1840), Montgomery County prosecuting attorney (1845-1849), U.S. Representative (1849-1853), chief judge of Maryland Court of Appeals (1861-1867), chief judge of sixth judicial circuit and associate judge of state court of appeals (1871 until death).

A firm believer in the Union and an equally strong foe of secession, his only political setback came in 1854 when he was the Whig candidate for governor, losing to a Democrat at a time when the state was torn by strife over slavery. The Whig party was destroyed, but not Bowie. Presiding over the appeals court during the war years, he won state-wide renown and respect for his fairness and, when he was due for mandatory retirement because of age, the Democratic-controlled legislature continued his tenure for life. The four-year break in service (1867-1871) was due only to postwar adoption of a new state constitution and reorganization of the judicial system.

BOWIE, ROBERT (b March 1750, Prince Georges County, Md.; d Jan. 8, 1818, Nottingham, Md.). Farmer, Revolutionary officer with George Washington in New York, Maryland Democratic-Republican. State house of delegates (1785-1790, 1801-1803), Prince Georges County justice of the peace (1793-1803, 1807-1811), governor (1803-1806, 1811-1812) an office in which he was a leading advocate of the hostilities that became known as the War of 1812.

BOWIE, SYDNEY JOHNSTON (b July 26, 1865, Talladega, Ala.; d May 7, 1928, Birmingham, Ala.). Lawyer, auto dealer, political leader, Alabama Democrat. Talladega city clerk (1885, 1886), alderman (1891), state Democratic executive committee (1894-1899), chairman of 1901 session when Calhoun County constitution was ratified, U.S. Representative (1901-1907), Birmingham Board of Education (1915-1919), chairman of state educational commission (1920), chairman of state delegation to Democratic National Convention (1920), state harbor commissioner (1922, 1923).

BOWIE, THOMAS FIELDER (b April 7, 1808, Queen Anne, Md.; d Oct. 30, 1869, Upper Marlboro, Md.). Lawyer, Maryland Whig turned Democrat. Prince Georges County deputy attorney general (1833-1842), state house of delegates (1842-1846), unsuccessful candidate for governor (1843), state consti-

tutional convention (1851), Whig presidential elector for Scott-Graham (1852), U.S. Representative as a Democrat (1855-1859).

BOWLER, JAMES BERNARD (b Feb. 5, 1875, Chicago, Ill.; d July 18, 1957, Chicago). Professional bicycle racer, insurance broker, Illinois Democrat. Chicago City Council (1906-1923, 1928-1953), city compensation commissioner (1923-1927), city public vehicle license commissioner (1934), U.S. Representative (1953 until death).

BOWLIN, JAMES BUTLER (b Jan. 16, 1804, Spotsylvania County, Va.; d July 19, 1874, St. Louis, Mo.). Lawyer, publisher, diplomat, Missouri Democrat. Chief clerk of state house of representatives (1836), member of the house (1836, 1837), St. Louis district attorney (1838), criminal court judge (1839-1842), U.S. Representative (1843-1851), minister to New Granada (1855-1858), commissioner to Paraguay (1858-1859).

BOWLING, WILLIAM BISMARCK (b Sept. 24, 1870, Calhoun County, Ala.; d Dec. 27, 1946, Lafayette, Ala.). Teacher, lawyer, jurist, Alabama Democrat. Fifth judicial circuit solicitor (1905-1920). U.S. Representative (1920-1928), fifth judicial circuit judge (1928 until death).

BOWMAN, FRANK LLEWELLYN (b Jan. 21, 1879, Masontown, Pa.; d Sept. 15, 1936, Washington, D.C.). Bank teller, coal miner, lawyer, West Virginia Republican. Morgantown postmaster (1911-1915), mayor (1916, 1917), U.S. Representative (1925-1933), member of Veterans' Administration's Board of Appeals (1935 until death).

BOX, JOHN CALVIN (b March 28, 1871, Houston County, Tex.; d May 17, 1941, Jacksonville, Tex.). Minister, lawyer, Texas Democrat. Cherokee county court judge (1898-1901), mayor of Jacksonville (1902-1905), Democratic state committee (1908-1910), chairman of board of education (1913-1918), U.S. Representative (1919-1931).

BOYCE, WILLIAM WATERS *(b Oct. 24, 1818, Charleston, S.C.; d Feb. 3, 1890, Fairfax County, Va.).* Lawyer, South Carolina Democrat. U.S. Representative (1853-1860) as a States' Rights Democrat, delegate to Confederate Provisional Congress (1861), member of Confederate Congress (1862-1864).

BOYD, ADAM *(b March 21, 1746, Mendham, N.J.: d Aug. 15, 1835, Hackensack, N.J.).* New Jersey Democrat. Member of Bergen County Board of Freeholders and Justices (1773, 1784, 1791, 1794, 1798), sheriff (1778-1781, 1789), state assembly (1782, 1783, 1787, 1794, 1795), common pleas court judge (1803-1805, 1813-1833), U.S. Representative (1803-1805, 1808-1813).

BOYD, LINN *(b Nov. 22, 1800, Nashville, Tenn.; d Dec. 17, 1859, Paducah, Ky.).* Farmer, Kentucky Democrat who in 1826 moved onto the Jackson Purchase and quickly became the settlers' main voice in both the state and national capital. State representative (1827-1832), U.S. Representative (1835-1837, 1839-1855), speaker House (1851-1855), lieutenant governor (1859 until death). As a congressman, Boyd was a steadfast supporter of Andrew Jackson, chairman of the Military Affairs Committee during the Mexican War, chairman of the Committee on Territories, and prime advocate of the 1850 Compromise.

BOYD, SEMPRONIUS HAMILTON *(b May 28, 1828, Williamson County, Tenn.; d June 22, 1894, Springfield, Mo.).* Missouri Republican with a host of venturesome interests: prospector in the 1849 California gold rush, gold camp teacher, Missouri lawyer, wagon maker, railroad builder, Union Army colonel, Emancipationist congressman and diplomat. Mayor of Springfield (1856), U.S. Representative (1863-1865, 1869-1871), fourteenth judicial district judge (1865), GOP National Committee member (1864-1868), GOP National Convention delegate (1864), minister to Siam (1890-1892).

BOYKIN, FRANK WILLIAM *(b Feb. 21, 1885, Bladon Springs, Ala.).* Farmer, livestock, timber and real estate dealer, Alabama Democrat who occupied a congressional seat for twenty-eight years (1925-1963), the last ten as dean of his home state's delegation, serving as chairman of the Merchant Marine and Fisheries Committee and a member of the Veterans' Affairs Committee.

BOYLAN, JOHN JOSEPH *(b Sept. 20, 1878, New York City; d Oct. 5, 1938, New York City).* Postal clerk, real estate operator, New York Democrat. State assembly (1909-1913), state senate (1913-1922), U.S. Representative (1923 until death).

BRACKENRIDGE, HENRY MARIE *(b May 11, 1786, Pittsburgh, Pa.; d. Jan. 18, 1871, Pittsburgh).* Lawyer, author, journalist, linguist, political liberal, and a waggish Pennsylvania Whig who at the age of seven, under parental directive, rode a flatboat from Pittsburgh to Ste. Genevieve, La., to study French.

In 1811, after a research voyage up the Missouri River to gather material for a book, he settled in the Orleans Territory (Louisiana) where he studied Spanish law, helped to found its judicial system, and was appointed first deputy attorney general and then district judge. During the War of 1812 he spied on the British for the United States, was promised a diplomatic appointment, went to Washington to accept it and, when it did not materialize, began practicing law in Baltimore and became a member of the Maryland legislature where he championed the admission of Jews to public office.

In 1817 he was named secretary of a mission sent to study the politics of South America, was judge for the western district of Florida (1821-1832), then he returned to Pennsylvania where he founded the town of Tarentum and was chosen a U.S. Representative (1840-1841) to fill a vacancy and served on the Mexican treaty commission.

His literary works include: *Views of Louisiana, History of the Late War* (of 1812), *The Voyage to South America, Speeches on the Jew Bill, Letters to the Public, History of the Western Insurrection in Western Pennsylvania,* and *Recollections of Persons and Places in the West.* Son of Hugh H. Brackenridge.

BRACKENRIDGE, HUGH HENRY *(b 1748, near Campbeltown, Scotland; d June 25, 1816, Carlisle, Pa.).* Teacher, author, minister, Revolutionary Army chaplain, patriot, lawyer, newspaper publisher and Pennsylvania Democratic-Republican. State assembly (1786-1787), founder of the *Pittsburgh Gazette* (1786), state supreme court justice (1799 until death).

This elder Brackenridge's literary works included: *The Battle of Bunker's Hill, The Death of General Montgomery, Six Political Discourses, Law Miscellanies, The Standard of Liberty,* and *Modern Chivalry.* Father of Henry M. Brackenridge.

BRADBURY, JAMES WARE *(b June 10, 1802, Parsonsfield, Maine; d Jan. 7, 1901, Augusta, Maine).* Educator and founder (1829) of New England's first normal school at Effingham, N.H., lawyer, newspaper editor, historian. Maine Democrat who nevertheless supported Lincoln, even to leading a walkout of delegates to the 1861 state convention that denounced the Civil War. Augusta prosecuting attorney (1834-1838), Polk-Dallas presidential elector (1844), U.S. Senate (1847-1853).

BRADFORD, AUGUSTUS WILLIAMSON *(b Jan. 9, 1806, Bel Air, Md.; d March 1, 1881, Baltimore, Md.).* Lawyer, Maryland Whig turned Unionist and Civil War governor (1862-1865) who strongly opposed the presence of federal troops at the polls yet recruited militiamen for the Northern cause and called the 1864 state convention at which Maryland abolished slavery.

BRADFORD, WILLIAM *(baptized March 29, 1590, Austerfield, Yorkshire, England, d May 9, 1657, Plymouth, Mass.).* Merchant, writer, and member of the Separatist Church; came to America in 1620 aboard the *Mayflower;* signer of the Mayflower Compact, which provided for democratic rule in Plymouth Colony; was reelected governor every year from 1622 through 1656, except for 1633, 1634, 1636, and 1644 when he served as deputy governor. When Plymouth, New Haven, Connecticut, and Massachusetts Bay colonies formed the United Colonies of America (1643) he four times was a delegate to the congress, twice serving as its president. He was the author of *Mourt's Relations* (with Edward Winslow), the *Letter Book,* and the *History of Plymouth Plantation.* (Not to be confused with William Bradford of New York.)

BRADFORD, WILLIAM *(b May 20, 1663, Barnwell, Leicestershire, England; d May 23, 1752, New York City).* Pioneer printer of England's middle colonies, setting up his first shop in Oxford, Pennsylvania (1685). Moved to Philadelphia and added a bookstore in 1688, bringing down upon himself the wrath of political and religious leaders for publishing material without their consent. He left Pennsylvania and, in 1693, became the crown's official printer in New York where his published documents included digests of assembly business and state laws and the first history of the colony, and founded (1725) the city's first newspaper, the

New York Gazette. Grandfather of the younger William Bradford—see next entry. (Not to be confused with William Bradford of Massachusetts.)

BRADFORD, WILLIAM *(b Jan. 19, 1721, New York City; d Sept. 25, 1791, Philadelphia, Pa.).* Grandson of the foregoing who learned his trade well, becoming known as the "patriot printer of 1776." He was a particularly vigorous foe of the Stamp Act, an early crusader for a continental congress, and then its official printer. Publications he founded included the *Weekly Advertiser* (1742-1793), *American Magazine and Monthly Chronicle* (1757-1758) and *General Repository* (1769).

BRADLEY, FREDERICK VAN NESS *(b April 12, 1898, Chicago, Ill.; d May 24, 1947, New London, Conn.).* Salesman, purchasing agent, Michigan Republican. U.S. Representative (1939 until death).

BRADLEY, STEPHEN ROW *(b Feb. 20, 1754, Wallingford, Conn.; d Dec. 9, 1830, Walpole, N.H.).* Revolutionary Army officer, one of the first two lawyers permitted to practice in Vermont, an ardent advocate of statehood there who was chosen one of a delegation that presented its case to the Continental Congress, and, when Vermont became the first state (after the original thirteen) to be admitted to the Union, became one of its first two senators, drawing a four-year term. State's attorney for Cumberland County (1780), Westminster register of probate (1782), Windham County judge (1783), state representative and speaker of the house (1785), associate judge of the Vermont Superior Court (1788-1791), Westminster City Council (1798), U.S. Senate (1791-1795, 1801-1813) and president pro tem (1802, 1803, 1808) where he sponsored legislation that made official a fifteen-star and fifteen-stripe national banner that was used (1795-1814) and known as Bradley's Flag. Father of William C. Bradley.

BRADLEY, THOMAS WILSON *(b April 6, 1844, Yorkshire, England; d May 30, 1920, Walden, N.Y.).* Banker, manufacturer, Union Army officer who was awarded the Congressional Medal of Honor "for gallantry at Chancellorsville." New York Republican. State assemblyman (1876), GOP National Convention delegate (1892, 1896, 1900), U.S. Representative (1903-1913).

BRADLEY, WILLIAM CZAR *(b March 23, 1782, Westminster, Vt.; d March 3, 1867, Westminster).* Lawyer, Vermont Democrat–Free-Soiler–Republican who supported the war policies of Madison, fought with John Quincy Adams, championed Jacksonian democracy, was a presidential elector for Fremont and Dayton (1856), and ran regularly but always unsuccessfully for governor; a man who preferred the political battle to the prize.

Windham County prosecuting attorney (1804-1811), state representative (1806, 1807, 1819, 1850), member of Governor's Council (1812), U.S. Representative (1813-1815, 1823-1827), U.S. agent who fixed the boundary between Maine and Canada (1815-1820) under the Treaty of Ghent, state constitutional convention delegate (1857). Son of Stephen R. Bradley.

BRADLEY, WILLIAM O'CONNELL *(b March 18, 1847, Lancaster, Ky.; d May 23, 1914, Washington, D.C.).* Lawyer, Union soldier at the age of fifteen, practicing lawyer at eighteen, Kentucky's first Republican governor (1895-1899). Garrard County prosecuting attorney (1870), Greeley-Brown presidential elector on the Liberal Republican ticket (1872), GOP National Convention delegate (1880, 1884, 1888, 1892, 1896, 1900, 1904), member of GOP National Committee (1890-1896), U.S. Senate (1909 until death).

BRADWELL, MYRA *(b Feb. 12, 1831, Manchester, Vt.; d Feb. 14, 1894, Chicago, Ill.).* Lawyer, editor, women's suffragist who promoted legislation favorable to women. Established (1868) the successful *Chicago Legal News*, acting as both editor and business manager. Studied law in her husband's office but was refused admission to the Illinois bar (1869), first because she was a married woman, then because she was a woman, a decision sustained by the U.S. Supreme Court. She was responsible (1882) for the passage of an Illinois act granting freedom in selecting a profession to all persons, irrespective of sex, and (1885) the state supreme court directed that she be granted a license to practice law.

BRADY, JOHN GREEN *(b May 25, 1848, New York City; d Dec. 17, 1918, Sitka, Alaska).* A young runaway who was taken in by an Indiana farm family and went on to become a teacher, lawyer, Alaska missionary, trading post manager, and founder of a movement that combined religious teachings with industrial instruction. Word of his deeds got back to Washington and he was appointed one of four U.S. commissioners to Alaska serving from 1884 until 1889. In 1897 he was named governor by President McKinley and served until 1906, a period that included the hectic Klondike gold rush days, and he did much to acquaint Americans with Alaska's tremendous natural resources.

BRAGG, EDWARD STUYVESANT *(b Feb. 20, 1827, Unadilla, N.Y.; d June 20, 1912, Fond du Lac, Wis.).* Lawyer, Union officer, diplomat, Wisconsin Democrat. Fond du Lac district attorney (1853), Democratic National Convention (1860, 1872, 1880, 1896), Fond du Lac postmaster (1866), state senate (1868, 1869), U.S. Representative (1877-1883, 1885-1887), minister to Mexico (1888-1889), consul general to Havana (1902-1903), consul general to Hong Kong (1903-1906).

BRAGG, THOMAS *(b Nov. 10, 1810, Warrenton, N.C.; d Jan. 21, 1872, Raleigh, N.C.).* Lawyer, member of Confederate cabinet, North Carolina Democrat. State house of commons (1842, 1843), presidential elector on Pierce-King ticket (1852), Democratic National Convention delegate (1844, 1848, 1852), governor (1855-1859), U.S. Senate (1859-1861) resigning and becoming attorney general of the Confederate States (1861-1863).

BRAMLETTE, THOMAS E. *(b Jan. 3, 1817, Cumberland County, Ky.; d Jan. 12, 1875, Louisville, Ky.).* Lawyer, Kentucky Whig-Union Democrat who stood firmly for preservation of the Union during the tense pre-Civil War days, supported the Northern cause during the war, even serving briefly as a federal officer, but after becoming governor (1863-1867) was one of Lincoln's most severe critics in the Blue Grass State. He welcomed back home men who had fought with the South and opposed any reprisals against them, and he strongly disapproved of the actions of Union troops stationed in Kentucky.

BRANCH, JOHN *(b Nov. 4, 1782, Halifax, N.C.; d Jan. 3, 1863, Enfield, N.C.).* Lawyer, North Carolina Democrat who held a diversity of high offices, both elective and appointive.

Commissioner of lands and dwellings evaluations and slave enumerator in third North Carolina district (1799), state senate (1811-1817, 1822, speaker 1815-1817), elected governor of North Carolina (1817-1820), appointed federal judge for western district of Florida (1822) by President Monroe, U.S. Senate (1823-1829), secretary of navy in President Jackson's cabinet (1829-1831), U.S. Representative (1831-1833), North Carolina constitutional convention delegate (1835), appointed governor of Florida (1844-1845) by President Tyler. Uncle of Lawrence O. Branch.

BRANCH, LAWRENCE O'BRYAN *(b Nov. 28, 1820, Enfield, N.C.; d Sept. 17, 1862, in Battle of Antietam, Sharpsburg,*

Md.). Newspaper editor-publisher, lawyer, railroad president, Indian fighter, Confederate general, North Carolina Democrat. Presidential elector on Pierce-King ticket (1852), U.S. Representative (1855-1861), appointed secretary of treasury by President Buchanan (1860) but declined. Nephew of John Branch, father of William A. B. Branch.

BRANCH, WILLIAM AUGUSTUS BLOUNT *(b Feb. 26, 1847, Tallahassee, Fla.; d Nov. 18, 1910, Washington, D.C.).* Lawyer, planter, Confederate soldier, North Carolina Democrat. U.S. Representative (1891-1895), state representative (1896). Son of Lawrence O. Branch.

BRAND, CHARLES HILLYER *(b April 20, 1861, Loganville, Ga.; d May 17, 1933, Athens, Ga.).* Banker, lawyer, Georgia Democrat. State senate (1894-1895) acting as president pro tempore, solicitor general for Georgia's western judicial circuit (1896-1904), superior court judge (1906-1917), U.S. Representative (1917 until death).

BRANDEGEE, AUGUSTUS *(b July 15, 1828, New London, Conn.; d Nov. 10, 1904, New London).* Lawyer, Connecticut Republican. State representative (1854, 1858, 1859, 1861), speaker (1861), presidential elector on Lincoln-Hamlin ticket (1860), U.S. Representative (1863-1867), GOP National Convention delegate (1864, 1880, 1884), Loyalist Convention (1866), New London corporation counsel (1897-1898). Father of Frank B. Brandegee.

BRANDEGEE, FRANK BOSWORTH *(b July 8, 1864, New London, Conn.; d Oct. 14, 1924, Washington, D.C.).* Lawyer, Connecticut Republican whose obstructionism was rivaled only by his conservatism. State representative (1888 and 1889, the latter term serving as speaker), New London corporation counsel (every year from 1889 until 1902, except for the two years that his

father held the post), GOP National Convention delegate (1888, 1892, 1900, 1904), chairman of state convention (1904), U.S. Representative (1902-1905), U.S. Senate (1905 until death), serving on the Judiciary, Foreign Relations, Patents and Library committees. Among the issues he sought to block: the League of Nations, the Child Labor Act, woman's suffrage, direct election of senators, the Federal Reserve system, prohibition, and income taxes. In his obituary, the *New York Times* spoke of his "consistent wrong-headedness." Son of Augustus Brandegee.

BRANDON, GERARD CHITTOCQUE *(b Sept. 15, 1788, near Natchez, Miss.; d March 28, 1850, near Natchez).* Lawyer, planter, Democrat, and the first native son ever to be elected governor of Mississippi (1825-1832). After that he refused to hold public office, but he had been a state representative and speaker, lieutenant governor, and a delegate to the 1817 and 1832 constitutional conventions—the only man who had attended both—and at the latter he fought against the bringing of more slaves into the state.

BRANNAN, SAMUEL *(b March 2, 1819, Saco, Maine; d May 5, 1889, Escondido, Calif.).* Printer, newspaper publisher, miller, real estate speculator, merchant. Mormon elder who headed a party of 238 travelers from New York to San Francisco (1846) by sea to become the first settlers to arrive in California after the U.S. seized it from Mexico. He founded San Francisco's first newspaper, the *California Star*, in 1847, was a member of its first city council, the first president of the Committee of Vigilance, which was organized in his office in 1851, and a founder of the Society of California Pioneers.

BRANTLEY, WILLIAM GORDON *(b Sept. 18, 1860, Blackshear, Ga.; d Sept. 11, 1934, Washington, D.C.).* Lawyer, Georgia Democrat. State representative

(1884, 1885), state senate (1886, 1887), Brunswick circuit court solicitor general (1888-1896), U.S. Representative (1897-1913), national convention (1912).

BRAXTON, CARTER *(b Sept. 16, 1736, near King and Queen Court House, Va.; d Oct. 10, 1797, Richmond, Va.).* Planter, patriot-statesman and signer of the Declaration of Independence. Virginia House of Burgesses (1761-1771, 1775), Continental Congress (1775-1776, 1777-1783, 1785), Virginia Council of State (1786-1791).

BRAYTON, CHARLES RAY *(b Aug. 16, 1840, Apponaug, R.I.; d Sept. 23, 1910, Providence, R.I.).* Lawyer, Union Army officer, and, after the Civil War, for about thirty years Rhode Island's Republican boss. Posts he held at various times included membership on the GOP National Committee, Providence postmaster and state police chief; as a lawyer he was on retainer by railroads and other large industrial interests, openly bought votes. The sheriff's office in Providence served as his headquarters.

BRECKINRIDGE, CLIFTON RODES *(b Nov. 22, 1846, near Lexington, Ky.; d Dec. 3, 1932, Wendover, Ky.).* Planter, cotton merchant, banker, Confederate Navy, Arkansas Democrat. U.S. Representative (1883-1894), minister to Russia (1894-1897), member of Dawes Commission for distribution of Indian lands (1900-1905), state constitutional convention (1917). Son of John C. Breckinridge.

BRECKINRIDGE, JAMES *(b March 7, 1763, Botetourt County, Va.; d May 13, 1833, Botetourt County).* Revolutionary soldier, lawyer, Virginia Federalist who associated with Jefferson in founding of the University of Virginia. State house of delegates (1789-1802, 1806-1808, 1820, 1821, 1823, 1824), U.S. Representative (1809-1817). Brother of John Breckinridge.

BRECKINRIDGE, JOHN *(b Dec. 2, 1760, Augusta County, Va.; d Dec. 14, 1806, near Lexington, Ky.).* Revolutionary soldier, lawyer, Kentucky Democrat. State attorney general (1795-1797), state representative (1798-1800), speaker (1799, 1800), U.S. Senate (1801-1805) resigning to become U.S. attorney general in Jefferson cabinet (1805 until death). Brother of James Breckinridge, grandfather of John C. and William C. P. Breckinridge.

BRECKINRIDGE, JOHN CABELL *(b Jan. 21, 1821, near Lexington, Ky.; d May 17, 1875, Lexington).* Lawyer, railroad executive, Confederate general, vice president of the United States, member of Confederate cabinet and the Southern Democratic candidate for president against Lincoln (Republican) and Douglas (Democratic) in 1860, receiving 848,356 popular and 72 electoral votes, Kentucky Democrat.

State representative (1849), U.S. Representative (1851-1855); vice president under President James Buchanan (1857-1861) when, although firmly dedicated to the Southern cause, he presided over the U.S. Senate with impartiality; U.S. Senate briefly in 1861, being expelled for joining the Confederate Army; secretary of war in Jefferson Davis cabinet (1861). Grandson of John Breckinridge, father of Clifton R. Breckinridge.

BRECKINRIDGE, WILLIAM CAMPBELL PRESTON *(b Aug. 28, 1837, Baltimore; Md.; d Nov. 18, 1904, Lexington, Ky.).* Lawyer, newspaper editor, college professor, Confederate officer assigned to guard Jefferson Davis and his cabinet, Kentucky Democrat. Fayette County attorney (1866), Democratic National Convention delegate (1876, 1888), U.S. Representative (1885-1895). Grandson of John Breckinridge.

BREEDING, JAMES FLOYD *(b Sept. 28, 1901, Brown County, Kans.).* Farmer-stockman, Kansas Democrat who served on the House Agriculture Committee. State representative (1947-1949, minority leader in latter year), Democratic nominee for lieutenant governor (1950), national convention delegate (1960), U.S. Representative (1957-1963).

BREESE, SIDNEY *(b July 15, 1800, Whitesboro, N.Y.; d June 28, 1878, Pinkneyville, Ill.).* Lawyer, muckraker newspaper editor, jurist, Illinois Democrat, foe of Stephen A. Douglas, officer in the Black Hawk War. Kaskaskia, Ill., postmaster (1821), third judicial circuit prosecuting attorney (1822-1826), U.S. district attorney for the state (1827-1829), second district circuit judge (1835-1841), state supreme court judge (1841, 1842), U.S. Senate (1843-1849) where he was chairman of the Public Lands Committee, state representative (1851 when he was speaker, and 1852), Illinois circuit court judge (1855-1857) and then once more on the supreme court bench (1857 until death) serving as chief justice (1867-1870, 1873, 1874). Always a staunch advocate of state ownership of public lands, he believed in the slogan "54-40 or fight," favored war with Mexico and annexation of Texas, but plugged for the turning over of state-held Illinois lead mines to private entrepreneurs.

BRENT, MARGARET *(b 1600, in England; d ca. 1670).* Early American feminist; held extensive estates in Virginia and Maryland, being the first woman in the latter colony to hold land in her own right; appointed by Governor Leonard Calvert executrix of his estates, possibly in recognition of the ability she displayed in helping him suppress a rebellion; appointed attorney for Lord Baltimore by the Provincial Court but turned down by Governor Greene of Maryland when she appealed (1648) for a place in the colonial assembly. Angered by this action, she left her home in Maryland (1650) and moved to Virginia.

BRENT, RICHARD *(b 1757, Stafford County, Va.; d Dec. 30, 1814, Washington, D.C.).* Virginia lawyer. State house of delegates (1788, 1793, 1794, 1800, 1801), U.S. Representative (1795-1799, 1801-1803), state senate (1808-1810), U.S. Senate (1809 until death).

BRENTS, THOMAS HURLEY *(b Dec. 24, 1840, Pike County, Ill.; d Oct. 23, 1916, Walla Walla, Wash.).* Northwest settler, merchant, lawyer, Republican. In Oregon: Canyon City postmaster (1863, 1864), Grand County clerk (1864-1866), Union-Republican convention (1866), state representative (1866), then studied law, began practice a year later in San Francisco, Calif., and three years later (1870) moved to Territory of Washington. In Washington: Walla Walla city attorney (1871, 1872), chairman of Republican territorial convention (1874), U.S. Representative (1879-1885), Walla Walla Superior Court judge (1896-1913).

BREWER, MARK SPENCER *(b Oct. 22, 1837, Addison Township, Mich.; d March 18, 1901, Washington, D.C.).* Lawyer, Michigan Republican, and a friend of two presidents, both of whom rewarded him for his political astuteness. Pontiac city attorney (1866, 1867), Oakland County circuit court commissioner (1866-1869), state senate (1872-1874), U.S. Representative (1877-1881, 1887-1891), appointed consul general to Berlin by President Garfield (1881-1885), GOP National Convention delegate (1896), appointed a U.S. Civil Service commissioner by President McKinley (1898 until death).

BREWSTER, WILLIAM *(b Jan. 1567, England; d April 10, 1644, Plymouth, Mass.).* Separatist, Puritan printer, church elder, member of the Mayflower party (1620), Plymouth Colony's only church officer until 1629, number two man to William Bradford in affairs of government.

BRICK, ABRAHAM LINCOLN (b May 27, 1860, St. Joseph County, Ind.; d April 7, 1908, Indianapolis, Ind.). Lawyer, Indiana Republican. St. Joseph and La Porte counties' prosecuting attorney (1886), GOP National Convention delegate (1896), U.S. Representative (1899 until death).

BRIDGES, HENRY STYLES (b Sept. 9, 1898, West Pembroke, Maine; d Nov. 26, 1961, Concord, N.H.). Teacher, magazine editor, banker, publisher, New Hampshire Republican who, at the time of death, was the senior Republican member of the U.S. Senate and had repeatedly demonstrated the reasons why he was called both the Gray Eminence of the Republican party and an "authentic American Tory."

His early political career was meteoric: at the age of twenty-six he was secretary of the New Hampshire Farm Bureau Federation (1922-1933), at thirty-two he was a member of the New Hampshire Public Service Commission (1930-1934), at thirty-six he was governor (1934-1936), at thirty-eight he was a U.S. Senator (1937 until death). In the intervening twenty-four years he was GOP floor leader (1952), president pro tem (1953-1955), chairman of the Senate Appropriations Committee and the Joint Congressional Committee on Foreign Economics Cooperation, and member of the Armed Services, Foreign Relations, and Military Affairs committees, besides being chairman of the GOP Policy Committee.

His tenure was one of consistent opposition to the New Deal and in some ways he was even consistent in his inconsistencies. He oposed Lend Lease, yet favored aid for victims of Nazi aggression; he was a foe of labor, even to dropping his first name so as not to be confused with leftist labor leader Harry Bridges; vigorously opposed union abuses, yet accepted $35,000 a year for serving as a neutral trustee of the United Mine Workers pension fund; he stood for clean government, yet was linked with such shadowy figures as Henry W. Grunewald and Bernard Goldfine; he was a candidate for the GOP presidential nomination in 1940, but worked vigorously for Wendell Willkie after his candidacy was unsuccessful.

BRIDGES, SAMUEL AUGUSTUS (b Jan. 27, 1802, Colchester, Conn.; d Jan. 14, 1884, Allentown, Pa.). Lawyer, Pennsylvania Democrat. Allentown town clerk (1837-1842), deputy state attorney general for Lehigh County (1837-1844), Democratic state convention delegate (1841), U.S. Representative (1848-1849, 1853-1855, 1877-1879).

BRIGGS, CLAY STONE (b Jan. 8, 1876, Galveston, Texas; d April 29, 1933, Washington, D.C.). Lawyer, Texas Democrat. State representative (1906-1908), tenth judicial district judge (1909-1919), U.S. Representative (1919 until death).

BRIGGS, FRANK OBADIAH (b Aug. 12, 1851, Concord, N.H.; d May 8, 1913, Trenton, N.J.). West Point graduate (1872, remaining in army until 1877), manufacturer, New Jersey Republican. Trenton school board (1884-1892), mayor (1899-1902), state board of education (1901, 1902), state treasurer (1902-1907), chairman of GOP state committee (1904-1911), U.S. Senate (1907-1913), GOP National Convention delegate (1908).

BRIGGS, GEORGE NIXON (b April 12, 1796, Adams, Mass.; d Sept. 11, 1861, Pittsfield, Mass.). Lawyer, Massachusetts Whig. Berkshire County register of deeds (1824-1831), Lanesboro town clerk (1824-1826), chairman of state highway commission (1826), U.S. Representative (1831-1843), governor of Massachusetts (1844-1851), state constitutional convention delegate (1853), common pleas court judge (1853-1858), member of New Granada Commission (1861) dying of an accidental gunshot wound on the day of his appointment.

BRIGHT, JESSE DAVID *(b Dec. 18, 1812, Norwich, N.Y.; d May 20, 1875, Baltimore, Md.).* Lawyer, coal company executive, leader of the proslavery wing in Indiana's Democratic party who was expelled from the U.S. Senate for writ- a letter addressed "To His Excellency, Jefferson Davis, President of the Con- federate States." Jefferson County pro- bate court judge (1834-1839), U.S. mar- shall for Indiana district (1840-1841), state senate (1841-1843), lieutenant gov- ernor (1843-1845), U.S. Senate (1845- 1862) and president pro tem three times, state representative (1866). His expulsion was voted (32-14), on Feb. 5, 1862, after twenty days of debate, on the charge of treason.

BRIGHT, JOHN MORGAN *(b Jan. 20, 1817, Fayetteville, Tenn.; d Oct. 3, 1911, Fayetteville).* Lawyer, Tennessee Demo- crat. State representative (1847, 1848), U.S. Representative (1871-1881).

BRINKERHOFF, JACOB *(b Aug. 31, 1810, Niles, N.Y.; d July 19, 1880, Mans- field, Ohio).* Lawyer, Ohio Democrat turned Free-Soiler turned Republican who throughout his political and judicial life was in the forefront of the fight against slavery anywhere in the United States and its territories, and the man reputed (rightly or wrongly) to have written the Wilmot Proviso. Richland County prosecuting attorney (1839- 1843), U.S. Representative (1843-1847), state supreme court justice (1856-1871).

BRISTOW, BENJAMIN HELM *(b June 20, 1832, Elkton, Ky.; d June 22, 1896, New York City).* Lawyer, Union Army officer, Kentucky Unionist Republican and prime mover for ratification of the Thirteenth (anti-slavery) Amendment, U.S. secretary of the treasury (1874- 1876) who broke up the nationwide tax-dodging Whiskey Ring, recipient of 126 fourth-ballot votes for the GOP presidential nomination (1876). State senate (1863-1865); U.S. attorney for Kentucky (1866-1870) fighting the Ku Klux Klan to a standstill and obtaining twenty-nine convictions, including one for murder, against its members; U.S. solicitor general (1870-1872), the Ameri- can Bar Association's second president (1879).

BRISTOW, JOSEPH LITTLE *(b July 22, 1861, Hazelgreen, Ky.; d July 14, 1944, near Fairfax, Va.).* Gentleman farmer, Kansas newspaper editor-publisher, a Republican leader in that state. Douglas County district court clerk (1886-1890), GOP state committee secretary (1894, 1898), Governor E. N. Morrill's private secretary (1895-1897), fourth assistant U.S. postmaster general (1897-1905), U.S. Senate (1909-1915), chairman of Kansas Utilities Commission (1915- 1918).

BRITTEN, FREDERICK ALBERT *(b Nov. 18, 1871, Chicago, Ill.; d May 4, 1946, Bethesda, Md.).* Construction contrac- tor, Illinois Republican. Chicago City Council (1908-1912), chairman of city civil service commission (1909), U.S. Representative (1913-1935), executive committee member of the Interparlia- mentary Union (1923-1934), member of GOP National Congressional Committee (1926), national convention delegate (1936).

BRODERICK, CASE *(b Sept. 23, 1839, Grant County, Ind.; d April 1, 1920, Holton, Kans.).* Farmer, lawyer, Kansas Republican. Mayor of Holton (1874, 1875), Jackson County prosecuting at- torney (1876-1880), state senate (1880- 1884), presidentially appointed associate justice of Idaho Territory Supreme Court (1884-1888), U.S. Representative from Kansas (1891-1899), presidential elector on Taft-Sherman ticket (1908).

BRODERICK, DAVID COLBRETH *(b Feb. 4, 1820, Washington, D.C.; d Sept. 16, 1859, San Francisco, Calif.).* New York saloon keeper and Tammany Hall ward leader who migrated to California in 1849, manufactured $4 and $8 gold pieces and sold them for $5 and $10, speculated in real estate, and was up to his neck in politics almost from the moment he got off the boat.

In New York City he presided over the charter convention (1846) and unsuccessfully ran for Congress. In California he was a delegate to the constitutional convention (1849), a state senator (1850, 1851), senate president (1851); in 1857 he was elected a U.S. Senator as part of a deal whereby he would trade off his seat to the then-incumbent, William M. Gwin, in exchange for federal patronage. President Buchanan wouldn't go along, however, and so he served until losing his life in a gun duel with Chief Justice David S. Terry of the California Supreme Court. The duel was over the slavery issue, which Terry favored, and Broderick opposed.

BRODHEAD, RICHARD *(b Jan. 5, 1811, Lehman Township, Pa.; d Sept. 16, 1863, Easton, Pa.).* Lawyer, Pennsylvania Democrat. State representative (1837-1839), Northampton County treasurer (1841), U.S. Representative (1843-1849), U.S. Senate (1851-1857).

BROMWELL, JACOB HENRY *(b May 11, 1848, Cincinnati, Ohio; d June 4, 1924, Wyoming, Ohio).* Teacher, lawyer, Ohio Republican. Wyoming mayor (1880-1886), Hamilton County assistant solicitor (1888-1892), U.S. Representative (1894-1903), common pleas court judge (1907-1913).

BROOKS, JAMES *(b Nov. 10, 1810, Portland, Maine; d April 30, 1873, Washington, D.C.).* Teacher, newspaper editor and Washington correspondent, founder of the *New York Daily Express* and its editor-in-chief (1836 until death), Maine and New York Whig-Democrat. In Maine: State representative (1835).

In New York: state assembly (1847), U.S. Representative (1849-1853, 1863-1866, 1867 until death).

BROOKS, OVERTON *(b Dec. 21, 1897, East Baton Rouge Parish, La.; d Sept. 16, 1961, Bethesda, Md.).* Lawyer, Louisiana Democrat. U.S. Representative (1937 until death).

BROOKS, PRESTON SMITH *(b Aug. 5, 1819, Edgefield, S.C.; d Jan. 27, 1857, Washington, D.C.).* Lawyer, South Carolina States' Rights Democrat who attacked and severely injured Congressman Charles Sumner of Massachusetts after the latter's "The Crime Against Kansas" speech (May 20, 1856). Brooks survived expulsion charges from the House through lack of the necessary two-thirds votes but nevertheless resigned (July 15, 1856) only to seek reelection to his own vacated position, win, he reseated (Aug. 1, 1856) and remain a U.S. Representative until death six months later. He had first become a Congressman on March 4, 1853. His only prior office was as a state representative (1844).

BROSIUS, MARRIOTT *(b March 7, 1843, Colerain Township, Pa.; d March 16, 1901, Lancaster, Pa.).* Lawyer, Pennsylvania Republican. U.S. Representative (1889 until death).

BROUGH, CHARLES HILLMAN *(b July 9, 1876, Clinton, Miss.; d Dec. 26, 1935, Washington, D.C.).* College teacher, lecturer, Arkansas Democrat during whose administration as governor (1916-1920) much legislation beneficial to women was enacted; for example, the right to vote in primaries even before the Nineteenth (suffrage) Amendment was adopted. Other progressive legislation enacted during his tenure provided for mothers' pensions, workers' health benefits, educational aid, and women's right to hold office. So popular was Brough that he was reelected (1918) without Republican opposition.

BROUGHTON, JOSEPH MELVILLE *(b Nov. 17, 1888, Raleigh, N.C.; d March 6, 1949, Washington, D.C.).* Teacher, newspaperman, farmer, North Carolina Democrat. State senate (1927-1929), governor (1941-1945); U.S. Senate to fill vacancy caused by death of Josiah W. Bailey, but he in turn died after serving only two months in 1949.

BROUSSARD, EDWIN SIDNEY *(b Dec. 4, 1874, Iberia Parish, La.; d Nov. 19, 1934, New Iberia).* Lawyer, Louisiana Democrat, and Spanish-American War officer who participated in Cuban campaign (1898-1899), and assistant secretary of the Taft Commission to the Philippine Islands (1899-1900). Prosecuting attorney for nineteenth judicial district (1903-1908); U.S. Senate (1921-1933), filling a seat formerly held by his brother, Robert F. Broussard.

BROUSSARD, ROBERT FOLIGNY *(b Aug. 17, 1864, Iberia Parish, La.; d April 12, 1918, New Iberia).* Lawyer, Louisiana Democrat, and brother of Edwin S. Broussard who showed him the way to Washington. Prosecuting attorney for nineteenth judicial district (1892-1897), U.S. Representative (1897-1915), U.S. Senate (1915 until death).

BROWDER, EARL RUSSELL *(b May 20, 1891, Wichita, Kanas; d June 27, 1973, Princeton, N.J.).* Self-educated descendant of a colonial American family, accountant, credit manager, U.S. agent for Soviet publications, writer, and a New York-based pacifist who joined the Socialist party in 1907 while still in Kansas, left in 1912 to become active in the Syndicalist League of America, was imprisoned (1917) for refusing to register for the draft, while in jail studied communism, joined the American Communist Party upon his release (1920), rose to become its na-

tional leader (1930-1945) and twice (1936, 1940) was its candidate for president of the United States, polling 80,159 votes the first time and 46,251 the second. He was again imprisoned (Feb. 1940-May 1942), this time for passport irregularity and, after release, became a vigorous supporter of the nation's position in World War II. He was removed as party leader for "swerving dangerously" from the Marxist-Leninist line and in 1946 was expelled from the party because of his criticism of its new leader. Author of *War or Peace with Russia* (1947).

BROWN, AARON VENABLE *(b Aug. 15, 1795, Brunswick County, Va.; d March 8, 1859, Washington, D.C.).* Tennessee Democrat who was the law partner of President Polk and served in the cabinet of President Buchanan. State senate (1821-1825), state representative (1831-1833), U.S. Representative (1839-1845), governor (1845-1847), Democratic National Convention delegate (1852), postmaster general (1857 until death).

BROWN, ALBERT GALLATIN *(b May 31, 1813, Chester District, S.C.; d June 12, 1880, Hinds County, Miss.).* Lawyer, planter, Confederate Army officer, Mississippi Democrat. State representative (1835-1839), U.S. Representative (1839-1841, 1847-1853), circuit superior court judge (1842, 1843), governor (1844-1848), U.S. Senate (1854-1861), Confederate senator (1862-1865). A friend said of him: "In politics, he had strategy without corruption"; in the forefront of most Congressional debates during his tenure in three separate chambers, seriously mentioned for the U.S. presidency in 1850.

BROWN, BEDFORD *(b June 6, 1795, Caswell County, N.C.; d Dec. 6, 1870, Caswell County).* Planter, North Carolina Democrat who opposed both abolition and secession and, consequently, a man who had his numerous ups and downs in politics. State house of commons (1815-1817, 1823), state senate (1828, 1829, 1842, 1858, 1860, 1868), U.S. Senate (1829-1840), Reconstruction Convention delegate (1865), Democratic National Convention delegate (1868).

BROWN, BENJAMIN GRATZ *(b May 28, 1826, Lexington, Ky.; d Dec. 13, 1885, Kirkwood, Mo.).* Lawyer, newspaper founder-editor who fought a duel in defense of his editorials, Union Army officer, Horace Greeley's running mate in 1872 presidential election, Missouri Liberal Republican turned Democrat who advocated voting rights for women in the District of Columbia as early as 1866, a man whose antislavery speech while a member of the state legislature is credited with giving birth to the Free-Soil movement.

State representative (1852-1858), a founder of the *Missouri Democrat* (1854), U.S. Senate (1863-1867), governor on the Liberal ticket (1871-1873). In the Senate he was a member of the Military Affairs and Indian Affairs committees, among others, and an advocate of such reforms as an eight-hour day for government workers, government operation of telegraph lines, a civil service merit system, and a prime mover in an attempt (1864) to prevent Lincoln's renomination. On voting rights, he had this to say: "I stand for universal suffrage, and as a matter of fundamental principle do not recognize the right of society to limit it on any ground of race, color, or sex." Grandson of John Brown of Virginia and Kentucky.

BROWN, ETHAN ALLEN *(b July 4, 1776, Darien, Conn.; d Feb. 24, 1852, Indianapolis, Ind., while attending a Democratic state convention).* Lawyer, diplomat, who made his mark both in Ohio and Indiana. His main political interest was roads and canals, which he described as "veins and arteries to the body politic that diffuse supplies, health, vigor, and animation to the whole system." In Ohio he was associate judge of the state supreme court (1810-1818), governor (1818-1822), U.S. Senator to fill an unexpired term (1822-1825) where he was chairman of the Committee on Roads and Canals, Ohio Canal commissioner (1825-1830), minister to Brazil (1830-1834), General Land Office commissioner in Washington (1835-1836). Then, that assignment done, he moved on to land in Rising Sun, Ind., that he had purchased a quarter-century earlier and became a member of the state house of representatives (1842) and a leader in Democratic affairs.

BROWN, FRED HERBERT *(b April 12, 1879, Ossippee, N.H.; d Feb. 3, 1955, Somersworth, N.H.).* Lawyer, New Hampshire's second Democratic governor (1923-1925) in the twentieth century. Somersworth city solicitor (1910-1914), state constitutional convention delegate (1912), presidential elector on the Wilson-Marshall ticket (1912), Somersworth mayor (1914-1922), U.S. attorney for New Hampshire (1914-1922), member state Public Service Commission (1925-1933), U.S. Senate (1933-1939), U.S. comptroller general (1939-1940), U.S. tariff commissioner (1940-1941).

BROWN, GEORGE WILLIAM *(b Oct. 13, 1812, Baltimore, Md.; d Sept. 5, 1890, Baltimore).* Lawyer, political independent who, as mayor of Baltimore (1859-1861) broke the mob rule that the Know-Nothing party held over the city. Though a foe of slavery and a believer in the Union, as the mayor of the largest city in a border state, he burned bridges to block a Northern force from marching through Baltimore. For this he was arrested and held in prison for fifteen months. Judge of Baltimore Supreme Bench (1872-1888).

BROWN, JAMES (b Sept. 11, 1766, near Staunton, Va.; d April 7, 1835, Philadelphia, Pa.). Lawyer, Indian fighter, diplomat, prominent both in Tennessee and Louisiana Territory. In Tennessee: secretary of state (1792). In Louisiana: territorial secretary and district attorney (1804), delegate to first constitutional convention (1812), U.S. Senate (1813-1817, 1819-1823), minister to France (1823-1829). Brother of John Brown of Virginia and Kentucky.

BROWN, JASON BREVOORT (b Feb. 26, 1839, Dillsboro, Ind.; d March 10, 1898, Seymour, Ind.). Lawyer, Indiana Democrat who served as secretary of Wyoming Territory (1873-1875). Indiana state representative (1862-1866), presidential elector for Seymour and Blair (1868), state senate (1870, 1880-1883), U.S. Representative (1889-1895).

BROWN, JOHN (b Sept. 12, 1757, Staunton, Va.; d Aug. 29, 1837, Frankfort, Ky.). Teacher, lawyer, Revolutionary soldier, Virginia officeholder who became Kentucky's first U.S. Senator and one of the western frontier's chief boosters. Member of Virginia Senate representing Kentucky district (1784-1788), Kentucky district delegate to Continental Congress (1787, 1788), U.S. Representative in First and Second Congresses (1789-1792); returned to Washington but as a member of the Senate when Kentucky became a state and served from 1792 until 1805; Senate president pro tem (1803-1805). Brother of James Brown and grandfather of Benjamin Gratz Brown. (Not to be confused with John Brown of Harper's Ferry fame—see next entry.)

BROWN, JOHN (b May 9, 1800, Torrington, Conn.; d Dec. 2, 1859, by hanging for treason, in Charleston, W.Va.). Tanner, wool dealer, abolitionist whose fanatical crusade ended when he led the guerrilla raid on the Harper's Ferry federal arsenal (Oct. 16, 1859) to seize weapons with which to arm escaped slaves.

In 1851 in Springfield, Mass., he formed militant Negroes into an armed band, called the U.S. League of Gileadites, to assist runaway slaves; in 1854 he moved his guerrilla operations to Kansas where two years later (May 24, 1856) he led a raid on proslavers on Pottawatomie Creek and killed five of them. In the Harper's Ferry operation, he led an eighteen-man force that included two of his five sons and five Negroes and occupied the arsenal for two days, waiting in vain for local Negroes to come to their aid. Colonel Robert E. Lee and a party of sailors and marines ended the occupation, killing his two sons and wounding Brown. A week later he was on trial for treason. (Not to be confused with John Brown of Virginia and Kentucky—see previous entry.)

BROWN, JOHN YOUNG (b June 28, 1835, Claysville, Ky.; d Jan. 11, 1904, Henderson, Ky.). Lawyer, Kentucky Democrat and Union supporter. In 1859, he was elected a U.S. Representative but, because of his age, could not be seated until 1860; in 1867-1869, he was banned because of alleged disloyalty arising from his criticism of the military conduct of federal troops occupying the South. The voters, however, returned him to the Senate (1873-1877). Retired to the private practice of law, but only until 1891 when he served as governor from 1891 to 1895.

BROWN, JOSEPH EMERSON (b April 15, 1821, Pickens District, S.C.; d Nov. 30, 1894, Atlanta, Ga.). Lawyer, railroad president, a Georgia Democrat turned Republican turned Democrat whom political bosses thought weak and controllable but who, as governor (1856-1865) frustrated them through use of the veto and his popularity with the voters. State senate (1849), Democratic presidential elector (1852), Blue Ridge circuit superior court judge (1855), chief justice of the state supreme court (1868-1870), U.S. Senate (1880-1891). His flirtation with the GOP came during Reconstruction.

BROWN, MILTON *(b Feb. 28, 1804, Lebanon, Ohio; d May 15, 1883, Jackson, Tenn.).* Lawyer, railroad president, Tennessee Whig. Chancery court judge (1835-1840), U.S. Representative (1841-1847).

BROWN, NORRIS *(b May 2, 1863, Maquoketa, Iowa; d Jan. 5, 1960, Seattle, Wash.).* Lawyer, Nebraska Republican. Buffalo County prosecuting attorney (1892-1896), state deputy attorney general (1900-1904), moving up to attorney general (1904-1906), U.S. Senate (1907-1913), GOP National Convention (1908).

BROWN, OLYMPIA *(b Jan. 5, 1835, Prairie Ronde, Mich.; d Oct. 23, 1926, Baltimore, Md.).* Ordained Universalist minister (1863), became active in the suffragist movement after meeting Susan B. Anthony (1866); elected president of the Wisconsin Woman's Suffrage Association (1887), serving for thirty years; lectured and campaigned extensively for suffrage. Married printer-newspaperman John Henry Willis (1873) but retained her maiden name.

BROWN, PAUL *(b March 31, 1880, Hartwell, Ga.; d Sept. 24, 1961, Elberton, Ga.).* Farmer, lawyer, Georgia Democrat who served more than a quarter century as a U.S. Representative (1933-1961). Before that he was state representative (1907, 1908), mayor of Lexington (1908-1914), Elbert County attorney (1928-1933), Democratic National Convention delegate (1932).

BROWN, ROBERT *(b Dec. 25, 1744, Weaversville, Pa.; d Feb. 26, 1823, Weaversville).* Blacksmith, farmer, Revolutionary soldier who was captured and held prisoner in New York's City Hall, Pennsylvania Democrat. State senate (1783-1787), U.S. Representative (1798-1815).

BROWN, WEBSTER EVERETT *(b July 16, 1851, Madison County, N.Y.; d Dec. 14, 1929, Chicago, Ill.).* Head of logging and paper-making enterprises, Wisconsin Republican. Mayor of Rhinelander (1894, 1895), U.S. Representative (1901-1907).

BROWN, WILLIAM GAY, SR. *(b Sept. 25, 1800, Kingwood, Va.; d April 19, 1884, Kingwood, W.Va.).* Lawyer, Virginia and West Virginia Democrat-Unionist whose home-town was in the former when he was born, in the latter when he died. In Virginia: state house of delegates (1832, 1840-1843), U.S. Representative (1845-1849, 1861-1863), state constitutional convention (1850, 1861), Democratic National Convention delegate (1860). When Virginia was partitioned (1863) and West Virginia became a state, he was returned to Congress once again and served until 1865.

BROWN, WILLIAM GAY, JR. *(b April 7, 1856, Kingwood, Va. [now W.Va.]; d March 9, 1916, Washington, D.C.).* Lawyer, banker, West Virginia Democrat. Presidential elector on Bryan-Kern ticket (1908), U.S. Representative (1911 until death).

BROWN, WILLIAM JOHN *(b Aug. 15, 1805, Mason County, Ky.; d March 18, 1857, near Indianapolis, Ind.).* Lawyer, editor, Indiana Democrat. State representative (1829-1832, 1841-1843), prosecuting attorney (1831-1835), Indiana secretary of state (1836-1840), U.S. Representative (1843-1845, 1849-1851), second assistant postmaster general (1845-1849), special postal agent for Indiana and Illinois (1853 until death).

BROWN, WILLIAM WALLACE *(b April 22, 1836, Summer Hill, N.Y.; d Nov. 4, 1926, Gradford, Pa.).* Lawyer, Pennsylvania Republican. State representative (1872-1876), U.S. Representative (1883-1887), Bradford city solicitor (1892-1897), Bradford city solicitor (1892-1897), War Department auditor (1897-1899), Navy Department auditor (1899-1907), assistant U.S. attorney general (1907-1910).

BROWN, WILLIAM WELLS *(b about 1816, Lexington, Ky.; d Nov. 6, 1884, Chelsea, Mass.).* An escaped slave who took the name of the Quaker who befriended him, became a self-educated physician, historian, author and spokesman for abolition, women's suffrage, temperance, and prison reform; considered the outstanding authority of his time on the Negro. Lecturer for the Western New York Anti-Slavery Society (1843-1849), American Peace Society delegate to Paris Peace Congress (1849). His written works included *The Black Man, His Antecedents, His Genius and His Achievements* (1863) and *The Negro in the American Rebellion, His Heroism and His Fidelity* (1867).

BROWNE, EDWARD EVERTS *(b Feb. 16, 1868, Waupaca, Wis.; d Nov. 23, 1945, Evanston, Ill.).* Lawyer, Wisconsin Republican. Waupaca County district attorney (1898-1905), GOP state convention delegate (1902, 1904, 1906), state senate (1907-1912), U.S. Representative (1913-1931), member of state conservation commission (1936-1941).

BROWNE, THOMAS McLELLAND *(b April 19, 1829, New Paris, Ohio; d July 17, 1891, Winchester, Ind.).* Lawyer, Union Army officer, Indiana Republican. Prosecuting attorney for thirteenth judicial circuit (1855-1860), secretary of the state senate (1861), state senate (1863), U.S. attorney for Indiana (1869-1872), unsuccessful candidate for governor (1872), GOP National Convention delegate (1876), U.S. Representative (1877-1891).

BROWNING, ORVILLE HICKMAN *(b Feb. 10, 1806, Cynthiana, Ky.; d Aug. 10, 1881, Quincy, Ill.).* Lawyer, Illinois Whig who was in on the founding of the Republican party. State senate (1836-1843), delegate to anti-Nebraska convention (1856) that laid foundation for the GOP, GOP National Convention delegate (1860), appointed U.S. Senator (1861-1863) to fill vacancy caused by death of Stephen A. Douglas, member of Union executive committee (1866), secretary of interior in cabinet of President Andrew Johnson (1866-1869), opposing his impeachment.

BROWNING, WILLIAM JOHN *(b April 11, 1850, Camden, N.J.; d March 24, 1920, Washington, D.C.).* Dry goods wholesaler, New Jersey Republican. Camden postmaster (1889-1894), chief clerk of the U.S. House of Representatives (1895-1911), U.S. Representative (1911 until death).

BROWNLOW, WALTER PRESTON *(b March 27, 1851, Abingdon, Va.; d July 8, 1910, Johnson City, Tenn.).* Locomotive engineer, newspaper editor-publisher, Tennessee Republican. GOP National Convention delegate (1880, 1884, 1896, 1900, 1904), Jonesboro postmaster (1881), doorkeeper of the U.S. House of Representatives (1881-1883), GOP National Committeeman (1884, 1896, 1900), U.S. Representative (1897 until death).

BROWNLOW, WILLIAM GANNAWAY *(b Aug. 29, 1805, Wytheville, Va.; d April 29, 1877, Knoxville, Tenn.).* Minister, editor of the *Knoxville Whig* (1849-1861) whose one-nation, antisecession editorials won him "the fighting parson" appellation and caused him to be arrested by the Confederacy; later an exile from his adopted state; he returned to become governor (1865-1869);

Whig turned Republican. After the 1860 Presidential election he wrote in an editorial: "Lincoln is chosen president, and whether with or without the consent and participation of the South, will be and ought to be inaugurated." The *Whig* was the last pro-Union newspaper in the South, being forced out of business in 1861.

Brownlow ultimately returned to Tennessee with a Union army, helped rally Unionists, held a nominating convention (1863) aimed at restoration of civilian government, became first a member of the central committee and then governor by acclamation, facing the growing Ku Klux Klan with 1,600 armed guards. Served in the U.S. Senate (1869-1875), where, because of illness, his career was relatively peaceful.

BRUCE, BLANCHE KELSO *(b March 1, 1841, Prince Edwards County, Va.; d March 17, 1898, Washington, D.C.).* A slave who had been tutored by his master's son, Bruce became a teacher in Missouri, a planter and land dealer in Mississippi, an important Republican figure, and the first Negro to serve a full term in the U.S. Senate (1875-1881) where he championed the rights of Indians, Chinese, blacks, and all minorities. Sergeant at arms of the state senate (1870), Bolivar County tax assessor and collector while also serving as sheriff (1872-1875), and on the Mississippi Board of Levee Commissioners; Garfield-appointed register of the Treasury (1881) and again, by Harrison appointment, (1897 until death); District of Columbia recorder of deeds (1891-1893).

BRUCE, WILLIAM CABELL *(b March 12, 1860, Staunton Hills, Va.; d May 9, 1946, Ruxton, Md.).* Lawyer, author, Maryland Democrat. State senate (1894-1896), its president (1896), head of Baltimore law department (1903-1908), city charter commission (1910), general counsel of state Public Service Commission (1910-1922), U.S. Senate (1923-1929).

BRUCKNER, HENRY *(b June 17, 1871, New York City; d April 14, 1942, New York City).* Manufacturer, banker, New York Democrat. State assembly (1901), Bronx borough commissioner of public works (1902-1905), U.S. Representative (1913-1917), Bronx borough president (1918-1933).

BRUMBAUGH, CLEMENT LAIRD *(b Feb. 28, 1863, Darke County, Ohio; d Sept. 28, 1921, Columbus, Ohio).* Educator, lawyer, Ohio Democrat. Greenville schools superintendent (1896-1900), state representative and minority leader (1900-1904), U.S. Representative (1913-1921).

BRUMM, CHARLES NAPOLEON *(b June 9, 1838, Pottsville, Pa.; d Jan. 11, 1917, Minersville, Pa.).* Lawyer, Union Army officer, Pennsylvania Republican. U.S. Representative (1881-1889, 1895-1899, 1906-1909), GOP National Convention delegate (1884), Schuylkill County common pleas judge (1909 until death). Father of George F. Brumm.

BRUMM, GEORGE FRANKLIN *(b Jan. 24, 1880, Minersville, Pa.; d May 29, 1934, Philadelphia, Pa.).* Lawyer, Pennsylvania Republican. A soldier on Mexican border (1916-1918) where he doubled as election commissioner for servicemen in Texas, U.S. Representative (1923-1927, 1929 until death). Son of Charles N. Brumm.

BRUNDIDGE, STEPHEN, JR. *(b Jan. 1, 1857, Searcy, Ark.; d Jan. 14, 1938, Searcy).* Lawyer, Arkansas Democrat. First judicial district prosecuting attorney (1886-1890), Democratic state central committee (1890-1892), U.S. Representative (1897-1909), unsuccessful candidate for governor (1908), for U.S. Senate (1918).

BRUNNER, WILLIAM FRANK *(b Sept. 15, 1887, Woodhaven, N.Y.; d April 23, 1965, Edgemere, N.Y.).* Insurance and real estate broker, New York City Democrat who, as president of the board of aldermen (1936-1938), served as acting mayor during the absence of Fiorello LaGuardia. State assembly (1922-1928), U.S. Representative (1929-1935), Queens County sheriff (1935-1936), commissioner of borough works (1941).

BRUNSDALE, CLARENCE NORMAN *(b July 9, 1891, Sherbrooke, N.Dak.).* Teacher, farmer, banker, North Dakota Republican. State senate (1927-1935, 1940-1951, its president pro tem 1943), majority leader (1945-1947), GOP National Committeeman (1948-1952), governor (1951-1957), GOP National Convention delegate (1940, 1948, 1956), U.S. Senate (1959-1960) to fill vacancy caused by death of William Langer.

BRYAN, GEORGE *(b Aug. 11, 1731, Dublin, Ireland; d Jan. 27, 1791, Philadelphia, Pa.).* Importer, Pennsylvania Conservative who defeated Benjamin Franklin for a seat in the state assembly (1764-1765) and was opposed to ratification of the U.S. Constitution (1787); after its adoption he helped to organize a revisionist convention (1788), out of which nothing meaningful emerged.

BRYAN, GUY MORRISON *(b Jan. 12, 1821, Herculaneum, Mo.; d June 4, 1901, Austin, Tex.).* Planter, Texas patriot who fought at San Jacinto (1836) and when Texas achieved statehood was one of its leading Democrats. State representative (1847-1853, 1873, 1879, 1887-1891), house speaker (1873), state senate (1853-1857), Democratic National Convention delegate (1856, 1860) the latter year as chairman of state delegation, U.S. Representative (1857-1859).

BRYAN, NATHAN PHILEMON *(b April 23, 1872, near Fort Mason, Fla.; d Aug. 8, 1935, Jacksonville, Fla.).* Lawyer, educator, jurist, Florida Democrat. Chairman of board of control of state institutions of higher education (1905-1909), U.S. Senate (1911-1917), judge of the U.S. Circuit Court of Appeals of fifth judicial circuit (1920 until death). Brother of William Jennings Bryan.

BRYAN, WILLIAM JENNINGS *(b March 19, 1860, Salem, Nebr.; d July 26, 1925, Dayton, Tenn.).* Lawyer, newspaper publisher, editorial writer, Nebraska Democrat and a Chautauqua lecturer with a gift for oratory that culminated in his famous "cross of gold" speech that won for him the Democratic presidential nomination (1896). U.S. Representative (1891-1895), a period in which his speaking skills and his positions on vital issues of the day, high among them free silver, made him titular leader of his party until the advent of Woodrow Wilson.

He was a delegate to the Democratic National Conventions of 1896, 1904, 1912, 1920, 1924 and the presidential nominee in 1900 and 1908 as well as 1896. In his first bid for the presidency he also had the endorsement of the Populist and Silver Republican parties and, out of more than 13 million popular votes cast, lost to the Republican, McKinley, by only about 600,000. The electoral vote was 271-176.

Bryan surrendered the mantle of leadership to Woodrow Wilson, campaigned for him, and served as secretary of state in his cabinet (1913-1915). Brother of Nathan P. Bryan.

BRYSON, JOSEPH RALEIGH *(b Jan. 18, 1893, Brevard, N.C.; d March 10, 1953, Bethesda, Md.).* Lawyer, South Carolina Democrat. State representative (1921-1924), state senate (1929-1932), U.S. Representative (1939 until death).

BUCHANAN, FRANK *(b Dec. 1, 1902, McKeesport, Pa.; d April 27, 1951, in U.S. Naval Hospital, Bethesda, Md.).* Teacher, auto dealer, economic consultant, Pennsylvania Democrat. Mayor of McKeesport (1942-1946), U.S. Representative (1946 until death). Husband of Vera D. Buchanan.

BUCHANAN, JAMES *(b April 23, 1791, Cove Gap, near Mercersburg, Pa.; d June 1, 1868, Wheatland, near Lancaster, Pa.).* Fifteenth president (Pennsylvania Federalist turned Democrat), 1857-1861; the last of the series of pre-Civil War presidents who, no matter what their attributes, were unequal to the task of closing the growing rift between North and South.

Eldest son of a successful storekeeper, James Buchanan graduated (1809) from Dickinson College, studied law and (1812) was admitted to the bar and practiced in Lancaster. A bachelor (the woman he hoped to marry died and no one took her place) whose orphaned niece, Harriet Lane, became his White House hostess. A volunteer in the War of 1812, he helped defend Baltimore from British attack.

Federalist state representative (1814, 1815), U.S. Representative (1821-1831), starting out as a Federalist then becoming (and remaining) a Democrat; appointed (1830) one of the managers in charge of impeachment proceedings against U.S. District Court Judge James H. Peck; Minister to Russia (1832-1834); elected to U.S. Senate to fill a vacancy, then twice reelected, serving from 1834 until he resigned in 1845 to accept position of secretary of state (1845-1849) in President Polk's cabinet, where he ably assisted in Polk's expansionist program.

Although a leading candidate for the Democratic presidential nomination in 1852, party controversy resulted in the nomination of dark horse Franklin Pierce who made him minister to Great Britain (1853-1856), during which period he collaborated with Pierre Soule (minister to Spain) and John Y. Mason (minister to France) in drawing up the Ostend Manifesto which urged that Cuba be annexed by the United States. Partly because he had been out of the United States and therefore not associated in the public mind with conflict over the Kansas-Nebraska Act, the Democratic party chose Buchanan as its standard bearer in the presidential election of 1856. The result was Buchanan 174, Republican candidate John C. Fremont 114 and American (Know-Nothing) party candidate Millard Fillmore 8 electoral votes.

As president, Buchanan favored western development and was knowledgeable in his promotion of a vigorous foreign policy, but these things were heavily overshadowed by the slavery problem. Like his predecessor, President Pierce, he supported legal rulings protecting property rights of slave owners in opposition to the humanistic demands of many of his fellow Northerners, and he accepted the Dred Scott decision as binding. During the last few weeks of his administration (after Lincoln had been elected his successor), the actual secession of Southern states began. Buchanan, a strict constructionist and well-versed in Constitutional law, was trapped in the vise of his conviction on the one hand that it was unlawful for states to secede; yet, on the other hand that he had no legal Constitutional right to use force to restrain them.

In retirement at "Wheatland," Buchanan supported the North in its conduct of the Civil War and prepared a defense of his actions as president.

BUCHANAN, JAMES PAUL *(b April 30, 1867, Midway, S.C.; d Feb. 22, 1937, Washington, D.C.).* Lawyer, Texas Democrat. Washington County justice of the peace (1889-1892), prosecuting attorney (1892-1899), district attorney for the twenty-first judicial district

(1899-1906), state representative (1906-1913), U.S. Representative (1913 until death).

BUCHANAN, VERA DAERR *(b July 20, 1902, Wilson, Pa.; d Nov. 26, 1955, McKeesport, Pa.).* Pennsylvania Democrat and widow of U.S. Representative Frank Buchanan. Upon his death she was chosen to replace him, and served until her death.

BUCK, FRANK HENRY *(b Sept. 23, 1887, Solano County, Calif.; d Sept. 17, 1942, Washington, D.C.).* Lawyer, oil- and lumberman, farmer, fruit grower, California Democrat. National convention delegate (1928, 1936, 1940), U.S. Representative (1933 until death).

BUCKALEW, CHARLES ROLLIN *(b Dec. 28, 1821, Fishing Creek Township, Pa.; d May 19, 1899, Bloomsburg, Pa.).* Lawyer, diplomat, Pennsylvania Democrat. Columbia County prosecuting attorney (1845-1847), state senate (1850-1853, 1857, 1858, 1869), presidential elector on the Buchanan-Breckinridge ticket (1856), state committee chairman (1857), minister to Ecuador (1858-1861), U.S. Senate (1863-1869), unsuccessful candidate for governor (1872), constitutional convention delegate (1873), U.S. Representative (1887-1891).

BUCKBEE, JOHN THEODORE *(b Aug. 1, 1871, Winnebago County, Ill.; d April 23, 1936, Rockford, Ill.).* Agriculturist, Illinois Republican. U.S. Representative (1927 until death).

BUCKINGHAM, WILLIAM ALFRED *(b May 28, 1804, Lebanon, Conn.; d Feb. 5, 1875, Norwich, Conn.).* Merchant, manufacturer, Connecticut Republican who served as governor (1858-1866) throughout the tense Civil War period and for whom a statue was unveiled in the statehouse. Norwich mayor (1849, 1850, 1856, 1857), presidential elector on the Fremont-Dayton ticket (1856), U.S. Senate (1869 until death).

BUCKLER, RICHARD THOMPSON *(b Oct. 27, 1865, Coles County, Ill.; d Jan. 23, 1950, Crookston, Minn.).* Agriculturist, Minnesota Farmer-Labor party leader who was active in Farm Bureau and Farmers Union affairs throughout his adult life. State senate (1915-1919, 1923-1927, 1931-1933), U.S. Representative (1935-1943).

BUCKLEY, CHARLES ANTHONY *(b June 23, 1890, New York City; d Jan. 22, 1967, New York City).* Building contractor, New York Democrat, Bronx borough Democratic boss more than thirteen years and a U.S. Representative more than thirty years (1935 until death).
    Alderman (1918-1923), state tax appraiser (1923-1929), city chamberlain (1929-1933), chairman of the Bronx county committee (1953 until death).

BUCKNER, AYLETT HAWES *(b Dec. 14, 1816, Fredericksburg, Va.; d Feb. 5, 1894, Mexico, Mo.).* Lawyer, newspaper editor, teacher, tobacco manufacturer, merchant, Missouri Democrat who attended Washington convention (1861) that sought to prevent Civil War. U.S. Representative (1873-1885).

BUDD, JAMES HERBERT *(b May 18, 1851, Janesville, Wis.; d July 30, 1908, Stockton, Calif.).* Lawyer, California Democrat. U.S. Representative (1883-1885), governor (1894-1898).

BULKELEY, MORGAN GARDNER *(b Dec. 26, 1837, East Haddam, Conn.; d Nov. 6, 1922, Hartford, Conn.).* Merchant, Union Army soldier, president of Aetna Life Insurance Co. (1879 until death), Connecticut Republican. Hartford City Council (1874), alderman (1875, 1876), first president of National League of Professional Base Ball Clubs (1876), mayor of Hartford (1880-1888), governor (1889-1893), GOP National Convention delegate (1888-1896), U.S. Senate (1905-1911).

BULLOCH, ARCHIBALD *(b about 1730, Charleston, S.C.; d Feb. 22, 1777, Savannah, Ga.).* Lawyer, the first Georgian to read the Declaration of Independence. Member of the committee named to sympathize officially with the citizens of Boston (1768), speaker of Georgia Royal Assembly (1772), president of Georgia provincial congress (1775-1776), member of Continental Congress (1775, 1776), president and commander in chief of Georgia from June 20, 1776 until Feb. 5, 1777, when state government was adopted. Theodore Roosevelt's great-great-grandfather.

BULLOCK, RUFUS BROWN *(b March 28, 1834, Bethlehem, N.Y.; d April 27, 1907, Atlanta, Ga.).* Telegraph expert, railroad executive, cotton manufacturer, Georgia Republican and Reconstruction period governor (1868-1871) who was charged with just about every crime of which a man in his position could be accused, became a fugitive, was at last captured (1876), tried, and acquitted on all counts for lack of evidence. He then staged a comeback in Georgia if not in politics, at least in the business world.

BULOW, WILLIAM JOHN *(b Jan. 13, 1869, Clermont County, Ohio; d Feb. 26, 1960, Washington, D.C.).* Lawyer, South Dakota Democrat. State senate (1899), Beresford city attorney (1902-1912, 1913-1927), mayor (1912-1913), Union County judge (1918), governor (1927-1931), Democratic National Convention delegate (1928), U.S. Senate (1931-1943).

BULWINKLE, ALFRED LEE *(b April 21, 1883, Charleston, S.C.; d Aug. 31, 1950, Gastonia, N.C.).* Lawyer, North Carolina Democrat. Gastonia prosecuting attorney (1913-1916), U.S. Representative (1921-1929, 1931 until death), U.S. adviser to International Civil Aviation Organization (1947).

BUNDY, HEZEKIAH SANFORD *(b Aug. 15, 1817, Marietta, Ohio; d Dec. 12, 1895, Wellston, Ohio).* Farmer, lawyer, iron dealer, Ohio Republican. State representative (1848, 1850), state senate (1855), presidential elector on Lincoln-Hamlin ticket (1860), U.S. Representative (1865-1867, 1873-1875, 1893-1895).

BURCH, THOMAS GRANVILLE *(b July 3, 1869, Henry County, Va.; d March 20, 1951, Martinsville, Va.).* Farmer, banker, insurance broker, Virginia Democrat. Member of state agriculture board (1910-1913), mayor of Martinsville (1912-1914), U.S. marshal (1914-1921), member of state government reorganization commission (1927), transportation and public utility advisory commission (1929), state board of education (1930, 1931), Democratic National Convention delegate (1908, 1912, 1924, 1932, 1936, 1940), U.S. Representative (1931-1946), U.S. Senate for six months in 1946 to fill vacancy caused by death of Carter Glass.

BURCHARD, HORATIO CHAPIN *(b Sept. 22, 1825, Marshall, N.Y.; d May 14, 1908, Freeport, Ill.).* Lawyer, Illinois Republican. State representative (1863-1866), U.S. Representative (1869-1879), director of U.S. Mints (1879-1885).

BURDICK, CLARK *(b Jan. 13, 1868, Newport, R.I.; d Aug. 27, 1948, Newport).* Lawyer, banker, Rhode Island Republican. Newport School Board (1899-1901), city solicitor (1901, 1902, 1907, 1908), state representative (1906-1908), GOP National Convention delegate (1912), chairman of Newport Representative Council (1906-1916), state senate (1915, 1916), mayor of Newport (1917, 1918), U.S. Representative (1919-1933).

BURDICK, USHER LLOYD *(b Feb. 21, 1879, Owatonna, Minn.; d Aug. 19, 1960, Washington, D.C.).* Teacher, lawyer, rancher, author who was raised among the Sioux Indians, North Dakota Republican-Independent. Benson County school superintendent (1900-1902), state representative (1907-1911), house speaker (1909), lieutenant governor (1911-1913), Williams County state's attorney (1913-1915), assistant U.S. attorney (1929-1932), U.S. Representative (1935-1945, 1949-1959). Father of U.S. Senator Quentin N. Burdick.

BURGES, TRISTAM *(b Feb. 26, 1770, Rochester, Mass.; d Oct. 13, 1853, East Providence, R.I.).* Professor of oratory, lawyer, Rhode Island Federalist-Whig. State representative (1811), chief justice of state supreme court (1815-1825), U.S. Representative (1825-1835), unsuccessful candidate for governor (1836) as a Whig.

BURGESS, GEORGE FARMER *(b Sept. 21, 1861, Wharton, Tex.; d Dec. 31, 1919, Gonzales, Tex.).* Farmer, lawyer, Texas Democrat. Gonzales County prosecuting attorney (1886-1889), presidential elector on Cleveland-Stevenson ticket (1892), U.S. Representative (1901-1917).

BURGIN, WILLIAM OLIN *(b July 28, 1877, McDowell County, N.C.; d April 11, 1946, Washington, D.C.).* Salesman, merchant, banker, lawyer, North Carolina Democrat. Mayor of Thomasville (1906-1910), state representative (1931), state senate (1933), U.S. Representative (1939 until death).

BURKE, AEDANUS *(b June 16, 1743, Galway, Ireland; d March 30, 1802, Charleston, S.C.).* Revolutionary soldier, lawyer, pamphleteer, South Carolina jurist-legislator who opposed ratification of U.S. Constitution, arguing that a president should be restricted to one term so as not to give rise to an Ameri-

can ruling class. State circuit court judge (1778-1780, 1783 until death), state representative (1779-1782), U.S. Representative (1789-1791).

BURKE, CHARLES HENRY *(b April 1, 1861, Genesee County, N.Y.; d April 7, 1944, Washington, D.C.).* Real estate investor, lawyer, South Dakota Republican state representative (1895, 1897), U.S. Representative (1899-1907, 1909-1915), commissioner of Indian affairs (1921-1929).

BURKE, EDMUND *(b Jan. 23, 1809, Westminster, Vt.; d Jan. 25, 1882, Newport, N.H.).* Newspaper editor, lawyer, New Hampshire Democrat. U.S. Representative (1839-1845), commissioner of patents (1846-1850), Democratic National Convention delegate (1844, 1852), presided over state convention (1867), state board of agriculture (1871).

BURKE, JAMES FRANCIS *(b Oct. 21, 1867, Petroleum Center, Pa.; d Aug. 8, 1932, Washington, D.C.).* Lawyer, Pennsylvania Republican who was extremely active in party's national affairs. Secretary of GOP National Committee (1892) resigning to become president of American Republican College League, officer or delegate to all national conventions (except for 1912) from 1892 to 1924, delegate to Parliamentary Peace Conference in Belgium (1905), U.S. Representative (1905-1915), U.S. director of war savings during World War I, general counsel to GOP National Committee (1927 until death), national convention parliamentarian (1928).

BURKE, MICHAEL EDMUND *(b Oct. 15, 1863, Beaver Dam, Wis.; d Dec. 12, 1918, Beaver Dam).* Lawyer, Wisconsin Democrat. Beaver Dam city clerk (1887-1889), state assembly (1891-1893), city attorney (1893-1908), state senate (1895-1899), Democratic National Convention (1904), mayor (1908-1910), U.S. Representative (1911-1917).

BURKE, THOMAS (b about 1747, Galway, Ireland; d Dec. 2, 1783, Orange County, N.C.). Lawyer, doctor, Revolutionary statesman and governor of North Carolina (1781-1782) who was kidnaped and held hostage by Tories. Provincial congress delegate (1775, 1776) serving on thirteen committees and drafting a resolution calling for North Carolina to join with the other colonies in a declaration of independence. Continental Congress (1776-1781), state house of commons (1777).

BURKE, WILLIAM JOSEPH (b Sept. 25, 1862, near London, England; d Nov. 7, 1925, Callery Junction, Pa.). Railroad conductor, labor leader, farmer, oil producer, Pennsylvania Republican. Member of Pittsburgh Greater City Council (1906-1910), state senate (1914-1917), Pittsburgh City Council (1918), U.S. Representative (1919-1923).

BURKETT, ELMER JOACOB (b Dec. 1, 1867, Mills County, Iowa; d May 23, 1935, Lincoln, Nebr.). Educator, lawyer, Nebraska Republican who served in both houses of Congress, declined the nomination for governor (1912), and failed to capture the nomination for vice president in the same year. State representative (1896-1898), U.S. Representative (1899-1905), U.S. Senate (1905-1911), GOP National Convention delegate (1908-1912).

BURLEIGH, EDWIN CHICK (b Nov. 27, 1843, Linneus, Maine; d June 16, 1916, Augusta, Maine). Teacher, surveyor, lumberman, publisher of the Kennebec Journal, Maine Republican. State land agent (1876-1878), state treasurer (1884-1888), governor (1889-1892), GOP National Convention delegate (1896), U.S. Representative (1897-1911), U.S. Senate (1913 until death).

BURLESON, ALBERT SIDNEY (b June 7, 1863, San Marcos, Tex.; d Nov. 24, 1937, Austin, Tex.). Lawyer, banker, rancher, conservative Texas Democrat who as a cabinet member did not hesitate to assail both labor and corporate interests; championed the cause of farmers and small businessmen; a deft politician who looked every inch the part, even to the wing collar. Assistant city attorney of Austin (1885-1890), twenty-sixth judicial district attorney (1891-1898), U.S. Representative (1899-1913); postmaster general (1913-1921)—his reward for helping Woodrow Wilson capture the presidential nomination. In that wartime position, he came as close as anyone ever did to censoring the American press, forcing many newspapers to cease publication by barring them from the mails for a variety of alleged security reasons.

BURLINGAME, ANSON (b Nov. 14, 1820, New Berlin, N.Y.; d Feb. 23, 1870, St. Petersburg, Russia). Lawyer, statesman, Massachusetts Republican who served three terms as a U.S. Representative (1855-1861), the first two as a member of the American (Know-Nothing) party before accepting a diplomatic position. State senate (1852), member of state constitutional convention (1853), ambassador to China (1861-1867), China's ambassador in negotiation of treaties with other powers (1867 until death), among them the Burlingame Treaty with the United States.

BURNET, DAVID GOUVERNEUR (b April 4, 1788, Newark, N.J.; d Dec. 5, 1870, Galveston, Tex.). Pioneer and first president of the republic of Texas (1836) who was replaced by and became a political foe of Sam Houston. Son of William Burnet.

BURNET, JACOB (b Feb. 22, 1770, Newark, N.J.; d May 10, 1853, Cincinnati, Ohio). Lawyer, banker, Ohio Federalist who did much to bring about statehood. Member of territorial council (1799-1802), state representative (1812, 1813), state supreme court judge (1821-

1828), U.S. Senate (1828-1831). Son of William Burnet.

BURNET, WILLIAM *(b Dec. 2, 1730, Newark, N.J.; d Oct. 7, 1791, Newark).* Physician, farmer, Revolutionary patriot, New Jersey delegate to Continental Congress (1780-1781), chairman of Essex County Committee of Public Safety (1775), surgeon general of the eastern district of the United States (1776-1783), presiding judge of the common pleas court (1776), Essex County's first judge (1781). Father of David G. and Jacob Burnet.

BURNETT, HENRY CORNELIUS *(b Oct. 5, 1825, Essex County, Va.; d Oct. 1, 1866, Hopkinsville, Ky.)* Lawyer, Confederate Army officer, Kentucky Democrat. U.S. Representative (1855 until expulsion in 1861), president of Kentucky conventions that enacted secession and set up state government, Provisional Confederate Congress (1861-1862), senator to first and second Confederate Congresses (1862-1865).

BURNETT, JOHN LAWSON *(b Jan. 20, 1854, Cedar Bluff, Ala.; d May 13, 1919, Gadsden, Ala.).* Lawyer, Alabama Democrat. State representative (1884), state senate (1886), U.S. Representative (1899 until death), member of U.S. Immigration Commission (1907-1910).

BURNETT, PETER HARDEMAN *(b Nov. 15, 1807, Nashville, Tenn.; d May 17, 1895, San Francisco, Calif.).* On his own from the age of fourteen, he worked at a variety of jobs in Tennessee and Missouri, taught himself the law, moved west to pioneer in both Oregon and California, and made his political contribution to both states. In Oregon he farmed, became a member of the legislative committee, was supreme court judge, and an elected member of the first legislature. In California, where he first went to mine for gold, he was judge of the superior court, was chosen the first governor (as a Democrat), an office he held from 1849 until 1851, climaxed his public career by serving as a state supreme court judge (1857-1858), and then devoted the rest of his days to earning a living (in the course of which he founded the Pacific Bank) and writing his memoirs.

BURNHAM, HENRY EBEN *(b Nov. 8, 1844, Dunbarton, N.H.; d Feb. 8, 1917, Manchester, N.H.).* Banker, lawyer, New Hampshire Republican. State representative (1873-1874), Hillsboro County treasurer (1875-1877), county probate court judge (1876-1879), constitutional convention delegate (1889), chairman of GOP state convention (1888), ballot law commissioner (1892-1900), U.S. Senate (1901-1913).

BURNSIDE, AMBROSE EVERETT *(b May 23, 1824, Liberty, Ind.; d Sept. 3, 1881, Bristol, R.I.).* West Point graduate, railroad executive, Union Army major general who received the thanks of Congress (1864) for "gallantry, good conduct, and soldierlike endurance" but resigned his commission as the result of a court of inquiry into the reasons for his loss of 4,000 men during the siege of Petersburg, Va.; Rhode Island Republican. Governor (1866-1868), U.S. Senate (1875 until death).

BURR, AARON *(b Feb. 6. 1756, Newark, N.J.; d Sept. 14, 1836, Port Richmond, Staten Island, N.Y.)* Lawyer, Revolutionary Army officer who distinguished himself at Quebec, Monmouth, and New Haven, went on to pursue what could have been a brilliant political career but instead ended up defending himself against charges of treason for trying to create a new nation in the Southwest; also the man who killed Alexander Hamilton in a duel (1804); New York Democrat and one of the first of New York City's Tammany leaders.

State assembly (1784, 1785, 1798, 1799), state attorney general (1789, 1790), Revolutionary claims commissioner (1791), U.S. Senate (1791-1797), president of state constitutional convention (1801), and then came his closest brush with destiny: Burr, along with Thomas Jefferson, John Adams, C. C. Pinckney, and John Jay were candidates for the two highest offices in the land—president and vice president. In those days the winner would be the former, the runner-up the latter. But Jefferson and Burr finished in a tie for first with 73 electoral votes each. The election was thrown into the House and on the thirty-sixth ballot Jefferson was chosen president, leaving the vice presidency for Burr, a position that he held (1801-1804). Whether the loss of the presidency caused sufficient rankle to stir thoughts of a separate empire in Burr's mind is subject for debate; nevertheless he did try to establish a new nation, was arrested, tried, and acquitted (1807).

BURROWS, JULIUS CAESAR (b Jan. 9, 1837, North East, Pa.; d Nov. 16, 1915, Kalamazoo, Mich.). Lawyer, educator, Union Army officer, Michigan Republican. Kalamazoo County prosecutor (1866-1870), U.S. Representative (1873-1875, 1879-1883, 1885-1895), GOP National Convention delegate (1884) and its temporary chairman (1908), U.S. Senate (1895-1911), vice chairman of National Monetary Commission (1908-1912).

BURT, ARMISTEAD (b Nov. 13, 1802, Clouds Creek, S.C.; d Oct. 30, 1883, Abbeville, S.C.). Farmer, lawyer, South Carolina Democrat. U.S. Representative (1843-1853), House speaker pro tem (1848), Democratic National Convention (1868).

BURTNESS, OLGER BURTON (b March 14, 1884, Grand Forks County, N.Dak.;

d Jan. 20, 1960, Grand Forks, N.Dak.). Lawyer, North Dakota Republican. Grand Forks County prosecutor (1911-1916), GOP National Convention (1916, 1936, 1948), state representative (1919, 1920), U.S. Representative (1921-1933), first judicial district judge (1950 until death).

BURTON, THEODORE ELIJAH (b Dec. 20, 1851, Jefferson, Ohio; d Oct. 28, 1929, Washington, D.C.). Lawyer, author, banker, lecturer, pacifist, Ohio Republican, and a power in the party. Cleveland City Council (1886-1888), U.S. Representative (1889-1891, 1895-1909, 1921-1928), U.S. Senate (1909-1915, 1928 until death), and throughout all of those congressional years a fighter against pork-barrel legislation.

His assignments were many, including chairman of the House Committee on the Inland Waterways Commission (1907-1909) and National Waterways Commission (1909-1912), membership on the National Monetary Commission (1908-1912), chairman of U.S. delegation to the control of arms convention in Switzerland (1925), president of the American Peace Society (1911-1915, 1925-1929), member of the Executive Council of the Interparliamentary Union (1904-1914, 1921-1929). In 1916 he received seventy-seven votes as Ohio's favorite-son candidate for the GOP presidential nomination; he was a delegate to the conventions of 1904, 1908, 1912, 1924 and temporary chairman and keynote speaker of the last.

BURWELL, WILLIAM ARMISTED (b March 15, 1780, Mecklenburg County, Va.; d Feb. 16, 1821, Washington, D.C.). President Jefferson's private secretary, Virginia Democrat. A member of the state house of delegates and then a U.S. Representative (1806 until death).

BUSHFIELD, HARLAN JOHN (b Aug. 6, 1882, Atlantic, Iowa; d Sept. 27, 1948,

Miller, S.Dak.). Lawyer, South Dakota Republican. Governor (1939-1942), U.S. Senate (1943 until death) and was succeeded by his wife, Vera Cahalan Bushfield, who resigned after two months.

BUTLER, ANDREW PICKENS *(b Nov. 19, 1796, Edgefield, S.C.; d May 25, 1857, Edgefield).* Lawyer, South Carolina States' Rights Democrat and a leader of the Calhoun faction both in state and national affairs. State senate (1824-1833), common pleas court judge (1835-1846), U.S. Senate (1846 until death) where he was chairman of the Judiciary Committee.

BUTLER, BENJAMIN FRANKLIN *(b Nov. 5, 1818, Deerfield, N.H.; d Jan. 11, 1893, Washington, D.C.).* Lawyer, Union Army major general, Massachusetts Democrat turned Republican turned Democrat who ran for governor with Greenback support and won (1883-1884) and for president on the Greenback and Anti-Monopolist ticket (1884) and lost, polling only 175,370 votes. State representative (1853), state senate (1859), Democratic National Convention delegate (1860), U.S. Representative (1867-1875, 1877-1879), one of the members named by the House to conduct impeachment proceedings (1868) against President Andrew Johnson.

BUTLER, BENJAMIN FRANKLIN *(b Dec. 14, 1795, Columbia County, N.Y.; d Nov. 8, 1858, Paris, France).* A New York Democrat–Free-Soiler–Republican who preferred the practice and teaching of law to public office but who served in Andrew Jackson's cabinet because his law partner, Vice President Martin Van Buren, asked him to, but then said no both to Van Buren and James Polk when they were in the White House. Albany County district attorney (1821-1824), state legislature (1827-1833), refused seat in U.S. Senate, U.S. attorney general (1833-1837) doubling also as secretary of war as Jackson's term drew to a close (October 1836-March 1837), organized law department in University of City of New York (1838), and taught for several years.

BUTLER, EZRA *(b Sept. 24, 1763, Lancaster, Mass.; d July 12, 1838, Waterbury, Vt.).* Hunter, trapper, farmer, clergyman, lawyer, Revolutionary soldier, Vermont National Republican-Democrat. Waterbury town clerk (1790) and a selectman, state representative (1794-1797, 1799-1804, 1807, 1808) and a member of the governor's council, first judge of the Chittenden County Court (1803-1806) and chief justice (1806-1811), Jefferson County chief justice (1812-1825) except for two years when he was a U.S. Representative (1813-1815), state constitutional convention delegate (1822), governor (1826-1828).

BUTLER, HUGH ALFRED *(b Feb. 28, 1878, Harrison County, Iowa; d July 1, 1954, Bethesda, Md.).* Construction engineer, grain miller, Nebraska Republican. Omaha Board of Education member (1919-1946), GOP National Committeeman (1936-1940), U.S. Senate (1941 until death).

BUTLER, MARION *(b May 20, 1863, Clinton, N.C.; d June 3, 1938, Takoma Park, Md.).* Teacher, newspaper publisher, cotton and tobacco grower, farm leader, lawyer, North Carolina Democrat-Populist-Republican. State senate (1890), Populist state chairman (1890), president of State Farmers' Alliance (1892, 1893), president of National Farmers' Alliance and Industrial Union (1894, 1895), chairman of People's party state committee (1894), U.S. Senate as a Populist (1895-1901), chairman of Populist National Executive Committee (1896-1904), GOP National Convention delegate (1912, 1916, 1920, 1924, 1928, 1932).

BUTLER, MATTHEW CALBRAITH *(b March 8, 1836, Greenville County, S.C.; d April 14, 1909, Columbia, S.C.).* Lawyer, Confederate major general, Spanish American War major general who supervised the evacuation of Cuba by Spanish forces (1898), South Carolina Democrat. State representative (1866), U.S. Senate (1877-1895).

BUTLER, PIERCE *(b July 11, 1744, County Carlow, Ireland; d Feb. 15, 1822, Philadelphia, Pa.).* A British Army officer stationed in Boston who resigned to cast his lot with the colonists and became a planter in Prince William's Parish, South Carolina, where he was chosen a delegate to the Continental Congress (1787, 1788), member of the convention that framed the federal Constitution (1787), and was elected to the U.S. Senate (1789-1796, 1802-1804).

BUTLER, THOMAS STALKER *(b Nov. 4, 1855, Uwehland Township, Pa.; d May 26, 1828, Washington, D.C.).* Lawyer, Pennsylvania Republican. Judge of fifteenth judicial district (1888), GOP National Convention delegate (1892), U.S. Representative for thirty years (1897 until death).

BUTTZ, CHARLES WILSON *(b Nov. 16, 1837, Stroudsburg, Pa.; d July 20, 1913, Lisbon, N.Dak.).* Lawyer, Union Army officer, Virginia, South Carolina, and North Dakota Republican. In Virginia: GOP National Convention delegate (1864), King William County commonwealth attorney (1866). In South Carolina: first judicial circuit solicitor (1872-1880), U.S. Representative for five months (1876-1877) filling a disputed vacancy. In North Dakota: Organized Ranson County and founded the town of Buttzville, state's attorney (1884-1886), state representative (1903-1909).

Buttzville, N.J., where he lived as a boy, is named for his family.

BYNUM, WILLIAM DALLAS *(b June 26, 1846, Greene County, Ind.; d Oct. 21, 1927, Indianapolis).* Lawyer, Indiana Democrat who helped organize the National, or Gold Standard, Democratic party and was its first chairman (1896-1898). Washington, Ind., city attorney after serving as its first city clerk (1871-1875) and then becoming mayor (1875-1879), presidential elector on the Tilden-Hendricks ticket (1876), state representative (1881-1885, speaker in last year), U.S. Representative (1885-1895) serving for a time as party whip, member of commission to codify U.S. criminal laws (1900-1906).

BYRD, HARRY FLOOD, SR. *(b June 10, 1887, Martinsburg, W.Va.; d Oct. 20, 1966, Berryville, Va.).* Fruit grower, newspaper publisher, Virginia Democrat denounced by his enemies as a ruthless machine boss but recognized by all as the dominant figure in state politics for fifty years. President of the Valley Turnpike Co. (1908-1918), state senator (1915-1925), state fuel commissioner (1918), chairman of Democratic state committee (1922), governor (1926-1930), Democratic National Committeeman (1928-1940), U.S. Senator (1933-1965), a position where he seemed always a voice out of the past. His hallmarks were racial segregation, states' rights conservatism, yet as governor he had been considered a progressive reformer.

A bitter foe of Franklin D. Roosevelt's New Deal policies, as chairman of the Senate Finance Committee he was able to carry that perverseness effectively into the Truman and Kennedy administrations and it was only when Johnson became president that he began to weaken. He relinquished his seat voluntarily, at the age of seventy-eight, but in so doing handpicked his fifty-one-year-old son, Harry, Jr., to succeed him. He died ten months after retirement.

BYRNE, WILLIAM THOMAS *(b March 6, 1876, Florida, N.Y.; d Jan. 27, 1952, Troy, N.Y.).* Lawyer, New York Democrat. State senate (1923-1926), U.S. Representative (1937 until death).

BYRNES, JAMES FRANCIS *(b May 2, 1879, Charleston, S.C.; d April 9, 1972, Columbia, S.C.).* Lawyer, South Carolina Democrat who devoted his life to government service, even to resigning his position as an associate justice of the U.S. Supreme Court (July 8, 1941-Oct. 3, 1942) in order to help more effectively in the nation's war effort as head of the Office of Economic Stabilization and then (May 27, 1943) as director of the Office of War Mobilization, resigning that post to become secretary of state (July 3, 1945) where he remained until 1947. Franklin D. Roosevelt called him "Assistant President." Second circuit solicitor (1908-1910), U.S. Representative (1911-1925), Democratic National Convention delegate (1920, 1932, 1936, 1940), U.S. Senate (1931-1941), governor (1951-1955).

BYRNS, JOSEPH WELLINGTON, SR. *(b July 20, 1869, Robertson County, Tenn.; d June 4, 1936, Washington, D.C.).* Lawyer, Tennessee Democrat. State representative (1895, 1897, 1899, speaker in 1899), state senate (1901), presidential elector on Parker-Davis ticket (1904), U.S. Representative (1909 until death), majority leader (1932-1935), speaker (1935 until death) and chairman of the Appropriations Committee. Thus, Byrns was a highly influential congressman who used that influence to bring about passage of much New Deal legislation and was able to boast at the end of the Seventy-third Congress (1934) that the House "in every single instance passed the president's recovery bills."

C

☆ ☆ ☆

CABELL, GEORGE CRAIGHEAD (b Jan. 25, 1836, Davnille, Va.; d June 23, 1906, Baltimore). Newspaper editor, lawyer, Confederate officer, Virginia Democrat Danville commonwealth attorney (1858-1861), U.S. Representative (1875-1887).

CABELL, WILLIAM H. (b Dec. 16, 1772, Cumberland County, Va.; d Jan. 12, 1853, Richmond, Va.) Lawyer, Virginia Democratic-Republican who served as a state legislator (1796-1804), as governor (1805-1808), and then as judge of the state court of appeals for forty years (1811-1851), the last nine of them as president.

CABET, ETIENNE (b Jan. 1, 1788, Dijon, France; d Nov. 8, 1856, St. Louis, Mo.). French lawyer, teacher, author, reformer who contracted to buy a million acres of land on the Red River in Texas to establish a utopian commune, recruited 500 Frenchmen, women, and children to colonize it and arrived only to find they had been cheated by American land speculators. Cabet then leased Nauvoo, a Mormon settlement in Illinois, renamed it Icaria, and was annually elected its president from 1849 until shortly before his death. The name Nauvoo exists today, but not Icaria.

CABOT, GEORGE (b Dec. 16, 1751, Salem, Mass.; d April 18, 1823, Boston, Mass.) Sea captain, merchant, trader, Massachusetts Federalist and adviser to Alexander Hamilton. State provincial congress (1775), delegate to state constitutional convention (1777) and convention ratifying the U.S. Constitution (1787), U.S. Senate (1791-1796), state executive council (1808), presiding officer of Hartford convention (1814).

CADILLAC, ANTOINE DE LA MOTHE (b about 1656, Gascony, France; d Oct. 18, 1730, Gascony) Founder of the French trading post called Detroit (1701), colonial governor of Louisiana (1713-1716).

CAFFERY, DONELSON (b Sept. 10, 1835, St. Mary Parish, La.; d Dec. 30, 1906, New Orleans) Confederate Army officer, sugar planter, lawyer, Louisiana Democrat who was active in the formation of the National (Gold Standard) Democratic party and vigorously opposed war with Spain. State constitutional convention (1879), state senate (1892, 1893), U.S. Senate (1892-1901).

CAIN, RICHARD HARVEY (b April 12, 1825, Greenbrier County, Va.; d Jan. 18, 1887, Washington, D.C.) A black man born of free parents; riverboat worker who studied for the ministry thus launching a career that culminated in service as bishop of the African Methodist Episcopal Church (1880 until death), publisher of *The Missionary*

131

Record, South Carolina Republican. State constitutional convention delegate (1868), state senate (1868-1872), U.S. Representative (1873-1875, 1877-1879).

CAINE, JOHN THOMAS *(b Jan. 8, 1829, Kirk Patrick Parish, Isle of Man; d Sept. 20, 1911, Salt Lake City, Utah).* Teacher, a founder and editor of the *Salt Lake Herald*, Utah Democrat who twice served in Congress as the candidate of the People's party. Secretary of territorial council (1856, 1857, 1859, 1860), constitutional convention delegate (1872, 1882), member of territorial council (1874, 1876, 1880, 1882), Salt Lake City recorder (1876, 1878, 1880, 1882), Utah Territory delegate to Congress (1882-1893) the last two terms (four years) wearing the People's party mantle, unsuccessful Democratic candidate to be the first governor when Utah became a state (1896) and was forced instead to settle for a seat in the first state senate.

CALDER, WILLIAM MUSGRAVE *(b March 3, 1869, Brooklyn, N.Y.; d March 3, 1945, Brooklyn)* Builder, Brooklyn Republican. Borough building commissioner (1902, 1903), delegate to every GOP National Convention from 1908 through 1940, U.S. Representative (1905-1915), U.S. Senate (1917-1923).

CALDERHEAD, WILLIAM ALEXANDER *(b Sept. 26, 1844, Perry County, Ohio; d Dec. 18, 1928, Enid, Oklahoma)* Union soldier, teacher, farmer, lawyer, Kansas Republican. Marshall County prosecutor (1889-1891), U.S. Representative (1895-1897, 1899-1911).

CALDWELL, ALEXANDER *(b March 1, 1830, Drakes Ferry, Pa.; d May 19, 1917, Kansas City, Mo.).* Army freight hauler with 5,000 men in his employ, wagon maker, railroad promoter, banker, land developer, Kansas Republican who served briefly in the U.S. Senate (1871-

1873), resigning as bribery charges were being heard against him.

CALDWELL, JOHN ALEXANDER *(b April 21, 1852, Fairhaven, Ohio; d May 24, 1927, Cincinnati)* Teacher, lawyer, Ohio Republican. U.S. Representative (1889-1894), mayor of Cincinnati (1894-1897), lieutenant governor (1899-1901), common pleas court judge (1902 until death) for a quarter-century.

CALHOUN, JOHN CALDWELL *(b March 18, 1782, near Calhoun Mills in what is now Mount Carmel, S.C.; d March 31, 1850, Washington, D.C.)* Statesman, lawyer, farmer, orator, author who described the U.S. Senate as "a diplomatic corps . . . sent here to protect the states' rights," South Carolina Democrat who was perhaps the South's leading citizen-champion in the first half of the nineteenth century, and the only vice president to resign until Spiro Theodore Agnew on Oct. 10, 1973, but for significantly different reasons: Calhoun chose to leave that second-highest office in the land because of policy differences with the President, Andrew Jackson; Agnew quit after pleading nolo contendere to federal tax evasion charges and being fined $10,000 and placed on three years' probation.

Calhoun's record of elective and appointive public office: state representative, filling his father's former seat (1808, 1809), U.S. Representative (1811-1817), secretary of war (1817-1825), vice president of the United States (1825-1832), U.S. Senate (1832-1843, 1845 until death), secretary of state (1844-1845).

As U.S. Representative he gained a national reputation as a war hawk, standing with Henry Clay and William Lowndes in advocating a policy that led to the War of 1812. As secretary of war he whipped the War Department into an efficient machine, advocated compulsory military service for all, calling the program a "draught"; coauthor of the

Monroe Doctrine. As vice president, he vigorously opposed the Tariff of Abominations, writing his *South Carolina Exposition and Protest* to bolster his case, pushed the cause of nullification so vigorously that President Jackson threatened to hang him "higher than Haman." Resigned to run for the Senate which he considered a more effective base of operations. As senator he took on capitalism as the foe of both the workingman and the farmer, reshaping the Democratic party to stand as a barrier between them and big business and big government but nevertheless endorsing the right of men to own slaves. As secretary of state he was no longer a war hawk, but spoke out for peace and one world, settled the dispute with England over Oregon, brought Texas into the Union.

His *Works of John C. Calhoun*, published posthumously (1854-1857), included *A Disquisition on Government* and the partially finished *A Discourse on the Constitution of the United States.*

CALHOUN, WILLIAM BARRON *(b Dec. 29, 1796, Boston, Mass.; d Nov. 8, 1865, Springfield, Mass.)* Lawyer, Massachusetts Whig. State representative (1825-1834, 1861, 1862), speaker (1829-1834), U.S. Representative (1835-1843), president of state senate (1846, 1847), Massachusetts secretary of state (1848-1851), state banking commissioner (1853-1855), presidential elector on the Clay-Frelinghuysen ticket (1844), mayor of Springfield (1859).

CALL, RICHARD KEITH *(b Oct. 24, 1792, near Petersburg, Va.; d Sept. 14, 1862, Tallahassee, Fla.)* Lawyer, railroad builder, Florida Democrat turned Whig who after many years in public office lived out his years fighting for preservation of the Union in the face of a rising secessionist movement in his state. Territorial council (1822), delegate to the U.S. Congress (1823-1825), territorial governor (1835-1840, 1841-

1844), unsuccessful Whig candidate for governor (1845) when Florida became a state. Uncle of Wilkinson Call.

CALL, WILKINSON *(b Jan. 9, 1834, Russellville, Ky.; d Aug. 24, 1910, Washington, D.C.)* Lawyer, Florida Democrat. Presidential elector for Greeley-Brown (1872) and Tilden-Hendricks (1876), Democratic National Convention delegate (1876), U.S. Senate (1879-1897). Nephew of Richard K. Call.

CALLENDER, JAMES THOMSON *(b 1758, Scotland; d July 17, 1803, Richmond, Va.)* Newspaper reporter and muckraking political writer who was regarded by Thomas Jefferson and others as a champion of liberty who had been unduly persecuted in England before coming to the United States where, as in his native land, he ran afoul of the sedition laws. His writings included *History of the United States for 1796* (1797) and *The Prospect Before Us* (1800).

CALVERT, CHARLES BENEDICT *(b Aug. 24, 1808, Riverdale, Md.; d May 12, 1864, Riverdale)* Farmer, Maryland Whig who, although a U.S. Representative for only one term (1861-1863), was a prime mover in formation of the U.S. Department of Agriculture. Before that he had founded the nation's first agricultural research college, the Maryland Agricultural College, in 1856.

CAMBRELENG, CHURCHILL CALDOM *(b Oct. 24, 1786, Washington, N.C.; d April 30, 1862, Huntington, N.Y.)* Merchant, New York Democrat who served eighteen years as a U.S. Representative (1821-1839) and was considered a somewhat unscrupulous supporter of Presidents Jackson and Van Buren, wielding a heavy hand as chairman of the Ways and Means, Commerce, and Foreign Affairs committees. Van Buren later rewarded him with the ambassadorship to Russia (1840-1841).

CAMERON, JAMES DONALD *(b May 14, 1833, Middletown, Pa.; d Aug. 30, 1918, Lancaster County, Pa.)* Railroad president who aided his father, Simon, in control of the Republican party in Pennsylvania as well as in the conduct of the family's various banking and business interests. His father persuaded President Grant to appoint him secretary of war (1876-1877); he placed federal troops at disposal of GOP bosses in Louisiana and Florida (1877) to help Hayes win their electoral votes; however, Hayes refused to continue him in the cabinet, and his father turned his U.S. Senate seat over to him, where he remained for twenty years (1877-1897). He also eventually succeeded his father as state GOP boss, serving as a national convention delegate (1868, 1876, 1880) and GOP national chairman (1879-1880).

CAMERON, RALPH HENRY *(b Oct. 21, 1863, Southport, Maine; d Feb. 12, 1953, Washington, D.C.).* Mine operator, rancher, Arizona Republican and the man who blazed and built the Bright Angel Trail into the Grand Canyon. Coconino County sheriff (1891, 1894-1898), national convention delegate (1896), chairman of county board of supervisors (1905-1907), U.S. delegate to Congress (1909 until Arizona became a state in 1912), U.S. Senate (1921-1927).

CAMERON, SIMON *(b March 8, 1799, Maytown, Pa.; d June 26, 1889, near Maytown).* Newspaper publisher, business entrepreneur, Pennsylvania Republican leader who left first the Democratic and then the People's party because of his convictions on the issues that led to the Civil War. Father of James Donald Cameron, who was his lieutenant, protégé, and understudy in affairs of both state and politics.

U.S. Senate (1845-1849, 1857-1861, 1867-1877), secretary of war in Lincoln's cabinet (1861-1862) resigning to organize Union forces, minister to Russia briefly in 1862, GOP National Convention delegate (1864), Loyalists' Convention (1866).

CAMP, ALBERT SIDNEY *(b July 26, 1892, Coweta County, Ga.; d July 24, 1954, Bethesda, Md.).* Lawyer, Georgia Democrat. National convention delegate (1924), state representative (1923-1928), U.S. Representative (1939 until death).

CAMPBELL, ALEXANDER *(b 1779, Frederick County, Va.; d Nov. 5, 1857, Ripley, Ohio)* A backwoods country doctor who traveled Ohio, taking an interest in political and civic affairs wherever he opened an office. Democrat turned Whig and vice president (1835) of Ohio's first antislavery society. State representative (1803, 1807-1809, 1819, 1832, 1833), its speaker (1808, 1809, 1819), U.S. Senate (1809-1813), presidential elector on the Monroe-Tompkins Democratic ticket (1820) and the Harrison-Granger Whig ticket (1836), state senate (1822-1824), unsuccessful candidate for governor (1826), mayor of Ripley (1838-1840).

CAMPBELL, ALEXANDER *(b Oct. 4, 1814, Franklin County, Pa.; d Aug. 8, 1898, LaSalle, Ill.)* Foundry superintendent, mine operator, Illinois Independent who was called Father of the Greenback party. Mayor of LaSalle (1852, 1853), state representative (1858, 1859), U.S. Representative (1875-1877).

CAMPBELL, GEORGE WASHINGTON *(b Feb. 9, 1769, Tongue, Sutherlandshire, Scotland; d Feb. 17, 1848, Nashville, Tenn.)* Teacher, lawyer, Tennessee Democrat-Republican who served for six months in 1814 as secretary of the treasury in President Madison's cabinet. U.S. Representative (1803-1809) sitting on tribunal that conducted impeachment proceedings against U.S. Supreme Court Associate Justice Samuel Chase, state appeals court judge (1809-1811), U.S. Senate (1811-1814, 1815-1818), minister to Russia (1818-1821).

CAMPBELL, GUY EDGAR *(b Oct. 9, 1871, Fetterman, W.Va.; d Feb. 17, 1940, Willoughby, Ohio)* Insurance broker, oil and gas producer, Pennsylvania Democrat-Republican who became what today might be called a Washington public relations man-lobbyist but then was called "advisor." U.S. Representative (1917-1933).

CAMPBELL, LEWIS DAVIS *(b Aug. 9, 1811, Franklin, Ohio; d Nov. 26, 1882, Hamilton, Ohio)* Printer, lawyer, farmer, Union Army officer, Ohio Whig who, as minister to Mexico (1866-1867), failed to settle the Maximilian-Juarez dispute. U.S. Representative (1849-1858, 1871-1873), state senate (1869-1870), state constitutional convention delegate (1873).

CAMPBELL, PHILIP PITT *(b April 25, 1862, Cape Breton, Nova Scotia; d May 26, 1941, Washington, D.C.)* Lawyer, Kansas Republican. U.S. Representative (1903-1923), GOP National Convention parliamentarian (1924).

CAMPBELL, TIMOTHY JOHN *(b Jan. 8, 1840, County Cavan, Ireland; d April 7, 1904, New York City)* Printer, lawyer, New York Democrat. State assembly (1868-1873, 1875, 1883), civil court justice (1875-1883), state senate (1884, 1885), U.S. Representative (1885-1889, 1891-1895).

CAMPBELL, WILLIAM BOWEN *(b Feb. 1, 1807, Sumner County, Tenn.; d Aug. 19, 1867, Wilson County, Tenn.)* Lawyer, farmer, banker, Indian fighter, Mexican War hero, briefly a Union Army general, Tennessee's last Whig governor (1851-1853), and an ardent antisecessionist who remained loyal to the Union even after secession yet did not lose his popularity. He was a state representative (1835, 1836), a U.S. Representative (1837-1843), and a fourth circuit judge (1847-1851, 1857)—all before secession. He remained in Tennessee throughout the Civil War, openly advocating a return to the Union and when that finally occurred was elected once again, this time as a Democrat, to the U.S. House of Representatives (1866-1867).

CAMPBELL, WILLIAM W. *(b June 10, 1806, Cherry Valley, N.Y.; d Sept. 7, 1881, Cherry Valley)* Lawyer, author, historian, and an enthusiastic supporter of the American (Know-Nothing) party who used as his campaign slogan "Americans should rule America" and while a U.S. Representative (1845-1847) tried to have naturalized citizens barred from the polling places, this at a time when Irish migration to the United States was at its peak. He also sat on the bench as New York City Superior Court judge (1849-1855) and state sixth district supreme court judge (1857-1865).

CANDLER, ALLEN DANIEL *(b Nov. 4, 1834, Homer, Ga.; d Oct. 26, 1910, Atlanta, Ga.)* Lawyer, manufacturer, railroad president, farmer, teacher, Georgia Democrat, Confederate Army officer who returned from the war with "one wife, one baby, one dollar, and one eye" to hold, among other offices, a U.S. Representative (1883-1891) and governor (1898-1902). His other positions: state representative (1873-1877), state senate (1878, 1879), Georgia secretary of state (1894-1898), compiler of state records (1903 until death).

CANDLER, EZEKIEL SAMUEL, JR. *(b Jan. 18, 1862, Belleville, Fla.; d Dec. 18, 1944, Corinth, Miss.)* Lawyer, Mississippi Democrat. Presidential elector on the Cleveland-Thurman ticket (1888), U.S. Representative (1901-1921), mayor of Corinth (1933-1937).

CANNON, CLARENCE (b April 11, 1879, Elsberry, Mo.; d May 12, 1964, Washington, D.C.) History professor, lawyer, a conservative Missouri Democrat, and parliamentarian of considerable note who first was sent to the U.S. House of Representatives as a member of the Sixty-eighth Congress in 1923 and was still there forty-one years later, a member of the Eighty-eighth Congress at the time of his death. His ties to the House began still earlier, however, as parliamentarian to the Sixty-fourth, Sixty-fifth, and Sixty-sixth Congresses—a period in which he wrote "A Synopsis of the Procedure of the House" (1918), and "Procedure in the House of Representatives" (1920); they, like "Cannon's Procedure," which came eight years later, were reissued through House resolution in 1935 and 1949. Additionally, Cannon was parliamentarian of all Democratic National Conventions from 1920 through 1960, editor-compiler of "Precedents of the House of Representatives," a regent of the Smithsonian Institution, chairman of the Appropriations Committee (where he battled effectively for economy), and member of the Joint Committee on Reduction of Nonessential Federal Expenditures.

CANNON, GEORGE QUAYLE (b Jan. 11, 1827, Liverpool, England; d April 12, 1901, Monterey, Calif.) Mormon missionary, editor of the Deseret News, Mormon leader and polygamist who was expelled from Congress because he practiced polygamy and later went to prison because of his religious beliefs. His case, and others like it, resulted in the manifesto (1890) advising Mormons not to contract "any marriage forbidden by the law of the land." Utah Republican, missionary to California (1849) and Hawaii (1850), U.S. Senate (1862) from the proposed state of Deseret whose admission to the Union was subsequently refused, territorial council (1865, 1866, 1869-1872), U.S.

Representative (1873-1881), his expulsion coming by a 123-79 vote of the House.

CANNON, JOSEPH GURNEY (b May 7, 1836, Guilford, N.C.; d Nov. 12, 1926, Danville, Ill.) Lawyer, Illinois Republican who by virtue of seniority more than ability exerted much influence upon the U.S. House of Representatives and brought the word "Cannonism" into the language as an expression of crudely iron-fisted partisan rule. He was in the House perhaps longer than any other man, but not once did he show a trace of traditional congressional manners; biographers describe him as "uncouth," "foul-mouthed," and "coarse." State's attorney for the twenty-seventh judicial district (1861-1868); U.S. Representative (1873-1891, 1893-1913, 1915-1923) or forty-six years in all, eight of them (1903-1911) as speaker, and holder of such assignments as chairman of the Appropriations Committee; permanent chairman of the GOP National Convention (1904) and recipient of fifty-eight votes for the presidential nomination (1908). It took a coalition of rebel Republicans and Democrats to strip him of some of his power in 1923.

CANNON, MARION (b Oct. 30, 1834, near Morgantown, W.Va.; d Aug. 27, 1920, Ventura, Calif.) Blacksmith, miner, farmer, California People's party Democrat. Nevada County recorder (1869-1871), first state president of the Farmers' Alliance (1890-1892); organizer of California People's party (1891), state representative on the National Supreme Council (1891-1892) and chairman of state delegation to national convention (1892), U.S. Representative (1893-1895).

CANNON, NEWTON (b May 22, 1781, Guilford County, N.C.; d Sept. 16, 1841, Nashville, Tenn.) Planter, Tennessee Democrat, and the state's first Whig governor (1835-1839). State representative (1811-1812), U.S. Representative (1814-1817, 1819-1823), member of U.S. commission to negotiate a treaty with the Chickasaw Indians (1819).

CANNON, RAYMOND JOSEPH *(b Aug. 26, 1894, Ironwood, Mich.; d Nov. 25, 1951, Milwaukee, Wis.)* Professional baseball player, lawyer, Wisconsin Democrat. U.S. Representative (1933-1939), unsuccessful candidate for gubernatorial nomination (1940, 1942).

CANTRILL, JAMES CAMPBELL *(b July 9, 1870, Georgetown, Ky.; d Sept. 2, 1923, Louisville, Ky.)* Farmer, Kentucky Democrat who died while campaigning for governor in the middle of his eighth term as U.S. Representative (1909 until death). Chairman of Scott County Democratic Committee (1895), state representative (1897, 1899), state senate (1901-1905), national convention delegate (1904).

CAPEHART, JAMES *(b March 7, 1847, Point Pleasant, W.Va.; d April 28, 1921, Cocoa, Fla.)* Farmer, stockbreeder, banker, fruitgrower, West Virginia Democrat. President of Mason County Court (1871, 1872, 1880-1885), Democratic National Convention delegate (1888), U.S. Representative (1891-1895).

CAPPER, ARTHUR *(b July 14, 1865, Garnett, Kans.; d Dec. 19, 1951, Topeka, Kans.)* Newspaper and magazine publisher, including *Capper's Weekly*, radio station owner, Kansas Republican who, as a U.S. Senator for thirty years (1919-1949), was leader of the farm bloc. GOP National Convention delegate (1908), governor (1915-1919).

CAPRON, ADIN BALLOU *(b Jan. 9, 1841, Mendon, Mass.; d March 17, 1911, Stillwater, R.I.)* Grain miller and dealer, Union Army officer, Rhode Island Republican. State representative (1887-1892) and speaker (1891, 1892), U.S. Representative (1897-1911).

CARAWAY, HATTIE WYATT *(b Feb. 1, 1878, Bakerville, Tenn.; d Dec. 21, 1950, Falls Church, Va.)* Teacher, Arkansas Democrat who was appointed to fill a vacancy in the U.S. Senate caused by the death of her husband, Thaddeus H. Caraway, on Nov. 13, 1931, and on Jan. 12, 1932, was elected in her own right, thus becoming the nation's first elected woman senator; reelected in 1938, and served until 1945. She remained in Washington, first as a member of the U.S. Employes' Compensation Commission (1945, 1946) and then as a member of the Employes' Compensation Appeals Board (1946 until death).

CARAWAY, THADDEUS HORATIUS *(b Oct. 17, 1871, Stoddard County, Mo.; d Nov. 6, 1931, Little Rock, Ark.).* Teacher, literary agent, farmer, lawyer, and a liberal Arkansas Democrat who did not hesitate to take on the Republican majority in Congress during his tenure, particularly on matters beneficial to agriculture. He was sparing of words, when asked to write his autobiography for the *Congressional Directory* contributing only two: "Democrat, Jonesboro." But, when he needed them, he knew how to use them, particularly in his speeches concerning the Harding administration, the oil scandals and the Teapot Dome affair, bringing about cancellation of naval oil reserve leases.
    Arkansas' second judicial circuit prosecuting attorney (1908-1912), U.S. Representative (1913-1921), U.S. Senate (1921 until death); fought for U.S. entry into the League of Nations, old age pensions and a soldier's bonus; was against lobbying and excessive campaign expenditure. In the forefront of the fight for New Deal legislation. Husband of Hattie W. Caraway.

CAREW, JOHN FRANCIS *(b April 16, 1873, Brooklyn, N.Y.; d April 10, 1951, Rockville Centre, N.Y.)* Lawyer, jurist, New York Democrat. State assembly (1904), Democratic state convention delegate (1912-1924) and national conventions (1912, 1924), U.S. Representative (1913-1929), state supreme court justice (1930 until mandatory retirement in 1943), becoming an official referee until death.

CAREY, JOSEPH MAULL *(b Jan. 19, 1845, Milton, Del.; d Feb. 5, 1924, Laramie, Wyo.)* Lawyer, rancher, Wyoming Progressive Republican who received the Democratic nomination for governor and who, as a territorial delegate to Congress (1885-1890), introduced the bill that permitted Wyoming to become a state and then served as its first U.S. Senator (1890-1895) and championed women's suffrage. U.S. attorney for the territory (1869-1871), associate justice of the territorial supreme court (1871-1876), U.S. Centennial Commissioner (1872-1876), GOP National Committeeman (1876-1897), mayor of Cheyenne (1881-1885), governor (1911-1915), a founder of the Progressive party (1912). Father of Robert D. Carey.

CAREY, ROBERT DAVIS *(b Aug. 12, 1878, Cheyenne, Wyo.; d Jan. 17, 1937, Cheyenne)* Farmer, rancher, banker who followed in his father's (Joseph M. Carey), footsteps as a Wisconsin Progressive Republican. Converse County GOP chairman (1908, 1909), state fair commission president (1909, 1910), Progressive National Committeeman (1912-1916), state highway commission chairman (1917, 1918), governor (1919-1923), GOP National Convention delegate (1924), Coolidge-appointed chairman of U.S. agricultural conference (1924), U.S. Senate (1930-1937).

CARLISLE, JOHN GRIFFIN *(b Sept. 5, 1835, Campbell County, Ky.; d July 31, 1910, New York City)* Teacher, lawyer, newspaper editor, Kentucky Democrat who served in the U.S. cabinet (1893-1897) and was one of the U.S. House of Representatives' outstanding speakers

(1883-1890) but was forced to become an exile from his home state because of his advocacy of sound money principles. State representative (1859-1861), state senate (1866-1871), national convention delegate (1868), lieutenant governor (1871-1875), U.S. Representative (1877-1890), U.S. Senate (1890-1893).

CARMACK, EDWARD WARD *(b Nov. 5, 1858, Sumner County, Tenn.; d Nov. 9, 1908, Nashville, Tenn.)* Lawyer, newspaper editor, Tennessee prohibitionist Democrat and campaigner for good government who was assassinated by antiprohibitionists. Columbia City attorney (1881), state representative (1884), national convention delegate (1896, 1900, 1904), U.S. Representative (1897-1901), U.S. Senate (1901-1907). His statue was placed on the State Capitol grounds.

CARMICHAEL, WILLIAM *(b ——, Queen Annes County, Md.; d Feb. 9, 1795, Madrid, Spain)* Diplomat, Revolutionary secret agent and Congressional courier (1776), and, as secretary to commission that sought French aid, is considered the man most responsible for Lafayette's siding with the Americans. Envoy to Prussia (1776), member of Continental Congress (1778-1780), secretary of Spanish legation (1779), chargé d'affaires at Madrid (1782-1794).

CARNEGIE, ANDREW *(b Nov. 25, 1835, Dunfermline, Scotland; d Aug. 11, 1919, Lenox, Mass.)* An immigrant factory hand who became a multimillionaire steel industrialist, friend of and adviser to presidents, philanthropist who described himself as a "distributor of wealth for the improvement of mankind," and an ardent worker for peace who sought in vain to prevent World War I. Among his monuments are the Pan American Union Building in Washington, D.C., to further hemispheric good will, and the Hague Peace Palace in the Netherlands as the locale for arbitration of international disputes; founder of the Carnegie Endowment for International Peace.

CARONDELET, FRANCISCO LUIS HECTOR, Baron de *(b about 1748, Noyelles, Flanders; d Aug. 10, 1807, Quito, Ecuador)* Spanish governor of West Florida and Louisiana (1791-1797) who built a canal from New Orleans to the Gulf of Mexico, but embarrassed his government by attempting to spread Spanish rule over all of the Mississippi Valley.

CARPENTER, CYRUS CLAY *(b Nov. 24, 1829, Susquehanna County, Pa.; d May 29, 1898, Fort Dodge, Iowa)* Fort Dodge's first schoolteacher, surveyor, farmer, Union Army officer who marched with Sherman to the sea, land broker, Iowa Republican who as governor (1872-1876) called railroad rates "the skeleton in the Iowa corn crib" and passed the Granger Law that regulated them. Webster County surveyor (1856), state representative (1858, 1860, 1884-1886), register of the state land office (1866-1868), second comptroller of the U.S. Treasury (1876-1877), state railroad commissioner (1878), U.S. Representative (1879-1883), Fort Dodge postmaster (1889-1893).

CARPENTER, MATTHEW HALE *(b Dec. 22, 1824, Moretown, Vt.; d Feb. 24, 1881, Washington, D.C.).* Lawyer who successfully represented the government before the Supreme Court in cases arising out of the Reconstruction, a strong supporter of the Union who, as a Wisconsin Democrat (who later turned Radical Republican), stumped for Douglas against Lincoln as the presidential candidate who could prevent secession. Rock County district attorney (1850-1854), U.S. Senate (1869-1875, 1879 until death) and four times chosen the Senate's president pro tem.

CARR, ELIAS *(b Feb. 25, 1839, Edgecombe County, N.C.; d July 22, 1900,*

Edgecombe County) Wealthy planter who was active in the Farmers' Alliance, North Carolina Democrat. As governor (1893-1897) he declared: "An efficient common school system is the only hope for an intelligent, thrifty laboring population upon our farms," called the state's roads a disgrace, and, despite his vast landholdings, advocated realty taxes to pay for both schools and roads.

CARRINGTON, EDWARD *(b Feb. 11, 1748, Goochland County, Va.; d Oct. 28, 1810, Richmond, Va.)* Revolutionary Army officer, Virginia delegate to the Continental Congress (1785, 1786), foreman of the jury at the treason trial of Aaron Burr (1807).

CARROLL (of Carrollton), CHARLES *(b Sept. 19, 1737, Annapolis, Md.; d Nov. 14, 1832, Baltimore, Md.)* Lawyer, Revolutionary leader and signer of the Declaration of Independence, Maryland Federalist. Maryland revolutionary convention delegate (1775), continental commissioner to Canada (1776), member of the Board of War (1776-1777), Continental Congress (1776, 1777, 1778), state senate (1777-1800), U.S. Senate (1789-1792). He was the last signer of the Declaration to die. Cousin of Daniel Carroll.

CARROLL, DANIEL *(b July 22, 1730, Upper Marlboro, Md.; d May 7, 1796, Rock Creek, now Forest Glen, Md.).* Wealthy land owner, Maryland Federalist, and friend of George Washington whom the latter appointed to the commission formed to choose the site of the nation's capital (1791-1795); thus his farm became Washington, D.C. Member of Continental Congress (1780-1784), signer of Articles of Confederation (1781), delegate to federal Constitutional Convention (1787), member of Maryland's first state senate and/or executive council (1788 until death), U.S. Representative (1789-1791). Cousin of Charles Carroll of Carrollton.

CARROLL, JOHN ALBERT *(b July 30, 1901, Denver, Colo.)* Lawyer, Colorado Democrat who served two years (1951, 1952) as a special assistant to President Truman. Assistant U.S. district attorney (1933, 1934), Denver district attorney (1937-1941), Rocky Mountain area attorney for the Office of Price Administration (1942-1943), U.S. Army overseas (1943-1945), U.S. Representative (1947-1951), U.S. Senate (1957-1963).

CARSON, SAMUEL PRICE *(b Jan. 22, 1798, Pleasant Gardens, N.C.; d Nov. 2, 1838, Hot Springs, Ark.)* Farmer, North Carolina Democrat who replanted his roots in Texas. In North Carolina: state senator (1822-1824, 1834), U.S. Representative (1825-1833), state constitutional convention delegate (1835). In Texas: delegate to convention that adopted the republic's constitution (1836), secretary of state of the Republic of Texas (1836-1838), and a commissioner to Washington (1836) to sue for recognition.

CARSS, WILLIAM LEIGHTON *(b Feb. 15, 1865, Pella, Iowa; d May 31, 1931, Duluth, Minn.)* Locomotive engineer from Minnesota who served one term as an independent U.S. Representative (1919-1921), ran unsuccessfully twice as a Democrat, and was elected twice again (1925-1929) on the Farmer-Labor ticket.

CARTER, CHARLES DAVID *(b Aug. 16, 1868, near Boggy Depot, Choctaw Nation, Indian Territory that is now Oklahoma; d April 9, 1929, Ardmore, Okla.)* The son of a stagecoach station operator, he was educated at Indian schools, became, successively, a ranch hand, store clerk, accountant, and a Democrat when Oklahoma became a state and served 10 terms as a U.S. Representative (1907-1927). Chickasaw Nation auditor of public accounts (1892-1894), member of Chickasaw Council (1895), Chickasaw Nation schools superintendent (1897), Indian Territory mining trustee by presidential appointment (1900-1904), secretary of Oklahoma's first Democratic executive committee (1906), state highway commissioner (1927-1929).

CARTER, THOMAS HENRY *(b Oct. 30, 1854, Scioto County, Ohio; d Sept. 17, 1911, Washington, D.C.)* Farmer, teacher, railroad man, lawyer, Republican who became Montana's first U.S. Representative after statehood (1889-1891), and a year later the man whom President Harrison picked to be chairman of the GOP National Committee and to manage his reelection campaign. Territorial delegate to Congress (1889), general land office commissioner (1891-1892), national convention delegate (1896, 1900, 1904), U.S. Senate (1895-1901, 1905-1911).

CARTERET, PHILIP *(b 1639, Isle of Jersey, England; d 1682, East Jersey).* He sailed from England to America, arrived in what is now Elizabeth, N.J., in 1665, became governor of New Jersey colony (1664-1674), convened the first session of its legislature (1668), and when it was divided into two provinces was made the first governor of East Jersey (1676-1682).

CARUTHERS, ROBERT LOONEY *(b July 31, 1800, Smith County, Tenn.; d Oct. 2, 1882, Lebanon, Tenn.)* Lawyer, law professor, newspaper editor, Cumberland University founder, and a Tennessee Whig who was elected governor (1862) but never served because of the occupation of the state by federal forces. State's attorney (1827-1832), state representative (1835), presidential elector on the Clay-Frelinghuysen ticket (1844), U.S. Representative (1841-1843), state supreme court judge (1852-1862), member of abortive peace-seeking convention (1861) that sought to avert the Civil War.

CARVILLE, EDWARD PETER *(b May 14, 1885, Mound Valley, Nev.; d June 27, 1956, Reno, Nev.)* Lawyer, Nevada Democrat. Elko County district attorney (1912-1918), district judge (1928-1934), U.S. attorney for Nevada (1934-1938), governor (1939-1945), U.S. Senate (1945-1947) to fill a vacancy.

CARY, WILLIAM JOSEPH *(b March 22, 1865, Milwaukee, Wis.; d Jan. 2, 1934, Milwaukee)* Telegraph operator, Wisconsin Republican. Milwaukee alderman (1900-1904), Milwaukee County sheriff (1904-1906), U.S. Representative (1907-1919), county clerk (1921-1933).

CASE, FRANCIS HIGBEE *(b Dec. 9, 1896, Everly, Iowa; d June 22, 1962, Bethesda, Md.)* Newspaper editor-publisher, South Dakota Republican. Member of state regents of education (1931-1933), U.S. Representative (1937-1951), U.S. Senate (1951-1962), serving on the Armed Services and Public Works committees. A furor was created in 1956 when he brought charges (resulting in FBI investigation and indictment) of bribery against representatives of oil interests trying to give him $2,500 as a "campaign contribution."

CASEY, JOHN JOSEPH *(b May 26, 1875, Wilkes-Barre Township, Pa.; d May 5, 1929, Balboa, Panama Canal Zone).* Union business agent, Pennsylvania Democrat. State representative (1907-1909), U.S. Representative (1913-1917, 1919-1921, 1923-1925, 1927 until death), member of secretary of labor's advisory council (1918); labor adviser and executive of the labor adjustment division, Emergency Fleet Corporation, U.S. Shipping Board during World War I.

CASS, LEWIS *(b Oct. 9, 1782, Exeter, N.H.; d June 17, 1866, Detroit, Mich.).* Teacher, lawyer, writer, War of 1812 general, statesman, Ohio and Michigan Democrat who numbered among his adversaries Aaron Burr, Daniel Webster, and Martin Van Buren, the last costing him the presidency of the United States (1848) when he ran on the Free-Soil ticket, thus dividing the Democratic votes and giving the victory to the Whig candidate, Zachary Taylor. In Ohio: state representative (1806) and U.S. Marshal (1807-1812). In Michigan: military and civil governor (1813-1831), President Jackson's secretary of war (1831-1836), minister to France (1836-1842), U.S. Senate (1845-1848, 1849-1857), President Buchanan's secretary of state (1857-1860), resigning because of the weak White House position on secession.

CASWELL, LUCIEN BONAPARTE *(b Nov. 27, 1827, Swanton, Vt.; d April 26, 1919, Fort Atkinson, Wis.)* Lawyer, banker, manufacturer, Wisconsin Republican who, in addition to his other functions, served on the Fort Atkinson School Board for sixty-five years. Jefferson County district attorney (1855, 1856), state assembly (1863, 1872, 1874), second district military enrollment commissioner (1863-1865), GOP National Convention delegate (1868), U.S. Representative (1875-1883, 1885-1891).

CATCHINGS, THOMAS CLENDINEN *(b Jan. 11, 1847, Hinds County, Miss.; d Dec. 24, 1927, Vicksburg, Miss.)* Lawyer, Confederate soldier, Mississippi Democrat. State senate (1875-1877), state attorney general (1877-1885), U.S. Representative (1885-1901).

CATT, CARRIE LANE CHAPMAN *(b Jan. 9, 1859, Ripon, Wis.; d Mar. 9, 1947, New Rochelle, N.Y.)* Suffragist and champion of peace. President of the National American Woman Suffrage Association, succeeding Susan B. Anthony (1900-1904, 1915-1920), leading the organization to the climax of its long fight when (1920) the Nineteenth Amendment was ratified. She then helped form the nucleus of the suffrage association into what is now the League of Women

Voters of the United States, with the objective of teaching American women to exercise wisely their newly acquired right to vote. President (1904-1923) of the International Woman Suffrage Alliance, chairman of the Conference on the Cause and Cure of War (1925-1932). In recognition of work for international disarmament, received $5,000 Pictorial Review Award.

CERMAK, ANTON JOSEPH (b May 9, 1873, Kladno, in what is now Czechoslovakia; d March 6, 1933, Miami, Fla., by an assassin's bullet fired at President-Elect Franklin Delano Roosevelt). A Horatio Alger-type businessman-banker who worked himself up from the coal mines and the canal tow paths, became active in Democratic politics in Illinois, was elected mayor of Chicago (1931) and in that capacity was at FDR's side when the assassin struck.

CHAFFEE, JEROME BUNTY (b April 17, 1825, Niagara County, N.Y.; d March 9, 1886, Salem Center, N.Y.) A farm boy who went west, struck it rich as a Colorado mining entrepreneur-banker-real estate dealer, became very active in Republican politics, and, as a delegate to Congress (1871-1875), is credited with being the man who did the most to have the territory admitted to the Union as a state and was rewarded by being chosen U.S. Senator (1876-1879).

CHAMBERLAIN, DANIEL HENRY (b June 23, 1835, West Brookfield, Mass.; d April 13, 1907, Charlottesville, Va.). Lawyer, orator, professor, who went South as an officer in a Massachusetts black regiment during the Civil War, stayed on and became a Republican governor of South Carolina (1874-1876), doing much to stem racial strife. Up for reelection with some Democratic support, both he and his opponent, Wade Hampton, claimed victory and both were sworn in, a situation that necessitated President Hayes's stepping in. Hampton

was declared the winner and Chamberlain went to New York to practice and to teach law at Cornell University.

CHAMBERLAIN, GEORGE EARLE (b Jan. 1, 1854, Adams County, Miss.; d July 9, 1928, Washington, D.C.) Lawyer, teacher, Oregon Democrat who, as chairman of the Senate Committee on Military Affairs during World War I, was sharply critical of the way the War Department was being run, thus bringing down upon himself the wrath of the White House. Linn County deputy clerk (1877-1879), state representative (1880-1882), third judicial district attorney (1884-1886), state attorney general (1891-1894), fourth judicial district attorney (1900-1902), governor (1903-1909) who did much to keep timber lands out of the hands of private interests, U.S. Senate (1909-1921), member of U.S. Shipping Board (1921-1923).

CHAMBERLAIN, JOSHUA LAWRENCE (b Sept. 8, 1828, Brewer, Maine; d Feb. 24, 1914, Portland, Maine) Professor of modern languages, president of Bowdoin College, Union Army officer who was awarded the Congressional Medal of Honor for bravery at Gettysburg, Republican governor of Maine (1867-1871).

CHAMBERS, EZEKIEL (b Feb. 28, 1788, Chestertown, Md.; d Jan. 30, 1867, Chestertown) Lawyer, Maryland Whig-Democrat and a politician who said he did not like politics. State senate (1822), U.S. Senate (1826-1834), second judicial circuit presiding judge and court of appeals judge (1834-1851), declined appointment as secretary of the navy (1852), unsuccessful candidate for governor (1864).

CHAMBERS, JOHN (b Oct. 6, 1780, Bromley Bridge, N.J.; d Sept. 21, 1852, Bourbon County, Ky.) Lawyer, Kentucky Whig who served as presidentially appointed governor of Iowa Territory (1841-1845), gaining renown for his ability to handle Indian affairs. State representative (1812, 1815, 1830, 1831), appeals court judge (1825-1827), U.S. Representative (1828-1829, 1835-1839), Sioux Indian treaty commissioner (1852).

CHAMPION, EPAPHRODITUS *(b April 6, 1756, Colchester, Conn.; d Dec. 22, 1834, East Haddam, Conn.)* Merchant, shipowner, exporter, importer, Revolutionary Army officer, Connecticut Federalist. State assembly (1791-1806), U.S. Representative (1807-1817).

CHANDLER, JOHN *(b Feb. 1, 1762, Epping, N.H.; d Sept. 25, 1841, Augusta, Maine)* Farmer, Revolutionary soldier who settled in the Maine district of Massachusetts after the war and when Maine became a state (1820) was elected U.S. Senator (1820-1829) as a Democrat. Before that he was Massachusetts state senator (1803-1805), U.S. Representative (1805-1809), Kennebec County sheriff, member of the general court (1819), and the Maine constitutional convention (1819-1820).

CHANDLER, JOSEPH RIPLEY *(b Aug. 22, 1792, Kingston, Mass.; d July 10, 1880, Philadelphia, Pa.)* Educator, editor of the *United States Gazette* and other publications, diplomat, philanthropist, and Pennsylvania Whig whose chief interests were prison reform and an end to religious intolerance, his speeches on the latter being published in book form. Philadelphia city council (1832-1848), state constitutional convention (1837), U.S. Representative (1849-1855), minister to the Two Sicilies (1858-1860), delegate to International Prison Congress (1872).

CHANDLER, WILLIAM EATON *(b Dec. 28, 1835, Concord, N.H.; d Nov. 20, 1917, Concord)* Lawyer, New Hampshire Republican who was appointed to high office by three presidents. State representative (1862-1864, 1881), house

speaker (1863, 1864), Lincoln-appointed Navy Department judge advocate general (1865) and first assistant secretary of the treasury (1865-1867), state constitutional convention (1876), Chester Arthur-appointed secretary of the navy (1882-1885), U.S. Senate (1887-1901), McKinley-appointed president of the Spanish Claims Treaty Commission (1901).

CHANDLER, ZACHARIAH *(b Dec. 10, 1813, Bedford, N.H.; d Nov. 1, 1879, Chicago, Ill.)* Teacher, merchant, banker, land dealer, Michigan Whig who helped to found the Republican party and for years was the state's undeniable political boss. As a U.S. Senator (1857-1875, Feb. 22, 1879, until death) he aligned himself with the radical, antislavery wing of the party, urged the fullest possible prosecution of the war against the South, and thought the Reconstruction Act much too lenient. Mayor of Detroit (1851-1852), unsuccessful Whig candidate for governor (1852), chairman of Republican National Executive Committee (1868, 1876).

CHAPMAN, JOHN GRANT *(b July 5, 1798, La Plata, Md.; d Dec. 10, 1856, Charles County, Md.)* Lawyer, planter, Maryland Whig who was president of the party's national convention (1856) in Baltimore. State house of delegates (1824-1832, 1843-1844) and its speaker (1826-1829, 1844), state senate (1832-1836), its president (1833-1836), unsuccessful gubernatorial candidate (1844), U.S. Representative (1845-1849), state constitutional convention president (1851).

CHAPMAN, REUBEN *(b July 15, 1799, Bowling Green, Va.; d May 16, 1882, Huntsville, Ala.).* Lawyer, wealthy planter, conservative Alabama Democrat who attempted ardently but in vain to reconcile the Northern and Southern wings of his party and, for his pains, was burned out and briefly imprisoned by Northern forces during the Civil War. State senator (1832-1835), U.S. Representative (1835-1847), governor (1847-1849), state representative (1855), delegate to Democratic peace convention (1860), Confederate representative to France (1862-1865).

CHAPMAN, VIRGIL MUNDAY *(b March 15, 1895, Middleton, Ky.; d March 8, 1951, Bethesda, Md., of auto-accident injuries.)* Lawyer, law journal editor, Kentucky Democrat. Irvine city attorney (1918-1920), U.S. Representative (1925-1929, 1931-1949), U.S. Senate (1949 until death).

CHAPMAN, WILLIAM WILLIAMS *(b Aug. 11, 1808, Clarksburg, Va.; d Oct. 18, 1892, Portland, Oregon)* Lawyer, Western frontiersman, Democrat. Michigan Territory prosecutor (1836), Wisconsin Territory district attorney (1837-1838), Iowa Territory delegate to Congress (1838-1840) and first Iowa constitutional convention delegate (1844), member of Oregon House of Representatives, a founder of the *Oregonian*, and Oregon surveyor general (1858).

CHASE, DUDLEY *(b Dec. 30, 1771, Cornish, N.H.; d Feb. 23, 1846, Randolph Center, Vt.)* Lawyer, farmer, Vermont Jeffersonian Democrat, and chief justice of the state supreme court (1817-1821) whose nephew, Salmon P. Chase, went him one better by becoming chief justice of the U.S. Orange County prosecutor (1803-1812), state representative (1805-1812, 1823, 1824) and speaker (1808-1812), state constitutional convention delegate (1814, 1822), U.S. Senate (1813-1817, 1825-1831).

CHASE, SALMON PORTLAND *(b Jan. 13, 1808, Cornish, N.H.; d May 7, 1873, New York City)* Teacher, schoolmaster, lawyer, civic reformer of Ohio who wore many political labels (in order: Whig, Democrat, Liberty party, Free-Soil, Free-Soil Democrat, Republican,

Liberal Republican), attained the highest judicial position in the land—Chief Justice of the United States (1864 until death) but never reached the pinnacle he so strongly coveted—the presidency.

A man who was incorruptible; the major reason for his many party mantles was his vigorous opposition to slavery— so much so that he was known as the "attorney general for runaway Negroes." He was a leading voice of the Liberal party, an organizer of both the Free-Soil party and the Anti-Nebraska party, which later became known as the Republican party, which nominated and elected him governor (1856-1860). It was during that period that he made his most vigorous bids for the presidency. But the fact that he was the GOP's most-prominent former Democrat did not help him sufficiently and he failed of nomination both in 1856 and 1860.

As a consolation, he agreed to become secretary of the treasury in Lincoln's cabinet (1861-1864) when he pulled the United States out of virtual bankruptcy by, among other things, issuing greenbacks (federal paper money) and helping to give birth to the National Banking System, which regulated U.S. monetary affairs until the Federal Reserve Act of 1913. However, he never was comfortable in that position, particularly because of his small respect for Lincoln and his deep dislike for Secretary of State William H. Seward, believing that neither prosecuted antislavery and the war against the South with sufficient vigor; in fact, it was Chase who, after many rejections, finally forced Lincoln to permit Negroes to bear arms.

Again in 1864 he sought the GOP presidential nomination only to again lose to Lincoln. Repeatedly before that, Chase had resigned as treasury secretary, repeatedly Lincoln had refused to accept because he wanted contrary viewpoints in his cabinet. But after his humbling for the third time at the nominating convention, Chase tendered his resignation once again, this time to see it accepted. And then Lincoln, upon the death of Chief Justice Roger B. Taney, confounded Chase (and the nation) by appointing him to preside over the Supreme Court; Lincoln's respect for Chase's ability and influence outweighed personal animosity.

Prior to all of that, this was Chase's path up the political ladder: Cincinnati City Council (1840), Liberty party National Convention delegate (1843, 1847), Free-Soil National Convention delegate (1848), U.S. Senator (1849-1855), resigning to become governor, being elected once again in 1861, only to resign two days after being seated to join the Lincoln cabinet.

As a Senator, Chase opposed the Compromise of 1850, fought against the Kansas-Nebraska Act of 1854, and took similarly steadfast positions wherever the issue of slavery (and that was the leading issue of the times) reared its head. Thus, history does not rate Chase as one of the most distinguished chief justices; partly because he had to rule upon many Civil War measures whose enactment he had helped to bring about.

In 1868 Chief Justice Chase presided over the impeachment trial of President Andrew Johnson and, in that same year, once again made a bid for the presidency, this time seeking the Democratic nomination only to lose out to Horatio Seymour. In 1872 he sought the Liberal Republican nomination but his health was too bad to make him a serious contender.

CHASE, SAMUEL *(b April 17, 1741, Princess Anne, Md.; d June 19, 1811, Washington, D.C.)* Lawyer, jurist, Maryland signer of the Declaration of Independence, and a Washington-appointed Associate Justice of the U.S. Supreme Court (1796 until death) who survived impeachment proceedings brought against him (1804) on charges of malfeasance growing out of the manner in which he had conducted two sedition

trials five years earlier (1799) and for a more-recent address to a Maryland grand jury. Tried by the Senate, he was acquitted (March 5, 1805) and returned to the bench. His defense attorney was Joseph Hopkinson of Pennsylvania. Member of the Maryland General Assembly (1764-1784), Continental Congress (1774-1778, 1784, 1785), special emissary to Canada to induce Canadians to join the revolution (1774), special state agent to England (1783) to recover Bank of England stock purchased when Maryland was a colony, Baltimore criminal court judge (1788), state general court judge (1791-1796).

CHAVES, JOSE FRANCISCO *(b June 27, 1833, Padillas, Mexico, now New Mexico; d Nov. 26, 1904, Pinoswell, N.Mex., by assassination)* Physician, rancher, Indian fighter, commander of New Mexico Volunteers who fought on side of Union in Civil War and provided escort for officials sent to organize New Mexico Territory (1863), historian, Republican who contributed much to the achievement of statehood (1912) but was slain eight years before his dream was realized. Territorial delegate to Congress (1865-1867, 1869-1871), member of territorial council (1875 until death) and eight times its president, second judicial district attorney (1875-1877), president of constitutional convention (1889), superintendent of public instruction (1903 until death).

CHAVEZ, DENNIS *(b April 8, 1888, Los Chavez, N.Mex.; d Nov. 18, 1962, Washington, D.C.)* Lawyer, New Mexico Democrat who served in the U.S. Senate more than a quarter-century (1935 until death) where he was chairman of the Public Works Committee and a member of the Appropriations Committee. His introduction to the Senate came while he was both a law student at Washington's Georgetown University and a clerk (1917-1920) in the office of the secretary of the Senate. Upon graduation, he returned home and began practicing law in Albuquerque. State representative (1923, 1924), member of Democratic National Committee (1933-1936), U.S. Representative (1931-1935) when he was appointed a senator to complete the term of Bronson M. Cutting who had died. After that he was reelected five times, the last time to a term that would have expired in 1965.

CHEATHAM, HENRY PLUMMER (b Dec. 27, 1857, Granville County, N.C.; d Nov. 29, 1935, Oxford, N.C.) Educator, farmer, lecturer, Republican who for many years was president of the Negro Association of North Carolina. Principal of the State Normal School at Plymouth (1883-1884), Vance County register of deeds (1884-1888), state convention delegate (1892), GOP National Convention delegate (1892, 1900), U.S. Representative (1889-1893), District of Columbia recorder of deeds (1897-1901), a founder of the North Carolina Colored Orphanage at Oxford (1887) and its superintendent (1907 until death).

CHEETHAM, JAMES (b 1772, Manchester ?, England; d Sept. 19, 1810, New York City) Coming to the United States after brief imprisonment during England's industrial revolution, he became a New York journalist and political pamphleteer who numbered Aaron Burr as one of his enemies and Thomas Paine as a not-very-agreeable acquaintance. His written works include A View of the Political Conduct of Aaron Burr and Life of Thomas Paine; a biographer has described the former work as "vindictive" and the latter as "distorted."

CHELF, FRANK LESLIE (b Sept. 22, 1907, Hardin County, Ky.) Lawyer, Kentucky Democrat. Marion County attorney (1933-1944), U.S. Army Air Corps (1942-1944), Democratic National Convention (1936), U.S. Representative (1945-1967) serving on the Judiciary Committee as well as the Joint Committee on Immigration and Nationality Policy.

CHENEY, EDNAH DOW LITTLEHALE (b June 27, 1824, Boston, Mass.; d Nov. 19, 1904, Jamaica Plain, Mass.) Author, lecturer, organizer, reformer who worked effectively for such causes as antislavery, the Freedman's Aid Society, and women's suffrage.

CHENOWETH, JOHN EDGAR (b Aug. 17, 1897, Trinidad, Colo.) Lawyer, merchant, railroadman, Colorado Republican. Assistant district attorney for third judicial district (1929-1933), Las Animas County judge (1933-1941), U.S. Representative (1941-1949, 1951-1965) serving on the Interior and Insular Affairs and Science and Astronautics committees.

CHEVES, LANGDON (b Sept. 17, 1776, Bulltown Fort, S.C. during a Cherokee Indian attack; d June 26, 1857, Columbia, S.C.) Lawyer, rice grower, president of the Bank of the United States (1819-1822) who put it back on a sound footing, South Carolina Democrat who declined appointments to the U.S. Supreme Court, to the Madison cabinet as secretary of the treasury, and to the U.S. Senate to fill a vacancy.

Charleston alderman (1802), state representative (1802-1810), presidential elector on the Madison ticket (1808), state attorney general (1808), U.S. Representative (1810-1815) succeeding Henry Clay as speaker (1814) and serving as chairman of the Ways and Means and Naval committees; state associate justice of law and appeal (1817-1819).

CHILTON, SAMUEL (b Sept. 7, 1804, Fauquier County, Va.; d Jan. 14, 1867, Warrenton, Va.) Lawyer, Virginia Whig who was appointed to defend John Brown at Harpers Ferry who in turn dismissed him for advising a plea of insanity. U.S. Representative (1843-

1845), state constitutional convention delegate (1850, 1851).

CHINDBLOM, CARL RICHARD *(b Dec. 21, 1870, Chicago, Ill.; d Sept. 12, 1956, Chicago)* Teacher, lawyer, Illinois Republican. GOP state convention delegate (1904, 1908, 1912, 1916), attorney for state board of health (1905, 1906), Cook County commissioner (1906-1910), county attorney (1912-1914), master in chancery (1916-1918), U.S. Representative (1919-1933), U.S. district court referee in bankruptcy (1934-1942).

CHIPERFIELD, ROBERT BRUCE *(b Nov. 20, 1899, Canton, Ill.)* Lawyer, Illinois Republican who served twelve terms as a U.S. Representative (1939-1963); member of Foreign Affairs Committee.

CHITTENDEN, MARTIN *(b March 12, 1763, Salisbury, Conn.; d Sept. 5, 1840, Williston, Vt.)* Farmer, merchant, Vermont Federalist. State representative (1790-1796), Chittenden County judge (1793-1795) and chief justice (1796-1813), U.S. Representative (1803-1813), governor (1814, 1815) who recalled the Vermont militia from New York, contending that it was purely a state force over which federal authorities had no jurisdiction. Son of Thomas Chittenden.

CHITTENDEN, THOMAS *(b Jan. 6, 1730, East Guilford, Conn.; d Aug. 25, 1797, Williston, Vt.)* Farmer, recipient of a land grant in Williston, where he moved and was soon in the forefront of Vermont efforts to gain statehood, becoming its first governor (1778-1797) and the man whom historians call the Father of Vermont. Father of Martin Chittenden.

CHOATE, JOSEPH HODGES *(b Jan. 24, 1832, Salem, Mass.; d May 14, 1917, New York City)* Lawyer, diplomat, a much-in-demand after-dinner speaker and a man of influence in New York Republican circles who did much to arouse the city against Boss Tweed and his Democratic cohorts. He spurned public office for himself but delivered political speeches for political figures beginning with John C. Fremont in 1856 and ending with Charles Evans Hughes in 1916. Ambassador to Great Britain (1899-1905).

CHOATE, RUFUS *(b Oct. 1, 1799, Essex, Mass.; d July 13, 1859, Halifax, Nova Scotia)* Lawyer, with Daniel Webster and others an organizer of the Whig party in Massachusetts, and an orator of considerable note in an age of orators who in an 1855 campaign speech called the infant Republican party "a sectional, anti-Union party." State representative (1825), state senate (1826), U.S. Representative (1831-1834), U.S. Senate (1841-1845) to complete term when Webster resigned, Whig National Convention delegate (1852), state constitutional convention (1853), state attorney general (1853).

CHRISMAN, JAMES STONE *(b Sept. 14, 1818, Monticello, Ky.; d July 29, 1881, Monticello)* Farmer, lawyer, Kentucky Democrat. State constitutional convention (1849), U.S. Representative (1853-1855), representative to First and Second Confederate Congresses (1862-1865), state representative (1869-1871).

CHRISTIANCY, ISAAC PECKHAM *(b March 12, 1812, Johnstown, N.Y.; d Sept. 8, 1890, Lansing, Mich.)* Lawyer, newspaper publisher, Michigan Free-Soiler who helped organize Republican party. Monroe County prosecutor (1841-1846), delegate to national Free-Soil convention (1848), unsuccessful candidate for governor (1852), state senate (1850-1852), delegate to first GOP National Convention (1856), associate judge of state supreme court (1858-1875), serving as chief justice (1872,

1873), U.S. Senate (1875-1879), minister to Peru (1879-1881).

CHRISTIANSON, THEODORE *(b Sept. 12, 1883, Lac qui Parie County, Minn.; d Dec. 9, 1948, Dawson, Minn.)* Lawyer, teacher, editor-publisher, manufacturer, public relations counselor nationally for retail grocers and retail druggists, Minnesota Republican. Dawson village counsel president (1910, 1911), state representative (1915-1925), governor (1925-1931), U.S. Representative (1933-1937).

CHRISTOPHER, GEORGE HENRY *(b Dec. 9, 1888, Bates County, Mo.; d Jan. 23, 1959, Washington, D.C.)* Farmer, Missouri Democrat. U.S. Representative (1949-1951, 1955 until death), assistant to director of Agricultural Conservation Program (1951-1952).

CHRISTOPHERSON, CHARLES ANDREW *(b July 23, 1871, Amherst Township, Minn.; d Nov. 2, 1951, Sioux Falls, S.Dak.)* Lawyer, banker, South Dakota Republican. Sioux Falls board of education (1908-1918), state representative (1912-1916), U.S. Representative (1919-1933), GOP state convention delegate (1938, 1940, 1942), GOP National Convention delegate (1944).

CHURCH, MARGUERITE STITT *(b Sept. 13, 1892, New York City)* Teacher, psychologist, lecturer, writer, widow of Ralph E. Church whom she succeeded in Congress, Illinois Republican. U.S. Representative (1951-1963) serving on the Foreign Affairs Committee. Participant, through presidential invitation, in 1960 White House Conference on Children and Youth.

CHURCH, RALPH EDWIN *(b May 5, 1883, Vermillion County, Ill.; d March 21, 1950, in Washington, D.C., while testifying before the House Committee on Expenditures in the Executive Department)* Lawyer, husband of Marguerite S. Church, Illinois Republican. State representative (1916-1932), U.S. Representative (1935-1941, 1943 until death), delegate to Interparliamentary Conference in Norway (1939).

CHURCHILL, THOMAS JAMES *(b March 10, 1824, Jefferson County, Ky.; d March 10, 1905, Little Rock, Ark.)*. Confederate general, Arkansas Democrat who served as state treasurer (1874-1880) and governor (1880-1882) in whose treasury accounts a $233,000 shortage was discovered, a fact that he blamed upon faulty bookkeeping.

CILLEY, JONATHAN *(b July 2, 1802, Nottingham, N.H.; d Feb. 24, 1838, near Washington, D.C., in a duel with Congressman William J. Graves of Kentucky)* Lawyer, newspaper editor, New Hampshire Jacksonian Democrat. State representative (1831-1836) and house speaker (1835, 1836), U.S. Representative (1837 until death).

CLAFLIN, WILLIAM *(b March 6, 1818, Milford, Mass.; d Jan. 5, 1905, Newton, Mass.)* Shoe manufacturer, Massachusetts Free-Soiler turned Republican who served on the GOP National Executive Committee for eleven years (1864-1875), four of them as chairman (1868-1872). State senate (1860, 1861) and its president (1861), lieutenant governor (1866-1868), governor (1869-1871), U.S. Representative (1877-1881). On one occasion while in Missouri on business, he bought a slave at auction and immediately set him free; he was Massachusetts' first governor to advocate women's voting rights and he created the state's first bureau of labor statistics.

CLAGETT, WYSEMAN *(b August, 1721, Bristol, England; d Dec. 4, 1784, Litchfield, N.H.)* Lawyer and king's attorney for New Hampshire (1765-1769) who cast his lot with the colonists and became active in affairs of the provincial congresses. Member of the Committee and Council of Public Safety (1776-1778), special justice of the superior court (1778-1781), New Hampshire's first and only solicitor general (1778-1784).

CLAGUE, FRANK *(b July 13, 1865, Warrensville, Ohio; d March 25, 1952, Redwood Falls, Minn.).* Teacher, lawyer, farmer, Minnesota Republican. Redwood County prosecutor (1895-1903), state representative (1903-1907) and speaker (1905), state senate (1907-1915), ninth judicial district judge (1919-1920), U.S. Representative (1921-1933).

CLAIBORNE, JOHN FRANCIS HAMTRAMCK *(b April 24, 1809, Natchez, Miss.; d May 17, 1884, near Natchez).* Newspaper editor, author, historian, Mississippi Democrat who at the age of twenty-five was elected to the U.S. House of Representatives (1835-1838) where, despite his brief stay due to illness, he gained a reputation as an orator who was not afraid to take on his elders in debate. He had already left his mark on the state legislature, having been elected a representative at the age of twenty-one (served 1830-1834). Son of Nathaniel Claiborne.

CLAIBORNE, NATHANIEL HERBERT *(b Nov. 14, 1777, Chesterfield, Va.; d Aug. 15, 1859, near Rocky Mount, Va.).* Farmer, Virginia Republican who gained a reputation as the unofficial watchdog of the state treasury and campaigner for government economy. Member state house of delegates (1810-1812), member of state executive council during War of 1812, state senate (1821-1825), U.S. Representative (1825-1837). Brother of William and father of John Claiborne.

CLAIBORNE, WILLIAM CHARLES COLE *(b 1775, Sussex County, Va.; d Nov. 23, 1817, New Orleans, La.)* Lawyer, Jef-

fersonian Democrat turned National Republican who left his political mark upon the states of Tennessee and Louisiana and the territories of Orleans and Mississippi.

In Tennessee: delegate to state constitutional convention (1796), superior court judge (1796-1797), U.S. Representative (1797-1801) although he was not yet twenty-five when elected. In Mississippi: presidentially appointed territorial governor (1801-1805) where (1803) he was given double duty with selection as a commissioner to take possession of the newly purchased Louisiana from the French. In Orleans: presidentially appointed territorial governor (1804-1812) where he and General Andrew Jackson could not agree on how best to defend New Orleans during the War of 1812. In Louisiana: the new state's first governor (1812-1816), and he was elected a U.S. Senator (1817) but died before the Congress convened.

Brother of Nathaniel Claiborne.

CLAPP, MOSES EDWIN *(b May 21, 1851, Delphi, Ind.; d March 6, 1929, near Accotink, Va.)* Lawyer, Minnesota Republican. St. Croix County, Wis., prosecutor (1878-1880), Minnesota attorney general (1887-1893), unsuccessful gubernatorial candidate (1896), U.S. Senate (1901-1917), staying on in Washington to practice law.

CLARK, ABRAHAM *(b Feb. 15, 1726, near what is now Elizabeth, N.J.; d Sept. 15, 1794, Rahway, N.J.).* Farmer, surveyor, lawyer and New Jersey signer of the Declaration of Independence who fought for inclusion of the Bill of Rights in the U.S. Constitution. Prior to 1774 he was the crown's high sheriff of Essex County and clerk of the Colonial Assembly, but he threw his support wholeheartedly into the Revolutionary cause, becoming first a member of the Committee on Public Safety and then its secretary (1775-1776). As a member of the Continental Congress (1776-

1778, 1779-1783, 1787-1789) he became known as "Congress Abraham" and rounded out his career by being sent to the Second and Third Congresses (1791 until death).

CLARK, CHAMP (see James Beauchamp Clark).

CLARK, CLARENCE DON (b April 16, 1851, Sandy Creek, N.Y.; d Nov. 18, 1930, Evanston, Wyo.) Lawyer, teacher, Wyoming Republican. Uinta County prosecutor (1882-1884), GOP National Convention delegate (1888, 1900, 1904, 1908, 1912), state constitutional convention delegate (1889), U.S. Representative (1890-1893), U.S. Senate (1895-1917), member International Joint Commission over water boundaries with Canada (1919-1929) and chairman of U.S. delegation (1923-1929).

CLARK, DANIEL (b Oct. 24, 1809, Stratham, N.H.; d Jan. 2, 1891, Manchester, N.H.) Teacher, lawyer, orator and New Hampshire Republican who used all of his debating skills to fight slavery and secession while a U.S. Senator (1857-1866). President of state constitutional convention (1876), federal judge for New Hampshire district (1866 until death).

CLARK, DAVID WORTH (b April 2, 1902, Idaho Falls, Idaho; d June 19, 1955, Los Angeles, Calif.) Lawyer, banker, radio station operator, Idaho Democrat. Assistant state attorney general (1933-1935), U.S. Representative (1935-1939), U.S. Senate (1939-1945).

CLARK, FRANK (b March 28, 1860, Eufaula, Fla.; d April 14, 1936, Washington, D.C.) Lawyer, Florida Democrat. Barton city attorney (1885, 1886), state representative (1889-1891, 1899), assistant U.S. attorney (1893), U.S. attorney for southern Florida district (1894-1897), state convention delegate (1888, 1890, 1892, 1896, 1900), state

Democratic chairman (1900), U.S. Representative (1905-1925), chairman of state delegation to national convention (1920), Coolidge-appointed Democratic member of U.S. Tariff Commission (1928-1930), Bureau of Internal Revenue attorney (1933 until death).

CLARK, JAMES (b Jan. 16, 1770, Bedford County, Va.; d Sept. 27, 1839, Frankfort, Ky.) Lawyer, Kentucky Clay Democrat turned Whig. State representative (1807-1808), appeals court judge (1810), U.S. Representative (1813-1816, 1825-1831), circuit court judge (1817-1824), state senate (1831-1835), governor (1836 until death).

CLARK, JAMES BEAUCHAMP "CHAMP" (b March 7, 1850 near Lawrenceburg, Ky., d March 2, 1921, Washington, D.C.). Newspaper editor, college president, lawyer, Missouri Democrat who was a leader in the revolt against House Speaker Joseph Cannon and succeeded him in that position (1911-1919), but who is best remembered for his spectacular battle for the presidential nomination (1912), leading all of his opponents for twenty-nine ballots, gaining a clear majority on eight of them but never able to gain the necessary two-thirds with the result that Woodrow Wilson became the compromise Democratic nominee.

City attorney of both Bowling Green and Louisiana, Mo., (1878-1881), presidential elector on the Hancock-English ticket (1880), Pike County prosecutor (1885-1889), state representative (1889, 1891), delegate to the Trans-Mississippi Congress (1891), U.S. Representative (1893-1895, 1897 until death) and minority leader (1907-1911), serving on the Foreign Affairs and Ways and Means committees; Democratic National Convention chairman (1904). His funeral services were held in the hall of the House. Father of Joel B. Clark.

CLARK, JEROME BAYARD (b April 5, 1882, Bladen County, N.C.; d Aug. 26,

1959, Fayetteville, N.C.) Lawyer, banker, North Carolina Democrat. State representative (1915), presidential elector on the Wilson-Marshall ticket (1916), state Democratic committeeman (1909-1919), member of state judicial conference (1924-1928), U.S. Representative (1929-1949).

CLARK, JOEL BENNETT "CHAMP" *(b Jan. 8, 1890, Bowling Green, Mo.; d July 13, 1954, Gloucester, Mass.)* Lawyer, author, World War I officer, jurist and, like his father, Champ Clark, a Missouri Democrat. Parliamentarian of U.S. House of Representatives (1913-1917), Democratic National Convention parliamentarian (1916) and delegate (1920, 1936, 1940), U.S. Senate (1933-1945), Smithsonian Institution regent (1940-1944), associate justice of the U.S. Court of Appeals for the District of Columbia (1945 until death).

CLARK, MYRON HOLLEY *(b Oct. 23, 1806, Naples, N.Y.; d Aug. 23, 1892, Canandaigua, N.Y.)*. Cabinetmaker, hardware merchant, New York Whig who was elected governor (1855-1856) as the candidate also of the Free Democracy, Anti-Nebraska, and Temperance parties and out of that coalition is said to have sprung the state's Republican party.

CLARK, WILLIAM *(b Aug. 1, 1770, Caroline County, Va.; d Sept. 1, 1838, St. Louis, Mo.)* Explorer of Lewis and Clark expedition fame who, after mapping the northern part of the Louisiana Purchase and finding a route to the Pacific, became governor of the Missouri Territory and superintendent of Indian affairs (1813-1820), both by presidential appointment.

CLARK, WILLIAM ANDREWS *(b Jan. 8, 1839, Connellsville, Pa.; d March 2, 1925, New York City)* Teacher, lawyer, mine laborer who acquired a fortune in various Montana mining, bank-

ing, and railroad enterprises and conducted a long feud with Marcus Daly for control of the Democratic party there. State constitutional convention president (1884, 1889), U.S. Senate (1901-1907) after previously being elected (1899) but not seated because of alleged voting frauds.

CLARKE, JAMES PAUL *(b Aug. 18, 1854, Yazoo City, Miss.; d Oct. 1, 1916, Little Rock, Ark.)* Lawyer, Arkansas Democrat who as a U.S. Senator (1903 until death) broke with his party over Panama Canal legislation and was given by Theodore Roosevelt a large share of the credit for its passage. State representative (1886-1888), state senate (1888-1892) and its president (1891), state attorney general (1892-1894), governor (1894-1896).

CLAY, CASSIUS MARCELLUS *(b Oct. 19, 1810, Madison County, Ky.; d July 22, 1903, Madison County)*. Distant relative of Henry Clay, a fierce foe of slavery and publisher of an abolitionist newspaper in Lexington, Ky., was run out of town and resumed publication in Cincinnati and Louisville. He was a founder of Kentucky's Emancipation party (1849), an early Republican, and ambassador to Russia (1861-1862).

CLAY, CLEMENT CLAIBORNE *(b Dec. 13, 1816, Huntsville, Ala.; d Jan. 3, 1882, Huntsville)* Lawyer, planter, Alabama Democrat who supported states' rights, was held without charge for a year as a plotter in Lincoln's assassination and then released without being brought to trial. He had surrendered voluntarily, riding 170 miles to do so, when he heard rumor of his involvement; died a broken man, protesting he had not had a chance to vindicate himself.

State representative (1842, 1844, 1845), county court judge (1846-1848), presidential elector on the Pierce-King ticket (1852), U.S. Senate (1853-1861) withdrawing to sit in the Confederate

Senate (1861-1863); member of secret Southern mission to arrange peace with the North, spending a year (1864-1865) in Canada in a vain effort to arrange safe-passage to Washington. Son of Clement Comer Clay.

CLAY, CLEMENT COMER *(b Dec. 17, 1789, Halifax County, Va.; d Sept. 9, 1866, Huntsville, Ala.)* Lawyer, Indian fighter, jurist, Alabama Democrat. Alabama territorial council (1817, 1818), circuit court judge (1819) and chief justice (1820-1823), state representative (1827, 1828) serving as speaker, U.S. Representative (1829-1835), governor (1835-1837), U.S. Senate (1837-1841), associate state supreme court judge (1843), and codifier of the laws of Alabama. Father of Clement Claiborne Clay.

CLAY, HENRY *(b April 12, 1777, Hanover County, Va.; d June 29, 1852, Washington, D.C.)* Lawyer, land speculator, three times a presidential candidate, Kentucky Jeffersonian Democrat turned Whig who did not hesitate to take firm positions on vital issues, yet, during his years in Congress, was known as the Great Compromiser and was considered one of the great statesmen of the pre-Civil War period. His entry into politics at the age of twenty-two was a ringing denunciation (1798) of the Alien and Sedition Acts; in 1806 he was appointed to fill a vacancy in the U.S. Senate although he was below the qualifying age of thirty-one.

State representative (1803, 1808, 1809) and its speaker in the last year, U.S. Senate (Nov. 19, 1806-March 3, 1807, Jan. 4, 1810-March 3, 1811, 1831-1842, 1849 until death), U.S. Representative (1811-1814, 1815-1821, 1823-1825) and speaker (1811-1814, 1815-1820, 1823-1825), a negotiator for peace with Great Britain (1814) although he had been the foremost hawk in War of 1812, John Quincy Adams' secretary of state (1825-1829), Whig presidential candidate (1824, 1832, 1844) receiving in the last year 105 electoral votes to James Polk's 170 and 1,300,097 popular votes to Polk's 1,338,464.

Some highspots in his career: successfully defended Aaron Burr (1806) in a Kentucky treason trial but never again spoke to him; architect of the "American System," a program for defense, transportation, and high protective tariffs; drafter of the Missouri Compromise (1820) by which Missouri entered the Union as a slave state, Maine entered as a free state and slavery was banned from then on in any new states north of 36°30'.

CLAY, MATTHEW *(b March 25, 1754, Halifax County, Va.; d May 27, 1815, Halifax Court House, Va.)* Revolutionary Army officer, Virginia Democrat. State house of delegates (1790-1794), U.S. Representative (1797-1813) serving sixteen years in a time when Congressmen seldom served more than one or two terms, was reelected to a ninth term (1815) but served only two months until death.

CLAYTON, HENRY De LAMAR *(b Feb. 10, 1857, Barbour County, Ala.; d Dec. 21, 1929, Montgomery, Ala.)* Lawyer, jurist, Alabama Democrat. Presidential elector for Cleveland-Thurman (1888) and Cleveland-Stevenson (1892), state representative (1890, 1891), U.S. attorney for middle Alabama district (1893-1896), permanent chairman of Democratic National Convention (1908), U.S. Representative (1897-1914), U.S. judge in Alabama's middle and northern districts (1914 until death).

CLAYTON, JOHN MIDDLETON *(b July 24, 1796, Dagsboro, Del.; d Nov. 9, 1856, Dover, Del.)* Lawyer, Delaware National Republican turned Whig. State representative (1824), Delaware secretary of state (1826-1828), U.S. Senate (1829-1836, 1845-1849, 1853 until death). Delaware's chief justice (1837-1839), secretary of state in President Taylor's

cabinet (1849-1850) where he nego-
tiated the Clayton-Bulwer treaty with
Great Britain which allowed the United
States to build a canal across Central
America. Nephew of Joshua Clayton.

CLAYTON, JOSHUA *(b July 20, 1744,
Bohemia Manor, Del.; d Aug. 11, 1798,
Philadelphia, Pa.)* Physician, Revolutionary Army officer, and Delaware's
first governor (1793-1796). Provincial
Congress delegate (1782-1784), state
representative (1785, 1787), president
of Delaware (1789-1793), U.S. Senate
(Jan. 19, 1798, until death seven months
later. Uncle of John M. Clayton).

CLAYTON, POWELL *(b Aug. 7, 1833,
Bethel, Pa.; d Aug. 25, 1914, Washington,
D.C.)* Civil engineer, Union army general and carpetbagger who relocated in
Arkansas (1865), became a planter,
promoter of the Reconstruction constitution (1868), and Republican boss for
the rest of his active life. He was
elected governor (1868-1871) during
which time the state house of representatives voted to impeach him for corrupt financial practices but the senate
dropped the charge. His other contributions to political life were membership
in the GOP National Committee, U.S.
Senate (1871-1877), GOP National Convention delegate (1872, 1896), ambassador to Mexico (1897-1905).

CLEMENTS, JUDSON CLAUDIUS *(b
Feb. 12, 1846, Villanow, Ga.; d June 18,
1917, Washington, D.C.)* Lawyer, Confederate Army officer, Georgia Democrat who became chairman of the Interstate Commerce Commission (1911
until death) after having been a member
since 1892. Walker County school commissioner (1871, 1872), state representative (1872-1876), state senate (1877-
1880), U.S. Representative (1881-1891).

CLEVELAND, CHAUNCEY FITCH *(b
Feb. 16, 1799, Canterbury, Conn.; d June
6, 1887, Hampton, Conn.)* Lawyer, Con-

necticut Democrat-War Republican-Democrat who as governor (1842-1844)
refused to extradite Thomas W. Dorr,
leader of Rhode Island's Dorr Rebellion, to face treason charges, contending that the man was a political
refugee. Between 1826 and 1866 he was
twelve times a state representative and
three times the house speaker, state's
attorney (1832), bank commissioner
(1838), U.S. Representative (1849-
1853), GOP National Convention delegate (1856, 1860), presidential elector
on Lincoln-Hamlin ticket (1860), delegate to peace convention (1861) that
tried to avert Civil War.

CLEVELAND, STEPHEN GROVER *(b
Mar. 18, 1837, Caldwell, N.J.; d June 24,
1908, Princeton, N.J.)* Twenty-second
and twenty-fourth president (New York
Democrat), 1885-1889, 1893-1897. Independent enemy of machine politics
strongly opposed by Tammany Hall; New
York governor.

Son of a Presbyterian clergyman who
moved his family (1841) to Fayetteville,
N.Y., then (1850) to Clinton where
(1853) he died. Grover clerked in a
general store, worked for the New York
Institution for the Blind, then headed
west to seek his fortune. He got as far
as Buffalo where he remained with an
uncle, obtaining a job as clerk in a law
office. He studied law and was admitted
to the bar in 1859. Partly because of
his widowed mother's need of his financial assistance, Cleveland (as was the
custom of the time) hired a substitute
when drafted for Civil War service. He
was an outdoorsman who liked to hunt
and fish and who remained a bachelor
until 1886 when, in a White House wedding, he married Frances Folsom who
was many years his junior. They had
five children.

Erie County assistant district attorney (1863), sheriff, "veto mayor" of
Buffalo (1882), reform governor (1883-
1884), incurring the enmity of Tammany
Hall and cooperating with assemblyman

Theodore Roosevelt in campaign for New York City municipal reform.

Cleveland's clean government record won him the presidential nomination at the 1884 Democratic Convention and the support of reform Republicans (the "mugwumps") who were unhappy over the nomination of James G. Blaine as their party's candidate. Blaine supporters gave the newspapers a story accusing Cleveland of being the father of an illegitimate child (Cleveland admitted the story's truth) and the tone was set for the mud-slinging campaign that followed. Cleveland might have lost the election had not one of Blaine's supporters antagonized many voters by referring to the Democrats as the party of "rum, Romanism, and rebellion." The results gave Cleveland 219 electoral votes against Blaine's 182. Running for reelection (1888), Cleveland received more popular votes than his Republican opponent, Benjamin Harrison, but lost the election, 168 to 233 electoral votes. The next time around (1892), he won the election 277-145, again running against Benjamin Harrison.

As president Cleveland tried to lower the tariff; remained independent, supporting the Civil Service Commission, and refused to knuckle under to party machine politics; vetoed many individual veterans' pension bills he considered invalid; suffered through the panic of 1893 (during which time he secretly underwent a successful operation for cancer of the jaw). He opposed inflation; split the party by his opposition to the silver Democrats during his second term; claiming interference with U.S. mails, Cleveland broke the Pullman strike of 1894 (led by Eugene V. Debs) by sending in troops, using federal injunctions, and arresting the leaders; enlarged the scope of the Monroe Doctrine by his firmness in the boundary dispute (1895) between Great Britain and Venezuela.

Retired to Princeton, N.J.; trustee of Princeton University; one of three men selected (1905) to reorganize the Equitable Life Assurance Society; prepared autobiographical essays (later printed as *Presidential Problems*) that he delivered as lectures.

CLEVENGER, CLIFF *(b Aug. 20, 1885, Brown County, Nebr.; d Dec. 13, 1960, Tiffin, Ohio)* Merchant, farmer, stockman, Ohio Republican who was a U.S. Representative for twenty years (1939-1959).

CLIFFORD, NATHAN *(b Aug. 18, 1803, Rumney, N.H.; d July 25, 1881, Cornish, Maine)* Singing teacher, lawyer, diplomat, Maine Democrat who was U.S. attorney general in Polk cabinet (1846-1848) and Buchanan-appointed associate justice of the U.S. Supreme Court (1858 until death).

State representative (1830-1834), house speaker (1832-1834), state attorney general (1834-1838), U.S. Representative (1839-1843), minister to Mexico (1848-1849) when treaty that made California part of the United States was negotiated.

CLINGMAN, THOMAS LANIER *(b July 27, 1812, Huntsville, N.C.; d Nov. 3, 1897, Morganton, N.C.)* Lawyer, explorer of North Carolina mountains, Confederate general. Southern Whig, and a moderate on slavery whose distrust of the motives of Northern Whigs drove him into the ranks of the Democratic party. North Carolina House of Commons (1836), state senate (1840), U.S. Representative (1843-1845, 1847-1858), U.S. Senate (1858-1861), Democratic National Convention delegate (1868).

CLINTON, DeWITT *(b March 2, 1769, Napanock, N.Y.; d Feb. 11, 1828, Albany, N.Y.)* Lawyer, historian, patron of the arts, humanitarian, Jeffersonian Democrat, a War of 1812 dove, James Madison's Peace party opponent for the presidency (1812), and the man who saw the Erie Canal through from dream to reality. New York City mayor (1803-1807, 1810, 1811, 1813, 1814) and New York governor (1817-1821, 1825 until death).

A leading politician-statesman of his time, he also served as private secretary to his uncle, Governor George Clinton (1790-1795); state assembly (1798), state senate (1798-1802, 1806-1811), state constitutional convention delegate (1801), member of Council of Appointments (1801, 1802, 1806, 1807), U.S. Senate (1802-1803) resigning to successfully run for the mayoralty, lieutenant governor from 1811 to 1813.

CLINTON, GEORGE *(b July 26, 1739, Little Britain, N.Y.; d April 20, 1812, Washington, D.C., while vice president, a position he had held since 1804 and under both Presidents Jefferson and Madison)* Lawyer, Revolutionary period leader, Continental Army general, a vigorous Anti-Federalist who fought against adoption of the federal Constitution for reasons he set forth in the *New York Journal's* famous Cato letters of 1787. Although considered a radical, he was seven times elected governor of New York (1777-1795, 1801-1804) as a States' Rights Democrat.

Ulster County district attorney (1765), state assembly (1768, 1800, 1801), N.Y. Committee of Correspondence member (1774), Continental Congress (1775-1776), president of the state convention that ratified the Constitution, an act he accepted gracefully since it already had won the ratification of a sufficient number of states for passage. He believed the Constitution would cause New York to lose many of its advantages to smaller states and, as one biographer put it, he "preferred to remain the most powerful citizen of New York rather than occupy a subordinate place under a national government in which his own state was not foremost." Uncle of DeWitt Clinton.

CLOPTON, DAVID *(b Sept. 29, 1820, Putnam County, Ga.; d. Feb. 5, 1892, Montgomery, Ala.)* Lawyer, Confederate soldier, and Alabama States' Rights Democrat who took the lead in the fight against carpetbaggers. His reward: nomination to the state house of representatives without his knowledge or consent. The reason he wasn't consulted: in both the U.S. and Confederate Congresses he had developed a distaste for legislative duties, preferring the quiet of the bench. U.S. Representative (1859-1861) resigning when Alabama seceded, Confederate Representative (1862-1864), state representative and speaker (1874), state supreme court judge (1884 until death).

CLOPTON, JOHN *(b Feb. 7, 1756, New Kent County, Va.; d Sept. 11, 1816, New Kent County)* Planter, lawyer, Revolutionary Army officer, Virginia Democrat who served twenty years in Congress. State house of delegates (1789-1791), U.S. Representative (1795-1799, 1801 until death). Virginia Privy Council (1799-1801).

CLYMER, GEORGE *(b March 16, 1739, Philadelphia, Pa.; d Jan. 23, 1813, Morrisville, Pa.)* Merchant, banker, Pennsylvania Federalist, signer of both the Declaration of Independence and the U.S. Constitution, and a key man in the financing of the Revolution. Member of Continental Congress (1776-1778, 1780-1783), state representative (1785-1788), federal Constitutional Convention delegate (1787), member of the First Congress (1789-1791). One of his financial chores was straightening out General Washington's commissary affairs.

COBB, AMASA *(b Sept. 27, 1823, Crawford County, Ill.; d July 5, 1905, Los Angeles, Calif.)* Miner, lawyer, Union Army general, Wisconsin and Nebraska Republican. In Wisconsin: Iowa County district attorney (1850-1854), state senate (1855, 1856), state adjutant general (1855-1858), state assembly (1860) and its speaker (1861), U.S. Representative (1863-1871). In Nebraska: mayor of Lincoln (1873), associate state supreme court justice (1878-1892) including four years as chief justice.

COBB, HOWELL *(b Sept. 7, 1815, Jefferson County, Ga.; d Oct. 9, 1868, New York City)* Lawyer, member of the wealthy planter class that dominated Southern political life in the pre-Civil War period, Confederate Army general, speaker of the U.S. House of Representatives during Henry Clay's Missouri Compromise debate. Georgia Democrat but a moderate who sided with the Unionists, thus becoming leader of what became known as Cobb Democrats who formed a Constitutional Union party coalition with Whigs and elected him governor by the largest majority ever given anyone up to that time. Nevertheless, when all efforts to hold the Union together failed, Cobb advocated immediate secession. Seriously considered for the presidency of the Confederacy but was not so chosen largely because of his lack of military know-how.

His political milestones include presidential elector on the Van Buren-Johnson ticket (1836), western Georgia judicial circuit solicitor general (1837-1841), U.S. Representative (1843-1845, 1855-1857) and speaker (1849-1851), governor (1851-1853), secretary of the treasury in the Buchanan cabinet (1857-1860), chairman of secessionist state convention that formed a Confederate government (1861).

COBB, THOMAS WILLIS *(b 1784, Columbia County, Ga.; d Feb. 1, 1830, Greensboro, Ga.)* Georgia lawyer. U.S. Representative (1817-1821, 1823-1824), U.S. Senate (1824-1828) resigning to become a state superior court judge (1828 until death).

COBB, WILLIAMSON ROBERT WINFIELD *(b June 8, 1807, Rhea County, Tenn; d Nov. 1, 1864, near Bellefontaine, Ala.).* Merchant, cotton grower, Alabama Democrat. U.S. Representative (1847-1861) resigning when Alabama seceded, elected to Confederate Congress (1863) but for unknown reasons did not take his seat.

COBBETT, WILLIAM *(b March 6, 1763, Farnham, Surrey, England; d June 18, 1835, Guildford, England)* Political pamphleteer, book store proprietor, journalist, farmer, author who wrote under the pseudonym "Peter Porcupine," twice fled England for America, bringing his biting pen along with him. His stays here, in Philadelphia, Pa. (1792-1800) and New Hyde Park, Long Island, N.Y., (1817-1819) were brief but he left his mark, publishing both *Porcupine's Gazette* and *Daily Advertiser* while in Pennsylvania and *The Rush-Light* while in New York and becoming loved by the Federalists and hated by the Democratic-Republicans. One of the forerunners of politically partisan journalism in the United States.

COCHRAN, CHARLES FREMONT *(b Sept. 27, 1846, Kirksville, Mo.; d Dec. 19, 1906, St. Joseph, Mo.)* Newspaper editor-publisher in Atchison, Kans., and St. Joseph, Mo., lawyer, Democrat. In Kansas: Atchison County prosecutor (1880-1884). In Missouri: U.S. Representative (1897-1905).

COCHRAN, JOHN JOSEPH *(b Aug. 11, 1880, Webster Groves, Mo.; d March 6, 1947, St. Louis, Mo.)* Newspaperman, lawyer, secretary to various U.S. Congressmen and Senators, Missouri Democrat. Clerk to the Senate Foreign Relations Committee (1917, 1918), U.S. Representative (1926-1947).

COCHRANE, JOHN *(b Aug. 27, 1813, Palatine, N.Y.; d Feb. 7, 1898, New York City)* Lawyer, Union Army general,

New York Democrat who flirted with the Free-Soil Movement, became first a Republican Unionist and then a Liberal Republican, and who (1864) ran for vice president with presidential candidate John C. Fremont, both withdrawing when their campaign did not attract sufficient support; he then backed Lincoln with whom he had had previous disagreements; ultimately returned to the Democratic ranks.

U.S. Representative (1857-1861) as a States' Rights Democrat, Democratic National Convention delegate (1860), chairman of Independent Republican National Convention that nominated him and Fremont (1864), state attorney general (1863-1865), sixth district internal revenue collector (1869), Liberal Republican National Convention (1872), leader of Tammany Hall (1889).

COCKE, JOHN *(b 1772, Brunswick, Va.; d Feb. 16, 1854, Rutledge, Tenn.)* Lawyer, farmer, Indian fighter, founder of school for deaf mutes, Tennessee representative (1796, 1797, 1807, 1809, 1812, 1837) and house speaker (1812, 1837), state senate (1799-1801, 1843), U.S. Representative (1819-1827).

COCKE, WILLIAM *(b 1747, Amelia County, Va.; d Aug. 22, 1828, Columbus, Miss.)* Lawyer, frontiersman who explored with Daniel Boone, Indian fighter who handed them a crushing defeat (1776) at Cocke's Fort, Tenn., officeholder in Virginia, Tennessee, Kentucky, North Carolina, and Mississippi. In Virginia: member of house of burgesses. In Tennessee: state constitutional convention delegate (1796), U.S. Senate (1796-1797, 1799-1805), first circuit judge (1809-1811). In Mississippi: member of territorial legislature (1813), then appointed Chickasaw Nation Indian agent (1814) by President James Madison. In Kentucky: member of house of delegates of short-lived Transylvania colony. In North Carolina: state legislator.

An orator but a poor grammarian, a man who tried (1784-1788) with others to form some of North Carolina's western counties into a state that would be called Franklin. He helped draft its constitution, he sat in its legislature, and he was chosen its delegate to the U.S. Congress. Father of John Cocke.

COCKRAN, WILLIAM BOURKE *(b Feb. 28, 1854, County Sligo, Ireland; d March 1, 1923, Washington, D.C.)* School principal, lawyer, orator of considerable note, and a maverick New York Democrat who did not hesitate to split with his party (he stumped for the opposition's William McKinley in 1896 and Theodore Roosevelt in 1912) over issues such as free silver and the conduct of Tammany Hall but always returning to the fold (he delivered Alfred Smith's nominating speech at the 1920 Democratic National Convention).

Spokesman for the anti-Tammany Irving Hall Democracy at the 1881 state convention but two years later Tammany's choice as counsel to the sheriff; U.S. Representative (1887-1889, 1891-1895, 1904-1909, 1921 until death), national convention delegate (1884, 1892, 1904, 1920), at the 1884 session delivering a blistering denunciation of Grover Cleveland that was heard above a thundering rainstorm at two o'clock in the morning.

COCKRELL, FRANCIS MARION *(b Oct. 1, 1834, Warrensburg, Mo.; d Dec. 13, 1915, Washington, D.C.)* Lawyer, Confederate general, Missouri Democrat who served thirty years (1875-1905) in U.S. Senate. Member of Interstate Commerce Commission (1905-1910), commissioner to reestablish boundary between Texas and New Mexico (1911), civilian member of War Department's Ordnance Board (1912 until death).

CODD, GEORGE PIERRE *(b Dec. 7, 1869, Detroit, Mich.; d Feb. 16, 1927, Detroit)* Lawyer, Michigan Republican who held many civic offices in Detroit including mayor (1905, 1906). Assistant city attorney (1894-1897), alderman (1902-1904), GOP National Convention delegate (1908), Wayne County circuit judge (1911-1921, 1924 until death), U.S. Representative (1921-1923).

COGSWELL, WILLIAM *(b Aug. 23, 1838, Bradford, Mass.; d May 22, 1895, Washington, D.C.)* Lawyer, Union Army general, Massachusetts Republican. Mayor of Salem (1867-1869, 1873, 1874), state representative (1870, 1871, 1881-1883), state senate (1885, 1886), GOP National Convention delegate (1892), U.S. Representative (1887 until death).

COHEN, JOHN SANFORD *(b Feb. 26, 1870, Augusta, Ga.; d May 13, 1935, Atlanta, Ga.)* New York and Georgia newspaperman, politically influential editor of the *Atlanta Journal*, which together with the *New York Herald* sponsored a national highway connecting New York City and Jacksonville, Fla., Georgia Democrat who supported William G. McAdoo for presidential nomination in 1924 and Franklin D. Roosevelt in 1932. National committee member (1924 until death) and its vice chairman (1932 until death), U.S. Senate to fill an unexpired term (1932-1933).

COKE, RICHARD *(b March 13, 1829, Williamsburg, Va.; d May 14, 1897, Waco, Texas)* Lawyer, Confederate officer, Texas Democrat who was removed from the state supreme court bench by General Sheridan for being "an impediment to reconstruction." District judge (1865), supreme court judge (1866-1867), governor (1874-1877), U.S. Senate (1877-1895).

COLDEN, CADWALLADER *(b Feb. 7, 1688, Ireland; d Sept. 28, 1776, Long Island, N.Y.)* Philosopher, scientist, author who migrated to Philadelphia (1710), then moved to New York (1718) where he became a Loyalist leader who

would not countenance opposition to the Stamp Act or other rebellions, yet managed to maintain his equilibrium while holding public office. Surveyor general (1720), Governor's Council (1721), lieutenant governor (1761 until death).

COLE, CORNELIUS *(b Sept. 17, 1822, Lodi, N.Y.; d Nov. 3, 1924, Hollywood, Calif.)* Lawyer, miner in the California gold rush of 1849, Union Army officer, California Republican who on June 27, 1922, close to his 100th birthday, visited Washington, D.C., and addressed the U.S. House of Representatives where he had served (1863-1865) before becoming a U.S. Senator (1867-1873). Sacramento City and County district attorney (1859-1862), GOP National Committeeman (1856-1860).

COLE, CYRENUS *(b Jan. 13, 1863, Marion County, Iowa; d Nov. 14, 1939, Washington, D.C.)* Newspaperman, author, Iowa Republican. U.S. Representative (1921-1933).

COLE, WILLIAM PURINGTON, JR. *(b May 11, 1889, Towson, Md.; d Sept. 22, 1957, Baltimore, Md.)* Civil engineer, lawyer, Maryland Democrat. U.S. Representative (1927-1929, 1931-1942), U.S. Customs Court judge (1942-1952), U.S. Court of Customs and Patent Appeals judge (1952 until death).

COLEMAN, WILLIAM *(b Feb. 14, 1766, Boston, Mass.; d July 14, 1829, New York City)* Lawyer, editor-proprietor of the *New York Evening Post*, and Federalist journalist who supported Alexander Hamilton, permitting Hamilton to dictate editorials. After Hamilton's death he became increasingly nonpartisan.

COLES, EDWARD *(b Dec. 15, 1786, Albemarle County, Va.; d July 7, 1868, Philadelphia, Pa.)* Son of a wealthy planter, private secretary to President

Madison (1809-1815), an abolitionist who, when his father died leaving him the plantation and all of its slaves, he set the slaves free and took them with him on an Ohio River boat to Illinois where he relocated largely because it was a free state. He became Illinois' second governor (1822-1826), running as a Democratic Republican; fought to stamp out the slavery that, although illegal, was being widely practiced.

COLFAX, SCHUYLER (b March 23, 1823, New York City; d Jan. 13, 1885, Mankato, Minn.) Newspaper editor, lecturer, Indiana Whig turned Republican, and vice president during the Grant administration (1869-1873). Whig National Convention delegate (1848, 1852), state constitutional convention delegate (1850), U.S. Representative on the GOP ticket (1855-1869).

COLLAMER, JACOB (b Jan. 8, 1792, Troy, N.Y.; d Nov. 9, 1865, Woodstock, Vt.) Lawyer, Vermont Whig turned Republican. State representative (1821, 1822, 1827, 1828), Windsor County state's attorney (1822-1824), superior court judge (1833-1842, 1850-1854), U.S. Representative as a Whig (1843-1849), postmaster general in Taylor cabinet (1849-1850), U.S. Senate as a Republican (1855 until death).

COLLIER, JAMES WILLIAM (b Sept. 28, 1872, Warren County, Miss.; d Sept. 28, 1933, Washington, D.C.) Lawyer, Mississippi Democrat who served virtually a quarter-century as a U.S. Representative (1909-1933), state representative (1896-1899), member of U.S. Tariff Commission (1933 until death).

COLLINS, PATRICK ANDREW (b March 12, 1844, County Cork, Ireland; d Sept. 13, 1905, Hot Springs, Va.) Lawyer, orator, Massachusetts Democrat who as an immigrant boy in New England during the Know-Nothing period learned the meaning of intolerance and fought it

throughout his political life. State representative (1868, 1869), state senate (1870, 1871), judge advocate general (1875), Democratic National Convention delegate (1876, 1880, 1888, 1892), U.S. Representative from 1883 until 1889 when, as he put it, he made good his escape; consul general in London (1893-1897), mayor of Boston (1902-1905).

COLMAN, LUCY NEWHALL (b July 26, 1817, Sturbridge, Mass.; d Jan. 18, 1906, Syracuse, N.Y.) Teacher who achieved integration of the "colored" school in Rochester, N.Y., in pre-Civil War days; antislavery lecturer sympathetic to the women's rights cause.

COLQUITT, ALFRED HOLT (b April 20, 1824, Monroe, Ga.; d March 26, 1894, Washington, D.C.) Lawyer, preacher, orator, Confederate Army officer, farmer, and as extreme a pro-Southern Georgia Democrat as his father, U.S. Senator Walter T. Colquitt, before him. As governor (1876-1882) he functioned so high-handedly that he made enemies of his allies while fighting reconstruction and carpetbaggers; his reelection campaign of 1880 was one of the most bitter in state history. U.S. Representative (1853-1855), state representative (1859), presidential elector for Breckinridge and Lane (1860), member of state secession convention (1861), U.S. Senate (1883 until death).

COLQUITT, WALTER TERRY (b Dec. 27, 1799, Halifax County, Va.; d May 7, 1855, Macon, Ga.) Lawyer, preacher, Georgia States' Rights Whig who became a Van Buren Democrat. State senator (1834, 1837), U.S. Representative (March 4, 1839–July 21, 1840), resigning rather than support William Henry Harrison for the presidency, switching his political affiliation and returning to the House to complete a vacancy (Jan. 3, 1842-March 3, 1843); U.S. Senate (1843-1848), member of the Nashville Convention (1850). Father of Alfred Holt Colquitt.

COLTON, CALVIN *(b Sept. 14, 1789, Longmeadow, Mass.; d March 13, 1857, Savannah, Ga.)* Minister who gave up the cloth to become an author and journalist; political pamphleteer who wrote under the name of Junius, largely in support of Whig policies. He was also Henry Clay's official biographer and, perhaps, ghost writer.

COLTON, DON BYRON *(b Sept. 15, 1876, Juab County, Utah; d Aug. 1, 1952, Salt Lake City)* Teacher, lawyer, farmer, sheep raiser, businessman, Utah Republican. GOP state convention delegate (1914-1924), state senate (1915-1917), GOP National Convention delegate (1904, 1924, 1928), U.S. Representative (1921-1933), unsuccessful candidate for U.S. Senate (1934) and governor (1940).

COMEGYS, JOSEPH PARSONS *(b Dec. 29, 1813, Kent County, Del.; d Feb. 1, 1893, Dover, Del.)* Lawyer and chief justice of the Delaware Supreme Court (1876 until death), Delaware Whig. Served six years as a state representative (1842-1848) and two months as a U.S. Senator (1856-1857) to fill a vacancy, declining all further offers to run for elective office. Delegate to Constitutional Union National Convention (1860) and Union National Convention (1866).

COMER, BRAXTON BRAGG *(b Nov. 7, 1848, Barbour County, Ala.; d Aug. 15, 1927, Birmingham, Ala.)* Planter, merchant, banker, cotton manufacturer, Alabama Democrat. President of state railway commission (1905, 1906), governor (1907-1911), U.S. Senate to fill vacancy caused by death of John H. Bankhead (March–November 1920).

COMINGO, ABRAM *(b Jan. 9, 1820, Mercer County, Ky.; d Nov. 10, 1889, Kansas City, Mo.)* Lawyer, Missouri

Democrat who served on presidentially appointed commission (1881) to arbitrate with Sioux Indians for possession of Dakota lands abutting the Black Hills. U.S. Representative (1871-1875).

COMSTOCK, ELIZABETH L. *(b Oct. 30, 1815, Maidenhead, Berkshire, England; d Aug. 3, 1891, Union Springs, N.Y.).* Eloquent Quaker who lectured for prison reform, women's rights, temperance, and the abolition of slavery; during the Civil War she comforted soldiers in hospitals and prison camps, helped slaves gain their freedom, and later helped to provide the temporary relief needed for the liberated slaves.

CONARD, JOHN *(b Nov. 1773, Chester Valley, Pa.; d May 9, 1857, Philadelphia, Pa.)* Lawyer, Pennsylvania Democrat whose advocacy of the War of 1812 earned him the soubriquet The Fighting Quaker. U.S. Representative (1813-1815), U.S. marshal for state's eastern district under Presidents Monroe, Adams, and Jackson.

CONBOY, SARA AGNES McLAUGHLIN *(b Apr. 3, 1870, Boston, Mass.; d Jan. 7, 1928)* Labor leader who, though a woman, was accepted into the inner councils of the American labor movement; worked effectively for legislation to protect children and women in industry.

CONDICT, LEWIS *(b March 3, 1772, Morristown, N.J.; d May 26, 1862, Morristown)* Physician, railroad president, New Jersey Anti-Federalist Whig. Morris County sheriff (1801-1803), state assembly (1805-1809, 1837, 1838 and four times speaker), U.S. Representative (1811-1817, 1821-1833), president of state medical society (1816, 1819), presidential elector on Harrison-Tyler ticket (1840).

CONDIT, JOHN *(b July 8, 1755, Orange, N.J.; d May 4, 1834, Orange).*

Physician, sportsman, Revolutionary Army surgeon, New Jersey Democrat of whom one biographer said: "Few men have served twenty years in Congress so inconspicuously." State general assembly (1788, 1789), U.S. Representative (1799-1803, 1819), U.S. Senate (1803-1817).

CONGER, EDWIN HURD (*b March 7, 1843, Knox County, Ill.; d May 18, 1907, Pasadena, Calif.*) Lawyer, stockman, banker, farmer, diplomat, Iowa Republican. Dallas County treasurer (1877-1881), state treasurer (1881-1885), U.S. Representative (1885-1890); minister to Brazil (1890-1893), to China (1898-1905), and to Mexico (1905).

CONGER, OMAR DWIGHT (*b April 1, 1818, Cooperstown, N.Y.; d July 11, 1898, Ocean City, Md.*) Lawyer, Michigan Republican. St. Clair County judge (1850), state senate (1855-1859), GOP National Convention delegate (1864, 1889), Lincoln-Johnson presidential elector (1864), state constitutional convention (1866), U.S. Representative (1869-1881), U.S. Senate (1881-1887).

CONKLING, ALFRED (*b Oct. 12, 1789, Amagansett, N.Y.; d Feb. 5, 1874, Oneida, N.Y.*) Lawyer, jurist, author, lecturer, New York and Nebraska Democrat but held no official position while in latter state. In New York: Montgomery County prosecutor (1818-1821), U.S. Representative (1821-1823), U.S. district judge (1825-1852), ambassador to Mexico (1852-1853). His written works included *Powers of the Executive Department of the United States* which had five printings, the first in 1866. Father of Frederick A. and Roscoe Conkling.

CONKLING, FREDERICK A. (*b Aug. 22, 1816, Canajoharie, N.Y.; d Sept. 18, 1891, New York City*) Merchant, Union officer, banker, insurance executive, writer, historian, philanthropist, New York Republican who served one term as a U.S. Representative (1861-1863) while also serving in the army. Son of Alfred and brother of Roscoe Conkling.

CONKLING, ROSCOE (*b Oct. 3, 1829, Albany, N.Y.; d April 18, 1888, New York City*) Corporation lawyer, campaign orator, New York Whig turned Union Republican whose control of federal patronage made him the state's undisputed GOP boss until President Garfield made appointments without consulting him and thus his foremost intrastate enemy, James G. Blaine, became U.S. secretary of state. Blaine's description of Conkling: "The finest torso in public life, a man of haughty disdain, of grandiloquent swell, of majestic, supereminent, overpowering turkey-gobbler strut."

Oneida County district attorney (1850), mayor of Utica (1858), U.S. Representative (1859-1863, 1865-1867), U.S. Senate (1867-1881) resigning over the appointment of Blaine and New York Customs House employees, going back before the state legislature for reelection only to be turned down. Thus came Conkling's retirement from politics, even to the refusal of Garfield's placating appointment (1882) as associate justice of the U.S. Supreme Court. Son of Alfred and brother of Frederick A. Conkling.

CONN, CHARLES GERARD (*b Jan. 29, 1844, Phelps, N.Y.; d Jan. 5, 1931, Los Angeles, Calif.*) Newspaper publisher, band instrument manufacturer, Union Army officer who was awarded the Congressional Medal of Honor, Indiana Democrat. Mayor of Elkhart (1880-1883), state representative (1889), U.S. Representative (1893-1895).

CONNALLY, THOMAS TERRY (*b Aug. 19, 1877, McLennan County, Texas; d Oct. 28, 1963, Washington, D.C.*) Lawyer, debater of considerable note, diplomat who played an important role in the creation of the United Nations and for nearly a half-century a leading Texas Democrat who served twelve years (1917-1929) as a U.S. Representative and twenty-four years (1929-1953) in the U.S. Senate.

Democratic National Convention delegate (1920, 1932, 1936, 1940, 1948) serving as chairman of state delegation (1936) and vice chairman (1948), chairman of state convention (1938), Interparliamentary Union delegate (1924, 1930, 1934, 1948), Empire Parliamentary Association delegate (1943), special Congressional advisor to the U.S. delegation to the Inter-American Conference on Problems of War and Peace (1945), vice chairman of U.S. delegation to the United Nations Conference on International Organization at San Francisco (1945), and U.S. representative to the first and second sessions of the UN General Assembly, advisor to the secretary of state at meetings of Council of Foreign Ministers at Paris and New York and the Paris Peace Conference (1946), delegate to the Inter-American Conference for the Maintenance of Continental Peace and Security (1947).

CONNERY, LAWRENCE JOSEPH *(b Oct. 17, 1895, Lynn, Mass.; d Oct. 19, 1941, Arlington, Va.)* Reporter on the *Lynn Item*, merchant mariner, secretary to his brother, Representative William P. Connery, Jr., lawyer, printer-stationer, Massachusetts Democrat who became a congressman upon William's death (1937) and served until his own death.

CONNERY, WILLIAM PATRICK, JR. *(b Aug. 24, 1888, Lynn, Mass.; d June 15, 1937, Washington, D.C.)* Actor, candy manufacturer, Massachusetts Democrat. U.S. Representative (1923 until death) who was succeeded by his brother, Lawrence J. Connery.

CONNOLLY, JAMES JOSEPH *(b Sept. 24, 1881, Philadelphia, Pa.; d Dec. 10, 1952, Philadelphia)* Real estate operator, transit investor, Pennsylvania Republican who was financial secretary of Philadelphia's GOP committee and seven terms a U.S. Representative (1921-1935).

CONNOR, HENRY WILLIAM *(b Aug. 5, 1793, Prince George County, Va.; d Jan. 6, 1866, Beatties Ford, N.C.).* Planter, Indian fighter, North Carolina Democrat. U.S. Representative (1821-1841), state senate (1848-1850).

CONRAD, CHARLES MYNN *(b Dec. 24, 1804, Winchester, Va.; d Feb. 11, 1878, New Orleans, La.)* Lawyer, Louisiana Jacksonian Democrat turned Whig over the Bank of the United States issue. U.S. Senate to fill a vacancy (1842-1843), state constitutional convention delegate (1844), U.S. Representative (1849-1850), secretary of war in the Fillmore cabinet (1850-1853), delegate to Provisional Confederate Congress (1861), member of Confederate Congress (1862-1864).

CONRAD, HOLMES *(b Jan. 31, 1840, Winchester, Va.; d Sept. 4, 1916, Winchester)* Teacher, law professor and lecturer, Confederate Army officer, leading member of the Virginia bar, and a leader in state Democratic affairs. Virginia legislator (1878-1882), assistant U.S. attorney general (1893-1895).

CONRAD, ROBERT TAYLOR *(b June 10, 1810, Philadelphia, Pa.; d June 27, 1858, Philadelphia)* Pennsylvania lawyer who showed far more interest in journalism, poetry, and playwriting, contributing many successful dramas to the American theater; also served as the Whig and Know-Nothing coalition mayor of Philadelphia (1854-1856) and criminal court judge.

CONRY, JOSEPH ALOYSIUS *(b Sept. 12, 1868, Brookline, Mass.; d June 22, 1943, Washington, D.C.)* Lawyer, Massachusetts Democrat who was decorated by the Russian czar. President of Boston Common Council (1896-1897), chairman of the board of aldermen (1898), U.S. Representative (1901-1903), consul of Russia (1912-1919) during which time Nicholas II honored him, special attorney for the U.S. Maritime Commission (1938-1939).

CONRY, MICHAEL FRANCIS *(b April 2, 1870, Shenandoah, Pa.; d March 2, 1917, Washington, D.C.)* Coal miner who was crippled in a mine accident, became a teacher and lawyer, moved to New York City and became active in Democratic affairs, serving as an assistant corporation counsel until going to Washington as a U.S. Representative (1909 until death).

CONWAY, JAMES SEVIER *(b Dec. 9, 1798, Greene County, Tenn.; d March 3, 1855, Lafayette County, Ark.)* A contractor who went west to survey government lands in the Arkansas Territory (1820) and by the time statehood was achieved (1836) was the owner of a large cotton plantation and more than 100 slaves. Active in Democratic-Republican (Democratic) politics, he became the state's first governor (1836-1840) and, according to one biographer, allowed a "piratical crew of fortune seekers to scuttle the financial fame of the state." Fortunately for Arkansas, his brother, Elias Nelson Conway, became the new governor (1852-1860) and straightened out the monetary mess.

CONWAY, MARTIN FRANKLIN *(b Nov. 19, 1827, Harford County, Md.; d Feb. 15, 1882, Washington, D.C.)* Printer who helped organize the National Typographical Union, then studied law, practiced in Kansas (1853) where he became both an active worker for statehood and agent for the Massachusetts Abolition Society; Kansas Republican.

Member of first legislative council (1854) and free state convention (1855), chief justice of the provisional

government's supreme court (1856, 1857), state constitutional convention president (1858); then, when statehood was achieved, U.S. Representative (1861-1863); member of abortive peace convention to avert Civil War (1861), U.S. consul at Marseille, France (1866-1869).

COOK, BURTON CHAUNCEY *(b May 11, 1819, Pittsford, N.Y.; d Aug. 18, 1894, Evanston, Ill.)* Lawyer, Illinois Republican who seconded Lincoln's nomination at the 1860 GOP presidential convention and nominated him for reelection in 1864. Ninth judicial district state's attorney (1846-1852), state senate (1852-1860), member of ill-fated peace convention that tried to avert Civil War (1861), U.S. Representative (1865-1871).

COOK, DANIEL POPE *(b 1794, Scott County, Ky.; d Oct. 16, 1827, Scott County)* Lawyer, Illinois newspaper editor, political figure for whom Cook County was named and the state's first attorney general (1819). U.S. Representative (1819-1827), President Adams' emissary to Cuba (1827) to report on political conditions there.

COOLEY, HAROLD DUNBAR *(b July 26, 1897, Nashville, N.C.; d Jan. 15, 1974, Wilson, N.C.).* North Carolina Democrat. Navy flyer in World War I, lawyer, Roosevelt-Garner presidential elector (1932) and a liberal, internationally minded U.S. Representative for more than thirty years (1934-1967) who for more than two decades was chairman of the House Agriculture Committee; a man so well liked by his tobacco-farmer constituents that he won reelection in 1956, the same year in which he refused to sign the Southern manifesto against racial integration. Delegate to Interparliamentary Conference in Cairo (1947) and Rome (1948) and a staunch advocate of foreign aid and reciprocal trade.

COOLIDGE, CALVIN *(b July 4, 1872, Plymouth Notch, Vt.; d Jan. 5, 1933, Northampton, Mass.)* Vice president (Massachusetts Republican) 1921-1923, until becoming thirtieth president, 1923-1929, after the death of President Harding; a man whose puritanical ethics were in contrast to the prevailing moral values during the jazz-age times of his administration, evidenced by such things as the open flaunting of Prohibition regulations and widespread stock market speculation; governor of Massachusetts.

Born John Calvin (he later dropped the first name), Coolidge was the son of a shrewd, hardworking storekeeper-farmer who also was a politician and a member of the Vermont legislature; his mother died when he was twelve years old. Attended the local school, Black River, and St. Johnsbury academies, and (1895) graduated from Amherst College, Amherst, Mass.; read law with a Northampton, Mass., firm, was admitted to the Massachusetts state bar (1897), and opened his own office in Northampton where he practiced law until 1919. Married Grace Anna Goodhue (1905) who taught at the Clarke School for the Deaf in Northampton. They had two sons, the younger of whom, Calvin, died (1924) while Coolidge was president.

Member of Northampton City Council (1899-1900); city solicitor and clerk of county courts; member state legislature (1907-1908, 1912-1915), serving as president of the senate for two terms; mayor of Northampton (1910-1911); lieutenant governor (1916-1918); governor (1919-1920) when his handling of the Boston police strike brought him nationwide publicity (he called out the state guard and, in reply to Samuel Gompers' criticism, stated: "There is no right to strike against the public safety by anybody, anywhere, at any time."). At the 1920 GOP National Convention, members of the convention rebelled and named Coolidge, rather than the choice of the political bosses,

to be Harding's running mate in an election the Republicans won with ease. After Harding's death in 1923, Coolidge became president, inheriting the Teapot Dome and other scandals from his predecessor's administration. At the convention of 1924, he was nominated on the first ballot, winning the election with 382 electoral votes against 136 for Democratic candidate John W. Davis and 13 for Progressive Robert M. La Follette.

As president Coolidge reflected his personal conviction that "the business of America is business," deferring to big business while twice vetoing legislation affording relief for farmers. Although times in general were prosperous, there can be little doubt that some of the seeds of the Great Depression were sown in the good years of the "roaring twenties." Coolidge chose not to run in 1928 and returned to Northampton where he wrote his *Autobiography* and (1930-1931) a series of syndicated newspaper articles.

COOPER, HENRY ALLEN *(b Sept. 8, 1850, Spring Prairie, Wis.; d March 1, 1931, Washington, D.C.)* Lawyer, Wisconsin Republican who served thirty-six years (1893-1919, 1921 until death) as a U.S. Representative. Racine County district attorney (1880-1886), GOP National Convention delegate (1884, 1908, 1924), state senator (1887-1889), and author of Wisconsin's Australian secret ballot law. (An Australian ballot is one printed at public expense, distributed only at the polling place, and is marked in secret.)

COOPER, HENRY ERNEST *(b Aug. 28, 1857, New Albany, Ind.; d May 14, 1929, Long Beach, Calif.)* Lawyer, California walnut grower who migrated to Hawaii (1891), was a leader (1893) in the successful revolt against the monarchy of Queen Liliuokalani, became minister of foreign affairs (1895-1900) of the Republic of Hawaii, was in the forefront of the movement for annexation by the United States, and was the first secretary (1900-1903) of the Territory of Hawaii. Called the Mark Hanna of Hawaii, other positions he filled (some of them simultaneously) in the provisional, republic, and territorial governments that followed the revolution were acting president, acting governor, superintendent of public instruction, chairman of the committee of safety, and, lastly before retirement, Oahu circuit court judge (1910-1914).

COOPER, JERE (b July 20, 1893, Dyer County, Tenn.; d Dec. 18, 1957, in U.S. Naval Hospital, Bethesda, Md.) Lawyer, Tennessee Democrat who was elected a U.S. Representative for fifteen consecutive terms (1929 until death). Dyersburg councilman and city attorney (1920-1928).

COOPER, JOHN (b Feb. 5, 1729, Gloucester County, N.J.; d April 1, 1785, Woodbury, N.J.) New Jersey patriot. Member of Gloucester County committee on correspondence (1774), Provincial Congress (1775, 1776) serving on committee that drafted New Jersey's first constitution, western New Jersey division treasurer (1775-1776), member of legislative council (1776-1780, 1784), Continental Congress (1776), Council of Safety (1778), county judge of the pleas (1779 until death).

COOPER, JOHN GORDON (b April 27, 1872, Wigan, England; d Jan. 7, 1955, Hagerstown, Md.) Railroad fireman and engineer, Ohio Republican who served eleven terms as a U.S. Representative (1915-1937). Delegate to GOP state convention (1910), state representative (1910-1912), chairman of state industrial commission's claims board (1937-1945).

COOPER, THOMAS (b Oct. 22, 1759, Westminster, England; d May 11, 1839, Columbia, S.C.) British philosopher, chemist, lawyer, agitator who brought his talents to the United States (1794), practiced law in Northumberland, Pa., and by 1800 had become a foremost Jeffersonian pamphleteer; one of his prime targets was the Sedition Law under which he was jailed and fined. Despite that, however, he was considered a member of the conservative wing of the Democratic party. In Pennsylvania he was Luzerne County commissioner (1801-1804), state judge (1804-1811), and professor of applied chemistry at Carlisle College (1811-1815). Then (1820-1834) he was president and professor at South Carolina College and, in that state, became an advocate of slavery and states' rights, always using his pen to promote his views powerfully.

COOPER, WILLIAM (b Dec. 2, 1754, Philadelphia, Pa.; d Dec. 22, 1809, Albany, N.Y.) New York Federalist and founder of Cooperstown, which today is the home of baseball's Hall of Fame. Otsego County Common Pleas Court judge, U.S. Representative (1795-1797, 1799-1801).

COOTE, RICHARD (b 1636, Ireland; d March 5, 1701, New York City) The Earl of Bellomont and colonial governor of Massachusetts, New Hampshire, and New York (1698-1701), cracking down on the hanky-panky going on between New York City's merchants and pirates and thus winning the support of the Leisler Democrats (see Jacob Leisler) but bringing down upon himself the wrath of the ruling classes.

COPELAND, ROYAL SAMUEL (b Nov. 7, 1868, Dexter, Mich.; d June 17, 1938, Washington, D.C.) Physician, medical writer and broadcaster, dean of the New York Flower Hospital and Medical College (1908-1918), Michigan and New York Democrat. In Michigan: mayor of Ann Arbor (1901-1903), president of park board (1905, 1906) and board of education (1907, 1908), state tuberculosis board member (1900-1908). In New York: member of U.S. Pension Examining Board (1917), commissioner of public health and president of the board of health (1918-1923), U.S. Senate (1923 until death), unsuccessful candidate for Democratic nomination for mayor of New York City (1937).

COPLEY, IRA CLIFTON *(b Oct. 25, 1864, Knox County, Ill.; d Nov. 1, 1947, Aurora, Ill.)* Illinois and California newspaper publisher who served six terms (1911-1923) as a Progressive Republican U.S. Representative from Illinois.

CORNBURY, EDWARD HYDE *(b 1661, England; d 1723, England)*. Viscount, and later the Earl of Clarendon; colonial governor of New York and New Jersey (1702-1708) who is best known for his arrogant ineptitude, dishonesty, and the acceptance of financial favors from the Anti-Leisler aristocracy (see Jacob Leisler).

CORNELL, ALONZO B. *(b Jan. 22, 1832, Ithaca, N.Y.; d Oct. 15, 1904, Ithaca)* Telegraph operator who became a Western Union executive, governor of New York (1879-1883) who pumped new vitality into state government but who is best remembered for his running feud with Roscoe Conkling over control of the Republican party.

CORNING, ERASTUS *(b Dec. 14, 1794, Norwich, Conn.; d April 9, 1872, Albany, N.Y.)* Iron manufacturer, New York Democrat. State senator (1842-1845), alderman and mayor of Albany (1834-1837), U.S. Representative (1857-1859, 1861-1863), delegate to peace conference (1861) that tried to avert Civil War, state constitutional convention delegate (1867). Grandfather of Parker Corning.

CORNING, PARKER *(b Jan. 22, 1874, Albany, N.Y.; d May 24, 1943, Albany)*. Manufacturer, New Jersey Democrat, U.S. Representative (1923-1937) and grandson of Erastus Corning.

CORTELYOU, GEORGE BRUCE *(b July 26, 1862, New York City; d Oct. 23, 1940, Huntington, N.Y.)* Stenographer who became private secretary to three presidents (Cleveland, McKinley, Theodore Roosevelt) and from there went on to become the holder of several cabinet positions, chairman of the Republican National Committee, Roosevelt's 1904 campaign manager, and president of a utility that today is New York's Consolidated Edison Company.

CORWIN, MOSES BLEDSO *(b Jan. 5, 1790, Bourbon County, Ky.; d April 7, 1872, Urbana, Ohio)* Farmer, lawyer, Ohio Whig. State representative (1838, 1839), U.S. Representative (1849-1851, 1853-1855). Brother of Thomas Corwin.

CORWIN, THOMAS *(b July 29, 1794, Bourbon County, Ky.; d Dec. 18, 1865, Washington, D.C.)* Lawyer, Ohio Whig turned Republican who served as governor, member of both houses of Congress, diplomat, and cabinet member, who argued vehemently against war with Mexico, declaring it would lead to civil war at home. Warren County prosecutor (1818-1828), state representative (1822, 1823, 1829), U.S. Representative (1831-1840, 1859-1861), governor (1840-1842), president of state Whig convention (1844), presidential elector on the Clay-Frelinghuysen ticket (1844), U.S. Senate (1845-1850), President Fillmore's secretary of the treasury (1850-1853), Lincoln-appointed minister to Mexico (1861-1864). Brother of Moses Bledso Corwin.

COSTIGAN, EDWARD PRENTISS *(b July 1, 1874, King William County, Va.; d Jan. 17, 1939, Denver, Colo.)* Lawyer, Republican with a keen interest in good government who became a founder of the Progressive party in Colorado (1912), ultimately (1930) donning the Democratic mantle and embracing Franklin D. Roosevelt's New Deal program. Progressive National Convention delegate (1912, 1916), unsuccessful Progressive candidate for governor (1912, 1914), Wilson-appointed member of U.S. Tariff Commission (1917-1928), Democratic state convention delegate (1930), U.S. Senate (1931-1937).

COTTON, AYLETT RAINS (b Nov. 29, 1826, Austintown, Ohio; d Oct. 30, 1912, San Francisco, Calif.) Teacher, lawyer, Iowa Republican who joined in the California gold rush of 1849, returned to Iowa to enter politics, and then went back to San Francisco to practice law. In Iowa, he was Clinton County judge (1851-1853), prosecutor (1854), mayor of Lyons (1855-1857), state constitutional convention (1857), state representative (1868-1870) and speaker (1870), U.S. Representative (1871-1875).

COUSINS, ROBERT GORDON (b Jan. 31, 1859, Cedar County, Iowa; d June 20, 1933, Iowa City, Iowa) Lawyer, writer, Chautauqua lecturer, Iowa Republican. State representative (1886), Cedar County prosecutor (1888-1890), presidential elector on the Harrison-Morton ticket (1888), U.S. Representative (1893-1909).

COUZENS, JAMES (b Aug. 26, 1872, Chatham, Canada; d Oct. 22, 1936, Detroit, Mich.) A poor boy who worked hard, saved $2,500 and invested it in automobiles as Henry Ford's business manager and virtual partner, parlaying it into $29 million, and meantime becoming a leading Michigan Republican who did not hesitate to criticize the policies of GOP Presidents Harding, Coolidge, and Hoover and support the New Deal. His reason for leaving Ford: "just making money nauseates me."

Detroit commissioner of street railways (1913-1915), metropolitan police commissioner (1916-1918), mayor of Detroit (1919-1922), U.S. Senate (1922 until death).

COVODE, JOHN (b March 18, 1808, Westmoreland County, Pa.; d Jan. 11, 1871, Harrisburg, Pa.) Farmer, manufacturer, coal shipper, anti-Masonic Whig turned Republican who, as a U.S. Representative from Pennsylvania (1854-1863, 1867 until death), instituted impeachment proceedings against President Johnson and who, throughout his political life, was known as Honest John.

COWAN, EDGAR (Sept. 19, 1815, Westmoreland County, Pa.; d Aug. 29, 1885, Greensburg, Pa.) Boat builder, teacher, lawyer, Pennsylvania Whig turned Republican who became a Union Nationalist because of falling out with the GOP, contending that the Civil War should be conducted only as the putting down of a rebellion and not as the conquering of secessionist states; thus he also argued that Reconstruction policies were much too harsh. Presidential elector on the Lincoln-Hamlin ticket (1860), U.S. Senate (1861-1867), Union National Convention delegate (1866). As a senator, Cowan stood by President Johnson during the latter's impeachment period and was appointed minister to Austria (1867). The Senate, however, took the view that the assignment was his reward and refused to confirm.

COWHERD, WILLIAM STROTHER (b Sept. 1, 1860, Jackson County, Mo.; d June 20, 1915, Pasadena, Calif.) Lawyer, Missouri Democrat. Mayor of Kansas City (1892), U.S. Representative (1897-1905).

COX, EDWARD EUGENE (b April 3, 1880, Mitchell County, Ga.; d Dec. 24, 1952, in U.S. Naval Hospital, Bethesda, Md.) Lawyer, Georgia Democrat.

Mayor of Camilla (1904-1906), Democratic National Convention delegate (1908), Albany circuit superior court judge (1912-1916), U.S. Representative (1925 until death).

COX, GEORGE BARNSDALE *(b April 29, 1853, Cincinnati, Ohio; d May 20, 1916)* Newsboy, shoeshine boy, bartender, saloonkeeper, and a molder of the Republican machine in Ohio, going to New York to study Tammany Hall bossism techniques and returning to dominate GOP affairs for twenty-two years (1888-1910) when he "retired" to his varied lucrative business interests. The only elective office he ever held was as a Cincinnati councilman (1877). But he had learned his Tammany Hall lessons well, earning these *Cincinnati Enquirer* tributes: his machine is "more complete, more exacting, and under more rigid discipline than Tammany Hall," and "No man had a chance to get on the Republican ticket without the approval of Cox." In 1911 Cox was indicted (but never tried) for perjury growing out of a Democratic-instituted state investigation that resulted in the return of nearly a quarter-million dollars to the state treasury.

COX, HANNAH PEIRCE *(b Nov. 12, 1797, Chester County, Pa.; d Apr. 15, 1876, Chester County)* Quaker reformer interested in women's betterment, temperance, peace, and the abolition of capital punishment who helped her husband, John Cox, conduct a station of the Underground Railroad; mistress of "Longwood" where members of a group of dedicated reformers including people such as William Lloyd Garrison and Lucretia Mott assembled and partook of her hospitality.

COX, JACOB DOLSON *(b Oct. 27, 1828, Montreal, Canada; d Aug. 4, 1900, Magnolia, Mass.)* Lawyer, Union Army general, railroad president, author, Ohio Republican who, as governor (1866-

1868), sought to segregate Negroes, a move that neither his party nor his state would countenance. Secretary of the Interior in Grant's first cabinet (1869-1870), U.S. Representative (1877-1879).

COX, JAMES MIDDLETON *(b March 31, 1870, Butler County, Ohio; d July 15, 1957, Dayton, Ohio)* Ohio, Florida, and Georgia newspaper publisher, radio and television station owner, Ohio Democrat who ran against Warren G. Harding for president (1920), receiving 9 million popular and 127 electoral votes. U.S. Representative (1909-1913), governor (1913-1915, 1917-1921), vice chairman of U.S. delegation to World Economic Conference (1933) and president of its monetary commission.

COX, SAMUEL SULLIVAN *(b Sept. 30, 1824, Zanesville, Ohio; d Sept. 10, 1889, New York City)* Newspaper editor-publisher, lawyer, diplomat, Ohio Democrat and New York Democrat turned Liberal Republican who was one of the leading Progressives of his day and an opponent of governmental infringements on personal freedoms. In Ohio: Democratic National Convention delegate (1864, 1868), U.S. Representative (1857-1868). In New York: U.S. Representative (1869-1873, 1873-1885, 1886 until death), minister to Turkey (1885-1886). In all he served thirty years as a congressman.

COX, WILLIAM ELIJAH *(b Sept. 6, 1861, Birdseye, Ind.; d March 11, 1942, Jasper, Ind.)* Lawyer, desk manufacturer, Indiana Democrat. Prosecutor for eleventh judicial district (1892-1898), U.S. Representative (1907-1919).

CRAFTS, SAMUEL CHANDLER *(b Oct. 6, 1768, Woodstock, Conn.; d Nov. 19, 1853, Craftsbury, Vt.)* Farmer, botanist, Vermont Whig. State constitutional convention (1793) and its president (1829), state representative (1796,

1800, 1801, 1802, 1803, 1805), clerk of the house (1798, 1799), Orleans County assistant judge (1800-1810, 1825-1828) and chief judge (1810-1816), state council (1809-1813, 1825, 1826), U.S. Representative (1817-1825), governor (1828-1831), county clerk (1836-1839), presidential elector on Harrison-Tyler ticket (1840), U.S. Senate to fill a vacancy (1842-1843).

CRAGIN, AARON HARRISON *(b Feb. 3, 1821, Weston, Vt.; d May 10, 1898, Washington, D.C.)* New Hampshire lawyer whose political loyalties were divided between the American (Know-Nothing) and Republican parties. State representative (1852-1855, 1859), two consecutive terms as a U.S. Representative—the first as a Know-Nothing, the second as a Republican (1855-1859), GOP National Convention delegate (1860); U.S. Senate as a Know-Nothing (1865-1877).

CRAIN, WILLIAM HENRY *(b Nov. 25, 1848, Galveston, Texas; d Feb. 10, 1896, Washington, D.C.)* Lawyer, Texas Democrat, state senate (1876-1878), twenty-third judicial district attorney (1872-1876), U.S. Representative (1885 until death).

CRANDALL, PRUDENCE *(b Sept. 3, 1803, Hopkinton, R.I.; d Jan. 28, 1889, Elk Falls, Kans.)* Quaker reformer, educator who attempted to establish (1833) a school for Negro children at Canterbury, Conn. When attempts at intimidation failed to stop her, a law was passed by the state legislature making what she was doing illegal. Thus she was arrested and imprisoned. Influential Abolitionists came to her aid and obtained skilled counsel who attempted to prove that the law was unconstitutional. They lost the case but appealed to the Supreme Court of Connecticut, which reversed the decision (1834) on the grounds of insufficient evidence.

CRANE, WINTHROP MURRAY *(b April 23, 1853, Dalton, Mass.; d Oct. 2, 1920, Dalton).* Massachusetts paper manufacturer who for twenty years (1892-1912) was a member of the Republican National Committee but would never serve as its chairman, governor (1900-1902) whose settling of a Boston teamsters' strike served as a model for President Theodore Roosevelt's handling of a national coal strike, and U.S. Senator (1904-1913) who was called the Senate's "most influential member" by President Taft. But all of his wisdom and influence failed him when, in the last two years of his life, despite his poor health, he sought in vain for the GOP to support U.S. entrance into the League of Nations. Some said his failure hastened his death.

GOP National Convention delegate (1892, 1896, 1904, 1908, 1916, 1920), lieutenant governor (1897-1899), declined appointment as Roosevelt's secretary of the treasury (1902).

A fellow senator, Chauncey M. Depew of New York, in writing his memoirs said of Crane: "He was one of the wonders of the Senate. He never made a speech. I do not remember that he made a motion. Yet his wisdom, tact, his sound judgment, his encyclopedic knowledge of public affairs and of public men made him an authority."

CRAVENS, JORDAN EDGAR *(b Nov. 7, 1830, Fredericktown, Mo.; d April 8, 1914, Fort Smith, Ark.)* Lawyer, Confederate Army officer, Arkansas Democrat. State representative (1860), Johnson County prosecutor (1865, 1866), state senate (1866-1868), presidential elector on the Greeley-Brown ticket (1872), U.S. Representative (1877-1883), circuit court judge (1890-1894). Cousin of William B. Cravens.

CRAVENS, WILLIAM BEN *(b Jan. 17, 1872, Fort Smith, Ark.; d Jan. 13, 1939, Washington, D.C.)* Lawyer, Arkansas Democrat. Fort Smith city attorney

(1898-1902), twelfth judicial district prosecutor (1902-1908), U.S. Representative (1907-1913, 1933 until death) and succeeded by his son, William Fadjo Cravens. Cousin of Jordan E. Cravens.

CRAVENS, WILLIAM FADJO (b Feb. 15, 1899, Fort Smith, Ark.) Lawyer, Arkansas Democrat who was elected a U.S. Representative to succeed his father, William B. Cravens, and remained for four more terms (thus serving 1939-1949). Before that he had been Fort Smith city attorney for ten years.

CRAWFORD, COE ISAAC (b Jan. 14, 1858, Allamakee County, Iowa; d April 25, 1944, Yankton, S.Dak.) Young Iowa lawyer who began practice (1883) in Dakota Territory and became a leader in territorial and, after statehood (1889), South Dakota Republican affairs. Hughes County prosecutor (1887, 1888), member of last territorial council (1889) and first state senate, attorney general (1892-1896), governor (1907-1909), GOP National Convention delegate (1908), U.S. Senate (1909-1915).

CRAWFORD, FRED LEWIS (b May 5, 1888, Dublin, Texas; d April 13, 1957, Washington, D.C.) Beet sugar producer, manufacturer, rancher, banker, transit operator, accountant in many states but, politically, a Michigan Republican who nine times was elected a U.S. Representative (1935-1953) before retiring to his farm in Maryland.

CRAWFORD, GEORGE WASHINGTON (b Dec. 22, 1798, Columbia, Ga.; d July 22, 1872, near Augusta, Ga.) Lawyer, Georgia Whig who presided over state secession convention (1861). State attorney general (1827-1831), state representative (1837-1842), U.S. Representative for one month (1843) to fill a vacancy, governor (1843-1847), secretary of war in Taylor cabinet (1849-1850).

CRAWFORD, MARTIN JENKINS (b March 17, 1820, Jasper County, Ga.; d July 23, 1883, Columbus, Ga.) Lawyer, farmer whose plantation was destroyed by Northern forces during the Civil War, Confederate officer, Georgia Democrat who was one of three-man commission chosen by Jefferson Davis to sue for peace. State representative (1845-1847), superior court judge (1854, 1875-1880), U.S. Representative (1855 until secession in 1861), Confederate Provisional Congress (1861-1862), state supreme court justice (1880 until death).

CRAWFORD, SAMUEL JOHNSON (b April 15, 1835, Lawrence County, Ind.; d Oct. 21, 1913) Lawyer, Union Army officer, farmer, author, Kansas Republican who became governor (1865-1868) before he was thirty. His only other fling at politics was as a state legislator (1861) before enlisting.

CRAWFORD, WILLIAM (b 1760, Paisley, Scotland; d Oct. 23, 1823, Adams County, Pa.) Physician, farmer, Pennsylvania Democrat. Associate Adams County judge (1801-1808), U.S. Representative (1809-1817).

CRAWFORD, WILLIAM HARRIS (b Feb. 24, 1772, Nelson County, Va.; d Sept. 15, 1834, Oglethorpe County, Ga.) Lawyer, planter, diplomat, cabinet member, Georgia Democrat who ran unsuccessfully for president of the United States in a year (1824) when there were four contestants (John Quincy Adams, Henry Clay, Crawford, and Andrew Jackson), no distinct party designations, and no electoral-vote majority; the contest was decided in the House of Representatives and the office went to Adams who had run second to Jackson, Crawford finishing fourth in the popular-vote column but third in electoral votes.

State representative (1803-1807), U.S. Senate (1807-1813), minister to France (1813-1815), secretary of war (1815-1816), secretary of the treasury (1816-

1825), state circuit court judge (1827 until death).

CREAL, EDWARD WESTER *(b Nov. 20, 1883, Larue County, Ky.; d Oct. 13, 1943, Hodgenville, Ky.)* Teacher, lawyer, newspaper publisher, Kentucky Democrat. Larue County schools superintendent (1910-1918), county attorney (1918-1928), commonwealth attorney (1929-1936), Democratic state executive committee member (1924-1940), U.S. Representative (1935 until death).

CREELY, JOHN VAUDAIN *(b Nov. 14, 1839, Philadelphia, Pa.; d ——)* Lawyer, Union Army officer, Pennsylvania Republican who mysteriously disappeared during his first term (1871-1873) as a U.S. Representative and was declared legally dead by a Philadelphia court on Sept. 28, 1900.

CRISP, CHARLES FREDERICK *(b Jan. 29, 1845, Sheffield, England; d Oct. 23, 1896, Atlanta, Ga.)* Lawyer, Free-Silver Democrat who was considered one of the ablest men Georgia ever sent to Washington and who died only a few weeks before his almost-inevitable election as a U.S. Senator. Southwestern judicial circuit solicitor general (1872-1877), superior court judge (1877-1882), U.S. Representative (1883 until death) and speaker of the House (1891-1895). Father of Charles R. Crisp.

CRISP, CHARLES ROBERT *(b Oct. 19, 1870, Ellaville, Ga.; d Feb. 7, 1937, Americus, Ga.)* Lawyer, Georgia Democrat who succeeded his father, Charles F. Crisp, as a member of Congress. Parliamentarian of the U.S. House of Representatives (1891-1895, 1911-1913), U.S. Representative (1896-1897, 1913-1932), Americus city court judge (1900-1912), Democratic National Convention parliamentarian (1912).

CRITTENDEN, JOHN JORDAN *(b Sept. 10, 1787, Woodford County, Ky.; d July 26, 1863, Frankfort, Ky.)* Lawyer, orator, proposer of the Crittenden Compromise (1860) to avert the Civil War, Kentucky statesman whose political ideals drove him repeatedly from one party label to another, a border state moderate on secession and slavery, a man who wanted to preserve the Union at all costs, the father of two sons who fought on opposite sides during the war.

State representative (1811-1817, 1825, 1829-1832) and six times speaker of the house, U.S. Senate (1817-1819, 1835-1841, 1842-1848, 1855-1861), U.S. district attorney (1827-1829), nominee for the U.S. Supreme Court but not confirmed (1828), U.S. attorney general (1841, 1850-1853), governor (1848-1850), U.S. Representative (1861 until death). Uncle of Thomas T. Crittenden.

CRITTENDEN, THOMAS THEODORE *(b Jan. 1, 1832, Shelby County, Ky.; d May 29, 1909, Kansas City, Mo.)* Lawyer, Union Army officer, Missouri Democrat. State attorney general (1864-1865), U.S. Representative (1873-1875, 1877-1879), governor (1881-1885), consul general at Mexico City (1893-1897). Nephew of John J. Crittenden.

CROCKETT, DAVID "DAVEY" *(b Aug. 17, 1786, State of Franklin, which later became Greene County, Tenn.; d March 6, 1836, in the Alamo, San Antonio, Texas)* Frontiersman, hunter, Indian scout, rifleman, anti-Jackson Tennessee Democrat turned Whig who gave his life for Texas independence. Although he had had only six months' schooling, he served as Giles County justice of the peace (1816-1820) (relying, he said, "on natural-born sense instead of law learning"), then moved further west in the state and became a member of the state house of representatives (1821-1823), ran for Congress as a joke, won, served three terms (1827-1831, 1833-1835), then headed still further west to aid the Texas cause. Father of John W. Crockett.

CROCKETT, JOHN WESLEY *(b July 10, 1807, Trenton, Tenn.; d Nov. 24, 1852, Memphis, Tenn.)* Lawyer, editor, merchant, Tennessee Whig who held many local and state offices before and after becoming a U.S. Representative (1837-1841). Son of Davey Crockett.

CROLY, HERBERT DAVID *(b Jan. 23, 1869, New York City; d May 17, 1930, Santa Barbara, Calif.)* Editor, author, founder of *The New Republic* (1914), and one of the nation's foremost writers on political affairs whom Walter Lippmann called "the first important political philosopher of the twentieth century." His books include *The Promise of American Life* (1909) and *Progressive Democracy* (1914).

CROMER, GEORGE WASHINGTON *(b May 13, 1856, Madison County, Ind.; d Nov. 8, 1936, Muncie, Ind.)* Muncie newspaper editor, lawyer, Indiana Republican. Prosecutor for the forty-sixth judicial circuit (1886-1890), GOP state committeeman (1892, 1894), mayor of Muncie (1894-1898), U.S. Representative (1899-1907).

CROSSER, ROBERT *(b June 7, 1874, Holytown, Scotland; d June 3, 1957, Bethesda, Md.)* Lawyer, teacher, Ohio Democrat who served nineteen terms as a U.S. Representative (1913-1919, 1923-1955), and before that as a state representative (1911, 1912).

CROSWELL, EDWIN *(b May 29, 1797, Catskill, N.Y.; d June 13, 1871, Princeton, N.J.)* Highly political journalist who was chosen by Martin Van Buren and others in the "Albany Regency," which controlled the Democratic party in New York state, to be editor of the *Albany Argus* (1823-1854) and state printer (1824-1839, 1844-1847).

CROUNSE, LORENZO *(b Jan. 27, 1834, Sharon, N.Y.; d May 13, 1909, Omaha, Nebr.)* Lawyer, Union Army officer who was severely wounded at Bull Run, jurist who upheld the right of Negroes to sit on juries, highly independent Nebraska Republican whose opposition to railroad interests cost him a seat in the U.S. Senate but won him the governorship (1892-1895). Member of Nebraska Territory House of Representatives (1866), state constitutional convention delegate (1866), associate justice of the state supreme court (1867-1873), U.S. Representative (1873-1877), Nebraska district internal revenue collector (1879-1883), assistant secretary of the U.S. treasury (1891-1892).

CROW, WILLIAM EVANS *(b March 10, 1870, German Township, Pa.; d Aug. 2, 1922, Uniontown, Pa.)* Newspaperman, lawyer, and a power in Pennsylvania Republican circles. Fayette County assistant district attorney (1896-1898) moving up to the top spot (1898-1901), GOP county committee chairman (1899-1901) and state chairman (1913, 1916, 1918), GOP National Convention delegate (1916, 1920), state senate (1907-1921) and president pro tem (1909, 1911), U.S. Senate (1921 until death).

CROWNINSHIELD, BENJAMIN WILLIAM *(b Dec. 27, 1772, Salem, Mass.; d Feb. 3, 1851, Boston, Mass.)* Merchant, banker, Massachusetts Democrat who served both Presidents Madison and Monroe as secretary of the navy (1814-1818). State representative (1811, 1821, 1833), state senate (1812), presidential elector on the Monroe-Tompkins ticket (1820), U.S. Representative (1823-1831). Brother of Jacob Crowninshield.

CROWNINSHIELD, JACOB *(b March 31, 1770, Salem, Mass.; d April 15, 1808, Washington, D.C.)* Sea captain, merchant, Massachusetts Democrat who could have been secretary of the navy, like his brother Benjamin W. Crowninshield, but had to refuse Jefferson's offer because of ill health. State senate (1801), U.S. Representative (1803 until death).

CROWTHER, FRANK *(b July 10, 1870, Liverpool, England; d July 20, 1955, Pueblo, Colo.)* Fabric designer, dentist, New Jersey and New York Republican who served twenty-four years in Congress and then retired to Colorado to play the violin and paint landscapes. In New Jersey: state assemblyman (1904, 1905), Middlesex County tax commissioner (1906-1909). In New York: president of Schenectady Common Council (1917, 1918), U.S. Representative (1919-1943).

CRUMP, EDWARD HULL *(b Oct. 2, 1874, Marshall County, Miss.; d Oct. 16, 1954, Memphis, Tenn.)* Wholesale merchant, harness and buggy manufacturer, farmer, banker, real estate operator, Tennessee Democrat who ruled Memphis with an iron fist, was one of the last big-city bosses and was known, appropriately, as Boss Crump. Democratic state convention delegate (1902, 1904), member of Memphis Board of Public Works (1905), city fire and police commission (1907), mayor (1910-1916, 1940), Democratic National Convention delegate (1912, 1924, 1928, 1936, 1940, 1944, 1948), Shelby County treasurer (1917-1923), state committeeman (1926-1930), national committeeman (1936-1945), U.S. Representative (1931-1935), Smithsonian Institution regent (1931-1935).

CRUMP, WILLIAM WOOD *(b Nov. 25, 1819, Henrico County, Va.; d Feb. 27, 1897, Richmond, Va.).* Lawyer, Richmond judge, Virginia legislator, a firm believer in states' rights and advocate of secession. Assistant secretary of the treasury of the Confederate States and, an expert on cross examination, one of the defense attorneys at Jefferson Davis' treason trial.

CRUMPACKER, EDGAR DEAN *(b May 27, 1851, Westville, Ind.; d May 19, 1920, Valparaiso, Ind.)* Lawyer, Indiana Republican. Prosecuting attorney for Indiana's thirty-first judicial district (1884-1888), state appellate judge (1891-1893), U.S. Representative (1897-1913).

CUFFE, PAUL *(b Jan. 17, 1759, Cuttyhunk, Mass.; d Sept. 9, 1817, Westport, Mass.).* Son of a slave, farmer, sea captain who with his brother, John, had much to do with Massachusetts' adoption (1781) of laws granting full citizenship rights to Negroes. In 1811-1812 he organized the Friendly Society whose purpose was to transport black families from the United States to Sierra Leone, Africa. By 1815 he had progressed to the point where, using his own money, he carried nine families (thirty-eight persons) to their new homes. Then his health failed and he could do no more. At about age twenty-one, he dropped his father's slave name, Slocum, and adopted his father's first name, Cuffe, as his last name.

CULBERSON, CHARLES ALLEN *(b June 10, 1855, Dadeville, Ala.; d March 19, 1925, Washington, D.C.)* Lawyer, Texas Democrat, and a leader in his party's affairs. Democratic state convention delegate (1890), state attorney general (1890-1894), governor (1894-1898), delegate to all national conventions (1896-1916), and twenty-four years as a U.S. Senator (1899-1923). Son of David B. Culberson.

CULBERSON, DAVID BROWNING *(b Sept. 29, 1830, Troup County, Ga.; d May 7, 1900, Jefferson, Texas)* Lawyer, Confederate Army officer, Texas Democrat who served eleven terms as a U.S. Representative (1875-1897), state representative (1859, 1864), state senate (1873-1875), McKinley-appointed commissioner to codify U.S. laws (1897 until death). Father of Charles A. Culberson.

CULBRETH, THOMAS *(b April 13, 1786, Kent County, Md.; d April 16, 1843, Greensboro, Md.)* Merchant, bank cashier, farmer, Maryland Democrat. Member of congressional committee at Hillsboro (1810), state house of delegates (1812, 1813), U.S. Representative (1817-1821), appointed chief judge of Caroline County Orphans' Court (1822), clerk of state executive council (1825-1838).

CULKIN, FRANCIS DUGAN *(b Nov. 10, 1874, Oswego, N.Y.; d Aug. 4, 1943, Oswego)* Newspaperman, lawyer, New York Republican. Oswego city attorney (1906-1910), Oswego County district attorney (1911-1921), county judge (1921-1928), U.S. Representative (1928 until death).

CULLEN, THOMAS HENRY *(b March 29, 1868, Brooklyn, N.Y.; d March 1, 1944, Washington, D.C.)* Marine insurance, shipper, New York Democrat. State assembly (1896-1898), state senate (1899-1918), delegate to six Democratic National Conventions, U.S. Representative for a quarter-century (1919 until death).

CULLOM, SHELBY MOORE *(b Nov. 22, 1829, Wayne County, Ky.; d Jan. 28, 1914, Washington, D.C.)* Lawyer, Illinois Republican leader with independent leanings who through seniority gained much power as a U.S. Senator (1883-1913), particularly as chairman of the Interstate Commerce and Foreign Relations committees and (1896) was in the running for the GOP presidential nomination.

Springfield city attorney (1855), presidential elector (1856), state representative (1856, 1860, 1861, 1873, 1874) and speaker (1860, 1873), U.S. Representative (1865-1871), GOP National Convention delegate (1872, 1884, 1892) placing Ulysses S. Grant's name in nomination (1872), governor (1877-1883) who created a furor by running for the U.S.

Senate while still holding that office.

CULPEPPER, JOHN *(b 1761,- Wadesboro, N.C.; d January, 1841, Darlington County, S.C.)* Minister, North Carolina Federalist. U.S. Representative (1807-1809, 1813-1817, 1819-1821, 1823-1825, 1827-1829).

CUMMING, ALFRED *(b Sept. 4, 1802, Augusta, Ga.; d Oct. 9, 1873, near Augusta)* Mayor of Augusta (1839) and a Georgia Democrat of political prominence who was chosen by President Buchanan to replace Brigham Young as governor of Utah Territory during the so-called Mormon War, serving from May 1857 until Lincoln's inauguration in 1861.

CUMMINGS, ALBERT BAIRD *(b Feb. 15, 1850, Greene County, Pa.; d July 30, 1926, Des Moines, Iowa)* Carpenter, teacher, surveyor, railroad builder who nevertheless fought against railroad domination of political affairs; lawyer, progressive Iowa Republican who rejected boss control. As a result the railroads and the party regulars fought him but the people elected him. State representative (1888-1890), governor (1902-1908), U.S. Senate (1908 until death) and Senate president pro tem (1919-1925). Delegate to every GOP convention, both state and national, from 1880 until he died, and a presidential elector (1892) on the Harrison-Reid ticket.

CUMMINGS, AMOS JAY *(b May 14, 1841, Conkling, N.Y.; d May 2, 1902, Baltimore, Md.)* An apprentice printer at twelve, a tramp printer who worked his way to New York City at fifteen, worked in the *Tribune* backshop, became Horace Greeley's night editor, then a founding editor of *The Evening Sun*, moved over to the *Evening Express*, which was controlled by Tammany leader John Kelly. New York Democrat and a U.S. Representative (1887-March 1889, November 1889-1894, 1895-1902) who several times made good his threat to return to journalism.

CUNNINGHAM, PAUL HARVEY *(b June 15, 1890, Indiana County, Pa.; d July 16, 1961, Brainerd, Minn.)* Lawyer, Iowa Republican. State representative (1933-1937), U.S. Representative (1941-1959).

CURRIER, FRANK DUNKLEE *(b Oct. 30, 1853, Canaan, N.H.; d Nov. 25, 1921, Canaan)* Lawyer, New Hampshire Republican. State representative (1879, 1899) and speaker (1899), GOP state committee secretary (1882-1890), state senate clerk (1883, 1885), GOP National Convention delegate (1884), state senate president (1887), U.S. Representative (1901-1913).

CURRY, CHARLES FORREST *(b March 14, 1858, Naperville, Ill.; d Oct. 10, 1930, Washington, D.C.)* Farmer, cattle rancher, timber and mining operator, California Republican. State assembly (1887, 1888), San Francisco city and county clerk (1894-1898), California secretary of state (1899-1910), U.S. Representative (1913 until death).

CURRY, GEORGE *(b April 3, 1863, near Bayou Sara, La.; d Nov. 27, 1947, Albuquerque, N.Mex.)* Ranch hand, merchant, stockman, hotel owner, active New Mexico Republican who, after serving in the Philippines as a cavalry officer, filled several governmental positions there. In New Mexico he was Lincoln County deputy treasurer (1886, 1887), county clerk (1888), county assessor (1890), sheriff (1892), member of territorial senate (1894, 1896) and president (1896), territorial governor (1907-1911), U.S. Representative (1912-1913) when statehood was gained, secretary to U.S. Senator Holm O. Bursum (1921, 1922), member of International Boundary Commission (1922-1927), state historian (1945 until death).

In the Philippine Islands he was gov-

ernor of Camarines Province (1901), Manila police chief (1902), governor of Isabela Province (1903-1905), governor of Samar Province (1905-1907).

CURRY, GEORGE LAW *(b July 2, 1820, Philadelphia, Pa.; d July 28, 1878)* Itinerant newspaperman who founded the *Oregon Free Press* (1846), suspending publication three years later when all of his subscribers joined in the California gold rush. He turned to farming and politics and became Oregon's last territorial governor (1854-1859); then failing by only one vote of becoming the new state's first U.S. Senator. Member of provisional legislature (1848-1849), chief clerk of the territorial council (1850-1851), delegate to territorial legislature's lower house (1851-1852), territorial secretary and acting governor (1853-1854).

CURRY, JABEZ LAMAR MONROE *(b June 5, 1825, Lincoln County, Ga.; d Feb. 12, 1903, Victoria, N.C.)* Texas Ranger, Confederate Army officer, college president-professor, preacher, author, diplomat, Alabama Democrat who used all of his oratorical skills to further public education not only in his home state but also throughout the country. State representative (1847, 1853, 1855), presidential elector on the Buchanan-Breckinridge ticket (1856), U.S. Representative (1857 until secession in 1861), Provisional Confederate Congress delegate and First Confederate Congress Representative, minister to Spain (1885-1888).

CURTIN, ANDREW GREGG *(b April 22, 1817, Bellefonte, Pa.; d Oct. 7, 1894, Bellefonte)* Lawyer, Pennsylvania Whig-Republican-Democrat and a powerful orator who stumped the countryside for presidential candidates of all three parties, and (1868) almost became Grant's vice presidential running mate. Presidential elector for Taylor-Fillmore (1848) and Scott-Graham (1852), secretary of Pennsylvania and superintendent of public instruction (1854-1856), governor (1861-1867), minister to Russia (1869-1872), U.S. Representative (1881-1887).

CURTIN, WILLARD SEVIER *(b Nov. 28, 1905, Trenton, N.J.)* Lawyer, Pennsylvania Republican. Bucks County district attorney (1949-1953), U.S. Representative (1957-1967) serving on the House Administration and Interstate and Foreign Commerce committees.

CURTIS, CHARLES *(b Jan. 25, 1860, Topeka, Kans.; d Feb. 8, 1936, Washington, D.C.)* Summertime jockey while a schoolboy, lawyer, conservative Kansas Republican, and an astute politician who served as congressman, senator, Herbert Hoover's vice president (1929-1933), although he had opposed Hoover's nomination, and a man who claimed he owed much of his success to the women around him, the most noted of whom was his half-sister, Dolly Gann.
Shawnee County prosecutor (1885-1889), U.S. Representative (1893-1907), U.S. Senate (1907-1913, 1915-1929), president pro tem of the Senate (1911), Republican whip (1915-1924), majority leader (1924-1929), unsuccessful candidate for reelection as vice president (1932), remaining in Washington to practice law after his term expired.

CURTIS, EDWARD UPTON *(b March 26, 1861, Roxbury, Mass.; d March 28, 1922, Boston, Mass.)* Lawyer, Massachusetts Republican. Reform mayor of Boston (1894-1895) and police commissioner (1918-1922) who precipitated the police strike of 1919, and ultimately broke it, by suspending all officers of a new police union and calling upon the governor, who had appointed him, either to back him all the way or accept his resignation.

CURTIS, GEORGE WILLIAM *(b Feb. 24, 1824, Providence, R.I.; d Aug. 31, 1892,* Staten Island, N.Y.) Journalist, author, orator, editor of *Harper's Weekly* (1863-1892) whose major interests were political reform, an end to slavery, and equal rights for women.

CURTIS, LAURENCE *(b Sept. 3, 1893, Boston, Mass.)* Lawyer, Massachusetts Republican. Secretary to U.S. Supreme Court Justice Oliver Wendell Holmes (1921, 1922), assistant U.S. attorney in Boston (1923-1930), city council (1930-1933), state representative (1933-1936), state senate (1936-1941), state treasurer (1947, 1948), GOP National Convention (1960), U.S. Representative (1953-1963) serving on the Foreign Affairs Committee and Joint Committee on Smithsonian Institution Museum of History and Technology Building.

CURTIS, THOMAS BRADFORD *(b May 14, 1911, St. Louis, Mo.)* Lawyer, Missouri Republican. St. Louis elections commissioner (1942), St. Louis County GOP Central Committee (1946-1950), U.S. Representative (1951-1969) serving on the Ways and Means Committee, Joint Economic Committee, and Joint Committee on Internal Revenue Taxation.

CUSHING, CALEB *(b Jan. 17, 1800, Salisbury, Mass.; d Jan. 2, 1879, Newburyport, Mass.)* Lawyer, diplomat, cabinet member, Massachusetts Whig-Democrat-Republican and a leader in all three parties, Mexican War general, jurist whom President Grant nominated (1874) to be chief justice of the United States but whom the Senate refused to confirm. He opposed slavery, but was not an abolitionist, holding that the North had no constitutional right to interfere in Southern affairs.
State representative (1825, 1833, 1834, 1845, 1846, 1850), state senate (1827), U.S. Representative (1835-1843), minister to China (1843-1845), twice unsuccessful candidate for governor (1847, 1848), mayor of Newbury-

port (1851, 1852), state supreme court judge (1852-1853), U.S. attorney general in the Pierce cabinet (1853-1857), Democratic National Convention chairman (1860), Johnson-appointed commissioner to codify U.S. laws (1866-1870).

CUSHING, THOMAS *(b March 24, 1725, Boston, Mass.; d Feb. 28, 1788, Boston)* Lawyer, merchant, Massachusetts patriot. Speaker of the provincial assembly (1761-1774), delegate to Provincial Congress (1774), member of Continental Congress (1774-1776), lieutenant governor (1780 until death), acting governor (1785), delegate to state constitutional convention (1788) that ratified federal Constitution.

CUSHMAN, FRANCIS WELLINGTON *(b May 8, 1867, Brighton, Iowa; d July 6, 1909, New York City)* Ranch hand, teacher, lawyer, Washington Republican. U.S. Representative (1899 until death).

CUTCHEON, BYRON M. *(b May 11, 1836, Pembroke, N.H.; d April 12, 1908, Ypsilanti, Mich.)* Teacher, lawyer, Union Army general who was awarded the Congressional Medal of Honor, Detroit newspaperman, Michigan Republican. State railroad control board member (1867-1883), presidential elector on the Grant-Colfax ticket (1868), Manistee city attorney (1870-1873), Manistee County prosecuting attorney (1873,

1874), Manistee postmaster (1877-1883), U.S. Representative (1883-1891).

CUTHBERT, ALFRED *(b Dec. 23, 1785, Savannah, Ga.; d July 9, 1856, Jasper County, Ga.)* Lawyer, Georgia Democrat. State representative (1810-1813), U.S. Representative (1813-1816, 1821-1827), state senate (1817-1819), U.S. Senate (1835-1843).

CUTTING, BRONSON MURRAY *(b June 23, 1888, Oakdale, N.Y.; d May 6, 1935, Atlanta, Mo., in a plane crash)* Santa Fe newspaper publisher, New Mexico Republican. Treasurer of Progressive state central committee (1912-1914) and chairman (1914-1916), U.S. Senate (1927 until death).

CUTTS, CHARLES *(b Jan. 31, 1769, Portsmouth, N.H.; d Jan. 25, 1846, Fairfax County, Va.)* Lawyer, New Hampshire Federalist. State representative (1803-1810) and speaker (1807, 1808, 1810), U.S. Senate to fill a vacancy (1810-1813), secretary of U.S. Senate (1814-1825).

CUTTS, RICHARD *(b June 28, 1771, Cutts Island, Mass., now Maine; d April 7, 1845, Washington, D.C.)* Lawyer, merchant, seafarer, Massachusetts Democrat. State representative (1799, 1800), U.S. Representative (1801-1813), second comptroller of the U.S. Treasury (1817-1829).

D

☆ ☆ ☆

DAGGETT, DAVID *(b Dec. 31, 1764, Attleboro, Mass.; d April 12, 1851, New Haven, Conn.)* Teacher, lawyer, Yale University law professor, Connecticut Federalist and pamphleteer who opposed democracy, universal suffrage and, as a jurist, in his charge to a jury (1833) said free Negroes were not U.S. citizens.

State representative (1791-1796, 1805) and speaker (1794-1796), state council (1797, 1809-1813), presidential elector (1804, 1808, 1812), New Haven County state's attorney (1811-1813), U.S. Senate (1813-1819), state supreme court judge (1826-1832) and chief judge (1832-1834), mayor of New Haven (1828-1830).

DAGGETT, ROLLIN MALLORY *(b Feb. 22, 1831, Richville, N.Y.; d Nov. 12, 1901, San Francisco, Calif.)* Printer who answered the lure of California gold (1849-1852), became a San Francisco newspaper publisher, moved on to Virginia City and the *Territorial Enterprise* and became active in Nevada politics as a Republican. Territorial council (1863), U.S. district court clerk (1867-1876), presidential elector on the Hayes-Wheeler ticket (1876), U.S. Representative (1879-1881), minister to Hawaii (1882-1885).

DAGUE, PAUL BARTRAM *(b May 19, 1898, Whitford, Pa.)* Pennsylvania Republican. Assistant superintendent of state highway department (1925-1935), Chester County sheriff (1944-1946), U.S. Representative (1947-1966) serving on the Agriculture Committee.

DALE, PORTER HINMAN *(b March 1, 1867, Island Pond, Vt.; d Oct. 6, 1933, Westmore, Vt.)* Teacher, lawyer, banker, Vermont Republican. Chief deputy collector of customs at Island Pond (1897-1910), GOP state convention chairman (1898, 1919), Brighton municipal court judge (1910), state senate (1910-1914), U.S. Representative (1915-1923), U.S. Senate (1923 until death).

DALLAS, ALEXANDER JAMES *(b June 21, 1759, Jamaica, British West Indies; d Jan. 16, 1817, Philadelphia, Pa.)* Lawyer, playwright, magazine editor, Pennsylvania Democrat who served as President Madison's secretary of the treasury (1814-1816) and acting secretary of war (1815), restored confidence in the dollar and replenished the bankrupt U.S. treasury. Secretary of the Commonwealth of Pennsylvania (1791-1794), U.S. attorney for Pennsylvania's eastern district (1801-1814). Father of George M. Dallas.

DALLAS, GEORGE MIFFLIN *(b July 10, 1792, Philadelphia, Pa.; d Dec. 31, 1864, Philadelphia)* Lawyer, diplomat, Pennsylvania Democrat who was vice president (1845-1849) under President Polk, casting the deciding vote that repealed the 1842 tariff bill. Private secretary to Albert Gallatin, U.S. minister to Russia, (1813-1814); solicitor of the United States Bank (1815-1817), mayor of Philadelphia (1829), U.S. district attorney for Pennsylvania's eastern district (1829-1831), U.S. Senate to fill a vacancy (1831-1833), state attorney general (1833-1835), minister to Russia (1837-1839), minister to England (1856-1861). Son of Alexander J. Dallas.

DALLINGER, FREDERICK WILLIAM *(b Oct. 2, 1871, Cambridge, Mass.; d Sept. 5, 1955, North Conway, N.H.)* Lawyer, lecturer, farmer, Massachusetts Republican. State representative (1894, 1895), state senate (1896-1899), Middlesex County public administrator (1897-1932), U.S. Representative (1915-1925, 1926-1932), U.S. Customs Court judge (1932-1942).

DALZELL, JOHN *(b April 19, 1845, New York City; d Oct. 2, 1927, Altadena, Calif.)* Corporation lawyer and Pennsylvania Republican whose wife, the former Mary Louise Duff, persuaded him that his place was in Congress and did much to keep him there for thirteen terms (1887-1913), made a reputation as a conservative and a parliamentarian and served as chairman of the House Rules Committee. GOP National Convention delegate (1904, 1908).

DANA, FRANCIS *(b June 13, 1743, Charlestown, Mass.; d April 25, 1811, Cambridge, Mass.)* Lawyer, diplomat, Massachusetts Federalist who regarded Jefferson and his Democrat-leaning followers as a threat to the nation. He served in many governmental roles including two years (1781-1783) in Russia —supposedly as a private citizen so as not to antagonize the British, but actually there to negotiate naval and commerce treaties. His secretary on that mission was John Quincy Adams.

Delegate to the Provincial Congress (1774), unofficial emissary to England (1774-1776) in a futile quest for understanding of the colonies' problems, state councilor (1776-1780), Continental Congress (1776-1778, 1784), signer of the Articles of Confederation (July 9, 1778), state supreme court judge (1785-1791) and chief justice (1791-1806).

DANA, RICHARD HENRY, JR. *(b Aug. 1, 1815, Cambridge, Mass.; d Jan. 6, 1882, Rome, Italy)* Sailor, author best known for *Two Years Before the Mast* (1840), less known for his role in the founding of the Free-Soil party, as a Massachusetts lawyer, or for his ability as a Harvard instructor in elocution. Free-Soil National Convention delegate (1848), state constitutional convention (1853), U.S. attorney for Massachusetts (1861-1866), one of the government lawyers (1867-1868) in the Jefferson Davis treason case, Grant-appointed minister to England (1876) but unconfirmed by the Senate because the president did not first clear the nomination with the Republican party.

DANA, SAMUEL WHITTLESEY *(b Feb. 13, 1760, Wallingford, Conn.; d July 21, 1830, Middletown, Conn.)* Lawyer, Connecticut Federalist. General assembly (1789-1796), U.S. Representative (1797-1810), U.S. Senate (1810-1821), mayor of Middletown (1822 until death) and also presiding judge of the Middlesex County Court (1825 until death).

DANAHER, JOHN ANTHONY *(b Jan. 9, 1899, Meriden, Conn.)* Lawyer and senior circuit judge of the U.S. Court of Appeals in the District of Columbia since Jan. 23, 1969. Assistant U.S. attorney for Connecticut district (1922-1934), Connecticut secretary of state (1933-1935), U.S. Senate (1938-1945), appointed to President's Commission on Internal Security and Individual Rights (1951) by Truman, to President's Conference on Administrative Procedure (1953) by Eisenhower, and to the U.S. Court of Appeals (1953).

DANE, NATHAN *(b Dec. 29, 1752, Ipswich, Mass.; d Feb. 15, 1835, Beverly, Mass.)* Lawyer, teacher, Massachusetts political figure who opposed the federal Constitution. State representative (1782-1785), Continental Congress (1785-1788), state senate (1790, 1791, 1794-1797), Essex County common pleas court judge (1794), commissioner charged with revising state laws (1795).

DANFORD, LORENZO *(b Oct. 18, 1829, Washington Township, Ohio; d June 19, 1899, St. Clairsville, Ohio)* Lawyer, Union Army officer, Ohio Republican after a brief fling at membership in the American (Know-Nothing) party. Presidential elector on the Fillmore-Donelson ticket (1856), Lincoln-Johnson ticket (1864), Harrison-Reid ticket (1892); Bemont County prosecutor (1857-1861), U.S. Representative (1873-1879, 1895 until death).

DANIEL, JOHN WARWICK *(b Sept. 5, 1842, Lynchburg, Va.; d June 29, 1910, Lynchburg)* Confederate Army officer, lawyer, Virginia Democrat. State house of delegates (1869-1872), state senate (1875-1881), presidential elector on the Tilden-Hendricks ticket (1876), delegate to five Democratic National Conventions (1880-1900), unsuccessful candidate for governor (1881), U.S. Representative (1885-1887), U.S. Senate (1887 until death).

DANIELS, JOSEPHUS *(b May 18, 1862, Washington, N.C.; d Jan. 15, 1948, Raleigh, N.C.)* Editor-publisher of the *Raleigh News and Observer*, long-time friend of William Jennings Bryan, Woodrow Wilson's secretary of the navy (1913-1921), confidante of Franklin Delano Roosevelt, diplomat, progressive North Carolina Democrat, and nationally a member of the party's inner circle.

Ambassador to Mexico (1933-1941) and the voice of FDR's Good Neighbor Policy aimed at bettering relations with Latin America.

DARBY, JOHN FLETCHER *(b Dec. 10, 1803, Person County, Mo.; d May 11, 1882, Warren County, Mo.)* Lawyer, banker, Missouri Whig who for six years (1835-1841) was mayor of St. Louis, State senate (1838), U.S. Representative (1851-1853).

DARRALL, CHESTER BIDWELL *(b June 24, 1842, Somerset County, Pa.; d Jan. 1, 1908, Washington, D.C.)* Physician, Union Army surgeon, merchant, planter, carpetbag Louisiana Republican. State senate (1868), delegate to GOP National Convention (1872, 1876), U.S. Representative (1869-1878, 1881-1883), register of U.S. Land Office in New Orleans (1883-1885).

DARROW, GEORGE POTTER *(b Feb. 4, 1859, Waterford, Conn.; d June 7, 1943, Philadelphia, Pa.)* Banker, paint manufacturer, insurance broker, Pennsylvania Republican. Philadelphia Common Council (1910-1915), U.S. Representative (1915-1937, 1939-1941).

DAVENPORT, JAMES *(b Oct. 12, 1758, Stamford, Conn.; d Aug. 3, 1797, Stamford)* Connecticut patriot, Revolutionary soldier. State representative (1785-1790), state senate (1790-1797), Fairfield County judge (1792-1796), U.S. Representative (1796 until death). Brother of John Davenport.

DAVENPORT, JAMES SANFORD *(b Sept. 21, 1864, Cherokee County, Ala.; d Jan. 3, 1940, Oklahoma City, Okla.)* Lawyer, Oklahoma pioneer who moved there (1890) when it was Muskogee, Indian Territory, and became an active Democratic politician. Member of territorial council (1897-1901) and speaker (1900-1901), Cherokee Nation attorney (1901-1907), mayor of Vinita (1903,

1904), U.S. Representative (1907-1909) when statehood was granted and again (1911-1917), judge of the state criminal court of appeals (1926 until death).

DAVENPORT, JOHN *(b Jan. 16, 1752, Stamford, Conn.; d Nov. 28, 1830, Stamford)* Teacher, lawyer, Continental Army officer, and a Connecticut Federalist. State representative (1776-1796), U.S. Representative (1799-1817). Brother of James Davenport.

DAVENPORT, THOMAS *(b ——, Cumberland County, Va.; d Nov. 18, 1838, Halifax County, Va.)* Lawyer, Virginia Federalist who served five terms as a U.S. Representative (1825-1835).

DAVEY, MARTIN LUTHER *(b July 25, 1884, Kent, Ohio; d March 31, 1946, Kent)* Tree surgeon, real estate operator, Ohio Democrat. Mayor of Kent (1913-1918), U.S. Representative (1918-1921, 1923-1929), Democratic National Convention delegate (1932, 1940), governor (1935-1939).

DAVEY, ROBERT CHARLES *(b Oct. 22, 1853, New Orleans, La.; d Dec. 26, 1908, New Orleans)* Merchant, Louisiana Democrat. State senate (1879, 1884, 1886, 1892) and president pro tem (1884, 1886), New Orleans recorders' court judge (1880-1888), U.S. Representative (1893-1895, 1897 until death).

DAVIDSON, JAMES HENRY *(b June 18, 1858, Colchester, N.Y.; d Aug. 6, 1918, Washington, D.C.)* Lawyer, teacher, Wisconsin Republican. Green Lake County district attorney (1888), Oshkosh city attorney (1895-1898), U.S. Representative (1897-1913, 1917 until death).

DAVIDSON, ROBERT HAMILTON McWHORTA *(b Sept. 23, 1832, Gadsden County, Fla.; d Jan. 18, 1908, Quincy, Fla.)* Lawyer, Confederate Army officer, Florida Democrat. State representative (1856-1859), state senate (1860-1862), state constitutional convention (1865), presidential elector for Greeley-Brown (1872), U.S. Representative (1877-1891), state railroad commissioner (1897, 1898).

DAVIE, WILLIAM RICHARDSON *(b June 20, 1756, Egremont, Cumberlandshire, England; d Nov. 29, 1820, Lancaster County, N.C.)* A Revolutionary Army soldier at twenty who, in seven years of war, rose to general before being severely wounded; lawyer, orator, "father" of the University of North Carolina and recipient of its first honorary degree, farmer, and Federalist in a heavily Democratic state yet so politically popular as to be elected governor (1798-1799). Halifax member of state legislature (1786-1798), chairman of boundary commission (1797), U.S. peace commissioner to France (1799), negotiator of Tuscarora Treaty (1802).

DAVILA, FELIX CARDOVA *(b Nov. 20, 1878, Vega Baja, P.R.; d Dec. 3, 1938, Condado, P.R.)* Lawyer, jurist, Puerto Rico Unionist who served fifteen years (1917-1932) as resident commissioner to the United States. Caguas municipal judge (1904), Manati municipal judge (1904-1908), Aguadillo district attorney (1908), Guayama district court judge (1908-1910), Arecibo district judge (1910-1911), and San Juan district judge (1911-1917), associate justice of the Puerto Rico Supreme Court (1932 until death).

DAVIS, CHARLES RUSSELL *(b Sept. 17, 1849, Pittsfield, Ill.; d July 29, 1930, Washington, D.C.)* Lawyer, Minnesota Republican. St. Peter city attorney and city clerk (1878-1898), Nicollet County prosecutor (1879-1889, 1901-1903), state representative (1889, 1890), state senate (1891-1895), U.S. Representative (1903-1925), then remaining in Washington to practice law.

DAVIS, CLIFFORD *(b Nov. 18, 1897, Hazlehurst, Miss.)* Lawyer, Tennessee Democrat. Memphis city judge (1923-1927), vice mayor and public safety commissioner (1928-1940), U.S. Representative for a quarter-century (1940-1965) serving on the Public Works Committee.

DAVIS, CUSHMAN KELLOGG *(b June 16, 1838, Henderson, N.Y.; d Nov. 27, 1900, St. Paul, Minn.)* Lawyer, Union Army officer, lecturer, Shakespearean scholar, Minnesota Republican who was more Bardian lecturer than toe-the-line politician. State representative (1867), U.S. attorney for Minnesota (1868-1873), governor (1874-1876), U.S. Senate (1887 until death), chairman of the Foreign Relations Committee; member of Spanish-American War peace commission in Paris (1898).

DAVIS, DAVID *(b March 9, 1815, Cecil County, Md.; d June 26, 1886, Bloomington, Ill.)* Lawyer, Supreme Court justice who resigned to run for the Senate, Illinois Whig-Republican-Independent Democrat and close friend of Abraham Lincoln, leading his supporters at the 1860 GOP National Convention and, after the assassination, acting as administrator of his estate; a man for whom a presidential groundswell grew (1872) with Labor Reformers, Liberal Republicans, and Democrats, each at their separate conventions, placing him in nomination. He appeared on the ballot with six other candidates and received one electoral vote.
State representative (1844), state constitutional convention (1847), eighth judicial district judge (1848-1862) with Lincoln often sitting for him, associate justice of the U.S. Supreme Court (1862-1877), U.S. Senate (1877-1883) and president pro tem (1881-1883).

DAVIS, EDMUND JACKSON *(b Oct. 2, 1827, St. Augustine, Fla.; d Feb. 7, 1883, Austin, Texas)* Texas lawyer who quit the Confederate cause when he failed to be chosen a delegate to the state secession convention, became a Union Army officer, president of the Reconstruction convention (1868-1869) where he advocated full Negro suffrage while stripping former Confederates of their voting rights, and (1870-1874) dictatorial Republican governor who appointed more than 8,000 people to governmental positions supposed to have been filled through popular election. When he lost a reelection bid, he declared the election laws unconstitutional and barricaded himself in the state capitol with a company of Negro troops to guard him, leaving only when President Grant refused to intervene.

DAVIS, EWIN LAMAR *(b Feb. 5, 1876, Bedford County, Tenn.; d Oct. 23, 1949, Washington, D.C.)* Lawyer, banker, Tennessee Democrat who was a member of the Federal Trade Commission (1933 until death) and its chairman (1935, 1940, 1945). Presidential elector on the Parker-Davis ticket (1904), delegate to all Democratic state conventions (1900-1910), seventh judicial circuit judge (1910-1918), U.S. Representative (1919-1933).

DAVIS, GARRETT *(b Sept. 10, 1801, Mount Sterling, Ky.; d Sept. 22, 1872, Paris, Ky.)* Kentucky lawyer, orator, farmer, close friend of Henry Clay, bitter foe of Roman Catholics, early supporter of Lincoln war policies but by 1864 so sharply critical of them that he narrowly averted expulsion from the Senate. He was a Whig turned Know-Nothing turned Democrat. State representative (1833-1835), U.S. Representative (1839-1847), declined Know-Nothing presidential nomination (1856), supported Constitutional Union ticket (1860), U.S. Senate (1861 until death).

DAVIS, HENRY GASSAWAY *(b Nov. 16, 1823, Baltimore, Md.; d March 11, 1916, Washington, D.C.)* West Virginia

Democrat who worked his way up from railroad brakeman to railroad builder, railroad president, coal mine operator, lumberman, banker, and vice presidential candidate (1904), the one thing that he tackled but did not win. State house of delegates (1865), national convention delegate (1868, 1872), state senate (1868, 1870), U.S. Senate (1871-1883), U.S. representative at Pan American conferences (1889, 1901), first chairman of Pan American Railway Committee (1901 until death).

DAVIS, JAMES CURRAN (b May 17, 1895, Franklin, Ga.) Lawyer, Georgia Democrat. State representative (1924-1928), state Department of Industrial Relations counsel (1928-1931), DeKalb County attorney (1931-1934), superior court judge (1934-1947), U.S. Representative (1947-1963) serving on District of Columbia, Post Office, and Civil Service committees.

DAVIS, JAMES JOHN (b Oct. 27, 1873, Tredegar, South Wales; d Nov. 22, 1947, Takoma Park, Md.) Steelworker, union officer, official of the Loyal Order of Moose, Indiana and Pennsylvania Republican who served as secretary of labor (1921-1930) for three presidents: Harding, Coolidge, Hoover. In Indiana: Elwood city clerk (1898-1902), Madison County recorder (1903-1907). In Pennsylvania: U.S. Senate (1930-1945).

DAVIS, JEFFERSON (b June 3, 1808, Fairview, Ky.; d Dec. 6, 1889, New Orleans, La.) West Point graduate, Indian fighter, Mexican War officer, cotton grower, Mississippi States' Rights Democrat and president of the Confederacy who was indicted for treason (1866) but never convicted, living out his years as a writer.

Presidential elector on the Polk-Dallas ticket (1844), U.S. Representative (1845-1846), U.S. Senate (1847-1851), unsuccessful candidate for governor (1851), President Pierce's sec-

retary of war (1853-1857), again a U.S. senator (1857-1861) resigning at secession after explaining his reasons in a stirring speech, chosen Confederate president (1861) by the Provisional Congress for a six-year term and inaugurated in 1862, taken prisoner by Union forces (1865) and paroled (1867).

DAVIS, JOHN (b Jan. 13, 1787, Northboro, Mass.; d April 19, Worcester, Mass.) Lawyer, Massachusetts Federalist-National Republican-Whig but, whatever the political tag, always a conservative. U.S. Representative (1825-1834), governor (1834, 1835, 1841-1843), U.S. Senate (1835-1841, 1845-1853).

DAVIS, JOHN WESLEY (b April 16, 1799, New Holland, Pa.; d Aug. 22, 1859, Carlisle, Ind.) Physician, diplomat, Indiana Democrat who served as Polk-appointed commissioner to China (1848-1851) and Pierce-appointed governor of the Oregon Territory (1853, 1854). Sullivan County surrogate (1829-1831), state representative (1831-1833, 1841-1843, 1851, 1852, 1857) and speaker (1831, 1841), Indian treaty commissioner (1834), U.S. Representative (1835-1837, 1839-1841, 1843-1847) and Speaker (1845-1847), Democratic National Convention delegate (1852).

DAVIS, JOHN WILLIAM (b April 13, 1873, Clarksburg, W.Va.; d March 24, 1955, Charleston, S.C.) Teacher, lawyer, diplomat, West Virginia Democrat who ran second to Calvin Coolidge in the 1924 presidential race, receiving 8,385,283 popular and 136 electoral votes. State house of delegates (1899), Democratic National Convention delegate (1904, 1932), member of Commission on Uniform State Laws (1909), U.S. Representative (1911-1913), solicitor general of the United States (1913-1918), ambassador to Great Britain (1918-1921), negotiator for exchange of prisoners of war with Germany (1918).

DAVIS, PAULINA KELLOGG WRIGHT *(b Aug. 7, 1813, Bloomfield, N.Y.; d Aug. 24, 1876, Providence, R.I.)* Lecturer, suffragist, editor who (1853) founded *Una,* first women's suffrage periodical.

DAVIS, REUBEN *(b Jan. 18, 1813, Winchester, Tenn.; d Oct. 14, 1890, Huntsville, Ala.)* Defied his preacher father's order not to practice law because lawyers "were wholly given up to the Devil," became a district attorney in Mississippi (1835-1839) at the age of twenty-two, and went on to become a Democratic congressman (1857 until secession in 1861). Confederate Army officer and a member of the Confederate Congress where, although he always had been known as a firebrand, he was sharply critical of Jefferson Davis' war policies. (They were not related.)

DAVIS, ROBERT WYCHE *(b March 15, 1849, Lee County, Ga.; d Sept. 15, 1929, Gainesville, Fla.)* Confederate soldier at fourteen, lawyer, newspaper editor, Florida Democrat. State representative (1884, 1885) and speaker (1885), U.S. Representative (1897-1905), register of U.S. land office at Gainesville (1914-1922), and mayor of Gainesville (1924, 1925).

DAWES, BEMAN GATES *(b Jan. 14, 1870, Marietta, Ohio; d May 15, 1953, Newark, Ohio)* Farmer, engineer, public utilities executive, railway builder, president and board chairman of the Pure Oil Co., founder of the Dawes Arboretum, Ohio Republican who served two terms as a U.S. Representative (1905-1909). Son of Rufus Dawes and brother of Vice President Charles G. Dawes.

DAWES, CHARLES GATES *(b Aug. 27, 1865, Marietta, Ohio; d April 23, 1951, Evanston, Ill.)* Public utilities executive, much-decorated World War I officer, board chairman of Chicago's City National Bank and Trust Co.; before moving to Illinois, a Nebraska lawyer who, at his own expense, fought so vigorously against the railroad monopoly's discriminatory farm-freight rates that he became known as "the people's advocate"; the organizer of Illinois' McKinley-for-President movement (1895), he became a member of the Republican Executive Committee and managed McKinley's western campaign; cowinner with Sir Austen Chamberlain, Britain's foreign secretary, of the Nobel Peace Prize (1925); author, statesman, diplomat, the U.S. Bureau of the Budget's first director (1921), coauthor of the Dawes Plan for German reparations, composer of *A Melody in A Minor* and other music, Illinois Republican who defeated Secretary of Commerce Herbert C. Hoover for the 1924 vice-presidential nomination (682½ to 234½) on the Coolidge ticket and served (1925-1929).

Among his other milestones: U.S. comptroller of the currency (1898-1901), Allied Reparation Commission chairman (1923), ambassador to Great Britain (1929-1932). Among his published works: *The Banking System of the United States and Its Relation to the Money and Business of the United States* (1894), *A Journal of the Great War* (1921), *Notes as Vice President* (1935), *How Long Prosperity* (1937), *Journal of the McKinley Years* (1950). Son of Rufus and brother of Beman G. Dawes.

DAWES, HENRY LAURENS *(b Oct. 30, 1816, Cummington, Mass.; d Feb. 5, 1903, Pittsfield, Mass.)* Teacher, newspaper editor, lawyer, Massachusetts Republican who is credited with the creation of the U.S. Weather Bureau. State representative (1848, 1849, 1852), state senate (1850), state constitutional convention (1853), western district attorney (1853-1857), U.S. Representative (1857-1875) serving as chairman of the Ways and Means and Appropriations committees, U.S. Senate

(1875-1893) and chairman of the Indian Affairs Committee.

DAWES, RUFUS *(b July 4, 1838, Malta, Ohio; d Aug. 2, 1899, Marietta, Ohio)* Wholesale lumber dealer, Union Army officer, Ohio Republican. U.S. Representative (1881-1883), father of Charles G. and Beman G. Dawes.

DAWSON, JOHN *(b 1762, Virginia; d March 31, 1814, Washington, D.C.).* Lawyer, Virginia Democrat, and a staunch supporter of Thomas Jefferson. State house of delegates (1786-1789), Continental Congress (1788, 1789), delegate to federal Constitution ratification convention (1788), presidential elector on the Washington ticket (1792), U.S. Representative (1797 until death).

DAYTON, ALSTON GORDON *(b Oct. 18, 1857, Philippi, Va., now W.Va.; d July 30, 1920, Battle Creek, Mich.)* Lawyer, West Virginia Republican. Upshur County prosecutor (1879), Barbour County prosecutor (1882-1886), U.S. Representative (1895-1905), federal judge for state's northern district (1905 until death).

DAYTON, ELIAS *(b May 1, 1737, Elizabethtown, now Elizabeth, N.J.; d Oct. 22, 1807, Elizabethtown)* Storekeeper, New Jersey patriot, French and Indian War and Revolutionary Army officer who saw much service in the field, Continental Congress (1778-1779), town recorder (1789), state general assembly (1791-1792, 1794-1796), mayor of Elizabethtown (1796-1805). Father of Jonathan Dayton.

DAYTON, JONATHAN *(b Oct. 16, 1760, Elizabethtown, now Elizabeth, N.J.; d Oct. 9, 1824, Elizabethtown)* Lawyer, Revolutionary officer, New Jersey Federalist who was indicted (1807) for conspiring with Aaron Burr but was never tried. State general assembly (1786,

1787, 1790) and speaker (1790), delegate to federal Constitutional Convention (1787) and the youngest signer of the Constitution, Continental Congress delegate (1787-1789), state council (1790), U.S. Representative (1791-1799) and speaker (1795-1799), U.S. Senate (1799-1805). Son of Elias Dayton.

DEANE, SILAS *(b Dec. 24, 1737, Groton, Conn.; d Sept. 23, 1789, aboard ship en route home from England).* Connecticut lawyer, merchant, general assembly delegate (1768-1775), and Continental Congress member (1774-1776) who became America's first foreign agent. He was assigned to purchase arms and other supplies from European countries, on a commission basis, to equip the Revolutionary Army; to obtain the personal services of military leaders; and to serve as ambassador to France with Benjamin Franklin and Arthur Lee to obtain French cooperation.

He was successful on all three missions. He assembled eight shiploads of supplies; enlisted Lafayette, Pulaski, Steuben, DeKalb, and other military leaders; and he negotiated (1778) two treaties in Paris. He also recruited some out-and-out mercenaries, however, who proved an embarrassment, and he was accused of charging Congress for supplies that actually had been gifts.

Deane was recalled and investigated; he returned to France to obtain proof of his innocence only to learn that he was persona non grata because of publication of some of his papers. He went to England and (1781) began writing letters home urging friends to give up the fight for independence. He died a poor man and there were reports that his death was suicide. Many years later (1842), Congress decided an injustice had been done him and, by way of restitution, gave his heirs $37,000.

DEARBORN, HENRY *(b Feb. 23, 1751, North Hampton, N.H.; d June 6, 1829,*

Roxbury, Mass.) Physician, general during the Revolutionary War and the War of 1812, diplomat, Massachusetts Democrat representing a Maine district. U.S. Representative (1793-1797), Jefferson's secretary of war (1801-1809), collector of the Port of Boston (1809-1812), ambassador to Portugal (1822-1824). Father of Henry A. S. Dearborn.

DEARBORN, HENRY ALEXANDER SCAM-MELL (b March 3, 1783, Exeter, N.H.; d July 29, 1851, Portland, Maine) Lawyer, author, Massachusetts political figure. Boston collector of customs (1812-1829), state constitutional convention (1820), state representative (1829), state senate (1830), U.S. Representative (1831-1833), state adjutant general (1834-1843) until dismissed for lending arms to Rhode Island to put down the Dorr Rebellion (see Thomas Dorr), mayor of Roxbury (1847-1851). Son of Henry Dearborn.

DE ARMOND, DAVID ALBAUGH (b March 18, 1844, Altoona, Pa.; d Nov. 23, 1909, Butler, Mo.) Lawyer, Missouri Democrat. Presidential elector on Cleveland-Hendricks ticket (1884), state senate (1879-1883), state supreme court commissioner (1884), twenty-second judicial circuit judge (1886-1890), U.S. Representative (1891 until death).

DEBERRY, EDMUND (b Aug. 14, 1787, Lawrenceville, now Mount Gilead, N.C.; d Dec. 12, 1859, Pee Dee Township, N.C.). Farmer, cotton and flour miller, North Carolina Whig. State senate (1806-1811, 1813, 1814, 1820, 1821, 1826-1828), U.S. Representative (1829-1831, 1833-1845, 1849-1851).

DEEMER, ELIAS (b Jan. 3, 1838, Durham, Pa.; d March 29, 1918, Williamsport, Pa.) Merchant, newspaper publisher, Union soldier, lumber manufacturer, banker, Pennsylvania Republican. President of Williamsport common coun-

cil (1888-1890), GOP National Convention delegate (1896), U.S. Representative (1901-1907), moved to Mississippi where he founded the town of Deemer.

DEGETAU, FEDERICO (b Dec. 5, 1862, Ponce, P.R.; d Jan. 20, 1914, Santurce, P.R.) Lawyer, author, Puerto Rico Republican who was sent to Spain to ask for autonomy. San Juan municipal council (1897, 1899, 1900) and mayor (1898), secretary of interior in Puerto Rico's first American cabinet (1899), resident commissioner to the United States (1901-1905).

DE LANCEY, JAMES, SR. (b Nov. 27, 1703, New York City; d July 30, 1760, New York City) Lawyer, merchant, and a power in New York politics, controlling both the council and the assembly at the same time, serving as lieutenant governor (1753 until death), and giving birth to the Episcopalian "De Lancey Party" that vied with the Presbyterian "Livingston Party" faction. The issue that first fashioned the rift was the chartering of King's College (now Columbia University) in 1754.

DELANEY, JOHN JOSEPH (b Aug. 21, 1878, Brooklyn, N.Y.; d Nov. 18, 1948, Brooklyn) Lawyer, New York Democrat. U.S. Representative (1918-1919, 1931 until death). Democratic state convention delegate (1922, 1924), deputy New York City commissioner of public markets (1924-1931).

DELANO, COLUMBUS (b June 4, 1809, Shoreham, Vt.; d Oct. 23, 1896, Mount Vernon, Ohio) Lawyer, farmer, banker, Ohio Whig turned Republican who was secretary of the interior (1870-1875) in President Grant's cabinet and accused of frauds in Indian affairs. U.S. Representative (1845-1847, 1865-1867, 1868-1869), GOP National Convention delegate (1860) when he seconded Lincoln's nomination and (1864), state representative (1863), internal revenue commissioner (1869-1870).

DELANY, MARTIN ROBINSON *(b May 6, 1812, Charles Town, Va., now W.Va.; d Jan. 24, 1885, Xenia, Ohio).* Physician, lecturer, journalist, son of free Negroes, and, during the Civil War, the first black major to serve in the U.S. Army; author of *The Condition, Elevation, Emigration and Destiny of the Colored People of the United States, Politically Considered* (1852); a leader in plans for migration to the Niger Valley in Africa, and a West Virginia Independent Republican who severely criticized Reconstruction era corruption and ran (1874) unsuccessfully for lieutenant governor.

DE LARGE, ROBERT CARLOS *(b March 15, 1842, Aiken, S.C.; d Feb. 14, 1874, Charleston, S.C.)* A slave who managed to acquire an education, then a farmer and South Carolina Republican whose tenure as a U.S. Representative (1871-1873) was marred by charges of election irregularities. State constitutional convention delegate (1868), state representative (1868-1870) and sinking fund commissioner, state land commissioner (1870-1871).

DE LEON, DANIEL *(b Dec. 14, 1852, island of Curaçao; d May 11, 1914, New York City)* Lawyer, teacher, newspaper editor. Columbia University lecturer on Latin American affairs and active member of New York's Socialist Labor Party who (1905) helped found the Industrial Workers of the World (IWW).

DEMING, HENRY CHAMPION *(b May 23, 1815, Colchester, Conn.; d Oct. 8, 1872, Hartford, Conn.)* Lawyer, writer, orator, Connecticut Republican whose experience as mayor of Hartford (1854-1858, 1860-1862) helped him to be an effective military mayor of New Orleans, La. (1862-1863) while an officer in the Union Army. Connecticut representative (1849, 1850, 1859-1861), state senate

(1851), U.S. Representative (1863-1867), Hartford district collector of internal revenue (1869 until death).

DEMPSEY, JOHN JOSEPH *(b June 22, 1879, White Haven, Pa.; d March 11, 1958, Washington, D.C.)* A railroad construction gang waterboy at thirteen who succeeded in a variety of commercial enterprises and became a leading New Mexico New Deal Democrat. State director for the National Recovery Administration (1933), Federal Housing Administration and National Emergency Council (1934); U.S. Representative (1935-1941, 1951 until death), member of U.S. Maritime Commission (1941), undersecretary of the interior (1941-1942), governor (1943-1947).

DEMPSEY, STEPHEN WALLACE *(b May 8, 1862, Hartland, N.Y.; d March 1, 1949, Washington, D.C.)* Lawyer, New York Republican. Assistant U.S. attorney (1889-1907), special assistant to the U.S. attorney general (1907-1912) in charge of prosecution of Standard Oil Co. and several railroads, U.S. Representative (1915-1931) remaining thereafter in Washington to practice law.

DENBY, EDWIN *(b Feb. 18, 1870, Evansville, Ind.; d Feb. 8, 1929, Detroit, Mich.)* University of Michigan football player of note, lawyer, banker, business entrepreneur, Michigan Republican whom President Harding, without prior consultation, appointed secretary of the navy (1921-1924) and who was involved in the Teapot Dome oil scandal.

Employee of Chinese imperial maritime customs service (1887-1894), state representative (1903), U.S. Representative (1905-1911), president of Detroit Charter Commission (1913, 1914). His last public position before Harding's surprise appointment was chief probation officer both in Detroit recorder's court and Wayne County circuit court (1920-1921). Said the *New York Times* of his part in the Teapot Dome investigation: "Stupidity is the (only) high crime and misdemeanor of which the Senate accuses Mr. Denby." Son of Charles Denby who was U.S. minister to China (1885-1898).

DENEEN, CHARLES SAMUEL *(b May 4, 1863, Edwardsville, Ill.; d Feb. 5, 1940, Chicago, Ill.)* Lawyer, Illinois Republican. State representative (1892), Chicago sanitary district attorney (1895, 1896), Cook County state's attorney (1896-1904), governor (1905-1913), U.S. Senate (1925-1931).

DENISON, EDWARD EVERETT *(b Aug. 28, 1873, Marion, Ill.; d June 17, 1953, Carbondale, Ill.)* Lawyer, banker, Illinois Republican. U.S. Representative (1915-1931).

DENNISON, WILLIAM *(b Nov. 23, 1815, Cincinnati, Ohio; d June 15, 1882, Columbus, Ohio)* Lawyer, businessman, Ohio Whig who was one of the state's pioneer Republicans. Acting chairman of Ohio delegation to GOP National Convention (1856) and chairman of Committee on Resolutions, governor (1860-1862), chairman of GOP National Convention (1864), postmaster general in Lincoln cabinet (1864-1866).

DENT, STANLEY HUBERT, JR. *(b Aug. 16, 1869, Eufaula, Ala.; d Oct. 6, 1938, Montgomery, Ala.)* Lawyer, Alabama Democrat who served as a U.S. Representative (1909-1921) and was chairman of the House Military Affairs Committee during World War I. State constitutional convention (1901), Montgomery County prosecutor (1902-1909), Democratic National Convention delegate (1908), president of state constitutional convention for repeal of the Eighteenth (prohibition) Amendment (1933).

DENTON, WINFIELD KIRKPATRICK *(b Oct. 28, 1896, Evansville, Ind.)* World War I aviator, lawyer, Indiana Democrat.

Vanderburgh County prosecuting attorney (1931-1936), state legislature (1937-1942) serving as caucus chairman (1939) and minority leader (1941), on budget committee (1940-1942), U.S. Army (1942-1945), U.S. Representative (1949-1953, 1955-1966) serving on Appropriations Committee.

DENVER, JAMES WILLIAM *(b Oct. 23, 1817, Winchester, Va.; d Aug. 9, 1892, Washington, D.C.)* Teacher, lawyer, publisher, Union Army general, California Democrat and the man for whom Denver, Colo., is named. California state senate (1852-1853), secretary of state (1853), U.S. Representative (1855-1857), U.S. commissioner of Indian affairs (1857). President Buchanan, seeking a strong man to put down the lawlessness rampant in the Kansas Territory, of which Colorado was then a part, appointed Denver territorial governor (1858). During that time gold was discovered on Cherry Creek, men rushed there, creating a boomtown that was named for the governor—the miners' way of thanking Denver for protecting them from claim jumpers, bandits, and confidence men.

DEPEW, CHAUNCEY MITCHELL *(b April 23, 1834, Peekskill, N.Y.; d April 5, 1928, New York City)* Lawyer who represented Cornelius Vanderbilt's railroad interests (often acting as lobbyist) and became president of the New York Central Railroad; New York Republican, raconteur, orator with a voice able to bring boisterous political conventions under control, and—his ultimate honor—a main speaker at the unveiling of the Statue of Liberty (1886).
  State assembly (1861-1862), New York secretary of state (1863-1864), appointed the first U.S. minister to Japan (1865) but refused when Commodore Vanderbilt convinced him that "railroads are the career for a young man,

not politics." Recipient of ninety-nine votes in balloting for GOP presidential nomination (1888), and delegate to all such conventions (1888-1924), U.S. Senate (1899-1911).

DE PRIEST, OSCAR *(b March 9, 1871, Florence, Ala.; d May 12, 1951, Chicago).* House painter, real estate dealer, and Illinois Republican who was Chicago's first Negro alderman (1915-1917), the first Negro ever to be elected a U.S. Representative from a northern state, and, the first Negro congressman elected in the twentieth century (1929-1935). Member Cook County Board of Commissioners (1904-1908), vice chairman of GOP county central committee (1932-1934), GOP National Convention delegate (1936), member of city council (1943-1947).

As a congressman, De Priest was regarded as the spokesman for America's eleven million black citizens until the Depression, when his Republican affiliations strained his political loyalties. He attempted the compromise strategy of remaining loyal to his party nationally, and supporting Democrats locally. However, he lost his 1934 reelection bid to Arthur W. Mitchell, the first Negro Democrat ever to be sent to Congress.

DERBIGNY, PIERRE AUGUSTE CHARLES BOURGUINON *(b 1767, Laon, France; d Oct. 6, 1829, Gretna, La.)* Louisiana National Republican who delivered, in French, the first Fourth of July speech (1804) ever made in New Orleans. Member of Louisiana's first state legislature (1812), state supreme court judge (1813-1820), governor (1828-1829).

DE ROUEN, RENE LOUIS *(b Jan. 7, 1874, St. Landry, now Evangeline, Parish, La.; d March 27, 1942, Baton Rouge, La.).* Merchant, banker, farmer, Louisiana Democrat. State constitutional convention delegate (1921), U.S. Representative (1927-1941).

DEROUNIAN, STEVEN BOGHOS *(b April 6, 1918, Sofia, Bulgaria)* Lawyer, New York Republican. North Hempstead councilman (1948-1952), alternate delegate to GOP National Conventions (1956, 1960), U.S. Representative (1953-1965) serving on the Ways and Means Committee.

DESHA, JOSEPH *(b Dec. 9, 1768, Monroe County, Pa.; d Oct. 11, 1842, Scott County, Ky.)* Frontiersman, farmer, Indian fighter to avenge killing of his two brothers; a hawk in the debate that preceded the War of 1812 and a general when the shooting started; Kentucky Democrat and a flowery orator whose credo, however, was "Think much and speak but little." State representative (1797, 1799-1802), state senate (1803-1807), U.S. Representative (1807-1819), governor (1824-1828).

His brother, Robert (1791-1849), was a U.S. Representative (1827-1831).

DEUSTER, PETER VICTOR *(b Feb. 13, 1831, Aix la Chappelle, Rhenish Prussia; d Dec. 31, 1904, Milwaukee, Wis.).* Printer, newspaperman who became a Milwaukee newspaper publisher, Wisconsin Democrat. State assembly (1863), state senate (1870, 1871), U.S. Representative (1879-1885), chairman of a commission named to diminish Oregon's Umatilla Indian Reservation (1887), U.S. consul at Crefeld, Germany (1896-1897).

DE VARGAS, DIEGO *(b about 1650, Madrid, Spain; d April 4, 1704, while fighting Apaches in New Mexico's Sandia Mountains. Full name: Don Diego Jose de Vargas Zapata y Lujon Ponce de Leon y Contreras)* Governor-captain general of New Mexico (1692-1697) who effectively dealt with Indian raiding parties and reconquered the province for Spain. Led settlers back to their homes but, in so doing, incurred the displeasure of the Santa Fe town council (cabildo). He was thrown into jail on their charges, replaced by Pedro Rodriguez Cubero by choice of the crown, vindicated himself, and was reappointed governor (1703 until death). As a reward, the king of Spain made him the Marquis de la Nava de Brazinas.

DE WOLF, JAMES *(b March 18, 1764, Bristol, R.I.; d Dec. 21, 1837, New York City)* Went to sea as a boy during the Revolution, became master of his own ship at twenty, by twenty-five had become a wealthy slave importer-trader, backed by Rhode Island's business and social leaders. His one ship had become a fleet, one ship of which was an armed brig, which he commanded in the War of 1812, then he turned to other pursuits: cotton manufacturing and politics, the latter as a Democrat. Rhode Island state representative (1817-1821, 1829-1837) and speaker of the house (1819-1821); U.S. Senate (1821-1835) where he opposed the spread of slavery.

DEXTER, SAMUEL *(b May 14, 1761, Boston, Mass.; d May 3, 1816, Athens, N.Y.)* Lawyer, Massachusetts Federalist who held several high offices but none of them for long. State representative (1788-1790), U.S. Representative (1793-1795), U.S. Senate (1799-1800), President Adams' secretary of war (seven months in 1800) and secretary of the treasury (four months in 1801).

DICK, CHARLES WILLIAM FREDERICK *(b Nov. 3, 1858, Akron, Ohio; d March 13, 1945, Akron)* Lawyer, Ohio Republican. Summit County auditor (1886-1894), secretary of GOP National Committee (1896-1900), U.S. Representative (1898-1904), U.S. Senate (1904-1911).

DICKERSON, MAHLON *(b April 17, 1770, Hanover, N.J.; d Oct. 5, 1853, Succasunna, N.J.)* Philadelphia lawyer who returned to New Jersey (to run his family's iron works) where he also showed a flair for Democratic politics, declining appointment as minister to

Russia (1834) in order to help his friend, Martin Van Buren, groom for the presidency. In Pennsylvania: Philadelphia Common Council (1802-1803), state commissioner of bankruptcy (1802), state attorney general (1805-1808), Philadelphia recorder (1808-1810). In New Jersey: member of the state assembly (1811-1813), state supreme court law reporter (1813, 1814) and justice (1813-1815), governor (1815-1817), U.S. Senate (1817-1833) and a fighter for high protective tariffs, vice president of state council (1833), secretary of the navy (1834-1838), U.S. district judge (1840), state constitutional convention delegate (1844). Brother of Philemon Dickerson.

DICKERSON, PHILEMON *(b Jan. 11, 1788, Succasunna, N.J.; d Dec. 10, 1862, Paterson, N.J.)* Lawyer and, like his brother, Mahlon, a New Jersey Democrat who served as governor (1836-1837). State assembly (1821-1822), U.S. Representative (1833-1836, 1839-1841), the state's last sergeant at law (1834), U.S. district judge (1841 until death), president of Paterson City Council (1851).

DICKINSON, CLEMENT CABELL *(b Dec. 6, 1849, Prince Edward Court House, Va.; d Jan. 14, 1938, Clinton, Mo.).* Teacher, lawyer, Missouri Democrat. Henry County prosecutor (1877-1882), Clinton city attorney (1882-1884), presidential elector on the Bryan-Sewall ticket (1896), state representative (1900-1902), state senate (1902-1906), U.S. Representative (1910-1921, 1923-1929, 1931-1935).

DICKINSON, DANIEL STEVENS *(b Sept. 11, 1800, Goshen, Conn.; d April 12, 1866, New York City)* Teacher, surveyor, lawyer, orator, New York Democrat who tried for the presidential nomination but received only sixteen votes at the 1860 national convention. After the opening shot of the Civil War was fired, he became a Republican.

Guilford postmaster (1827-1832), Binghamton's first president (1834), Democratic National Convention delegate (1835, 1844, 1848, 1852), state senate (1837-1840), lieutenant governor, senate president and court of errors president (1842-1844), presidential elector on the Polk-Dallas ticket (1844), U.S. Senate (1844-1851), state attorney general on the Union ticket (1861), a GOP National Convention delegate (1864), U.S. attorney for New York's southern district (1865 until death).

DICKINSON, DONALD McDONALD *(b Jan. 17, 1846, Port Ontario, N.Y.; d Oct. 15, 1917, Trenton, Mich.)* Lawyer, Michigan Democrat who supported Horace Greeley, became party head in the state, friend and supporter of Grover Cleveland, and the man in Michigan who had to be seen for a federal appointment. Never sought elective office but served as postmaster general in Cleveland's cabinet (1888-1903). In his honor the state legislature laid out a county and called it Dickinson.

DICKINSON, JOHN *(b Nov. 8, 1732, Talbot County, Md.; d Feb. 14, 1808, Wilmington, Del.)* Lawyer, patriot, delegate to the Continental Congress both from Pennsylvania and Delaware with a conservative point of view that put him in opposition to Benjamin Franklin, the Sugar Act, and the Stamp Act; a man who was opposed to the use of force and who voted against the Declaration of Independence because he favored reconciliation with the crown. However, only two Congressmen offered to bear arms after the Revolution began and he was one of them, becoming a brigadier general of Pennsylvania Militia.

In Delaware: member of the assembly of the Lower Counties (1760) as the state was then called, delegate to the Colonial Congress (1765), member of the Continental Congress (1776, 1777, 1779, 1780), president of the state of

Delaware (1781), member of federal Constitutional Convention and a signer of the document that resulted from it (1787). In Pennsylvania: member of the Continental Congress (1774-1776), president of Pennsylvania (1782-1785). Brother of Philemon Dickinson.

DICKINSON, PHILEMON *(b April 5, 1739, Talbot County, Md.; d Feb. 4, 1809, near Trenton, N.J.)* Superintendent of the family estates, Revolutionary Army officer, Delaware and New Jersey office-holder who served (1784) on commission that chose site on which Washington, D.C., now stands. In Delaware: delegate to Continental Congress (1782, 1783). In New Jersey: delegate to Provincial Congress (1776) and major general in command of New Jersey Militia throughout the war, vice president of council (1783, 1784), U.S. Senate (1790-1793). Brother of John Dickinson.

DICKSTEIN, SAMUEL *(b Feb. 5, 1885, near Vilna, Russia; d April 22, 1954, New York City)* Lawyer, New York Democrat, special deputy state attorney general (1911-1914), New York City alderman (1917), state assembly (1919-1922), U.S. Representative (1923-1945), state supreme court judge (1945 until death).

DIEKMA, GERRIT JOHN *(b March 27, 1859, Holland, Mich.; d Dec. 20, 1930, The Hague, Netherlands, while serving as ambassador)* Lawyer, diplomat, Michigan Republican who was manager of the party's speakers' bureau in 1912. State representative (1885-1891) and house speaker (1889), mayor of Holland (1895), chairman of state GOP central committee (1900-1910, 1927), GOP National Convention delegate (1896), member of Spanish Treaty Claims Commission (1901-1927), U.S. Representative (1908-1911), minister to the Netherlands (1929 until death).

DIES, MARTIN, SR. *(b March 13, 1870, Jackson Parish, La.; d July 13, 1922, Kerrville, Texas)* Lawyer, newspaper editor, rancher, Texas Democrat. Tyler County judge (1894), first judicial district attorney (1898-1900), U.S. Representative (1909-1919). Father of Martin Dies, Jr.

DIES, MARTIN, JR. *(b Nov. 5, 1900, Colorado, Texas; d Nov. 14, 1972, Lufkin, Texas)* Lawyer, rancher-farmer, East Texas Law School teacher, and a Texas Democrat who, as a U.S. Representative (1931-1945, 1953-1959), was the man most responsible for creation (1938) of the House Committee on Un-American Activities. He became chairman of what became known as the Dies Committee and won praise for exposure of Nazi bunds and camps, but later received much adverse criticism in the probing of alleged communism in unions, the motion picture industry, and the Works Progress Administration's Federal Theater. Son of the preceding.

DIETERICH, WILLIAM HENRY *(b March 31, 1876, Brown County, Ill.; d Oct. 12, 1940, Springfield, Ill.)* Lawyer, Illinois Democrat. Rushville city attorney (1903-1907), Rushville schools treasurer (1906-1908), Schuyler County judge (1906-1910), state representative (1917-1921), presidential elector on the Smith-Robinson ticket (1928), U.S. Representative (1931-1933), U.S. Senate (1933-1939).

DIETRICH, CHARLES HENRY *(b Nov. 26, 1853, Aurora, Ill.; d April 10, 1924, Hastings, Nebr.)* Merchant who delivered his wares via pack animals through the Black Hills, miner who struck it rich, banker, Nebraska Republican who served as governor less than a year (1901), resigning to become a U.S. Senator (1901-1905), and then retiring from both political and financial pursuits.

DILL, CLARENCE CLEVELAND *(b Sept. 21, 1884, Knox County, Ohio)* Newspaperman, teacher, lawyer, Washington Democrat. Spokane County deputy prosecutor (1911-1913), governor's private secretary (1913), state convention delegate (1912 when he was chairman, 1916, 1924, 1928, 1932) and national convention (1920, 1924, 1932), U.S. Representative (1915-1919), U.S. Senate (1923-1935), Columbia Basin commissioner (1945-1948), special assistant to the U.S. attorney general (1946-1953).

DILLARD, JAMES HARDY *(b Oct. 24, 1856, Nansemond County, Va.; d Aug. 2, 1940, Charlottesville, Va.)* Humanitarian who was one of the nation's leading educators, with a particular concern for bettering relations between the races and educational opportunities for blacks; created the Negro Rural School Fund (better known as the Jeanes Fund), the Phelps-Stokes Fund, and the John F. Slater Fund. He taught at such schools as Tulane, the University of Vermont, and Phillips Exeter Academy, and received honorary doctorates from such others as Harvard and Washington and Lee.

DILLINGHAM, PAUL, JR. *(b Aug. 10, 1799, Shutesbury, Mass.; d July 26, 1891, Waterbury, Vt.)* Lawyer, Vermont Democrat. Waterbury justice of the peace (1826-1844), town clerk (1829-1844), state representative (1833-1835, 1837-1840), Washington County prosecutor (1835-1838), state constitutional convention delegate (1836, 1857, 1870), state senate (1841, 1842, 1861), U.S. Representative (1843-1847), lieutenant governor (1862-1865), governor (1865, 1866). Father of William P. Dillingham.

DILLINGHAM, WILLIAM PAUL *(b Dec. 12, 1843, Waterbury, Vt.; d July 12, 1923, Montpelier, Vt.)* Lawyer, banker, Vermont Republican who as a U.S. Senator (1900 until death) sponsored the so-called Dillingham Bill imposing a quota system on immigration. Washington County prosecutor (1872-1876), state secretary of civil and military affairs (1866-1876), state representative (1876, 1884), state senate (1878, 1880), state tax commissioner (1882-1888), governor (1888-1890) by the largest vote margin ever to that time, chairman of U.S. Immigration Commission (1907-1910). Son of Paul Dillingham, Jr.

DILLON, CHARLES HALL (b Dec. 18, 1853, Jasper, Ind.; d Sept. 15, 1929, Vermillion, S.Dak.) Indiana, Iowa, and Dakota Territory lawyer, South Dakota Republican. GOP National Convention delegate (1900, 1908), state senator (1903-1911), U.S. Representative (1913-1919), associate justice of the state supreme court (1922-1926).

DIMOND, ANTHONY JOSEPH (b Nov. 30, 1881, Palatine Bridge, N.Y.; d May 28, 1953, Anchorage, Alaska) Prospector, miner, lawyer, Alaska Territory Democrat. U.S. commissioner at Chisana (1913, 1914), special assistant U.S. attorney for Alaska's third judicial division (1917), mayor of Valdez (1920-1922, 1925-1932), territorial senate (1923-1926, 1929-1932), delegate to Congress (1933-1945), district judge (1945 until death).

DINGELL, JOHN DAVID, SR. (b Feb. 2, 1894, Detroit, Mich.; d Sept. 19, 1955, Washington, D.C.) Newspaperman, pipeline builder, beef and pork wholesaler, Michigan Democrat who was an organizer and trustee of Colorado Springs Labor College and served nearly twelve terms as a U.S. Representative (1933 until death). He was then succeeded in Congress by his namesake son.

DINGLEY, NELSON, JR. (b Feb. 15, 1832, Durham, Maine; d Jan. 13, 1899, Washington, D.C.) Lawyer, editor-owner of the Lewiston Journal, Maine Republican. State representative (1862-

1865, 1868, 1873) and speaker (1863, 1864), governor (1874-1876), GOP National Convention delegate (1876, 1880), U.S. Representative (1881 until death).

DINSMOOR, SAMUEL (b July 1, 1766, Windham, N.H.; d March 15, 1835, Keene, N.H.) Lawyer, New Hampshire War Democrat. U.S. Representative (1811-1813), presidential elector on the Monroe ticket (1820), Cheshire County probate judge (1823-1831), member of New Hampshire-Massachusetts boundary commission (1825), governor (1831-1833).

DINSMORE, HUGH ANDERSON (b Dec. 24, 1850, Cave Springs, Ark.; d May 2, 1930, St. Louis, Mo.) Lawyer, farmer, Arkansas Democrat. Fourth judicial district prosecutor (1878-1884), presidential elector on the Cleveland-Hendricks ticket (1884), minister to Korea (1887-1890), U.S. Representative (1893-1905).

DIRKSEN, EVERETT McKINLEY (b Jan. 4, 1896, Pekin, Ill.; d Sept. 7, 1969, Washington, D.C.) World War I balloon-based field artillery observer in France, wholesale baker, lawyer with a flair for theatrics, Illinois Republican, and an orator of national prominence who, as minority leader of the U.S. Senate (1959 until death), was considered by many to be the voice of Republicanism. A man of considerable political skill and clout, whether on Senate floor or convention floor, when Dirksen spoke people listened to every word, uttered in a voice, according to one biographer, "now a whisper, now a deep growl, now rolling thunder." U.S. Representative (1933-1949), U.S. Senate (1951 until death).

Although a conservative and confirmed political partisan, on matters of national and international significance Dirksen forgot party labels and gave support to the president, Democrat or Republican. So it was with such issues as the nuclear test ban treaty, the 1964

Civil Rights Act, the 1965 Voting Rights Act, and the war in Vietnam. Presidents Kennedy and Johnson, Democrats both of them, looked to his advice and support and Dirksen, a man of pride and vanity, basked at the attention they gave him. It was different, though, with President Nixon, a Republican, and the shock, although not openly expressed or revealed, was considerable when the senator from Illinois was less called upon for advice and cooperation.

DISNEY, WESLEY ERNEST (b Oct. 31, 1883, Richland, Kans.; d March 26, 1961, Washington, D.C.) Lawyer, Oklahoma Democrat. Muskogee County attorney (1911-1915), state representative (1919-1924), U.S. Representative (1931-1945).

DITTER, JOHN WILLIAM (b Sept. 5, 1888, Philadelphia, Pa.; d Nov. 21, 1943, Lancaster County, Pa., in a plane crash). Lawyer, Pennsylvania Republican. U.S. Representative (1933 until death).

DIX, JOHN ADAMS (b July 24, 1798, Boscawen, N.H.; d April 21, 1879, New York City) New York lawyer, railroad president who was on his way to becoming a power nationally as a leader of the Democratic party when the proslavery wing prevented him from becoming U.S. secretary of state. Soon after he became, briefly, a Free-Soiler and then a Republican. As President Buchanan's secretary of the treasury for two months in 1861, he wired a subordinate in New Orleans: "If anyone attempts to haul down the American flag, shoot him on the spot," then resigned to become a Union Army general for the next four years.

State adjutant general (1831-1833), New York secretary of state (1833-1839), secretary of Democratic National Convention (1832), state representative (1842), U.S. Senate (1845-1849) to fill a vacancy, unsuccessful Free-Soil gubernatorial candidate (1848), assistant U.S. treasurer (1853), New York City post-master (1860-1861), minister to France (1866-1869), governor (1873-1875), unsuccessful candidate for mayor of New York City (1876).

DIXON, JAMES (b Aug. 5, 1814, Enfield, Conn.; d March 27, 1873, Hartford, Conn.) Lawyer, president of the Hartford Life Insurance Co., poet, conservative Connecticut Whig who turned Republican, then had a falling out with the GOP "radical" wing over President Johnson's policies, failed to win GOP nomination for a third term as U.S. Senator (1857-1869), and ran, unsuccessfully, as a Democrat. In the Senate, he opposed acquisition of Cuba (1859) as a proslavery Democratic trick. State representative (1837, 1838, 1844, 1854) and speaker (1837), U.S. Representative (1845-1849).

DIXON, JOSEPH MOORE (b July 31, 1867, Snow Camp, N.C.; d May 22, 1934, Missoula, Mont.) Lawyer, newspaper publisher, dairy farmer, Montana Republican-Progressive. Missoula County's assistant prosecutor (1893-1895) and prosecutor (1895-1897), state representative (1900), GOP National Convention (1904, 1916), U.S. Representative (1903-1907), U.S. Senate (1907-1913), chairman of National Progressive Convention (1912), governor (1921-1925), first assistant secretary of the interior (1929-1933).

DIXON, LINCOLN (b Feb. 9, 1860, Vernon, Ind.; d Sept. 16, 1932, Lyndon, Ky.) Lawyer, Indiana Democrat who was appointed and reappointed to the U.S. Tariff Commission by Republican Presidents Coolidge and Hoover and served from 1927 until death. Sixth judicial circuit prosecutor (1884-1892), Democratic state committeeman (1897-1904, 1920-1927), U.S. Representative (1905-1919), Democratic National Convention delegate (1920, 1924) and the man in charge of the party's western campaign (1924) the year its candidate, John W. Davis, lost to Coolidge.

DIXON, NATHAN FELLOWS, SR. *(b Dec. 13, 1774, Plainfield, Conn.; d Jan. 29, 1842, Washington, D.C.)* Lawyer, banker, Rhode Island Whig. State representative (1813-1830), U.S. Senate (1839 until death). Father of Nathan F. Dixon, Jr.

DIXON, NATHAN FELLOWS, JR. *(b May 1, 1812, Westerly, R.I.; d April 11, 1881, Westerly)* Lawyer, banker, Rhode Island Whig turned Republican. State representative (1841-1849, 1851-1854, 1858-1862, 1871-1877), governor's council (1842), presidential elector on the Clay-Frelinghuysen ticket (1844), U.S. Representative as a Whig (1849-1851) and as a Republican (1863-1871), delegate to Union National Convention (1866). Son of the preceding, father of the following.

DIXON, NATHAN FELLOWS, III *(b Aug. 28, 1847, Westerly, R.I.; d Nov. 8, 1897, Westerly)* Lawyer, banker, Rhode Island Republican. U.S. attorney for Rhode Island district (1877-1885), U.S. Representative for one month in 1885 to fill a vacancy, state senator (1885-1889), U.S. Senate (1889-1895). Son of Nathan F. Dixon, Jr.

DOBBIN, JAMES COCHRANE *(b Jan. 17, 1814, Fayetteville, N.C.; d Aug. 4, 1857, Fayetteville)* Lawyer, North Carolina Democrat who, as secretary of the navy (1853-1857) in the Pierce cabinet, helped introduce steam vessels to the fleet. U.S. Representative (1845-1847), state house of commons (1848, 1850, 1852) and speaker (1850), Democratic National Convention delegate (1852).

DOCKERY, ALEXANDER MONROE *(b Feb. 11, 1845, Daviess County, Mo.; d Dec. 26, 1926, Gallatin, Mo.)* Physician, banker, Missouri Democrat. Gallatin city councilman (1878-1881) and mayor

(1881-1883), Democratic state convention chairman (1886, 1901), U.S. Representative (1883-1899), governor (1901-1905), Democratic National Convention delegate (1904), third assistant postmaster general (1913-1921).

DODD, THOMAS JOSEPH *(b May 15, 1907, Norwich, Conn.; d May 24, 1971, Old Lyme, Conn.)* Lawyer, FBI agent (1933, 1934), executive trial counsel at the Nuremburg Nazi war crime trials (1945, 1946), and a conservative Connecticut Democrat who became the sixth member (1967) of the U.S. Senate ever censured by that body. The reason: alleged diversion of campaign funds to his personal use.

State director of National Youth Administration (1935-1938), Democratic National Convention delegate (1936, 1948, 1952), assistant U.S. attorney general (1938-1945) helping to shape the Justice Department's first civil rights section and prosecuting Ku Klux Klan cases, unsuccessful candidate for party's gubernatorial nomination (1946, 1948), U.S. Representative (1953-1957), U.S. Senate (1959-1971).

DODDRIDGE, PHILIP *(b May 17, 1773, Bedford County, Va.; d Nov. 19, 1832, Washington, D.C.)* Lawyer, orator, Virginia politician in a period when tidewater versus western sectionalism was a primary issue, a leading spokesman for the latter. The result was separation and statehood for West Virginia but not until thirty-one years after his death. Member of Virginia House of Delegates (1815, 1816, 1822, 1823, 1828, 1829), state constitutional convention delegate (1829), U.S. Representative (1829 until death).

DODGE, AUGUSTUS CAESAR *(b Jan. 2, 1812, Ste. Genevieve, Mo.; d Nov. 20, 1883, Burlington, Iowa)* A frontier youth who worked side by side with his father, Henry Dodge, in the family lead mines in Illinois, fought beside him in the Black Hawk and other Indian wars and then sat beside him in Washington, his father having been sent there from the Wisconsin Territory, when he, Augustus, was elected as a Democrat from the Iowa Territory. What little schooling he had was taught him by his wife, Clara Ann Hertich, daughter of the Ste. Genevieve schoolmaster.

Public land office registrar in Burlington (1838-1840), delegate to Congress (1840-1846) then, when Iowa gained statehood, its first U.S. Senator (1848-1855); minister to Spain (1855-1859), unsuccessful candidate for governor (1859), Democratic National Convention delegate (1864), mayor of Burlington (1874, 1875). By then tired of political life, he embarked upon a new career: lecturing at pioneer gatherings.

DODGE, HENRY (b Oct. 2, 1782, Vincennes, Ind.; d June 19, 1867, Burlington, Iowa) Lead mine operator, Indian fighter and colonel of U.S. Dragoons, Wisconsin Democrat but before that succeeding his father, Isaac, as sheriff of southern Louisiana's Ste. Genevieve district (1805-1821) and marshal of the Missouri Territory (1813-1821). In Wisconsin he was territorial governor (1836-1841, 1845-1848), delegate to Congress (1841-1845) then, after statehood, U.S. Senate (1848-1857). Father of Augustus C. Dodge.

DOHENY, EDWARD LAURENCE (b Aug. 10, 1856, near Fond du Lac, Wis.; d Sept. 8, 1935, Beverly Hills, Calif.). Mule train driver and prospector for gold who switched to oil and struck it fabulously rich. One of his partners in the oil business was Albert B. Fall and they and Harry F. Sinclair were the prime participants in the Teapot Dome oil scandal. Doheny admitted "lending" Fall (Warren Harding's secretary of the interior) $100,000 and both were indicted for bribery and conspiracy. Doheny was acquitted but the government cancelled his oil leases and

forced him to repay profits made from them.

DOLE, SANFORD BALLARD (b April 23, 1844, Honolulu, Hawaii; d June 9, 1926, Honolulu). Son of missionaries, Massachusetts-educated lawyer who returned to Hawaii and, in his word, "sought through legislative work, the newspapers, personal appeal and individual influence to avert the catastrophe that seemed inevitable if such tendencies (of the monarchy that then prevailed) were not restrained." All that failed, however, and he somewhat reluctantly joined the revolution, becoming head of the provisional government (1893-1894) and minister of foreign affairs. Then, when attempts for annexation by the United States failed, he became president of the Republic of Hawaii (1894-1900) until an annexation treaty could be negotiated, at which time he became first governor of the new Territory of Hawaii (1900-1903) and then U.S. district judge (1903-1915). Before the revolution he was a reform member of the Hawaiian legislature (1884-1887), associate justice of the supreme court (1887-1893).

DOLLIVER, JONATHAN PRENTISS (b Feb. 6, 1858, Preston County, Va., now W.Va.; d Oct. 15, 1910, Fort Dodge, Iowa) Lawyer, orator, convention keynoter, much-in-demand campaign speaker, Iowa Republican who began his political career as a conservative and slowly was converted to La Follette liberalism. Fort Dodge city solicitor (1880-1887), U.S. Representative (1889-1900), U.S. Senate (1900 until death).

DOLPH, JOSEPH NORTON (b Oct. 19, 1835, Dolphsburg, N.Y.; d March 10, 1897, Portland, Oreg.) Lawyer, railroad executive, Indian fighter, Oregon Republican. Portland city attorney (1864, 1865), U.S. district attorney (1865-1868), state senate (1866, 1868, 1872, 1874), U.S. Senate (1883-1895), and, in both of the latter offices, a good friend of the railroads. Yet he was a liberal, favoring womens' suffrage and the Sherman Anti-Trust Act.

DOMINICK, FREDERICK HASKELL *(b Feb. 20, 1877, Peak, S.C.; d March 11, 1960, Newberry S.C.)* Lawyer and a power in South Carolina's Democratic party. State representative (1900-1902), delegate to every Democratic state convention (except for 1914) between 1900 and death and Newberry County committee chairman (1906-1914), assistant state attorney general (1913-1916), national convention delegate (1920, 1924), U.S. Representative (1917-1933), assistant to the U.S. attorney general during World War II.

DONAHEY, ALVIN VICTOR *(b July 7, 1873, Cadwallader, Ohio; d April 8, 1946, Columbus, Ohio)* Journeyman printer who showed a flair for politics and varied business enterprises: insurance, banking, and manufacturing. Ohio Democrat. Goshen Township clerk (1898-1903), Tuscarawas County auditor (1905-1909), state constitutional convention delegate (1912), state auditor (1912), three-term governor (1923-1929) after losing in an earlier try (1920), U.S. Senate (1935-1941).

DONELSON, ANDREW JACKSON *(b Aug. 25, 1799, near Nashville, Tenn.; d June 26, 1871, Memphis, Tenn.)* Named for the man who later became president and raised by him from childhood, Donelson throughout all of his life was Jackson's protege: West Point graduate and Jackson's aide during the Seminole campaign, confidential secretary during his presidential tries (1824, 1828, 1832), private secretary during the White House years. A lawyer, and obviously a Democrat, he did not suffer when Jackson's power waned. Tyler picked him to negotiate with the new Texas Republic and Polk retained him to finish the job, then named him minister to Prussia

(1846-1849); in 1856 he was the vice-presidential candidate on the Fillmore ticket.

DONGAN, THOMAS *(b 1634, Castletown, County Kildare, Ireland; d Dec. 14, 1715, London, England)* Professional soldier of the crown who was considered, according to a biographer, "one of the very best of all the colonial governors," administering over New York (1683-1688). The "Dongan Charter" granting the colonists new liberties (among them elections and religious tolerance) was adopted by a representative assembly he had convened. He became, after the death of an older brother, the Earl of Limerick.

DONNELLY, IGNATIUS *(b Nov. 3, 1831, Philadelphia, Pa.; d Jan. 1, 1901, Minneapolis, Minn.)* Lawyer, author, land speculator, farmer, orator, Minnesota politician who was, in order, Republican, Liberal Republican, Granger, Greenbacker, Populist. His prediction for the future of politics in America: a struggle "between the few who seek to grasp all power and wealth, and the many who seek to preserve their rights as American citizens and freemen." Lieutenant governor (1859-1863), U.S. Representative (1863-1869), People's party candidate for vice president (1890).

DOOLEY, EDWIN BENEDICT *(b April 13, 1905, Brooklyn, N.Y.)* Public relations and advertising counselor, journalist, New York Republican. Mamaroneck village trustee (1942-1946), mayor (1950-1956), U.S. Representative (1957-1963) serving on the Public Works Committee.

DOOLITTLE, DUDLEY *(b June 21, 1881, Cottonwood Falls, Kans.; d Nov. 14, 1957, Emporia, Kans.)* Lawyer, banker, Kansas Democrat. Chase County prosecutor (1908-1912), Strong City mayor (1912), U.S. Representative (1913-1919), U.S. Treasury representative in Italy

(1919), federal prohibition director for Kansas (1920), member of Democratic National Committee (1925), Farm Credit Administration general agent (1934-1938).

DOOLITTLE, JAMES ROOD *(b Jan. 3, 1815, Hampton, N.Y.; d July 23, 1897, Providence, R.I.)* Lawyer, gifted orator who stumped for many presidential candidates, New York and Wisconsin antislave but states' rights Democrat-Republican-Democrat, close friend and staunch supporter of Abraham Lincoln. An example of his style, in the opening words of a speech at an 1864 campaign rally: "I believe in God Almighty! Under Him I believe in Abraham Lincoln!"

In New York: Wyoming County district attorney (1847-1850) and a leader in the Democrats' so-called Barnburning faction, writing an 1847 state convention resolution that became a model presidential plank for both the Free-Soilers (1848) and Republicans (1856): "The Democrats of New York declare their uncompromising hostility to the extension of slavery into territory now free, or which may be hereafter acquired by any action of the government of the United States." In Wisconsin: first judicial circuit judge (1853-1856), U.S. Senate (1857-1869), as a Republican, unsuccessful Democratic candidate for governor (1871). The reason for the shift back to the Democratic ranks: the radical GOP wing turned all its guns against him when he supported Andrew Johnson's reconstruction policies and voted against impeachment.

DOOLITTLE, WILLIAM HALL *(b Nov. 6, 1848, Erie County, Pa.; d Feb. 26, 1914, Tacoma, Wash.)* Union soldier, lawyer, Nebraska and Washington Republican. In Nebraska: state representative (1874-1876), assistant U.S. attorney (1876-1880). In Washington: U.S. Representative (1893-1897).

DOREMUS, FRANK ELLSWORTH *(b Aug. 31, 1865, Vanango County, Pa.; d Sept. 4, 1947, Howell, Mich.)* Founder-editor of the *Portland, (Mich.) Review*, lawyer, Michigan Democrat. State representative (1890-1892), Portland postmaster (1895-1899), Detroit assistant corporation counsel (1903-1907), city comptroller (1907-1910), U.S. Representative (1911-1924), mayor of Detroit (1923, 1924).

DORGAN, THOMAS ALOYSIUS *(b April 29, 1877, San Francisco, Calif.; d May 2, 1929)* Sports writer and cartoonist, known as Tad, who applied his brush for a time on William Randolph Hearst's *New York Journal* as a political satirist assigned to lampoon Tammany Hall. In 1905 Hearst ran against Tammany candidate George B. McClellan for mayor, Tad cartoons showed him, a Tammany tiger, in prison stripes, almost swinging the vote to Hearst. McClellan won, but only by the thinnest margin in Tammany history.

DORR, THOMAS WILSON *(b Nov. 5, 1805, Providence, R.I.; d Dec. 27, 1854, Providence)* Lawyer, political reformer who led his Dorrite followers in a successful lifetime fight to rewrite Rhode Island's archaic constitution and liberalize voting regulations but, for him, it culminated in the so-called Dorr Rebellion of 1842, imprisonment on treason charges promulgated by the state's establishment, ultimate pardon and restoration of all civil rights (1851), but only when he was a broken man. His only officially recognized elective office was the state general assembly (1834), but, unofficially, his Peoples' party supporters elected him governor (1842) and it was the vain attempts to seat him that brought on the Rebellion of May 18—a march on the Providence arsenal and the popgun-size firing of an ancient cannon at its Establishment defenders.

DORSEY, CLEMENT *(b 1778, Anne Arundel County, Md.; d Aug. 6, 1848, Leonardstown, Md.)* Maryland lawyer. U.S. Representative (1825-1831), fifth circuit court judge (1832 until death).

DORSEY, STEPHEN WALLACE *(b Feb. 28, 1842, Benson, Vt.; d March 20, 1916, Los Angeles, Calif.)* Ohio tool manufacturer, railroad executive in Arkansas where he also was an influential member of the Republican inner circle, New Mexico and Colorado cattle ranch and mine operator; but, most of all, a grand-scale promoter who was indicted (1881) in the star route postal scandals involving a half-million dollars in government funds. U.S. Senator from Arkansas (1873-1879), chairman of GOP state executive committee (1876), secretary of the GOP National Committee (1880).

DOTY, JAMES DUANE *(b Nov. 5, 1799, Salem, N.Y.; d June 13, 1865, Salt Lake City, Utah)* Lawyer, Mississippi River explorer, land speculator, Democrat–Free-Soiler who made his contribution to development of the West by helping to divide the Michigan Territory into the three territories of Michigan, Iowa, and Wisconsin; laying out the capital of Wisconsin and naming it Madison; holding office in Michigan, Wisconsin, and Utah. In Michigan: secretary of the legislative council, court clerk and U.S. judge for the northern part of the territory (1823-1832). In Wisconsin: delegate to Congress (1839-1841), territorial governor (1841-1844), first state constitutional convention delegate (1846) and, after statehood, U.S. Representative (1849-1853). In Utah: superintendent of Indian affairs (1861-1863), treasurer and territorial governor (1863 until death).

DOUGHERTY, JOHN *(b Feb. 25, 1857, Iatan, Mo.; d Aug. 1, 1905, Liberty, Mo.).* Newspaper editor-publisher, lawyer, Missouri Democrat. Liberty city attorney (1881-1886), Clay County prosecutor (1888-1895), U.S. Representative (1899-1905).

DOUGHTON, ROBERT LEE *(b Nov. 7, 1863, Laurel Springs, N.C.; d Oct. 1, 1954, Laurel Springs)* Farmer, banker, North Carolina Democrat who served forty-two years as a U.S. Representative (1911-1953). Before that he was on the state board of agriculture (1903-1909), state senate (1908, 1909), state prison board (1909-1911).

DOUGLAS, FRED JAMES *(b Sept. 14, 1869, Clinton, Mass.; d Jan. 1, 1949, Utica, N.Y.)* Physician-surgeon, New York Republican. Utica Board of Education (1910-1920), mayor (1922-1924), public safety commissioner (1928, 1929); U.S. Representative (1937-1945).

DOUGLAS, HELEN GAHAGAN *(b Nov. 25, 1900, Boonton, N.J.)* Actress, opera singer, lecturer, author who once was called one of "the ten most beautiful women in America," wife of actor Melvyn Douglas, mother of three, liberal California Democrat who ran unsuccessfully against Richard M. Nixon for the U.S. Senate (1950) in a campaign that contributed to his "tricky Dick" image.

Member of Works Progress Administration's national advisory committee and National Youth Administration's state committee (1939-1940), Democratic National Committeewoman (1940-1944), vice chairman of state central committee and chairman of its women's division (1940-1944), member of board of governors of state Housing and Planning Association (1942-1943), Roosevelt-appointed member of Office of Civil Defense's voluntary participation committee, and Truman-appointed alternate delegate to the United Nations Assembly, U.S. Representative (1945-1951). Her professional credits included: *Mary Queen of Scotland* (1934) and *First Lady* (1952) on the stage, the movie *She* (1935); and author of *The Eleanor Roosevelt We Remember* (1963).

DOUGLAS, STEPHEN ARNOLD (*b April 23, 1813, Brandon, Vt.; d June 3, 1861, Chicago, Ill.)* Known as The Little Giant, lawyer, teacher, orator, Illinois Democrat who privately thought slavery a cancer but publicly compromised the issue so as not to offend the South and because he thought it an aid to the nation's "manifest destiny" economic development; author of the Kansas-Nebraska Act, which allowed the people of the two territories through "popular sovereignty" to decide the slavery question for themselves; Lincoln's adversary in the debates of 1858 on the meaning of the Dred Scott decision; Lincoln's presidential opponent (1860) receiving 1,376,000 popular votes but only 12 electoral votes.

Morgan circuit state's attorney (1835), state representative (1836, 1837), land office registrar (1837), Illinois secretary of state (1840, 1841), state supreme court judge (1840-1843), U.S. Representative (1843-1847), U.S. Senate (1847 until death), unsuccessful candidate for Democratic presidential nomination (1852, 1856, 1860).

DOUGLASS, FREDERICK *(b about 1817, Tuckahoe, Md., of an unknown white father and a slave mother; d Feb. 20, 1895, near Washington, D.C.)* An escaped house servant-slave (1838) who worked on the docks of New York and then New Bedford, Mass., where he became an active abolitionist and self-educated lecturer, editor-publisher of *The North Star*, author (*Narrative of the Life of Frederick Douglass*, 1845), advisor to John Brown and thus forced to flee the country, recruiter of black troops to fight on the side of the Union, and, during Reconstruction, a spokesman for suffrage and equal rights for freedmen. His rewards, honors and offices included: secretary of the Santo Domingo Commission (1871), District of Columbia marshal (1877-1881) and recorder of deeds (1881-1886), minister to Haiti (1889-1891). His name at birth was Frederick Augustus Washington Bailey, later Frederick Johnson, and then the name that history knows him by—Frederick Douglass.

DOUGLASS, JOHN JOSEPH *(b Feb. 9, 1873, East Boston, Mass.; d April 5, 1939, West Roxbury, Mass.)* Author, playwright, lawyer, Massachusetts Democrat. State representative (1899, 1900, 1906, 1913), state constitutional convention delegate (1917, 1918), Democratic National Convention delegate (1928, 1932), U.S. Representative (1925-1935), Boston commissioner of penal institutions (1935 until death).

DOVENER, BLACKBURN BARRETT *(b April 20, 1842, Tays Valley, Va., now W.Va.; d May 9, 1914, Glen Echo, Md.)*. Ohio River boat captain, lawyer, Confederate Army officer, West Virginia Republican. State house of delegates (1883, 1884), U.S. Representative (1895-1907).

DOWELL, CASSIUS CLAY *(b Feb. 29, 1864, Warren County, Iowa; d Feb. 4, 1940, Washington, D.C.)* Lawyer, Iowa Republican. State representative (1894-1898), state senate (1902-1912), U.S. Representative (1915-1935, 1937 until death).

DOWNEY, SHERIDAN *(b March 11, 1884, Laramie, Wyo.; d Oct. 25, 1961, San Francisco, Calif.)* Lawyer, California Democrat who served as a U.S. Senator (1939-1950) before withdrawing from politics because of ill health. Son of Stephen W. Downey.

DOWNEY, STEPHEN WHEELER *(b July 25, 1839, Western Port, Md.; d Aug. 3, 1902, Denver, Colo.)* Lawyer, Wyoming Republican. Albany County prosecutor (1869, 1870, 1899 until death), territorial council (1871, 1875, 1877), treasurer (1872-1875) and auditor (1877-1879), delegate to Congress (1879-1881), territorial representative (1886, 1890), president of University of Wyoming at Laramie (1891-1897). Then, after statehood, state representative (1893, 1895) and speaker (1895), state constitutional convention (1889). Father of Sheridan Downey.

DOYLE, CLYDE GILMAN *(b July 11, 1887, Oakland, Calif.; d March 14, 1963, Arlington, Va.)* Lawyer, California Democrat. President of Long Beach Board of Freeholders (1921, 1922), U.S. Representative (1945-1947, 1949 until death) serving on the Armed Services and Un-American Activities committees; briefly, immediately prior to his death, acting head of the latter.

DRAKE, CHARLES DANIEL *(b April 11, 1811, Cincinnati, Ohio; d April 1, 1892, Washington, D.C.)* Naval midshipman, lawyer, and a publicly unpopular Missouri political leader of the chaotic 1850s and 1860s who wore the Whig, Know-Nothing, Democrat, radical Unionist, and radical Republican party labels. Finally making it to the U.S. Senate (1867-1870) only to serve half a term before resigning to become, as his reward for sponsoring harsh Reconstructionist measures, chief justice of the Court of Claims (1870 until death).

DRAKE, FRANCIS MARION *(b Dec. 30, 1830, Rushville, Ill.; d Nov. 20, 1903, Centerville, Iowa)* A man who answered the California lure of gold, returned to his family home in Iowa, struck it rich as a railroad builder, and became interested in politics—Republican Governor (1896-1898)—and philanthropy—Drake University is named for him.

DRANE, HERBERT JACKSON *(b June 20, 1863, Franklin, Ky.; d Aug. 11, 1947, Lakeland, Fla.)* One of the founders of Lakeland, railroad builder, real estate operator, citrus grower, Florida Democrat. Mayor of Lakeland (1888-1892), Polk County commissioner (1896-1899),

state representative (1903-1905), state senate (1913-1917) and its president (1913-1915), U.S. Representative (1917-1933), member of Federal Power Commission (1933-1937).

DRAPER, ANDREW SLOAN *(b June 21, 1848, Westford, N.Y.; d April 27, 1913).* Teacher, lawyer, author, New York Republican who became state superintendent of public instruction (1886-1892) over the objections of educational leaders who did not consider it a job for a politician. But Draper gave up politics for education, served as superintendent of schools in Cleveland, Ohio (1893-1894), became president of the University of Illinois (1894-1904), and then was reclaimed by his native state to be its first commissioner of education (1904 until death), and to him goes the lion's share of the credit for the creation of New York's Department of Education. His only purely political office was as a member of the state legislature (1881-1882).

DRAPER, EBEN SUMNER *(b June 17, 1858, Hopedale, Mass.; d April 9, 1914, Greenville, S.C.)* Massachusetts Republican leader and cotton machinery manufacturer who broke an Industrial Workers of the World (IWW) strike (1913) at the family's mills. Chairman of state GOP committee (1893-1899), chairman of state delegation to national convention (1896) where he supported the gold plank, presidential elector (1900), lieutenant governor (1906-1908), governor (1909-1911).

DRAPER, MARGARET GREEN *(b ——; d c. 1807, London, Eng.)* Publisher (after her husband's death on June 5, 1774) of Boston Loyalist newspaper *The Massachusetts Gazette and Weekly News-Letter.* It was suspended (Feb. 22, 1776) when the British evacuated and Margaret Draper, whose Boston property was confiscated by the Americans, lived out her life in England, where she received a pension from the British government.

DRAPER, WILLIAM HENRY *(b June 24, 1841, Rochdale, Mass.; d Dec. 7, 1921, Troy, N.Y.)* Merchant, manufacturer, New York Republican. Lansingburgh village trustee (1885-1895), Rensselaer County jury commissioner (1896-1900), U.S. Representative (1901-1913).

DRAYTON, WILLIAM *(b Dec. 30, 1776, St. Augustine, Fla.; d May 24, 1846, Philadelphia, Pa.)* Lawyer, South Carolina Union Democrat who declined appointment by President Jackson as either secretary of war or ambassador to England. State representative (1806-1808), U.S. Representative (1825-1833), president of the Bank of the United States (1840, 1841).

DREWRY, PATRICK HENRY *(b May 24, 1875, Petersburg, Va.; d Dec. 21, 1947, Petersburg)* Lawyer, bank director, Virginia Democrat. State senate (1912-1920), Democratic state convention delegate (1912, 1916, 1920, 1924) and national convention (1916), chairman of state Economy and Efficiency Commission (1916-1918), U.S. Representative (1920 until death), member of Democratic National Congressional Committee (1923-1927).

DRISCOLL, MICHAEL EDWARD *(b Feb. 9, 1851, Syracuse, N.Y.; d Jan. 19, 1929, Syracuse)* Lawyer, lecturer, New York Republican. GOP state convention chairman (1906), U.S. Representative (1899-1913).

DRIVER, WILLIAM JOSHUA *(b March 2, 1873, Mississippi County, Ark.; d Oct. 1, 1948, Osceola, Ark.)* Lawyer, banker, Arkansas Democrat. State representative (1897-1899), second judicial circuit judge (1911-1918), state constitutional convention delegate (1918), U.S. Representative (1921-1939), Democratic National Convention delegate (1932).

DROMGOOLE, GEORGE COKE *(b May 15, 1797, Lawrenceville, Va.; d April 27, 1847, Brunswick County, Va.)* Lawyer, Virginia Democrat. State representative (1823-1826), state senate (1826-1835), state constitutional convention delegate (1829), U.S. Representative (1835-1841, 1843 until death).

DRYDEN, JOHN FAIRFIELD *(b Aug. 7, 1839, Temple, Maine; d Nov. 24, 1911, Newark, N.J.)* Financier, founder of many banks and the Prudential Insurance Co. and its president (1881-1911); a man who firmly believed that life insurance could be an answer to many economic problems of the poor, New Jersey Republican who bucked entrenched party interests to become a U.S. Senator (1901-1907). Presidential elector on the McKinley-Hobart ticket (1896) and McKinley-Roosevelt ticket (1900).

DUANE, JAMES *(b Feb. 6, 1733, New York City; d Feb. 1, 1797, Duanesburg, N.Y.)* Lawyer, colonial conservative who nevertheless favored independence, mayor of New York City (1784-1789) who competently handled the task of cleaning up the ravages of occupying British forces. Chancery court clerk (1762), New York attorney general (1767), boundary commissioner (1768, 1784), Indian commissioner (1774), provincial convention delegate (1775), member of the Revolutionary Committee of One Hundred (1775), Continental Congress (1774-1784), Provincial Congress (1776, 1777), state senate (1782-1785, 1788-1790), delegate to state constitutional ratifying convention (1788), New York's first U.S. district judge (1789-1794).

DUANE, WILLIAM *(b May 17, 1760, near Lake Champlain, N.Y., but raised in Ireland; d Nov. 24, 1835, Philadelphia, Pa.)* Newspaperman in Ireland, India, and England who returned to the United States, settled in Philadelphia, became an associate of Benjamin Franklin Bache on the *Aurora*, upon the latter's death turning it into the most powerful Jeffersonian journal in the land. A bold editor, he risked all in writing about what he thought was right, facing down threats of deportation and personal injury, even going to jail on charges of inciting to seditious riot (1799).

DUBOIS, FRED THOMAS *(b May 29, 1851, Palestine, Ill.; d Feb. 14, 1930, Washington, D.C.)* Early Idaho settler who did much to bring statehood to the territory, a Republican until the issue of free silver, which he favored, drove him into the Democratic party. U.S. marshal of Idaho (1882-1886), delegate to Congress (1887-1890), GOP National Convention delegate (1888) and chairman of first and second state delegations to the 1892 and 1896 conventions, U.S. Senate as a Republican (1891-1897) and as a Silver Republican (1901-1907) and during the latter term becoming a Democrat. Delegate to Democratic National Conventions (1904, 1908, 1912), civilian member of the U.S. Board of Ordnance and Fortifications (1918-1920), Coolidge-appointed Democratic member of the International Joint Boundary Commission (1924 until death).

DUBOIS, WILLIAM EDWARD BURGHARDT *(b Feb. 23, 1868, Great Barrington, Mass.; d Aug. 27, 1963, Accra, Ghana)* College professor, author, lecturer, a founder of the National Association for the Advancement of Colored People (1909) and editor of *The Crisis* (1909-1934) and for more than fifty years a monumental and often controversial leader of Negro thought. He received his bachelor's degree at Fisk, both his master's degree and doctorate at Harvard, taught at Wilberforce, Pennsylvania, and Atlanta universities and was the first Negro ever elected to the National Institute of Arts and Letters. Upon formation of the United Nations, he became head of its Council on

Afro-American Affairs (1945) and chairman of the Peace Information Center in New York (1949).

A man of peace but politically a radical, Dr. DuBois joined the Socialist party in 1911, switched to the Democrats to help Wilson's presidential bid, then to the American Labor party and was its candidate for U.S. Senator from New York (1950); two years before his death and after moving to and becoming a citizen of Ghana he finally enrolled in the Communist party. As a result of that leftist progression, there was great furor in Great Barrington when a monument to his memory was proposed. Finally, however (1969), a five-acre park was dedicated on the site of the house in which he was born.

DUCHE, JACOB *(b Jan. 31, 1737, Philadelphia, Pa.; d Jan. 3, 1798, Philadelphia)* Clergyman and ardent Pennsylvania Loyalist who, after the Revolution, showed such enthusiasm for independence that he was made chaplain of the Continental Congress. But in 1777 he renounced his Revolutionary sympathies and even wrote General Washington a letter urging him to urge the Congress to recall the Declaration of Independence. As a result, he was removed as chaplain, his property was confiscated, he fled to England, but pined for America and returned (1792) to live out his years.

DUDLEY, CHARLES EDWARD *(b May 23, 1780, Johnston Hall, England; d Jan. 23, 1841, Albany, N.Y.)* Merchant, scientist, New York Democrat and member of the "Albany Regency" who completed the term of Martin Van Buren when he resigned from the U.S. Senate (1829-1833). Presidential elector on the Monroe-Tompkins ticket (1816), state senate (1820-1825), mayor of Albany (1821-1824, 1828, 1829).

DUDLEY, EDWARD BISHOP *(b Dec. 15, 1769, Onslow County, N.C.; d Oct. 30,*

1855, Wilmington, N.C.) Founder and president of the Wilmington & Weldon Railroad, National Republican who was North Carolina's first governor (1837-1841) to be chosen by the people and not by the legislature. State house of commons (1811, 1813, 1816, 1817, 1834, 1835), state senate (1814), U.S. Representative (1829-1831).

DULLES, JOHN FOSTER *(b Feb. 25, 1888, Washington, D.C.; d May 24, 1959, Washington)* Lawyer, statesman, New York Republican and, as President Eisenhower's secretary of state (1953 until a month before death), brought the word "brinkmanship" into the language and whose Southeast Asia containment policies were said to have done much to bring on the Vietnam war.

Special State Department agent in Central America (1917), Army intelligence officer in World War I, assistant to War Trade Board chairman (1918), counsel to American Peace Commission (1918, 1919), member of Reparations Commission and Supreme Economic Council (1919), legal advisor for Polish Financial Stabilization Plan (1927), U.S. representative at Berlin debt conferences (1933), delegate to San Francisco Conference on World Organization (1945).

Advisor to secretary of state at Council of Foreign Ministers (1945, 1947, 1949), representative to the United Nations General Assembly (1946-1949) and chairman of U.S. delegation in Paris (1948), U.S. Senate for four months in 1949 to fill vacancy created by resignation of Robert F. Wagner but then defeated by Herbert Lehman in try for election to balance of term, again a UN representative (1950), consultant to secretary of state (1951, 1952).

DUNBAR, MOSES *(b June 14, 1746, Wallingford, Conn.; d March 19, 1777, Hartford, by hanging)* Clergyman and Connecticut Loyalist who was impris-

oned early in the Revolution because of his beliefs, then fled to Long Island, became a captain in Lord Howe's army, attempted to recruit other Connecticut colonists for the Crown, was betrayed, tried for treason, and executed on a hilltop that later became part of the Trinity College campus.

DUNCAN, JAMES *(b May 5, 1857, Kincardine, Scotland; d Sept. 14, 1928, Quincy, Mass.)* Stonecutter, labor journalist, associate of Samuel Gompers, first vice president of the American Federation of Labor (1894-1925). Republican and a friend and advisor to many presidents. In 1917, in the wake of the Bolshevik revolution, President Wilson appointed him labor member of a special diplomatic mission to Russia; in 1919 he was a member of the American Labor Mission to the Paris peace conference.

DUNCAN, JOSEPH *(b Feb. 22, 1794, Paris, Ky.; d Jan. 15, 1844, Jacksonville, Ill.)* Farmer, Indian fighter, Illinois Democrat turned Whig with a frontiersman's blunt, no-nonsense approach to politics. Jackson County justice of the peace (1821-1823), state senate (1824-1826), U.S. Representative (1827-1834), governor (1834-1838).

DUNIWAY, ABIGAIL JANE SCOTT *(b Oct. 22, 1834, near Groveland, Ill.; d Oct. 11, 1915)* Newspaper editor, author, teacher, suffragist, pioneer who crossed the country to Oregon by ox team. As a widow responsible for the support of her six children, Abigail Duniway came to realize the inequalities existing between the sexes and from 1870, when she helped to organize an Equal Rights Society in Albany, Oregon, she devoted her life to the cause of equal rights for women. In Portland (1871) and with the help of her young sons (the oldest was sixteen), she launched *The New Northwest*, a newspaper in which she used the columns to champion the rights of women. She endured much abuse in the lecturing and organizing work that she also carried on (becoming the recognized leader of the women's suffrage movement in the Northwest), but she had her moment of triumph when she personally drew up the proclamation, signed by the governor of Oregon, announcing the passage of the suffrage amendment in that state (1912).

DUNLAP, JOHN *(b 1747, Strabane, County Tyrone, Ireland; d Nov. 27, 1812, Philadelphia, Pa.)* Printer, bookseller, publisher of the *Pennsylvania Packet and Daily Advertiser* which was the first daily newspaper in the United States (1784); printer to Congress and printer of the Declaration of Independence and the Constitution.

DUNLAP, ROBERT PINCKNEY *(b Aug. 17, 1794, Brunswick, Maine; d Oct. 20, 1859, Brunswick)* Lawyer, Maine Democrat. State representative (1821-1823), president of Bowdoin College's Board of Overseers (1821 until death), state senate (1824-1828, 1831-1833) four of those years as senate president, executive councilor (1829-1833), governor (1834-1838), U.S. Representative (1843-1847), Portland's collector of customs (1848, 1849), and Brunswick's postmaster (1853-1857).

DUNMORE, JOHN MURRAY *(b 1732, Scotland; d March 5, 1809, Ramsgate, England)* His titles: Earl of Dunmore, Viscount Fincastle, Baron of Blair, Baron of Moulin, Baron of Tillymont—and what American historians most care about— the colonial governor of Virginia (1771-1775) responsible for what became known as Lord Dunmore's War (1774). During his stay in the colonies, he served as governor of New York (1770-1771), followed by brief social popularity in Virginia, and then his cancelling of the House of Burgesses in the next three years because of revolutionary

goings-on. As for the war that bore his name, he mounted it to put down Indian uprisings in the west and ended it by seizing frontier lands for himself.

DUNN, POINDEXTER *(b Nov. 3, 1834, Wake County, N.C.; d Oct. 12, 1914, Texarkana, Tex.)* Lawyer, cotton grower, railroad builder, Arkansas Democrat, Confederate Army officer. State representative (1858), presidential elector on the Greeley-Brown (1872) and Tilden-Hendricks (1876) tickets, U.S. Representative (1879-1889).

DUNNELL, MARK HILL *(b July 2, 1823, Buxton, Maine; d Aug. 9, 1904, Owatonna, Minn.)* Educator, lawyer, Maine and Minnesota Republican. In Maine: state representative (1854), state senate (1855), state superintendent of common schools (1855, 1857-1859), GOP National Convention delegate (1856), U.S. consul at Vera Cruz, Mexico, (1861, 1862). In Minnesota: state representative (1867), state schools superintendent (1867-1870), U.S. Representative (1871-1883, 1889-1891), GOP National Convention delegate (1892).

DU PONT, HENRY ALGERNON *(b July 30, 1838, Eleutherean Mills, Del.; d Dec. 31, 1926, near Wilmington, Del.)* West Point graduate, Union Army officer, railroad executive, farmer, writer, Delaware Republican who served as a U.S. senator (1905-1917) years after reluctantly giving up his military career and joining the family's powder-making firm, E. I. du Pont de Nemours & Company, which his father headed. Cousin of Thomas C. du Pont.

DU PONT, THOMAS COLEMAN *(b Dec. 11, 1863, Louisville, Ky.; d Nov. 11, 1930, Wilmington, Del.)* Mining engineer, industrialist with wide interests, Delaware Republican who served as a member of the GOP National Committee from 1908 until death, thus compiling an unexceeded record of continuous service in that position. U.S. Senate (1921-1922, 1925-1928). Cousin of Henry A. du Pont.

DUPRÉ, HENRY GARLAND *(b July 28, 1873, Opelousas, La.; d Feb. 21, 1924, Washington, D.C.)* Lawyer, Louisiana Democrat. Assistant New Orleans city attorney (1900-1910), state representative (1900-1910) and house speaker (1908-1910), Democratic state convention chairman (1908), U.S. Representative (1910 until death).

DURELL, EDWARD HENRY *(b July 14, 1810, Portsmouth, N.H.; d March 29, 1887, Schoharie, N.Y.)* Lawyer, Louisiana Unionist turned Republican who vigorously opposed secession and cooperated with the federal forces when they occupied New Orleans, thus becoming the Lincoln-appointed U.S. judge (1863-1874) who acted as intermediary between North and South and somehow managed to remain neutral both in the Civil War and the Reconstruction. But, in 1872, he ruled a Democratic election board illegal and ordered the U.S. marshal to permit only "authorized persons" to enter the statehouse. Thus Republicans gained control of the state government and Durell, who a year earlier had been praised by the Louisiana bar as "a tried, faithful, able, learned and incorruptible judge," was investigated by a U.S. Senate committee that condemned him—a federal judge who interceded in a state election —for action "without parallel in judicial proceedings."

Member of New Orleans common council (1854-1860) who wrote the city charter (1856), drafter of wartime form of municipal government (1862) by direction of the military governor, and president of bureau of finance, federally appointed mayor of New Orleans (1863), president of state constitutional government (1864), delegate to GOP National Convention (1864), went to Washington (1867) and succeeded in having Louisi-

ana exempted from confiscation penalties while also turning down offer of ambassadorship to Austria.

DURFEE, JOB *(b Sept. 20, 1790, Tiverton, R.I.; d July 26, 1847, Tiverton).* Lawyer, Rhode Island Populist-Democrat. State representative (1816-1820, 1826-1829) and speaker (1827-1829), U.S. Representative (1821-1825), associate justice of the state supreme court (1833-1835) and chief justice (1835 until death).

DURFEE, NATHANIEL BRIGGS *(b Sept. 29, 1812, Tiverton, R.I.; d Nov. 9, 1872, Tiverton)* Farmer, fruit grower, Rhode Island Know-Nothing–Republican. State representative (1843-1854), U.S. Representative (1855-1859).

DURKEE, CHARLES *(b Dec. 10, 1805, Royalton, Vt.; d Jan. 14, 1870, Omaha, Nebr.)* Merchant, farmer, lumberman, one of the founders of Southport (now Kenosha), Wis., Wisconsin Free-Soiler– Republican who served as governor, by presidential appointment, of the Utah Territory (1865-1869). Member of Wisconsin territorial legislature (1836-1838, 1847, 1848), U.S. Representative (1849-1853), U.S. Senate (1855-1861).

DUVAL, WILLIAM POPE *(b 1784, Mount Comfort, Va.; d March 19, 1854, Washington, D.C.)* Self-educated lawyer, Indian fighter, Kentucky Democrat, Florida pioneer, and the territory's first civil governor (1822-1834) who was Washington Irving's "Ralph Ringwood." U.S. Representative (1813-1815) from Kentucky.

DUVALL, GABRIEL *(b Dec. 6, 1752, Prince Georges County, Md.; d March 6, 1844, Prince Georges County)* Lawyer, Maryland Democrat and Madison-appointed associate justice of the U.S. Supreme Court (1812-1835), resigning because of deafness. Member of governor's council (1783, 1784), U.S. Representative (1794-1796), chief justice of the Maryland general court (1796-1802), presidential elector (1796, 1800), first comptroller of the U.S. Treasury (1802-1811).

DWIGHT, JOHN WILBUR *(b May 24, 1859, Dryden, N.Y.; d Jan. 19, 1928, Washington, D.C.)* Iowa, Wisconsin, South Dakota, Minnesota farmer, lumber operator, land speculator, and Virginia railway executive and through it all remaining a New York Republican. GOP National Convention delegate (1888, 1892, 1900, 1904, 1920), U.S. Representative (1902-1913).

DWIGHT, THEODORE *(b Dec. 15, 1764, Northampton, Mass.; d June 12, 1846, New York City)* Lawyer, author who was one of the Connecticut Wits; Hartford, Albany, and New York newspaper editor-publisher; Connecticut Federalist. State council member (1809-1815), U.S.

Representative (1806-1807), secretary of the Hartford convention (1814). Cousin of Aaron Burr.

DWORSHAK, HENRY CLARENCE *(b Aug. 29, 1894, Duluth, Minn.; d July 23, 1962, Washington, D.C.)* Printer, newspaper editor-publisher, Idaho Republican, a leader of the conservative bloc and staunch opponent of what he called "socialistic spending." U.S. Representative (1939-1946), U.S. Senate (1946 until death) serving on the Appropriations and Interior and Insular Affairs Committees and the Joint Committee on Atomic Energy.

DYER, LEONIDAS CARSTARPHEN *(b June 11, 1871, Warren County, Mo.; d Dec. 15, 1957, St. Louis, Mo.)* Lawyer, Missouri Republican who was commander in chief of the Spanish War Veterans (1915-1916). U.S. Representative (1911-1914, 1915-1933).

E

☆ ☆ ☆

EAMES, BENJAMIN TUCKER *(b June 4, 1818, Dedham, Mass.; d Oct. 6, 1901, East Greenwich, R.I.)* Bookkeeper, teacher, lawyer, Rhode Island Republican. State senate (1854-1857, 1863, 1864, 1884, 1885), commissioner to revise the state laws (1857), state representative (1859, 1860, 1868, 1869, 1879-1881), U.S. Representative (1871-1879).

EARLE, ELIAS *(b June 19, 1762, Frederick County, Va.; d May 19, 1823, Centerville, S.C.)* Georgia metals prospector and one of the South's earliest ironmasters, South Carolina Democrat. State senate (1800), U.S. Representative (1805-1807, 1811-1815, 1817-1821).

EARLY, PETER *(b June 20, 1773, Madison County, Va.; d Aug. 15, 1817, Greene County, Ga.)* Georgia jurist who served as governor (1813-1815). U.S. Representative (1803-1807), first judge of Ocmulgee circuit superior court (1807-1813), state senate (1815 until death).

EARNSHAW, MANUEL *(b Nov. 19, 1862, Cavite, Philippine Islands; d Feb. 13, 1936, Manila)* Waterfront engineer and a political independent who served as resident commissioner to the United States (1913-1917).

EASTON, NICHOLAS *(b 1593, Wales; d Aug. 15, 1675, Newport, R.I.)* A Massachusetts colonist (1634) who relocated in what is now Portsmouth, Rhode Island, moved to Newport where he built the first house (1639) and became a pillar in the life of the settlement, holding several offices, among them governor (1672-1674). His son, John, an author, also was governor (1690-1695).

EATON, CHARLES AUBREY *(b March 29, 1868, Nova Scotia; d Jan. 23, 1953, Washington, D.C.)* Clergyman, journalist, New Jersey Republican who served fourteen terms as U.S. Representative (1925 until three weeks before death).

EATON, JOHN HENRY *(b June 18, 1790, Halifax County, N.C.; d Nov. 17, 1856, Washington, D.C.)* Lawyer, Florida land speculator, Tennessee Democrat, strong supporter of Andrew Jackson and author of his exceedingly subjective biography, but who ended up causing a stir in Washington society, to say nothing of upsetting Jackson's cabinet when its leaders, and the wives of cabinet members, would not accept his second wife, Peggy O'Neale, who was much too bright and carefree a spirit. As a result, Eaton, who was secretary of war in that cabinet (1829-1831), resigned in a huff and the cabinet split down the middle; those more loyal to Vice President Calhoun than to the president also resigning, but using the states' rights issue as their reason.

208

To placate his protege, Jackson tried unsuccessfully to have Eaton named U.S. senator (a post he had held, 1818-1829) and then appointed him governor of the Florida Territory (1834-1836) and minister to Spain (1836-1840).

EATON, WILLIAM ROBB *(b Dec. 17, 1877, Pugwash, Nova Scotia; d Dec. 16, 1942, Denver, Colo.)* Lawyer, Colorado Republican. Second judicial district attorney (1909-1913), state senate (1915-1918, 1923-1926), U.S. Representative (1929-1933).

EBERHARTER, HERMAN PETER *(b April 29, 1892, Pittsburgh, Pa.; d Sept. 9, 1958, Arlington, Va.)* Lawyer, Pennsylvania Democrat. State representative (1935, 1936), U.S. Representative (1937 until death).

ECTON, ZALES NELSON *(b April 1, 1898, Weldon, Iowa; d March 3, 1961, Bozeman, Mont.)* Rancher, Montana Republican. State representative (1933-1937), state senate (1937-1946), chairman of state GOP central committee (1940-1944), U.S. Senate (1947-1953).

EDDY, FRANK MARION *(b April 1, 1856, Pleasant Grove, Minn.; d Jan. 13, 1929, St. Paul, Minn.)* Teacher, newspaperman, writer, lecturer, Minnesota Republican and the state's first native son to be elected U.S. Representative (1895-1903).

EDEN, CHARLES *(b 1673, England; d March 26, 1722, Bertie County, N.C.).* Colonial governor of North Carolina (1714 until death).

EDEN, JOHN RICE *(b Feb. 1, 1826, Bath County, Ky.; d June 9, 1909, Sullivan, Ill.)* Lawyer, Illinois Democrat. Seventeenth judicial district prosecutor (1856-1860), U.S. Representative (1863-1865, 1873-1879, 1885-1887).

EDEN, ROBERT *(b Sept. 14, 1741, Durham, England; d Sept. 2, 1784, Annapolis, Md.)* Colonial governor of Maryland (1768-1776) who, faced with arrest for anti-Revolution sentiments, was rushed out of Maryland aboard a British warship, returning in a nonofficial capacity at the end of the war.

EDGE, WALTER EVANS *(b Nov. 20, 1873, Philadelphia, Pa.; d Oct. 29, 1956, New York City)* New Jersey Republican who made a career out of politics and public service. State senate journal clerk (1897-1899), secretary of state senate (1901-1904), presidential elector on Roosevelt-Fairbanks ticket (1904), state assemblyman (1910), state senate (1911-1916) and senate president (1915), governor (1917-1919, 1944-1947), GOP National Convention delegate eleven times (1916-1956), U.S. Senate (1919-1929), ambassador to France (1929-1933).

EDGERTON, ALFRED PECK *(b Jan. 11, 1813, Plattsburg, N.Y.; d May 14, 1897, Hicksville, Ohio)* Land manager who opened up new areas for settlement in northwest Ohio, financial agent, canal manager, Ohio Democrat. State senator (1845, 1846), U.S. Representative (1851-1855), chairman of U.S. Civil Service Commission (1885). Brother of Joseph K. Edgerton.

EDGERTON, JOSEPH KETCHUM *(b Feb. 16, 1818, Vergennes, Vt.; d Aug. 25, 1893, Fort Wayne, Ind.)* Lawyer, financier with interests in railroading, banking, and manufacturing, Indiana Democrat. U.S. Representative (1863-1865). Brother of Alfred P. Edgerton.

EDGERTON, SIDNEY *(b Aug. 17, 1818, Cazenovia, N.Y.; d July 19, 1900, Akron, Ohio)* Teacher, lawyer, Ohio Free-Soiler turned Republican who served as chief U.S. judge of the Idaho Territory (1863), helped to establish the Montana Territory and was its first territorial governor (1865, 1866). In Ohio he was delegate to first Free-Soil National Convention (1848) and delegate to first GOP National Convention (1856), Summit County prosecutor (1852-1856), U.S. Representative (1859-1863).

EDMONDS, GEORGE WASHINGTON (b Feb. 22, 1864, Pottsville, Pa.; d Sept. 28, 1939, Philadelphia, Pa.) Pharmacist, fuel wholesaler, Pennsylvania Republican. Philadelphia common council (1896-1902), U.S. Representative (1913-1925, 1933-1935).

EDMUNDS, GEORGE FRANKLIN (b Feb. 1, 1828, Richmond, Vt.; d Feb. 27, 1919, Pasadena, Calif.) Lawyer, Vermont Republican. State representative (1854-1859) three of those years as speaker of the house, state senator and presiding officer of the senate (1861, 1862), U.S. Senate (1866-1891) and its president pro tem (1883-1885).

EDMUNDSON, HENRY ALONZO (b June 14, 1814, Blacksburg, Va.; d Dec. 16, 1890, Shawsville, Va.) Lawyer, Confederate Army officer, farmer, Virginia Democrat. U.S. Representative (1849-1861).

EDWARDS, CHARLES GORDON (b July 2, 1878, Daisy, Ga.; d July 13, 1931, Atlanta, Ga.) Lawyer, farmer, Confederate Army officer, Georgia Democrat. U.S. Representative (1907-1917, 1925 until death), member of Savannah Harbor Commission (1920-1924), and a trustee of Southern Methodist College at McRae, Ga.

EDWARDS, EDWARD IRVING (b Dec. 1, 1863, Jersey City, N.J.; d Jan. 26, 1931, Jersey City) Lawyer, banker, New Jersey Democrat. State comptroller of the treasury (1911-1917), state senate (1918-1920), governor (1920-1923), U.S. Senate (1923-1929).

EDWARDS, HENRY WAGGAMAN (b October, 1779, New Haven, Conn.; d July 22, 1847, New Haven) Lawyer, Connecticut Democrat. U.S. Representative (1819-1823), U.S. Senate (1823-1827), state senate (1827-1829), speaker of state house of representatives (1830), governor (1833-1834, 1835-1838). Son of Pierrepont Edwards.

EDWARDS, JOHN (b 1748, Stafford County, Va.; d 1837, Bourbon County, Ky.) An early settler in what is now Fayette County, Ky., but then was in Virginia, and thus a political figure in both states. In Virginia: member of state house of delegates (1781-1783, 1785, 1786), delegate to eighth convention convened to define the boundaries of the proposed state of Kentucky (1785-1788). In Kentucky: member of convention that drafted state constitution (1792), one of the new state's first U.S. senators (1792-1795), state representative (1795), state senate (1796-1800). (Not to be confused with the next John Edwards, who was born in Kentucky but did not hold political office there.)

EDWARDS, JOHN (b Oct. 24, 1805, Louisville, Ky.; d April 8, 1894, Washington, D.C.) A lawyer, newspaperman and very much the wanderer, dabbling in politics wherever he lit. He remained in Arkansas long enough to be elected a U.S. Representative (March 1871–Feb. 1872) as a Liberal Republican but only long enough for his election to be successfully contested. In Indiana he was a state representative (1845, 1846); in California, an alcalde (chief administrative and judical officer) (1849); back in Indiana, a state senator (1853); in Iowa, where (for him) he stayed quite a long time, member of the constitutional convention (1855), state representative (1856-1860) and house speaker (1858-1860), founder-editor of the Patriot (1857), officer in the Iowa Volunteers during the Civil War; in Arkansas,

Johnson-appointed U.S. internal revenue assessor (1866-1869). His last recorded residence was Washington, D.C. (Not to be confused with John Edwards of Virginia and Kentucky—see previous entry.)

EDWARDS, JOHN CUMMINS *(b June 24, 1804, Frankfort, Ky.; d Oct. 14, 1888, Stockton, Calif.)* In Missouri, a lawyer; in California, a rancher, merchant, real estate operator, and in both states a Democrat. In Missouri: secretary of state (1830-1835, 1857), Cole County district judge (1832-1837), state representative (1836), state supreme court judge (1837-1839), U.S. Representative (1841-1843), governor (1844-1848). In California: mayor of Stockton (1851).

EDWARDS, NINIAN *(b March 17, 1775, Montgomery County, Md.; d July 20, 1833, Belleville, Ill.)* Lawyer, saw and grist mill operator, merchant, Kentucky and Illinois Democrat who held many offices (elective, appointive, judicial) but was not noted for his brilliance and whose reckless charges against Treasury Secretary William H. Crawford cost him a diplomatic post. In Kentucky: State representative (1796, 1797), general court judge (1803), circuit court judge (1804), presidential elector on the Jefferson-Clinton ticket (1804), appeals court judge (1806). In Illinois: Madison-appointed territorial governor (1809-1818), U.S. Senate (1818-1824), Monroe-appointed minister to Mexico (1824) but recalled while en route there, state governor (1826-1831). Nephew of Kentucky's John Edwards.

EDWARDS, PIERREPONT *(b April 8, 1750, Northampton, Mass.; d April 5, 1826, Bridgeport, Conn.)* Lawyer, Revolutionary Army soldier, Connecticut patriot, drafter of state constitution (1818), and administrator of Benedict Arnold's estate. Member of Continental Congress (1787, 1788), state representative (1789, 1790) and house speaker,

U.S. district judge (1806 until death). Father of Henry W. Edwards.

EDWARDS, THOMAS OWEN *(b March 29, 1810, Williamsburg, Ind.; d Feb. 5, 1876, Wheeling, W.Va.)* Physician, Ohio Whig who while serving as a U.S. Representative (1847-1849) attempted in vain to save the life of his fellow congressman, former President John Quincy Adams, who suffered a stroke while making a House speech.

EDWARDS, WELDON NATHANIEL *(b Jan. 25, 1788, Gaston, N.C.; d Dec. 18, 1873, Warren County, N.C.)* Lawyer, planter, conservative North Carolina Democrat who presided over the state secession convention in 1861. State representative (1814, 1815), U.S. Representative (1816-1827), state senate (1833-1844) and its president (1850).

EGAN, MAURICE FRANCIS *(b May 24, 1852, Philadelphia, Pa.; d Jan. 15, 1924, Brooklyn, N.Y.)* Author, wit, journalist who wrote "10,000 to 15,000 words a week" for the varied publications to which he contributed, professor of literature at Catholic and Notre Dame universities, diplomat who loved the good life, a man of no particular political stripe but adviser, "unofficially," to Presidents McKinley, Roosevelt, Taft, and Wilson. His only official position was minister to Denmark (1907-1918).

EGAN, PATRICK *(b Aug. 13, 1841, Ballymahon, County Longford, Ireland; d Sept. 30, 1919, New York City)* A political refugee (Fenian) from Ireland, he settled in Lincoln, Nebr., became a grain elevator operator, real estate dealer, a leading light in the Philadelphia Irish convention (1883) that gave birth to the Irish National League of America, and a power in Republican politics who delivered a large bloc of votes for Benjamin Harrison (1888) and was then appointed minister to Chile, serving until the end of Harrison's stay in the White House.

EICHER, EDWARD CLAYTON *(b Dec. 16, 1878, Washington County, Iowa; d Nov. 29, 1944, Alexandria, Va.).* Lawyer, Iowa Democrat. Democratic National Convention delegate (1932), U.S. Representative (1933-1938) resigning to become a Roosevelt-appointed member of the Securities and Exchange Commission (1938-1942) and leaving while chairman to be seated as the chief justice of the U.S. District Court for the District of Columbia (1942 until death).

EISENHOWER, DWIGHT DAVID "IKE" *(b Oct. 14, 1890, Denison, Texas; d Mar. 28, 1969, Walter Reed Army Hospital, Washington, D.C.).* Thirty-fourth president (Republican), 1953-1961, a military man who had no prior political experience; temporary chairman of U.S. Joint Chiefs of Staff; five-star general (1944) and chief of staff of the U.S. Army (1945-1948); supreme commander (World War II) of Allied Expeditionary Forces in Europe (1943-1945), where he demonstrated an exceptional ability to smooth ruffled feathers and led the invasion that brought about Germany's surrender; supreme commander of NATO forces in Europe (1951-1952); president of Columbia University (1948-1950); wrote (1948) best seller entitled *Crusade in Europe*; while president, suffered and recovered from three major illnesses; found relaxation in painting and golf.

Dwight Eisenhower was third in a family of six sons (a seventh died in infancy), all of whom were successes in adult life. When Dwight was about a year old, the family moved to Abilene, Kansas, where his father took a job in a creamery and the boys learned to take turns doing the family chores: building the fire, tending the garden, the chickens, and the family cow. After graduating from high school (1909), Dwight worked at various jobs around Abilene, then, after taking a competitive examination, received appointment to the U.S. Military Academy at West Point where he was an outstanding football player

until he broke his leg and was forced to quit. He graduated (1915) sixty-first in a class of 164.

Years later, at the Command and General Staff School, Fort Leavenworth, Kansas, he was to finish at the top of a class of 275 carefully selected officers. In World War I, Eisenhower was commander of a tank training center near Gettysburg, Penn. After that, he saw service in a variety of posts including the Canal Zone and the Philippines. During Louisiana army maneuvers in 1941, Eisenhower established a reputation as a tactician and came to the attention of Chief of Staff George C. Marshall who, shortly after Pearl Harbor, summoned him to Washington and appointed him chief of the War Plans Division of the War Department General Staff. From then on, it was a swift climb to the top.

Married Mamie Geneva Doud (1916) and the couple had two sons, one of whom died in infancy.

Although in 1948 Eisenhower turned down invitations by both major parties to consider entering the presidential race, he changed his mind in 1952 and retired from the army in order to campaign for the Republican nomination, winning it on the first ballot. He was immensely popular with the people and (with running mate Richard M. Nixon) went on to defeat Democratic candidate Adlai E. Stevenson, 442 to 89 electoral votes. His winning score in the 1956 election, again running against Stevenson and with Nixon as vice presidential candidate, was 457 to 73.

During his presidency, the Supreme Court ruled segregation in the nation's public schools was unconstitutional and Eisenhower sent federal troops to Little Rock, Ark., to force compliance with the ruling. Eisenhower refused to speak out directly against Senator Joseph R. McCarthy's Communist witch-hunting activities even though he wasn't immune to the senator's attacks. Also during this time, the Korean War was brought to an end; Russia and the United States were engaged in a space and nuclear weapons race and efforts to reach agreement on regulations of nuclear testing were unsuccessful. Eisenhower became a world traveler in an attempt to promote peace and friendship but his plans to return Soviet Premier Khrushchev's 1959 visit to the United States were halted when a U.S. U-2 spy plane was shot down while flying over Russia. Under the Southeast Asia (SEATO) alliance (1954), the United States extended economic and military aid to South Vietnam; the Eisenhower Doctrine (1957) pledged American military aid to any Middle East nation threatened by Communist aggression; in 1961, Eisenhower broke off diplomatic relations with Cuba.

In retirement he lived on his farm in Gettysburg, a respected elder statesman who supported Nixon's presidential campaigns and wrote his own memoirs.

ELBERT, SAMUEL *(b 1743, Prince William Parish, S.C.; d Nov. 2, 1788, Savannah, Ga.)* Merchant, Indian trader, Revolutionary Army officer, Georgia patriot. Continental Congress delegate (1784), governor (1785-1786).

ELDREDGE, CHARLES AUGUSTUS *(b Feb. 27, 1820, Bridport, Vt.; d Oct. 26, 1896, Fond du Lac, Wis.)* Lawyer, Wisconsin Democrat. State senate (1854-1856), U.S. Representative (1863-1875).

ELIOT, THOMAS DAWES *(b March 20, 1808, Boston, Mass.; d June 14, 1870, New Bedford, Mass.)* Lawyer, Massachusetts Whig–Free-Soiler–Republican. State representative (1839), state senate (1846), U.S. Representative as a Whig (1854-1855) and as a Republican (1859-1869), Free-Soil National Convention delegate (1855).

ELKINS, DAVIS *(b Jan. 24, 1876, Washington, D.C.; d Jan. 5, 1959, Richmond, Va.)* Railroad and utilities executive, banker, West Virginia Republican. U.S. Senator less than a month in 1911 to fill a vacancy caused by the death of his father, Stephen B. Elkins, he ran for the office in his own right, was elected and served (1919-1925).

ELKINS, STEPHEN BENTON *(b Sept. 26, 1841, Perry County, Ohio; d Jan. 4, 1911, Washington, D.C.)* Lawyer who began practice in New Mexico Territory (1864) after arriving in Messila in a covered wagon from Missouri where he had been raised, learned the Spanish language, became a political leader, an outstanding advocate of statehood, and the holder of many high offices as a New Mexico, New York, and West Virginia Republican; Union Army officer, landowner, mine operator, railroad executive.

In New Mexico: territorial representative (1864, 1865), district attorney (1866, 1867) and attorney general (1867); U.S. district attorney for the territory (1867-1870), delegate to Congress (1873-1877). In New York: Secretary of war in the Harrison cabinet (1891-1892). In West Virginia: U.S. Senate (1895 until death). Father of Davis Elkins.

ELLENDER, ALLEN JOSEPH *(b Sept. 24, 1891, Montegut, La.; d July 27, 1972, in U.S. Naval Hospital, Bethesda, Md.).* Louisiana lawyer and potato farmer who served in the U.S. Senate for thirty-five years (1937 until death) and whom a *New York Times* obituary writer described as "a peppery, outspoken Dixie Democrat who mingled Southern conservatism with some liberal attitudes that often came as a surprise to Senators generally known as liberals."

Houma city attorney (1913-1915), Terrebonne Parish district attorney (1915, 1916), state constitutional convention delegate (1921), state representative (1924-1936), floor leader (1928-1932), and house speaker (1932-1936). As a senator, he was chairman of the Agricultural Committee and (1971) succeeded Richard B. Russell of Georgia as Senate president pro tem.

ELLERY, CHRISTOPHER *(b Nov. 1, 1768, Newport, R.I.; d Dec. 2, 1840, Middletown, R.I.)* Lawyer, Rhode Island Democrat, Newport County superior court clerk (1794-1798), U.S. Senate to complete an unexpired term (1801-1805), U.S. commissioner of loans in Providence (1806), Newport collector of customs (1820-1834). Nephew of William Ellery.

ELLERY, WILLIAM *(b Dec. 22, 1727, Newport, R.I.; d Feb. 15, 1820, Newport).* Merchant, Rhode Island naval officer who became a lawyer twenty-three years after graduating from Harvard in 1747, signer of the Declaration of Independence whose home was burned in retaliation by the British, Federalist who was very much part of the states' rights movement in Rhode Island. Newport County common pleas court clerk (1768-1769), member of the Continental Congress (1776-1781, 1783-1785), member of the nation's first admiralty board (1779-1782), chief justice of the superior court (1785) but did not take the bench because he was needed in Congress, commissioner of Rhode Island's Continental Loan Office (1786-1790), Newport customs collector (1790 until death). Uncle of Christopher Ellery.

ELLIOTT, CARL ATWOOD *(b Dec. 20, 1913, Vina, Ala.)* Lawyer, Alabama Democrat. U.S. Representative (1949-1965) serving on the Rules Committee.

ELLIOTT, JAMES *(b Aug. 18, 1775, Gloucester, Mass.; d Nov. 10, 1839, Newfane, Vt.)* Indian fighter, self-educated lawyer, poet, and publisher of the *Freeman's Journal* in Philadelphia, a great admirer of Jefferson and yet a Federalist who represented Vermont in the Eighth, Ninth and Tenth Congresses (1803-1809). Windham County court

clerk (1817-1835), state representative (1818, 1819, 1837, 1838), probate court registrar (1822-1834), Windham County state's attorney (1837 until death).

ELLIOTT, JOHN MILTON *(b May 20, 1820, Scott County, Va.; d March 26, 1879, Frankfort, Ky., by assassination).* Lawyer, Kentucky Democrat who served as a U.S. Representative (1853-1859), representative in the First and Second Confederate Congresses, state representative (1861), circuit judge (1868-1874), and appeals court judge (1876 until death).

ELLIOTT, RICHARD NASH *(b April 25, 1873, Fayette County, Ind.; d March 21, 1948, Washington, D.C.)* Teacher, lawyer, Indiana Republican. Fayette County attorney (1897-1906), state representative (1905-1909), Connersville city attorney (1905-1909), GOP National Convention delegate (1916), state GOP convention chairman (1930), U.S. Representative (1917-1931), assistant U.S. comptroller general (1931-1943).

ELLIOTT, ROBERT BROWN *(b Aug. 11, 1842, of West Indian parents in Boston, Mass.; d Aug. 9, 1884, New Orleans, La.)* British-educated editor of the *Charleston Leader*, South Carolina Republican who later forsook politics to practice law in New Orleans. State constitutional convention delegate (1868), state representative (1868-1870, 1874-1876) and speaker in the latter term, assistant state adjutant general (1869-1871), U.S. Representative (1871-1874).

ELLIOTT, SARAH BARNWELL *(b 1848, Georgia; d Aug. 30, 1928, Sewanee, Tenn.)* Author, playwright, Tennessee suffragist leader.

ELLIS, EDGAR CLARENCE *(b Oct. 2, 1854, Vermontville, Mich.; d March 15, 1847, St. Petersburg, Fla.)* Minnesota educator who taught Latin at Carleton College (1881, 1882), then became a lawyer in Missouri and active in the Democratic party. Fergus Falls, Minn., schools superintendent (1882-1885), U.S. Representative from Missouri (1905-1909, 1921-1923, 1925-1927, 1929-1931).

ELLIS, EZEKIEL JOHN (b Oct. 15, 1840, Covington, La.; d April 25, 1889, Washington, D.C.) Lawyer, Confederate Army officer who was captured at Missionary Ridge, Louisiana Democrat. State senate (1866-1870), U.S. Representative (1875-1885).

ELLIS, HUBERT SUMMERS (b July 6, 1887, Hurricane, W.Va.; d Dec. 3, 1959, Huntington, W.Va.) Insurance business, salesman, West Virginia Republican, U.S. Representative (1943-1949), state Federal Housing Administration director (1954-1958).

ELLIS, JOHN WILLIS (b Nov. 23, 1820, Rowan County, N.C.; d July 7, 1861, Raleigh, N.C.) Lawyer, North Carolina Democrat who in his first inaugural address as governor (1858 until death) warned that the South could lose its constitutional rights because of slavery. As the state's chief executive, he favored secession, urged creation of the Confederacy, reorganized the state militia, and when the first Civil War shot was fired convened the state legislature in special session, saw an ordinance of secession adopted at the convention that followed, and died in the midst of making war preparations. He was a member of the state house of commons (1844, 1846, 1848) and superior court judge (1848-1858).

ELLIS, SETH HOCKETT (b Jan. 3, 1830, Martinsville, Ohio; d June 23, 1904, Waynesville, Ohio) Quaker farmer who all his life was a leader in the Ohio Grange, which he helped to found, and, as a Union Reformer, made two unsuccessful bids for high office: for governor (1899) and president (1890).

ELLSWORTH, FRANKLIN FOWLER (b July 10, 1879, St. James, Minn.; d Dec. 23, 1942, Minneapolis, Minn.) Lawyer, Minnesota Republican. St. James city attorney (1904, 1905), Watonwan County prosecutor (1905-1909), U.S. Representative (1915-1921), unsuccessful candidate for governor (1920, 1924).

ELLSWORTH, OLIVER (b April 29, 1745, Windsor, Conn.; d Nov. 26, 1807, Windsor) Lawyer, one of the two Connecticut delegates at the federal Constitutional convention (1787) who persuaded the deadlocked conferees to accept the Connecticut Compromise as a means of determining who, how many, and how chosen the members of the U.S. Senate and House of Representatives should be. Later, when party lines were drawn, he became a Federalist and a chief justice of the United States (1796), resigning because of poor health (1799). Member of Connecticut general assembly (1775, 1776), state attorney (1777), Continental Congress (1777-1784), Governor's Council (1780-1785, 1801-1807), superior court judge (1785-1789), U.S. Senate (1789-1796), resigning to become chief justice. Father of William W. Ellsworth.

ELLSWORTH, WILLIAM WOLCOTT (b Nov. 10, 1791, Windsor, Conn.; d Jan. 15, 1868, Hartford, Conn.) Lawyer, Trinity College law professor, Connecticut Whig. U.S. Representative (1829-1834), governor (1838-1842), state supreme court judge (1847-1861). Son of Oliver Ellsworth.

ELMER, EBENEZER (b Aug. 23, 1752, Cedarville, N.J.; d Oct. 18, 1843, Bridgeton, N.J.) Physician, New Jersey Democrat. State general assembly (1789-1795) and speaker (1791, 1795), U.S. Representative (1801-1807), vice president of state council (1807), Bridgeton collector of customs (1808-1817, 1822-1832), vice president of Burlington College (1808-1817, 1822-1832). Brother of Jonathan Elmer.

ELMER, JONATHAN *(b Nov. 29, 1745, Cedarville, N.J.; d Sept. 3, 1817, Bridgeton, N.J.)* Physician who was graduated from the University of Pennsylvania's first medical class (1769), New Jersey Federalist. Cumberland County high sheriff (1772), Continental Congress (1776-1778, 1781-1784, 1787, 1788), state council (1780, 1784), College of New Jersey trustee (1782-1795), county surrogate (1784-1802), U.S. Senate (1789-1791), presiding judge of the county court of common pleas (1802-1804). Brother of Ebenezer Elmer.

ELMER, LUCIUS QUINTIUS CINCINNATUS *(b Feb. 3, 1793, Bridgeton, N.J.; d March 11, 1883, Bridgeton)* Lawyer, New Jersey Democrat. State prosecutor (1824), general assembly (1820-1823) and speaker (1823), Cumberland County prosecutor of the pleas (1824), U.S. attorney for the state (1824-1829), U.S. Representative (1843-1845), state attorney general (1850-1852), state supreme court justice (1852-1869). Son of Ebenezer Elmer.

ELMER, WILLIAM PRICE *(b March 2, 1871, Robertsville, Mo.; d May 11, 1956, Salem, Mo.)* Lawyer, historian, bank director, and a power in the Missouri Republican party. Dent County prosecutor (1895, 1896, 1905, 1906), state representative (1903, 1904, 1921, 1922, 1929-1933), Salem city attorney (1920-1930), GOP National Convention delegate (1904, 1908, 1912, 1920), GOP county chairman (1908-1944), U.S. Representative (1943-1945), University of Missouri Board of Curators (1949-1955).

ELMORE, FRANKLIN HARPER *(b Oct. 15, 1799, Laurens District, S.C.; d May 28, 1850, Washington, D.C.)* Lawyer, banker, South Carolina States' Rights Democrat who was appointed (April 11, 1850) to occupy the U.S. Senate seat emptied by John C. Calhoun's death but died six weeks after arriving in Washington. Southern circuit solicitor (1822-1836), U.S. Representative (1836-1839).

ELSTON, JOHN ARTHUR *(b Feb. 10, 1874, Woodland, Calif.; d Dec. 15, 1921, Washington, D.C.)* Educator, lawyer, California Progressive Republican. Governor's executive secretary (1903-1907), trustee of the State Institution for the Deaf and Blind (1911-1914), U.S. Representative (1915 until death).

ELY, SMITH, JR. *(b April 17, 1825, Hanover, N.J.; d July 1, 1911, Livingston, N.J.)* Merchant, New York Democrat. School commissioner (1856-1860), state senate (1858, 1859), New York County supervisor (1860-1870), U.S. Representative (1871-1873, 1875-1876) resigning to become mayor of New York City (1877, 1878).

ELY, WILLIAM *(b Aug. 14, 1765, Longmeadow, Mass.; d Oct. 9, 1817, Springfield, Mass.)* Lawyer, Massachusetts Federalist who served five terms as a U.S. Representative (1805-1815); state representative (1801-1803, 1815, 1816).

EMERSON, HENRY IVORY *(b March 15, 1871, Litchfield, Maine; d Oct. 28, 1953, East Cleveland, Ohio)* Lawyer, Ohio Republican. Cleveland councilman (1902, 1903), U.S. Representative (1915-1921).

EMOTT, JAMES, SR. *(b March 9, 1771, Poughkeepsie, N.Y.; d April 7, 1850, Poughkeepsie)* Lawyer, jurist, New York Federalist. Onondaga County land commissioner to settle military-reservation title disputes (1797), state assemblyman (1804, 1814-1817) and assembly speaker (1804, 1814), U.S. Representative (1809-1813), Dutchess County Common Pleas Court judge (1817-1823), second judicial circuit judge (1827-1831), Father of James Emott, Jr.

EMOTT, JAMES, JR. *(b April 23, 1823, Poughkeepsie, N.Y.; d Sept. 11, 1884, Poughkeepsie)* Lawyer, banker, New York Whig, a founder of the Association of the Bar of the City of New York, and a reformer who served on the Committee of Seventy that broke up the Tweed Ring. Dutchess County district attorney (1849), first mayor of Poughkeepsie (1854), second judicial district supreme court justice (1856-1864) being elected with Republican support. Son of James Emott, Sr.

ENDECOTT, JOHN *(b 1588, Dorchester, England; d March 15, 1665, Boston, Mass.)* First governor of the Massachusetts Bay Colony (1629-1630), serving again (1644-1645, 1649-1650, 1651-1654, 1655-1665), and always the harshly intolerant Puritan who particularly persecuted the Quakers.

ENDICOTT, WILLIAM CROWNING-SHIELD *(b Nov. 19, 1826, Salem, Mass.; d May 6, 1900, Boston, Mass.).* Lawyer, Massachusetts Whig-Democrat who, as Grover Cleveland's secretary of war (1885-1889) was praised for creating the "Endicott Board of Fortifications" on the Atlantic coast and damned for agreeing (1887) that Civil War-captured Confederate flags should be returned to their respective states. Salem Common Council (1852, 1853, 1857), city solicitor (1858-1863), judge of the state supreme judicial court (1873-1882), unsuccessful candidate for governor (1884).

ENGEL, ALBERT JOSEPH *(b Jan. 1, 1888, New Washington, Ohio; d Dec. 2, 1959, Grand Rapids, Mich.)* Lawyer, tree farmer, Michigan Republican. Missaukee County prosecutor (1916, 1917, 1919, 1920), World War I officer (1917-1919), state senate (1921, 1922, 1927-1932), U.S. Representative (1935-1951).

ENGLE, CLAIR *(b Sept. 21, 1911, Bakersfield, Calif.; d July 30, 1964,* Washington, D.C.) Lawyer, California Democrat. Tehama County district attorney (1934-1942), state senate (1943), U.S. Representative (1943-1959), Democratic National Convention (1948), U.S. Senate (1959 until death) serving on the Armed Services and Commerce Committees. One of the most colorful (typical comment: "I'm sure going to throw a skunk into your henhouse"), outspoken, and active of American legislators (known as "Congressman Fireball"). Shortly before his death and partially paralyzed, he was wheeled twice into the chamber to vote, first to end debate on the historic civil rights bill of 1964, the second time helping to bring about its passage.

ENGLEBRIGHT, HARRY LANE *(b Jan. 2, 1884, Nevada City, Nev.; d May 13, 1943, in U.S. Naval Hospital, Bethesda, Md.)* Mining engineer, California Republican. U.S. Representative (1926 until death). Son of William F. Englebright.

ENGLEBRIGHT, WILLIAM FELLOWS *(b Nov. 23, 1855, New Bedford, Mass.; d Feb. 10, 1915, Oakland, Calif.)* Mining engineer, California Republican. U.S. Representative (1906-1911). Father of Harry L. Englebright.

ENGLISH, JAMES EDWARD *(b March 13, 1812, New Haven, Conn.; d March 2, 1890, New Haven)* Banker, manufacturer, Connecticut Democrat who served briefly as a U.S. Senator (Nov. 27, 1875–May 17, 1876) to fill a vacancy but many more years as governor (1867-1869, 1870-1871) and U.S. Representative (1861-1865). He was also New Haven selectman (1847-1861) and member of common council (1848, 1849), state representative (1855, 1872), state senate (1856-1858), National Union Convention delegate (1866), presidential elector on the Tilden-Hendricks (1876) and Cleveland-Hendricks tickets (1884).

ENGLISH, THOMAS DUNN *(b June 29, 1819, Philadelphia, Pa.; d April 1, 1902, Newark, N.J.)* Lawyer, physician, journalist, playwright, poet whose best-known poem perhaps is "Ben Bolt" (1843), friendly adversary of Edgar Allan Poe, and a New Jersey Democrat who delighted in crusading against Know-Nothingism not only in the Garden State but also in New York and Virginia where he had previously resided. New Jersey assemblyman (1863, 1864), U.S. Representative (1891-1895).

ENGLISH, WILLIAM EASTIN *(b Nov. 3, 1850, Scott County, Ind.; d April 29, 1926, Indianapolis, Ind.)* Lawyer, wounded Spanish-American War officer who became the first elected commander in chief of the United Spanish War Veterans of the United States, Indiana Democrat turned Republican. State representative (1880), U.S. Representative (May 1884–March 1885) after successfully contesting his predecessor's election, Democratic National Convention delegate (1892, 1896), Indianapolis Park Commission chairman (1898-1900) and president of the Indianapolis Board of Safety (1904-1906), GOP National Convention delegate (1912), state senator (1916 until death). Son of William H. English.

ENGLISH, WILLIAM HAYDEN *(b Aug. 27, 1822, Lexington, Ind.; d Feb. 7, 1896, Indianapolis)* Author, lawyer, Indiana Democrat who ran unsuccessfully for vice president (1880). Secretary of state constitutional convention (1850), member and speaker of the state house of representatives (1851, 1852), U.S. Representative (1853-1861), Smithsonian Institution regent (1853-1861). Father of William E. English.

EPPES, JOHN WAYLES *(b April 7, 1773, Chesterfield County, Va.; d Sept. 13, 1823, Buckingham County, Va.).* Nephew and supporter of Thomas Jef-

ferson, lawyer, planter, Virginia Democrat. State house of delegates (1801-1803), U.S. Representative (1803-1811, 1813-1815), U.S. Senate (1817-1819) resigning because of poor health.

ERICKSON, JOHN EDWARD *(b March 14, 1863, Stoughton, Wis.; d May 25, 1946, Helena, Mont.)* Lawyer, Montana Democrat. Teton County attorney (1897-1905), eleventh judicial district judge (1905-1915), Democratic National Convention delegate (1920), Democratic state chairman (1920-1924), governor (1925-1933), U.S. Senate to fill a vacancy (1933-1934).

ERMENTROUT, DANIEL *(b Jan. 24, 1837, Reading, Pa.; d Sept. 17, 1899, Reading)* Lawyer, Pennsylvania Democrat. Berks County district attorney (1862-1865), Reading city solicitor (1867-1870), school board member (1868-1876), Democratic National Convention delegate (1868, 1880), chairman of county standing committee (1869, 1872, 1873), state senate (1873-1880), U.S. Representative (1881-1889, 1897 until death), delegate to all Democratic state conventions (1895-1899).

ERNST, RICHARD PRETLOW *(b Feb. 25, 1858, Covington, Ky.; d April 13, 1934, Baltimore, Md.)* Lawyer, banker, trustee of four colleges (Centre, University of Kentucky, Pikeville, and Western College for Women), Kentucky Republican. Covington councilman (1888-1892), U.S. Senate (1921-1927).

ERRETT, RUSSELL *(b Nov. 10, 1817, New York City; d April 7, 1891, Carnegie, Pa.)* Self-educated newspaperman, Union soldier, Pennsylvania Republican. Pittsburgh comptroller (1860), clerk of the state senate (1860, 1861, 1872-1876), state senate (1867), internal revenue assessor (1869-1873), U.S. Representative (1877-1883), U.S. pension agent (1883-1887).

ESCH, JOHN JACOB (b March 20, 1861, Norwalk, Wis.; d April 27, 1941, LaCrosse, Wis.) Lawyer, teacher, Wisconsin Republican. Sparta city treasurer (1885), GOP state convention delegate (1894, 1896), U.S. Representative (1899-1921), member of Interstate Commerce Commission (1921-1928) and its chairman (1927-1928).

ESLICK, EDWARD EVERETT (b April 19, 1872, Giles County, Tenn.; d June 14, 1932, Washington, D.C., while addressing the U.S. House of Representatives) Lawyer, banker, farmer, Tennessee Democrat who, together with his wife, the former Willa McCord Blake, comprised an extremely active husband-and-wife political team. He was a presidential elector on the Bryan-Sewall (1896), Bryan-Stevenson (1900) and Parker-Davis (1904) tickets; U.S. Representative (1925 until death).

ESLICK, WILLA McCORD BLAKE (b Sept. 8, 1878, Fayetteville, Tenn.; d Feb. 18, 1961, Pulaski, Tenn.) A woman who was active in civic and political affairs, Tennessee Democrat. Member of the Giles County Council of National Defense during World War I, member of State Democratic Committee, U.S. Representative (August 1932-March 1933) to complete the term upon the death of her husband, Edward E. Eslick.

ESTOPINAL, ALBERT (b Jan. 30, 1845, St. Bernard Parish, La.; d April 28, 1919, New Orleans) Confederate soldier, commission merchant, planter, Louisiana Democrat. St. Bernard Parish sheriff (1872-1876), state representative (1876-1880), state constitutional convention delegate (1879, 1898), state senate (1880-1900), lieutenant governor (1900-1904), chairman of Democratic state central committee (1908), U.S. Representative (1908 until death).

EUSTIS, GEORGE (b Sept. 28, 1828, New Orleans, La.; d March 15, 1872,

Cannes, France) Lawyer, diplomat, Louisiana Know-Nothing. U.S. Representative (1855-1859), secretary of Confederate legation in Paris during the Civil War, remaining in France afterward and negotiating a postal treaty for the United States. Brother of James B. Eustis.

EUSTIS, JAMES BIDDLE (b Aug. 27, 1834, New Orleans, La.; d Sept. 9, 1899, Newport, R.I.) Lawyer, judge advocate in the Confederate Army, University of Louisiana law professor, Louisiana Democrat. State representative (1872), state senator (1874-1878), U.S. Senate (1876-1879, 1885-1891), ambassador to France (1893-1897). Brother of George Eustis.

EUSTIS, WILLIAM (b June 10, 1753, Cambridge, Mass.; d Feb. 6, 1825, Boston) Physician, Revolutionary Army surgeon, Massachusetts Democrat who defeated John Quincy Adams in the 1802 congressional race by a vote of 1,899 to 1,840, secretary of war at the outbreak of the War of 1812, "in whom," Henry Clay said, "there exists no sort of confidence." State representative (1788-1794), U.S. Representative (1801-1805, 1820-1823); secretary of war in both the Jefferson and Madison cabinets (1807-1813) resigning, some say by request, and being soothed by appointment as minister to the Netherlands (1814-1818); governor (1823 until death) after being defeated in three earlier tries.

EVANS, ALEXANDER (b Sept. 13, 1818, Elkton, Md.; d Dec. 5, 1888, Elkton) Lawyer, Maryland Whig. U.S. Representative (1847-1853).

EVANS, CHARLES ROBLEY (b Aug. 9, 1866, Breckenridge, Ill.; d Nov. 30, 1954, Kearney, Nebr.) Prospector, mining operator, Nevada Democrat. U.S. Representative (1919-1921), U.S. Capitol guide (1934-1948).

EVANS, GEORGE *(b Jan. 12, 1797, Hallowell, Maine; d April 6, 1867, Portland, Maine)* Lawyer, Maine Whig whom John Quincy Adams, a congressional debating adversary, described as "one of the ablest and most eloquent orators in Congress." His main interest was public finance, but he was unusually knowledgeable on many matters of state. State representative (1825-1829) and speaker (1829), U.S. Representative (1829-1841), U.S. Senate (1841-1847) serving as Finance Committee chairman, member of Mexican claims commission (1849, 1850), Maine attorney general (1850, 1854, 1856).

EVANS, HENRY CLAY *(b June 18, 1843, Juanita County, Pa.; d Dec. 12, 1921, Chattanooga, Tenn.)* Union Army soldier, railroad car builder, Tennessee Republican who gained national prominence when he was elected governor (1894) only to have a legislative recount go against him. Mayor of Chattanooga (1881, 1882) and organizer of its school system, U.S. Representative (1889-1891), first assistant U.S. postmaster general (1891-1893), U.S. pension commissioner (1897-1902), U.S. consul to London (1902-1905), Chattanooga's first commissioner of health and education (1911-1915).

EVANS, HIRAM KINSMAN *(b March 17, 1863, Walnut Township, Iowa; d July 9, 1941, Corydon, Iowa)* Lawyer, jurist, Iowa Republican. Wayne County prosecutor (1891-1895), state representative (1896, 1897), University of Iowa regent (1897-1904), mayor of Corydon (1901-1903), third judicial district judge (1904-1923), U.S. Representative (1923-1925), state parole board member (1927-1933).

EVANS, JOHN MORGAN *(b Jan. 7, 1863, Sedalia, Mo.; d March 12, 1946, Washington, D.C.)* Lawyer, Montana Democrat. Missoula police court judge (1889-1894), U.S. land office registrar (1894-1898), mayor of Missoula in Montana's first city commission form of government (1911, 1912), U.S. Representative (1913-1921, 1923-1933).

EVANS, ROBERT EMORY *(b July 15, 1856, Coalmont, Pa.; d July 8, 1925, Lincoln, Nebr.)* Machinist, lawyer, Nebraska Republican. Winnegago Industrial School superintendent (1889-1891), Dakota County prosecutor (1895), eighth judicial circuit judge (1895-1899), GOP National Convention delegate (1912), U.S. Representative (1919-1923), state supreme court judge (1924 until death).

EVANS, WALTER *(b Sept. 18, 1842, Barren County, Ky.; d Dec. 30, 1923, Louisville, Ky.)* Union Army officer, self-educated lawyer and the first Kentucky Republican to represent his district in Congress (1895-1899). GOP National Convention delegate (1868, 1872, 1880, 1884), state representative (1871), state senate (1873), commissioner of internal revenue (1883-1885), U.S. district judge (1899 until death).

EVANS, WILLIAM ELMER *(b Dec. 14, 1877, Laurel County, Ky.; d Nov. 12, 1959, Los Angeles, Calif.)* Lawyer, rancher, banker, real estate operator, California Republican. GOP National Convention delegate (1924), U.S. Representative (1927-1935).

EVARTS, WILLIAM MAXWELL *(b Feb. 6, 1818, Boston, Mass.; d Feb. 28, 1901, New York City)* Lawyer, statesman who negotiated with England to stop building Confederate warships, president of the New York City Bar Association when it was fighting Tweed Ring corruption, chief defense counsel (1868) at President Johnson's impeachment proceedings, New York Republican. Assistant U.S. attorney (1849-1853), chairman of state delegation to GOP National Convention (1860), state constitutional convention delegate (1867, 1868), attorney general in the Grant cabinet (1868-1869), secretary of state in the Hayes cabinet (1877-1881), delegate to International Monetary Conference in Paris (1881), U.S. Senate (1885-1891).

EVELEIGH, NICHOLAS *(b about 1748, Charleston, S.C.; d April 16, 1791, Philadelphia, Pa.)* Farmer, South Carolina patriot, Revolutionary army officer. State representative (1781), member of Continental Congress (1781, 1782), member of state legislative council (1783), first comptroller of the U.S. Treasury (1789 until death).

EVERETT, EDWARD *(b April 11, 1794, Dorchester, Mass.; d Jan. 15, 1865, Boston, Mass.)* Clergyman, professor of Greek literature at Harvard, diplomat, brilliant public speaker who shared the platform with Lincoln at Gettysburg (1863), but a vacillating Massachusetts figure whose political career was marred by his reluctance to make decisions. U.S. Representative as a National Republican (1825-1835), governor (1836-1840), ambassador to England (1841-1845), president of Harvard (1846-1849), secretary of state in Fillmore cabinet upon death of Daniel Webster (Nov. 6, 1852–March 3, 1853), U.S. Senator (1853-1854) as a Unionist who resigned after not voting on the Kansas-Nebraska Act, unsuccessful vice presidential candidate on the Constitutional-Union ticket (1860), presidential elector as a Republican on the Lincoln-Johnson ticket (1864).

EVERETT, HORACE *(b July 17, 1779, Foxboro, Mass.; d Jan. 30, 1851, Windsor, Vt.)* Lawyer, Vermont Whig. Windsor County prosecutor (1813-1818), state representative (1819, 1820, 1822, 1824, 1834), state constitutional convention delegate (1828), U.S. Representative (1829-1843).

EVERETT, ROBERT ASHTON *(b Feb. 24, 1915, Obion County, Tenn.; d Jan. 26, 1969.)* Tennessee Democrat. Administrative assistant to Senator Tom Stewart (1945-1949), administrative assistant to Governor Gordon Browning (1950-1952), U.S. Representative (1958 until death) serving on the Public Works and Veterans' Affairs committees.

EVINS, JOHN HAMILTON *(b July 18, 1830, Spartanburg District, S.C.; d Oct. 20, 1884, Spartanburg)* Lawyer, Confederate Army officer, South Carolina Democrat. State representative (1863, 1864), Democratic National Convention delegate (1876), U.S. Representative (1877 until death).

EWING, THOMAS, SR. *(b Dec. 28, 1789, Ohio County, Va., now W.Va.; d Oct. 26, 1871, Lancaster, Ohio)* A farmboy who loved books and toiled in the salt works to further his education, lawyer who became known as "the logician of the West," advisor to Presidents Lincoln and Johnson, Ohio Whig who turned Democrat as a sign of protest against Reconstruction policies. U.S. Senate (1831-1837, 1850-1851), secretary of the treasury in Harrison and Tyler cabinets (1841) resigning when the latter twice vetoed a national bank bill, secretary of the interior in the Taylor cabinet (1849-1850) who urged the location of a mint near the California gold fields and construction of a railroad to the Pacific, delegate to Washington convention (1861) aimed at averting the Civil War, delegate to Union National Convention (1865). Father of Thomas Ewing, Jr.

EWING, THOMAS, JR. *(b Aug. 7, 1829, Lancaster, Ohio; d Jan. 21, 1896, New York City)* Private secretary to President Zachary Taylor (1849, 1850), lawyer, Union Army officer, Kansas and Ohio Whig who, like his namesake father, became a Democrat because of what he considered improper Reconstruction policies. In Kansas: delegate to the Leavenworth Constitutional Convention (1858), delegate to the peace convention (1861) that vainly tried to avert the Civil War, chief justice of the Kansas Supreme Court (1861, 1862). In Ohio: state constitutional convention delegate (1873, 1874), U.S. Representative (1877-1881), unsuccessful candidate for governor (1879) losing to Charles Foster, the Republican candidate.

F

☆ ☆ ☆

FAIR, JAMES GRAHAM *(b Dec. 3, 1831, County Tyrone, Ireland; d Dec. 28, 1894, San Francisco, Calif.)* California and Nevada prospector who struck it fabulously rich with the Bonanza and other gold and silver mines said to have yielded $200 million, meanwhile also trying his hand at real estate, manufacturing, and Democratic politics in Nevada. U.S. Senate (1881-1887).

FAIRBANKS, CHARLES WARREN *(b May 11, 1852, Union County, Ohio; d June 4, 1918, Indianapolis, Ind.)* Associated Press correspondent, lawyer, a leader in the Republican party both nationally and in Indiana, Theodore Roosevelt's vice president (1905-1909), and unsuccessful candidate for the same office when Charles Evans Hughes was the presidential nominee (1916). Ohio Wesleyan University trustee (1885), state GOP convention chairman (1892, 1898), temporary chairman of and keynoted speaker at GOP National Convention (1896) and again a delegate in 1900 and 1904, chairman of U.S. delegation to Joint High Commission that adjusted differences with Canada (1898), U.S. Senate (1897-1905) where he was considered the spokesman for his close friend, President McKinley.

FAIRCHILD, GEORGE WINTHROP *(b May 6, 1854, Oneonta, N.Y.; d Dec. 31, 1924, New York City)* Publisher of the Oneonta Herald, farmer, banker, manufacturer, New York Republican. U.S. Representative (1907-1919).

FAIRCHILD, JOHN *(b Jan. 30, 1797, Saco, Maine; d Dec. 24, 1847, Washington, D.C.)* Lawyer, Maine Democrat. U.S. Representative (1835-1838), resigning to become governor (1839-1843) and once again resigning, this time to become a U.S. Senator (1843 until death).

FAIRFIELD, LOUIS WILLIAM *(b Oct. 15, 1858, Auglaize County, Ohio; d Feb. 20, 1930, Joliet, Ill.)* Teacher, lecturer, newspaper editor, Indiana Republican. Vice president of Tri-State College (1885-1917), U.S Representative (1917-1925).

FALCONER, JACOB ALEXANDER *(b Jan. 26, 1869, Ontario, Canada; d July 1, 1928, Wingdale, N.Y.)* Lumberman, Washington Progressive. Mayor of Everett (1897, 1898), state representative (1904-1908) and house speaker (1907), state senate (1909-1912), U.S. Representative (1913-1915). He was also a road builder in Texas, ship broker in New York, oil and gas wildcatter in New Mexico.

FALL, ALBERT BACON *(b Nov. 26, 1861, Franklin, Ky.; d Nov. 30, 1944, El Paso, Tex.)* Teacher, lawyer, rancher

223

with mine, lumber, and railroad interests, New Mexico Republican who resigned as secretary of the interior in Harding cabinet (1921-1923) because of involvement with Harry F. Sinclair and Edward L. Doheny in Teapot Dome and Elk Hills oil-leasing scandals, was convicted (1929) of accepting a $100,000 bribe and jailed (1931-1932). Before that he served in the New Mexico Territory as representative (1891, 1892), associate supreme court justice (1893), attorney general (1897, 1907), territorial council member (1897). Then, after statehood, U.S. Senate (1912-1921).

FARAN, JAMES JOHN *(b Dec. 29, 1808, Cincinnati, Ohio; d Dec. 12, 1892, Cincinnati)* Editor-publisher of the *Cincinnati Enquirer* (1844-1881), lawyer, Ohio Democrat. State representative (1835-1839), house speaker (1838-1839), state senate (1839-1843), U.S. Representative (1845-1849), mayor of Cincinnati (1855-1857), city postmaster (1855-1859), Democratic National Convention delegate (1860).

FARGO, WILLIAM GEORGE *(b May 20, 1818, Pompey, N.Y.; d Aug. 3, 1881, Buffalo, N.Y.)* Messenger, stagecoach operator, and a cofounder of Wells, Fargo & Co., which had its beginnings in Buffalo and spread west to the goldfields of California. A New York Democrat, his only elective office was as mayor of Buffalo during the Civil War years (1862-1866).

FARIS, GEORGE WASHINGTON *(b June 9, 1854, Jasper County, Ind.; d April 17, 1914, Washington, D.C.)* Lawyer, Indiana Republican. U.S. Representative (1895-1901) who shortly thereafter transferred his law practice to the nation's capital.

FARLEY, JAMES INDUS *(b Feb. 24, 1871, Steuben County, Ind.; d June 16, 1948, Bryn Mawr, Pa.)* Teacher, automobile dealer, farmer, Indiana Democrat. National convention delegate (1928), U.S. Representative (1933-1939).

FARNSWORTH, JOHN FRANKLIN *(b March 27, 1820, Eaton, Canada; d July 14, 1897, Washington, D.C.)* Lawyer, Union Army officer, Illinois Republican. U.S. Representative (1857-1861, 1863-1873) with decided radical leanings during Reconstruction.

FARRINGTON, JOSEPH RIDER *(b Oct. 15, 1897, Washington, D.C.; d June 19, 1954, Washington)* Philadelphia and Washington newspaperman who became president-general manager of the *Honolulu Star-Bulletin* (1939 until death), Hawaii Republican. Secretary of territorial legislative commission (1933), territorial senate (1934-1942), delegate to the U.S. Congress (1943 until death) when he was succeeded by his wife, the former Mary Elizabeth Pruett. Son of Wallace R. Farrington.

FARRINGTON, MARY ELIZABETH PRUETT *(b May 30, 1898, Tokyo, Japan)*. Newspaper correspondent (1918-1957), publisher of the *Honolulu Star-Bulletin*, Hawaii Republican who was active in the national affairs of GOP women, serving as president of both the League of Republican Women in Washington (1946-1948) and of the National Federation of Women's Republican Clubs (1949-1953). Additionally, she was a GOP National Convention delegate (1952) who two years later was elected a delegate to the U.S. Congress to fill the vacancy caused by the death of her husband, Joseph R. Farrington, then was reelected and so served three years (1954-1957).

FARRINGTON, WALLACE RIDER *(b May 3, 1871, Orono, Maine; d Oct. 6, 1933)* Newspaperman who put muscle into the *Honolulu Star-Bulletin*, a founder of the Republican party in Hawaii, and Harding-appointed territorial governor (1921-1929). Father of Joseph Rider Farrington.

FARWELL, CHARLES BENJAMIN *(b July 1, 1823, Painted Post, N.Y.; d Sept. 23, 1903, Lake Forest, Ill.)* Surveyor, farmer, land speculator, banker, dry goods wholesaler, Illinois Republican. Member of state equalization board (1867), chairman of Cook County Board of Supervisors (1868), U.S. Representative (1871-1876, 1881-1883). U.S. Senate (1887-1891).

FASSETT, JACOB SLOAT *(b Nov. 13, 1853, Elmira, N.Y.; d April 21, 1924, Vancouver, British Columbia)* Editor-publisher of the *Elmira Daily Advertiser* (1879-1896), lawyer, banker, lumberman, New York Republican and an upstate crusader against political corruption in New York City. Chemung County district attorney (1878, 1879), state senate (1884-1891) and president pro tem (1889-1891), GOP National Convention delegate (1880, 1892, 1916) and temporary chairman (1892), secretary of GOP National Committee (1888-1892), unsuccessful candidate for governor (1891), state constitutional convention delegate (1904), U.S. Representative (1905-1911), chairman of GOP advisory committee (1918).

FAULK, ANDREW JACKSON *(b Nov. 26, 1814, Milford, Pa.; d Sept. 4, 1898, Yankton, S.Dak.)* Newspaperman, lawyer, Indian trader, Pennsylvania Democrat turned Republican over the issue of slavery, Johnson-appointed governor of the Dakota Territory and superintendent of Indian affairs (1866-1869) who urged exploitation of the Black Hills mineral deposits and did much to open the area to white settlers.

FAULKNER, CHARLES JAMES, SR. *(b July 6, 1806, Martinsburg, Va., now W.Va.; d Nov. 1, 1884, near Martinsburg)* Lawyer, farmer, railroad president, Virginia and West Virginia Demo-

crat who advocated gradual abolition of slavery. Appointed minister to France in 1859 by President Buchanan, served until 1861 when he returned and was imprisoned as a Southern sympathizer, released after two months, then became a Confederate Army officer on Stonewall Jackson's staff.

In Virginia: member of house of delegates (1829-1834, 1848, 1849), Virginia-Maryland boundary commissioner (1832), state senate (1838-1842), state constitutional convention (1850), U.S. Representative (1851-1859). In West Virginia: state constitutional convention delegate (1872), U.S. Representative (1875-1877). Father of Charles J. Faulkner, Jr.

FAULKNER, CHARLES JAMES, JR. *(b Sept. 21, 1847, near Martinsburg, Va. which became part of W.Va. during his lifetime; d Jan. 13, 1929, near Martinsburg)* Confederate Army cadet, lawyer, planter, West Virginia Democrat. Thirteenth judicial circuit judge (1880), U.S. Senate (1887-1899), Democratic state convention chairman (1888, 1892), member of the International Joint High Commission of the United States and Great Britain (1898). Son of Charles J. Faulkner, Sr.

FAUST, CHARLES LEE *(b April 24, 1879, Logan County, Ohio; d Dec. 17, 1928, in U.S. Naval Hospital, Bethesda, Md.)* Teacher, lawyer, Missouri Republican. St. Joseph city counselor (1915-1919), U.S. Representative (1921 until death).

FAY, FRANCIS BALL *(b June 12, 1793, Southboro, Mass.; d Oct. 6, 1876, South Lancaster, Mass.)* Merchant, Massachusetts Whig of little education but a man who got the unheralded things done. For example, he founded the state's first reform school and Southboro's first public library. Southboro postmaster (1817-1832), Worcester County deputy sheriff (1824-1830), member of state general court (1830, 1831, 1834-1836, 1840), state senate (1843-1845, 1848, 1868), U.S. Representative to fill a vacancy (1852-1853), mayor of Chelsea (1857).

FEATHERSTONE, LEWIS PORTER *(b July 28, 1851, Oxford, Miss.; d March 14, 1922, Longview, Texas)* Planter, railroad builder. Arkansas Union Laborite and farm leader. State representative (1887, 1888), president of the State Wheel, a farmers' organization (1887, 1888), U.S. Representative (1890-1891) after successfully contesting the election of William H. Cate.

FEE, JOHN GREGG *(b Sept. 9, 1816, Bracken County, Ky.; d Jan. 11, 1901, Berea, Ky.)* Dedicated Kentucky Abolitionist clergyman who was disinherited by his slave-owner parents because of his views, shot at and set upon by mobs, exiled from Kentucky (1859-1863), but through it all stuck to his cause, establishing not only Abolitionist churches in defiance of his superiors but also founding Berea College (1855).

FELCH, ALPHEUS *(b Sept. 28, 1804, Limerick, Maine; d June 13, 1896, Ann Arbor, Mich.)* Lawyer, Michigan Democrat who was president of board commissioned (1853-1856) to settle Spanish and Mexican war claims. State representative (1835-1837), state banking commissioner (1838, 1839), state auditor general (1842), associate justice of state supreme court (1842-1845), governor (1846-1847) resigning to become a U.S. Senator (1847-1853).

FELL, JOHN *(b Feb. 5, 1721, New York City; d May 15, 1798, Coldenham, N.Y.)* Farmer, overseas trader, New Jersey patriot known as a "great Tory hunter" who was captured by loyalist raiders and held prisoner in the New York City jail (April 23, 1777-Jan. 7, 1778). New Jersey common pleas judge

(1766-1774), member of Provincial Congress (1775), chairman of both the Bergen County committee of safety and the Standing Committee of Correspondence, member of provincial council (1776), member of Continental Congress (1778-1780) and the state council (1782, 1783).

FELLOWS, FRANK *(b Nov. 7, 1889, Bucksport, Maine; d Aug. 27, 1951, Bangor, Maine)* Lawyer, Maine Republican. U.S. Representative (1941 until death).

FELLOWS, JOHN R. *(b July 29, 1832, Troy, N.Y.; d Dec. 7, 1896, New York City)* Lawyer who, although a Northerner, was very much on the side of the South; Confederate Army officer, Arkansas and New York Democrat. In Arkansas: presidential elector on the Constitutional-Union ticket of Bell and Everett (1860), delegate to state secession convention (1861), state senate (1866, 1867). In New York: assistant New York County district attorney (1869-1872, 1885-1887) and district attorney (1888-1890, 1894 until death), U.S. Representative (1891-1893).

FELTON, REBECCA LATIMER *(b June 10, 1835, De Kalb County, Ga.; d Jan. 24, 1930, Atlanta)* Writer who for twenty-eight years contributed to the *Atlanta Journal*, teacher, lecturer, and mother of five who worked side by side with her husband, William H. Felton, against Georgia's political hierarchy and, many years after his death, became the first woman to serve in the U.S. Senate—but only for two days and at the age of eighty-seven. It happened like this: Senator Thomas E. Watson died on Sept. 26, 1922, and on Oct. 3 Governor Thomas W. Hardwick, in a gesture of Southern chivalry, appointed Mrs. Felton to sit until a successor could be elected and sworn. She did not take the oath, however, until Nov. 21, attended the session of that day and the next when Walter F. George was sworn.

Congressional secretary to her husband (1875-1881), delegate to the Tennessee Centennial Exposition (1887), member of board of lady managers of the Chicago Exposition (1890-1894), chairman of the woman's executive board of the Cotton States and International Exposition (1894, 1895), general agriculture juror at the Louisiana Purchase Exposition (1894, 1895, 1904), Progressive Republican National Convention delegate (1912), and then, as a Democrat, those two historic days in the Senate in 1922.

FELTON, WILLIAM HARRELL *(b June 19, 1823, Oglethorpe County, Ga.; d Sept. 24, 1909, Cartersville, Ga.)* Physician, teacher, farmer, clergyman, Confederate Army surgeon, Georgia Whig turned independent Democrat who devoted his political life to fighting the entrenched conservative machine. State representative (1851, 1884-1890), U.S. Representative (1875-1881). Two years after his death, his wife's *My Memoirs of Georgia Politics*, a book that named names and identified skeletons, was published. Husband of Rebecca L. Felton.

FENN, EDWARD HART *(b Sept. 12, 1856, Hartford, Conn.; d Feb. 23, 1939, Washington, D.C.)* Hartford newspaperman, Connecticut Republican. State representative (1907, 1915), state senate (1909, 1911), state fish and game commissioner (1912-1916), U.S. Representative (1921-1931).

FENN, STEPHEN SOUTHMYD *(b March 28, 1820, Watertown, Conn.; d April 13, 1892, Blackfoot, Idaho)* Miner, rancher, lawyer, farmer, Idaho Democrat. Member of territorial council (1864-1867), first judicial district attorney (1869), territorial representative and speaker of the house (1872), delegate to Congress (1876-1879).

FENNER, ARTHUR *(b Dec. 10, 1745, Providence, R.I.; d Oct. 15, 1805, Providence)* A Continental Congress-appointed member of the Committee of Inspection (1774-1776) and for many years clerk of Providence's Common Pleas Court who was a leader of the Antifederalist party that opposed Rhode Island's adoption of the federal Constitution. The state's freemen, seeking to close an ever-widening breach over the issues, decided upon a compromise with an Antifederalist to become governor, and a Federalist to be deputy governor, and the General Assembly to decide who should fill each position. It chose Fenner to be governor and thus he became Rhode Island's fourth governor (1790-1791). It was on May 5, 1790, that the Assembly made that choice, then on May 29 it met again to decide once and for all whether Rhode Island should ratify the Constitution. Ratification won by a vote of 34 to 32 and all state officers—with Fenner first among them—took an oath to support the newly adopted Constitution. In 1791 he ran for reelection, was the victor, and served until death. Father of James Fenner.

FENNER, JAMES *(b Jan. 22, 1771, Providence, R.I.; d April 17, 1846, near Providence)* Rhode Island's first governor elected after enactment of the 1842 constitution forced upon the state by the Dorr Rebellion (see Thomas Dorr), Democrat, and a politician through and through. U.S. Senate (1805-1807), governor (1807-1811, 1824-1831, 1843-1845), presidential elector on the Monroe-Tompkins (1816, 1820) and Van Buren-Johnson (1836) tickets, president of Rhode Island Historical Society (1822, 1823), president of state constitutional convention (1842). Son of Arthur Fenner.

FENNO, JOHN *(b Aug. 12, 1751, Boston, Mass.; d Sept. 14, 1798, Philadelphia, Pa.)* Skilled at Penmanship and secretary to General Artemas Ward, he tried his hand at trade, went heavily into debt, turned to journalism and found his niche as founder-editor-publisher (1789) of the strongly Federalist, Hamilton-supported *Gazette of the United States*, only to have his career cut short in the Philadelphia yellow fever epidemic of 1798. Fenno was very much the gentleman but that did not prevent him from becoming embroiled in the journalistic battles of the day, with the Jeffersonian press lined up on the other side. In one exchange that turned into a donnybrook he was caned by Benjamin Franklin Bache, editor of the rival *Aurora*.

FENTON, IVOR DAVID *(b Aug. 3, 1889, Mahanoy City, Pa.)* Physician, Pennsylvania Republican. U.S. Representative (1939-1963) serving on the Appropriations Committee.

FENTON, REUBEN EATON *(b July 4, 1819, Carroll, N.Y.; d Aug. 25, 1885, Jamestown, N.Y.)* Lawyer, merchant, banker, lumberman, Democrat who helped found Republican party in New York and chairman of its first state convention (1855). Carroll supervisor (1846-1852), U.S. Representative (1853-1855, 1857-1864), governor (1865-1868), U.S. Senate (1869-1875), chairman of U.S. commission to International Monetary Conference in Paris (1878).

FERGUSON, MIRIAM A. "MA" *(b June 13, 1875, Bell Co., Texas; d June 25, 1961, Austin, Texas)* Democratic governor of Texas (1925-1927, 1933-1935). Installed in 1925 just fifteen days later than Governor Nellie T. Ross of Wyoming, thereby losing the right to call herself first woman governor in the United States. Wife of Democratic Texas Governor James Edward Ferguson who was elected in 1914 as the champion of the businessman and poor independent farmer and impeached for misuse of state funds in 1917. He was found guilty

on several charges and removed from office but was said to perform the functions of the position during his wife's tenure. "Ma's" goals in running for office in 1924 were to clear her husband's name and break the Ku Klux Klan grip on the state.

FERNALD, BERT MANFRED *(b April 3, 1858, West Poland, Maine; d Aug. 23, 1946, West Poland)* Teacher, farmer, food canner, Maine Republican. State representative (1896-1898), state senate (1898-1902), governor (1909-1911), U.S. Senate (1916 until death).

FERNANDEZ, ANTONIO MANUEL *(b Jan. 17, 1902, Springer, N.Mex.; d Nov. 7, 1956, Albuquerque, N.Mex.)* Lawyer, New Mexico Democrat. Eighth judicial district court reporter (1925-1930) and assistant district attorney (1933), state representative (1935), chief tax attorney for the State Tax Commission (1935, 1936), first assistant state attorney general (1937-1941), member of state's first Public Service Commission (1941, 1942), U.S. Representative (1943 until death).

FERRIS, SCOTT *(b Nov. 3, 1877, Neosho, Mo.; d June 8, 1945, Oklahoma City, Okla.)* Lawyer, farmer, oil business, Oklahoma Democrat. State representative (1904, 1905), U.S. Representative (1907-1921), Democratic National Convention delegate (1912, 1916), unsuccessful candidate for U.S. Senate (1920), Democratic National Committeeman (1924-1940).

FERRIS, WOODBRIDGE NATHAN *(b Jan. 6, 1853, Spencer, N.Y.; d March 23, 1928, Washington, D.C.)* Educator, banker, founder and president of the Ferris Institute (1884 until death), Michigan Democrat. Pittsfield (Ill.) schools superintendent (1879-1884), governor of Michigan (1913-1916), U.S. Senate (1923 until death).

FERRY, ELISHA PEYRE *(b Aug. 9, 1825, Monroe, Mich.; d Oct. 14, 1895, Seattle, Wash.)* Lawyer, banker, Illinois Republican leader and first mayor of Waukegan; became friendly with Ulysses S. Grant during the Civil War thus embarking upon a new career in the territory and state of Washington. When Grant became president he appointed Ferry surveyor-general of Washington Territory (1869-1872), then governor (1872-1880) and, after statehood, the first state governor (1889-1893). Ferry County is named for him.

FERRY, ORRIS SANFORD *(b Aug. 15, 1823, Bethel, Conn.; d Nov. 21, 1875, Norwalk, Conn.)* Editor of the *Yale Literary Magazine* in his college years, lawyer, Union Army officer, Connecticut Republican who, as a U.S. Senator, voted for President Johnson's impeachment and filed an opinion; when Horace Greeley ran for president, Ferry called it "mere midsummer madness." Probate judge (1849), state senate (1855, 1856), Fairfield County prosecutor (1856-1859), U.S. Representative (1859-1861), U.S. Senator (1867 until death) elected to a first term as the organization candidate but, upon losing that support for refusing to toe the line, was reelected by a coalition of liberal Republicans and Democrats.

FERRY, THOMAS WHITE *(b June 10, 1827, Mackinac Island, Mich.; d Oct. 13, 1896, Grand Haven, Mich.)* Son of the missionary-founder of Grand Haven, merchant, lumberman, Michigan Republican who as president pro tem of the U.S. Senate presided (1877) over the sixteen joint Congressional meetings needed to decide the Hayes-Tilden presidential election. State representative (1850-1852), state senate (1856), GOP National Convention delegate (1860), U.S. Representative (1865-1871), U.S. Senator (1871-1883) who was noted for his financial expertise, Senate president pro tem (1875-1879).

FESS, SIMEON DAVISON *(b Dec. 11, 1861, Allen County, Ohio; d Dec. 23, 1936, Washington, D.C.)* Lawyer, educator, lecturer, editor, author, Ohio Republican who was a power in the party, Dean of Ohio Northern University's College of Law (1896-1900) and university president (1900-1902), president of Antioch College (1907-1917), state constitutional convention delegate (1912), U.S. Representative (1913-1923), chairman of GOP National Congressional Committee (1918-1922), U.S. Senate (1923-1935), GOP National Convention delegate (1924) and temporary chairman of the 1928 convention where he delivered the keynote speech, chairman of the GOP National Committee (1930-1932).

FESSENDEN, SAMUEL CLEMENT *(b March 7, 1815, New Gloucester, Maine; d April 18, 1882, Stamford, Conn.)* Clergyman, lawyer, Maine Republican, U.S. Representative (1861-1863), U.S. Patent Office examiner (1865-1879), U.S. consul at St. John, New Brunswick, Canada (1879-1881). Brother of Thomas and William Fessenden.

FESSENDEN, THOMAS AMORY DEBLOIS *(b Jan. 23, 1826, Portland, Maine; d Sept. 28, 1868, Auburn, Maine).* Lawyer, Maine Republican. GOP National Convention delegate (1856, 1868), state representative (1860, 1868), Androscoggin County prosecutor (1861, 1862), U.S. Representative to fill a vacancy for four months (Dec. 1862-March 1863), presidential elector on the Grant-Colfax ticket (1868). Brother of Samuel and William Fessenden.

FESSENDEN, WILLIAM PITT *(b Oct. 16, 1806, Boscawen, N.H.; d Sept. 9, 1869, Portland, Maine)* Lawyer, Maine Whig turned Republican with two brothers who also served their state and nation carrying on their father's antislavery traditions. State representative (1832, 1840, 1845, 1846, 1853, 1854), Whig

National Convention delegate (1840, 1848, 1852), U.S. Representative (1841-1843), U.S. Senate (1854-1864, 1865 until death) serving as chairman of the Senate Finance Committee, Lincoln's secretary of the treasury (1864-1865), delegate to North-South peace conference (1861).

A skilled debater and man of conviction, he accompanied Daniel Webster on his 1837 Western tour but in 1852 would not support him for the presidency; as a senator he vigorously opposed the Kansas-Nebraska Bill, sought a moderate Reconstruction program, and fought Andrew Johnson's impeachment. Brother of Samuel and Thomas Fessenden.

FEW, WILLIAM *(b June 8, 1748, near Baltimore, Md.; d July 16, 1828, Fishkill, N.Y.)* Lawyer, banker, Continental Army officer, Georgia and New York Democrat. In Georgia: State representative (1777, 1779, 1783, 1793), member of executive council (1777, 1778), Richmond County presiding judge and surveyor general (1778), Continental Congress (1780-1788), an original trustee of the University of Georgia (1785), federal Constitutional convention delegate (1787) and state ratifying convention delegate (1788), U.S. Senate (1789-1793), state circuit court judge (1794-1797). In New York: State assemblyman (1802-1805), state prison inspector (1802-1810), U.S. commissioner of loans (1804), New York City alderman (1813, 1814).

FIELD, MOSES WHELOCK *(b Feb. 10, 1828, Watertown, N.Y.; d March 14, 1889, Hamtramck, Mich.)* Merchant, farmer, Michigan Republican who had a lot to do with the formation of the Independent Greenback party and the man who issued the call to its 1876 national convention. Detroit alderman (1863-1865), U.S. Representative (1873-1875), University of Michigan regent (1888).

FIELDS, WILLIAM JASON *(b Dec. 29, 1874, Willard, Ky.; d Oct. 21, 1954, Grayson, Ky.)* Lawyer, farmer, real estate-insurance broker, Kentucky Democrat. U.S. Representative (1911-1923), governor (1923-1927), commonwealth attorney for thirty-seventh judicial district (1932-1935), member of state workmen's compensation board (1936-1944).

FILENE, EDWARD ALBERT *(b Sept. 3, 1860, Salem, Mass.; d Sept. 26, 1937, Paris, France)* Son of a Yiddish immigrant from Poland, founder with his brother of a Boston department store, Massachusetts Democrat, friend of and adviser to presidents and premiers, economist, author, and reformer on the local, state, national, and international levels, many of whose major hopes were stymied by the moneyed men around him. For example, he was a prime mover in the formation of the U.S. Chamber of Commerce, seeing it as an instrument for the public good, only to break with it years later over what he considered its class-interest policies; he tried to turn operation of the department store over to its employees through their Filene Cooperative Association but was blocked by the store's board of directors.

His lifetime dedication to reform began in 1909 in Boston, encompassed the "Boston 1915," and accomplished much in the way of health and educational improvements but little in the way of politics; nationally, he advocated high wages, unemployment and health insurance—all as an aid to the economy —only to draw criticism from the people in power; internationally, he created a European peace-plan contest that drew more than 15,000 responses.

There were also these successful accomplishments: creation of the bargain basement to offer merchandise to less-affluent shoppers, installment buying, credit unions, the Consumer Distribution Corporation, and, in particular, the Twentieth Century Fund.

An ardent New Dealer, his last major public appearance was for the delivery of a 1936 election-eve speech in behalf of Franklin Delano Roosevelt.

FILLMORE, MILLARD *(b Jan. 7, 1800, Cayuga County, N.Y.; d Mar. 8, 1874, Buffalo)* Handsome, six-foot vice president who became thirteenth president (New York Whig) on Zachary Taylor's death, serving from July 9, 1850, to 1853.

Fillmore helped his parents with the hard work of their New York frontier farm, then, at fifteen, was apprenticed to a harsh and demanding clothier from whom he eventually bought his freedom. There was very little time for schooling in his childhood, but Fillmore still managed to read for the law and (1823) was admitted to the bar of Erie County. Married Abigail Powers (1826), a pretty schoolteacher who had encouraged him in his studies and who bore him two children. She died (1853) and (1858) Fillmore married widow Caroline Carmichael McIntosh.

With the backing of political leader Thurlow Weed, elected to New York State Legislature (1829-1831). U.S. Representative (1833-1835, 1837-1843), generally following the leadership of Henry Clay. Became (1840) chairman of the House Ways and Means Committee, and played a leading role in drafting the protective tariff bill of 1842. Unsuccessful Whig candidate for governor of New York (1844); state comptroller (1847-1849). With Clay's backing, he became popular war-hero Zachary Taylor's running mate in the presidential election of 1848. As vice president, Fillmore presided calmly and fairly over the angry Senate debates on slavery that stirred emotions across party lines. As president, he felt that compromise on the slavery issue was the only course that would preserve the nation and therefore signed the measures comprising the Compromise of 1850 (suggested by Clay and which many thought President Taylor, had he lived, would have vetoed), including the Fugitive Slave Act which damned Fillmore in the eyes of the Abolitionists. It is thought by many that, with the stroke of the pen, he committed political suicide, not only for himself but for the Whig party as well. He lost the 1852 Whig presidential nomination to Mexican War hero General Winfield Scott. He was nominated (1856) by the American party (the Know-Nothings) but ran a poor third. He then retired from active politics.

FINDLAY, JAMES *(b Oct. 12, 1770, Mercersburg, Pa.; d Dec. 28, 1835, Cincinnati, Ohio)*. Lawyer, a Democrat who migrated to Cincinnati in 1793 and became the Ohio Territory's first U.S. marshal (1802). Member of the territorial legislative council (1798), U.S. receiver of public moneys (1800), state representative (1803), Cincinnati mayor (1805, 1806, 1810, 1811), War of 1812 officer who was decorated for gallantry, U.S. Representative (1825-1833), unsuccessful candidate for governor (1834). Brother of John and William Findlay.

FINDLAY, JOHN *(b March 31, 1766, Mercersburg, Pa.; d Nov. 5, 1838, Chambersburg, Pa.)* Pennsylvania Democrat. Franklin County chief clerk (1809-1821), War of 1812 officer, U.S. Representative (1821-1827), Chambersburg postmaster (1829 until death). Brother of James and William Findlay.

FINDLAY, WILLIAM *(b June 20, 1768, Mercersburg, Pa.; d Nov. 12, 1846, Harrisburg, Pa.)* Farmer, lawyer, Pennsylvania Democrat and the brother (see James and John Findlay) who went farthest politically. State representative (1797, 1804-1807), state treasurer (1807-1817), governor (1817-1820), U.S. Senate (1821-1827), director of the U.S. Mint (1827-1841).

FINDLEY, WILLIAM *(b 1741 or 1742, Ireland; d April 4, 1821, near Greensburg, Pa.)* A 1763 migrant to America, he became almost immediately a fierce advocate of independence while working simultaneously as a weaver, teacher, and farmer, with time out for military service in the Revolution. Settling in western Pennsylvania, he showed all the traits of a born politician, siding with the frontier people against the vested interests. Thus he opposed ratification of the federal Constitution, Hamilton's monetary policies, and, because he thought a tax on liquor was discriminatory, played a leading part in the Whiskey Insurrection of 1794; Pennsylvania Democrat.

Westmoreland county council of censors (1783), general assembly (1785, 1786), state supreme executive council (1789, 1790), state representative (1790, 1791), state constitutional convention delegate (1790), U.S. Representative (1791-1799, 1803-1817), state senate (1799-1802), and author of *History of the Insurrection in the Four Western Counties of Pennsylvania* which was published in 1796 to explain what the Whiskey Rebellion was all about.

FINLEY, DAVID EDWARD *(b Feb. 28, 1861, Trenton, Ark.; d Jan. 26, 1917, Charlotte, N.C.)* Lawyer, South Carolina Democrat. State representative (1890-1892), state senate (1892-1896), University of South Carolina trustee (1890-1896), U.S. Representative (1899 until death).

FISH, HAMILTON, SR. *(b Aug. 3, 1808, New York City; d Sept. 7, 1893, Garrison, N.Y.)* Lawyer, landowner, New York Whig-Republican, and President Grant's secretary of state (1869-1877) whose tenure was one Cuban crisis after another. New York City and County commissioner of deeds (1832-1833), U.S. Representative (1843-1845), lieutenant governor (1848), governor (1849, 1850), U.S. Senate (1851-1857). Son of Nicholas Fish who named him after his lifelong friend, Alexander Hamilton. Father of Hamilton Fish, Jr.

FISH, HAMILTON, JR. *(b April 17, 1849, Albany, N.Y.; d Jan. 15, 1936, Aiken, S.C.)* Private secretary to his father while the latter was President Grant's secretary of state (1869-1871), lawyer, financier, New York Republican. State assemblyman (1874-1896) and assembly speaker (1895, 1896), assistant U.S. treasurer (1903-1908), U.S. Representative (1909-1911).

FISH, HAMILTON, III *(b Dec. 7, 1888, Garrison, N.Y.)* Famous Harvard football player during his college years, financier, oil developer, author, much-decorated World War I captain of Negro infantry but one of the nation's leading World War II isolationists and vigorous anti-Communist who was suspected of having Nazi bund connections; New York Republican who served twelve terms as a U.S. Representative (1920-1945) and then lost the support of the state's GOP heirarchy because he interjected religion into his campaign for a thirteenth term. State assemblyman (1914-1916).

FISH, NICHOLAS *(b Aug. 28, 1758, New York City; d June 20, 1833)* Lifelong friend of Alexander Hamilton, son-in-law of Peter Stuyvesant, lawyer, Revolutionary Army officer, son of well-to-do parents but the Fish credited with building the family fortune; New York Federalist. State adjutant general (1784-1788), appointed New York district supervisor of revenue by President Washington (1793), New York City alderman and leader of the Tammany opposition (1806-1817); chairman of the Columbia College Board of Trustees, president of the New York Society of the Cincinnati, executor of Alexander Hamilton's will.

FISHER, DAVID *(b Dec. 3, 1794, Somerset County, Pa.; d May 7, 1886, Mount Holly, Ohio)* Lay preacher, newspaper editor-publisher, Ohio Whig, and U.S. Representative (1847-1849) into whose arms John Quincy Adams fell when he suffered a stroke while delivering a speech. State representative (1834), unsuccessful candidate for governor (1844).

FISHER, GEORGE PURNELL *(b Oct. 13, 1817, Milford, Del.; d Feb. 10, 1899, Washington, D.C.)* Lawyer, Delaware Whig turned Union Republican. State representative (1843, 1844). Delaware secretary of state (1846), confidential clerk to U.S. Secretary of State John M. Clayton (1849), Taylor-appointed commissioner to adjudicate claims against Brazil (1850-1852), state attorney general (1857-1860), U.S. Representative (1861-1863); Lincoln-appointed judge of the District of Columbia, and then also D.C.'s district attorney and serving in both posts (1863-1875), Harrison-appointed first auditor of the Treasury Department (1889-1893).

FISHER, HUBERT FREDERICK *(b Oct. 6, 1877, Milton, Fla.; d June 16, 1941, New York City)* Lawyer, nurseryman, Tennessee Democrat. National convention delegate (1912), state senate (1913, 1914), U.S. attorney for state's western district (1914-1917), U.S. Representative (1917-1931).

FISK, CLINTON BOWEN *(b Dec. 8, 1828, in the western New York frontier; d July 9, 1890, New York City)* Self-educated musician, banker, Union Army officer, New York Republican turned Prohibitionist who opened a school for Negroes in Nashville, Tenn. (1866), which prospered and quickly became known as Fisk University, a monument to the man who devoted his postwar life to the education of freedmen. He took two flings at elective political office: Prohibitionist candidate for governor of New Jersey (1886) and for president of the United States (1888).

FISK, JAMES *(b Oct. 4, 1763, Greenwich, Mass.; d Nov. 17, 1844, Swanton, Vt.)* Self-educated preacher, lawyer, farmer, Massachusetts and Vermont Jeffersonian Democrat. In Massachusetts: member of the general assembly (1785). In Vermont: State representative (1800-1805, 1809, 1810, 1815), Orange County judge (1802-1809, 1816), chairman of Canadian boundary committee (1804), U.S. Representative (1805-1809, 1811-1815), state supreme court judge (1815, 1816), U.S. Senate to fill a vacancy (Nov. 4, 1817-Jan. 8, 1818), federal collector of revenue for Vermont (1818-1826).

FITCH, THOMAS *(b Jan. 27, 1838, New York City; d Nov. 12, 1923, Decoto, Calif.).* Newspaperman, lawyer, California and Nevada Republican. In California: member of state assembly (1862, 1863). In Nevada: delegate to state convention that drafted constitution (1864), Washoe County district attorney (1865, 1866), U.S. Representative (1869-1871).

FITZGERALD, JOHN FRANCIS "HONEY FITZ" *(b Feb. 11, 1863, Boston, Mass.; d Oct. 2, 1950, Boston, Mass.)* Newspaper publisher, insurance broker, investment banker, and a power in Massachusetts' Democratic party. Member of Boston Common Council (1892), state senate (1893, 1894), U.S. Representative (1895-1901) and six months in 1919 when his election was successfully contested, mayor of Boston (1906, 1907, 1910-1914), chairman of state delegation to Democratic National Convention (1912), unsuccessful candidate for governor (1922), presidential elector (1924, 1936, 1940, 1944), member of Port of Boston Authority (1934-1948). Grandfather of John, Robert and Edward Kennedy.

FITZGERALD, JOHN JOSEPH *(b March 10, 1872, Brooklyn, N.Y.; d May 13, 1952, Brooklyn)* Lawyer, New York Democrat. Delegate to all national conventions (1900-1928), U.S. Representative (1899-1917), Kings County judge (1932-1942).

FITZPATRICK, BENJAMIN *(b June 30, 1802, Greene County, Ga.; d Nov. 25, 1869, near Wetumpka, Ala.)* Lawyer, planter, Alabama States' Rights Democrat who refused to be the vice presidential running mate of Stephen A. Douglas in the 1860 presidential election. Montgomery circuit solicitor (1822, 1823), governor (1841-1845), U.S. Senate (1848-1849 to fill a vacancy, 1853-1855 to fill another vacancy, 1855-1861, resigning upon secession), president of state constitutional convention (1865).

FITZPATRICK, JAMES MARTIN *(b June 27, 1869, West Stockbridge, Mass.; d April 10, 1949, New York City)* Miner, transit worker, real estate operator, New York Democrat. New York City alderman (1919-1927), U.S. Representative (1927-1945).

FLANAGAN, JAMES WINRIGHT *(b Sept. 5, 1805, Gordonsville, Va.; d Sept. 28, 1887, Longview, Tex.)* Merchant, lawyer, rancher who poled a flatboat from Kentucky to Texas via the Ohio, Mississippi, and Red rivers with his wife, Polly, and son, Webster, settled in Henderson and gained renown as a political maverick, first as a Whig and then as a Republican in a Democratic state.

State representative (1851, 1852), state senate (1855, 1856), state constitutional convention delegate (1866, 1868), lieutenant governor (1869-1870), U.S. Senate (1870-1875), GOP National Convention delegate (1872, 1876, 1880). Father of Webster Flanagan.

FLANAGAN, WEBSTER *(b Jan. 9, 1832, Claverport, Ky.; d May 5, 1924)* Texas lawyer, railroad builder, rancher, foe of secession who however joined the Confederate army when it came, and at war's end wrote this letter to President Johnson's Reconstruction governor: "I want an office, and a good one. I think I am entitled to it, and I know you are willing to make an appointment where there is merit. I was one of the few who braved the secession storm in my country. . . . I would like to be one of the assessors or collectors of revenue. . . . If not that, anything that will pay."

And so began a political career that culminated with young Flanagan becoming the clearly recognized leader of Republicanism in Texas. Only once did he seek elective office, running purely for the honor in a gubernatorial race that all Texas knew no Republican could win. He much preferred holding appointive positions and being a power to be reckoned with—for example, at GOP National Conventions. The convention of 1880 best-personified his approach to politics. Accused by a Massachusetts delegate of having "an eye to the offices," he replied: "What are we here for, except for the offices?" Son of James W. Flanagan.

FLANDERS, ALVAN *(b Aug. 2, 1825, Hopkinton, N.H.; d March 14, 1884, San Francisco, Calif.)* Machinist, merchant, cofounder of the *San Francisco Daily Times*, California and Washington Territory Republican. In California: state representative (1861). In Washington: Wallula's first postmaster (1865-1867), delegate to Congress (1867-1869), Grant-appointed territorial governor (1869-1870).

FLANDERS, BENJAMIN FRANKLIN *(b Jan. 26, 1816, Bristol, N.H.; d March 13, 1896, Lafayette Parish, La.)* New Orleans editor, railroad executive, banker, Louisiana Unionist-Republican at the time of the Civil War. New Orleans alderman (1847, 1852), schools superintendent (1850), city treasurer (1862),

U.S. Representative (four months in 1862-1863), special U.S. Treasury agent for Louisiana, Texas, Mississippi, Alabama, and western Florida (1863, 1866), military governor of Louisiana (1867, 1868), mayor of New Orleans (1870-1872), assistant U.S. treasurer at New Orleans (1873-1882).

FLANNAGAN, JOHN WILLIAM, JR. *(b Feb. 20, 1885, Louisa County, Va.; d April 27, 1955, Bristol, Va.)* Lawyer, banker, Virginia Democrat who served as congressional adviser to the UN Food and Agriculture Organization (1945). Buchanan County commonwealth attorney (1916, 1917), U.S. Representative (1931-1949).

FLEMING, WILLIAM HENRY *(b Oct. 18, 1856, Augusta, Ga.; d June 9, 1944, Augusta)* Lawyer, Georgia Democrat. Augusta and Richmond County schools superintendent (1877-1880), state representative (1888-1896) and speaker (1894, 1895), president of state bar association (1894, 1895), U.S. Representative (1897-1903).

FLETCHER, DUNCAN UPSHAW *(b Jan. 6, 1859, Sumter County, Ga.; d June 17, 1936, Washington, D.C.)* Lawyer, Georgia Democrat who sat in the U.S. Senate for a quarter-century (1909 until death) where he sponsored the Fletcher-Rayburn Act (1934) that created the Securities and Exchange Commission. As a member and chairman of the Commerce Committee and chairman of the Banking and Currency Committee he did much to bring about farm loan legislation and became an authority and adviser to presidents on both domestic and foreign land mortgaging. He was the only one of Georgia's top Democrats to stump for Alfred E. Smith in the 1928 presidential campaign that turned on the issue of religion.

Jacksonville councilman (1887), state representative (1893), mayor of Jacksonville (1893-1895, 1901-1903) who supervised reconstruction after the May 3, 1901, fire that virtually destroyed the city, chairman of Duval County Board of Public Instruction (1900-1907), president of the Gulf Coast Inland Waterways Association and the Mississippi to Atlantic Waterways Association (1908, 1909).

FLETCHER, LOREN *(b April 10, 1833, Mount Vernon, Maine; d April 15, 1919, Atlanta, Ga.)* Stonecutter, lumber and flour manufacturer, banker, Minnesota Republican. State representative (1872-1886) and speaker (1880-1886), U.S. Representative (1893-1903, 1905-1907).

FLETCHER, THOMAS BROOKS *(b Oct. 10, 1879, Mechanicstown, Ohio; d July 1, 1945, Washington, D.C.)* Redpath lecturer, Chautauqua worker, newspaperman in several Ohio cities including editor-publisher of the *Marion Daily Tribune* (1910-1922), and a Democrat who served as a U.S. Representative (1925-1929, 1933-1939).

FLETCHER, THOMAS CLEMENT *(b Jan. 22, 1827, Herculaneum, Mo.; d March 25, 1899, Washington, D.C.)* Member of a slave-owning family but a foe of slavery, lawyer, Union Army officer, Missouri Democrat turned Republican who strongly supported Lincoln's nomination at the 1860 GOP National Convention and served as governor (1865-1869) during a stormy Reconstruction period.

FLICK, JAMES PATTON *(b Aug. 28, 1845, Bakerstown, Pa.; d Feb. 25, 1929, Bedford, Iowa)* Union soldier, lawyer, Iowa Republican. Taylor County recorder (1869, 1870), state representative (1878, 1879), third judicial district attorney (1880-1886), U.S. Representative (1889-1893).

FLOOD, HENRY DE LA WARR *(b Sept. 2, 1865, Appomattox County, Va.; d Dec.*

8, 1921, Washington, D.C.) Lawyer, Virginia Democrat who as chairman of the House Committee on Foreign Affairs (1913-1919) wrote the resolution declaring war with Germany. State house of delegates (1887-1891), state senate (1891-1903), Appomattox County prosecutor (1891, 1895, 1899), presidential elector on the Cleveland-Stevenson ticket (1892), U.S. Representative (1901 until death). Uncle of Harry Flood Byrd.

FLORENCE, THOMAS BIRCH (b Jan. 26, 1812, Philadelphia, Pa.; d July 3, 1875, Washington, D.C.) Hatter, newspaper editor-publisher, Pennsylvania Democrat. U.S. Representative (1851-1861).

FLOWER, ROSWELL PETTIBONE (b Aug. 7, 1835, Theresa, N.Y.; d May 12, 1899, Eastport, N.Y.) Jeweler, manufacturer, banker, stockbroker, New York Democrat whom Tammany Hall offered as a presidential candidate and whom opponents referred to as "that flamboyant millionaire." U.S. Representative (1881-1883, 1889-1891), governor (1891-1895), chairman of Gold Democrat delegation to national convention (1896) where, as temporary chairman, he asserted: "This gathering is notice to the world that the Democratic party has not yet surrendered to Populism and Anarchy."

FLOYD, JOHN (b April 24, 1783, Jefferson County, Ky., which then was in Virginia; d Aug. 17, 1837, Monroe County, Va., which now is in West Virginia) Physician, Virginia Democrat who in 1832 was the Nullifiers' candidate for president, receiving North Carolina's eleven electoral votes. Montgomery County justice of the peace (1807), War of 1812 surgeon, state delegate (1814, 1815), U.S. Representative (1817-1829), governor (1830-1834), a position in which he vigorously defended states' rights and slavery.

FLOYD, JOHN CHARLES (b April 14, 1858, Sparta, Tenn.; d Nov. 4, 1930, Yellville, Ark.) Teacher, lawyer, Arkansas Democrat. State representative (1889-1891), fourteenth judicial circuit prosecutor (1890-1894), U.S. Representative (1905-1915).

FLOYD, WILLIAM (b Dec. 17, 1734, Brookhaven, N.Y.; d Aug. 4, 1821, Westernville, N.Y.) Wealthy landowner whose property was seized by the British, Revolutionary Army officer, patriot, and signer of the Declaration of Independence who at the age of sixty-nine took up a pioneer's life in western New York. Member of Continental Congress (1774-1777, 1778-1783), state senate (1777, 1778, 1784-1788, 1808), U.S. Representative in the First Congress (1789-1791), presidential elector (1792, 1800, 1804, 1820), state constitutional convention delegate (1801).

FLYNN, DENNIS THOMAS (Feb. 13, 1861, Phoenixville, Pa.; d June 19, 1939, Oklahoma City, Okla.) Raised in an orphanage from the age of three, he went on to become an Iowa and Kansas newspaper publisher and an Oklahoma Territory lawyer who was active in Republican affairs, serving as Oklahoma's first member on the GOP National Committee. Postmaster in Kiowa, Kansas (1884-1885); then in Oklahoma, Guthrie postmaster (1889-1892), delegate to Congress (1893-1897, 1899-1903), GOP National Convention delegate (1912).

FOCHT, BENJAMIN KURTZ (b March 12, 1863, New Bloomfield, Pa.; d March 27, 1937, Washington, D.C.) Newspaper editor-publisher, Pennsylvania Republican. GOP state convention delegate (1889), state representative (1893-1897), state senate (1901-1905), state water supply commissioner (1912-1914), U.S. Representative (1907-1913, 1915-1923, 1933 until death), commonwealth deputy secretary (1928, 1929).

FOGARTY, JOHN EDWARD *(b March 23, 1913, Providence, R.I.; d Jan. 10, 1967, Washington, D.C.)* Bricklayer, labor leader, Rhode Island Democrat. U.S. Representative (1941-1944, 1945-1967) serving on the Appropriations Committee, chairman (1949-1967) of Subcommittee on Labor, Health, Education and Welfare. Honored many times for his work in behalf of improved public health.

FOLSOM, NATHANIEL *(b Sept. 18, 1726, Exeter, N.H.; d May 26, 1790, Exeter)* New Hampshire patriot and Continental Army officer who, even as the nation was being born, not only recognized the evils of slavery but foresaw its dangers for the country. Member of the Continental Congress (1774, 1775, 1777-1780), executive councilor (1778), president of state constitutional convention (1783).

FOOT, SOLOMON *(b Nov. 19, 1802, Cornwall, Vt.; d March 28, 1866, Washington, D.C.)* Teacher, lawyer, Vermont Whig turned Republican who, as a U.S. Senator (1851 until death), often presided as president pro tem and gained a reputation as a parliamentarian whom a constituent described as "master of us all." State representative (1833, 1836-1838) and speaker (1837, 1838), state constitutional convention delegate (1836), county prosecutor (1836-1842), U.S. Representative (1843-1847).

FOOTE, HENRY STUART *(b Feb. 28, 1804, Fauquier County, Va.; d May 19, 1880, Nashville, Tenn.)* Lawyer, Mississippi Democrat-Unionist who very much opposed Jefferson Davis and the secession, thus moving on first to California as a Reformer, then to Tennessee, and finally to Washington, D.C., as a Republican, but with brief returns to Mississippi. In Mississippi: Presidential elector on the Polk-Dallas Democratic ticket (1844), U.S. Senate (1847-1852) as a

Unionist, governor (1852-1854) as a Union Democrat. In California: unsuccessful candidate for the U.S. Senate, failing by one vote. In Tennessee: member of the First and Second Confederate Congresses where he continued to oppose Davis and resigned when Lincoln's peace proposals were rebuffed; an episode that landed him in a Confederate jail for a brief period. In Washington: stump speaker for the Hayes-Wheeler Republican presidential ticket (1876), Hayes-appointed superintendent of the New Orleans mint (1878 until death).

FOOTE, SAMUEL AUGUSTUS *(b Nov. 8, 1780, Cheshire, Conn.; d Sept. 15, 1846, Cheshire)* Lawyer, shipper, farmer, Connecticut Whig whose resolution (1829) on public lands triggered Webster-Hayne debate. State representative (1817, 1818, 1821-1823, 1825, 1826) and speaker the latter two years, U.S. Representative (1819-1821, 1823-1825, 1833-1834), U.S. Senate (1827-1833), governor (1834, 1835), presidential elector on the Clay-Frelinghuysen ticket (1844).

FORAKER, JOSEPH BENSON *(b July 5, 1846, Highland County, Ohio; d May 10, 1917, Cincinnati, Ohio)* Union Army officer, lawyer, and Republican leader who three times nominated fellow Ohioans for the presidency at GOP National Conventions—John Sherman (1884) and William McKinley (1896, 1900). The end of his political career was hastened when the Hearst press published letters (1908) disclosing that he had received $29,500 as an employee of Standard Oil while holding public office. Foraker contended the money was for legal services.

Cincinnati Superior Court judge (1879-1882); GOP National Convention delegate, twice as chairman of the Ohio contingent (1884, 1888, 1892, 1896, 1900); governor (1885-1889), GOP state convention chairman (1886, 1890, 1896,

1900), U.S. Senate (1897-1909) losing his reelection bid as a result of the newspaper story. He remained out of politics until 1914 when, in an attempt at a comeback, he sought nomination for the U.S. Senate once again, only to be defeated in the primaries by Warren G. Harding.

FORD, NICHOLAS *(b June 21, 1833, Wicklow, Ireland; d June 18, 1897, Miltonvale, Kans.)* Miner, merchant, Missouri Liberal Republican who followed the ore lure to Nevada and was a member of Virginia City's first city council. In Missouri: state representative (1875), U.S. Representative (1879-1883), unsuccessful candidate for governor (1884).

FORD, THOMAS *(b Dec. 5, 1800, Fayette County, Pa.; d Nov. 3, 1850, Peoria, Ill.)* Lawyer, author, Illinois Democrat who as governor (1842-1846) constantly had to call out the militia because of clashes between Mormons and Christians in the west. His book, *History of Illinois from its Commencement as a State in 1818 to 1847*, tells the story of the times. State's attorney (1829-1835), circuit judge (1835-1837, 1839-1842), Chicago municipal court judge (1837-1838).

FORD, THOMAS FRANCIS *(b Feb. 18, 1873, St. Louis, Mo.; d Dec. 26, 1958, South Pasadena, Calif.)* Newspaperman, magazine editor, lecturer, California Democrat. Los Angeles councilman (1931-1933), U.S. Representative (1933-1945).

FORDNEY, JOSEPH WARREN *(b Nov. 5, 1853, Blackford County, Ind.; d Jan. 8, 1932, Saginaw, Mich.)* From chore boy in lumber camps, he rose to become the owner of extensive interests in lumber, banks, and farms with a flair for politics; an Illinois Republican who served twelve terms as a U.S. Representative (1899-1923), was a member

(and later chairman) of the Ways and Means Committee with high protective tariffs as his chief interest, thus giving his name to the Fordney-McCumber Tariff of 1922. Earlier, as a Saginaw alderman (1896-1900), he did much to diversify the city's industry, thus giving it a more solid economic base; GOP National Convention delegate (1908).

FORNES, CHARLES VINCENT *(b Jan. 22, 1844, Erie County, N.Y.; d May 22, 1929, Buffalo, N.Y.)* Woolens importer and jobber, banker, New York Democrat. President of the New York City Board of Aldermen (1902-1907), U.S. Representative (1907-1913).

FORNEY, DANIEL MUNROE *(b May, 1784, Lincoln County, N.C.; d Oct. 15, 1847, Lowndes County, Ala.)* Farmer, businessman, North Carolina Democrat. U.S. Representative (1815-1818), Monroe-appointed commissioner to meet with the Creek Indians (1820), state senator (1823-1826). Son of Peter Forney.

FORNEY, PETER *(b April 21, 1756, Lincoln County, N.C.; d Feb. 1, 1834, Lincoln County, N.C.)* Revolutionary army officer, iron manufacturer, North Carolina Democrat. State house of commons (1794-1796), state senate (1801, 1802), presidential elector on the Jefferson-Clinton (1804), Madison-Clinton (1808), Monroe-Tompkins (1816), and Jackson-Calhoun (1824, 1828) tickets; U.S. Representative (1813-1815). Father of Daniel and grandfather of William H. Forney.

FORNEY, WILLIAM HENRY *(b Nov. 9, 1823, Lincolnton, N.C.; d Jan. 16, 1894, Jacksonville, Ala.)* Lawyer, Confederate officer who was wounded thirteen times in the Civil War and crippled for life at Gettysburg, Alabama Democrat. University of Alabama trustee (1851-1860), state representative (1859, 1860), state senate (1865, 1866), U.S.

Representative (1875-1893). Grandson of Peter Forney.

FORREST, URIAH *(b 1756, St. Marys County, Md.; d July 6, 1805, near Georgetown, D.C.)* Revolutionary officer who lost a leg at Brandywine, Maryland Federalist. Member of Continental Congress (1786, 1787), U.S. Representative in the Third Congress (1793-1794), clerk of the District of Columbia circuit court (1800 until death).

FORRESTER, ELIJAH LEWIS *(b Aug. 16, 1896, Lee County, Ga.)* Lawyer, Georgia Democrat. Leesburg City Court solicitor (1920-1933), mayor of Leesburg (1922-1931), Lee County attorney (1928-1937), southwestern judicial circuit solicitor general (1937-1950), Democratic National Conventions (1948-1952), U.S. Representative (1951-1965) serving on the Judiciary Committee.

FORSYTH, JOHN *(b Oct. 22, 1780, Fredericksburg, Va.; d Oct. 21, 1841, Washington, D.C.)* Lawyer, orator who was skilled on the debating platform, statesman who got the Spanish to ratify 1819 treaty and the French to pay indemnities as specified in 1831 treaty, Georgia Democrat fiercely loyal to Andrew Jackson.

State attorney general (1808), U.S. Representative (1813-1818, 1823-1827), U.S. Senate (1818-1819, 1829-1834), minister to Spain (1819-1823), governor of Georgia (1827-1829), secretary of state in the Jackson and Van Buren cabinets (1834-1841).

FORTEN, JAMES *(b Sept. 2, 1766; d Mar. 4, 1842)* Abolitionist, freeborn Negro descendant of several generations of Pennsylvanians. When nine years old, in order to help his widowed mother, he dropped out of the Quaker school he had been attending and went to work, eventually becoming a well-to-do sailmaker and one of the foremost Negroes of his day. During the Revolu-

tionary War, as a teenage sailor aboard a Philadelphia privateer, he was captured, imprisoned, and eventually exchanged. In the War of 1812, with Richard Allen and Absalom Jones (founders of the African Methodist Episcopal Church), he organized a force of 2,500 free Negroes to defend Philadelphia against the British.

Actively involved in bettering conditions for Negroes, he refused to provide rigging for slave-ship owners and opposed colonization programs aimed at resettling Negroes in Africa. Besides the abolition of slavery, he was interested in other reforms as well, such as temperance and women's suffrage.

Granddaughter Charlotte Forten (1837-1914), a teacher, author and poet, served as an agent with the Freedmen's Aid Society at Port Royal, St. Helena Island, during the Civil War.

FORWARD, CHAUNCEY *(b Feb. 4, 1793, Old Granby, Conn.; d Oct. 19, 1839, Somerset, Pa.)* Lawyer, Pennsylvania Democrat. State representative (1820-1822), U.S. Representative (1826-1831), Somerset County chief clerk and recorder (1831 until death). Brother of Walter Forward.

FORWARD, WALTER *(b Jan. 24, 1783, East Granby, Conn.; d Nov. 24, 1852, Pittsburgh, Pa.)* Left home at seventeen, worked his way to the thriving town of Pittsburgh (pop. 5,000), studied law, held state and local office, became editor of a Democratic newspaper (*Tree of Liberty*), grew disillusioned and thus helped to form (1834) the Whig party. U.S. Representative (1822-1825), state constitutional convention delegate (1837), Harrison-appointed first comptroller of the treasury (1841), Tyler-appointed secretary of the treasury (1841-1843), Taylor-appointed chargé d'affaires to Denmark (1849-1851), president judge of the Allegheny County Court (1851 until death). Brother of Chauncey Forward.

FOSS, EUGENE NOBLE *(b Sept. 24, 1858, West Berkshire, Mass.; d Sept. 13, 1939, Boston, Mass.)* Manufacturer, real estate operator, Massachusetts Democrat. U.S. Representative to fill a vacancy (1910), resigning to become governor (1911-1913). Brother of George E. Foss.

FOSS, FRANK HERBERT *(b Sept. 20, 1865, Augusta, Maine; d Feb. 15, 1947, Fitchburg, Mass.)* Industrial builder, banker, Massachusetts Republican. Fitchburg councilman (1906-1912), water commissioner (1913-1915) and mayor (1917-1920); GOP state committeeman (1915-1946) and chairman (1921-1924), delegate to all GOP state conventions (1915-1946), U.S. Representative (1925-1935).

FOSS, GEORGE EDMUND *(b July 2, 1863, West Berkshire, Vt.; d March 15, 1936, Chicago, Ill.)* Lawyer, Illinois Republican. U.S. Representative (1895-1913, 1915-1919). Brother of Eugene N. Foss.

FOSTER, ABIEL *(b Aug. 8, 1735, Andover, Mass; d Feb. 6, 1806, Canterbury, N.H.)* Clergyman who was forced out of his eighteen-year (1761-1779) pioneer pastorate in Canterbury because of factionalism and then turned wholly to public service, actively supporting the Revolution, holding many New Hampshire provincial offices, becoming a Federalist upon the drawing of party lines, and serving as U.S. Representative in the First Congress (1789-1791) and later in four others (1795-1803).

Deputy to the provincial congress (1775), member of the Continental Congress (1783-1785), Rockingham County common pleas judge (1784-1788), state senate (1791-1794) and its president (1793).

FOSTER, ABIGAIL KELLEY *(b Jan. 15, 1810, Pelham, Mass.; d Jan. 14, 1887, Worcester, Mass.)* Abolitionist and one of the early pioneers, along with Susan B. Anthony et al., in the women's suffrage movement. A courageous, radical lecturer whose meetings were sometimes broken up by mobs. Married to radical abolitionist Stephen Symonds Foster.

FOSTER, ADDISON GARDNER *(b Jan. 28, 1837, Belchertown, Mass.; d Jan. 11, 1917, Tacoma, Wash.)* Grain, real estate, lumber, mine, and rail executive, Washington Republican who served in the U.S. Senate (1899-1905).

FOSTER, CHARLES *(b April 12, 1828, Seneca County, Ohio; d Jan. 9, 1904, Springfield, Ohio)* Businessman, banker, Ohio Republican who served as President Harrison's secretary of the treasury (1891-1893). U.S. Representative (1871-1879), governor (1880-1884).

FOSTER, DAVID JOHNSON *(b June 27, 1857, Barnet, Vt.; d March 21, 1912, Washington, D.C.)* Lawyer, Vermont Republican. Chittenden County prosecutor (1886-1890), state senate (1892-1894), state tax commissioner (1894-1898), chairman of the board of railroad commissioners (1898-1900), U.S. Representative (1901 until death).

FOSTER, DWIGHT *(b Dec. 7, 1757, Brookfield, Mass.; d April 29, 1823, Brookfield)* Lawyer, Massachusetts Federalist. Worcester County justice of the peace (1781-1823), state representative (1791, 1792, 1808, 1809), common pleas court special justice and county sheriff (1792), U.S. Representative (1793-1800), state constitutional convention delegate (1799), U.S. Senate to fill a vacancy (1800-1803), chief justice of the court of common pleas (1801-1811). Brother of Theodore Foster.

FOSTER, LAFAYETTE SABINE *(b Nov. 22, 1806, Franklin, Conn.; d Sept. 19, 1880, Norwich, Conn.)* Teacher, lawyer, Yale law professor, editor of the *Re-*

publican, a Whig periodical, Connecticut Whig turned Republican. State representative (1839, 1840, 1846-1848, 1854) including three years as speaker, unsuccessful Whig gubernatorial candidate (1850, 1851), mayor of Norwich (1851, 1852), U.S. Senate as a Republican (1855-1867) and president pro tem of the Senate (1865-1867) his wit doing much to relieve tense moments, associate justice of the state supreme court (1870-1876).

FOSTER, MARTIN DAVID *(b Sept. 3, 1861, Edwards County, Ill.; d Oct. 20, 1919, Olney, Ill.)* Physician who was a member of the board of U.S. examining surgeons (1885-1889, 1893-1897), Illinois Democrat. Mayor of Olney (1895, 1902), U.S. Representative (1907-1919).

FOSTER, MURPHY JAMES *(b Jan. 12, 1849, Franklin, La.; d June 12, 1921, near Franklin)* Lawyer, Louisiana Democrat who successfully led a fight to end a governmentally sanctioned but privately operated state lottery and later, in a successful gubernatorial reelection bid, defeated the Lily White Republican candidate and so served as governor for eight years (1892-1900). State senate (1879-1895) and president pro tem (1888-1890), U.S. Senate (1901-1913), collector of the port of New Orleans (1914 until death).

FOSTER, STEPHEN SYMONDS *(b Nov. 17, 1809, Canterbury, N.H.; d Sept. 8, 1881, Worcester, Mass.)* Farmer, preacher, but outspoken foe of organized religion, ardent abolitionist, fighter for women's suffrage (his wife was Abigail Kelley, a pioneer in the movement), and an all-round reformer who showed such dedication while a student at Dartmouth when he chose jail rather than compulsory military service and, upon completion of his sentence, embarked upon a crusade against prison horrors. A friend, delivering his funeral oration, summed up his life:

"New England needed something to shake it and stun it into listening. He was the man and offered himself for martyrdom."

FOSTER, THEODORE *(b April 29, 1752, Brookfield, Mass.; d Jan. 13, 1828, Providence, R.I.)* Lawyer, Rhode Island Federalist who was elected a U.S. Senator (1790-1803) as a Law and Order candidate and for whom the town of Foster was named. He supported Aaron Burr in the 1800 presidential campaign (which was won by Thomas Jefferson). Providence town clerk (1775-1787), state representative (1776-1782, 1812-1816), admiralty court judge (1785), Brown University trustee (1794-1822). Brother of Dwight Foster.

FOSTER, THOMAS FLOURNOY *(b Nov. 23, 1790, Greensboro, Ga.; d Sept. 14, 1848, Columbus, Ga.)* Lawyer, Georgia Democrat. State representative (1822-1825), U.S. Representative (1829-1835, 1841-1843).

FOULKE, WILLIAM DUDLEY *(b Nov. 20, 1848, New York City; d May 30, 1935, Richmond, Ind.)* Newspaper editor-publisher, author, lecturer, Indiana Theodore Roosevelt Republican who most of all was a reformer with civil service and women's suffrage as his main interests. His only elective office was as a state senator (1883-1885), but he was a U.S. Civil Service commissioner (1901-1903), member of the National Civil Service Reform League from 1885 —chairing many investigative committees and serving as president (1923-1924), founder and first president of the Indiana Civil Service Reform Association, president of the American Woman's Suffrage Association (1885-1890) and of the National Municipal League (1910-1915).

FOWLER, CHARLES NEWELL *(b Nov. 2, 1852, Lena, Ill.; d May 27, 1932, Orange, N.J.)* Lawyer, banker, mortgage lender,

New Jersey Republican. U.S. Representative (1895-1911), GOP state committeeman (1898-1907).

FOWLER, JOHN *(b 1755, Virginia; d Aug. 22, 1840, Lexington, Ky.)* Revolutionary Army officer, Virginia and Kentucky patriot. In Virginia: delegate to Danville convention, Constitutional ratification convention, house of delegates (1787). In Kentucky: U.S. Representative (1797-1807), Lexington postmaster (1814-1822).

FOWLER, JOSEPH SMITH *(b Aug. 31, 1820, Steubenville, Ohio; d April 1, 1902, Washington, D.C.)* Educator, lawyer, Tennessee Republican-Unionist-Democrat who opposed slavery and secession, supported presidential candidates Lincoln (1864) and Greeley (1872), backed many radical Reconstruction measures, and denounced the Johnson impeachment proceedings as the work of "mere politicians" not noted "for their prudence, wisdom or patriotism."

Franklin College (Tenn.) mathematics professor (1845-1849), president of Howard Female College (Tenn.) (1856-1861), state comptroller (1862-1865) doing much to rebuild the government, GOP National Convention delegate (1864), U.S. Senate (1866-1871), presidential elector on the Greeley-Brown ticket (1872).

FRANCIS, DAVID ROWLAND *(b Oct. 1, 1850, Richmond, Ky.; d Jan. 15, 1927, St. Louis, Mo.)* Grain merchant, Missouri Democrat who was ambassador to Russia (1916-1918), a period encompassing the Revolution, but he stuck to his post, moving the embassy from place to place, living on trains, supporting the Kerensky government, and remaining under the Bolsheviks.

Democratic National Convention delegate (1884), mayor of St. Louis (1885-1889), governor of Missouri (1889-1893), secretary of the interior in the Cleveland cabinet (1896) just long enough to set 21 million acres aside as forest reserves, thus raising the hackles of the lumber industry and its Washington lackeys.

FRANCIS, JOHN BROWN *(b May 31, 1791, Philadelphia, Pa.; d Aug. 9, 1864, Warwick, R.I.)* Merchant, farmer, Rhode Island independent whose political labels included National Republican, Law and Order, Anti-Masonic, Democrat. State representative (1821-1829), Brown University trustee (1828-1857) and chancellor (1841-1854), state senate (1831, 1842, 1845-1856), governor (1833-1838), U.S. Senate to fill a vacancy (1844-1845). Grandson of John Brown.

FRANK, GLENN *(b Oct. 1, 1887, Queen City, Mo.; d Sept. 15, 1940, in an auto accident near Greenleaf, Wis.).* Preacher of the Billy Sunday and Chautauqua school, magazine editor, author, educator, reformer, syndicated newspaper columnist, research assistant to Boston reformer Edward A. Filene, politically a liberal with independent leanings who numbered Herbert Hoover among his friends and Franklin D. Roosevelt and Senator Robert M. La Follette among his foes. In fact, it was while seeking the Republican nomination for the Senate in order to run against La Follette that he was killed.

Editor in chief of the *Century* magazine (1921-1925), president of the University of Wisconsin (1925-1937), chairman of the Republican program committee (1937) and author of the pamphlet, *A Program for a Dynamic America*; chairman of the platform committee that wrote the isolationist foreign policy plank that came out of the 1940 GOP National Convention.

FRANKLIN, BENJAMIN *(b Jan. 17, 1706, Boston, Mass.; d April 17, 1790, Philadelphia, Pa.)* Apprentice candle- and soapmaker in his father's tallow works, then printer in the shop of a brother he could not stand so he trekked to

Philadelphia at the age of seventeen and history knows the rest: founder-publisher of the *Pennsylvania Gazette* (1728) and *Poor Richard's Almanac* (1732), self-taught scholar-linguist, debater, philosopher, scientist, inventor who proved the relationship between lightning and electricity, and—for what we know him best and owe him most—politician, statesman, diplomat.

Clerk of the Pennsylvania assembly (1736-1751), member of the provincial assembly (1744-1754), Philadelphia postmaster (1737-1753), delegate to the Albany Congress (1754) that adopted his "Plan of Union," deputy postmaster general of the British North American Colonies (1753-1774), Pennsylvania's agent to England (1757-1762, 1764-1775), member of the Continental Congress (1775, 1776) and signer of the Declaration of Independence, president of the Pennsylvania constitutional convention (1776), diplomatic commissioner and minister to France (1776-1785), negotiator with John Jay and John Adams of peace treaty with Britain (1781-1783) of which he later said: "There never was a good war nor a bad peace."

Back to the United States again to hold the offices of governor of Pennsylvania (1785-1788), president of the University of Pennsylvania's board of trustees, delegate to the Federal Constitutional convention (1787) where his arguments for a single legislative body and unpaid executives were rejected but his humor, good will, and dedication did not wane.

FRANKLIN, BENJAMIN JOSEPH *(b March, 1839, Maysville, Ky.; d May 18, 1898, Phoenix, Ariz.)* Teacher, lawyer, Confederate Army officer, farmer, Missouri Democrat who capped his political career by serving as the presidentially appointed governor of the Arizona Territory (1896-1897). Jackson County, Mo., prosecutor (1871-1875), U.S. Representative (1875-1879), U.S. consul at Hankow (now Wuhan), China (1885-1890).

FRANKLIN, JESSE *(b March 24, 1760, Orange County, Va.; d Aug. 31, 1823, Surry County, N.C.)* A school dropout at twelve, a Revolutionary Army officer at seventeen who was captured and hanged—fortunately with a bridle that broke and so he escaped to live and became a leading North Carolina Democrat. State house of commons (1793, 1794, 1797, 1798), state senate (1805, 1806), U.S. Representative (1795-1797), U.S. Senate (1799-1805, 1806-1813) and president pro tem (1804), Chickasaw Indian treaty commissioner (1817), governor (1820, 1821). Brother of Meshack Franklin.

FRANKLIN, MESHACK *(b 1772, Surry County, N.C.; d Dec. 18, 1839, Surry County)* North Carolina Democrat. State house of commons (1800, 1801), U.S. Representative (1807-1815), state senate (1828, 1829, 1838). Brother of Jesse Franklin.

FRANKLIN, WILLIAM *(b 1731, Philadelphia, Pa.; d Nov. 16, 1813, England)*. Son of Benjamin Franklin who took him to England when he was stationed there, where William was educated and became enamored of the British cause. He became the crown-appointed last royal governor of New Jersey (1763), had a bitter falling out with his father, was arrested by the New Jersey Provincial Congress (1776), released (1778), and returned to England (1782) never again to return to his native land. Two years later, however, he was reconciled with his father. And thus Benjamin Franklin wrote his famous autobiography—mainly for William's eyes to see.

FRAZIER, JAMES BERIAH, SR. *(b Oct. 18, 1856, Pikeville, Tenn.; d March 28, 1937, Chattanooga, Tenn.)* Lawyer, Tennessee Democrat. Presidential elector on the Bryan-Stevenson ticket (1900), governor (1903-1905), U.S. Senate (1905-1911).

FRAZIER, JAMES BERIAH, JR. *(b June 23, 1890, Chattanooga, Tenn.)* Lawyer, Tennessee Democrat. U.S. attorney for Tennessee's eastern district (1933-1948), U.S. Representative (1949-1963) serving on the Ways and Means Committee.

FRAZIER, LYNN JOSEPH *(b Dec. 21, 1874, Steele County, Minn.; d Jan. 11, 1947, Riverdale, Md.)* Farmer, Nonpartisan League governor of North Dakota (1917-1921) and, as a Republican, a three-term U.S. Senator (1923-1941).

FREAR, JAMES ARCHIBALD *(b Oct. 24, 1861, Hudson, Wis.; d May 28, 1939, Washington, D.C.)* Lawyer, Wisconsin Republican. Hudson city attorney (1894, 1895), St. Croix County district attorney (1896-1901), state assemblyman (1903), state senate (1905), Wisconsin secretary of state (1907-1913), U.S. Representative (1913-1935) and then remaining in Washington to practice law.

FREE, ARTHUR MONROE *(b Jan. 15, 1879, San Jose, Calif.; d April 1, 1953, San Jose)* Lawyer, California Republican. Mountain View city attorney (1904-1910), Santa Clara County district attorney (1907-1919), GOP state convention delegate (1914, 1920-1936), U.S. Representative (1921-1933).

FREEMAN, JONATHAN *(b March 21, 1745, Mansfield, Conn.; d Aug. 20, 1808, Hanover, N.H.)* Farmer, New Hampshire Federalist who was treasurer of Dartmouth College for more than forty years. Executive councillor (1789-1797), state representative (1787-1789), state senate (1789-1794), constitutional convention delegate (1791) and member of state council, Dartmouth College overseer (1793-1808), U.S. Representative (1797-1801) where for a time he sat beside his nephew, Nathaniel Freeman, Jr.

FREEMAN, NATHANIEL, JR. *(b May 1, 1766, Sandwich, Mass.; d Aug. 22, 1800, Sandwich)* Massachusetts lawyer, justice of the peace (1793), U.S. Representative (1795-1799). Nephew of Jonathan Freeman.

FREEMAN, RICHARD PATRICK *(b April 24, 1869, New London, Conn.; d July 8, 1944, Newington, Conn.)* Lawyer, Connecticut Republican. Special U.S. Interior Department agent in Oregon and Washington (1896-1898), New London prosecuting attorney (1898-1901), U.S. Representative (1915-1933).

FRELINGHUYSEN, FREDERICK *(b April 13, 1753, Somerset County, N.J.; d April 13, 1804, Millstone, N.J.)* Lawyer, Minuteman major, Revolutionary Army officer, Indian fighter, and the first of a long line of Frelinghuysens to hold office in New Jersey.

Member of the Provincial Congress at the age of twenty-two (1775, 1776), Continental Congress (1778, 1779, 1782, 1783), common pleas court clerk (1781-1789), state assembly (1784, 1800-1804), delegate to state convention that ratified federal Constitution (1787), member of state council (1790-1792), U.S. Senator as a Federalist (1793-1796) with time out in 1794 to serve as a major general in putting down the Whiskey Insurrection, Princeton College trustee (1802-1804).

FRELINGHUYSEN, FREDERICK THEODORE *(b Aug. 4, 1817, Millstone, N.J.; d May 20, 1885, Newark, N.J.)* Lawyer, New Jersey Republican who, as secretary of state in President Arthur's cabinet (1881-1885), reversed some of the decisions made by his predecessor, James G. Blaine, the GOP candidate for president in 1884.

Newark city attorney (1849) and councilman (1850), Rutgers College trustee (1851-1885), delegate to North-South peace convention (1861), state attorney general (1861-1866) resigning to fill a vacancy in the U.S. Senate (1866-1869, 1871-1877), president of American Bible Society (1884, 1885). Grandson of Frederick Frelinghuysen.

FRELINGHUYSEN, JOSEPH SHERMAN *(b March 12, 1869, Raritan, N.J.; d Feb. 8, 1948, Tucson, Ariz.)* Insurance executive, New Jersey Republican. Chairman of Somerset County GOP executive committee (1902-1905), state senate (1906-1912), its president pro tem (1909, 1910) and acting governor; GOP state committeeman (1914-1916), president of the state agriculture board (1912-1925) and state board of education (1915-1919), U.S. Senate (1917-1923), GOP National Convention delegate (1916-1928, 1936, 1944), Rutgers College trustee (1918-1928). Nephew of Frederick T. Frelinghuysen.

FRELINGHUYSEN, THEODORE *(b March 28, 1787, Millstone, N.J.; d April 12, 1862, New Brunswick, N.J.)* Lawyer, educator, New Jersey Adams Democrat turned Whig who was Henry Clay's vice presidential running mate in the 1844 presidential election and before that, as a U.S. Senator, the maker of a six-hour speech against the removal of Indians from their lands that won him national acclaim (although it did not save the Indians their homes).

State attorney general (1817-1829), vice president of American Sunday School Union (1826-1860), U.S. Senate (1829-1835), mayor of Newark (1837, 1838), New York University chancellor (1839-1850), president of the American Board of Commissioners for Foreign Missions (1841-1857), president of the American Tract Society (1842-1848), president of the American Bible Society (1846-1861), president of Rutgers College (1850 until death). Son of Frederick Frelinghuysen.

FREMONT, JOHN CHARLES *(b Jan. 21, 1813, Savannah, Ga.; d July 13, 1890,*

New York City) The illegitimate son of a French refugee father and a Virginia tidewater mother; a military man with political leanings, civil engineer, and explorer who five times crossed the continent (three times for the army and twice for tycoons seeking railroad routes, his father-in-law, Senator Thomas H. Benton of Missouri among them); the first Republican candidate for president (1856), carrying all but five northern states and polling 1,339,932 popular and 114 electoral votes to James Buchanan's 1,832,955 and 174; the man who has more Western places named for him than anybody; the man whom one biographer described as "one of the most controversial figures in U.S. history."

In 1845, he led an expedition into California, planted the American flag atop a peak in the Gabilan Mountains (now Fremont State Park) only to be made to withdraw since no war yet existed with Mexico. In 1846, with the war then on, new orders from Washington sent him back to California to aid in the conquest. He was made commandant and governor of the new territory only to be court martialed, convicted, and dismissed on a charge of mutiny. President Polk later issued a pardon. In 1850-1851 with California in the Union and Fremont a civilian he served as U.S. Senator as a Free-Soil Democrat. From 1861 until 1864, a Lincoln-appointed major general in the Union Army, he served as commander of the western military district, where he took it upon himself to issue an emancipation order, then as commander of the mountain district where he became the darling of the Radical Republicans who nominated him as their 1864 presidential candidate in order to block Lincoln's reelection. Smoke-filled-room talks, however, caused his name to be withdrawn. Then came the comparatively quiet years of his life as governor of the Arizona Territory (1878-1883).

FRENCH, BURTON LEE *(b Aug. 1, 1875, Carroll County, Ind.; d Sept. 12, 1954, Hamilton, Ohio)* Lawyer, Idaho Republican who served more than a quarter-century as a congressman, but not consecutively, and then became a professor of government. State representative (1898-1902), U.S. Representative (1903-1909, 1911-1915, 1917-1933), delegate to Interparliamentary Union Conventions (1930 in London, 1931 in Bucharest), Truman-appointed member of Federal Loyalty Review Board (1947-1953).

FRENCH, EZRA BARTLETT *(b Sept. 23, 1810, Landaff, N.H.; d April 24, 1880, Washington, D.C.)* Maine newspaper editor and lawyer who aided in the organization of the Republican party (1856). State representative (1838-1840), state senate (1842-1845), bank commissioner (1856), U.S. Representative (1859-1861), delegate to North-South peace convention (1861), second auditor of the U.S. Treasury (1861 until death).

FRENCH, RICHARD *(b June 20, 1792, Madison County, Ky.; d May 1, 1854, Covington, Ky.)* Lawyer, Kentucky Democrat. State representative (1820-1826), presidential elector on the Jackson-Calhoun ticket (1828), circuit court judge (1829), U.S. Representative (1835-1837, 1843-1845, 1847-1849).

FROMENTIN, ELIGIUS *(b—, France; d Oct. 6, 1822, New Orleans, La.)* French priest who fled to America during the Reign of Terror, taught school and studied law in Pennsylvania and Maryland, gave up the priesthood and practiced law in New Orleans. Clerk to the Orleans Territory House of Representatives (1807-1811), secretary of the state constitutional convention (1812), secretary of the state senate (1812, 1813), U.S. Senate (1813-1819), New Orleans criminal court judge (1821); U.S. judge for west and part of east Florida (1821-1822).

FRYE, WILLIAM PIERCE *(b Sept. 2, 1830, Lewiston, Maine; d Aug. 8, 1911, Lewiston)* Lawyer, Maine Republican, a politician and an office-holder who really did his homework and consequently a man of power and influence in all that he tackled; as one Washington colleague described him: "Emphatically a man of work."

State representative (1861, 1862, 1867), mayor of Lewiston (1866, 1867), state attorney general (1867-1869), Bowdoin College trustee, presidential elector on the Lincoln-Johnson ticket (1864), GOP National Convention delegate (1872, 1876, 1880) and member of national executive committee; U.S. Representative (1871-1881) when, said James G. Blaine, "his rank as a debater was soon established and he exhibited a degree of care and industry not often found among Representatives"; U.S. Senate (1881 until death), president pro tem (1896 until death), chairman of the Commerce Committee, member of the Foreign Relations and Appropriations Committees.

FULLER, ALVAN TUFTS *(b Feb. 27, 1878, Boston, Mass.; d April 30, 1958, Boston)* Automobile dealer, Massachusetts Republican who, according to the *Biographical Directory of the American Congress*, "did not accept compensation for services while in public office." State representative (1915), GOP National Convention delegate (1916), U.S. Representative (1917-1921) resigning to become lieutenant governor (1921-1924), governor (1925-1929).

FULLER, CHARLES EUGENE *(b March 31, 1849, Boone County, Ill.; d June 25, 1926, Rochester, Minn.)* Lawyer, banker, Illinois Republican. Belvidire city attorney (1875, 1876), Boone County prosecutor (1876-1878), state senate (1878-1882, 1888-1892), state representative (1882-1888), seventeenth judicial circuit judge (1897-

1903), U.S. Representative (1903-1913, 1915 until death).

FULLER, CLAUDE ALBERT (b Jan. 20, 1876, Prophetstown, Ill.; d Jan. 8, 1968). Lawyer, banker, farmer, Arkansas Democrat. Eureka Springs city clerk (1898-1902), state representative (1903-1905), mayor of Eureka Springs (1906-1910, 1920-1928), fourth judicial district prosecutor (1910-1914), Eureka Springs School Board president (1916-1928), delegate to all Democratic state conventions (1903-1943) and most national conventions (1908-1960), U.S. Representative (1929-1939).

FULLER, THOMAS JAMES DUNCAN (b March 17, 1808, Hardwick, Vt.; d Feb. 13, 1876, Faquier County, Va.) Lawyer, Maine Democrat. U.S. Representative (1849-1857), Buchanan-appointed second auditor of the U.S. Treasury (1857-1861).

FULLER, TIMOTHY (b July 11, 1778, Chilmark, Mass.; d Oct. 1, 1835, Groton, Mass.) Teacher, lawyer, Massachusetts Democrat. State senate (1813-1817), U.S. Representative (1817-1825), state representative (1825-1828, 1831), state councillor (1828).

FULMER, HAMPTON PITTS (b June 23, 1875, Orangeburg County, S.C.; d Oct. 19, 1944, Washington, D.C.) Farmer, merchant, banker, South Carolina Democrat who served as a state representative (1917-1920), as U.S. Representative (1921 until death), and was succeeded (Nov. 1944–Jan. 1945) by his wife, the former Willa Lybrand.

FULTON, CHARLES WILLIAM (b Aug. 24, 1853, Lima, Ohio; d Jan. 27, 1918, Portland, Oregon) Lawyer, Oregon Republican. State senate (1878, 1890, 1898, 1902), senate president (1893, 1901), presidential elector on the Harrison-Morton ticket (1888) and the messenger who carried Oregon's electoral college vote to Washington, U.S. Senate (1903-1909), declined presidential appointment as minister to China (1909).

FULTON, WILLIAM SAVIN (b June 2, 1795, Cecil County, Md.; d Aug. 15, 1844, Little Rock, Ark.) Lawyer, Arkansas Democrat. Jackson-appointed secretary of Arkansas Territory (1829-1835) and territorial governor (1835-1836); after statehood, U.S. Senate (1836 until death).

FUNSTON, EDWARD HOGUE (b Sept. 16, 1836, Clark County, Ohio; d Sept. 10, 1911, Iola, Kans.) Union Army officer, farmer, Kansas Republican. State representative (1873-1876) and house speaker (1875), state senate (1880-1884) and president pro tem (1880), U.S. Representative (1884-1894) when his election in the midst of a fifth term was successfully contested.

FYAN, ROBERT WASHINGTON (b March 11, 1835, Bedford Springs, Pa.; d July 28, 1896, Marshfield, Mo.) Lawyer, Union Army officer, Missouri Democrat. Webster County attorney (1859), circuit attorney (1865, 1866), fourteenth judicial circuit judge (1866-1883), state constitutional convention delegate (1875), U.S. Representative (1883-1885, 1891-1895).

G

☆ ☆ ☆

GABALDON, ISAURO *(b Dec. 8, 1875, San Isidoro, Philippine Islands; d Dec. 21, 1942, Manila)* Lawyer, Philippine Islands nationalist. Governor of Province of Nueva Ecija (1906, 1912-1916), Philippine representative (1907-1911), Philippine Senate (1916-1919), resident commissioner to the United States (1920-1928).

GADSDEN, CHRISTOPHER *(b Feb. 16, 1723, Charleston, S.C.; d Sept. 15, 1805, Charleston)* A man of commerce and a pre-Revolution patriot who was a South Carolina delegate to the Colonial Congress that met in New York in 1765, a member of the First Continental Congress (1774-1776), a Revolutionary Army officer who helped defend Charleston, a framer of the state constitution (1778), lieutenant governor (1778-1780), and, to cap his career, a man who was elected governor (1781) but who declined to serve. Grandfather of James Gadsden.

GADSDEN, JAMES *(b May 15, 1788, Charleston, S.C.; d Dec. 26, 1858, Charleston)* War of 1812 engineering officer and Indian fighter who explored the Southwest and built Gulf Coast defenses; Southern nationalist and railroad tycoon who envisioned a Southern rail network reaching to the Pacific that would permit direct trade with Europe and thus make the South independent of the North. While minister to Mexico (1853-1856) he negotiated the $10 million Gadsden Purchase that, among other territorial gains, provided land for additional railroad right of way. Also a planter and a Democrat, his only elective office was as a member of Florida's first territorial legislative council (1824). Grandson of Christopher Gadsden.

GAGE, MATILDA JOSLYN *(b Mar. 24, 1826, Cicero, N.Y.; d Mar. 18, 1898, Chicago, Ill.)* An active organizer, effective lecturer and writer in the field of women's rights, she spoke to congressional committees several times on the subject of suffrage. Edited the feminist *National Citizen* in Syracuse, New York, and collaborated (1881-1886) with Susan B. Anthony and Elizabeth Cady Stanton on the first three volumes of *History of Woman Suffrage.* One of the organizers of the New York State Woman's Suffrage Association and the National Woman's Suffrage Association, she served both as an officer for many years.

GAGE, THOMAS *(b 1721, Firle, England; d April 2, 1787, England).* French and Indian War officer who fought with General Edward Braddock, commander in chief of North America (1763-1773), and last royal governor of Massachusetts (1774-1775), he being the man whose deeds precipitated the shots fired at Lexington and Concord and Bunker Hill.

GAILLARD, JOHN (b Sept. 5, 1765, St. Stephens District, S.C.; d Feb. 26, 1826, Washington, D.C.) Planter, conservative South Carolina Democrat, and very much a power in the U.S. Senate, made possible by the fact that as president pro tem for most of the years from 1814 until death. Two vice presidents died leaving the chair for him to occupy. There, among other things, he was a War of 1812 hawk and staunch advocate of all measures having to do with the advancement of slavery. State representative (1794-1796), state senate (1796-1804) where he showed his ability to seize and to hold the reins tight, U.S. Senate (1804 until death).

GAINES, JOHN POLLARD (b Sept. 22, 1795, Augusta, Va., now W.Va.; d Dec. 9, 1857, Marion County, Oregon) Lawyer, Kentucky Whig who while serving as an officer in the Mexican War was captured whereupon his home district elected him a U.S. Representative (1847-1849) although he was a prisoner of war in Mexico City. When they failed to reelect him, he accepted appointment as governor of the Oregon Territory (1850-1853) and lived out his life there as a farmer.

GAINES, JOHN WESLEY (b Aug. 24, 1860, Wrencoe, Tenn.; d July 4, 1926, Nashville, Tenn.) Physician, lawyer, Tennessee Democrat. Presidential elector on the Cleveland-Stevenson ticket (1892), U.S. Representative (1897-1909).

GAINES, JOSEPH HOLT (b Sept. 3, 1864, Washington, D.C.; d April 12, 1951, Montgomery, W.Va.) Lawyer, West Virginia Republican. U.S. attorney for the state (1897-1901), U.S. Representative (1901-1911).

GALE, GEORGE (b June 3, 1756, Somerset County, Md.; d Jan. 2, 1815, Cecil County, Md.). Revolutionary soldier, delegate to the Maryland convention that ratified federal Constitution (1788), member of the First Congress (1789-1791). Father of Levin Gale.

GALE, LEVIN (b April 24, 1784, Elkton, Md.; d Dec. 18, 1834, Elkton) Maryland lawyer who served one term in the state senate (1816) and one as a U.S. Representative (1827-1829) and then decided that he had had enough of elective office. Son of George Gale.

GALES, JOSEPH, SR. (b Feb. 4, 1761, Eckington, England; d Aug. 24, 1841, Raleigh, N.C.) British reformer and newspaper publisher who was forced to flee England for supporting such people and causes as Thomas Paine, Joseph Priestley, abolition, and the French Revolution, ultimately arriving in North Carolina with all his banners still unfurled. Stopped over in Philadelphia where, as a reporter for the American Daily Advertiser, he recorded congressional proceedings verbatim, then moved on to North Carolina where—his liberal banners still very much flying— he founded (1799) the pro-Jefferson Raleigh Register, occupied the mayor's chair for nineteen years, served as state printer (1800-1832), and then moved to Washington to join his son, Joseph, Jr. There father and son together compiled (1834) the first two volumes of the Annals of Congress, then Gales, Sr., became secretary of the Peace Society and the treasurer of the American Colonization Society while Gales, Jr., continued with the Annals until 1856.

GALES, JOSEPH, JR. (b April 10, 1786, Eckington, England; d July 21, 1860, Washington, D.C.) By no means the reformer that his father was but very much the reporter-journalist-scholar that his parents had taught him to be, making Washington, D.C., the sphere of his operations where, professionally, he was publisher of the authoritative *National Intelligencer* and, politically, variously a Republican, Whig, and Constitutional Democrat. Limited only to local office because of the city's status, the highest position he achieved was that of mayor of Washington (1827-1830). In his writings, the younger Gales supported national free education, religious liberalism, Clay's American System, and the United States Bank. *Intelligencer* files today are considered the most authoritative record of Congressional proceedings covering the years 1807-1833. Additionally, with his brother-in-law, William W. Seaton, he compiled and published the 29-volume *Register of Debates in Congress* covering the years 1825-1837 and the 38-volume *American State Papers* for the years 1832-1861.

GALLAGHER, THOMAS *(b July 6, 1850, Concord, N.H.; d Feb. 24, 1930, San Antonio, Texas)* Iron molder, hatter, banker, Illinois Democrat and a wheel in Chicago. City council (1893-1897), board of education (1897-1903), chairman of Cook County Central Committee (1902), president of county committee (1906, 1907) and member of executive committee (1909, 1911, 1913), U.S. Representative (1909-1921).

GALLAGHER, WILLIAM JAMES *(b May 13, 1875, Minneapolis, Minn.; d Aug. 13, 1946, Rochester, Minn.).* Newspaper proofreader, truck driver, street sweeper for Hennepin County and the city of Minneapolis from 1919 until retirement in 1942 and then went on to become a U.S. Representative as a Democrat (1945 until death). He was so well liked that he had been nominated for a second term when death took him.

GALLATIN, ALBERT *(b Jan. 29, 1761, Geneva, Switzerland; d Aug. 12, 1849,* *Astoria, Queens, N.Y.)* Came to the United States at nineteen, spent ten years as, variously, French instructor at Harvard, frontier trader, land speculator, and western Pennsylvania farmer, developing a keen interest in politics, aligning himself strongly with the Jeffersonian Democrats, and thus embarking upon a career of statesmanship and diplomacy. Biographers describe him as "one of the greatest of U.S. secretaries of the treasury" (1802-1814) under both Presidents Jefferson and Madison, and one of the chief architects of the Treaty of Ghent (1814) that brought peace with Britain. However, two things militated against him: his Swiss birth (in 1793 he was denied a seat in the U.S. Senate on a strictly party vote that ruled he had not been a U.S. citizen long enough) and his role in western Pennsylvania's Whiskey Rebellion in which he urged moderation.

Pennsylvania constitutional convention delegate (1789), state representative (1790-1792) when he gave Pennsylvania a plan for ridding itself of debt, U.S. Representative (1795-1801), minister to France (1815-1823), minister to Great Britain (1826-1827). Then, his active years of politics and diplomacy behind him, he became president (1831-1839) of the National Bank of New York which later was called the Gallatin Bank, helped to found New York University, and wrote extensively on the three subjects that he knew best: politics, banking, and education.

GALLEGOS, JOSE MANUEL *(b Oct. 30, 1815, Rio Arriba County, N.Mex.; d April 21, 1875, Santa Fe)* Theologian, New Mexico Democrat whose place of birth was then part of Mexico and who did much to achieve independence. Member of the New Mexico Legislative Assembly during sovereignty of the Mexican Republic (1843-1846), member of first territorial council (1851), delegate to U.S. Congress (1853-1856, 1871-1873), speaker of territorial house of representatives (1860-1862) when he was imprisoned by Texas Confederate troops, territorial treasurer (1865, 1866), superintendent of Indian affairs (1868).

GALLINGER, JACOB HAROLD *(b March 28, 1837, Cornwall, Canada; d Aug. 17, 1918, Franklin, N.H.)* Printer, physician who chose Concord, N.H., as the place to practice, became a powerful New Hampshire Republican and sat for twenty-seven years in the U.S. Senate (1891 until death) where, although almost always extremely orthodox, he did support women's suffrage and hastened adoption of the Nineteenth Amendment. But, as for such things as civil service reforms, he contemptuously called that "Sunday school politics." As chairman of the Senate's District of Columbia committee, he vowed to make Washington the world's most beautiful city.

State representative (1872, 1873, 1891), state constitutional convention delegate (1876), state senate (1878-1880) and senate president (1879, 1880), state surgeon general (1879, 1880), GOP state committee chairman (1882-1890, 1898-1908), chairman of state GOP National Convention delegation (1888, 1900, 1904, 1908), U.S. Representative (1885-1889).

GALLIVAN, JAMES AMBROSE *(b Oct. 22, 1866, Boston, Mass.; d April 3, 1928, Arlington, Mass.).* Newspaperman, Massachusetts machine Democrat who first was chosen a U.S. Representative in 1914 to complete the term vacated by James M. "Boss" Curley and remained in Congress for the rest of his life. State representative (1895, 1896), state senate (1897, 1898), Boston street commissioner (1900-1914).

GALLOWAY, JOSEPH *(b about 1729, West River, Md.; d Aug. 29, 1803, Watford, Hertfordshire, England).* Pennsylvania lawyer, merchant, land promoter, philosopher, pamphleteer, and colonial statesman who strongly advocated settlement of differences with England by negotiation rather than by war, then, when forced to make a choice, sided with the British. For this he was convicted of treason and his property confiscated. Upon the fall of Philadelphia (1778) to the Revolutionary forces he moved to England where he became the spokesman for American Tories. His many written works remain today as source material for historians looking into the Revolution. Member of the Pennsylvania colonial house of representatives (1757-1775) and speaker (1766-1774), delegate to First Continental Congress (1775), General Howe-appointed civil administrator of Philadelphia (1776-1778), and police superintendent.

GAMBLE, JOHN RANKIN *(b Jan. 15, 1848, Alabama, N.Y.; d Aug. 14, 1891, Yankton, S.Dak.)* Lawyer, South Dakota pioneer who worked hard for statehood, was elected a U.S. Representative (1891) after it was achieved, but died before Congress convened. Yankton County district attorney (1876-1878), U.S. attorney for the Dakota Territory (1878), member of territorial house of representatives (1877-1879) and territorial council (1881-1885). Brother of Robert J. Gamble, uncle of Ralph A. Gamble.

GAMBLE, RALPH ABERNETHY *(b May 6, 1885, Yankton, S.Dak.; d March 4, 1959, St. Michaels, Md.)* Lawyer, Republican who chose sophisticated New York as the place to practice, rather than follow in the footsteps of his father, Robert J., and uncle, John R., who staked their claim in South Dakota. Mamaroneck town counsel (1918-1933), Larchmont town counsel (1926-1928), U.S. Representative (1937-1956).

GAMBLE, ROBERT JACKSON *(b Feb. 7, 1851, Genesee County, N.Y.; d Sept.*

22, 1924, Sioux Falls, S.Dak.) Lawyer, historian, South Dakota Republican. District attorney for Dakota Territory's second judicial district (1880), Yankton city attorney (1881, 1882), territorial council (1885), GOP state convention chairman (1892, 1893), U.S. Representative (1895-1897, 1899-1901), U.S. Senate (1901-1913). Brother of John R. Gamble and father of Ralph Gamble.

GAMBRILL, STEPHEN WARFIELD (b Oct. 2, 1873, Howard County, Md.; d Dec. 19, 1938, Washington, D.C.) Lawyer, Maryland Democrat. Member of state house of delegates (1920-1922), state senate (1924), U.S. Representative (1924 until death).

GANDY, HARRY LUTHER (b Aug. 13, 1881, Churubusco, Ind.; d Aug. 15, 1957, Los Gatos, Calif.) Newspaper publisher, rancher, coal executive, South Dakota Democrat. U.S. Commissioner at Wasta (1910-1913) and publisher of the Wasta Gazette (1910-1918), state senate (1911), receiver of public moneys at Rapid City's U.S. land office (1913-1915), U.S. Representative (1915-1921).

GANSEVOORT, LEONARD (b July 14, 1751, Albany, N.Y.; d Aug. 26, 1810, Albany). Lawyer, Revolutionary cavalry officer who served as president of New York for one month in 1777. Provincial Congress (1775, 1776), Albany County clerk (1777, 1778), state assemblyman (1778, 1779, 1788), Continental Congress (1787, 1788), state senate (1791-1793), Albany County judge (1794-1797), member of council of appointment (1797), probate court judge (1799 until death).

GARBER, MILTON CLINE (b Nov. 30, 1867, Humboldt, Calif.; d Sept. 12, 1948, Alexandria, Minn.) Lawyer who homesteaded in Oklahoma with his father and brother upon opening of the Cherokee Strip, founded the town that bears

their name, opened the Garber oil fields, and became one of the territory's and state's foremost Republicans while also branching into agriculture and newspaper publishing in and around Enid.

Garfield County probate judge (1902-1906), Roosevelt-appointed associate justice of the territorial supreme court and fifth judicial district trial judge (1906-1907) until Oklahoma became a state; then elected twentieth judicial district judge (1908-1912), mayor of Enid (1919-1921), U.S. Representative (1923-1933).

GARCELON, ALONZO (b May 6, 1813, Lewiston, Maine; d Dec. 8, 1906, Medford, Mass.) Teacher, farmer, surgeon who is said to have performed Maine's first mastoid operation, railroad president, road builder, cofounder and editor of the Lewiston Falls Journal, Union Army officer who fought at Bull Run, and a man who had as varied a political career as was his private life, serving several parties: Whig, Democrat, Free-Soiler, Republican before becoming the Greenback Democrat governor of Maine (1879-1880). State representative (1853, 1857), state senate (1854-1856), mayor of Lewiston (1871).

GARD, WARREN (b July 2, 1873, Hamilton, Ohio; d Nov. 1, 1929, Hamilton). Lawyer, Ohio Democrat. Butler County prosecutor (1898-1903), common pleas court judge (1907-1912), U.S. Representative (1913-1921).

GARDENER, HELEN HAMILTON (b Jan. 21, 1853, Winchester, Va.; d July 26, 1925, Washington, D.C.) An independent woman who broke away from political and religious traditions, author, suffragist, and first woman member of the U.S. Civil Service Commission (appointed in 1920 by President Wilson). She was vice president of the National American Woman's Suffrage

Association and, as vice chairman of the organization's congressional committee, was effective in winning the support of legislators.

GARDNER, AUGUSTUS PEABODY *(b Nov. 5, 1865, Boston, Mass.; d Jan. 4, 1918, Camp Wheeler, Macon, Ga.)* Harvard Law School graduate who never practiced, but devoted his life to, according to the *Biographical Directory of the American Congress*, "the management of his estate" and Massachusetts Republicanism. State senator (1900, 1901), U.S. Representative (1902-1917), World War I officer serving at Governors Island and Camp Wheeler.

GARDNER, FRANK *(b May 8, 1872, Finley Township, Ind.; d Feb. 1, 1937, Scottsburg, Ind.)* Lawyer, Indiana Democrat. Scott County auditor (1903-1911) and attorney (1911-1917), Democratic county committee chairman (1912-1922), U.S. Representative (1923-1929), sixth judicial circuit judge (1930 until death).

GARDNER, HENRY JOSEPH *(b June 14, 1818, Dorchester, Mass.; d July 21, 1892, Milton, Mass.)* Merchant, Massachusetts Whig who helped to found the Know-Nothing party there. Member of Boston Common Council (1850) and its president (1852-1853), general court (1851-1852), constitutional convention delegate (1853), three-term governor (1855-1858) being first elected in a year when Bay State Know-Nothings swept virtually all elective offices.

GARDNER, JOHN JAMES *(b Oct. 17, 1845, Atlantic County, N.J.; d Feb. 7, 1921, Indian Mills, N.J.)* Union soldier, real estate and insurance broker, farmer, New Jersey Republican. Atlantic City alderman (1867), mayor (1868-1872, 1874, 1875), both city councilman and county coroner (1876), state senate (1878-1893) and its president (1883),

GOP National Convention delegate (1884), U.S. Representative (1893-1913).

GARDNER, JOSEPH *(b 1752, Honeybrook Township, Pa.; d 1794, Elkton, Md.)* Physician, Pennsylvania patriot. Continental Army officer, Pennsylvania committee of safety (1776-1777), state assembly (1776-1778), executive council (1779), Continental Congress (1784, 1785).

GARDNER, WASHINGTON *(b Feb. 16, 1845, Morrow County, Ohio; d March 31, 1928, Albion, Mich.)* Lawyer, clergyman, Albion College professor, Michigan Republican. Michigan secretary of state (1894-1899), U.S. Representative (1899-1911), pension commissioner (1921-1925).

GARFIELD, JAMES ABRAM *(b Nov. 19, 1831, Orange, Ohio; d Sept. 19, 1881, Elberon, N.J., after being shot on July 2, 1881)* Twentieth president, Mar. 4, 1881-Sept. 19, 1881 (Ohio Republican). Nearly six feet tall and broad shouldered, Garfield had been canal boatman, college president, lay preacher, Union Army general, U.S. Representative.

Garfield's father, a pioneer farmer in Cuyahoga County, Ohio, died soon after James, the youngest of four children, was born. Mrs. Garfield kept the family together and James helped by working on the farm until he was sixteen. Then he went to Cleveland and became a canal boatman. Through hard work and sacrifices he managed to get a good education, graduating from the Western Reserve Eclectic Institute (now Hiram College), at Hiram, Ohio, and from Williams College, Williamstown, Mass., returning to Hiram, first as teacher then (1857-1861) as president. Studied law and (1860) was admitted to the bar. Married classmate Lucretia Rudolph (1858), with whom he had seven children, two of whom died in infancy.

When the Civil War broke out, Garfield used his considerable ability as an orator to stimulate enlistments and helped assemble a regiment, the Forty-second Ohio Volunteer Infantry, of which he became lieutenant colonel, then colonel, in spite of the fact that he had no military experience. He had a very active military career: fought at Shiloh, was chief of staff of the Army of the Cumberland, and served in the Chickamauga campaign. He advanced rapidly in rank, retiring as a major general in 1863 to reenter politics (some say at Lincoln's request).

Member of Ohio legislature (1859-1861), elected nine successive times as U.S. Representative (1863-1880), and to the U.S. Senate in 1880 (he never took this seat, but was inaugurated as president instead) in spite of the fact that on two occasions the finger of scandal pointed his way—his name was among those of a group of congressmen listed in Oakes Ames' memorandum book as having accepted gifts of stock in the Crédit Mobilier company; his critics accused him of being guilty of conflict of interest when he accepted a retaining fee for services rendered to the De-Golyer company which was seeking a paving contract from the government. Garfield denied the first allegation and proof was not convincing. His answer to the second one was that he had no connection with the governmental department that would make the paving award.

Served on Appropriations and Ways and Means committees and, in 1876, became the leader of the Republican party in the House. With the exception of tariff bills, he regularly voted the GOP line. In 1877 he was a member of the electoral commission created by act of Congress and his vote helped elect Hayes president.

Garfield would like to have thrown his hat into the ring as a possible presidential candidate at the GOP convention in 1880 but he was dissuaded and, instead, became convention manager for John Sherman. The other principal contenders were Ulysses S. Grant and James G. Blaine. Although Garfield worked hard, he was unable to obtain the necessary votes for his candidate and, on the thirty-fifth ballot, some of the Sherman delegates shifted their support to him. He was unanimously nominated on the next ballot and went on, with running mate Chester A. Arthur, to win the election against Democratic nominee Winfield S. Hancock, 214 to 155 electoral votes. The ill-feeling that developed between Garfield and the Grant-Conkling faction (the "Stalwarts") during the convention continued after the election, when the Stalwarts felt Garfield was slighting them in the appointments he made. Just four months after taking office, while at the Washington railway station, Garfield was shot by Charles J. Guiteau, an erratic, disappointed office-seeker who claimed to be a member of the Stalwart faction. It was more than two months later that the president died from the effects of the bullet wound and, on June 30, 1882, Guiteau was hanged.

GARLAND, AUGUSTUS HILL (b June 11, 1832, Tipton County, Tenn.; d Jan. 26, 1899, Washington, D.C.) Lawyer, teacher, Arkansas Whig-Constitutional Unionist who opposed secession but voted for it and became a Democrat after Fort Sumter was bombarded (1861).

Presidential elector on the Bell-Everett ticket (1860), member of Provisional Congress (1861), Confederate Congress as a representative (1861-1864) and senator (1864-1865), governor (1874-1876), U.S. Senate (1877-1885), U.S. attorney general in the Cleveland cabinet (1885-1889).

GARLAND, MAHLON MORRIS (b May 4, 1856, Pittsburgh, Pa.; d Nov. 19, 1920, Washington, D.C.) Metal worker, union leader and a vice president of the American Federation of Labor, Pennsylvania Republican. Member of Pittsburgh select council (1886, 1887), U.S. collector of customs at Pittsburgh (1898-1915), U.S. Representative (1915 until death).

GARLAND, RICE *(b about 1795, Lynchburg, Va.; d 1861, Brownsville, Texas).* Lawyer, Louisiana Whig. U.S. Representative (1834-1840), state supreme court judge (1840-1846).

GARNER, JOHN NANCE *(b Nov. 22, 1868, Red River County, Texas; d Nov. 7, 1967, Uvalde, Texas)* Lawyer, Texas Democrat who was a U.S. Representative thirty years (1903-1933) resigning to become vice president during Franklin D. Roosevelt's first two terms (1933-1941). Uvalde County judge (1893-1896), state representative (1898-1902), Democratic National Convention delegate (1900, 1916, 1924) and national committeeman (1934-1941).

A power in the House, he was legislative whip when Champ Clark was speaker, President Wilson's liaison when Claude Kitchin deserted him, ranking Democrat on the Ways and Means Committee, speaker in the Seventy-Second Congress and, in 1932, defeated both Roosevelt and Alfred E. Smith in the California presidential primary. For three ballots he was in the running for the nomination at the national convention but ultimately had to settle for second place.

During his tenure as vice president, he opposed FDR on many issues, among them the so-called packing of the Supreme Court, a third term, and New Deal spending policies.

GARNET, HENRY HIGHLAND *(b 1815, New Market, Md.; d Feb. 13, 1882, Liberia, Africa)* A slave who broke bondage (1824), began formal education in New York two years later, became a clergyman and an ardent abolitionist, and was well on his way to becoming the outstanding Negro of his time when in 1843, in Buffalo, N.Y., he told a national black convention that slaves should take up arms against their masters.

His chief critic at that meeting was Frederick Douglass and thereafter Garnet devoted more time to his ministerial duties than to the antislavery movement although by no means forsaking it. The highspot of his career perhaps came in 1865 when, as pastor of Washington's 15th Street Presbyterian Church, he preached a sermon *(A Memorial Discourse)* in the House of Representatives commemorating adoption of the Thirteenth (antislavery) Amendment.

Appointed ambassador to Liberia by President Garfield in 1881, he died while performing his duties there.

GARNETT, JAMES MERCER *(b June 8, 1770, Essex County, Va.; d April 23, 1843, near Loretto, Va.)* Virginia planter, educator who conducted a boys' school on his plantation, a founder of the State Agricultural Society, vice president of the Virginia Colonization Society, and a Democrat who, coincidentally, was a member of the grand jury that indicted (1807) Aaron Burr for treason.

Member state house of delegates (1800, 1801, 1824, 1825), U.S. Representative (1805-1809), delegate to antitariff conventions (1821, 1831). Brother of Robert S. and grandfather of Muscoe R. H. Garnett.

GARNETT, MUSCOE RUSSELL HUNTER *(b July 25, 1821, Essex County, Va.; d Feb. 14, 1864, Essex County)* Lawyer, Virginia Democrat who was active in the secession movement there. State constitutional convention delegate (1850, 1851), Democratic National Convention delegate (1852, 1856), state house of delegates (1853-1856), member of the University of Virginia Board of Visitors (1855-1859), U.S. Representative (1856-1861), delegate to both Virginia secession and state constitutional conventions (1861), member of the First Confederate Congress (1862 until death). Grandson of James M. Garnett.

GARNETT, ROBERT SELDEN *(b April 26, 1789, Essex County, Va.; d Aug. 15, 1840, Essex County)* Lawyer, Virginia Democrat. State house of delegates (1816, 1817), U.S. Representative (1817-1827). Brother of James M. Garnett.

GARRARD, JAMES *(b Jan. 14, 1749, Stafford County, Va.; d Jan. 19, 1822, Mt. Lebanon, Ky.)* Clergyman, Revolutionary Army officer, Democrat who was active in drive toward statehood for Kentucky and was its second governor (1796-1804).

GARRETT, DANIEL EDWARD *(b April 28, 1869, Robertson County, Tenn.; d Dec. 13, 1932, Washington, D.C.)* Lawyer, Tennessee and Texas Democrat. In Tennessee: State representative (1892-1896), state senate (1902, 1904). In Texas: U.S. Representative (1913-1915, 1917-1919, 1921 until death).

GARRETT, FINIS JAMES *(b Aug. 26, 1875, Weakley County, Tenn.; d May 25, 1956, Washington, D.C.)* Newspaperman, teacher, lawyer, Tennessee Democrat. Master in chancery (1900-1905), delegate to all Democratic state conventions (1896-1925) and national (1924), U.S. Representative (1905-1929) and minority floor leader (1923-1929), Coolidge-appointed judge of the U.S. Court of Customs and Patent Appeals (1929-1937), and Roosevelt-appointed presiding judge of the same court (1937-1955).

GARRETT, THOMAS *(b Aug. 21, 1789, Upper Darby, Pa.; d Jan. 25, 1871, Wilmington, Del.)* Hardware merchant, tool maker, Delaware Abolitionist who devoted his life to helping slaves to escape. He helped to free 2,700 blacks,

but had to endure a $10,000 reward on his head in Maryland, trial and conviction in Delaware (1848), and fines so heavy they cost him all his property. However, upon adoption of the Fifteenth (equal rights) Amendment (1870), Negroes celebrated by drawing him through the streets of Wilmington in an open carriage and, when he died, they carried him to his grave on their shoulders.

GARRISON, WILLIAM LLOYD *(b Dec. 10, 1805, Newburyport, Mass.; d May 24, 1879, New York City)* Printer, newspaper editor, pamphleteer, reformer, and one of the foremost of all Abolitionists. His objective was immediate emancipation, and his cause took him all over the United States and abroad. In his most famous editorial, published in the first issue of Boston's *Liberator* (Jan. 1, 1831), he wrote: "I am in earnest, I will not equivocate, I will not excuse, I will not retreat a single inch, and I will be heard!" A man who took nothing for granted, he advocated dissolution of the nation, contending the Constitution sanctioned slavery; he withheld support from Lincoln until after the Emancipation Proclamation (1863), before that criticizing him for his hesitation.

Only upon the end of the Civil War did Garrison feel that his mission had been accomplished and he then took up other causes (women's suffrage, prohibition, free trade), but with not nearly his old vigor.

GARVEY, MARCUS MOZIAH, JR. *(b Aug. 17, 1887, St. Ann's Bay, Jamaica; d June 10, 1940, London, England).* Black nationalist who founded (1914) the Universal Negro Improvement Association (UNIA) in Jamaica, migrated to New York (1916), launched a Harlem branch of the UNIA (1917), began publication of the *Negro World*, and devoted all of his literary, oratorical, and organizational skills to the redemption of homelands in Africa. Thus he established the Black Star (steamship) Line, acquired three vessels, and at a UNIA international convention in New York (1920) was authorized, in somewhat vague terms, to free Africa from white domination. But from then on he was beset with problems: he was convicted and imprisoned for using the mails to defraud in the sale of Black Star stock and upon release (1927) was deported to Jamaica; meantime Liberia reneged on UNIA colonization plans and in 1935 he moved to London to live out his years.

GARY, JULIAN VAUGHAN (b Feb. 25, 1892, Richmond, Va.) Teacher, lawyer, Virginia Democrat. Counsel and executive assistant to state tax board (1919-1924), state house of delegates (1926-1934), U.S. Representative (1945-1965) serving on the Appropriations Committee.

GASQUE, ALLARD HENRY (b March 8, 1873, near Hyman, S.C.; d June 17, 1938, Washington, D.C.) Educator, South Carolina Democrat. Florence County superintendent of education (1902-1923), member of Democratic state executive committee (1912-1920) and chairman of county committee (1919-1923), U.S. Representative (1923 until death). His widow, the former Elizabeth Hawley, served four months (1938-1939) to complete his term.

GASTON, WILLIAM (b Sept. 19, 1778, New Bern, N.C.; d Jan. 23, 1844, Raleigh, N.C.) Lawyer, North Carolina Federalist. State senate (1800, 1812, 1818, 1819), state representative (1807-1809, 1824, 1827, 1828, 1829, 1831) and house speaker (1808), presidential elector on the Pinckney-King ticket (1808), U.S. Representative (1813-1817), state supreme court judge (1833 until death), state constitutional convention delegate (1835).

GATHINGS, EZEKIEL CANDLER (b Nov. 10, 1903, Prairie, Miss.) Lawyer, Arkansas Democrat who was a U.S. Representative for thirty years (1939-1969) and before that was a state senator (1935-1939). He was a member of the House Agriculture Committee.

GAVIN, LEON HARRY (b Feb. 25, 1893, Buffalo, N.Y.; d Sept. 14, 1963, Washington, D.C.) New York Republican who served twenty years (1943-1963) as a U.S. Representative; member of the Armed Services Committee. Received recognition (1954) from Izaak Walton League and other prominent organizations for his championship of the national forest system.

GAY, EDWARD JAMES (b Feb. 3, 1816, Liberty, Va.; d May 30, 1889, Iberville Parish, La.). Manufacturer, planter, first president of the Louisiana Sugar Exchange, and a Democrat of that state. U.S. Representative (1885 until death). His namesake grandson's biography follows.

GAY, EDWARD JAMES (b May 5, 1878, Iberville Parish, La.; d Dec. 1, 1952, New Orleans, La.) Planter, manufacturer, Louisiana Democrat. State representative (1904-1918), Democratic National Convention delegate (1904, 1920), U.S. Senate to fill a vacancy (1918-1921), member of the Louisiana State University Board of Supervisors and building committee chairman (1921-1928), electoral college member at large (1941, 1945). Grandson of the preceding.

GAYLE, JOHN (b Sept. 11, 1792, Sumter District, S.C.; d July 28, 1859, near Mobile, Ala.) Lawyer, Alabama Democrat turned Whig who was active in politics almost from the day he completed his studies until the day of his death, beginning when President Monroe appointed him a member of the Alabama Territory's first council (1817,

1818). His political career included positions as first judicial district solicitor (1819), state representative (1822, 1823, 1829) and house speaker (1829), state supreme court judge (1823), governor (1831-1835), U.S. Representative (1847-1849), U.S. district judge (1849 until death).

GAYOSO DE LEMOS, MANUEL (b about 1752, Spain; d July 18, 1799, Louisiana) Diplomat, Spanish governor of the Natchez District (1789-1797), and governor of Louisiana (1797 until death) who was constantly at odds with the United States over territorial rights, even to preparing for war, and sided with James Wilkinson and Kentucky dissidents who wanted what was then the West to become a separate nation.

GEAR, JOHN HENRY (b April 7, 1825, Ithaca, N.Y.; d July 14, 1900, Washington, D.C.) Iowa pioneer merchant and one of that state's first Republicans. Mayor of Burlington (1863), state representative (1871-1873), governor (1878-1881), GOP National Convention delegate (1892, 1896), U.S. Representative (1887-1891, 1893-1895), assistant secretary of the U.S. Treasury (1892-1893), U.S. Senate (1895 until death).

GEARHART, BERTRAND WESLEY (b May 31, 1890, Fresno, Calif.; d Oct. 11, 1955, San Francisco) Lawyer, California Republican. Fresno County assistant district attorney and district attorney (1917-1923), state athletic commissioner (1931), state constitutional convention delegate (1933), U.S. Representative (1935-1949).

GEARY, JOHN WHITE (b Dec. 30, 1819, Westmoreland County, Pa.; d Feb. 8, 1873, Westmoreland County). Teacher, store clerk, farmer, lawyer, and a military engineer in the West who was San Francisco's first mayor (1850), governor of the Kansas Territory (1856-1857), and Republican gover-

nor of Pennsylvania (1867-1873). Assigned by President Polk to establish mail service on the West Coast, he was appointed postmaster of San Francisco (1849), helped to bring about California's status as a free state, and was chairman of the Democratic National Committee. He accepted the Kansas position after refusing a similar one in the Utah Territory. At the time, Kansas was on the verge of civil war over slavery and he agreed to try to put down the anarchy and rebellion rampant there. He ended the revolt in three weeks mainly by dismissing the pro-slavery militia and substituting in its place federal troops. During the Civil War he fought for the Union at Chancellorsville and Gettysburg and in other battles and was wounded at Cedar Mountain. Returning to his Westmoreland farm very much the hero, he stepped boldly and imposingly (he stood almost six-foot-six) onto the political scene and in his two terms as governor asserted his independence of the legislature by vetoing 390 bills.

GEDDES, GEORGE WASHINGTON (b July 16, 1824, Mount Vernon, Ohio; d Nov. 9, 1892, Mansfield, Ohio) Lawyer, Ohio Democrat. Sixth judicial district common pleas judge (1856-1873), U.S. Representative (1879-1887).

GEHRMANN, BERNARD JOHN (b Feb. 13, 1880, Gnesen, Germany; d July 12, 1958, Mellen, Wis.) Farmer, agricultural teacher-lecturer, farm agent, and a Wisconsin Republican turned Progressive. Ashland County School Board clerk (1916-1934), chairman of the Mellen Town Board (1921-1932), conductor of farmers' institutes for University of Wisconsin's College of Agriculture (1920-1933), state assemblyman (1927-1933, 1946, 1948, 1950, 1952), GOP National Convention delegate (1932), state senate (1933, 1934, 1954-1957), U.S. Representative as a Progressive (1935-1943).

GEISSENHAINER, JACOB AUGUSTUS *(b Aug. 28, 1839, New York City; d July 20, 1917, Mount Pocono, Pa.)* Lawyer, New Jersey Democrat. U.S. Representative (1889-1895).

GELSTON, DAVID *(b July 4, 1744, Bridgehampton, N.Y.; d Aug. 21, 1828, New York City)* Merchant, farmer, New York political leader who signed the articles of association (1775). Suffolk County delegate to provincial congress (1775-1777), state constitutional convention delegate (1777), state assemblyman (1777-1785) and assembly speaker (1784, 1785), Continental Congress (1789), council of appointment (1792, 1793), state senate (1791-1794, 1798, 1802), canal commissioner (1792), New York County surrogate (1787-1801), collector of the Port of New York (1801-1820).

GENTRY, MEREDITH POINDEXTER *(b Sept. 15, 1809, Rockingham County, N.C.; d Nov. 2, 1866, Nashville, Tenn.).* Lawyer, planter, Tennessee Whig turned Democrat. State representative (1835-1839), U.S. Representative (1839-1843, 1845-1853), unsuccessful candidate for governor (1855), member of Confederate Congress (1862-1863).

GEORGE, HENRY, SR. *(b Sept. 2, 1839, Philadelphia, Pa.; d Oct. 29, 1897, New York City, where his body lay in state and was viewed by 100,000 people)* Radical Republican, Democrat, and any meaningful liberal label of the place and the moment. Son of a customhouse clerk, he grew up to become a world-renowned leader in the fields of journalism, economics, protest and reform—all of them based first upon the things that he experienced or saw as a foremast boy on a ship in the Orient trade beginning at the age of fifteen, and then as a journeyman printer on newspapers in the California and Canadian gold fields. His first known written work was a eulogy to President Lincoln, after the assassination, for the *Alta California,* and his major written work was *Progress and Poverty* (1879). His particular targets were poverty, slavery, and land speculation; and his prime panacea was the single tax. An unsuccessful candidate for mayor of New York City in 1886, where it was widely believed that his defeat was due to election frauds, his second try for the mayoralty ended with his sudden death due to a stroke.

GEORGE, HENRY, JR. *(b Nov. 3, 1862, Sacramento, Calif.; d Nov. 14, 1916, Washington, D.C.)* Aide to his father and then, in his own right, journalist, foreign correspondent, Democrat who picked up the elder George's Jefferson party banner in the 1897 New York City mayoralty election but lost. U.S. Representative (1911-1915).

GEORGE, JAMES ZACHARIAH *(b Oct. 20, 1826, Monroe County, Ga.; d Aug. 14, 1897, Mississippi City, Miss.)* Soldier who served in Mexico (1847) under Colonel Jefferson Davis, Confederate Army officer, lawyer, Mississippi Democrat who voted for and signed the ordinance of secession. Before that, as state supreme court reporter (1854-1861) he compiled ten volumes of court reports. After the Civil War he was chairman of the Democratic state executive committee (1875, 1876), chief justice of the state supreme court (1879-1881), U.S. Senator (1881 until death). One major reason for his rise in politics was his leadership in the fight to restore native white supremacy in Mississippi and the unseating of Adelbert Ames (1876) as its last Republican governor.

GEORGE, MELVIN CLARK *(b May 13, 1849, Noble County, Ohio; d Feb. 22, 1933, Portland, Oregon)* Lawyer, Oregon Republican. State senate (1876-1880) and president (1878), U.S. Representative (1881-1885), circuit court judge (1897-1907), presidential elector on the Harding-Coolidge (1920) and Coolidge-Dawes (1924) tickets.

GEORGE, WALTER FRANKLIN *(b Jan. 29, 1878, Webster County, Ga.; d Aug. 4, 1957, Vienna, Ga.)* Lawyer, Georgia Democrat who was a U.S. Senator thirty-five years (1922-1957), for many years chairman of the Senate Foreign Relations Committee, and during the last months of his life, President Eisenhower's special ambassador to the North Atlantic Treaty Organization (NATO). Before his Washington days he was solicitor general of the Cordele judicial circuit (1907-1912), superior court judge (1912-1917), state appeals court judge (1917), associate state supreme court justice (1917-1922).

GEORGE, WILLIAM REUBEN *(b June 4, 1866, West Dryden, N.Y.; d April 25, 1936, at the George Junior Republic, near West Dryden)* New York jewelry and firearms manufacturer who founded the Junior Republic (1895) to teach children the art of government and participatory democracy. It began with five summers of taking New York City slum youngsters to the country only to find that they had come to expect it as their due. At its peak, the Junior Republic (open only to persons between the ages of fourteen and twenty-one) had its own currency, farm, shops and stores, political parties, elections, and government officials from president on down to street cleaner—all of it located on 400 acres of land. It was a model for other junior republics in many states and abroad but it had its political problems, particularly from official bureaucracy bent on to-the-letter enforcement of child labor laws.

GERLACH, CHARLES LEWIS *(b Sept. 14, 1895, Bethlehem, Pa; d May 5, 1947, Allentown, Pa.)* Fuel and appliance dealer, Pennsylvania Republican. State

committeeman (1936, 1937), U.S. Representative (1939 until death).

GERRY, ELBRIDGE *(b July 17, 1744, Marblehead, Mass.; d Nov. 23, 1814, Washington, D.C.)* Exporter, importer, follower of Samuel Adams, signer of the Declaration of Independence and the Articles of Confederation, Massachusetts Anti-Federalist and vice president of the United States (1813 until death) having been elected on the Democratic James Madison ticket.

Massachusetts colonial house of representatives (1772-1775), Continental Congress (1776-1781, 1782-1785), federal constitutional convention delegate (1787) where he at first refused to sign the document, contending it placed too much power in the hands of the president; U.S Representative in the First and Second Congresses (1789-1793), governor of Massachusetts (1810, 1811).

GERRY, PETER GOELET *(b Sept. 18, 1879, New York City; d Oct. 31, 1957, Providence, R.I.)* Lawyer, Rhode Island Democrat. Member of Newport Representative Council (1912), Democratic National Convention delegate (1912, 1916, 1932) and National Committeeman (1932-1936), U.S. Representative (1913-1915), U.S. Senate (1917-1929, 1935-1947). Great-grandson of Elbridge Gerry.

GERVAIS, JOHN LEWIS *(b year unknown but apparently in France; d Aug. 18, 1798, Charleston, S.C.)* Merchant, landowner, planter who arrived in South Carolina from Europe in 1764 and soon was an active advocate of independence. Delegate to provincial convention and Provincial Congress (1775, 1776), council of safety (1775, 1776, 1781), congressionally appointed deputy postmaster general for South Carolina (1778), Revolutionary Army officer who helped to defend Charleston (1780), state senate president (1781, 1782), Continental Congress (1782, 1783),

South Carolina commissioner of public accounts (1794, 1795).

GETZ, JAMES LAWRENCE *(b Sept. 14, 1821, Reading, Pa.; d Dec. 25, 1891, Reading)* Lawyer, publisher of the *Reading Gazette and Democrat*, Pennsylvania Democrat. State representative (1856, 1857) and speaker (1857), U.S. Representative (1867-1873), city comptroller (1888 until death).

GEYER, HENRY SHEFFIE *(b Dec. 9, 1790, Frederick, Md.; d March 5, 1859, St. Louis, Mo.)* Lawyer, orator, Whig who played an important role in Missouri's struggle for statehood. Territorial assembly (1818), constitutional convention delegate (1820), state representative (1820-1824) with three of those years as speaker, refused Fillmore appointment as secretary of war (1850), U.S. Senate (1851-1857).

GEYER, LEE EDWARD *(b Sept. 9, 1888, Wetmore, Kans.; d Oct. 11, 1941, Washington, D.C.)* Teacher, high school football coach, California Democrat. State representative (1934-1936), U.S. Representative (1939 until death), Democratic National Convention delegate (1940).

GIBBONS, JAMES SLOAN *(b July 1, 1810, Wilmington, Del.; d Oct. 17, 1892, New York City)* Philadelphia merchant, New York banker, but most of all an author and abolitionist who is best remembered for writing "We Are Coming, Father Abraham," which first was published in the *New York Evening Post* (July 16, 1862) and became the Civil War's most famous song. Active in the American Anti-Slavery Society and a Quaker, his home was looted and his papers destroyed during New York City's July 1863 draft riots.

GIBBONS, THOMAS *(b Dec. 15, 1757, Savannah, Ga.; d May 16, 1826, New York City)* Georgia lawyer and Revo-

lutionary period Tory whose property and person were spared only because his father and brother were patriots. Upon war's end he became active in Savannah politics and served as mayor (1791-1792, 1794-1795, 1799-1801), then moved to New Jersey and broke a monopolistic hold on ferryboat service between Elizabethtown and Manhattan —going all the way to the U.S. Supreme Court to do so.

GIBBONS, WILLIAM *(b April 8, 1726, Bear Bluff, S.C.; d Sept. 27, 1800, Savannah, Ga.)* Lawyer and one of the six Sons of Liberty who, upon hearing of the battle at Lexington, broke into the crown's powder magazine in Savannah (May 14, 1775), took 600 pounds of explosives, and thus brought the Revolution to Georgia. Provincial Congress delegate and member of committee of safety (1775), executive council (1777-1781), Chatham County associate justice (1781, 1782), Continental Congress (1784, 1785), state representative (1783, 1785-1789, 1791-1793) serving as speaker (1783, 1786, 1787), state constitutional convention president (1789), inferior court justice (1790-1792).

GIBSON, CHARLES HOPPER *(b Jan. 19, 1842, Queen Annes County, Md.; d March 31, 1900, Washington, D.C.).* Lawyer, Maryland Democrat. Commissioner in chancery (1869-1870), Talbot County state's attorney (1871-1880), U.S. Representative (1885-1891), U.S. Senate (1891-1897). Cousin of Henry R. Gibson.

GIBSON, ERNEST WILLARD *(b Dec. 29, 1872, Londonderry, Vt.; d June 20, 1940, Washington, D.C.)* Lawyer, vice president of Norwich College, Vermont Republican. State representative (1906), state senator and president pro tem (1908), GOP National Convention delegate (1912), U.S. Representative (1923-1933), U.S. Senate (1933 until death).

GIBSON, HENRY RICHARD *(b Dec. 24, 1837, Kent Island, Md.; d May 25, 1938, Washington, D.C.)* Union soldier, Knoxville newspaper editor, author, lawyer, Tennessee Republican. State constitutional convention delegate (1870), state senate (1871, 1872), state representative (1874, 1875), U.S. pension agent at Knoxville (1883-1885), second chancery division chancellor (1886-1894), medical-law professor at Tennessee Medical College (1889-1906), author of *Gibson's Suits in Chancery* (1891), U.S. Representative (1895-1905), associate reviser of the *Code of Tennessee* (1918) which he had first helped to edit and compile (1896). Cousin of Charles H. Gibson.

GIBSON, PARIS *(b July 1, 1830, Brownfield, Maine; d Dec. 16, 1920, Great Falls, Mont.)* Maine real estate operator, farmer who moved to Minnesota and built the first flour mill and then a woolen mill in Minneapolis, and then on to northern Montana where he introduced sheep raising on a large scale, established the city of Great Falls, used its waters for power, opened iron mines, built railroads, and was an active Democrat, rekindling an interest in politics that he had shown in Maine where he had been a state representative (1852). Thirty years later, in Montana, first mayor of Great Falls (1882), state constitutional convention delegate (1889), state senate (1890), U.S. Senate (1901-1905) to fill a vacancy.

GIBSON, RANDALL LEE *(b Sept. 10, 1832, Woodford County, Ky.; d Dec. 15, 1892, Hot Springs, Ark.)*. Wealthy sugar planter, Confederate officer, lawyer, Louisiana Democrat who had much to do with the removal of federal troops from Louisiana, establishment of the Mississippi River Commission, and the founding of Tulane University, becoming president of its first board of administrators. U.S. Representative (1875-1883), U.S. Senate (1883 until death) and also administrator of the Howard Memorial Library, trustee of the Peabody Fund, and regent of the Smithsonian Institution.

GIBSON, WALTER MURRAY *(b 1823 at sea; d Jan. 21, 1888, San Francisco, Calif.)* Shipmaster, author, lecturer, and an adventurer whose exploits landed him in prison for sixteen months in Dutch Sumatra, advised Brigham Young to sell the Salt Lake Territory to the United States and reestablish the Mormon colony in Hawaii, went to Hawaii (1861) to expedite the plan and used church money to buy land in his own name, established the newspaper *Nuhou* (which means "Hawaii for the Hawaiians"), became the kingdom's premier in 1882, and remained in power until 1887 when he was deposed by the revolution.

GIDDINGS, DeWITT CLINTON *(b July 18, 1827, Susquehanna County, Pa.; d Aug. 19, 1903, Brenham, Tex.)* Confederate soldier, lawyer, banker, Texas Democrat. State constitutional convention delegate (1866), U.S. Representative (1872-1875, 1877-1879), Democratic National Convention delegate (1884, 1888, 1892).

GIDDINGS, JOSHUA REED *(b Oct. 6, 1795, Tioga Point, Pa.; d May 27, 1864, Montreal, Canada)* Teacher, lawyer, orator, Ohio Whig–Free-Soiler–Republican and an unrelenting enemy of slavery who urged war if need be to set slaves free, carrying on his fight vigorously, vocally, through twenty years in Congress. There, too, he opposed the Mexican War and annexation of Texas, seeing both as a ploy for the spreading of slavery.

As a U.S. Representative (1838-1859), he struck up a friendship with Abraham Lincoln who religiously studied his speeches and gleaned from them many ideas that he later executed as president. When Giddings' failing health prevented him from running for reelection, Lincoln appointed him consul to Canada (1861 until death).

GIFFORD, CHARLES LACEILLE *(b March 15, 1871, Cotuit, Mass.; d Aug. 23, 1947, Cotuit)* Cape Cod real estate broker, oysterman, cranberry grower, Massachusetts Republican who served a quarter-century as a U.S. Representative (1922 until death).

GIFFORD, OSCAR SHERMAN *(b Oct. 20, 1842, Watertown, N.Y.; d Jan. 16, 1913, Canton, S.Dak.)* Union soldier, lawyer, South Dakota Republican who was active politically both before and after statehood. In the Dakota Territory he was Lincoln County district attorney (1874), mayor of Canton (1881, 1882), state constitutional convention delegate (1883), delegate to Congress (1885-1889). U.S. Representative (1889-1891) when South Dakota became a state.

GILBERT, GEORGE GILMORE *(b Dec. 24, 1849, Taylorsville, Ky.; d Nov. 9, 1909, Louisville, Ky.)* Teacher, lawyer, Kentucky Democrat. Spencer County prosecutor (1876-1880), state senate (1885-1889), Democratic National Convention delegate (1896), U.S. Representative (1899-1907). Father of Ralph W. E. Gilbert.

GILBERT, NEWTON WHITING *(b May 24, 1862, Worthington, Ohio; d July 5, 1939, Santa Ana, Calif.)* Lawyer, Indiana Republican who was sent to the Philippine Islands by Theodore Roosevelt and found a new way of life there. Steuben County surveyor (1886-1892), state senate (1896-1900), lieutenant governor (1900-1904), U.S. Representative (1905-1906) resigning to become judge of the court of first instance at Manila (1906-1908), member of the Philippine Commission (1908, 1909), president of the Philippine University

Board of Regents (1908, 1909), secretary of public instruction for the Philippine Islands (1909) and vice governor (1909-1913). Then, upon returning to the United States, delegate from New York to the GOP National Convention of 1916.

GILBERT, RALPH WALDO EMERSON *(b Jan. 17, 1882, Taylorsville, Ky.; d July 30, 1939, Louisville, Ky.)* Lawyer, Kentucky Democrat. Shelby County judge (1910-1917), U.S. Representative (1921-1929, 1931-1933), state representative (1929, 1933), state senate (1936 until death). Son of George G. Gilbert.

GILCHRIST, FRED CRAMER *(b June 2, 1868, California, Pa.; d March 10, 1950, Laurens, Iowa)* Teacher, lawyer, Iowa Republican. Superintendent of schools in Laurens and Rolfe (1886-1890) and Pocahontas County (1890-1892), state representative (1902-1904), president of Laurens Board of Education (1905-1928), state senate (1923-1931), U.S. Representative (1931-1945).

GILES, WILLIAM BRANCH *(b Aug. 12, 1762, Amelia County, Va.; d Dec. 4, 1830, Amelia County)* Lawyer, Virginia Anti-Federalist who served in the first five U.S. Congresses (1790-1798) and again in the seventh (1801-1803), presidential elector on the Jefferson-Burr Democratic ticket (1800), state house of delegates (1798-1800, 1816, 1817, 1826, 1827), U.S. Senate (1803-1815), governor (1827-1830), state constitutional convention delegate (1829, 1830).

GILES, WILLIAM FELL *(b April 8, 1807, Harford County, Md.; d March 21, 1879, Baltimore, Md.)* Lawyer, Maryland Democrat who devoted much of his life to the American Colonization Society and to the removal of Maryland's free Negroes to Liberia. State house of delegates (1838-1840), U.S. Representative (1845-1847), U.S. district judge for Maryland (1853 until death).

GILL, JOHN, JR. *(b June 9, 1850, Baltimore, Md.; d Jan. 17, 1918, Baltimore).* Lawyer, Maryland Democrat. State delegate (1874-1877), state senate (1882-1886, 1904, 1905), delegate to all Democratic state conventions (1880-1908) and national (1884, 1888, 1892), Baltimore police commissioner (1888-1897), U.S. Representative (1905-1911), appeal tax court judge (1912-1918).

GILLESPIE, DEAN MILTON *(b May 3, 1884, Salina, Kans.; d Feb. 2, 1949, Baltimore, Md.)* Rancher, auto and oil dealer, Colorado Republican. U.S. Representative (1944-1947).

GILLESPIE, OSCAR WILLIAM *(b June 20, 1858, Clarke County, Miss.; d Aug. 23, 1927, Fort Worth, Tex.)* Lawyer, Texas Democrat. Tarrant County assistant attorney (1886-1888) and prosecuting attorney (1890-1894), U.S. Representative (1903-1911).

GILLET, CHARLES WILLIAM *(b Nov. 26, 1840, Addison, N.Y.; d Dec. 31, 1908, New York City)* Union soldier, manufacturer, New York Republican. Addison postmaster (1878-1886), U.S. Representative (1893-1905).

GILLETT, FREDERICK HUNTINGTON *(b Oct. 16, 1851, Westfield, Mass.; d July 31, 1935, Springfield, Mass.)* Lawyer, Massachusetts Republican who as a U.S. Representative for thirty-two years (1893-1925) and speaker (1919-1925) led the drive for appropriation procedures reforms that led to the Budget Act of 1921. Assistant state attorney general (1879-1882), state representative (1890-1891) and, to cap his career in Washington, U.S. Senate (1925-1931), an office he sought only because President Coolidge asked him to run.

GILLETT, JAMES NORRIS *(b Sept. 20, 1860, Viroqua, Wis.; d April 20, 1937, Berkeley, Calif.)* Lawyer, California Republican. Eureka city attorney (1889-

1895), state senate (1897-1899), U.S. Representative (1903-1906) resigning to become governor (1907-1911).

GILLETTE, WILSON DARWIN *(b July 1, 1880, Bradford County, Pa.; d Aug. 7, 1951, Towanda, Pa.)* Auto dealer, Pennsylvania Republican. State representative (1930-1941), U.S. Representative (1941 until death).

GILLON, ALEXANDER *(b 1741, Rotterdam, Holland; d Oct. 6, 1794, Orangeburg District, S.C.)* Merchant ships' captain, Revolutionary naval officer who captured two British privateers in Charleston harbor and then was commissioned commodore in the South Carolina Navy (1778) and sent abroad to purchase ships and recruit men, a delicate mission that he handled like a bulldozer and thus aroused the antagonism of two other Americans abroad: Benjamin Franklin, who put roadblocks in his way, and John Paul Jones who called him "The Red Ribboned Commodore." Still Gillon did succeed in obtaining and outfitting one ship that he renamed the *South Carolina*, took her to sea, seized several ships, and participated in the capture of the Bahamas (1782). However, Gillon's skill as a sailor is questionable since it is known that during a storm a passenger aboard the *South Carolina* had to take command. Nevertheless, when the war was over, he returned home a hero, took an interest in politics, was chosen a delegate to the state convention (1788) that ratified the federal Constitution and was elected a U.S. Representative (1793 until death).

GILMAN, CHARLES JERVIS *(b Feb. 26, 1824, Exeter, N.H.; d Feb. 5, 1901, Brunswick, Maine)* Lawyer, New Hampshire Whig and Maine Whig turned Republican. In New Hampshire: state representative (1851, 1852). In Maine: state representative (1854, 1855) and member of Whig committee, then, as a

Republican, U.S. Representative (1857-1859), GOP National Convention delegate (1860). Grand-nephew of John T. Gilman.

GILMAN, CHARLOTTE PERKINS STETSON *(b July 3, 1860, Hartford, Conn.; d Aug. 17, 1935, Pasadena, Calif.)* Feminist, editor, writer, lecturer, great-granddaughter of Lyman Beecher and grand-niece of Harriet Beecher Stowe, who carried the family tradition of reform into a new era. Concerned with the labor movement and women's rights, her philosophy, radical for the times, that women must achieve financial independence before they can fully develop their potential, is presented in *Women and Economics* (1898), translated into six languages and probably the best known of her many written works. Incurably ill, she died a suicide.

GILMAN, JOHN TAYLOR *(b Dec. 19, 1753, Exeter, N.H.; d Sept. 1, 1828, Exeter)* Farmer, shipbuilder, financier, 1775 Minuteman, and a Federalist whom one biographer calls "probably the ablest member of a family long prominent in New Hampshire affairs." Exeter selectman (1777, 1778), state representative (1779, 1781, 1810, 1811), delegate to convention of states in Hartford (1780), Continental Congress (1782, 1783), state treasurer (1791), moderator (1791-1794, 1806, 1807, 1809-1811, 1817, 1818, 1820-1825), the state's second governor (1794-1805) and again (1813-1816), presidential elector on the Clinton-Ingersoll Peace party ticket (1812), Dartmouth College trustee (1817-1819), board president of Phillips Exeter Academy (1795-1827) and donor of much of its campus. Brother of Nicholas Gilman, grand-uncle of Charles J. Gilman.

GILMAN, NICHOLAS *(b Aug. 3, 1755, Exeter, N.H.; d May 2, 1814, Philadelphia, Pa.)* Financier, Revolutionary

Army officer, New Hampshire Federalist turned Democrat. Member of Continental Congress (1786-1788), constitutional convention delegate (1787), U.S. Representative in the first four Congresses as a Federalist (1789-1797), Federalist presidential elector (1793, 1797); then, as a Democrat, Jefferson-appointed commissioner in bankruptcy (1802-1804), U.S. Senate (1805 until death). Brother of John T. Gilman.

GILMER, GEORGE ROCKINGHAM *(b April 11, 1790, Wilkes County, Ga.; d Nov. 16, 1859, Lexington, Ga.)* Teacher, lawyer, author, historian, Georgia National Republican-Democrat-Whig, and Indian fighter who built a fort that flourished and became the city of Atlanta. State representative (1818, 1819, 1824), U.S. Representative (1821-1823, 1827-1829, 1833-1835), governor (1829-1831) as a National Republican and as a Whig (1837-1839), presidential elector on the White-Tyler ticket (1836) and the Harrison-Tyler ticket (1840).

GILMER, JOHN ADAMS *(b Nov. 4, 1805, Guilford County, N.C.; d May 14, 1868, Greensboro, N.C.)* Teacher, lawyer, Southern Unionist–Whig–Know-Nothing who opposed secession yet sided with the South when the chips were down, even to declining a seat in the Lincoln cabinet. State senate (1846-1856), U.S. Representative (1857-1861), Second Confederate Congress (1864), Union National Convention of Conservatives delegate (1866) in Philadelphia.

GILMER, THOMAS WALKER *(b April 6, 1802, Gilmerton, Va.; d Feb. 28, 1844, in a naval accident on the Potomac River).* Lawyer, newspaper editor, Virginia Democrat who helped to organize the Whig party there and who, as governor (1840-1841), resigned in a dispute with the state legislature over the extradition of prisoners. U.S. Representative (1841-1844) when he resigned to become secretary of the navy in the Tyler cabinet and two weeks later was killed when a gun exploded aboard the USS *Princeton.*

GILMER, WILLIAM FRANKLIN "DIXIE" *(b June 7, 1901, Mount Airy, N.C.; d June 9, 1954, Oklahoma City, Okla.).* Lawyer, Oklahoma Democrat who years later returned to Washington to serve as a U.S. Representative (1949-1951) in the same chambers where he had been a page boy (1911-1919). At death he was Oklahoma's safety commissioner.

GIST, JOSEPH *(b Jan. 12, 1775, Union District, S.C.; d March 8, 1836, Pinckneyville, S.C.)* Lawyer, South Carolina Democrat. State representative (1801-1819), South Carolina College trustee (1809-1821), U.S. Representative (1821-1827).

GIST, WILLIAM HENRY *(b Aug. 22, 1807, Charleston, S.C.; d Sept. 30, 1874, Union District, S.C.)* Lawyer, wealthy planter and South Carolina Democrat who, as governor (1858-1860) led the fight for secession. State representative (1840-1844), state senate (1844-1856).

GLASS, CARTER *(b Jan. 4, 1858, Lynchburg, Va.; d May 28, 1946, Washington, D.C.)* Editor-publisher of the *Lynchburg Daily News* and *Daily Advance*, conservative Virginia Democrat who spent forty-four years of his life on Capitol Hill where, as chairman of the Senate Banking and Currency Committee, he drafted the Glass-Owens Federal Reserve Act (1913) and thus sired the Federal Reserve System.

Clerk of the Lynchburg city council (1881-1901), member of Board of Visitors of the University of Virginia (1898-1906), state senate (1899-1903), state constitutional convention delegate (1901), U.S. Representative (1902-1918), secretary of the treasury in the Wilson cabinet (1918-1920), U.S. Senate (1920 until death), chairman of the Democratic National Convention platform committee (1920).

Very much a figure to be reckoned with in national affairs, Glass was even a stronger foe of Roosevelt's New Deal policies than he was a supporter of Wilson, most of whose ideas he wrote into the 1920 platform. He called many of FDR's ideas "Communistic" and fought them bitterly as chairman of the Appropriations Committee. Among FDR's programs he disliked were lowering of the gold content of the dollar, federal spending for welfare, the 1937 plan to pack the Supreme Court, and the National Industrial Recovery Act. And, when Roosevelt asked him to again serve as treasury secretary, he said no.

GLEN, HENRY *(b July 13, 1739, Schenectady, N.Y.; d Jan. 6, 1814, Schenectady)* New York patriot, upstate political leader, and deputy quartermaster general during the Revolution. Schenectady County clerk (1767-1809), member of first three Provincial Congresses (1774-1776), state assembly (1786, 1787, 1810), U.S. Representative (1793-1801).

GLENN, MILTON WILLITS *(b June 18, 1903, Atlantic City, N.J.; d Dec. 14, 1967).* Lawyer, New Jersey Republican. Margate City municipal magistrate (1940-1943), Atlantic County freeholder (1946-1951), state assembly (1950-1957), U.S. Representative (1957-1965) serving on the Merchant Marine and Fisheries and Interstate and Foreign Commerce committees.

GLOVER, DAVID DELANO *(b Jan. 18, 1868, Prattsville, Ark.; d April 5, 1952, Malvern, Ark.)* Farmer, merchant, teacher, lawyer, Arkansas Democrat. State representative (1909, 1911), seventh judicial district prosecutor (1913-1917), U.S. Representative (1929-1935).

GLYNN, JAMES PETER *(b Nov. 12, 1867, Winsted, Conn.; d March 6, 1930, on a train near Washington, D.C.)* Lawyer, Connecticut Republican. Winsted town clerk (1892-1902), town court prosecutor (1899-1902), postmaster (1902-1914), U.S. Representative (1915-1923, 1925 until death).

GLYNN, MARTIN HENRY *(b Sept. 27, 1871, Kinderhook, N.Y.; d Dec. 14, 1924, Albany, N.Y.)* Editor-publisher of the *Albany Times-Union*, lawyer, orator, New York Democrat who was elected to the U.S. House of Representatives at the age of twenty-seven where (1899-1901) he showed an astute interest in labor legislation, and later, as governor (1913-1914), brought about the state's workmen's compensation laws and its primary election system. State comptroller (1906-1908), lieutenant governor (1912-1913), temporary chairman of two Democratic state conventions (1912, 1916) and the national convention of 1916 where, in his keynote speech, he used the phrase "he kept us out of war" in eulogizing Woodrow Wilson and thus created a campaign slogan.

GODWIN, HANNIBAL LAFAYETTE *(b Nov. 3, 1873, Harnett County, N.C.; d June 9, 1929, Dunn, N.C.)* Lawyer, North Carolina Democrat. Mayor of Dunn (1897), state senate (1903), presidential elector on the Parker-Davis ticket (1904), member of Democratic state executive committee (1904-1906), U.S. Representative (1907-1921).

GOEBEL, HERMAN PHILIP *(b April 5, 1853, Cincinnati, Ohio; d May 4, 1930, Cincinnati)* Lawyer, Ohio Republican. State representative (1875, 1876), Hamilton County probate court judge (1884-1890), U.S. Representative (1903-1911).

GOEBEL, WILLIAM *(b Jan. 4, 1856, Carbondale, Pa.; d Feb. 3, 1900)* Lawyer, Kentucky Democrat who, as a state senator (1887-1899) brought about much reform legislation including the heatedly fought Goebel Election Law of 1898. In 1899 he was nominated for governor, was the center of the state's most bitter election contest ever with the final tally going to his Republican opponent. Goebel charged fraud, the issue went to the Democratic-controlled legislature and, on Jan. 30, 1900, while the decision was still pending, he was shot by an assassin and, before his death four days later, he was officially declared governor. As a result, Kentucky was violently split, there was danger of riot and threat of revolt, but ultimately common sense prevailed.

GOFF, GUY DESPARD *(b Sept. 13, 1866, Clarksburg, W. Va.; d Jan 7, 1933, Thomasville, Ga.)* Lawyer, West Virginia and Wisconsin Republican who several times served briefly as an assistant or special assistant to the U.S. attorney general in 1917, 1920, 1921, 1922, and 1923. Also the prosecutor for Wisconsin's Milwaukee County (1895), that state's eastern district attorney (1911-1915), first general counsel and then member of the U.S. Shipping Board (1920-1921), and then back to his native state to become a U.S. Senator (1925-1931). Son of Nathan Goff.

GOFF, NATHAN *(b Feb. 9, 1843, Clarksburg, Va., now W.Va.; d April 24, 1920, Clarksburg)* Lawyer, Virginia Republican who fought on the side of the Union in the Civil War, and when West Virginia became a state (1863) was one of its most active political leaders.

State house of delegates (1867, 1868), U.S. attorney for West Virginia (1868-1882) with two months out in 1881 to serve as President Hayes' secretary of the navy, GOP National Convention delegate (1872, 1876, 1880), U.S. Representative (1883-1889), elected governor (1888) by popular vote but lost by legislative action, U.S. fourth judicial circuit court judge (1892-1913),

U.S. Senate (1913-1919). Father of Guy D. Goff.

GOLDFOGLE, HENRY MAYER *(b May 23, 1856, New York City; d June 1, 1929, New York City)* Lawyer, New York Democrat. Fifth district court judge (1887, 1893), municipal court judge (1888-1900), Democratic National Convention delegate (1892, 1896), U.S. Representative (1901-1915, 1919-1921), president of New York City Board of Taxes and Assessments (1921 until death).

GOLDMAN, EMMA *(b June 27, 1869, Kovno, Lithuania; d May 14, 1940, Toronto, Canada)* Anarchist propagandist, writer, and editor; lecturer; literary and drama critic; nurse. Spent her early youth in Russia where revolution was brewing and terrorist acts not uncommon, emigrated to Rochester, N.Y. in 1885, became a factory worker, and began attending socialist meetings. Espoused anarchism (1889), influenced to some extent by New York anarchist paper *Die Freiheit* and the bloody Chicago Haymarket Square riots over demands for an eight-hour working day (1886) and the subsequent trial and punishment of eight anarchist leaders (four were hanged). With Alexander Berkman she founded and edited an anarchist journal, *Mother Earth* (1906-1917). Although dedicated to propagandizing the radical principles in which she profoundly believed, such as doing away with government so it could be replaced by the voluntary cooperation of mankind, she also practiced nursing and lectured eloquently on current social problems and modern European drama. Her speaking tours covered Europe as well as the United States. Subjected to frequent police interference, she was convicted of inciting to riot and spent almost a year in prison (1893-1894), again imprisoned for fifteen days (1916) for publicly advocating birth control and for two years (1917-1919) for obstruct-

ing the draft. On her release in 1919, a federal court took away the U.S. citizenship she acquired through marriage and she was deported, along with Berkman, to Russia. She disagreed with the Russian Bolsheviks on their methods and left there in 1921, moving from country to country, residing in England (where she obtained citizenship by marriage), France, and Spain. She continued to lecture, write *(My Disillusionment in Russia* [1923] is one of her well-known books), and work for causes she considered worthy (she was anti-Franco during the Spanish Civil War). She returned once to the United States on a speaking tour, but only after promising to refrain from mentioning political issues.

GOLDSBOROUGH, CHARLES *(b July 15, 1765, Dorchester County, Md.; d Dec. 13, 1834, near Cambridge, Md.).* Lawyer, Federalist, and member of a Maryland family that sent many men to public office. State senate (1791-1795, 1799-1801), U.S. Representative (1805-1817), governor (1818, 1819), and the last Federalist to so serve in Maryland.

GOLDSBOROUGH, PHILLIPS LEE *(b Aug. 6, 1865, Princess Anne, Md.; d Oct. 22, 1946, Baltimore)* Lawyer, banker, Maryland Republican. Dorchester County state's attorney (1892-1898), state comptroller (1898, 1899), state collector of internal revenue (1902-1911), governor (1912-1915), U.S. Senate (1929-1935), Republican National Committee member (1932-1936), director of the Federal Deposit Insurance Corporation (1935 until death).

GOLDSBOROUGH, ROBERT *(b Dec. 3, 1733, Dorchester County, Md.; d Dec. 22, 1788, near Cambridge, Md.)* Lawyer, Maryland patriot. Dorchester County high sheriff (1761-1765), Maryland burgess (1765), attorney general (1766), member of Continental Congress (1774, 1775), council of safety (1775), delegate to provincial constitutional convention (1776), state senate (1777).

GOLDSBOROUGH, ROBERT HENRY (b Jan. 4, 1779, Talbot County, Md.; d Oct. 5, 1836, near Easton, Md.) Planter, a founder of the Easton Gazette (1817), Maryland Federalist-Whig-National Republican. State house of delegates (1804, 1825), U.S. Senate (1813-1819, 1835 until death), presidential elector on the Clay-Sergeant ticket (1832).

GOLDSBOROUGH, THOMAS ALAN (b Sept. 16, 1877, Greensboro, Md.; d June 16, 1951, Washington, D.C.) Lawyer, Maryland Democrat. Caroline County prosecutor (1908), U.S. Representative (1921-1939), regent of the Smithsonian Institution (1932-1939), associate justice of the District of Columbia U.S. district court (1939 until death).

GOMPERS, SAMUEL (b Jan. 27, 1850, London, England; d Dec. 13, 1924, San Antonio, Texas) Labor leader whose politics was trade unionism from the time he was fourteen and joined the Cigarmakers' Union in New York. He was highly active in formation of the American Federation of Labor and served as its president from its founding in 1866 until death (except for one year). He sought above all else to exert moral influence, he detested socialism, believed strongly that labor and capitalism must work together, and was against political action on the part of unions although sometimes he was forced to compromise that principle.

GOOD, JAMES WILLIAM (b Sept. 24, 1866, Linn County, Iowa; d Nov. 18, 1929, Washington, D.C.) Lawyer, Iowa Republican who was secretary of war in the Hoover cabinet for eight months (March 5, 1929, until death). Cedar Rapids city attorney (1906-1908), U.S. Representative (1909-1921).

GOODE, JOHN, JR. (b May 27, 1829, Bedford County, Va.; d July 14, 1909, Norfolk, Va.) Lawyer, orator, Confederate Army officer who twice was a member of the Confederate Congress, and a Virginia Democrat of national political stature. State house of delegates (1852, 1866, 1867), Democratic presidential elector (1852, 1856, 1884) and president of the Electoral College in the latter year, delegate to state secessionist convention (1860), Democratic National Executive Committeeman (1868-1876) and national convention delegate (1868, 1872, 1884, 1892), U.S. Representative (1875-1881), Cleveland-appointed U.S. solicitor general (1885-1886), member of U.S. and Chilean Claims Commission (1893), state constitutional convention president (1901, 1902).

GOODE, PATRICK GAINES (b May 10, 1798, Cornwall, Va.; d Oct. 17, 1862, Sidney, Ohio) Clergyman, lawyer, Ohio Whig. State representative (1833-1835), U.S. Representative (1837-1843), common pleas court judge (1844-1851).

GOODE, WILLIAM OSBORNE (b Sept. 16, 1798, Inglewood, Va.; d July 3, 1859, Boydton, Va.) Lawyer, Virginia Democrat. State house of delegates (1822, 1824-1832, 1839, 1840, 1845, 1846, 1852) serving three terms as speaker, state constitutional convention delegate (1829, 1830, 1850), U.S. Representative (1841-1843, 1853 until death).

GOODELL, WILLIAM (b Oct. 25, 1792, Coventry, N.Y.; d Feb. 14, 1878, Janesville, Wis.) Rhode Island, North Carolina, Virginia, and New York merchant, lecturer, preacher, newspaper and periodicals editor, and above all else a reformer and Abolitionist of national repute who helped found the Liberty party (1840), the Liberty League (1857), and the National Prohibition party.

GOODHUE, BENJAMIN (b Sept. 20, 1748, Salem, Mass.; d July 28, 1814, Salem) Merchant who operated privateers during the Revolution, Massachusetts Federalist. State representative (1780-1782), state senate (1786-1788), state constitutional convention delegate (1779, 1780), U.S. Representative in the first four Congresses (1789-1796) and then a U.S. Senator (1796-1800).

GOODING, FRANK ROBERT *(b Sept. 16, 1859, Tiverton, England; d June 24, 1928, Gooding, Idaho)* Farmer, miner, mail carrier, woodcutter, and charcoal merchant who became one of Idaho's leading Republicans. State senate (1900-1904), chairman of GOP state central committee (1902), governor (1905-1909), U.S. Senate (1921 until death in the town to which he gave his name).

GOODLOE, WILLIAM CASSIUS *(b June 27, 1841, Madison County, Ky.; d Nov. 10, 1889, Lexington, Ky.)* Private secretary to his great-uncle, Cassius M. Clay, when latter was minister to Russia; Union Army officer, orator with a biting tongue and arrogant manner who made politics his business. He helped to found the Republican party in Kentucky (1867) when he also became the founding publisher of the *Kentucky Statesman*, and he died in the Lexington post office at the hands of his rival for state control of the party, Armistead M. Swope, who also was killed in the struggle.

State representative (1872), state senate (1873), minister to Belgium (1878-1880), U.S. collector of internal revenue for Kentucky (July 1889 until death).

GOODNIGHT, ISAAC HERSCHEL *(b Jan. 31, 1849, Allen County, Ky.; d July 24, 1901, Franklin, Ky.)* Lawyer, Kentucky Democrat. State representative (1877, 1878), Democratic state convention chairman (1891), U.S. Representative (1889-1895), seventh circuit judge (1897 until death).

GOODNOW, ISAAC TICHENOR *(b Jan. 17, 1814, Whigingham, Vt.; d March 20,*

1894, Manhattan, Kans.) College professor and foe of slavery who led a party of 200 Free-Soil colonists (1855) from Boston to Kansas where they founded the town of Manhattan and Bluemont Central College, which became (1863) the Kansas State Agricultural College. Delegate to Free State Convention (1855) and the 1858 convention that drafted the Leavenworth Constitution, state representative (1861, 1862), state superintendent of public instruction (1862-1866).

GOODRICH, CHAUNCEY *(b Oct. 20, 1759, Durham, Conn.; d Aug. 18, 1815, Hartford, Conn.)* Lawyer, Connecticut Federalist, and, with his brother, Elizur, a member of the state oligarchy. State representative (1793, 1794), U.S. Representative (1795-1801), member of state executive council (1802-1807), U.S. Senate (1807-1813) resigning to become both lieutenant governor and mayor of Hartford (1813 until death).

GOODRICH, ELIZUR *(b March 24, 1761, Durham, Conn.; d Nov. 1, 1849, New Haven, Conn.)* Lawyer, Yale law professor, Connecticut Federalist. State representative (1795-1802) serving as clerk for six sessions and speaker for two, presidential elector on the Adams ticket (1796), U.S. Representative (1799-1801) resigning to accept presidential appointment as New Haven collector of customs (1801-1803), member of governor's council (1803-1818), probate court judge (1802-1818), chief county court judge (1805-1818), mayor of New Haven (1803-1822), secretary of Yale College (1818-1846). Brother of Charles Goodrich.

GOODWIN, GODFREY GUMMER *(b Jan. 11, 1873, Nicollet County, Minn.; d Feb. 16, 1933, Washington, D.C.)* Lawyer, Minnesota Republican. Isanti County prosecutor (1898-1907, 1913-1925), president of Cambridge Board of Education (1914-1917), U.S. Representative (1925 until death).

GOODWIN, JOHN NOBLE *(b Oct. 18, 1824, South Berwick, Maine; d April 29, 1887, Paraiso Springs, Calif.)* Lawyer, Maine and Arizona Republican whom President Lincoln named to serve as first governor of the Arizona Territory (1863-1866) a few months after appointing him its chief justice. In Maine: state senate (1854), U.S. Representative (1861-1863). In Arizona: delegate to the Thirty-ninth Congress (1865-1867).

GOODWIN, WILLIAM SHIELDS *(b May 2, 1866, Warren, Ark.; d Aug. 9, 1937, Warren)* Lawyer, Arkansas Democrat. State representative (1895), presidential elector on the Bryan-Stevenson ticket (1900), state senate (1905-1909), University of Arkansas trustee (1907-1911), U.S. Representative (1911-1921).

GOODWYN, PETERSON *(b 1745, Dinwiddie County, Va.; d Feb. 21, 1818, Dinwiddie County)* Planter, lawyer, Revolutionary Army officer, Virginia Democrat. Member state house of delegates (1789-1802), U.S. Representative (1803 until death).

GORDON, GEORGE WASHINGTON *(b Oct. 5, 1836, Pulaski, Tenn.; d Aug. 9, 1911, Memphis, Tenn.)* Civil engineer, Confederate army officer, lawyer, Tennessee Democrat who served as a special Indian agent in Arizona and Nevada (1887-1890). Memphis schools superintendent (1890-1907), U.S. Representative (1907 until death).

GORDON, JOHN BROWN *(b Feb. 6, 1832, Upson County, Ga.; d Jan. 9, 1904, Miami, Fla.)* Lawyer, lecturer, author of *Reminiscences of the Civil War* (1903), railroad builder, Georgia Democrat who fought brilliantly throughout the Civil War and led the last charge at Appomattox, thus becoming the idol of the people back home. Then he threw himself into the thick of the fight to restore home rule.

An influential man politically, Gordon,

with Alfred H. Colquitt and Joseph E. Brown, constituted the so-called new triumvirate of Georgia Democracy who believed that the state's future lay more in industry than in agriculture.

Union National Convention delegate (1866), Democratic gubernatorial candidate (1868) losing to the Republican Reconstructionist R. B. Bullock; Democratic National Convention delegate (1868, 1872), presidential elector on the Seymour-Blair (1868) and Greeley-Brown (1872) tickets, U.S. Senate (1873-1880, 1891-1897), governor (1886-1890), commander in chief of the United Confederate Veterans (1890 until death).

GORDON, LAURA DE FORCE *(b Aug. 17, 1838, North East, Erie County, Pa.; d Apr. 6, 1907)* After accompanying her doctor husband to New Orleans, then by wagon train to White Plains, Nevada (where she was the first white woman), then on to California, Mrs. Gordon set about building an unusual career for a woman of her time. She published (1873), the *Stockton (Calif.) Weekly Leader*, which was so successful it soon became the *Daily Leader*, supporting the Democratic party. Mrs. Gordon moved the paper (1875) to Sacramento where she sold it. Becoming interested in law, she first helped secure passage of a bill permitting women to practice law in California, then, after being refused admission to the newly founded Hastings College of Law, she and another woman student took the matter to court and won the case. She was one of the first women admitted (1879) to the California bar as well as one of the first admitted to practice (1887) before the Supreme Court of the United States. She was also an active supporter of women's suffrage.

GORDON, THOMAS SYLVY *(b Dec. 17, 1893, Chicago, Ill.; d Jan. 22, 1959, Chicago)* Banking and office management, Illinois Democrat. Chicago west parks commissioner (1933-1936) and vehicle licenses commissioner (1936-1939), Democratic National Convention delegate (1936), city treasurer (1939-1942), U.S. Representative (1943-1959).

GORDON, WILLIAM *(b Dec. 15, 1862, Ottawa County, Ohio; d Jan. 16, 1942, Cleveland, Ohio)* Teacher, lawyer, lumber dealer, Ohio Democrat. Ottawa County deputy treasurer (1887-1891), school examiner (1890-1896) and prosecutor (1895-1901), Democratic National Convention delegate (1896), Democratic state committeeman (1903, 1904), U.S. Representative (1913-1919).

GORE, THOMAS PRYOR *(b Dec. 10, 1870, Webster County, Miss.; d March 16, 1949, Washington, D.C.)* Lawyer, blind Texas and Oklahoma Populist-Democrat. Populist National Convention delegate and Congressional candidate from Texas (1896); member of Oklahoma territorial council (1903-1905), U.S. Senate upon achievement of statehood (1907-1921) and again (1931-1937), Democratic National Convention delegate (1912) and national committeeman (1912-1916).

GORHAM, BENJAMIN *(b Feb. 13, 1775, Charlestown, Mass.; d Sept. 27, 1855, Boston)* Lawyer, Massachusetts legislator. State representative (1814-1818, 1841), state senate (1819-1821, 1823-1825), U.S. Representative (1820-1823, 1827-1831, 1833-1835). Son of Nathaniel Gorham.

GORHAM, NATHANIEL *(b May 27, 1738, Charlestown, Mass.; d June 11, 1796, Charlestown)* Merchant, Genesee Valley (N.Y.) land speculator, Massachusetts patriot who was a member (1782-1783, 1785-1787) and president (1786-1787) of the Continental Congress. Member of provincial legislature (1771-1775), delegate to Provincial Congress (1774, 1775), member of board of

war (1778-1781), state constitutional convention delegate (1779), state senate (1780, 1781), delegate to federal constitutional convention (1787) and the state's ratifying convention (1788), Middlesex common pleas court judge (1785-1796), then resigning to become part of a cartel that sought to make millions in the Genesee Country but instead caused him to die of apoplexy. Father of Benjamin Gorham.

GORMAN, ARTHUR PUE *(b March 11, 1839, Woodstock, Md.; d June 4, 1906, Washington, D.C.)* Congressional page, canal executive, Maryland Democrat and Stephen A. Douglas protégé (serving as his private secretary) who learned his political lessons well. For example, years later, although he disagreed with Grover Cleveland's policies and opposed his nomination, he managed his election campaigns both in 1884 and 1892. Fifth Maryland district collector of internal revenue (1866-1869), state house of delegates (1869-1875) and speaker (1873, 1874), state senate (1875-1881), U.S. Senate (1881-1899, 1903 until death) serving variously as caucus chairman, majority leader, and minority leader.

GORMAN, WILLIS ARNOLD *(b Jan. 12, 1816, near Flemingsburg, Ky.; d May 20, 1876, St. Paul, Minn.)* Lawyer, Indiana Democrat who was appointed governor of the Minnesota Territory (1853-1857) thus replanting his roots there, serving as a brigadier general in the Union Army and becoming active in the drive for statehood and in state politics—even to breaking his cane on the head of a Republican delegate to the 1857 constitutional convention. In Indiana: state senate clerk (1837, 1838), U.S. Representative (1849-1853). In Minnesota: state representative (1858), St. Paul prosecutor (1869-1875).

GORSKI, MARTIN *(b Oct. 30, 1886, Poland; d Dec. 4, 1949, Chicago, Ill.).*

Lawyer, Illinois Democrat. Assistant state's attorney (1918-1920), master in chancery of Cook County Superior Court (1929-1942), U.S. Representative (1943 until death).

GRAFF, JOSEPH VERDI *(b July 1, 1854, Terre Haute, Ind.; d Nov. 10, 1921, Peoria, Ill.)* Merchant, lawyer, banker, Illinois Republican, GOP National Convention delegate (1892), U.S. Representative (1895-1911).

GRAHAM, GEORGE SCOTT *(b Sept. 13, 1850, Philadelphia, Pa.; d July 4, 1931, Islip, N.Y.)* Lawyer, University of Pennsylvania professor of criminal law and procedure (1887-1898), Pennsylvania Republican. Member of Philadelphia's select council (1877-1880), Philadelphia County district attorney (1880-1899), GOP National Convention delegate (1892, 1924), U.S. Representative (1913 until death).

GRAHAM, JAMES *(b Jan. 7, 1793, Lincoln County, N.C.; d Sept. 25, 1851, Rutherford County, N.C.)* Lawyer, farmer, North Carolina Whig. State representative (1822, 1823, 1824, 1828, 1829), U.S. Representative (1833-1843, 1845-1847). Brother of William A. Graham.

GRAHAM, WILLIAM ALEXANDER *(b Sept. 5, 1804, Vesuvius Furnace, N.C.; d Aug. 11, 1875, Saratoga Springs, N.Y.)* Lawyer, statesman, North Carolina Whig who though a Southerner through and through remained a Union man and fought secession—so much so that in the 1860 presidential election New York and Pennsylvania electors were urged to vote for him in hopes of preventing a breakup of the states. Yet when the split did come, he sided with the South and served in the Confederate Congress where he still remained a moderate who worked for peace. His political career had many meaningful milestones: member of the state house of commons (1836, 1838, 1840) and speaker in the latter two sessions; Whig U.S. Senator from a Democratic state (1840-1843); governor (1845-1849) when he did much to build railroads and improve the state's transportation facilities; secretary of the navy in the Fillmore cabinet (1850-1852) when he advocated Perry's Japanese expedition, exploration of the Amazon, and a shakeup in naval personnel; Winfield Scott's vice presidential running mate (1852); state senate (1854, 1862, 1865). Brother of James Graham.

GRAHAM, WILLIAM HARRISON *(b Aug. 3, 1844, Allegheny, Pa.; d March 2, 1923, Pittsburgh, Pa.)* Union soldier, leather merchant, banker, Pennsylvania Republican. State representative (1875-1878), Allegheny County recorder of deeds (1882-1891), U.S. Representative (1898-1903, 1905-1911), member of county board of viewers (1911-1923).

GRANAHAN, KATHRYN ELIZABETH *(b ——, Easton, Pa.)* Social worker, Pennsylvania Democrat, and the first Philadelphia woman to serve in Congress (1956-1963). First elected upon the death of her husband, William Thomas Granahan, she became a member of the Post Office, Civil Service, and Government Operations committees and chairman of the Subcommittee on Postal Operations. Delegate to Democratic National Convention (1960).

GRANAHAN, WILLIAM THOMAS *(b July 26, 1895, Philadelphia; d May 25, 1956, Darby, Pa.)* Builder, Pennsylvania Democrat. State Democratic committee (1938-1942), state inheritance tax supervisor (1940, 1941), chief disbursing officer of the state treasury (1941-1944), U.S. Representative (1945-1947, 1949 until death).

GRANGER, DANIEL LARNED DAVIS *(b May 30, 1852, Providence, R.I.; d Feb. 14, 1909, Washington D.C.)* Lawyer,

Rhode Island Democrat. Reading clerk of the state house of representatives (1887-1890), Providence treasurer (1890-1901) and mayor (1901, 1902), U.S. Representative (1903 until death).

GRANGER, FRANCIS *(b Dec. 1, 1792, Suffield, Conn.; d Aug. 31, 1868, Canandaigua, N.Y.)* Lawyer, a leader both nationally and in New York of the Anti-Masonic movement, and later top man of the Silver Grays (so-called for the hair that grew to his shoulders), the conservative wing of the Whig party.

State assemblyman (1826-1828, 1830-1832), unsuccessful candidate for governor on both the Anti-Masonic and National Republican tickets (1830, 1832), Anti-Masonic National Convention delegate (1830), U.S. Representative (1835-1837, 1839-March, 1841; November, 1841-1843), Whig and Anti-Masonic candidate for vice president (1836) the final decision going against him in the Senate, postmaster general in the Harrison cabinet (March-September, 1841), delegate to 1861 peace-between-states conference where he was a strong advocate of compromise.

GRANT, GEORGE McINVALE *(b July 11, 1897, Louisville, Ala.)* Lawyer, Alabama Democrat. Pike County solicitor (1927-1937), U.S. Representative for twenty-seven years (1938-1965), serving on the Agriculture Committee.

GRANT, ULYSSES S. *(b April 27, 1822, Point Pleasant, near New Richmond, Ohio; d July 23, 1885, Mt. McGregor, near Saratoga, N.Y.; buried in Grant's Tomb, New York City)* Eighteenth president, (Republican) 1869-1877, with no previous political experience but who had been Civil War commander of the Union armies.

Grant's father, Jesse, was a poorly educated tanner and farmer who moved his family to Georgetown, Ohio, when his son was about a year old. Grant attended school regularly, although he was also required to work hard on his father's farm where he developed a great fondness for horses and outdoor life. Attended West Point (1839-1843) where he excelled in riding and where his name was mistakenly recorded as Ulysses Simpson (he was christened Hiram Ulysses), which name he thereafter used, preferring the initials it gave him to the former H.U.G. Married Julia Dent (1848), daughter of a Missouri planter who bore him a daughter and three sons, one of whom was Frederick Dent Grant (1850-1912) who became minister to Austria-Hungary (1889-1893), New York City police commissioner (1895-1897), and brigadier-general of volunteers in the Spanish American War.

Served under Generals Zachary Taylor and Winfield Scott in the Mexican War. Resigned from the army (1854) after being transferred to the Pacific Coast where his wife was unable to follow him and where (now a captain) he is said to have been reprimanded for drowning his loneliness with alcohol. He returned to his wife and family in St. Louis but, though he tried his hand at a number of trades, did not meet with success. When the Civil War broke out, he was appointed colonel, then brigadier general of the Twenty-first Illinois Volunteers. With the help of Union gunboats (February 1862), he captured Forts Henry and Donelson, thereby attracting Lincoln's attention and resulting in his promotion to major general of volunteers. He got into serious trouble at the battle of Shiloh in the following April but more than redeemed himself at Vicksburg (1862-1863) with a remarkable campaign resulting in a victory that put the Mississippi River in control of the North and cut the Confederacy in half. Grant was promoted to major general in the regular army and soon after was put in charge of most of the Union troops between the Allegheny Mountains and the Mississippi River. He went on to defeat

General Braxton Bragg at Chattanooga and to be put in charge of all Union armies, with the rank of lieutenant general. He coordinated the armies in a way that made it possible for them to smash the Confederate forces and, in April 1865, the Civil War was over. In 1866, Grant was made general of the army.

Appointed secretary of war (1867) when President Johnson suspended Stanton, Grant cooperated with Congress and angered Johnson by turning the office back to Stanton.

Nominated by the Republican party on the first ballot at the presidential convention of 1868, Grant was easily elected, with 214 electoral votes against 80 received by Horatio Seymour, his Democratic opponent. Grant's skill as a general did not carry over into the office of the president, perhaps in part because he tried to run both jobs in much the same way and also because he appointed friends to fill positions without regard for their qualifications or reliability (giving them his loyal support when they got into trouble in spite of the way they misused his trust)— perhaps, most of all, because of the confusion, the passions, the corruption, and the general difficulty of those post-Civil War years. Reconstruction was badly managed, the panic of 1873 occurred during Grant's administration, and there were numerous scandals involving his friends and associates. But foreign relations were well-handled by Secretary of State Hamilton Fish, with Grant's support.

He went along with the Radical Republican punitive approach to Reconstruction. The "Liberal" Republicans who disapproved and wanted to see a change in the administration joined with the Democrats in support of Horace Greeley against Grant in the 1872 presidential election, but Grant again won easily, with a larger plurality than he received in 1868.

After retirement from office, Grant spent two years touring Europe with his family. His friends tried to nominate him at the 1880 presidential campaign to run for a third term but without success. Shortly before Grant's death (from cancer of the throat), and in order to provide the now impoverished ex-president with funds, Congress (after a great deal of delay and controversy) reappointed him to the position of general he had given up when he became president. In the meantime, Grant had found a way to earn money on his own: by writing his memoirs, and doing it so well (in spite of his painful illness) that they are considered outstanding among narratives of military history.

GRAVES, WILLIAM JORDAN (b 1805, New Castle, Ky.; d Sept. 27, 1848, Louisville, Ky.) Lawyer, Missouri Whig who killed fellow Congressman Jonathan Cilley of Maine in a duel (1838) outside Washington. State representative (1834, 1843), U.S. Representative (1835-1841), presidential elector on the Clay-Frelinghuysen ticket (1844).

GRAY, FINLY HUTCHINSON (b July 21, 1863, Fayette County, Ind.; d May 8, 1947, Connersville, Ind.) Lawyer, lecturer, Indiana Democrat. Mayor of Connersville (1904-1910), U.S. Representative (1911-1917, 1933-1939).

GRAY, GEORGE (b May 4, 1840, New Castle, Del.; d Aug. 7, 1925, Wilmington, Del.) Lawyer, Delaware Democrat whose judicial and diplomatic skills made him invaluable to the nation both at home and abroad. For example, he was chairman of the Roosevelt-appointed committee that settled the Pennsylvania coal strike of 1902; he was a member of the Permanent Court of Arbitration (1900-1924) by successive appointments of Presidents McKinley, Roosevelt, Taft, and Wilson.

State attorney general (1879-1884), Democratic National Convention delegate (1876, 1880, 1884, 1892, 1896), U.S. Senate (1885-1899) serving, among other assignments, on the Foreign Relations Committee; member of Quebec commission (1898) to settle U.S.-Canadian differences, member of Paris commission (1898) that arranged U.S.-Spanish peace terms, judge of the U.S. Circuit Court of Appeals for the Third Circuit (1899-1914), helped settle U.S.-British North Atlantic coast fisheries dispute (1909), American member of international commission for advancement of peace (1915), head of U.S. delegation to Pan-American Scientific Congress (1915), member of joint U.S.-Mexican commission (1916); a trustee of the Carnegie Endowment for International Peace, and member of the Smithsonian Institution Board of Regents during most of his public life.

GRAYSON, WILLIAM (b 1740, Prince William County, Va.; d March 12, 1790, Dumfries, Va.) Lawyer, Washington's aide-de-camp during the Revolution, Virginia leader who opposed adoption of the federal Constitution contending that it discriminated against the South.

Member of board of war (1780, 1781), Continental Congress (1784-1787), delegate to state constitutional convention (1788), U.S. Senate (1789 until death). Father of William J. Grayson.

GRAYSON, WILLIAM JOHN (b Nov. 2, 1788, Beaufort, S.C.; d Oct. 4, 1863, Newberry, S.C.) Planter, lawyer, writer who was a frequent contributor to the Southern Quarterly Review, and a South Carolina Whig. State representative (1822-1826), state senate (1826-1831), Beaufort County commissioner of equity (1831-1833), U.S. Representative (1833-1837), Charleston collector of customs (1841-1853). Son of William Grayson.

GREELEY, HORACE (b Feb. 3, 1811, Amherst, N.H.; d Nov. 29, 1872, Pleas-antville, N.Y.) Apprentice printer at the age of fourteen who became the founding editor-publisher of the New Yorker and the New York Tribune, reformer who opposed slavery, favored the Free-Soil movement, deplored the death penalty, supported labor, evinced a crusading journalist's interest in politics, and wore a variety of political labels, among other things becoming a radical abolitionist leader of the Republican party in New York, yet remaining cool to Lincoln's 1864 presidential reelection bid.

U.S. Representative as a Whig (December 1848–March 1849) to fill a vacancy, GOP National Convention delegate (1860) from Oregon when New York denied him a seat, unsuccessful candidate for U.S. Senate (1861), presidential elector on the Lincoln-Johnson ticket (1864), state constitutional convention delegate (1867) the same year that he enraged fellow Northerners by posting bail for the imprisoned Jefferson Davis; unsuccessful GOP candidate for Congress (1870), unsuccessful candidate of the Liberal Republicans and Democrats for the U.S. presidency (1872) receiving 2,843,446 votes to Grant's 3,596,745.

GREEN, DUFF (b Aug. 15, 1791, Woodford County, Ky.; d June 10, 1875, near Dalton, Ga.) St. Louis, New York, and Washington newspaper editor, land speculator, railroad, mining, and industrial developer; friend and adviser to presidents, among other things "holding" a seat in Jackson's so-called Kitchen Cabinet, wearing no particular political label and seeking no elective office, yet true to his origins remaining loyal to the South no matter to which state his varied interests took him.

GREEN, HENRY DICKINSON (b May 3, 1857, Reading, Pa.; d Dec. 29, 1929, Reading) Lawyer, Reading newspaper editor, Texas oil operator, Pennsylvania Democrat. State representative (1883-

1886), state senator (1889-1896), U.S. Representative (1899-1903).

GREEN, JAMES STEPHEN *(b Feb. 28, 1817, Fauquier County, Va.; d Jan. 19, 1870, St. Louis, Mo.)* Lawyer who broke the grip of his political mentor, Thomas H. Benton, upon the Democratic party in Missouri (1849) and in the U.S. Senate (1857-1861) was an eloquent and forceful foe of squatter sovereignty. Presidential elector on the Polk-Dallas ticket (1844), state constitutional convention delegate (1845), U.S. Representative (1847-1851), Pierce-appointed chargé d' affaires to Colombia (1853-1854).

GREEN, NORVIN *(b April 17, 1818, New Albany, Ind.; d Feb. 12, 1893, Louisville, Ky.)* Physician, Kentucky Democrat who preferred telegraphy to medicine and politics, forsaking both to form a nationwide system that became Western Union. State representative (1850-1853, 1867), presidential elector on the Pierce-King ticket (1852).

GREEN, ROBERT STOCKTON *(b March 25, 1831, Princeton, N.J.; d May 7, 1895, Elizabeth, N.J.)* Lawyer, New Jersey Democrat. Elizabeth city attorney (1857-1868) and prosecutor of the borough courts (1857), Democratic National Convention delegate (1860, 1880, 1888), Union County surrogate (1862-1867), Elizabeth councilman (1863-1873), presiding common pleas court judge (1868-1873), member of state constitutional amendment commission (1873), U.S. Representative (1885-1887), governor (1887-1889), state vice chancellor (1890-1895), appeals court judge (1894 until death).

GREEN, THEODORE FRANCIS *(b Oct. 2, 1867, Providence, R.I.; d May 19, 1966, Providence)* Lawyer, Brown University instructor in Roman law (1894-1897), business executive, liberal Rhode Island Democrat who as governor (1933-1936) broke the back of the Republican machine that long had controlled the state and went on to Washington to become a U.S. Senator (1937-1961) at the age of seventy and remaining until the age of ninety-four, thus being the oldest person ever to be a member of the U.S. Congress. Chairman of the Providence Planning Commission (1917-1919), state representative (1907), Democratic National Convention delegate (1912-1944), presidential elector on the Wilson-Marshall ticket (1912), Democratic state convention chairman (1914, 1924, 1926), Democratic National Committeeman (1936-1946), chairman of the Senate Foreign Relations Committee (1957-1959).

GREEN, WILLIAM RAYMOND *(b Nov. 7, 1856, Colchester, Conn.; d June 11, 1947, Bellport, N.Y.)* Lawyer, Iowa Republican. Fifteenth judicial district court judge (1894-1911), U.S. Representative (1911-1928), judge of the U.S. Court of Claims (1928-1942).

GREENE, FRANK LESTER *(b Feb. 10, 1870, St. Albans, Vt.; d Dec. 17, 1930, St. Albans)* Newspaperman, Vermont Republican. President of Vermont Press Association (1904, 1905), member of state constitutional amendment commission (1908), GOP National Convention (1908) and state convention delegate (1910, 1914) serving as chairman (1914), U.S. Representative (1912-1923), Smithsonian Institution regent (1917-1923), U.S. Senate (1923 until death).

GREENE, WILLIAM STEDMAN *(b April 28, 1841, Tremont, Ill.; d Sept. 22, 1924, Fall River, Mass.)* Real estate dealer, Massachusetts Republican. Member of Fall River Common Council (1876-1879) and its president (1877-1879), mayor (1880, 1881, 1886, 1895-1897), postmaster (1881-1885), state prison superintendent (1888-1893), U.S. Representative (1898 until death).

GREENUP, CHRISTOPHER *(b 1750, Westmoreland County, Va.; d April 27, 1818, Frankfort, Ky.)* Lawyer, Revolutionary Army officer, Indian fighter, and political figure who took part in the move to separate Kentucky from Virginia. Member of Virginia House of Delegates (1785), delegate to separation conventions (1785, 1788), U.S. Representative from Kentucky (1792-1797), state representative (1798), state senate clerk (1799-1802), circuit court judge (1802-1804), governor as a Jeffersonian Democrat (1804-1808), presidential elector on the Madison-Clinton ticket (1808), Franklin County justice of the peace (1812), and an original trustee of Transylvania University.

GREENWAY, ISABELLA SELMES *(b March 22, 1886, Boone County, Ky.; d Dec. 18, 1953, Tucson, Ariz.)* A New Mexico homesteader (1910) who operated a cattle ranch there and was chairman of the Women's Land Army (1918) before moving to Arizona where she operated both a resort and an airline while also becoming politically active, serving as Democratic National Committeewoman and U.S. Representative (1933-1937).

GREENWOOD, ALFRED BURTON *(b July 11, 1811, Franklin County, Ga.; d Oct. 4, 1889, Bentonville, Ark.)* Lawyer, Arkansas Democrat. State representative (1842-1845), state prosecutor (1845-1851), circuit judge (1851-1853), U.S. Representative (1853-1859), commissioner of Indian affairs (1859-1861), Confederate representative (1862-1865).

GREEVER, PAUL RANOUS *(b Sept. 28, 1891, Lansing, Kans.; d Feb. 16, 1943, Cody, Wyo., while cleaning a shotgun).* Lawyer, banker, Wyoming Democrat. Mayor of Cody (1930-1932), University of Wyoming trustee (1933-1934), U.S. Representative (1935-1939).

GREGG, ALEXANDER WHITE *(b Jan. 31, 1855, Centerville, Tex.; d April 30, 1919, Palestine, Tex.)* Lawyer, Texas Democrat. State senate (1886-1888), U.S. Representative (1903 until a month before death).

GREGG, ANDREW *(b June 10, 1755, Carlisle, Pa.; d May 20, 1835, Bellefonte, Pa.)* Tutor, merchant, farmer, banker, Pennsylvania political leader who served as a U.S. Representative (1791-1807) and U.S. Senator (1807-1813) where he was elected president pro tem (1809). Pennsylvania secretary of state (1820-1823).

GREGORY, NOBLE JONES *(b Aug. 30, 1897, Mayfield, Ky.)* Banker, Kentucky Democrat. Secretary-treasurer of the Mayfield Board of Education, U.S. Representative (1937-1959). Brother of William V. Gregory.

GREGORY, WILLIAM VORIS *(b Oct. 21, 1877, Graves County, Ky.; d Oct. 10, 1936, Mayfield, Ky.).* Lawyer, teacher, Kentucky Democrat. Mayfield schools superintendent (1898-1900), county surveyor (1902-1910), county judge (1913-1919), U.S. attorney for the western district (1919-1923), U.S. Representative (1927 until death). Brother of Noble J. Gregory.

GRIEST, WILLIAM WALTON *(b Sept. 22, 1858, Christiana, Pa.; d Dec. 5, 1929, Mount Clemens, Mich.)* Teacher, newspaperman, utilities executive, Pennsylvania Republican. Delegate to all GOP National Conventions (1896-1928), Pennsylvania secretary of state (1899-1903), U.S. Representative (1909 until death).

GRIFFIN, ANTHONY JEROME *(b April 1, 1866, New York City; d Jan. 13, 1935, New York City)* Lawyer, newspaperman, New York Democrat. State senate (1911-1915), state constitutional convention delegate (1915), U.S. Representative (1918 until death).

GRIFFIN, ISAAC *(b Feb. 27, 1756, Kent County, Del.; d Oct. 12, 1827, Nicholson Township, Pa.; in a fall from a farm wagon)* Farmer, Continental Army officer, Pennsylvania Democrat. Justice of the peace (1794), state representative (1807-1812), U.S. Representative (1813-1817). Great-grandfather of Eugene McLanahan Wilson.

GRIFFIN, JOHN KING *(b Aug. 13, 1789, Laurens County, S.C.; d Aug. 1, 1841, Laurens County)* Planter, South Carolina Whig and advocate of states' rights. State representative (1816-1818), state senate (1820-1824, 1828), U.S. Representative (1831-1841).

GRIGGS, JAMES MATHEWS *(b March 29, 1861, Lagrange, Ga.; d Jan. 5, 1910, Dawson, Ga.)* Teacher, lawyer, newspaperman, Georgia Democrat. Pataula judicial circuit solicitor general (1888-1893) and judge (1893-1896), Democratic National Convention delegate (1892), U.S. Representative (1897 until death), chairman of Democratic Congressional Campaign Committee (1904-1908).

GRIMES, JAMES WILSON *(b Oct. 20, 1816, Deering, N.H.; d Feb. 7, 1872, Burlington, Iowa)* Lawyer, Iowa Republican. Territorial representative (1838, 1845), governor (1854-1858), U.S. Senate (1859-1869), delegate to Washington search-for-peace conference (1861).

GRIMKÉ, ANGELINA EMILY *(b Feb. 20, 1805, Charleston, S.C.; d Oct. 26, 1879, Hyde Park, Mass.)* See Grimké, Sarah Moore.

GRIMKÉ, SARAH MOORE *(b Nov. 26, 1792, Charleston, S.C.; d Dec. 23, 1873, Hyde Park, Mass.)* Abolitionist and women's rights reformer. Encouraged to develop her mind by her father, John Faucheraud Grimké, senior associate judge of the South Carolina Supreme Court, Sarah evaluated the slavery she saw all around her both with the sensitive compassion of her nature and the reason of her mind and knew that it was wrong. She influenced the thinking of her younger sister, Angelina Emily Grimké, and eventually the two, repelled by the inhumanity of slavery and frustrated by their inability to do anything about it, left their wealthy, aristocratic Southern family, moved to the North and became Quakers. First Angelina, then the more timid Sarah, joined the antislavery movement (and the women's rights movement that had become its natural offshoot), writing and lecturing for the cause. They were shy at first, but with their deep sincerity and first-hand knowledge of their subject and the help of abolitionist leader Theodore Dwight Weld, whom Angelina married in 1838, they soon became among the most effective of the movement's lecturers—especially Angelina, who in 1838 appeared three times before the Massachusetts legislative committee dealing with antislavery petitions.

GRINNELL, JOSIAH BUSHNELL *(b Dec. 22, 1821, New Haven, Vt.; d March 31, 1891, Grinnell, Iowa)* Clergyman who delivered the first antislavery sermon ever uttered in a Washington pulpit, was banished to New York by his parishioners, became a friend of Horace Greeley who advised him to "go West, young man, go West" and so relocated in Iowa where he founded both the town of Grinnell and Grinnell University, became a highly successful railroad builder, banker, lawyer, and one of the state's leading Republicans. State senate (1856-1860), GOP National Convention delegate (1860), U.S. Representative (1863-1867).

GRISWOLD, MATTHEW *(b June 6, 1833, Lyme, Conn.; d May 19, 1919, Erie,*

Pa.) Teacher, farmer, manufacturer, Republican who served as a Connecticut state representative (1862, 1865) before moving to Pennsylvania and serving as a U.S. Representative (1891-1893, 1895-1897). Grandson of Roger Griswold.

GRISWOLD, ROGER *(b May 21, 1762, Lyme, Conn.; d Oct. 25, 1812, Norwich, Conn.)* Lawyer, Connecticut Federalist who declined appointment to Adams cabinet as secretary of war (1801). U.S. Representative (1795-1805), state supreme court judge (1807), lieutenant governor (1809-1811), governor (1811 until death). Grandfather of Matthew Griswold.

GRONNA, ASLE JORGENSON *(b Dec. 10, 1858, Elkader, Iowa; d May 4, 1922, Lakota, N.Dak.)* Teacher, farmer, businessman, North Dakota Republican. Territorial representative (1889), chairman of Nelson County GOP central committee (1902-1906), University of North Dakota regent (1902), U.S. Representative (1905-1911), U.S. Senator (1911-1921).

GROOME, JAMES BLACK *(b April 4, 1838, Elkton, Md.; d Oct. 5, 1893, Baltimore)* Lawyer, Maryland Democrat. State constitutional convention delegate (1867), member of state house of delegates (1871, 1872, 1873-1874), presidential elector on the Greeley-Brown ticket (1872), governor (1874-1876), U.S. Senate (1879-1885), Baltimore collector of customs (1889-1893).

GROSVENOR, CHARLES HENRY *(b Sept. 20, 1833, Pomfret, Conn.; d Oct. 30, 1917, Athens, Ohio)* Lawyer, Union Army officer, Ohio Republican. State representative (1874-1878) twice serving as speaker, GOP National Convention delegate (1896, 1900), U.S. Representative (1885-1891, 1893-1907), chairman of Chickamauga and Chattanooga National Park Commission (1910 until death).

GROUT, WILLIAM WALLACE *(b May 24, 1836, Compton, Quebec, Canada; d Oct. 7, 1902, Kirby, Vt.)* Lawyer, Union Army officer, farmer, Vermont Republican. Orleans County prosecutor (1865, 1866), state representative (1868-1870), state senate (1876), U.S. Representative (1881-1883, 1885-1901).

GROVE, WILLIAM BARRY *(b Jan. 15, 1764, Fayetteville, N.C.; d March 30, 1818, Fayetteville)* Lawyer, banker, North Carolina Federalist. State house of commons (1786, 1788, 1789), federal Constitution ratification convention delegate (1788, 1789), U.S. Representative (1791-1803).

GROVER, LA FAYETTE *(b Nov. 29, 1823, Bethel, Maine; d May 10, 1911, Portland, Ore.)* Lawyer who began practice in the Oregon Territory (1851) and grew with the area, becoming one of its leading Democrats. In the territory he served as second judicial district prosecutor and territorial auditor of public accounts (1851, 1852), territorial representative (1853) and speaker (1855), Rogue River Indian War auditor of spoliation claims (1854) and Oregon and Washington costs (1856), delegate to convention that framed state constitution (1857). After statehood, he was one of Oregon's first U.S. Representatives (Feb. 15 to March 3, 1859), governor (1870-1877), U.S. Senate (1877-1883).

GROW, GALUSHA AARON *(b Aug. 31, 1823, Ashford, Conn.; d March 31, 1907, Glenwood, Pa.)* Lawyer; railroad, lumber, oil and coal developer; a leading advocate of homesteading legislation, Pennsylvania Free-Soil Democrat who became one of the most vocal new Republicans of the pre-Civil War period. U.S. Representative (1851-1863, 1894-1903) and speaker of the House (1861-1863), GOP National Convention delegate (1864, 1884, 1892).

GRUNDY, FELIX *(b Sept. 11, 1777, Berkeley County, Va.; d Dec. 19, 1840, Nashville, Tenn.)* Lawyer in whose office James K. Polk studied for the bar, Kentucky and Tennessee Democrat who was one of the foremost advocates of the War of 1812. In Kentucky: state constitutional convention delegate (1799), state representative (1800-1805), state supreme court judge (1806) and chief justice (1807). In Tennessee: U.S. Representative as a War Democrat (1811-1814), state representative (1815-1819), U.S. Senate (1829-1838, 1839 until death), U.S. attorney general in the Van Buren cabinet (1838-1839).

GUDGER, JAMES MADISON, JR. *(b Oct. 22, 1855, Madison County, N.C.; d Feb. 29, 1920, Asheville, N.C.)* Lawyer, North Carolina Democrat. State senate (1900), sixteenth district state solicitor (1901, 1902), U.S. Representative (1903-1907, 1911-1915). Father of Katherine G. Langley.

GUERNSEY, FRANK EDWARD *(b Oct. 15, 1866, Dover, Maine; d Jan. 1, 1927, Boston, Mass.)* Lawyer, banker, Maine Republican. Piscataquis County treasurer (1890-1896), state representative (1897-1899) and senator (1903), GOP National Convention delegate (1908), U.S. Representative (1908-1917).

GUEVARA, PEDRO *(b Feb. 23, 1879, Santa Cruz, Philippine Islands; d Jan. 19, 1937, Manila)* Filipino freedom fighter who took part in the revolt against Spanish rule, helped promote the Biakna-bato peace agreement (1897), then served throughout the Spanish-American War and Philippine Insurrection and, when they were over, helped to maintain the peace; journalist, lawyer, and politically a Nationalist. Philippine representative (1909-1912) and senator (1916-1922), chairman of the Philippine delegation to the Far Eastern Bar Conference in Peking, China (1921), resident commissioner to the United States (1923-1936).

GUFFEY, JOSEPH F. *(b Dec. 29, 1870, Guffey's Station, Pa.; d March 6, 1959, Washington, D.C.)* Utilities executive, oil producer, Pennsylvania Democrat who was a national committeeman (1920-1932) and a U.S. Senator (1935-1947).

GUGGENHEIM, SIMON *(b Dec. 30, 1867, Philadelphia, Pa.; d Nov. 2, 1941, New York City)* Philanthropist-financier who made a fortune in mining and smelting and, among his other charities, created the John Simon Guggenheim Foundation in memory of his son; Colorado Republican. Presidential elector on the Roosevelt-Fairbanks ticket (1904), U.S. Senate (1907-1913).

GUNN, JAMES *(b March 13, 1753, Virginia; d July 30, 1801, Louisville, Ga.).* Lawyer, Revolutionary Army officer, Georgia patriot who was twice elected to the Continental Congress (1788, 1789) but did not serve. U.S. Senate (1789-1801). (Not to be confused with James Gunn of Idaho—see next entry.)

GUNN, JAMES *(b March 6, 1843, County Fermanagh, Ireland; d Nov. 5, 1911, Boise, Idaho)* Teacher, Union Army officer, itinerant journalist in Colorado (where he was mayor of Georgetown for three years), Nevada, California, and Idaho where he set his roots and became an active Populist. Member of state's first senate (1890), editor of the *Boise Sentinel* (1892-1897), U.S. Representative (1897-1899). (Not to be confused with James Gunn of Georgia—see previous entry.)

GUTHRIE, JAMES *(b Dec. 5, 1792, Nelson County, Ky.; d March 13, 1869, Louisville, Ky.)* Lawyer, real estate speculator, road builder, railroad executive who gave Union forces full use of his Louisville & Nashville line (1861-1865) to aid in conquest of the Confederate Southwest, Kentucky Unionist Democrat who founded and was president of the University of Louisville.

Commonwealth attorney (1820), state representative (1827-1829), state senate (1831-1840), state constitutional convention president (1849), U.S. secretary of the treasury in the Pierce cabinet (1853-1857), delegate to peace-between-states conference (1861), Democratic National Convention delegate (1864), U.S. Senate (1865-1868) resigning because of health, Union National Convention delegate (1866).

GUYER, ULYSSES SAMUEL (b Dec. 13, 1868, Lee County, Ill.; d June 5, 1943, Bethesda, Md., Naval Hospital) Educator, lawyer, Kansas Republican. St. John schools superintendent (1896-1901), Kansas City city court judge (1907-1909), mayor (1909-1910), U.S. Representative (1924-1925, 1927 until death).

GWIN, WILLIAM McKENDREE (b Oct. 9, 1805, Sumner County, Tenn.; d Sept. 3, 1885, New York City) Lawyer, physician, farmer, Mississippi and California Democrat whose sympathies for the South during the Civil War got him into trouble with both the United States and Mexican governments when his scheme to relocate Southerners in Chihuahua and Sonora won the support of Napoleon III but not of Emperor Maximilian who shipped him back to the states where he was imprisoned for eight months (1865-1866). Thus ended a political career that had taken him from Mississippi as U.S. marshal (1833), U.S. Representative (1841-1843); to California where he was a leading advocate of statehood, a constitutional convention delegate (1849), then one of the new state's first U.S. Senators (1850-1855, 1857-1861); to obscurity in New York after the Civil War.

GWINNETT, BUTTON (b 1732, Down Hatherly, Gloucestershire, England; d May 19, 1777, near Savannah, Ga.). Merchant, trader, planter, Georgia patriot, and signer of the Declaration of Independence who died of wounds received in a duel three days earlier with General Lachlan McIntosh. Delegate to Provincial Congress (1776), member of Continental Congress (1776, 1777), state constitutional convention delegate (1777), Georgia's acting president and commander in chief (February-March, 1777).

H

☆ ☆ ☆

HABERSHAM, JOHN *(b Dec. 23, 1754, near Savannah, Ga.; d Dec. 17, 1799, near Savannah)* Georgia merchant, Revolutionary Army officer who was twice taken prisoner, Washington-appointed Indian agent, one of the commissioners named to adjust the Georgia-South Carolina boundary, and member of the board of trustees that established the University of Georgia. His only political office: member of the 1785 Continental Congress. Brother of Joseph and uncle of Richard W. Habersham.

HABERSHAM, JOSEPH *(b July 28, 1751, Savannah, Ga.; d Nov. 17, 1815, Savannah)* Despite his father's loyalty to the crown, one of Georgia's first and most fiery revolutionists (1774), member of the Council of Safety and Provincial Council (1775), and a leader in the first overt acts of the Revolutionary War: seizure of Savannah's royal powder magazine and a ship from London loaded with military stores. He became an officer in the Continental Army and then, the strife over, settled down to becoming Georgia's leading merchant with a dedication to public service. Delegate to the Continental Congress (1783, 1784), delegate to the federal Constitution ratifying convention (1788), mayor of Savannah (1792); Washington-appointed U.S. postmaster general and serving also throughout the John Adams administration (1795-1801), president of the Branch Bank of the United States in Savannah (1802 until death). Brother of John and uncle of Richard W. Habersham.

HABERSHAM, RICHARD WYLLY *(b Dec. 1786, Savannah, Ga.; d Dec. 2, 1842, Clarksville, Ga.)* Lawyer, Georgia States' Rights Democrat who was chosen governor by a coalition of Whigs and Democrats while on his deathbed. U.S. Representative (1839 until death). Nephew of John and Joseph Habersham.

HADLEY, LINDLEY HOAG *(b June 19, 1861, Parke County, Ind.; d Nov. 1, 1948, Wallingford, Conn.)* Lawyer, Washington State Republican. U.S. Representative (1915-1933) and then remaining on in Washington, D.C., to practice law.

HAGEN, HARLAN FRANCIS *(b Oct. 8, 1914, Lawton, N.Dak.)* Lawyer, California Democrat. Hanford City Council (1948), state assembly (1949-1952), alternate delegate to Democratic National Convention (1956) and delegate (1960), U.S. Representative (1953-1967) serving on the Agriculture and Merchant Marine and Fisheries committees.

HAIGHT, HENRY HUNTLY *(b May 20, 1825, Rochester, N.Y.; d Sept. 2, 1878, San Francisco, Calif.)* Lawyer, California political figure who began his career

283

as a Democrat, switched to Republicanism, and then back to the Democratic fold. As governor (1867-1871) he opposed voting rights for Negroes and supported laws (the so-called yellow peril legislation) prohibiting Chinese from entering the United States. The University of California was established during his administration and he later served on the board of regents.

HAINER, EUGENE JEROME *(b Aug. 16, 1851, Funfkirchen, Hungary; d March 17, 1929, Omaha, Nebr.)* Lawyer, banker, farmer, creamery operator, Nebraska Republican. U.S. Representative (1893-1897).

HALE, EUGENE *(b June 9, 1836, Turner, Maine; d Oct. 28, 1918, Washington, D.C.)* Lawyer, ultraconservative Maine Republican who during thirty years in the U.S. Senate (1881-1911) opposed just about every reform ever proposed, became expert on naval affairs but disillusioned after the Spanish-American War because he viewed growing sea strength as a sign of spreading American imperialism, declined to be postmaster general in the Grant cabinet and secretary of the navy in the Hayes cabinet, and after retirement from politics lived out his years as member of the National Monetary Commission. Hancock County prosecutor (1858-1866), state representative (1867, 1868, 1880), U.S. Representative (1869-1879) and chairman of the GOP Congressional Campaign Committee. Father of Frederick Hale.

HALE, FLETCHER *(b Jan. 22, 1883, Portland, Maine; d Oct. 22, 1931, in U.S. Naval Hospital, Brooklyn, N.Y.)* Lawyer, New Hampshire Republican. Laconia city solicitor (1915), Belknap County solicitor (1915-1920), state constitutional convention delegate (1918), state tax commissioner (1920-1925), U.S. Representative (1925 until death).

HALE, FREDERICK *(b Oct. 7, 1874, Detroit, Mich.; d ———)* Lawyer, Maine Republican. State representative (1904), GOP National Committee member (1912-1918), U.S. Senate (1917-1941). Son of Eugene Hale.

HALE, JOHN PARKER *(b March 31, 1806, Rochester, N.H.; d Nov. 19, 1873, Dover, N.H.)* Lawyer, lecturer with a ready wit and firm convictions, and a New Hampshire political figure whose career was by no means run of the mill. For example, as a Democrat, he was drummed out of the party because of his abolitionist views, ran for the U.S. Senate as an independent, and became the first antislavery candidate ever elected to that body; turned Republican, he became one of the country's foremost GOP spokesmen and was re-elected senator; as a legislator, he was responsible for the elimination of flogging and grog rations in the navy; as chairman of the Senate's Naval Affairs Committee he was accused of influence peddling but survived the scandal; in 1848 he accepted the Liberty party nomination for the presidency but later withdrew in favor of the Free-Soiler, Van Buren; in 1852 he ran for the presidency as the candidate of the Free-Soil party and received 155,825 votes; in 1865 Lincoln appointed him minister to Spain, a post that he filled until 1869 when he was recalled for allegedly dallying with the queen.

State representative (1832) and speaker (1846), U.S. attorney (1834-1841), U.S. Representative (1843-1845) when he disregarded instructions from home and voted against Texas annexation because of the slavery issue and so was read out of the Democratic party, U.S. Senate (1847-1853, 1855-1865).

HALL, BOLLING *(b Dec. 25, 1767, Dinwiddie County, Va.; d Feb. 25, 1836, Autauga County, Ala.)* Revolutionary soldier at sixteen, planter, Georgia Democrat, and War of 1812 hawk. State representative (1800-1802, 1804-1806), U.S. Representative (1811-1817).

HALL, HILAND *(b July 20, 1795, Bennington, Vt.; d Dec. 18, 1885, Springfield, Mass.)* Lawyer, historian who wrote *The History of Vermont* (1868), abolitionist, Vermont Whig turned Republican. State representative (1827), Benton County clerk (1828, 1829), U.S. Representative (1833-1843), state bank commissioner (1843-1846), state supreme court judge (1846-1850), second comptroller of the treasury (1850-1851), U.S. land commissioner for California (1851-1854), governor (1858-1860), delegate to search-for-peace convention (1861), president of Vermont Historical Society (1859-1865).

HALL, JOHN *(b Nov. 27, 1729, Anne Arundel County, Md.; d March 8, 1797, near Annapolis, Md.)* Lawyer, planter, Maryland patriot who served in the Continental Congress (1775, 1777, 1780, 1783, 1784).

HALL, LYMAN *(b April 12, 1724, Wallingford, Conn.; d Oct. 19, 1790, Burke County, Ga.)* Minister, physician, one of the New England Congregationalists who founded Sunbury, Georgia, a town that became the hub of revolutionary thinking with Hall as the leader who later, while a member of the Continental Congress (1775-1778), signed the Declaration of Independence. He also served as governor (1783-1784).

HALL, PHILO *(b Dec. 31, 1865, Wilton, Minn.; d Oct. 7, 1938, Brookings, S.Dak.).* Lawyer, South Dakota Republican. Brookings County prosecutor (1892-1898), state senate (1901-1903), state attorney general (1902-1906), U.S. Representative (1907-1909), GOP state convention delegate (1923).

HALL, THOMAS *(b June 6, 1869, Cliff Mine, Mich.; d Dec. 4, 1958, Bismarck, N.Dak.)* Railroad worker, newspaper-man, rancher, farmer, North Dakota Republican. Fargo city assessor (1903-1907), state secretary of Progressive Republican Committee (1906-1912), railroad commission secretary (1910-1914), North Dakota secretary of state (1912-1924, 1942-1954), U.S. Representative (1924-1933).

HALL, THOMAS H. *(b June, 1773, Prince George County, Va.; d June 30, 1853, Tarboro, N.C.)* Physician, farmer, North Carolina Democrat. U.S. Representative (1817-1825, 1827-1835), state senate (1836).

HALL, URIEL SEBREE *(b April 12, 1852, Randolph County, Mo.; d Dec. 30, 1932, Columbia, Mo.)* Lawyer, farmer, Missouri Democrat, and an educator with an interest in athletics as well as in academics. U.S. Representative (1893-1897), president of Pritchett College (1897-1901), founder of the Hall West Point-Annapolis Coaching School and its president-supervisor (1918-1930). Son of William A. and nephew of Willard P. Hall.

HALL WILLARD PREBLE *(b May 9, 1820, Harper's Ferry, Va.; d Nov. 2, 1882, St. Joseph, Mo.)* Lawyer, farmer, Mexican War officer and coauthor of Kearny Code of civil law for New Mexico, Missouri Democrat. Presidential elector on the Polk-Dallas ticket (1844), U.S. Representative (1847-1853), delegate to constitutional convention that determined to keep Missouri in the Union (1861), provisional lieutenant governor (1861-1864), governor (1864, 1865). Brother of William A. and uncle of Uriel S. Hall.

HALL, WILLIAM *(b Feb. 11, 1775, Surry County, N.C.; d Oct. 7, 1856, Sumner County, Tenn.)* Farmer, Indian fighter, Tennessee Democrat. State representative (1797-1805), state senate (1821-1829) and speaker (1827-1829), governor (1829) to fill the unexpired term of Sam

Houston who resigned, U.S. Representative (1831-1833).

HALL, WILLIAM AUGUSTUS *(b Oct. 15, 1815, Portland, Maine; d Dec. 15, 1888, Randolph County, Mo.)* Lawyer, farmer, Missouri Democrat. Presidential elector on the Polk-Dallas ticket (1844), circuit court judge (1847-1861), state constitutional convention delegate (1861), U.S. Representative (1862-1865), Democratic National Convention delegate (1864). Father of Uriel S. and brother of Willard P. Hall.

HALLECK, CHARLES ABRAHAM *(b Aug. 22, 1900, Demotte, Ind.).* Lawyer, Indiana Republican who served more than thirty years in Congress, many of them as his party's majority or minority leader. Prosecuting attorney for thirtieth judicial circuit (1924-1934), U.S. Representative (1935-1969), majority leader in the Eightieth and Eighty-third Congresses, minority leader in the Eighty-sixth through Ninetieth Congresses. For a time, as minority leader, he and Everett Dirksen, his counterpart in the Senate, held periodic news conferences to refute the claims of the opposition in what came to be known as Ev and Charlie sessions.

HAMER, THOMAS LYON *(b July 1800, Northumberland County, Pa.; d Dec. 2, 1846, Monterey, Mexico, of disease while a brigadier general in the Mexican War)* Teacher, lawyer, Ohio Democrat who, as a U.S. Representative (1833-1839), nominated Ulysses S. Grant for West Point. State representative (1825, 1828) and speaker (1829). Uncle of Thomas R. Hamer.

HAMER, THOMAS RAY *(b May 4, 1864, Vermont, Ill.; d Dec. 22, 1950, Phoenix, Ariz.)* Lawyer, farmer, banker, Idaho Republican who, as a Spanish-American War private rose to lieutenant colonel (1898-1901), was wounded in the Philippines but remained there to serve first as military governor of the island of Cebu and then as associate justice of the Philippine Islands Supreme Court. Back home: GOP state convention delegate (1908, 1912), U.S. Representative (1909-1911). Nephew of Thomas L. Hamer.

HAMILL, JAMES ALPHONSUS *(b March 30, 1877, Jersey City, N.J.; d Dec. 15, 1941, Jersey City)* Lawyer, New Jersey Democrat who was decorated Chevalier of the French Legion of Honor for his work in French literature. State assemblyman (1902-1905), Democratic National Convention delegate (1908), U.S. Representative (1907-1921), Jersey City corporation counsel (1932-1941).

HAMILTON, ALEXANDER *(b Jan. 11, 1755 or 1757, Nevis, in what then was the Danish West Indies; d July 12, 1804, New York City, of wounds inflicted the day before by Aaron Burr in a Weehawken, N.J., duel)* Political scientist, soldier, lawyer, statesman, author of the bulk of *The Federalist* papers that gave rise to the Federalist party.

The common-law son of Rachel Fawcette Levine and James Hamilton, he began work in a Nevis counting house at thirteen, headed it at fifteen, came to New York to be educated at seventeen, wrote two important pamphlets that contributed to the Revolution before he was twenty-one, and thus launched his short-lived career as one of those men who shaped the course of the nation; but always a conservative both in politics and economics. He felt "the rich and the well-born," with a president and senate serving for life, should govern what he referred to as the "American empire." He thought the Constitutional Convention (1787) to which he was a delegate "a mere waste of time" that was producing "motley and feeble" measures, yet the best to be obtained under the circumstances. And so he spoke long and eloquently for the Constitution's adoption at the New York ratifying convention (1788) and thus saw it carried by a vote of 30 to 27.

A man of intense pride and some conceit, Hamilton also suffered from imagined slights, a hot temper, and outspoken opinions. During the 1800 electoral tie between Jefferson and Burr for the presidency that threw the decision before the House, Hamilton called the former a "demagogue" and the latter "despicable." Thus he supported Jefferson as the lesser of two evils. But his spoken and written views of Burr did not stop there and so it was that the duel came about, a one-sided encounter since Hamilton did not fire.

Artillery captain in the Continental Army (1776, 1777), aide de camp to General Washington with the rank of lieutenant colonel (1777-1781) and leader of a storming party at the Battle of Yorktown, member of Continental Congress (1782, 1783, 1787, 1788), member of Annapolis Convention (1786), state assemblyman (1787), the nation's first secretary of the treasury in the Washington cabinet (1789-1795).

HAMILTON, EDWARD LaRUE *(b Dec. 9, 1857, Niles Township, Mich.; d Nov. 2, 1923, St. Joseph, Mich.)* Lawyer, Michigan Republican who served a quarter-century as a U.S. Representative (1897-1921).

HAMILTON, JAMES, JR. *(b May 8, 1786, Charleston, S.C.; drowned Nov. 15, 1857, on a voyage from New Orleans to Galveston)* South Carolina lawyer who served in the U.S. House of Representatives as a States' Rights Free Trader (1822-1829), and was a Democrat governor (1830-1832).

HAMILTON, WILLIAM THOMAS *(b Sept. 8, 1820, Boonsboro, Md.; d Oct. 26, 1888, Hagerstown, Md.)* Lawyer, antisecessionist Maryland Democrat who during the Civil War was a leader in the so-called Peace Party there. Member of state house of delegates

(1848), presidential elector on the Cass-Butler ticket (1848), U.S. Representative (1849-1855), U.S. Senate (1869-1875), governor (1879-1883).

HAMLIN, COURTNEY WALKER *(b Oct. 27, 1858, Brevard, N.C.; d Feb. 16, 1950, Santa Monica, Calif.)* Lawyer, Missouri Democrat. U.S. Representative (1903-1905, 1907-1919).

HAMLIN, HANNIBAL *(b Aug. 27, 1809, Paris, Maine; d July 4, 1891, Bangor, Maine)* Farmer, printer, lawyer, Maine Democrat turned Republican who was vice president during the Lincoln administration (1861-1865). State representative (1836-1840, 1847) and speaker (1837, 1839, 1840), U.S. Representative (1843-1847), U.S. Senate (1848-Jan. 8, 1857), governor (Jan. 8-Feb. 20, 1857) and again U.S. Senate (1857-1861) until resigning to become vice president, minister to Spain (1881-1882).

HAMMER, WILLIAM CICERO *(b March 24, 1865, Randolph County, N.C.; d Sept. 26, 1930, Asheboro, N.C.)* Educator, lawyer, editor-publisher of the *Asheboro Courier*, North Carolina Democrat. Asheboro superintendent of public instruction (1891-1895, 1899-1901), mayor, councilman, and school commissioner (1895-1899), superior court solicitor (1901-1914), U.S. attorney (1914-1920), U.S. Representative (1921 until death).

HAMMOND, JAMES HENRY *(b Nov. 15, 1807, Newberry District, S.C.; d Nov. 13, 1864, Beach Island, S.C.)* Lawyer, farmer, South Carolina Democrat and orator with a will of his own and a willingness to speak his thoughts and suit his actions to his words. For example, although himself a member of the U.S. Senate (1857 until retiring on Nov. 11, 1860, because of Lincoln's election as president) he termed it "a vulgar set of sharpshooters, country court lawyers, and newspaper politicians." His best-remembered speech (delivered March 4, 1858, after William H. Seward had boasted that the North would rule a conquered South): "You dare not make war on cotton. . . . No power on earth dares make war upon it. . . . Cotton is king."

U.S. Representative as a States' Rights Free Trader (1835-1836), governor (1842-1844).

HAMMOND, WINFIELD SCOTT *(b Nov. 17, 1863, Southboro, Mass.; d Dec. 30, 1915, Clinton, La.)* Educator, lawyer, Minnesota Democrat. Watonwan County prosecutor (1895, 1896, 1900-1905), member of state board of normal school directors (1896-1900), U.S. Representative (1907-1914), governor (1914 until death).

HAMPTON, WADE *(b 1752, Virginia; d Feb. 4, 1835, Columbia, S.C.)* South Carolina patriot who was a Revolutionary officer, found the military life so much to his liking that he was still in the army in the War of 1812, and managed to be not only an active Democrat but also a farmer who was said to be the wealthiest planter in the United States (in 1830 he owned 3,000 slaves). U.S. Representative (1795-1797, 1803-1805), presidential elector on the Jefferson-Burr ticket (1801). Grandfather of the following.

HAMPTON, WADE *(b March 28, 1818, Charleston, S.C.; d April 11, 1902, Columbia, S.C.)* Planter, Confederate officer who took cavalry command upon death of J. E. B. Stuart, South Carolina Democrat during whose gubernatorial years (1876-1879) white supremacy was restored. U.S. Senate (1879-1891), U.S. railroad commissioner (1893-1897). Grandson of the preceding.

HANCOCK, CLARENCE EUGENE *(b Feb. 13, 1885, Syracuse, N.Y.; d Jan. 3, 1948, Washington, D.C.)* Lawyer, Wesleyan University trustee, New York Republican. U.S. Representative (1927-1947).

HANCOCK, JOHN *(b Jan. 12, 1737, Quincy, Mass.; d Oct. 8, 1793, Quincy).* Boston merchant who inherited a fortune at twenty-seven, then turned his talents to politics, became a symbol of the pre-Revolutionary patriotic movement, a militia commander during the war, and the first man to sign the Declaration of Independence.

Member of the provincial legislature (1766-1772), Provincial Congress president (1774), member of the Continental Congress (1775-1780, 1785, 1786) and its president (1775-1777), delegate to state constitutional convention (1780), governor (1780-1785, 1787 until death). (Not to be confused with John Hancock of Texas—see next entry.)

HANCOCK, JOHN *(b Oct. 24, 1824, Jackson County, Ala.; d July 19, 1893, Austin, Tex.)* Lawyer, rancher, Texas Democrat who refused to take the oath of allegiance to the Confederate States and so was expelled from the state house of representatives (he served 1860-1861) and lived out the Civil War years in the North. Texas second judicial district judge (1851-1855), state constitutional convention delegate (1866), U.S. Representative (1871-1877, 1883-1885). (Not to be confused with John Hancock of Massachusetts—see previous entry.)

HAND, THOMAS MILLET *(b July 7, 1902, Cape May, N.J.; d Dec. 26, 1956, Cold Spring, N.J.)* Lawyer, real estate broker, publisher of the *Cape May Star and Wave* (1940 until death), New Jersey Republican. Cape May County clerk of the Board of Chosen Freeholders (1924-1928), county prosecutor (1928-1933), mayor of Cape May (1937-1944), U.S. Representative (1945 until death).

HANLY, JAMES FRANKLIN *(b April 4, 1863, Champaign County, Ill.; d Aug. 1, 1920, Tuscarawas County, Ohio, in an automobile accident)* Teacher, lawyer, editor, Indiana Republican and dry lecturer who was the Prohibition party's candidate for president (1916) and polled 220,506 votes. State senate (1890, 1891), U.S. Representative (1895-1897), governor (1905-1909).

HANNA, JOHN ANDRE *(b 1762, Flemington, N.J.; d July 23, 1805, Harrisburg, Pa.)* Lawyer, Pennsylvania Anti-Federalist and military leader who commanded the Dauphin County Brigade during the Whisky Insurrection of 1793. Delegate to state convention that ratified federal Constitution (1787), secretary of the Anti-Federal conference (1788), state representative (1791), U.S. Representative (1797 until death).

HANNA, LOUIS BENJAMIN *(b Aug. 9, 1861, New Brighton, Pa.; d April 23, 1948, Fargo, N.Dak.)* Lumberman, merchant, farmer, banker, Fargo College trustee, North Dakota Republican. State representative (1895-1897), state senate (1897-1901, 1905-1909), chairman of GOP state central committee (1902-1908), GOP National Convention delegate (1904), U.S. Representative (1909-1913), governor (1913-1917), chairman of state GOP campaign committee (1924).

HANNA, MARCUS "MARK" ALONZO *(b Sept. 24, 1837, New Lisbon, Ohio; d Feb. 15, 1904, Washington, D.C.)* Business entrepreneur, banker, and leading official of Cleveland street railway system who openly backed candidates favorable to his interests, William McKinley's mentor who saved him from financial disaster in the 1893 panic and then gained for him the 1896 presidential nomination on the first ballot. He was rewarded with the chairmanship of the GOP National Committee, and then raised campaign funds by assessing business and banking interests. He always defended labor's right to organize and played a major role in settlement of the 1902 coal strike.
  GOP national convention delegate

(1884, 1888, 1896), U.S. Senate, first by appointment and then by election (1897 until death). Hanna was being prominently mentioned for the 1904 GOP presidential nomination when he died.

HANNEGAN, EDWARD ALLEN *(b June 25, 1807, Hamilton County, Ohio; d Feb. 25, 1859, St. Louis, Mo.)* Teacher, farmhand, lawyer, orator, Indiana Democrat and fierce advocate of Oregon-country expansionism who sent the cry "54° 40′ or fight" ringing throughout the land. State representative (1832, 1833, 1841, 1842), U.S. Representative (1833-1837), Laporte Land Office register (1839), U.S. Senate (1843-1849), minister to Prussia (March, 1949) until recalled (January, 1850) because of his blunt talk and a taste for rum.

HANSBROUGH, HENRY CLAY *(b Jan. 30, 1848, Randolph County, Ill.; d Nov. 16, 1933, Washington, D.C., and his ashes were sprinkled under an elm tree on the Capitol grounds)* Printer, newspaper publisher, North Dakota Republican. Mayor of Devils Lake (1885-1888), GOP National Convention delegate (1888, 1892, 1900) and national committeeman (1888-1896), U.S. Representative (1889-1891), U.S. Senate (1891-1909).

HANSON, ALEXANDER CONTEE *(b Feb. 27, 1786, Annapolis, Md.; d April 23, 1819, Howard County, Md.)* Lawyer, Maryland Federalist, and founding editor-publisher of the *Republican* (Baltimore) whose plant was destroyed by a mob two days after the start of the War of 1812 because of editorials criticizing the administration. U.S. Representative (1813-1816), U.S. Senate (1816 until death). Grandson of John Hanson.

HANSON, JOHN *(b April 3, 1715, Mulberry Grove, Md.; d Nov. 15, 1783, Oxon Hill, Md.)* Farmer, Maryland patriot who was president of the Continental

Congress (1781-1782), a signer of the Articles of Confederation and nine times a member of the state house of delegates. State senate (1757-1773), delegate to General Congress at Annapolis (1774), Frederick County treasurer (1775), member of Maryland convention (1775) that issued Freemen declaration, member of Continental Congress (1780-1783). Grandfather of Alexander C. Hanson.

HARALSON, HUGH ANDERSON (b Nov. 13, 1805, Greene County, Ga.; d Sept. 25, 1854, Lagrange, Ga.) Lawyer, farmer, Georgia Democrat. State representative (1831, 1832), state senate (1837, 1838), U.S. Representative (1843-1851).

HARALSON, JEREMIAH (b April 1, 1846, Muscogee County, Ga.; d about 1916, near Denver, Colo., in a hunting accident) Self-educated slave who relocated in Alabama after the Emancipation, became a farmer, preacher (and later a Colorado miner), and showed a keen interest in politics as a Republican. Alabama representative (1870), state senate (1872), U.S. Representative (1875-1877) after agreeing to a runoff election and successfully refuting a charge of fraud.

HARDIN, BENJAMIN (b Feb. 29, 1784, Westmoreland County, Pa.; d Sept. 24, 1852, Bardstown, Ky.) Lawyer, Kentucky Whig. State representative (1810, 1811, 1824, 1825), state senate (1828-1832), U.S. Representative (1815-1817, 1819-1823, 1833-1837), Kentucky secretary of state (1844-1847), state constitutional convention delegate (1849).

HARDING, WARREN GAMALIEL (b Nov. 2, 1865, Blooming Grove, Ohio; d Aug. 2, 1923, San Francisco, Calif.). Twenty-ninth president (Ohio Republican), 1921-1923, who died in office; administration remembered for Teapot Dome and other scandals; U.S. Senator.

Oldest of eight children born to farmer father who later became a doctor, Harding attended Caledonia public schools then Ohio Central College (1879-1882) at Iberia, briefly studied law, taught school, worked in the insurance business, and then went to work on a newspaper. He liked newspaper work and, with a friend (whom he later bought out), purchased a struggling weekly, the Marion Star, which prospered and eventually became a daily.

The tall, handsome, easy-going Harding was likable and fit easily into the social and civic life of Marion. He married (1891) divorcee Florence Kling De Wolfe, daughter of a Marion banker, whose ambitions had an influence on Harding's future. The couple had no children of their own but Mrs. Harding had a son by her former husband.

Member of state legislature (1899-1903); with the assistance of Harry M. Daugherty (political manipulator who thereafter became his close associate) nominated and elected lieutenant governor (1904-1905); unsuccessful GOP candidate for governor (1910); an eloquent speaker, Harding was chosen to nominate William Howard Taft at the national convention of 1912; U.S. Senate (1915 until he resigned to become president in 1921), where he was a member of the Foreign Relations Committee; temporary chairman (1916) of GOP National Convention, making the keynote speech. At the 1920 GOP National Convention, Harding was chosen as a dark-horse presidential candidate (with Calvin Coolidge as his running mate). He conducted a front-porch campaign in which he gave the impression to both those in favor and those against the League of Nations (a principal issue of the election) that he was on their side and promised a return to "normalcy" to a country weary of war and Wilson's idealism. He easily defeated Democratic candidate James M. Cox.

As President, Harding's most outstanding achievement in foreign affairs was the Washington Disarmament Conference (1921). He brought an end to the League of Nations question by making treaties with Germany and her allies that excluded the League Covenant.

On the home front, Harding's irresponsibility in appointments resulted in some of the worst corruption to occur in any administration. Secretary of the Interior Albert B. Fall was convicted of accepting a bribe from private oil interests (the Teapot Dome scandal); although he was not convicted, Attorney General Harry M. Daugherty was brought to trial for corrupt actions. Before these and other scandals became public knowledge, Harding set out on a speaking tour of the West and Alaska (June 1923) to try to restore some of the popularity that was slipping away from his administration. On the return journey, he became ill in Seattle with what at the time was thought to be food poisoning and died a few days later in San Francisco where doctors said he was suffering from pneumonia. No autopsy was performed so exact cause of death was not determined.

HARDWICK, THOMAS WILLIAM *(b Dec. 9, 1872, Thomasville, Ga.; d Jan. 31, 1944, Sandersville, Ga.)* Lawyer, Georgia Democrat. State representative (1890-1899, 1901, 1902), Washington County prosecutor (1895-1897), U.S. Representative (1903-1914), U.S. Senate (1914-1919), governor (1921-1923), special assistant to the U.S. attorney general (1923-1924).

HARDY, GUY URBAN *(b April 4, 1872, Abingdon, Ill.; d Jan. 26, 1947, Canon City, Colo.)* Teacher, newspaper editor-publisher, Colorado Republican. Canon City postmaster (1900-1904), president of the National Editorial Association (1918, 1919), U.S. Representative (1919-1933).

HARDY, PORTER, JR. *(b June 1, 1903, Bon Air, Va.)* Accountant, businessman, farmer, Virginia Democrat. U.S. Representative (1947-1969) serving on the Armed Services and Government Operations committees.

HARDY, RUFUS *(b Dec. 16, 1855, Monroe County, Miss.; d March 13, 1943, Corsicana, Tex.)* Lawyer, Texas Democrat. Navarro County prosecutor (1880-1884), thirteenth judicial district attorney (1884-1888), district judge (1888-1896), chairman of the Texas Sound Money Democracy (1896), U.S. Representative (1907-1923).

HARLAN, ANDREW JACKSON *(b March 29, 1815, Clinton County, Ohio; d May 19, 1907, Savannah, Mo.)* Lawyer, Indiana Democrat who was voted out of the party for voting against repeal of the Missouri Compromise while a U.S. Representative (1853-1855), declined renomination by the People's party, migrated to the Dakota Territory and became the Republican speaker of the territorial house of representatives (1861), remained there until driven out by Indians, moved to Missouri where he was a state representative (1864-1868) and house speaker (1867, 1868), and then on to Kansas where he was postmaster of Wakeeney (1890-1894).

HARLAN, JAMES *(b Aug. 26, 1820, Clark County, Ill.; d Oct. 5, 1899, Mount Pleasant, Iowa)* Lawyer, Iowa Whig–Free-Soiler–Republican whose most-lasting claim to fame is that he fired Walt Whitman from a clerk's job while secretary of the interior in the Andrew Johnson cabinet (1865-1867). State superintendent of public instruction (1847), president of Iowa Wesleyan University (1853-1855), U.S. Senate (1857-1865, 1867-1873), delegate to search-for-peace convention (1861), delegate to Philadelphia loyalist convention (1866), presiding judge of the court of commissioners of *Alabama* claims (1882-1885).

HARMANSON, JOHN HENRY *(b Jan. 15, 1803, Norfolk, Va.; d Oct. 24, 1850, New Orleans, La.)* Farmer, lawyer, Louisiana Democrat. State senate (1844), U.S. Representative (1845 until death).

HARMER, ALFRED CROUT *(b Aug. 8, 1825, Germantown, Pa.; d March 6, 1900, Germantown)* Shoe manufacturer, coal wholesaler with railroad interests, Pennsylvania Republican. Philadelphia councilman (1856-1860) and recorder of deeds (1860-1863), GOP National Convention delegate (1865); U.S. Representative (1871-1875, 1877 until death) for a total of almost thirty years in Congress.

HARNETT, CORNELIUS *(b April 20, 1723, Chowan County, N.C.; d April 20, 1781, while a British prisoner in Wilmington, N.C.)* Merchant, a leading Southern statesman during the Revolutionary period whom history often refers to as "the Samuel Adams of North Carolina."

Member of the colonial assembly (1754-1775), chairman of the Cape Fear Sons of Liberty and leader of North Carolina's Stamp Act resistance (1765, 1766), Committee of Correspondence (1773, 1774), Wilmington Committee of Safety chairman (1774, 1775), member of the Provincial Congress (1775, 1776) and its president (1776); president of the provincial council (1775, 1776) and thus the new government's chief executive, member of the Continental Congress (1777-1780) and signer of the Articles of Confederation.

HARPER, ALEXANDER *(b Feb. 5, 1786, near Belfast, Ireland; d Dec. 1, 1860, Zanesville, Ohio).* Lawyer, Ohio Whig. State representative (1820, 1821), pres-

ident-judge of the common pleas court (1822-1836), U.S. Representative (1837-1839, 1843-1847, 1851-1853).

HARPER, ROBERT GOODLOE *(b January, 1765, near Fredericksburg, Va.; d Jan. 14, 1825, Baltimore, Md.)* Revolutionary soldier at fifteen, surveyor, teacher, lawyer, War of 1812 general, South Carolina and Maryland Democrat turned Federalist whose interest in politics turned to Negro colonization in Africa and, as a founding member of the American Colonization Society, suggested Liberia and Monrovia as the names for the colony and its capital. In South Carolina: state representative (1790-1795), U.S. Representative (1795-1801) and the Federalist floor leader (1797-1801). In Maryland: U.S. Senate (1816) resigning because of his other interests.

HARRELD, JOHN WILLIAM *(b Jan. 24, 1872, Butler County, Ky.; d Dec. 26, 1950, Oklahoma City, Okla.)* Teacher, lawyer, oil producer, Oklahoma Republican. Butler County prosecutor (1892-1896), referee in bankruptcy (1908-1915), U.S. Representative (1919-1921), U.S. Senate (1921-1927).

HARRINGTON, VINCENT FRANCIS *(b May 16, 1903, Sioux City, Iowa; d Nov. 29, 1943, Rutlandshire, England, while an Army Air Corps major)* University of Portland (Oreg.) instructor and athletic director, mortgage company executive, Iowa Democrat. State senate (1933-1937), U.S. Representative (1937-1942) resigning to enter military service.

HARRIS, BENJAMIN GWINN *(b Dec. 13, 1805, St. Marys County, Md.; d April 4, 1895, near Leonardtown, Md.)* Lawyer, Maryland Democrat who while a U.S. Representative (1863-1867) was sentenced by a military court to three years at hard labor and prohibited from ever again holding federal office for giving shelter to two Confederate soldiers. President Johnson remitted the sentence.

HARRIS, BENJAMIN WINSLOW *(b Nov. 10, 1823, East Bridgewater, Mass.; d Feb. 7, 1907, East Bridgewater)* Lawyer, Massachusetts Republican. State senate (1857), state representative (1858), southeastern district attorney (1858-1866), second district internal revenue collector (1866-1873), U.S. Representative (1873-1883), Plymouth County probate judge (1887-1906). Father of Robert O. Harris.

HARRIS, ISHAM GREEN *(b Feb. 10, 1818, Franklin County, Tenn; d July 8, 1897, Washington, D.C.)* Lawyer, Confederate Army officer, and Tennessee Democrat who, as governor (1857-1862), led the movement for secession and had much to do with the legislature's adoption of a declaration of independence after Fort Sumter was fired upon. State senate (1847), presidential elector (1848, 1856), U.S. Representative (1849-1853), U.S. Senate (1877 until death) serving as president pro tem (1893-1895).

HARRIS, JOHN THOMAS *(b May 8, 1823, Browns Gap, Va.; d Oct. 14, 1899, Harrisonburg, Va.)* Lawyer, Virginia Democrat. Rockingham County commonwealth attorney (1852-1859), presidential elector (1856, 1888), U.S. Representative (1859-1861, 1871-1881), state delegate (1863-1865), twelfth judicial district judge (1866-1869), Democratic state convention chairman (1884).

HARRIS, OREN *(b Dec. 20, 1903, Belton, Ark.)* Lawyer, Arkansas Democrat. Union County deputy prosecuting attorney (1933-1936), thirteenth judicial district prosecuting attorney (1936-1940), Democratic state convention delegate (1936, 1940), national convention (1944), U.S. Representative (1941-

1966) serving as chairman of the Interstate and Foreign Commerce Committee.

HARRIS, ROBERT ORR *(b Nov. 8, 1854, Boston, Mass.; d June 13, 1926, Brockton, Mass.)* Lawyer, Massachusetts Republican. State representative (1889), southeastern district attorney (1891-1901), superior court associate judge (1902-1911), U.S. Representative (1911-1913), U.S. attorney (1921-1924). Son of Benjamin W. Harris.

HARRIS, SAMPSON WILLIS *(b Feb. 23, 1809, Elbert County, Ga; d April 1, 1857, Washington, D.C.)* Lawyer, Alabama Democrat. State representative (1834, 1835), eighth circuit solicitor (1841), state senate (1844, 1845), U.S. Representative (1847-1857).

HARRIS, WILLIAM ALEXANDER, SR. *(b Aug. 24, 1805, Fauquier County, Va.; d March 28, 1864, Pike County, Mo.).* Lawyer, Washington newspaper editor, Virginia Democrat. State house of delegates (1830-1831), presidential elector on the Van Buren-Johnson ticket (1840), U.S. Representative (1841-1843), chargé d'affaires to Argentina (1846-1851), U.S. Senate printer (1857-1859). Father of the following.

HARRIS, WILLIAM ALEXANDER, JR. *(b Oct. 29, 1841, Loudon County, Va.; d Dec. 20, 1909, Chicago, Ill.)* Civil engineer, rancher, Confederate Army officer, Kansas Populist-Democrat. U.S. Representative as a Populist (1893-1895), state senate (1896), U.S. Senate as a Democrat (1897-1903), unsuccessful candidate for governor (1906). Son of the preceding.

HARRIS, WILLIAM JULIUS *(b Feb. 3, 1868, Cedartown, Ga.; d April 18, 1932, Washington, D.C.)* Banker, insurance broker, Georgia Democrat. Private secretary to U.S. Senator Alexander S. Clay (1904-1909), state senate (1911, 1912), chairman of state Democratic committee (1912, 1913), U.S. Census Bureau director and acting secretary of the U.S. Department of Commerce (1913-1915), member of the Federal Trade Commission (1915-1918) and its chairman (1917-1918), U.S. Senate (1919 until death).

HARRISON, BENJAMIN *(b April 5, 1726, Charles City County, Va.; d April 24, 1791, Charles City County)* Manager of family estate, father of one President (William Henry Harrison) and great-grandfather of another (Benjamin Harrison), one of Virginia's most eloquent Revolutionary statesmen, and a signer of the Declaration of Independence.

Member of colonial house of burgesses (1749-1775) and member of the committee that drew up remonstrances to the king and to Parliament (1764), Virginia revolutionary convention delegate (1775), member of the Continental Congress (1774-1778) when, as chairman of the Committee of the Whole House, he reported the resolution (June 10, 1776) declaring the colonies to be free and independent; state delegate (1776-1782, 1787-1791) and house speaker (1778-1782, 1785, 1786), governor (1782-1784), delegate to state convention that ratified U.S. Constitution (1788).

HARRISON, BENJAMIN *(b Aug. 20, 1833, North Bend, Ohio; d Mar. 13, 1901, Indianapolis, Ind.).* Twenty-third president (Indiana Republican) 1889-1893; Union Army officer; grandson of President William Henry Harrison, and namesake of a great-grandfather who signed the Declaration of Independence; U.S. Senator; lawyer.

Harrison grew up on a 600-acre farm near North Bend, belonging to his father, U.S. Representative John Scott Harrison. Attended Farmers College; graduated (1852) from Miami University, Oxford, Ohio; read law in Cin-

cinnati; admitted to the bar (1853), then (1854) moved to Indianapolis, Ind., where he practiced law, worked hard, and became very successful. For forty years he served as an elder of the Presbyterian Church. Married Caroline Lavinia Scott (1853). The couple had two children. Caroline died in the White House (1892) and (1896) Harrison married her widowed niece, Mrs. Mary Scott Lord Dimmick, by whom he had one child.

Early in the Civil War Harrison was commissioned second lieutenant of Indiana Volunteers and, after helping to raise the Seventieth Indiana Infantry Regiment, became its colonel. Attached to Sherman's army (1864), his command participated in the bloody battles of the Atlanta campaign. Brevetted brigadier general (1865).

Secretary (1858) to the Republican state central committee; Indianapolis city attorney (1857); reporter (1860-1864) of the Indiana Supreme Court, being reelected at the end of the Civil War to serve an additional four years; drafted by his party (1876) as its candidate for governor. "Kid-glove" Harrison, as he was labeled by the Democrats, lost the election to their candidate, James Douglas ("Blue Jeans") Williams, but gained recognition and friends throughout the state; appointed a member (1879-1881) of the newly created Mississippi River Commission; chairman Republican state convention (1878); as chairman (1880) of Indiana delegation to the GOP National Convention he played an important part in nominating Garfield, but turned down the cabinet post Garfield offered him; as U.S. Senator (1881-1887) he served as chairman of the Committee on Territories and gained the support of many veterans by backing pension legislation; defeated for reelection (1886) to the Senate, he was chosen (1888) as GOP presidential candidate to run against Democratic incumbent Grover Cleveland, with tariff as the main issue of the campaign. Although Cleveland received roughly 100,000 more popular votes than did Harrison, the outcome in the electoral college was reversed, with Harrison winning, 233 to 168. Although Harrison was renominated in 1892 to again run against Cleveland, he was defeated. The tariff again was an issue and the first effects of the Panic of 1893 were beginning to be felt.

As president, Harrison went along with regular Republican measures; the highly protective McKinley Tariff Act was passed as well as the Sherman Silver Purchase Act that increased the amount of silver the treasury had to buy each month. He also sent a Hawaiian annexation treaty to the Senate that Cleveland (when he succeeded Harrison) withdrew before it had been voted on.

Harrison retired to his Indianapolis law practice. He served as Venezuela's senior counsel to present its case in a boundary dispute with Great Britain before a Paris arbitration tribunal. He lectured and wrote. Some of his lectures were compiled into a book, *Views of an Ex-President* (1901), and a series of articles was published as the widely sold *This Country of Ours* (1897).

HARRISON, BURR POWELL *(b July 2, 1904, Winchester, Va.)* Lawyer, Virginia Democrat. Attorney for Frederick County (1932-1940), state senate (1940-1942), judge of the seventeenth judicial circuit and the Winchester corporation court (1942-1946), U.S. Representative (1946-1963) serving on the Ways and Means Committee.

HARRISON, BYRON PATTON "PAT" *(b Aug. 29, 1881, Crystal Springs, Miss.; d June 22, 1941, Washington, D.C.)* Lawyer, teacher, Mississippi Democrat. Second district attorney (1905-1910), state Democratic convention delegate (1916), Democratic National Convention delegate (1908, 1920, 1924) and tem-

porary chairman of the latter, U.S. Representative (1911-1919), U.S. Senate (1919 until death) and its president pro tem (1941).

HARRISON, CARTER HENRY *(b Feb. 15, 1825, Fayette County, Ky.; d Oct. 28, 1893, Chicago, Ill., by assassination).* Grand-nephew of Benjamin Harrison who forsook his Kentucky plantation to venture into Chicago real estate, developed a late interest in politics and unknown talents for oratory; author, lawyer, Illinois Democrat who died at the hands of a frustrated jobseeker. Cook County commissioner (1874-1876), U.S. Representative (1875-1879), mayor of Chicago (1879-1887, 1893 until death), unsuccessful candidate for governor (1884), editor-publisher of the *Chicago Times* (1891-1893).

HARRISON, FRANCIS BURTON *(b Dec. 18, 1873, New York City; d Nov. 21, 1957, Flemington, N.J.)* Lawyer, New Jersey Democrat and expert on Philippine affairs who served as adviser to the first four presidents of the new Philippine Republic after independence in 1946. U.S. Representative (1903-1905, 1907-1913), governor general of the Philippine Islands (1913-1921), adviser to the president of the Philippine Commonwealth (1935, 1936, 1942), U.S. commissioner of civil service claims in Manila (1946-1947).

HARRISON, JOHN SCOTT *(b Oct. 4, 1804, Vincennes, Ind.; d May 25, 1878, near North Bend, Ohio)* Farmer, Ohio Whig who served two terms as a U.S. Representative (1853-1857). Son of President William Henry Harrison; father of President Benjamin Harrison.

HARRISON, THOMAS WALTER *(b Aug. 5, 1856, Leesburg, Va.; d May 9, 1935, Winchester, Va.)* Lawyer, editor of the *Winchester Times*, Virginia Democrat. State senate (1887-1894), seventeenth judicial district circuit court judge (1895-1916), state constitutional convention delegate (1901, 1902), U.S. Representative (1916-1922, 1923-1929).

HARRISON, WILLIAM HENRY *(b Feb. 9, 1773, Berkeley Plantation, Charles City County, Va.; d April 4, 1841, White House, Washington, D.C.)* Ninth president (Whig), serving one month in 1841; Indian fighter, U.S. Army general, and public official who negotiated a number of treaties with the Indians.

Son of Benjamin Harrison, a well-to-do planter and Virginia governor, he entered Hampden-Sydney College at fourteen, dropped out to study medicine, but gave that up to join the army as an ensign (1791). Married Anna Symmes (1795) who bore him ten children, one of whom was to become the father of Benjamin Harrison, twenty-third president. Made captain (1797) and given command of Fort Washington.

Secretary of Northwest Territory (1798), territorial delegate to the U.S. Congress (1799-1800) who played an important part in obtaining the Harrison Land Act of 1800 and also in the division of the Northwest Territory into the two territories of Ohio and Indiana; governor of Indiana Territory (1801-1813) and also Indian commissioner. In November 1811, Harrison led about 1,000 men against the Shawnee in the victorious but indecisive battle against their encampment on the banks of Tippecanoe Creek (the source of the nickname "Tippecanoe" which was given to Harrison during the presidential campaign of 1840). Major general in the War of 1812 in command of the Army of the Northwest (1812-1814) and defeated British and Indians (Oct. 5, 1813) at the Battle of the Thames. U.S. Representative from Ohio (1816-1819); Ohio state senate (1819-1821); U.S. Senate from Ohio (1825-1828), resigning to become minister to Colombia under John Quincy Adams and recalled (1829) by President Jackson.

Harrison did surprisingly well as Whig presidential candidate against Van Buren in 1836 so the Whigs ran him again in the campaign of 1840, this time accompanied by a ballyhoo campaign (the first of its kind) that could make today's public relations experts sit up and take notice. The catchy campaign slogan, "Tippecanoe and Tyler too" (John Tyler was Harrison's vice presidential running mate), used by supporters wearing coonskin caps and occupying campaign headquarters built to look like log cabins helped bring out an unprecedented number of voters to cast their ballots for a man presented as a rugged Indian-fighting, cider-drinking frontier hero in opposition to Van Buren who was ridiculed (no more accurately) as an effete aristocrat. The strain of the campaign was too much for Harrison and he died of pneumonia just one month after his inauguration.

HARRISON, WILLIAM HENRY *(b Aug. 10, 1896, Terre Haute, Ind.)* Lawyer, Indiana and Wyoming Republican, and descendant of two U.S. presidents (great-great-grandson of William Henry Harrison and grandson of Benjamin Harrison). Indiana state representative (1927-1929), Wyoming state representative (1945-1950), secretary to Wyoming Interim Committee (1947-1950), U.S. Representative (1951-1955, 1961-1965, 1967-1969) serving on the Appropriations Committee, regional administrator of Housing and Home Finance Agency (1955-1956).

HART, EDWARD JOSEPH *(b March 25, 1893, Jersey City, N.J.; d April 20, 1961, West Allenhurst, N.J.)* Lawyer, New Jersey Democrat. Secretary to the U.S. Excise Commission (1913-1917), chief field deputy of the Internal Revenue Bureau (1916-1921), assistant Jersey City corporation counsel (1930-1934), Democratic state committee chairman (1944-1949), Democratic National Convention delegate (1940, 1944), U.S.

Representative (1935-1955), state Public Utility Commissioner (1955-1960).

HART, JOHN *(b about 1707, Stonington, Conn.; d May 11, 1779, Hunterdon County, N.J.)* Farmer, New Jersey signer of the Declaration of Independence whose estate was devastated by British troops. Member of Provincial Assembly (1761-1771), Hunterdon County judge (1768-1775), member of Provincial Congress (1775) and its vice president (1776), member of Committee of Safety (1775, 1776), Continental Congress (1776), member and speaker of the first state assembly and those that immediately followed (1776, 1777, 1778), chairman of the state council of safety (1777, 1778).

HARTLEY, THOMAS *(b Sept. 7, 1748, Reading, Pa.; d Dec. 21, 1800, Yorktown, Pa.)* Lawyer, Continental Army officer, Indian fighter whose forces avenged Pennsylvania's Wyoming massacre (1778) with a vengeance. Delegate to Pennsylvania provincial convention (1775), state representative (1778), member of Council of Censors (1783), delegate to state convention that ratified U.S. Constitution (1787), U.S. Representative in the first six Congresses (1789 until death).

HARTMAN, CHARLES SAMPSON *(b March 1, 1861, Monticello, Ind.; d Aug. 3, 1929, Great Falls, Mont.)* Lawyer, diplomat, Montana Republican turned Democrat. Gallatin County probate judge (1884-1886), state constitutional convention delegate (1889), U.S. Representative (1893-1899), GOP National Convention delegate (1896), Democratic National Convention delegate (1900), minister to Ecuador (1913-1922), twelfth Montana judicial district judge (1927 until death).

HARVEY, JAMES MADISON *(b Sept. 21, 1833, Monroe County, Va.; d April 15, 1894, near Junction City, Kans.)* Civil engineer who surveyed government lands in New Mexico, Utah, Nevada, and Oklahoma; farmer, Union Army officer, Kansas Republican. State representative (1865, 1866), state senate (1867, 1868), governor (1868-1872), U.S. Senate (1874-1877) to fill a vacancy.

HARVEY, JONATHAN *(b Feb. 25, 1780, Sutton, N.H.; d Aug. 23, 1859, North Sutton, N.H.)* New Hampshire farmer, state representative (1811-1816, 1831-1834, 1838-1840), state senate (1816-1823) and its president (1817-1823), member of executive council (1823-1825), U.S. Representative (1825-1831). Brother of Matthew Harvey.

HARVEY, MATTHEW *(b June 21, 1781, Sutton, N.H.; d April 7, 1866, Concord, N.H.)* Lawyer, New Hampshire Democrat. State representative (1814-1820) and three times house speaker, U.S. Representative (1821-1825), state senate president (1825-1827), member of the executive council (1828, 1829), governor (1830-1831), U.S. district judge (1831 until death). Brother of Jonathan Harvey.

HARVEY, RALPH *(b Aug. 9, 1901, Henry County, Ind.)* Agricultural instructor, farmer, Indiana Republican. Henry County councilman (1932-1942), state representative (1942-1947), U.S. Representative (1947-1959, 1961-1965), member of House Agriculture Committee.

HASKELL, CHARLES NATHANIEL *(b March 13, 1860, Leipsic, Ohio; d July 5, 1933, Oklahoma City, Okla.)* Railroad and telephone line builder, Oklahoma Democrat who served as the state's first governor (1907-1911).

HASKINS, KITTREDGE *(b April 8, 1836, Dover, Vt.; d Aug. 7, 1916, Brattleboro, Vt.)* Lawyer, Union Army officer, Vermont Republican. GOP state committeeman (1869-1872), state's attorney (1870-1872), state representative (1872-1874, 1896-1900) and house speaker (1898-1900), U.S. attorney (1880-1887), state senate (1892-1894), chairman of state commission to establish boundary with Massachusetts (1892-1900), U.S. Representative (1901-1909), Brattleboro municipal court judge (1910) and postmaster (1912-1915).

HASTINGS, WILLIAM WIRT *(b Dec. 31, 1866, Benton County, Ark.; d April 8, 1938, Muskogee, Okla.)* Cherokee Indian, teacher, lawyer, Oklahoma Democrat who on Jan. 22, 1936, was designated by President Roosevelt as chief of the Cherokees for a day in order to sign treaty papers that were a culmination of his long fight while a member of Congress for legislation favorable to his people. Cherokee Nation attorney general (1891-1895), national attorney for the Cherokee Tribe (1907-1914), delegate to both national and state Democratic conventions (1912), presidential elector on the Wilson-Marshall ticket (1912), U.S. Representative (1915-1921, 1923-1935).

HATCH, WILLIAM HENRY *(b Sept. 11, 1833, Scott County, Ky.; d Dec. 23, 1896, Marion County, Mo.)* Lawyer, Confederate Army officer, farmer, Missouri Democrat who, as chairman of the House Agriculture Committee, was responsible for the Hatch Act (1887), first oleomargarine act (1886), meat inspection act (1890), and a leader in the move to raise the Department of Agriculture to cabinet status. U.S. Representative (1879-1895).

HATCHER, ROBERT ANTHONY *(b Feb. 24, 1819, Buckingham County, Va.; d Dec. 4, 1886, Charleston, Mo.)* Lawyer, Confederate Army officer, Missouri Democrat. State representative (1850, 1851), state convention delegate (1862), member of Confederate Congress (1864, 1865), U.S. Representative (1873-1879).

HAUGEN, GILBERT NELSON *(b April 21, 1859, Rock County, Wis.; d July 18, 1933, Northwood, Iowa)* Real estate operator, banker, Iowa Republican who served seventeen terms as a U.S. Representative (1899-1933). Worth County treasurer (1887-1893), state representative (1894-1898). As chairman of the House Agriculture Committee (1919-1931), he was largely responsible for passage of farm-surplus legislation, largely through agitation for the McNary-Haugen bill that Congress twice passed only to see it twice vetoed (1927, 1928).

HAUGEN, NILS PEDERSON *(b March 9, 1849, Modum, Norway; d April 23, 1931, Madison, Wis.)* Lawyer, tax expert, and progressive Wisconsin Republican who helped Governor Robert M. La Follette achieve needed tax reforms. State assemblyman (1879, 1880), state railroad commissioner (1882-1887), U.S. Representative (1887-1895), member of the state tax commission (1901-1921) and its chairman (1911-1921), president of the National Tax Association (1919, 1920), adviser to the Montana Equalization Board (1921-1923).

HAVEN, SOLOMON GEORGE *(b Nov. 27, 1810, Chenango County, N.Y.; d Dec. 24, 1861, Buffalo, N.Y.)* Lawyer, New York Whig. Erie County district attorney (1844-1846), mayor of Buffalo (1846, 1847), U.S. Representative (1851-1857).

HAWES, HARRY BARTOW *(b Nov. 15, 1869, Covington, Ky.; d July 31, 1947, Washington, D.C.)* Lawyer who represented the Republic of Hawaii in U.S. annexation, Missouri Democrat who gave up active political life in order to devote his energies to wildlife conservation. Member of Democratic Notification Committee (1904, 1916), U.S. Representative (1921-1926), U.S. Senate (1926-1933) and coauthor of the Hawes-Cutting bill granting independence to the Philippines.

HAWES, RICHARD *(b Feb. 6, 1797, Caroline County, Va.; d May 25, 1877, Paris, Ky.)* Lawyer, Indian fighter, Kentucky Whig whom Confederate sympathizers installed as provisional governor (1862-1865). State representative (1828, 1829, 1834), U.S. Representative (1837-1841), Bourbon County judge (1866), master commissioner of the circuit and common pleas courts (1867 until death).

HAWKINS, BENJAMIN *(b Aug. 15, 1754, in what is now Warren County, N.C.; d June 6, 1816, Crawford County, Ga.).* Washington's French interpreter during the Revolution, North Carolina Federalist, and a man of wealth and position who gave up the soft life to serve as Indian agent and commissioner and became known as "the beloved man of the Four Nations." Member of state house of commons (1778, 1779, 1784), Continental Congress (1781-1784, 1786, 1787) with time out in 1785 to negotiate treaties with the Creeks and Cherokees, delegate to state convention that ratified U.S. Constitution (1789), U.S. Senate (1789-1795), Washington-appointed commissioner to represent all Indian tribes south of the Ohio River (1796 until death).

HAWLEY, JOHN BALDWIN *(b Feb. 9, 1831, Hawleyville, Conn.; d May 24, 1895, Hot Springs, S.Dak.)* Lawyer, Union Army officer, Illinois Republican. Rock Island postmaster (1865-1866), U.S. Representative (1869-1875), assistant secretary of the treasury (1877-1880).

HAWLEY, JOSEPH ROSWELL *(b Oct. 31, 1826, Stewartsville, N.C.; d March 17, 1905, Washington, D.C.)* Lawyer, Union Army officer, editor of the *Hartford Courant*, Connecticut Free-Soiler who helped to organize the Republican party there. Governor (1866-1867), GOP National Convention chairman (1868) and delegate (1872, 1876, 1880), presidential elector on the Grant-Colfax ticket (1868), U.S. Representative (1872-1875, 1879-1881), U.S. Senate (1881-1905).

HAWLEY, WILLIS CHATMAN *(b May 5, 1864, Benton County, Oreg.; d July 24, 1941, Salem, Oreg.)* Educator, lawyer, businessman, Oregon Republican who served more than a quarter-century in Congress. President of Oregon State Normal School at Drain (1888-1891), president of Willamette University (1893-1902) and professor of history and economics for sixteen years, U.S. Representative (1907-1933).

HAY, JAMES *(b Jan. 9, 1856, Millwood, Va.; d June 12, 1931, Madison, Va.).* Lawyer, Virginia Democrat. Commonwealth attorney (1883-1896), state delegate (1885-1889), Democratic state committeeman and delegate to the national convention (1888), state senate (1893-1897), U.S. Representative (1897-1916), judge of the U.S. Court of Claims (1916-1927).

HAY, JOHN MILTON *(b Oct. 8, 1838, Salem, Ind.; d July 1, 1905, Lake Sunapee, N.H.)* Newspaperman, poet, author, Republican who lived most of his adult life in New York and Washington, D.C., but whose career began in his uncle's law office in Springfield, Ill.—next door to Abraham Lincoln's—to thus launch a career of statesmanship whose first position (as a Lincoln appointee) was titled "pension office clerk" but whose duties were that of assistant private secretary to the president with offices and residence in the White House. The secretary was John G. Nicolay and their joint outstanding contribution to American history was *Abraham Lincoln: A History* (10 volumes, 1890) and *Abraham Lincoln: Complete Works* (2 volumes, 1894).

After Lincoln's assassination, he was secretary of the Paris legation (1865-1867), chargé d'affaires in Vienna (1867-

1868), secretary of the Madrid legation (1869-1870), *New York Tribune* editorial writer (1870-1875), assistant secretary of state (1879-March, 1881), *Tribune* editor for six months (1881), and then spent years in writing and travel until 1896 when he served as a personal adviser to another good friend, William McKinley, in the presidential campaign. He became ambassador to Great Britain (1897-1898) and then secretary of state (1898-1905)—seven momentous years for the United States during which Hay negotiated a peace treaty with Spain, pressed for an "open door" policy with China, delineated the Alaskan-Canadian boundary with Great Britain, signed a series of treaties that made the Panama Canal possible, and settled disputes with Germany over Samoa and with Germany and England over Venezuela.

HAY, MARY GARRETT *(b Aug. 29, 1857, Charlestown, Ind.; d Aug. 29, 1928, New Rochelle, N.Y.)* A woman with a strong sense of political and civic responsibility and active in many organizations, she took an early interest in the temperance movement but this soon broadened to include women's suffrage. A local and state suffrage association official, she went on to become an organizer on the national level, campaigning effectively in many states, including New York, where, partly through her efforts, women's suffrage was won in 1917.

HAYDEN, CARL *(b Oct. 2, 1877, Hayden's Ferry, now Tempe, Ariz.; d Jan. 25, 1972, Mesa, Ariz.)* Merchant, flour miller, Arizona Democrat who served fifteen years as a U.S. Representative and forty-two years in the U.S. Senate before reluctantly retiring at ninety because of advancing infirmities. Tempe councilman (1902-1904), Democratic National Convention delegate (1904), Maricopa County treasurer (1904-1906) and sheriff (1907-1912). Upon Arizona's

admission to the Union, the first man from the new state to be elected to the U.S. House of Representatives (1912-1927), after that came the beginning of the longest stay in U.S. Senate history —March 1927 to May 1968.

One of the Senate's most untiring workhorses, Hayden once was described by Lyndon B. Johnson as the most influential member of both houses of Congress and yet by the *New York Times* as "one man who has never been affected by the arrogance of power." He was chairman of the Appropriations Committee at retirement, before that of the Committee on Rules and Administration, and among many other things is credited with major contributions to the federal roadbuilding program.

Asked once by Franklin D. Roosevelt why he showed so much interest in roads, Hayden is said to have replied: "Because Arizona has two things people will drive thousands of miles to see —the Grand Canyon and the Petrified Forest. They can't get there without roads."

HAYES, EVERIS ANSON *(b March 10, 1855, Waterloo, Wis.; d June 3, 1942, San Jose, Calif.)* Lawyer, miner, fruit grower, California Republican and publisher of the *San Jose Daily Mercury Herald* who served seven terms as a U.S. Representative (1905-1919).

HAYES, RUTHERFORD BIRCHARD *(b Oct. 4, 1822, Delaware, Ohio; d Jan. 17, 1893, Fremont, Ohio)* Nineteenth president (Ohio Whig turned Republican), 1877-1881, who was awarded the election by an electoral commission appointed by Congress after fraud was charged. Civil War general in the Union Army; governor of Ohio; U.S. Representative; lawyer.

Hayes' father died before he was born and the boy's prosperous uncle, Sardis Birchard, helped in his upbringing. He attended private schools in Ohio and Connecticut, graduated from Kenyon College, Gambier, Ohio (1842), and Harvard Law School (1845). He returned to Ohio, was admitted to the bar (1845), and began practice in Lower Sandusky (now Fremont). In 1849 Hayes opened a law office in Cincinnati where he distinguished himself in several criminal trials, enjoyed the cultural life of the community, joined the Sons of Temperance and Odd Fellows, and attended the Episcopal church. By 1852 he had saved enough money to marry attractive Lucy Webb (as White House hostess she would permit no alcoholic beverages to be served and was nicknamed "Lemonade Lucy"). The couple had eight children, three of whom died in infancy.

Hayes had hoped to see hostilities averted through negotiation, but when the Civil War broke out he gave his services in varied ways to the Union Army, including a stint as judge-advocate, trying court-martial cases. But he saw a good deal of action, too, and was severely wounded at South Mountain. First commissioned as major of a regiment of Ohio volunteers, he was eventually (1865) brevetted a major general of volunteers.

Delegate to Republican state convention (1855); city solicitor of Cincinnati (1857-1859). While still in the army, Hayes was nominated to run for the U.S. House of Representatives and was elected even though he refused to leave his post to campaign. Served from 1865 to July 20, 1867, when he resigned to become governor of Ohio (1868-1872, 1876-1877) and, in 1877, resigned as governor to become president.

A split between Republican liberals and the regular party leaders made Hayes the compromise choice for his party's nomination for the presidential candidacy at the 1876 convention. The political turmoil that existed in the country as the result of post-Civil War reconstruction policies was reflected in the election. When Hayes' Democratic opponent, New York reformer Samuel J. Tilden appeared to have won, the Republicans charged fraud in the election returns from South Carolina, Florida, Louisiana, and Oregon. Congress appointed a commission composed of Supreme Court justices, U.S. Senators and Congressmen and it voted, on party lines (Mar. 2, 1877), that Hayes had won by one electoral vote. There seems little doubt that a deal was made between Republican and Southern Democratic leaders and one of Hayes' first acts as president was to withdraw federal troops from the South.

He fought staunchly for civil service reform and a sound fiscal policy. His actions alienated many members of his party just as they did workingmen when he called out federal troops to suppress the railroad strike of 1877.

Hayes did not seek his party's nomination for re-election in 1880. In retirement, he turned to his Ohio home; was trustee of the Peabody Educational Fund, the National Prison Association, and Ohio State University.

HAYNE, ROBERT YOUNG *(b Nov. 10, 1791, St. Paul's Parish, S.C.; d Sept. 24, 1839, Asheville, N.C.)* Lawyer, railroad promoter and president, South Carolina Democrat who engaged in famous debate (1830) with Daniel Webster over the burning issue of the period: the power of the states versus the power of the federal government—nullification. State representative (1814-1818) and house speaker (1818), state attorney general (1818-1822), U.S. Senate (1823-1832) resigning to make way so that his nullification fight could be continued by John C. Calhoun with Haynes moving into the governor's seat (1832-1834); mayor of Charleston (1835-1837), president of the Knoxville convention (1836), president of the Louisville, Cincinnati & Charleston Railroad (1836-1839).

HAYS, CHARLES *(b Feb. 2, 1834, Greene County, Ala.; d June 24, 1879,*

Greene County) Planter, Confederate Army officer, Alabama Democrat. Delegate to Democratic National Convention (1860), state constitutional convention delegate (1867), state senate (1868), U.S. Representative (1869-1877).

HEALD, WILLIAM HENRY *(b Aug. 27, 1864, Wilmington, Del.; d June 3, 1939, Wilmington)* Lawyer, banker, Delaware Republican. National bank examiner for Montana, Idaho, Washington and Oregon (1888-1892), Wilmington postmaster (1901-1905), U.S. Representative (1909-1913), University of Delaware trustee (1915 until death), presidential elector on the Hughes-Fairbanks ticket (1916).

HEALEY, ARTHUR DANIEL *(b Dec. 29, 1889, Somerville, Mass.; d Sept. 16, 1948, Somerville)* Lawyer, Massachusetts Democrat. U.S. Representative (1933-1942) resigning to become a U.S. district judge (1942 until death).

HEALEY, JAMES CHRISTOPHER *(b Dec. 24, 1909, Bronx, N.Y.)* Lawyer, New York Democrat. Attorney for State Labor Relations Board (1938-1940), assistant U.S. attorney for the southern district of N.Y. (1941-1943), U.S. Navy (1943-1946), assistant New York City corporation counsel (1946-1949), counsel to Bronx borough president (1949-1956), U.S. Representative (1956-1965) serving on the Interstate and Foreign Commerce Committee.

HEARST, GEORGE *(b Sept. 3, 1820, Franklin County, Mo.; d Feb. 28, 1891, Washington, D.C.)* Mining school graduate who crossed the plains on foot to prospect in California and upon that foundation built a fortune; mine operator and speculator, rancher, publisher of the *San Francisco Examiner*, California Democrat. State assemblyman (1865, 1866), unsuccessful gubernatorial candidate (1882), U.S. Senate (1886, 1887 until death). Father of William Randolph Hearst.

HEARST, WILLIAM RANDOLPH *(b April 29, 1863, San Francisco, Calif.; d Aug. 14, 1951, Beverly Hills, Calif.)* Head of a vast publishing empire that began in 1886 when his father, George Hearst, gave him the *San Francisco Examiner*, and always a man with a keen interest in politics not only as critical observer and commentator but also as active participant. New York Democrat. U.S. Representative (1903-1907), Municipal Ownership candidate for mayor of New York (1905) reportedly winning the vote but losing the ballot count to Tammany Hall, unsuccessful candidate for governor (1906), unsuccessful Independent candidate for mayor again (1909).

HEATWOLE, JOEL PRESCOTT *(b Aug. 22, 1856, Waterford Mills, Ind.; d April 4, 1910, Northfield, Minn.)* Newspaper editor-publisher of the *Northfield News*; Minnesota Republican. Secretary of GOP state central committee (1886, 1888) and chairman (1890), national convention delegate (1888), state university regent (1890), mayor of Northfield (1894), U.S. Representative (1895-1903).

HEDGE, THOMAS *(b June 24, 1844, Burlington, Iowa; d Nov. 28, 1920, Burlington)* Lawyer, Union soldier, Iowa Republican. U.S. Representative (1899-1907).

HEDGEMAN, ANNA ARNOLD *(b ——, Marshalltown, Iowa)* Negro sociologist, teacher, and civil rights leader. Consultant on racial problems for the Brooklyn Emergency Relief Bureau, executive director (1944-1948) of National Council for the Fair Employment Practices Commission, assistant to administrator (1949-1953) of Federal Security Agency (now Department of Health, Education and Welfare), member (1954-1959) of New York City Mayor Robert F. Wagner's "cabinet," providing liaison with eight city departments.

HEDRICK, ERLAND HAROLD *(b Aug. 9, 1894, Barn, W.Va.; d Sept. 20, 1954, Beckley, W.Va.)* Physician, West Virginia Democrat. Veterans' Administration medical examiner (1919-1944), city and county health officer (1927-1932), U.S. Representative (1945-1953).

HEFLIN, JAMES THOMAS *(b April 9, 1869, Louina, Ala.; d April 22, 1951, Lafayette, Ala.)* Lawyer, Alabama Democrat. Mayor of Lafayette (1893, 1894), register in chancery (1894-1896), state representative (1896-1900), member of Democratic state executive committee (1896-1902), state constitutional convention delegate (1901), Alabama secretary of state (1902-1904), delegate to state Democratic convention (1900) and national (1908), U.S. Representative (1904-1920), U.S. Senate (1920-1931), special assistant to the U.S. attorney general (1936-1937), special representative of the Federal Housing Administration (1935-1936, 1939-1942).

HEIDINGER, JAMES VANDAVEER *(b July 17, 1882, Wayne County, Ill.; d March 22, 1945, Phoenix, Ariz.)* Lawyer, Illinois Republican. Wayne County judge (1914-1926), assistant state attorney general (1927-1933), GOP National Convention delegate (1928), U.S. Representative (1941 until death).

HEITFELD, HENRY *(b Jan. 12, 1859, St. Louis, Mo.; d Oct. 21, 1938, Spokane, Wash.)* Idaho rancher, fruit grower who was elected U.S. Senator as a Populist (1897-1903). State senate (1894-1897), unsuccessful candidate for governor (1904), mayor of Lewiston (1905-1909) and register of the U.S. Land Office there (1914-1922), county commissioner (1930-1936) and twice the chairman of the board.

HELGESEN, HENRY THOMAS *(b June 26, 1857, near Decorah, Iowa; d April 10, 1917, Washington, D.C.)* Merchant, farmer, lumber dealer, North Dakota Republican. State agriculture and labor commissioner (1889-1892), member of Milton Board of Education (1893-1896) and its president (1893, 1894), University of North Dakota regent (1897-1901, 1907-1913), U.S. Representative (1911 until death).

HELM, HARVEY *(b Dec. 2, 1865, Danville, Ky.; d March 3, 1919, Columbus, Miss.)* Lawyer, Kentucky Democrat. State representative (1894), Lincoln County attorney (1897-1905), Democratic National Convention delegate (1900), U.S. Representative (1907 until death).

HELVERING, GUY TRESILLIAN *(b Jan. 10, 1878, Felicity, Ohio; d July 4, 1946, Washington, D.C.)* Lawyer, banker, Kansas Democrat. Marshall County prosecutor (1907-1911), U.S. Representative (1913-1919), mayor of Salina (1926-1930), state Democratic chairman (1930-1934), state highway director (1931, 1932), Roosevelt-appointed commissioner of internal revenue (1933-1943), U.S. district judge (1943 until death).

HEMENWAY, JAMES ALEXANDER *(b March 8, 1860, Boonville, Ind.; d Feb. 10, 1923, Miami, Fla.)* Lawyer, Indiana Republican. Second judicial district prosecutor (1886-1890), GOP state committeeman (1890), U.S. Representative (1895-1905) resigning to become U.S. Senator (1905-1909).

HEMPHILL, JOHN *(b Dec. 18, 1803, Chester District, S.C.; d Jan. 7, 1862, Richmond, Va.)* Teacher, lawyer, Indian fighter, Democratic editor of a nullification newspaper (1832, 1833) who migrated to the new Republic of Texas (1838) and embarked upon a political-judicial career and became known as "the John Marshall of Texas."

Fourth judicial district judge (1840-1842), Mier expedition adjutant general (1842), chief justice of the Texas

Supreme Court (1846-1858), U.S. Senate (1859-1861) and one of fourteen who met (Jan. 6, 1861) and recommended that their states immediately secede and so was expelled from the Senate six months later, member of the Confederate Congress (1861 until death). Uncle of John J. Hemphill.

HEMPHILL, JOHN JAMES *(b Aug. 25, 1849, Chester, S.C.; d May 11, 1912, Washington, D.C.)* Lawyer, South Carolina Democrat. State representative (1876-1882), U.S. Representative (1883-1893). Nephew of John Hemphill and great-uncle of Congressman Robert W. Hemphill.

HEMPHILL, JOSEPH *(b Jan. 7, 1770, Thornburg Township, Pa.; d May 29, 1842, Philadelphia, Pa.)* Lawyer, porcelain manufacturer, Pennsylvania Federalist turned Jackson Democrat who as chairman of the House Committee on Slave Trade held that Missouri's treatment of free Negroes was unconstitutional (1820). State representative (1797-1800, 1805, 1831, 1832), U.S. Representative (1801-1803, 1819-1826) as a Federalist and as a Jackson Democrat (1829-1831), first president-judge of the Philadelphia district court (1811-1819).

HENDERSON, CHARLES BELKNAP *(b June 8, 1873, San Jose, Calif.; d Nov. 8, 1954, San Francisco, Calif.)* Lawyer, telephone and railroad executive, Nevada Democrat who was one of Torrey's Rough Riders in the Spanish-American War. Elko County district attorney (1901-1905), state representative (1905-1907), University of Nevada regent (1907-1917), U.S. Senate to fill a vacancy (1918-1921), Reconstruction Finance Corporation director (1934-1941) and chairman (1941-1947).

HENDERSON, DAVID BREMNER *(b March 14, 1840, Old Deer, Scotland; d Feb. 25, 1906, Dubuque, Iowa)* Union Army officer, lawyer, Iowa Republican who served ten terms in the U.S. House of Representatives (1883-1903), the last two as speaker (1899-1903). Third district internal revenue collector (1865-1869), assistant U.S. attorney for the northern district (1869-1871).

HENDERSON, JAMES PINCKNEY *(b March 31, 1808, Lincolnton, N.C.; d June 4, 1858, Washington, D.C.)* Lawyer, Republic of Texas diplomat who upon statehood became the first governor of Texas (1846-1847), States' Rights Democrat. The republic's attorney general (1836), secretary of state (1837), envoy to Europe (1837-1839), special minister to U.S. to negotiate annexation (1844); delegate to state constitutional convention (1845), U.S. Senate (1857 until death).

HENDERSON, JOHN BROOKS *(b Nov. 16, 1826, Pittsylvania County, Va.; d April 12, 1913, Washington, D.C.).* Teacher, lawyer, Missouri statesman who considered himself a States' Rights Democrat but opposed secession as "a damnable heresy," blamed the Civil War on northern Republicans, yet stuck by the Union throughout it even to introducing the Thirteenth (emancipation) Amendment (1864) because he felt that it would pass only if introduced by a border-state senator. His other chief interests were the Alaska purchase and a better break for Indians.

State representative (1848-1856), presidential elector on the Buchanan-Breckinridge (1856) and Douglas-Johnson (1860) tickets, Democratic National Convention delegate (1860), Union delegate to state secession convention (1861) where he argued long, eloquently, and successfully, to keep Missouri from seceding; U.S. Senate (1862-1869), chairman of a peace commission that successfully negotiated a treaty (1867) with hostile Indian tribes.

The price that he knew he would, and did, pay for his position on slavery, secession, and preservation of the

Union was political oblivion once his term in the Senate was over.

HENDERSON, JOHN STEELE *(b Jan. 6, 1846, Rowan County, N.C.; d Oct. 9, 1916, Salisbury, N.C.)* Confederate soldier, lawyer, North Carolina Democrat. Rowan County register of deeds (1866-1868), state constitutional convention delegate (1875), state representative (1876), state senate (1878, 1900, 1902), member of commission to codify state laws (1881), presiding justice of the county inferior court (1884-1885), U.S. Representative (1885-1895), Salisbury alderman (1900).

HENDERSON, THOMAS *(b Aug. 15, 1743, Freehold, N.J.; d Dec. 15, 1824, Freehold)* Physician, Minuteman, Revolutionary Army officer, New Jersey Federalist. Monmouth County surrogate (1776), member of Provincial Council (1777), elected delegate to Continental Congress (1779) but declined to serve, state assemblyman (1780-1784), master in chancery (1790), vice president of state council (1793, 1794), acting governor (1794), U.S. Representative (1795-1797), common pleas judge (1783-1799), member of state council (1812, 1813).

HENDERSON, THOMAS JEFFERSON *(b Nov. 29, 1824, Brownsville, Tenn.; d Feb. 6, 1911, Washington, D.C.)* Lawyer, Union Army officer, Illinois Republican. State representative (1855, 1856), state senate (1857-1860), presidential elector on the Grant-Colfax ticket (1868), fifth district internal revenue collector (1871), U.S. Representative (1875-1895).

HENDRICKS, THOMAS ANDREWS *(b Sept. 7, 1819, near Zanesville, Ohio; d Nov. 25, 1885, Indianapolis, Ind.)* Lawyer, Indiana Democrat who opposed entry of Negroes into the state; as a U.S. Senator (1863-1869) supported the war yet opposed the Lincoln administra-

tion on such matters as the draft and emancipation; briefly Grover Cleveland's vice president (March 4, 1885, until death). State representative (1848), state senate (1849), state constitutional convention delegate (1851), U.S. Representative (1851-1855), general land office commissioner (1855-1859), unsuccessful candidate for governor (1860), governor (1873-1877), vice presidential candidate on the Tilden ticket (1876). Nephew of William Hendricks.

HENDRICKS, WILLIAM *(b Nov. 12, 1782, Ligonier Valley, Pa.; d May 16, 1850, Madison, Ind.)* Printer-publisher who set up the second press in the Indiana Territory, lawyer, Indiana Democrat, secretary of the Vincennes general assembly (1814, 1815) that preceded statehood in 1816, secretary of first state constitutional convention (1816), U.S. Representative (1816-1822) resigning to become governor (1822-1825) and again resigning, this time to become U.S. Senator (1825-1837), Indiana University trustee (1829-1840). Uncle of Thomas A. Hendricks.

HENEY, FRANCIS JOSEPH *(b March 17, 1859, Lima, N.Y.; d Oct. 31, 1937, Santa Monica, Calif.).* Lawyer, graft and corruption fighter who at first was an ally but later a foe of Hiram Johnson, a California progressive who switched political identity between progressive Democrat and progressive Republican several times and helped to found the state's Progressive party; a man of firm convictions, but never able to garner enough votes for election to public office. A colorful personality, in his younger days he had been teacher, cowboy, miner, Indian trader, and cattle rancher throughout the West. Twice in the course of his legal activities he was involved in gunplay, once killing the defendant in a divorce action in self defense and another time (1908) being shot in the neck while successfully prosecuting San Francisco political boss Abe Ruef on graft charges.

HENNINGS, THOMAS CAREY, JR. *(b June 25, 1903, St. Louis, Mo.; d Sept. 13, 1960, Washington, D.C.)* Lawyer, lecturer, Missouri Democrat. St. Louis assistant circuit attorney (1929-1934), U.S. Representative (1935-1940), St. Louis circuit attorney (1941-1944), U.S. Senate (1951 until death).

HENRY, EDWARD STEVENS *(b Feb. 10, 1836, Gill, Mass.; d Oct. 10, 1921, Rockville, Conn.)* Merchant, banker, Connecticut Republican. State representative (1883), state senate (1887, 1888), GOP National Convention delegate (1888), state treasurer (1889-1893), mayor of Rockville (1894, 1895), U.S. Representative (1895-1913).

HENRY, JOHN *(b November 1750, Dorchester County, Md.; d Dec. 16, 1798, Dorchester County)* Lawyer, Maryland Democrat turned Federalist who before the drawing of party lines served in the Continental Congress (1778-1781, 1784-1787), U.S. Senate (1789-1797) as a Democrat, resigning to become governor (1797-1798) as a Federalist.

HENRY, PATRICK *(b May 29, 1736, Studley, Va.; d June 6, 1799, Red Hill, Va.).* Merchant, lawyer, orator of considerable note, Virginia patriot who, as every history student knows, cried "give me liberty or give me death!" during an impassioned speech (Virginia convention, 1775) in favor of armed resistance to British rule. But, what is not so well-known, he turned down offers of high office perhaps more than any other American, past or present. Among them: U.S. Senator, secretary of state, chief justice of the United States, ambassador to France. Another fact, also not so well-known, is that he strongly opposed the federal Constitu-

tion because of a firm conviction that it would infringe upon individual and state rights.

Member of the colonial house of burgesses (1765), Continental Congress (1774-1776), governor (1776-1779, 1784-1786), delegate to state convention that ratified the Constitution despite his opposition (1788).

HENRY, ROBERT LEE *(b May 12, 1864, Linden, Tex.; d July 9, 1931, Houston, Tex.)* Lawyer, Texas Democrat. Mayor of Texarkana (1890-1891), assistant Texas attorney general (1891-1896), U.S. Representative (1897-1917). Great-great-great grandson of Patrick Henry.

HEPBURN, WILLIAM PETERS *(b Nov. 4, 1833, Wellsville, Ohio; d Feb. 7, 1916, Clarinda, Iowa).* Lawyer, Union Army officer, Iowa Republican who during his years in Washington was an uncompromising foe of pork-barrel legislation while being the leading champion and coauthor of the 1906 Pure Food and Drug Act. Marshall County prosecutor (1856), eleventh judicial district attorney (1856-1861), clerk of the state house of representatives (1858), GOP National Convention delegate (1860, 1888, 1896), presidential elector on the Hayes-Wheeler (1876) and Harrison-Morton (1888) tickets, U.S. Representative (1881-1887, 1893-1909), solicitor of the treasury during the Benjamin Harrison administration (1889-1893).

HERBERT, HILARY ABNER *(b March 12, 1834, Laurens, S.C.; d March 5, 1919, Tampa, Fla.)* Lawyer, Confederate Army officer, Alabama Democrat who as secretary of the navy (1893-1897) in the Cleveland cabinet won congressional approval of a strong sea force. U.S. Representative (1877-1893).

HEREFORD, FRANK *(b July 4, 1825, Fauquier County, Va.; d Dec. 21, 1891, Union, W.Va.)* Lawyer, California and West Virginia Democrat. In California:

Sacramento County district attorney (1855-1857). In West Virginia: U.S. Representative (1871-1877), U.S. Senate to fill a vacancy (1877-1881), presidential elector on the Cleveland-Thurman ticket (1888).

HERLONG, ALBERT SYDNEY, JR. *(b Feb. 14, 1909, Manistee, Ala.)* Lawyer, Florida Democrat. Lake County judge (1937-1949), Leesburg city attorney (1946-1948), U.S. Representative (1949-1969) serving on the Ways and Means Committee.

HERMANN, BINGER *(b Feb. 19, 1843, Lonaconing, Md.; d April 15, 1926, Roseburg, Oreg.)* Teacher, lawyer, Oregon Republican. State representative (1866-1868), state senate (1868-1870), deputy internal revenue collector (1868-1871), receiver of public moneys (1871-1873), general land office agent (1897-1903), U.S. Representative (1885-1897, 1903-1907).

HERNANDEZ, BENIGNO CARDENAS *(b Feb. 13, 1862, Taos, N.Mex.; d Oct. 18, 1954, Los Angeles, Calif.)* Merchant, rancher, New Mexico Republican. Probate clerk and ex-officio recorder of deeds for Rio Arriba County (1900-1904), sheriff (1904-1906), county treasurer and tax collector (1908-1912), Santa Fe land office receiver (1912, 1913), GOP National Convention delegate (1912-1916), U.S. Representative (1915-1917, 1919-1921), collector of internal revenue (1921-1933), member of Selective Service Board (1940-1947).

HERNANDEZ, JOSEPH MARION *(b Aug. 4, 1793, St. Augustine, Fla., which then was a Spanish colony; d June 8, 1857, Matanzas Province, Cuba)* Sugar planter, Indian fighter who led the 1837 expedition that resulted in the capture of Chief Osceola, Florida Territory Whig. Delegate to Seventeenth U.S. Congress (1822-1823).

HERRICK, MANUEL *(b Sept. 20, 1876, Perry, Ohio; disappeared Jan. 11, 1952, in a Sierra blizzard and his body was found Feb. 29 in a snowbank near his mining claim eight miles from Quincy, Calif.)* Oklahoma farmer-cattle rancher and California miner who preferred the rugged life to politics—a fact of which he became convinced as a one-term Republican U.S. Representative from the Cherokee Strip (1921-1923).

HERRING, CLYDE LaVERNE *(b May 3, 1879, Jackson, Mich.; d Sept. 15, 1945, Washington, D.C.)* Rancher, farmer, automobile dealer, Iowa Democrat. National committeeman (1924-1928), governor (1933-1937), Democratic National Convention delegate (1940), U.S. Senate (1937-1943).

HERSEY, IRA GREENLIEF *(b March 31, 1858, Hodgdon, Maine; d May 6, 1943, Washington, D.C.)* Lawyer, Maine Republican. State representative (1909-1912), state senate (1913-1916) and its president the last two years, U.S. Representative (1917-1929), Aroostook County probate judge (1934-1942).

HERTER, CHRISTIAN ARCHIBALD *(b March 28, 1895, Paris, France; d Dec. 30, 1967, Washington, D.C.)* Magazine editor-publisher, diplomat, lecturer, Massachusetts Republican who devoted most of his adult life to government service; the man who placed Richard Nixon's name in nomination for the vice presidency (1956) in order to head off Harold E. Stassen who wanted him, Herter, to be Dwight D. Eisenhower's running mate. The highmark of his career, secretary of state in the Eisenhower cabinet (1959-1961).

Attache to the U.S. embassy in Berlin (1916) and for two months in charge of the U.S. legation in Brussels; served in State Department at home (1917-1919); assistant commissioner and secretary of diplomatic mission that drew up a prisoner-of-war agreement with Germany, and secretary of the American Peace Commission (1918), executive secretary of the European Relief Council (1920), personal assistant to Secretary of Commerce Herbert Hoover (1921-1924), Harvard University overseer (1940-1944, 1946-1952), state representative (1931-1943) and house speaker (1939-1943), deputy director of the Office of Facts and Figures in Washington (1941, 1942), U.S. Representative (1943-1953), GOP National Convention delegate (1948), governor (1953-1957), U.S. undersecretary of state to John Foster Dulles (1957-1959).

HEWES, JOSEPH *(b Jan. 23, 1730, Kingston, N.J.; d Nov. 10, 1779, Philadelphia, Pa.).* Merchant, shipper, North Carolina signer of the Declaration of Independence who acted as chairman of the marine committee during the Revolution, a position tantamount now to secretary of the navy, and as such armed American vessels and appointed John Paul Jones to command one of them. Member of state house of commons (1766-1775, 1778, 1779), committee of correspondence (1773), Continental Congress (1774-1777, 1779 until death).

HEWITT, ABRAM STEVENS *(b July 31, 1822, Haverstraw, N.Y.; d Jan. 18, 1903, New York City)* Lawyer, iron works operator with Peter Cooper, organizer-manager of the Cooper Union for the advancement of science and art, New York Democrat. U.S. Representative (1875-1879, 1881-1886), mayor of New York City (1887, 1888), Palisades Interstate Park Commissioner (1900 until death), Columbia University trustee (1901 until death).

HEYBURN, WELDON BRINTON *(b May 23, 1852, Delaware County, Pa.; d Oct. 17, 1912, Washington, D.C.)* Lawyer, Idaho Republican. Delegate to convention that framed state constitution

(1889), GOP National Convention delegate (1888, 1892, 1900, 1904), GOP National Committeeman (1904-1908), U.S. Senate (1903 until death).

HEYWARD, THOMAS, JR. *(b July 28, 1746, St. Helena's Parish, which later became St. Luke's, S.C.; d March 6, 1809, St. Luke's Parish, S.C.).* Planter, Continental Army officer, South Carolina signer of the Declaration of Independence. Member of commons house of assembly (1772), provincial convention delegate (1774), Council of Safety (1775, 1776), general assembly (1776-1778), Continental Congress (1776-1778), state constitutional convention committee (1776), state representative (1778-1784) except for a year when he was a prisoner of war, circuit court judge (1779-1789), state constitutional convention delegate (1790).

HIBBARD, ELLERY ALBEE *(b July 31, 1826, St. Johnsbury, Vt.; d July 24, 1903, Laconia, N.H.)* Lawyer, banker, New Hampshire Democrat. State house of representatives clerk (1852-1854), Laconia moderator (1862, 1863), state representative (1865, 1866), U.S. Representative (1871-1873), state supreme court judge (1873-1874). Cousin of Harry Hibbard.

HIBBARD, HARRY *(b June 1, 1816, Concord, Vt.; d July 28, 1872, Somerville, Mass.)* Lawyer, New Hampshire Democrat. Assistant clerk and clerk of the state house of representatives (1840-1842), a member (1843-1845) and speaker (1844, 1845); state senate (1845, 1847, 1848) and its president (1847, 1848), Democratic National Convention delegate (1848, 1856), U.S. Representative (1849-1855). Cousin of Ellery A. Hibbard.

HICKENLOOPER, BOURKE BLAKEMORE *(b July 21, 1896, Blockton, Iowa; d Sept. 4, 1971, Shelter Island, N.Y.)* Lawyer,

Iowa Republican who, during his twenty-four years as a U.S. Senator (1945-1969), became known to his colleagues as "the consummate skeptic," yet his name was attached to a host of significant laws, chief among them the Atomic Energy Act of 1954. State representative (1934-1937), lieutenant governor (1939-1942), governor (1943-1945). While senator, he was chairman of the Joint Congressional Committee on Atomic Energy, senior GOP member of the Foreign Relations Committee, member of the Agriculture, Aeronautical and Space Science and Banking committees, and chairman of the Senate Republican Policy Committee.

HICKEY, ANDREW JAMES *(b Aug. 27, 1872, Albion, N.Y.; d Aug. 20, 1942, Buffalo, N.Y.)* Lawyer, Indiana Republican. U.S. Representative (1919-1931).

HICKS, THOMAS HOLLIDAY *(b Sept. 2, 1798, Dorchester County, Md.; d Feb. 14, 1865, Washington, D.C.).* Farmer, merchant who wore many party mantles and as Know-Nothing governor of Maryland (1858-1862) delayed calling a special session of the legislature to discuss secession until an April 1861 riot took the matter out of his hands and the arrival of federal troops left the secessionists powerless to act. Friends said delay was his strategy to block secession. Foes said he was afraid of physical harm, no matter how he acted. He was also a Democrat, Whig, and Republican. Dorchester County sheriff (1824), state delegate (1836), member of governor's council (1837), county register of wills (1838-1851, 1855-1861), state constitutional convention delegate (1851), U.S. Senate (1862 until death).

HIESTAND, EDGAR WILLARD *(b Dec. 3, 1888, Chicago, Ill.)* Merchant, California Republican. U.S. Representative (1953-1963) serving on the Administration, and Education and Labor committees.

HIESTER, DANIEL *(b June 25, 1747, Berks County, Pa.; d March 7, 1804, Washington, D.C.)* Farmer, sawmill and gristmill operator, Continental Army officer, Pennsylvania and Maryland Anti-Federalist. In Pennsylvania: member of supreme executive council (1784-1786), commissioner of Connecticut land claims (1787), U.S. Representative in the first four Congresses (1789-1796). In Maryland: U.S. Representative in the Seventh and Eighth Congresses (1801 until death). Cousin of Joseph Hiester, uncle of William Hiester.

HIESTER, JOSEPH *(b Nov. 18, 1752, Berne Township, Pa.; d June 10, 1832, Reading, Pa.)* Merchant, Continental Army officer who was captured and held aboard the prison ship *Jersey* (1776), Pennsylvania political leader who was elected to Congress as a Federalist and governor (1820-1824) as an Independent Democrat. Member of state conference (1776), delegate to state convention that ratified federal Constitution (1787) and to state constitutional convention (1790), state representative (1787-1790), state senate (1790-1794), U.S. Representative (1797-1805, 1815-1820). Cousin of Daniel Hiester.

HIESTER, WILLIAM *(b Oct. 10, 1790, Berne Township, Pa.; d Oct. 13, 1853, New Holland, Pa.)* Farmer, merchant, Pennsylvania Whig. Lancaster County justice of the peace (1823-1828), U.S. Representative (1831-1837), state constitutional convention delegate (1837), state senate (1840-1842) and senate speaker (1842). Nephew of Daniel Hiester.

HILDEBRANDT, FRED HERMAN *(b Aug. 2, 1874, West Bend, Wis.; d Jan. 26, 1956, Bradenton, Fla.)* Railroad brakeman and conductor, South Dakota Democrat. State representative (1922, 1923), chairman of state Game and Fish Commission (1927-1931), U.S. Representative (1933-1939), Democratic National Convention delegate (1944).

HILL, BENJAMIN HARVEY *(b Sept. 14, 1823, Hillsborough, Ga.; d Aug. 16, 1882, Atlanta, Ga.).* Lawyer and a Georgia moderate who tried several political labels (Democrat, Whig, Know-Nothing, Constitutional Unionist) in hope of finding a middle ground on such issues as secession but, once it was a fact, became Jefferson Davis' legislative voice in the Confederate Senate (1861-1865) and, after the Civil War, one of the foremost foes of the Reconstruction acts.

State representative (1851), state senate (1859, 1860), presidential elector (1856) on the Know-Nothing Fillmore-Donelson ticket (1856) the Constitutional Union Bell-Everett tickets (1860), delegate to state secession convention (1861), delegate to Confederate Provisional Congress (1861), U.S. Representative (1875-1877), U.S. Senate (1877 until death).

HILL, DAVID BENNETT *(b Aug. 29, 1843, Havana, now Montour Falls, N.Y.; d Oct. 20, 1910, Albany, N.Y.).* Lawyer, astute New York Democrat who knew well how to keep upstate and New York City politicians at loggerheads with each other to the advantage of himself, thus, among other things, enabling him to control federal patronage while U.S. Senator (1892-1897) though President Cleveland wanted that for himself. But his most memorable contribution to the American political scene came when William Jennings Bryan won the Democratic presidential nomination (1896). Said Hill: "I am a Democrat still. Very still."

Elmira city attorney (1864), delegate to all Democratic state conventions (1868-1881) and presiding officer (1877, 1881), state assemblyman (1871-1872), mayor of Elmira (1882), Democratic National Convention delegate (1884, 1896, 1900, 1904), New York State Bar Association president (1886, 1887), lieutenant governor (1883, 1884), governor (1885-1892).

HILL, EBENEZER J. *(b Aug. 4, 1845, Redding, Conn.; d Sept. 27, 1917, Norwalk, Conn.)* Union Army soldier, businessman, banker, Connecticut Republican. GOP National Convention delegate (1884), state senator (1886, 1887), U.S. Representative (1895-1913, 1915 until death).

HILL, ISAAC *(b April 6, 1788, West Cambridge, Mass.; d March 22, 1851, Washington, D.C.)* Editor-publisher of the *New Hampshire Patriot*, New Hampshire Democrat, and member of Andrew Jackson's Kitchen Cabinet whom James Buchanan three decades later called the best-informed man on American affairs he had ever known. State senate (1820-1822, 1827), state representative (1826), second comptroller of the U.S. Treasury (1829, 1830), U.S. Senate (1831-1836), governor (1836-1839), U.S. subtreasurer at Boston (1840, 1841).

HILL, JOHN BOYNTON PHILIP CLAYTON *(b May 2, 1879, Annapolis, Md.; d May 23, 1941, Washington, D.C.)* Lawyer, Maryland Republican. U.S. attorney (1910-1915), GOP National Convention delegate (1916), U.S. Representative (1921-1927).

HILL, JOSHUA *(b Jan. 10, 1812, Abbeville District, S.C.; d March 6, 1891, Madison, Ga.)* Georgia .lawyer who was torn between love for country and love for the South, thus switching his political allegiance from Whig to Know-Nothing to Constitutional Union to Union Republican, and during the Civil War struggling in vain for peace. As a Whig: national convention delegate (1844). As a Know-Nothing: U.S. Representative (1857-1861). As a Constitutional Unionist: national convention delegate (1860), unsuccessful candidate for governor (1863). As a Union Republican: elected a U.S. Senator in 1868 but did not qualify until 1871, served until 1873, and did not stand for reelection.

HILL, NATHANIEL PETER *(b Feb. 18, 1832, Montgomery, N.Y.; d May 22, 1900, Denver Colo.)* Brown University chemistry professor (1860-1864) who went to Colorado to investigate mineral resources, liked what he found, and stayed to become a mining and smelting operator, real estate speculator, publisher of the *Denver Republican* and an active Republican. Mayor of Black Hawk (1871), territorial council member (1872, 1873), U.S. Senate (1879-1885).

HILL, SAMUEL BILLINGSLEY *(b April 2, 1875, Franklin, Ark.; d March 16, 1958, Bethesda, Md.)* Lawyer, Washington Democrat. Douglas County prosecutor (1907-1911), Douglas and Grant counties superior court judge (1917-1924), U.S. Representative (1923-1936) resigning to become a member of the U.S. Board of Tax Appeals (1936-1953).

HILLEGAS, MICHAEL *(b April 22, 1729, Philadelphia, Pa.; d Sept. 29, 1804, Philadelphia)* Sugar refiner, merchant, Pennsylvania patriot who was one of the nation's first two treasurers and a man who used much of his personal fortune to finance the Revolution. He and George Clymer were appointed continental treasurers (July 29, 1775) of the united colonies but the job became solely his (Aug. 6, 1776) when Clymer was seated in the Continental Congress. Then on Sept. 6, 1777, Hillegas was appointed treasurer of the United States and served until Sept. 11, 1789, the first man to hold that office.

Some of his other public offices included a commissioner to locate and construct Fort Mifflin (1762), member of provincial assembly (1765-1775), commissioner to improve Delaware River navigation (1771), member of the Philadelphia Committee of Observation (1774), Pennsylvania Committee of Safety treasurer (1775), Philadelphia alderman (1793 until death).

HILLHOUSE, JAMES *(b Oct. 21, 1754, Montville, Conn.; d Dec. 29, 1832, New Haven, Conn.)* Lawyer, Revolutionary Army officer, Connecticut Federalist who while a U.S. Senator (1796-1810) submitted seven constitutional amendments aimed at preventing the concentration of power in the hands of the president, whoever he might be. None were adopted.

State representative (1780-1785), treasurer of Yale College (1782-1832), member of state council (1789-1790), U.S. Representative (1791-1796), U.S. Senate (1796-1810) and president pro tem (1801). Son of William Hillhouse.

HILLHOUSE, WILLIAM *(b Aug. 25, 1728, Montville, Conn.; d Jan. 12, 1816, Montville)* Connecticut lawyer, Revolutionary officer. State representative (1756-1760, 1763-1785), Continental Congress (1783-1786), common pleas court judge (1784-1806), state senate (1785-1808), New London district probate judge (1786-1807). Father of James Hillhouse.

HILLQUIT, MORRIS *(b Aug. 1, 1869, Riga, Latvia; d Oct. 7, 1933, New York City)* Lawyer, orator, writer, New York Socialist who early in life was a Social Democrat, then switched to the Socialist Labor party, aligning himself with Eugene Debs and his Social Democratic Party of America when a rift developed over cooperation with labor and becoming a main spokesman for the Socialist party that ultimately emerged (1901). His many bids for elective office—twice for mayor of New York, five times for the U.S. Congress—were unsuccessful but he always received an unusually high number of votes.

HINDS, ASHER CROSBY *(b Feb. 6, 1863, Benton, Maine; d May 1, 1919, Washington, D.C.)* Newspaperman, Maine Republican. Clerk to the speaker of the U.S. House of Representatives (1889-1891) and clerk at the speaker's table (1895-1911), editor of the House *Rules, Manual and Digest* (1899) and *Hinds' Precedents* (1908), U.S. Representative (1911-1917).

HINSHAW, EDMUND HOWARD *(b Dec. 8, 1860, Greensboro, Ind.; d June 15, 1932, Los Angeles, Calif.)* Lawyer, motion-picture theater operator, Nebraska Republican. Fairbury public schools superintendent (1887, 1888), Fairbury city clerk and attorney (1889, 1890), Jefferson County attorney (1895-1899), U.S. Representative (1903-1911).

HINSHAW, JOHN CARL WILLIAMS *(b July 28, 1894, Chicago, Ill.; d Aug. 5, 1956, in U.S. Naval Hospital, Bethesda, Md.)* Investment banker, real estate broker, California Republican. U.S. Representative (1939 until death).

HISCOCK, FRANK *(b Sept. 6, 1834, Pompey, N.Y.; d June 18, 1914, Syracuse, N.Y.)* Lawyer, New York Republican. Onandaga County district attorney (1860-1863), state constitutional convention delegate (1867), GOP National Convention delegate (1876), U.S. Representative (1877-1887) resigning to become U.S. Senator (1887-1893).

HITCHCOCK, ETHAN ALLEN *(b Sept. 19, 1835, Mobile, Ala.; d April 9, 1909, Washington, D.C.)* Importer, glass and metals manufacturer, Missouri Republican, and close friend of President McKinley who appointed him secretary of the interior (1898-1907), a post in which he quickly and effectively established himself as a conservationist and friend of the Indians. He exposed wide frauds in the handling of public lands, cleaned out the General Land Office, and had more than a thousand people in twenty states indicted, among them many government officials. Prior to his cabinet years, Hitchcock was briefly minister to Russia (1897-1898).

HITCHCOCK, FRANK HARRIS *(b Oct. 5, 1867, Amherst, Ohio; d Aug. 5, 1935, Tucson, Ariz.)* Lawyer, Ohio Republican who made politics his professional career beginning with his appointment (1903) as assistant secretary of the GOP National Committee. By 1905 he was assistant postmaster general, in February 1908 he resigned to manage William H. Taft's presidential campaign and thus later also became chairman of the committee. His reward was the usual for faithful service in high places: U.S. postmaster general in the Taft cabinet and dispenser of patronage (1909-1913). He went into private practice in New York (1914) but did not forsake politics, managing the preconvention campaigns of Charles Evans Hughes (1916) and Leonard Wood (1920). In 1928 he moved to Arizona, invested in newspapers and mines, and served as that state's GOP National Committeeman (1932-1933).

HITCHCOCK, GILBERT MONELL *(b Sept. 18, 1859, Omaha, Nebr.; d Feb. 3, 1934, Washington, D.C.)* Lawyer, Nebraska Republican with Populist leanings that carried him first into the Fusionist camp and then into the Democratic party, influential publisher of the *Omaha World-Herald* who hired William Jennings Bryan to edit it (1896). U.S. Representative (1903-1905, 1907-1911), U.S. Senate (1911-1923), Democratic National Convention delegate and chairman of the platform committee (1932). As a senator, he at first opposed Woodrow Wilson on many issues, both foreign and domestic, but after becoming chairman of the Foreign Relations Committee (1918) he also became the president's spokesman in the Senate. Son of Phineas Warren Hitchcock.

HITCHCOCK, HERBERT EMERY *(b Aug. 22, 1867, Maquoketa, Iowa; d Feb. 17, 1958, Mitchell, S.Dak.)* Lawyer, banker, Yankton College trustee, South Dakota Democrat. State's attorney (1902-1906), state senate (1909, 1911, 1929), Mitchell School Board president (1924-1934), Democratic state executive committee chairman (1934-1937) and national convention delegate (1908, 1928, 1932, 1936, 1940), U.S. Senate to fill a vacancy (1936-1938).

HITCHCOCK, PHINEAS WARREN *(b Nov. 30, 1831, New Lebanon, N.Y.; d July 10, 1881, Omaha, Nebr.)* Lawyer, Nebraska Republican. GOP National Convention delegate (1860), U.S. marshal (1861-1864), delegate to the U.S. Congress (1865-1867). Nebraska and Iowa surveyor general (1867-1869), U.S. Senator from Nebraska (1871-1877). Father of Gilbert M. Hitchcock.

HITT, ROBERT ROBERTS *(b Jan. 16, 1834, Urbana, Ohio; d Sept. 19, 1906, Narragansett Pier, R.I.)* Court reporter and stenographer who, at Lincoln's insistence, reported the Lincoln-Douglas debates (1858); diplomat, Illinois Republican. Among his assignments: official stenographer for the state legislature (1858-1860), federal Civil War reporter who covered the inquiry into Fremont's Missouri conduct, reporter for the joint Congressional committee that investigated the Ku Klux Klan (1872), first secretary of the Paris legation and temporary chargé d'affaires (1874-1881). Assistant secretary of state (1881-1882), U.S. Representative (1882 until death) for many years serving as chairman of the Foreign Affairs Committee, Smithsonian Institution regent (1893 until death), McKinley-appointed commissioner to establish government for the Hawaiian Islands (1898).

HOAR, EBENEZER ROCKWOOD *(b Feb. 21, 1816, Concord, Mass.; d Jan. 31, 1895,* *Concord)* Lawyer, Massachusetts anti-slavery Whig turned Republican who served in the Grant cabinet and was nominated by Grant as an associate justice of the Supreme Court but failed to win Senate confirmation. State senate (1846), common pleas judge (1849-1855), state supreme court judge (1859-1869), U.S. attorney general (1869-1870), U.S. Representative (1873-1875), member of Harvard University Board of Overseers. Son of Samuel, father of Sherman, and brother of George F. Hoar.

HOAR, GEORGE FRISBIE *(b Aug. 29, 1826, Concord, Mass.; d Sept. 30, 1904, Worcester, Mass.)* Lawyer, Massachusetts Republican. Worcester city solicitor (1860), state representative (1852), state senate (1857), U.S. Representative (1869-1877), Harvard University overseer (1874-1880, 1896 until death), state GOP convention chairman (1871, 1877, 1882, 1885); GOP National Convention delegate (1876, 1880, 1884, 1888), presiding in 1880 and chairman of his state delegation (1880, 1884, 1888); Smithsonian Institution regent (1880), U.S. Senate (1877 until death). Son of Samuel, father of Rockwood, and brother of Ebenezer R. Hoar.

HOAR, ROCKWOOD *(b Aug. 24, 1855, Worcester, Mass.; d Nov. 1, 1906, Worcester)* Lawyer, Clark University trustee, Massachusetts Republican. Middle district assistant district attorney (1884-1887), Worcester Common Council member (1887-1891), U.S. Representative (1905 until death). Grandson of Samuel, son of George F., and nephew of Ebenezer R. Hoar.

HOAR, SAMUEL *(b May 18, 1778, Lincoln, Mass.; d Nov. 2, 1856, Concord, Mass.)* Lawyer, the first of three generations of Hoars to contribute to the Massachusetts political scene. An Abolitionist, he was sent by the state legislature to South Carolina (1844) to test the constitutionality of acts prohibiting Negro sailors on Massachusetts ships from entering the southern state but never had the opportunity to argue the case in court, because on the day of his arrival in Charleston the South Carolina legislature, with only one dissent, voted to expel him and they did.

At that time he was a Whig, before that he had been a Federalist, and later —as with so many Northerners of the period—switched first to the Free-Soil movement and then to Republicanism, in fact presiding over the state convention (1855) that brought the GOP to Massachusetts.

State constitutional convention delegate (1820), U.S. Representative (1835-1837), presidential elector on the Free-Soil ticket (1848). Father of Ebenezer R. and George F., grandfather of Rockwood and Sherman Hoar.

HOAR, SHERMAN *(b July 30, 1860, Concord, Mass.; d Oct. 7, 1898, Concord)* Massachusetts lawyer and the only one of five family members who held public office to don a Democratic cloak. President of the state's Young Men's Democratic Club (1884), U.S. Representative (1891-1893), U.S. attorney for the state (1893-1897), director of the Massachusetts Volunteer Aid Association until death during the Spanish-American War. Grandson of Samuel, son of Ebenezer R., and nephew of George F. Hoar.

HOBART, GARRET AUGUSTUS *(b June 3, 1844, Monmouth County, N.J.; d Nov. 21, 1899, Paterson, N.J.)* Teacher, lawyer, New Jersey Republican who was vice president (1897 until death) when William McKinley was in the White House. Paterson city counsel (1871, 1872), state assemblyman (1872-1876) and speaker (1874), state senator (1876-1882) and president (1881, 1882), GOP National Convention delegate (1876, 1880), GOP National Committeeman (1884-1896).

HOBBS, SAMUEL FRANCIS *(b Oct. 5, 1887, Selma, Ala.; d May 31, 1952, Selma)* Lawyer, Alabama Democrat. Fourth judicial circuit judge (1921-1926), Muscle Shoals Commission chairman (1931), state National Recovery Administration Committee chairman (1933), U.S. Representative (1935-1951).

HOBBY, OVETA CULP *(b 1931, Killeen, Tex.)* Presented with the Distinguished Service Medal for her work in organizing and directing World War II Women's Auxiliary Army Corps; first secretary of health, education and welfare (1953-1955), serving in President Eisenhower's cabinet. Returned to Texas in 1955 where she became editor and chairman of the board of the *Houston Post*, published by husband William Pettus Hobby.

HOCH, HOMER *(b July 4, 1879, Marion, Kans.; d Jan. 30, 1949, Topeka, Kans.).* Lawyer, Kansas Republican, and editor of the *Marion Record*. GOP National Convention delegate (1928), U.S. Representative (1919-1933), State Corporation Commission chairman (1933-1939), member of state supreme court (1938 until death).

HOEVEN, CHARLES BERNARD *(b March 30, 1895, Hospers, Iowa)* Lawyer, Iowa Republican. Sioux County attorney (1925-1937), state senate (1937-1941, its president 1939-1941), chairman of GOP state convention (1940), chairman of GOP state judicial convention (1942), U.S. Representative (1943-1965) serving on the Agriculture Committee.

HOEY, CLYDE ROARK *(b Dec. 11, 1877, Shelby, N.C.; d May 12, 1954, Washington, D.C.)* Editor of the *Cleveland* (N.C.) *Star*, lawyer, North Carolina Democrat. State representative (1898-1902), state senate (1902-1904), assistant U.S. attorney for the western district of North Carolina (1913-1919), U.S.

Representative (1919-1921), governor (1937-1941), Democratic National Committeeman (1941-1944), U.S. Senate (1945 until death).

HOFFMAN, CLARE EUGENE *(b Sept. 10, 1875, Vicksburg, Pa.; d Nov. 3, 1967, Allegan, Mich.)* Lawyer, Michigan Republican, isolationist opposed to New Deal social reform who served twenty-eight years (1935-1963) as a U.S. Representative; member of Government Operations and Education and Labor committees. Allegan County prosecuting attorney (1904-1910).

HOFFMAN, ELMER JOSEPH *(b July 7, 1899, DuPage County, Ill.)* Farmer, truckman, Illinois Republican. DuPage County sheriff (1939-1942, 1947-1950), chief deputy sheriff (1943-1946), county probation officer (1951), state treasurer (1952-1958), U.S. Representative (1959-1965) serving on the Rules Committee.

HOFFMAN, HAROLD GILES *(b Feb. 7, 1896, South Amboy, N.J.; d June 4, 1954, New York City)* Newspaperman, banker, New Jersey Republican. South Amboy city treasurer (1920-1925), state assemblyman (1923, 1924), mayor of South Amboy (1925, 1926), delegate to GOP state convention (1934-1937) and national convention (1936), U.S. Representative (1927-1931), state motor vehicle commissioner (1931-1935), governor (1935-1938), executive director of the state unemployment compensation commission (1938 until death, with time out for World War II military service).

HOLADAY, WILLIAM PERRY *(b Dec. 14, 1882, Vermilion County, Ill.; d Jan. 29, 1946, Georgetown, Ill.)* Lawyer, Illinois Republican. Vermilion County assistant prosecutor (1905-1907), state representative (1909-1923), U.S. Representative (1923-1933).

HOLBROOK, EDWARD DEXTER *(b May 6, 1836, Elyria, Ohio; d June 18, 1870,* *Idaho City, Idaho, of gunshot wounds).* Lawyer, Idaho Territory Democrat who was a delegate to the thirty-ninth and fortieth Congresses (1865-1869).

HOLBROOK, FREDERICK *(b Feb. 15, 1813, Warehouse Point, Conn.; d April 28, 1909, Brattleboro, Vt.).* One of the nation's first scientific farmers, agricultural writer, and designer of a plow (1867) that was revolutionary for its day. Vermont Republican who while governor (1861-1863) devised a plan that was accepted nationally for the recruiting of Union Army volunteers. State senate (1849-1850). In addition to his agricultural and political interests, he was a bank president and music director for half a century at Brattleboro's Centre Congregational Church.

HOLCOMB, SILAS ALEXANDER *(b Aug. 25, 1858, Gibson County, Ind.; d April 25, 1920, Bellingham, Wash.)* Teacher, country lawyer with a keen awareness of the needs of penny-pinched farmers, Nebraska Populist who twice was elected third-party governor (1895-1899) and, in the words of one biographer, "proved to be the conservative leader of a radical party." District judge (1891-1893), state supreme court justice (1899-1905), member of the board of commissioners of state institutions (1913-1920).

HOLCOMBE, GEORGE *(b March 1786, Hunterdon County, N.J.; d Jan. 14, 1828, Allentown, N.J.)* Physician, New Jersey Democrat. State assemblyman (1815, 1816), U.S. Representative (1821 until death).

HOLCOMBE, JAMES PHILEMON *(b Sept. 20, 1820, Powhatan County, Va.; d Aug. 22, 1873, Capon Springs, W.Va.).* Lawyer, writer, orator, University of Virginia professor, Virginia States' Rights Democrat who nevertheless sought to avert the Civil War but, once it had begun, served as a Confederate secret agent in Canada. State secessionist convention delegate (1861), member of the Confederate Congress (1862-1864).

HOLLAND, EDWARD EVERETT *(b Feb. 26, 1861, Nansemond County, Va.; d Oct. 23, 1941, Suffolk, Va.)* Lawyer, banker, Virginia Democrat. Mayor of Suffolk (1885-1887), Nansemond County commonwealth attorney (1887-1907), state senate (1907-1911, 1930-1941), U.S. Representative (1911-1921), Democratic National Convention delegate (1920, 1924).

HOLLAND, ELMER JOSEPH *(b Jan. 8, 1894, Pittsburgh, Pa.; d Aug. 9, 1968, Washington, D.C.)* Sales manager, Pennsylvania Democrat. State representative (1934-1942), Pittsburgh superintendent of highways and sewers (1940-1942), U.S. Representative (1942-1943, 1956 until death), state senate (1943-1956). A labor-oriented legislator and a senior member of Education and Labor Committee.

HOLLAND, JAMES *(b 1754, Anson County, N.C.; d May 19, 1823, Maury County, Tenn.)* Farmer, lawyer, North Carolina Anti-Federalist. Tryon County sheriff (1777-1778), Rutherford County justice of the peace (1780-1800) and comptroller (1782-1785), state senate (1783, 1787), state house of commons (1786, 1789), delegate to state convention that adopted federal Constitution (1789), member of University of North Carolina's first Board of Trustees (1789-1795), U.S. Representative (1795-1797, 1801-1811), Maury County, Tenn., justice of the peace (1812-1818).

HOLLAND, SPESSARD LINDSEY *(b July 10, 1892, Bartow, Fla.; d Nov. 6, 1971, Bartow)* Teacher, lawyer, World War I flyer, Emory University and Southern College trustee, conservative Florida Democrat who classified himself as a "moderate liberal" and had much to do with passage of the Twenty-fourth Amendment that removed racial barriers to voting. Polk County prosecutor (1919, 1920), county judge (1921-1929), state senate (1932-1940), Florida's wartime governor (1941-1945) and U.S. Senate for a quarter-century (1946-1970).

HOLLIDAY, ELIAS SELAH *(b March 5, 1842, Aurora, Ind.; d March 13, 1936, Brazil, Ind.)* Teacher, lawyer, Indiana Republican. Mayor of Brazil (1877-1880, 1887, 1888), city attorney (1884), presidential elector on the Blaine-Logan ticket (1884), city councilman (1892-1896), U.S. Representative (1901-1909).

HOLMAN, RUFUS CECIL *(b Oct. 14, 1877, Portland, Oregon; d Nov. 27, 1959, Portland)* Farmer, businessman, paper box manufacturer, Oregon Republican. Member of Portland Charter Commission (1912), member-chairman of Multnomah County Commission and the Columbia River Interstate Bridge Commission (1913-1921), port commissioner (1931), state treasurer (1931-1939), U.S. Senate (1939-1945).

HOLMAN, WILLIAM STEELE *(b Sept. 6, 1822, near Aurora, Ind.; d April 22, 1897, Washington, D.C.)* Lawyer, skilled parliamentarian and orator, Indiana Democrat who in sixteen terms in Congress was known variously—depending upon which side of the aisle one sat—as "the watchdog of the treasury," "the great objector," and "hayseed statesman." Probate judge (1843-1846), prosecutor (1847-1849), state constitutional convention delegate (1850), state representative (1851, 1852), common pleas judge (1852-1856), U.S. Representative (1859-1865, 1867-1877, 1881-1895, 1897 for a month until death).

HOLMES, ADONIRAM JUDSON *(b March 2, 1842, Wooster, Ohio; d Jan. 21, 1902, Clarinda, Iowa)* Union Army officer, lawyer, Iowa Republican. Mayor of Boone (1880, 1881), state representative (1882, 1883), U.S. Representative (1883-1889), House sergeant at arms (1889-1891), county attorney (1896-1899).

HOLMES, BAYARD TAYLOR (b July 29, 1852, North Hero, Vt.; d April 3, 1924, Fairhope, Ala.) Surgeon, University of Illinois professor, medical writer, Illinois Socialist, and unsuccessful candidate for mayor of Chicago (1895).

HOLMES, DAVID (b March 10, 1769, Mary Ann Furnace, Pa.; d Aug. 20, 1832, Jordan's Sulphur Springs, Va.) Lawyer, Virginia and Mississippi Democrat. In Virginia: U.S. Representative (1797-1809). In Mississippi: territorial governor (1809-1817) and, upon admission to the Union, the first state governor (1817-1820).

HOLMES, GABRIEL (b 1769, Sampson County, N.C.; d Sept. 26, 1829, Sampson County) Lawyer, North Carolina Democrat. State house of commons (1794, 1795), state senate (1797-1802, 1812, 1813), governor (1821-1824), U.S. Representative (1825 until death).

HOLMES, ISAAC EDWARD (b April 6, 1796, Charleston, S.C.; d Feb. 24, 1867, Charleston) Lawyer, farmer, Democrat who was one of the founders of the South Carolina Association (1823), an organization formed to counter Northern abolitionist sentiments. State representative (1826-1833), U.S. Representative (1839-1851).

HOLMES, JOHN (b March 14, 1773, Kingston, Mass.; d July 7, 1843, Portland, Maine) Lawyer, writer, wit, Massachusetts and Maine politician who was called the Duke of Somersaults when he transferred his allegiance from Federalist to Democrat (1811) and it's not known what he was called when he became a Whig (1824). In Massachusetts, where he successfully advocated partition that would give statehood to Maine: state representative (1802, 1803), state senate (1813, 1814), Madison-appointed commissioner to divide Passamaquoddy Bay islands between U.S. and Britain (1814, 1815), U.S. Representative (1817-1820), chairman of Maine constitutional convention (1816). In Maine: U.S. Senate (1820-1827, 1829-1833), state representative (1835-1838), U.S. attorney (1841 until death).

HOLMES, OLIVER WENDELL, JR. (b March 8, 1841, Boston, Mass.; d March 6, 1935, Washington, D.C.) Massachusetts lawyer, legal writer, Union Army officer, Harvard lecturer-professor who was associate justice of the state supreme judicial court (1883-1899) and chief justice (1899-1902) before being appointed associate justice of the U.S. Supreme Court by Theodore Roosevelt where he remained until retirement in 1932.

In the twenty years on the state bench he rendered about 1,300 opinions and in the thirty years that followed as a member of the highest court in the land, where he was classified as a liberal, his opinions were so profound that one biographer described him not merely as "a commanding American legal figure" but as "a significant figure in the history of civilization."

Many of his decisions, which showed the same command of words that made his father one of the literary greats, provide food for thought today. For example, in a 1928 wire-tap case he held in a dissenting view that "we have to choose, and for my part I think it a less evil that some criminals should escape than that the government should play an ignoble part."

HOLMES, PEHR GUSTAF (b April 9, 1881, Sweden; d Dec. 19, 1952, Venice, Fla.) Manufacturer, banker, insurance broker, Massachusetts Republican. Worcester councilman (1908-1911), alderman (1913-1916) and mayor (1917-1919), member of Governor's Council (1925-1928), U.S. Representative (1931-1947).

HOLTEN, SAMUEL *(b June 9, 1738, Danvers, Mass.; d Jan. 2, 1816, Danvers).* Physician, Massachusetts Anti-Federalist who devoted his legislative energies largely to the army's medical and surgical needs during the Revolution. Member of the Provincial Congress (1774-1775), Committee of Safety (1775), Continental Congress (1778-1780, 1782-1787) and its president pro tem (1785), state constitutional convention delegate (1779), state senate (1780-1782, 1784, 1786, 1789, 1790), member of Governor's Council (1780-1782, 1784, 1786, 1789-1792, 1795, 1796), state representative (1787), signer of the Articles of Confederation (1788), U.S. Representative (1793-1795), Essex County probate judge (1796-1815).

HOLTZMAN, LESTER *(b June 1, 1913, New York City)* Lawyer, New York Democrat. U.S. Representative (1953-1962) serving on the Judiciary Committee.

HOOKER, CHARLES EDWARD *(b 1825, Union, S.C.; d Jan 8, 1914, Jackson, Miss.)* Lawyer, Confederate Army officer who lost an arm at Vicksburg, Mississippi Democrat who was elected but removed as state attorney general (1865) by Union military authorities and was elected again (1868). River district attorney (1850-1854), state representative (1859), U.S. Representative (1875-1883, 1887-1895, 1901-1903), Democratic National Convention delegate (1884).

HOOKER, ISABELLA BEECHER *(b Feb. 22, 1822, Litchfield, Conn; d Jan. 25, 1907, Hartford, Conn.)* Reformer prominent in early women's suffrage movement, lecturer, organizer, younger sister of Harriet Beecher Stowe. Her interest in humanity was stimulated by the atmosphere of the famous Beecher home but her personal brand of reforming zeal found its direction in husband John Hooker's law office where he read to her from Blackstone. She made frequent appearances before legislative committees, once (1870) presenting to the Connecticut legislature a bill making husband and wife equal in property rights. She persisted until a similar bill, drawn up by her husband, was passed (1877).

HOOKER, WARREN BREWSTER *(b Nov. 24, 1856, Perrysburg, N.Y.; d March 5, 1920, Fredonia, N.Y.)* Lawyer, New York Republican. Chautauqua County special surrogate (1878-1881), Pomfret town supervisor (1889, 1890), U.S. Representative (1891-1898) resigning to become state supreme court justice (1898-1913) and member of the appellate division (1902-1909).

HOOKS, CHARLES *(b Feb. 20, 1768, Bertie County, N.C.; d Oct. 18, 1843, near Montgomery, Ala.)* Planter, North Carolina Democrat. Member of state house of commons (1801-1805), state senate (1810, 1811), U.S. Representative (1816-1817, 1819-1825).

HOOPER, JESSIE ANNETTE JACK *(b Nov. 8, 1865, Winneshiek County, Iowa; d May 8, 1935, Oshkosh, Wis.).* Suffragist and peace advocate. Grew up in New Hampton, Iowa; after marriage (1888), moved to Oshkosh, Wisconsin, where she responded to the need for charitable work and also became an active member and an officer of the Wisconsin Woman's Suffrage Association, campaigning in the Wisconsin legislature for reforms affecting the welfare of women and children; a board member of the National Woman's Suffrage Association, she lobbied in Congress to help secure passage of the Nineteenth Amendment and, when the amendment passed, she campaigned in a number of states for its ratification. First president of the Wisconsin branch of the League of

Women Voters. Though unsuccessful (1922) in an attempt, as Democratic candidate, to unseat incumbent Senator Robert M. La Follette, she did carry populous Milwaukee County. Recording secretary (1929-1932) of Conference for the Cause and Cure of War.

HOOPER, JOSEPH LAWRENCE *(b Dec. 22, 1877, Cleveland, Ohio; d Feb. 22, 1934, Washington, D.C.)* Lawyer, Michigan Republican. Calhoun County circuit court commissioner (1901-1903) and prosecutor (1903-1907), Battle Creek city attorney (1916-1918), U.S. Representative (1925 until death).

HOOPER, SAMUEL *(b Feb. 3, 1808, Marblehead, Mass.; d Feb. 14, 1875, Washington, D.C.)* Businessman, Massachusetts Republican. State representative (1851-1853), state senate (1858), U.S. Representative (1861 until death).

HOOPER, WILLIAM *(b June 17, 1742, Boston, Mass.; d Oct. 14, 1790, Hillsboro, N.C.)* Lawyer, orator, Revolutionary leader and signer of the Declaration of Independence whose utterances roused the people and caused him to be disbarred for a year by the British, North Carolina Federalist who strongly urged ratification of the U.S. Constitution. Member of the colonial assembly (1773-1776), Continental Congress (1774-1777), state assemblyman (1777, 1778).

HOOPER, WILLIAM HENRY *(b Dec. 25, 1813, Cambridge, Md.; d Dec. 30, 1882, Salt Lake City, Utah)* Merchant, trader, miner, banker, and Democrat who planted roots in the Utah Territory in 1850 and became a leading political figure. Territorial secretary (1857, 1858), congressional delegate (1859-1861, 1865-1873), territorial senator (1862).

HOOVER, HERBERT CLARK *(b Aug. 10, 1874, West Branch, Iowa; d Oct. 20, 1964, New York City)* Thirty-first president (Liberal Republican), 1929-1933, who administered during the first years of the Great Depression; secretary of commerce; international rags-to-riches engineer; humanitarian.

Son of a Quaker farmer who also was village blacksmith, Hoover was orphaned at an early age and raised by relatives, first in Iowa, then in Newburg, Oregon. He worked his way through Stanford University, graduating in 1895, and very soon achieved a meteoric success in the field of engineering, which took him to many countries and brought him adventure and personal wealth. In Tientsin, China, at the outbreak of the Boxer Rebellion, he directed construction of barricades to protect members of the foreign colony. With him in China was his wife, the former Lou Henry, banker's daughter and fellow Stanford graduate (1898) whom he married in 1899. In London at the outbreak of World War I, he helped stranded Americans get back to the United States, then, deserting his private career for public service, he gained an international reputation as a humanitarian for his phenomenal success as director of massive war relief in Europe, both during and after hostilities.

Appointed U.S. food administrator during World War I by President Wilson (1917-1919); favored American entry into the League of Nations. Considered by both Democrats and Republicans (1919) as a possible presidential candidate, Hoover made it clear that his affiliation was with the latter. Able secretary of commerce under both Presidents Harding and Coolidge (1921-1928), he organized seven-state pact for Colorado River irrigation and Hoover Dam. When nominated by his party as its presidential candidate in 1928, the popular Hoover rode the tide of postwar prosperity to an easy victory, receiving 444 electoral votes to Democratic opponent Alfred E. Smith's 87. In the election of 1932, the results were reversed when Democrat Franklin D. Roosevelt defeated Hoover 472 to 59 electoral votes.

During his presidency, Hoover supported conservation and started White House conferences on housing and on child health and protection, but much of the program he envisioned was to remain nothing more than a dream because, shortly after he became president, the stock market crashed and the Great Depression was upon the country. Although Hoover felt that government, as much as possible, should be indirect, he approved federally administered public works programs to help relieve the hardship of widespread unemployment and bank foreclosures. His main thrust, however, was an attempt to restore confidence and stimulate private enterprise and state and local action and, toward this end, the Reconstruction Finance Corporation (RFC) was established (1932). Twelve million were unemployed by July 1932 and many people, encouraged by Hoover's political enemies and failing to realize that he was not personally responsible for the Depression, made him the object of their frustration and anger.

In the field of foreign affairs, Hoover promoted disarmament, took steps to improve relations with Latin America, and persuaded Congress to approve a moratorium on war debts and reparation payments.

In retirement, certain that had he been given more time as president his methods would have won out against the Depression, Hoover was an outspoken critic of Roosevelt's New Deal. In time, the people's attitude toward him softened and he became a respected elder statesman, accepting and successfully carrying out important assignments: coordinator of European Food Program (1947), chairman of Commission for Reorganization of the Executive Branch (1947-1949) for President Truman, chairman of the second Commission on Reorganization (1953-1955)

for President Eisenhower, founded Hoover Institution on War, Revolution and Peace at Stanford University. His books include *The Challenge to Liberty* (1934), three volumes of *Memoirs* (1951-1952) and *The Ordeal of Woodrow Wilson* (1958).

HOPKINS, ALBERT JARVIS *(b Aug. 15, 1846, DeKalb County, Ill.; d Aug. 23, 1922, Aurora, Ill.)* Lawyer, Illinois Republican. Kane County prosecutor (1872-1876), member of GOP state central committee (1878-1880), presidential elector on the Blaine-Logan ticket (1884), U.S. Representative (1885-1903), U.S. Senate (1903-1909), GOP National Convention delegate (1904, 1908).

HOPKINS, HARRY LLOYD *(b Aug. 17, 1890, Sioux City, Iowa; d Jan. 29, 1946, New York City)* Social worker, New York Democrat, and one of Franklin D. Roosevelt's closest friends and perhaps his most trusted adviser, even to living in the White House during much of World War II. Head of New York's Temporary Emergency Relief Administration (1931), the Federal Emergency Relief Administration (1933), and the Works Progress Administration (1935) distributing to the jobless more than $8 billion by 1938; U.S. secretary of commerce (1938-1940), lend-lease administrator (1941), adding to those duties membership on the War Production Board and the Anglo-American Munitions Assignment Board (1942). Politically, he was the string, the framework, and the tail to the FDR kite, the man responsible for the 1940 draft-Roosevelt movement. Upon Roosevelt's death, Truman retained him as a special adviser and credited him with saving the San Francisco United Nations Conference (1945).

HOPKINS, STEPHEN *(b March 7, 1707, Providence, R.I.; d July 13, 1785, Providence)* Farmer, surveyor, merchant, newspaper editor, Rhode Island patriot, colonial governor, and signer of the Declaration of Independence. Chief justice of the superior court (1751-1754, 1773), delegate to the Colonial Congress (1754), colonial governor (1755, 1756, 1758-1761, 1763, 1764, 1767), Continental Congress (1774-1780).

HOPKINSON, FRANCIS *(b Sept. 21, 1737, Philadelphia, Pa.; d May 9, 1791, Philadelphia)* A man of many talents and firsts: lawyer who received the first diploma from the University of Pennsylvania (1757), musician who composed the first native American secular song (1759), allegorist whose *A Pretty Story* (1774) bared American grievances and *The New Roof* (1787) supported the Constitution, artist who is said to have designed the first American flag (1777), New Jersey signer of the Declaration of Independence, New Jersey and Pennsylvania jurist. In Pennsylvania: secretary of commission that negotiated treaty with Indians (1761), an event that he commemorated in the poem *The Treaty*; member of Navy Board at Philadelphia (1776-1777), continental loan office treasurer (1778), admiralty court judge (1779-1789), delegate to state convention that ratified U.S. Constitution (1787), U.S. judge for the eastern district (1789-1791). In New Jersey: Salem port customs collector (1763-1766), member of Provincial Council (1774-1776) and executive council (1775), Continental Congress (1776). Father of Joseph Hopkinson.

HOPKINSON, JOSEPH *(b Nov. 12, 1770, Philadelphia, Pa.; d Jan. 15, 1842, Philadelphia)* Lawyer who was associated with Daniel Webster in one celebrated case of the time and was counsel for Supreme Court Justice Samuel Chase (1804, 1805) in his impeachment trial before the U.S. Senate; also a song writer who gave the country "Hail Columbia" (1798); Pennsylvania Federalist except for one brief period (1820-

1823) in New Jersey where he served in the state assembly. In Pennsylvania: U.S. Representative (1815-1819), federal judge for the state's eastern district (1828-1842), state constitutional convention chairman (1837), secretary of the University of Pennsylvania Board of Trustees (1790, 1791) and a trustee (1806-1819, 1822-1842). Son of Francis Hopkinson.

HORAN, WALTER FRANKLIN *(b Oct. 15, 1898, Wenatchee, Wash.)* Fruit grower, Washington Republican. U.S. Representative (1943-1965) serving on the Appropriations Committee.

HORNER, HENRY *(b Nov. 30, 1878, Chicago, Ill.; d Oct. 6, 1940, Winnetka, Ill.)* Lawyer, Illinois Democrat and foe of machine rule who as governor (1933-1940) pulled the state through the Depression years. Before that he had been Cook County probate judge (1914-1932) with a remarkable amount of human sympathy.

HORSEY, OUTERBRIDGE *(b March 5, 1777, near Laurel, Del.; d June 9, 1842, Frederick County, Md.).* Lawyer, Delaware Federalist. State representative (1800-1802), state attorney general (1806-1810), U.S. Senate (1810-1821).

HORTON, FRANK OGILVIE *(b Oct. 18, 1882, Muscatine, Iowa; d Aug. 17, 1948, Sheridan, Wyo.)* Rancher, Wyoming Republican. State representative (1921-1923), state senate (1923-1931) and its president (1931), GOP National Convention delegate (1928, 1936) and National Committeeman (1937-1948), U.S. Representative (1939-1941).

HOUGHTON, ALANSON BIGELOW *(b Oct. 10, 1863, Cambridge, Mass.; d Sept. 15, 1941, South Dartmouth, Mass.).* A founder and president of the Corning Glass Works, New York Republican. Trustee of Hobart and Stephens colleges, the Carnegie and Bamberger foundations, and the Princeton Institute. Presidential elector on the Roosevelt-Fairbanks (1904), Hughes-Fairbanks (1916), and Coolidge-Dawes (1924) tickets, U.S. Representative (1919-1922) resigning to become ambassador to Germany (1922-1925) and ambassador to England (1925-1929).

HOUK, JOHN CHILES *(b Feb. 26, 1860, Clinton, Tenn.; d June 3, 1923, Fountain City, Tenn.)* Lawyer, Tennessee Republican who was secretary of the state GOP committee for four years and assistant doorkeeper of the U.S. House of Representatives (1889-1891) while his father, Leonidas C. Houk, was a Congressman and whom, upon death, he replaced (1891-1895). After that a state senator (1896, 1910, 1916, 1918, 1920).

HOUK, LEONIDAS CAMPBELL *(b June 8, 1836, Sevier County, Tenn.; d May 25, 1891, Knoxville, Tenn.)* Cabinetmaker, preacher, Union Army officer, lawyer, writer, Tennessee Union Republican who as a circuit court judge (1866-1870) dismissed all treason cases brought before him contending that Tennessee, having seceded, was not a state during the Civil War. Presidential elector on the Lincoln-Johnson (1864), Grant-Wilson (1872), and Hayes-Wheeler (1876) tickets; state constitutional convention delegate (1865), GOP National Convention delegate (1868, 1880, 1884, 1888), state representative (1873-1875), U.S. Representative (1879 until death) being succeeded by his son, John C. Houk.

HOUSE, EDWARD MANDELL *(b July 26, 1858, Houston, Tex.; d March 28, 1938, New York City)* Cotton planter, businessman, Texas Democrat who refused ever to seek elective office but was famous as Woodrow Wilson's friend and closest adviser; known as Colonel House, an honorary title bestowed upon him while a member of the governor's staff (1892-1904) which he did not like but which nevertheless stayed with him for the rest of his life.

He served Wilson throughout the World War I years, maintaining close contact with Allies as chief of the U.S. mission to the Interallied Conference, formulator of the fourteen-point peace plan and drafter of the League of Nations Covenant. House and Wilson had a falling out in 1919, but for the next two decades the Colonel remained prominent as an elder statesman, adviser to both U.S. and European leaders and a champion of Franklin D. Roosevelt's 1932 presidential bid.

HOUSE, JOHN FORD *(b Jan. 9, 1827, Williamson County, Tenn.; d June 28, 1904, Clarksville, Tenn.)* Lawyer, Confederate soldier, Tennessee Constitutional Unionist who, upon secession, cast his lot with the South, ultimately becoming a Democrat. State representative (1853), presidential elector on the Constitutional Union ticket of Bell and Everett (1860), Democratic National Convention delegate (1868), state constitutional convention delegate (1870), U.S. Representative (1875-1883).

HOUSTON, GEORGE SMITH *(b Jan. 17, 1808, Williamson County, Tenn.; d Dec. 31, 1879, Athens, Ala.)* Lawyer, Alabama Union Democrat. State representative (1832), Florence judicial district state's attorney (1836), U.S. Representative (1841-1849, 1851-1861), Union National Convention delegate (1866), governor (1874-1878), U.S. Senate (March 3, 1879 until death).

HOUSTON, JOHN WALLACE *(b May 4, 1814, Concord, Del.; d April 26, 1896, Georgetown, Del.)* Lawyer, Delaware Whig. Delaware secretary of state (1841-1844), U.S. Representative (1845-1851), associate superior court judge (1855 until death), delegate to abortive peace-between-states conference (1861) Uncle of Robert G. Houston.

HOUSTON, ROBERT GRIFFITH *(b Oct. 13, 1867, Milton, Del.; d Jan. 29, 1946, Lewes, Del.)* Farmer, lawyer, publisher of the *Sussex Countian*, banker, Delaware Republican. Collector of customs (1900-1904), member of first State Anti-Tuberculosis Commission (1911-1914) and Commission for the Feeble Minded (1918-1936), assistant state attorney general (1920-1924, 1933-1935), U.S. Representative (1925-1933). Nephew of John W. Houston.

HOUSTON, SAMUEL *(b March 2, 1793, Timber Ridge Church, Va.; d July 26, 1863, Huntsville, Tex.)* Adopted Cherokee Indian, store clerk, Creek Indian fighter, lawyer, orator, Tennessee Democrat who moved later to the Cherokee Nation in what is now Oklahoma and then to Texas (1833) where he was the first president of the republic (1836-1838), returning again to that office (1841-1844) with the years in between spent as a member of the Texas Congress (1938-1840). In Tennessee: district attorney (1819), state adjutant general (1820), U.S. Representative (1823-1827), governor (1827-1829). In Texas: delegate to constitutional convention (1833) where he was chosen commander in chief of the Texas Army in the war for independence from Mexico that culminated with his victory over Santa Ana at San Jacinto (1836); member of the Republic's Congress (1838-1840); upon admission to the Union, one of the new state's first two U.S. Senators (1846-1859), governor (1859-1861) as an anti-secessionist Union Democrat being deposed for refusing to take the oath of allegiance to the Confederate States.

HOUSTON, VICTOR STEWART KALEOALOHA *(b July 22, 1876, San Francisco, Calif.; d July 31, 1959, Honolulu, Hawaii)* Annapolis graduate and U.S. Navy officer who retired in 1926, became active in Hawaiian Island Republican circles, and returned to active duty (1941-1945) during World War II. Delegate to the U.S. Congress (1927-1933), GOP National Convention delegate (1928-1932), member of Hawaiian Homes Commission (1945-1951).

HOUSTON, WILLIAM CANNON *(b March 17, 1852, Bedford County, Tenn.; d Aug. 30, 1931, near Woodbury, Tenn.).* Planter, newspaper publisher, lawyer, Tennessee Democrat. State representative (1877-1879, 1881-1885, 1879), Democratic state executive committeeman and chairman of party's state convention (1888), presidential elector on the Cleveland-Thurman ticket (1888), eighth judicial circuit judge (1894-1904), U.S. Representative (1905-1919).

HOUSTOUN, JOHN *(b Aug. 31, 1744, Waynesboro, Ga.; d July 20, 1796, near Savannah, Ga.)* Lawyer, Georgia patriot who was one of the four founders of the Sons of Liberty. Delegate to Provincial Congress (1775), member of Continental Congress (1775-1777, 1779) who was at home in Georgia when Declaration of Independence was signed, governor (1778, 1784), Georgia's chief justice (1786), Chatham County justice of the peace (1787), mayor of Savannah (1789, 1790), superior court judge (1792).

HOWARD, BENJAMIN *(b 1760, Lexington, Ky., which then was in Virginia; d Sept. 18, 1814, St. Louis, Mo.)* Kentucky lawyer who was the Madison-appointed governor of the Louisiana District at the time it became the Missouri Territory and continued as the chief executive officer, in both posts serving from April 10, 1810 until March 12, 1813, when he resigned to become an army general. Missouri's Howard County is named for him. In Kentucky: State representative (1801, 1802), U.S. Representative (1807-1810).

HOWARD, BENJAMIN CHEW *(b Nov. 5, 1791, near Baltimore, Md.; d March 6,*

1872, Baltimore) Lawyer, Maryland Democrat who was appointed official U.S. Supreme Court reporter (1843-1862) and wrote twenty-four volumes of Supreme Court Reports in a manner that was described as "models of clarity, diction, and thoroughness" by representatives of the legal profession. Baltimore councilman (1820), member of state house of delegates (1824), U.S. Representative (1829-1833, 1835-1839), U.S. emissary to settle Ohio-Michigan boundary dispute (1835), delegate to save-the-peace conference (1861). Son of John E. Howard.

HOWARD, EDGAR (b Sept. 16, 1858, Osceola, Iowa; d July 19, 1951, Columbus, Neb.) Lawyer, Nebraska newspaperman who purchased the Columbus Telegram (1900) and converted it from a weekly to a daily, Democrat. State representative (1894-1896), Sarpy County probate judge (1896-1900), lieutenant governor (1917-1919), U.S. Representative (1923-1935).

HOWARD, EVERETTE BURGESS (b Sept. 19, 1873, Morgantown, Ky.; d April 3, 1950, Midland, Tex.) Kentucky, Oklahoma, and Missouri newspaperman who struck it rich in the Oklahoma and Texas oil and gas fields, planted his roots in Tulsa, and became active in politics as a Democrat. Member of the state board of public affairs (1911-1915), state auditor (1915-1919), U.S. Representative (1919-1921, 1923-1925, 1927-1929).

HOWARD, JACOB MERRITT (b July 10, 1805, Shaftsbury, Vt.; d April 2, 1871, Detroit, Mich.) Lawyer, orator, Michigan Whig who drafted the platform for the first convention (1854) of a new political party to which he gave the name "Republican." Detroit city attorney (1834), state representative (1838), U.S. Representative (1841-1843), state attorney general (1855-1861), U.S. Senate (1862-1871) where he became the

bluntly outspoken leader of the GOP's radical wing, favoring among other things the fullest possible punishment of the South.

HOWARD, JOHN EAGER (b June 4, 1752, near Baltimore, Md.; d Oct. 12, 1827, near Baltimore) Planter, Revolutionary Army officer, Maryland Federalist who was the vice presidential candidate (1816) in the party's last national campaign. Continental Congress (1784-1788), governor (1789-1791), state senate (1791-1795), declined appointment as President Washington's secretary of war (1795), U.S. Senate (1796-1803). Father of Benjamin C. Howard.

HOWARD, WILLIAM ALANSON (b April 8, 1813, Hinesburg, Vt.; d April 10, 1880, Washington, D.C.) Lawyer, Michigan Republican whom President Hayes appointed governor of Dakota Territory (1878 until death). Detroit city treasurer (1848-1850), U.S. Representative (1855-1859, 1860-1861), GOP state central committee chairman (1860, 1861), Detroit postmaster (1861-1866), declined appointment as minister to China (1869), railroad lands commissioner (1869-1878), GOP National Convention delegate (1868, 1872, 1876).

HOWARD, WILLIAM MARCELLUS (b Dec. 6, 1857, Berwick City, La.; d July 5, 1932, Augusta, Ga.) Lawyer, Georgia Democrat. Northern circuit solicitor general (1884-1896), U.S. Representative (1897-1911), Smithsonian Institution regent (1905-1912), an original trustee of the Carnegie Endowment for International Peace (1910), U.S. Tariff Board member (1911-1913).

HOWE, JULIA WARD (b May 27, 1819, New York City; d Oct. 17, 1910, Middletown, R.I.) Minor poet, essayist, editor, reformer, lecturer. Organizer whose early activities were involved with abolition and women's rights but who later in life espoused causes directed at improving a great many areas of human existence, including the founding of a world peace organization. Descendant of Richard Ward and Samuel Ward, both Rhode Island colonial governors, exceptionally well-educated daughter of a wealthy banker, she married (1843) humanitarian Samuel Gridley Howe. The couple associated with many of the leading intellectuals and reformers of the time and were drawn into the abolitionist movement. They edited an antislavery paper, *The Commonwealth*, and their home became a center for abolitionist activity.

In December 1861, while visiting a Civil War army camp near Washington, Julia watched a Northern army go into battle singing "John Brown's Body." Stirred by the sight, she was later moved to write the words of "The Battle Hymn of the Republic" to the same tune.

One of the first vice presidents of the New England Woman's Club, organized in 1868, she served as its president most of the time from 1871 to 1910. Active in the women's suffrage movement, she joined with Lucy Stone and others of the movement's leaders in forming the American Woman's Suffrage Association. Instrumental in organizing and the opening speaker at the World's Congress of Women in Behalf of International Peace held in New York in 1870. A year later she became president of the newly formed American Branch of the Woman's International Peace Association.

HOWE, LOUIS McHENRY *(b Jan. 14, 1871, Indianapolis, Ind.; d April 18, 1936, Washington, D.C.)* Albany correspondent for the *New York Telegram* (1911) who met a young and promising state senator, Franklin Delano Roosevelt, and became his secretary and political strategist-adviser. Among his achievements, he taught Eleanor Roosevelt how to be a successful campaigner.

Upon Howe's death, she wrote his lasting eulogy which began: "There has never been a story of greater devotion to another man's success. . . ."

HOWE, TIMOTHY OTIS *(b Feb. 24, 1816, Livermore, Maine; d March 25, 1883, Kenosha, Wis.)* Lawyer, Wisconsin Union Republican who was postmaster general in the Arthur cabinet (1881 until death). Circuit and state supreme court judge (1850-1855), U.S. Senate (1861-1879), delegate to International Monetary Conference in Paris (1881). Before moving to Wisconsin (1845) he was a state representative in Maine in the same year.

HOWELL, BENJAMIN FRANKLIN *(b Jan. 27, 1844, Cedarville, N.J.; d Feb. 1, 1933, New Brunswick, N.J.)* Union soldier, merchant, banker, New Jersey Republican. Middlesex County surrogate (1882-1892), U.S. Representative (1895-1911), GOP National Convention delegate (1896), U.S. immigration commissioner (1907-1910).

HOWELL, CLARK *(b Sept. 21, 1863, Barnwell County, S.C.; d Nov. 14, 1936, Atlanta, Ga.)* Editor of the *Atlanta Constitution*, Georgia Democrat who was active in state politics, was recognized nationally by a string of presidents and, as a close friend of Franklin D. Roosevelt, organized the nation's first Roosevelt-for-President clubs.

HOWELL, DAVID *(b Jan. 1, 1747, Morristown, N.J.; d July 21, 1824, Providence, R.I.)* Rhode Island lawyer, jurist, civic and political leader but—more than that—a Brown University educator with this chronology: tutor (1766-1769), professor of natural philosophy (1769-1779), fellow (1773-1824), secretary (1780-1806), professor of law (1790-1824), acting president (1791, 1792). His judicial and political offices: justice of the peace (1779), common pleas judge (1780), Continental Congress (1782-

1785), state supreme court justice (1786, 1787), state attorney general (1789), U.S. district court judge (1812 until death). Father of Jeremiah Brown Howell.

HOWELL, JEREMIAH BROWN *(b Aug. 28, 1771, Providence, R.I.; d Feb. 5, 1822, Providence)* Lawyer, Rhode Island Federalist. U.S. Senate (1811-1817). Son of David Howell.

HOWELL, JOSEPH *(b Feb. 17, 1857, Brigham City, Utah; d July 18, 1918, Logan, Utah)* Teacher, merchant, real estate dealer, banker, Utah Republican. Mayor of Wellsville (1882-1884), member of the territorial house of representatives (1886-1892) and, after statehood, University of Utah regent (1896-1900), state senate (1896-1900), U.S. Representative (1903-1917).

HUBBARD, ASAHEL WHEELER *(b Jan. 19, 1819, Haddam, Conn.; d Sept. 22, 1879, Sioux City, Iowa)* Teacher, lawyer, railroad builder, real estate operator, banker, who served in the Indiana House of Representatives (1847-1849) before moving to Iowa and becoming an active Republican. Fourth judicial district judge (1859-1862), U.S. Representative (1863-1869). Father of Elbert H. Hubbard.

HUBBARD, ELBERT HAMILTON *(b Aug. 1849, Rushville, Ind.; d June 4, 1912, Sioux City, Iowa)* Lawyer, Iowa Republican. State representative (1882), state senate (1900-1902), U.S. Representative (1905 until death). Son of Asahel W. Hubbard.

HUBBELL, JAY ABEL *(b Sept. 15, 1829, Avon, Mich.; d Oct. 13, 1900, Houghton, Mich.)* Lawyer, Michigan Republican. Houghton County prosecutor (1861-1867), U.S. Representative (1873-1883), state senate (1885-1887), twelfth judicial circuit judge (1894-1899).

HUCK, WINNIFRED SPRAGUE MASON *(b Sept. 14, 1882, Chicago, Ill.; d Aug. 24, 1936, Chicago)* Journalist, lecturer, Illinois Republican who succeeded her father, William E. Mason, as U.S. Representative (1922-1923).

HUDDLESTON, GEORGE, SR. *(b Nov. 11, 1869, Wilson County, Tenn.; d Feb. 29, 1960, Birmingham, Ala.)* Lawyer, Alabama Democrat, U.S. Representative (1915-1937).

HUDSPETH, CLAUDE BENTON *(b May 12, 1877, Medina, Tex.; d March 19, 1941, San Antonio, Tex.)* Publisher of the *Ozona Kicker*, rancher, oil and land operator, lawyer, Texas Democrat. State representative (1902-1906), state senator (1906-1918) and four times senate president, U.S. Representative (1919-1931).

HUFF, GEORGE FRANKLIN *(b July 16, 1842, Norristown, Pa.; d April 18, 1912, Washington, D.C.)* Mine operator, industrialist, Pennsylvania Republican. GOP National Convention delegate (1880), state senate (1884-1888), U.S. Representative (1891-1893, 1895-1897, 1903-1911).

HUGHES, CHARLES EVANS *(b April 11, 1862, Glens Falls, N.Y.; d Aug. 27, 1948, Osterville, Mass.)* Latin and Greek teacher while studying law, professor of law at Cornell University (1891-1893), author, New York Republican who was Woodrow Wilson's presidential opponent (1916), and—as he is best-remembered—as the Hoover-appointed Chief Justice of the United States (1930-1941). He was considered one of the greatest jurists of his time. Governor (1907-1910), Taft-appointed associate justice of the Supreme Court (1910) resigning (1916) upon receiving the GOP presidential nomination; in that race Hughes received 8,533,507 popular and 254 electoral votes to Wilson's 9,127,695 popular and 277 electoral votes; Harding-appointed secretary of state (1921-1925), member of the Permanent Court of Arbitration at The Hague (1926-1930), Permanent Court of International Justice judge (1928-1930).

As chief justice, Hughes opposed Roosevelt's creation of new government agencies, contending they would usurp functions of the courts. He did, on the other hand, support much of the New Deal social program. Many of his written opinions became legal classics. Among his published books are *Conditions of Progress in Democratic Government* (1909), *The Pathway of Peace, and Other Addresses* (1925), *The Supreme Court of the United States* (1927), and *Pan-American Peace Plans* (1929).

HUGHES, CHARLES JAMES, JR. *(b Feb. 16, 1853, Kingston, Mo.; d Jan. 11, 1911, Denver, Colo.)* Lawyer, Harvard and University of Denver professor, Colorado Democrat. Presidential elector on the Bryan-Stevenson ticket (1900), Democratic National Convention delegate (1904, 1908), U.S. Senate (1909 until death).

HUGHES, JAMES ANTHONY *(b Feb. 27, 1861, Ontario, Canada; d March 2, 1930, Marion, Ohio)* Traveling salesman, timber man, real estate dealer, West Virginia and Kentucky Republican. In Kentucky: state representative (1888-1890). In West Virginia: state senate (1894-1898), delegate to GOP state convention (1896, 1898) and to all national conventions (1892-1924), Huntington postmaster (1896-1900), U.S. Representative (1901-1915, 1927 until death).

HUGHES, JAMES HURD *(b Jan. 14, 1867, Kent County, Del.; d Aug. 29, 1953, Lewes, Del.)* Lawyer, farmer, banker, Delaware Democrat. Delaware secretary of state (1897-1901), presidential elector on the Wilson-Marshall ticket (1912), unsuccessful candidate for governor (1916), U.S. Senate (1937-1943).

HUGHES, WILLIAM *(b April 3, 1872, Drogheda, Ireland; d Jan. 30, 1918, Trenton, N.J.)* Court reporter, lawyer, New Jersey Democrat. U.S. Representative (1903-1905, 1907-1912), Passaic County common pleas judge by appointment of Governor Woodrow Wilson (1912-1913), U.S. Senate (1913 until death).

HULL, CORDELL *(b Oct. 2, 1871, Olympus, Tenn.; d July 23, 1955, in U.S. Naval Hospital, Bethesda, Md.)* Lawyer, Tennessee Democrat who won the Nobel Peace Prize (1945) for his part in organizing the United Nations, and was secretary of state in the Roosevelt cabinet (1933-1944). Democratic state convention delegate (1890), state representative (1893-1897), army captain in the Spanish-American War, fifth judicial circuit judge (1903-1906), U.S. Representative (1907-1921, 1923-1931), chairman of the Democratic National Executive Committee (1921-1924), U.S. Senate (1931-1933).

HULL, HARRY EDWARD *(b March 12, 1864, Allegany County, N.Y.; d Jan. 16, 1938, Washington, D.C.)* Bookkeeper, grain merchant, brick manufacturer, telephone company president, Iowa Republican. Williamsburg alderman (1887-1889), mayor (1889-1901), and postmaster (1901-1914); U.S. Representative (1915-1925), Coolidge-appointed commissioner general of immigration (1925-1933).

HULL, JOHN ALBERT TIFFIN *(b May 1, 1841, Sabina, Ohio; d Sept. 26, 1928, Clarendon, Va.)* Union Army officer, lawyer, farmer, banker, Iowa Republican. Secretary of the state senate (1872-1878), Iowa secretary of state (1878-1884), lieutenant governor (1885-1889), U.S. Representative (1891-1911).

HULL, MERLIN *(b Dec. 18, 1870, Warsaw, Ind.; d May 17, 1953, LaCrosse, Wis.)* Lawyer, farmer, publisher of the *Jackson County Journal* (1904-1926) and *Banner-Journal* (1926-1953), Wisconsin Republican-Progressive-Republican. Jackson County district attorney (1907-1909), state assemblyman (1909-1915) and speaker (1913), secretary of state (1917-1921), U.S. Representative (1929-1931, 1935 until death).

HUMPHREY, WILLIAM EWART *(b March 31, 1862, Montgomery County, Ind.; d Feb. 14, 1934, Washington, D.C.).* Lawyer, Washington Republican. Seattle corporation counsel (1898-1902), U.S. Representative (1903-1917), Coolidge-appointed member of the Federal Trade Commission (1925-1933).

HUMPHREYS, BENJAMIN GRUBB, SR. *(b Aug. 25, 1808, Claiborne County, Miss.; d Dec. 20, 1882, Leflore County, Miss.)* West Point cadet who was expelled for participating in a Christmas Eve (1826) student riot, Mississippi planter, insurance agent, antisecessionist Whig who nevertheless served as a Confederate officer during the Civil War, then became a Democrat and the first elected governor in the postwar period, serving (1865-1868) until he was ousted forcibly by the U.S. military. Earlier he had been a state legislator (1838-1846).

HUMPHREYS, BENJAMIN GRUBB, JR. *(b Aug. 17, 1865, Claiborne County, Miss.; d Oct. 16, 1923, Greenville, Miss.)* Merchant, lawyer, Mississippi Democrat. Leflore County superintendent of education (1892-1896), fourth district attorney (1895-1903), U.S. Representative (1903 until death), Democratic National Convention delegate (1920). Father of William Y. Humphreys.

HUMPHREYS, CHARLES *(b Sept. 19, 1714, Haverford, Pa.; d March 11, 1786, Haverford)* Pennsylvania miller who served in the Provincial Congress (1764-1774) and the Continental Congress (1774-1776), but refused to sign the Declaration of Independence because, as a Quaker, he did not believe in war.

HUMPHREYS, WILLIAM YERGER *(b Sept. 9, 1890, Greenville, Miss.; d Feb. 26, 1933, Greenville)* Lawyer, Mississippi Democrat who became a U.S. Representative upon the death of his father, Benjamin Grubb Humphreys, Jr., (1923-1925) but did not seek renomination or reelection. Washington County prosecutor (1928 until death).

HUNT, GEORGE WYLIE PAUL *(b Nov. 1, 1859, Huntsville, Mo.; d Dec. 24, 1934, Phoenix, Ariz.)* Prospector, miner, construction hand, cowboy and itinerant worker who roamed the West, finally settled in Arizona, became a rancher and firm friend of labor, a highly progressive Democrat who did much to achieve statehood, became nationally known and a living legend of the Southwest. Arizona's first governor after it became a state and the only man ever to hold that office for six terms (1912-1919, 1923-1929, 1931-1933). Wilson-appointed minister to what was then Siam but is now Thailand (1920-1921).

HUNT, JONATHAN *(b Aug. 12, 1787, Vernon, Vt.; d May 15, 1832, Washington, D.C.)* Lawyer, banker, Vermont National Republican. State representative (1811, 1816, 1817, 1824), U.S. Representative (1827 until death).

HUNT, LESTER CALLAWAY *(b July 8, 1892, Isabel, Ill.; d June 19, 1954, Washington, D.C.)* Dentist, Wyoming Democrat. President of state board of dental examiners (1924-1928), state representative (1933, 1934), Wyoming secretary of state (1935-1943), governor (1943-

1949), chairman of governors' conference (June 1948), U.S. Senate (1949 until death).

HUNT, WASHINGTON *(b Aug. 5, 1811, Windham, N.Y.; d Feb. 2, 1867, New York City)* Lawyer, farmer, New York Whig turned Democrat who was offered the Democratic vice presidential nomination (1860) but declined. Niagara County common pleas judge (1836-1841), U.S. Representative (1843-1849), state comptroller (1849, 1850), governor (1850-1852), temporary chairman of the last Whig National Convention(1856), Democratic National Convention delegate (1864).

HUNTER, ROBERT MERCER TALIAFERRO *(b April 21, 1809, Essex County, Va.; d July 18, 1887, near Lloyds, Va.)* Lawyer, Virginia States' Rights Whig turned Democrat who unsuccessfully sought the Democratic presidential nomination (1860), Southern statesman who was one of the peace commissioners that met with Abraham Lincoln at Hampton Roads (1865), a man who declined appointment as secretary of state in the cabinets of Presidents Pierce and Buchanan. Member of state house of delegates (1833), state senate (1835-1837), U.S. Representative (1837-1843, 1845-1847) and House speaker (1839-1841), U.S. Senate (1847-1861) and author of the 1857 tariff act. In the Confederacy, provisional congressman (1861), secretary of state (1861-1862), Senate (1862-1865) often serving as president pro tem. After the war, state treasurer (1877), Tappahannock tax collector (1885).

HUNTER, WHITESIDE GODFREY *(b Dec. 25, 1841, near Belfast, Ireland; d Nov. 2, 1917, Louisville, Ky.)* Physician, Union Army surgeon, oil lands and utilities speculator, Kentucky Republican. State representative (1874-1878), GOP National Convention delegate (1880, 1892), minister to Guatemala and Honduras (1897-1902), U.S. Representative (1887-1889, 1895-1897, 1903-1905).

HUNTER, WILLIAM *(b Nov. 26, 1774, Newport, R.I.; d Dec. 3, 1849, Newport).* Lawyer, diplomat, Rhode Island Federalist. State representative (1799-1811, 1822-1826), U.S. Senate (1811-1821), Jackson-appointed chargé d'affaires (1834-1841) and Tyler-appointed minister (1841-1843) to Brazil.

HUNTINGTON, BENJAMIN *(b April 19, 1736, Norwich, Conn.; d Oct. 16, 1800, Rome, N.Y.)* Connecticut lawyer. Windham County surveyor (1764), state representative (1771-1780) and house speaker (1778, 1779), clerk of the house (1776, 1777), delegate to Provincial Congress (1778), Continental Congress (1780-1784, 1787, 1788), state senator (1781-1790, 1791-1793), mayor of Norwich (1784-1796), U.S. Representative in the First Congress (1789-1791), state superior court judge (1793-1798).

HUNTINGTON, JABEZ WILLIAMS *(b Nov. 8, 1788, Norwich, Conn.; d Nov. 1, 1847, Norwich)* Lawyer, teacher, Connecticut Whig. State representative (1829), U.S. Representative (1829-1834), state supreme court of errors judge (1834-1840), U.S. Senate (1840 until death).

HUNTINGTON, SAMUEL *(b July 3, 1731, Windham, Conn.; d Jan. 5, 1796, Norwich, Conn.)* Cooper, lawyer, Connecticut signer of the Declaration of Independence. Executive councillor (1763), colonial assemblyman (1765), crown attorney (1765), superior court judge (1774-1784) and its chief justice in the last year, member of Continental Congress (1776-1784) and its president (1779-1781), lieutenant governor (1785), governor (1786 until death).

HUNTON, EPPA *(b Sept. 22, 1822, Fauquier County, Va.; d Oct. 11, 1908, Rich-*

mond, Va.) Teacher, lawyer, Confederate Army officer, Virginia Democrat. Prince William County commonwealth attorney (1849-1861), member of the state convention (1861), U.S. Representative (1873-1881), U.S. Senate to fill a vacancy (1892-1895).

HURLBUT, STEPHEN AUGUSTUS (b Nov. 29, 1815, Charleston, S.C.; d March 27, 1882, Lima, Peru) Lawyer, Union officer who was one of the founders of the Grand Army of the Republic, diplomat, Illinois Whig-Republican. State constitutional convention delegate (1847), Whig presidential elector (1848), state representative (1859, 1861, 1867), commander in chief of the GAR (1866-1868), GOP presidential elector (1868), minister to Colombia (1869-1872), U.S. Representative (1873-1877), minister to Peru (1881 until death).

HUSTING, PAUL OSCAR (b April 25, 1866, Fond du Lac, Wis.; d Oct. 21, 1917, Rush Lake, Wis., by accident while duck hunting) Lawyer with two big interests in life—politics and conservation of natural resources. Wisconsin Democrat who cooperated closely with the La Follette Progressives and the man largely credited with carrying the state

for Woodrow Wilson in 1912. Dodge County district attorney (1902-1906), state senate (1907-1913), the first man from Wisconsin sent to the U.S. Senate (1915 until death) by direct vote of the people.

HUTCHINSON, ANNE (b c 1591, Alford, Lincolnshire, England; d 1643, in what is now Pelham Bay Park, N.Y.) A kindly, intellectual student of the Bible and mother of fourteen children, she emigrated (1634) with her husband and family to Massachusetts Bay. There the Puritans were attracted in increasing numbers to the informal meetings she held in her home where she presented her religious views that were based on the idea that salvation depended on faith alone rather than on one's deeds. Accused of practicing "antinomianism" she was tried for "traducing the ministers and their ministry," found guilty, and banished from the colony. The Hutchinsons moved (1638), along with some of Anne's followers, to Rhode Island where there was greater religious freedom and where she and William Coddington founded what is now Portsmouth. After quarrelling with Coddington, she moved on to Long Island, then to what is now Pelham Bay, where she was killed in an Indian uprising.

I

☆ ☆ ☆

IGLESIAS, SANTIAGO (born Santiago Iglesias Pantin) *(b Feb. 22, 1872, La Coruña, Spain; d Dec. 5, 1939, Washington, D.C.)* Cabinetmaker in Spain, labor leader in Cuba, and thereafter a lifetime resident of Puerto Rico where he was the founding editor of three labor newspapers and a labor leader who became resident commissioner to the United States as a Coalitionist (1933 until death).

INGALLS, JOHN JAMES *(b Dec. 29, 1833, Middleton, Mass.; d Aug. 16, 1900, East Las Vegas, N.Mex.)* Lawyer, farmer, journalist who was one of the founders of the *Kansas Magazine*, nationally known orator with a biting tongue, Kansas Republican whose role as party leader was more titular than factual. Secretary of the territorial council (1860), state senate secretary (1861), state senator (1862), U.S. Senate (1873-1891) and president pro tem (1887-1891).

INGERSOLL, RALPH ISAACS *(b Feb. 8, 1789, New Haven, Conn.; d Aug. 26, 1872, New Haven)* Lawyer, Connecticut Democrat. State representative (1820-1825) and house speaker (1824, 1825), U.S. Representative (1825-1833), New Haven County state's attorney (1833), minister to Russia (1846-1848), mayor of New Haven (1851).

INGERSOLL, ROBERT GREEN *(b Aug. 11, 1833, Dresden, N.Y.; d July 21, 1899, Dobbs Ferry, N.Y.)* Lawyer, lecturer known as "the great agnostic," Union Army officer, Illinois Democrat turned Republican, and a campaign orator of national note who delivered the nominating speech for James G. Blaine at the GOP National Convention (1876). The nomination went to Rutherford B. Hayes, but Blaine was known forevermore as "the plumed knight" and Ingersoll could not begin to keep up with all the speaking engagements that came his way.

INGHAM, SAMUEL DELUCENNA *(b Sept. 16, 1779, Bucks County, Pa.; d June 5, 1860, Trenton, N.J.)* Paper manufacturer, coal field developer, Pennsylvania Democrat who resigned as Andrew Jackson's secretary of the treasury (1829-1831) in the furor that raged over the social acceptance of the former Peggy O'Neale, the wife of Secretary of War John H. Eaton. U.S. Representative (1813-1818, 1822-1829), chief clerk of the Bucks County courts (1818, 1819), secretary of the commonwealth (1819-1820).

IRELAND, JOHN *(b Jan. 1, 1827, near Millerstown, Ky.; d March 15, 1896, Seguin, Texas).* Lawyer, Confederate Army officer, Texas Democrat who while

331

governor (1883-1887) bungled the handling of fence-cutting and labor strikes but did see to it that the state capitol was properly built. He was Seguin's first mayor (1858-1860), state representative (1872), state senate (1873-1874), associate justice of the state supreme court (1875, 1876) and several times lost elections to national office.

IRVING, WILLIAM *(b Aug. 15, 1766, New York City; d Nov. 9, 1821, New York City)* Merchant, fur trader, contributor of poems and essays to *Salmagundi*, which was published by his younger brother, Washington Irving, the light of his life whose literary career he helped to finance and to foster. As a New York Democrat, he was a U.S. Representative (1814-1819).

IVERSON, ALFRED, SR. *(b Dec. 3, 1798, Waynesboro, Ga.; d March 5, 1873, East Macon, Ga.)* Lawyer, planter, Georgia Democrat, and ardent believer in Southern rights and, ultimately, secession, who argued that it was the federal government's duty to protect slavery both in the states where it existed and in territories to which some men wanted it spread. State representative (1827-1830), state superior court judge (1835-1837, 1849-1853), state senate (1843, 1844), presidential elector on the Polk-Dallas ticket (1844), U.S. Representative (1847-1849), U.S. Senate (1855-1861).

IVES, IRVING McNEIL *(b Jan. 24, 1896, Bainbridge, N.Y.; d Feb. 24, 1962, Norwich, N.Y.)* Banker, insurance broker, Hamilton College and Cornell University trustee, New York Republican. Member of state assembly (1930-1946), minority leader (1935), speaker (1936), majority leader (1937-1946); chairman of New York State Temporary Commission Against Discrimination (1944, 1945), dean of New York State School of Industrial and Labor Relations (1945-1947), U.S. Senate (1947-1959).

J

☆ ☆ ☆

JACKSON, ANDREW *(b March 15, 1767, probably in Waxhaw, South Carolina; d June 8, 1845, at the Hermitage near Nashville, Tenn.).* Seventh president (Tennessee Democrat), 1829-1837; came from obscure, poor background to become a colorful military hero, school teacher, lawyer, legislator, planter, and horse racer.

Jackson's father probably died shortly before his birth, his mother died when he was fourteen, and most of his early years he shifted for himself, becoming a self-reliant but fun-loving young man who briefly studied the law and was admitted (1787) to the North Carolina bar. Hot-headed, he fought many a duel, at least once because of the unconventional nature of his marriage (1791) to Rachel Donelson Robards which (apparently without the couple realizing their error) took place before Rachel's first husband obtained a divorce. Jackson and his wife (they had no children but adopted her nephew, Andrew Jackson, Jr.) made their home at the Hermitage, a cotton plantation near Nashville.

Appointed public prosecutor (1788) in western North Carolina (later Tennessee); delegate to Tennessee state constitutional convention (1796), U.S. Representative (1796-1797) and U.S. Senate (1797-1798, 1823-1825); popular Tennessee Superior Court judge (1798-1804).

Major general in command of the Tennessee militia (1802) and commissioned major general in U.S. Army during War of 1812. Defeated Chief Red Eagle (bringing an end to the British-inspired Creek uprising) at the Battle of Horseshoe Bend. At Battle of New Orleans, defeated vastly superior enemy forces and won the only great victory of the war—15 days after peaceful settlement had been reached at Ghent. "Old Hickory," as the tall, straight, impressive Jackson was affectionately called by his troops, became the people's beloved hero. It didn't dim his glory in their eyes when (1817-1818) as commander of U.S. troops in the Seminole War, he either exceeded his authority or misunderstood orders and created a serious international problem by pursuing the Indians into Spanish-held Florida and capturing forts there. Governor of Florida (March to July 1821).

Jackson became a leader of the Democratic party with a strong (if somewhat emotional) appeal to the Western settler, the Eastern laborer, the small man. Ran for president in 1824, polling the most votes in a four-way race, but did not receive a majority so election went to the House and John Quincy Adams won when Henry Clay (one of the four contestants) withdrew and turned his support over to Adams. Jackson's claim that a deal had been made was unsubstantiated but aroused sympathy. He ran again in 1828, this time winning easily with 178 electoral votes to John Quincy Adams' 83. He won again in 1832, with 219 electoral votes to 49 for Henry Clay. His beloved Rachel died shortly before his first term began.

As president, Jackson believed in party loyalty, rewarded it with government jobs, a procedure that came to be called the "spoils system," and helped develop "Jacksonian" democracy. Controversy developed between him and his South Carolinian vice president, John C. Calhoun, one aggravation being the Eaton affair in which Mrs. Peggy O'Neale Eaton, wife of the secretary of war, was snubbed by Mrs. Calhoun. When Calhoun (who resigned in December 1832) argued that South Carolina had the right to nullify and ignore federal tariff regulations because it considered them unconstitutional, Jackson stood by the Union and counteracted by threatening to use the Force Bill. A compromise tariff saved the situation. But Jackson refused to enforce a Supreme Court ruling that would have prevented the state of Georgia from removing the Cherokee Indians. He vetoed a recharter bill for the Second Bank of the United States in July 1832 (thereby making it a major issue in the 1832 election), removed the funds and put them in state banks. Issued the Specie Circular (1836), requiring public land payments to be made in coin, not paper money. This slowed down land speculation but was a factor in hastening the Panic of 1837.

In retirement at the Hermitage, Jackson continued to exert a strong influence on the Democratic party.

JACKSON, CLAIBORNE FOX *(b April 4, 1806, Fleming County, Ky.; d Dec. 6, 1862, near Little Rock, Ark.)* Merchant, proslavery Missouri Democrat who switched allegiance from U.S. Senator Thomas H. Benton to membership in the so-called Central Clique whose policies were set forth in the Jackson Resolutions that were passed by the state assembly (1848). As governor (1861) he did not openly favor secession, but did oppose coercion.

JACKSON, EDWARD BRAKE *(b Jan. 25, 1793, Clarksburg, Va., now W.Va.; d Sept. 8, 1826, Bedford Springs, Pa.).* Physician, Virginia Democrat. State house of delegates (1815-1818), U.S. district court clerk (1819), U.S. Representative (1820-1823). Son of George and brother of John G. Jackson.

JACKSON, GEORGE *(b Jan. 9, 1757, Cecil County, Md.; d May 17, 1831, Zanesville, Ohio)* A lawyer in Virginia, a farmer in Ohio, and a Revolutionary army officer who held office in both. In Virginia: justice of the peace (1784), state house of delegates (1785-1791, 1794), delegate to the state convention that ratified the U.S. Constitution (1788), U.S. Representative (1795-1797, 1799-1803). In Ohio: State representative (1809-1812), state senate (1817-1819). Father of Edward B. and John G. Jackson.

JACKSON, HOWELL EDMUNDS *(b April 8, 1832, Paris, Tenn.; d Aug. 8, 1895, West Meade, Tenn.)* Lawyer, Tennessee Democrat who much preferred the softness of judicial robes to the rough and tumble of politics and so happily served as associate justice of the U.S. Supreme Court (1893 until death). State representative (1880), U.S. Senate (1881-1886) resigning to accept appointment as U.S. circuit judge for the sixth federal circuit (1886-1893).

JACKSON, JABEZ YOUNG *(b July 1790, Savannah, Ga.; d Clarkesville, Ga.).* Georgia Union Democrat. U.S. Representative (1835-1839). Son of the following James Jackson, uncle of the other.

JACKSON, JAMES *(b Sept. 21, 1757, Devonshire, England; d March 19, 1806,*

Washington, D.C.) Lawyer, Georgia Democrat, Revolutionary Army officer who accepted the keys to Savannah from the British (1782) and so was given a house by a grateful state assembly. Clerk of the Savannah court (1776, 1777), delegate to state's first constitutional convention (1777), U.S. Representative in the First Congress (1789-1791), U.S. Senate (1793-1795, 1801 until death), presidential elector on the Jefferson-Clinton ticket (1797), governor (1798-1801). Father of Jabez Y. and grandfather of the following entry.

JACKSON, JAMES *(b Oct. 18, 1819, Jefferson County, Ga.; d Jan. 13, 1887, Atlanta, Ga.)*. Lawyer, jurist, Georgia Democrat who was judge advocate on the staff of General Thomas J. (Stonewall) Jackson during the Civil War. State senate secretary (1842), state representative (1845, 1847), superior court judge (1846-1859), U.S. Representative (1857-1861) resigning upon Georgia's secession, associate justice of the state supreme court (1875-1889) and then chief justice (1889 until death). Grandson of the preceding, nephew of Jabez Y. Jackson. No known relationship with General Jackson.

JACKSON, JOHN GEORGE *(b Sept. 22, 1777, Buckhannon, Va.; d March 28, 1825, Clarksburg, Va.; both municipalities are now in W.Va.)*. Civil engineer, Virginia Democrat who while in Congress was wounded in a duel with Congressman Joseph Pearson, a North Carolina Federalist. Surveyor of public lands in what is now Ohio (1793), member of state house of burgesses (1798-1801), U.S. Representative (1803-1810, 1813-1817), member of state house of delegates (1811, 1812) and the first U.S. judge for Virginia's western district (1819 until death). Son of George and brother of Edward B, Jackson.

JACKSON, RICHARD, JR. *(b July 3, 1764, Providence, R.I.; d April 18, 1838, Providence)* Manufacturer, insurance executive, Rhode Island Federalist. U.S. Representative (1808-1815), Brown University trustee (1809-1838).

JACKSON, SAMUEL DILLON *(b May 28, 1895, Allen County, Ind.; d March 8, 1951, Fort Wayne, Ind.)* Lawyer, Indiana Democrat who was a power in party affairs although he never held high elective office. Allen County prosecutor (1924-1928), chairman of Democratic state speakers' bureau (1934) and state convention (1936), state attorney general (1940), appointed to U.S. Senate to fill a vacancy (1944), unsuccessful candidate for governor (1944), permanent chairman of the Democratic National Convention (1944).

JACKSON, WILLIAM *(b Sept. 2, 1783, Newton, Mass.; d Feb. 26, 1855, Newton)* Soap and candle manufacturer, banker, newspaper publisher, Massachusetts Whig who was one of the founders of the Liberty party (1846), and a man of many intense interests, among them construction of railroads, abolition of slavery, spreading of the Biblical Word, better education opportunities for women, and temperance; the latter was such a strong interest that he ended the practice of serving daily allotments of rum to his employes, adding the money so saved to their pay envelopes instead. State representative (1829-1832), secretary of the Newton Female Academy (1831), U.S. Representative (1833-1837), founding president of the American Missionary Society (1846-1854).

JACKSON, WILLIAM HUMPHREYS *(b Oct. 15, 1839, Wicomico County, Md.; d April 3, 1915, Salisbury, Md.)*. Farmer, lumber manufacturer, Maryland Republican. U.S. Representative (1901-1905, 1907-1909). Father of William P. Jackson.

JACKSON, WILLIAM PURNELL *(b Jan. 11, 1868, Salisbury, Md.; d March 7, 1939, Salisbury)* Businessman, banker, railroad director, Maryland Republican. GOP National Committee member (1908-1932), U.S. Senate to fill a vacancy (1912-1914). Son of William H. Jackson.

JACOBS, ORANGE *(b May 2, 1827, Livingston County, N.Y.; d May 21, 1914, Seattle, Wash.)* Lawyer, Washington Territory Republican. Associate justice of the territorial supreme court (1869-1071) and chief justice (1871-1875), delegate to the U.S. Congress (1875-1879), mayor of Seattle (1880), member of territorial council (1885-1887) and Seattle charter revision commission (1889), city corporation counsel (1890), Kings County superior court judge (1896-1900).

JACOBSEN, BERNHARD MARTIN *(b March 26, 1862, Schleswig-Holstein, Germany; d June 30, 1936, Rochester, Minn.).* Merchant, industrial financier, Iowa Democrat. Clinton postmaster (1914-1923), U.S. Representative (1931 until death). Father of William S. Jacobsen.

JACOBSEN, WILLIAM SEBASTIAN *(b Jan. 15, 1887, Clinton, Iowa; d April 10, 1955, Dubuque, Iowa)* Physical education instructor, merchant, business manager, Iowa Democrat who was a delegate to all of his party's state conventions (1932-1944) and national conventions (1936, 1944). U.S. Representative (1937-1943), War Assets Administration liaison officer (1945-1947), Clinton's acting postmaster (1951-1954). Son of Bernhard M. Jacobsen.

JACOWAY, HENDERSON MADISON *(b Nov. 7, 1870, Dardanelle, Ark.; d Aug. 4, 1947, Little Rock, Ark.)* Lawyer, Indian lands distributor, banker, Arkansas Democrat. Fifth judicial district prosecutor (1904-1908), member of state

Democratic central committee (1910-1912), U.S. Representative (1911-1923), Social Security Board counsel for the states of Arkansas, Missouri, Oklahoma, and Kansas (1936-1945).

JAMES, ADDISON DAVIS *(b Feb. 27, 1850, Butler County, Ky.; d June 10, 1947, Penrod, Ky.).* Physician, Kentucky Republican. State constitutional convention delegate (1890), state representative (1891-1893), state senate (1895), U.S. marshal for the state (1897-1905), U.S. Representative (1907-1909). Grandfather of John A. Whitaker (which see).

JAMES, BENJAMIN FRANKLIN *(b Aug. 1, 1885, Philadelphia, Pa.; d Jan. 26, 1961, Bryn Mawr, Pa.)* Printing executive, Pennsylvania Republican. Radnor Township commissioner (1929-1936), state representative (1939-1947), U.S. Representative (1949-1959).

JAMES, CHARLES TILLINGHAST *(b Sept. 15, 1805, West Greenwich Center, R.I.; d Oct. 17, 1862, Sag Harbor, N.Y.).* Inventor who specialized in cotton mills, went on to rifled cannons, and died when a shell he had manufactured exploded. Thus ended a career that had seen him a U.S. Senator (1851-1857) as a Protective Tariff Democrat from Rhode Island.

JAMES, OLLIE MURRAY *(b July 27, 1871, Crittenden County, Ky.; d Aug. 28, 1918, Baltimore, Md.)* Lawyer, who at sixteen had been a state legislative page, and a Kentucky Democrat who was one of the most popular political orators of his time. Twice he was chairman of the Kentucky delegation to the Democratic National Convention (1896, 1904) the first time when only twenty-five. A delegate to the 1908 convention, he delivered a memorable speech seconding the nomination of William Jennings Bryan and in 1912 was permanent chairman of the convention that nominated

Woodrow Wilson. U.S. Representative (1903-1913), U.S. Senate (1913 until death).

JAMES, WILLIAM FRANCIS *(b May 23, 1873, Morristown, N.J.; d Nov. 17, 1945, Arlington, Va.)* Real estate-insurance broker, Michigan Republican. Hancock alderman (1906-1908) and mayor (1908, 1909), state senate (1910-1914), U.S. Representative (1915-1935).

JARMAN, PETE *(b Oct. 31, 1892, Greensboro, Ala.; d Feb. 17, 1955, Washington, D.C.)* Alabama Democrat whose adult life was spent in public service. Sumter County probate office clerk (1913-1917), World War I officer who was wounded in action, assistant state examiner of accounts (1919-1930), Alabama secretary of state (1931-1934), assistant state comptroller (1935, 1936), state Democratic executive committeeman (1927-1930), U.S. Representative (1937-1949), ambassador to Australia (1949-1953).

JARRETT, WILLIAM PAUL *(b Aug. 22, 1877, Honolulu; d Nov. 10, 1929, Honolulu)* Law enforcement officer and Hawaiian Democrat who was a delegate to the U.S. Congress (1923-1927) before statehood. Deputy sheriff and sheriff of the city and county of Honolulu (1906-1914), territorial high sheriff and warden of Oahu Prison (1914-1922), manager of the Lunalilo Home for Aged Hawaiians (1927 until death).

JARVIS, LEONARD *(b Oct. 19, 1781, Boston, Mass.; d Oct. 18, 1854, Surry, Maine)* Maine Democrat. Hancock County sheriff (1821-1829), Penobscot district collector of customs (1829-1831), U.S. Representative (1829-1837), Port of Boston navy agent (1838-1841).

JAY, JOHN *(b Dec. 12, 1745, New York City; d May 17, 1829, Bedford, N.Y.).* Lawyer, farmer, statesman, conservative New York patriot who was the first chief justice of the United States by appointment of President Washington (1789-1795), during which time he was sent to London (1794) where he negotiated and signed the Jay Treaty which affected British, French, and Spanish territorial claims and American expansion. Member of the Continental Congress (1774-1777, 1778, 1789) and its president (1778, 1789), delegate to the 1776 convention that on his motion unanimously approved the Declaration of Independence, an architect of the New York state constitution (1777), chief justice of the state (1777, 1778), minister to Spain (1779), negotiator for peace with Great Britain (1781) and a signer of the Treaty of Paris, treaty negotiator with the European powers (1783-1784), secretary of foreign affairs (1784-1789), minister to England (1794-1795), governor (1795-1801).

JEFFERSON, THOMAS *(b April 13, 1743, at "Shadwell" in what is now Albemarle County, Va.; d July 4, 1826, at "Monticello," Albemarle County, Va.).* Third president (Virginia Democratic Republican), 1801-1809; Revolutionary leader, author of many important documents and letters (principal author of the Declaration of Independence, which he also signed), lawyer, educator, scientist, farmer, architect, visionary leader of the Democratic-Republican party who opposed actions weighted in favor of aristocrats (he thought the United States should remain a country of farms augmented by commerce), supported the Constitution though somewhat fearful of the power it gave to centralized government and dissatisfied until the Bill of Rights was added; though a slave owner, he helped curtail the spread of slavery by his influence on the Northwest Ordinance of 1787.

Son of a Virginia planter-surveyor, he graduated from College of William and Mary (1762) and then studied law for five years under George Wythe. A man devoted to his wife (well-to-do widow

Martha Wayles Skelton whom he married in 1772) and family and with a zest for living though saddened by the early deaths of four of his six children and that of Mrs. Jefferson in 1782.

Member Virginia legislature (1769-1774, 1782), winning early reputation as a skillful draftsman of resolutions and addresses. Wrote: *A Summary View of the Rights of British America, Set Forth in some Resolutions Intended for the Inspection of the Present Delegates of the People of Virginia, now in Convention* and *Bill for Establishing Religious Freedom*; member Virginia's delegation to the Continental Congress (1775, 1776, 1783-1785); governor of Virginia (1779-1781), serving through the difficult war years; spent next five years in Europe, first assisting Benjamin Franklin and John Adams in negotiating trade treaties, then (1785-1789) serving as minister to France. He witnessed the beginning of the French Revolution and developed deep and lasting sympathies for the French people and their cause; secretary of state under Washington (1789-1793) and increasingly in conflict with Alexander Hamilton, fellow cabinet member and Federalist party leader; lost presidential bid of 1796 to Federalist John Adams by three electoral votes, thus becoming vice president. Differing philosophies and party pressures forced the two former friends into enemy camps. In 1800, members of the Electoral College apparently intended to elect Jefferson president and Aaron Burr vice president but the two men instead (due to electoral rules that were later changed) wound up with a tie vote that the House of Representatives resolved in Jefferson's favor after 36 stormy ballots and Alexander Hamilton's intervention in behalf of Jefferson, whom he mistrusted less than he did Burr. Fittingly, Jefferson was the first president to be inaugurated in Washington, D.C., a city he had helped to plan.

As president, Jefferson freed the political prisoners arrested under the Alien and Sedition Acts passed during Adams' administration (and in response to which Jefferson had secretly written the famous Kentucky Resolutions); cut spending and reduced taxes; although in favor of strict Constitutional interpretation, under pressure of emergency he approved stretching that document's authority in order to negotiate for the purchase from France of the Louisiana Territory (1803), a purchase that greatly increased the size of the nation. Reelected in 1804 (162 electoral votes to Federalist C. C. Pinckney's 14) to what turned out to be a stormy second term. Aaron Burr, arrested and accused of treason, was acquitted by a jury charged by Jefferson's political enemy (and distant relative), Federalist Chief Justice John Marshall; Europe was involved in the Napoleonic Wars and, in a desperate attempt to keep his country out of the conflict, Jefferson resorted to trade embargoes that brought financial distress to many Americans, including Jefferson himself.

In retirement at Monticello (1809-1826), he founded the University of Virginia at nearby Charlottesville; carried on a prolific correspondence with people from many walks of life, including John Adams. The two former presidents, who renewed their friendship of Revolutionary days after Jefferson's retirement, both died on the same day.

JENCKES, THOMAS ALLEN *(b. Nov. 2, 1818, Cumberland, R.I.; d Nov. 4, 1875, Cumberland)* Lawyer, Rhode Island Republican. State legislative clerk (1840-1844), state constitutional convention secretary (1842), state adjutant general (1845-1855), state representative (1854-1857), state law-revision commissioner (1855), U.S. Representative (1863-1871).

JENIFER, DANIEL *(b 1723, Charles County, Md.; d Nov. 16, 1790, Annapolis, Md.)* Maryland patriot who was active in pre-Revolutionary movements. Member of provincial court (1766), Governor's Council (1773), president of Council of Safety (1775-1777), state senate president (1777-1780), member of the Continental Congress (1778-1782), delegate to federal Constitutional Convention and a signer of that instrument (1778). Uncle of the younger Daniel Jenifer.

JENIFER, DANIEL *(b April 15, 1791, Charles County, Md.; d Dec. 18, 1855, Mulberry Grove, Md.)* Lawyer, Maryland National Republican. U.S. Representative (1831-1833, 1835-1841), minister to Austria (1841-1845), county register of wills (1846-1851). Nephew of the elder Daniel Jenifer.

JENKINS, ALBERT GALLATIN *(b Nov. 10, 1830, Cabell County, Va.; d May 21, 1864, near Dublin, Va., of wounds received in the Battle of Cloyds Mountain)* Lawyer who preferred to be a farmer, Confederate Army officer, Virginia Democrat. Democratic National Convention delegate (1856), U.S. Representative (1857-1861), delegate to the Confederate Provisional Congress (1861).

JENKINS, JOHN JAMES *(b Aug. 24, 1843, Weymouth, England; d June 8, 1911, Chippewa Falls, Wis.)* Union soldier, lawyer, Wisconsin Republican who also served as U.S. attorney for the Wyoming Territory (1876-1880), and Taft-appointed judge of Puerto Rico (1910 until death). Sauk County circuit court clerk (1867-1870), state assemblyman (1872), Chippewa County judge (1872-1876), U.S. Representative (1895-1909).

JENKINS, THOMAS ALBERT *(b Oct. 28, 1880, Oak Hill, Ohio; d Dec. 21, 1959, Worthington, Ohio)* Lawyer, Ohio Republican who served seventeen terms as a U.S. Representative (1925-1959). Lawrence County prosecutor (1916-1920), state senate (1923, 1924), GOP state convention delegate (1920, 1924).

JENKINS, TIMOTHY *(b Jan. 29, 1799, Barre, Mass.; d Dec. 24, 1859, Martinsburg, N.Y.)* New York Democrat turned Republican and a lawyer who represented the Oneida Indians in their dealings with the state (1838-1845) while part of that time also serving as Oneida County's district attorney (1840-1845). U.S. Representative (1845-1849, 1851-1853), GOP National Convention delegate (1856).

JENNINGS, JOHN, JR. *(b June 6, 1880, Jacksboro, Tenn.; d Feb. 27, 1956, Knoxville, Tenn.)* Lawyer, Tennessee Republican. Campbell County superintendent of public instruction (1903, 1904), county attorney (1911-1918), GOP National Convention delegate (1912, 1936, 1944), special assistant to the U.S. attorney general (1918, 1919), second chancery division judge (1918-1923), U.S. Representative (1939-1951).

JENNINGS, JONATHAN *(b 1784, Hunterdon County, N.J.; d July 26, 1834, near Charlestown, Ind.)* A Northwest Territory pioneer who practiced law and was a land-office clerk, newspaperman, and farmer there, became active in politics, cast his lot with the Democrats, and represented both the territory and state of Indiana in Congress besides serving as its first elected governor (1816-1822). As a territory: delegate to the U.S. Congress (1809-1816), state constitutional convention president (1816). As a state: Indian land treaty commissioner (1818, 1832), U.S. Representative (1822-1831).

JOHANSEN, AUGUST EDGAR *(b July 21, 1905, Philadelphia, Pa.)* Journalist, clergyman, Michigan Republican. Calhoun County Tax Allocation Board (1949, 1950), administrative assistant to Congressman Paul W. Shafer (1951-1954), U.S. Representative (1955-1965) serving on the Un-American Activities and Post Office and Civil Service committees.

JOHNS, KENSEY, JR. *(b Dec. 10, 1791, New Castle, Del.; d March 28, 1857, New Castle)* Lawyer, Delaware Federalist. U.S. Representative (1827-1831), state chancellor (1832 until death).

JOHNSON, ALBERT *(b March 5, 1869, Springfield, Ill.; d Jan. 17, 1957, American Lake, Wash.)* Newspaperman who rose from cub reporter to editor of important papers in Missouri, Connecticut, Washington State, and Washington, D.C., before becoming editor-publisher of the *Grays Harbor Washingtonian* in Hoquiam, Wash., where he was also active in Republican politics. U.S. Representative (1913-1933).

JOHNSON, ANDREW *(b Dec. 29, 1808, Raleigh, N.C.; d July 31, 1875, at home of daughter, near Elizabethton, Tenn.).* Seventeenth president (Tennessee Democrat who was elected vice president on the Republican ticket), 1865-1869, taking office when Abraham Lincoln was assassinated; unsuccessfully impeached; hot-tempered friend of the working classes who, as U.S. Representative and Senator worked to make Western lands available to them for homesteading; Alaska was purchased during his presidential administration.

Son of a bank porter and sexton who died in 1811, Johnson had no formal schooling but was apprenticed to a tailor when still a boy. Although he ran away from his employer, he learned the tailoring trade and moved with his family to eastern Tennessee (1826) where he established his own shop in Greeneville. He soon met and married Eliza McCardle who helped him improve the scanty education he had given himself and bore him five children. He liked to debate and became a leader of working class people, championing their causes.

Greeneville alderman (1828-1830), mayor (1830-1834), member of state legislature (1835-1837, 1839-1841), U.S. Representative (1843-1853), gerrymandered out of a chance to win reelection to the House, he ran for governor and won (1853-1857), U.S. Senate (1857-1862) where he supported the principle of popular sovereignty to determine whether a territory should be slave or free but he was outspokenly opposed to secession. Resigned as senator to accept appointment as military governor of Tennessee, with the rank of brigadier general of volunteers. After the state was taken away from the Confederate Army, Johnson dealt skillfully with a difficult situation and carried through a workable program of reconstruction in which he pushed for amendments that would bring about the abolition of slavery in the state.

Elected vice president (1864) on the ticket headed by Abraham Lincoln (having been nominated by the Republicans in an attempt to overcome the stigma of sectionalism and win Democratic support); upon the death of Lincoln, became president (April 15, 1865). He defied Congress and attempted, in many ways, to carry out Southern reconstruction along the lines Lincoln had wanted but he did not want to grant equal civil rights to Negroes. The conflict that developed led to Johnson's impeachment and a trial before the Senate which, by only one vote, failed to convict.

The stubborn Johnson was not broken in spirit by the insurmountable difficulties of his tenure as president. Upon expiration of his term, he again ran (1869), albeit unsuccessfully, for election to the U.S. Senate; again unsuccessfully (1872), as an independent candidate for U.S. Representative; finally his tenacity was rewarded and he was elected to the U.S. Senate (1875) but died a few months after taking office.

JOHNSON, ANTON JOSEPH *(b Oct. 20, 1878, Peoria, Ill.; d April 16, 1958, Macomb, Ill.)* Farmer, dairyman, Republican who was president of the Illinois Milk Dealers' Association (1931-

1936) and head of the Illinois Dairy Products Association (1937). U.S. Representative (1939-1949), mayor of Macomb (1949-1951).

JOHNSON, BEN *(b May 20, 1858, Nelson County, Ky.; d June 4, 1950, Bardstown, Ky.)* Lawyer, Kentucky Democrat. State representative (1885) and house speaker (1887), fifth district internal revenue collector (1893-1897), state senate (1905-1906), U.S. Representative (1907-1927), Democratic National Convention president (1912, 1920), state highway commissioner (1927-1936).

JOHNSON, CAVE *(b Jan. 11, 1793, Robertson County, Tenn.; d Nov. 23, 1866, Clarksville, Tenn.)* Lawyer, Kentucky Democrat, and a friend and adviser of President Polk who was rewarded by being made postmaster general (1845-1849), introduced postage stamps to the U.S. mails. Montgomery County prosecutor (1817), U.S. Representative (1829-1837, 1839-1845), seventh judicial circuit court judge (1850, 1851), president of the state Bank of Tennessee (1854-1860).

JOHNSON, EDWIN STOCKTON *(b Feb. 26, 1857, Owen County, Ind.; d July 19, 1933, Platte, S.Dak.)* Banker, farmer, real estate operator, money lender, lawyer, South Dakota Republican turned Democrat. As a Republican: Douglas County prosecutor (1892, 1893), state senate (1894, 1895). As a Democrat: chairman of Democratic state central committee (1902-1904), national committeeman (1904-1916), unsuccessful gubernatorial candidate (1912), U.S. Senate (1915-1921).

JOHNSON, GEORGE WILLIAM *(b Nov. 10, 1869, Jefferson County, W.Va.; d Feb. 24, 1944, Martinsburg, W.Va.).* Lawyer, farmer, fruit grower, West Virginia Democrat. Martinsburg city attorney (1900), U.S. Representative (1923-1925, 1933-1943).

JOHNSON, HENRY *(b Sept. 14, 1783, Virginia; d Sept. 4, 1864, Pointe Coupee Parish, La.)* Lawyer who practiced in the Orleans Territory (1809) and became active in the drive for statehood, casting his lot with the Louisiana Whigs. Parish Court district judge (1811), delegate to first state constitutional convention (1812), U.S. Senate (1818-1824, 1844-1849), governor (1824-1828), U.S. Representative (1834-1839).

JOHNSON, HERSCHEL VESPASIAN *(b Sept. 18, 1812, Burke County, Ga.; d Aug. 16, 1880, Jefferson County, Ga.).* Lawyer, planter, moderate Georgia states' rights Democrat who opposed secession but supported the Confederacy and in 1860 was the vice presidential running mate of Stephen A. Douglas. State Democratic convention delegate (1841), presidential elector on the Polk-Dallas (1844) and Pierce-King (1852) tickets, U.S. Senate (1848-1849) and elected again (1866) but was not permitted to be seated, Democratic National Convention delegate (1848, 1852, 1856), Ocmulgee circuit superior court judge (1849-1853), governor (1853-1857), state secession convention delegate (1861), senator in the Confederate Congress (1862-1865), state constitutional convention president (1865), middle circuit judge (1873 until death).

JOHNSON, HIRAM WARREN *(b Sept. 2, 1866, Sacramento, Calif.; d Aug. 6, 1945, in U.S. Naval Hospital, Bethesda, Md.)* Lawyer who first came into the limelight (1908) in prosecution of Abe Ruef, a California political boss; a Republican reformer in that state and a founder of its Progressive party, becoming Theodore Roosevelt's vice presidential running mate (1912) and was touted for the same spot on the Harding ticket (1920) but would not accept second place.

Governor (1911-1917), U.S. Senate (1917 until death) with a reputation as a conservative and isolationist who voted against U.S. entry into World War I but for entry into World War II, supported Franklin D. Roosevelt for president (1932) and was sympathetic to the New Deal but opposed FDR's Supreme Court bill (1937) and his third-term bid (1940).

JOHNSON, JACOB *(b Nov. 1, 1847, Aalborg, Denmark; d Aug. 15, 1925, Salt Lake City, Utah)* Lawyer, farmer, Utah Republican. U.S. district attorney (1880-1888), U.S. commissioner (1881-1893), Sanpete County probate judge (1888-1890) and prosecutor (1892-1894), territorial representative (1893-1895), seventh judicial district judge (1896-1905), GOP National Convention delegate (1912), U.S. Representative (1913-1915).

JOHNSON, JAMES *(b Jan. 1, 1774, Orange County, Va.; d Aug. 14, 1826, Washington, D.C.)* Businessman, Kentucky Democrat. State senate (1808), presidential elector on the Monroe-Tompkins ticket (1820), U.S. Representative (1825 until death). Brother of John T. and Richard M. and uncle of Robert W. Johnson.

JOHNSON, JAMES WELDON *(b June 17, 1871, Jacksonville, Fla.; d June 26, 1938, in a Wiscasset, Maine, automobile accident)* Teacher, newspaper editor, lawyer who was the first Negro admitted to the Florida bar (1897), lyricist, song-and-dance man, novelist, New York Republican who campaigned for Theodore Roosevelt (1904), foreign service officer whose diplomatic career was cut short by prejudice, field secretary of the National Association for the Advancement of Colored People (1916-1930), and author of the poem "Lift Every Voice and Sing," which many consider to be the Negro national anthem.

A main figure in the emergence of the NAACP as a force to be reckoned with in U.S. life, politics, and democracy, Johnson's honors included honorary degrees from Talladega College and Atlanta and Howard universities and the Spingarn Medal (1925) that is awarded annually for "the highest or noblest achievement by an American Negro."

JOHNSON, JOHN TELEMACHUS *(b Oct. 5, 1788, Great Crossings, Ky.; d Dec. 17, 1856, Lexington, Mo.)* Lawyer, clergyman-evangelist who helped establish Bacon College (1836), was editor of the *Christian Messenger, Gospel Advocate*, and the *Christian*, Kentucky Jackson Democrat who served five terms as a state representative. U.S. Representative (1821-1825). Brother of James and Richard M. and uncle of Robert W. Johnson.

JOHNSON, JOSEPH *(b Dec. 19, 1785, Orange County, N.Y.; d Feb. 27, 1877, Bridgeport, W.Va.)* Farmer, Virginia Democrat. Member of state house of delegates (1815, 1816, 1818-1822, 1847, 1848), U.S. Representative (1823-1827, 1833, 1835-1841, 1845-1847), Democratic National Convention delegate (1844), state constitutional convention delegate (1850, 1851), governor for part of 1851 and then elected to a full term (1852-1856), presidential elector on the Douglas-Johnson ticket (1860).

JOHNSON, JOSEPH TRAVIS *(b Feb. 28, 1858, Brewerton, S.C.; d May 8, 1919, Spartanburg, S.C.)* Lawyer, South Carolina Democrat. U.S. Representative (1901-1915), resigning to accept appointment as a federal judge in South Carolina (1915 until death).

JOHNSON, JUSTIN LEROY *(b April 8, 1888, Wausau, Wis.; d March 26, 1961, Stockton, Calif.)* World War I pilot, lawyer, California Republican. San Joaquin County deputy district attorney (1920, 1921), Stockton city attorney (1923-1933), city planning commissioner (1934-1941), GOP National Convention delegate (1936, 1948), U.S. Representative (1943-1957).

JOHNSON, LESTER R. *(b June 16, 1901, Brandon, Wis.; d ——)*. Lawyer, Wisconsin Democrat. Chief clerk of state assembly (1936-1939), member of state banking commission (1942), Jackson County district attorney (1943-1946, 1953), Democratic National Convention delegate (1952, 1960), U.S. Representative (1953-1965) serving on the Agriculture Committee.

JOHNSON, LYNDON BAINES *(b Aug. 27, 1908, on a farm near Stonewall, Gillespie County, Texas; dead on arrival at San Antonio Airport en route to Brooke Army Medical Center after suf- fering a heart attack at his ranch home in Johnson City, Texas, Jan. 22, 1973, the day before a Vietnam cease-fire agreement was announced)*.

Populist Texas Democrat, thirty-sixth president (1963-1969) who followed the lead of the president whom he probably admired most, Franklin D. Roosevelt, and instituted more social legislation (he called his program the Great Society) than any chief executive ever before him, only to see his accomplishments negated and his place in history tarnished by the nation's growing involvement in the Vietnam war, an escalation made possible by congressional adoption of the Tonkin Gulf resolution (1964) on his urging; "A man," one historian nearly a decade later described him, "whose advisors led him down the slippery path on Vietnam."

A poor boy but "born into politics" (his father and both grandfathers served in the Texas legislature), he began his career as a teacher and in 1931 embarked upon his life's work as a volunteer for Richard M. Kleberg, Sr., one of the owners of the mammoth King Ranch, in the latter's successful bid for a Congressional seat and first went to Washington as his secretary (1932-1935) where he quickly became the protege of an old family friend, Sam Rayburn, one of the most powerful members the House of Representatives had ever known. Then came nearly two years as Texas state director of the National Youth Administration (1935-1937) and Johnson, not yet thirty, was on his way.

Upon the death of Congressman James P. Buchanan, he ran successfully for the vacated seat, was reelected to six successive terms (1937-1949); on Dec. 9, 1941, two days after Pearl Harbor, he was commissioned a lieutenant commander in the U.S. Navy and thus became the first member of either house to enter the military in World War II. Almost immediately he was dispatched to the South Pacific on a mission for President Roosevelt, and resumed his seat in Congress July 27, 1942, when FDR summoned all legislators who had enlisted back to Washington.

Democratic National Convention delegate (1940, 1944, 1948); U.S. Senator (1947-1961), winning that office for the first time by only eighty-seven votes and thus acquiring the nickname "Landslide Lyndon"; Democratic whip (1951-1953), minority leader (1953-1954), and then majority leader (1954-1961)—a position in which he was the youngest to so serve in Senate history, yet in which he quickly proved one of the best, in so doing also earning several more appellations, among them arm-twister, wheeler-dealer, horse-trader, and, the only one that he accepted kindly, the Great Persuader.

At his party's 1960 presidential convention in Los Angeles, Johnson was nominated for the office of vice president, a move calculated to balance a ticket that had John F. Kennedy, a New Englander, as the Democrats' presidential nominee. The ticket won, Johnson was sworn and so served from January 1961, until that fateful day in Dallas

(Nov. 22, 1963) when an assassin's bullet struck Kennedy down and the boy who was "born to politics" took the presidential oath on the flight back to Washington.

In 1964, after carrying on in the socially conscious tradition of Roosevelt, Truman, and Kennedy, Johnson easily won reelection in his own right, defeating U.S. Senator Barry Goldwater by the most overwhelming popular-vote majority ever accorded any president. His Jan. 20, 1965, inaugural address best described his humanitarian hopes for the nation when he said: "In a land of great wealth, families must not live in hopeless poverty. In a land rich in harvest, children must not go hungry. In a land of healing miracles, neighbors must not suffer and die untended. In a great land of learning and scholars, young people must be taught to read and write."

But then came the "slippery path" to Vietnam and Johnson, as the years went on and U.S. involvement and casualties mounted, found himself more and more isolated from an increasingly torn and restless people. And so on March 31, 1968, he went on television to tell the people that he would not run for reelection.

JOHNSON, MAGNUS (b Sept. 19, 1871, Varmland, Sweden; d Sept. 13, 1936, Litchfield, Minn.) Glassblower in Sweden who after migrating to the United States became a lumberjack, farmer, agricultural reformer, Populist-Republican, and ultimately a leader in Minnesota's Farmer Labor party. A man with a foghorn voice that never required a loudspeaker, he was known as both "Magnavox Johnson" and "Yenerally Speaking Yohnson," a powerful champion of the dirt farmer and the workingman who elected him a U.S. Senator (1923-1925) to fill a vacancy despite stiff opposition from both Republican and Democratic candidates. President of the State Union of the

American Society of Equity (1911-1914), vice president of the Equity Cooperative Exchange (1912-1926), state representative (1915-1919), GOP National Convention delegate (1916), state senate (1919-1923), unsuccessful gubernatorial candidate (1922, 1926), U.S. Representative (1933-1935) who failed to be reelected because of gerrymandering of his district, state superintendent of public stockyards (1934-1936).

JOHNSON, MARTIN NELSON (b March 3, 1850, Racine County, Wis.; d Oct. 21, 1909, Fargo, N.Dak.) Teacher, lawyer, farmer and an Iowa Republican who planted roots in the Dakota Territory (1882). In Iowa: State representative (1877), state senate (1878-1882), presidential elector on the Hayes-Wheeler ticket (1876). In Dakota Territory and North Dakota: Nelson County prosecutor (1886-1890), state constitutional convention delegate and chairman of first state GOP convention (1889), U.S. Representative (1891-1899), U.S. Senate (March, 1909, until death eight months later).

JOHNSON, REVERDY (b May 21, 1796, Annapolis, Md.; d Feb. 10, 1876, Annapolis) Lawyer, Maryland Whig turned Democrat. State deputy attorney general (1816, 1817), state senate (1821-1829, 1860, 1861), U.S. Senate (1845-1849 as a Whig, 1863-1868 as a Democrat), U.S. attorney general in the Taylor cabinet (1849-1850), delegate to peace-between-states conference (1861), minister to England (1868, 1869).

JOHNSON, RICHARD MENTOR (b Oct. 17, 1781, Bryants Station, Ky.; d Nov. 19, 1850, Frankfort, Ky.) Lawyer, War of 1812 officer who reportedly killed the Indian chief, Tecumseh, in the Battle of the Thames, Kentucky Democrat who was appointed vice president by the Senate (1837) when none of the four official candidates received the necessary number of electoral votes and served until 1841. State representative (1804-1807, 1819, 1841, 1842), U.S. Representative (1807-1819, 1829-1837), U.S. Senate (1819-1829). Brother of James and John T., and uncle of Robert W. Johnson.

JOHNSON, ROBERT WARD *(b July 22, 1814, Scott County, Ky.; d July 26, 1879, Little Rock, Ark.)* Lawyer, secessionist Arkansas Democrat, and member of the noted Johnson family said to have ruled both the territory and the state from 1836 until the Civil War caused its dynasty to crumble. His father, U.S. Judge Benjamin Johnson, sat on the bench there for much of that period. Little Rock circuit prosecutor (1840-1842) while doubling as ex-officio state attorney general, U.S. Representative (1847-1853), U.S. Senate (1853-1861), delegate to the Provisional Government of the Confederate States (1862) and a Confederate senator throughout the Civil War. Nephew of James, John T. and Richard M. Johnson.

JOHNSON, ROYAL CLEAVES *(b Oct. 3, 1882, Cherokee, Iowa; d Aug. 2, 1939, Washington, D.C.)* Lawyer, World War I infantry officer who was wounded in action and awarded the Croix de Guerre, South Dakota Republican. Assistant state's attorney of Hyde County (1906, 1907) rising to state's attorney (1908, 1909), state attorney general (1910-1914), U.S. Representative (1915-1933).

JOHNSON, THOMAS *(b Nov. 4, 1732, Albert County, Md., d Oct. 26, 1819, Frederick, Md.).* Lawyer, Revolutionary Army officer and the Continental Congressman (1774-1777) who nominated George Washington to be commander in chief of the armed forces (1775); Maryland's first governor after statehood (1777-1779), associate justice of the U.S. Supreme Court (1791-1793), and a member of the commis-

sion that chose the site of the nation's capital city and named it Washington. Delegate to the provincial assembly (1762) and a member of the Committee of Correspondence and the Council of Safety, delegate to Annapolis convention (1774), delegate to Maryland's first constitutional convention (1776), member of state house of delegates (1780, 1786, 1787), delegate to state convention that ratified federal Constitution (1788), chief justice of the state's general court (1790, 1791). He missed out on the signing of the Declaration of Independence because he was not in Philadelphia when that historic event took place.

JOHNSON, TOM LOFTIN *(b July 18, 1854, Georgetown, Ky.; d April 10, 1911, Cleveland, Ohio)* Street railway executive, manufacturer, Ohio Democrat who was mayor of Cleveland for ten years (1899-1909) and an unsuccessful gubernatorial candidate (1903). U.S. Representative (1891-1895).

JOHNSON, WILLIAM COST *(b Jan. 14, 1806, Frederick County, Md.; d April 14, 1860, Washington, D.C.)* Lawyer, Maryland Whig. State representative (1831, 1832), U.S. Representative (1833-1835, 1837-1843), state constitutional convention delegate (1836).

JOHNSON, WILLIAM SAMUEL *(b Oct. 7, 1727, Stratford, Conn.; d Nov. 14, 1819, Stratford)* Lawyer, Connecticut patriot who was the first president of New York's Columbia College (1787-1800). Colonial representative (1761, 1765), delegate to Stamp Act Congress (1765), agent to England to determine state title to Indian lands (1767-1771), member of Governor's Council (1766, 1771-1775), Connecticut Supreme Court judge (1772-1774), member of the Continental Congress (1784-1787), Constitutional Convention delegate (1787), U.S. Senate (1789-1791).

JOHNSTON, JOSIAH STODDARD *(b Nov. 24, 1784, Salisbury, Conn.; d May 19, 1833, in a steamboat explosion on the Red River in Louisiana)* Lawyer, farmer, Louisiana Democrat and supporter of Henry Clay. Member of first territorial legislature (1805-1812), state representative (1812) and district judge (1812-1821), U.S. Representative (1821-1823), U.S. Senate (1824 until death).

JONES, ALLEN *(b Dec. 24, 1739, Edgecombe, now Halifax, County, N.C.; d Nov. 10, 1798, Northampton County, N.C.).* Planter, Revolutionary Army officer, North Carolina patriot. Member of colonial assembly (1773-1775), delegate to five Provincial Congresses (1774-1776), state senate (1777-1779, 1783, 1784, 1787), Continental Congress (1779, 1780), delegate to state convention that rejected federal Constitution (1788). Brother of Willie Jones.

JONES, ANDRIEUS ARISTIEUS *(b May 16, 1862, Abion County, Tenn.; d Dec. 20, 1927, Washington, D.C.)* Teacher, lawyer, New Mexico Democrat who was first assistant secretary of the interior (1913-1916). Mayor of Las Vegas (1893, 1894), special assistant U.S. attorney (1894-1898), Democratic National Convention delegate (1896), Democratic state chairman (1906-1908, 1911) and national committeeman (1908-1922), U.S. Senate (1917 until death).

JONES, ANSON *(b Jan. 20, 1798, Great Barrington, Mass.; d Jan. 9, 1858, Houston, Tex.)* Pioneer Texas physician with an interest in politics and served as the last president of the Republic of Texas (1844-1846).

JONES, CHARLES WILLIAM *(b Dec. 24, 1834, Balbriggan, Ireland; d Oct. 11, 1897, Dearborn, Mich.)* Carpenter, lawyer, Florida Democrat. Democratic National Convention delegate (1872), state representative (1874), U.S. Senate (1875-1887).

JONES, GEORGE WASHINGTON *(b March 15, 1806, King and Queen County, Va.; d Nov. 14, 1884, Fayetteville, Tenn.)* Saddlemaker, Tennessee Democrat. Justice of the peace (1832-1835), state representative (1835-1839), state senate (1839-1841), Lincoln County court clerk (1840-1843), U.S. Representative (1843-1859), delegate to peace-between-states convention (1861), Confederate Representative (1862-1864), state constitutional convention delegate (1870).

JONES, JAMES KIMBROUGH *(b Sept. 29, 1839, Marshall County, Miss.; d June 1, 1908, Washington, D.C.)* Confederate soldier, planter, lawyer, Arkansas Democrat, and advocate of free silver. State senate (1873-1879), Democratic National Convention delegate (1896, 1900) and national committee chairman in the same years, U.S. Representative (1881-1885), U.S. Senate (1885-1903).

JONES, JEHU GLANCY *(b Oct. 7, 1811, Caernarvon Township, Pa.; d March 24, 1878, Reading, Pa.)* Clergyman, lawyer, Pennsylvania Democrat who helped his friend, James Buchanan, obtain the presidential nomination and was rewarded by being made minister to Austria (1858-1861). Berks County district attorney (1847-1849), Democratic state convention delegate (1848, 1849, 1855) and its president (1855), Democratic National Convention delegate (1848, 1856) and its vice president (1848), U.S. Representative (1851-1853, 1854-1858).

JONES, JOHN PERCIVAL *(b Jan. 27, 1829, Herefordshire, England; d Nov. 27, 1912, Los Angeles, Calif.)* Miner and developer of mineral resources first in California and then in Nevada, where he also struck it rich politically as a Republican U.S. Senator for thirty years (1873-1903). Before that he had been a California state senator (1863-1867).

JONES, JOHN WINSTON *(b Nov. 22, 1791, Amelia County, Va.; d Jan. 29, 1848, Chesterfield County, Va.)* Lawyer, teacher, planter, Virginia Democrat. Fifth circuit prosecutor (1818-1835), state constitutional convention delegate (1829, 1830), U.S. Representative (1835-1845) and speaker of the House (1843-1845), speaker of the state house of delegates (1846).

JONES, PAUL CARUTHERS *(b March 12, 1901, Kennett, Mo.)* Newspaper publisher, radio station manager, Missouri Democrat. Kennett City Council (1931-1933), mayor (1933-1935), Board of Education (1934-1946), state representative (1935-1937), state senate (1937-1944), chairman of state highway commission (1945-1948), U.S. Representative (1948-1969) serving on the Agriculture and House Administration committees and Joint Committee on the Library.

JONES, SAMUEL MILTON *(b Aug. 8, 1846, Carnarvonshire, Wales; d July 12, 1904, Toledo, Ohio)* Immigrant boy who rose from oil-field laborer to wealthy inventor-manufacturer of oil-producing equipment, advocated trade unionism, the eight-hour day, a minimum wage, and vacations for his employes, and, as an independent Ohio Republican, showed the same zeal for reform in politics. His only public office was as mayor of Toledo (1897 until death) when he reintroduced most if not all of his private-worker benefits to city employes, plus civil service. Through books and speeches he spread his theories throughout the country and became known as Golden Rule Jones. One of his books is *The New Right; A Plea for Fair Play Through a More Just Social Order* (1899).

JONES, WALTER *(b Dec. 18, 1745, Williamsburg, Va.; d Dec. 31, 1815, Westmoreland County, Va.)* Physician, Virginia Democrat. Member of state

house of delegates (1785-1787, 1802, 1803), state constitutional convention delegate (1788), U.S. Representative (1797-1799, 1803-1811).

JONES, WESLEY LIVSEY *(b Oct. 9, 1863, Moutrie County, Ill.; d Nov. 19, 1932, Seattle, Wash.)* Lawyer, Washington Republican who as chairman of the Senate Commerce Committee (1919-1930) was a staunch defender of the free enterprise system particularly as it applied to private industry. U.S. Representative (1899-1909), U.S. Senate (1909 until death).

JONES, WILLIAM *(b 1760, Philadelphia, Pa.; d Sept. 6, 1831, Bethlehem, Pa.)* Revolutionary soldier at the age of sixteen who switched to the sea, commanded privateers, at war's end became a shipping merchant in Philadelphia, and donned the mantle of Thomas Jefferson's Democrat-Republican party. U.S. Representative (1801-1803), secretary of the navy in the Madison cabinet (1813-1814), president of the Bank of the United States (1816-1819), and Philadelphia collector of customs (1827-1829).

JONES, WILLIAM ATKINSON *(b March 21, 1849, Warsaw, Va.; d April 17, 1918, Warsaw)* Lawyer, Virginia Democrat who was a U.S. Representative for more than a quarter-century (1891 until death). Democratic National Convention delegate (1880, 1896, 1900).

JONES, WILLIAM CAREY *(b April 5, 1855, Remsen, N.Y.; d June 14, 1927, Spokane, Wash.)* Lawyer, Washington territorial and state political figure who first was a Republican and then was a Democrat, rating high in both parties, and always a staunch advocate of free silver. He was city attorney in Madelia, Minn. (1882, 1883), before moving to Washington where he was Cheney city attorney (1884-1889), twelfth territorial district prosecutor (1886-1889), state attorney general (1889-1897), delegate to every territorial and state GOP convention (1884-1894) and all Democratic state conventions (1904-1924), chairman of the state central committee of the Free Coinage Republican party (1896), U.S. Representative as a Free Silver Republican (1897-1899).

JONES, WILLIAM THEOPILUS *(b Feb. 20, 1842, Corydon, Ind.; d Oct. 9, 1882, Corydon)* Lawyer, Union soldier, Wyoming Territory Republican. Presidential elector on the Grant-Colfax ticket (1868), associate justice of the territorial supreme court (1869), delegate to Congress (1871-1873).

JONES, WILLIE *(b Dec. 24, 1740, Northampton County, N.C.; d June 18, 1801, Raleigh, N.C.)* Farmer with strongly anti-British views, a firm believer in colonial rights, and a leader of North Carolina opposition to the federal Constitution because of the fear that it would stand in the way of political democracy. Member of the Provincial Congress (1774, 1776), chairman of the Committee of Safety (1776) and the new state's ex-officio governor until one could be elected, Constitutional Convention delegate (1776), member of state house of commons (1776-1778), Continental Congress (1780, 1781), delegate to state convention that refused to ratify U.S. Constitution (1788). Brother of Allen Jones.

JONKMAN, BARTEL JOHN *(b April 28, 1884, Grand Rapids, Mich.; d June 13, 1955, Grand Rapids)* Lawyer, Michigan Republican. Kent County assistant prosecutor (1915-1920) and prosecutor (1929-1936), U.S. Representative (1940-1949).

JOSEPH, ANTONIO *(b Aug. 25, 1846, Taos, N.Mex.; d April 19, 1910, Ojo Caliente, N.Mex.)* Merchant, hotel and land owner, New Mexico Democrat who attended all state and national political conventions during his adult life. Territorial representative (1882), delegate to the U.S. Congress (1885-1895), territorial senate (1896-1898) and senate president (1898).

JOY, CHARLES FREDERICK *(b Dec. 11, 1849, Jacksonville, Ill.; d April 13, 1921, St. Louis, Mo.)* Lawyer, Missouri Republican. U.S. Representative (1894, 1895-1903), St. Louis recorder of deeds (1907-1921).

JUDD, NORMAN BUEL *(b Jan. 10, 1815, Rome, N.Y.; d Nov. 10, 1878, Chicago, Ill.)* New York newspaperman turned lawyer who migrated to Chicago (1836) and drafted its first charter and became its first city attorney (1837-1839), alderman (1842-1844) and state senator (1844-1860)—all as a Democrat.

After switching to the fledgling Republican party, he managed Abraham Lincoln's campaign (1860) for the presidential nomination and delivered the convention speech that won the designation for Lincoln. As a reward he was appointed minister to Berlin (1861-1865). After that he was U.S. Representative (1867-1871), Chicago port collector (1872 until death). He also became quite a railroad tycoon, thanks to his legal talent and use of political connections.

JUDD, WALTER HENRY *(b Sept. 25, 1898, Rising City, Nebr.)* Teacher, physician, medical missionary who after several years in the Orient returned to the United States (1938) and lectured extensively to warn of Japanese preparations for war. Then, as a Minnesota Republican, he successfully ran for the U.S. House of Representatives and served for twenty years (1943-1963) earning for himself a reputation as a conservative-minded expert on foreign affairs.

JULIAN, GEORGE WASHINGTON *(b May 5, 1817, Wayne County, Ind.; d July 7, 1899, Indianapolis)* Lawyer, writer, abolitionist leader and Indiana Free-Soiler turned Republican who was the Free-Soil candidate for vice president (1852) on the ticket with John P. Hale that polled only 155,825 popular votes. As a Free-Soiler: delegate to the national convention (1848), presidential elector on the Van Buren-Adams ticket (1848), U.S. Representative (1849-1851). As a Republican: first national convention delegate and chairman of its committee on organization (1856), U.S. Representative (1861-1871), Cleveland-appointed surveyor general of New Mexico (1885-1889).

K

★ ★ ★

KAHN, FLORENCE PRAG *(b Nov. 9, 1868, Salt Lake City, Utah; d Nov. 16, 1948, San Francisco, Calif.)* California Republican who first was chosen a U.S. Representative to fill the vacancy caused by the death of her husband, Julius, but then proved that women can do all right on their own, being five times re-elected and serving twelve years in all (1925-1937).

KAHN, JULIUS *(b Feb. 28, 1861, Kuppenheim, Germany; d Dec. 18, 1924, San Francisco, Calif.)* Actor, lawyer, California Republican who believed firmly in military preparedness and wrote the Selective Draft Act of 1917. State assemblyman (1892), U.S. Representative (1899-1903, 1905 until death) who was succeeded by his wife, the former Florence Prag (which see).

KALANIANAOLE, JONAH KUHIO *(b March 26, 1871, Koloa, Kauai, Hawaii; d Jan. 7, 1922, Waikiki, Honolulu, Hawaii).* Son of High Chief David Kahalepouli Piikoi and Princess Kinoiki Kekaulike, proclaimed a prince (1884), served a year in prison (1895) for participating in the royalist revolt against the Republic of Hawaii, visited Africa (1899-1902) and fought on the side of the British in the Boer War, returned to Hawaii, accepted the new politics there, affiliating briefly with the Home Rule party but then leading a "young Turk" revolt against its tight-fisted bigotry, then turned to Republicanism and ten times was elected a delegate to the U.S. Congress from the territory of Hawaii (1903 until death).

KALBFLEISCH, MARTIN *(b Feb. 8, 1804, Flushing, Holland; d Feb. 12, 1873, Brooklyn, N.Y.)* Chemist, paint and chemical manufacturer, New York Democrat. New York City health warden (1832), school trustee (1836), supervisor of Bushwick (1852-1854), Brooklyn alderman (1855-1861), mayor of Brooklyn (1862-1864, 1867-1871), U.S. Representative (1863-1865), Union National Convention delegate (1866).

KANE, ELIAS KENT *(b June 7, 1794, New York City; d Dec. 12, 1835, Washington, D.C.)* Lawyer, Illinois Democrat who was active in the move for statehood. Delegate to first state constitutional convention (1818) and the first Illinois secretary of state (1820-1824), state representative (1824), U.S. Senate (1825 until death).

KARSTEN, FRANK MELVIN *(b Jan. 7, 1913, San Antonio, Tex.)* Missouri Democrat. Secretary to Congressman John Joseph Cochran (1934-1946), U.S. Representative (1947-1969) serving on the Ways and Means Committee.

350

KASSON, JOHN ADAM *(b Jan. 11, 1822, Charlotte, Vt.; d May 19, 1910, Washington, D.C.)* Lawyer, diplomat, Iowa Free-Soiler turned Republican who played a key role in drafting the GOP platform (1860) on which Lincoln sought the presidency. First assistant postmaster general (1861, 1862), U.S. commissioner to the International Postal Congress (1863) out of which came the International Postal Union, U.S. Representative (1863-1867, 1873-1877, 1881-1884), U.S. commissioner to negotiate postal pacts with seven European nations (1867), state representative (1868-1872), minister to Austria-Hungary (1877-1881), minister to Germany (1884-1885), special envoy to the Congo International Conference (1885) and the Samoan International Conference (1889), U.S. special commissioner to negotiate reciprocity treaties (1897), member of U.S.-British Joint High Commission to settle differences in Canada (1898).

KAUFMAN, DAVID SPANGLER *(b Dec. 18, 1813, Boiling Springs, Pa.; d Jan. 31, 1851, Washington, D.C.)* Lawyer, Indian fighter, Texas pioneer and, after statehood, a Democrat. Member of Texas House of Representatives (1839-1843) and senate (1843-1845), chargé d'affaires to the United States (1845), U.S. Representative (1846 until death).

KEAN, HAMILTON FISH *(b Feb. 27, 1862, Union County, N.J.; d Dec. 27, 1941, New York City)* Banker, farmer, and a power in New Jersey Republican affairs. Secretary-treasurer of the Union County GOP committee (1884-1906) doubling as chairman (1900-1906), state committeeman (1905-1919), national committeeman (1919-1928), GOP National Convention delegate (1916, 1932), U.S. Senate (1929-1935). Brother of the younger John and great-grandson of the elder John Kean.

KEAN, JOHN *(b 1756, Charleston, S.C.; d May 4, 1795, Philadelphia, Pa.)* Merchant, South Carolina patriot who was taken prisoner (1780) when the British captured Charleston and, after release, was commissioned by General Washington to audit accounts of the Revolutionary Army. Continental Congress (1785-1787). Then, when the Bank of the United States was organized (1791), he was appointed its cashier by President Washington and so served in Philadelphia until death. Great-grandfather of both the preceding and following entries.

KEAN, JOHN *(b Dec. 4, 1852, Ursino, N.J.; d Nov. 4, 1914, Ursino)* Banker, manufacturer, lawyer, New Jersey Republican. U.S. Representative (1883-1885, 1887-1889), GOP state committee chairman (1891, 1892), unsuccessful candidate for governor (1892), U.S. Senate (1899-1911). Brother of Hamilton F. and great-grandson of John Kean.

KEARNS, CARROLL DUDLEY *(b May 7, 1900, Youngstown, Ohio)* Teacher, concert artist, Pennsylvania Republican. U.S. Representative (1947-1963). Served on the District of Columbia and Education and Labor committees.

KEARNS, CHARLES CYRUS *(b Feb. 11, 1869, Tonica, Ill.; d Dec. 17, 1931, Amelia, Ohio)* New Mexico and Arkansas newspaperman before settling down to practice law in Ohio and becoming an active Republican there. Clermont County prosecutor (1906-1909), U.S. Representative (1915-1931).

KEARNS, THOMAS *(b April 11, 1862, Ontario, Canada; d Oct. 18, 1918, Salt Lake City, Utah)* Farmer, freight hauler, mine operator, Utah Republican. Park City councilman (1895), state constitutional convention delegate (1895), GOP National Convention delegate (1896, 1900), U.S. Senate (1901-1905).

KEE, JOHN *(b Aug. 22, 1874, Glenville, W.Va.; d May 8, 1951, Washington, D.C.).* Lawyer, West Virginia Democrat who was chairman of the House Committee on Foreign Affairs at the time of his death. State senate (1923-1927), U.S. Representative (1933 until death).

KEEFE, FRANK BATEMAN *(b Sept. 23, 1887, Winneconne, Wis.; d Feb. 5, 1952, Neenah, Wis.)* Lawyer, teacher, banker, Wisconsin Republican. Winnebago County prosecutor (1922-1928), U.S. Representative (1939-1951).

KEFAUVER, CAREY ESTES *(b July 26, 1903, Monroe County, Tenn.; d Aug. 10, 1963, in U.S. Naval Hospital, Bethesda, Md., after suffering a heart attack during debate on the Senate floor)* Great Smokies farm-raised lawyer described in his *New York Times* obituary as "the crusading Tennessee Democrat with the ready handshake and homespun personality," coming into the national limelight with his investigations of organized crime (1950, 1951), twice making of him a serious contender for the Democratic presidential nomination (1952, 1956) and Adlai Stevenson's vice presidential running mate (1956). State commissioner of finance and taxation (1939), U.S. Representative (1939-1949), U.S. Senate (1949 until death).

KEIFER, JOSEPH WARREN *(b Jan. 30, 1836, Clark County, Ohio; d April 22, 1932, Springfield, Ohio)* Lawyer, Union Army officer, Antioch College trustee, banker, orator, Ohio Republican whom one biographer described as "a mediocre speaker" of the U.S. House of Representatives (1881-1883) and "a professional veteran." State senate (1868, 1869), commander of the Ohio Grand Army of the Republic (1871, 1872), GOP National Convention delegate (1876), U.S. Representative (1877-1885, 1905-1911), Spanish-American War officer (1898-1899), first commander in chief of the Spanish War Veterans (1900, 1901).

KEITT, LAURENCE MASSILLON *(b Oct. 4, 1824, Orangeburg, S.C.; d June 4, 1864, near Richmond, Va., as the result of wounds received the day before in the Battle of Cold Harbor)* Lawyer, slavery leader, secessionist, Confederate Army officer, independent South Carolina Democrat, and a bombastic orator with a fierce wrath whom contemporaries often referred to as "Old Tempestuous." U.S. Representative (1853-1860), state secessionist convention delegate (1861), member of Confederate Provisional Congress (1861).

KELLEY, AUGUSTINE BERNARD *(b July 9, 1883, New Baltimore, Pa.; d Nov. 20, 1957, Bethesda, Md.)* Mining engineer who applied his professional knowledge to the coal fields of Pennsylvania where politically he was an active Democrat. Member of Greensburg Board of Education (1935, 1936), U.S. Representative (1941 until death).

KELLEY, PATRICK HENRY *(b Oct. 7, 1867, Silver Creek Township, Mich.; d Sept. 11, 1925, Washington, D.C.).* Teacher, lawyer, Michigan Republican. Member of state board of education (1901-1905), state superintendent of public instruction (1905-1911), lieutenant governor (1907-1911), U.S. Representative (1913-1923).

KELLEY, WILLIAM DARRAH *(b April 12, 1814, Philadelphia, Pa.; d Jan. 9, 1890, Washington, D.C.)* Jeweler's apprentice, lawyer, lecturer, debater, author whose books include *Lincoln and Stanton* (1885), Pennsylvania Democrat who became a Republican as a result of his opposition to slavery and as a congressman favored full suffrage for freedmen and the use of Negro soldiers in the Union Army. His nickname was Pig Iron because of his advocacy of high duties on iron and steel. Deputy prosecutor for the city and county of Philadelphia (1845, 1846), common pleas court judge (1846-1856), GOP National Convention delegate (1860), U.S. Representative for fifteen terms (1861 until death) and chairman of the House Ways and Means Committee (1881-1883).

KELLOGG, FRANK BILLINGS *(b Dec. 22, 1856, Potsdam, N.Y.; d Dec. 21, 1937, St. Paul, Minn.)* Farmhand who became one of the nation's foremost trust-busting lawyers numbering Standard Oil among his trophies, diplomat, Minnesota Republican who as Calvin Coolidge's secretary of state (1925-1929) negotiated the Kellogg-Briand Peace Pact (1928), and was awarded the Nobel Peace Prize (1930). Rochester, Minn., city attorney (1878-1881), Olmsted County attorney (1882-1887), U.S. delegate to the Universal Congress of Lawyers and Jurists (1904), GOP National Committeeman (1904-1912), GOP National Convention delegate (1904, 1908, 1912), American Bar Association president (1912, 1913), U.S. Senate (1917-1923), delegate to the Fifth International Conference of American States (1923), ambassador to Great Britain (1923-1925), associate judge of the Permanent Court for International Justice (1930-1935).

KELLOGG, WILLIAM PITT *(b Dec. 8, 1831, Orwell, Vt.; d Aug. 10, 1918, Washington, D.C.)* Teacher, lawyer, Union Army officer, Illinois Republican who relocated in Louisiana and won the dubious distinction of being one of that state's most vigorous carpetbag politicians. While in Illinois: presidential elector on the Lincoln-Hamlin ticket (1860), Lincoln-appointed collector of the Port of New Orleans (1865-1868). In Louisiana: delegate to all GOP National Conventions (1868-1896), U.S. Senate (1868-1872, 1877-1883), governor (1873-1877), U.S. Representative (1883-1885).

KELLY, EDNA FLANNERY *(b Aug. 20, 1906, East Hampton, N.Y.)* Widow of New York City Court Justice Edward L. Kelly, New York Democrat who served twenty years in elective national office. Member of Kings County Democratic Executive Committee (1944-1951), her party's associate research director in state legislature (1943), chief research director (1944-1949), U.S. Representative (1949-1969) serving on Foreign Affairs Committee, its subcommittee on Europe, and as member of Committee on Standards of Official Conduct; delegate to eighteenth General Assembly of the United Nations.

KELLY, JAMES KERR *(b Feb. 16, 1819, Center County, Pa.; d Sept. 15, 1903, Washington, D.C.)* Lawyer, deputy attorney general in Mifflin County, Pa., until gold lured him to California (1849), then on to the Oregon Territory (1851) where he planted Democratic roots. Commissioner to codify territorial laws (1852), territorial legislature (1853-1857) and twice its president, officer in the Yakima Indian War (1855, 1856), state constitutional convention delegate and a framer of that document (1857), state senate (1860-1864), unsuccessful candidate for governor (1866), U.S. Senate (1871-1877), chief justice of the state supreme court (1878-1882).

KELLY, MELVILLE CLYDE *(b Aug. 4, 1883, Bloomfield, Ohio; d April 29, 1935, Punxsutawney, Pa., of accidental gunshot wounds)* Publisher of the *Braddock Leader* and *Daily News-Herald*, Pennsylvania Republican. State representative (1910-1913), U.S. Representative (1913-1915, 1917-1935).

KEM, OMER MADISON *(b Nov. 13, 1855, Hagerstown, Ind.; d Feb. 13, 1942, Cottage Grove, Oreg.)* Fruit grower, cattle raiser, Nebraska and Colorado Populist before moving on to Oregon and developing utility interests. In Nebraska: Deputy treasurer of Custer County (1890, 1891), U.S. Representative (1891-1897). In Colorado: state representative (1907).

KENDALL, CHARLES WEST *(b April 22, 1828, Searsmont, Maine; d June 25, 1914, Mt. Rainier, Md.)* Gold miner, editor-publisher of the *San Jose (Calif.) Tribune* (1855-1859), lawyer, orator, California and Nevada Democrat. In California: state assemblyman (1861, 1862). In Nevada: U.S. Representative (1871-1875). Later he moved to Colorado where he wrote articles on politics and economics. Then on to Maryland and a position as assistant librarian in the Interstate Commerce Commission, Washington, D.C. (1892 until death).

KENDALL, NATHAN EDWARD *(b March 17, 1868, Lucas County, Iowa; d Nov. 5, 1936, Des Moines, Iowa)* Lawyer, Iowa Republican. Albia city attorney (1890-1892), Monroe County prosecutor (1893-1897), state representative (1899-1909) and speaker of the house (1909), U.S. Representative (1909-1913), governor (1921-1925).

KENDALL, SAMUEL AUSTIN *(b Nov. 1, 1859, Greenville Township, Pa.; d Jan. 8, 1933, in the House Office Building, Washington, D.C.)* Teacher; lumber, coal mine, and railroad executive, Pennsylvania Republican. Public schools superintendent in Jefferson, Iowa (1884-1898), member of Pennsylvania House of Representatives (1899-1903), U.S. Representative (1919 until death).

KENDRICK, JOHN BENJAMIN *(b Sept. 6, 1857, Cherokee County, Tex.; d Nov. 3, 1933, Sheridan, Wyo.)* A cattleman who knew all the rigors of range life and months-long drives, becoming one of Wyoming's and Montana's foremost ranchers; the only working cowboy up to that time ever admitted to the Wyoming Stock Growers' Association of which he was vice president (1911) and president (1912, 1913). A Wyoming Democrat in a strongly Republican state, he was a state senator (1910-1914), Democratic National Convention delegate (1912, 1916), governor (1915-

1917), and U.S. Senator (1917 until death) after the people wrote in his name and won him the nomination although the Republican state legislature had refused to elect him.

KENNA, JOHN EDWARD *(b April 10, 1848, Kanawha County, Va., later W.Va.; d Jan. 11, 1893, Washington, D.C.)* Confederate soldier, lawyer, West Virginia Democrat. Kanawha County prosecutor (1872-1877), U.S. Representative (1877-1883), U.S. Senate (1883 until death).

KENNEDY, AMBROSE JEROME *(b Jan. 6, 1893, Baltimore, Md.; d Aug. 29, 1950, Baltimore)* Insurance broker, Maryland Democrat. Baltimore councilman (1922-1926), state senate (1928, 1929), Democratic National Convention delegate (1928, 1932), state parole commissioner (1929-1932), U.S. Representative (1932-1941).

KENNEDY, ANTHONY *(b Dec. 21, 1810, Baltimore, Md.; d July 4, 1892, Annapolis, Md.)* Lawyer, farmer, a Whig in Virginia, a Unionist in Maryland. In Virginia: state house of delegates (1839-1843), Jefferson County Court magistrate (1840-1850). In Maryland: state house of delegates (1856). U.S. Senate (1857-1863), state constitutional convention delegate (1867). Brother of John P. Kennedy.

KENNEDY, CHARLES AUGUSTUS *(b March 24, 1869, Montrose, Iowa; d Jan. 10, 1951, Montrose)* Nurseryman, banker, Iowa Republican. Mayor of Montrose (1890-1895), state representative (1903-1905), U.S. Representative (1907-1921).

KENNEDY, JOHN FITZGERALD *(b May 29, 1917, Brookline, Mass.; d Nov. 22, 1963, Dallas, Texas; assassinated while riding in a motorcade)* Thirty-fifth president (Massachusetts Democrat), 1961-1963; good-looking, effective speaker with a winning personality and a sense of humor, he was the youngest man and the first Roman Catholic elected president; World War II hero; newspaper reporter; U.S. Representative and Senator; author of *Why England Slept* (1940) and Pulitzer prize-winning *Profiles in Courage* (1956), both best-selling books.

Second child in a family of nine children born to Rose and financier Joseph Patrick Kennedy (an ambassador to Great Britain during Franklin D. Roosevelt's administration), his maternal grandfather was Boston mayor John F. (Honey Fitz) Fitzgerald. Other well-known members of John Kennedy's family are brothers Robert F. (which see) and Edward M. When John was a child, the active, sports-loving family moved from the Boston suburbs to New York City suburbs. After elementary school, John spent a year at Canterbury School in New Milford, Conn., four years at Choate School, Wallingford, Conn., a short time at the London School of Economics, a short time at Princeton University (leaving because of illness), then (1936) he enrolled at Harvard University and, in spite of the fact that he had been an average student through most of his educational experience, graduated *cum laude* in 1940. He topped it all off with a period of study at the Stanford University Graduate School of Business. Married beautiful and glamorous Jacqueline Lee Bouvier (1953) who tastefully refurnished the White House. The couple had three children, one of whom died shortly after birth.

Navy PT boat commander during World War II and awarded the Navy and Marine Corps Medal and the Purple Heart. After the war, tried his hand at journalism then, in order to carry on for older brother Joe who died during the war, turned to politics. U.S. Representative (1947-1953) who was critical of the administration because it did not do more to prevent the loss of China to communism but supported Truman's Fair Deal program; U.S. Senate (1953-1960) where, although he became increasingly liberal on many issues, he straddled the fence on McCarthyism; very nearly defeated Estes Kefauver for the vice presidential nomination in 1956; nominated presidential candidate on the first ballot at the 1960 Democratic National Convention, Kennedy defeated Republican opponent Richard M. Nixon in a campaign that included a unique series of television debates between the two candidates. The score: 303 electoral and 34,221,485 popular votes for Kennedy; 219 electoral and 34,108,684 popular votes for Nixon.

During his presidency, although much of Kennedy's broad progressive domestic program was blocked by Congress, the Trade Expansion Act was passed (1962) and he was able to advance the cause of civil rights by use of his executive powers and the help of brother Robert who was attorney general; the Peace Corps was established (1961) with brother-in-law Sargent Shriver at its head; space exploration advanced rapidly; the Alliance for Progress was jointly signed (1961) by the United States and all Latin American countries except Cuba. American troops and equipment were sent to South Vietnam and Thailand (military advisers to Laos) to help those countries resist the spread of communism. Confronted with one crisis after another, Kennedy displayed admirable composure in dealing with them. For example, when the Soviet Union built missile sites in Cuba (1962), Kennedy successfully confronted Premier Khrushchev who backed down and had the sites dismantled and the missiles returned to Russia. Although the nuclear arms race between Russia and the United States continued during the Kennedy administration, negotiation led (1963) to a limited test-ban treaty.

KENNEDY, JOHN LAUDERDALE *(b Oct. 27, 1854, Ayrshire, Scotland; d Aug. 30, 1946, Pacific Palisades, Calif.)* Lawyer, banker and a Republican power in Nebraska. Presidential elector on the Mc-Kinley-Roosevelt ticket (1900), U.S. Representative (1905-1907), Omaha fire and police commissioner and chairman of the board (1907, 1908), GOP state committee chairman (1911, 1912), federal fuel administrator for the state (1917-1919), president of the Omaha Chamber of Commerce (1924, 1925).

KENNEDY, JOHN PENDLETON *(b Oct. 25, 1795, Baltimore, Md.; d Aug. 18, 1870, Newport, R.I.)* Novelist, historian, lawyer, Maryland Whig who was secretary of the navy in the Fillmore cabinet (1852-1853). State delegate (1821-1823) and speaker of the house (1846), U.S. Representative (1838-1839, 1841-1845), presidential elector on the Harrison-Tyler ticket (1840). Brother of Anthony Kennedy.

KENNEDY, MARTIN JOHN *(b Aug. 29, 1892, New York City; d Oct. 27, 1955, New York City)* Real estate-insurance broker, New York Democrat. Chairman of New York City School Board (1918-1924), state senate (1924-1930), U.S. Representative (1930-1945).

KENNEDY, ROBERT FRANCIS *(b Nov. 20, 1925, Brookline, Mass.; d June 6, 1968, Los Angeles, Calif.)* Brother of John F. Kennedy and, like him, the victim of an assassin's bullet; author of *The Enemy Within* (1960), Massachusetts and New York Democrat, a leader of the party's liberal wing and his brother's most influential adviser, serving as his campaign manager both in his run for a U.S. Senate seat (1952) and the presidency (1960).

In Massachusetts: attorney with the U.S. Department of Justice's criminal division (1951-1952), first counsel and then chief counsel of the U.S. Senate Permanent Subcommittee on Investigations (1953-1959), U.S. attorney general (1960-1964) and the first in history to serve as a member of his brother's cabinet. In New York: U.S. Senate

(1964 until death), candidate for the Democratic presidential nomination (1968).

As subcommittee attorney, he worked on Joseph McCarthy's probe of alleged Communist infiltration into government and then, as chief counsel, he much improved his image by delving into corrupt labor-management practices. As attorney general, he markedly stepped up enforcement of existing equal rights laws. As senator, he vigorously opposed Lyndon B. Johnson's Vietnam policies, became a late starter in the Democratic presidential primaries and had captured several states, including California, when the assassin's bullet struck.

KENNEY, RICHARD ROLLAND *(b Sept. 9, 1856, Laurel, Del.; d Aug. 14, 1931, Dover, Del.)* Lawyer, Delaware Democrat. State librarian (1879-1881), state adjutant general (1887-1891), Democratic state committeeman (1890-1917) and national convention delegate (1892, 1900, 1904), national committeeman (1896-1908), U.S. Senate (1895-1901), counsel to the state house of representatives (1921), Kent County prosecutor (1921-1925), member of state board of supplies (1921-1923), member-secretary of the state public lands commission (1913-1929).

KENT, JOSEPH *(b Jan. 14, 1779, Calvert County, Md.; d Nov. 24, 1837, near Bladensburg, Md.)* Maryland physician-farmer who at least three times changed political hats: from Federalist to Democrat to Republican to National Republican. U.S. Representative as a Federalist (1811-1815) and as a Democrat (1819-1826), presidential elector on the Democratic Monroe-Tompkins ticket (1816), Republican governor (1826-1829), vice president of the Republican National Convention (1831) that nominated Henry Clay for the U.S presidency, U.S. Senate as a National Republican (1833 until death).

KENYON, WILLIAM SQUIRE *(b June 10, 1869, Elyria, Ohio; d Sept. 9, 1933, Sebasco Estates, Maine)* Lawyer, progressive Iowa Republican who, as a U.S. Senator (1911-1922), organized and led the Western and Southern farm bloc. A friend of labor and a foe of unethical business practices, he headed committees that investigated steel and coal strikes, and devised legal codes that spelled out duties and obligations of both capital and labor.

His love, however, was more for judicial robes than for politics and he readily resigned from the Senate to accept Harding appointment as eighth circuit judge of the U.S. Circuit Court of Appeals (1922 until death) during which time he cancelled the oil leases involved in the Teapot Dome scandals. Such rulings were in keeping with his earlier traditions as a hard-hitting prosecutor, particularly as special assistant to U.S. Attorney General George W. Wickersham (1910-1911) when he dug deep into railroad rebate and packing house abuses.

Webster County prosecutor (1892-1896) where he set a record for convictions, eleventh judicial district judge (1900-1902), declined appointment to Coolidge Cabinet as secretary of the navy, accepted Hoover appointment (1929) as a member of the National Commission on Law Observance and Enforcement, better known as the Wickersham Commission. Liberal Republicans (1928) unsuccessfully urged him to seek the presidential nomination.

KERN, JOHN WORTH *(b Dec. 20, 1849, Alto, Ind.; d Aug. 17, 1917, Asheville, N.C.)* Lawyer of some note as a debater, progressive Indiana Democrat who was nominated by acclamation at the 1908 national convention to be William Jennings Bryan's vice presidential running mate and in 1912 the most-junior U.S. Senator ever chosen Democratic floor leader. Kokomo city attorney (1871-1884), state supreme court

reporter (1885-1889), state senate (1893-1897), special assistant U.S. district attorney (1893-1894), Indianapolis city solicitor (1897-1901), unsuccessful gubernatorial candidate (1900, 1904), U.S. Senate (1911-1917).

KERNAN, FRANCIS *(b Jan. 14, 1816, Wayne, N.Y.; d Sept. 7, 1892, Utica, N.Y.).* Lawyer, New York Free-Soiler turned Democrat who helped Samuel Tilden fight the state's infamous Tweed Ring. State appeals court reporter (1854-1857), state assemblyman (1861), U.S. Representative (1863-1865), state constitutional convention delegate (1867, 1868), candidate for governor (1872) who lost, some said, because of his Catholic religion; U.S. Senate (1875-1881), state university regent (1870-1892).

KERR, JOHN HOSEA *(b Dec. 31, 1873, Yanceyville, N.C.; d June 21, 1958, Warrenton, N.C.)* Lawyer, North Carolina Democrat who was a U.S. Representative more than a quarter-century (1923-1953). Mayor of Warrenton (1897, 1898), third district solicitor (1906-1916), superior court judge (1916-1923), Democratic National Convention delegate (1932, 1940), chairman of U.S. delegation to Inter-American Travel Congress (1941).

KERR, MICHAEL CRAWFORD *(b March 15, 1827, Titusville, Pa.; d Aug. 19, 1876, Rockbridge Alum Springs, Va.)* Lawyer, Indiana Democrat. New Albany city attorney (1854), Floyd County prosecutor (1855), state representative (1856, 1857), state supreme court reporter (1862-1865), U.S. Representative (1865-1873) and speaker of the house (1875 until death).

KERR, ROBERT SAMUEL *(b Sept. 11, 1896, Ada, Okla., which then was Indian Territory; d Jan. 1, 1963, Washington, D.C.)* Public and Sunday school teacher, lawyer who drilled for oil on a shoestring and struck it rich to, some say, the tune of $35 million; orator, Oklahoma Democrat who as a U.S. Senator (1949 until death) was one of the most powerful of his time doing, among other more national things, much to wipe out his state's dust-bowl conditions but never forgetting the industry that made him. State supreme court special justice (1931), president of the Oklahoma County juvenile council (1935, 1936), state parole board member (1935-1938), Oklahoma's first native-born governor (1943-1947), Democratic National Committeeman (1940-1948) and delegate to all national conventions (1940-1960) and the keynote speaker in 1944, chairman of the Southern Governors Conference (1945, 1946).

KETCHAM, JOHN CLARK (b Jan. 1, 1873, Toledo, Ohio; d Dec. 4, 1941, Hastings, Mich.) Teacher, banker, Michigan Republican. Barry County schools commissioner (1899-1907), GOP county committee chairman (1902-1908), Hastings postmaster (1907-1914), master of the state Grange (1912-1920), U.S. Representative (1921-1933), state insurance commissioner (1935-1937), counsel for the Michigan Chain Store Bureau (1938-1941).

KETCHAM, JOHN HENRY (b Dec. 21, 1832, Dover Plains, N.Y.; d Nov. 4, 1906, New York City) Farmer, Union Army officer, New York Republican who served thirty years in Congress but not consecutively. Dutchess County supervisor (1854, 1855), state assemblyman (1856, 1857), state senator (1860, 1861), U.S. Representative (1865-1873, 1877-1893, 1897 until death), GOP National Convention delegate (1876, 1896), District of Columbia commissioner (1874-1877).

KEY, DAVID McKENDREE (b Jan. 27, 1824, Greene County, Tenn.; d Feb. 3, 1900, Chattanooga, Tenn.) Lawyer, Confederate Army officer, who, as a U.S. Senator (1875-1877), sought to restore good relations between North and South and thus caused President Hayes, an Ohio Republican, to appoint him, a Tennessee Democrat, first to the cabinet as postmaster general (1877-1880) and then to the federal district court bench (1880-1894). Presidential elector on the Buchanan-Breckinridge (1856) and Breckinridge-Lane (1860) tickets, state constitutional convention delegate (1870), third chancery division chancellor (1870-1875).

KEY, PHILIP BARTON (b April 12, 1757, Cecil County, Md.; d July 28, 1815, Georgetown, D.C.) Lawyer-farmer who fought on the side of the British in the Revolutionary War yet later made his mark in politics as a Maryland Federalist. Member of state house of delegates (1794-1799), U.S. Representative (1807-1813). His nephew was Francis Scott Key who wrote "The Star Spangled Banner."

KEYES, HENRY WILDER (b May 23, 1863, Newbury, Vt.; d June 19, 1938, North Haverhill, N.H.) Farmer, banker, New Hampshire Republican. State representative (1891-1895, 1915-1917), state senate (1903-1905), treasurer of the state license commission (1903-1915), chairman of state excise commission (1915-1917), governor (1917-1919), U.S. Senate (1919-1937).

KIDDER, JEFFERSON PARISH (b June 4, 1815, Braintree, Vt.; d Oct. 2, 1883, St. Paul, Minn.) Farmer, teacher, lawyer, Vermont Democrat, Minnesota and Dakota Territory Republican. In Vermont: State constitutional convention delegate (1843), state attorney (1843-1847), state senate (1847, 1848), lieutenant governor (1853, 1854), Democratic National Convention delegate (1856). In Minnesota: state representative (1863, 1864). In Dakota: Lincoln-appointed associate justice of the territorial supreme court and reappointed by Presidents Grant, Hayes, and Arthur

(1865-1875, 1879 until death) with time out to serve as an elected delegate to the U.S. Congress (1875-1879).

KIESS, EDGAR RAYMOND *(b Aug. 26, 1875, Warrensville, Pa.; d July 20, 1930, Eagles Mere, Pa.)* Teacher, newspaper publisher, real estate developer, Pennsylvania Republican. State representative (1904-1910), Pennsylvania State College trustee (1912-1930), U.S. Representative (1913 until death).

KILBURN, CLARENCE EVANS *(b April 13, 1893, Malone, N.Y.)* Banker, New York Republican who was a U.S. Representative for a quarter-century (1940-1965) serving on the Banking and Currency Committee and Joint Economic Committee.

KILGORE, CONSTANTINE BUCKLEY *(b Feb. 20, 1835, Newnan, Ga.; d Sept. 23, 1897, Ardmore, Okla.)* Lawyer, Confederate Army officer who was wounded and captured at Chickamauga; Texas Democrat whom President Cleveland appointed judge (1895) for the southern district of Indian Territory, now Oklahoma, and so served for the two remaining years of his life. Rusk County justice of the peace (1869), state constitutional convention delegate (1875), presidential elector on the Hancock-English ticket (1880), state senate (1884-1886) and senate president (1885), U.S. Representative (1887-1895).

KILGORE, HARLEY MARTIN *(b Jan. 11, 1893, Brown, W.Va.; d Feb. 28, 1956, in U.S. Naval Hospital, Bethesda, Md.).* Teacher, lawyer, West Virginia Democrat. Organizer of Raleigh County's first high school (1915) and its principal for a year, World War I officer, county criminal court judge (1933-1941), U.S. Senate (1941 until death), Democratic National Convention delegate (1944, 1948, 1952).

KILLINGER, JOHN WEINLAND *(b Sept. 18, 1824, Annville, Pa.; d June 30, 1896,* *Lebanon, Pa.)* Lawyer, Pennsylvania Republican. Lebanon County prosecutor (1848, 1849), state representative (1850, 1851), state senate (1854-1857), GOP National Convention delegate (1856), U.S. Representative (1859-1863, 1871-1875, 1877-1881), internal revenue assessor (1864-1866).

KINCHELOE, DAVID HAYES *(b April 9, 1877, McLean County, Ky.; d April 16, 1950, Washington, D.C.)* Lawyer, Kentucky Democrat. McLean County prosecutor (1902-1906), presidential elector on the Wilson-Marshall ticket (1912), U.S. Representative (1915-1930), U.S. Customs Court judge (1930-1948).

KINDRED, JOHN JOSEPH *(b July 15, 1864, Southampton County, Va.; d Oct. 23, 1937, Astoria, Queens, N.Y.)* Lawyer, farmer, physician who specialized in mental disorders, New York Democrat. U.S. Representative (1911-1913, 1921-1929), professor of medical jurisprudence at Florida's John B. Stetson University (1933-1937).

KING, ADAM *(b 1790, York, Pa.; d May 6, 1835, York)* Physician, editor-publisher of the *York Gazette* (1818-1835), Pennsylvania Democrat. York County court clerk (1818-1826), U.S. Representative (1827-1833).

KING, CECIL RHODES *(b Jan. 13, 1898, Fort Niagara, N.Y.)* Businessman, California Democrat who served as a U.S. Representative for twenty-seven years (1942-1969) and before that as a state assemblyman for ten years (1932-1942). In Congress he was a member of the House Ways and Means Committee, the Joint Committee on Internal Revenue Taxation, and the Joint Committee on Reduction of Nonessential Federal Expenditures.

KING, CYRUS *(b Sept. 6, 1772, Scarboro, Mass., now Maine; d April 25, 1817, Saco, Maine)* Private secretary to his half-brother, Rufus King, when the latter was minister to England (1796), lawyer, a founder of Maine's Thornton Academy, Maine Federalist. U.S. Representative (1813-1817). Brother of William King.

KING, EDWARD JOHN *(b July 1, 1867, Springfield, Mass.; d Feb. 17, 1929, Washington, D.C.)* Lawyer, Illinois Republican. Galesburg city attorney (1893, 1894), state representative (1907-1914), U.S. Representative (1915 until death).

KING, GEORGE GORDON *(b June 9, 1807, Newport, R.I.; d July 17, 1870, Newport)* Lawyer, Rhode Island Whig. Member and speaker of the state house of representatives (1845, 1846), presidential elector on the Taylor-Fillmore ticket (1848), U.S. Representative (1849-1853).

KING, JAMES GORE *(b May 8, 1791, New York City; d Oct. 3, 1853, near Weehawken, N.J.)* Lawyer, merchant, banker, Erie Railroad president (1835), New Jersey Whig. New York Chamber of Commerce member (1817-1853), vice president (1841-1845), president (1845-1848); U.S. Representative (1849-1851). Son of Rufus and brother of John A. King.

KING, JOHN ALSOP *(b Jan. 3, 1788, New York City; d July 7, 1867, Jamaica, N.Y.)* Lawyer, farmer, and one of the founders of both the Queens County and New York State Agricultural Societies, New York Whig turned Republican. State assembly (1819-1821, 1832, 1838, 1840), state senate (1823-1825) resigning to become secretary of the legation at London (1825) and chargé d'affaires (1826) while his father, Rufus King, was minister to England; Whig National Convention delegate (1839, 1852), U.S. Representative (1849-1851), governor (1857, 1858), delegate to the first GOP National Convention (1856), presidential elector on the Lincoln-Hamlin ticket (1860), delegate to the peace convention (1861) that sought to avert the Civil War.

KING, MARTIN LUTHER, JR. *(b Jan. 15, 1929, Atlanta, Ga.; d April 4, 1968, Memphis, Tenn., by assassination)* Atlanta clergyman, lecturer, and foremost nonviolent leader of the Negro drive for equal rights in the 1950s and 1960s. As such he was the man who led the historic Montgomery, Ala., bus boycott (1956), the prime organizer and first president of the Southern Christian Leadership Conference (1957 until death), keynote speaker at the tens-of-thousands strong March on Washington (1963), and was involved in similar demonstrations that made him widely known and respected by many in the United States and abroad. Additionally he was one of the nation's, and perhaps the world's, leading advocates of peace, a dedicated foe of American military involvement in Vietnam, and the youngest person to be awarded the Nobel Peace Prize (1964).

KING, PRESTON *(b Oct. 14, 1806, Ogdensburg, N.Y.; d Nov. 12, 1865, New York Harbor, N.Y. in a fall from a ferryboat)* Lawyer, publisher of the *St. Lawrence Republican*, New York Democrat–Free-Soiler–Republican who preferred states' rights to federal centralization yet opposed the spread of slavery and compromise with the South. Ogdensburg postmaster (1831-1834), state assemblyman (1835-1838), U.S. Representative (1843-1847 as a Democrat, 1849-1853 as a Free-Soiler), Free-Soil National Convention delegate (1848), U.S. Senate as a Republican (1857-1863), GOP National Convention delegate and presidential elector on the Lincoln-Johnson ticket (1864), collector of the Port of New York (Aug. 15, 1865, until death).

KING, RUFUS *(b March 24, 1755, Scarboro, in what then was Massachusetts but now is Maine; d April 29, 1827, Jamaica, Queens, N.Y.)* Lawyer, diplomat, Revolutionary Army officer, orator who used all his speaking skills to advocate a strong central government at the 1787 federal Constitutional Convention, Massachusetts and New York Federalist who was considered one of the ablest U.S. Senators of his time but three times failed in bids for still higher office: twice for vice president and once for president.

In Massachusetts: state representative (1782), Continental Congressman (1784-1787), delegate to the state convention that ratified the federal Constitution. In New York: state assemblyman (1789, 1790), U.S. Senate (1789-1796, 1813-1825), minister to Great Britain (1796-1803, 1825-1826). C. C. Pinckney's vice presidential running mate (1804, 1808), presidential candidate (1816) receiving 34 electoral votes to James Monroe's 183.

Half-brother of Cyrus and William, father of James G. and John A King.

KING, SAMUEL WILDER *(b Dec. 17, 1886, Honolulu, Hawaii; d March 24, 1959, Honolulu)* Naval officer, real estate-insurance broker, territory of Hawaii Republican. Honolulu supervisor (1932-1934), U.S. Congressional delegate (1935-1943), GOP National Convention delegate (1936, 1940, 1948, 1952), Hawaiian Emergency Housing Committee member (1946), chairman of Statehood Commission (1949-1953), constitutional convention president (1950), Homes Commission chairman (1952), Eisenhower-appointed territorial governor (1953-1957).

KING, WILLIAM *(b Feb. 9, 1768, Scarboro, Mass., now Maine; d June 17, 1852, Bath, Maine)* Deprived of the family wealth that went to his brother, Cyrus, and half-brother, Rufus, yet a self-made man who became Maine's leading ship builder-owner-merchant, real estate holder, and one of the owners of the state's first cotton mill. Politically, a Democrat turned Whig and the man most responsible for winning Maine's separation from Massachusetts and the new state's first governor (1820-1821) receiving 21,083 of the 22,014 votes cast. While Maine was still a part of Massachusetts: Topsham representative in the state general court (1795, 1799), Bath representative (1804-1806), senator from Lincoln County (1807-1811, 1818-1819). After statehood and the governorship: commissioner to effect a treaty with Spain (1821-1824), Bath collector of customs (1830-1834), unsuccessful Whig candidate for governor (1835). Additionally, during his lifetime, this King was a trustee of Waterville (now Colby) College (1821-1848), overseer of Bowdoin College (1797-1821) and trustee (1821-1849). The people of Bath knew him as The Sultan and his statue now stands in Maine's Capitol.

KING, WILLIAM HENRY *(b June 3, 1863, Fillmore, Utah; d Nov. 27, 1949, Salt Lake City, Utah)* A church missionary in Great Britain (1880-1883) who returned to the United States to hold a variety of Fillmore and Millard County elective offices while qualifying for the bar, was active in the drive for statehood, and then took an equally active part in Democratic affairs. Territorial legislator (1887, 1888), president of the territorial council (1891), associate territorial supreme court justice (1894-1896); and after statehood, U.S. Representative (1897-1899, 1900-1901), U.S. Senate (1917-1941).

KING, WILLIAM RUFUS de VANE *(b April 7, 1786, Sampson County, N.C.; d April 18, 1853, King's Bend, Ala.)* Lawyer, planter, diplomat who prevented France from interfering with the annexation of Texas; North Carolina and Alabama Democrat who served almost as many years, twenty-nine, as a U.S. Senator (1819-1844, 1848-1852) as he did days as Franklin Pierce's vice president (March 4, 1853 until death six weeks later).

In North Carolina: member of state house of commons (1807-1809), Wilmington city solicitor (1810), U.S. Representative (1811-1816). In 1818 he moved to Alabama, became active in the campaign for statehood and was sent to Washington as one of the new state's first senators, taking time out to serve as minister to France (1844-1846) during a period made ticklish by the Texas situation and threats of interference both from Britain and France.

In the Senate he was, at different times, chairman of the Foreign Relations and Public Lands committees, and its presiding officer for many years. He was sworn in as vice president, by special act of Congress, in Cuba where he had gone in hope of recovering from tuberculosis and died in his plantation home the day after returning to the United States, thus never having been in Washington during his brief vice-presidential tenure.

KINKAID, MOSES PIERCE *(b Jan. 24, 1856, Monongalia County, W.Va.; d July 6, 1922, Washington, D.C.)* Lawyer, Nebraska Republican. State senate (1883), district judge (1887-1900), U.S. Representative (1903 until death).

KINZER, JOHN ROLAND *(b March 28, 1874, East Earl Township, Pa.; d July 25, 1955, Lancaster, Pa.)* Lawyer, Pennsylvania Republican. Lancaster County solicitor (1912-1923), GOP National Convention delegate (1928), U.S. Representative (1930-1947).

KIRBY, WILLIAM FOSGATE *(b Nov. 16, 1867, Miller County, Ark.; d July 26, 1934, Little Rock, Ark.)* Lawyer, jurist, author of *Kirby's Digest of the Statutes of Arkansas* (1904), Arkansas Democrat. State representative (1893, 1897),

state senate (1899-1901), state attorney general (1907-1909), associate justice of the state supreme court (1910-1916, 1926 until death), U.S. Senate (1916-1921).

KIRKWOOD, SAMUEL JORDAN *(b Dec. 20, 1813, Harford County, Md.; d Sept. 1, 1894, Iowa City, Iowa).* Farmer, teacher, miller, lawyer, banker, railroad president, Ohio Whig and Iowa Republican who, as governor (1860-1864, 1876-1877), put down the Civil War proslavery Copperhead movement (Northerners who were sympathetic to the South during the Civil War) in the latter state. In Ohio: Richland County prosecutor (1845-1849), state constitutional convention delegate (1850, 1851). In Iowa: State senate (1856-1859), U.S. Senate (1866-1867, 1877-1881), secretary of the interior in the Garfield cabinet (1881-1882).

KITCHELL, AARON *(b July 10, 1744, Hanover, N.J.; d June 25, 1820, Hanover)* Blacksmith, New Jersey Democrat. U.S. Representative (1791-1797, 1799, 1801), U.S. Senate (1805-1809), state assemblyman (1781, 1782, 1786-1790, 1793, 1794, 1797, 1801-1804, 1809), presidential elector on the Monroe-Tompkins ticket (1816).

KITCHIN, ALVIN PAUL *(b Sept. 13, 1908, Scotland Neck, N.C.)* Lawyer, FBI agent, North Carolina Democrat. U.S. Representative (1957-1963) serving on the Armed Services Committee. Grandson of William H., nephew of Claude and William W. Kitchin.

KITCHIN, CLAUDE *(b March 24, 1869, Halifax County, N.C.; d May 31, 1923, Wilson, N.C.)* Lawyer, North Carolina Democrat who as a U.S. Representative (1901 until death) used ridicule like a stiletto to gain a reputation as the most effective debater in the House. He was majority leader (1915-1919) and chairman of the Ways and Means Committee. Son of William H., and brother of William W. and uncle of Alvin P. Kitchin.

KITCHIN, WILLIAM HODGES *(b Dec. 22, 1837, Lauderdale County, Ala.; d Feb. 2, 1901, Scotland Neck, N.C.).* Confederate Army officer, lawyer, North Carolina Democrat. U.S. Representative (1879-1881). Father of Claude and William W. and grandfather of Alvin P. Kitchin.

KITCHIN, WILLIAM WALTON *(b Oct. 9, 1866, Halifax County, N.C.; d Nov. 9, 1924, Scotland Neck, N.C.)* Editor of the *Scotland Neck Democrat,* lawyer, North Carolina Democrat. Chairman of the Halifax County executive committee (1890), state senate (1892), U.S. Representative (1897-1909) resigning to become governor (1909-1913). Son of William H., brother of Claude, uncle of Alvin P. Kitchin.

KITTERA, JOHN WILKES *(b November, 1752, East Earl Township, Pa.; d June 6, 1801, Lancaster, Pa.)* Lawyer, Pennsylvania Federalist. U.S. Representative (1791-1801). Father of Thomas Kittera.

KITTERA, THOMAS *(b March 21, 1789, Lancaster, Pa.; d June 16, 1839, Philadelphia, Pa.)* Lawyer, Pennsylvania Federalist. State deputy attorney general (1817, 1818), Philadelphia deputy attorney general (1824-1826), city council president (1824-1826), U.S. Representative to fill a vacancy (1826-1827). Son of John Wilkes Kittera.

KITTREDGE, ALFRED BEARD *(b March 28, 1861, Nelson, N.H.; d May 4, 1911, Hot Springs, Ark.)* Lawyer, South Dakota Republican. Chairman of the Minnehaha County GOP Committee (1887), state senate (1889-1891), GOP National Committeeman (1892-1896), U.S. Senate (1901-1909).

KLEBERG, RICHARD MIFFLIN, SR. *(b Nov. 18, 1887, Kleberg County, Texas;* *d May 8, 1955, Hot Springs, Ark.).* Rancher, banker, Texas Democrat who at time of death was chairman of the board of the vast King Ranch Corporation. Texas College of Arts and Industry board president (1929-1931), U.S. Representative (1931-1944), state game and fish commissioner (1951-1955). Nephew of Rudolph Kleberg.

KLEBERG, RUDOLPH *(b June 26, 1847, Cat Spring, Texas; d Dec. 28, 1924, Austin, Texas)* Confederate cavalryman, lawyer, founder-publisher of the *Cuero Star,* Texas Democrat. DeWitt County prosecutor (1876-1890), state senate (1882-1886), U.S. attorney for the western Texas district (1885), U.S. Representative (1896-1903), official reporter for the court of criminal appeals (1905 until death). Uncle of Richard M. Kleberg, Sr.

KNIGHT, NEHEMIAH RICE *(b Dec. 31, 1780, Cranston, R.I.; d April 18, 1854, Providence, R.I.)* Banker, Rhode Island Anti-Federalist turned Democrat. Common pleas court clerk (1805-1811), circuit court clerk and collector of customs (1812-1817), governor (1817-1821), U.S. Senate (1821-1841).

KNOTT, JAMES PROCTOR *(b Aug. 29, 1830, Raywick, Ky.; d June 18, 1911, Lebanon, Ky.)* Lawyer, orator with a great gift for satire, educator, Missouri and Kentucky Democrat who was briefly imprisoned (1862) while in the former state for refusing to take the oath of allegiance to the federal government although he did not by any means carry his Southern sympathies to extremes. In Missouri: state representative (1857-1859), state attorney general (1859-1860) resigning when he failed to bring feuding for- and against-secession factions together. In Kentucky: U.S. Representative (1867-1871, 1875-1883), governor (1883-1887), state constitutional convention delegate (1891); Centre College civics and economics professor

(1892-1894), organizer and first dean of its law school (1894-1901).

KNOWLAND, JOSEPH RUSSELL *(b Aug. 5, 1873, Alameda, Calif.; d Feb. 1, 1966, Piedmont, Calif.)* Wholesale lumberman, shipper, banker, publisher of the *Oakland Tribune*, California Republican who for many years was one of the powers behind the scenes, making (and some said breaking) officeholders on levels high and low. U.S. Representative (1904-1915), state park commission chairman (1936-1960).

KNOX, PHILANDER CHASE *(b May 6, 1853, Brownsville, Pa.; d Oct. 12, 1921, Washington, D.C.)* Lawyer, Pennsylvania Republican who served in the cabinets of three presidents and as Taft's secretary of state (1909-1913) widened the scope of the Monroe Doctrine to include Asian nations; the words that guided much of his policies —dollar diplomacy. Assistant U.S. attorney (1876), state bar association president (1897), McKinley-appointed U.S. attorney general and continuing under Roosevelt (1901-1904), U.S. Senate (1904-1909, 1917 until death).

KNOX, VICTOR ALFRED *(b Jan. 13, 1899, Chippewa County, Mich.).* Farmer, plumbing contractor, Michigan Republican. Soo Township treasurer (1923, 1924), county supervisor (1925-1931), state legislature (1937-1952; temporary speaker and GOP floor leader 1943-1946; speaker 1947-1952), U.S. Representative (1953-1965) serving on the Ways and Means Committee.

KNUTSON, HAROLD *(b Oct. 20, 1880, Skien, Norway; d Aug. 21, 1953, Wadena, Minn.)* Newspaper editor-publisher in Minnesota who sixteen times was sent to Washington by his Republican constituents; his papers were the *Royalton Banner, Foley Independent*, and *Wadena Pioneer Journal*. GOP state convention delegate (1902,

1904, 1910), GOP National Convention delegate (1940), president of Northern Minnesota Editorial Association (1910, 1911), U.S. Representative (1917-1949).

KOCIALKOWSKI, LEO PAUL *(b Aug. 16, 1882, Chicago, Ill.; d Sept. 27, 1958, Chicago)* Businessman, Illinois Democrat. Cook County tax appraisal and delinquent tax supervision (1916-1932), Democratic National Convention delegate (1928), U.S. Representative (1933-1943), county civil service commissioner (1945-1949).

KOPP, WILLIAM FREDERICK *(b June 20, 1869, Des Moines County, Iowa; d Aug. 24, 1938, Mt. Pleasant, Iowa).* Lawyer, Iowa Republican. Henry County prosecutor (1895-1899), Mt. Pleasant postmaster (1906-1914), Iowa Wesleyan College trustee (1908-1938), state representative (1915-1917), U.S. Representative (1921-1933).

KOWALSKI, FRANK *(b Oct. 18, 1907, Meriden, Conn.)* Writer, inventor, soldier (1925-1958) retiring as a colonel; Connecticut Democrat. U.S. Representative (1959-1963) serving on the Armed Services Committee.

KRAMER, CHARLES *(b April 18, 1879, Paducah, Ky.; d Jan. 20, 1943, Los Angeles, Calif.)* Lawyer, California Democrat. U.S. Representative (1933-1943).

KREIDER, AARON SHENK *(b June 26, 1863, South Annville Township, Pa.; d May 19, 1929, Annville, Pa.)* Farmer, merchant, banker, shoe manufacturer, Pennsylvania Republican who founded the town of Lawn (1886). Annville commissioner (1909-1912), GOP state convention delegate (1910), president of the National Association of Shoe Manufacturers (1913-1916), U.S. Representative (1913-1923) and Lebanon Valley College board president.

KUNKEL, JOHN CRAIN *(b July 21, 1898, Harrisburg, Pa.)* Banker, farmer, Pennsylvania Republican. U.S. Representative (1939-1951, 1961-1967), Dauphin County commissioner (1952-1956).

KUNZ, STANLEY HENRY *(b Sept. 26, 1864, Nanticoke, Pa.; d April 23, 1946, Chicago, Ill.)* Horse breeder, Illinois Democrat. State representative (1888-1890), state senate (1902-1906), Chicago councilman (1891-1921), Cook County Democratic committeeman (1891-1925), Democratic National Convention delegate (1912, 1916, 1924), U.S. Representative (1921-1931, 1932-1933).

KURTZ, JACOB BANKS *(b Oct. 31, 1867, Delaware Township, Pa.; d Sept. 18, 1960, Altoona, Pa.)* Lawyer, Pennsylvania Republican. Blair County district attorney (1905-1912), chairman of county committee of public safety during World War I, U.S. Representative (1923-1935), GOP National Convention delegate (1936, 1940, 1948), Altoona city solicitor (1944-1946).

KVALE, OLE JUULSON *(b Feb. 6, 1869, Winnesheik County, Iowa; d Sept. 11, 1929, near Otter Tail Lake, Minn.)* Minnesota clergyman who four times ran for Congress as an Independent Republican and was successful each time (the last three his name also appeared on the Farmer-Labor ticket) and thus served as a U.S. Representative (1923 until death) when he was succeeded by his son, Paul J. Kvale.

KVALE, PAUL JOHN *(b March 27, 1896, Orfordville, Wis.; d June 14, 1960, Minneapolis, Minn.)* Newspaperman who was an editor on the *Swift County News* and the *Minneapolis Tribune*, Minnesota Farmer-Laborite. Secretary to his father, Congressman Ole J. Kvale (1922-1929), U.S. Representative first to fill his father's unexpired term and then four times in his own right (1929-1939).

KYLE, JAMES HENDERSON *(b Feb. 24, 1854, Greene County, Ohio; d July 1, 1901, Aberdeen, S.Dak.)* South Dakota clergyman whose introduction to politics was purely accidental: the last-minute substitute orator at an Aberdeen Independence Day celebration, he delivered a speech that so stirred the people that the Populist party convened right then and there and nominated him for the state senate without his knowledge. State senate (1890), U.S. Senate (1891 until death), chairman of U.S. Industrial Commission (1898-1901).

L

☆ ☆ ☆

LACEY, JOHN FLETCHER *(b May 30, 1841, New Martinsville, Va., now W.Va.; d Sept. 29, 1913, Oskaloosa, Iowa).* Farmer, bricklayer, Union Army officer, lawyer, Iowa Republican who was one of the nation's earliest conservationists, serving as chairman of the Forestry Committee while a U.S. Representative (1889-1891, 1893-1907). State representative (1870), Oskaloosa councilman (1880-1883), state GOP convention chairman (1898).

LADD, EDWIN FREEMONT *(b Dec. 13, 1859, Starks, Maine; d June 22, 1925, Baltimore, Md.)* Chemist who conducted a life-long campaign against food additives and adulteration, North Dakota Nonpartisan Republican. New York State Experiment Station chemist (1884-1890) and then dean of the school of chemistry and pharmacy at North Dakota Agricultural College for many years and college president (1916-1921), chief chemist at the North Dakota Agricultural Experiment Station (1890-1916), editor of the *North Dakota Farmer* (1899-1904), state food commissioner (1902-1921), U.S. Senate (1921 until death).

LA FOLLETTE, ROBERT MARION, SR. *(b June 14, 1855, Primrose, Wis.; d June 18, 1925, Washington, D.C.)* Lawyer, reformer, statesman, Wisconsin Republican who almost continually bucked entrenched interests and won; a leader in the Progressive movement who sought the presidential nomination (1912) but lost out to Theodore Roosevelt as the result of a nervous breakdown, tried again with success (1924) but only polled 4,831,289 popular and 13 electoral votes in the general election.

Dane County district attorney (1880-1884), U.S. Representative (1885-1891), GOP National Convention delegate (1896, 1904, 1912), governor (1901-1906), U.S. Senate (1906 until death). A leader of the Senate insurgents, he strove successfully for meaningful rail legislation, sponsored the La Follette Seamen's Act, opposed the Payne-Aldrich Tariff and, though against U.S. entry into World War I, supported most war measures once participation became a fact; his most notable dissent was with the draft.

LA FOLLETTE, ROBERT MARION, JR. *(b Feb. 6, 1895, Madison, Wis.; d Feb. 24, 1953, Washington, D.C., by suicide because of worry about his health).* Private secretary to his father (1919-1925), publishing house and broadcasting executive, author, economic-research consultant and, like his father, a highly independent Wisconsin Progressive Republican. Chairman of the GOP state central committee (1920-1924), vice chairman of the Progressive National Executive Committee during his father's presidential campaign (1924), U.S. Senate to succeed his father and staying on in his own right for nearly a quarter-century (1925-1947).

LA FOLLETTE, WILLIAM LEROY *(b Nov. 30, 1860, Thorntown, Ind.; d Dec. 20, 1934, Colfax, Wash.)* Fruit grower, stockman, Washington Republican. State representative (1899-1901), U.S. Representative (1911-1919).

LA GUARDIA, FIORELLO HENRY *(b Dec. 11, 1882, New York City; d Sept. 20, 1947, New York City)* Lawyer, foreign service officer, Republican-Socialist-Progressive who as Fusionist mayor (1934-1945) did quite a job of cleaning up New York City after years of Tammany Hall misrule and malpractice. A short man, he was known to the people as the Little Flower, winning his way into their hearts by such ways as reading the Sunday comics to children over radio every week during a newspaper strike.

American consular service attache in Budapest, Hungary, and Trieste, Austria (1901-1904), and agent at Fiume, Austria (1904-1906), Immigration Service interpreter at Ellis Island (1907-1910), deputy state attorney general (1915-1917), U.S. Representative (1917-1919, 1923-1933), with time out during World War I to command American air forces on the Italian-Austrian front. President of the city board of aldermen (1920, 1921), U.S. delegate to the Interparliamentary Conference in Berlin (1928) and London (1930), president of the U.S. Conference of Mayors (1936-1945), U.S. director of Civil Defense (1941-1942) and chairman of the U.S. section of the Permanent U.S.-Canada Joint Defense Board, U.S. delegate to the International Civil Aviation Conference (1944), special ambassador to Brazil (1946), director general of the United Nations Relief and Rehabilitation Administration (1946).

LAMAR, LUCIUS QUINTUS CINCINNATUS *(b Sept. 17, 1825, Putnam County, Ga.; d Jan. 23, 1893, Vineville, Ga.)* Lawyer, educator, orator, diplomat, jurist, and a Mississippi Democrat dedicated to the preservation of states' rights who drafted its ordinance of secession but who, in the postwar era, threw his efforts into reconciliation between South and North.

University of Mississippi professor of mathematics (1852), political economy, and social science (1866) and law (1867); Georgia state representative during a brief return to his home state (1853), U.S. Representative (1857-1860, 1873-1877), delegate to state secession convention (1861), Confederate Army officer who was sent on a special mission to Russia, France, and England (1863), state constitutional convention delegate (1865, 1868, 1875, 1877, 1881), U.S. Senate (1877-1885), Democratic National Convention delegate (1880), secretary of the interior in the Cleveland cabinet (1885-1888), Cleveland-appointed associate justice of the U.S. Supreme Court (1888 until death).

Uncle of William B. and nephew of Mirabeau B. Lamar.

LAMAR, MIRABEAU BUONAPARTE *(b Aug. 16, 1798, Warren County, Ga.; d Dec. 19, 1859, Richmond, Texas)* Merchant, writer, orator, poet, secretary to Democratic Governor George M. Troup of Georgia (1823-1827) and editor of the *Columbus (Ga.) Enquirer* before moving on to Texas to join the fight for independence, becoming the Texas republic's second president (1838-1841) in a campaign that was marked by the suicide of his two main opponents. Secretary of war in the provisional cabinet of President David G. Burnet (1836) and then the new republic's vice president during Sam Houston's first term (1836-1838). As president, he opened negotiations leading to recognition by England, Holland, and France, personally selected the site of the capital city of Austin (1840), and introduced a comprehensive educational system. Uncle of the preceding, granduncle of the following.

LAMAR, WILLIAM BAILEY *(b June 12, 1853, Jefferson County, Fla.; d Sept 26, 1928, Thomasville, Ga.)* Lawyer, Florida Democrat. Jefferson County circuit court clerk (1877-1881), county judge (1883-1886), state representative (1887) but declined to be speaker, state attorney general (1889-1903), U.S. Representative (1903-1909), national commissioner to the Panama-Pacific International Exposition in San Francisco (1915). Grand-nephew of Mirabeau B. and nephew of Lucius Q. C. Lamar.

LAMB, JOHN *(b June 12, 1840, Sussex County, Va.; d Nov. 21, 1924, Richmond, Va.).* Confederate Army officer, merchant, Virginia Democrat. U.S. Representative (1897-1913).

LAMBERT, JOHN *(b Feb. 24, 1746, Lambertville, N.J.; d Feb. 4, 1823, near Lambertville)* Farmer, New Jersey Democrat. State assemblyman (1780-1785, 1788), member of state council (1790-1804) and its vice president (1801-1804), acting governor (1802, 1803), U.S. Representative (1805-1809), U.S. Senate (1809-1815).

LAMBERTSON, WILLIAM PURNELL *(b March 23, 1880, Fairview, Kans.; d Oct. 26, 1957, Fairview)* Farmer, Kansas Republican. State representative (1909-1911, 1919-1921), speaker pro tem (1911), speaker (1919); state senate (1913-1915), chairman of State Efficiency and Economy Commission (1917), member of state board of administration (1923-1925), U.S. Representative (1929-1945), mayor of Fairview (1949-1952), chairman of Brown County Board of Commissioners (1953-1956).

LANDIS, CHARLES BEARY *(b July 9, 1858, Millville, Ohio; d April 24, 1922, Asheville, N.C.)* Newspaper editor, Indiana Republican. President of the Indiana Republican Editorial Association (1894, 1895), U.S. Representative (1897-1909). Brother of Frederick Landis.

LANDIS, FREDERICK *(b Aug. 18, 1872, Sevenmile, Ohio; d Nov. 15, 1934, Logansport, Ind.)* Lawyer, writer, lecturer, Indiana Republican who was one of the organizers of the state's Progressive party, temporary chairman of its first convention, its unsuccessful candidate for governor, and National Progressive Convention delegate (all in 1912). U.S. Representative (1903-1907); unsuccessful candidate for governor (1928) this time as a Republican once again. Brother of Charles B. Landis.

LANE, AMOS *(b March 1, 1778, near Aurora, N.Y.; d Sept. 2, 1849, Lawrenceburg, Ind.)* Lawyer, Indiana Democrat. State representative (1816, 1817, 1839) and house speaker in the latter year, U.S. Representative (1833-1837). Father of James H. Lane.

LANE, HARRY *(b Aug. 28, 1855, Corvallis, Oreg.; d May 23, 1917, San Francisco, Calif.)* Physician, Oregon Democrat. Oregon State Insane Asylum superintendent (1887-1891), mayor of Portland (1905-1909), U.S. Senate (1913 until death). Grandson of Joseph and nephew of LaFayette Lane.

LANE, HENRY SMITH *(b Feb. 24, 1811, Bath County, Ky.; d June 18, 1881, Crawfordsville, Ind.)* Lawyer, banker, Indiana Whig turned Republican who resigned less than a week after being inaugurated as governor (1861) in order to sit in the U.S. Senate instead (1861-1867). State senate (1837), state representative (1838, 1839), U.S. Representative (1840-1843), chairman of the first GOP National Convention (1856) and delegate (1860, 1868, 1872), special Indian commissioner (1869-1871), Mississippi River improvement commissioner (1872).

LANE, JAMES HENRY *(b June 22, 1814, Lawrenceburg, Ind.; d July 11, 1866, near Fort Leavenworth, Kans., by suicide).* Lawyer, Indiana Democrat who migrated to the Kansas Territory (1855), became active in the antislavery Free State movement there and commander of Lane's Army of the North that staged atrocity raids on proslavery bulwarks (1856). In Indiana: lieutenant governor (1849), U.S. Representative (1853-1855). In Kansas: delegate to the Topeka constitutional convention (1856) and president of the Leavenworth constitutional convention (1857), U.S. Senate as a Republican (1861 until death). Son of Amos Lane.

LANE, JOSEPH *(b Dec. 14, 1801, Buncombe County, N.C.; d April 19, 1881, Roseburg, Oreg.)* Farmer, soldier, Indiana Democrat who was rewarded for his heroism in the Mexican War by being appointed governor of the Oregon Territory (1849-1850) where he did well politically until 1860 when he ran for vice president with J. C. Breckinridge on a platform that advocated secession. In Indiana: state representative (1822, 1823, 1831-1833, 1838, 1839), state senate (1844-1846). In Oregon: delegate to Congress (1851-1859) until statehood, then U.S. Senate (1859-1861). Father of LaFayette Lane, grandfather of Harry Lane.

LANE, LaFAYETTE *(b Nov. 12, 1842, Vanderburg County, Ind.; d Nov. 23, 1896, Roseburg, Oregon)* Lawyer, Oregon Democrat. State representative (1864), state code commissioner (1874), U.S. Representative (1875-1877). Son of Joseph and uncle of Harry Lane.

LANE, THOMAS JOSEPH *(b July 6, 1898, Lawrence, Mass.)* Lawyer, Massachusetts Democrat. State representative (1927-1938), state senate (1939-1941), U.S. Representative (1941-1963) serving on the Judiciary Committee.

LANE, WILLIAM CARR *(b Dec. 1, 1789, Fayette County, Pa.; d Jan. 6, 1863, St. Louis, Mo.).* Physician, army surgeon, Missouri Democrat-Whig who was elected the first mayor of St. Louis (1823) and reelected seven times. Fifteen years later President Fillmore appointed him governor of the New Mexico Territory (1852-1853).

LANGDON, JOHN *(b June 25, 1741, Portsmouth, N.H.; d Sept. 18, 1819, Portsmouth)* Merchant, Revolutionary Army officer who pledged his fortune to equip troops, New Hampshire Democrat. Member of the Continental Congress (1775, 1776, 1783) and speaker of the New Hampshire House of Representatives many times, president of New Hampshire (1785) and governor (1788, 1805, 1809-1811), federal Constitutional Convention delegate (1787), U.S. Senate (1789-1801) in the First Congress and the Senate's first president pro tem, declined Madison appointment as secretary of the navy (1811) and nomination for vice president (1812). Brother of Woodbury Langdon.

LANGDON, WOODBURY *(b 1739, Portsmouth, N.H.; d Jan. 13, 1805, Portsmouth)* Merchant who was one of New Hampshire's leading figures both before and during the Revolution. State representative (1778, 1779), Continental Congress (1779, 1780), state executive council (1781-1784), state superior court judge (1782-1791). Brother of John Langdon.

LANGER, WILLIAM *(b Sept. 30, 1886, Everest Township, N.Dak.; d Nov. 8, 1959, Washington, D.C.)* Lawyer, North Dakota Republican. State attorney general (1916-1920), twice governor (1933-1934 as the Nonpartisan League candidate and 1937-1939 wearing the Independent label), U.S. Senate (1941 until death).

LANGLEY, JOHN WESLEY *(b Jan. 14, 1868, Floyd County, Ky.; d Jan. 17, 1932, Pikeville, Ky.)* Teacher, lawyer, Kentucky Republican. State representative (1886-1890), U.S. Representative (1907-1926). Husband of Katherine Gudger Langley.

LANGLEY, KATHERINE GUDGER *(b Feb. 14, 1888, Madison County, N.C.; d Aug. 15, 1948, Pikeville, Ky.)* Teacher, leader in Kentucky's Republican party. Pike County Red Cross chairman during World War I, first chairman of the state Woman's Republican Central Committee (1920) and vice chairman of the overall central committee (1920-1922), GOP National Convention alternate delegate (1920) and delegate (1924), U.S. Representative (1927-1931), third Kentucky district railroad commissioner (1939-1942). Wife of John W. Langley, daughter of James M. Gudger, Jr. of North Carolina.

LANGSTON, JOHN MERCER *(b Dec. 14, 1829, Louisa, Va.; d Nov. 15, 1897, Washington, D.C.)* Lawyer, writer, educator, lecturer, foreign service officer, Ohio Liberty party member and Virginia Republican of Negro, Indian, English ancestry who recruited black troops to fight on the side of the North. In Ohio: Brownhelm township clerk (1855), Oberlin councilman (1865-1867) and school board trustee (1867, 1868). In Washington, D.C.: Freedman's Bureau inspector general (1868-1869), law department-dean of the new Howard University (1869-1876) and the school's vice president (1872-1876), minister resident and consul general to Haiti and chargé d'affaires to Santo Domingo (1877-1885). In Virginia: GOP National Convention delegate (1876), president of the Virginia Normal and Collegiate Institute (1885 until death), GOP state convention delegate (1890), U.S. Representative (1890-1891). His autobiography, *From the Virginia Plantation to the National Capital*, was published in 1894.

LANGWORTHY, EDWARD *(b 1738, Savannah, Ga.; d Nov. 2, 1802, Baltimore, Md.).* A waif who was raised in the Bethesda Orphan House, later becoming a teacher there; newspaperman, writer, and a Georgia patriot who helped to organize the colony's Council of Safety (1775) and served as its secretary, member of the Continental Congress (1777-1779) and signer of the Articles of Confederation, Baltimore clerk of the customs (1795 until death).

LANHAM, SAMUEL WILLIS TUCKER *(b July 4, 1846, Spartanburg District, N.C.; d July 29, 1908, Weatherford, Texas).* Teacher, lawyer, Confederate soldier, Texas Democrat. Weatherford district attorney (1871-1876), presidential elector on the Hancock-English ticket (1880), U.S. Representative (1883-1893, 1897-1903), governor (1903-1907).

LANKFORD, RICHARD ESTEP *(b July 22, 1914, Wilmington, Del.)* Lawyer, farm manager, Maryland Democrat. State house of delegates (1948-1954), state legislative council (1953), U.S. Representative (1955-1965). Member of House Armed Services and Government Operations committees.

LARRABEE, WILLIAM HENRY *(b Feb. 21, 1870, Montgomery County, Ind.; d Nov. 16, 1960, New Palestine, Ind.).* Teacher, physician, Indiana Democrat. Hancock County Health Board secretary (1917, 1918), New Palestine councilman (1916-1920), state representative (1923-1925), U.S. Representative (1931-1943).

LARRAZOLO, OCTAVIANO AMBROSIO *(b Dec. 7, 1859, Allende, Chihuahua, Mexico; d April 7, 1930, Albuquerque, N.Mex.)* Teacher, lawyer, Texas and New Mexico Democrat turned Republican who championed the cause of the Chicano peoples and had written into the New Mexico constitution (1910) provisions guaranteeing the rights of

Spanish-speaking voters against disfranchisement and the use of the Spanish language. In Texas: U.S. district and circuit courts clerk in El Paso (1885-1888), western district attorney (1892-1895). In New Mexico: governor (1919-1921), state representative (1927, 1928), U.S. Senate (1928-1929).

LARRINAGA, TULIO *(b Jan. 15, 1847, Trujillo Alto, P.R.; d April 28, 1917, San Juan, P.R.)* Civil engineer, architect who worked on New York's Grand Central Terminal, served as architect for the city of San Juan, and built Puerto Rico's first railroad (1880). A Unionist, he was the island's assistant secretary of the interior (1898-1900), delegate to Washington (1900-1902), member of the Arecibo house of delegates (1902), resident commissioner to the United States (1905-1911), U.S. delegate to the Third Pan American Congress (1906), member of Puerto Rico's executive council (1911).

LARSEN, WILLIAM WASHINGTON *(b Aug. 12, 1871, Hagan, Ga.; d Jan. 5, 1938, Dublin, Ga.)* Teacher, lawyer, farmer, Georgia Democrat. Swainsboro city court prosecutor (1899-1905), councilman (1905-1909), state Democratic convention delegate (1902, 1906, 1912), superior court judge (1914, 1915), U.S. Representative (1917-1933), University of Georgia trustee (1927-1938), Farm Credit Administration regional manager (1933-1936), state unemployment insurance commissioner (1937 until death).

LATIMER, ASBURY CHURCHWELL *(b July 31, 1851, Abbeville County, S.C.; d Feb. 20, 1908, Washington, D.C.).* Farmer, South Carolina Democrat. Anderson County Democratic Committee chairman (1890-1892), U.S. Representative (1893-1903), U.S. Senate (1903 until death) also serving as an immigration commissioner (1907 until death).

LAURANCE, JOHN *(b 1750, Cornwall, England; d Nov. 11, 1810, New York City)* Lawyer, Revolutionary Army aide to General Washington who presided at the court-martial of Major John André (a British spy who was eventually hanged), New York Federalist. Regent of the University of the State of New York and trustee of Columbia College (1784-1810), delegate to the Continental Congress (1785-1787), state senate (1789), U.S. Representative in the First and Second Congresses (1789-1793), Washington-appointed U.S. judge for the New York district (1794-1796), U.S. Senate (1796-1800).

LAURENS, HENRY *(b March 6, 1724, Charleston, S.C.; d Dec. 8, 1792, near Charleston)* South Carolina merchant, planter, Indian fighter, Revolutionary patriot who was captured at sea (1779) while en route to his assigned post as minister to Holland and held prisoner in the Tower of London for fifteen months before being exchanged for Lord Cornwallis. Commons house of assembly (1757-1775), Provincial Congress (1775-1776) and its president (1775), general committee president (1775), Council of Safety president (1775, 1776), vice president of South Carolina (1776, 1777), delegate to the Continental Congress (1777-1779) and its president (1778), one of the peace commissioners who signed the preliminary Treaty of Paris (1782).

LAWRENCE, GEORGE PELTON *(b May 19, 1859, Adams, Mass.; d Nov. 21, 1917, New York City)* Lawyer, Massachusetts Republican. Northern Berkshire district judge (1885-1894), state senator (1895-1897) and senate president (1896, 1897), U.S. Representative (1897-1913), state public service commissioner (1913).

LAWRENCE, WILLIAM *(b June 26, 1819, Mt. Pleasant, Ohio; d May 8, 1899,*

Kenton, Ohio) Teacher, lawyer, Union Army officer, banker, Ohio Republican, and the congressman mainly responsible for the enabling legislation that created the Department of Justice. Logan County bankruptcy commissioner (1842), county prosecutor (1845), editor of the *Logan Gazette* (1845-1847), state representative (1846, 1847), state senate (1847-1854), supreme court reporter (1851), common pleas and district court judge (1857-1864), an editor of the *Western Law Monthly* (1859-1862), U.S. Representative (1865-1871, 1873-1877), first comptroller of the U.S. Treasury (1880-1885).

LAZARO, LADISLAS *(b June 5, 1872, near Ville Platte, La.; d March 30, 1927, Washington, D.C.)* Physician, farmer, Louisiana Democrat. State senate (1908-1912), U.S. Representative (1913 until death).

LEACH, DeWITT CLINTON *(b Nov. 23, 1822, Clarence, N.Y.; d Dec. 21, 1909, Springfield, Mo.)* Teacher, Michigan-Missouri newspaper editor-publisher who covered the "under the oaks" convention (1854) at which the Republican party was born and thereafter was a Michigan Republican. State representative (1849, 1850), state constitutional convention delegate (1850, 1867), state librarian (1855-1857), U.S. Representative (1857-1861), Lincoln-appointed Indian agent for the state (1861-1865).

LEASE, MARY ELIZABETH CLYENS *(b Sept. 11, 1853, Ridgway, Pa.; d Oct. 29, 1933, Callicoon, N.Y.)* Daughter of an Irish political exile, wife of a pharmacist, and mother of four children. Admitted to the Kansas bar in the mid 1880s and active with the Populists in the 1890 campaign; an effective agitator for the Irish cause and an advocate, successively, of women's suffrage, prohibition, evolution, birth control and Roosevelt Progressivism.

LEATHERWOOD, ELMER O. *(b Sept. 4, 1872, Pike County, Ohio; d Dec. 24, 1929, Washington, D.C.)* Lawyer, business executive, Utah Republican. Third judicial district attorney (1908-1916), GOP National Convention delegate (1924), U.S. Representative (1921 until death).

LEAVITT, HUMPHREY HOWE *(b June 18, 1796, Suffield, Conn.; d March 15, 1873, Springfield, Ohio)* Teacher, store clerk, lawyer, Ohio Democrat who was a Jackson-appointed federal district judge for thirty-seven years (1834-1871). Jefferson County prosecutor (1823-1829), state representative (1825, 1826), state senate (1827, 1828), common pleas and supreme court clerk (1828, 1829), U.S. Representative (1830-1834) when he resigned to accept the judicial appointment.

LEAVY, CHARLES HENRY *(b Feb. 16, 1884, York County, Pa.; d Sept. 25, 1952, Tacoma, Wash.)* Teacher, lawyer, Washington Democrat. Pend Oreille County prosecutor (1915-1918), special assistant U.S. attorney (1918-1921), Spokane County prosecutor (1922-1926), Central Valley High School board member (1923-1927), presidential elector on the Davis-Bryan ticket (1924), superior court judge (1926-1936), U.S. Representative (1937-1942) resigning to become a federal judge (1942-1952).

LEE, ARTHUR *(b Dec. 20, 1740, Westmoreland County, Va.; d Dec. 12, 1792, Urbana, Va.)* Virginia physician, lawyer, who for many years before the Revolution also served as a foreign service officer for the colonies. Massachusetts agent in England and France (1770), congressional correspondent in London (1775), commissioner to France (1776) and Spain (1777), member of the Virginia House of Delegates (1781-1783, 1785, 1786), delegate to the Continental Congress (1781-1784), member of the treasury board (1785-1789). Brother of Francis L. and Richard H. Lee.

LEE, CHARLES *(b 1758, Prince Warren County, Va.; d June 24, 1815, Fauquier County, Va.)* Lawyer, friend of George Washington, Virginia Federalist who was one of Aaron Burr's defense lawyers. Collector of the Port of Alexandria (1789-1793), state assemblyman (1793-1795), U.S. attorney general in the Washington and Adams cabinets (1795-1801).

LEE, FITZHUGH *(b Nov. 19, 1835, Fairfax County, Va.; d April 28, 1905, Washington, D.C.)* West Point graduate, Confederate cavalry officer, farmer, Virginia Democrat. Governor (1886-1890), consul general to Havana (1896-1898) in the days preceding the Spanish-American War in which he served as a major general. Nephew of Robert E. Lee.

LEE, FRANCIS LIGHTFOOT *(b Oct. 14, 1734, Westmoreland County, Va.; d Jan. 11, 1797, Richmond County, Va.)* Virginia patriot who signed the Declaration of Independence. Member of the house of burgesses (1758-1775) and signer of the Westmoreland declaration against the Stamp Act, delegate to the Continental Congress (1775-1780), member of the state house of delegates (1780, 1781), state senate (1778-1782). Brother of Arthur and Richard H. Lee.

LEE, GORDON *(b May 29, 1859, Ringgold, Ga.; d Nov. 7, 1927, Chickamauga, Ga.)* Farmer, manufacturer, Georgia Democrat. State representative (1894, 1895), state senate (1902-1904), U.S. Representative (1905-1927), Democratic National Convention delegate (1924).

LEE, HENRY *(b Jan. 29, 1756, Prince William County, Va.; d March 25, 1818, Cumberland Island, Ga.)* Daring Revo-lutionary Army cavalry officer who became known as Light-Horse Harry; Virginia Federalist who delivered the joint-session eulogy that characterized George Washington as "first in war, first in peace, and first in the hearts of his countrymen." Continental Congress delegate (1785-1788), delegate to the state convention that ratified the federal Constitution (1788), governor (1791-1794), commander of the U.S. forces that put down the Whisky Insurrection (1794), U.S. Representative (1799-1801).

Brother of Richard Bland Lee and grandfather of William H. F. Lee (whose father was General Robert E. Lee).

LEE, RICHARD BLAND *(b Jan. 20, 1761, Prince William County, Va.; d March 12, 1827, Washington, D.C.)*. Planter, Virginia Federalist. State house of delegates (1784-1788, 1796, 1799-1806), U.S. Representative in the First, Second, and Third Congress (1789-1795), Madison-appointed commissioner to settle claims growing out of War of 1812 losses (1816), Monroe-appointed Washington, D.C., Orphan's Court judge (1819 until death). Brother of Henry Lee.

LEE, RICHARD HENRY *(b Jan. 20, 1732, Westmoreland County, Va.; d June 19, 1794, Westmoreland County)*. Virginia lawyer who was one of the colony's foremost foes of the Stamp Act, signer of the Declaration of Independence, and author of the nation's first Thanksgiving Day proclamation (1777). County justice of the peace (1757), member of the house of burgesses (1758-1775), Continental Congress delegate (1774-1780, 1784-1787) and its president (1784), member of state house of delegates (1777, 1780, 1785), delegate to state convention that ratified the federal Constitution (1788), U.S. Senate (1789-1792). Brother of Arthur and Francis L. Lee.

LEE, WILLIAM HENRY FITZHUGH *(b May 31, 1837, Arlington, Va.; d Oct. 15, 1891, Ravensworth, Va.)* Son of General Robert E. Lee and himself a Confederate cavalry officer who was wounded at Brandy Station and later taken prisoner; planter, Virginia Democrat. State senate and its presiding officer (1875-1878), U.S. Representative (1887 until death). Grandson of Henry Lee.

LEFFLER, ISAAC *(b Nov. 7, 1788, Washington County, Pa.; d March 8, 1866, Charlton, Iowa)* Lawyer, Virginia Democrat who pioneered in Iowa (1835) while it was part of the Michigan Territory, remained when it became part of the Wisconsin Territory, and fought hard, and successfully, for a further division into the Iowa Territory. In Virginia: state house of delegates (1817-1819, 1823-1827, 1832, 1833), state public works commissioner (1827), U.S. Representative (1827-1829). In Michigan Territory: chief justice of the Des Moines County first judicial council (1836). In Wisconsin Territory: Des Moines County delegate to the first territorial legislature (1836, 1837) and speaker in the latter year, unsuccessful Whig candidate for Congress (1837). In Iowa Territory: trustee of the university at Belmont (1838), territorial representative (1841), Tyler-appointed U.S. marshal for the territory (1843-1845). In Iowa State: Fillmore-appointed receiver of public moneys for the Charlton land district (1852-1853). Brother of Shepherd Leffler.

LEFFLER, SHEPHERD *(b April 24, 1811, Washington County, Pa.; d Sept. 7, 1879, Des Moines County, Iowa)* Lawyer who practiced in the Michigan Territory section that became known as Iowa and where he was a leading Democrat. As a territory: representative (1839, 1841), territorial council member (1841-1843, 1845), constitutional convention president (1844) and delegate (1846). As a state: U.S. Representative (1846-1851). Brother of Isaac Leffler.

LEGARÉ, GEORGE SWINTON *(b Nov. 11, 1869, Rockville, S.C.; d Jan. 31, 1913, Charleston, S.C.)* Lawyer, South Carolina Democrat. Charleston corporation counsel (1898-1903), U.S. Representative (1903 until death).

LEGARÉ, HUGH SWINTON *(b Jan. 2, 1797, Charleston, S.C.; d June 20, 1843, Boston, Mass.)* Lawyer, founding editor of the *Southern Review* (1828-1832), foreign service officer, South Carolina Union Democrat who was U.S. attorney general in the Tyler cabinet (1841 until death). State representative (1820-1822, 1824-1830), state attorney general (1830-1832), chargé d'affaires to Brussels (1832-1836), U.S. Representative (1837-1839), ad interim U.S. secretary of state for the six weeks before his death while also serving as attorney general.

LEHLBACH, FREDERICK REIMOLD *(b Jan. 31, 1876, New York City; d Aug. 4, 1937, Washington, D.C.)* Lawyer, New Jersey Republican. Member of Newark Board of Education (1900-1903), state assemblyman (1903-1905), state board of equalization of taxes clerk (1905-1908), assistant Essex County prosecutor (1908-1913), U.S. Representative (1915-1937). Nephew of Herman Lehlbach.

LEHLBACH, HERMAN *(b July 3, 1845, Heilig-Kreuz-Steinach, Baden, Germany; d Jan. 11, 1904, Newark, N.J.)* Civil engineer, New Jersey Republican. State assembly (1884-1886), U.S. Representative (1885-1891), Essex County sheriff (1893-1896). Uncle of Frederick R. Lehlbach.

LEHMAN, HERBERT HENRY *(b March 28, 1878, New York City; d Dec. 5, 1963,*

New York City, of a heart attack while preparing to go to Washington to receive the Presidential Medal of Freedom, the nation's highest peacetime civilian award) Textile manufacturer, investment banker, philanthropist whose gifts included the Children's Zoo in Central Park, humanitarian who was director of the United Nations Relief and Rehabilitation Administration (1943-1946) which helped more than 500 million victims of World War II, liberal New York Democrat whom Franklin D. Roosevelt called "that good right arm of mine."

Delegate to all Democratic National Conventions (1928-1956), lieutenant governor (1929-1932), governor (1933-1942), director of the State Department's Relief and Rehabilitation Operations (1943), member of the Public Advisory Board of the Economic Cooperation Administration (1948), U.S. Senate (1949-1957).

LEIB, MICHAEL *(b Jan. 8, 1760, Philadelphia, Pa.; d Dec. 22, 1822, Philadelphia)* Physician, Revolutionary Army surgeon, Pennsylvania Democrat, and Philadelphia boss whose arrogance wrecked the party there. Member of state prison society (1789), committee of correspondence (1793), state representative (1797, 1798, 1817, 1818), U.S. Representative (1799-1806), presidential elector on the Madison-Clinton ticket (1808), U.S. Senate (1809-1814), Philadelphia postmaster (1814), chief clerk of the U.S. district court in Philadelphia (1822).

LEIGH, BENJAMIN WATKINS *(b June 18, 1781, Chesterfield County, Va.; d Feb. 2, 1849, Richmond, Va.)* Lawyer, Virginia Whig whose political career was wrecked by his integrity. State delegate (1811-1813, 1830, 1831), state constitutional convention delegate (1829, 1830), state appeals court reporter (1829-1841), U.S. Senate (1834-1836) in which latter role he insisted

upon censuring Andrew Jackson despite a legislative directive to forget the Bank of the United States mess.

LEISLER, JACOB *(b March, 1640, Frankfurt, Germany; d May 16, 1691, New York City, by hanging)* Soldier, merchant, colonial governor of New York (1689-1691) who might be described as the first American Populist; certainly a man who left his imprint on politics for decades to come.

He came to the United States as a twenty-year-old soldier, married a wealthy widow three years later, traveled in her circles, ran her businesses, and found that he had little stomach for the aristocracy. When the Protestants, William and Mary, replaced James, a Catholic, as England's ruling monarchs, Leisler headed a New York Committee of Safety (1688) to protect the colony against a rumored Catholic conspiracy and possible French-Indian attack. He rallied farmers, workers, and other antiaristocrats and soon the protection became a revolution.

Leisler became governor and promptly introduced a host of political and social reforms, establishing a representative assembly and permitting the people of New York City to choose a mayor by popular vote (Peter Delanoy, 1689-1691, was their choice and it is significant that New York did not have another popular election until 1834). Meantime, the aristocrats reached William and Mary who sent an armada to help Henry Sloughter replace Leisler as governor, using what force was necessary. Leisler surrendered and Sloughter, exceeding his orders, hanged him for treason.

LEMKE, WILLIAM *(b Aug. 13, 1878, Albany, Minn.; d May 30, 1950, Fargo, N.Dak.)* Lawyer, North Dakota Nonpartisan League Republican who was the Union party candidate for president (1936) polling 882,479 votes. GOP state committee chairman (1916-1920), member of the national executive committee of the National Nonpartisan League (1917-1921), state attorney general (1921, 1922), U.S. Representative (1933-1941, 1943 until death).

LENROOT, IRVINE LUTHER *(b Jan. 31, 1869, Superior, Wis.; d Jan. 26, 1949, Washington, D.C.)* Lawyer, Wisconsin Republican. GOP state convention delegate (1900, 1902, 1904), member of the state assembly (1901-1907) and its speaker (1903-1907), U.S. Representative (1909-1918), U.S. Senate (1918-1927), Hoover-appointed judge of the U.S. Court of Customs and Patent Appeals (1929-1944).

LESINSKI, JOHN, SR. *(b Jan. 3, 1885, Erie, Pa.; d May 27, 1950, Dearborn, Mich.)* Builder, realty and building supply businesses, Michigan Democrat. National convention delegate (1936, 1940, 1944), state convention in same years, U.S. Representative (1933 until death).

LESINSKI, JOHN, JR. *(b Dec. 28, 1914, Detroit, Mich.)* Building supply business, Michigan Democrat. U.S. Representative (1951-1965) serving on the Appropriations Committee.

LESTER, RUFUS EZEKIEL *(b Dec. 12, 1837, Burke County, Ga.; d June 16, 1906, Washington, D.C.)* Lawyer, Confederate soldier, Georgia Democrat. State senator (1870-1879) the last three years as senate president, mayor of Savannah (1883-1889), U.S. Representative (1889 until death).

LETCHER, JOHN *(b March 29, 1813, Lexington, Va.; d Jan. 26, 1884, Lexington).* Lawyer, newspaper editor, Virginia Democrat (1860-1864) who was a prime mover in bringing about the peace-between-the-states convention in Washington (1861) that unfortunately failed to avert the Civil War. Presidential elector on the Cass-Butler ticket

(1848), state constitutional convention delegate (1850), U.S. Representative (1851-1859), member of state house of delegates (1875-1877), member of the Virginia Military Institute Board of Visitors (1866-1880) and its president for ten years.

LETCHER, ROBERT PERKINS *(b Feb. 10, 1788, Goochland County, Va.; d Jan. 24, 1861, Frankfort, Ky.)* Lawyer, a Kentucky legislator who was first a Clay Democrat and then a Whig. State representative (1813-1815, 1817, 1836-1838) and house speaker (1838), U.S. Representative (1823-1833, 1834-1835), presidential elector on the Harrison-Granger ticket (1836), governor (1840-1844), minister to Mexico (1849-1852).

LEVER, ASBURY FRANCIS *(b Jan. 5, 1875, Lexington County, S.C.; d April 28, 1940, near Charleston, S.C.).* Teacher, lawyer, banker, South Carolina Democrat who sponsored much important farm legislation while chairman of the House Agricultural Committee (1913-1919). Private secretary to Congressman J. William Stokes (1897-1901), Democratic state convention delegate (1896, 1900), state representative (1900-1901), U.S. Representative (1901-1919), member of the Federal Farm Loan Board (1919-1922), then one of its field representatives, and ultimately becoming public relations director of the Farm Credit Administration until death.

LEVIN, LEWIS CHARLES *(b Nov. 10, 1808, Charleston, S.C.; d March 14, 1860, Philadelphia, Pa.)* Lawyer, Pennsylvania Know-Nothing who was editor-publisher of the *Sun*, a penny daily native American newspaper in Philadelphia. U.S. Representative (1845-1851).

LEVY, JEFFERSON MONROE *(b April 16, 1852, New York City; d March 6, 1924, New York City)* Lawyer, New York Democrat who was a nephew of

Uriah P. Levy, the first Jew ever to reach the rank of commodore in the U.S. Navy. U.S. Representative (1899-1901, 1911-1915).

LEWELLING, LORENZO DOW *(b Dec. 21, 1846, Salem, Iowa; d Sept. 3, 1900, Wichita, Kans.)* Teacher, Quaker non-combat Union Army veteran, Iowa newspaper publisher, orator, Kansas Populist who was elected governor (1893-1895) with Democratic support and introduced many reforms despite Republican opposition in the legislature. State senate (1896 until death).

LEWIS, DAVID JOHN *(b May 1, 1869, Nuttals Bank, Pa.; d Aug. 12, 1952, Cumberland, Md.)* Coal miner, lawyer, Maryland Democrat. State senate (1902-1906), U.S. Representative (1911-1917, 1931-1939), member of the U.S. Tariff Commission (1917-1925), member of the National Mediation Board (1939-1943).

LEWIS, DIXON HALL *(b Aug. 10, 1802, Dinwiddie County, Va.; d Oct. 25, 1848, New York City)* Lawyer, Alabama States' Rights Democrat. State representative (1825-1827), U.S. Representative (1829-1844), U.S. Senate (1844 until death).

LEWIS, ELIJAH BANKS *(b March 27, 1854, Coney, Ga.; d Dec. 10, 1920, Montezuma, Ga.)* Merchant, banker, Georgia Democrat. State senate (1894, 1895), U.S. Representative (1897-1909).

LEWIS, FRANCIS *(b March, 1713, Liandaff, Wales; d Dec. 30, 1803, New York City)* Merchant, French and Indian fighter who was captured, imprisoned in France, and subsequently given 5,000 acres of land by a grateful colonial government; New York signer of the Declaration of Independence. Delegate to the Stamp Act Congress (1765), member of the Continental Congress (1774-

1779), provincial convention delegate (1775), member of the Committee of One Hundred (1775), member of the Provincial Congress (1776, 1777), admiralty commissioner (1779). Father of Morgan Lewis.

LEWIS, FRED EWING *(b Feb. 8, 1865, Allentown, Pa.; d June 27, 1949, Allentown)* Lawyer, banker, Pennsylvania Republican. Mayor of Allentown (1896, 1902, 1932-1936), U.S. Representative (1913-1915).

LEWIS, JAMES HAMILTON *(b May 18, 1863, Danville, Va.; d April 9, 1939, Washington, D.C.)* Lawyer, Washington and Illinois Democrat who did special war work in France (1918) and was knighted by the kings of Belgium and Greece. In Washington: served on joint commission to settle Alaska-Canadian boundaries (1889, 1890), U.S. Representative (1897-1899), U.S. commissioner to regulate customs laws with Canada (1899). In Illinois: Chicago corporation counsel (1905-1907), U.S. Senate (1913-1919, 1931 until death). He also was an unsuccessful candidate for governor in both Washington (1892) and Illinois (1908).

LEWIS, JOHN FRANCIS *(b March 1, 1818, Lynnwood, Va.; d Sept. 2, 1895, Lynnwood)* Farmer, antisecessionist Virginia Republican who was a delegate to the state convention called for that purpose (1861) but refused to sign the enabling ordinance. Lieutenant governor as a True Republican (1869), U.S. Senate (1870-1875), western district U.S. marshal (1878-1882), and again lieutenant governor, this time being elected on the Readjuster ticket (1882-1886).

LEWIS, JOSEPH, JR. *(b 1772, Virginia; d March 30, 1834, Clifton, Va.)* Virginia Federalist. State house of delegates (1799-1803, 1817, 1818), U.S. Representative (1803-1817).

LEWIS, LAWRENCE *(b June 22, 1879, St. Louis, Mo.; d Dec. 9, 1943, Washington, D.C.)* Newspaperman, Harvard English instructor, lawyer, Colorado Democrat. State civil service commissioner (1917-1918), U.S. Representative (1933 until death).

LEWIS, MORGAN *(b Oct. 16, 1754, New York City; d April 7, 1844, New York City).* Revolutionary Army officer, lawyer, and one of the first New Yorkers to cast his lot with Thomas Jefferson's new Democratic-Republican (Democratic) party. State assembly (1789-1794), attorney general (1791-1792), supreme court justice (1792-1801) and chief justice (1801-1804), governor (1804-1807) decisively defeating Aaron Burr for the latter office in what one chronicler of the times described as "a campaign of unexampled virulence." He was also president of the New York Historical Society (1832-1836), president-general of the Society of the Cincinnati (1839-1844), and one of the founders of New York University. Son of Francis Lewis.

L'HOMMEDIEU, EZRA *(b Aug. 30, 1734, Southold, N.Y.; d Sept. 27, 1811, Southold)* Lawyer, farmer, New York Federalist, and follower of John Jay. Delegate to the Provincial Congress (1775-1777), state assemblyman (1777-1783), Continental Congress (1779-1783, 1787, 1788), state senate (1784-1792, 1794-1809), Suffolk County clerk (1784 until death), regent of the University of the State of New York (1787 until death), state constitutional convention delegate (1801).

LIBONATI, ROLAND VICTOR *(b Dec. 29, 1900, Chicago, Ill.; d ——).* Lawyer, Illinois Democrat who founded and operated a camp for underprivileged children in Wisconsin. Illinois general assembly and/or state senate (1942-1958, Democratic whip 1944-1957, minority leader 1957, 1958), U.S. Representative (1958-1965) and a member of the Judiciary and Veterans' Affairs committees.

LIGON, THOMAS WATKINS *(b May 10, 1810, Farmville, Va.; d Jan. 12, 1881, Howard County, Md.)* Lawyer, Maryland Democrat whose opposition to Know-Nothingism cut short his political life. State house of delegates (1843), U.S. Representative (1845-1849), governor (1854-1858).

LINCOLN, ABRAHAM *(b Feb. 12, 1809, Hardin, now Larue, County, Ky.; d April 15, 1865, Washington, D.C. after having been shot by assassin John Wilkes Booth while attending Ford's Theater on April 14)* Sixteenth president (Illinois Whig turned Republican), 1861-1865, whose administration took the country through the Civil War years. Six feet four inches tall, a powerful wrestler and log splitter, and a skillful lawyer. A gaunt, homely, melancholy man, yet a man who loved people, had a keen wit and the ability to tell a story well.

Son of frontier farmer Thomas Lincoln, who (1816) moved his family from Kentucky to what is now Spencer County, Indiana. Life was hard and Abe learned at an early age to help his father with the work. In 1818, Abe's mother, Nancy Hanks Lincoln, died, but was soon replaced with a stepmother (Sarah, a widow with three children of her own) who was kind to the boy. Although as a child Lincoln attended a few log cabin schools, the total time he spent in them probably did not amount to more than one year. But he was eager to learn and read and reread the few books available to him. His knowledge was added to in a practical way when (1828) he and another young man ferried a flatboat of produce down the Ohio and Mississippi rivers to New Orleans. In 1830, the Lincolns moved on again, this time to land near Decatur, Illinois. After helping get the family settled, young Abe left home to make his own way in the world. He settled for a time in New Salem, Illinois, where he worked at a number of different jobs. It was in New Salem that Lincoln met innkeeper's daughter Ann Rutledge but the well-known stories romanticizing his despair when she died are probably exaggerated. He served as a volunteer (1832) during the Black Hawk War but saw no action. He studied law, was admitted to the Illinois bar (1837) and, that same year, moved to Springfield, Ill., where he became a practicing attorney.

In Springfield, he met Mary Todd, a well-educated member of a prominent Kentucky family. After a difficult courtship, he and Mary married and had four sons (one of whom died in 1850 and one while Lincoln was president).

Unsuccessful candidate for Illinois House of Representatives (1832), member of state legislature (1834-1842), U.S. Representative (1847-1849) who opposed the Mexican War but voted to send supplies to the troops then in the field, unsuccessful candidate for election to U.S. Senate (1855). Lincoln became active in the newly formed Republican party that attracted many Whigs and Free-Soilers who were unhappy over the fact that the Kansas-Nebraska Act of 1854 (strongly supported by Democratic senator from Illinois, Stephen A. Douglas) could permit slavery to spread into the western territories. Although an unsuccessful Republican candidate for the U.S. Senate (1858), Lincoln won national prominence with his campaign speeches and the seven debates that matched his speaking skill against that of incumbent Douglas. Lincoln expressed some of the convictions that motivated him during his acceptance speech at the 1858 Illinois Republican convention when he said: "A house divided against itself cannot stand. I believe this government cannot endure permanently, half slave and half free."

Chosen on the third ballot (over William H. Seward and Salmon P. Chase) to be the Republican party's presidential candidate in 1860, Lincoln won the election against a badly divided Democratic party. Although he did not receive a majority of the popular vote, his total electoral vote was 180 as opposed to the combined total of 123 received by the other three candidates—Senator Douglas, Vice President Breckinridge, and John Bell. (When he ran again in 1864, against Democratic opponent General George B. McClellan, he won easily with a popular majority of more than 400,000.)

Soon after Lincoln's election, the Southern states started seceding from the Union. His inaugural address was conciliatory in tone, but when he sent provisions to Fort Sumter in Charleston Harbor, the Confederates fired on the fort (April 12, 1861) and Lincoln called (April 15) for 75,000 volunteers, proclaiming that a state of insurrection existed. The Civil War had begun and it took all of Lincoln's great ability to lead the country through to its conclusion in April 1865. His relations with his cabinet and with Congress were far from harmonious.

Many of the ablest military officers were Southerners and new leaders had to be found. He assumed a staggering burden of work most executives would have left to others to do—seeing callers, personally making thousands of appointments, writing letters and his own speeches. The most notable of these, the Gettysburg address (Nov. 19, 1863) clearly stated his concept of the meaning of the war.

On Sept. 22, 1862, after victory at Antietam, Lincoln issued the preliminary Emancipation Proclamation, declaring that slaves held within areas that were in rebellion against the Union, on and after Jan. 1, 1863, would be free and abolition of slavery became at that point an acknowledged aim of the war.

Lincoln's plans for reconstruction of

the war-torn South with "malice toward none" and "charity for all" ended with his assassination.

LINCOLN, ENOCH *(b Dec. 28, 1788, Worcester, Mass.; d Oct. 8, 1829, Augusta, Maine)* Poet, student of Indian life and languages, lawyer in the part of Massachusetts that became Maine, and a leading Democrat in both states. In Massachusetts: U.S. district attorney (1815-1818), U.S. Representative (1818-1821). In Maine: U.S. Representative (1821-1826), governor (1827 until death). Son of Levi Lincoln, Sr., brother of Levi, Jr.

LINCOLN, LEVI, SR. *(b May 15, 1749, Hingham, Mass.; d April 14, 1820, Worcester, Mass.)* Minuteman, trial lawyer who argued eloquently and successfully against the legality of slavery, Massachusetts Democrat who held two positions in Jefferson's cabinet but refused appointment to the U.S. Supreme Court. Worcester County probate judge and court clerk (1775-1781), state constitutional convention delegate (1779), delegate to the Continental Congress (1781) but declined to serve, state representative (1796), state senate (1797, 1798), U.S. Representative (1800-1801) to fill an unexpired term, U.S. attorney general (1801-1804) and acting secretary of state for two months in 1801, member of the Governor's Council (1806, 1810, 1811), lieutenant governor (1807-1808), governor (1808-1809), declined Madison appointment as associate justice (1809) because of failing eyesight. Father of Levi Jr. and Enoch Lincoln.

LINCOLN, LEVI, JR. *(b Oct. 25, 1782, Worcester, Mass.; d May 29, 1868, Worcester)* Lawyer, Massachusetts Democrat-National Republican-Whig-Republican who was the first elected mayor of Worcester (1848). State senate (1812, 1813), state representative (1814-1822) and house speaker (1822),

state constitutional convention delegate (1820), lieutenant governor (1823), associate justice of the state supreme court (1824), governor (1825-1834), U.S. Representative (1834-1841), collector of the Port of Boston (1841-1843), again a state senator (1844, 1845) and senate president (1845), presidential elector on the Whig Taylor-Fillmore ticket (1848) and Republican Lincoln-Johnson ticket (1864). Brother of Enoch Lincoln.

LINCOLN, ROBERT TODD *(b Aug. 1, 1843, Springfield, Ill.; d July 25, 1926, Manchester, Vt.)* Son of Abraham Lincoln who entered Harvard (1859) with a letter to the university president from Stephen A. Douglas introducing "the son of a friend with whom I have lately been canvassing the State of Illinois"; Union Army officer on the staff of General Grant, lawyer, Illinois Republican who numbered many large corporations among his clients, among them the Pullman Company of which he later became president (1897) and then chairman of the board (1911). While its attorney, workers went on strike (1894), Lincoln obtained an injunction, and his conduct was unfavorably compared with his father's emancipation of the slaves. His political credits: leader of the Grant delegation to the state GOP convention (1880) in a vain bid for a third term, Garfield-appointed secretary of war (1881-1885), Harrison-appointed minister to England (1889-1893).

LIND, JOHN *(b March 25, 1854, Kanna, Sweden; d Sept. 18, 1930, Minneapolis, Minn.)* Teacher, lawyer, and a highly independent Minnesota progressive who began his political career as a Republican and ended it as a Democrat. U.S. land office receiver at Tracy (1881-1885), U.S. Representative (1887-1893 as a Republican and 1903-1905 as a Democrat), governor (1898-1900 as a Democrat), President Wilson's personal representative in the overthrow of

Mexico's Huerta government (1913), a task that he tried to accomplish peacefully but in which he failed.

LINDBERGH, CHARLES AUGUSTUS, SR. *(b Jan. 20, 1859, Stockholm, Sweden; d May 24, 1924, Crookston, Minn.).* Father of the trans-Atlantic flyer, farmer, lawyer, progressive Minnesota Republican who also was active in the Nonpartisan and Farmer-Labor movements. Morrison County prosecutor (1891-1893), U.S. Representative (1907-1917).

LINDSAY, GEORGE HENRY *(b Jan. 7, 1837, New York City; d May 25, 1916, Brooklyn, N.Y.)* Real estate-investment counselor, New York Democrat. State assemblyman (1882-1886), Kings County coroner (1886-1892), U.S. Representative (1901-1913). Father of George W. Lindsay.

LINDSAY, GEORGE WASHINGTON *(b March 28, 1865, Brooklyn, N.Y.; d March 15, 1938, Brooklyn)* Real estate operator, New York Democrat. Democratic state committeeman and assembly district leader (1919-1934), state insurance department investigator (1914-1920), assemblyman (1920), deputy tenement house commissioner (1921-1923), U.S. Representative (1923-1935). Son of George H. Lindsay.

LINTHICUM, JOHN CHARLES *(b Nov. 26, 1867, Linthicum Heights, Md.; d Oct. 5, 1932, Baltimore, Md.)* Educator, lawyer, Maryland Democrat. Member of state house of delegates (1904, 1905), state senate (1906-1909), presidential elector on the Bryan-Kern ticket (1908), U.S. Representative (1911 until death), Democratic National Convention delegate (1924).

LITTAUER, LUCIUS NATHAN *(b Jan. 20, 1859, Gloversville, N.Y.; d March 2, 1944, Westchester County, N.Y.).* Glove manufacturer, financier, philanthropist, New York Republican. U.S. Representative (1897-1907), delegate to all GOP state conventions (1897-1912), GOP National Convention delegate (1900, 1904, 1908, 1928), regent of the University of the State of New York (1912-1914).

LITTLE, JOHN SEBASTIAN *(b March 15, 1853, Jenny Lind, Ark.; d Oct. 29, 1916, Little Rock, Ark.)* Lawyer, Arkansas Democrat. State representative (1884), circuit judge (1887-1890), state judicial convention chairman (1893), U.S. Representative (1894-1907), governor (1907-1908).

LITTLE, MALCOLM (see Malcolm X)

LITTLE, PETER *(b Dec. 11, 1775, Petersburg, Pa.; d Feb. 5, 1830, Freedom, Md.).* Watchmaker, farmer, Maryland Democrat. State house of delegates (1806, 1807), U.S. Representative (1811-1813, 1816-1829).

LITTLEFIELD, CHARLES EDGAR *(b June 21, 1851, Lebanon, Maine; d May 2, 1915, New York City)* Lawyer, Maine Republican. State representative (1885-1887) and house speaker (1887), state attorney general (1889-1893), GOP National Convention delegate (1892, 1896), U.S. Representative (1899-1908).

LITTLEPAGE, ADAM BROWN *(b April 14, 1859, Kanawha County, Va., now W.Va.; d June 29, 1921, Charleston, W.Va.)* Lawyer, West Virginia Democrat who was general counsel for the United Mine Workers there. State senate (1906-1910), U.S. Representative (1911-1913, 1915-1919).

LIVERMORE, ARTHUR *(b July 29, 1766, Londonderry, N.H.; d July 1, 1853, Campton, N.H.)* Lawyer, jurist, New Hampshire Federalist turned Democrat. State representative (1794, 1795), Rockingham County solicitor (1796-1798), superior court associate justice (1798-1809) and chief justice (1809-1813), presidential elector on the Federalist ticket (1800), state supreme court associate justice (1813-1816), U.S. Representative as a Democrat (1817-1821, 1823-1825), state senate (1821, 1822), Grafton County probate judge (1822, 1823), chief justice of the court of common pleas (1825–1832). Son of Samuel and brother of Edward St. Loe Livermore.

LIVERMORE, EDWARD ST. LOE *(b April 5, 1762, Portsmouth, N.H.; d Sept. 15, 1832, Tewksbury, Mass.)* Lawyer, New Hampshire and Massachusetts Federalist. In New Hampshire: U.S. district attorney (1789-1797), Rockingham County state solicitor (1791-1793), associate justice of the state supreme court (1797-1799), Portsmouth naval port officer (1799-1802). In Massachusetts: U.S. Representative (1807-1811). Son of Samuel and brother of Arthur Livermore.

LIVERMORE, SAMUEL *(b May 14, 1732, Waltham, Mass.; d May 18, 1803, Holderness, N.H.)* Lawyer who moved to New Hampshire (1758) soon after being admitted to the bar and where he was politically active for the rest of his life. Member of the general court from Londonderry (1768-1770), state's attorney (1775-1778), delegate to the Continental Congress (1780-1782, 1785), chief justice of the state supreme court (1782-1789), state constitutional convention delegate (1788) and president (1791), U.S. Representative in the First and Second Congresses (1789-1793), U.S. Senate (1793-1801). Father of Arthur and Edward S. Livermore.

LIVINGSTON, EDWARD *(b May 26, 1764, Livingston Manor, N.Y.; d May 22, 1836, Barrytown, N.Y.)* Member of one of New York's leading colonial families, lawyer, diplomat, New York and Louisi-

ana Democrat, moving to the latter state after making good the money taken from the city coffers by an underling while mayor of New York City, a post that he held while also serving as U.S. district attorney there (1801-1803). However, trouble plagued him and he ran into difficulties with Thomas Jefferson over land rights in Louisiana while also living down accusations of favoring Aaron Burr, Jefferson's rival for the presidency (1801) when the contest went before the House of Representatives. However, he became a national hero when he organized the people of Louisiana against British invasion in the War of 1812 and served as an aide to Andrew Jackson in the Battle of New Orleans.

Also, in New York: U.S. Representative (1795-1801). In New Orleans: reviser of the state criminal codes (1821-1825) aiming them at prevention rather than punishment, state representative (1820), U.S. Representative (1823-1829), U.S. Senate (1829-1831) resigning to become secretary of state in the Jackson cabinet (1831-1833), minister to France (1833-1835).

The family relationship between several of the succeeding Livingstons is as follows:

Philip and William Livingston were brothers as were their nephews, Edward and Robert; Walter was Philip's son and the father of Henry W. There were other prominent Livingstons but their prominence ran more to other fields than they did to politics. See *The Livingstons of Livingston Manor* (1910).

LIVINGSTON, HENRY WALTER *(b 1768, Linlithgo, N.Y.; d Dec. 22, 1810, Livingston Manor, N.Y.)* New York lawyer who was secretary to Gouverneur Morris (which see), U.S. ambassador to France (1792-1794), and Columbia County common pleas judge before showing the family interest in politics. State assemblyman (1802, 1810), U.S. Representative (1803-1807).

LIVINGSTON, LEONIDAS FELIX *(b April 3, 1832, Newton County, Ga.; d Feb. 11, 1912, Washington, D.C.)* Confederate soldier, farmer, Georgia Democrat. State representative (1876, 1877, 1879-1881), state senate (1882, 1883), U.S. Representative (1891-1911).

LIVINGSTON, PHILIP *(b Jan. 15, 1716, Albany, N.Y.; d June 12, 1778, York, Pa., while attending the sixth session of the Continental Congress)* Merchant, educator, New York signer of the Declaration of Independence. New York City alderman (1754-1762), provincial representative (1763-1769) and speaker of the house (1768), member of New York Committee of Correspondence, delegate to the Stamp Act Congress (1765), register in chancery (1768, 1769), Continental Congress delegate (1774 until death), New York Provincial Convention president (1775), state assemblyman (1776), state senate (1777).

LIVINGSTON, ROBERT R. *(b Nov. 27, 1746, New York City; d Feb. 26, 1813, Clermont, N.Y.)* New York lawyer, diplomat, one of the five committeemen who wrote the Declaration of Independence and the man who administered the oath taken by George Washington upon becoming the first president of the United States; also the partner of Robert Fulton in the building of the first steamboat. New York City recorder (1773-1775), provincial convention member (1775), Continental Congress delegate (1775-1777, 1779-1781), state constitutional convention delegate (1777), secretary of foreign affairs (1781-1783), state chancellor (1777-1801), minister to France (1801-1804).

LIVINGSTON, WALTER *(b Nov. 27, 1740; d May 14, 1797, New York City).* Member of the Livingston family about whom least is recorded. Provincial convention delegate and member of the First Provincial Congress (1775), Albany County judge (1774, 1775), New

York commissary of stores and provisions and general of the northern department (1775-1776), state assemblyman (1777-1779) and speaker (1778), New York-Massachusetts boundary commissioner (1784), regent of the University of the State of New York (1784-1787), Continental Congress delegate (1784, 1785), U.S. Treasury commissioner appointee (1785).

LIVINGSTON, WILLIAM *(b Nov. 30, 1723, Albany, N.Y.; d July 25, 1790, Elizabeth, N.J.)* Lawyer, founding editor-publisher of the *Independent Reflector* (1752), a signer of the federal Constitution and the first governor of the state of New Jersey (1776 until death). New York-Massachusetts (1754) and New York-New Jersey (1764) boundary commissioner. Member of the New York Provincial Assembly from Livingston Manor, N.Y. (1759-1761), moving to Elizabeth (then known as Elizabethtown) in 1772. In New Jersey: brigadier general in the militia (1775-1776), federal constitutional convention delegate (1787).

LLOYD, EDWARD, SR. *(Dec. 15, 1744, Talbot County, Md.; d July 8, 1796, Talbot County)* Wealthy Maryland land-owner-planter who was known as The Patriot because of his dedication to the Independence cause. Member of the general assembly (1771-1774), Committee of Correspondence (1774), Committee of Safety (1775), provincial convention (1776) and member of its executive council (1777-1779), state delegate (1780), state senate (1781, 1786, 1791), Continental Congress (1783-1784), state constitutional convention that ratified federal Constitution (1788).

LLOYD, EDWARD, JR. *(b July 22, 1779, Talbot County, Md.; d June 2, 1834, Annapolis, Md.)* Wealthy landowner-planter, Maryland Democrat. State delegate (1800-1805), U.S. Representative

(1806-1809), governor (1809-1811), state senator (1811-1815, 1826-1831) and senate president during the latter years, presidential elector (1812), U.S. Senate (1819-1826).

LLOYD, HENRY DEMAREST *(b May 1, 1847, New York City; d Sept. 28, 1903, Chicago, Ill., while spearheading a campaign for municipal ownership of street railways)* Lawyer, author, journalist, and one of the country's foremost muckrakers who cut his eye teeth by helping to oust New York's Tammany Hall from power (1871); New York Liberal Republican, Illinois Socialist. His books included *Story of a Great Monopoly* (1881), which was an exposé of Standard Oil and the railroads, *Strike of Millionaires Against Miners* (1890), and *Wealth Against Commonwealth* (1894). He gained the knowledge to write such books as financial editor and editorial writer on the *Chicago Tribune* before switching to socialism.

LLOYD, JAMES TILGHMAN *(b Aug. 28, 1857, Canton, Mo.; d April 3, 1944, Quincy, Ill., of auto accident injuries).* Teacher, lawyer, Missouri Democrat who for a time was active in Washington, D.C., municipal affairs. In Missouri: Lewis County deputy sheriff (1879-1881), deputy circuit clerk and recorder (1881-1882), Shelby County prosecutor (1889-1893), U.S. Representative (1897-1917), Democratic National Convention delegate (1908), chairman of Democratic congressional committee (1908-1912). In Washington, D.C., where he remained to practice law: board of education president (1924-1925), Chamber of Commerce president (1925).

LOAN, BENJAMIN FRANKLIN *(b Oct. 4, 1819, Hardinsburg, Ky.; d March 30, 1881, St. Joseph, Mo.)* Missouri lawyer who was elected a U.S. Representative as an Emancipationist (1863-1867) and as a Radical (1867-1869) but couldn't make it when he tried as a Republican (1876).

LOBECK, CHARLES OTTO *(b April 6, 1852, Andover, Ill.; d Jan. 30, 1920, Omaha, Nebr.)* Traveling salesman, real estate and insurance broker, Nebraska Republican turned Democrat. State senate (1892), Omaha councilman (1897-1903), presidential elector on the Bryan-Stevenson ticket (1900), city controller (1903-1911), U.S. Representative (1911-1919).

LOCKE, DAVID ROSS *(b Sept. 20, 1833, Vestal, N.Y.; d Feb. 15, 1888, Toledo, Ohio)* Journalist who climaxed his career while editor and part owner of the *Toledo Blade*, antislavery political satirist who created a Thomas Nast cartoon character named Petroleum V. Nasby to zero in on Copperheads (Northerners who sympathized with the South during the Civil War) and Democrats. His most famous reader was Abraham Lincoln.

LOCKE, MATTHEW *(b 1730, northern Ireland; d Sept. 7, 1801, Salisbury, N.C.)* Wagoneer, planter, Revolutionary Army officer who, as a delegate to the North Carolina convention (1789) called to ratify the federal Constitution, voted against it, believing that the best government is the one that governs least. So, too, as a Jefferson Democrat in the U.S. House of Representatives (1793-1799) he was a continuing foe of the Federalist policies of Presidents Washington and Adams. North Carolina treasury commissioner (1771), Rowan County safety committee member (1774), provincial congressman (1775), colonial congressman (1776), state constitutional convention delegate (1776), state house of commons (1777-1781, 1783-1792), state senate (1781, 1782).

LOCKWOOD, BELVA ANN BENNETT *(b Oct. 24, 1830, Royalton, N.Y.; d May 19,*

1917, Washington, D.C.) Twice widowed teacher whose many activities included women's suffrage, temperance, and peace and who took up the study of law in her middle years. Admitted to the bar at the age of forty-three, she worked to secure passage of a law (1879) making it possible for women to practice before the U.S. Supreme Court, then became the first woman to do so. Many important achievements followed: nominated by the National Equal Rights party (1884, 1888) as their presidential candidate; sponsored a bill before Congress (1900) forbidding further encroachment upon North Carolina Cherokee territories, and was attorney of record in the Cherokees' case against the U.S. government in which they won a $5 million judgment; prepared (1903) an amendment (granting suffrage to women in Arizona, New Mexico, and Oklahoma) to the Statehood Bill before Congress; represented the United States at the International Congress of Charities, Correction, and Philanthropy in Geneva; lectured eloquently for women's suffrage; was a member of the nominating committee for the Nobel Peace Prize; delegate (1889) to the Universal Peace Congress in Paris; member (1892) of the International Peace Bureau in Berne, Switzerland. Fittingly, the National League of Women Voters placed her name on their New York State honor roll.

LODGE, HENRY CABOT (b May 12, 1850, Boston, Mass.; d Nov. 9, 1924, Cambridge, Mass.) Editor, author, lecturer, historian, lawyer, but most of all a Massachusetts Republican whose first interest was politics on the national level. As a U.S. Senator (1893 until death) he was a friend and supporter of Theodore Roosevelt and foe of Woodrow Wilson, especially on the question of the League of Nations, which the president favored—and the United States did not join the League.

State representative (1880-1881), U.S. Representative (1887-1893); GOP National Convention delegate (1884-1924 except for 1912), convention chairman (1900, 1908, 1920), resolutions committee chairman (1904-1916); U.S. immigration commissioner (1907-1910), Harvard University overseer (1911 until death) and alumni president (1914), president of state historical society (1915), Senate majority leader (1918 until death), member of Conference on Limitation of Armaments (1921).

He is the author of Alexander Hamilton (1882), Daniel Webster (1883), The Life and Letters of George Cabot (1887), and the two-volume George Washington (1888-1889). His great grandfather was George Cabot, his grandson is Henry Cabot Lodge, Jr., Richard Nixon's vice presidential running mate (1960) and U.S. Senator (1937-1944, 1946-1953), the first senator since the Civil War to resign to enter combat.

LOFT, GEORGE WILLIAM (b Feb. 6, 1865, New York City; d Nov. 6, 1943, Baldwin, N.Y.) Candy manufacturer, banker, New York Democrat. Presidential elector on the Wilson-Marshall (1912) and Davis-Bryan tickets (1924), U.S. Representative (1913-1917).

LOGAN, GEORGE (b Sept. 9, 1753, Stenton, Pa.; d April 9, 1821, Philadelphia, Pa.) Physician, scientific farmer who founded the Pennsylvania Society for the Promotion of Agriculture and wrote many booklets on the subject, friend of Benjamin Franklin, and a Pennsylvania Quaker whose love for peace led him to go to Paris (1798) on his own to seek a better understanding between the United States and France. As a result, Congress passed the Logan Act which made it illegal for private people to do such a thing ever again. U.S. Senate (1801-1807) as a Jefferson Democrat.

LOGAN, JOHN ALEXANDER *(b Feb. 9, 1826, Murphysboro, Ill.; d Dec. 26, 1886, Washington, D.C.)* Lawyer, Union Army officer, Illinois Democrat turned Republican who was one of the congressmen named to conduct impeachment proceedings against President Andrew Johnson. As a Democrat: Jackson County court clerk (1849), state representative (1852, 1853, 1856, 1857), third judicial district prosecutor (1853-1857), presidential elector on the Buchanan-Breckinridge ticket (1856), U.S. Representative (1859-1862). As a Republican: U.S. Representative (1867-1871) resigning to become a U.S. Senator (1871-1877, 1879 until death).

LOGUEN, JERMAIN WESLEY *(b 1813, Davidson County, Tenn.; d Sept. 30, 1872, Saratoga Springs, N.Y.)* Unschooled son of a slave mother and a white father, he escaped (1834) ultimately to become a bishop of the African Methodist Episcopal Zion Church, an outspoken antislavery lecturer, master of a school for Negro children in Utica, N.Y., and manager of the Syracuse stop on the Underground Railroad helping about 1,500 slaves to escape.

LONDON, MEYER *(b Dec. 29, 1871, Kalvaria, Russia; d June 6, 1926, New York City, of auto accident injuries)*. Lawyer, reformer, pacifist, orator, labor leader whose special sphere was the garment industry; New York Socialist and a vigorous foe of communism who, as a U.S. Representative, (1915-1919, 1921-1923) opposed both the draft and U.S. entry into World War I.

LONERGAN, AUGUSTINE *(b May 20, 1874, Thompson, Conn.; d Oct. 18, 1947, Washington, D.C.)* Lawyer, Connecticut Democrat. Hartford planning commissioner and assistant corporation counsel (1910-1912), U.S. Representative (1913-1915, 1917-1921, 1931-1933), Democratic state convention chairman (1918, 1934) and national convention delegate (1920), U.S. Senate (1933-1939).

LONG, CHESTER ISAIAH *(b Oct. 12, 1860, Greenwood Township, Pa.; d July 1, 1934, Washington, D.C.)* Teacher, lawyer, Kansas Republican. State senate (1889-1893), U.S. Representative (1895-1897, 1899-1903), U.S. Senate (1903-1909), chairman of commission to revise state statutes (1921-1923).

LONG, GEORGE SHANNON *(b Sept. 11, 1883, Tunica, La.; d March 22, 1958, in U.S. Naval Hospital, Bethesda, Md.)*. Dentist, lawyer, Oklahoma and Louisiana Democrat. In Oklahoma: state representative (1920-1922). In Louisiana: superintendent of Louisiana Colony and Training School (1948-1950), institutional inspector (1950-1952), Democratic National Convention delegate (1948), U.S. Representative (1953 until death). Brother of Huey P. Long.

LONG, HUEY PIERCE *(b Aug. 30, 1893, Winn Parish, La.; d Sept. 10, 1935, Baton Rouge, La.)* Democratic lawyer who was the Kingfish of Louisiana politics until an assassin's bullet cut short his life. He battled with the vested interests for state legislation of benefits to the poor such as toll-free roads and bridges, free textbooks in both parochial and public schools, an end to poll taxes. On the national scene he was a foe of Roosevelt's New Deal, offering as a substitute his own "Share Our Wealth" program that would take from the rich and give to the poor.

State public service commissioner (1918-1928) and commission chairman (1924-1928), Democratic National Committeeman (1928 until death), governor (1928-1932), U.S. Senate (1932 until death).

The irony of his assassination is that although Long was the virtual dictator of Louisiana, the man who shot him did so for personal reasons, not political. Perhaps an insight into what manner of man he was are the two books that he wrote: *Every Man a King* (1933) and *My First Days in the White House* (1935). Brother of George S. Long.

LONG, JEFFERSON FRANKLIN *(b March 3, 1836, Crawford County, Ga.; d Feb. 5, 1900, Macon, Ga.)* A slave who became a successful merchant tailor and Georgia Republican. U.S. Representative (1870-1871), GOP National Convention delegate (1880).

LONG, JOHN DAVIS *(Oct. 27, 1838, Buckfield, Maine; d Aug. 28, 1915, Hingham, Mass.)* Lawyer, teacher, Massachusetts Republican. State representative (1875-1878) and house speaker (1876, 1877), lieutenant governor (1879), governor (1880-1882), U.S. Representative (1883-1889), secretary of the navy in the McKinley cabinet (1897-1902).

LONGFELLOW, STEPHEN *(b June 23, 1775, Gorham, Maine, which then was in Massachusetts; d Aug. 2, 1849, Portland, Maine)* Lawyer, Massachusetts and, after partition, Maine Federalist. In Massachusetts: Member of state general court and delegate to the Hartford Convention (1814, 1815), presidential elector on the King-Howard ticket. In Maine: U.S. Representative (1823-1825), state representative (1826), Bowdoin College overseer (1811-1817), president of state historical society (1834). Father of the poet, Henry Wadsworth Longfellow.

LONGWORTH, NICHOLAS *(b Nov. 5, 1869, Cincinnati, Ohio; d April 9, 1931, Aiken, S.C.)* Lawyer, Ohio Republican who was House floor leader (1923-1925) and speaker (1925-1931). Member of Cincinnati Board of Education (1898), state representative (1899, 1900), state senate (1901-1903), U.S. Representative (1903-1913, 1915 until death). Son-in-law of Theodore Roosevelt.

LOOFBOUROW, FREDERICK CHARLES *(b Feb. 8, 1874, Atlantic, Iowa; d July 8, 1949, Salt Lake City, Utah)* Lawyer, Utah Republican. Third judicial district attorney (1905-1911) and judge (1911-1916) U.S. Representative (1930-1933).

LORIMER, WILLIAM *(b April 27, 1861, Manchester, England; d Sept. 13, 1934, Chicago, Ill.)* Real estate operator, banker, manufacturer, Illinois Republican boss who was ousted from the U.S. Senate after serving three years (1909-1912) as the result of a resolution declaring that his election was due to "corrupt methods and practices." GOP National Convention delegate (1892), U.S. Representative (1895-1901, 1903-1909). His power base was Cook County's newly naturalized immigrants.

LORING, GEORGE BAILEY *(b Nov. 8, 1817, North Andover, Mass.; d Sept. 13, 1891, Salem, Mass.)* Surgeon who helped to revamp the U.S. marine hospital system (1849), farmer, stock breeder who founded the New England Agricultural Society (1849); Massachusetts political leader (first a Democrat, then a Republican) who served well as U.S. commissioner of agriculture (1881-1885) for Presidents Garfield and Arthur and had much to do with elevating the department to cabinet status.

Salem postmaster (1853-1858), state representative (1866, 1867), state GOP committee chairman (1869-1876), state senate member and president (1873-1876), GOP National Convention delegate (1868, 1872, 1876), U.S. centennial commissioner (1872), U.S. Representative (1877-1881), U.S. minister to Portugal (1889-1890).

LOSER, JOSEPH CARLTON *(b Oct. 1, 1892, Nashville, Tenn.)* Lawyer, Tennessee Democrat. Nashville assistant city attorney (1923-1929), assistant district attorney general of the tenth judicial circuit (1929-1934), district attorney (1934-1956), Democratic National Convention delegate (1944,

1952, 1956), presidential elector (1956), secretary of Democratic state executive committee (1954-1958), U.S. Representative (1957-1963) and a member of the Judiciary and District of Columbia committees.

LOUCKS, HENRY LANGFORD *(b May 24, 1846, Hull, Canada; d Dec. 29, 1928, Clearlake, S.Dak.)* Merchant who homesteaded in Deuel County, Dakota Territory (1884), turned to farming and became the moving force behind the farmer-homesteaders' political activities, publishing the *Dakota Ruralist*, heading first the territorial and then the national Farmers' Alliance, organizing the Independent party and leading it into the Populist fold and forming for many years a forceful fusion with the Democrats that, among other accomplishments, brought about the election of James H. Kyle to the U.S. Senate (1891). In 1890 Loucks was the Farmers' Alliance-Knights of Labor unsuccessful gubernatorial candidate and in 1892 he was president of the People's (Populist) party National Convention.

LOUD, EUGENE FRANCIS *(b March 12, 1847, Abington, Mass.; d Dec. 19, 1908, San Francisco, Calif.)* Seaman, Union soldier, miner, customs service clerk, California Republican. State assemblyman (1884), U.S. Representative (1891-1903).

LOUD, GEORGE ALVIN *(b June 18, 1852, Bracebridge, Ohio; d Nov. 13, 1925, Myrtle Point, Mich., in an auto accident)* Railroad and lumber executive, Michigan Republican. U.S. Representative (1903-1913, 1915-1917).

LOUDENSLAGER, HENRY CLAY *(b May 22, 1852, Mauricetown, N.J.; d Aug. 12, 1911, Paulsboro, N.J.)* Produce commission merchant, New Jersey Republican who was a U.S. Representative for the last nineteen years of his life (1893 until death).

LOUGHRIDGE, WILLIAM *(b July 11, 1827, Youngstown, Ohio; d Sept. 26, 1889, near Reading, Pa.)* Lawyer, Iowa Republican. State senator (1857-1860), sixth judicial circuit judge (1861-1867), U.S. Representative (1867-1871, 1873-1875).

LOVEJOY, ELIJAH PARISH *(b Nov. 9, 1802, Albion, Maine; d Nov. 7, 1837, Alton, Ill.)* Teacher, clergyman, antislavery Missouri and Illinois newspaper editor and Whig who is remembered in history as the Martyr Abolitionist. While editor of the *St. Louis Observer*, a Presbyterian weekly, he was forced by an unsympathetic populace to leave that rowdy river port and he moved his press to Illinois, only to be greeted by a mob that dumped it in the river. However, he would not be silenced and succeeded in setting up shop and resuming publication with the *Alton Observer*. His editorial policies remained fiercely abolitionist and he was subjected to constant harassment. Time and again his presses were smashed and, when a new one arrived from Ohio, Lovejoy braved a mob that tried to burn the warehouse in which it was temporarily stored. A fatal bullet was his reward. Brother of Owen Lovejoy.

LOVEJOY, OWEN *(b Jan. 6, 1811, Albion, Maine; d March 25, 1864, Brooklyn, N.Y.)* An abolitionist Illinois clergyman who confined his utterances to the pulpit in keeping with his vow at the side of his dying brother, Elijah, "never to forsake the cause." He became the state's most-meaningful foe of slavery, was elected to the state legislature in 1854, met Abraham Lincoln there and for the next two years urged him to become the force about whom a new party and its "ragtag, bobtail" gang could rally. The rest is history. As for Lovejoy, he remained not only Lincoln's major representative in Illinois but also a Republican U.S. Representative (1857 until death).

LOVERING, WILLIAM CROAD *(b Feb. 25, 1835, Woonsocket, R.I.; d Feb. 4, 1910, Washington, D.C.)* Cotton manufacturer, street railway president, Union soldier, Massachusetts Republican. GOP National Convention delegate (1880), GOP state convention president (1892), U.S. Representative (1897 until death).

LOW, ISAAC *(b April 13, 1735, Raritan Landing, N.J.; d July 25, 1791, Isle of Wight, England)* Merchant, liberal New York pre-Revolutionary leader who was a delegate to the Stamp Act Congress (1765), the Provincial Congress (1775), and the First Continental Congress (1774, 1775), but who, however, did not believe the colonies should be independent of England. Accused of treason, he took refuge in the British-held New York City garrison where not only did he continue in business but also helped to found the Chamber of Commerce and was its president from 1775 until moving to England in 1783.

LOW, SETH *(b Jan. 18, 1850, Brooklyn, N.Y.; d Sept. 17, 1916, Bedford Hills, N.Y., where he had founded the Bedford Farmers' Cooperative Association).* Ship operator, merchant, New York Republican, and a reformer who felt the nation's two major priorities were labor and Negro rights and strove to achieve them in his lifetime. Thus he cooperated with Booker T. Washington, was a Tuskegee Institute trustee, and a member of the Colorado Coal Commission assigned by President Wilson to investigate labor difficulties in that state.

In New York, he was the GOP mayor of Brooklyn (1881-1885), Independent mayor of New York (1901-1903), and the president of Columbia College (1890-1901) who brought into its university complex Barnard, Teachers' College, and the College of Physicians and Surgeons and purchased its Morningside Heights location.

LOWNDES, THOMAS *(b Jan. 22, 1766, Charleston, S.C.; d July 8, 1843, Charleston)* Lawyer, planter, South Carolina Federalist. State representative (1796-1800), U.S. Representative (1801-1805). Brother of William Lowndes.

LOWNDES, WILLIAM *(b Feb. 11, 1782, St. Bartolomew's Parish, S.C.; d Oct. 27, 1822, at sea while en route to England)* Lawyer, planter, South Carolina Democrat who was nominated for the U.S. presidency (1821) but declined as he also did offers of cabinet posts and foreign missions by Presidents Madison and Monroe. State representative (1806-1810), U.S. Representative (1811-1822). Brother of Thomas Lowndes.

LOWRIE, WALTER *(b Dec. 10, 1784, Edinburgh, Scotland; d Dec. 14, 1868, New York City)* Teacher, surveyor, farmer, Pennsylvania Democrat. State representative (1811, 1812), state senate (1813-1819), U.S. Senate (1819-1825) and secretary of the senate (1825-1836), secretary of the Presbyterian Board of Foreign Missions (1836 until death).

LOZIER, RALPH FULTON *(b Jan. 28, 1866, Ray County, Mo.; d May 28, 1945, Kansas City, Mo.)* Lawyer, farmer, Missouri Democrat. Carrollton city attorney (1915-1944), Democratic National Convention delegate (1928), U.S. Representative (1923-1935), seventh judicial circuit judge (1936).

LUCE, ROBERT *(b Dec. 2, 1862, Auburn, Maine; d April 7, 1946, Waltham, Mass.)* Lawyer, journalist, author, Massachusetts Republican. State representative (1899, 1901-1908), GOP state convention president (1910), chairman of commission on cost of living (1910, 1916, 1917), lieutenant governor (1912), member of state teachers' retirement board (1914-1919), state constitutional convention delegate (1917-1919), state Republican Club president (1918), U.S. Representative (1919-1935, 1937-1941), Smithsonian Institution regent (1929-1931).

LUDLOW, LOUIS LEON *(b June 24, 1873, Fayette County, Ind.; d Nov. 28, 1950, Washington, D.C.)* Author, journalist who was Washington correspondent for Indiana and Ohio newspapers for most of his working life, Indiana Democrat who, as a congressman, sponsored a constitutional amendment for a referendum on any war in which the United States or any American nation was invaded or attacked by a non-American country. U.S. Representative (1929-1949).

LUMPKIN, JOHN HENRY *(b June 13, 1812, Lexington, Ga.; d July 10, 1860, Rome, Ga.)* Private secretary to his uncle, Governor Wilson Lumpkin; lawyer, Georgia Democrat. State representative (1835), Cherokee circuit solicitor general (1838), U.S. Representative (1843-1849, 1855-1857), Rome circuit superior court judge (1850-1853), unsuccessful gubernatorial candidate (1857), Democratic National Convention delegate (1860).

LUMPKIN, WILSON *(b Jan. 14, 1783, Pittsylvania County, Va.; d Dec. 28, 1870, Athens, Ga.)* Teacher, lawyer, planter, Georgia Democrat who carried his advocacy of states' rights to extremes that included even noninterference with the deportation of Indians. State representative (1808-1812), U.S. Representative (1815-1817, 1827-1831), governor (1831-1835), Cherokee treaty commissioner (1836-1837), U.S. Senate (1837-1841), then leaving public office to farm and to rehabilitate the state railroad. Uncle of John Henry Lumpkin.

LUNA, TRANQUILINO *(b Feb. 25, 1849, Los Lunas, N.Mex.; d Nov. 20, 1892, Peralta, N.Mex.)* Rancher, New Mexico Territory Republican. GOP National Convention delegate (1880, 1888), delegate to Congress (1881-1884), Valencia County sheriff (1888-1892).

LUNDEEN, ERNEST *(b Aug. 4, 1878, Union County, S.Dak.; d Aug. 31, 1940, in a plane crash near Lovettsville, Va.).* Lawyer, progressive Minnesota Republican turned Farmer-Laborite who was an isolationist on foreign affairs but extremely liberal on domestic matters. As a Republican: state representative (1910-1914), national convention delegate (1912, 1916), U.S. Representative (1917-1919) voting against conscription and entry into World War I. As a Farmer-Laborite: U.S. Representative (1933-1937), U.S. Senate (1937 until death).

LYNCH, JOHN ROY *(b Sept. 10, 1847, Concordia Parish, La.; d Nov. 2, 1939, Chicago, Ill.)* Son of a white man and black woman who, after his father's death, was raised in slavery; after emancipation became a self-educated photographer, farmer, lawyer, major in the U.S. Army, and a much-respected Mississippi Republican who was the first Negro to serve as temporary chairman of a national presidential convention —elevated to that position (1884) by a group of young Republicans led by Theodore Roosevelt and Henry Cabot Lodge. The respect in which he was held crossed party lines, as evidenced by the fact that he twice was offered positions by Democratic administrations.

Justice of the peace (1869), state representative (1869-1873) and house speaker in the last term, GOP National Convention delegate (1872, 1884, 1888, 1892, 1900), U.S. Representative (1873-1877, 1882-1883), GOP state executive committee chairman (1881-1889) and national committeeman (1884-1889), fourth auditor of the U.S. Treasury by appointment of President Harrison (1889-1893), army officer (1898-1911), living out the rest of his life as an attorney in Chicago.

LYNCH, THOMAS, SR. *(b 1727, St. James' Parish, S.C.; d December 1776, Annapolis, Md.)* One of the South's largest rice growers and a South Carolina patriot who was prevented by illness from signing the Declaration of Independence while a member of the Continental Congress (1774-1776)—an historic honor that however fell to his namesake son. Commons house of assembly (1751-1757, 1761-1763, 1765, 1768, 1772), Colonial Congress delegate (1765), general committee member (1769-1774), delegate to the First and Second Provincial Congress (1775, 1776), member of the state's first general assembly (1776).

LYNCH, THOMAS, JR. *(b Aug. 5, 1749, Prince George's Parish, S.C.; d 1779, at sea with all hands aboard a ship that disappeared while on a voyage to France)* Lawyer, planter, Revolutionary Army officer and South Carolina signer of the Declaration of Independence. Member of the First and Second Provincial Congresses (1774-1776), constitutional committee (1776), general assembly (1776), Continental Congress delegate (1776, 1777). Son of Thomas Lynch, Sr.

LYNCH, WALTER ALOYSIUS *(b July 7, 1894, New York City; d Sept. 10, 1957, Belle Harbor, Queens, N.Y.)* Lawyer, New York Democrat. New York City magistrate (1930), state constitutional convention delegate (1938), U.S. Representative (1940-1951), state supreme court justice (1955 until death).

LYNDE, WILLIAM PITT *(b Dec. 16, 1817, Sherburne, N.Y.; d Dec. 18, 1885, Milwaukee, Wis.)* Lawyer, Wisconsin Democrat. State attorney general (1844), U.S. district attorney (1845), U.S. Representative (1848-1849, 1875-1879), mayor of Milwaukee (1860), state assemblyman (1866), state senate (1869, 1870).

LYON, CALEB *(b Dec. 7, 1822, Greig, N.Y.; d Sept. 8, 1875, Roseville, Staten Island, N.Y.)* World traveler, poet, author, lecturer, and artist who was described by one of his biographers as a "polished misfit," and definitely a man who got around, but only as far as he wanted to go. Appointed consul general to Shanghai (1847), he got as far as California, entrusted a deputy to act for him, and stayed on in San Francisco long enough to serve as a secretary of the constitutional convention (1849) and design the state seal. Then back to New York where he was an assemblyman (1850) and state senator (1851) as a Whig and U.S. Representative (1853-1855) as an Independent. Then on to Idaho to be the Lincoln-appointed territorial governor (1864-1865) as a Republican who successfully negotiated a treaty with the Shoshone Indians. Then home to his estate on Staten Island to putter with his pottery and poetry and to write a book on Revolutionary-period ceramics.

LYON, CHITTENDEN *(b Feb. 22, 1787, Fair Haven, Vt.; d Nov. 23, 1842, Eddyville, Ky.)* Merchant, farmer, Kentucky Democrat for whom Lyon County is named. State representative (1822-1824), state senate (1827-1835), U.S. Representative (1827-1835). Son of Matthew Lyon.

LYON, MATTHEW *(b July 14, 1746, County Wicklow, Ireland; d Aug. 1, 1822, Spadra Bluff, Ark.)* Definitely one of the rugged individualists who built the nation: printer, newspaper publisher, one of the Green Mountain Boys' Revolutionary officers, mill builder and operator, founder of the town of Fair Haven, Vt. (1783), the Vermont presidential elector whose decisive vote elected Thomas Jefferson over Aaron Burr, leader of a settler band into the Kentucky wilderness, and the first congressman ever jailed (for four months in 1798) for engaging in fisticuffs on the House floor with a fellow congressman. State representative (1779-1783, 1786-1796), U.S. Representative (1797-1801) as a Jeffersonian Democrat from Vermont.

Then he led a settler band into the Kentucky wilderness (1801) where he was a prehostilities foe of the War of 1812 but, once it was begun, a builder of gunboats for the government; served in state house of representatives (1802), U.S. Representative (1803-1811). Finally, he went on to the Arkansas Territory (1820 until death) to serve as U.S. factor to the Cherokee Nation. Father of Chittenden Lyon.

M

☆ ☆ ☆

McADOO, WILLIAM *(b Oct. 25, 1853, County Donegal, Ireland; d June 7, 1930, New York City)* Lawyer, newspaper reporter, writer, New Jersey and New York Democrat. In New Jersey: state assemblyman (1882), U.S. Representative (1883-1891). In New York: Cleveland-appointed assistant secretary of the navy (1893-1897), New York City police commissioner (1904, 1905) and chief magistrate (1910 until death).

McADOO, WILLIAM GIBBS *(b Oct. 31, 1863, Cobb County, Ga.; d Feb. 1, 1941, Washington, D.C.)* A prime mover in construction of the rapid-transit tunnel between New York and New Jersey; Tennessee, New York, and California lawyer, author, steamship line executive who twice (1920-1924) was a major contender for the Democratic presidential nomination. In Tennessee: Deputy clerk of the U.S. Circuit Court (1882-1885) while studying law at the University of Tennessee. In New York: Democratic National Convention delegate (1912, 1932, 1936), vice chairman of the Democratic National Committee (1912), secretary of the treasury in the Wilson cabinet (1913-1918) doing much in the creation of the Federal Reserve System and the Federal Farm Loan Board; during World War I headed four Liberty Loan drives that netted more than $18 million, and served as director general of railways (1917-1919). In Cal-ifornia: U.S. Senate (1933-1938). His second wife was Woodrow Wilson's daughter, Eleanor.

McANDREWS, JAMES *(b Oct. 22, 1862, Woonsocket, R.I.; d Aug. 31, 1942, Chicago, Ill.)* Businessman, Illinois Democrat who was Chicago's building commissioner before achieving higher office. U.S. Representative (1901-1905, 1913-1921, 1935-1941).

McARTHUR, CLIFTON NESMITH *(b June 10, 1879, The Dalles, Oreg.; d Dec. 9, 1923, Portland, Oreg.)* Newspaper reporter, farmer, lawyer, Oregon Republican. Secretary of the GOP state central committee (1908), secretary to Governor Frank W. Benson (1908-1911), state representative (1909-1913) and twice house speaker, U.S. Representative (1915-1923).

McARTHUR, DUNCAN *(b June 14, 1772, Dutchess County, N.Y.; d April 29, 1839, Chillicothe, Ohio)* Indian fighter who doubled as a spy, surveyor who laid out the town of Chillicothe, War of 1812 brigadier general who commanded Fort Meigs and invaded Canada, Ohio Democrat turned National Republican. State representative (1804, 1817, 1818, 1826) and house speaker (1817, 1818), state senate (1805-1814, 1821-1823, 1829, 1830), governor (1830, 1832).

McBRIDE, GEORGE WYCLIFFE *(b March 13, 1854, Yamhill County, Oreg.; d June 18, 1911, Portland, Oreg.)* Merchant, Oregon Republican. State representative and speaker (1882), Oregon secretary of state (1886-1895), U.S. Senate (1895-1901). Brother of John R. McBride.

McBRIDE, JOHN ROGERS *(b Aug. 22, 1832, Franklin County, Mo.; d July 20, 1904, Spokane, Wash.)* Lawyer, Oregon Republican who helped bring law and order to the Idaho Territory. Yamhill County schools superintendent (1854), state constitutional convention delegate (1857), state senate (1860-1862), U.S. Representative (1863-1865), Lincoln-appointed chief justice of the Idaho Territory (1865-1869) when he became the Grant-appointed U.S. Assay Office superintendent at Boise. Then he returned to the practice of law in Idaho, Utah, and Washington and served as a GOP National Committeeman for twelve years (1880-1892). Brother of George W. McBride.

McCALL, SAMUEL WALKER *(b Feb. 28, 1851, East Providence, Pa.; d Nov. 4, 1923, Winchester, Mass.)* Lawyer, editor of the *Boston Daily Advertiser*, novelist, Massachusetts Republican. State representative (1888, 1889, 1892), GOP National Convention delegate (1888, 1902, 1916), U.S. Representative (1893-1913).

McCARRAN, PATRICK ANTHONY *(b Aug. 8, 1876, Reno, Nev.; d Sept. 28, 1954, Hawthorne, Nev.)* Farmer, stockman, lawyer, Nevada Democrat who gave his name to an alien immigration act that tightened loyalty regulations (1952), some said too harshly. State legislator and representative in an irrigation congress (1903), Nye County district attorney (1907-1909), state supreme court associate justice (1913-1917) and chief justice (1917-1918), member of state board of pardons (1913-1919) and a parole commissioner (1913-1918), chairman of state board of bar examiners (1919-1932), U.S. Senate (1933 until death).

McCARTHY, JOSEPH RAYMOND *(b Nov. 14, 1908, Grand Chute, Wis.; d May 2, 1957, in U.S. Naval Hospital, Bethesda, Md.)* Chicken farmer, grocery clerk, movie usher, lawyer, World War II Marine officer, Wisconsin Republican who devoted most of his U.S. Senate tenure (1947 until death) to conducting highly publicized investigations of alleged Communists which many classified as nothing more than witch hunts. Tenth state judicial circuit judge (1939-1942).

McCLEARY, JAMES THOMPSON *(b Feb. 5, 1853, Ingersoll, Ontario, Canada; d Dec. 17, 1924, LaCrosse, Wis.).* Educator, farmer, writer, Minnesota Republican. President of Wisconsin State Educational Association (1891), U.S. Representative (1893-1907), secretary of the American Iron and Steel Institute (1911-1920).

McCLELLAN, GEORGE BRINTON, JR. *(b Nov. 23, 1865, Dresden, Saxony; d Nov. 30, 1940, Washington, D.C.)* Educator, newspaperman, orator, author, lawyer, historian, New York Democrat, and a progress-minded Tammany Hall sachem until his independence, and some say honesty, put him in the political soup. His father was the Civil War general and some said that until they'd had enough of his opposition, Tammany leaders tolerated him because of his famous name. Treasurer of the New York and Brooklyn Bridge (1889-1893), president of the New York City Board of Aldermen (1893-1894), delegate to all Democratic city, state, and national conventions (1890-1903), U.S. Representative (1895-1903) resigning to become mayor of New York (1903-1910) defeating Seth Low for his first term and William Randolph Hearst for his second, university lecturer on civic affairs (1908-1912), Princeton University professor of economic history (1912-1931).

McCLELLAND, ROBERT *(b Aug. 1, 1807, Greencastle, Pa.; d Aug. 30, 1880, Detroit, Mich.)* Lawyer, Michigan Democrat who resigned as governor (1851-1853) to become secretary of the interior in the Pierce cabinet (1853-1857). State constitutional convention delegate (1835, 1850, 1867), University of Michigan regent (1837, 1850), state representative (1837, 1839, 1843; the last year as house speaker), mayor of Monroe (1841), U.S. Representative (1843-1849), Democratic National Convention (1848, 1852, 1868) and state convention delegate (1850).

McCLERNAND, JOHN ALEXANDER *(b May 30, 1812, Breckinridge County, Ky.; d Sept. 20, 1900, Springfield, Ill.).* Farmer, Indian fighter, river trader, founder of the *Shawneetown* (Ill.) *Democrat* (1835), lawyer, Union Army general, Illinois Democrat. State representative (1836, 1840, 1842, 1843), presidential elector on the Van Buren-Johnson (1840) and Pierce-King (1852) tickets, U.S. Representative (1843-1851, 1859, 1861). Sangamon district circuit judge (1870-1873), president of the Democratic National Convention (1876).

McCLINTIC, JAMES VERNON *(b Sept. 8, 1878, Robertson County, Tex.; d April 22, 1948, on a train near Chicago, Ill.).* Traveling salesman, merchant, homesteader, lawyer, Oklahoma Democrat. Snyder city clerk (1908), Kiowa County clerk (1909), state representative (1911), state senate (1913, 1914), U.S. Representative (1915-1935), executive assistant to the governor (1935-1940), special assistant to the U.S. secretary of the interior (1941-1944), member of the War Department's readjustment division (1944, 1945).

McCLURG, JOSEPH WASHINGTON *(b Feb. 22, 1818, near Lebanon, Mo.; d Dec. 2, 1900, London, Mo.)* Teacher, Union Army officer, merchant, steamboat and leadmine operator, Missouri Emancipationist, Radical Republican, Republican whose support of carpetbag policies drove the state into the Democratic column for the next three decades. Said the *St. Louis Dispatch* (July 17, 1868) of him: "McClurg is the embodiment of all that is narrow, bigoted, revengeful, and ignorant in the Radical Party." St. Louis County deputy sheriff (1841-1844), leader of an ox-team caravan to the California gold fields (1849-1852), state convention delegate (1861-1863), U.S. Representative first as an Emancipationist then as a Radical (1865-1868), governor as a Republican (1869-1871), register of the Springfield Land Office (1889).

McCOMAS, LOUIS EMORY *(b Oct. 28, 1846, Washington County, Md.; d Nov. 10, 1907, Washington, D.C.)* Lawyer, law professor, Maryland Republican who during his years in Congress actively supported civil service reform while even more vigorously opposing the importation of alien labor. U.S. Representative (1883-1891), GOP National Convention delegate (1892, 1900) and secretary of the GOP National Committee (1892), Harrison-appointed associate justice of the District of Columbia Supreme Court (1892-1898), U.S. Senate (1899-1905), Roosevelt-appointed District of Columbia Court of Appeals justice (1905 until death).

McCONNELL, WILLIAM JOHN *(b Sept. 18, 1839, Commerce, Mich.; d March 30, 1925, Moscow, Idaho)* California, Oregon, and Idaho cattleman, merchant, banker, teacher and a Republican political figure in Oregon and Idaho. In Oregon: state senate president (1882), GOP National Convention delegate (1884). In Idaho: deputy U.S. marshall

(1865-1867), constitutional convention delegate (1890), U.S. Senate (1890-1891), governor (1892-1896), Indian inspector (1897-1901), Immigration Service inspector (1909 until death).

McCOOK, ANSON GEORGE *(b Oct. 10, 1835, Steubenville, Ohio; d Dec. 30, 1917, New York City)* Ohio drug store clerk, teacher, Union Army officer, internal revenue assessor for the seventeenth district, California and Nevada miner, New York lawyer who founded the *Law Journal* and planted Republican roots. U.S. Representative (1877-1883), secretary of the U.S. Senate (1883-1893), New York City chamberlain (1895-1898).

McCORMICK, JOSEPH MEDILL *(b May 16, 1877, Chicago, Ill.; d Feb. 25, 1925, Washington, D.C.)* Member of the Chicago newspaper family, becoming editor-publisher of the *Chicago Tribune* and part owner of two Cleveland newspapers, staunch supporter of Theodore Roosevelt, but leading the Progressives back into the Republican party (1916) when U.S. involvement in World War I loomed large. Though not nearly so reactionary a conservative as others in his family, he nevertheless opposed the Treaty of Versailles and the League of Nations. Vice chairman of the Progressive National Campaign Committee (1912-1914), state representative (1912-1916), GOP state convention chairman (1916), GOP National Convention delegate (1916), U.S. Representative (1917-1919), U.S. Senate (1919 until death).

McCORMICK, NELSON B. *(b Nov. 20, 1847, Greene County, Pa.; d April 10, 1914, Phillipsburg, Kans.)* Homesteader, lawyer, Kansas Populist turned Democrat. Phillips County deputy prosecutor (1886-1888) and prosecutor (1890-1894, 1910-1914), U.S. Representative (1897-1899), Democratic state convention delegate (1904, 1908).

McCORMICK, RICHARD CUNNINGHAM *(b May 23, 1832, New York City; d June 2, 1901, Jamaica, Queens, N.Y.)* New York newspaperman who covered the Civil War for the *Evening Post* and the *Commercial Advertiser* (1861, 1862), then, after being sent west by President Lincoln, established the *Prescott Arizona Miner* (1864) and the *Tucson Arizona Citizen* (1870); in Arizona, a Unionist turned Republican, the party he stayed with upon returning to New York. First chief clerk of the U.S. Department of Agriculture (1862), Lincoln-appointed secretary of the Arizona Territory (1863-1864) and Johnson-appointed territorial governor (1866-1869), delegate from Arizona to the U.S. Congress (1869-1875), GOP National Convention delegate (1872, 1876, 1880), first assistant secretary of the treasury (1877), U.S. Representative from New York (1895-1897).

McCORMICK, RUTH HANNA *(b March 27, 1880, Cleveland, Ohio; d Dec. 31, 1944, Chicago, Ill.).* Active worker for the suffrage amendment (1913 until adoption), wife of Joseph Medill McCormick but a newspaperwoman in her own right in Rockford, Ill.; dairy and breeding farm operator, Illinois Republican who was both an associate member of the GOP National Committee and chairman of its first woman's executive committee (1919-1924), in the latter year becoming the first elected national committeewoman from Illinois (1924-1928), then, in a pioneer try for elective office was chosen U.S. Representative (1929-1931). A widow, in Congress she met and married Congressman Albert Gallatin Simms of New Mexico (which see).

McCORMICK, WASHINGTON JAY *(b Jan. 4, 1884, Missoula, Mont.; d March 7, 1949, Missoula)* Lawyer, writer, Montana Republican. State representative (1918-1920), U.S. Representative (1921-1923).

McCOY, ISAAC *(b June 13, 1784, Fayette County, Pa.; d June 21, 1846, Louisville, Ky.)* Baptist missionary who worked among the Indians in Indiana, became convinced that they could never live equitably with the white man, and convinced Washington that a separate Indian state should be set up west of the Mississippi. Then, as the appointee of Secretary of War John C. Calhoun, he became Indian agent and surveyor (1830), assisted eastern Indians in their westward trek, surveyed reservations in Kansas and Oklahoma's Cherokee Outlet and a site for the Indian state capital. But that was as far as his plans progressed, the white man having other ideas for the land. In 1842 McCoy became corresponding secretary and general agent for the Indian Mission Association and so served until death.

He set forth hopes and much of his experiences in *Remarks on the Practicability of Indian Reform* (1827), *History of Baptist Indian Mission* (1840), and a series of reports published as the *Annual Register of Indian Affairs* (1835-1838).

McCOY, WILLIAM *(b ——, Fauquier County, Va.; d 1864, Charlottesville, Va.)* Virginia Democrat who served more than twenty years as a U.S. Representative (1811-1833), yet a man about whom little is recorded. Member of the state house of delegates (1798-1804), state constitutional convention delegate (1829-1830).

McCRACKEN, ROBERT McDOWELL *(b March 15, 1874, Vincennes, Ind.; d May 16, 1934, Emmett, Idaho, as the result of auto accident injuries while campaigning)* U.S. surveyor's clerk, lawyer, Idaho Republican. Chief clerk of the state house of representatives (1903), Bingham County prosecutor (1904-1906), state representative (1906-1910), U.S. Representative (1915-1917).

McCRARY, GEORGE WASHINGTON *(b Aug. 29, 1835, Vanderburg County, Ind.; d June 23, 1890, St. Joseph, Mo.)* Lawyer, trout fisherman, Iowa Republican who as secretary of war in the Hayes cabinet (1877-1879) ordered troops to pursue marauding Mexican gangs across the border, an action that brought about U.S. recognition of the Diaz government. He also withdrew troop support from Louisiana and South Carolina carpetbaggers. State representative (1857), state senate (1861-1865), U.S. Representative (1869-1877), U.S. judge for the eighth judicial circuit (1880-1884).

McCREARY, JAMES BENNETT *(b July 8, 1838, Richmond, Ky.; d Oct. 8, 1918, Richmond)* Confederate Army officer, lawyer, Kentucky Democrat who as governor (1875-1879, 1912-1916) had more luck in the establishment of a state normal school and college of agriculture than he did with attempts to put an end to mountain feuds. Democratic National Convention delegate (1868, 1900, 1904, 1908, 1912), state representative (1869-1873) and house speaker (1871, 1873), International Monetary Conference delegate (1892), U.S. Representative (1885-1897), state Democratic campaign committee chairman (1900), U.S. Senate (1903-1909).

McCREERY, WILLIAM *(b 1750, Ulster, Ireland; d March 8, 1814, Baltimore County, Md.)* Maryland farmer. U.S. Representative (1803-1809), state senate (1811 until death).

McCULLOCH, PHILIP DODDRIDGE, JR. *(b June 23, 1851, Murfreesboro, Tenn.; d Nov. 26, 1928, Marianna, Ark.)* Lawyer, Arkansas Democrat. First judicial district prosecutor (1878-1884), Lee County Democratic central committee chairman (1875-1893), presidential elector on the Cleveland-Thurman ticket

(1888), Democratic state convention delegate (1890), U.S. Representative (1893-1903).

McCUMBER, PORTER JAMES *(b Feb. 3, 1858, Crete, Ill.; d May 18, 1933, Washington, D.C.)* Teacher, lawyer, North Dakota Republican who served twenty-four years (1899-1923) in the U.S. Senate and, as chairman of its Finance Committee, sponsored the Fordney-McCumber Tariff. Richland County state's attorney (1883-1885), territorial representative (1885) and senator (1887), member of International Boundary Commission (1925 until death).

McDONALD, JOSEPH EWING *(b Aug. 29, 1819, Butler County, Ohio; d June 21, 1891, Indianapolis, Ind.)* Indiana lawyer who helped rejuvenate the Democratic party there after the Civil War. Prosecutor (1843-1847), U.S. Representative (1849-1851), unsuccessful gubernatorial candidate (1864), U.S. Senate (1875-1881).

McDONOUGH, GORDON LEO *(b Jan. 2, 1895, Buffalo, N.Y.).* Chemist, California Republican. Los Angeles County Board of Supervisors (1933-1944), U.S. Representative (1945-1963) serving on Banking and Currency and Merchant Marine and Fisheries committees and Joint Committee on Defense Production.

McDOUGALL, ALEXANDER *(b 1731, Islay, Scotland; d June 9, 1786, New York City)* Privateer (1756-1763), rabidly patriotic pre-Revolutionary pamphleteer, Continental Army officer who succeeded Benedict Arnold as West Point commander, and, after the war, an increasingly conservative New York merchant who became the first president of both the New York Society of the Cincinnati and the bank of New York. Delegate to the Continental Congress (1781, 1782, 1784, 1785), state senate (1783 until death).

McDOUGALL, JAMES ALEXANDER *(b Nov. 19, 1817, Bethlehem, N.Y.; d Sept. 3, 1867, Albany, N.Y.)* Lawyer, Illinois and California Democrat-Unionist who explored the South and Far West and finally settled in San Francisco. In Illinois: State attorney general (1842-1846). In California: attorney general (1850-1851), U.S. Representative (1853-1855), U.S. Senate (1861-1867), Democratic National Convention delegate (1864), Union National Convention delegate (1866).

McDOWELL, ALEXANDER *(b March 4, 1845, Franklin, Pa.; d Sept. 30, 1913, Sharon, Pa.).* Union soldier, editor-publisher of the *Venango* (Pa.) *Citizen*, banker, Pennsylvania Republican who served as clerk of the U.S. House of Representatives (1895-1911) after being a member (1893-1895). Sharon School Board treasurer (1880-1913) and borough treasurer (1880-1909), GOP National Convention delegate (1900, 1904, 1908).

McDOWELL, HARRIS BROWN, JR. *(b Feb. 10, 1906, New Castle County, Del.).* Farmer, real estate operator, Delaware Democrat. Member state board of agriculture (1937-1940), state representative (1940-1942), Delaware Farm Bureau (1941-1948), state senate (1942-1946), Delaware secretary of state (1949-1953), New Castle County Zoning Commission (1953, 1954), national convention delegate (1944, 1948, 1952, 1956, 1960), U.S. Representative (1955-1957, 1959-1967) serving on Foreign Affairs and Veterans' Affairs committees.

McDUFFIE, GEORGE *(b Aug. 10, 1790, Columbia County, Ga.; d March 11, 1851, Cherry Hill, S.C.)* Lawyer, president of South Carolina College, South Carolina Democrat, and vigorously outspoken advocate of nullification who believed that import duties levied on the South guaranteed the North 40 out of every 100 bales of cotton, a quarrelsome orator who while a U.S. Representative (1821-1834) proposed direct election of presidents. And, because he was so talented a speaker, he always spoke before a jammed chamber and his audiences listened, although they did not always act as he wished. State representative (1818-1820), governor (1834-1836), U.S. Senate (1842-1846).

McDUFFIE, JOHN (b Sept. 25, 1883, River Ridge, Ala.; d Nov. 1, 1950, Mobile, Ala.) Lawyer, Alabama Democrat. State representative (1907-1911), first judicial district prosecutor (1911-1919), U.S. Representative (1919-1935) resigning to become a U.S. district judge (1935 until death).

McENERY, SAMUEL DOUGLAS (b May 28, 1837, Monroe, La.; d June 28, 1910, New Orleans, La.) Confederate Army officer, lawyer, Louisiana Democrat. Lieutenant governor (1880-1881), governor (1881-1888), associate justice of the state supreme court (1888-1897), U.S. Senate (1897 until death).

McFADDEN, LOUIS THOMAS (b July 25, 1876, Granville Center, Pa.; d Oct. 1, 1936, New York City) Banker, anti-Semitic Pennsylvania Republican who while chairman of the House Committee on Banking and Currency (1920-1931) put his name and his effort behind passage of the McFadden-Pepper Act (1927) that gave national banks more muscle to meet the growing threat of state banks. Always a sharp critic, he proposed (1932) that President Hoover be impeached because of his moratorium on war debts, castigated the Federal Reserve Board for "having caused the greatest depression we have ever known" and, in open House debate (1933), charged that Jews were responsible for repeal of the gold clause. U.S. Representative (1915-1935).

MacGREGOR, CLARENCE (b Sept. 16, 1872, Newark, N.Y.; d Feb. 18, 1952, Buffalo, N.Y.) Lawyer, New York Republican. State assemblyman (1908-1912), U.S. Representative (1919-1928), state supreme court justice (1928-1942), and then an official referee of the same court (1943 until death).

McGREGOR, J. HARRY (b Sept. 30, 1896, Jefferson County, Ohio; d Oct. 7, 1958, Coshocton, Ohio) General contractor, Ohio Republican. State representative (1935-1940), minority whip (1937-1939), majority leader and speaker pro tem (1939, 1940), U.S. Representative (1940 until death).

McGROARTY, JOHN STEVEN (b Aug. 20, 1862, Foster Township, Pa.; d Aug. 7, 1944, Los Angeles, Calif.) Knight of St. Gregory, journalist, author, dramatist who was elected California's poet laureate in 1933, yet could never completely subject his interest in politics to the arts. And so, as a Democrat, his California constituency sent him to the U.S. House of Representatives (1935-1939).

McGUIRE, BIRD SEGLE (b Oct. 13, 1865, Belleville, Ill.; d Nov. 9, 1930, Tulsa, Okla.) Cattleman, teacher, lawyer who first settled in Kansas, then moved on to the Oklahoma Territory and helped it to become a state; Republican. In Kansas: Chautauqua County prosecutor (1890-1894). In Oklahoma: assistant U.S. attorney (1897-1902) and delegate to Congress (1903-1907) while a territory and then, after statehood, U.S. Representative (1907-1915).

McHENRY, JAMES (b Nov. 16, 1753, Ballymena, County Antrim, Ireland; d May 3, 1816, Fayetteville, Md.) Physician who was General Washington's secretary during part of the Revolution (1778-1780) and then transferred to General Lafayette's staff until the end of the war; strong advocate of the federal Constitution, supporter of Alexander Hamilton, and a Maryland Federalist. State senate (1781-1786), member of the Continental Congress (1783-1786), federal Constitutional Convention delegate (1787), secretary of war in the Washington cabinet (1796-1800).

McINTIRE, CLIFFORD GUY *(b May 4, 1908, Perham, Maine)* Farmer, Maine Republican. Regional manager for Farm Credit Administration (1933-1947), U.S. Representative (1951-1965) serving on the Agriculture Committee.

McKAY, JAMES IVER *(b 1793, Elizabethtown, N.C.; d Sept. 4, 1853, Goldsboro, N.C.)* Lawyer, North Carolina Democrat who as chairman of the House Ways and Means Committee (1843-1847) was known as Old Money Bags because of his insistence upon the strictest possible economy in government, even to dispensing with a committee clerk, yet strongly supporting expenditures that he deemed necessary to the nation's good. State senate (1815-1819, 1822, 1826, 1830), U.S. Representative (1831-1849).

McKEAN, SAMUEL *(b April 7, 1787, Bradford County, Pa.; d Dec. 14, 1841, West Burlington, Pa.)* Merchant, founder of the *Bradford Gazette*, Pennsylvania Democrat who believed slavery was none of the government's business. Bradford County commissioner (1814), state representative (1815-1819), U.S. Representative (1823-1829), state senate (1829), Pennsylvania secretary of state (1830-1834), presidential elector on the Jackson-Wilkins ticket (1832), U.S. Senate (1833-1839).

McKEAN, THOMAS *(b March 19, 1734, New London, Pa.; d June 24, 1817, Philadelphia, Pa.)* Lawyer, radical foe of the Stamp Act, signer of the Declaration of Independence, a powerful early-day politician who helped give rise to the spoils system, maintained homes in both Delaware and Pennsylvania and held office in both, sometimes simultaneously; at first a Democrat but turned ultimately to the Federalist banner, not so much because of conviction but rather because that was where he could find the strongest support.

In Delaware: Sussex County deputy attorney general (1756-1758), assemblyman (1762-1775) and house speaker (1772), trustee of the New Castle County loan office (1764-1776), delegate to the Stamp Act Congress (1765) and to the General Congress (1765), delegate to the Continental Congress (1774-1776, 1778-1783) and its president (1781), state representative (1776, 1777) and house speaker (1777), president of the state of Delaware (1777). In Pennsylvania: Chief justice (1777-1799), delegate to the state convention that ratified the federal Constitution (1789) and state constitutional convention delegate (1789), governor (1799-1808).

McKELLAR, KENNETH DOUGLAS *(b Jan. 29, 1869, Richmond, Ala.; d Oct. 25, 1957, Memphis, Tenn.)* Lawyer, Tennessee Democrat who served more than forty years in Washington. Presidential elector on the Parker-Davis ticket (1904), Democratic National Convention delegate (1908), U.S. Representative (1911-1917), U.S. Senator (1917-1953) and Senate president pro tem (1945-1947, 1949-1953).

McKENNA, JOSEPH *(b Aug. 10, 1843, Philadelphia, Pa.; d Nov. 21, 1926, Washington, D.C.)* Lawyer, California Republican whom President McKinley appointed associate justice of the U.S. Supreme Court in the face of wide criticism but who served competently for more than a quarter-century (1898-1925) showing unexpected social vision. Solano County district attorney (1866-1868), state representative (1875,

1876), U.S. Representative (1885-1892), U.S. ninth judicial circuit judge (1892-1897), attorney general in the McKinley cabinet (1897-1898).

McKENZIE, JOHN CHARLES *(b Feb. 18, 1860, Woodbine Township, Ill.; d Sept. 17, 1941, Elizabeth, Ill.)* Teacher, grain dealer, lawyer, banker, Illinois Republican. State representative (1892-1896), state claims commissioner (1896-1900), state senate (1900-1911) and senate president pro tem (1903-1905), U.S. Representative (1911-1925).

McKEOWN, THOMAS DEITZ *(b June 4, 1878, Blackstock, S.C.; d Oct. 22, 1951, Ada, Okla.)* Lawyer, farmer, oil producer, Oklahoma Democrat. Seventh district judge (1910-1914), fifth division supreme court commission presiding judge (1915, 1916), U.S. Representative (1917-1921, 1923-1935), Democratic state convention delegate (1942), Pontotoc County attorney (1946) and county judge (1947 until death).

McKIM, ALEXANDER *(b Jan. 10, 1748, Brandywine, Del.; d Jan. 18, 1832, Baltimore, Md.)* Merchant, Revolutionary Army cadet-cavalryman who fought under Lafayette in the Virginia campaign of 1791, and a Maryland Democrat who served both as presiding judge of the Baltimore County Orphans' Court and justice of the court of quarter sessions. State house of delegates (1778), U.S. Representative (1809-1815). Uncle of Isaac McKim.

McKIM, ISAAC *(b July 21, 1775, Baltimore, Md.; d April 1, 1838, Baltimore).* Merchant who was one of the organizers of the Baltimore & Ohio Railroad and an importer whose clipper ships operated around the world, Maryland Democrat. State senate (1821-1823), U.S. Representative (1823-1825, 1833 until death). Nephew of Alexander McKim.

McKINLEY, JOHN *(b May 1, 1780, Culpeper County, Va.; d July 19, 1852, Louisville, Ky.)* Lawyer, Alabama Democrat who was an extremely conscientious associate justice of the U.S. Supreme Court (1837 until death) often driving himself to fulfill his obligations despite increasingly worsening health. U.S. Senate (1826-1831 and one month in 1837), U.S. Representative (1833-1835).

McKINLEY, WILLIAM *(b Jan. 29, 1843, Niles, Ohio; d Sept. 14, 1901, Buffalo, N.Y., having been shot on Sept. 6 by anarchist Leon Czolgosz while attending the Pan-American Exposition).* Twenty-fifth president (Ohio Republican), 1897-1901, who administered during the Spanish-American War; Union Army officer; U.S. Representative; Ohio governor; lawyer; kindly man who got along well with people.

Seventh of nine children born to a small-scale iron foundryman who moved his family to Poland, Ohio (1852), where McKinley attended a private school. He entered Allegheny College, Meadville, Pa. (1860), but ill health forced him to drop out and he subsequently taught school. Enlisted as a private at the outbreak of the Civil War in the Twenty-third Ohio Volunteer Infantry under Rutherford B. Hayes; advanced in rank, serving for a time as mess sergeant; brevetted major (1865). Studied law, attended Albany (N.Y.) Law School and was admitted to the Ohio bar in 1867, opening an office in Canton, which became his permanent residence. Married Ida Saxton, daughter of influential local banker (1871). The McKinleys had two daughters, both of whom had early deaths. Mrs. McKinley suffered from chronic ill health but through all their heartbreaks the couple remained unusually devoted.

Stark County prosecuting attorney (1869-1871), GOP delegate to national conventions (1884, 1888, 1892) serving twice as chairman of committee on resolutions; U.S. Representative (1877-1884 [his election was successfully contested and he lost his seat in 1884], 1885-1891) and member of powerful House Ways and Means Committee, becoming (1889) its chairman; espoused the cause of country's industrial leaders whose interests were best served by a high protective tariff and was chief architect of the highly controversial McKinley Tariff Act. The unpopularity of the act lost him his seat in elections of 1890 but, with help of Mark Hanna (which see), Cleveland industrialist and boss of Ohio Republican Party, he was twice elected governor, serving from 1892-1896; nominated by the Republicans (1896) for the presidency, again with the help of Hanna who adroitly managed a campaign in which McKinley read carefully drafted speeches to groups who gathered at his front porch. McKinley defeated Democratic candidate William Jennings Bryan (who toured the country eloquently advocating free silver), receiving a popular majority and 271 to 176 electoral votes. Times were good in 1900 and McKinley, on the basis of "the full dinner pail" and with Theodore Roosevelt as his vice presidential running mate, again defeated Bryan who campaigned against imperialism, this time with 292 to 155 electoral votes.

During McKinley's presidency, the Dingley Tariff Bill, with its controversially high duties, was passed (1897), the Hawaiian Islands were annexed, a gold standard act was passed, and the destruction of the battleship *Maine* (1898) in the Havana harbor helped McKinley decide to ask Congress for a declaration of war against Spain.

McKINLEY, WILLIAM BROWN *(b Sept. 5, 1856, Petersburg, Ill.; d Dec. 7, 1926, Martinsville, Ind.)* Public utilities executive who developed the Illinois Traction System, philanthropist and a worker for world peace, Illinois Republican. University of Illinois trustee

(1902-1905), GOP National Convention delegate (1908), U.S. Representative (1905-1913, 1915-1921), U.S. Senate (1921 until death).

McKINNEY, JOHN FRANKLIN *(b April 12, 1827, Miami County, Ohio; d June 13, 1903, Piqua, Ohio)* Lawyer who was a post-1850 power in the Ohio Democratic party. Delegate to all Democratic national conventions (1850-1888), U.S. Representative (1863-1865, 1871-1873), Democratic state executive committee chairman (1879-1880).

McLACHLAN, JAMES *(b Aug. 1, 1852, Argyllshire, Scotland; d Nov. 21, 1940, Los Angeles, Calif.)* Lawyer, California Republican who while attending college in New York was the Tompkins County school commissioner (1877). In California: Los Angeles County district attorney (1890-1892), U.S. Representative (1895-1897, 1901-1911), member of the National Monetary Commission (1911, 1912).

McLAIN, FRANK ALEXANDER *(b Jan. 29, 1852, Amite County, Miss.; d Oct. 10, 1920, Gloster, Miss.)* Lawyer, Mississippi Democrat. State representative (1881-1883), district attorney (1883-1896), state constitutional convention delegate (1890), U.S. Representative (1898-1909), state supreme court commissioner (1910-1912).

McLANE, LOUIS *(b May 28, 1786, Smyrna, Del.; d Oct. 7, 1857, Baltimore, Md.)* Lawyer, Delaware Democrat who moved to Maryland after becoming president of the Baltimore & Ohio Railroad (1837-1847), holder of two positions in the Jackson cabinet shifting from treasury to state when he and the president could not agree on the rechartering of the Bank of the United States. U.S. Representative (1817-1827), U.S. Senate (1827-1829) resigning to become ambassador to England (1829-1831) a position to which he later returned (1845-1846) and negotiated the Oregon Territory boundary, secretary of the treasury (1831-1833), secretary of state (1833-1834), Maryland constitutional convention delegate (1850). Father of Robert M. McLane.

McLANE, ROBERT MILLIGAN *(b June 23, 1815, Wilmington, Del.; d April 16, 1898, Paris, France)* West Point graduate, lawyer, diplomat, Maryland Democrat who while minister to Mexico (1859-1860) negotiated a treaty with Juarez that was, however, not subsequently ratified in Washington.

Member of state house of delegates (1845), U.S. Representative (1847-1851, 1879-1883), presidential elector on the Pierce-King ticket (1852), minister to China, Japan, Korea, and Siam (1853-1854), Democratic National Convention delegate (1856, 1876), state senate (1877), governor (1884-1885), minister to France (1885-1889). Son of Louis McLane.

McLAUGHLIN, JAMES CAMPBELL *(b Jan. 26, 1858, Beardstown, Ill.; d Nov. 29, 1932, Marion, Va.)* Lawyer, Michigan Republican who served a quarter-century (1907 until death) as a U.S. Representative. Muskegon County prosecutor (1887-1901), state tax commissioner and assessor (1901-1906) who took part in Michigan's first assessment of railroad property.

McLAUGHLIN, MELVIN ORLANDO *(August 8, 1876, Osceola, Iowa; d June 18, 1928, York, Nebr.)* Clergyman, teacher, York College president (1913-1918), mine investment broker, Nebraska Republican. U.S. Representative (1919-1927).

McLAURIN, ANSELM JOSEPH *(b March 26, 1848, Brandon, Miss.; d Dec. 22, 1909, Brandon)* Lawyer, Confederate Army officer, Mississippi Democrat who believed that men who beat their

wives should not be allowed to vote. Raleigh district attorney (1871), state representative (1879), presidential elector on the Cleveland-Thurman ticket (1888), state constitutional convention delegate (1890), U.S. Senate (1894-1895, 1901 until death), governor (1895-1900), U.S. Immigration Commission member (1908 until death).

McLAURIN, JOHN LOWNDES *(b May 9, 1860, Red Bluff, S.C.; d July 29, 1934, near Bennettsville, S.C.)* Lawyer, planter, South Carolina Democrat who devised the state warehouse system for the storing and financing of cotton. State representative (1890), state attorney general (1891-1897), U.S. Representative (1891-1897), U.S. Senate (1897-1903), state senate (1914, 1915), state warehouse commissioner (1915-1917).

MACLAY, SAMUEL *(b June 17, 1741, Lurgan Township, Pa.; d Oct. 5, 1811, Buffalo Township, Pa.)* Farmer, surveyor who fought in the Revolution, Pennsylvania Democrat. Franklin County associate judge (1792-1795), U.S. Representative (1795-1797), state senate (1797-1803) and speaker (1801-1803), U.S. Senate (1803-1809). Brother of William and father of William P. Maclay.

MACLAY, WILLIAM *(b July 20, 1737, New Garden, Pa.; d April 16, 1804, Harrisburg, Pa.)* Indian fighter, French and Indian War and Revolutionary Army officer, surveyor, lawyer who, according to at least one biographer, was the first Jefferson Democrat. He and Robert Morris were chosen the two U.S. Senators to represent Pennsylvania in the First Congress, they drew lots to determine which would take the long-term seat, Morris won and as a result Maclay served only two years (1789-1791). Jefferson, a senator from Virginia, did not arrive to take his seat for eleven months and it was left to Maclay to lead the Democratic forces in their opposition to the Federalist, Hamilton, and his financial proposals. No official records of Congressional proceedings and debate—all carried on behind closed doors—were kept in those early days and thus there was no documentation of what the First Congress did or said until 1880 when it was discovered that Maclay had kept a diary that is now invaluable to historians.

Chief clerk of the Northumberland County courts (1772), Provincial Assembly (1781), Indian commissioner (1784-1785), common pleas judge, member of the executive council (1786, 1788), state representative (1795, 1803, 1804), presidential elector (1796), Dauphin County judge (1801-1803). Brother of Samuel and uncle of William P. Maclay.

MACLAY, WILLIAM BROWN *(b March 20, 1812, New York City; d Feb. 19, 1882, New York City)* Latin teacher, lawyer, associate editor of the *New York Quarterly Review* (1836), New York Democrat. State assemblyman (1840-1842), U.S. Representative (1843-1849, 1857-1861).

MACLAY, WILLIAM PLUNKETT *(b Aug. 23, 1774, Northumberland County, Pa.; d Sept. 2, 1842, Milroy, Pa.).* Surveyor, farmer, Pennsylvania Democrat. Mifflin County chief clerk (1808-1814), state representative (1815), U.S. Representative (1816-1821), state constitutional convention delegate (1837). Son of Samuel and nephew of William Maclay.

McLEAN, GEORGE PAYNE *(b Oct. 7, 1857, Simsbury, Conn.; d June 6, 1932, Simsbury)* Lawyer, Connecticut Republican. State representative (1883, 1884), member of commission to revise state statutes (1885), state senate (1886), U.S. attorney (1892-1896), governor (1901-1903), U.S. Senate (1911-1929).

McLEAN, JOHN *(b March 11, 1785, Morris County, N.J.; d April 4, 1861, Cincinnati, Ohio)* Self-educated lawyer, weekly newspaper publisher, Ohio Democrat-Whig-Republican who was frequently mentioned for the presidency; an associate justice of the U.S. Supreme Court (1829 until death) who in a Dred Scott case minority opinion held that slavery was not a right but rather a matter of force supported by local law. U.S. Representative (1813-1816), associate judge of the state supreme court (1816-1822), U.S. general land office commissioner (1822), postmaster general in the Monroe and Adams cabinets (1823-1829), recipient of 196 votes for the presidential nomination at the GOP National Convention of 1856.

McLEOD, CLARENCE JOHN *(b July 3, 1895, Detroit, Mich.; d May 15, 1959, Detroit)* Lawyer, Michigan Republican. U.S. Representative (1920-1921, 1923-1937).

McMANES, JAMES *(b April 13, 1822, County Tyrone, Ireland; d Nov. 23, 1899, Philadelphia, Pa.)* Millhand, real estate operator, Pennsylvania Whig-People's Republican-Republican who as a municipal gas works trustee managed to rule Philadelphia with an iron political fist for about twenty years (beginning in 1865) and amassed a fortune in utilities, banking, and various other enterprises but paid back about $500,000 to depositors when one of his banks failed. A mayor and a governor-maker, his slip from the throne began at the 1880 GOP National Convention when he split with the Pennsylvania delegation and refused to support President Grant for a third term.

McMILLAN, BENTON *(b Sept. 11, 1845, Monroe County, Ky.; d Jan. 8, 1933, Nashville, Tenn.)* Lawyer, insurance broker, Tennessee Democrat. State representative (1874), state agent for the purchase of territory from Kentucky (1875), presidential elector on the Tilden-Hendricks ticket (1876), special circuit court judge (1877), U.S. Representative (1879-1899), governor (1899-1903), minister to Peru (1913-1919) and Guatemala (1919-1922).

McMILLAN, JAMES *(b May 12, 1838, Hamilton, Ontario, Canada; d Aug. 10, 1902, Manchester, Mass.)* Railroad and Great Lakes shipping executive and a power in Michigan Republican affairs, serving as chairman of the GOP state central committee, president of the Detroit Park Commission, member of the Detroit Board of Estimate, presidential elector on the Blaine-Logan ticket (1884) and U.S. Senate (1889 until death).

McMILLAN, SAMUEL JAMES RENWICK *(b Feb. 22, 1826, Brownsville, Pa.; d Oct. 3, 1897, St. Paul, Minn.)* Lawyer, Indian fighter, jurist, Minnesota Republican. First judicial district judge (1858-1864), associate state supreme court justice (1864-1874) and chief justice (1874-1875), U.S. Senate (1875-1887).

McMILLAN, THOMAS SANDERS *(b Nov. 27, 1888, Allendale County, S.C.; d Sept. 29, 1939, Charleston, S.C.).* Teacher, lawyer, farmer, South Carolina Democrat. State representative (1917-1924) and house speaker (1921-1924), U.S. Representative (1925 until death) when he was succeeded by his widow, Clara Gooding McMillan (1939-1941); executive committee member of the Interparliamentary Union (1937-1939) and Oslo convention delegate (1939).

McNAMARA, PATRICK VINCENT *(b Oct. 4, 1894, North Weymouth, Mass.; d April 30, 1966, U.S. Naval Hospital, Bethesda, Md.).* Construction business, Michigan Democrat. Director of Detroit area Office of Price Administration (1942-1945), city council (1946, 1947), board of education (1949-1955), U.S.

Senate (1955 until death) where he was chairman of the Public Works Committee and member of the Labor and Public Welfare Committee.

McNARY, CHARLES LINZA *(b June 12, 1874, Marion County, Oreg.; d Feb. 25, 1944, Fort Lauderdale, Fla.)* Lawyer, Oregon Republican who was Wendell Willkie's vice presidential running mate in the 1940 presidential election. Third judicial district deputy district attorney (1906-1913), Willamette University law department dean (1908-1913), associate justice of the state supreme court (1913-1915), chairman of the GOP state central committee (1916, 1917), U.S. Senator (1917 until death) and Senate minority leader (1933 until death).

MACON, NATHANIEL *(b Dec. 17, 1757, Warren County, N.C.; d June 29, 1837, Warren County)* Revolutionary soldier, planter, North Carolina Democrat who served thirty-eight years in Washington (1791-1828), and received twenty-four electoral votes for vice president of the United States (1825). State senate (1780-1782, 1784, 1785), U.S. Representative (1791-1815) and House speaker (1801-1807), U.S. Senator (1815-1828) and twice Senate president pro tem, state constitutional convention president (1835), presidential elector on the Van Buren-Johnson ticket (1836).

MACON, ROBERT BRUCE *(b July 6, 1859, Phillips County, Ark.; d Oct. 9, 1925, Marvell, Ark.)* An orphan boy at nine who became a successful farmer, lawyer, Arkansas Democrat. State representative (1883-1887), circuit court clerk (1892-1896), first judicial district prosecutor (1898-1902), U.S. Representative (1903-1913).

McPHERSON, EDWARD *(b July 31, 1830, Gettysburg, Pa.; d Dec. 14, 1895, Gettysburg)* Newspaper editor, political historian, Pennsylvania Republican who served as clerk of the U.S. House of Representatives (1863-1875, 1881-1883, 1889-1891) after two terms as a member (1859-1863). Permanent president of the GOP National Convention (1876), director of the U.S. Bureau of Engraving and Printing (1877, 1878).

McPHERSON, JOHN RHODERIC *(b May 9, 1833, York, N.Y.; d Oct. 8, 1897, Jersey City, N.J.)* Farmer, livestock dealer, New Jersey Democrat. Jersey City alderman (1864-1870) and board president three of those years, state senate (1871-1873), presidential elector on the Tilden-Hendricks ticket (1876), U.S. Senate (1877-1895), Democratic National Convention delegate (1884, 1888, 1892).

McQUEEN, JOHN *(b Feb. 9, 1804, Robeson County, N.C.; d Aug. 30, 1867, Society Hill, S.C.)* Lawyer, South Carolina Democrat who served as a U.S. Representative (1849-1861) and during the Civil War was a member of the First Confederate Congress.

McRAE, JOHN JONES *(b Jan. 10, 1815, Sneedsboro, now McFarlan, N.C.; d May 31, 1868, Belize, British Honduras)* Lawyer, newspaper publisher, Mississippi Democrat who was appointed to the U.S. Senate to fill a vacancy created by the resignation of Jefferson Davis (Dec. 1851-March 1852). State representative (1848-1850) and house speaker in the latter year, governor (1854-1858), U.S. Representative (1858-1861), member of the Confederate Congress (1862-1864).

McRAE, THOMAS CHIPMAN *(b Dec. 21, 1851, Mt. Holly, Ark.; d June 2, 1929, Prescott, Ark.)* Lawyer, banker, conservation-minded Arkansas Democrat who bucked the entrenched interests in a fight for recovery of public lands. State election commissioner (1874), state representative (1877), presidential elector on the Hancock-English ticket (1880), Democratic state convention

chairman (1884, 1902), Democratic National Convention delegate (1884), U.S. Representative (1885-1903), state bankers' association president (1909, 1910), and state bar association president (1917, 1918), state constitutional convention delegate (1918), governor (1921-1925). As a reward for long and faithful service to his party, he was elected (1926) a life member of its state conventions.

McREYNOLDS, SAMUEL DAVIS *(b April 16, 1872, Bledsoe County, Tenn.; d July 11, 1939, Washington, D.C.)* Lawyer, Tennessee Democrat who for sixteen years (1923 until death) was an influential U.S. Representative—as a member of the Immigration and Naturalization Committee supported the tight restrictions contained in the Johnson Act of 1924, and then as chairman of the Foreign Relations Committee (1932 until death) considered an able spokesman for the Roosevelt administration. Sixth judicial circuit district attorney (1894, 1896), sixth circuit criminal court judge (1903-1923), delegate to the International Monetary Conference in London (1933).

McSWAIN, JOHN JACKSON *(b May 1, 1875, Laurens County, S.C.; d Aug. 6, 1936, Columbia, S.C.)* Lawyer, South Carolina Democrat who served eight terms as a U.S. Representative (1921 until death).

MACK, RUSSELL VERNON *(b June 13, 1891, Hillman, Mich.; d March 28, 1960, Washington, D.C., on the House floor).* Publisher of the *Hoquiam Daily Washingtonian* (1934-1950) and a Washington Republican who served as a U.S. Representative from 1947 until death.

MACY, WILLIAM KINGSLAND *(b Nov. 21, 1889, New York City; d July 15, 1961, Islip, N.Y.)* Financier, food broker, newspaper publisher, radio station owner, and a powerful New York

Republican who was active in the probe of the State Banking Department (1929) and had much to do with bringing about the Seabury investigation of New York City corruption (1931, 1932). Suffolk County GOP committee chairman (1926-1951) and state GOP chairman (1930-1934), national convention delegate (1928, 1932, 1940, 1944, 1948), state convention delegate (1928-1946), regent of the University of the State of New York (1941-1953), state senate (1946), U.S. Representative (1947-1951).

MADDEN, MARTIN BARNABY *(b March 20, 1855, Darlington, England; d April 27, 1928, Washington, D.C., in a House committee room)* Quarry operator, banker, Illinois Republican who was a delegate to every national convention (1896-1924), usually serving on the resolutions committee; coauthor (1900) of the plank calling for construction of the Panama Canal. Chicago councilman (1889-1897) and council president (1891-1893), Chicago GOP committee chairman (1890-1896), U.S. Representative (1905 until death).

MADDOX, JOHN W. *(b June 3, 1848, Chattooga County, Ga.; d Sept. 27, 1922, Rome, Ga.)* Farmer, lawyer, insurance executive, Georgia Democrat whose first taste of politics was as deputy sheriff of the county in which he was born. Mayor of Summerville (1877), county commissioner (1878-1880), state representative (1880-1884), state senate (1884-1886), Rome circuit superior court judge (1886-1892), U.S. Representative (1893-1905), mayor of Rome (1906, 1907), state superior court judge (1908-1912).

MADISON, JAMES *(b March 16, 1751, Port Conway, Va.; d June 28, 1836, Montpelier, Orange County, Va.).* Fourth president (Virginia Democratic-Republican), 1809-1817; declared war on Britain in 1812; was Constitution's chief architect and kept notes published as the *Journal of the Federal Convention* which are the main source of information about the framing of that document; wrote many of the *Federalist* papers that helped obtain Constitution's acceptance by the states; strongly supported passage of the first ten amendments known as the Bill of Rights. Early supporter of Federalist Alexander Hamilton, then, with close friend Thomas Jefferson, became a leader of the opposition Democratic-Republican party. At the end of his second term as president, approved many measures initially supported by the Federalists.

Raised at his comfortably well-off father's Virginia plantation, Montpelier, and the eldest of a large family, Madison graduated from Princeton College in 1771. Married (1794) Dolly Payne Todd, a pretty young widow who became renowned for her charm as a White House hostess and who was a great help and comfort to Madison. The Madisons had no children but raised Dolly's son by her previous marriage.

Member Virginia Legislature (1776-1777, 1784-1786, 1799-1800) where he helped write state constitution, proposed amendment (adopted at a later time) to separate church and state. He was not reelected in 1778 because, it's said, he refused to treat the voters to free rum; served that year on Governor Patrick Henry's advisory council. He was delegate to Continental Congress (1780-1783, 1786-1788); delegate to Constitutional Convention (1787); as U.S. Representative (1789-1797) opposed Hamilton's proposals for creation of a national bank and other measures that would tend to strengthen the central government. In protest against the Alien and Sedition Acts (1798), he wrote the Virginia Resolutions, which were used at a later date as arguments for states' rights in a way that exceeded Madison's intentions.

As secretary of state (1801-1809), he worked closely with President Jefferson and, when he himself became president (defeating Federalist candidate C. C. Pinckney by 122 to 47 electoral votes in 1808), he tried to avoid war with France and England and continued Jefferson's policy of depriving U.S. goods to belligerents who infringed on U.S. neutrality rights. Failure of this policy, a tricky maneuver by Napoleon, and pressure from "war hawks" led by Henry Clay and John C. Calhoun, who hoped for American expansion into Canada and Florida, finally pushed Madison into the War of 1812—a war for which the United States was unprepared, during which Britain set fire to the Capitol, and because of which New England threatened to secede, yet Madison was reelected to a second term (he received 128 electoral votes to Federalist candidate De Witt Clinton's 89). At war's end there was a spirit of nationalism in the land and westward movement brought prosperity.

In retirement at Montpelier, the elder statesman and Dolly Madison entertained graciously but were forced to sell part of the farm to meet expenses; when Jefferson died, Madison succeeded him as rector of the University of Virginia (1826); cochairman of Virginia state constitutional convention (1829).

MAGEE, WALTER WARREN *(b May 23, 1861, Groveland, N.Y.; d May 25, 1927, Syracuse, N.Y.)* Lawyer, New York Republican. Onondaga County supervisor (1892, 1893), Syracuse corporation counsel (1904-1914), U.S. Representative (1915 until death).

MAGINNIS, MARTIN *(b Oct. 27, 1841, near Pultneyville, N.Y.; d March 27, 1919, Los Angeles, Calif.).* Union Army officer, miner, publisher of the *Helena Daily Gazette*, Montana Democrat who led a band of 150 hardy Minnesota men across the northern route into the Montana Territory (1866). Delegate to Congress (1873-1885), state commissioner of mineral land (1890-1893).

MAGNUSON, DONALD HAMMER *(b March 7, 1911, Spokane County, Wash.).* Newspaperman, Washington Democrat. U.S. Representative (1953-1963) serving on the Appropriations Committee.

MAGOFFIN, BERIAH *(b April 18, 1815, Harrodsburg, Ky.; d Feb. 28, 1885, Harrodsburg)* Lawyer, Kentucky Democrat who as governor (1859-1862) tried to maintain the state's neutrality at the start of the Civil War, failed to do so, and resigned. After the war he fell into even deeper disrepute with his party when he endorsed Kentucky's ratification of the Thirteenth Amendment and spoke out in favor of equal rights for Negroes. Democratic National Convention delegate (1848, 1856, 1860).

MAGOON, HENRY STERLING *(b Jan. 31, 1832, Monticello, Wis.; d March 3, 1889, Darlington, Wis.)* Ancient languages professor, lawyer, Republican who was the first native of Wisconsin to serve as a U.S. Representative (1875-1877) and, before that, as state senator (1871, 1872).

MAHON, THADDEUS MACLAY *(b May 21, 1840, Green Village, Pa.; d May 31, 1916, Scotland, Pa.)* Union soldier who was wounded in action (1864), lawyer, railroad president, Pennsylvania Republican. State representative (1870-1872), U.S. Representative (1893-1907).

MAHONE, WILLIAM *(b Dec. 1, 1826, Southampton County, Va.; d Oct. 8, 1895, Washington, D.C.)* Confederate Army officer who was hailed as a hero; railroad builder-executive who was called the Railroad Ishmael; the mainspring behind Virginia's Readjuster Movement (a form of populism) that provided the base upon which he became the state's undisputed Republican boss. Another appellation was King of the Lobby, which he earned while a U.S. Senator (1881-1887) through his ability to trade his one vote for patronage and important committee assignments.

MALCOLM X *(b May 19, 1925, Omaha, Nebr.; d Feb. 21, 1965, New York City by assassination while about to deliver a speech in a Harlem ballroom).* A man with a ghetto background who rose from waiter, marijuana pusher, burglar, and drug addict to found the fiercely nationalistic Organization of Afro-American Unity and became a much-in-demand lecturer before collegiate and white civic-minded audiences.

Born Malcolm Little, he became a follower of Elijah Muhammad and the Black Muslim sect while in prison (1946-1952), changed his name to Malcolm X, diligently studied Negro culture and history, emerged a forceful speaker, and remained faithful to the movement until expelled (1963) for declaring the John Kennedy assassination was a case of "chickens coming home to roost." Shortly thereafter his new organization was formed and was steadily gaining in national stature when a bullet cut short his life. He was buried under the name Al Hajj Malik al-Shabazz which he had adopted (1964) upon making a pilgrimage to Mecca.

MALLARY, ROLLIN CAROLAS *(b May 27, 1784, Cheshire, Conn.; d April 16, 1831, Baltimore, Md.)* Lawyer, Vermont Democrat. Secretary to the governor and council (1807, 1809-1812, 1815-1819), Rutland County state's attorney (1811-1813, 1815, 1816), U.S. Representative (1820 until death).

MALLORY, STEPHEN RUSSELL, SR. *(b 1812, Trinidad, West Indies; d Nov. 9, 1873, Pensacola, Fla.)* Lawyer, Seminole Indian fighter, Florida Democrat who as Confederate secretary of the navy during the Civil War succeeded in making the Southern fleet as strong as it was despite great obstacles. Monroe County judge (1837-1845), collector of the Port of Key West (1845), U.S. Senate (1851-1861).

MALLORY, STEPHEN RUSSELL, JR. *(b Nov. 2, 1848, Columbia, S.C.; d Dec. 23, 1907, Pensacola, Fla.)* Confederate Navy midshipman, Latin and Greek instructor at Georgetown College (1869-1871), lawyer, Florida Democrat. U.S. Representative (1891-1895), U.S. Senate (1897 until death).

MALONE, GEORGE WILSON *(b Aug. 7, 1890, Fredonia, Kans.; d May 19, 1961, Washington, D.C.)* Civil and hydraulic engineer, Nevada Republican. U.S. Senate (1947-1959) and then remaining in Washington as a consultant engineer.

MALONEY, FRANCIS THOMAS *(b March 31, 1894, Meriden, Conn.; d Jan. 16, 1945, Meriden)* Newspaperman, real estate-insurance broker, Connecticut Democrat. Mayor of Meriden (1929-1933), U.S. Representative (1933-1935), U.S. Senate (1935 until death).

MANDERSON, CHARLES FREDERICK *(b Feb. 9, 1837, Philadelphia, Pa.; d Sept. 28, 1911, Liverpool, England).* Severely wounded Union Army officer, lawyer who was president of the American Bar Association (1900), Nebraska Republican who as a U.S. Senator (1883-1895) in the days before the automobile strongly urged a federally built system "of great highways or boulevards that shall connect metropolitan centers." Stark County attorney (1867-1869) and Omaha City attorney for six years, state constitutional convention delegate (1871-1874), president pro tem of the U.S. Senate (1891-1893).

MANGUM, WILLIE PERSON *(b May 10, 1792, Orange, now Durham, County, N.C.; d Sept. 7, 1861, Red Mountain, now Rougemont, N.C.)* Lawyer, debater of note, North Carolina Democrat who broke with Andrew Jackson (which see) over the Bank of the United States issue and became a Whig. Recipient (1837) of South Carolina's eleven electoral votes for the presidency. North

Carolina state representative (1823-1826), U.S. Senate (1831-1836, 1840-1853) and president pro tem (1842-1845).

MANKIN, HELEN DOUGLAS (b Sept. 11, 1896, Atlanta, Ga.; d July 25, 1956, near College Park, Ga., in an auto accident) Lawyer, Georgia Democrat who was an ambulance driver (1918, 1919) in France during World War I. State assemblywoman (1937-1946), U.S. Representative (1946-1947).

MANLOVE, JOE JONATHAN (b Oct. 1, 1876, Jasper County, Mo.; d Jan. 31, 1956, Joplin, Mo.) Lawyer, farmer, real estate operator, Missouri Republican. Executive secretary of the Ozark Playgrounds Association (1920-1922), U.S. Representative (1923-1933).

MANN, HORACE (b May 4, 1796, Franklin, Mass.; d Aug. 2, 1859, Yellow Springs, Ohio) Lawyer, educator, humanitarian, antislavery Massachusetts Whig turned Free-Soiler who while president of the state senate (1835-1837) signed a historic educational bill creating a state board of education, became its secretary (1837-1848), and completely revised the public school system making it into a model for the nation. State representative (1827-1833), commissioner for the revision of state statutes (1835), state senate (1833-1837), U.S. Representative to fill a vacancy caused by the death of John Quincy Adams and then reelected (1848-1853), president of Antioch College (1853 until death). For ten of the years (1838-1848) that he served as board of education secretary, Mann also was editor of the Common School Journal, a semimonthly magazine that he established in order to better U.S. opinion on matters concerning public education.

MANN, JAMES ROBERT (b Oct. 20, 1856, McLean County, Ill.; d Nov. 30, 1922, Washington, D.C.) Lawyer, Illinois Republican who served a quarter-century as a U.S. Representative (1897 until death). Chicago councilman (1892-1896), state GOP convention chairman (1894), Cook County GOP convention chairman (1895, 1902), House minority leader (1911-1917). As a congressman he was associated with such lasting legislation as the women's suffrage amendment, the white-slave law known as the Mann Act, and the Pure Food and Drug Act of 1906.

MANSFIELD, JOSEPH JEFFERSON (b Feb. 9, 1861, Wayne, Va., now W.Va.; d July 12, 1947, in U.S. Naval Hospital, Bethesda, Md.) Farm laborer, freight clerk, a big man in Colorado County and Eagle Lake, Texas, establishing that city's first newspaper; Democrat who served thirty years as a U.S. Representative (1917 until death). Eagle Lake prosecutor (1888) and mayor (1889), Colorado County prosecutor (1892-1896), ex-officio county schools superintendent (1896-1910), county judge (1896-1916).

MANTLE, LEE (b Dec. 13, 1851, Birmingham, England; d Nov. 18, 1934, Los Angeles, Calif.) Telegraph operator, stagecoach agent, founder-manager-editor of the Inter Mountain, mine and real estate operator, Montana Republican with four years out (1896-1900) to organize and lead the Silver Republican party. Butte alderman (1881), territorial representative (1882, 1884, 1888) and house speaker in the latter year, GOP National Convention delegate (1884, 1896), mayor of Butte (1892), U.S. Senate (1895-1899).

MANZANARES, FRANCISCO ANTONIO (b Jan. 25, 1843, Abiguiu, N.Mex.; d Sept. 17, 1904, Las Vegas, N.Mex.). Merchant, wholesale grocer, New Mexico Democrat who successfully contested the election of Tranquilino Luna and completed his term as a delegate to Congress (March, 1884-March, 1885). Valencia County commissioner (1896, 1897).

MAPES, CARL EDGAR *(b Dec. 26, 1874, Eaton County, Mich.; d Dec. 12, 1939, New Orleans, La., while there as a House subcommittee member to take testimony on an oil conservation bill).* Lawyer, Michigan Republican who served fourteen terms (1913 until death) as a U.S. Representative. Kent County assistant prosecutor (1900-1904), state representative (1905-1907), state senate (1909-1913).

MARCANTONIO, VITO *(b Dec. 10, 1902, New York City; d Aug. 9, 1954, New York City)* Lawyer, New York Republican who embraced the American Labor party, a coalition of trade unionists, liberal Democrats, and leftists that dissolved after twenty years (1936-1956). As a Republican: assistant U.S. attorney (1930, 1931), U.S. Representative (1935-1937). As an American Laborite: U.S. Representative (1939-1951), unsuccessful candidate for mayor (1949).

MARCHANT, HENRY *(b April 9, 1741, Martha's Vineyard, Mass.; d Aug. 30, 1796, Newport, R.I.)* Lawyer who was prominent in Rhode Island's pre-Revolution affairs, a frequent visitor to England who kept in close touch with the nonconformists, radicals, and merchants there who called themselves the Friends of America; signer of the Articles of Confederation. Rhode Island attorney general (1771-1777), Continental Congress delegate (1777-1780, 1783, 1784), prime mover in the state convention (1789) that ratified the federal Constitution. His reward for the latter was appointment by President Washington to the federal bench (1790-1796).

MARCY, WILLIAM LEARNED *(b Dec. 12, 1786, Southbridge, Mass.; d July 4,* *1857, Ballston Spa, N.Y.).* Lawyer, statesman who negotiated twenty-four treaties with foreign countries, New York Democrat who helped to organize the so-called Albany Regency that held power for so long. Troy recorder (1816-1818), state adjutant general (1821) and comptroller (1823-1829) who did much to hold down the public debt, associate justice of the state supreme court (1829-1831), U.S. Senate (1831-1833), governor (1833-1839) who, though not an abolitionist, refused to extradite those who were, prime mover in the state's first geological survey and settler of the boundary dispute with New Jersey, Mexican claims commissioner (1839-1842), Democratic state convention president (1843), secretary of war in the Polk cabinet (1845-1849) and President Pierce's secretary of state (1853-1857).

MARSH, BENJAMIN FRANKLIN *(b 1839, Wythe Township, Ill.; d June 2, 1905, Warsaw, Ill.)* Union officer, lawyer, farmer, Illinois Republican. U.S. Representative (1877-1883, 1893-1901, 1903 until death), state railroad and warehouse commissioner (1889-1893), GOP National Convention delegate (1888).

MARSH, GEORGE PERKINS *(b March 15, 1801, Woodstock, Vt.; d July 24, 1882, Vallombrosa, Italy)* Lawyer, diplomat who was an authority on languages, Vermont Whig. Member of governor's council (1835), U.S. Representative (1843-1849), Taylor-appointed minister to Turkey (1849-1853) and head of a special mission to Greece (1852), state fish commissioner (1857) and railroad commissioner (1857-1859), Lincoln-appointed ambassador to Italy (1861 until death).

MARSHALL, FRED *(b March 13, 1906, Union Grove Township, Minn.)* Farmer, Minnesota Democrat. Member of state Agriculture Administration Committee

(1937-1941), state director of the Farm Security Administration (1941-1948), U.S. Representative (1949-1963) serving on the Appropriations Committee.

MARSHALL, HUMPHREY *(b 1760, Orlean, Va.; d July 1, 1841, Franklin County, Ky.)* Wealthy landowner, attorney, planter, author of *The History of Kentucky* (1812), and a Kentucky Federalist who somehow managed to survive in a state full of Jeffersonian Democrats, before statehood vigorously opposing separation from Virginia and voting against it at the Danville convention (1787). State representative (1793, 1807, 1808, 1823), U.S. Senate (1795-1801). Some of the major donnybrooks that he survived were a ducking in the Kentucky River, stoning by a mob in Frankfurt, a gun duel with Henry Clay, exposure of Aaron Burr's duplicity. Grandfather of the younger Humphrey Marshall, father of Thomas A. Marshall, and cousin of John Marshall.

MARSHALL, HUMPHREY *(b Jan. 13, 1812, Frankfort, Ky.; d March 28, 1872, Louisville, Ky.)* West Point graduate who was a brigadier general in the Confederate army, farmer, lawyer, Kentucky Whig turned Know-Nothing. U.S. Representative (1849-1852, 1855-1859), minister to China (1852-1854), member of the second Confederate Congress (1864-1865). Grandson of the elder Humphrey Marshall.

MARSHALL, JOHN *(b Sept. 24, 1755, Germantown, Va.; d July 6, 1835, Philadelphia, Pa.)* The fourth chief justice of the United States (1801 until death) and one of the ablest of all time, certainly the man who has left the most lasting imprint on the Supreme Court. Revolutionary Army officer at twenty-two, lawyer, statesman, a leader among Virginia Federalists although a distant relative of Thomas Jefferson; refused offers of high federal position by President Washington, among them attorney general.

Delegate to the state house of burgesses (1780, 1782-1788), member of the executive council (1782-1795), delegate to the state convention (1788) that ratified the U.S. Constitution, special commissioner to France in the "XYZ Affair" (1797-1798), U.S. Representative (1799-1800), secretary of state in the Adams cabinet (1800-1801). Cousin of the elder Humphrey Marshall.

MARSHALL, SAMUEL SCOTT *(b March 12, 1821, Gallatin County, Ill.; d July 26, 1890, McLeansboro, Ill.)* Lawyer, Illinois Democrat. State representative (1846, 1847), third judicial circuit state's attorney (1847, 1848) and circuit judge (1851-1854, 1861-1864), Democratic National Convention delegate (1860, 1864, 1880), Union National Convention Delegate (1866), U.S. Representative (1855-1859, 1865-1875), president of the Board of Managers of Hamilton College (1875-1880).

MARSHALL, THOMAS ALEXANDER *(b Jan. 15, 1794, near Versailles, Ky.; d April 17, 1871, Louisville, Ky.).* Lawyer who taught law at Transylvania College (1836-1849), Kentucky Whig turned Unionist. State representative (1827, 1828, 1863), U.S. Representative (1831-1835), state court of appeals judge (1835-1856) and the same court's chief justice ten years later (1866, 1867). Son of the elder and uncle of the younger Humphrey Marshall.

MARSHALL, THOMAS FRANK *(b March 7, 1854, Hannibal, Mo.; d Aug. 20, 1921, Detroit Lakes, Minn.)* Merchant, banker, surveyor, North Dakota Republican. Mayor of Oakes (1888-1892) GOP National Convention delegate (1892), U.S. Representative (1901-1909).

MARSHALL, THOMAS RILEY *(b March 14, 1854, North Manchester, Ind.; d June 1, 1925, Washington, D.C.)* Lawyer, reform governor of Indiana (1909-1913), vice president of the United States (1913-1921), and a Democratic wit who gave the nation such slogans as "what this country needs is a good five-cent cigar" and "Democrats, like poets, are born not made." One biographer describes him as "the most popular vice president the country ever had." He was loyal to such a degree that when Woodrow Wilson was ill he refused to consider the thought of being made president in his place.

MARTIN, ALEXANDER *(b 1740, Amwell Township, N.J.; d Nov. 10, 1807, Rockingham County, N.C.)* North Carolina lawyer, planter, who gave up positions under the crown to join the Continental Army and fight at such places as Germantown and Brandywine. Member of the colonial assembly (1774, 1775), state senate (1779-1782), acting governor (1781, 1782), governor (1782-1784, 1789-1792), delegate to state convention called to ratify the U.S. Constitution (1787), University of North Carolina trustee (1790-1807) and board president (1792, 1793), U.S. Senate (1793-1799).

MARTIN, AUGUSTUS NEWTON *(b March 23, 1847, Butler County, Pa.; d July 11, 1901, in Marion, Ind., Soldiers' Home Hospital)* Union soldier at sixteen, teacher, lawyer, Indiana Democrat. State representative (1875), state supreme court reporter (1876-1880), U.S. Representative (1889-1895).

MARTIN, CHARLES HENRY *(b Oct. 1, 1863, Edwards County, Ill.; d Sept. 22, 1946, Portland, Oregon)* West Point graduate and career army officer who upon retirement as a major general (1927) resided in Oregon and became actively interested in politics, as a Democrat. U.S. Representative (1931-1935), governor (1935-1939). In the army he saw combat in the Spanish-American War, Philippine Insurrection,

and the Boxer campaign in China; served as assistant chief of staff (1922-1924), and commanded the Panama Canal Department (1925-1927).

MARTIN, EBEN WEVER *(b April 12, 1855, Maquoketa, Iowa; d May 22, 1932, Hot Springs, S.Dak.)* Lawyer, South Dakota Republican. Territorial representative (1884, 1885), president of Deadwood Board of Education (1886-1900), U.S. Representative (1901-1907, 1908-1915).

MARTIN, JOHN ANDREW *(b April 10, 1868, Cincinnati, Ohio; d Dec. 23, 1939, Washington, D.C.)* Railroad construction hand, locomotive fireman, publisher of the *La Junta (Colo.) Times*, lawyer, Colorado Democrat. La Junta councilman (1895, 1896), state representative (1901, 1902), Pueblo city attorney (1905-1906, 1916-1917), U.S. Representative (1909-1913, 1933 until death).

MARTIN, JOSEPH WILLIAM, JR. *(Nov. 3, 1884, North Attleboro, Mass.; d March 7, 1968, Hollywood, Fla.)* One of seven children of a widowed mother, newsboy at seven who rose to publisher of the *North Attleboro Chronicle* (1908 until death), a power in Massachusetts and national Republican affairs during most of his adult life, conservative U.S. Representative for forty-two years (1925-1967) who regarded Roosevelt's New Deal as a form of fascism and Truman's Fair Deal as only slightly better, although he did vote for such measures as the Fair Labor Standards Act, the Norris-LaGuardia Anti-Injunction Act, and Social Security; considered one of the most skillful political technicians of his time, his credo was: "You've got to follow in order to lead," a tenet that he adhered to during twenty years in which he served almost continuously as House GOP leader (1939-1959) when he was replaced by Charles A. Halleck at a caucus in which the secret vote was 74-70 against him. His feelings about that rejection are spelled out in his autobiography *My First 50 Years in Politics.*

State representative (1912-1914), state senate (1914-1917), chairman of state railway investigating commission (1917), chairman of state legislative campaign committee (1917), presidential elector on the Harding-Coolidge ticket (1920), executive secretary of the GOP state executive committee (1922-1925), GOP National Convention chairman (1916, 1936, 1940, 1948, 1952, 1956) and permanent chairman (1940, 1944, 1948, 1952, 1956, 1960), GOP National Committee Chairman (1940-1942), House speaker (1946-1948, 1952-1954).

MARTIN, LUTHER *(b Feb. 9, 1744, New Brunswick, N.J.; d July 10, 1826, New York City, an impoverished, paralytic, alcoholic in the home of the friend whom he had defended against charges of treason, Aaron Burr)* Teacher, brilliant lawyer, Maryland patriot who vigorously prosecuted Loyalists during the Revolution, dedicated opponent of the federal Constitution, which he felt provided far too much centralization, and yet a Federalist because of his continuing feud with Thomas Jefferson. Member of the Annapolis convention (1774), state attorney general (1778-1805, 1818-1820), Continental Congress member (1784, 1785), federal constitutional convention delegate (1787) and state ratifying convention (1788), chief justice of the court of oyer and terminer for the city and county of Baltimore (1814).

MARTIN, THOMAS STAPLES *(b July 29, 1847, Scottsville, Va.; d Nov. 12, 1919, Charlottesville, Va.)* Lawyer, Virginia Democrat who, though a quiet man, as a U.S. Senator (1895 until death) knew politics inside out and so ruled his party in his home state.

MARTIN, WHITMELL PUGH *(b Aug. 12, 1867, Assumption Parish, La.; d April 6, 1929, Washington, D.C.)* Chemist, lawyer, Louisiana Progressive-Democrat. Kentucky Military Institute chemistry professor (1889, 1890), Lafourche Parish schools superintendent (1894-1900), twentieth district attorney (1900-1906), district judge (1906-1914), U.S. Representative (1915 until death).

MASON, JAMES MURRAY *(b Nov. 3, 1798, Analostan Island, Va.; d April 28, 1871, Alexandria, Va.)* Lawyer, Virginia Democrat who considered the conflict between North and South that preceded the Civil War as a clash between industrial and agricultural systems, author of the Fugitive Slave Law of 1850, Confederate statesman who almost, through no fault of his own, started a war between the United States and England. It happened like this: As the South's diplomatic commissioner to Britain and France, he was en route to Europe when the English mail steamer, *Trent,* on which he was a passenger, was stopped by a U.S. man-of-war (Nov. 8, 1861) that seized and took him to Boston where he was held prisoner until Jan. 2, 1862; only his release on orders from Washington staved off the threatened conflict.

State constitutional convention delegate (1829), state delegate (1826-1832), presidential elector on the Jackson-Van Buren ticket (1832), U.S. Representative (1837-1839), U.S. Senate (1847-1861) serving ten of those years as chairman of the Foreign Relations Committee.

MASON, JOHN YOUNG *(b April 18, 1799, Greensville County, Va.; d Oct. 3, 1859, Paris, while U.S. Minister to France, a post to which he had been appointed in 1854)* Lawyer, Virginia Democrat who served in the cabinets of Presidents Tyler and Polk. State delegate (1823-1827), state senate (1827-1831), U.S. Representative (1831-1837),

U.S. district judge (1837), state constitutional convention delegate (1829, 1850), secretary of the navy (1844-1845, 1846-1849), U.S. attorney general (1845-1846).

MASON, NOAH MORGAN *(b July 19, 1882, Glamorganshire, Wales; d Mar. 29, 1965, Joliet, Ill.)* Teacher, Illinois Republican who was a U.S. Representative twenty-six years (1937-1963). Oglesby schools superintendent (1908-1936), city commissioner (1918-1926), member of State Normal School Board (1926-1930), state senate (1930-1936). In Congress he was a member of the House Ways and Means Committee, the Joint Committee on Internal Revenue Taxation, and the Joint Committee on Reduction of Nonessential Federal Expenditures.

MASON, SAMSON *(b July 24, 1793, Fort Ann, N.Y.; d Feb. 1, 1869, Springfield, Ohio)* Lawyer, Ohio Whig. Clark County prosecutor (1822), state senate (1829-1831, 1862-1864), president judge of the court of common pleas (1834), U.S. Representative (1835-1843), state representative (1845, 1846), U.S. attorney (1850-1853), state constitutional convention delegate (1850).

MASON, STEVENS THOMSON *(b Oct. 27, 1811, Loudoun County, Va.; d Jan. 4, 1843, New York City)* The Boy Governor of Michigan (1835-1840), acquiring the name in this way: In 1830 he accompanied his father, John Thomson Mason, to the territory where the latter served as secretary until President Jackson sent him on a secret mission to Texas and Mexico (1831). Then Jackson, much to the irritation of the people, appointed young Mason, then only nineteen, to his father's created post and so he served until 1835. Meanwhile he studied for the law, the people learned to like him, he filled in occasionally as governor ex officio, registered as a Democrat, and took the lead in the drive for statehood. And the people, showing how their minds could change, elected him the state's first governor at the age of twenty-four. A year after leaving office he moved to New York where he practiced law until death. In 1905, the people of Michigan arranged to have his body reinterred in Detroit's Capitol Square.

MASON, WILLIAM ERNEST *(b July 7, 1850, Franklinville, N.Y.; d June 16, 1921, Washington, D.C., when his daughter, Winnifred Sprague Mason Huck, succeeded him in Congress).* Teacher, lawyer, Illinois Republican. State representative (1879), state senate (1882-1885), U.S. Representative (1887-1891, 1917 until death), U.S. Senate (1897-1903).

MASSINGALE, SAMUEL CHAPMAN *(b Aug. 2, 1870, Quitman, Miss.; d Jan. 17, 1941, Washington, D.C.)* Lawyer, Oklahoma Democrat. Member of the territorial council (1902), U.S. Representative (1935 until death).

MATHEWS, GEORGE *(b Aug. 30, 1739, Augusta County, Va.; d Aug. 30, 1812, Augusta, Ga.)* Farmer, Revolutionary soldier who was wounded and captured at Brandywine, governor of Georgia (1787-1788, 1793-1796) and a member of the House in the First Congress (1789-1791). In the episode for which he is most remembered, he was the instigator of an insurrection whose aim was to separate west from east Florida through armed invasion (which he led in 1811) and to gain independence from Spain.

MATHEWS, JOHN *(b 1744, Charleston, S.C.; d Nov. 17, 1802, Charleston)* Indian fighter, lawyer, South Carolina patriot and Continental Army officer. Member of the commons house of assembly (1772), the General Committee of Ninety-Nine (1774) and the First and Second Provincial Congresses (1775-

1776); associate circuit court judge (1776), state representative (1776-1780, 1784) and house speaker (1777, 1778), Continental Congress delegate (1778-1782), governor (1782, 1783), chancery court judge (1784), equity court judge (1791-1797).

MATLACK, TIMOTHY *(b 1730, Haddonfield, N.J.; d April 14, 1829, Holmesburg, Pa.)* Merchant, Quaker who nevertheless commanded a battalion of Philadelphia Associators during the Revolution, a founder of the Society of Free Quakers (1781), and, as assistant secretary of the Continental Congress with great skill in penmanship, probably the man who prepared the official Declaration of Independence. Provincial conference delegate (1775), state constitutional convention delegate (1776) where he was appointed secretary of state, a member of the Committee of Safety and keeper of the great seal, member of the University of Pennsylvania's first Board of Trustees (1779), Continental Congress delegate (1780, 1781), master of the state rolls (1800-1809).

MATSON, COURTLAND CUSHING *(b April 25, 1841, Brookville, Ind.; d Sept. 4, 1915, Chicago, Ill.)* Lawyer, Indiana Democrat. U.S. Representative (1881-1889).

MATTHEWS, DONALD RAY "BILLY" *(b Oct. 3, 1907, Micanopy, Fla.)* Teacher, Florida Democrat. State representative (1935), U.S. Army (1942-1946), U.S. Representative (1953-1967) serving on the Appropriations Committee.

MATTHEWS, STANLEY *(b July 21, 1824, Cincinnati, Ohio; d March 22, 1889, Washington, D.C.)* Editor of the *Cincinnati Herald* (1846-1879), sponsored the Matthews Resolution that made silver legal tender, and a man whom the Senate failed to confirm as associate justice of the U.S. Supreme Court when nominated by President

Hayes (Jan. 26, 1881) but who was approved when renominated two months later (March 14, 1881) and was seated in May, serving until death. Hamilton County assistant prosecutor (1845), state house clerk (1848-1850), common pleas judge (1850-1852), U.S. attorney (1858-1861), Cincinnati Superior Court judge (1863-1864), presidential elector (1864, 1868).

MATTOCKS, JOHN *(b March 4, 1777, Hartford, Conn.; d Aug. 14, 1847, Peacham, Vt.)* Lawyer, vehemently anti-slavery Vermont Whig who (and this has nothing to do with slavery) found out just how unpopular a man can become when, as governor (1843, 1844), he tried to have Thanksgiving observed on Dec. 25, thus, cried his outraged opponents, attempting to turn Christmas into a Pumpkin Pie Holiday. State representative (1807, 1815, 1816, 1823, 1824), U.S. Representative (1821-1823, 1825-1827, 1841-1843), state supreme court judge (1833, 1834), state constitutional convention delegate (1836).

MAVERICK, FONTAINE MAURY *(b Oct. 23, 1895, San Antonio, Texas; d June 7, 1954, San Antonio)* Lawyer, World War I officer who was awarded the Silver Star and Purple Heart, homebuilder, liberal Texas Democrat. Bexar County tax collector (1929-1931), Democratic National Convention delegate (1928, 1940), U.S. Representative (1935-1939), mayor of San Antonio (1939-1941), divisional director and later vice chairman of the War Production Board, and chairman of the Smaller War Plants Corporation during World War II.

MAXEY, SAMUEL BELL *(b March 30, 1825, Tomkinsville, Ky.; d Aug. 16, 1895, Eureka Springs, Ark.)* West Point graduate and friend of the Indians who organized three brigades of them to fight on the side of the South in the

Civil War, Confederate Army officer, lawyer, Texas Democrat. In Kentucky before moving to Texas: County and circuit courts clerk and master in chancery (1852-1856). In Texas: Lamar County district attorney (1858, 1859), Confederate commander of the Indian Territory military district and superintendent of Indian affairs (1863-1865), U.S. Senate (1875-1887).

MAXWELL, AUGUSTUS EMMETT (b Sept. 21, 1820, Elberton, Ga.; d May 5, 1903, Chipley, Fla.) Lawyer, railroad president, Florida Democrat who was a Confederate senator (1862-1865) during the Civil War. State attorney general (1846, 1847), state representative (1847) and secretary of state (1848), state senate (1849, 1850), U.S. Representative (1853-1857), U.S. Navy agent (1857-1861), state supreme court judge (1865, 1866).

MAXWELL, SAMUEL (b May 20, 1825, Lodi, N.Y.; d Feb. 11, 1901, Fremont, Nebr.) Teacher, lawyer, farmer and a Nebraska pioneer who was a delegate to the first Republican territorial convention there, switched to Populism and was elected a U.S. Representative (1897-1899) on a fusion ticket. Territorial representative (1859, 1860, 1864, 1865), delegate to territorial constitutional convention (1864, 1865) and state constitutional convention (1875), member of the first state house of representatives (1866), member of a governor's committee to select capitol building plans and university lands (1867), state supreme court justice (1873-1894) much of that time serving as chief justice.

MAY, ANDREW JACKSON (b June 24, 1875, Floyd County, Ky.; d Sept. 6, 1959, Prestonsburg, Ky.) Teacher, lawyer, farmer, mine and bank executive in Kentucky who served eight terms as a U.S. Representative (1931-1947). Floyd

County attorney (1901-1909), special circuit court judge in Johnson and Martin counties (1925, 1926).

MAYBANK, BURNET RHETT (b March 7, 1899, Charleston, S.C.; d Sept. 1, 1954, Flat Rock, N.C.) Cotton exporter and a South Carolina Democrat who was a leader in political affairs at all levels. Charleston alderman (1927-1931) and mayor (1931-1938), a state advisor to the U.S. Public Works Administration (1933-1934), state Public Service Authority chairman (1934-1939) and bank control board member (1933-1934), governor (1939-1941), U.S. Senate (1941 until death).

MAYNARD, HORACE (b Aug. 30, 1814, Westboro, Mass.; d May 3, 1882, Knoxville, Tenn.) University of East Tennessee (now Tennessee) math professor (1839-1844), lawyer, orator whose doubts about a nation torn drove him from Whig to Know-Nothing to Republican to Unionist and to Radical Republicanism in Tennessee. Presidential elector on the Whig's Scott-Graham (1852) and the GOP's Lincoln-Johnson tickets (1864), U.S. Representative (1857-1863 as a Know-Nothing and 1866-1875 as a Republican), military government state attorney general (1863-1865), Southern Loyalist Convention delegate (1866), unsuccessful gubernatorial candidate (1874), minister to Turkey (1875-1880), postmaster general in the Hayes cabinet (1880-1881).

MAYS, JAMES HENRY (b June 29, 1868, Morristown, Tenn.; d April 19, 1926, near Wendell, Idaho) Kansas miner and lumberman; Illinois, Iowa, and Utah insurance salesman; Michigan, Indiana, and Utah lawyer; Idaho rancher; Utah industrialist, staying put in Utah long enough to be three times elected a U.S. Representative (1915-1921) as a Democrat.

MEACHAM, JAMES *(b Aug. 16, 1810, Rutland, Vt.; d Aug. 23, 1856, Rutland).* Clergyman, Vermont Whig. Middlebury College professor (1846-1850), U.S. Representative (1849 until death).

MEADER, GEORGE *(b Sept. 13, 1907, Benton Harbor, Mich.)* Lawyer, Michigan Republican. Washtenaw County prosecuting attorney (1941-1943), assistant counsel to U.S. Senate special committee investigating national defense program (1943-1945), chief counsel (1945-1947), chief counsel of U.S. Senate Banking and Currency Subcommittee investigating the Reconstruction Finance Corporation (1950), U.S. Representative (1951-1965) serving on the Government Operations and Judiciary committees.

MEDARY, SAMUEL *(b Feb. 25, 1801, Montgomery County, Pa.; d Nov. 7, 1864, Columbus, Ohio)* Founder-publisher of the *Ohio Sun* and *Ohio Statesman*, using the former to gain power in state Democratic circles and the latter to entrench himself as boss of the party for a decade or more. Outspoken on national matters in his editorial columns, he backed Texas annexation, Oregon's reoccupation, the Mexican War, and the Kansas-Nebraska Act. He held several local and state offices, ranging from school trustee to state legislator before moving on to more nationally noted positions: temporary chairman of the Democratic National Convention (1856), governor of the Minnesota Territory (1857-1858), governor of the Kansas Territory (1858-1860).

MEDILL, JOSEPH *(b April 6, 1823, near St. John, New Brunswick, Canada; d March 16, 1899, San Antonio, Tex.).* Ohio abolitionist-journalist who, with his brothers, bought the *Coshocton (Ohio) Whig* (1849), immediately changed its name to *Coshocton Republican*, nine years later purchased an interest in the *Chicago Tribune*, became

active in the formation of a new national party and, some say, urged upon it (1856) the title of his old newspaper. And thus, it is said, the Republican party got its name. Be that as it may, Medill became a close friend of Abraham Lincoln and helped to win him the 1860 presidential nomination. He himself was a member of the Illinois constitutional assembly (1869), a U.S. Civil Service commissioner under President Grant, and mayor of Chicago in the term that immediately followed the great fire of 1871.

MEIGS, RETURN JOHNATHAN, JR. *(b Nov. 16, 1764, Middletown, Conn.; d March 29, 1825, Marietta, Ohio)* Lawyer who first practiced in what was then the Northwest Territory, Indian fighter, Ohio Democrat. Territorial judge (1802, 1803), chief justice of the Ohio Supreme Court (1803, 1804), Louisiana Supreme Court judge (1805, 1806), U.S. judge in the Michigan Territory (1807, 1808). And then in Ohio; U.S. Senate (1808-1810), fusionist governor (1810-1814), postmaster general in the Madison and Monroe cabinets (1814-1823).

MERCER, CHARLES FENTON *(b June 16, 1778, Fredericksburg, Va.; d May 4, 1858, Howard, Va.)* Orphan boy who paid off his father's debts, lawyer, a founder and first president of the Chesapeake & Ohio Canal Co. (1828-1833), Virginia Federalist turned Whig who strongly opposed the slave trade and did much to further the colonization of free Negroes in Liberia during his nearly quarter-century (1817-1839) as a U.S. Representative.

MERCER, DAVID HENRY *(b July 9, 1857, Benton County, Iowa; d Jan. 10, 1919, Omaha, Nebr.)* Lawyer, Nebraska Republican who was something of a power in the party for many years, serving as chairman of Omaha city and county committees and then moving up to U.S. Representative (1893-1903), secretary of the GOP state central committee (1896) and chairman (1897, 1898), secretary of the GOP National Congressional Committee (1896).

MERCER, JAMES *(b Feb. 26, 1736, Stafford County, Va.; d Oct. 31, 1793, Richmond, Va.)* French and Indian fighter, lawyer, Virginia patriot who was active in pre-Revolution affairs. Member of house of burgesses (1762-1776), Virginia conventions (1774, 1775, 1776), Committee of Public Safety (1775, 1776), state constitutional convention (1776), Continental Congress (1779, 1780), judge of the general court (1779-1789), and the first Virginia Court of Appeals (1789 until death). Half-brother of John F. Mercer.

MERCER, JOHN FRANCIS *(b May 17, 1759, Stafford County, Va.; d Aug. 30, 1821, Philadelphia, Pa.)* Continental Army officer, Virginia lawyer who later moved to Maryland where he continued his political activities, enrolling in Jefferson's new Democratic-Republican party. Virginia delegate to the Continental Congress (1782-1785). In Maryland: federal convention delegate (1787) where he strongly opposed the centralized powers contained in the proposed U.S. Constitution and carried his opposition to the state ratifying convention (1788), state house of delegates (1788, 1789, 1791, 1792, 1800, 1803-1806), U.S. Representative (1792-1794), governor (1801-1803). Half-brother of James Mercer.

MERRITT, MATTHEW JOSEPH *(b April 2, 1895, New York City; d Sept. 29, 1946, Malba, Queens, N.Y.)* Real estate and insurance broker, New York Democrat, U.S. Representative (1935-1945).

MERRITT, SAMUEL AUGUSTUS *(b Aug. 15, 1827, Staunton, Va.; d Sept. 8, 1910, Salt Lake City, Utah)* Lawyer, mine operator, California, Idaho Territory, and Utah Territory Democrat. In California: Mariposa County clerk and public administrator (1850), state representative (1851, 1852), state senate (1857-1862). In Idaho: delegate to Congress (1871-1873). In Utah: Salt Lake City attorney (1888-1890), Democratic National Committeeman (1892), chief justice of the territorial supreme court (1894-1896).

MERRITT, SCHUYLER *(b Dec. 16, 1853, New York City; d April 1, 1953, Stamford, Conn.)* Lock and key manufacturer, banker, Connecticut Republican. State constitutional convention delegate (1904), Connecticut Board of Education member (1910-1916), GOP National Convention delegate (1916), U.S. Representative (1917-1931, 1933-1937).

MERROW, CHESTER EARL *(b Nov. 15, 1906, Center Ossipee, N.H.)* Educator, lecturer, news commentator, New Hampshire Republican. State representative (1939, 1940), U.S. Representative (1943-1963), delegate to United Nations Educational and Cultural Conference in London (1945), congressional advisor to first conference of U.N. Educational, Scientific and Cultural Organization in Paris (1946) and member of U.S. delegation to the organization (1946-1949); member of House Foreign Affairs Committee.

METCALF, JESSE HOUGHTON *(b Nov. 16, 1860, Providence, R.I.; d Oct. 9, 1942, Providence)* Textile manufacturer, Brown University trustee, Rhode Island Republican. State representative (1889-1891, 1907), Providence councilman (1888-1892), Metropolitan Park Commission chairman (1909-1924), member of penal and charitable board (1917-1923), GOP National Committeeman (1935-1940), U.S. Senate (1924-1937).

METCALF, VICTOR HOWARD *(b Oct. 10, 1853, Utica, N.Y.; d Feb. 20, 1936,*

Oakland, Calif.) Lawyer, banker, California Republican who held two positions in the Theodore Roosevelt cabinet. U.S. Representative (1899-1904), resigning to become secretary of commerce and labor (1904-1906), and quitting that to become secretary of the navy (1906-1908).

METCALFE, THOMAS *(b March 20, 1780, Fauquier County, Va.; d Aug. 18, 1855, Nicholas County, Ky.)* Stone mason, farmer, antisecessionist Kentucky Democrat-National Republican-Whig. State representative (1812-1816), U.S. Representative (1819-1828), governor (1828-1832), state senate (1834), president of state Board of Improvement (1840), U.S. Senate to fill a vacancy (June 1848-March 1849).

MEYER, ADOLPH *(b Oct. 19, 1842, Natchez, Miss.; d March 8, 1908, New Orleans, La.)* Confederate Army officer, planter, banker, Louisiana Democrat. U.S. Representative (1891 until death).

MEYER, HERBERT ALTON *(b Aug. 30, 1886, Chillicothe, Ohio; d Oct. 2, 1950, in U.S. Naval Hospital, Bethesda, Md.).* Lawyer, oil marketing executive, publisher of the *Independence (Kans.) Daily Reporter,* Kansas Republican. Assistant to the U.S. secretary of the interior (1915-1917), U.S. Representative (1947 until death).

MICHAELSON, MAGNE ALFRED *(b Sept. 7, 1878, Kristiansand, Norway; d Oct. 26, 1949, Chicago, Ill.)* Teacher, banker, Illinois Republican. Chicago councilman (1915-1918), state constitutional convention delegate (1920), U.S. Representative (1921-1931).

MICHENER, EARL CORY *(b Nov. 30, 1876, Seneca County, Ohio; d July 4, 1957, Adrian, Mich.)* Lawyer, Michigan Republican who served thirty years (1919-1933, 1935-1951) as a U.S. Representative. Lenawee County assistant prosecutor (1907-1910).

MIDDLETON, ARTHUR *(b June 26, 1742, Berkeley County, S.C.; d Jan. 1, 1787, near Charleston, S.C.)* Lawyer, planter, one of five South Carolinians who stole weapons (April 21, 1776) from a public storehouse with which to fight the British, signer of the Declaration of Independence, Revolutionary militiaman who was captured (1780) during the siege of Charleston, political leader who advocated the property seizure and expulsion of loyalists but opposed their tarring and feathering.

Berkeley County justice of the peace (1765, 1776-1786), member of provincial house of commons (1765-1768, 1772-1775), provincial convention delegate (1774, 1775), member of Council of Safety (1775, 1776), delegate to Provincial Congress that drafted state constitution (1776), delegate to the Continental Congress (1776-1778, 1781-1783), state representative (1778-1780, 1785, 1786), state senate (1781, 1782), member of the privy council (1782). Son of the elder Henry Middleton, father of the younger Henry Middleton.

MIDDLETON, HENRY *(b 1717, near Charleston, S.C.; d June 13, 1784, Charleston)* Owner of 20 plantations, 50,000 acres of land, and 800 slaves, South Carolina patriot who however shared none of his son Arthur's passion for action, believing that colonial differences with the British could be negotiated and in fact resigned from the Continental Congress (February 1776) when he found himself very much in the minority. Justice of the peace and quorum (1742-1780), member of the provincial house of commons (1742-1755) and its speaker (1745-1747, 1754, 1755), Indian affairs commissioner (1755), member of the King's Provincial Council (1755-1770), provincial convention delegate (1774), delegate to the Continental Congress (1774-1776) and its second president (1774-1775), Council of Safety (1775, 1776), member of the Provincial Congress (1775, 1776), member of the transition government council (1776-1778), state senate (1778-1780) taking protection from the British after the surrender of Charleston but without loss of reputation or holdings. Father of Arthur Middleton, grandfather of the younger Henry Middleton—see next entry.

MIDDLETON, HENRY *(b Sept. 28, 1770, London, England; d June 14, 1846, Charleston, S.C.)* Planter, diplomat, South Carolina Democrat who did not go along with Calhoun's nullification theory and so helped to found and to lead the Union party there. State representative (1802-1810), state senate (1810), governor (1810-1812), U.S. Representative (1815-1819), minister to Russia (1820-1830), antitariff convention delegate (1831), Union Convention vice president (1833). Son of Arthur Middleton, grandson of the elder Henry Middleton.

MIFFLIN, THOMAS *(b Jan. 10, 1744, Philadelphia, Pa.; d Jan. 19, 1800, Lancaster, Pa.)* Merchant, one of the youngest and most radical members of the First Continental Congress, Continental Army officer who for a time was an aide to General Washington (later involved in the cabal that tried to replace Washington), Pennsylvania Democrat. Member of American Philosophical Society (1765-1799), colonial legislator (1772-1774), Continental Congress (1774-1776, 1782-1784) and its president (1783), University of Pennsylvania trustee (1778-1791), state representative (1785-1788, 1799-1800), serving as speaker from 1785 to 1788, federal Constitutional Convention delegate (1787), president of the state supreme executive council (1788-1790) and the state constitutional convention (1790), governor (1790-1799).

MILLEDGE, JOHN *(b 1757, Savannah, Ga.; d Feb. 9, 1818, near Augusta, Ga.).* Young lawyer who, upon hearing the news from Lexington and Concord, helped break into a Savannah warehouse and steal 600 pounds of powder, some of which allegedly was used at Bunker Hill; Revolutionary soldier, Georgia Democrat who donated the site for the University of Georgia. Attorney general (1780), state representative (1782), U.S. Representative (1792-1793, 1795-1799, 1801-1802), governor (1802-1806), U.S. Senator (1806-1809) and Senate president pro tem (1809).

MILLER, FRIEDA SEGELKE *(b April 16, 1889, La Crosse, Wis.)* Labor expert who championed improved working conditions, especially for women, and U.S. government official. Social economy teacher, Bryn Mawr College (1916-1917); New York state labor commissioner (1929-1938); New York state industrial commissioner (1938-1943); special assistant to U.S. ambassador to England, John G. Winant (1943-1944); director of U.S. Department of Labor's Women's Bureau (1944-1953); U.S. representative at the 1946 conference of the International Labour Organisation and, that same year, U.S. delegate to United Nations General Assembly.

MILLER, JACOB WELSH *(b Aug. 29, 1800, German Valley, N.J.; d Sept. 30, 1862, Morristown, N.J.)* Lawyer, New Jersey Whig. Member of state assembly (1832) and state council (1838-1840), U.S. Senate (1841-1853).

MILLER, JAMES MONROE *(b May 6, 1852, Three Springs, Pa.; d Jan. 20, 1926, Council Grove, Kans.)* Lawyer, Kansas Republican. Morris County prosecutor (1880-1888), presidential elector on the Blaine-Logan ticket (1884), state representative (1894, 1895), U.S. Representative (1899-1911).

MILLER, JOHN *(b Nov. 25, 1781, Berkeley County, Va., now W.Va.; d March 18, 1846, near Florissant, Mo.).* Newspaper publisher, writer, Missouri Democrat who as governor (1825-1832) advocated state and federal policing of the Santa Fe Trail against brigands and the establishment of state colleges and libraries. Franklin Land Office register (1818-1825), U.S. Representative (1837-1843).

MILLER, JOHN FRANKLIN *(b Nov. 21, 1831, South Bend, Ind.; d March 8, 1886, Washington, D.C.)* Lawyer, Union Army officer, Indiana and California Republican. In Indiana: state senate (1860). In California: San Francisco port collector (1867-1871), delegate to the second state constitutional convention (1878-1879), U.S. Senate (1881 until death). Uncle of the following.

MILLER, JOHN FRANKLIN *(b June 9, 1862, St. Joseph County, Ind.; d May 28, 1936, Seattle, Wash.)* Lawyer, Washington Republican. King County prosecutor (1890-1894) and deputy prosecutor (1905-1908), mayor of Seattle (1908-1910), U.S. Representative (1917-1931). Nephew of the preceding.

MILLER, STEPHEN DECATUR *(b May 8, 1787, Lancaster District, S.C.; d March 8, 1838, Raymond, Miss.)* Lawyer, cotton grower, South Carolina Democrat who believed in Calhoun's theory of nullification and while governor (1828-1830) did much to turn the people against Congress, then was elected to U.S. Senate as a Nullifier and served from 1831 to 1833 when he resigned, supposedly because of poor health. U.S. Representative (1817-1819), state senate (1822-1828), delegate to state nullification conventions (1830, 1832).

MILLER, THOMAS EZEKIEL *(b June 17, 1849, Ferrebeville, S.C., of free Negro parents; d April 8, 1938, Charleston, S.C.)* Railroad newsboy who studied for the law and became interested both in education and politics, South Carolina Republican. Beaufort County school superintendent (1872), state representative (1874, 1876, 1878, 1894), state executive committeeman (1878-1880), state senate (1880), U.S. Representative (1890-1891), state constitutional convention delegate (1895), president of the State Colored College (1896-1911), the first such institution in South Carolina.

MILLER, WARNER *(b Aug. 12, 1838, Hannibal, N.Y.; d March 21, 1918, New York City)* Briefly a Union soldier, developer of a new process for making paper out of wood pulp, a highly nationalistic New York Republican who strongly favored exclusion of Chinese from American shores, and a power in his party being a delegate to all national conventions (1872, 1884-1896), and all state and county conventions for forty years, and Herkimer County GOP chairman for ten years. State assemblyman (1874, 1875), U.S. Representative (1879-1881), U.S. Senate (1881-1887), chairman of the state's special tax commission (1906).

MILLER, WILLIAM JENNINGS *(b March 12, 1899, North Andover, Mass.; d Nov. 22, 1950, Wethersfield, Conn.).* World War I soldier who lost both legs in a plane crash in France (1918) and was hospitalized until 1931, then went into the insurance business in Connecticut and became interested in politics as a Republican. U.S. Representative (1939-1941, 1943-1945, 1947-1949).

MILLIGAN, JACOB LeROY *(b March 9, 1889, Richmond, Mo.; d March 9, 1951, Kansas City, Mo.)* Lawyer, Missouri Democrat. U.S. Representative (1920-1921, 1923-1935), Democratic National Convention delegate (1928), president of Kansas City Police Board (1949-1950).

MILLIGAN, JOHN JONES *(b Dec. 10, 1795, Bohemia Manor, Md.; d April 20, 1875, Philadelphia, Pa.)* Lawyer, Delaware Whig who sat on the state superior court bench for a quarter-century (1839-1864). Before that he was a U.S. Representative (1831-1839).

MILLIKEN, SETH LLEWELLYN *(b Dec. 12, 1831, Montville, Maine; d April 18, 1897, Washington, D.C.)* Lawyer, Maine Republican. State representative (1857, 1858), supreme judicial court clerk (1859-1871), GOP National Convention delegate (1876, 1884), presidential elector on the Hayes-Wheeler ticket (1876), U.S. Representative (1883 until death).

MILLIKIN, EUGENE DONALD *(b Feb. 12, 1891, Hamilton, Ohio; d July 26, 1958, Denver, Colo.)* Lawyer, oil company president, Colorado Republican. Executive secretary to Governor George A. Carlson (1915-1917), U.S. Senate (1941-1957).

MILLS, OGDEN LIVINGSTON *(b Aug. 23, 1884, Newport, R.I.; d Oct. 11, 1937, New York City)* Lawyer, author, lecturer, wealthy New York Republican who chose politics as a career and was considered an expert on fiscal matters yet lost a public debate (1925) with Governor Alfred E. Smith concerning a $100 million bond issue; a foe of Roosevelt's New Deal liberalism, but a liberal by his own standards, and a man who was seriously considered for the GOP presidential nomination (1936) that ultimately went to Governor Alfred M. Landon of Kansas. GOP National Convention delegate (1912, 1916, 1920) and chairman of the policies and platform committee (1920), state senate (1914-1917), World War I infantry captain, U.S. Representative (1921-1927), Smith's unsuccessful gubernatorial opponent (1926); Coolidge-appointed undersecretary of the treasury (1927-1932) and continuing under Hoover then, when Secretary Andrew W. Mellon was made ambassador to England, being elevated to the top spot (1932-1933).

MILLS, ROGER QUARLES *(b March 30, 1832, Todd County, Ky.; d Sept. 2, 1911, Corsicana, Tex.)* Lawyer, Confederate Army officer who was wounded at Missionary Ridge and Atlanta, Texas Democrat who while a U.S. Representative (1873-1892) wrote the Mills Tariff Reduction Bill (1887). U.S. Senate (1892-1899).

MILLSON, JOHN SINGLETON *(b Oct. 1, 1808, Norfolk, Va.; d March 1, 1874, Norfolk)* Lawyer, Virginia Democrat. Presidential elector on the Polk-Dallas (1844) and Cass-Butler (1848) tickets, U.S. Representative (1849-1861).

MINOR, EDWARD SLOMAN *(b Dec. 13, 1840, Point Peninsula, N.Y.; d July 26, 1924, Sturgeon Bay, Wis.)* Hardware merchant, horticulturist, Union Army officer, Wisconsin Republican. State assemblyman (1877, 1881, 1882), state senator (1883-1886) and senate president during his last term, Sturgeon Bay and Lake Michigan Ship Canal superintendent (1884-1891), state fish commissioner (1891-1894), mayor of Sturgeon Bay (1894, 1918), U.S. Representative (1895-1907), Sturgeon Bay postmaster (1911-1915).

MITCHELL, GEORGE EDWARD *(b March 3, 1781, Elkton, Md.; d June 28, 1832, Washington, D.C.)* Physician, War of 1812 army officer who was in command at the successful defense of Fort Oswego, N.Y., Maryland Democrat. Member of state house of delegates (1808) and president of the executive council (1809-1812), U.S. Representative (1823-1827, 1829 until death).

MITCHELL, JOHN HIPPLE *(b June 22, 1835, Washington County, Pa.; d Dec. 8, 1905, Portland, Oregon)* Lawyer, Willamette University professor (1867), Oregon Republican whom one biographer described as "an adroit, disreputable, and very popular political leader." Portland corporation attorney (1861), state senator (1862-1866) and senate president (1864-1866), U.S. Senate (1873-1879, 1885-1897, 1901 until death).

MITCHELL, NATHANIEL *(b 1753, Sussex County, Del.; d Feb. 21, 1814, Laurel, Del.)* Farmer, Revolutionary Army officer, Delaware Federalist. Delgate to the Continental Congress (1786-1788), Sussex County chief clerk (1788-1805), Federalist presidential elector who voted for Adams and Pinckney (1800), governor (1805-1808), state representative (1808), state senate (1810-1812).

MITCHILL, SAMUEL LATHAM *(b Aug. 20, 1764, Hempstead, N.Y.; d Sept. 7, 1831, New York City)* Physician, lawyer, educator, New York Democrat. Commissioner to purchase Iroquois Indian land (1788), state assemblyman (1791, 1798), one of the founders of the State Society for the Promotion of Agriculture (1793), Columbia College professor of chemistry and natural history (1792), editor of the *N.Y. Medical Repository* (1797-1813), U.S. Representative (1801-1804, 1810-1813), U.S. Senate (1804-1809), founding president of the Lyceum of Natural History (1817-1823), New York College of Physicians and Surgeons professor of natural history (1808-1820) and botany and materia medica (1820-1826), vice president of Rutgers Medical School (1826-1830).

MONDELL, FRANKLIN WHEELER *(b Nov. 6, 1860, St. Louis, Mo.; d Aug. 6, 1939, Washington, D.C.)* Orphan boy who made good in a rugged way, working in the West as a miner, store clerk, gandy dancer, and a variety of other jobs and ventures, ultimately signing on to prospect for coal and oil for a rail-road, opened Wyoming's rich Cambria coal mines, founded the town of Newcastle, became an ultraconservative law-and-order Wyoming Republican who was wounded while leading a posse and carried two slugs in his body for the rest of his life.

At the age of sixty-four he became a lawyer and in that same year the *New York Times*, in describing his role as permanent chairman of the 1924 GOP National Convention, said: "The word 'reactionary' is a mild one as applied to (his) pre-Adamite views." On giving up public life, Mondell became a lobbyist for the Wyoming Wool Growers Association. Mayor of Newcastle (1888-1895), member of the first state senate (1890-1892) and president of the second (1892-1894), GOP National Convention delegate (1892, 1900, 1904, 1908, 1912), U.S. Representative (1895-1897, 1899-1923) and majority leader (1919-1923), assistant General Land Office commissioner (1897-1899), War Finance Corporation director (1923-1925).

MONEY, HERNANDO De SOTO *(b Aug. 26, 1839, Zeiglersville, Miss.; d Sept. 18, 1912, Harrison County, Miss.).* Lawyer, Confederate soldier, planter, newspaper editor, Mississippi Democrat who successfully fought the carpetbaggers, was elected a U.S. Representative (1875-1885, 1893-1897) and a U.S. Senator (1897-1911). As chairman of the House Committee on Post Offices and Post Roads he took the lead in bringing an end to the star route system of mail handling and reduced first-class rates from three to two cents.

MONROE, JAMES *(b April 28, 1758, Westmoreland County, Va.; d July 4, 1831, New York City)* Fifth president (Virginia Democratic-Republican), 1817-1825, for whom Monroe Doctrine was named.

Son of a moderately wealthy Virginia planter, Monroe attended the College of William and Mary for two years but dropped out at the outbreak of the Revolutionary War to join a Virginia regiment. He fought in numerous battles and rose to rank of lieutenant colonel. Became Thomas Jefferson's protégé, studying law with him (1780-1783). Married Elizabeth Kortright (1786), who bore him two daughters, and built a home for his family, "Ash Lawn," near Jefferson's Monticello.

Member Virginia Assembly (1782, 1786, 1810, 1811); delegate to the Continental Congress (1783-1786). As a delegate to Virginia's convention to consider the federal Constitution (1788), he opposed ratification, fearing the document would place too much power in a centralized government at the expense of individual states' rights. After ratification, he lost to Madison in a bid for a congressional seat but was appointed to fill an unexpired term in the U.S. Senate and was reelected for the following term, serving from 1790 until his resignation in 1794. He became a staunch supporter of the Democratic-Republicans in their opposition to Federalist policies such as broad interpretation of the Constitution, a strong centralized government, and anything that seemed to favor industrial development over agrarian interests.

Monroe then began a diplomatic career that had its ups and downs. Because of his pronounced sympathy for revolutionary France, Washington sent him there as minister plenipotentiary (1794) but, in trying to offset the bad effects of the Jay Treaty with Britain, Monroe was accused of jeopardizing U.S. neutrality and (1796) was recalled; after serving as governor of Virginia (1799-1802, during which time his friendship with Madison developed), President Jefferson sent him back to France to negotiate with Napoleon for the purchase of New Orleans. He (with Robert Livingston) took advantage of Napoleon's offer to sell the entire vast area that made up the Louisiana Territory to the United States. Then went to

London with William Pinkney (1803-1807) and spent several years of unsuccessful negotiation over freedom of the seas. Again he became governor of Virginia (1811), but resigned to become Madison's secretary of state (1811-1817) and, for a time (1814-1815) also secretary of war. There were prosperous good times in the land after the War of 1812 came to an end and Monroe, as Madison's choice, easily won the presidential election of 1816 with 183 electoral votes to Federalist Rufus King's 34.

As president, he established the Monroe Doctrine (with the aid of Secretary of State John Quincy Adams), warning Europe that the United States would not permit future colonization in North and South America; postponed the slavery crisis by his approval of the Missouri Compromise admitting Missouri as a slave state, Maine as a free one, and establishing 36° 30′ north latitude as the dividing line between slave and free soil; concluded a treaty demilitarizing the boundary between the United States and Canada, and acquired Florida from Spain. The years of his presidency were called the "Era of Good Feeling" (even though there was a panic in 1819 and political conflicts were brewing that surfaced later) and, in the election of 1820, only one electoral vote was cast against him.

In retirement, he first moved to Virginia where he renewed friendships with Madison and Jefferson and was elected to state constitutional convention (1829); personal finances were a serious problem and, near the end of his life, he moved to New York City to live with his daughter.

MONTAGUE, ANDREW JACKSON (b Oct. 3, 1862, Campbell County, Va.; d Jan. 24, 1937, Urbanna, Va.). Lawyer, orator, educator who was a lifetime worker for world peace, independent Virginia Democrat who succeeded in weakening the grip of the existing political machine of Thomas S. Martin (which see), was elected governor (1902-1906), won a battle for direct primaries and then learned, through the ballot box, that though he had weakened the grip, he had not broken it and the Martin organization returned to power.

U.S. attorney for Virginia's western district (1893-1898), state attorney general (1898-1902), Democratic National Convention delegate (1904), unsuccessful candidate for the Democratic nomination for U.S. Senate with Martin the victor (1905), U.S. delegate to the Third Conference of American Republics (1906), Richmond College Law School dean (1906-1909), U.S. delegate to the Third International Conference on Maritime Law (1909, 1910); trustee of Carnegie Institute and officer, from assistant treasurer to president, of the Carnegie Endowment for International Peace (1910-1929); U.S. Representative (1913 until death), president of the American Society for Judicial Settlement of International Disputes (1917), president of the American Peace Society (1920-1924), president of the American group of the Interparliamentary Union (1930-1935).

MONTOYA, NESTOR *(b April 14, 1862, Old Albuquerque, N.Mex.; d Jan. 13, 1923, Washington, D.C.)* Journalist who was the founder, editor, and publisher of the Spanish newspaper *La Bandera Americana* (The American Flag), New Mexico Republican. Territorial representative (1892-1903) and house speaker (1903), territorial senate (1905, 1906), state press association president (1908-1923), delegate to convention that drafted and adopted state constitution (1910), University of New Mexico regent (1916-1919), Bernalillo County clerk (1919-1920), U.S. Representative (1921 until death).

MOODY, GIDEON CURTIS *(b Oct. 16, 1832, Cortland, N.Y.; d March 17, 1904,* *Los Angeles, Calif.)* Lawyer, Union Army officer, Indiana and South Dakota Republican. In Indiana: Floyd County prosecutor (1854), state representative (1861). In the Dakota Territory: territorial representative (1867-1869, 1874-1875) and house speaker (1868-1869, 1874-1875), GOP National Convention delegate (1868, 1888) associate justice of the territorial supreme court (1878-1883); then, upon division into North and South Dakota: delegate to the latter's constitutional conventions (1883, 1885) and one of the state's first two U.S. Senators (1889-1891).

MOODY, WILLIAM HENRY *(b Dec. 23, 1853, Newbury, Mass.; d July 2, 1917, Haverhill, Mass.)* Lawyer, Massachusetts Republican whose trust-busting efforts while U.S. attorney general (1904-1906) won him nomination by Theodore Roosevelt as an associate justice of the Supreme Court and confirmation despite stiff Senate opposition because of his crackdown. He served from 1906 until 1910 when poor health forced his retirement. Haverhill city solicitor (1888-1890), eastern district attorney (1890-1895), U.S. Representative (1895-1902), secretary of the navy (1902-1904).

MOON, JOHN AUSTIN *(b April 22, 1855, Albermarle County, Va.; d June 26, 1921, Chattanooga, Tenn.)* Lawyer, Tennessee Democrat who was a U.S. Representative nearly a quarter-century (1897 until death). Chattanooga city attorney (1881, 1882), state Democratic executive committeeman (1888), special circuit judge (1889-1891) and regular judge (1891 until resigning to go to Congress).

MOON, REUBEN OSBORNE *(b July 22, 1847, Jobstown, N.J.; d Oct. 25, 1919, Philadelphia, Pa.)* Lawyer, lecturer, professor of oratory and a Pennsylvania Republican whose silver syllables won him election five times as a U.S. Representative (1903-1913) but failed him when he sought renomination for a sixth term.

MOONEY, CHARLES ANTHONY (b Jan. 5, 1879, St. Marys, Ohio; d May 29, 1931, Cleveland, Ohio) Life insurance broker, Ohio Democrat. State senate (1915-1919), U.S. Representative (1919-1921, 1923 until death). Democratic National Convention delegate (1920, 1924, 1928).

MOONEY, WILLIAM (b 1756, apparently New York City; d Nov. 27, 1831, New York City) Upholsterer, wallpaper dealer, New York Democrat who was one of the founders and first grand sachem of the New York Society of Tammany (1789 until death) which at first was a philanthropic-social organization but quickly found that there was profit in politics and came to be known as Tammany Hall. It compiled a long record of corruption and graft at all levels that ran into the hundreds of millions of dollars with Mooney getting his share. Among other things, as New York City's almshouse superintendent, he added to its expenditures lavish living for his family, wines and whiskeys and, according to his ledgers, "trifles for Mrs. Mooney"—a phrase that ultimately became a rallying cry for foes of Tammany.

MOORE, ANDREW (b 1752, Rockbridge County, Va.; d April 14, 1821, Lexington, Va.) Lawyer, Continental Army officer, Virginia Democrat who was a strong supporter of James Madison on all except the tariff, and a man who did much to help found Washington and Lee University. Member of state house of delegates (1780-1783, 1785-1788, 1799, 1800), delegate to state convention that ratified the federal Constitution (1788), U.S. Representative (1789-1797, 1804), state senate (1800, 1801), U.S. Senate (1804-1809).

MOORE, ARTHUR HARRY (b July 3, 1879, Jersey City, N.J.; d Nov. 18, 1952, Branchburg Township, N.J.). Lawyer, New Jersey Democrat who was a close follower and, some said, political puppet of mayor Frank ("I am the Law") Hague who for many years held sway over Jersey City politics with influence that stretched throughout Hudson County and the state. Secretary to the mayor of Jersey City (1908-1911), city collector (1911-1913), city commissioner (1913-1925), governor (1926-1928, 1932-1934, 1938-1940), U.S. Senate but only for half a term (1935-1938) resigning to run for governor for the third time.

MOORE, CHARLES ELLIS (b Jan. 3, 1884, Guernsey County, Ohio; d April 2, 1941, Cambridge, Ohio) Lawyer, banker, Ohio Republican. Guernsey County prosecutor (1914-1918), U.S. Representative (1919-1933).

MOORE, GABRIEL (b 1785, Stokes County, N.C.; d June 9, 1845, Caddo, Tex.) Lawyer, Alabama Democrat. Speaker of the territorial house of representatives (1817), state constitutional convention delegate (1819), president of the state senate (1821), U.S. Representative (1821-1829), governor (1829-1831), U.S. Senate (1831-1837).

MOORE, JOSEPH HAMPTON (b March 8, 1864, Woodbury, N.J.; d May 2, 1950, Philadelphia, Pa.) Lawyer, newspaperman, banker, and a highly active Pennsylvania Republican who served as president of the Allied Republican Clubs of Philadelphia, the Pennsylvania State League, and the National League of Republican Clubs (1900-1906). Chief clerk to the Philadelphia city treasurer (1894-1897), secretary to the mayor (1900), city treasurer (1901-1903), chief of the U.S. Bureau of Manufactures (1905), president of the Atlantic Deeper Waterways Association (1907-1947), U.S. Representative (1906-1920), mayor of Philadelphia (1920-1923, 1932-1935), GOP National Convention delegate (1920), U.S. delegate to the International Navigation Congress (1926).

MOORE, LITTLETON WILDE *(b March 25, 1835, Marion County, Ala.; d Oct. 29, 1911, Lagrange, Tex.)* Lawyer, Confederate Army officer, Texas Democrat. State constitutional convention delegate (1875), district judge (1876-1885), U.S. Representative (1887-1893), twenty-third judicial district judge (1901 until death).

MOORE, NICHOLAS RUXTON *(b July 21, 1756, Baltimore County, Md.; d Oct. 7, 1816, Baltimore)* Member of Maryland's first military company organized for the Revolution in which he fought as a captain, Democrat who helped to put down the Whiskey Insurrection. State house of delegates (1801, 1802), U.S. Representative (1803-1811, 1813-1815).

MOORE, THOMAS *(b 1759, Spartanburg District, S.C.; d July 11, 1822, Spartanburg County)* Revolutionary soldier at sixteen and a brigadier general in the War of 1812, South Carolina planter who served seven terms as a U.S. Representative (1801-1813, 1815-1817).

MOORES, MERRILL *(b April 21, 1856, Indianapolis, Ind.; d Oct. 21, 1929, Indianapolis, of auto-accident injuries).* Lawyer, Indiana Republican. Marion County GOP committee chairman (1892-1896), assistant state attorney general (1894-1903), state and city bar association president (1908), state commissioner of the National Conference on Uniform State Laws (1909-1925), member of the Interparliamentary Union executive council (1919), U.S. Representative (1915-1925).

MOREHEAD, CHARLES SLAUGHTER *(b July 7, 1802, Nelson County, Ky.; d*

Dec. 21, 1868, near Greenville, Miss.). Lawyer who owned plantations in Kentucky, Mississippi, and Louisiana; Kentucky Whig turned Know-Nothing who, as governor (1855-1859), advocated neutrality between North and South only to be arrested and imprisoned later (1861) by federal authorities for publicly criticizing the cutting off of trade with the South. State representative (1828, 1829, 1832-1842, 1844, 1853) and house speaker (1841, 1842, 1844), state attorney general (1830-1835), U.S. Representative (1847-1851), presidential elector on the Scott-Graham ticket (1852), delegate to peace between-the-states convention (1861).

MOREHEAD, JOHN HENRY *(b Dec. 3, 1861, Lucas County, Iowa; d May 31, 1942, St. Joseph, Mo.)* Teacher, farmer, merchant, banker, real estate operator, Nebraska Democrat. Richardson County treasurer (1896-1899), mayor of Falls City (1900), state senate (1910-1912), lieutenant governor (1912-1913), governor (1913-1917), U.S. Representative (1923-1935), Democratic National Convention delegate (1940).

MORGAN, CHARLES HENRY *(b July 5, 1842, Cuba, N.Y.; d Jan. 4, 1912, Joplin, Mo.)* Union Army officer, lawyer, mine operator, Missouri Democrat turned Republican. Barton County prosecutor (1868-1872), state representative (1872-1874), U.S. Representative (1875-1879, 1883-1885, 1893-1895) as a Democrat and (1909-1911) as a Republican, Democratic National Convention delegate (1880), presidential elector on the Cleveland-Thurman Democratic ticket (1888).

MORGAN, DICK THOMPSON *(b Dec. 6, 1853, Prairie Creek, Ind.; d July 4, 1920, Danville, Ill.)* Mathematics professor, lawyer, Indiana and Oklahoma Republican. In Indiana: state representative (1880, 1881). In Oklahoma: register of the U.S. Land Office at Woodward (1904-1908), U.S. Representative (1909 until death).

MORGAN, EDWIN DENNISON *(b Feb. 8, 1811, Washington, Mass.; d Feb. 14, 1883, New York City)* Merchant, wholesale grocer, Union Army officer, philanthropist, New York Republican turned Union Republican and back to straight Republican again, and something of a power in the party who started his political career by serving on the Hartford, Conn., City Council (1832) before moving to New York City. Alderman (1849), state senate (1850-1855), state immigration commissioner (1855-1858), GOP National Convention vice president (1856) and delegate (1860), GOP National Committee chairman (1856-1864, 1872), governor (1859-1862), chairman of the Union congressional committee (1864), U.S. Senate (1863-1869), closing out his political career by refusing to be secretary of the treasury in the Arthur cabinet (1881).

MORGAN, JOHN TYLER *(b June 20, 1824, Athens, Tenn.; d June 11, 1907, Washington, D.C.)* Lawyer, Confederate Army officer, Alabama Democrat who served thirty years in U.S. Senate (1877 until death) and strongly advocated the repossession of lands granted to railroads and fought for states' rights. Presidential elector on the Breckenridge-Lane (1860) and Tilden-Hendricks (1876) tickets, delegate to state secessionist convention (1861).

MORIN, JOHN MARY *(b April 18, 1868, Philadelphia, Pa.; d March 3, 1942, Baltimore, Md.).* Factory and mill hand, merchant, hotel operator, banker, Pennsylvania Republican. Pittsburgh councilman (1904-1906), delegate to all GOP state conventions (1905-1912), Pittsburgh director of public safety (1909-1913), U.S. Representative (1913-1929),

U.S. employees compensation commissioner (1928 until death).

MORRIL, DAVID LAWRENCE *(b June 10, 1772, Epping, N.H.; d Jan. 28, 1849, Concord, N.H.)* Physician, clergyman, newspaper editor and a man who combined scholarship with politics; New Hampshire Democrat and an ardent enemy of slavery. State representative (1808-1817) and house speaker (1816), U.S. Senate (1817-1823), state senate president (1823, 1824), governor (1824-1827), editor of the *New Hampshire Observer* (1831-1833).

MORRILL, ANSON PEASLEE *(b June 10, 1803, Belgrade, Maine; d July 4, 1887, Augusta, Maine)* Woolen mill owner, railroad president, Maine Democrat who quit the party over the slavery issue and became the state's first Republican governor (1855-1856). State representative (1833, 1880), Somerset County sheriff (1839), land agent (1850-1853), GOP National Convention delegate (1856), U.S. Representative (1861-1863). Brother of Lot M. Morrill.

MORRILL, EDMUND NEEDHAM *(b Feb. 12, 1834, Westbrook, Maine; d March 14, 1909, San Antonio, Tex.).* Sawmill operator, Union Army officer, banker, educator who founded the Morrill Free Public Library at Hiawatha, Kans., and the Hiawatha Academy; ultraconservative Kansas Republican who while governor (1895-1897) allegedly said of farmers seeking relief from high mortgage interest rates and the drought: "When the government has protected the individual in his life and property, he ought to hustle for himself to get bread." Member of territorial legislature (1857, 1858), Brown County district court clerk (1866-1870) and county clerk (1866-1873), state senator (1872-1874, 1876-1880) and senate president pro tem (1877), U.S. Representative (1883-1891), manager of Leavenworth soldiers' home (1890).

MORRILL, JUSTIN SMITH *(b April 14, 1810, Strafford, Vt.; d Dec. 28, 1898, Washington, D.C.)* Merchant, farmer, horticulturist, Vermont antislavery Whig turned Union Republican who served in Washington for forty-three years and wrote the Land Grant College Act that Buchanan vetoed (1857) and Lincoln signed (1862). U.S. Representative (1855-1867), U.S. Senate (1867 until death).

MORRILL, LOT MYRICK *(b May 3, 1813, Belgrade, Maine; d Jan. 10, 1883, Augusta, Maine)* Teacher, lawyer, skilled debater, Maine Democrat turned Republican who declined to be Grant's secretary of war but served in the Grant and Hayes cabinets as secretary of the treasury (1876-1877). State senator (1854, 1856) and senate president (1856), governor (1858-1860), U.S. Senate (1861-March 1869, Oct. 1869-1876) being named to the first term to fill the seat vacated by Lincoln's vice president, Hannibal Hamlin; Portland, Maine, collector of customs (1877 until death).

Before converting to Republicanism, he was a power in Maine's Democratic circles serving as chairman of the party's state committee (1849-1856) and as one of the state's most effective lobbyists whose legal and oratorical skills were much in demand by interests seeking special consideration. His reason for leaving the fold after the Democratic National Convention of 1856: "the platform is a flagrant outrage upon the country and an insult to the North." In Washington, he led the debate (1862) that resulted in passage of the emancipation act and (1866) he was prominent in the fight for Negro suffrage. Brother of Anson P. Morrill.

MORRIS, DANIEL *(b Jan. 4, 1812, Fayette, N.Y.; d April 22, 1889, Penn Yan, N.Y.)* Lawyer, New York Republican. Yates County district attorney (1847-1850), state assembly (1859), U.S. Representative (1863-1867).

MORRIS, GOUVERNEUR *(b Jan. 31, 1752, Morrisania, now a part of New York City; d Nov. 6, 1816, Morrisania).* Lawyer, author of *Observations on the American Revolution,* signer of the Articles of Confederation, one of three men (John Jay and Robert Livingston were the others) who wrote New York's first state constitution (1776), state militia officer, a patriot who divided his time between New York and Pennsylvania and, when party lines were drawn, became one of Alexander Hamilton's staunchest Federalists with his home state as his base. Perhaps his greatest and most-lasting contribution: As assistant U.S. minister of finance (1781-1785) he devised the decimal coinage plan and gave the name "cent" to the basic coin of the U.S. monetary system.

Member of New York provincial congress (1775-1777), the committee that designed the state seal (1777), the first state council of safety (1777) and the first state assembly (1777, 1778); New York delegate to the Continental Congress (1777, 1778), Pennsylvania delegate to the federal Constitutional Convention (1787), commissioner to England (1789), minister to France (1792-1794), U.S. Senate (1800-1803), chairman of the Erie Canal Commission (1810-1813).

An historian's interesting footnote: Morris was in France (1789) when the French Revolution erupted and his subsequent *Diary of the French Revolution* covering the years 1789-1793 was published in 1939. Half-brother of Lewis Morris, uncle of Lewis R. Morris.

MORRIS, LEWIS *(b April 8, 1726, Morrisania, N.Y.; d Jan. 22, 1798, Morrisania)* Farmer, signer of the Declaration of Independence, New York Federalist who had been a crown-appointed admiralty court judge (1760-1774) when he resigned in protest of British policy. Provincial convention delegate (1775), delegate to the Continental Congress

(1775-1777), state provincial congress (1776, 1777), Westchester County judge and member of the committee on the detection of conspiracies (1777), state senate (1777-1781, 1784-1788), member of the council of appointments (1786) and one of the University of New York's first regents (1784 until death), delegate to state convention that ratified federal Constitution (1788), presidential elector on the Adams-Pinckney ticket (1796). Half brother of Gouverneur Morris, uncle of Lewis R. Morris.

MORRIS, LEWIS ROBERT *(b Nov. 2, 1760, Scarsdale, N.Y.; d Dec. 29, 1825, Springfield, Vt.)* Farmer, large landowner, Vermont Federalist who while a U.S. Representative (1797-1803) withheld his thirty-sixth-ballot vote and thus delivered Vermont to Thomas Jefferson in his contest with Aaron Burr for the presidency. Secretary of foreign affairs (1781-1783), member of Springfield meeting-house committee (1785), tax collector (1786, 1787), Windsor County Court clerk (1789-1796) and judge (1801), clerk of the state house of representatives (1790, 1791) and one of the committee that presented Vermont's statehood plea to Congress (1791), state constitutional convention secretary (1793), state representative (1795-1797, 1803-1808). Nephew of Gouverneur and Lewis Morris.

MORRIS, ROBERT *(b Jan. 20, 1734, Liverpool, England; d May 8, 1806, Philadelphia, Pa.)* Pennsylvania patriot, signer of the Declaration of Independence, probably America's major merchant of the times, the man who, probably more so than anyone, made the Revolution financially possible, and founder of the nation's first national bank who, ironically, was declared bankrupt after unwise speculation in western lands and spent three years in debtor's prison (1798-1801)—this after declining to serve as President Wash-

ington's secretary of the treasury. Signer of the nonimportation agreement (1765), member of the Continental Congress (1776-1778), state assembly (1778-1780), the new nation's superintendent of finance (1781-1784), state representative (1785-1787), constitutional convention delegate (1787), U.S. Senate (1789-1795) in the First Congress. Father of Thomas Morris.

MORRIS, THOMAS *(b Feb. 26, 1771, Philadelphia, Pa.; d March 12, 1849, New York City)* New York lawyer. State assembly (1794-1796), U.S. Representative (1801-1803), U.S. marshal for New York's southern district (1816, 1820, 1825, 1829). Son of Robert Morris.

MORRISON, JAMES HOBSON *(b Dec. 8, 1908, Hammond, La.)* Lawyer, Louisiana Democrat who ran unsuccessfully for governor in 1939 and 1944. U.S. Representative (1943-1967).

MORRISON, WILLIAM RALLS *(b Sept. 14, 1825, Prairie du Long, Ill.; d Sept. 29, 1909, Waterloo, Ill.)* California gold miner, Union Army officer who was badly wounded in the siege of Fort Donelson; Illinois Union Democrat who advocated tariff reforms and was a member (1887-1897) and chairman (1892-1897) of the Interstate Commerce Commission. Monroe County circuit court clerk (1852-1854), state representative (1854-1860, 1870, 1871) and house speaker (1859, 1860), U.S. Representative (1863-1865, 1873-1887), Democratic National Convention delegate (1856, 1868, 1884, 1888), Union National Convention delegate (1866).

MORROW, JEREMIAH *(b Oct. 6, 1771, near Gettysburg, Pa.; d March 22, 1852, Twenty-mile Stand, Ohio)* Farmer, surveyor who settled early in the Northwest Territory where he became a prime mover in the drive for Ohio statehood, an advocate of the sale of public lands in small parcels at bargain-basement prices, and the father of the state's canal-building program. Democrat turned Whig. Territorial representative (1801, 1802, 1829, 1835), state constitutional convention delegate (1802), state senate (1803, 1827), U.S. Representative (1803-1813 as a Democrat and 1840-1843 as a Whig), U.S. Senate (1813-1819), presidential elector on the Monroe-Tompkins ticket (1820), state canal commissioner (1822), governor (1822-1826).

MORROW, JOHN *(b April 19, 1865, Lafayette County, Wis.; d Feb. 25, 1935, Santa Fe., N.Mex.)* Teacher, lawyer, banker, rancher, landowner, New Mexico Democrat. Colfax County schools superintendent (1892-1896), territorial representative (1897, 1898), Raton city attorney (1900, 1901), board of education president (1903-1923), Democratic National Convention delegate (1908), New Mexico Normal University regent (1921, 1922), U.S. Representative (1923-1929).

MORTON, JACKSON *(b Aug. 10, 1794, Spotsylvania County, Va.; d Nov. 20, 1874, Santa Rosa County, Fla.)* Lumber business, Florida Whig. Member of the legislative council (1836) and president (1837), constitutional convention delegate (1838), navy agent at Pensacola (1841-1845); after statehood, presidential elector on the Taylor-Fillmore ticket (1848), U.S. Senate (1849-1855), deputy to the Confederate Provisional Congress (1861) and member of the Confederate Congress (1862-1865). Brother of Jeremiah Morton.

MORTON, JEREMIAH *(b Sept. 3, 1799, Fredericksburg, Va.; d Nov. 28, 1878, Orange County, Va.)* Lawyer, planter, Virginia Theological Seminary trustee, Virginia Whig. U.S. Representative (1849-1851), state secession convention delegate (1861). Brother of Jackson Morton.

MORTON, JOHN *(b 1724, Ridley Township, Pa.; d April 1777, Ridley Park, Pa.).* Surveyor, Pennsylvania signer of the Declaration of Independence. Delaware County justice of the peace (1757), member of the colonial assembly (1756-1766, 1769-1775) and its speaker (1771-1775), delegate to the Stamp Act Congress (1765), high sheriff (1766-1770), president judge of the county general sessions and common pleas court (1770-1774), associate justice of the Pennsylvania Supreme Court of Appeals (1774-1775), member of the Continental Congress (1774-1777).

MORTON, LEVI PARSONS *(b May 16, 1824, Shoreham, Vt.; d May 16, 1920, Rhinebeck, N.Y.)* Teacher, merchant, banker, land speculator, New York Republican who was vice president during the Harrison administration (1889-1893). U.S. Representative (1879-1881), minister to France (1881-1885), governor (1895-1897).

MORTON, MARCUS *(b Dec. 19, 1784, Freetown, Mass.; d Feb. 6, 1864, Taunton, Mass.)* Lawyer, Massachusetts Democrat turned Free-Soiler and a champion of the working classes who might be described as one of the nation's first political figures with a trust-busting bent; a man who regularly ran for governor from 1828 through 1843, twice was elected and served (1840-1841, 1843-1844); a man who declined the vice presidential spot on the Free-Soil party's Van Buren ticket (1848) because he was not yet convinced that he should bolt the Democratic fold. State senate clerk (1811), U.S. Representative (1817-1821), executive councillor (1823), lieutenant governor (1824-1825) serving briefly as the state's chief executive upon the death of Governor William Eustis, state supreme court judge (1825-1840), Boston collector of customs (1845-1849), state constitutional convention delegate (1853), state representative (1858).

MORTON, OLIVER HAZARD PERRY THROCK (b Aug. 4, 1823, Salisbury, Ind.; d Nov. 1, 1877, Indianapolis, Ind.). Hatter, lawyer, Indiana Democrat who left his party because of the Kansas-Nebraska Act, helped to found the Republican party nationally. As governor (1861-1867) wholeheartedly supported the Civil War and stymied Copperhead (Northerners who sympathized with the South during the Civil War) plots; as U.S. Senator (1867 until death) uncompromisingly backed Reconstruction; a serious contender for the GOP presidential nomination (1876).

MOSELEY, JONATHAN OGDEN (b April 9, 1762, East Haddam, Conn.; d Sept. 9, 1838, Saginaw, Mich.) Lawyer, Connecticut Federalist. State representative (1794-1804), East Haddam justice of the peace (1794-1817), Middlesex County state's attorney (1801-1805), U.S. Representative (1805-1821).

MOSES, GEORGE HIGGINS (b Feb. 9, 1869, Lubec, Maine; d Dec. 20, 1944, Concord, N.H.) Editor of the Concord Evening Monitor (1892-1918), writer, New Hampshire Republican. Private secretary to Governor David H. Goodell (1889-1891) and Governor John McLane (1905), secretary to the GOP state committee chairman (1890), member-secretary of the state forestry commission (1893-1907), member of the Concord Board of Education (1902, 1903, 1906-1909, 1913-1916), U.S. minister to Greece and Montenegro (1909-1912), GOP National Convention delegate (1908, 1916), U.S. Senator (1918-1933) and Senate president pro tem (1925-1933).

MOSES, JOHN (b June 12, 1885, Strand, Norway; d March 3, 1945, Rochester, Minn., two months after being sworn as a U.S. Senator). A Norwegian college boy who worked up the hard way after coming to the United States: laborer, farmhand, clerk, freight claims investigator, State Teachers College secretary (1911-1913), lawyer, farmer, banker, North Dakota Democrat. Mercer County state's attorney (1919-1923, 1927-1933), governor (1939-1945) and U.S. Senate only to die while undergoing an operation.

MOTT, GORDON NEWELL (b Oct. 21, 1812, Zanesville, Ohio; d April 27, 1887, San Francisco, Calif.) Ohio lawyer who moved to Texas to aid in the fight for independence, then on to California during the 1849 gold rush, and ultimately sent to the Nevada Territory by President Lincoln to serve as associate supreme court justice (1861-1863); resigned to serve as a delegate to the U.S. Congress (1863-1864) as a Republican. In California: Sutter County judge (1850), district judge (1851-1854).

MOTT, JAMES WHEATON (b Nov. 12, 1883, Clearfield County, Pa.; d Nov. 12, 1945, Bethesda, Md.) Newspaperman, lawyer, Oregon Republican. Astoria city attorney (1922-1928, 1930-1932), state corporation commissioner (1931-1932), U.S. Representative (1933 until death).

MOTT, LUCRECIA COFFIN (Jan. 3, 1793, Nantucket Island, Mass.; d Nov. 11, 1880, near Philadelphia, Pa.) Liberal and eloquent Quaker preacher favoring temperance and the abolition of slavery (her home was a station on the Underground Railroad), mother of six, early pioneer in women's rights, and one of the movement's guiding spirits. The position held by her sex was forcefully brought home to Lucrecia Mott when, as a teacher in a Friends boarding school, she received but half the pay given to men teachers; again, as a delegate to the world antislavery convention held in London in 1840, she was refused recognition and seating because of her sex. In 1848, she joined Elizabeth Cady Stanton, another woman rebuffed at the London meeting, in organizing the first women's rights convention ever held in the United States.

MOTT, LUTHER WRIGHT *(b Nov. 30, 1874, Oswego, N.Y.; d July 10, 1923, Oswego)* Banker, New York Republican. State superintendent of banks, resigning after serving only five days in 1907; GOP National Convention delegate (1908), state bankers' association president (1910, 1911), U.S. Representative (1911 until death).

MOULDER, MORGAN MOORE *(b Aug. 31, 1904, Linn Creek, Mo.)* Lawyer, Missouri Democrat. Camden County prosecuting attorney (1928-1938), special assistant to the U.S. attorney for western district of Missouri (1943-1946), eighteenth judicial circuit court judge (1947-1948), U.S. Representative (1949-1963) serving on the Un-American Activities and Interstate and Foreign Commerce committees.

MOUTON, ALEXANDER *(b Nov. 19, 1804, Attakapas District, La.; d Feb. 12, 1885, near Vermillionville, now Lafayette, La.)* Lawyer, planter, Louisiana Democrat who presided over the state secession convention (1861). State representative (1827-1832, 1836) and house speaker (1831, 1832), presidential elector (1828, 1832, 1836), U.S. Senate (1837-1842), governor (1842-1846), southwestern railroad convention president (1852), head of a vigilance committee (1858) formed to rid Lafayette Parish of outlaws, Democratic National Convention delegate (1860).

MUDD, SYDNEY EMANUEL, SR. *(b Feb. 12, 1858, Charles County, Md.; d Oct. 21, 1911, Philadelphia, Pa.)* Lawyer, Maryland Republican. State house of delegates (1879, 1881) and speaker (1895), presidential elector on the Garfield-Arthur ticket (1880), U.S. Representative (1890-1891, 1897-1911), GOP National Convention delegate (1896). Father of the following.

MUDD, SYDNEY EMANUEL, JR. *(b June 20, 1885, Charles County, Md.; d Oct. 11, 1924, Baltimore, Md.)* Lawyer and professor of criminal law at Georgetown University Law School (1910), Maryland Republican. District of Columbia assistant district attorney (1911-1914), U.S. Representative (1915 until death). Son of the preceding.

MUHLENBERG, FREDERICK AUGUSTUS CONRAD *(b Jan. 1, 1750, Trappe, Pa.; d June 5, 1801, Lancaster, Pa.)* Clergyman, member of a well-known Pennsylvania family and a man who early embraced Alexander Hamilton's Federalist philosophy but gradually switched to Thomas Jefferson's Democratic-Republicanism. Member of the Continental Congress (1770, 1780), state representative (1780-1783) and house speaker, president of the state convention that ratified the federal Constitution (1787), U.S. Representative (1789-1797) and speaker in the First and Third Congresses, unsuccessful candidate for governor (1793, 1796), president of the state council of censors, state land office receiver general (1800 until death). Brother of John P. G. Muhlenberg.

MUHLENBERG, HENRY AUGUSTUS *(b July 21, 1823, Reading, Pa.; d Jan. 9, 1854, Washington, D.C.)* Lawyer, Pennsylvania Democrat. State senate (1849-1852), U.S. Representative (1853 until death). Son of Henry A. P. Muhlenberg.

MUHLENBERG, HENRY AUGUSTUS PHILIP *(b May 13, 1782, Lancaster, Pa.; d Aug. 11, 1844, Reading, Pa.)* Clergyman, Pennsylvania Democrat. U.S. Representative (1829-1838), unsuccessful gubernatorial candidate (1835, 1837), minister to Austria (1838-1840), Democratic nominee for governor (1844) but died before election day. Father of Henry A. and nephew of John P. G. Muhlenberg.

MUHLENBERG, JOHN PETER GABRIEL (b Oct. 1, 1746, Trappe, Pa.; d Oct. 1, 1807, Providence, Pa.) Clergyman, Continental Army officer, Pennsylvania Democrat whose pre-Revolutionary ministerial duties took him to Virginia where he was a member of the house of burgesses (1774) and Dunmore County Committee of Safety chairman. In Pennsylvania: member of the state supreme executive council (1784) and its vice president (1785-1787), U.S. Representative in the First, Third, and Sixth Congresses (1789-1791, 1793-1795, 1799-1801), U.S. Senate for four months (1801), resigning to accept appointment by President Jefferson as state supervisor of revenue (1801) and Philadelphia collector of customs (1802 until death). Brother of Frederick A. C. and uncle of Henry A. P. Muhlenberg.

MULLER, NICHOLAS (b Nov. 15, 1836, Grand Duchy of Luxemburg; d Dec. 12, 1917, New Brighton, N.Y.) Railroad ticket agent, banker, New York Democrat. State assemblyman (1875, 1876), Democratic state central committeeman (1875), U.S. Representative (1877-1881, 1883-1887, 1899-1902) and when not in Washington between 1888 and 1904 a holder of a variety of New York City jobs, among them president of the police and excise boards, and quarantine and tax commissioner.

MULTER, ABRAHAM JACOB (b Dec. 24, 1900, New York City) Lawyer, New York Democrat. U.S. Representative from 1947 until his resignation Dec. 31, 1967, upon his election as a New York State Supreme Court justice. In Congress he had served on the District of Columbia and Banking and Currency committees and as a member of the Joint Committee on Defense Production.

MURCH, THOMPSON HENRY (b March 29, 1838, Hampden, Maine; d Dec. 15, 1886, Danvers, Mass.) Sailor, stonecutter, labor leader, merchant, who was elected a U.S. Representative (1879-1883) from Maine on the Greenback Labor Reformer ticket.

MURDOCK, VICTOR (b March 18, 1871, Burlingame, Kans.; d July 8, 1945, Wichita, Kans.) Newspaperman who was editor of the Wichita Eagle for most of his working years, Kansas Republican who became chairman of the National Committee for the Progressive party (1915, 1916). State appellate court clerk (1895-1897), U.S. Representative (1903-1915), member of the Federal Trade Commission (1917-1924) and chairman (1919, 1920, 1922, 1923), federal meat commissioner (1918).

MURPHY, BENJAMIN FRANKLIN (b Dec. 24, 1867, Steubenville, Ohio; d March 6, 1938, Takoma Park, Md.). Glassworker, merchant, banker, real estate operator, Ohio Republican. U.S. Representative (1919-1933).

MURPHY, HENRY CRUSE (b July 5, 1810, Brooklyn, N.Y.; d Dec. 1, 1882, Brooklyn) Lawyer, founding editor-publisher of the Brooklyn Eagle, historian, author and collector of early Americana works, anti-Tammany New York Democrat who lost the presidential nomination to Franklin Pierce (1852), and a man of foresight who had much to do with the construction of the Brooklyn Bridge and the development of Coney Island as a seaside resort. Kings County prosecutor (1841, 1842), mayor of Brooklyn (1842, 1843), state constitutional convention delegate (1846, 1867, 1868), U.S. Representative (1843-1845, 1847-1849), minister to the Netherlands (1857-1861), state senate (1861-1873).

MURRAY, GEORGE WASHINGTON (b Sept. 22, 1853, Sumter County, S.C.; d April 21, 1926, Chicago, Ill.) Born into slavery and orphaned by the time of the Emancipation, he acquired an education the hard way, taught school for fourteen years and became interested in politics when, somewhat against his will, he was chosen South Carolina, Sumter County Republican chairman (1888) and went on to become the only Negro to serve in the Fifty-third Congress. His main political interest was better educational opportunities for Negroes, his main personal interest, the invention of farming implements, and he was also involved in real estate, writing, and lecturing. Charleston collector of customs (1890-1892), U.S. Representative (1893-1895, 1896-1897).

MURRAY, JAMES EDWARD *(b May 3, 1876, Ontario, Canada; d March 23, 1961, Butte, Mont.)* Lawyer, banker, Montana Democrat who served more than a quarter-century in U.S. Senate (1934-1961). Silver Bow County attorney (1906-1908), chairman of the state advisory board to the Public Works Administration (1933, 1934), Democratic National Convention delegate (1920, 1932, 1936, 1940, 1944, 1948).

MURRAY, REID FRED *(b Oct. 16, 1887, Ogdensburg, Wis.; d April 29, 1952, Bethesda, Md.)* Farm agent, professor of animal husbandry, cattle and farm dealer, Wisconsin Republican who served seven terms as U.S. Representative (1939 until death).

MURRAY, THOMAS JEFFERSON *(b Aug. 1, 1894, Jackson, Tenn.)* Teacher, lawyer, Tennessee Democrat. District attorney general for state's twelfth judicial circuit (1922-1933), chairman of Madison County Democratic executive committee (1924-1933), member of state executive committee (1923, 1924), national convention delegate (1928, 1932, 1936), U.S. Representative (1943-1967) and chairman of the Post Office and Civil Service committees.

MURRAY, WILLIAM HENRY *(b Nov. 21, 1869, Grayson County, Tex.; d Oct. 15, 1956, Oklahoma City, Okla.)* Texas newspaperman-lawyer who moved to the Indian Territory (now Oklahoma) in 1898, was involved in ranching, writing, and politics as a Democrat and did much to achieve statehood. Legal adviser to the governor of the Chickasaw Nation (1898-1901), member of the Choctaw-Chickasaw Coal Commission (1903), Oklahoma Code Commission chairman (1903), vice president of the Sequoyah constitutional convention (1905), president of the Oklahoma constitutional convention (1906), chairman of the first Democratic state convention (1907), state representative (1907-1909) and house speaker during the first legislative session, Democratic National Convention delegate (1908, 1912, 1916, 1932), U.S. Representative (1913-1917), governor (1931-1935).

Between 1917 and 1931 he spent much of the time in South America helping to colonize southeast Bolivia.

MUTCHLER, HOWARD *(b Feb. 12, 1859, Northampton County, Pa.; d Jan. 4, 1916, Easton, Pa.)* Editor-publisher of Easton's *Northampton Democrat* and a Pennsylvania Democrat who became a U.S. Representative upon the death of his father, Congressman William Mutchler (served 1893-1894), waited seven years and ran successfully in his own right (1901-1903).

MUTCHLER, WILLIAM *(b Dec. 21, 1831, Palmer Township, Pa. d June 23, 1893, Easton, Pa.)* Lawyer, Pennsylvania Democrat. Northampton County sheriff (1854-1860) and chief clerk (1861-1867), internal revenue assessor (1867-1869), Democratic state committee chairman (1869, 1870), Democratic National Convention delegate (1876 until death), U.S. Representative (1875-1877, 1881-1885, 1889 until death). Father of Howard Mutchler.

MYERS, FRANCIS JOHN *(b Dec. 18, 1901, Philadelphia, Pa.; d July 5, 1956, Philadelphia)* Lawyer, Pennsylvania Democrat. Secretary to the Philadelphia district attorney (1929-1931), Home Owners' Loan Corporation attorney (1934, 1935), state deputy attorney general (1937), U.S. Representative (1939-1945), U.S. Senate (1945-1951), Democratic National Convention delegate (1948).

MYERS, HENRY LEE *(b Oct. 9, 1862, near Boonville, Mo.; d Nov. 11, 1943, Billings, Mont.)*. Lawyer, Montana Democrat. State Democratic convention delegate (1894, 1898, 1900), Ravalli County prosecutor (1895-1899), state senate (1899-1903), fourth judicial district judge (1907-1911), U.S. Senate (1911-1923), Democratic National Convention delegate (1912), associate state supreme court justice (1927-1929).

N

☆ ☆ ☆

NASH, ABNER *(b Aug. 8, 1740, Prince Edward County, Va.; d Dec. 2, 1786, New York City, while attending a session of Congress).* Planter, lawyer, North Carolina patriot whom the royal governor considered one of the province's "foremost patrons of revolt and anarchy" and who became its second state governor (1780, 1781). Member of state house of commons (1777, 1778, 1782) and speaker (1777), state senate (1779, 1780) and senate president (1779), delegate to the Continental Congress (1782 until death).

NASH, CHARLES EDMUND *(b May 23, 1844, Opelousas, La.; d June 21, 1913, New Orleans, La.)* Bricklayer, Union Army soldier who lost a leg at Fort Blakely, Louisiana Republican who was the first, and perhaps only, Negro from that state to serve in Congress. Customs inspector (1865), U.S. Representative (1875-1877), Washington, La., postmaster (1882).

NAST, THOMAS *(b Sept. 27, 1840, Landau, Germany; d Dec. 7, 1902, Guayaquil, Ecuador)* Cartoonist who covered the Civil War for *Harper's Weekly* and whom President Lincoln called "our best recruiting sergeant," then a specialist in political lampooning who created the Republican elephant, Democratic donkey, and Tammany tiger—the latter to attack New York's corrupt Tweed Ring. Never himself a candidate

for political office, he did accept appointment by President Roosevelt (1902) as U.S. consul to Guayaquil, Ecuador, only to quickly fall victim to the climate and die.

NEEDHAM, JAMES CARSON *(b Sept. 17, 1864, Carson City, Nev., in a covered wagon; d July 11, 1942, Modesto, Calif.).* Lawyer, California Republican. War Department clerk in Washington, D.C. (1887-1888), U.S. Representative (1899-1913), state superior court judge (1919-1935).

NEELY, MATTHEW MANSFIELD *(b Nov. 9, 1874, Grove, W.Va.; d Jan. 18, 1958, in U.S. Naval Hospital, Bethesda, Md.).* Lawyer, West Virginia Democrat who was in public office for fifty years in positions from mayor to governor and U.S. Senator. Mayor of Fairmont (1908-1910), state house of delegates clerk (1911-1913), U.S. Representative (1913-1921, 1945-1947), U.S. Senate (1923-1929, 1931-1941, 1949 until death), governor (1941-1945).

NELL, WILLIAM COOPER *(b Dec. 20, 1816, Boston, Mass.; d May 25, 1874, Boston)* Journalist-author who devoted his life to the antislavery cause, brought about the end of separate schools for colored children, served as an aide to Frederick Douglass on the *North Star* publication, and was the first Negro ever to hold a federal government position—that of clerk in the Boston post office (1861 until death). His literary works include *Services of Colored Americans in the Wars of 1776 and 1812* (1851), and *The Colored Patriots of the American Revolution* (1855) to which Harriet Beecher Stowe wrote an introduction.

NELSON, CHARLES PEMBROKE *(b July 2, 1907, Waterville, Maine)* Lawyer, University of Florida at Gainesville teacher (1957-1959), Maine Republican who was secretary to his father, Congressman John E. Nelson (1931, 1932). Augusta city solicitor (1934-1942), GOP National Convention delegate (1936), chief of the state arson division (1941, 1942), Army Air Corps officer (1942-1946), state bar examiner (1946-1948), mayor of Augusta (1947, 1948), U.S. Representative (1949-1957), state highway commission's chief trial attorney (1959), West Bath town moderator (1960).

NELSON, HUGH *(b Sept. 30, 1768, Yorktown, Va.; d March 18, 1836, Albemarle County, Va.)* Lawyer, Virginia Democrat and a neighbor, close friend, and advisor to Presidents Monroe and Jefferson. State senate (1786-1791), speaker of the house of delegates (1793), member of the state assembly (1805-1809), general court judge (1809-1811), presidential elector on the Madison-Clinton ticket (1808), U.S. Representative (1811-1823), U.S. minister to Spain (1823-1824). Son of Thomas Nelson, Jr.

NELSON, JEREMIAH *(b Sept. 14, 1769, Rowley, Mass.; d Oct. 2, 1838, Newburyport, Mass.)* Merchant, shipper, insurance executive, Massachusetts Federalist. Member of the state general court (1803, 1804), U.S. Representative (1805-1807, 1815-1825, 1831-1833), chairman of the Newburyport Board of Selectmen (1811).

NELSON, JOHN EDWARD *(b July 12, 1874, China, Maine; d April 11, 1955, Augusta, Maine)* Lawyer, Maine Republican. U.S. Representative (1922-1933), Colby College trustee (1926-1931). Father of Charles P. Nelson.

NELSON, JOHN MANDT *(b Oct. 10, 1870, Burke, Wis.; d Jan. 29, 1955, Madison, Wis.)* Lawyer, editor of *The State* (1897-1898), Wisconsin Republican who worked at a variety of government jobs while gaining an education. Dane County schools superintendent (1892-1894), bookkeeper in the office of the Wisconsin secretary of state (1894-1897), state treasury correspondent (1898-1902); then U.S. Representative (1906-1919, 1921-1933).

NELSON, KNUTE *(b Feb. 2, 1843, Voss, Norway; d April 28, 1923, on a train near Timonium, Md.)* Lawyer, Union soldier who was wounded and captured at Port Huron; Wisconsin and Minnesota Republican with a conservative bent who favored, however, a federal income tax and low tariffs and (1902) sponsored legislation creating the Commerce and Labor Department. In Wisconsin: member of the state assembly (1868, 1869). In Minnesota: Douglas County attorney (1872-1874), state senate (1875-1878), presidential elector on the Garfield-Arthur ticket (1880), University of Minnesota regent (1882-1893), U.S. Representative (1883-1889), governor (1893-1895), U.S. Senate (1895 until death). One of the highspots of his nearly thirty years in the Senate: On his eightieth birthday he received messages of congratulation from the king of Norway and the president of the Norwegian Congress.

NELSON, ROGER *(b 1759, near Frederick, Md.; d June 7, 1815, Frederick).* Revolutionary Army officer who was wounded at Camden, lawyer, Maryland Democrat. Member of state house of delegates (1795, 1801, 1802), state senate (1803-1804), U.S. Representative (1804-1810), and one of the managers of the impeachment proceedings brought against Supreme Court Justice Samuel Chase, fifth state judicial circuit judge (1810 until death).

NELSON, SAMUEL *(b Nov. 10, 1792, Hebron, N.Y.; d Dec. 13, 1873, Cooperstown, N.Y.)* Lawyer, New York Democrat who was a Tyler-appointed associate justice of the U.S. Supreme Court (1845-1872). His specialties were international, maritime, admiralty, and patent laws, the former leading President Grant (1871) to name him to the Joint High Commission set up to settle the *Alabama* claims. Before the Supreme Court appointment, he was presidential elector on the Monroe ticket (1820), Cortland postmaster (1820-1824), state constitutional convention delegate (1821) where he argued against the ownership of property as a condition for voting, sixth circuit judge (1823-1831), associate justice of the state supreme court (1831-1837) and chief justice (1837-1845).

NELSON, THOMAS, JR. *(b Dec. 26, 1738, Yorktown, Va.; d Jan. 4, 1789, Hanover County, Va.).* Friend of Patrick Henry, merchant, planter, Virginia signer of the Declaration of Independence who sacrificed his fortune to the Revolutionary cause and commanded Virginia forces in the field. Member of the house of burgesses and delegate to the first provincial convention (1774), member of the Continental Congress (1775-1777, 1779, 1780), governor (1781). Father of Hugh Nelson.

NELSON, THOMAS AMOS ROGERS *(b March 19, 1812, Kingston, Tenn.; d Aug. 24, 1873, Knoxville, Tenn.)* Lawyer, Tennessee Whig-Unionist-Democrat who while a Congressman was taken off a Washington-bound train by Confederate raiders and held prisoner in Virginia

for a short time; one of President Andrew Johnson's impeachment-trial attorneys. Presidential elector on the Clay-Frelinghuysen (1844) and Taylor-Fillmore (1848) tickets, diplomatic commissioner to China (1851), U.S. Representative (1859-1863), Union National Convention delegate (1866), Democratic National Convention delegate (1868), state supreme court judge (1870-1871).

NELSON, WILLIAM LESTER *(b Aug. 4, 1875, Cooper County, Mo.; d Dec. 31, 1946, Columbia, Mo.)* Teacher, farmer, newspaperman, agricultural writer, Missouri Democrat. State representative (1901-1903, 1905-1907), assistant secretary to the state board of agriculture (1908-1918), U.S. Representative (1919-1921, 1925-1933, 1935-1943), assistant war food administrator (1943).

NESMITH, JAMES WILLIS *(b July 23, 1820, New Brunswick, Canada, while his parents were visiting there from Maine; d June 17, 1885, Rickreall, Oreg.)* A Maine farmboy who drifted West and joined the great migration (1843) to the west coast where he was one of the first Oregon colonists, studied for the law, farmed, raised stock, fought Indians, embarked on a political career, developed skills as a debator, became a Douglas Democrat and a strong supporter of Lincoln during the Civil War— all this only to see his public career cut short because of his close friendship with Andrew Johnson. Judge of the Oregon provisional government (1845-1848), U.S. marshal (1853-1855), superintendent of Indian affairs for the Oregon and Washington territories (1857-1861), U.S. Senate (1861-1867), Polk County road supervisor (1868), U.S. Representative (1873-1875).

NEUBERGER, MAURINE BROWN *(b Jan. 9, 1907, Cloverdale, Oreg.)* Widow of Richard L. Neuberger who succeeded him as U.S. Senator (1960-1967), writer, photographer, Oregon Democrat with a great interest in consumer affairs, equality for women, and disarmament. Among the positions she held in those areas: chairman of the Citizens Advisory Council on Status of Women, consumer relations consultant to the Food and Drug Administration, member of the general advisory committee on arms control and disarmament, member of the President's Consumer Advisory Council. Before going to Washington, she was a member of the state house of representatives (1951-1955).

NEUBERGER, RICHARD LEWIS *(b Dec. 26, 1912, Multnomah County, Oreg.; d March 9, 1960, Portland Oreg.)* Author, newspaperman who was a correspondent for the *New York Times* (1939-1954), Oregon Democrat. State representative (1941, 1942), military aide to the U.S. delegation to the United Nations Conference (1945), state senate (1949-1954), U.S. Senate (1955 until death). Husband of Maurine B. Neuberger.

NEW, ANTHONY *(b 1747, Gloucester County, Va.; d March 2, 1833, Todd County, Ky.)* Lawyer, Revolutionary Army officer, farmer, Virginia and Kentucky Democrat. In Virginia: U.S. Representative (1793-1805). In Kentucky: U.S. Representative (1811-1813, 1817-1819, 1821-1823).

NEW, HARRY STEWART *(b Dec. 31, 1858, Indianapolis, Ind.; d May 9, 1937, Baltimore, Md.)* Newspaperman who rose from reporter to publisher of the *Indianapolis Journal* (1878-1903), quarry operator, builder, Indiana Republican who abided by the rules and became postmaster general in the cabinets of Presidents Harding and Coolidge (1923-1929). Before that he was state senator (1896-1900), GOP National Convention delegate (1896, 1912, 1920, 1924), GOP National Committee member (1900-1912) and chairman (1907, 1908), U.S. Senator (1917-1923).

NEWBOLD, THOMAS *(b Aug. 2, 1760, Springfield Township, N.J.; d Dec. 18, 1823, Springfield Township)* Farmer, banker, New Jersey Democrat. State assemblyman (1797, 1820-1822), presidential elector (1804) who cast his vote for Thomas Jefferson, U.S. Representative (1807-1813).

NEWELL, "DOC" ROBERT *(b March 30, 1807, Muskingum County, Ohio; d Nov. 1869, Lewiston, Idaho)* Trapper who was one of the first four men to travel to Oregon by wagon, settled near what is now the town of Hillsboro, became a river boatman, merchant, and a political leader, served on the legislative committee (1843) that drew up a provisional constitution, and was a member of the house of representatives during the life of the provisional government. He joined the California gold rush of 1848-1849, returned to Oregon (1850), served as an Indian scout (1855-1856), sat in the state legislature (1860-1862); then went on to Idaho where he was an army-post commissioner and Indian agent (1862 until death).

NEWELL, WILLIAM AUGUSTUS *(b Sept. 5, 1817, Franklin, Ohio; d Aug. 8, 1901, Allentown, N.J.)* Physician, New Jersey Whig-Republican who besides being governor of that state (1857-1860) was the Garfield-appointed governor of the Washington Territory (1880-1884). U.S. Representative (1847-1851, 1865-1867), GOP National Convention delegate (1864), U.S. Indian inspector (1884-1885).

NEWLANDS, FRANCIS GRIFFITH *(b Aug. 28, 1848, Natchez, Miss.; d Dec. 24, 1917, Washington, D.C.)* Nevada lawyer who was one of free silver's strongest advocates, serving for many years as vice chairman of the National Silver Committee and switching his political affiliations from Silver party to Republican and ultimately to Democrat (1891) because of his dislike for GOP financial policies. U.S. Representative (1893-1903), U.S. Senate (1903 until death).

NEWTON, THOMAS, JR. *(b Nov. 21, 1768, Norfolk, Va.; d Aug. 5, 1847, Norfolk, Va.)* Lawyer, Virginia Democrat who spent most of his adult life in Congress where he supported all legislation that would increase U.S. commerce. State house of delegates (1796-1799), U.S. Representative (1801-1833).

NEWTON, WALTER HUGHES *(b Oct. 10, 1880, Minneapolis, Minn.; d Aug. 10, 1941, Minneapolis)* Lawyer, writer, Minnesota Republican who was President Hoover's secretary (1929-1933) and a Roosevelt-appointed member of the Federal Home Loan Bank Board (1933-1934). Hennepin County first assistant prosecutor (1914-1918), U.S. Representative (1919-1929), Smithsonian Institution regent (1924-1931), federal referee in bankruptcy (1938 until death).

NIBLACK, WILLIAM ELLIS *(b May 19, 1822, Dubois County, Ind.; d May 7, 1893, Indianapolis, Ind.)* Teacher, surveyor, lawyer, Indiana Democrat who favored the Northern point of view during the Civil War but supported the McClellan presidential nomination (1864) on a peace platform. State representative (1849, 1850, 1862, 1863), state senate (1850-1853), circuit court judge (1854-1859), U.S. Representative (1857-1861, 1865-1875), Democratic National Committeeman (1864-1872) and national convention delegate (1864, 1868, 1876), state supreme court judge (1877-1889).

NICHOLAS, JOHN *(b about 1757, Williamsburg, Va.; d Dec. 31, 1819, Geneva, N.Y.)* Lawyer, farmer, Virginia and New York Democrat. In Virginia: U.S. Representative (1793-1801). In New York: state senate (1806-1809), common pleas court judge (1806-1819). Brother of William C. and uncle of Robert C. Nicholas.

NICHOLAS, ROBERT CARTER *(b 1793, Hanover, Va.; d Dec. 24, 1857, Terrebonne Parish, La.)* Sugar planter, Louisiana Democrat. U.S. Senate to fill a vacancy (1836-1841), Louisiana secretary of state (1843-1846). Nephew of John and William C. Nicholas.

NICHOLAS, WILSON CARY *(b Jan. 31, 1761, Williamsburg, Va.; d Oct. 10, 1820, near Charlottesville, Va.)* Revolutionary Army officer who was commander of Washington's Life Guard, planter, friend and political ally of Thomas Jefferson, and a Virginia Democrat who helped to frame the anti-Federalist resolutions (1798), later became involved in western land speculations and saw his financial bubble burst (1819) with Jefferson not escaping unharmed. Member of the state house of delegates (1784-1788, 1789, 1794-1800), delegate to the state constitutional convention that ratified the federal Constitution (1788), U.S. Senate (1799-1804), collector of Norfolk port (1804-1807), U.S. Representative (1807-1809), governor (1814-1817). Brother of John, uncle of Robert C. Nicholas.

NICHOLLS, FRANCIS REDDING TILLOU *(b Aug. 20, 1834, Donaldsonville, La.; d Jan. 4, 1912, near Thibodeaux, La.).* West Point graduate, lawyer, planter, antisecessionist Louisiana Democrat who nevertheless fought on the side of the Confederacy, losing an arm at Winchester and a foot at Chancellorsville.

After the war, very much the hero, he led the political fight to rid the state of Carpetbag rule, ran for governor and, when the ruling forces declared his Republican opponent elected, set up a de facto government that ultimately was recognized by the federal government. And so he held office (1877-1880) until a New Orleans cadre of professional politicians took control of the Democratic party statewide.

He remained in political retirement for the next eight years, returning once again to politics only when the Louisiana lottery became a national scandal. Again he was elected governor (1888-1892) and succeeded in driving the lottery out of existence. Only then did he accept reward—appointment as chief justice of the Louisiana Supreme Court (1892-1904), but a new state constitution, which he favored, caused his demotion to associate justice, a position that he held until 1911 when he retired because of poor health.

NICHOLS, JOHN CONOVER (b Aug. 31, 1896, Joplin, Mo.; d Nov. 7, 1945, Asmara, Eritrea, in an airplane crash). Lawyer, airline executive, Oklahoma Democrat. U.S. Representative (1935-1943).

NICHOLSON, JOHN ANTHONY (b Nov. 17, 1827, Laurel, Del.; d Nov. 4, 1906, Dover, Del.) Lawyer, Delaware Democrat. Kent County free schools superintendent (1851), U.S. Representative (1865-1869).

NICHOLSON, JOSEPH HOPPER (b May 15, 1770, Chestertown, Md.; d March 4, 1817, Baltimore, Md.) Lawyer, Maryland Democrat who raised, financed, and commanded an artillery company during the War of 1812 that took part in the defense of Fort McHenry. Member of the state house of delegates (1796-1798), U.S. Representative (1799-1806), chief justice of the sixth judicial district and associate justice of the state court of appeals (1806 until death).

NICHOLSON, SAMUEL DANFORD (b Feb. 22, 1859, Prince Edward Island, Canada; d March 24, 1923, Denver, Colo.) Mine laborer who worked himself up to president of a string of mines and discoverer of the zinc ore named for him: Nicholsoiti; Colorado Populist turned Republican. Mayor of Leadville (1893-1897), U.S. Senate (1921 until death).

NICOLAY, JOHN GEORGE (b Feb. 26, 1832, Essingen, Germany; d Sept. 26, 1901, Washington, D.C.) Printer's apprentice who became editor-publisher of the Pittsfield (Ill.) Free Press, became a close, lifelong friend of John Hay (which see), met Abraham Lincoln and served as his private secretary (with Hay as his assistant), and together the two of them wrote his biography: Abraham Lincoln, a History (1890). U.S. consul in Paris (1865-1869), marshal of the U.S. Supreme Court (1872-1887).

NICOLLS, RICHARD (b 1624, Bedfordshire, England; d May 28, 1672, off coast of England in the battle of Solebay). Lawyer who was appointed the first English governor of New York (1664-1668) and brought about the surrender of New Amsterdam without bloodshed.

NILES, JOHN MILTON (b Aug. 20, 1787, Windsor, Conn.; d May 31, 1856, Hartford, Conn.) Lawyer, founder of the Hartford Times (1817), author, Connecticut Jacksonian Democrat turned Republican. Associate judge of the Hartford County court (1821-1826), state representative (1826), Hartford postmaster (1829-1836), U.S. Senate (1835-1839, 1843-1849), unsuccessful candidate for governor (1839), U.S. postmaster general in the Van Buren cabinet (1840-1841).

NIXON, GEORGE STUART (b April 2, 1860, Placer County, Calif.; d June 5, 1912, Washington, D.C.) Railroad telegrapher, opera-house builder, banker, mine operator, rancher, Nevada Republican. State representative (1891), U.S. Senate (1905 until death).

NOAH, MORDECAS MANUEL (b July 19, 1785, Philadelphia, Pa.; d March 22, 1851, New York City) Newspaperman who founded New York's Evening Star, playwright, lawyer, New York Democrat turned Whig who tried in vain to establish a colony called Ararat for Jewish refugees on Grand Island in the Niagara River. Consul to Tunis (1813-1815), New York County sheriff (1822), surveyor of the Port of New York (1829-1833), associate judge of the court of sessions (1841-1842).

NOBLE, JAMES *(b Dec. 16, 1785, Clarke County, Va.; d Feb. 26, 1831, Washington, D.C.)* Lawyer who chose Indiana as the land of opportunity, operated a ferryboat on the Ohio River, became skilled in oratory, and was instrumental in bringing about statehood, serving as one of Indiana's first two U.S. Senators (1816 until death). Franklin County prosecutor (1810, 1811), circuit court judge (1815), state constitutional convention delegate (1816).

NOLAN, JOHN IGNATIUS *(b Jan. 14, 1874, San Francisco, Calif.; d Nov. 18, 1922, San Francisco)* Iron molder, labor leader, California Republican. San Francisco city and county supervisor (1911), secretary of the San Francisco Labor Council (1912), U.S. Representative (1913 until death after being reelected to a sixth term). Husband of Mae Ella Nolan.

NOLAN, MAE ELLA *(b Sept. 20, 1886, San Francisco, Calif.)* California Republican who served as a U.S. Representative (1923-1925) to fill the vacancy caused by the death of her husband, John I. Nolan.

NORBECK, PETER *(b Aug. 27, 1870, Clay County, S.Dak. which was then Dakota Territory; d. Dec. 20, 1936, Redfield, S.Dak.)* Farmer, well driller, progressive South Dakota Republican who had much to do with the creation of the Mount Rushmore National Monument. State senate (1909-1915), lieutenant governor (1915, 1916), governor (1917-1921), delegate to all GOP National Conventions (1916-1932), U.S. Senate (1921

until death). Politically he followed the lead of such men as Theodore Roosevelt and Robert La Follette, worked continually to better the farmers' lot and, as a conservationist, played a major role in passage of the Migratory Bird Act (1929).

NORBLAD, ALBIN WALTER, JR. *(b Sept. 12, 1908, Escanaba, Mich.; d Sept. 20, 1964, U.S. Naval Hospital, Bethesda, Md.)* Lawyer, Oregon Republican. State representative (1935-1937), GOP National Convention (1940), Army Air Corps (1942-1945), U.S. Representative (1946 until death) serving on the Armed Services Committee.

NORRELL, WILLIAM FRANK *(b Aug. 29, 1896, Milo, Ark.; d Feb. 15, 1961, Washington, D.C.)* Lawyer, Arkansas Democrat. State senator (1930-1938) and senate president for four of those years, U.S. Representative (1939 until death).

NORRIS, GEORGE WILLIAM *(b July 11, 1861, Sandusky County, Ohio; d Sept. 2, 1944, McCook, Nebr.)* Teacher, lawyer, Nebraska Republican who began his political career by serving three terms as Furnas County attorney before moving on to bigger things. Fourteenth district judge (1895-1902), U.S. Representative (1903-1913), U.S. Senate (1913-1943) running for his last term as an Independent Republican.

NORRIS, ISAAC *(b Oct. 23, 1701, Philadelphia, Pa.; d July 13, 1766, Philadelphia)* Merchant, dedicated pacifist and leader of the Quaker party in Pennsylvania who proposed this Biblical quotation (Lev. 25:10) that is inscribed upon the Liberty Bell: "Proclaim liberty throughout the land unto all the inhabitants thereof." Philadelphia Common Council (1727-1730) and alderman (1730-1742), member of the Pennsylvania assembly (1734-1766) and speaker (1750-1764), delegate to the Albany Indian Conferences (1745, 1754).

NORRIS, MOSES, JR. *(b Nov. 8, 1799, Pittsfield, N.H.; d Jan. 11, 1855, Washington, D.C.)* Lawyer, New Hampshire Democrat. State representative (1837-1840, 1842) and house speaker (1847, 1848), member of the state council (1841, 1842), U.S. Representative (1843-1847), U.S. Senate (1849 until death).

NORTON, MARY TERESA *(b March 7, 1875, Jersey City, N.J.; d Aug. 2, 1959, Greenwich, Conn.)* New Jersey Democrat who was the first woman to serve a quarter-century in either the U.S. Senate or the House of Representatives, sitting (1925-1951) in the latter. President of the Queen's Daughters Day Nursery Association of Jersey City (1916-1927); vice chairman of the state Democratic committee (1921-1931) and chairman (1932-1935) while also serving as vice chairman of Hudson County committee; county freeholder (1922), Democratic National Convention delegate (1924-1948), delegate to International Labor Conference in Paris (1945), consultant to the Women's Advisory Committee on Defense Manpower (1951, 1952).

NORTON, PATRICK DANIEL *(b May 17, 1876, Ishpeming, Mich.; d Oct. 14, 1953, Minot, N.Dak.)* Lawyer, banker, farmer, stock raiser, North Dakota Republican. Ramsey County schools superintendent (1905-1907), chief clerk of the state house of representatives (1907, 1908), Adams County prosecutor (1907-1911), North Dakota secretary of state (1911-1913), U.S. Representative (1913-1919), national bank receiver (1924-1927), GOP National Convention delegate (1928) and delegate to all state conventions (1920-1940).

NOYES, JOHN *(b April 2, 1764, Atkinson, N.H.; d Oct. 26, 1841, near Putney, Vt.)* Dartmouth College tutor (1797-1799) who numbered Daniel Webster among his pupils, merchant, Vermont Federalist who held several state and local offices and served one term as a U.S. Representative (1815-1817) and then retired to farm life and his books.

NYE, JAMES WARREN *(b June 10, 1815, DeRuyter, N.Y.; d Dec. 25, 1876, White Plains, N.Y.)* Lawyer, New York Republican who was appointed governor of the Washoe (Nevada) Territory (1861-1864) by Abraham Lincoln, remained after Nevada became a state and was one of its first two U.S. Senators (1864-1873). In New York: Madison County district attorney (1839) and judge (1840-1848), unsuccessful Congressional candidate on the Anti-Slavery ticket (1846), first president of New York City's Metropolitan Police Board (1857-1860).

O

☆ ☆ ☆

OATES, WILLIAM CALVIN *(b Nov. 30, 1835, Pike County, Ala.; d Sept. 9, 1910, Montgomery, Ala.)* Lawyer, teacher, journalist, Confederate Army officer who lost an arm at Richmond, Alabama Democrat. National convention delegate (1868), state representative (1870-1872), state constitutional convention delegate (1875), U.S. Representative (1881-1894), governor (1894-1896) after election in one of the state's most exciting campaigns.

O'BRIEN, GEORGE DONOGHUE *(b Jan. 1, 1900, Detroit, Mich.; d Oct. 25, 1957, Washington, D.C.)* Lawyer, Michigan Democrat. U.S. Representative (1937-1939, 1941-1947, 1949-1955), Democratic National Convention delegate (1944), District of Columbia assistant corporation counsel (1955 until death).

O'BRIEN, LEO WILLIAM *(b Sept. 21, 1900, Buffalo, N.Y.)* Newspaperman, radio-TV commentator, New York Democrat. Member of Albany Port District Commission (1935-1952), U.S. Representative (1952-1966) serving on the Interior and Insular Affairs and Interstate and Foreign Commerce committees.

O'CONNELL, JOHN MATTHEW *(b Aug. 10, 1872, Westerly, R.I.; d Dec. 6, 1941, Westerly)* Teacher, dentist, Rhode Island Democrat. State representative (1929-1932), U.S. Representative (1933-1939).

O'CONNOR, JAMES *(b April 4, 1870, New Orleans, La.; d Jan. 7, 1941, Covington, La.)* Lawyer, Louisiana Democrat. State constitutional convention delegate (1898, 1913), state representative (1900-1912), Orleans Parish assistant city attorney (1918-1919), U.S. Representative (1919-1931).

O'CONNOR, JAMES FRANCIS *(b May 7, 1878, near California Junction, Iowa; d Jan. 15, 1945, Washington, D.C.).* Lawyer, banker, rancher, Montana Democrat. Sixth judicial district judge (1912), speaker of the state house of representatives (1917-1918), Federal Trade Commission special counsel (1918), U.S. Representative (1937 until death).

O'CONNOR, JOHN JOSEPH *(b Nov. 23, 1885, Raynham, Mass.; d Jan. 26, 1960, Washington, D.C.)* Lawyer, New York Democrat. Secretary of the Democratic delegation to the state constitutional convention (1915), state assemblyman (1920-1923), Child Welfare Commission legislative secretary (1921, 1922), delegate to all state and county Democratic conventions (1919-1938), Democratic National Convention delegate (1936), U.S. Representative (1923-1939); when

446

his own party failed to nominate him for an eighth term, the Republicans did, but to no avail—he lost the election.

O'CONOR, HERBERT ROMULUS *(b Nov. 17, 1896, Baltimore, Md.; d March 4, 1960, Baltimore)* Lawyer, newspaperman, banker, Maryland Democrat. Assistant state's attorney (1920-1922), people's counsel to the Public Service Commission (1923), state's attorney (1923-1934), attorney general (1935-1939), governor (1939-1946), Governors' Conference chairman (1942), chairman of Interstate Commission on Potomac River Basin (1943-1945), president and national chairman of Council of State Governments (1943), national chairman of the Interstate Commission on Postwar Reconstruction and Development (1943-1946), U.S. Senate (1947-1953).

O'DAY, CAROLINE LOVE GOODWIN *(b June 22, 1875, Perry, Ga.; d Jan. 4, 1943, Rye, N.Y.)* Artist, New York Democrat. Vice chairman of state Democratic committee (1916-1920) and associate chairman (1923-1942), Democratic National Convention delegate (1924, 1928, 1932, 1936), state social welfare commissioner (1923-1934), U.S. Representative (1935-1943).

ODDIE, TASKER LOWNDES *(b Oct. 24, 1870, Brooklyn, N.Y.; d Feb. 17, 1950, San Francisco, Calif.)* Lawyer who went west (1898), settled in Nevada, raised crops and cattle, and developed some of the most productive gold and silver mines in the Tonopah and Goldfield districts; all of this while also staking a political claim as a Republican. Nye County district attorney (1901, 1902), state senate (1903-1906), governor (1911-1915), U.S. Senate (1921-1933).

ODELL, BENJAMIN BAKER, JR. *(b Jan. 14, 1854, Newburgh, N.Y.; d May 9, 1926, Newburgh)* Successful businessman and a New York Republican who helped

Theodore Roosevelt along his political way by proposing him for governor (1899, 1900) and then, while holding that office himself (1901-1904), applied business tactics to state business and thus gave New York one of its soundest administrations. He was a member of the GOP state executive committee for twenty-five years, ten of those years as chairman, and thus he was able to defy boss rule, choosing his own appointees and making his own decisions. U.S. Representative (1895-1899).

O'DONNELL, JAMES *(b March 25, 1840, Norwalk, Conn.; d March 17, 1915, Jackson, Mich.)* Union soldier, publisher of the *Jackson Daily Citizen*, Michigan Republican who originated the nation's rural free mail delivery system. Jackson city recorder (1863-1866), presidential elector on the Grant-Wilson ticket (1872), mayor (1876, 1877), U.S. Representative (1885-1893).

O'FERRALL, CHARLES TRIPLETT *(b Oct. 21, 1840, Brucetown, Va.; d Sept. 22, 1905, Richmond, Va.)* Confederate cavalry officer, lawyer, writer, Virginia Democrat who as governor (1894-1898) made a determined but only temporarily successful effort to put an end to lynching. Member of house of delegates (1871-1873), Rockingham County judge (1874-1880), U.S. Representative (1884-1893).

OGLESBY, RICHARD JAMES *(b July 25, 1824, Floydsburg, Ky.; d April 24, 1899, Elkhart, Ill.)* Union Army officer, lawyer, miner, farmer, Illinois Republican. State senate (1860), governor (1865-1869, 1873, 1885-1889), U.S. Senate (1873-1879).

O'HARA, BARRATT *(b April 28, 1882, Saint Joseph, Mich.; d Aug. 11, 1969, Washington, D.C.)* Newspaperman, lawyer, movie maker, radio commentator, Illinois Democrat. Lieutenant governor (1913-1917), chairman of state senate vice and wage investigations (1913-1915), unsuccessful gubernatorial candidate (1920), U.S. Representative (1949-1951, 1953-1969), member of House Foreign Affairs Committee.

O'HARA, JAMES EDWARD *(b Feb. 26, 1844, New York City; d Sept. 15, 1905, New Bern, N.C.)* Howard University-educated lawyer, North Carolina Republican who was one of six Negro delegates to the state constitutional convention (1875) after first coming to public notice as transcription clerk of the 1868 convention. U.S. Representative (1883-1887).

OLDER, FREMONT *(b Aug. 30, 1856, Freedom Township, Wis.; d March 3, 1935, near Stockton, Calif., of a heart attack while driving)* Crusading California and Nevada newspaperman who left his greatest mark upon San Francisco where he was editor of first the *Bulletin* and then the *Call.* Among his causes: an end to the political domination of the state and city by the Southern Pacific Railroad, prison reform, the acquittal of Thomas J. Mooney and other alleged anarchists (1916), and the breaking of political boss Abraham Ruef.

OLDFIELD, PEARL PEDEN *(b Dec. 2, 1876, Cotton Plant, Ark.)* Arkansas Democrat who served as a U.S. Representative (1929-1931) upon the death of her husband, William A. Oldfield.

OLDFIELD, WILLIAM ALLAN *(b Feb. 4, 1874, Franklin, Ark.; d Nov. 19, 1928, Washington, D.C.)* Lawyer, teacher, Arkansas Democrat who served ten terms in the U.S. House of Representatives (1909 until death) and then was succeeded by his widow, Pearl Peden Oldfield. Before going to Congress he had been Independence County's prosecuting attorney (1902-1906).

OLDS, EDSON BALDWIN *(b June 3, 1802, Marlboro, Vt.; d Jan. 24, 1869,* *Lancaster, Ohio)* Teacher, merchant, physician, Ohio Democrat who was charged with disloyalty and briefly imprisoned (1862) during the Civil War and while in jail was elected a state representative (1862-1866), a position that he had held many times before (1842, 1843, 1845, 1846). State senator (1846-1848) and senate president (1846, 1847), U.S. Representative (1849-1855).

O'LEARY, JAMES ALOYSIUS *(b April 23, 1889, New Brighton, N.Y.; d March 16, 1944, West Brighton, N.Y.)* Lawyer, real estate-insurance broker, ice manufacturer, New York Democrat. U.S. Representative (1935 until death).

OLIVER, WILLIAM BACON *(b May 23, 1867, Eutaw, Ala.; d May 27, 1948, New Orleans, La.)* Lawyer, Alabama Democrat who was a power in the party as chairman for many years of the Tuscaloosa County central committee. Sixth judicial circuit solicitor (1898-1909), University of Alabama Law School dean (1909-1913), Democratic National Convention delegate (1924), U.S. Representative (1915-1937), special assistant to the U.S. attorney general (1939-1944).

OLMSTED, MARLIN EDGAR *(b May 21, 1847, Ulysses Township, Pa.; d July 19, 1913, New York City)* Lawyer, Pennsylvania Republican who as chairman of the House Committee on Insular Affairs secured for Puerto Rico legislation already applicable to Hawai and the Philippines. State constitutional convention delegate (1891), U.S. Representative (1897-1913).

OLSON, FLOYD BJERSTJERNE *(b Nov. 13, 1891, Minneapolis, Minn.; d Aug. 22, 1936, of cancer in the Mayo Clinic, Rochester, Minn.)* Itinerant salesman, fisherman, longshoreman who roamed as far from home as Alaska, Industrial Workers of the World member, lawyer, Minnesota Democrat turned Farmer Laborite, and orator with a great gift for sarcasm whose words usually were far more radical than his deeds. Hennepin County assistant attorney (1919-1920), county attorney (1920-1928), governor (1931-1936). A reluctant supporter of Franklin D. Roosevelt, he often was spoken of as the presidential candidate of a third-party ticket that never materialized.

O'NEALE, MARGARET "PEGGY" (b 1796, Washington, D.C.; d Nov. 8, 1879, Washington, D.C.) Daughter of a Washington tavernkeeper in whose inn John H. Eaton of Tennessee took lodging upon being elected to the U.S. Senate (1818) as did his friend, Andrew Jackson, five years later. Jackson became President; Eaton became his secretary of war. Peggy's husband, John B. Timberlake, a Navy purser, died at sea (1828) and she and Eaton soon after were married.

This, to say the least, threw the wives of the other cabinet members into a dither. They were, in the language of the times, scandalized. They would have nothing to do with Peggy O'Neale. They urged their husbands to have nothing to do with her husband. As a result, all Washington joined in the social donnybrook. Jackson stood by his friends, John and Peggy, and the cabinet faded away. Eaton was named governor of Florida and then U.S. minister to Spain and where he went Peggy O'Neale went with him. He died in 1856; Peggy married an Italian gigolo-type, Antonio Buchignani, who ran off with her fortune and her granddaughter, and Peggy died forlorn and destitute.

O'NEILL, CHARLES (b March 21, 1821, Philadelphia, Pa.; d Nov. 25, 1893, Philadelphia) Lawyer, Pennsylvania Republican. State representative (1850-1852, 1860), state senate (1853), U.S. Representative (1863-1871, 1873 until death).

O'NEILL, JOHN JOSEPH (b June 25, 1846, St. Louis, Mo.; d Feb. 19, 1898, St. Louis) Gold pen manufacturer, lawyer, Missouri Democrat. State representative (1872-1878), municipal assemblyman (1879-1881), U.S. Representative (1883-1889, 1891-1893, 1894-1895).

ORR, JAMES LAWRENCE (b May 12, 1822, Craytonville, S.C.; d May 5, 1873, St. Petersburg, Russia, while U.S. minister to that country) Lawyer, newspaperman, and a man torn by the same conflicts that tore the nation. At first against secession and then for it, a Confederate senator-soldier, yet a commissioner who went to Washington to negotiate a provisional government for his home state of South Carolina and a Democrat who urged acceptance of Reconstruction and finally turned to Radical Republicanism after being elected governor as a Conservative.

State representative (1844-1848), U.S. Representative (1849-1859) and speaker (1857-1859), southern rights convention delegate (1851), Democratic National Convention delegate (1860) and the state secession convention in the same year, Confederate senator (1861), state constitutional convention delegate (1865), governor (1865-1868), state convention president (1866), Union National Convention delegate (1866), eighth judicial circuit judge (1868-1870), GOP state convention delegate (1872) and national convention in the same year, and staunch supporter of the presidential candidacy of Ulysses S. Grant. His reward was appointment as ambassador to Russia (December 1872, until death).

ORTH, GODLOVE STEIN (b April 22, 1817, Lebanon, Pa.; d Dec. 16, 1882, Lafayette, Ind.) Lawyer, orator, Indiana Whig who turned to Know-Nothingism, then to the People's party, and finally to Republicanism; a man who, according to one biographer, placed party solidarity above principle, a man who not once voted for an unpopular cause. State senator (1843-1848) and senate president (1845), presidential elector on the Taylor-Fillmore ticket (1848), delegate to the peace-between-states convention (1861), U.S. Representative (1863-1871, 1873-1875, 1879 until death), minister to Austria-Hungary (1875-1876).

OSBORNE, JOHN EUGENE *(b June 19, 1858, Westport, N.Y.; d April 24, 1943, Rawlins, Wyo.)* Physician, rancher, banker, Wyoming Democrat who for twenty years (1900-1920) was member of the Democratic National Committee. Member of the Wyoming territorial legislature (1883-1885), chairman of the territory's prison-building commission (1888), mayor of Rawlins (1888), the state of Wyoming's third governor (1893-1895), Democratic National Convention delegate (1896), U.S. Representative (1897-1899), first assistant secretary of state (1913-1917).

OSGOOD, SAMUEL *(b Feb. 3, 1748, Andover, Mass.; d Aug. 12, 1813, New York City)* Minuteman officer during the Revolution, merchant who applied his knowledge of business and finance to legislative matters, Massachusetts Democrat who opposed the U.S. Constitution as placing too much power in the hands of the federal government, yet served as the nation's first postmaster general (1789-1791) when he resigned and moved to New York. In Massachusetts: delegate to the Essex County convention (1774), member of the Provincial Congress (1775-1778), member of the Continental Congress (1780-1784), state representative (1784), one of the first three commissioners of the U.S. Treasury (1785-1789). In New York: state assemblyman (1800-1803), state supervisor (1801), Port of New York naval officer (1803 until death).

O'SHAUNESSY, GEORGE FRANCIS *(b May 1, 1868, Galway, Ireland; d Nov. 28, 1934, Providence, R.I.)* Lawyer, New York and Rhode Island Democrat. In New York: state deputy attorney general (1904, 1905), New York City assistant corporation counsel (1906). In Rhode Island: state representative (1910), U.S. Representative (1911-1919), collector of internal revenue (1919-1921).

OSMERS, FRANK CHARLES, JR. *(b Dec. 30, 1907, Leonia, N.J.)* Jeweler, publisher, real estate broker, New Jersey Republican. Haworth Borough Council (1930-1934), mayor (1935, 1936), state assembly (1935-1937), U.S. Representative (1939-1943, 1951-1965), U.S. Army (1943-1946), member of House Armed Services Committee.

OSTERTAG, HAROLD CHARLES *(b June 22, 1896, Attica, N.Y.)* Railroad executive, New York Republican. State assembly (1932-1950), member of Board of Managers of the Council of State Governments (1935-1950), GOP state convention delegate (1930-1958), national conventions (1952, 1956, 1960), U.S. Representative (1951-1965) serving on the Appropriations Committee.

OTERO, MARIANO SABINO *(b Aug. 29, 1844, Peralta, N.Mex.; d Feb. 1, 1904, Albuquerque, N.Mex.)* Rancher, banker, manufacturer who declined Democratic nomination as a delegate to Congress from New Mexico Territory (1877), but accepted the Republican nomination at the following congressional election, won and so served (1879-1881). Before that he was Bernalillo County probate judge (1871-1879). Nephew of Miguel A. Otero.

OTERO, MIGUEL ANTONIO *(b June 21, 1829, Valencia, N.Mex.; d May 30, 1882, Las Vegas, N.Mex.)* Teacher, lawyer, merchant, railroad builder, New Mexico Territory Democrat who declined Lincoln appointment (1861) as minister to Spain, instead accepting the post of territorial secretary (1861-

1862) and acting governor. Territorial representative (1852-1854), attorney general (1854), delegate to the U.S. Congress (1856-1861), Democratic National Convention delegate (1860). Uncle of Mariano S. Otero.

OTIS, HARRISON GRAY *(b Oct. 8, 1765, Boston, Mass.; d Oct. 28, 1848, Boston)* Lawyer, orator who was a strong defender of freedom of speech, Massachusetts Federalist turned Whig who was one of the leaders of the Hartford convention (1814) where he successfully argued against breaking away from the federal government. State representative (1796) and house speaker (1802-1804), Washington appointee as U.S. attorney for the state (1796) and John Adams appointee (1801-1802) for the same job, U.S. Representative (1797-1801), state senator (1805-1816) and senate president (1805, 1808-1810), Harvard University overseer (1810-1823) and fellow (1823-1825), common pleas court judge (1814-1818), mayor of Boston (1829-1832). Son of Samuel A. Otis.

OTIS, SAMUEL ALLYNE *(b Nov. 24, 1740, Barnstable, Mass.; d April 22, 1814, Washington, D.C.)* Massachusetts merchant who began his public service as collector of clothing for the Continental Army (1777) and ended it as secretary of the U.S. Senate (1789 until death). In between, he served as state representative (1776, 1784-1787) and house speaker (1784), delegate to the Massachusetts convention that drafted the first state constitution, Continental Congress (1787, 1788). Father of Harrison G. Otis.

OTJEN, THEOBALD *(b Oct. 27, 1851, West China, Mich.; d April 11, 1924, Milwaukee, Wis.)* Lawyer, Wisconsin Republican. Milwaukee councilman (1887-1894), library trustee (1887-1891) and museum trustee (1891-1894), U.S. Representative (1895-1907).

OURY, GRANVILLE HENDERSON *(b March 12, 1825, Abingdon, Va.; d Jan. 11, 1891, Tucson, Ariz.)* Missouri lawyer, California gold miner (1849-1856), who landed in Tucson, Arizona (1856), led a party to the rescue of the Crabbe expedition under siege in Sonora, Mexico (1857), and stayed on to become a power in territorial politics as a Democrat. Delegate to the Confederate Congress (1862) resigning to serve as an officer in the Confederate Army (1862-1864), territorial representative (1866, 1873, 1875) and house speaker (1866, 1873), territorial attorney general (1869-1871), Maricopa district attorney (1871-1873), Pinal County district attorney (1879, 1889, 1890), delegate to the U.S. Congress (1881-1885), Democratic National Convention delegate (1884).

OUTHWAITE, JOSEPH HODSON *(b Dec. 5, 1841, Cleveland, Ohio; d Dec. 9, 1907, Columbus, Ohio)* Educator, lawyer, Ohio Democrat. Franklin County prosecutor (1874-1878), county children's home trustee (1879-1883), Columbus sinking fund trustee (1883-1890), U.S. Representative (1885-1895), civilian member of the Board of Ordnance and Fortification (1895-1899), Ohio State University trustee (1896-1898) and law school dean (1904 until death).

OVERMAN, LEE SLATER *(b Jan. 3, 1854, Salisbury, N.C.; d Dec. 12, 1930, Washington, D.C.)* Teacher, lawyer, banker, railroad executive, North Carolina Democrat who was author of the so-called Overman Law (1918) that widened the president's power to transfer government functions from one department to another. State representative (1883, 1885, 1887, 1893, 1899) and house speaker (1893), Democratic state convention president (1900, 1911), presidential elector on the Bryan-Stevenson ticket (1900), U.S. Senate (1903 until death) with funeral services conducted in the Senate chambers.

OVERSTREET, JAMES WHETSTONE *(b Aug. 28, 1866, Screven County, Ga.; d Dec. 4, 1938, Sylvania, Ga.)* Lawyer, Georgia Democrat. State representative (1898, 1899), state Democratic executive committee member (1905, 1906), Sylvania city judge (1902-1906), U.S. Representative (1906-1907, 1917-1923), Democratic National Convention delegate (1912).

OVERSTREET, JESSE *(b Dec. 14, 1859, Franklin, Ind.; d May 27, 1910, Indianapolis, Ind.)* Lawyer, Indiana Republican. GOP state committeeman (1892), U.S. Representative (1895-1909).

OVERTON, JOHN HOLMES *(b Sept. 17, 1875, Marksville, La.; d May 14, 1948, Bethesda, Md.)* Lawyer, Louisiana Democrat. U.S. Representative (1931-1933), U.S. Senate (1933 until death).

OWEN, ROBERT DALE *(b Nov. 9, 1800, Glasgow, Scotland; d June 24, 1877, Lake George, N.Y.)* Reformer, teacher, newspaper editor, lecturer, author who published New York's *Free Enquirer* (1828-1832) as the voice of a group who believed in equitable distribution of wealth, more liberal divorce laws, emancipation of slaves, and other social legislation, then returned to the communal-type town of New Harmony, Indiana, which he had helped his father to found (1825) and became interested in politics; Indiana Democrat. While a U.S. Representative (1843-1847) proposed measures upon which the Oregon boundary dispute was resolved and the Smithsonian Institution was founded. State representative (1835-1838), Pierce-appointed chargé d'affaires to the Two Sicilies (1853-1854) and minister (1854-1858). While in Italy he became a Spiritualist and worked thereafter to raise it above cultism and to find for it a basis of scientific fact. His many published works include *Footfalls on the Boundary of Another World* (1860), *The Wrong of Slavery* (1864), *The Debatable Land Between This World and the Next* (1872), and his autobiography *Threading My Way* (1874).

OWEN, ROBERT LATHAM *(b Feb. 3, 1856, Lynchburg, Va.; d July 19, 1947, Washington, D.C.)* Lawyer, banker, Indian Territory (now the state of Oklahoma) and Oklahoma Democrat who was chairman of the National Popular Government League for thirty-four years (1913 until death). Democratic National Committeeman (1892-1896) and national convention delegate (1892, 1896, 1924), vice chairman of the Oklahoma Democratic campaign committee (1906); then, a month after statehood in November 1907, becoming one of Oklahoma's first two U.S. Senators, serving December 1907-1925.

OWEN, RUTH BRYAN *(b Oct. 2, 1885, Jacksonville, Ill.; d July 26, 1954, Copenhagen, Denmark)* Nurse, author, lecturer, educator, Florida Democrat, and a humanitarian whose good works included three years in the West Indies (1910-1912), three years in England (1912-1915), membership on the executive committee of the American Women's War Relief Fund which operated the American Women's War Hospital, and war nurse with the Voluntary Aid Detachment in the Egypt-Palestine campaign (1915-1918).

Vice president of the Board of Regents of the University of Miami (1925-1928) and member of the faculty (1926-1928), U.S. Representative (1929-1933), delegate to the Interparliamentary Union (1930), Roosevelt-appointed minister to Denmark (1933-1936), special assistant in the Division of Public Liaison of the State Department at the San Francisco Conference (1945), member of the Federal Reformatory for Women advisory board (1938-1954), trustee of the Starr Commonwealth for Boys (1941-1954). Daughter of William Jennings Bryan.

P

☆ ☆ ☆

PACA, WILLIAM *(b Oct. 31, 1740, Queen Anne, now Harford, County, Md.; d Oct. 23, 1799, Queen Anne County).* Lawyer, planter, Maryland signer of the Declaration of Independence who contributed financially to the Revolution and before that a leader in the fight against proprietary rule and a framer of the state constitution. Member of the provincial assembly (1771-1774) and the first and second Continental Congress (1774-1779), state senate (1777-1779), chief judge of the superior court (1778-1780), chief justice of the court of appeals in prize and admiralty cases (1780-1782), Maryland's third state governor (1782-1785) who among other accomplishments helped found Washington College and laid the cornerstone for its first building (1783); delegate to the state convention that ratified the federal Constitution (1788) but not before he had offered twenty-eight amendments to it.

PACHECO, ROMUALDO *(b Oct. 31, 1831, Santa Barbara, Calif.; d Jan. 23, 1899, Oakland, Calif.)* Son of a Mexican army officer who was killed at Cahuenga Pass (1831), sea captain, rancher, who took the oath of allegiance to the United States when California was admitted to the Union and devoted much effort to bringing native Californians and U.S. settlers together; Republican. State senator (1851, 1861), state assemblyman (1853-1855, 1868-1870), state treasurer (1863-1866), lieutenant governor (1871-1875), governor (1875), U.S. Representative (1877-1878, 1879-1883), minister to the Central American states (1890-1891) and to Honduras and Guatemala (1891-1893).

PACKER, ASA *(b Dec. 29, 1805, Mystic, Conn.; d May 17, 1879, Philadelphia, Pa.)* Carpenter, merchant, canal boat builder and operator who later built and ran the Lehigh Valley Railroad and then used much of his fortune to found and endow Lehigh University (1866), Pennsylvania Democrat. State representative (1842, 1843), Carbon County associate judge (1843, 1844), U.S. Representative (1853-1857), Democratic National Convention delegate (1868).

PADDOCK, ALGERNON SIDNEY *(b Nov. 9, 1830, Glens Falls, N.Y.; d Oct. 17, 1897, Beatrice, Nebr.)* Teacher, lawyer who began practice in Omaha, Nebraska Territory (1857), also had flings at journalism, manufacturing, farming, and the brokerage business while showing keen interest in politics as a Republican. Delegate to the first territorial convention (1859), GOP National Convention delegate (1860, 1864), secretary and acting governor of the territory (1861-1867), U.S. Senate (1875-1881, 1887-1893), Utah Territory elections commissioner (1882-1886).

453

PADGETT, LEMUEL PHILLIPS *(b Nov. 28, 1855, Columbia, Tenn.; d Aug. 2, 1922, Washington, D.C.)* Lawyer, Tennessee Democrat. Presidential elector on the Cleveland-Hendricks ticket (1884), state senate (1898), U.S. Representative (1901 until death).

PAGÁN, BOLIVAR *(b May 16, 1897, Guayanilla, P.R.; d Feb. 9, 1961, San Juan, P.R.)* Lawyer, writer, editor, Puerto Rican Coalitionist who was resident commissioner to the United States (1939-1945). Fajardo judge (1922), insular elections commissioner (1923-1951), San Juan city treasurer (1925-1929), public service associate commissioner (1930-1933), Puerto Rican senate (1933-1939, 1945-1953) and president pro tem and majority leader (1933-1939).

PAGE, CARROLL SMALLEY *(b Jan. 10, 1843, Westfield, Vt.; d Dec. 3, 1925, Hyde Park, Vt.)* Hide dealer, banker, Vermont Republican. State representative (1869-1872), state senate (1874-1876), GOP state committee secretary (1872-1890) and chairman (1886-1890), GOP National Convention delegate (1880, 1912), governor (1890-1892), U.S. Senate (1908-1923).

PAGE, HORACE FRANCIS *(b Oct. 20, 1833, Orleans County, N.Y.; d Aug. 23, 1890, San Francisco, Calif.)* Teacher, lawyer, mail contractor, mine, sawmill, livery stable, and stage coach operator, California Republican. U.S. Representative (1873-1883), GOP National Convention delegate (1884).

PAGE, JOHN *(b April 17, 1744, Gloucester County, Va.; d Oct. 11, 1808, Richmond, Va.)* Planter, Revolutionary Army officer who earlier had served under George Washington in the French and Indian War, Virginia Democrat, and a lifelong friend of Thomas Jefferson. State constitutional convention delegate and lieutenant governor (1776), member of state house of delegates (1781-1783, 1785-1788, 1797, 1798, 1800, 1801), U.S. Representative in the first four Congresses (1789-1797), Jeffersonian presidential elector (1800), governor (1802-1805), Brother of Mann Page. (Not to be confused with John Page of New Hampshire—see next entry.)

PAGE, JOHN *(b May 21, 1787, Haverhill, N.H.; d Sept. 8, 1865, Haverhill).* Farmer, New Hampshire Democrat who served fourteen terms as a Haverhill selectman. Assistant U.S. tax assessor (1813) and assessor (1815), state representative (1818-1820, 1835), Grafton County register of deeds (1827, 1829-1835), member of Governor's Council (1836, 1838), U.S. Senate to fill a vacancy (1836-1837), governor (1840-1842). (Not to be confused with John Page of Virginia—see previous entry.)

PAGE, MANN *(b 1749, Gloucester County, Va.; d 1781, Spotsylvania County, Va.)* Lawyer, estate manager, member of the Virginia House of Burgesses and the Continental Congress (1777). Brother of John Page of Virginia.

PAGE, ROBERT NEWTON *(b Oct. 26, 1859, Cary, N.C.; d Oct. 3, 1933, Aberdeen, N.C.)* Lumber and railroad executive, banker, North Carolina Democrat. Mayor of Aberdeen (1890-1898), state representative (1901, 1902), U.S. Representative (1903-1917).

PAINE, ROBERT TREAT *(b March 11, 1731, Boston, Mass.; d May 12, 1814, Boston)* Clergyman, lawyer, gunpowder maker, Massachusetts signer of the Declaration of Independence, and a Federalist who had been one of the prosecutors in the Boston Massacre trials (1770) and later became the state's first attorney general (1777-1790). State convention delegate (1768), colonial representative (1773), Provincial Congress delegate (1774, 1775), Continental Congress member (1774-

1778), state representative (1777), member of the Governor's Council (1779, 1780), a drafter of the state constitution (1779-1780), state supreme court judge (1790-1804).

PAINE, THOMAS *(b Jan. 29, 1737, Thetford, England; d June 8, 1809, New York City)* An arrival in America (1774) under the sponsorship of Benjamin Franklin to become editor of the *Pennsylvania Magazine* (1775-1777), a staunch advocate of independence and supporter of the Revolution, and a writer who probably is American history's best-known pamphleteer; perhaps the most-stirring words to come from his pen: "These are the times that try men's souls. The summer soldier and the sunshine patriot will, in this crisis, shrink from the service of their country. Tyranny, like hell, is not easily conquered" (from *The American Crisis* [1776]). He was among the first to call for a strong federal Constitution, helped to plan the financing of the Revolution, and continued until death to propagandize for reform and the rights of man not only in the United States but also in England and France. Said Thomas Jefferson of him: "[He] labored as any man living" to further "the original sentiments of democracy."

PALMER, ALEXANDER MITCHELL *(b May 4, 1872, Luzerne County, Pa.; d May 11, 1936, Washington, D.C.)* Lawyer, banker, corporate executive, Pennsylvania Democratic leader of national repute who as alien property custodian (1917-1919) was sharply scored for the manner in which he handled $600 million worth of confiscated property, and then as U.S. attorney general (1919-1921) was even more intensely criticized for the use of war-emergency powers in an attempt to put down the 1919 coal strike and for his raids upon the homes of alleged radicals. All of these factors combined to cost him the Democratic presidential nomination at the 1920 na-

tional convention when he and William G. McAdoo were chief opponents of the ultimate victor, James M. Cox. He remained a party regular however, campaigning for John W. Davis (1924) and Alfred E. Smith (1928) and helping to write most of Franklin D. Roosevelt's platform (1932). U.S. Representative (1909-1915), Democratic National Convention delegate (1912, 1916), Democratic National Committeeman (1912-1920).

PALMER, JOHN McAULEY *(b Sept. 13, 1817, Eagle Creek, Ky.; d Sept. 25, 1900, Springfield, Ill.)* Teacher, lawyer, Illinois Democrat who helped to found the Republican party there, fought as a colonel and general in the Union Army during the Civil War, served as Republican governor (1869-1873), then returned to the Democratic fold and rounded out his political career by running for president as a National (Gold) Democrat (1896) and garnering only 133,148 popular votes.

Macoupin County probate judge (1843-1847), state constitutional convention delegate (1847), county judge (1849-1852), state senate (1852-1854, 1855-1856), state founding GOP convention chairman (1856) and national convention delegate in the same year, presidential elector on the Lincoln-Hamlin ticket (1860), delegate to the peace-between-states convention (1861), Democratic National Convention delegate (1884), U.S. Senate (1891-1897).

PALMER, WILLIAM ADAMS *(b Sept. 12, 1781, Hebron, Conn.; d Dec. 3, 1860, Danville, Vt.)* Lawyer, farmer, Vermont Democrat and anti-Masonic leader. Caledonia County court clerk (1807-1815), state representative (1811, 1812, 1818, 1825, 1826, 1829), county probate judge (1811-1817), state supreme court judge (1816-1818), U.S. Senate (1818-1825), county assistant judge (1826-1828), state constitutional convention delegate (1828, 1836, 1850), governor (1831-1835).

PANTIN, SANTIAGO IGLESIAS (see Iglesias, Santiago)

PARK, FRANK *(b March 3, 1864, Tuskegee, Ala.; d Nov. 20, 1925, Fort Lauderdale, Fla.)* Teacher, civil engineer, lawyer, Georgia Democrat who was chairman of the Worth County executive committee (1891-1902), county court judge (1898-1903), second district Democratic congressional committee chairman (1902-1904), Sylvester city court judge (1903-1908) and judge of the Albany judicial circuit (1908-1913), board chairman of the State Agricultural and Mechanical School (1911-1915), U.S. Representative (1913-1925).

PARKER, ALTON BROOKS *(b May 14, 1852, Cortland, N.Y.; d May 10, 1926, New York City)* Lawyer, New York Democrat who was chosen the party's presidential candidate (1904) on the first ballot and lost the election to Theodore Roosevelt because, it was said, campaign strategists played down his liberal leanings and presented him to the voters as a conservative. As a result, he got 5,084,223 popular and 140 electoral votes to Teddy's 7,628,461 and 366 votes.

Although for many years the Democratic state chairman, Parker never before or after sought elective political office, preferring to serve on the judicial bench, beginning as Ulster County surrogate (1877-1890) and ending as chief justice of the state court of appeals (1897-1904).

PARKER, JAMES *(b March 3, 1776, Bethlehem, N.J.; d April 1, 1868, Perth Amboy, N.J.)* Surveyor, lands manager, lawyer, New Jersey Democrat. State assembly (1806-1810, 1812, 1813, 1815, 1816, 1818, 1827), mayor of Perth Amboy (1815 and again thirty-five years later in 1850), presidential elector on the Jackson-Calhoun ticket (1824), Perth Amboy collector of customs (1829-1833), U.S. Representative (1833-1837),

state constitutional convention delegate (1844). Grandfather of Richard W. Parker.

PARKER, JAMES SOUTHWORTH *(b June 3, 1867, Great Barrington, Mass.; d Dec. 19, 1933, Washington, D.C.)*. Teacher, farmer, harness racehorse breeder, New York Republican. State assemblyman (1904, 1905, 1908-1912), U.S. Representative (1913 until death).

PARKER, JOHN MILLIKEN *(b March 16, 1863, Bethel Church, Miss.; d May 20, 1939, Pass Christian, Miss.)* Cotton broker, political reformer who began his career as a Louisiana Democrat, headed a Good Government League and was its unsuccessful candidate for governor (1912), became a Progressive supporter of Theodore Roosevelt in the same year and that movement's unsuccessful gubernatorial candidate (1916) as well as vice presidential nominee, only to be forced to give up the campaign when Roosevelt declined the presidential nomination. Parker then returned to the Democratic fold, threw his support to Woodrow Wilson and four years later, still very much the reformer, again ran for the governor's office, this time successfully. He served (1920-1924) and, among other things, sponsored legislation that weakened the New Orleans political coterie and did not hesitate to use the state militia to quell Ku Klux Klan violence.

PARKER, JOSIAH *(b May 11, 1751, Isle of Wight County, Va.; d March 18, 1810, Macclesfield, Va.)* Wealthy landowner by royal and U.S. government grant, planter, Revolutionary Army officer who fought at Trenton, Princeton, and Brandywine; supporter of Patrick Henry, Anti-Federalist Virginia Democrat who was a representative in the first five Congresses (1789-1801). Member of the Virginia convention and Committee of Safety (1775) and the house of delegates (1780, 1781), Portsmouth naval officer (1786).

PARKER, RICHARD *(b Dec. 22, 1810, Richmond, Va.; d Nov. 10, 1893, Winchester, Va.)* Lawyer, Virginia Democrat who, while thirteenth judicial circuit judge (1851-1869), sentenced John Brown to death for insurrection (1859). U.S. Representative (1848-1851).

PARKER, RICHARD WAYNE *(b Aug. 6, 1848, Morristown, N.J.; d Nov. 28, 1923, Paris, France)* Lawyer, New Jersey Republican who inherited his interest in politics but not his political leanings from his grandfather, James Parker. State assemblyman (1885, 1886), U.S. Representative (1895-1911, 1914-1919, 1921-1923), GOP National Convention delegate (1916).

PARKS, TILMAN BACON *(b May 14, 1872, Lafayette County, Ark.; d Feb. 12, 1950, Washington, D.C.)* Lawyer, Arkansas Democrat. State representative (1901, 1903, 1909), presidential elector on the Parker-Davis ticket (1904), temporary chairman of the Democratic state convention (1910), eighth judicial circuit prosecutor (1914-1918), U.S. Representative (1921-1937).

PARRIS, ALBION KEITH *(b Jan. 19, 1788, Hebron, Mass., now Maine; d Feb. 22, 1857, Portland, Maine)* Lawyer, Massachusetts and, after division into separate states, Maine Democrat. In Massachusetts: Oxford County prosecutor (1811), state representative (1813), state senate (1814), U.S. Representative (1815-1818), U.S. judge for the Maine district (1818-1820), delegate to the Maine constitutional convention (1819). In Maine: Cumberland County probate judge (1820, 1821), governor (1822-1827), U.S. Senate (1827-1828) resigning to become a state supreme court judge (1828-1836), second comptroller of the U.S. Treasury (1836-1850), mayor of Portland (1852). Cousin of Virgil D. Parris.

PARRIS, VIRGIL DELPHINI *(b Feb. 18, 1807, Buckfield, Maine; d June 13, 1874,*

Paris, Maine) Lawyer, Maine Democrat. Assistant secretary of the state senate (1831) and member (1842, 1843), state representative (1832-1837), U.S. Representative running as a States' Rights Democrat (1838-1841), U.S. marshal for the state (1844-1848), special mail agent for New England (1853), Kittery Navy Yard naval storekeeper (1856), Democratic National Convention delegate (1852, 1872). Cousin of Albion K. Parker.

PASCO, SAMUEL *(b June 28, 1834, London, England; d March 13, 1917, Tampa, Fla.)* Educator, lawyer, Confederate soldier who was wounded and captured at Missionary Ridge; a leading postwar Florida Democrat. Jefferson County circuit court clerk (1866-1868), Democratic state committee chairman (1876-1878) and a committeeman for many years beginning in 1872, presidential elector on the Hancock-English ticket (1880), state constitutional convention president (1885), state representative (1886, 1887) and house speaker (1887), U.S. Senate (1887-1899), member of the Isthmian Canal Commission (1899-1905).

PATERSON, WILLIAM *(b Dec. 24, 1745, Antrim, Ireland; d Sept. 9, 1806, Albany, N.Y.)* Lawyer, New Jersey Federalist who was one of the signers of the Constitution and an associate justice of the Supreme Court of the United States (1793 until death). Delegate and secretary to the Provincial Congress (1775, 1776), state senate (1776, 1777), state constitutional convention delegate (1776), state attorney general (1776-1783), delegate to the federal Constitutional Convention (1787) where he presented the New Jersey Plan which represented the views of the small states, U.S. Senate (1789-1790) resigning to become governor (1790-1793).

PATTEN, JOHN *(b April 26, 1746, Kent County, Del.; d Dec. 26, 1800, near*

Dover, Del.) Delaware farmer, Revolutionary Army officer, member of the Continental Congress (1785, 1786), U.S. Representative (1793-1794, 1795-1797).

PATTERSON, JOSIAH *(b April 14, 1837, Morgan County, Ala.; d Feb. 10, 1904, Memphis, Tenn.)* Lawyer, Confederate cavalry commander, Alabama and Tennessee Democrat but never held office in the former. In Tennessee: State representative (1882), presidential elector on the Cleveland-Thurman ticket (1888), U.S. Representative (1891-1897). Father of Malcolm R. Patterson.

PATTERSON, MALCOLM RICE *(b June 7, 1861, Somerville, Ala.; d March 8, 1935, Sarasota, Fla.)* Lawyer, Tennessee Democrat. Shelby County district attorney (1894-1900), U.S. Representative (1901-1906) resigning to become governor (1906-1910), first circuit court judge (1923-1934). Son of Josiah Patterson.

PATTERSON, THOMAS MacDONALD *(b Nov. 4, 1839, County Carlow, Ireland; d July 23, 1916, Denver, Colo.)* Printer, jeweler, Union soldier, lawyer who settled in Denver (1872) and became an influence in Colorado territorial and state affairs as a Democrat-Populist, not the least of the reasons for his influence being the fact that he also became the owner of the *Rocky Mountain News* and *Denver Times.* As a territory: Denver city attorney (1873-1874), delegate to Congress (1875-1876). As a state: U.S. Representative (1877-1879), Democratic National Committeeman (1874-1880), Democratic National Convention delegate (1876, 1880, 1888, 1892), Populist National Convention delegate (1895), U.S. Senate (1901-1907). Throughout it all, a friend of labor and the common man.

PATTON, NAT *(b Feb. 26, 1884, Houston County, Tex.; d July 27, 1957, Crockett, Tex.)* Farmer, lawyer, Texas Democrat. Houston County judge (1918-1922), state senate (1929-1934), Democratic state convention delegate (1924, 1935), U.S. Representative (1935-1945).

PAYNE, HENRY B. *(b Nov. 30, 1810, Hamilton, N.Y.; d Sept. 9, 1896, Cleveland, Ohio)* Lawyer, Ohio Democrat. Cleveland city clerk (1836), presidential elector on the Cass-Butler ticket (1848), Democratic National Convention delegate (1856, 1860, 1872), U.S. Representative (1875-1877), U.S. Senator (1885-1891). Grandfather of Frances P. Bolton, great-grandfather of Oliver P. Bolton.

PAYNE, SERENO ELISHA *(b June 26, 1843, Hamilton, N.Y.; d Dec. 10, 1914, Washington, D.C.)* Lawyer, New York Republican who was a U.S. Representative for nearly thirty years (1883-1887, 1889 until death). Before that he was Auburn city clerk (1867, 1868), supervisor (1871, 1872), Cayuga County district attorney (1873-1879), president of the Auburn Board of Education (1879-1882).

PAYNTER, THOMAS HANSON *(b Dec. 9, 1851, Lewis County, Ky.; d March 8, 1921, Frankfort, Ky.)* Lawyer, farmer, Kentucky Democrat. Greenup County prosecutor (1876-1882), U.S. Representative (1889-1895), resigning to become a state appeals court judge (1895-1906), and resigning that for a seat in the U.S. Senate (1907-1913).

PAYSON, LEWIS EDWIN *(b Sept. 17, 1840, Providence, R.I.; d Oct. 4, 1909, Washington, D.C.)* Lawyer, Illinois Republican. Livingston County Court judge (1869-1873), U.S. Representative (1881-1891).

PEABODY, NATHANIEL *(b March 1, 1741, Topsfield, Mass.; d June 27, 1823, Exeter, N.H.)* Physician, Revolutionary Army officer, New Hampshire patriot who made the mistake of going broke and consequently spent twenty years in a debtor's prison. Chairman of the Committee of Safety (1776), state representative (1776-1779, 1781-1785, 1787-1790, 1793-1796) and house speaker (1793), member of the Continental Congress (1779, 1780), state constitutional convention delegate (1782, 1783), state senator (1785, 1786, 1790-1793), councillor (1784, 1785).

PEARCE, DUTEE JERAULD *(b April 3, 1789, Prudence, R.I.; d May 9, 1849, Newport, R.I.)* Lawyer, Rhode Island Democrat who held a variety of offices in Newport before moving up the political ladder. State attorney general (1819-1825), presidential elector on the Monroe-Tompkins ticket (1820), U.S. Representative (1825-1837).

PEARCE, JAMES ALFRED *(b Dec. 8, 1804, Alexandria, Va.; d Dec. 20, 1862, Chestertown, Md.)* Lawyer, planter, Maryland Whig-Democrat who sought in vain for a solution to the secessionist question. State house of delegates (1831), U.S. Representative (1835-1839, 1841-1843), U.S. Senate (1843 until death).

PEARRE, GEORGE ALEXANDER *(b July 16, 1860, Cumberland, Md.; d Sept. 19, 1923, Cumberland)* Lawyer, Maryland Republican. State senate (1890-1892), Allegany County prosecutor (1895-1899), U.S. Representative (1899-1911).

PEARSON, JOSEPH *(b 1776, Rowan County, N.C.; d Oct. 27, 1834, Salisbury, N.C.)* Lawyer, North Carolina Federalist who shot Congressman John G. Jackson, a Virginia Democrat, in the hip in a duel while a U.S. Representative (1809-1815).

PEASE, ELISHA MARSHALL *(b Jan. 3, 1812, Enfield, Conn.; d Aug. 26, 1883, Lampasas, Texas)* A country store and postal clerk who left Connecticut for the lure of Texas, arrived in 1835 and immediately embarked upon a public career that lasted the rest of his life. In the struggle for independence, he fought in the first skirmish at Gonzales, then as secretary of the provisional government, he helped write the new republic's constitution (1836), and next through a progression of elective offices he culminated his career with his election as governor (1853-1857). He was then a Democrat but his feelings concerning slavery and secession drove him to Unionism and then to Republicanism.

PEAVEY, HUBERT HASKELL *(b Jan. 12, 1881, Adams, Minn.; d Nov. 21, 1937, Washburn, Wis.)* A young man who tried his hand at a variety of things (mainly real estate development) in Nebraska, Kansas, Oklahoma, and South Dakota before taking root as a newspaperman and Republican politician in Wisconsin. Washburn alderman (1911) and mayor (1912, 1920-1922), state assemblyman (1913-1915), became editor-publisher of the *Washburn News* (1915), U.S. Representative (1923-1935).

PECK, GEORGE WILBUR *(b Sept. 28, 1840, Henderson, N.Y.; d April 16, 1916, Milwaukee, Wis.)* Author of the *Peck's Bad Boy* books, humorist, lecturer, newspaperman who was the founding editor of the *Milwaukee Sun*, and a Wisconsin Democrat. Mayor of Milwaukee (1890), governor (1891-1895).

PEEL, SAMUEL WEST *(b Sept. 13, 1831, Independence County, Ark.; d Dec. 18, 1924, Bentonville, Ark.)* Lawyer, Confederate Army officer, Arkansas Democrat. Carroll County circuit court clerk (1858-1860), fourth judicial circuit prosecutor (1873-1876), U.S. Representative (1883-1893).

PEERY, WILLIAM *(b ——; d Dec. 17, 1800, Cold Spring, Del.)* Farmer, lawyer, Delaware patriot who recruited, equipped, and commanded a company of soldiers in the Revolution. State representative (1782, 1784, 1787, 1793, 1794), member of the Continental Congress (1785, 1786), Sussex County treasurer (1785-1796).

PEFFER, WILLIAM ALFRED *(b Sept. 10, 1831, Cumberland County, Pa.; d Oct. 7, 1912, Grenola, Kans.)* Pennsylvania, Indiana, and Missouri farmer, California gold miner, Union Army officer, and finally a Kansas lawyer-journalist-author who became editor of the *Kansas Farmer* (1881) and made it into the state's most influential agricultural publication and the voice of the Farmers' Alliance, meanwhile embracing the Republican, then the Populist, and once again the Republican party. State senate (1874-1876), presidential elector on the Garfield-Arthur ticket (1880), U.S. Senate (1891-1897).

PENDLETON, EDMUND *(b Sept. 9, 1721, Caroline County, Va.; d Oct. 23, 1803, Richmond, Va.)* Lawyer, Virginia civic and political leader who opposed Patrick Henry yet was very much a patriot, among other things presiding over the Virginia convention (1776) that recommended a declaration of independence. Justice of the peace (1751), member of the house of burgesses (1752-1774), Committee of Correspondence (1773), colonial convention (1774), First Continental Congress (1774, 1775), governor of the young colony (1774-1776), Committee of Safety (1775), first speaker of the state house of delegates (1776, 1777), general and chancery court judge (1777), appeals court presiding judge (1779-1803), state constitutional convention president (1788). Uncle of John Penn.

PENDLETON, GEORGE HUNT *(b July 19, 1825, Cincinnati, Ohio; d Nov. 24, 1889, Brussels, Belgium)* Lawyer, railroad president, and an Ohio Democrat who was a leader of the party's pre-

Civil War peace wing and George B. McClellan's vice presidential running mate in the 1864 presidential election; a man who participated fully in the rough-and-tumble politics of the day, yet through it all lived up to his nickname: Gentleman George.

State senate (1854-1856), U.S. Representative (1857-1865), Loyalist Convention delegate (1866), unsuccessful gubernatorial candidate (1869) losing to Rutherford B. Hayes, U.S. Senate (1879-1885) and chairman of the Civil Service Committee (1883) and proponent of many reforms that the political spoilsmen did not care for, Cleveland-appointed minister to Germany (1885 until death). Son of Nathaniel G. Pendleton, son-in-law of Francis Scott Key.

PENDLETON, NATHANAEL GREENE *(b Aug. 25, 1793, Savannah, Ga.; d June 16, 1861, Cincinnati, Ohio)* Lawyer, Ohio Whig. State senate (1825-1829), U.S. Representative (1841-1843). Father of George H. Pendleton.

PENINGTON, JOHN BROWN *(b Dec. 20, 1825, near New Castle, Del.; d June 1, 1902, Dover, Del.)* Teacher, lawyer, Delaware Democrat. State representative (1857) and clerk of the house (1859, 1863, 1871), Democratic National Convention delegate (1860), U.S. attorney for the Delaware district (1868-1872), state attorney general (1874-1878), U.S. Representative (1887-1891).

PENN, JOHN *(b May 17, 1741, near Port Royal, Va.; d Sept. 14, 1788, Granville County, N.C.)* Lawyer, planter, North Carolina signer of the Declaration of Independence, and member of the Board of War (1780-1781). Member of the Provincial Congress (1775) and the Continental Congress (1775-1780), one of North Carolina's three ratifiers of the Articles of Confederation, tax receiver (1784). Nephew of Edmund Pendleton.

PENN, WILLIAM *(b Oct. 14, 1644, London, England; d July 30, 1718, near London)* British naval officer, lawyer, manager of his father's estate, author and Quaker missionary who founded the city of Philadelphia and the Commonwealth of Pennsylvania.

PENNINGTON, ALEXANDER CUMMING McWHORTER *(b July 2, 1810, Newark, N.J.; d Jan. 25, 1867, New York City)*. Lawyer, New Jersey Whig. State assembly (1837, 1838), Newark alderman (1837-1840), U.S. Representative (1853-1857). Cousin of William Pennington.

PENNINGTON, WILLIAM *(b May 4, 1796, Newark, N.J.; d Feb. 16, 1862, Newark)* Lawyer, New Jersey Democrat turned Whig who served five terms as governor (1837-1843) and later managed to stir up considerable controversy in Congress, although only a U.S. Representative for one term (1859-1861), when he was chosen house speaker as the compromise choice of warring factions. U.S. district court clerk (1815-1826), state assemblyman (1828), sergeant at law (1834). Cousin of Alexander C. M. Pennington.

PENNOYER, SYLVESTER *(b July 6, 1831, Groton, N.Y.; d May 31, 1902, Portland, Oreg.)* Lawyer, lumberman, newspaper editor-publisher, real estate speculator, Oregon Democrat-Populist who climbed to political power on the backs of Chinese laborers. Governor (1887-1895), mayor of Portland (1896-1898).

PENROSE, BOIES *(b Nov. 1, 1860, Philadelphia, Pa.; d Dec. 31, 1921, Washington, D.C.)* Lawyer, Pennsylvania Republican, and political boss who was said to have more interest in power than in profit to the extent that he cultivated political connections to the neglect of his law clients. State representative (1884-1886), state senate (1886-1897), U.S. Senate (1897 until

death), GOP National Convention delegate (1900, 1904, 1908), state GOP chairman (1903-1905), national committeeman (1904-1912).

PEREA, FRANCISCO *(b Jan. 9, 1830, Los Padillas, Mexico, now N.Mex.; d May 21, 1913, Albuquerque, N.Mex.)*. Stock raiser, drover boss, mule-train operator, spa proprietor, Perea's Battalion officer during the Civil War, New Mexico Republican who was in Ford's Theater when Lincoln was assassinated. Member of the territorial council (1858, 1866, 1884), GOP National Convention delegate (1864), congressional delegate (1863-1865), Jemez Springs postmaster (1894-1905). Cousin of Pedro Perea.

PEREA, PEDRO *(b April 22, 1852, Bernalillo, N.Mex.; d Jan. 11, 1906, Bernalillo)*. Stockman, banker, New Mexico Territory Republican. Member of the council of the territorial legislature (1889, 1891, 1895), GOP National Convention delegate (1896), delegate to the U.S. Congress (1899-1901). Cousin of Francisco Perea.

PERKINS, BISHOP WALDEN *(b Oct. 18, 1841, Rochester, Ohio; d June 20, 1894, Washington, D.C.)* New Mexico and California prospector, Union Army officer, lawyer, editor of the *Oswego (Kans.) Register*, Kansas Republican. Labette County prosecutor (1869) and probate court judge (1870-1882), U.S. Representative (1883-1891), U.S. Senate (1892-1893) to fill a vacancy caused by the death of Preston B. Plumb.

PERKINS, FRANCES *(b Apr. 10, 1882, Boston, Mass.; d May 14, 1965, New York City)* First woman cabinet member, serving as U.S. secretary of labor (1933-1945) in Franklin D. Roosevelt's cabinet, contributing to the social reform legislation of the New Deal; executive secretary of New York City Consumers' League (1910-1912), executive secretary of New York Committee on Safety (1912-1917), lobbied in Albany for better factory conditions and maximum working hour laws for women, member New York State Industrial Board (1923-1929) becoming its chairman (1926-1929), industrial commissioner, under Governor Roosevelt, to direct the enforcement of factory and labor laws in New York State (1929-1933). She resigned as secretary of labor in 1945 and was made a member of the U.S. Civil Service Commission (1946-1952).

PERKINS, GEORGE CLEMENT *(b Aug. 23, 1839, Kennebunkport, Maine; d Feb. 26, 1923, Oakland, Calif.)* West Coast steamship operator, whaler, merchant, miner, farmer, banker, patron of the sciences and art—all this after first getting the taste for adventure and the sea when he shipped out at the age of twelve as a cabin boy aboard a sailing vessel; California Republican who in addition to public office was president of both the San Francisco Art Association and Chamber of Commerce, and director of the California Academy of Sciences and other public institutions. State senate (1869-1877), governor (1879-1883), U.S. Senate (1893-1915).

PERKINS, GEORGE DOUGLAS *(b Feb. 29, 1840, Holly, N.Y.; d Feb. 3, 1914, Sioux City, Iowa)* Printer, Union soldier, Iowa journalist who worked for the Associated Press, founded the *Cedar Falls Gazette*, was editor and then publisher of the *Sioux Falls Journal*, and cultivated an interest in politics as a Republican. State senate (1874-1876), state immigration commissioner (1880-1882), U.S. marshal for Iowa's northern district (1883-1885), U.S. Representative (1891-1899), GOP National Convention delegate (1876, 1880, 1888, 1908, 1912), unsuccessful candidate for governor (1904).

PERKINS, JAMES BRECK *(b Nov. 4, 1847, St. Croix Falls, Wis.; d March 11,*

1910, Washington, D.C.) Lawyer, historian, author, whose interest in French history was approached only by his interest in politics, New York Republican. Rochester city attorney (1874-1880), state assemblyman (1898-1900), U.S. Representative (1901 until death).

PERKINS, JOHN, JR. *(b July 1, 1819, Natchez, Miss.; d Nov. 28, 1885, Baltimore, Md.)* Lawyer, cotton planter, Louisiana Democrat who was chairman of the state secessionist convention (1861). Circuit court judge (1851-1853), U.S. Representative (1853-1855), Confederate senator (1862-1865).

PERKINS, RANDOLPH *(b Nov. 30, 1871, Dunellen, N.J.; d May 25, 1936, Washington, D.C.)* Lawyer, New Jersey Republican. Mayor of Westfield (1903-1905), state assemblyman (1905-1911) and assembly speaker (1907), Bergen County GOP chairman (1911-1916), U.S. Representative (1921 until death).

PETERS, ANDREW JAMES *(b April 3, 1872, West Roxbury, Mass.; d June 26, 1938, Jamaica Plain, Mass.)* Lawyer, Massachusetts Democrat. State representative (1902), state senate (1904, 1905), U.S. Representative (1907-1914) resigning to become assistant secretary of the U.S. Treasury (1914-1917), mayor of Boston (1918-1922).

PETERS, JOHN ANDREW *(b Oct. 9, 1822, Ellsworth, Me.; d April 2, 1904, Bangor, Me.)* Lawyer, Maine Republican who much preferred the bench to the bar and partisan politics. State senate (1862, 1863), state representative (1864), state attorney general (1864-1866), U.S. Representative (1867-1873), state supreme judicial court judge (1873-1883) and chief justice (1883-1900). Uncle of younger John Andrew Peters.

PETERS, JOHN ANDREW *(b Aug. 13, 1864, Ellsworth, Me.; d Aug. 22, 1953,*

Ellsworth) Nephew of the elder John A. Peters who pretty much followed in his uncle's footsteps: lawyer, jurist, Maine Republican. Ellsworth municipal court judge (1896-1908), state representative (1909, 1911, 1913) and house speaker (1913), U.S. Representative (1913-1922) resigning to become U.S. district judge (1922-1947), GOP National Convention delegate (1916).

PETERS, RICHARD, JR. *(b June 22, 1743, near Philadelphia, Pa.; d Aug. 22, 1828, Philadelphia)* Lawyer, Revolutionary Army officer, Pennsylvania patriot who even in that trying period advocated something far in advance of the times: scientific farming. Register of the admiralty (1771-1776), secretary of the Continental Board of War and one of its leaders (1776-1781), member of the Continental Congress (1782, 1783), state assemblyman and speaker (1787-1790), state senate and speaker (1791), U.S. district judge (1792-1828) some of whose rulings laid the groundwork for the 1798 Sedition Act.

PETERS, SAMUEL RITTER *(b Aug. 16, 1842, Walnut Township, Pickaway County, Ohio; d April 21, 1910, Newton, Kans.)* Union Army officer, lawyer, Missouri and Kansas newspaperman, and Republican politician. In Missouri: Editor of the *Memphis Reveille* (1868-1873), GOP National Convention delegate (1872), mayor of Memphis (1873). In Kansas: state senate (1874-1875), ninth judicial district judge (1875-1883), U.S. Representative (1883-1891), member of the board of managers of the state reformatory (1895-1899), Newton postmaster (1898-1910), editor of the *Newton Daily Kansas Republican* (1899).

PETERSON, HUGH *(b Aug. 21, 1898, Montgomery County, Ga.; d Oct. 3, 1961, Sylva, N.C.)* Lawyer, farmer, journalist, Georgia Democrat. Mayor of Ailey (1922), state representative (1923-1931), state senate (1931, 1932), U.S. Representative (1935-1947).

PETTIGREW, RICHARD FRANKLIN *(b July 23, 1848, Ludlow, Vt.; d Oct. 5, 1926, Sioux Falls, S.Dak.)* Teacher, lawyer, surveyor, real estate broker, highly independent Republican in the Dakota Territory and then in South Dakota who was against sale of public forest lands, for public ownership of the railroads and telegraph lines, and who walked out of the GOP National Convention (1896) and supported instead the Democratic presidential candidate William Jennings Bryan. In the territory: member of the territorial house of representatives (1872) and the territorial council (1877, 1879, 1885), delegate to the U.S. Congress (1881-1883). After statehood: U.S. Senate (1889-1901).

PETTIS, SPENCER DARWIN *(b 1802, Culpeper County, Va.; d Aug. 28, 1831, St. Louis, Mo., as the result of a duel in which both he and his opponent, Major Thomas Biddle, were mortally wounded—the duel was caused by differences over the United States Bank which then was a national political issue)* Lawyer, Missouri Democrat. Missouri secretary of state (1826-1828), U.S. Representative (1829 until death).

PETTIT, JOHN *(b June 24, 1807, Sackets Harbor, N.Y.; d Jan. 17, 1877, Lafayette, Ind.)* Lawyer, jurist, Indiana Democrat who also served as chief justice of the U.S. courts in the Kansas Territory (1859-1861). In Indiana: State representative (1838, 1839), U.S. attorney (1839-1843), U.S. Representative (1843-1849), state constitutional convention delegate (1850), presidential elector on the Pierce-King ticket (1852), U.S. Senate to fill a vacancy (1853-1855), state supreme court judge (1870 until death).

PETTUS, EDMUND WINSTON *(b July 6, 1821, Limestone County, Ala.; d July 27, 1907, Hot Springs, N.C.)* Lawyer, Confederate Army officer, Alabama Democrat who served as envoy to

Mississippi during formation of the Confederacy. Democratic National Convention delegate (1876, 1896), U.S. Senate (1897 until death).

PFOST, GRACIE BOWERS *(b March 12, 1906, Harrison, Ark. d Aug. 11, 1965, Baltimore, Md.)* Milk products chemist, real estate operator, Idaho Democrat. Canyon County clerk, recorder, and auditor (1929-1939), county treasurer (1941-1951), Democratic National Convention delegate (1944, 1948, 1952, 1956, 1960), U.S. Representative (1953-1963) serving on the Interior and Insular Affairs and Public Works committees and nicknamed Hell's Belle for her stubborn support of the Hell's Canyon dam project. After being defeated for Senate post (1962) she was named special assistant for housing for the elderly in Federal Housing Administration.

PHELPS, JOHN SMITH *(b Dec. 22, 1814, Simsbury, Conn.; d Nov. 20, 1886, St. Louis, Mo.)* Lawyer, Union Army officer whom Lincoln appointed (1862) military governor of Arkansas, Missouri Democrat. State representative (1840), U.S. Representative (1845-1863), governor (1877-1881).

PHELPS, SAMUEL SHETHAR *(b May 13, 1793, Litchfield, Conn.; d March 25, 1855, Middlebury, Vt.)* Lawyer, Vermont Whig. State representative (1821-1832), state supreme court judge (1832-1838), state senate (1838, 1839), U.S. Senate (1839-1851, 1853-1854).

PHELPS, WILLIAM WALTER *(b Aug. 24, 1839, New York City; d June 17, 1894, Englewood, N.J.)* Lawyer, diplomat, banker, railroad director, New Jersey Republican. U.S. Representative (1873-1875, 1883-1889), GOP National Convention delegate (1880, 1884), minister to Austria (1881-1882), U.S. representative at the International Congress on the Samoan Question (1889), minister to

Germany (1889-1893), special judge of the state court of errors and appeals (1893).

PHILLIPS, WILLIAM ADDISON *(b Jan. 14, 1824, Paisley, Scotland; d Nov. 30, 1893, Fort Gibson, Indian Territory, now Oklahoma)* Farmer, lawyer, historian, *New York Tribune* correspondent (1845-1862) who used Kansas as his base and became prominent as an antislavery writer and friend of the Indians who served as commander of the Cherokee Indian Regiment in the Civil War and later became attorney for the Cherokees in Washington, Kansas Republican. He also founded the city of Salinas and was the first supreme court justice under the Leavenworth constitution. Cherokee County prosecutor (1865), state representative (1865), U.S. Representative (1873-1879).

PHIPPS, LAWRENCE COWLE *(b Aug. 30, 1862, Amwell Township, Pa.; d March 1, 1958, Santa Monica, Calif.)* Industrialist, financier, Colorado Republican. President of the Colorado Taxpayers' Protective League (1913), GOP National Convention delegate (1920, 1924, 1928, 1936), U.S. Senate (1919-1931).

PIATT, DONN *(b June 29, 1819, Cincinnati, Ohio; d Nov. 12, 1891, near West Liberty, Ohio)* Lawyer, Union Army officer who was reprimanded by Lincoln for ordering that a brigade of colored troops be recruited only from slaves, Ohio Democrat turned Republican, but most of all an Ohio, New York, and Washington, D.C., journalist with a crushing invective and sometimes overzealous pen who delighted in exposing the frailties and corrupt practices of men in both parties and who was indicted (the charges of inciting rebellion and insurrection were later dropped) for stating editorially of Hayes' inauguration: "If a man thus returned to power can ride in safety from the executive mansion to the Capitol to be inaugurated, we are fitted for the slavery that will follow inauguration."

He served in Ohio as Hamilton County common pleas judge (1852-1853), secretary of the U.S. legation in France (1853-1855), member of the Ohio legislature (1866). The publication for which he was best known was Washington's weekly *Capital* of which he was a cofounder and editor (1871-1880). Then he turned to free-lance writing. His books include *Memories of Men Who Saved the Union* (1887), which was comprised of essays on Lincoln, Grant, Sherman, Seward, Chase, and others—some of the essays sharply biting. He also wrote short stories, poems, plays, a novel, and biography.

PICKENS, ISRAEL *(b Jan. 30, 1780, Mecklenburg, now Cabarrus, County, N.C.; d April 24, 1827, near Matanzas, Cuba)* Lawyer, North Carolina and Alabama Democrat. In North Carolina: State senate (1809), U.S. Representative (1811-1817) when he was appointed U.S. Land Office register (1817-1821) in the Mississippi Territory, which included the present state of Alabama. Then, in Alabama: governor (1821-1825), U.S. Senate (1826) to fill a vacancy.

PICKERING, TIMOTHY *(b July 17, 1745, Salem, Mass.; d Jan. 29, 1829, Salem).* Lawyer, pamphleteer, merchant, farmer, Massachusetts patriot who was quartermaster general of the army (1780-1783) and after the Revolution a fierce Pennsylvania Federalist whose hero was Alexander Hamilton; a diplomat with a flair for the undiplomatic whose criticism of and attacks upon John Adams for resisting war with France hastened the end of the party.

In Massachusetts: Salem selectman and assessor (1772-1777), member of the Committee on State of Rights and Colonists (1773), Committee of Safety (1774, 1775), town clerk (1774-1776), register of deeds, Essex County common pleas court and provincial maritime court judge (1775-1777) and state legislature (1776), leaving all to enter the army as a colonel; member of the Board of War (1777-1780). In Pennsylvania: State constitutional convention delegate (1789-1790) and then the holder of three positions in succession in Washington's cabinet—postmaster general (1791-1794), secretary of war (1795), and then secretary of state until removed by Adams in 1800. Then back to Massachusetts where he was appointed chief justice of the common pleas and general sessions courts (1802-1803), U.S. Senate (1803-1811), state executive council (1812), U.S. Representative (1813-1817), chairman of the Salem School Committee (1821).

PICKLER, JOHN ALFRED *(b Jan. 24, 1844, Washington County, Ind.; d June 13, 1910, Faulkton, S.Dak.)* Union Army officer, lawyer, real estate operator, Missouri, Iowa, Dakota Territory, and South Dakota Republican. In Missouri: Adair County district attorney (1872-1874). In Iowa: presidential elector on the Garfield-Arthur ticket (1880), state legislator (1881-1883). In the territory: member of the Dakota legislature (1884). In South Dakota: U.S. Representative (1889-1897).

PIERCE, BENJAMIN *(b Dec. 25, 1757, Chelmsford, Mass.; d April 1, 1839, Hillsborough, N.H.)* Father of President Franklin Pierce but himself a boy of little schooling, he worked as a farm laborer, enlisted in the Massachusetts militia soon after the first shots were fired at Lexington, engaged in many battles, survived Valley Forge, and was mustered out (1784) a lieutenant. Then he became a land agent who opened new tracts in New Hampshire and Vermont, picked out a frontier farm for himself in Hillsborough (1786) and there he became a prosperous farmer and tavernkeeper, an intensely active supporter of Thomas Jefferson, a leader in the Democratic-Republican party, and, his ultimate achievement, governor (1827-1830). Member of the lower house of the state legislature (1789-1802), state constitutional convention delegate (1791), Governor's Council (1803-1809, 1814-1817), Hillsborough County sheriff (1809-1813, 1818-1827), presidential elector on the Jackson-Calhoun ticket (1828).

PIERCE, FRANKLIN *(b Nov. 23, 1804, Hillsborough, N.H.; d Oct. 8, 1869, Concord, N.H.)* Fourteenth president (New Hampshire Democrat), 1853-1857. Good looking, with a friendly personality that attracted people to him; served as colonel of volunteers in Mexican War and was commissioned brigadier general (1847).

Son of Benjamin Pierce who was a Revolutionary War veteran and twice (1827, 1830) governor of New Hampshire. Graduated Bowdoin College (1824), studied law and was admitted to the bar in 1827. Married (1834) Jane Means Appleton, daughter of the former president of Bowdoin. The couple had three children, all of whom died in childhood, one son being killed in a train accident before his parents' eyes shortly before Pierce's inauguration as president.

Member of state legislature (1829-1833, serving as speaker of house of representatives in 1832 and 1833); U.S. Representative (1833-1837); U.S. Senate (1837-1842) when, because of family pressures, he resigned and resumed practice of law in Concord and became state leader of the Democratic party; declined President Polk's invitation to serve as attorney general; member state constitutional convention (1850), serving as its president.

In the presidential election campaign of 1852, the Democrats were hopelessly split into factions led by Stephen A. Douglas, William L. Marcy, James Buchanan, and Lewis Cass, a situation that made it possible for Pierce, as a dark-horse candidate to win the nomination on the forty-ninth ballot (although a

Northerner he was acceptable to the South because he supported the slavery compromise measures of 1850 viewing the whole matter as a legal, rather than a moral, issue). He went on to win the election, defeating his erstwhile Mexican War superior, Whig candidate General Winfield Scott, with a score of 254 to 42 electoral votes.

As president, Pierce carried out few of his plans. Hoping to unite the party, he chose strong representatives from all sections of the country to serve in his cabinet. Though he did his best to ease the tensions over slavery, his best in those troubled times wasn't good enough. He supported the Kansas-Nebraska Act (repealing the Missouri Compromise, which had prohibited slavery in the territories north of the line of 36° 30′, leaving it up to the citizens of the new territories to determine whether or not they would permit slavery) in hope of gaining support from Southern leaders for his program. But passage of the act served to inflame the issue of slavery and was a contributing factor when, in the 1856 presidential campaign, Pierce was rejected by his party as a candidate. His ambitious expansionist plans (which included the annexation of Cuba) did not materialize, although he did succeed in completing the Gadsden Purchase—a narrow strip of land from Mexico, intended as the right of way for a southern railroad route to the Pacific. Also on the plus side, a reciprocity treaty with Canada and Commodore Perry's successful Japanese expedition.

After retirement from the presidency, his open disapproval of Lincoln and the Civil War made Pierce an unpopular man.

PIERCE, GILBERT ASHVILLE *(b Jan. 11, 1839, East Otto, N.Y.; d Feb. 15, 1901, Chicago, Ill.)* Union Army officer, lawyer, journalist who in 1891 purchased the *Minneapolis Tribune* and became its editor in chief, Indiana, Dakota Territory, North Dakota, and Minnesota Republican. In Indiana: State representative (1868), assistant financial clerk to the U.S. Senate (1869-1871). In the territory: governor (1884-1886). In North Dakota: one of the state's first two U.S. senators (1889-1891). In Minnesota: minister to Portugal (three months in 1893).

PIERCE, RICE ALEXANDER *(b July 3, 1848, Dresden, Tenn.; d July 12, 1936, Union City, Tenn.)* Confederate soldier, lawyer, Tennessee Democrat. Mayor of Union City (1872), twelfth judicial circuit attorney general (1874-1883), U.S. Representative (1883-1885, 1889-1893, 1897-1905), Democratic state campaign committee chairman (1929).

PIERCE, WALTER MARCUS *(b May 30, 1861, Grundy County, Ill.; d March 27, 1954, Eola Hills, Oreg.)* Teacher, farmer, banker, lawyer, Oregon Democrat. Umatilla County schools superintendent (1886-1890), county clerk (1890-1894), state senate (1903-1907, 1917-1921), governor (1923-1927), Oregon State College regent (1905-1927), delegate to all Democratic state conventions (1890-1908), Democratic National Convention delegate (1920, 1932, 1936) and national committeeman (1932-1936), U.S. Representative (1933-1943).

PILCHER, JOHN LEONARD *(b Aug. 27, 1898, Thomas County, Ga.)* Farmer, merchant, farm services businesses, Georgia Democrat. State senate (1940-1944), state purchasing agent (1948, 1949), U.S. Representative (1953-1965) serving on the Foreign Affairs Committee.

PILES, SAMUEL HENRY *(b Dec. 28, 1858, Livingston County, Ky.; d March 11, 1940, Los Angeles, Calif.)* Lawyer, Washington Republican. Third judicial district assistant prosecutor while a territory (1887-1889), Seattle city attorney (1888, 1889), U.S. Senate (1905-1911), minister to Colombia (1922-1928).

PILLION, JOHN RAYMOND *(b Aug. 10, 1904, Conneaut, Ohio)* Lawyer, farmer, businessman, New York Republican. Lackawanna city court judge (1932-1936), Lackawanna corporation counsel and tax attorney (1936-1941), state assembly (1941-1950), U.S. Representative (1953-1965) and a member of the Appropriations Committee.

PILLSBURY, JOHN SARGENT *(b July 29, 1828, Sutton, N.H.; d Oct. 18, 1901, Minneapolis, Minn.)* General store clerk, merchant, tailor, hardware dealer, and finally a flour miller in partnership with his brother, George, and two nephews, building it into the world's largest such business and yet a man with political and civic interests, casting his lot with Minnesota's Republican party and holding a variety of local, county, and state offices before being elected governor (1876-1882). One of his best-known civic deeds was rescuing the University of Minnesota from bankruptcy (1864).

PINCKNEY, CHARLES *(b Oct. 26, 1757, Charles Town, now Charleston, S.C.; d Oct. 29, 1824, Charleston)* Lawyer, planter, Revolutionary soldier who was captured by the British (1780) and one of South Carolina's most prominent political figures contributing much to the Articles of Confederation as leader of an amendment movement, the drafting of the federal Constitution, and the acquisition of Louisiana; South Carolina Federalist turned Democrat and Thomas Jefferson's campaign manager there. State representative (1779-1784, 1786-1789, 1792-1796, 1805, 1806, 1810-1814), member of the Continental Congress (1777, 1778, 1784-1787), federal Constitutional Convention delegate (1787), president of the state constitutional convention (1788, 1790), governor (1789-1792, 1796, 1798, 1806-1808), U.S. Senate (1798-1801) resigning to become minister to Spain (1801-1804), U.S. Representative (1819-1821). Father of Henry L. Pinckney.

PINCKNEY, CHARLES COTESWORTH *(b Feb. 25, 1746, Charleston, S.C.; d Aug. 16, 1825, Charleston)* Lawyer, Continental army officer who was captured at Charleston, and a South Carolina Federalist who was Alexander Hamilton's vice presidential running mate (1800) and twice thereafter was a candidate for president, losing to Thomas Jefferson (1804) and James Madison (1808). In 1796 Washington appointed him minister to France but the French, angered over Jay's Treaty, refused to receive him. In 1797 he was sent back to France as part of a commission to settle outstanding grievances. French officials sought a bribe before negotiating and Pickney retorted sharply: "It is No! No! Not a six-pence!" and since has been widely misquoted until now his words are twisted into the slogan: "Millions for defense but not one cent for tribute!" Thus ended the mission; John Adams published the commission's report but substituted the letters X,Y,Z for the French agents' names and an undeclared naval war with France followed. Brother of Thomas Pinckney and second cousin of Charles Pinckney.

PINCKNEY, HENRY LAURENS *(b Sept. 24, 1794, Charleston, S.C.; d Feb. 3, 1863, Charleston)* Lawyer, founding editor-publisher of the *Charleston Mercury* (1819), South Carolina Democrat who strongly championed nullification both from the political stump and in his editorials. State representative (1816-1832), Charleston intendant (1830-1832), mayor (1837-1840) and port collector (1841, 1842), U.S. Representative (1833-1837), St. Philip's and St. Michael's parishes tax collector (1845-1863). Son of Charles Pinckney.

PINCKNEY, THOMAS *(b Oct. 23, 1750, Charleston, S.C.; d Nov. 2, 1828, Charleston)* Lawyer, planter, Revolutionary Army officer who was wounded and captured at the Battle of Camden, South Carolina Federalist whose career in many ways paralleled that of his second cousin, Charles Pinckney. Governor (1787-1789), presiding officer of the state convention that ratified the federal Constitution (1788), state representative (1791), minister to Great Britain (1792-1796) and envoy to Spain (1794-1795) who settled boundary differences both with Florida and Louisiana and obtained navigational freedom on the Mississippi, U.S. Representative (1797-1801), president general of the Society of the Cincinnati (1825-1828). Brother of Charles C. Pinckney.

PIÑERO, JESÚS T. *(b April 16, 1897, Carolina, P.R.; d Nov. 19, 1952, Loiza, P.R.)* Farmer, sugar-cane and dairy products manufacturer, Puerto Rico Popular Democrat. President of the Carolina municipal assembly (1928-1932), member of Puerto Rico House of Representatives (1940-1944), Popular Democrat Convention delegate (1940), resident commissioner to the United States (1945-1946) resigning to become governor (1946-1948).

PINKNEY, WILLIAM *(b March 17, 1764, Annapolis, Md.; d Feb. 25, 1822, Washington, D.C.)* Physician who did not practice, preferring the law and bombastic oratory to medicine, diplomat of some note, an authority on the U.S. Constitution, and a Maryland Democrat who contributed to the Missouri Compromise. State constitutional convention delegate (1788), state house of delegates (1789-1792, 1795), U.S. Representative (1791, 1815-1816), member of the state executive council (1792-1795), commissioner to London under the Jay Treaty (1796-1804), state attorney general (1805), joint minister to England with James Monroe (1806-1807) and sole minister (1807-1811), state senate (1811), U.S. attorney general in the Madison cabinet (1811-1814), minister to Russia and special envoy to Naples (1816-1818), U.S. Senate (1819 until death).

PITKIN, FREDERICK WALKER (b Aug. 31, 1837, Manchester, Conn.; d Dec. 18, 1886, Pueblo, Colo.) Lawyer and an advocate of good health who traveled many states seeking what to him was the right climate, finally settled upon Colorado where he rose to political prominence as a Republican. As a law-and-order frontier governor (1879-1883) he had much to do with the putting down of a Ute uprising (1879), their banishment from the state, and the smothering of a Leadville miners' strike (1880).

PITKIN, TIMOTHY (b Jan. 21, 1766, Farmington, Conn.; d Dec. 18, 1847, New Haven, Conn.) Lawyer, author said to be an authority on commerce, Connecticut Federalist. State representative (1790, 1792, 1794-1805) who was clerk of the house (1800-1802) and speaker (1803-1805) and again a member (1819-1830); U.S. Representative (1805-1819), state constitutional convention delegate (1818).

PITNEY, MAHLON (b Feb. 5, 1858, Morristown, N.J.; d Dec. 9, 1924, Washington, D.C.) Lawyer, New Jersey Republican who as a Taft-appointed associate justice of the U.S. Supreme Court (1912-1922) was known for his conservative, antilabor views. U.S. Representative (1895-1899), state senator (1899-1901) and senate president (1901), associate justice of the state supreme court (1901-1908) and state chancellor (1908-1912).

PITTENGER, WILLIAM ALVIN (b Dec. 29, 1885, Montgomery County, Ind.; d Nov. 26, 1951, Duluth, Minn.) Lawyer,

Minnesota Republican. State representative (1917-1920), U.S. Representative (1929-1933, 1935-1937, 1939-1947).

PITTMAN, KEY (b Sept. 19, 1872, Vicksburg, Miss.; d Nov. 10, 1940, Reno, Nev.) Seattle lawyer who joined the Klondike gold rush (1897-1901) and took time out from mining to help form the Alaskan consent government and serve as Nome's first prosecutor (1899); then, when his claims petered out, moved to Nevada (1902) to become one of the state's leading Democrats who as a U.S. Senator (1913 until death) supported the miners and the mining industry. Some of his contributions were the Pittman Act (1918), the World Economic Conference's silver pact (1933), and the Silver Purchase Act (1934).

PLAISTED, HARRIS MERRILL (b Nov. 2, 1828, Jefferson, N.H.; d Jan. 31, 1898, Bangor, Maine) Union Army officer, lawyer, writer, Maine Republican turned Greenback Democrat and editor-publisher of Augusta's New Age (1883 until death), which he used to further the interests of William Jennings Bryan and bimetallism. State representative (1867, 1868), GOP National Convention delegate (1868), state attorney general (1873-1875), U.S. Representative (1875-1877), governor (1881-1883).

PLATER, GEORGE (b Nov. 8, 1735, St. Marys County, Md.; d Feb. 10, 1792, Annapolis, Md.) Lawyer, Revolutionary naval officer, Maryland Federalist. Member of the Maryland Assembly (1758), provincial court judge (1771-1773), councilman (1773, 1774), Annapolis convention delegate (1776), delegate to the Continental Congress (1778-1781), president of the state convention that ratified the U.S. Constitution (1788); elector in the first presidential election, casting his vote for Washington; governor (1791 until death). Father of Thomas Plater.

PLATER, THOMAS (b May 9, 1769, Annapolis, Md.; d May 1, 1830, Poolesville, Md.) Maryland lawyer who, as an officer in the state militia (1794), helped put down the Whisky Insurrection. U.S. Representative (1801-1805). Son of George Plater.

PLATT, ORVILLE HITCHCOCK (b July 19, 1827, Washington, Conn.; d April 21, 1905, Washington, Conn.) Lawyer, Connecticut Republican with a reputation for conservatism who as U.S. Senator for a quarter-century (1879 until death) consistently supported the man in the White House, no matter what his politics. One of his most lasting contributions was procurement of an international copyright agreement (1891) that did much to minimize literary piracy. State senate clerk (1855, 1856), Connecticut secretary of state (1857), state senate (1861, 1862), state representative (1864, 1869) and house speaker in the latter year, New Haven County state's attorney (1877-1879).

PLATT, THOMAS COLLIER (b July 15, 1833, Owego, N.Y.; d March 6, 1910, New York City) Druggist, banker, timberland speculator, express company executive, and New York Republican boss of national repute who had his differences with Presidents Garfield and Harrison and whose political power was finally eclipsed by Theodore Roosevelt. U.S. Representative (1873-1877), U.S. Senate for two months in 1881, resigning with Roscoe Conkling because Garfield did not place federal patronage for New York in their hands; president of the State Board of Quarantine Commissioners (1880-1888), GOP National Convention delegate (1876, 1880, 1884, 1888, 1892, 1896, 1900, 1904), U.S. Senate (1897-1909).

PLEASANTS, JAMES (b Oct. 24, 1769, Powhatan County, Va.; d Nov. 9, 1836, Goochland County, Va.) Political foe of Andrew Jackson, lawyer, planter,

Virginia Democrat. Member of the state house of delegates (1797-1802), U.S. Representative (1811-1819), U.S. Senate (1819-1822) resigning to become governor (1822-1825), state constitutional convention delegate (1829, 1830). Cousin of Thomas Jefferson.

PLUMB, PRESTON B. (b Oct. 12, 1837, Delaware County, Ohio; d Dec. 20, 1891, Washington, D.C.) Newspaperman who was one of the founders (1857) of the town of Emporia, where he then edited and published the Kansas News, Union Army officer, lawyer, banker and a Kansas Republican. Free State Convention secretary (1857), Leavenworth constitutional convention delegate (1859), state representative (1862, 1867, 1868) and house speaker (1868), U.S. Senate (1877 until death).

PLUMER, WILLIAM, SR. (b June 25, 1759, Newburyport, Mass.; d Dec. 22, 1850, Epping, N.H.) Lawyer, journalist, author, farmer, historian, New Hampshire Federalist who switched to the Democrat-Republican fold after becoming a friend and supporter of Thomas Jefferson. State representative (1788-1791, 1797-1800) and house speaker (1791, 1797), U.S. Senate (1802-1807), state senate member and president (1810, 1811), governor (1812, 1813, 1816-1819), presidential elector on the Monroe-Tompkins ticket (1820). Father of the following.

PLUMER, WILLIAM, JR. (b Feb. 9, 1789, Epping, N.H.; d Sept. 18, 1854, Epping). Lawyer, historian, author and a New Hampshire Democrat whose works included a biography of his father (see preceding). U.S. commissioner of loans (1816, 1817), state representative (1818), U.S. Representative (1819-1825), state senate (1827, 1828).

POINDEXTER, GEORGE (b 1779, Louisa County, Va.; d Sept. 5, 1855, Jackson, Miss.) Virginia lawyer who migrated to Mississippi and made his political contribution to both territorial and state affairs as a Democrat. As a territory: attorney general (1802-1805), member of the general assembly (1805), delegate to the U.S. Congress (1807-1813), U.S. district judge (1813-1817). As a state: U.S. Representative (1817-1819), governor (1819-1821), U.S. Senate (1830-1835).

POINDEXTER, MILES *(b April 22, 1868, Memphis, Tenn.; d Sept. 21, 1946, Greenlee, Va.)* Lawyer, Washington Republican. Walla Walla County prosecutor (1892), Spokane County assistant prosecutor (1898-1904), superior court judge (1904-1908), U.S. Representative (1909-1911), U.S. Senate (1911-1923), minister to Peru (1923-1928).

POINSETT, JOEL ROBERTS *(b March 2, 1779, Charleston, S.C.; d Dec. 12, 1851, Sumter County, S.C.)* Lawyer, amateur horticulturist, South Carolina Union Democrat who was considered an expert on Latin American affairs and so was sent by President Monroe (1809) to Chile and Rio de la Plata to investigate the chances of success of a revolt against Spain; later, as first U.S. minister to Mexico (1825-1829), he was noted for two things: the development from a native bloom of the flower that came to be known as the Poinsettia, and expulsion for meddling in Mexican politics. State representative (1816-1820), U.S. Representative (1821-1825), secretary of war in the Van Buren cabinet (1837-1841).

POLAND, LUKE POTTER *(b Nov. 1, 1815, Westford, Vt.; d July 2, 1887, Lamoille County, Vt.)* Lawyer, banker, Vermont Republican who was chairman of House committees that investigated the Ku Klux Klan, the Credit Mobilier railroad construction fund scandal, and the Carpetbag administration in Arkansas. Register of probate (1839, 1840),

state constitutional convention delegate (1843), Lamoille County prosecutor (1844, 1845), state supreme court judge (1848-1860) and chief justice (1860-1865), U.S. Senate to fill a vacancy (1865-1867), U.S. Representative (1867-1875, 1883-1885), state representative (1878).

POLK, JAMES GOULD *(b Oct. 6, 1896, Penn Township, Ohio; d April 28, 1959, Washington, D.C.)* Educator, farmer, Ohio Democrat. New Vienna High School principal (1919-1920), New Vienna schools superintendent (1920-1922), Hillsboro High School principal (1923-1928), U.S. Representative (1931-1941, 1949 until death), special Department of Agriculture assistant (1942-1946).

POLK, JAMES KNOX *(b Nov. 2, 1795, Mecklenburg County, N.C.; d June 15, 1849, Nashville, Tenn.)* Eleventh president (Tennessee Democrat), 1845-1849, he was first "dark horse" presidential candidate chosen by a major political party; protégé and faithful supporter of Andrew Jackson, he became known as Young Hickory but lacked Jackson's warmth and emotional appeal.

Born on a North Carolina frontier farm, but his family moved to Duck River Valley in what became Maury County, central Tennessee. Graduated from University of North Carolina (1818), read law with Felix Grundy and was admitted to the bar in 1820. Married Sarah Childress (1824) who allowed no hard liquor or dancing in the White House. They had no children.

Chief clerk, Tennessee Senate (1821-1823); member state house of representatives (1823-1825) where he gained reputation of being a clear-thinking debater; U.S. Representative (1825-1839) and speaker (1835-1839), becoming a leader of the Jackson forces. In an attempt to regain control of Tennessee for Jacksonian Democrats, ran successfully for governor, serving from 1839 to 1841, but lost the elections of 1841 and 1843. His big chance came when Van Buren came out in opposition to Texas annexation, then became deadlocked with Lewis Cass in the 1844 Democratic National Convention; Polk (with Jackson's support) was given the presidential nomination. He won with 170 electoral votes to Whig candidate Henry Clay's 105.

Although he generally continued Jacksonian policy, as president Polk was unquestionably his own man. Though frail, he worked very hard and achieved his specified goals in spite of the growing angry controversy between abolitionists and proslavers who turned much of the government's business into factional squabbles. He reduced the tariff and federal appropriations for internal improvement and restored Van Buren's independent treasury system. But it was in definitely settling disputes over borders and expanding the country's size that Polk made his most important contributions. The northern boundary of the Oregon Territory was set along the forty-ninth parallel, thus ending the "54° 40′ or fight" controversy with Britain in peaceful compromise. After diplomatic relations with Mexico broke down, Polk ordered American troops to advance to the Rio Grande, the Mexican army retaliated, and conflict resulted. Congress declared war on Mexico (May 12, 1846). Mexico was decisively beaten (peace treaty was ratified by the Senate on March 10, 1848), New Mexico and California were ceded to the United States for payment of $15 million, and the question of which country owned Texas was definitely settled.

Polk refused to run for reelection. His strength apparently used up, he became ill and died three months after retiring.

POLK, WILLIAM HAWKINS *(b May 24, 1815, Maury County, Tenn.; d Dec. 16, 1862, Nashville, Tenn.)* Lawyer, Tennessee Democrat who was minister to the Kingdom of Naples (1845-1847)

when his brother, James, was president. U.S. Representative (1851-1853).

POLLOCK, JAMES *(b Sept. 11, 1810, Milton, Pa.; d April 19, 1890, Lock Haven, Pa.)* Lawyer, Pennsylvania Whig turned Know-Nothing who, as director of the Philadelphia Mint (1861-1866, 1873), thought up the "In God We Trust" motto on U.S. coins. Northumberland County deputy attorney general (1836), U.S. Representative (1844-1849), governor (1855-1858), delegate to the peace-between-states convention (1861), Philadelphia naval officer (1879).

POOL, JOHN *(b June 16, 1826, Pasquotank County, N.C.; d Aug. 16, 1884, Washington, D.C.)* Lawyer, planter, North Carolina Unionist Whig turned Republican turned Democrat who while a U.S. Senator (1868-1873) had much to do with the introduction of anti-Ku Klux Klan legislation. State senate (1856, 1858, 1864, 1865), unsuccessful Whig candidate for governor (1860), state constitutional convention delegate (1865). Uncle of Walter F. Pool.

POOL, WALTER FRESHWATER *(b Oct. 10, 1850, near Elizabeth City, N.C.; d Aug. 25, 1883, Elizabeth City)* Lawyer, North Carolina Republican. U.S. Representative (March 4, 1883, until death). Nephew of John Pool.

POPE, JOHN *(b 1770, Prince William County, Va.; d July 12, 1845, Springfield, Ky.)* Lawyer, Kentucky Democrat who served as territorial governor of Arkansas (1829-1835), presidential elector (1800), state representative (1802, 1806, 1807), U.S. Senator (1807-1813) and Senate president pro tem (1811), state senate (1825-1829), U.S. Representative (1837-1843).

PORTER, ALBERT GALLATIN *(b April 20, 1824, Lawrenceburg, Ind.; d May 3, 1897, Indianapolis, Ind.)* Law partner of Benjamin Harrison, Indiana Republican. Indianapolis city attorney (1851-1853), state supreme court reporter (1853-1857), city councilman (1857-1859), U.S. Representative (1859-1863), first comptroller of the U.S. Treasury (1878-1880), governor (1881-1885), GOP National Convention delegate (1888), minister to Italy (1889-1892).

PORTER, STEPHEN GEYER *(b May 18, 1869, Columbiana County, Ohio; d June 27, 1930, Pittsburgh, Pa.)* Lawyer, Pennsylvania Republican, and a man of influence in the field of foreign policy as a U.S. Representative (1911 until death) and chairman (1919 until death) of the House Foreign Affairs Committee. Allegheny city solicitor (1903-1906), GOP state convention chairman (1912).

POST, MORTON EVEREL *(b Dec. 25, 1840, West Henrietta, now Rochester, N.Y.; d March 19, 1933, Alhambra, Calif.).* Colorado muleskinner, Montana miner, Wyoming Territory rancher-banker, California fruitgrower, and a Democrat. In Montana: Democratic National Convention delegate (1864). In Wyoming: Laramie County commissioner (1870-1876), member of the legislative council (1878-1880), delegate to Congress (1881-1885).

POST, PHILIP SIDNEY *(b March 19, 1833, Florida, N.Y.; d Jan. 6, 1895, Washington, D.C.)* Lawyer, Union Army officer who was wounded at Nashville (1864) and awarded the Congressional Medal of Honor (1893), Illinois Republican. Consul to Vienna (1866-1874), consul general to Austria-Hungary (1874-1879), state commander of the Grand Army of the Republic (1886), U.S. Representative (1887 until death).

POSTON, CHARLES DEBRILLE *(b April 20, 1825, Hardin County, Ky.; d June 24, 1902, Phoenix, Ariz.)* A Kentucky and Tennessee clerk who moved to California during the gold rush, became a San Francisco customs house clerk

(1850-1853), and then moved to Arizona where he found his niche as a silver-mine operator and a Republican. His first position there (1863) was superintendent of Indian affairs and civilian aide to General Heintzelman. Also, territorial delegate to Congress (Dec. 1864-March 1865), Land Office register at Florence (1878), consular agent in El Paso, Texas (1890).

POTTER, CLARKSON NOTT *(b April 25, 1825, Schenectady, N.Y.; d Jan. 23, 1882, New York City)* Civil engineer, surveyor, lawyer, New York Democrat who was president of the American Bar Association (1881, 1882). U.S. Representative (1869-1875, 1877-1879), Democratic state convention chairman (1875, 1877) and national convention delegate (1872, 1876), Union College trustee (1863-1882).

POTTER, ELISHA REYNOLDS, SR. *(b Nov. 5, 1764, Little Rest, now Kingston, R.I.; d Sept. 26, 1835, South Kingston, R.I.)* Blacksmith, farmer, Revolutionary soldier, lawyer, writer, Rhode Island Federalist. State representative (1793-1796, 1798-1808, 1816, 1817, 1819-1835) and house speaker (1795, 1796, 1802, 1806-1808), U.S. Representative (1796, 1797, 1809-1815).

POTTER, ELISHA REYNOLDS, JR. *(b June 20, 1811, Little Rest, now Kingston, R.I.; d April 10, 1882, Kingston, R.I.).* Lawyer, Rhode Island Whig. State adjutant general (1833-1837), state representative (1838-1840), U.S. Representative (1843-1845), state senate (1847-1852, 1861-1863), state public schools commissioner (1849-1854), associate justice of the state supreme court (1868 until death).

POU, EDWARD WILLIAM *(b Sept. 9, 1863, Tuskegee, Ala.; d April 1, 1934, Washington, D.C.)* Lawyer, North Carolina Democrat who served thirty-three years in the U.S. House of Representatives (1901 until death) where, as Rules Committee chairman, he did much to advance the legislative programs of Woodrow Wilson and Franklin D. Roosevelt. State Democratic executive committee chairman (1886), presidential elector on the Cleveland-Thurman ticket (1888), fourth judicial district solicitor (1890-1901), Democratic National Convention delegate (1916).

POWDERLY, TERENCE VINCENT *(b Jan. 22, 1849, Carbondale, Pa.; d June 24, 1924, Washington, D.C.)* Lawyer, orator, official of the Machinists and Blacksmiths' Union and the Knights of Labor in Pennsylvania (1871 until death), and a reformer who believed neither in strikes nor in labor's formal entry into politics. But he was very much opposed to the pay system as we know it, advocating in its stead distribution of profits among those who produce a given product. U.S. commissioner-general of immigration (1897-1902), special representative of the Department of Commerce and Labor (1906-1907), Bureau of Immigration information chief (1907-1921).

POWELL, ADAM CLAYTON, JR. *(b Nov. 29, 1908, New Haven, Conn.; d April 4, 1972, Miami, Fla.)* Clergyman, writer, lecturer, and a New York Democrat who for twenty-two years (1945-1967) was a U.S. Representative and was both a symbol and a spokesman for blacks in the United States.

An early-day civil rights activist. Long before going to Washington there had been many other milestones in his life of which his Harlem constituency could well be proud: editor of *The People's Voice,* New York City councilman (1941-1944), Columbia University Extension School instructor, cofounder of the National Negro Congress.

His major achievement as a congressman was chairman of the House Committee on Education and Labor (1960-1967), thus enabling him to play a major part in passage of forty-eight important pieces of social legislation, among them the 1961 Minimum Wage Bill, the Manpower Development and Training Act, the Anti-Poverty Bill, the Juvenile Delinquency Act, the Vocational Educational Act, and the National Defense Educational Act.

His credo as once expressed to an interviewer: "As a member of Congress, I have done nothing more than any other member and, by the grace of God, I intend to do not one bit less."

His downfall came in 1966 when his affairs were investigated by a select committee of House members who recommended public censure and loss of seniority. But the full House on March 1, 1967, went much further and by a vote of 307 to 116 excluded Powell from the Ninetieth Congress. Blacks contended that the decision was purely racist and two months later at a special election overwhelmingly chose him to fill his own vacated seat. In January 1969 the House voted, 251 to 160, to reseat him but fined him $25,000 for the alleged misuse of payroll and travel funds and stripped him of his seniority. Six months after that, the Supreme Court ruled that the House exclusion action of 1967 was unconstitutional. Powell, his faith in American jurisprudence restored but a much-subdued man, returned to Washington but his heart obviously was no longer in his work and he lost his bid for renomination at the next primary election, albeit by a narrow margin—150 votes in a six-man race.

POWELL, LAZARUS WHITEHEAD *(b Oct. 6, 1812, Henderson County, Ky.; d July 3, 1867, near Henderson, Ky.).* Lawyer, Kentucky Union Democrat who strongly argued that his state remain neutral and just as strongly fought against military meddling into civic affairs during the Civil War. State representative (1836), presidential elector on the Polk-Dallas ticket (1844), governor (1851-1855), U.S. Senate (1859-1865), Union National Convention delegate (1866).

POWELL, PAULUS (b 1809, Amherst County, Va.; d June 10, 1874, Amherst, Va.) Virginia Democrat. Member of the state house of delegates (1843-1849, 1863, 1864), U.S. Representative (1849-1859).

POWER, THOMAS CHARLES (b May 22, 1839, Dubuque County, Iowa; d Feb. 16, 1923, Helena, Mont.) Civil engineer, teacher, Dakota surveyor, Missouri River trader and steamship operator, Montana rancher, banker, merchant, Montana Republican. Delegate to the territory's first constitutional convention (1883), GOP National Convention delegate (1888) and after statehood a U.S. Senator (1890-1895).

POWERS, CALEB (b Feb. 1, 1869, Whitley County, Ky.; d July 25, 1932, Baltimore, Md.) Lawyer, Kentucky Republican who was convicted of complicity in the assassination of Governor William Goebel (1900), pardoned (1908), and then elected four times a U.S. Representative (1911-1919). Knox County schools superintendent (1894-1899), Kentucky secretary of state (1899), GOP National Convention delegate (1912).

POWERS, HORACE HENRY (b May 29, 1835, Morristown, Vt.; d Dec. 8, 1913, Morrisville, Vt.) Lawyer, University of Vermont trustee (1883 until death), Vermont Republican. State representative (1858, 1874) and house speaker (1874), Lamoille County prosecutor (1861, 1862), council of censors member (1869), state constitutional convention delegate (1870), state senate (1872, 1873), state supreme court judge (1874-1890), GOP National Convention delegate (1892), U.S. Representative (1891-1901).

POWERS, LLEWELLYN (b Oct. 14, 1836, Pittsfield, Maine; d July 28, 1908, Houlton, Maine) Lawyer, Maine Republican. Aroostook County prosecutor (1864-1871), collector of customs (1868-1872), state representative (1873-1876, 1883, 1892, 1895) and house speaker in the latter year, U.S. Representative (1877-1879, 1901 until death), governor (1896-1900).

PRALL, ANNING SMITH (b Sept. 17, 1870, Port Richmond, N.Y.; d July 23, 1937, Boothbay Harbor, Maine) New York Democrat who held political jobs that ranged from New York City Board of Education member-president (1918-1921) to Federal Communications Commission chairman (1935 until death). City tax and assessment commissioner (1922, 1923), Democratic National Convention delegate (1924), U.S. Representative (1923-1935).

PRATT, THOMAS GEORGE (b Feb. 18, 1804, Georgetown, Md., now Washington, D.C.; d Nov. 9, 1869, Baltimore, Md.) Lawyer, Maryland Whig who, owing to his Southern sympathies, became a Civil War Democrat and ultimately a Unionist. Member of the state house of delegates (1832-1835), presidential elector on the Harrison-Tyler ticket (1836), executive council president (1836), state senate (1838-1843), governor (1845-1848), U.S. Senate (1850-1857), Democratic National Convention delegate (1864), Union National Convention delegate (1866).

PRESTON, PRINCE HULON, JR. (b July 5, 1908, Monroe, Ga.; d Feb. 8, 1961, Savannah, Ga.) Lawyer, Georgia Democrat. State representative (1935-1938), U.S. Representative (1947-1961).

PRICE, HIRAM (b Jan. 10, 1814, Washington County, Pa.; d May 30, 1901, Washington, D.C.) Farmer, bookkeeper, merchant, banker, railroad executive,

Iowa Republican who was U.S. commissioner of Indian affairs during the Garfield administration (1881-1885). U.S. Representative (1863-1869, 1877-1881).

PRICE, RODMAN McCAMLEY *(b May 5, 1816, Newton, N.J.; d June 7, 1894, Oakland, N.J.)* Lawyer, ferryboat and quarry operator, New Jersey Republican who was a Navy officer during the Mexican War and, as prefect and alcalde (administrative and judicial official) of Monterey (1846), was the first U.S. citizen to exercise judicial functions in California; naval agent (1848-1850) and delegate to California's first constitutional convention. In New Jersey: U.S. Representative (1851-1853), governor (1854-1857) gaining a reputation as "the father" of the state's public school system, delegate to the peace-between-states convention (1861).

PRICE, THOMAS LAWSON *(b Jan. 19, 1809, near Danville, Va.; d July 15, 1870, Jefferson City, Mo.)* Manufacturer, merchant, stage line operator, railroad builder, banker, land speculator, planter, and a pro-Union Missouri Democrat who did much to revitalize the party there after the Civil War. Lieutenant governor (1849-1850), state representative (1860-1862), U.S. Representative (1862-1863), Democratic National Convention delegate (1864, 1868).

PRIEST, JAMES PERCY *(b April 1, 1900, Carters Creek, Tenn.; d Oct. 12, 1956, Nashville, Tenn.)* Teacher, newspaperman, Tennessee Democrat. U.S. Representative (1941 until death).

PRINCE, GEORGE WASHINGTON *(b March 4, 1854, Tazewell County, Ill.; d Sept. 26, 1939, Los Angeles, Calif.).* Lawyer, Illinois Republican. Galesburg city attorney (1881-1883), Knox County GOP committee chairman (1884), state representative (1888-1892), U.S. Representative (1895-1913).

PRINCE, LeBARON BRADFORD *(b July 3, 1840, Flushing, N.Y.; d Dec. 8, 1922, Flushing)* Lawyer, orator, author, and a New York Republican whose most-lasting contributions were to New Mexico where as a presidentially appointed official he staked out a new life for himself and, in many respects, for the territory. There he became, in addition to his judicial and political chores, a newspaper correspondent, miner, fruit-grower, historian, and chronicler of much that went on to bring about New Mexico's transition to statehood.

In New York: delegate to all GOP state conventions (1867-1879) and the 1868 and 1876 national conventions, state assemblyman (1871-1875), state senate (1876-1877). In New Mexico: chief justice (1879-1882), governor (1889-1893). He formulated the territory's first public school code, was a founder of the University of New Mexico, and organized a constitutional convention where fundamental laws were formulated.

PROCTOR, REDFIELD *(b June 1, 1831, Proctorsville, Vt.; d March 4, 1908, Washington, D.C.)* Lawyer, Union Army officer, quarry operator, Vermont Republican who served as secretary of war in the Harrison cabinet (1889-1891) when he resigned to become a U.S. Senator (1891 until death). State representative (1867, 1868, 1888), state senator and senate president pro tem (1874, 1875), lieutenant governor (1876-1878), governor (1878-1880), GOP National Convention delegate (1884, 1888, 1896).

PUGH, JAMES LAWRENCE *(b Dec. 12, 1820, Burke County, Ga.; d March 9, 1907, Washington, D.C.)* Lawyer, planter, Confederate soldier, Alabama Democrat. Presidential elector (1848, 1856, 1876), U.S. Representative (1859-1861), member of the Confederate Congress (1861-1865), state Democratic convention president (1874), state constitutional convention delegate (1875), U.S. Senate (1880-1897).

PUJO, ARSÉNE PAULIN *(b Dec. 16, 1861, Calcasieu Parish, La.; d Dec. 31, 1939, New Orleans, La.)* Lawyer, Louisiana Democrat who as chairman of the House Banking and Currency Committee (1911-1913) conducted investigations of trusts that led to major reforms.

State constitutional convention delegate (1898), U.S. Representative (1903-1913), member of the National Monetary Commission (1908-1912).

PURNELL, FRED SAMPSON *(b Oct. 25, 1882, Fountain County, Ind.; d Oct. 21, 1939, Washington, D.C.)* Lawyer, Indiana Republican. Attica city attorney (1910-1914), U.S. Representative (1917-1933).

Q

☆ ☆ ☆

QUAY, MATTHEW STANLEY (b Sept. 30, 1833, Dillsburg, Pa.; d May 28, 1904, Beaver, Pa.) Lawyer, Union Army officer, editor of the Beaver Radical (1867-1872), much-hated and much-feared Pennsylvania Republican boss whose two passions were politics and good books. Chief clerk of Beaver County (1856-1860), state representative (1865-1867), commonwealth secretary (1872-1878, 1879-1882), Philadelphia city recorder and state GOP chairman (1878, 1879), GOP National Convention delegate (1872, 1876, 1880, 1888, 1892), state treasurer (1885-1887), U.S. Senate (1887-1899, 1901 until death). GOP National Committee chairman (1888).

QUEZON, MANUEL LUIS (b Aug. 19, 1878, Baler, Tayabas Province, Philippine Islands; d Aug. 1, 1944, Saranac Lake, N.Y., two years after escaping from invading Japanese forces via a U.S. submarine) Lawyer, Philippine nationalist who was president of the commonwealth (1935 until death). Tayabas provincial governor (1906, 1907), delegate to the first assembly and his party's floor leader (1907, 1908), resident commissioner to the United States (1909-1916), member-president of the Philippine Senate (1916-1935).

QUIN, PERCY EDWARDS (b Oct. 30, 1872, Amite County, Miss.; d Feb. 4, 1932, Washington, D.C.) Teacher, lawyer, Mississippi Democrat. McComb City city attorney (1895), Democratic state convention chairman (1889, 1912), state representative (1900-1902), U.S. Representative (1913 until death).

QUINCY, JOSIAH, SR. (b Feb. 23, 1744, Boston, Mass.; d April 26, 1775, aboard ship homeward bound from England where he had gone in Sept. 1774 on a secret mission to present the case of the colonies) Member of a prominent Massachusetts family, lawyer, orator, writer on matters political and patriotic in the journals of the times and under several pseudonyms whose words were generally heeded throughout the colonies. His most prominent case as an attorney was, with John Adams, in defense of British soldiers put upon by a mob in what became known as the Boston Massacre (March 5, 1770). His strong lawyer's conviction that every man is entitled to his day in court was the reason for his taking the case, which was prosecuted by his older brother, Samuel, who was then solicitor-general of Massachusetts. Father of the following.

478

QUINCY, JOSIAH, JR. *(b Feb. 4, 1772, Boston, Mass.; d July 1, 1864, Quincy, Mass.)* Lawyer, Harvard University president (1829-1845), Massachusetts Federalist. State senate (1804, 1805, 1813-1820), U.S. Representative (1805-1813), state representative (1821, 1822) and house speaker (1822), state constitutional convention delegate (1820), Boston municipal court judge (1822), mayor of Boston (1823-1829) whose administration began erection of the Bunker Hill monument. Son of the preceding.

R

☆ ☆ ☆

RABAUT, LOUIS CHARLES *(b Dec. 5, 1886, Detroit, Mich.; d Nov. 12, 1961, Hamtramck, Mich.)* Lawyer, builder, Michigan Democrat. Democratic National Convention delegate (1936, 1940), U.S. Representative (1935-1947, 1949 until death) and Interparliamentary Union delegate (1939).

RADCLIFF, JACOB *(b April 20, 1764, Rhinebeck, N.Y.; d May 6, 1844, Troy, N.Y.)* Lawyer, Columbia College trustee (1805-1817), and a New York Federalist who with two others leased a plot of land (1804) on the New Jersey side of New York Harbor for $6,000 and on it founded a municipality they called Jersey City. In New York: state assemblyman (1794-1795), assistant state attorney general (1796-1798), state supreme court justice (1798-1804), member of the Committee of Correspondence (1808, 1812), mayor of New York City (1810, 1815-1817), state constitutional convention delegate (1821).

RAGON, HEARTSILL *(b March 20, 1885, Dublin, Ark.; d Sept. 15, 1940, Fort Smith, Ark.)* Lawyer, Arkansas Democrat. State representative (1911-1913), district attorney (1916-1920), Democratic state convention secretary (1918) and chairman (1920), Democratic National Convention delegate (1920), U.S. Representative (1923-1933) resigning to become U.S. judge for the western district of Arkansas (1933 until death).

RAINEY, HENRY THOMAS *(b Aug. 20, 1860, Carrollton, Ill.; d Aug. 19, 1934, St. Louis, Mo.)* Lawyer, farmer, Illinois Democrat and staunch supporter of Woodrow Wilson and Franklin Delano Roosevelt who, as House speaker (1933 until death) pushed through the first New Deal measures. Greene County master in chancery (1887-1895), U.S. Representative (1903-1921, 1923 until death).

RAINEY, JOSEPH HAYNE *(b June 21, 1832, Georgetown, S.C.; d Aug. 2, 1887, Georgetown)* Son of slaves who had purchased their freedom, barber, banker, broker, he escaped to the West Indies during the Civil War, returning then to South Carolina where he became a leader in the Republican party, which sent him to Congress where he thus became the first Negro in U.S. history to sit in the House of Representatives (1870-1879); an able spokesman for Indians and Chinese as well as blacks. Member of the state GOP executive committee (1867-1870), state constitutional convention delegate (1868), state senate (1870), internal revenue agent (1879-1881).

RAINS, ALBERT M. *(b March 11, 1902, Groveoak, Ala.)* Lawyer, Alabama

480

Democrat. Etowah County deputy solicitor (1930-1935), Gadsden city attorney (1935-1944), state representative (1942-1944), U.S. Representative (1945-1965) serving on the Banking and Currency Committee and the Joint Committee on Defense Production.

RAKER, JOHN EDWARD *(b Feb. 22, 1863, Knox County, Ill.; d Jan. 22, 1926, Washington, D.C.)* Lawyer, California Democrat. Modoc County district attorney (1895-1899), superior court judge (1903-1910), Democratic state central committee chairman (1908-1910), Democratic National Convention delegate (1908), U.S. Representative (1911 until death).

RAMSAY, ROBERT LINCOLN *(b March 24, 1877, Durham, England; d Nov. 14, 1956, Wheeling, W.Va.)* Lawyer, West Virginia Democrat. Follansbee city attorney (1905-1930), Brooks County prosecutor (1908-1912, 1916-1920), member of West Virginia University Board of Governors (1927-1930), U.S. Representative (1933-1939, 1941-1943, 1949-1953), special assistant to the U.S. attorney general (1943-1945), state assistant attorney general (1945-1948).

RAMSEY, ALEXANDER *(b Sept. 8, 1815, near Harrisburg, Pa.; d April 22, 1903, St. Paul, Minn.)* Lawyer, historian, land speculator, Pennsylvania Whig who became a Minnesota pioneer (giving Ramsey County its name) when President Taylor sent him there to be its territorial governor (1849-1853) and to negotiate treaties with the Sioux. He then remained on into statehood and played a leading role in the establishment of the Republican party in Minnesota. In Pennsylvania: secretary to the electoral college (1840), clerk of the state house of representatives (1841), U.S. Representative (1843-1847). In Minnesota: mayor of St. Paul (1855), state governor (1860-1863),

U.S. Senate (1863-1875), secretary of war in the Hayes cabinet (1879-1881), chairman of the Edmunds Commission that dealt with Mormonism in Utah (1882-1886), state historical society president (1849-1863, 1891-1903).

RAMSEYER, CHRISTIAN WILLIAM *(b March 13, 1875, Butler County, Ohio; d Nov. 1, 1943, Washington, D.C.)* Educator, lawyer, Iowa Republican. Davis County prosecutor (1911-1915), U.S. Representative (1915-1933), U.S. Court of Claims commissioner (1933 until death).

RANDALL, SAMUEL JACKSON *(b Oct. 10, 1828, Philadelphia, Pa.; d April 13, 1890, Washington, D.C.)* Merchant, Union Army officer, Pennsylvania Democrat who served more than a quarter-century as U.S. Representative (1863 until death), among other things baring Reconstruction scandals in the Grant administration and gaining national note with the slogan: "Retrenchment and Reform." Speaker of the House (1876-1881).

RANDELL, CHOICE BOSWELL *(b Jan. 1, 1857, Murray County, Ga.; d Oct. 19, 1945, Sherman, Tex.)* Lawyer, Texas Democrat. U.S. Representative (1901-1913).

RANDOLPH, EDMUND JENNINGS *(b Aug. 10, 1753, Williamsburg, Va.; d Sept. 12, 1813, Clarke County, Va.).* Lawyer, military aide to General Washington (1775), Virginia Democrat who introduced the Virginia Plan at the federal constitutional convention (1787) and drafted his own version of what he was convinced the Constitution should be, yet later voted to ratify the final document at the state constitutional convention (1788); also the first U.S. attorney general (1789-1794), then became secretary of state (1794-1795) in the Washington cabinet only to resign under a cloud a year later because of alleged misdoings concerning the Jay Treaty which was negotiated during his administration but over his protests. That took him out of politics but not out of the limelight—he was chief defense counsel at Aaron Burr's treason trial (1807). Virginia attorney general (1776), member of the Continental Congress (1779-1782), governor (1786-1788), member of the state house of delegates (1788, 1789).

RANDOLPH, JOHN *(b June 2, 1773, Cawsons, Va.; d May 24, 1833, Philadelphia, Pa.).* Lawyer who preferred to be known as John Randolph of Roanoke, a sickly man yet an authority on parliamentary law and an extreme extrovert who was most at home on the debating platform. However, when words failed him he fought a harmless duel with Henry Clay (1826) and so lived to debate and to serve another day; Virginia States' Rights Democrat and always a strict constitutional constructionist. U.S. Representative (1815-1817, 1819-1825, 1827-1829, 1833). U.S. Senate (1825-1827) to fill a vacancy, state constitutional convention delegate (1829), U.S. minister to Russia briefly in 1830 when illness forced his resignation.

RANDOLPH, THEODORE FITZ *(b June 24, 1826, Mansfield, Pa.; d Nov. 7, 1883, Morristown, N.J.)* Merchant, mine operator, president of the Morris & Essex Railroad, New Jersey Democrat. State assemblyman (1859), state senate (1862, 1863), governor (1869-1872), U.S. Senate (1875-1881).

RANDOLPH, THOMAS MANN *(b Oct. 1, 1768, Goochland County, Va.; d June 20, 1828, at Monticello, the home of his father-in-law, Thomas Jefferson).* Planter, Virginia Democrat. State senate (1793, 1794), U.S. Representative (1803-1807), member of the state house of delegates (1819, 1820, 1823-1825), governor (1819-1822).

RANKIN, JEANNETTE *(b June 11, 1880, Missoula County, Mont.; d May 18, 1973, Carmel, Calif.)* Social worker in Washington State (1910), California (1911), Montana (1912-1914), and New Zealand (1915); pacifist, lecturer, rancher, and a Montana Republican who did much to further the cause of women's rights and, appropriately, was the first member of her sex to be elected a U.S. Representative (1917-1919, 1941-1943), thus being in Congress for the vote on whether to declare war in both World Wars I and II and both times she voted no. Both times she ran for office on peace and suffragist platforms and, after her first victory, declared: "I knew the women would stand behind me. I am deeply conscious of the responsibility. I will not only represent the women of Montana, but also the women of the country, and I have plenty of work cut out for me." True to her words, she introduced (among other measures) the first bill to grant women citizenship independent of their husbands, and authored the first bill for government-sponsored instruction of hygiene in maternity and infancy.

RANKIN, JOHN ELLIOTT *(b March 29, 1882, Itawamba County, Miss.; d Nov. 26, 1960, Tupelo, Miss.)* Lawyer, lecturer, farmer, real estate operator, newspaper contributor, and an outspokenly conservative Mississippi Democrat who time and time again as a U.S. Representative for thirty-two years (1921-1953) showed that he was anti-Negro, anti-Jewish, antiunion, and anti-Communist. Membership on the House Un-American Activities Committee and chairmanship of the House Veterans Committee provided him with ample opportunity to sound off on all of them. However, his actions did not always match his words; for example, he screamed about the "New Deal-Communist cabal" yet was coauthor of the bill that created the New Deal's

Tennessee Valley Authority; he denounced "Communist Jews" but defended its chairman David Lilienthal when under attack as a pro-Communist. Lee County prosecutor (1911-1915), Democratic National Convention delegate (1932, 1936, 1940).

RANSDELL, JOSEPH EUGENE (b Oct. 7, 1858, Alexandria, La.; d July 27, 1954, Lake Providence, La.) Lawyer, printing executive, cotton and pecan grower, real estate operator, Louisiana Democrat who served thirty-two years in Washington. Eighth judicial district attorney (1884-1896), member of the fifth district levee board (1896-1899), state constitutional convention delegate (1898), U.S. Representative (1899-1913), U.S. Senate (1913-1931), member of the board of supervisors of Louisiana State University and Agricultural College at Baton Rouge (1940-1944).

RANSIER, ALONZO JACOB (b Jan. 3, 1834, Charleston, S.C.; d Aug. 17, 1882, Charleston) A Negro born of free parents, he worked as a shipping clerk but found a short-lived niche in South Carolina politics as a Republican during the Reconstruction, rising to the position of lieutenant governor (1870) and serving a term as U.S. Representative (1873-1875) only to end his days by working as a laborer. Friends of Equal Rights Convention delegate (1865) who delivered its message to Congress: "Provide federal protection for Negroes"; member of the "Outside Congress," a strong lobbying group (1865-1868); state executive committee chairman (1868), state constitutional convention delegate (1868-1869), presidential elector on the Grant-Colfax ticket (1868), president of the Southern States Convention (1871), GOP National Convention delegate (1872), U.S. internal revenue collector (1875-1876).

RANSLEY, HARRY CLAY (b Feb. 5, 1863, Philadelphia, Pa.; d Nov. 7, 1941, Philadelphia) Merchant, Philadelphia Republican who wielded a bit of power there, among other things serving sixteen years as a member of the Select Council, eight of them as its president. State representative (1891-1894), GOP National Convention delegate (1912), Philadelphia County sheriff (1916-1920), GOP city committee chairman (1916-1919), U.S. Representative (1920-1937).

RANSOM, MATT WHITAKER (b Oct. 8, 1826, Warren County, N.C.; d Oct. 8, 1904, Northampton County, N.C.) Lawyer, planter, North Carolina Whig turned Democrat who opposed secession but fought on the side of the South during the Civil War, rising to major general and being three times wounded. Presidential elector on the Scott-Graham ticket (1852), state attorney general (1852-1855), member of the state house of commons (1858-1860), peace commissioner to the Confederate Provisional Congress (1861), U.S. Senate (1872-1895), U.S. minister to Mexico (1895-1897), Democratic National Convention delegate (1876, 1896).

RAPIER, JAMES THOMAS (b Nov. 13, 1837, Florence, Ala.; d May 31, 1883, Montgomery, Ala.) A Negro with unusual advantages (his father was a successful planter), he was educated by private tutors and abroad, became a successful journalist (editor-publisher of the Montgomery Sentinel), cotton grower, and a founder of Alabama's Republican party, but most of all a labor leader who was the driving force in bringing together the state's black workers and sharecroppers for their common good. The Ku Klux Klan and the rebirth of the Democratic party in the South put an end to his political career. State constitutional convention delegate (1867), unsuccessful candidate for Alabama secretary of state (1870), internal revenue assessor (1871), U.S. Representative (1873-1875), second district internal revenue collector (1878 until death).

RAUCH, GEORGE WASHINGTON *(b Feb. 22, 1876, Salamonie Township, Ind.; d Nov. 4, 1940, Marion, Ind.)* Lawyer, Indiana Democrat. U.S. Representative (1907-1917), federal bank receiver (1930-1939).

RAWLINS, JOSEPH LAFAYETTE *(b March 28, 1850, Mill Creek, Utah; d May 24, 1926, Salt Lake City)* University of Deseret professor (1873-1875), lawyer, Utah Democrat. U.S. Representative (1893-1895), Democratic National Convention delegate (1896-1900), U.S. Senate (1897-1903).

RAY, GEORGE WASHINGTON *(b Feb. 3, 1844, Otselic, N.Y.; d Jan. 10, 1925, Norwich, N.Y.)* Union soldier, lawyer, New York Republican who was the party's Chenango County chairman and a state committeeman (1880). U.S. Representative (1883-1885, 1891-1902) resigning to become a U.S. district judge (1902 until death).

RAY, JOHN HENRY *(b Sept. 27, 1886, Mankato, Minn.)* Lawyer, banker, New York Republican. U.S. Representative (1953-1963) serving on Judiciary and Merchant Marine and Fisheries committees.

RAYBURN, SAM *(b Jan. 6, 1882, Roane County, Tex.; d Nov. 16, 1961, Bonham, Tenn.).* Lawyer, Texas Democrat who was both a U.S. Representative (1913 until death) and Speaker of the House (1940-1947, 1949-1953, 1955 until death) longer than anyone in history, both tenures going far beyond mere fulfillment of boyhood dreams while working on his father's cotton farm. Rayburn came a long way from those early days: champion of Roose-

velt's New Deal, Truman's Fair Deal, and Kennedy's New Frontier programs; permanent chairman of three Democratic National Conventions (1948, 1952, 1956), presidential hopeful Lyndon Johnson's floor manager at the 1960 convention. In short, a man of stature, statesmanship, and party loyalty, yet a man who did not hesitate to excuse himself from the fray when he disagreed with policy or objective. State representative (1907-1913) and house speaker (1911, 1912).

RAYMOND, HENRY JARVIS *(b Jan. 24, 1820, Lima, N.Y.; d June 18, 1869, New York City)* Newspaperman who was Horace Greeley's assistant on the *New York Tribune*, broke with him (1843), founded the *New York Times* (Sept. 18, 1851), and continued to show his deep interest in politics and reform but with more moderation as set forth in the Volume One, Number One statement of policy: "We do not mean to write as if we were in a passion—unless that shall really be the case; and we shall make it a point to get into a passion as rarely as possible." Raymond's interest in politics went beyond that of the critical journalist, so much so that he was a leader in New York's Whig party, switched to the Free-Soil movement when the Know-Nothings took over, and ultimately becoming a founder of the Republican party nationally (1856) and author of its statement of principle.

State assemblyman (1850, 1851, 1862) and assembly speaker (1851, 1862), Whig National Convention delegate (1852), lieutenant governor (1854), GOP National Convention delegate (1860), U.S. Representative (1865-1867).

RAYNER, ISIDOR *(b April 11, 1850, Baltimore, Md.; d Nov. 25, 1912, Washington, D.C.)* Lawyer, Maryland Democrat. Member of state house of delegates (1878-1884), state senate

(1884-1886), U.S. Representative (1887-1889, 1891-1895), state attorney general (1899-1903), U.S. Senate (1905 until death).

READ, GEORGE *(b Sept. 18, 1733, Cecil County, Md.; d Sept. 21, 1798, New Castle, Del.)* Lawyer, Delaware signer of the Declaration of Independence and a delegate to the federal Constitutional Convention, attorney general for lower Delaware (1763), member of the Continental Congress (1774-1777), president of the state constitutional convention (1776) and Delaware's first and only vice president, state representative (1779, 1780), U.S. Court of Appeals judge (1782), U.S. Senate (1789-1793), Delaware's chief justice (1793 until death).

REAGAN, JOHN HENNINGER *(b Oct. 8, 1818, Sevierville, Tenn.; d March 6, 1905, Palestine, Tex.)* Indian fighter, surveyor, lawyer, Texas Democrat who was Confederate postmaster general during the Civil War but later, although for a time it cost him politically, advised his fellow Texans to accept emancipation and all that went with it as facts of life. Deputy surveyor of public lands (1839-1843), state representative (1847-1849), district court judge (1852-1857), U.S. Representative (1857-1861, 1875-1887), state secessionist convention delegate (1861) and deputy to the Confederate Provisional Congress, Confederate acting secretary of the treasury (briefly in 1865), state constitutional convention delegate (1875), U.S. Senate (1887-1891), resigning to become a member of the Texas Railroad Commission (1891-1897) and its chairman (1897-1903).

REAVIS, CHARLES FRANK *(b Sept 5, 1870, Falls City, Nebr.; d May 26, 1932, Lincoln, Nebr.)* Lawyer, Nebraska Republican. Richardson County district attorney (1894-1896), U.S. Representative (1915-1922), resigning to become

special assistant to the U.S. attorney general in the prosecution of war-fraud cases (1922-1924).

REDFIELD, WILLIAM COX *(b June 18, 1858, Albany, N.Y.; d June 13, 1932, New York City)* Printer, stationer, manufacturer, banker, investment and insurance executive, and a New York Democrat who tried mightily but in vain to be his party's vice presidential candidate (1912), yet worked just as strenuously to bring about Woodrow Wilson's presidential victory. Gold Democrat National Convention delegate (1896), Brooklyn public works commissioner responsible for the replacement of 100 miles of cobblestone streets with asphalt and concrete (1902, 1903), U.S. Representative (1911-1913), secretary of commerce in the Wilson cabinet (1913-1919).

REECE, BRAZILLA CARROLL *(b Dec. 22, 1889, Johnson County, Tenn.; d March 19, 1961, Bethesda, Md.)* Educator, lawyer, banker, publisher, Tennessee Republican who was chairman of the GOP National Committee (1946-1948) and a congressman for thirty-four years but not consecutively. Director of the New York University School of Business Administration (1919, 1920), U.S. Representative (1921-1931, 1933-1947, 1951 until death), GOP National Convention delegate (1928, 1932, 1936, 1940, 1944, 1948), Smithsonian Institution regent (1945, 1946).

REED, CHAUNCEY WILLIAM *(b June 2, 1890, West Chicago, Ill.; d Feb. 9, 1956, Bethesda, Md.)* Lawyer, Illinois Republican. DuPage County state's attorney (1920-1935), GOP county central committee chairman (1926-1934), U.S. Representative (1935 until death).

REED, CLYDE MARTIN *(b Oct. 19, 1871, Champaign County, Ill.; d Nov. 8, 1949, Parsons, Kans.)* U.S. Railway Mail Service employee who rose from mail handler to superintendent (1889-1917), Parsons newspaper publisher, and a Kansas Republican. Secretary to Governor Henry J. Allen (1919), member of the state industrial court (1920), state Public Utilities Commission chairman (1921-1924), governor (1929-1931), U.S. Senate (1939 until death).

REED, DANIEL ALDEN *(b Sept. 15, 1875, Sheridan, N.Y.; d Feb. 19, 1959, Washington, D.C.)* Lawyer, banker, lecturer, New York Republican who served twenty-one consecutive terms as a U.S. Representative (1919 until death). State excise department attorney (1903-1909), special U.S. emissary to France (1917, 1918), Interparliamentary Union delegate four times starting in 1948.

REED, JAMES ALEXANDER *(b Nov. 9, 1861, Richland County, Ohio; d Sept. 8, 1944, Oscoda County, Mich.)* Lawyer, Missouri Democrat. Kansas City counselor (1897, 1898), Jackson County prosecutor (1898-1900), mayor of Kansas City (1900-1904), Democratic National Convention delegate (1908, 1912, 1916, 1920, 1924), U.S. Senate (1911-1929).

REED, JOHN, SR. *(b Nov. 11, 1751, Framingham, Mass.; d Feb. 17, 1831, West Bridgewater, Mass.).* Clergyman, Navy chaplain, Massachusetts Federalist. U.S. Representative (1795-1801). Father of the following.

REED, JOHN, JR. *(b Sept. 2, 1781, West Bridgewater, Mass.; d Nov. 25, 1860, West Bridgewater)* Educator, lawyer, Massachusetts Federalist turned Whig. U.S. Representative (1813-1817, 1821-1841), lieutenant governor (1845-1851). Son of the preceding.

REED, JOSEPH *(b Aug. 27, 1741, Trenton, N.J.; d March 5, 1785, Philadelphia,* *Pa.)* Lawyer, land dealer, iron trader, Revolutionary Army officer, New Jersey and Pennsylvania patriot, and a founder of the University of Pennsylvania. In New Jersey: deputy secretary (1767-1770). In Pennsylvania: member of Committee of Correspondence (1774), president of the Pennsylvania convention (1775), delegate to the Continental Congress (1777, 1778), supreme executive council president (1778-1781), University of Pennsylvania trustee (1782-1785).

REED, STUART FELIX *(b Jan. 8, 1866, Barbour County, W.Va.; d July 4, 1935, Washington, D.C.)* Teacher, lawyer, newspaperman, writer, West Virginia Republican. Editor of the *Clarksburg Telegram* (1890-1898), state senate (1895-1899), Clarksburg postmaster (1897-1901), president of the Broaddus College Board of Trustees (1901-1908), International Tax Conference delegate (1909), West Virginia secretary of state (1909-1917), U.S. Representative (1917-1925).

REED, THOMAS BRACKETT *(b Oct. 18, 1839, Portland, Maine; d Dec. 7, 1902, Washington, D.C.)* Lawyer, writer, Maine Republican who was a power in the party and in the nation, the promulgator of the Reed House Rules that among other things gave the majority the ability to govern, a debater with a great gift for sarcasm who once described a statesman as "a successful politician who is dead," McKinley's principal opponent in the 1896 fight for the GOP presidential nomination who was convinced that he lost only because of a doublecross—yet he was an all-out supporter of the McKinley administration for the next two years until expansionist policies and annexation of Hawaii caused him to resign in disgust after serving nearly a quarter-century (1877-1899) as a U.S. Representative and House speaker (1889-1891, 1895-1899). Acting assistant U.S.

Navy paymaster (1864-1865), state representative (1868, 1869), state senate (1870), state attorney general (1870-1872), Portland city solicitor (1874-1877).

REEDER, WILLIAM AUGUSTUS *(b Aug. 28, 1849, Cumberland County, Pa.; d Nov. 7, 1929, Beverly Hills, Calif.).* Teacher, farmer, banker, real estate operator, Kansas Republican. Beloit public schools principal (1871-1879), U.S. Representative (1899-1911).

REID, CHARLES CHESTER *(b June 15, 1868, Clarksville, Ark.; d May 20, 1922, Little Rock, Ark.)* Lawyer, Arkansas Democrat. Conway County prosecutor (1894-1898), U.S. Representative (1901-1911).

REID, DAVID SETTLE *(b April 19, 1813, Rockingham County, N.C.; d June 19, 1891, Reidsville, N.C.)* Lawyer, North Carolina Democrat. State senate (1835-1842), U.S. Representative (1843-1847), governor (1851-1854), U.S. Senate (1854-1859), peace-between-states convention delegate (1861), state constitutional convention delegate (1875).

REID, FRANK R. *(b April 18, 1879, Aurora, Ill.; d Jan. 25, 1945, Aurora).* Lawyer, Illinois Republican. Kane County prosecutor (1904-1908), state's attorney (1904-1908), assistant U.S. attorney (1908-1910), state representative (1911-1912), Kane County GOP central committee chairman (1914-1916), League of Illinois Municipalities secretary (1916, 1917), U.S. Representative (1923-1935).

REILLY, MICHAEL KIERAN *(b July 15, 1869, Empire, Wis.; d Oct. 14, 1944, Neptune, N.J.)* Lawyer, Wisconsin Democrat. Fond du Lac County district attorney (1899, 1900), Fond du Lac city attorney (1905-1910), Democratic National Convention delegate (1908,

1924), U.S. Representative (1913-1917, 1930-1939).

RENCHER, ABRAHAM *(b Aug. 12, 1798, Wake County, N.C.; d July 6, 1883, Chapel Hill, N.C.)* Lawyer, capitalist, agriculturist, North Carolina Democrat whom President Buchanan appointed territorial governor of New Mexico (1857-1861). U.S. Representative (1829-1839, 1841-1843), minister to Portugal (1843-1847), presidential elector on the Pierce-King ticket (1852).

REVELS, HIRAM RHODES *(b Sept. 27, 1827, Fayetteville, N.C.; d Jan. 16, 1901, Aberdeen, Miss.)* The first Negro to serve in the U.S. Senate (1870-1871), Revels was born of free parents, learned the barber's trade, went to Quaker schools in Indiana and Ohio and Knox College in Illinois, became a clergyman and lecturer among his people in Ohio, Indiana, Illinois, Kansas, Missouri, Kentucky, and Tennessee; a teacher and an educator; the Civil War recruiter of two black regiments in Maryland, a third in Missouri (where he also established a freedman's school), and chaplain of a fourth in Mississippi. He finally settled in Mississippi to organize Negro churches and reluctantly entered politics as a Republican but not a Reconstructionist, so much so in fact that he later joined the Democrats in driving the Carpetbaggers out, explaining his reasons in an open letter to President Grant that was published in the *Jackson Daily Times* (1875). Natchez alderman (1866), state senate (1870), acting Mississippi secretary of state (1873), Alcorn Agricultural College president (1871-1874, 1876-1882).

REYBURN, JOHN EDGAR *(b Feb. 7, 1845, New Carlisle, Ohio; d Jan. 4, 1914, Washington, D.C.).* Lawyer, manufacturer, Pennsylvania Republican. State representative (1871, 1874-1876), state senator (1876-1892) and senate president pro tem (1883), U.S. Representative (1890-1897, 1906-1907), presidential elector on the Roosevelt-Fairbanks ticket (1904), mayor of Philadelphia (1907-1911). Father of William S. Reyburn.

REYBURN, WILLIAM STUART *(b Dec. 17, 1882, Philadelphia, Pa.; d July 25, 1946, New Haven, Conn.)* Washington, D.C., lawyer, Pennsylvania Republican. State representative (1909-1911), U.S. Representative to fill a vacancy (1911-1913). Son of John E. Reyburn.

RHEA, JOHN *(b 1753, County Londonderry, Ireland; d May 27, 1832, Sullivan County, Tenn.)* North Carolina patriot who fought at King's Mountain, lawyer, planter who was in on the birth of Tennessee as a state where he became an active Democrat. In North Carolina: Sullivan County Court clerk (1785-1790), member of the house of commons, delegate to the state convention that ratified the federal Constitution (1789). In Tennessee: Constitutional Convention delegate (1796), Greene County attorney general (1796), state representative (1796, 1797), U.S. Representative (1803-1815, 1817-1823), U.S. commissioner to negotiate a treaty with the Choctaw Indian Nation (1816).

RHEA, JOHN STOCKDALE *(b March 9, 1855, Russellville, Ky.; d July 29, 1924, Russellville).* Lawyer, Kentucky Democrat-Populist. Logan County prosecutor (1882), presidential elector on the Cleveland-Hendricks (1884) and Cleveland-Thurman (1888) tickets, Democratic National Convention delegate (1892, 1896), U.S. Representative (1897, 1902, 1903-1905), circuit court judge (1913-1922).

RHETT, ROBERT BARNWELL, changed from Smith *(b Dec. 24, 1800, Beaufort, S.C.; d Sept. 14, 1876, St. James Parish, La.)* Lawyer, publisher of the *Charleston Mercury*, South Carolina Democrat, states' rights extremist, and ardent champion of secession who carried his dream of a separate and free South to the grave. Appointed to the U.S. Senate (Dec. 18, 1850) upon the death of John C. Calhoun, whose lead he closely followed, Rhett resigned (May 7, 1852) in protest against the outcome of a state convention that went only so far as to affirm South Carolina's right to secede, thereafter devoting his political energies to the formation of a Southern Confederacy.

A delegate to the state secession convention (1860), he went in a similar role to the Confederate Provisional Congress (1861) and came away a bitter man when he failed to win not only the Southern presidency but even a seat in the Confederate cabinet. He then opposed Jefferson Davis as vigorously as he had the Union and ultimately moved to Louisiana. In South Carolina: state representative (1826-1832), state attorney general (1832-1835), U.S. Representative (1837-1849), Nashville convention delegate (1850). In Louisiana: Democratic National Convention delegate (1868).

RHODES, GEORGE MILTON *(b Feb. 24, 1898, Reading, Pa.)* Printer, labor leader, Pennsylvania Democrat. Member of Reading Housing Authority (1938-1948), local rationing board and war manpower committee (1942-1946), Democratic National Convention delegate (1952, 1956), U.S. Representative (1949-1969) and a member of the Ways and Means Committee.

RICE, ALEXANDER HAMILTON *(b Aug. 30, 1818, Newton Lower Falls, Mass.; d July 22, 1895, Boston, Mass.)* Paper manufacturer, Massachusetts Republican. Mayor of Boston (1856, 1857), U.S. Representative (1859-1867), Philadelphia Loyalist Convention delegate (1866), GOP National Convention delegate (1868), governor (1876-1879).

RICE, EDMUND *(b Feb. 14, 1819, Waitsfield, Vt.; d July 11, 1889, White Bear Lake, Minn.)* Michigan lawyer who joined his brother, Henry M. Rice, in Minnesota (1849) and helped him to forge the territory into a state; railroad tycoon; Democrat. In Michigan: chancery court register (1841) and master in chancery (1845). In Minnesota: third circuit supreme court clerk (1849), territorial representative (1851), Ramsey County commissioner (1856), state senate (1864-1866, 1874-1876), state representative (1867, 1872, 1877, 1878), mayor of St. Paul (1881-1883, 1885-1887), U.S. Representative (1887-1889).

RICE, HENRY MOWER *(b Nov. 29, 1817, Waitsfield, Vt.; d Jan. 15, 1894, San Antonio, Tex.)* Minnesota pioneer, Indian trader, and friend of the Indian who negotiated treaties with the Winnebago and Chippewa tribes (1847), with the Sioux (1851), and with still others many years later as a U.S. commissioner (1887, 1888); Minnesota Democrat. Delegate to the U.S. Congress (1853-1857), U.S. Senate (1858-1863), University of Minnesota regent (1851-1859), unsuccessful gubernatorial candidate (1865), Ramsey County treasurer (1878-1884). Brother of Edmund Rice.

RICE, WILLIAM WHITNEY *(b March 7, 1826, Deerfield, Mass.; d March 1, 1896, Worcester, Mass.)* Teacher, lawyer, Massachusetts Republican. Worcester County insolvency judge (1858), mayor of Worcester (1860), middle district attorney (1869-1874), state representative (1875), U.S. Representative (1877-1887).

RICH, CHARLES *(b Sept. 13, 1771, Warwick, Mass.; d Oct. 15, 1824, Shoreham, Vt.)* Lawyer, Vermont Democrat. State representative (1800-1811), Addison County judge for six years, U.S. Representative (1813-1815, 1817 until death).

RICHARDS, CHARLES LENMORE *(b Oct. 3, 1877, Austin, Nev.; d Dec. 22, 1953, Reno, Nev.)* Lawyer, Nevada Democrat who served as chairman of the party's state committee (1922). Nye County district attorney (1903, 1904), state representative (1919), Nevada councillor to the U.S. Chamber of Commerce (1923-1924), U.S. Representative (1923-1925).

RICHARDSON, HARRY ALDEN *(b Jan. 1, 1853, Camden, Del.; d June 16, 1928, Dover, Del.)* Food products manufacturer, banker, utilities executive, Delaware Republican. State senate (1888), unsuccessful gubernatorial candidate (1890), GOP National Convention delegate (1908, 1912), U.S. Senate (1907-1913).

RICHARDSON, JAMES DANIEL *(b March 10, 1843, Rutherford County, Tenn.; d July 24, 1914, Murfreesboro, Tenn.)* Confederate soldier, lawyer, writer, Tennessee Democrat who gave up politics to devote his time, talents, and energies to Masonry. State representative and house speaker (1871), state senate (1873, 1874), Democratic National Convention delegate (1876, 1896, 1900) and permanent chairman (1900), Democratic Congressional Committe chairman (1900), U.S. Representative (1855-1905), editor-compiler of the ten-volume government publication *A Compilation of the Messages and Papers of the Presidents* (1896-1899), and the two-volume *A Compilation of the Messages and Papers of the Confederacy* (1905).

RICHARDSON, WILLIAM *(b May 8, 1839, Athens, Ala.; d March 31, 1914, Atlantic City, N.J.)* Confederate soldier who was badly wounded at Chickamauga, lawyer, Alabama Democrat. State representative (1865-1867), Madison County probate and county courts judge (1875-1886), presidential elector on the Cleveland-Thurman ticket (1888),

Democratic National Convention delegate (1904), U.S. Representative (1900 until death).

RICHARDSON, WILLIAM ALEXANDER *(b Jan. 16, 1811, Fayette County, Ky.; d Dec. 27, 1875, Quincy, Ill.)* Teacher, lawyer, newspaperman, Illinois Democrat who twice succeeded Stephen A. Douglas. State's attorney (1834, 1835), state representative (1836-1838, 1844-1846) and house speaker (1844), state senate (1838-1842), presidential elector on the Polk-Dallas ticket (1844), U.S. Representative, initially to fill the vacancy caused by Douglas' resignation and then elected in his own right (1847-1856, 1861-1863), Democratic National Convention delegate (1860, 1868), U.S. Senate to fill the vacancy caused by Douglas' death (1863-1865).

RICHARDSON, WILLIAM MERCHANT *(b Jan. 4, 1774, Pelham, N.H.; d March 15, 1838, Chester, N.H.)* Lawyer, jurist, New Hampshire Federalist who for twenty-two years was chief justice of the state superior court (1816 until death). U.S. Representative (1811-1814), U.S. attorney (1814-1816).

RICHMOND, DEAN *(b March 31, 1804, Barnard, Vt.; d Aug. 27, 1866, New York City)* Salt manufacturer, grain forwarder, ship operator, railroad tycoon whose corporations merged into the New York Central; New York Barnburner–Free-Soiler–Democrat and finally a National Unionist who hoped to bring Democrats and conservative Republicans together—this after serving as chairman of the state Democratic committee for sixteen years (1850-1866). He never sought elective office, feeling that his poor education and profane speech would work against him, but was very much a man to be reckoned with in a smoke-filled room, whether the topic under discussion was the next governor or the next president.

RICKETTS, EDWIN DARLINGTON *(b Aug. 3, 1867, Perry County, Ohio; d July 3, 1937, Logan, Ohio)* Teacher, lawyer, Ohio Republican. U.S. Representative (1915-1917, 1919-1923), GOP National Convention delegate (1928).

RIDDLE, ALBERT GALLATIN *(b May 28, 1816, Monson, Mass.; d May 16, 1902, Washington, D.C.)* Carpenter, lawyer, orator who was a man to be reckoned with on the debating platform and a fiercely antislavery Ohio Whig who issued the call (1848) for a mass meeting that culminated in formation of the state's Free-Soil party with him as the leader until the Republican party came into being and provided him with a more-lasting political base. Geauga County prosecutor (1840-1846), state representative (1848-1850), U.S. Representative (1861-1863), U.S. consul at Matanzas, Cuba (1863, 1864), District of Columbia law officer (1877-1889).

RIDDLE, GEORGE READ *(b 1817, New Castle, Del.; d March 29, 1867, Washington, D.C.)* Civil engineer whose specialties were canals and railroads and who, as a bit of a departure, accepted a commission (1849) to retrace Mason's and Dixon's line, Delaware Democrat. State deputy attorney general (1849, 1850), U.S. Representative (1851-1855), U.S. Senate (1864 until death).

RIDGELY, HENRY MOORE *(b Aug. 6, 1779, Dover, Del.; d Aug. 6, 1847, Dover)* Lawyer, Delaware Federalist. Delaware secretary of state (1817-1827), U.S. Representative (1811-1815), U.S. Senate (1827-1829) to fill a vacancy.

RIEHLMAN, ROY WALTER *(b Aug. 26, 1899, Otisco, N.Y.)* Merchant, baker, New York Republican. Nedrow postmaster (1921-1923), Tully Board of Education (1933-1938), Onondaga County supervisor (1938-1943), county clerk

(1943-1946), U.S. Representative (1947-1965) serving on the Government Operations and Science and Astronautics committees.

RILEY, JOHN JACOB *(b Feb. 1, 1895, Orangeburg, S.C.; d Jan. 1, 1962, Myrtle Beach, S.C.)* Teacher, real estate operator, South Carolina Democrat. State convention delegate (1928-1944), U.S. Representative (1945-1949, 1951-1962) and a member of the Appropriations Committee.

RINGGOLD, SAMUEL *(b Jan. 15, 1770, Chestertown, Md.; d Oct. 18, 1829, Frederick, Md.)* Farmer, land speculator, Maryland Democrat. Member of state house of delegates (1795), state senate (1801-1806), Washington County levy court judge (1806-1810, 1822-1826), U.S. Representative (1810-1815, 1817-1821).

RIORDAN, DANIEL JOSEPH *(b July 7, 1870, New York City; d April 28, 1923, Washington, D.C.)* Real estate operator, New York Democrat. U.S. Representative (1899-1901, 1906 until death), state senate (1902-1906).

RITCHIE, ALBERT CABELL *(b Aug. 29, 1876, Richmond, Va.; d Feb. 24, 1936, Baltimore, Md.)* Lawyer, Maryland Democrat whose battles for the consumer against the price-fixing policies of utility companies gave him a ride up the political escalator that culminated with fifteen consecutive years as governor (1920-1935). In that position he broadened his fight for reforms to include all bureaucratic entrenched interests and brought about many lasting reforms in many areas while lowering taxes. His main national interest was the repeal of Prohibition. Assistant city solicitor of Baltimore (1903-1908), assistant people's counsel for the state Public Service Commission (1910-1914), state attorney general (1915-1919).

RIVERA, LUIS MUÑOZ *(b July 17, 1859, Barranquitas, P.R.; d Nov. 15, 1916, San Juan, P.R.)* Poet, newspaper publisher whose publications included New York's *Puerto Rico Herald*; a lifelong fighter for home rule and free trade who was the prime mover in the founding of the island's Liberal (1897), Federal (1900), and Unionist (1902) parties. Special home-rule representative to Spain (1896), Puerto Rico secretary of state and cabinet president (1897-1899) and organizer of the insular police force, member of the Puerto Rico House of Delegates (1906-1910), resident commissioner to the United States (1911 until death).

RIVERS, LUCIUS MENDEL *(b Sept. 28, 1905, Gumville, S.C.; d Dec. 28, 1970, Birmingham, Ala., seventeen days after undergoing open-heart surgery)* Lawyer, South Carolina Democrat, a U.S. Representative thirty years (1941 until death); hard-working, hard-drinking chairman of the House Armed Services Committee, and a believer in a mighty America who was a strong defender and champion of the military establishment, its armament, its top brass, its lowest enlisted man. A man who, however, remembering his home constituency, ringed Charleston, S.C., with more job-providing military installations than the South and most of the North (if not all) had ever known. State representative (1933-1936), Democratic National Convention delegate (1936).

RIVES, WILLIAM CABELL *(b May 4, 1792, Nelson County, Va.; d April 25, 1868, Albemarle County, Va.)* Lawyer, planter, Virginia Democrat-Whig who, when the chips were down, chose the Confederacy. State constitutional convention delegate (1816), member of the state house of delegates (1817-1820, 1822, 1823), U.S. Representative (1823-1829), U.S. minister to France (1829-1832, 1849-1853), U.S. Senate (1832-1834, 1836-1845), delegate to peace-between-the-states convention (1861), Confederate Provisional Congress delegate (1861) and member of the Second Confederate Congress.

RIXEY, JOHN FRANKLIN *(b Aug. 1, 1854, Culpeper County, Va.; d Feb. 8, 1907, Washington, D.C.)* Lawyer, Virginia Democrat. Culpeper County commonwealth attorney (1879-1891), U.S. Representative (1897 until death).

ROACH, WILLIAM NATHANIEL *(b Sept. 25, 1840, Washington, D.C.; d Sept. 7, 1902, New York City)* Dakota Territory mail contractor, farmer, North Dakota Democrat. As a territory: mayor of Larimore (1883-1887), territorial representative (1885). As a state: unsuccessful gubernatorial candidate in the first state election (1889) and again in 1891, U.S. Senate (1893-1899).

ROANE, JOHN *(b Feb. 9, 1766, King William County, Va.; d Nov. 15, 1838, King William County)* Planter, Virginia Democrat. Presidential elector on the Washington ticket (1789), member of state house of delegates (1788-1790, 1792), state constitutional convention delegate (1788), U.S. Representative (1809-1815, 1827-1831, 1835-1837). Father of John J. Roane.

ROANE, JOHN JONES *(b Oct. 31, 1794, Essex County, Va.; d Dec. 18, 1869, Washington, D.C.)*. Farmer, Virginia Democrat. House of delegates (1820-1823), U.S. Representative (1831-1833), U.S. Patent Office clerk (1836-1851), special Treasury Department agent (1855-1867). Son of John Roane.

ROBB, EDWARD *(b March 19, 1857, Brazeau, Mo.; d March 13, 1934, Perryville, Mo.)* Lawyer, Missouri Democrat. Perry County prosecutor (1880-1884), state representative (1884-1886), state assistant attorney general (1889-1893), U.S. Representative (1897-1905), Democratic National Convention delegate (1908).

ROBBINS, ASHER *(b Oct. 26, 1757, Wethersfield, Conn.; d Feb. 25, 1845, Newport, R.I.)* Teacher, lawyer, Rhode Island Whig. U.S. attorney (1812), state assemblyman (1818-1825, 1840, 1841), U.S. Senate (1825-1839), Newport postmaster (1841 until death).

ROBERTS, EDWIN EWING *(b Dec. 12, 1870, Pleasant Grove, Calif.; d Dec. 11, 1933, Reno, Nev.)* Teacher, lawyer, newspaper publisher, Nevada Republican. Ormsby County district attorney (1900-1910), U.S. Representative (1911-1919), GOP National Convention delegate (1912, 1924), mayor of Reno (1923 until death).

ROBERTS, ELLIS HENRY *(b Sept. 30, 1827, Utica, N.Y.; d Jan. 8, 1918, Utica)*. Educator, editor-publisher of the *Utica Morning Herald*, banker, New York Republican who was a sound-money man and U.S. treasurer (1897-1905). GOP National Convention delegate (1864, 1868, 1876), state assemblyman (1866), U.S. Representative (1871-1875), assistant treasurer of the United States (1889-1893).

ROBERTS, ERNEST WILLIAM *(b Nov. 22, 1858, East Madison, Maine; d Feb. 27, 1924, Washington, D.C.)* Lawyer, Massachusetts Republican. Chelsea councilman (1887, 1888), state representative (1894, 1896), state senate (1897, 1898), U.S. Representative (1899-1917).

ROBERTS, JONATHAN *(b Aug. 16, 1771, near Norristown, Pa.; d July 24, 1854, King of Prussia, Pa.)* Farmer, Pennsylvania Democrat turned Whig because of disagreement with Andrew Jackson and his policies. State representative (1799, 1800), state senate (1811, 1812), U.S. Representative (1811-1814) resigning to become U.S. Senator (1814-1821), Philadelphia customs collector (1841).

ROBERTS, KENNETH ALLISON *(b Nov. 1, 1912, Piedmont, Ala.)* Lawyer, Alabama Democrat. State senate (1942), U.S. Navy (1942-1945), Piedmont city attorney and member of state board of veterans affairs (1948-1950), U.S. Representative (1951-1963) serving on the Interstate and Foreign Commerce Committee.

ROBERTS, WILLIAM RANDALL (b Feb. 6, 1830, County Cork, Ireland; d Aug. 9, 1897, New York City) Dry goods clerk who became a millionaire Bowery merchant, president of the Fenian Brotherhood (1865-1867) who organized raids across the border into Canada (1866) and with that as a base became a power in New York's Tammany Hall until 1881 when he was one of several who broke away to form the New York County Democracy. U.S. Representative (1871-1875), city alderman (1877), minister to Chile (1885-1889), the latter in return for supporting Grover Cleveland.

ROBERTSON, ALICE MARY (b Jan. 2, 1854, Tullahassee Mission, Indian Territory, now Tullahasee, Okla.; d July 1, 1931, Muskogee, Okla.) Educator, social worker, historian, Washington correspondent for the Muskogee News, and a humanitarian who devoted most of her life's work to bettering the lot of the Creek Indians among whom she was born of missionary parents. A somewhat reluctant politician, she agreed to run for office on the Republican ticket and so served one term as a U.S. Representative (1921-1923). She also served as clerk in the U.S. Indian office in Washington (1873-1879), founder of the Nuyaka Mission School and Henry Kendall College, which now is the University of Tulsa; government supervisor of Creek Indian schools (1900-1905), Muskogee postmistress (1905-1913).

ROBERTSON, A. WILLIS (b May 27, 1887, Martinsburg, W.Va.) Lawyer, Virginia Democrat. State senate (1916-1922), Rockbridge County Common-

wealth's attorney (1922-1928), chairman of state Game and Inland Fisheries Commission (1926-1932), U.S. Representative (1933-1946), U.S. Senate (1946-1967) serving as chairman of the Banking and Currency Committee and the Joint Committee on Defense Production and as a member of the Senate Appropriations Committee.

ROBERTSON, CHARLES RAYMOND (b Sept. 5, 1889, near Madison, Wis.; d Feb. 18, 1951, Bismarck, N.Dak.) Merchant, paint manufacturer, North Dakota Republican who was a member of the party's state executive committee. GOP National Convention delegate (1940), U.S. Representative (1941-1943, 1945-1949), member of the Hoover Commission and state chairman for the Hoover Report (1949 until death).

ROBERTSON, EDWARD WHITE (b June 13, 1823, Davidson County, Tenn.; d Aug. 2, 1887, Baton Rouge, La.) Lawyer, Confederate Army officer, Louisiana Democrat. State Representative (1847-1849, 1853), state auditor of public accounts (1857-1862), U.S. Representative (1877-1883, 1887 until death later in the same year when he was succeeded by his son, Samuel M. Robertson).

ROBERTSON, JOHN (b April 13, 1787, Dinwiddie County, Va.; d July 5, 1873, near Lynchburg, Va.) Lawyer, writer, orator with a reputation as a "stinging" debater and a man who would never suppress a thought nor an opinion; a stickler for the Constitution. Virginia Democrat turned Whig. State house of delegates (1816-1819), state attorney general (1823-1834), U.S. Representative (1834-1839), twenty-first judicial circuit judge (1841-1861) and Richmond and Henrico counties chancery court judge (1851-1861), delegate to the Washington peace convention that vainly sought to stave off the Civil War (1861). Chief among his four published works was a metrical romance, *Virginia, or the Fatal Patent* (1825). Brother of Thomas B. and Wyndham Robertson.

ROBERTSON, SAMUEL MATTHEWS *(b Jan. 1, 1852, Plaquemine, La.; d Dec. 24, 1911, Baton Rouge, La.)* Lawyer, college professor, Louisiana Democrat who succeeded his father (Edward W. Robertson) as U.S. Representative to thus begin a twenty-year stay in that office (1887-1907). Superintendent of the Louisiana School for the Deaf and Dumb (1908-1911).

ROBERTSON, THOMAS BOLLING *(b Feb. 27, 1779, Dinwiddie County, Va.; d Oct. 5, 1828, White Sulphur Springs, Va.)* Virginia lawyer whom Thomas Jefferson appointed secretary of the Louisiana Territory (1807-1811) thus launching him on a political career as a Democrat in that state. After statehood: U.S. Representative (1812-1818), governor (1820-1822), state attorney general (1822), U.S. district judge (1825-1827). Brother of John and Wyndham Robertson.

ROBERTSON, WYNDHAM *(b Jan. 26, 1803, near Richmond, Va.; d Feb. 11, 1888, Abingdon, Va.)* Lawyer, writer, planter, Virginia Whig, and an ardent antisecessionist who, however, warned the North that Virginia would stand with the other Southern states. State executive council (1830-1836), governor (1836-1837), state house of delegates (1838-1841, 1859-1865). His most important literary endeavor was *Pocahontas, alias Matooka, and her Descendants through her Marriage with John Rolfe* (1887). Brother of John and Thomas B. Robertson.

ROBESON, GEORGE MAXWELL *(b March 16, 1829, Oxford Furnace, N.J.; d Sept. 27, 1897, Trenton, N.J.)* Lawyer, Union Army officer, New Jersey Republican whose years as secretary of the navy in the Grant cabinet (1869-1877)

were punctuated by a congressional investigation of charges that he was overly extravagant with government funds—but nothing came of the investigation. Camden County prosecutor by appointment although he did not live there (1858), state attorney general (1867-1869), U.S. Representative (1879-1883).

ROBINSON, GEORGE DEXTER *(b Jan. 20, 1834, Lexington, Mass.; d Feb. 22, 1896, Chicopee, Mass.)* Teacher, lawyer, Massachusetts Republican. State representative (1874), state senate (1876), U.S. Representative (1877-1884), governor (1884-1887).

ROBINSON, JAMES CARROLL *(b Aug. 19, 1823, Edgar County, Ill.; d Nov. 3, 1886, Springfield, Ill.)* Farmer, lawyer, Illinois Democrat. U.S. Representative (1859-1865, 1871-1875), state livestock commissioner (1886).

ROBINSON, JAMES McCLELLAN *(b May 31, 1861, Allen County, Ind.; d Jan. 16, 1942, Los Angeles, Calif.)* Lawyer, Indiana Democrat. Thirty-eighth judicial circuit prosecutor (1886-1890), U.S. Representative (1897-1905).

ROBINSON, JAMES WILLIAM *(b Jan. 19, 1878, Coalville, Utah)* Lawyer, educator, Utah Democrat who was Utah County food administrator during World War I. County attorney (1918-1921), University of Utah regent (1925-1935), U.S. Representative (1933-1947), U.S. director of grazing (1947-1949).

ROBINSON, JONATHAN *(b Aug. 11, 1756, Hardwick, Mass.; d Nov. 3, 1819, Bennington, Vt.)* Lawyer, Vermont jurist. Bennington town clerk (1795-1801), state representative (1789-1802, 1818), state probate court judge (1795-1798, 1815-1819), chief justice of the state supreme court (1801-1807), U.S. Senate first to fill a vacancy and then reelected in his own right (1807-1815). Brother of Moses Robinson.

ROBINSON, JOSEPH TAYLOR *(b Aug. 26, 1872, Lonoke, Ark.; d July 14, 1937, Washington, D.C.)* Lawyer, Arkansas Democrat who served as governor for two months in 1913 and then resigned to take a seat in the U.S. Senate where he remained for nearly a quarter-century (1913 until death). State assemblyman (1895), presidential elector on the Bryan-Stevenson ticket (1900), U.S. Representative (1903-1913).

ROBINSON, MOSES *(b March 20, 1741, Hardwick, Mass.; d May 26, 1813, Bennington, Vt.)* Lawyer, Revolutionary Army officer who was chief justice of Vermont (1778-1781, 1782-1784, 1785-1789) and a member of the Governor's Council (1778-1785), governor (1789, 1790), U.S. Senate (1791-1796), state representative (1802). Brother of Jonathan Robinson.

ROBINSON, THOMAS JOHN BRIGHT *(b Aug. 12, 1868, New Diggings, Wis.; d Jan. 27, 1958, Hampton, Iowa)* Farmer, banker, real estate and investment broker, Iowa Republican. State senate (1912-1916), U.S. Representative (1923-1933).

ROBSION, JOHN MARSHALL, SR. *(b Jan. 2, 1873, Bracken County, Ky.; d Feb. 17, 1948, Barbourville, Ky.).* Teacher, lawyer, banker, Kentucky Republican. GOP National Convention delegate (1916), U.S. Representative (1919-1930, 1935 until death), U.S. Senate to complete a vacated term (11 months in 1930). Father of the following.

ROBSION, JOHN MARSHALL, JR. *(b Aug. 28, 1904, Barboursville, Ky.)* Congressional secretary (1919-1928) while studying for the bar, lawyer, Kentucky Republican. Chief of U.S. Pension Bureau's law division (1929-1935), state GOP general counsel (1938-1942), U.S. Army (1942-1946), part of that time on the staff of General Mark Clark, state special circuit judge (1946-1952), U.S. Representative (1953-1959), unsuccessful gubernatorial candidate (1959). Son of the preceding.

ROCKWELL, FRANCIS WILLIAMS *(b May 26, 1844, Pittsfield, Mass.; d June 26, 1929, Pittsfield)* Lawyer, banker, Massachusetts Republican. Special justice of the central Berkshire district court (1873-1875), state representative (1879), state senate (1881, 1882), U.S. Representative (1884-1891), GOP National Convention delegate (1900), member of the Greylock Reservation Commission (1898-1926). Son of Julius Rockwell.

ROCKWELL, JULIUS *(b April 26, 1805, Colebrook, Conn.; d May 19, 1888, Berkshire County, Mass.)* Lawyer, Massachusetts Whig-Republican. State representative (1834-1838, 1858) serving four of those years as house speaker, state bank commissioner (1838-1840), U.S. Representative (1843-1851), state constitutional convention delegate (1853), U.S. Senate to fill a vacancy (1854-1855), presidential elector on the Fremont-Dayton ticket (1856), state superior court judge (1859-1886). Father of Francis W. Rockwell.

ROCKWELL, ROBERT FAY *(b Feb. 11, 1886, Cortland, N.Y.; d Sept. 29, 1950, Maher, Colo.)* Cattle rancher, fruit grower, Colorado Republican. State representative (1916-1920), state senate (1920-1924, 1938-1941), lieutenant governor (1922-1924), unsuccessful candidate for governor (1930), state agriculture commissioner (1932-1946), U.S. Representative (1941-1949).

RODENBERG, WILLIAM AUGUST *(b Oct. 30, 1865, Randolph County, Ill.; d Sept. 10, 1937, Alpena, Mich.)* Teacher, lawyer, business investor, Illinois Republican. GOP national convention delegate (1896, 1908, 1916, 1920), U.S.

Representative (1899-1901, 1903-1913, 1915-1923), U.S. Civil Service commissioner (1901-1902).

RODEY, BERNARD SHANDON *(b March 1, 1856, County Mayo, Ireland; d March 10, 1927, Albuquerque, N.Mex.).* Office worker, lawyer, New Mexico Territory Republican whose political career took him far afield. Albuquerque city attorney (1887, 1888), territorial senator and author of the bill creating the University of New Mexico (1889), constitutional convention delegate (1890), delegate to the U.S. Congress (1901-1905), GOP National Convention delegate (1908), U.S. district judge in Puerto Rico (1906-1910), U.S. attorney in Alaska (1910-1913), special assistant U.S. attorney for Washington's western district to aid in the prosecution of Alaskan coal frauds (1912-1913).

RODNEY, CAESAR *(b Oct. 7, 1728, Dover, Del.; d June 29, 1784, Dover).* Farmer, signer of the Declaration of Independence, Revolutionary Army general, president of Delaware (1778-1782), and one of many Delaware Rodneys who made their political contribution to the history of the colony and the state. The number of lower court judgeships that he held are too numerous to mention, but these are the other positions he held and offices he filled that are worthy of note: high sheriff of Kent County (1755-1758), captain of the county militia (1756), superintendent of the printing of Delaware currency (1759), assemblyman (1762-1769), loan office superintendent (1769), associate justice of the Delaware Supreme Court (1769-1777), member of the Continental Congress (1774-1776, 1777, 1778, 1782, 1783). Brother of Thomas, cousin of George B., and uncle of Caesar A. Rodney.

RODNEY, CAESAR AUGUSTUS *(b Jan. 4, 1772, Dover, Del.; d June 10, 1824, Buenos Aires, while serving as U.S. minister to Argentina, a position that he had held from Jan. 27, 1823).* Lawyer, diplomat, Delaware Democrat who was U.S. attorney general in the cabinets of both Presidents Jefferson and Madison (1807-1811). U.S. Representative (1803-1805, 1821-1822), member of the Delaware Committee of Safety (1813), state senate (1815), commissioner to investigate the propriety of U.S. recognition of the new South American republics (1817-1818), U.S. Senate (1822-1823) resigning to take the Argentine appointment. Son of Thomas and nephew of Caesar Rodney.

RODNEY, DANIEL *(b Sept. 10, 1764, Lewes, Del.; d Sept. 2, 1846, Lewes).* Merchant, Delaware Federalist whose relationship to the other Rodneys is unknown. Common pleas court associate judge (1793-1806), presidential elector on the Pinckney-King ticket (1808), governor (1814-1817), U.S. Representative to complete Caesar A. Rodney's unexpired term (1822-1823) and U.S. Senate (1826-1827) to fill another vacancy, but the total extent of his tenure in Washington was only seven months.

RODNEY, GEORGE BRYDGES *(b April 2, 1803, Lewes, Del.; d June 18, 1883, New Castle, Del.)* Lawyer, Delaware Whig. Register in chancery and clerk of the Sussex County Orphans' Court (1826-1830), U.S. Representative (1841-1845), delegate to the peace-between-states convention (1861). Cousin of Caesar and Thomas Rodney.

RODNEY, THOMAS *(b June 4, 1744, Kent County, Del.; d Jan. 2, 1811, Natchez, Miss., while serving as U.S. judge for the Mississippi Territory from 1803)* Revolutionary officer, farmer who was a Delaware delegate to the Continental Congress (1781-1783, 1785-1787), justice of the peace (1770, 1778), member of the assembly to elect delegates (1774), Council of

Safety (1775), Kent County chief justice (1778) and register of wills (1779), state assemblyman and house speaker (1787), county almshouse superintendent (1802), associate justice of the state supreme court (1802-1803) resigning to accept the Mississippi appointment. Brother of Caesar, father of Caesar A., cousin of George B. Rodney.

ROGERS, DWIGHT LAING (b Aug. 17, 1886, Tattnall County, Ga.; d Dec. 1, 1954, Fort Lauderdale, Fla.) Lawyer, Florida Democrat. State representative (1930-1938) and house speaker pro tem (1933), U.S. Representative (1945 until death).

ROGERS, EDITH NOURSE (b March 19, 1881, Saco, Maine; d Sept. 10, 1960, Boston, Mass.). Widow of John J. Rogers who succeeded him as a U.S. Representative, intending to remain in office only for one term, but was still there at death thirty-five years later. An Independent Republican from Massachusetts, her chief interest was in the welfare of servicemen and veterans, an interest that she first showed in World War I when she served overseas as a hospital aide. During World War II, she visited hospitals overseas, introduced the bill that created the Women's Army Corps, and had much to do with the drafting of the GI Bill of Rights. She served Presidents Harding, Coolidge, and Hoover as their personal dollar-a-year inspector of veterans' hospitals. She was a presidential elector on the Coolidge-Dawes ticket (1924), and, as a congresswoman, was among the first in Washington to protest Hitler's persecution of the Jews.

ROGERS, JOHN JACOB (b Aug. 18, 1881, Lowell, Mass.; d March 28, 1925, Washington, D.C.) Textile heir, lawyer, Massachusetts Republican. U.S. Representative (1913 until death). Husband of Edith Nourse Rogers.

ROGERS, WALTER EDWARD (b July 19, 1908, Texarkana, Ark.) Lawyer, Texas Democrat. Pampa city attorney (1938-1940), thirty-first judicial district attorney (1943-1947), U.S. Representative (1951-1967) serving on the Interior and Insular Affairs and Interstate and Foreign Commerce committees.

ROLLINS, EDWARD HENRY (b Oct. 3, 1824, Somersworth, N.H.; d July 31, 1889, Isle of Shoals, N.H.) Merchant, banker, railroad tycoon and a New Hampshire Whig turned Know-Nothing who had much to do with the founding of the Republican party there which he then proceeded to rule with something of an iron fist for many years while fighting against reform and for the harshest kind of Reconstruction for the South. State representative (1855-1857) and house speaker (1856, 1857), chairman of the state delegation to the GOP National Convention (1860), U.S. Representative (1861-1867), U.S. Senate (1877-1883).

ROMERO, TRINIDAD (b June 15, 1835, Sante Fe, N.Mex., which then was still part of Mexico; d Aug. 28, 1918, Las Vegas, N.Mex.) Merchant, freight hauler via ox teams from Kansas City to Santa Fe, rancher, New Mexico Territory Republican. Territorial representative (1863), San Miguel County probate judge (1869, 1870), delegate to the U.S. Congress (1877-1879).

ROOSEVELT, ANNA ELEANOR (b Oct. 11, 1884, New York City; d Nov. 7, 1962, New York City) Teacher, lecturer, newspaper columnist, author who donated all of her earnings to charity; niece of Theodore Roosevelt (who gave the bride away), distant cousin and wife of Franklin Delano Roosevelt; First Lady who very much blossomed forth as a quasi-political figure in her own right, showing great statesmanship, diplomacy, compassion, and stature as a champion of the poor and the downtrodden.

Director of women's activities in Alfred E. Smith's presidential bid (1928), assistant director of the office of Civil Defense under Fiorello La Guardia (1941-1942), Truman-appointed U.S. delegate to the United Nations (1945-1952), and chairman of the U.N. Economic and Social Council's Human Rights Commission.

Critics of Mrs. Roosevelt often called her leftist, pro-Communist, and worse, but those stances were best answered by Communist newspapers that characterized her as "a garrulous, feeble, old woman, consumed with an anti-Soviet fever" and Gallup polls that year after year showed her to be the world's most-admired woman. Said Claire Booth Luce of her: "No woman has ever so comforted the distressed or so distressed the comfortable."

ROOSEVELT, FRANKLIN DELANO *(b Jan. 30, 1882, Hyde Park, N.Y.; d April 12, 1945, of a cerebral hemorrhage at Warm Springs, Ga., shortly after his fourth inauguration)* Thirty-second president (New York Democrat), elected to an unprecedented four terms (1933-1945), whose administration started during the darkest days of the Great Depression and continued almost to the end of World War II; governor of New York; assistant secretary of the navy; lawyer; one of the most controversial presidents; a colorful, strong-willed man, both in public office and private life, who refused to let an attack of poliomyelitis (1921) that crippled both legs put an end to his political career.

Son of wealthy parents, a descendent of New York aristocracy and fifth cousin of Theodore Roosevelt, Franklin Roosevelt received his early education from private tutors, then attended preparatory school at Groton. Graduated from Harvard in 1904, he studied at Columbia University Law School and (1907) was admitted to the bar. Married distant cousin (she was Theodore

Roosevelt's niece) Anna Eleanor Roosevelt (1905) with whom he had six children (one died in infancy) and who was not only a valuable helpmeet but also became a prominent personality in her own right (which see).

Member New York State Legislature (1911-1912) where (as well as at the 1912 Democratic convention that nominated Woodrow Wilson for president) he opposed Tammany leaders; assistant secretary of the navy in Wilson's cabinet (1913-1920) where he gained invaluable experience and associations that, along with the Roosevelt name, led to his nomination (1920) as Democratic candidate James M. Cox's running mate in his unsuccessful bid for the presidency; made a dramatic return from his crippling bout with polio by placing Alfred E. Smith's name in nomination for president (1924) at the Democratic National Convention (and again in 1928); as governor of New York (1929-1932) he experimented with methods that later were used in New Deal legislation and provided the first direct unemployment aid to be given by any state; elected president in 1932 with 472 electoral votes to Herbert C. Hoover's 59, in 1936 with 523 to Alfred M. Landon's 8, in 1940 with 449 to Wendell L. Willkie's 82, and in 1944 with 432 to Thomas E. Dewey's 99.

As president, Roosevelt reassured the nation that "the only thing we have to fear is fear itself," and he used his radio fireside chats to develop a strong rapport with people from coast to coast; he declared a bank holiday that lasted until banks could be inspected and those that were sound reopened; he called Congress into special session to start work on the tremendous amount of legislation that was needed to get his New Deal moving; legislation designed primarily to alleviate the suffering of those most acutely affected by the depression. He, with his advisers (some of whom were called the Brain Trust) broke with precedent and created bold new programs, such as the Agricultural Adjustment Act (AAA), the National Industrial Recovery Act (NIRA), the Tennessee Valley Authority (TVA), the Emergency Relief Administration (ERA), the Works Progress Administration (WPA), the United States Housing Authority, and the Fair Labor Standards Act.

When the Supreme Court declared some of the New Deal measures unconstitutional, Roosevelt retaliated by trying, unsuccessfully, to pack the Court. Roosevelt was faced in the late thirties with a recession (at one time over 10 million were unemployed) that lingered until the outbreak of World War II brought the production activity of U.S. rearmament and greatly increased purchases of supplies by nations fighting the Axis.

In the field of foreign relations, Roosevelt, following the precedent established by President Hoover in his dealings with Latin America, proclaimed the Good Neighbor Policy and relations with nations south of the U.S. border continued to improve. After France's surrender to Germany (1940), Roosevelt, seeking to defend America by aiding the Allies, promoted the Lend-Lease Act and, in a shipboard meeting (1941) joined Winston Churchill in adopting the Atlantic Charter. On Dec. 7, 1941, Japan attacked the U.S. fleet at Pearl Harbor, Hawaii, and, when Germany and Italy declared war on the United States four days later, the U.S. was plunged into World War II. Roosevelt met with Churchill, Stalin, and other Allied leaders in Casablanca, French Morocco; Quebec, Canada; Teheran, Iran; and Yalta in the Crimea to determine war (and peace) policies.

Roosevelt died shortly before Germany's surrender. His efforts toward the creation of a world organization of which the United States would be a member bore fruit when (also after his death) the Senate ratified U.S. entrance into the United Nations.

ROOSEVELT, THEODORE (b Oct. 27, 1858, New York City; d Jan. 6, 1919, Oyster Bay, N.Y.). Vice president (1901 until assassination of President McKinley); twenty-sixth president (New York Republican), 1901-1909, and one of the most colorful with a dramatic appeal that still is felt; though never a radical, he was sympathetic to the movements attempting to bring about needed social change and honest government and fought against the corruption of politics by big business; won the Nobel Peace Prize, yet furthered U.S. standing as a world power and carried out his slogan: "Speak softly and carry a big stick"; New York governor; conservationist, hunter, explorer, and prolific writer (two of his books were Naval History of the War of 1812 and Winning of the West).

One of four children born to Theodore and Martha Bulloch Roosevelt, Theodore (fondly known to Americans as Teddy) was descended from Klaes Martensen van Roosevelt and related to both Franklin D. and Eleanor Roosevelt. Because of poor health as a child (he later built up his body through exercise that became an important aspect of his practice and philosophy of life) he was taught by private tutors; graduated from Harvard (1880) where he was a member of Phi Beta Kappa. Married Alice Hathaway Lee (1880) who bore him one daughter (Alice Lee who became Mrs. Nicholas Longworth), then, in 1884, she and Teddy's mother died within a few hours of each other. Grief-stricken, Roosevelt retired for a time to his ranch in the Dakota Territory where he gained knowledge of the ways of the West. Married (1886) Edith Kermit Carow with whom he had five children, one of whom, Theodore Roosevelt, Jr., became assistant secretary of the navy, governor of Puerto Rico, and governor-general of the Philippines.

A moderate reform member of New York State Legislature (1882-1884); unsuccessful candidate (1886) for mayor of New York City; appointed a member of U.S. Civil Service Commission (1889-1895) by President Benjamin Harrison; championed public decency as a New York City police commissioner (1895-1897); supported William McKinley in the presidential campaign of 1896 and (1897) was appointed assistant secretary of the navy, resigning when war was declared with Spain and, with Leonard Wood, organized the famous Rough Rider regiment, becoming its colonel and a national hero.

Governor of New York (1899-1900) where his reform policies, though moderate, worried the GOP political leadership so that, to get him out of the state, he was made McKinley's running mate and (1900) elected vice president, becoming president (1901) when McKinley was assassinated and elected in his own right (1904), defeating Democratic candidate Alton B. Parker by 196 electoral votes.

During his presidency, a treaty was signed with Panama and construction begun on the Panama Canal; the Sherman Anti-Trust Act was enforced; Roosevelt persuaded operators and miners to arbitrate the coal strike of 1902; the U.S. Department of Commerce and Labor was established; important legislation was passed including the Reclamation Act (1902), Elkins Act (1903), Pure Food and Drug and Federal Meat Inspection Acts (1906), and Hepburn Act (1906).

After retirement from the presidency, Roosevelt organized the Progressive (or "Bull Moose") party and (1912) ran unsuccessfully as its presidential candidate against incumbent William Howard Taft (whose nomination Roosevelt had engineered in 1908) and Woodrow Wilson. He was shot by a fanatic during the campaign but recovered. When World War I broke out he strongly advocated preparedness, speaking out against U.S. isolation. When the United States entered the war, his request to raise and command a division of volunteers was turned down and he devoted his energies to supporting the war effort at home.

ROOT, ELIHU (b Feb. 15, 1845, Clinton, N.Y.; d Feb. 7, 1937, New York City). Teacher, lawyer, statesman, author, New York Republican who served many presidents, and dedicated his life to public service; recipient of many high awards, including the Nobel Peace Prize (1912); holder of many high offices, including president of the Carnegie Endowment for International Peace (1910-1925), and vital assignments, including advisor on the Covenant of the League of Nations and counsel of the League to the advisory commission of international jurists that convened at The Hague (1920) to plan for a permanent court of international justice. His last undertaking before retirement was as a delegate to Geneva (1929) to revise the statutes of the Permanent Court of International Justice.

U.S. attorney for the southern district of New York and personal counsel to President Arthur (1883-1885), state constitutional convention chairman (1894, 1915), secretary of war in the McKinley cabinet (1899-1904), member of the Alaskan Boundary Tribunal (1903), secretary of state in the Roosevelt cabinet (1905-1909), U.S. Senate (1909-1915), GOP National Convention chairman (1904, 1912), GOP state convention chairman (1908, 1910, 1913, 1914, 1916, 1920, 1922), U.S. counsel in the North Atlantic Fisheries arbitration (1910), member of the Permanent Court of Arbitration at The Hague (1910), Wilson-appointed ambassador to head a special mission to Russia (1917), U.S. Commissioner Plenipotentiary to the Conference on Limitations of Armament (1921, 1922), president of the New York college of presidential electors (1925).

ROOT, ERASTUS *(b March 16, 1773, Hebron, Conn.; d Dec. 24, 1846, New York City)* Teacher, lawyer, New York Democrat who turned Whig after refusing to support Andrew Jackson's presidential candidacy (1832). State assemblyman (1798-1802, 1818-1822, 1826-1828, 1830) and assembly speaker (1827, 1828), U.S. Representative (1803-1805, 1809-1811, 1815-1817, 1831-1833), member of commission to revise state laws (1811), state senate (1812-1815, 1840-1844), state constitutional convention delegate (1821), lieutenant governor (1822-1824), Whig state convention delegate (1846).

ROOT, JESSE *(b Dec. 28, 1736, Coventry, Conn.; d March 29, 1822, Coventry).* Clergyman, lawyer, Revolutionary Army officer, Connecticut jurist who was a superior court judge (1789-1796) and chief justice (1796-1807). Delegate to the Continental Congress (1778-1783), state's attorney (1785-1789), state representative (1807-1809), presidential elector (1808), state constitutional convention delegate (1818).

ROSS, EDMUND GIBSON *(b Dec. 7, 1826, Ashland, Ohio; d May 8, 1907, Albuquerque, N.Mex.)* Newspaperman who published several Kansas papers, Union Army officer, railroad promoter who gave the Atchison, Topeka and Santa Fe Railroad its name, lawyer, Kansas Republican turned Democrat who also served as Cleveland-appointed governor of the New Mexico Territory (1885-1889). In Kansas: state constitutional convention delegate (1859-1861), U.S. Senate (1866-1871), Democratic National Convention delegate (1876). In New Mexico: immigration secretary of the Bureau of Immigration (1894-1896).

ROSS, GEORGE *(b May 10, 1730, New Castle, Del.; d July 14, 1779, near Philadelphia, Pa.)* Pennsylvania lawyer torn by his loyalties and thus first a Tory, then a Whig, and when the chips were down very much the patriot and signer of the Declaration of Independence. Colonial assemblyman (1768, 1776), state convention delegate (1774), member of the Continental Congress (1774-1777), admiralty court judge (April 1779 until death).

ROSS, NELLIE TAYLOE *(b 1880, St. Joseph, Mo.)* On the death of her husband, Democratic Governor William B. Ross of Wyoming (1924) she, also a Democrat, was elected to fill his unexpired term (1925-1927), making her the first woman elected to that position in the United States. Appointed director of the U.S. Mint (1933-1953), another first for a woman.

ROSS, THOMAS RANDOLPH *(b Oct. 26, 1788, New Garden Township, Pa.; d June 28, 1869, near Lebanon, Ohio).* Lawyer, farmer, Ohio Democrat. U.S. Representative (1819-1825).

ROUSE, ARTHUR BLYTHE *(b June 20, 1874, Burlington, Ky.; d Jan. 25, 1956, Lexington, Ky.)* Lawyer, bus line operator, Kentucky Democrat. First state racing commission secretary (1907-1911), state Democratic executive committee member (1903-1910), U.S. Representative (1911-1927), chairman of Democratic National Congressional Committee (1921-1924), U.S. court clerk (1935-1953).

RUBEY, THOMAS LEWIS *(b Sept. 27, 1862, Lebanon, Mo.; d Nov. 2, 1928, Lebanon)* Teacher, banker, Missouri Democrat. Lebanon schools superintendent (1886-1891), state representative (1891, 1892), state senate (1901-1903) and senate president (1903), lieutenant governor (1903-1905), U.S. Representative (1911-1921, 1923 until death).

RUCKER, ATTERSON WALDEN (b April 3, 1847, Harrodsburg, Ky.; d July 19, 1924, Jefferson County, Colo.). Confederate soldier, Missouri lawyer who transferred his practice to Colorado where he became interested in mining and agriculture with a fling at Democratic politics. U.S. Representative (1909-1913).

RUCKER, WILLIAM WALLER (b Feb. 1, 1855, Alleghany County, Va.; d May 30, 1936, Keytesville, Mo.) Teacher, lawyer, farmer, Missouri Democrat who was a U.S. Representative for virtually a quarter-century (1899-1923). Charlton County prosecutor (1886, 1892), twelfth circuit judge (1892-1899).

RUFFIN, EDMUND (b Jan. 5, 1794, Prince George County, Va.; d June 18, 1865, Amelia County, Va., by his own hand when he saw that the Southern cause was lost) Agricultural researcher-experimenter whose contributions served farmers everywhere, planter, writer, publisher, Virginia Whig turned Democrat whose firm beliefs in slavery and secession were so deeply rooted and so coherently and widely expressed that he was chosen to fire the first shot at Fort Sumter—the shot that began the Civil War. Among his published broadsides were four pamphlets setting forth his views on slavery, and Anticipations of the Future, a book published in 1860 that enunciated his views on the need for secession and, in the words of one biographer, "the glories of an independent South."

RUFFIN, THOMAS (b Sept. 9, 1820, Louisburg, N.C.; d Oct. 13, 1863, in a prison camp at Alexandria, Va., from wounds received in action at Bristoe Station) Lawyer, Confederate Army officer, North Carolina Democrat. Seventh Missouri judicial circuit judge (1844-1848), U.S. Representative (1853-1861), Confederate Provisional Congress delegate (1861).

RUGGLES, BENJAMIN (b Feb. 21, 1783, Abington, Conn.; d Sept. 2, 1857, St. Clairsville, Ohio) Lawyer, farmer, Ohio Democrat turned Whig. Third judicial circuit common pleas court president judge (1810-1815), U.S. Senate (1815-1833), presidential elector on the Harrison-Granger ticket (1836).

RUGGLES, JOHN (b Oct. 8, 1789, Westboro, Mass.; d June 20, 1874, Thomaston, Maine) Lawyer, orator, writer, Maine Democrat, but most of all an inventor who wrote the measure that resulted (1836) in the reorganization of the U.S. Patent Office. State representative (1823-1831) and house speaker (1825-1829, 1831), supreme judicial circuit justice (1831-1834), U.S. Senate (1835-1841).

RUPPERT, JACOB, JR. (b Aug. 5, 1867, New York City; d Jan. 13, 1939, New York City) Brewer, president of the New York Yankees baseball club (1914 until death), New York Democrat. U.S. Representative (1899-1907), president of the U.S. Brewers Association (1911-1914).

RUSH, BENJAMIN (b Dec. 24, 1745, near Philadelphia, Pa.; d April 19, 1813, Philadelphia). Physician, pioneer in chemistry, educator, author on medical, social, and political topics, Pennsylvania signer of the Declaration of Independence, reformer who believed firmly in the abolition of slavery, Revolutionary Army physician-general who resigned because of differences with George Washington. Delegate to the Continental Congress (1776, 1777), delegate to the state convention that adopted the federal Constitution (1787), treasurer of the U.S. Mint at Philadelphia (1799 until death).

RUSK, HARRY WELLES (b Oct. 17, 1852, Baltimore, Md.; d Jan. 28, 1926, Baltimore) Lawyer, Maryland Democrat who was Baltimore's party leader

(1898-1908). Member of state house of delegates (1876, 1878, 1880), state senate (1882-1884), Democratic National Convention delegate (1884), U.S. Representative (1886-1897).

RUSK, JEREMIAH McLAIN *(b June 17, 1830, Malta, Ohio; d Nov. 21, 1893, Viroqua, Wis.)* Farmer, Union Army officer, Wisconsin Republican who was U.S. secretary of agriculture in the Harrison cabinet (1889-1893). Viroqua sheriff (1855-1857) and coroner (1857), state assemblyman (1862), state bank comptroller (1866-1869), U.S. Representative (1871-1877), governor (1882-1889).

RUSK, THOMAS JEFFERSON *(b Dec. 5, 1803, Pendleton District, S.C.; d July 29, 1857, Nacogdoches, Tex.).* Teacher, lawyer, Indian fighter, signer of the Texas declaration of independence (1836), secretary of war for the new republic who took command when Sam Houston was wounded in the Battle of San Jacinto, firm advocate of statehood, and a Democrat. Member of the second Texas congress, chief justice of the Texas Supreme Court (1838-1842), president of the convention that confirmed annexation to the United States (1845), U.S. Senate (1846 until death).

RUSSELL, BENJAMIN EDWARD *(b Oct. 5, 1845, Monticello, Fla.; d Dec. 4, 1909, Bainbridge, Ga.)* Confederate drummer boy who rose to lieutenant and was captured at Sailors Creek, editor-publisher of the *Bainbridge Democrat*, Georgia Democrat. State constitutional convention delegate (1877), Democratic National Convention delegate (1880), mayor of Bainbridge (1881, 1882), state representative (1882, 1883), Bainbridge postmaster (1885-1890), U.S. Representative (1893-1897).

RUSSELL, CHARLES ADDISON *(b March 2, 1852, Worcester, Mass.; d Oct. 23, 1902, Killingly, Conn.)* Worcester newspaper editor, woolen manufacturer, Connecticut Republican. State representative (1883), Connecticut secretary of state (1885, 1886), U.S. Representative (1887 until death).

RUSSELL, GORDON JAMES *(b Dec. 22, 1859, Huntsville, Ala.; d Sept. 14, 1919, Kerrville, Tex.).* Teacher, lawyer, Texas Democrat. Van Zandt County judge (1890-1892), seventh judicial district attorney (1892-1896) and judge (1896-1904), U.S. Representative (1902-1910), U.S. judge (1910 until death).

RUSSELL, JOSEPH JAMES *(b Aug. 23, 1854, Mississippi County, Mo.; d Oct. 22, 1922, Charleston, Mo.)* Lawyer, Missouri Democrat. Mississippi County school commissioner (1878, 1879), county prosecutor (1880-1884), Democratic National Convention delegate (1884), presidential elector on the Cleveland-Hendricks ticket (1884), state representative (1886-1890) and house speaker pro tem (1886, 1888), U.S. Representative (1907-1909, 1911-1919).

RUSSELL, RICHARD BREVARD *(b Nov. 2, 1897, Winder, Ga.; d Jan. 21, 1971, Washington, D.C.)* Lawyer, debater of note, Georgia Democrat who in thirty-eight years (1933 until death) became one of the most powerful and most sagacious U.S. Senators the nation had ever known. Harry Truman and Mike Mansfield, the Senate majority leader at the time of his death, said he would have been president if he came from another part of the country. However, he did try and at the 1952 Democratic National Convention received 294 votes for the nomination but the choice went to Adlai E. Stevenson of Illinois. Apologized a leading Democrat: "At this time of racial crisis, we just can't put a Southerner on top of the ticket." An ironical note to this: When offered the post of Senate majority leader (1953), Russell turned it down and tapped Lyndon Johnson for the job and thus put Johnson on the road to the presidency.

As example of Russell's ability to smell out national and international crises, he warned President Eisenhower (1954) against involvement in Vietnam. Later he called the war "one of the great tragedies of our history," although he supported it once the United States was in it.

Russell began his political career early in life, becoming a state representative (1921-1931) at the age of twenty-three and governor (1931-1933) at the age of thirty-three. His most influential assignments in Washington were chairman of the Senate Armed Services Committee and the Military Expenditures Subcommittee of the Senate Appropriations Committee.

RUSSELL, WILLIAM *(b 1782, Ireland; d Sept. 28, 1845, Scioto County, Ohio).* Farmer, Ohio Jackson Democrat turned Whig. State representative (1809, 1810, 1811-1813), U.S. Representative (1827-1833, 1841-1843).

RUTHERFURD, JOHN *(b Sept. 20, 1760, New York City; d Feb. 23, 1840, Edgerston, N.J.).* Lawyer, farmer, surveyor who laid out New York City north of Fourteenth Street (1807-1811) and was commissioned to determine the New York-New Jersey-Pennsylvania boundary lines (1826-1833), New Jersey Federalist. Presidential elector (1788), state assemblyman (1788, 1789), U.S. Senate (1791-1798), president of East Jersey Board of Proprietors (1804-1840), Anti-Masonic National Convention delegate (1831).

RUTLEDGE, EDWARD *(b Nov. 23, 1749, Christ Church Parish, S.C.; d Jan. 23, 1800, Charleston, S.C.)* South Carolina lawyer who at first opposed independence but then had a change of heart, signed the Declaration of Independence, served in the Revolution as an officer, and was captured at Charleston. Though politically a conservative Federalist, he cast his presidential elector vote for Thomas Jefferson (1796). Member of the Continental Congress (1774-1777), delegate to the First and Second Provincial Congresses (1775, 1776), member of the first Board of War (1776), member of the general assembly (1778), state representative (1782, 1786, 1788, 1792), state constitutional convention delegate (1790), refused Washington appointment to the U.S. Supreme Court (1794), governor (1798 until death). Brother of John Rutledge, Sr.

RUTLEDGE, JOHN, SR. *(b 1739, Christ Church Parish, S.C.; d July 23, 1800, Charleston, S.C.)* Lawyer with a brilliant judicial mind, a man who believed that rule belonged in the hands of the wealthy, yet very much the patriot who was the youngest delegate to the Stamp Act Congress (1765) and chairman of a committee that drafted a petition to the House of Lords; president and commander in chief of South Carolina (1776-1778); presided over the U.S. Supreme Court, but only for the August 1795 term because the Senate refused to confirm his nomination as chief justice because of his vehement attacks upon the Jay Treaty. Member of the provincial assembly (1762), attorney general pro tem (1764, 1765), member of the Continental Congress (1774-1776, 1782, 1783), state chancellor (1787), state constitutional convention delegate (1787), and delegate to the state convention that ratified the federal Constitution (1788), recipient of South Carolina's electoral vote for vice president (1789), associate justice of the U.S. Supreme Court (1789-1791), chief justice of South Carolina (1790-1795). Father of the following. Brother of Edward Rutledge.

RUTLEDGE, JOHN, JR. *(b 1766, Charleston, S.C.; d Sept. 1, 1819, Philadelphia, Pa.)* Lawyer, planter, South Carolina Federalist. State representative (1788-1794, 1811), U.S. Representative (1797-1803). Son of the preceding.

RYAN, ELMER JAMES *(b May 26, 1907, Rosemount, Minn.; d Feb. 1, 1958, in an auto accident near Somerset, Wis.)* Lawyer, Minnesota Democrat. South St. Paul city attorney (1933-1934), Democratic National Convention delegate (1936, 1940), U.S. Representative (1935-1941).

RYAN, THOMAS *(b Nov. 25, 1837, Oxford, N.Y.; d April 5, 1914, Muskogee, Okla.)* Lawyer, Union soldier, Kansas Republican. Shawnee County prosecutor (1865-1873), assistant U.S. attorney (1873-1877), U.S. Representative (1877-1889), minister to Mexico (1889-1893), first assistant secretary of the interior (1897-1907), resident representative of the secretary of the interior in Oklahoma (1907 until death).

RYAN, WILLIAM HENRY *(b May 10, 1860, Hopkinton, Mass.; d Nov. 18, 1939, Buffalo, N.Y.)* Merchant, insurance and bonding business, banker, New York Democrat. Erie County supervisor (1894-1899) and board chairman (1898), U.S. Representative (1899-1909), Democratic National Convention delegate (1904, 1924), member of the Allegany State Park Commission (1930-1939).

S

☆ ☆ ☆

SABATH, ADOLPH JOACHIM *(b April 4, 1866, Zabori, Austria-Hungary; d Nov. 6, 1952, in U.S. Naval Hospital, Bethesda, Md.)* Lawyer, Illinois Democrat who was a U.S. Representative forty-five years (1907 until death) a delegate to all Democratic National Conventions (1896-1944) and all state conventions (1890-1952). Chicago ward committeeman and district leader (1892-1944), justice of the peace (1895), police magistrate (1897-1906), member of the Democratic central and executive committees (1909-1920).

SABIN, ALVAH *(b Oct. 23, 1793, Georgia, Vt.; d Jan. 22, 1885, Sycamore, Ill.)* Clergyman, abolitionist who was a delegate to the first Anti-Slavery National Convention. Vermont Whig who for forty years was pastor of the Georgia Baptist Church while also being highly active politically. State representative (1826-1835, 1838-1840, 1847-1849, 1851, 1861, 1862), state senate (1841, 1843, 1845), Vermont secretary of state (1841), U.S. Representative (1853-1857), Franklin County commissioner (1861-1862).

SABIN, DWIGHT MAY *(b April 25, 1843, LaSalle County, Ill.; d Dec. 22, 1902, Chicago, Ill.)* Union soldier, farmer, and businessman specializing in coal, lumber, and the manufacture of farm machinery and railroad cars, Minnesota Republican who was chairman of the GOP National Committee (1883, 1884). State senate (1872-1875), state representative (1878, 1881), GOP National Committeeman and National Convention delegate (1872, 1876, 1880, 1884), U.S. Senate (1883-1889).

SACKETT, FREDERIC MOSLEY *(b Dec. 17, 1868, Providence, R.I.; d May 18, 1941, Baltimore, Md.)* Coal mine operator, cement manufacturer, utilities tycoon and a Kentucky Republican who was ambassador to Germany (1930-1933) during the upsurge of Hitler. President of the Louisville Board of Trade (1917, 1922, 1923), director of the Louisville branch of the Federal Reserve Bank (1917-1924), member of the state Board of Charities and Corrections (1919-1924), U.S. Senate (1925-1930).

SADOWSKI, GEORGE GREGORY *(b March 12, 1903, Detroit, Mich.; d Oct. 9, 1961, Utica, Mich.)* Lawyer, real estate operator, builder, golf club owner, Michigan Democrat. State senate (1931, 1932), Democratic state central committee member (1930-1936), Democratic National Convention delegate (1932, 1936, 1940, 1944, 1948), U.S. Representative (1933-1939, 1943-1951).

ST. GEORGE, KATHARINE PRICE COL-
LIER *(b——, Bridgenorth, England).*
Member of Daughters of the American
Revolution, New York Republican with
a long and active interest in politics.
Member of Tuxedo Park Town Board
(1926-1949), Orange County GOP Committee (1942-1948 when she served
variously as treasurer, vice chairman,
and chairman), GOP National Convention delegate (1944), Tuxedo Park
Board of Education (1926-1946) and its
president (1930-1946), U.S. Representative (1947-1965) serving as a member
of the Rules and Post Office and Civil
Service committees.

SALOMON, HAYM *(b 1740, Lissa,
Poland; d Jan. 6, 1785, Philadelphia, Pa.).*
A Polish fighter for independence who
was forced to flee to England (1772),
ultimately made his way to America
and became an equally fervent American patriot and successful New York
commission merchant-broker who used
his fortune to help finance the Revolution. Twice (1776, 1778) jailed by the
British for his outspoken Whig beliefs,
fears that he was a spy, and suspicion
that he plotted to burn the king's fleet
and supply warehouses. While held cap-
tive he devised a new underground plot
to induce Hessian soldiers to desert.
Ultimately he escaped, made his way to
Philadelphia, appeared before Congress
in a plea for a more-active role but
was turned down (some biographers
say because he was a Jew). Undaunted,
he then spent more than $1 million for
the U.S. cause. He died penniless and
it was years later that his sacrifices
became known.

SALTONSTALL, LEVERETT *(b Sept. 1,
1892, Chestnut Hill, Mass.)* Massachusetts Republican, Middlesex County
assistant district attorney (1921-1922),
member Newton Board of Aldermen
(1920-1922), state representative
(1923-1936, speaker 1929-1936), governor (1939-1944). Elected to U.S. Senate

(1944-1967) to complete term of Henry
Cabot Lodge, Jr., who resigned to enter
army and then was reelected three
times.

SANDERS, ARCHIE DOVELL *(b June
17, 1857, Stafford, N.Y.; d July 15, 1941,
Rochester, N.Y.)* Produce merchant,
New York Republican who, at death,
was chairman of the Genesee County
GOP Committee. Stafford highway commissioner (1894), supervisor (1895),
state assemblyman (1895, 1896), GOP
National Convention delegate (1896,
1924), twenty-eighth district internal
revenue collector (1898-1913), GOP
state committeeman (1900, 1901),
state senate (1914, 1915), U.S. Representative (1917-1933).

SANDERS, EVERETT *(b March 8,
1882, Clay County, Ind.; d May 12, 1950,
Washington, D.C.)* Lawyer, Indiana
Republican who was President Coolidge's secretary (1925-1929) and GOP
National Chairman (1932-1934). U.S
Representative (1917-1925), director of
the GOP National Speakers' Bureau
(1924).

SANDERS, JARED YOUNG, SR. *(b Jan.
29, 1869, St. Mary Parish, La.; d March
23, 1944, Baton Rouge, La.)* Lawyer,
Louisiana Democrat who was first
elected to office as an antilottery candidate. State representative (1892-
1904) and house speaker (1900-1904),
state constitutional convention delegate (1898, 1921), lieutenant governor
(1904-1908), governor (1908-1912), U.S.
Representative (1917-1921). Father of
the following.

SANDERS, JARED YOUNG, JR. *(b
April 20, 1892, Franklin, La.; d Nov. 29,
1960, Baton Rouge, La.)* Lawyer,
banker, Louisiana Democrat. State representative (1928-1932), state senate
(1932-1934), U.S. Representative (1934-
1937, 1941-1943), Democratic National
Convention delegate (1940, 1944). Son
of the preceding.

SANDERS, MORGAN GURLEY *(b July 14, 1878, Van Zandt County, Tex.; d Jan. 7, 1956, Corsicana, Tex.)* Teacher, newspaper publisher, lawyer, Texas Democrat. State representative (1902-1906), Van Zandt County prosecutor (1910-1914), seventh judicial district attorney (1915, 1916), U.S. Representative (1921-1939).

SANDERS, NEWELL *(b July 12, 1850, Owen County, Ind.; d Jan. 26, 1939, Lookout Mountain, Tenn.)* Bookstore owner, farm implement manufacturer, railroad director, Republican who was the first member of that party from Tennessee to serve in the U.S. Senate in forty years (April 1912-January 1913) when he was appointed to fill a vacancy. Chattanooga alderman (1882-1886), GOP state executive committee chairman (1894-1912), GOP National Convention chairman (1900, 1908, 1912, 1916, 1920, 1924).

SANDERS, WILBUR FISKE *(b May 2, 1834, Leon, N.Y.; d July 7, 1905, Helena, Mont.)* New York teacher, lawyer, Union Army officer who settled in that part of Idaho that later became Montana, became a mine operator, stock raiser, and Republican leader, serving as one of Montana's first U.S. Senators (1890-1893) when it became a state. As a territory: GOP National Convention delegate (1868, 1872, 1876, 1884), territorial representative (1873-1879).

SANDLIN, JOHN NICHOLAS *(b Feb. 24, 1872, Webster Parish, La.; d Dec. 25, 1957, Minden, La.)* Lawyer, Louisiana Democrat. Second district attorney (1904-1910) and judge (1910-1920), Democratic National Convention delegate (1916), U.S. Representative (1921-1937).

SANFORD, NATHAN *(b Nov. 5, 1777, Bridgehampton, N.Y.; d Oct. 17, 1838, Flushing, N.Y.)* Lawyer, New York Democrat. U.S. bankruptcy commis-

sioner (1802), U.S. attorney (1803-1816), state assemblyman (1810, 1811) and assembly speaker (1811), state senate (1812-1815), U.S. Senate (1815-1821, 1826-1831), chancellor of New York (1823-1826).

SANTANGELO, ALFRED EDWARD *(b June 4, 1912, New York City)* Lawyer, New York Democrat. Assistant district attorney in Manhattan (1945), state senate (1947-1950, 1953-1956), U.S. Representative (1957-1963) serving on the Appropriations Committee.

SARGENT, AARON AUGUSTUS *(b Sept. 28, 1827, Newburyport, Mass.; d Aug. 14, 1887, San Francisco, Calif.).* Lawyer, publisher of the *Nevada City Journal,* California Know-Nothing who helped to organize the Republican party there while displaying keen mastery of the machine politician's trade and ultimately went on to Congress where he was coauthor of the first Pacific railroad bill and unabashed champion of the railroads. Nevada County district attorney (1855, 1856), state senate (1856), GOP National Convention delegate (1860), U.S. Representative (1861-1863, 1869-1873), U.S. Senate (1873-1879), minister to Germany (1882-1884).

SATTERFIELD, DAVE EDWARD, JR. *(b Sept. 11, 1894, Richmond, Va.; d Dec. 27, 1946, Richmond)* Lawyer, Virginia Democrat. Richmond commonwealth attorney (1922-1933), U.S. Representative (1937-1945).

SAULSBURY, ELI *(b Dec. 29, 1817, Mispillion Hundred, Del.; d March 22, 1893, Dover, Del.)* Lawyer, Delaware Democrat who sometimes engaged in political rivalry with his brothers, Gove and Willard Saulsbury, Sr. For example, in 1871 he and Gove, whose term as governor was about to expire, vied for the U.S. Senate seat that Willard was about to vacate. Faced with a tough family decision (this was before senators were elected by popular vote), Willard threw his support to Eli and Gove thus retired from political life. All were Democrats.

Eli: Democratic National Convention delegate (1864), U.S. Senate (1871-1889).

Gove: Democratic National Convention delegate (1856), state senator (1862, 1863, 1864, 1865) and senate speaker (1865), acting governor (1865), governor (1866-1871).

Willard: State attorney general (1850-1855), Democratic National Convention delegate (1856, 1864), U.S. Senate (1859-1871), state chancellor (1874 until death).

SAULSBURY, GORE. See Saulsbury, Eli.

SAULSBURY, WILLARD, JR. *(b April 17, 1861, Georgetown, Del.; d Feb. 20, 1927, Wilmington, Del.)* Lawyer, banker, businessman, Delaware Democrat who, even more than his father, was a power in the party. Democratic county executive committee chairman (1892-1900), state committee member (1892-1919) and chairman (1900-1906), national committeeman (1908-1920), national convention delegate (1896, 1904, 1912, 1916, 1920), U.S. Senate (1913-1919) and Senate president pro tem (1916-1919), member of the advisory committee of the Conference on Limitation of Armaments (1921, 1922), member of the Pan American Conference (1923).

SAULSBURY, WILLARD, SR. See Saulsbury, Eli.

SAUND, DALIP SINGH *(b Sept. 20, 1899, Amritsar, India)* Farmer, businessman, California Democrat who came to the United States in 1920, graduated from college in 1922 as a math major, helped found and was first president of the India Association of America which sought citizenship rights for migrants from East India, became a citizen in 1949, and thus began an active interest in politics. In 1950 he was elected justice court judge in the Westmorland judicial district but was not seated because he had been a citizen less than a year, tried again in 1952, won once more and served until 1957 when he became a U.S. Representative (1957-1963), member of the House Foreign Affairs and Interior and Insular Affairs committees.

SAUNDERS, ALVIN *(b July 12, 1817, Fleming County, Ky.; d Nov. 1, 1899, Omaha, Nebr.)* Itinerant farmhand who picked up an education in his travels, finally settled in Iowa where he became a successful merchant and banker, and ended in Nebraska (sent there by Abraham Lincoln to be governor of the territory, 1861-1867) where he had much to do with the bringing about of statehood and ascendancy of the GOP. In Iowa: Mount Pleasant postmaster (1839-1846), state constitutional convention delegate (1846) and the youngest man present, state senate (1854-1861), GOP state convention delegate (1860) and state delegation chairman to the national convention (1860), and then an active campaigner for Lincoln. In Nebraska: GOP National Convention delegate (1868), U.S. Senate (1877-1883). Grandfather of William Henry Harrison of Wyoming.

SAUNDERS, EDWARD WATTS *(b Oct. 20, 1860, Franklin County, Va.; d Dec. 16, 1921, Franklin County)* Lawyer, Virginia Democrat. Member of the state house of delegates (1887-1901) and speaker (1899), circuit court judge (1901-1906), U.S. Representative (1906-1920), state supreme court of appeals judge (1920 until death).

SAUNDERS, ROMULUS MITCHELL *(b March 3, 1791, near Milton, N.C.; d April 21, 1867, Raleigh, N.C.)* Lawyer, North Carolina Democrat who came within one vote of being elected governor (1840), losing to the Whig candidate, William A. Graham (which see). Member of the state house of commons (1815, 1817, 1819, 1850-1852), University of North Carolina trustee (1819-1864), U.S. Representative (1821-1827, 1841-1845), state attorney general (1828-1831), superior court judge (1835-1840, 1852-1856), minister to Spain (1846-1849).

SAWYER, LEMUEL *(b 1777, Camden County, N.C.; d Jan. 9, 1852, Washington, D.C.)* Lawyer, author, playwright, North Carolina Democrat. Member of the state house of commons (1800, 1801), presidential elector on the Jefferson-Clinton ticket (1804), U.S. Representative (1807-1813, 1817-1823, 1825-1829).

SAWYER, PHILETUS *(b Sept. 22, 1816, Whiting, Vt.; d March 29, 1900, Oshkosh, Wis.)* Lumber tycoon, banker, railroad investor, and a powerful Wisconsin Republican who helped give the U.S. Senate a reputation as a millionaires' club; La Follette's prime target in his campaign against corruption and boss rule in Wisconsin. One of the most rugged in an era of rugged individualists, he was known as the "grand old man of Oshkosh." State assemblyman (1857, 1861), mayor of Oshkosh (1863, 1864), GOP National Convention delegate (1864, 1876, 1880), U.S. Representative (1865-1875), U.S. Senate (1881-1893).

SAYERS, JOSEPH DRAPER *(b Sept. 23, 1841, Grenada, Miss.; d May 15, 1929, Austin, Tex.)* Confederate Army officer, teacher, lawyer, Texas Democrat. State senate (1873-1879), Democratic state executive committee chairman (1875-1878), lieutenant governor (1879, 1880), U.S. Representative (1885-1899), governor (1899-1903), University of Texas regent (1913), chairman of the state industrial accident board (1914, 1915), state legal examiner (1923-1925), state pardon board member (1927 until death).

SCALES, ALFRED MOORE *(b Nov. 26, 1827, Reidsville, N.C.; d Feb. 9, 1892, Greensboro, N.C.)* Lawyer, banker, Confederate private who rose to brigadier general, North Carolina Democrat. Rockingham County solicitor (1853), member of state house of commons (1852, 1853, 1856, 1857), U.S. Representative (1857-1859, 1875-1884), presidential elector on the Breckinridge-Lane ticket (1860), state representative (1866-1869), governor (1884-1888).

SCHAEFER, EDWIN MARTIN *(b May 14, 1887, Belleville, Ill.; d Nov. 8, 1950, St. Louis, Mo.)* Chemical engineer, plant superintendent, Illinois Democrat. St. Clair County assistant recorder of deeds (1928-1930), county treasurer (1930-1932), Democratic state convention delegate (1928, 1932, 1936), U.S. Representative (1933-1943).

SCHALL, THOMAS DAVID *(b June 4, 1878, Reed City, Mich.; d Dec. 22, 1935, Washington, D.C., after being struck by an automobile)* Lawyer who did not let accidental blindness (1907) stand in the way of his career, entered Minnesota politics as a Republican and served as a U.S. Representative (1915-1925), U.S. Senator (1925 until death).

SCHENCK, PAUL FORNSHELL *(b April 19, 1899, Miamisburg, Ohio).* Teacher, real estate operator, Ohio Republican. Dayton recreation director (1929-1935), board of education (1941-1950, president for seven years), vice chairman of Dayton Safety Council (1946, 1947), executive secretary of Dayton Defense Council (1942-1945), U.S. Representative (1951-1965) serving on the House Administration and Interstate and Foreign Commerce committees and as a member of the Joint Committee on Printing and the Joint Committee on the Library.

SCHENCK, ROBERT CUMMING *(b Oct. 4, 1809, Franklin, Ohio; d March 23, 1890, Washington, D.C.)* Lawyer, teacher, diplomat, Union Army officer, Ohio Whig turned Republican. State representative (1839-1843), U.S. Representative (1843-1851, 1863-1871), minister to Brazil with accreditation to Uruguay, Paraguay, and the Argentine Confederation (1851-1853), Philadelphia Loyalist Convention delegate (1866), minister to Great Britain (1870-1876). He resigned from the army to begin his second tour in Congress where he became chairman of the House Military Affairs Committee, a violently outspoken foe of Copperheads (Northerners who sympathized with the South during the Civil War) and a leader in the opposition to President Johnson.

SCHERER, GORDON HARRY *(b Dec. 26, 1906, Cincinnati, Ohio)* Lawyer, Ohio Republican. Hamilton County assistant prosecuting attorney (1933-1940), Cincinnati safety director (1943, 1944), city planning commission (1945, 1946), city council (1945-1949), U.S. Representative (1953-1963) and a member of the Public Works and House Un-American Activities committees.

SCHNEIDER, GEORGE JOHN *(b Oct. 30, 1877, Grand Chute, Wis.; d March 12, 1939, Toledo, Ohio)* Papermaker, labor leader, Wisconsin Republican-Progressive and a follower of Robert La Follette. Vice president of the International Brotherhood of Paper Makers (1909-1927), state Federation of Labor executive board member (1921-1928), U.S. Representative (1923-1933, 1935-1939).

SCHUETZ, LEONARD WILLIAM *(b Nov. 16, 1887, Posen, Germany; d Feb. 13, 1944, Washington, D.C.)* Stenographer, meat packing and construction company executive, Illinois Democrat. U.S. Representative (1931 until death.)

SCHUREMAN, JAMES *(b Feb. 12, 1756, New Brunswick, N.J.; d Jan. 22, 1824, New Brunswick)* Merchant, Revolutionary soldier, New Jersey civic and political leader who became a Federalist when party lines were drawn; member of the First and other Congresses. Member of the general assembly (1783-1785, 1788), Provincial Congress delegate (1786), member of the Continental Congress (1786, 1787), U.S. Representative (1789-1791, 1797-1799, 1813-1815), president of New Brunswick (1792), U.S. Senate (1799-1801), mayor of New Brunswick (1801-1813, 1821 until death), member of the state council (1808, 1810).

SCHURZ, CARL *(b March 2, 1829, Liblar, Germany; d May 14, 1906, New York City)* A leading student participant in the revolution of 1848, he was forced to flee Germany, ultimately reached the United States and made for himself a lasting place in history as a statesman, political orator, lecturer, lawyer, newspaperman, author, champion of the underdog, political reformer, and a Republican who was a leader first in the Liberal Republican movement and then of the Mugwumps; however, a poor military tactician as evidenced by his leadership of Wisconsin volunteers in battle on the side of the Union in the Civil War. His home states changed as his jobs changed: Pennsylvania, Wisconsin, Michigan, Missouri, New York.

In Wisconsin: Foe of slavery, strong supporter of GOP presidential candidate John C. Fremont (1856) and deliverer of the state to him, chairman of the state delegation to the GOP National Convention (1860) and vigorous campaigner for Lincoln, minister to Spain (1861-1862); conducted an inspection of the South for President Johnson (1865), but his report was not well received because it recommended that voting rights be extended to Negroes; delegate to and keynote speaker of the GOP National Convention (1868).

In Missouri: U.S. Senate (1869-1875) when he split with Grant over government corruption and became a leader in the Liberal Republican movement, permanent president of its Cincinnati convention (1872) and supporter of Horace Greeley for president although he had wanted the nomination for himself despite his foreign birth, supporter of Rutherford B. Hayes (1876), secretary of the interior in the Hayes cabinet (1877-1881).

In New York: a leader of the opposition to James G. Blaine and prime mover in the Mugwump rift (1884), president of the National Civil Service Reform League (1892-1901).

SCHWABE, GEORGE BLAINE *(b July 26, 1886, Arthur, Mo.; d April 2, 1952, Alexandria, Va.)* Lawyer, Oklahoma Republican. Mayor of Nowata (1913, 1914) and member of the board of education there (1918-1922), state representative (1918-1922) and house speaker (1921, 1922), chairman of Tulsa County GOP committee (1928-1936), GOP National Convention delegate (1936), U.S. Representative (1945-1949, 1951 until death).

SCHWARTZ, HENRY HERMAN *(b May 18, 1869, Mercer County, Ohio; d April 24, 1955, Casper, Wyo.)* Newspaperman, lawyer, South Dakota and Wyoming Democrat who was a U.S. Land Office field service executive in Washington State, Montana, and Washington, D.C. (1897-1910). In South Dakota: state representative (1896, 1897), special assistant to the U.S. attorney general (1907). In Wyoming: delegate to all Democratic state conventions (1927-1935), president of the Casper Board of Education and the Natrona County High School Board (1928-1934), state senate (1933-1935), Democratic state committee chairman (1932-1936), Democratic

National Convention delegate (1928, 1932), U.S. Senate (1937-1943), member of the National Mediation Board (1943-1947).

SCHWELLENBACH, LEWIS BAXTER *(b Sept. 20, 1894, Superior, Wis.; d June 10, 1948, Washington, D.C.)* Lawyer, Washington Democrat who was U.S. secretary of labor in the Truman cabinet (1945 until death). State American Legion commander (1922), University of Washington regent (1933, 1934) and president of the board (1933), Democratic state convention chairman (1924) and King County committee chairman (1928-1930), unsuccessful candidate for governor (1932), delegate to the International Parliamentary Union at The Hague (1938), U.S. Senate (1935-1940) resigning to become a U.S. district judge (1940-1945).

SCOFIELD, GLENNI WILLIAM *(b March 11, 1817, Dewittville, N.Y.; d Aug. 30, 1891, Warren, Pa.)* Teacher, lawyer, Pennsylvania Republican. Warren County district attorney (1846-1848), state representative (1849-1851), state senate (1857-1859), eighteenth judicial district president judge (1861-1863), U.S. Representative (1863-1875), U.S. register of the treasury (1878-1881), associate justice of the U.S. Court of Claims (1881-1891).

SCOTT, CHARLES FREDERICK *(b Sept. 7, 1860, Allen County, Kans.; d Sept. 18, 1938, Iola, Kans.)* Newspaperman who became editor of the *Iola Register* (1882), lecturer, Kansas Republican who was the party's national publicity director (1912). University of Kansas regent (1891-1900), state senate (1892-1896), presidential elector on the McKinley-Hobart ticket (1896), U.S. Representative (1901-1911), delegate to the International Institute of Agriculture in Rome (1911), GOP National Convention delegate (1916, 1932).

SCOTT, FRANK DOUGLAS *(b Aug. 25, 1878, Alpena, Mich.; d Feb. 12, 1951, Palm Beach, Fla.)* Lawyer, Michigan Republican. Alpena city attorney (1903, 1904), city prosecutor (1906-1910), state senate (1911-1914) and senate president pro tem (1913, 1914), U.S. Representative (1915-1927).

SCOTT, JOHN *(b May 18, 1785, Hanover County, Va.; d Oct. 1, 1861, Ste. Genevieve, Mo.).* Lawyer who settled in Missouri and became politically active both in the territory and in the state. As a territory: delegate to Congress (1816-1821). As a state: U.S. Representative (1821-1827).

SCOTT, JOHN MORIN *(b 1730, New York City; d Sept. 14, 1784, New York City)* Lawyer, Revolutionary general, a founder of the Sons of Liberty, and unsuccessful candidate in the election (1777) that chose George Clinton as New York's first state governor. City alderman (1756-1761), member of the general committee (1775) and the Provincial Congress (1775-1777), state constitutional convention delegate (1776), state senate (1777-1782), New York secretary of state (1778-1784), member of the Continental Congress (1780-1783).

SCOTT, NATHAN BAY *(b Dec. 18, 1842, Guernsey County, Ohio; d Jan. 2, 1924, Washington, D.C.)* Union soldier, glass manufacturer, banker, West Virginia Republican. Wheeling councilman (1881-1883) and council president, state senate (1883-1890), GOP National Executive Committeeman (1888), internal revenue commissioner (1898-1899), U.S. Senate (1899-1911).

SCOTT, RALPH JAMES *(b Oct. 15, 1905, Surry County, N.C.)* Lawyer, North Carolina Democrat. State representative (1937), twenty-first judicial district solicitor (1938-1956), U.S. Rep-

resentative (1957-1967) serving on the Education and Labor Committee.

SCOTT, WILLIAM KERR *(b April 17, 1896, Haw River, N.C.; d April 16, 1958, Burlington, N.C.)* Dairy farmer, North Carolina Democrat. Alamance County farm agent (1920-1930), state Grange master (1930-1933), Farm Debt Adjustment Program regional director (1934-1936), state agriculture commissioner (1937-1948), U.S. commissioner to Mexico to study hoof and mouth disease (1947), governor (1949-1952), U.S. Senate (1954 until death).

SCRANTON, GEORGE WHITFIELD *(b May 11, 1811, Madison, Conn.; d March 24, 1861, Scranton, Pa.)* Teamster, merchant, farmer, railroad builder, iron manufacturer who experimented in smelting, coal mine operator who founded the city of Scranton; Pennsylvania Republican. U.S. Representative (1859 until death). Second cousin of Joseph A. Scranton.

SCRANTON, JOSEPH AUGUSTINE *(b July 26, 1838, Madison, Conn.; d Oct. 12, 1908, Scranton, Pa.)* Founding editor-publisher of the *Scranton Republican*, Pennsylvania Republican. Internal revenue collector (1862-1866), GOP National Convention delegate (1872), Scranton postmaster (1874-1881), U.S. Representative (1881-1883, 1885-1887, 1889-1891, 1893-1897), Lackawanna County treasurer (1901-1903). Second cousin of George W. Scranton.

SCRUGHAM, JAMES GRAVES *(b Jan. 19, 1880, Lexington, Ky.; d June 23, 1945, San Diego, Calif.)* Engineer, educator, editor-publisher of the *Nevada State Journal* (1927-1932), Nevada Democrat. University of Nevada mechanical engineering professor (1903-1914) and Engineering College dean (1914-1917), state engineer and public service commissioner (1917-1923), governor (1923-1927), special adviser to the secretary of the interior on Colorado River development projects (1927), U.S. Representative (1923-1942) resigning to fill a U.S. Senate vacancy (1942 until death).

SCUDDER, NATHANIEL *(b May 10, 1733, Monmouth Court House, N.J.; d Oct. 17, 1781, Monmouth County, N.J.)*. New Jersey physician, Revolutionary Army officer who was killed in action at Black Point. Member of the Committee of Safety, delegate to the Provincial Congress (1774), member-speaker of the general assembly (1776), member of the Continental Congress (1777-1779), Princeton College trustee (1778-1781).

SCULLY, THOMAS JOSEPH *(b Sept. 19, 1868, South Amboy, N.J.; d Dec. 14, 1921, South Amboy)* Towing and transportation executive, New Jersey Democrat. Presidential elector on the Bryan-Kern ticket (1908), mayor of South Amboy (1909, 1910, 1921), U.S. Representative (1911-1921), Democratic National Convention delegate (1912).

SEARS, WILLIAM JOSEPH *(b Dec. 4, 1874, Smithville, Ga.; d March 30, 1944, Kissimmee, Fla.)* Lawyer, Florida Democrat. Mayor of Kissimmee (1907-1911), Osceola County public instruction superintendent (1905-1915), U.S. Representative (1915-1929, 1933-1937), associate member of the U.S. Board of Veterans' Appeals (1937-1942).

SEARS, WILLIS GRATZ *(b Aug. 16, 1860, Willoughby, Ohio; d June 1, 1949, Omaha, Nebr.)* Lawyer, jurist, Nebraska Republican. Burt County prosecutor (1895-1901), state representative (1901-1904) and house speaker (1901), fourth judicial district judge (1903-1923, 1932-1948), U.S. Representative (1923-1931).

SEAVER, EBENEZER *(b July 5, 1763, Roxbury, Mass.; d March 1, 1844, Roxbury)* Farmer, Massachusetts Democrat. State representative (1794-1802, 1822, 1823, 1826), U.S. Representative (1803-1813).

SEBASTIAN, WILLIAM KING *(b 1812, Centerville, Tenn.; d May 20, 1865, Memphis, Tenn.)* Lawyer, cotton grower, Arkansas Democrat who was expelled from the U.S. Senate when Arkansas seceded from the Union, took no part in Confederate movements during the Civil War but did not live to see his expulsion revoked (1877) and compensation paid to his children. Helena prosecutor (1835-1837), circuit judge (1840-1843), state supreme court associate justice (1843-1845), member-president of the state senate (1846-1847), presidential elector on the Polk-Dallas ticket (1846), U.S. Senate (1848-1861).

SEDDON, JAMES ALEXANDER *(b July 13, 1815, Falmouth, Va.; d Aug. 19, 1880, Goochland County, Va.)* Lawyer, follower of John C. Calhoun, active secessionist, and a Virginia Democrat who was the Confederate States' secretary of war (1862-1865). U.S. Representative (1845-1847, 1849-1851), peace-between-states convention delegate (1861), member of Provisional Confederate Congress (1861).

SEDGWICK, THEODORE *(b May 9, 1746, West Hartford, Conn.; d Jan. 24, 1813, Boston, Mass.)* Military secretary to General John Thomas in the invasion of Canada (1776), lawyer who (1783) argued vigorously against slavery in the defense of a runaway, and a Massachusetts Federalist who later just as vigorously opposed Shays's Rebellion (1786-1787). State representative (1780, 1782, 1783, 1787, 1788) and house speaker (1787, 1788), state senate (1784-1785), delegate to the Continental Congress (1785-1788), delegate to the state convention that adopted the federal Constitution (1788), U.S. Representative (1789-1796, 1799-1801) and House speaker (1799-1801), U.S.

Senate to fill a vacancy (1796-1799) and Senate president pro tem (1798), state supreme court judge (1802 until death).

SEELYE, JULIUS HAWLEY *(b Sept. 14, 1824, Bethel, Conn.; d May 12, 1895, Amherst, Mass.)* Clergyman, lecturer, Massachusetts educator who gave most of his life to Amherst College except for a year (1872) as a lecturer in India and two years (1875-1877) as an Independent U.S. Representative. Professor of philosophy at Amherst (1858-1876) and college president (1876-1890).

SEGER, GEORGE NICHOLAS *(b Jan. 4, 1866, New York City; d Aug. 26, 1940, Washington, D.C.)* Builder, New Jersey Republican. Member of the Passaic Board of Education (1906-1911) and mayor (1911-1919), GOP National Convention delegate (1916), president of the New Jersey League of Municipalities (1917-1918), Passaic director of finance (1919-1923), U.S. Representative (1923 until death).

SELLS, SAM RILEY *(b Aug. 2, 1871, Bristol, Tenn.; d Nov. 2, 1935, Johnson City, Tenn.)* Lawyer, lumberman, brick manufacturer, Tennessee Republican. State senate (1909-1911), U.S. Representative (1911-1921), GOP National Convention delegate (1912, 1916).

SELVIG, CONRAD GEORGE *(b Oct. 11, 1877, Rushford, Minn.; d Aug. 2, 1953, Santa Monica, Calif.)* Teacher, writer, lecturer, Minnesota Republican. Harmony and Glencoe schools superintendent (1901-1910), GOP state convention delegate (1908), U.S. Representative (1927-1933).

SENEY, GEORGE EBBERT *(b May 29, 1832, Uniontown, Pa.; d June 11, 1905, Tiffin, Ohio)* Lawyer, Union Army officer, Ohio Democrat. Presidential elector on the Buchanan-Breckinridge ticket (1856), common pleas judge (1857),

Democratic National Convention delegate (1876), U.S. Representative (1883-1891).

SENEY, JOSHUA *(b March 4, 1756, Queen Annes County, Md.; d Oct. 20, 1798, Queen Annes County)* Maryland farmer, lawyer who started his political career as high sheriff (1779) of his home county. Member of the state house of delegates (1785-1787) and the Continental Congress (1787, 1788), U.S. Representative in the First and Second Congresses (1789-1792) resigning to become chief justice of Maryland's third judicial district (1792-1796), presidential elector supporting Washington and Adams (1792).

SERGEANT, JOHN *(b Dec. 5, 1779, Philadelphia, Pa.; d Nov. 23, 1852, Philadelphia)* Lawyer, Pennsylvania Federalist-National Republican-Whig and an intellectual who many times refused high position, among them: associate justice of the U.S. Supreme Court, ambassador to Great Britain, and a seat on the Harrison cabinet. Philadelphia deputy attorney general (1800), state bankruptcy commissioner (1801), state representative (1808-1810), U.S. Representative (1815-1823, 1827-1829, 1837-1841), state canal commission (1825), envoy to the Panama Congress (1826), unsuccessful National Republican candidate for vice president (1832), state constitutional convention president (1838). Son of Jonathan D. Sergeant.

SERGEANT, JONATHAN DICKINSON *(b 1746, Newark, N.J.; d Oct. 8, 1793, Philadelphia, Pa.)* Lawyer who held office in the days of the Revolution in both New Jersey and Pennsylvania. In New Jersey: Somerset County surrogate (1769), state provincial convention secretary (1774); Provincial Congress member during parts of 1775 and 1776, its treasurer and safety committee chairman during the same 1775 period; member of the committee that drafted the first state constitution (1776); Continental Congress (Feb. 14-June 22, 1776) resigning after only a few months, being reelected in November and serving until Sept. 6, 1777 when he resigned once again, this time to accept office in Pennsylvania where he was state attorney general (1777-1780), member of the Council of Public Safety (1777), and state counsel in the Wyoming land controversy with Connecticut (1782). Father of John Sergeant.

SEVERANCE, LUTHER (b Oct. 26, 1797, Montague, Mass.; d Jan. 25, 1855, Augusta, Me.) Printer and a Maine Whig who founded the Kennebec Journal (1825). State representative (1829, 1839, 1840, 1842, 1848), state senate (1835, 1836), U.S. Representative (1843-1847), vice president of the Whig National Convention (1848), U.S. commissioner to the Sandwich Islands (1850-1854).

SEVIER, AMBROSE HUNDLEY (b Nov. 10, 1801, Greene County, Tenn.; d Dec. 31, 1848, Pulaski County, Ark.) Lawyer, planter, Whig, and an early Arkansas settler who worked tirelessly for statehood. As a territory: clerk of the house of representatives (1821-1823), a member (1823-1827), and speaker (1827); delegate to Congress (1828-1836); then, upon admission to the Union, one of the new state's first U.S. Senators (1836-1848), minister to Mexico to successfully negotiate a peace treaty (March-June 1848).

SEVIER, JOHN (b Sept. 23, 1745, Rockingham County, Va.; d Sept. 24, 1815, near Fort Decatur, Ala.) Early backwoods pioneer in that part of North Carolina that is now eastern Tennessee, Indian fighter, Revolutionary Army officer, and a planter with an interest in a variety of businesses and a constant quasi-official military leader whose rampages often skirted on the edge of out-lawism. In and out of the people's favor, he left his political mark as both a North Carolina and Tennessee Democrat and, a prime mover in the short-lived but never recognized state of Franklin as its governor (1785-1788). In North Carolina: Watauga County clerk and district judge (1777-1780), U.S. Representative in the First Congress (1789-1791). In Tennessee: the new state's first governor (1796-1801), state senate (1810-1811), U.S. Representative (1811 until death).

SEWARD, WILLIAM HENRY (b May 16, 1801, Florida, N.Y.; d Oct. 16, 1872, Auburn, N.Y.) Lawyer, Anti-Masonic, antislavery New York Whig turned Republican, secretary of state in Lincoln and Johnson cabinets (1861-1869), and a man who definitely left his mark upon American history. For example, he kept European nations out of the Civil War; acquired Alaska from Russia; was a major contender with Lincoln (1860) for the GOP presidential nomination; warned in the Compromise of 1850 debate that slavery had to be ended "within the framework of the Union" if war was to be avoided; insisted while governor (1838-1842) that there be Catholic teachers in the New York City public schools system because of the city's heavy Irish population.

State senate (1830-1834), U.S. Senate (1849-1861), and then his long tenure as secretary of state that ended with Grant's inauguration and which he capped by embarking upon a worldwide tour where he was given high honors by all the foreign courts at which he called.

On the night of Lincoln's assassination, Seward also was brutally attacked and left a partial cripple for life.

SEWELL, WILLIAM JOYCE (b Dec. 6, 1835, Castlebar, Ireland; d Dec. 27, 1901, Camden, N.J.) Merchant, railroad executive, commander of New Jersey volunteers during the Civil War who was wounded and received the Congressional Medal of Honor for action at Chancellorsville, and for many years after the war, New Jersey's undisputed Republican chieftain. State senator (1872-1880) and senate president (1876, 1879, 1880), U.S. Senate (1881-1887, 1895-1901), GOP National Convention delegate (1876, 1880, 1884, 1888, 1892, 1896, 1900).

SEYMOUR, EDWARD WOODRUFF *(b Aug. 30, 1832, Litchfield, Conn.; d Oct. 16, 1892, Litchfield)* Lawyer, Connecticut Democrat. State representative (1859, 1860, 1870, 1871), state senate (1876), U.S. Representative (1883-1887), state supreme court judge (1889 until death). Son of Origen S. Seymour.

SEYMOUR, HORATIO *(b May 31, 1778, Litchfield, Conn.; d Nov. 21, 1857, Middlebury, Vt.)* Lawyer, Vermont Democrat-Whig. Middlebury postmaster (1800-1809), member of the state executive council (1809-1814), Addison County state's attorney (1810-1813, 1815-1819), U.S. Senate (1821-1833), unsuccessful Whig candidate for governor (1836), probate court judge (1847-1856). Uncle of Origen Storrs Seymour.

SEYMOUR, ORIGEN STORRS *(b Feb. 9, 1804, Litchfield, Conn.; d Aug. 12, 1881, Litchfield)* Lawyer, Connecticut Democrat who twice ran unsuccessfully for governor (1864, 1865). County clerk (1836-1844), state representative (1842, 1849, 1850, 1880) and speaker (1850), U.S. Representative (1851-1855), state supreme court judge (1870-1873) and chief justice (1873-1874), chairman of committee to settle Connecticut-New York boundary dispute (1876). Father of Edward W. and nephew of Horatio Seymour.

SEYMOUR, THOMAS HART *(b Sept. 29, 1807, Hartford, Conn.; d Sept. 3, 1868, Hartford)* Lawyer, editor of the *Jeffersonian* (1837-1838), and a leader in an important political faction known as the Connecticut Peace Democrats. Probate judge (1836-1838), U.S. Representative (1843-1845), Mexican War officer (1846-1848), governor (1850-1853), presidential elector on the Pierce-King ticket (1852), minister to Russia (1853-1858). His portrait was removed by the state senate (1862) because he wanted to avoid war with the South. But he did receive thirty-eight first-ballot votes for the presidential nomination at the Democratic National Convention (1864).

SHACKLEFORD, DORSEY WILLIAM *(b Aug. 27, 1853, Saline County, Mo.; d July 15, 1936, Jefferson City, Mo.).* Teacher, lawyer, Missouri Democrat. Cooper County prosecutor (1882-1886, 1890-1892), fourteenth judicial circuit judge (1892-1899), U.S. Representative (1899-1919).

SHAFER, JACOB K. *(b Dec. 26, 1823, Rockingham County, Va.; d Nov. 22, 1876, Eureka, Nev.)* Lawyer, California and Idaho Democrat. In California: fifth judicial district attorney (1850), mayor of Stockton (1852), San Joaquin County judge (1853-1862). In Idaho Territory: delegate to the U.S. Congress (1869-1871).

SHAFER, PAUL WERNTZ *(b April 27, 1893, Elkhart, Ind.; d Aug. 17, 1954, Washington, D.C.)* Lawyer, Indiana and Michigan newspaperman, Michigan Republican. Battle Creek municipal judge (1929-1936), U.S. Representative (1937 until death).

SHAFROTH, JOHN FRANKLIN *(b June 9, 1854, Fayette, Mo.; d Feb. 20, 1922, Denver, Colo.)* Lawyer, Colorado Republican-Silver Republican-Democrat who very much represented the Western position when it came to conservation versus grazing and mineral rights and a man who did something quite unusual in American politics: he resigned as U.S. Representative (1895-1904) because he was convinced that his opponent, Robert W. Bonynge, was the rightful election winner. Denver city attorney (1887-1891), governor (1908-1912), U.S. Senate (1913-1919), War Minerals Relief Commission chairman (1919-1921).

SHALLENBERGER, ASHTON COKAYNE *(b Dec. 23, 1862, Toulon, Ill.; d Feb. 22, 1938, Franklin, Nebr.)* Stockraiser, farmer, banker, Nebraska Democrat. Democratic state convention temporary chairman (1897-1919), U.S. Representative (1901-1903, 1915-1919, 1923-1929, 1931-1935), governor (1908-1911), Democratic National Convention delegate (1920).

SHALLENBERGER, WILLIAM SHADRACK *(b Nov. 24, 1839, Mount Pleasant, Pa.; d April 15, 1914, Washington, D.C.)* Merchant, Union soldier who was wounded at Chancellorsville, Gettysburg, and the Wilderness; Pennsylvania Republican. Beaver County GOP Committee chairman (1872, 1874), U.S. Representative (1877-1883), second assistant U.S. postmaster general (1897-1907).

SHANKS, JOHN PETER CLEAVER *(b June 17, 1826, Martinsburg, Va., now W.Va.; d Jan. 23, 1901, Portland, Ind.)*. Lawyer, Union Army officer, Indiana Republican. State representative (1855, 1879), U.S. Representative (1861-1863, 1867-1875).

SHANNON, JOSEPH BERNARD *(b March 17, 1867, St. Louis, Mo.; d March 28, 1943, Kansas City, Mo.)* Lawyer, Missouri Democrat. Kansas City Justice court constable (1890-1892), city market-master (1892-1894), Democratic state committee chairman (1910) and national convention delegate (1908, 1912, 1920, 1924, 1928, 1932, 1940), state constitutional convention dele-

gate (1922, 1923), U.S. Representative (1931-1943).

SHANNON, THOMAS *(b Nov. 15, 1786, Washington County, Pa.; d March 16, 1843, Barnesville, Ohio)* Farmer, merchant, Ohio Democrat. State representative (1819-1822, 1824, 1825), U.S. Representative for four months (1826-1827) to fill a vacancy, state senate (1829, 1837-1841). Brother of Wilson Shannon.

SHANNON, WILSON *(b Feb. 24, 1802, Mount Olivet, Ohio; d Aug. 31, 1877, Lawrence, Kans.)* Lawyer, Ohio Democrat. Belmont County prosecutor (1833-1835), state prosecutor (1835), governor (1838-1840, 1842-1844), minister to Mexico (1844, 1845), U.S. Representative (1853-1855), governor of Kansas Territory (1855, 1856), relocating there permanently. Brother of Thomas Shannon.

SHARON, WILLIAM *(b Jan. 9, 1821, Smithfield, Ohio; d Nov. 13, 1885, San Francisco, Calif.)* Lawyer, merchant, silver miner, banker, real estate operator in California, and a Nevada Republican who served one term in the U.S. Senate (1875-1881).

SHARP, SOLOMON P. *(b 1780, Abingdon, Va.; d Nov. 7, 1825, Frankfort, Ky.)*. Farmer, lawyer, Kentucky Democrat who was assassinated. State representative (1809-1811, 1817, 1818, 1825), U.S. Representative (1813-1817), state attorney general (1820-1824).

SHARP, WILLIAM GRAVES *(b March 14, 1859, Mt. Gilead, Ohio; d Nov. 17, 1922, Elyria, Ohio)* Lawyer, industrialist, Ohio Democrat. Lorain County prosecutor (1885-1888), presidential elector on the Cleveland-Stevenson ticket (1892), Democratic National Convention delegate (1904), U.S. Representative (1909-1914), ambassador to France (1914-1919).

SHAW, ANNA HOWARD *(b Feb. 14, 1847, Newcastle-upon-Tyne, England; d July 2, 1919, Moylan, Pa.)* Suffragist, lecturer, reformer, ordained minister, doctor of medicine, wilderness pioneer. Endured hardships as a young girl living with her family in Michigan wilderness; taught school at fifteen; entered high school at twenty-three; preached and gave temperance lectures to earn meager living while attending Albion (Mich.). College (1873-1876); almost starved in unheated attic when she went on to Boston University's Theological School (1876-1878); preached for seven years but, because of her sex, was not ordained until 1880; during those seven years earned her M.D. degree at Boston University Medical School.

She came to believe that the efforts of women struggling at that time for reforms could only succeed if they first obtained the vote, met feminist leader Susan B. Anthony in 1888, became her close associate, and from that time until 1915 when she felt the fight was won, devoted her life to obtaining suffrage for women.

Even among the group of unusual women who were the suffragist leaders, Dr. Shaw was outstanding, both in her effective eloquence and her remarkable endurance. She traveled widely, lecturing, attending conventions (in Europe as well as the United States), appeared before congressional committees, campaigned in any state considering a suffrage measure. Vice president at large of the National American Woman Suffrage Association (1892-1904), president of the organization (1904-1915); chairman of the women's committee of the Council of National Defense (1917-1919) and awarded the Distinguished Service Medal for her work.

On a speaking tour around the United States with William Howard Taft and A. Lawrence Lowell, president of Harvard University (1919), advocating the League of Nations and a treaty of peace under League auspices, she contracted pneumonia and died shortly thereafter.

SHAW, HENRY *(b 1788, Windham County, Vt.; d Oct. 17, 1857, Peekskill, N.Y.)* Lawyer, Massachusetts and New York Federalist turned National Republican. In Massachusetts: U.S. Representative (1817-1821), state representative (1824-1830, 1833), state senate (1835), presidential elector on the Clay-Sergeant National Republican ticket (1832), unsuccessful gubernatorial candidate (1845). In New York: New York City Board of Education (1849) and member of the city's common council (1850-1851), state assemblyman (1853). Son of Samuel Shaw.

SHAW, SAMUEL *(b Dec., 1768, Dighton, Mass.; d Oct. 23, 1827, Clarendon Springs, Vt.)* Physician, Vermont Democrat who was jailed for denouncing President Adams with too bitter a bite. State representative (1800-1807), U.S. Representative (1808-1813). Father of Henry Shaw.

SHEAKLEY, JAMES *(b April 24, 1829, Sheakleyville, Pa.; d Dec. 10, 1917, Greenville, Pa.)* Cabinetmaker, California '49er, Pennsylvania merchant, petroleum producer, and a Democrat there with time out to serve and to practice law for twenty years in Alaska. In Pennsylvania: U.S. Representative (1875-1877), mayor of Greenville (1909-1913), justice of the peace (1914 until death). In Alaska: Cleveland-appointed U.S. commissioner of schools (1887-1892), Democratic National Convention delegate (1892), territorial governor (1893-1897).

SHELDEN, CARLOS DOUGLAS *(b June 10, 1840, Walworth, Wis.; d June 24, 1904, Houghton, Mich.)* Union army officer, real estate and mining operator, Michigan Republican. State representative (1892), state senate (1894), U.S. Representative (1897-1903).

SHEPPARD, HARRY RICHARD *(b Jan. 10, 1885, Mobile, Ala.; d April 28, 1969, Washington, D.C.)* Lawyer, railroad worker, Alaska goldminer, film consultant in selection of settings for silent films, businessman, California Democrat who served as a U.S. Representative for twenty-eight years (1937-1965) and was a member of the Appropriations Committee when his last term expired.

SHEPPARD, JOHN LEVI *(b April 13, 1852, Bluffton, Ala.; d Oct. 11, 1902, Texarkana, Texas)* Lawyer, Texas Democrat. Fifth judicial district attorney (1882-1888) and judge there (1888-1896), Democratic state convention temporary chairman (1892), Bimetallic Convention delegate (1893), Democratic National Convention delegate (1896), U.S. Representative (1899 until death) when he was succeeded by his son, Morris.

SHEPPARD, MORRIS *(b May 28, 1875, Wheatville, Tex.; d April 9, 1941, Washington, D.C.)* Lawyer, Texas Democrat who succeeded his father, John Levi Sheppard, as a U.S. Representative (1902), served through reelection until 1913 when he was elected to the U.S. Senate and remained there more than a quarter-century (1913 until death).

SHEPPERD, AUGUSTINE HENRY *(b Feb. 24, 1792, Rockford, N.C.; d July 11, 1864, Salem, now Winston-Salem, N.C.).* Lawyer, North Carolina Democrat turned Whig. State representative (1822-1826), presidential elector on the Jackson-Calhoun Democratic ticket (1824) and the Clay-Frelinghuysen Whig ticket (1844), U.S. Representative as a Democrat (1827-1839) and as a Whig (1841-1843, 1847-1851).

SHERBURNE, JOHN SAMUEL *(b 1757, Portsmouth, N.H.; d Aug. 2, 1830, Portsmouth, N.H.)* Revolutionary Army officer who lost a leg at Butts Hill, and a New Hampshire lawyer who sat for more than a quarter-century as a U.S. district judge there (1804 until death). U.S. Representative (1793-1797), U.S. attorney (1801-1804).

SHERLEY, JOSEPH SWAGAR *(b Nov. 28, 1871, Louisville, Ky.; d Feb. 13, 1941, Louisville)* Lawyer, Kentucky Democrat. U.S. Representative (1903-1919), U.S. Railroad Administration Finance Division director (1919-1920).

SHERMAN, JAMES SCHOOLCRAFT *(b Oct. 24, 1855, Utica, N.Y.; d Oct. 30, 1912, Utica)* Lawyer, banker, businessman, New York Republican who was vice president in the Taft administration (1909 until death). Mayor of Utica (1884), GOP National Convention delegate (1892), state GOP convention chairman (1895, 1900), U.S. Representative (1887-1891, 1892-1909).

SHERMAN, JOHN *(b May 10, 1823, Lancaster, Ohio; d Oct. 22, 1900, Washington, D.C.)* Lawyer, Ohio Whig-Republican who served in the cabinets of two presidents and succeeded a third in the Senate; the man who led in planning the national banking system and the nation's foremost expert of his time on finance. Whig National Convention secretary (1848) and delegate (1852), president of the first Ohio state GOP convention (1855), U.S. Representative (1855-1861), U.S. Senate (1861-1877) and again (1881-1897) having been appointed to fill the seat vacated when Garfield was elected president, secretary of the treasury in the Hayes cabinet (1877-1881), secretary of state in the McKinley cabinet (1897-1898).

SHERMAN, ROGER *(b April 19, 1721, Newton, Mass.; d July 23, 1793, New Haven, Conn.)* Shoemaker, surveyor, lawyer, and a Connecticut patriot whose accomplishments were many. He was the only member of the Continental Congress who signed all four great state papers (the Declaration of 1774, the Declaration of Independence which he had helped to write, the Articles of Confederation, and the federal Constitution), introducer of the Connecticut Compromise, and a grim holdout for the sale of public lands to settlers rather than to speculators; a man whom John Adams described as "an old Puritan, as honest as an angel and as firm in the cause of American independence as Mount Atlas."

Member of the Connecticut Assembly (1755, 1756, 1758-1761, 1764-1766), Litchfield County justice of the peace (1755-1761) and of the quorum (1759-1761) and the same positions in New Haven County (1765, 1766), state senate (1766-1785), superior court judge (1766, 1767, 1773-1788), Council of Safety (1777-1779), Continental Congress delegate (1774-1781, 1783, 1784), mayor of New Haven (1784 until death), U.S. Constitutional Convention delegate (1787), U.S. Representative in the First Congress (1789-1791), U.S. Senate (1791 until death).

SHERWOOD, ISAAC R. *(b Aug. 13, 1835, Stanford, N.Y.; d Oct. 15, 1925, Toledo, Ohio)* Lawyer, Union Army private who rose to brigadier general, editor of several Ohio papers, author, and an Ohio Republican turned Democrat because he believed in greenbacks; as a congressman, he did not believe in U.S. involvement in World War I. Williams County probate judge (1860-1861), Ohio secretary of state (1868, 1870), organizer of the state's bureau of statistics (1869), U.S. Representative as a Republican (1873-1875) and as a Democrat (1907-1921, 1923-1925), Lucas County probate judge (1878, 1881).

SHIEL, GEORGE KNOX *(b 1825, Ireland; d Dec. 12, 1893, Salem, Oregon).* Lawyer, Oregon Democrat. U.S. Representative (1861-1863).

SHIELDS, JAMES *(b May 10, 1810, County Tyrone, Ireland; d June 1, 1879, Ottumwa, Iowa)* Lawyer, Mexican War general and Union Army general in the Civil War, and a man who indeed did get around—probably the only man in history to serve in the U.S. Senate from three different states (Illinois, Minnesota, and Missouri) besides holding high political office in Oregon; Democrat. In Illinois: State representative (1836), state auditor (1839), state supreme court judge (1843), land office commissioner (1845-1847), U.S. Senate (1849-1855). In Oregon: Polk-appointed governor of the territory (1848-1849). In Minnesota: U.S. Senate (1858-1859) upon admission to the Union. In Missouri: State representative (1874, 1879), state attorney general (1877), U.S. Senate to fill a vacancy (two months in 1879).

SHIELDS, JOHN KNIGHT *(b Aug. 15, 1858, Grainger County, Tenn.; d Sept. 30, 1934, near Knoxville, Tenn.)* Lawyer, Tennessee Democrat who was highly independent of the machine. Twelfth chancery division chancellor (1893, 1894), Democratic National Convention delegate (1896, 1904), state supreme court associate justice (1902-1910) and chief justice (1910-1913), U.S. Senate (1913-1925), and a decided isolationist who helped lead the fight against entry into the League of Nations.

SHIPSTEAD, HENRIK *(b Jan. 8, 1881, Burbank, Minn.; d June 26, 1960, Alexandria, Minn.)* Dentist, Minnesota Farmer Laborite-Republican. Member of the Glenwood Charter Commission (1911, 1912) and mayor (1911-1913), state representative (1917), U.S. Senate (1923-1947).

SHIVELY, BENJAMIN FRANKLIN *(b March 20, 1857, St. Joseph County, Ind.; d March 14, 1916, Washington, D.C.).* Teacher, journalist, lawyer, Indiana

Democrat who first was sent to Congress as a National Anti-Monopolist. Secretary of the National Anti-Monopoly Association (1883), Indiana University board president (1884), U.S. Representative (1884-1885, 1887-1893), unsuccessful candidate for governor (1896), U.S. Senate (1909 until death).

SHORT, DEWEY *(b April 7, 1898, Galena, Mo.)* Southwestern College professor, clergyman, Missouri Republican who received 108 votes for the vice presidential nomination (1940), inspected Nazi atrocity camps (1945), and was assistant secretary of the army (1957-1961). U.S. Representative (1929-1931, 1935-1957), Interparliamentary Union delegate (1939, 1947), alternate delegate to the signing of the U.S.-Japanese security pact (1951).

SHORTRIDGE, SAMUEL MORGAN *(b Aug. 3, 1861, Mt. Pleasant, Iowa; d Jan. 15, 1952, Atherton, Calif.)* Lawyer, California Republican. Presidential elector (1888, 1900, 1908), U.S. Senate (1921-1933).

SHOTT, HUGH IKE *(b Sept. 3, 1866, Staunton, Va.; d Oct. 12, 1953, Bluefield, W.Va.)* Editor-publisher of the *Bluefield Daily Telegraph* (1893 until death). West Virginia Republican. Bluefield postmaster (1903-1912), U.S. Representative (1929-1933), U.S. Senate to fill a vacancy (Nov. 18, 1942-Jan. 3, 1943).

SHOUP, GEORGE LAIRD *(b June 15, 1836, Kittanning, Pa.; d Dec. 21, 1904, Boise, Idaho)* Farmer, stock raiser, Union scout and later a Colorado Volunteer Cavalry officer during the Civil War, merchant, miner; a Colorado, Montana, and Idaho pioneer who finally settled down in the latter, helped to found Salmon City and served as the territory's last governor (1889-1890) and the state's first governor; then one of Idaho's first U.S. Senators (1890-

1901); Republican. In Colorado: delegate to convention that prepared constitution for the proposed state (1864). In Idaho: Lemhi County treasurer (1868), county commissioner (1868, 1869) and schools superintendent (1871); territorial representative (1874), territorial council (1878); GOP National Convention delegate (1880) and National Committeeman (1880-1884, 1888-1892).

SHREVE, MILTON WILLIAM *(b May 3, 1858, Chapmanville, Pa.; d Dec. 23, 1939, Erie, Pa.)* Lawyer, banker, manufacturer, Pennsylvania Republican. Erie County district attorney (1899-1902), state representative (1907-1912) and house speaker (1911-1912), U.S. Representative (1913-1915, 1919-1933).

SHUFORD, ALONZO CRAIG *(b March 1, 1858, Catawba County, N.C.; d Feb. 8, 1933, Chapel Hill, N.C.)* Farmer who early in life joined the Farmers' Alliance and made it his main interest, serving as a lecturer, delegate to the 1892 labor conference in St. Louis, and vice president of the State Alliance (1894); Populist and Progressive. Populist Convention delegate (1892), U.S. Representative (1895-1899), presidential elector on the La Follette-Wheeler ticket (1924).

SIBLEY, HENRY HASTINGS *(b Feb. 20, 1811, Detroit, Mich.; d Feb. 18, 1891, St. Paul, Minn.)* Son of Northwest and Michigan Territory pioneer Solomon Sibley and very much a pioneer in his own right, but in the Wisconsin and Minnesota territories. Indian fighter, Union Army officer, builder of the first stone house in Minnesota which the Daughters of the American Revolution still preserve, banker, railroad builder, utilities executive; Democrat. He first went (1828) to Wisconsin to become a fur trader in Mackinac, moving on to the mouth of the Minnesota River (1834) and becoming a leader in the formation of first the Minnesota territory and then the state.

In Wisconsin: justice of the peace (1831), delegate to the U.S. Congress (1848-1849). In Minnesota: delegate to the U.S. Congress (1849-1853), member of the territorial legislature (1855) and state constitutional convention president (1857); then, upon statehood, the first governor (1858-1860), state university regent (1860-1869) and board president (1876-1891), president of the Minnesota Historical Society (1879-1891), president of U.S. commission to settle Ojibway Indian damage claims (1883).

SIBLEY, JOSEPH CROCKER *(b Feb. 18, 1850, Friendship, N.Y.; d May 19, 1926, near Franklin, Pa.)* A man of many talents and political convictions, bringing them all to fruit in Pennsylvania. Oil refiner who developed products that he induced Standard Oil to buy, teacher, farmer who pioneered in the science of agriculture, developer of prize Jersey milk cows and one of the breed's foremost judges in the U.S. His political labels, in order of appearance: Low-tariff Republican, successful congressional candidate of a Democrat-People's Party-Prohibitionist coalition, Democrat, and unsuccessful congressional candidate of a Democrat-Populist coalition, a man who was mentioned as the Bimetallic League's presidential candidate (1896), and then a Republican again. Mayor of Franklin (1879), U.S. Representative (1893-1895 thanks to the coalition, 1899-1901 as a Democrat, 1901-1907 as a Republican).

SIBLEY, SOLOMON *(b Oct. 7, 1769, Sutton, Mass,; d April 4, 1846, Detroit, Mich.)* Lawyer who first practiced in that part of the Northwest Territory that is now Marietta, Ohio, then moved on to Detroit which later became part of the Michigan Territory. In 1799 he was a member of the Northwest Territory legislature. Other offices in Michi-

gan Territory: mayor of Detroit (1806), president of the Detroit Board of Trustees (1815), territorial auditor (1814-1817), U.S. attorney (1815-1823), delegate to the U.S. Congress (1820-1823), territorial supreme court judge (1824-1827). Father of Henry Hastings Sibley.

SICKLES, DANIEL EDGAR *(b Oct. 20, 1825, New York City; d May 3, 1914, New York City)* Lawyer, Union Army general who stopped Stonewall Jackson at Chancellorsville, lost a leg and gained a Congressional Medal of Honor at Gettysburg, yet was criticized by General Meade for allegedly making an improper tactical decision, and through it all a somewhat unstable New York Democrat. For example, he killed Francis Scott Key's son in a duel, then pleaded temporary insanity; as U.S. minister to Spain (1869-1875) he became known there as the Yankee King because of his blunt approach to diplomatic problems. On the affirmative side, he acquired for New York City the land that is now known as Central Park.

New York City corporation counsel (1853), secretary of the London legation (1853-1855), state senate (1856, 1857), U.S. Representative (1857-1861, 1893-1895), special emissary to the South American republics (1865), military governor of the Carolinas (1865-1867) but removed for applying too much high-handed vigor to the execution of his duties, state Civil Service Commission chairman (1888, 1889), city sheriff (1890).

SIEGEL, ISAAC *(b April 12, 1880, New York City; d June 29, 1947, New York City)* Lawyer, New York Republican. Special attorney general for the prosecution of election frauds (1909, 1910), U.S. Representative (1915-1923), GOP National Convention delegate (1916, 1920, 1924, 1936), city magistrate (1939-1940), domestic relations court justice (1940 until death).

SILER, EUGENE *(b June 26, 1900, Williamsburg, Ky.)* Lawyer, Kentucky Republican. State appeals court judge (1945-1949), unsuccessful candidate for governor (1951), U.S. Representative (1955-1965) and served on the Banking and Currency Committee.

SILSBEE, NATHANIEL *(b Jan. 14, 1773, Salem, Mass.; d July 14, 1850, Salem).* Sailor, sea captain, ship owner, merchant. Massachusetts Democrat turned Whig who was chairman of the Senate Commerce Committee (1833-1835). U.S. Representative (1817-1821), state representative (1821), state senate member-president (1823-1825), presidential elector voting for Adams (1824) and Daniel Webster (1836), U.S. Senate (1826-1835), Whig state convention delegate-president (1832).

SIMMONS, FURNIFOLD McLENDEL *(b Jan. 20, 1854, Jones County, N.C.; d April 30, 1940, New Bern, N.C.).* Planter, lawyer, North Carolina Democrate who bossed the state—as a white supremacist—from 1892 until 1928 when he made the mistake of opposing Al Smith, the party's candidate for the presidency. U.S. Representative (1887-1889), fourth district internal revenue collector (1893-1901), Democratic National Committeeman (1924-1928), U.S. Senate (1901-1931).

SIMMS, ALBERT GALLATIN *(b Oct. 8, 1882, Washington, Ark.)* Accountant, lawyer, banker, farmer, rancher, New Mexico Republican who, while a U.S. Representative (1929-1931), met and married Congresswoman Ruth Hanna McCormick. Albuquerque councilman and Bernalillo County Board of Commissioners chairman (1920-1922), state representative (1925-1927), GOP National Committee member (1932-1934).

SIMON, JOSEPH *(b Feb. 7, 1851, Bechtheim, Germany; d Feb. 14, 1935, Portland, Oreg.)* Lawyer, Oregon Republican. Portland city councilman (1877-1880), GOP state committee secretary (1878) and chairman (1880, 1884, 1886), state senator (1880-1898) and senate president (1889, 1891, 1895, 1897, 1898), GOP National Convention delegate (1892, 1900) and National Committeeman (1892-1896), U.S. Senate (1898-1903), mayor of Portland (1909-1911).

SIMPSON, JEREMIAH *(b March 31, 1842, Prince Edward Island, Canada; d Oct. 23, 1905, Wichita, Kans.)* Sailor, Union soldier, farmer, Kansas Republican-Populist. U.S. Representative (1891-1895, 1897-1899).

SIMPSON, RICHARD MURRAY *(b Aug. 30, 1900, Huntingdon, Pa.; d Jan. 7, 1960, Bethesda, Md.)* Insurance broker, Pennsylvania Republican. U.S. Representative (1937 until death).

SIMPSON, SIDNEY ELMER *(b Sept. 20, 1894, Carrollton, Ill.; d Oct. 26, 1958, Pittsfield, Ill.)* Bus operator, Illinois Republican who held a variety of local positions before being elected a U.S. Representative (1943 until death). His widow, Edna Oakes Simpson, then served (1959-1961).

SIMS, THETUS WILLRETTE *(b April 25, 1852, Wayne County, Tenn.; d Dec. 17, 1939, Washington, D.C.)* Lawyer, Tennessee Democrat. Perry County superintendent of public instruction (1882-1884), presidential elector on the Cleveland-Stevenson ticket (1892), U.S. Representative (1897-1921).

SINCLAIR, JAMES HERBERT *(b Oct. 9, 1871, Ontario, Canada; d Sept. 5, 1943, Miami, Fla.)* Banker, farmer, real estate operator, North Dakota Republican. Cooperstown schools superintendent (1896-1898), Griggs County register of deeds (1899-1905), state representative (1915-1919), U.S. Representative

(1919-1935), GOP member of the Special Mexican Claims Commission (1936-1939).

SINGLETON, OTHO ROBARDS *(b Oct. 14, 1814, Jessamine County, Ky.; d Jan. 11, 1889, Washington, D.C.)* Lawyer, Mississippi Democrat who was a U.S. Representative both before and after the Civil War (1853-1855, 1857-1861, 1875-1887). Also, state representative (1846, 1847), state senate (1848-1854), presidential elector on the Pierce-King ticket (1852), member of the Confederate Congress (1861-1865).

SINNOTT, NICHOLAS JOHN *(b Dec. 6, 1870, The Dalles, Oregon; d July 20, 1929, Washington, D.C.)* Lawyer, Oregon Republican. State senate (1909, 1911), U.S. Representative (1913-1928) resigning to become a judge of the U.S. Court of Claims (1928 until death).

SIROVICH, WILLIAM IRVING *(b March 18, 1882, York, Pa.; d Dec. 17, 1939, New York City)* Physician, lecturer, editor, playwright who somehow found time to delve into politics as a New York Democrat. Fifth district school board member (1906-1926), Peoples Hospital superintendent (1910-1927), state pension commissioner who probed widows' pensions (1913), state charities convention member (1914), child welfare commissioner (1919-1931), U.S. Representative (1927 until death).

SISSON, THOMAS UPTON *(b Sept. 22, 1869, Attala County, Miss.; d Sept. 26, 1923, Washington, D.C.)* Lawyer, Mississippi Democrat. Principal of Carthage High School (1889, 1890) and Kosciusko grade schools (1890-1892), state senate (1898), presidential elector on the Bryan-Stevenson ticket (1900), fifth judicial district attorney (1903-1907), U.S. Representative (1909-1923).

SKINNER, HARRY *(b May 25, 1855, Perquimans County, N.C.; d May 19, 1929, Greenville, N.C.)* Lawyer who was active in the American Bar Association and a North Carolina Democrat whose interest in bettering the lot of farmers and workers drove him to the Populist cause. His newspaper article, under the headline "The Hope of the South" (1889), put forth a plan for fixing the price of cotton and was said to be the forerunner of the "subtreasury" scheme for farm-product pricing. First congressional district Democratic executive committee chairman (1880-1890) and the same position in Pitt County (1880-1892), state representative (1891, 1892), Pitt County Populist Executive Committee chairman and state central committee member (1892-1896), University of North Carolina trustee (1890-1896), U.S. Representative (1895-1899), eastern district U.S. attorney (1902-1910), state bar association president (1915, 1916). Brother of Thomas G. Skinner.

SKINNER, RICHARD *(b May 30, 1778, Litchfield, Conn.; d May 23, 1833, Manchester, Vt.)* Lawyer, Middlebury College trustee who was interested in public education, Vermont Democrat. Bennington County state's attorney (1801-1813, 1819), Manchester district probate judge (1806-1813), U.S. Representative (1813-1815), state supreme court assistant judge (1815, 1816), state representative (1815) and speaker of the house (1818), governor (1820-1823), chief justice of the state supreme court (1823-1828).

SKINNER, THOMAS GREGORY *(b Jan. 22, 1842, Perquimans County, N.C.; d Dec. 22, 1907, Baltimore, Md.)* Confederate Army officer, lawyer, North Carolina Democrat who was a delegate to most of the party's state conventions between 1870 and 1902. U.S. Representative (1883-1887, 1889-1891), Democratic National Convention delegate (1892, 1904), state senate (1899, 1900). Brother of Harry Skinner.

SLADE, WILLIAM *(b May 9, 1786, Cornwall, Vt.; d Jan. 18, 1859, Middlebury, Vt.)* Lawyer, Vermont Democrat turned Whig, and a vigorous antislavery pamphleteer who helped found the *Columbian Patriot* (1813) in order to circulate his views more widely. Democratic presidential elector on the Madison-Gerry ticket (1812), U.S. State Department clerk (1823-1829), U.S. Representative (1831-1843), state supreme court reporter (1843, 1844), governor (1844-1846).

SLATER, JAMES HARVEY *(b Dec. 28, 1826, Sangamon County, Ill.; d Jan. 28, 1899, La Grande, Oreg.).* Pioneer Oregon lawyer and newspaper publisher, Democrat. Benton County territorial district court clerk (1853-1856), territorial assemblyman (1857, 1858), state representative (1859), fifth judicial district attorney (1868), Democratic presidential elector on the Seymour-Blair ticket (1868), U.S. Representative (1871-1873), U.S. Senate (1879-1885), state railroad commissioner (1889-1891).

SLAYDEN, JAMES LUTHER *(b June 1, 1853, Mayfield, Ky.; d Feb. 24, 1924, San Antonio, Tex.)* Rancher, cotton merchant, fruit grower, mine manager, Texas Democrat, an original trustee of the Carnegie Endowment for International Peace who also served as president of the American Peace Society. State representative (1892), U.S. Representative (1897-1919). Uncle of Maury Maverick.

SLEMONS, WILLIAM FERGUSON *(b March 15, 1830, Weakley County, Tenn.; d Dec. 10, 1918, Monticello, Ark.)* Lawyer, Confederate cavalry officer, Arkansas Democrat. State convention delegate (1861), district attorney (1866-1868), U.S. Representative (1875-1881),

Drew County judge (1903-1907), justice of the peace (1908-1918).

SLEMP, CAMPBELL *(b Dec. 2, 1839, Lee County, Va.; d Oct. 13, 1907, Big Stone Gap, Va.)* Farmer, real estate operator, Confederate Army officer, Virginia Republican. Presidential elector on the Harrison-Morton (1888) and Harrison-Reid (1892) tickets, U.S. Representative (1903 until death). Father of Campbell B. Slemp.

SLEMP, CAMPBELL BASCOM *(b Sept. 4, 1870, Turkey Cove, Va.; d Aug. 7, 1943, Knoxville, Tenn.).* Lawyer, mathematics professor, Virginia Republican who succeeded his father, Campbell, as a U.S. Representative in 1907 and served until 1923 when he became secretary to President Coolidge (1923-1925). GOP state chairman (1905-1918).

SMALL, JOHN HUMPHREY *(b Aug. 29, 1858, Washington, N.C.; d July 13, 1946, Washington, D.C.)* Teacher, lawyer, newspaper editor, North Carolina Democrat. State senate reading clerk (1881), Beaufort County superintendent of public instruction (1881), solicitor of the county's interior court (1882-1885) and attorney for its board of commissioners (1888-1896), Washington, N.C., councilman (1887-1890) and mayor (1889, 1890), Democratic elector on the Bryan-Sewall ticket (1896), U.S. Representative (1899-1921).

SMALLS, ROBERT *(b April 5, 1839, Beaufort, S.C.; d Feb. 22, 1915, Beaufort)* A slave at the outbreak of the Civil War, he managed to enlist in the Confederate Navy, became a member of the crew of the *Planter*, smuggled his wife and three children aboard, took command of the steamer, and delivered her to the squadron blockading Charleston Harbor. Thus he became a hero to the Union, was appointed a pilot in the navy by President Lincoln, and by 1864 had risen to the rank of captain. Though a modest man and poorly educated, in 1866 he turned to politics as a South Carolina Republican and as a crowning glory to his career served longer as a U.S. Representative than any other Negro Reconstruction congressman (1875-1879, 1882-1887). State constitutional convention delegate (1868), state representative (1868), state senate (1870-1872), GOP National Convention delegate (1872, 1876), officer in the state militia (1865-1877) rising to major general, collector of Beaufort port (1897-1913).

SMILIE, JOHN *(b Ireland, 1741; d Dec. 30, 1812, Washington, D.C.)* An immigrant lad who settled in Pennsylvania in 1760, fought in the Revolution, and became interested in politics as a Democrat. State representative (1784-1786), state constitutional convention delegate (1790), state senate (1790-1793), U.S. Representative (1793-1795, 1799 until death), presidential elector (1796).

SMITH, ABBY HADASSAH *(b June 1, 1797, Glastonbury, Conn.; d July 23, 1878, Glastonbury)* Like her sister, Julia Evelina Smith, a highly educated Connecticut farm woman who from 1869 on devoted her life to the suffrage movement, from 1873 on refused to pay taxes until given the right to vote and so had her property repeatedly confiscated—a fact that led Julia to write *Abby Smith and Her Cows, with a Report of the Law Case Decided Contrary to Law* (1877).

SMITH, ADDISON TAYLOR *(b Sept. 5, 1862, Guernsey County, Ohio; d July 5, 1956, Washington, D.C.)* Lawyer, educator, Idaho Republican. Secretary to U.S. Senators George L. Shoup (1891-1901) and Weldon B. Heyburn (1903-1912), GOP state central committee chairman (1904-1911), Boise U.S. Land Office register (1907, 1908), member of GOP National Congressional Committee (1917-1927), U.S. Representative (1913-1933), associate member of the Board of Veterans' Appeals (1934-1942), director of the Columbia Institution for the Deaf, now Gallaudet College (1937 until death).

SMITH, ALFRED EMANUEL *(b Dec. 30, 1873, New York City; d Oct. 4, 1944, New York City)* Son of a struggling East Side Irish family, he went to work as a laborer in New York's Fulton Fish Market at the age of twelve, showed an early interest in politics with a flair for speaking, became the champion of the working man, and rose to become a four-term Democratic governor (1918-1920, 1922-1928), and Herbert Hoover's rival for the U.S. presidency (1928) losing in a prosperous Republican year with his Roman Catholicism and wet stand on prohibition also working against him.

State assemblyman (1904-1915), majority leader (1911-1913), speaker (1913-1915); state constitutional convention delegate (1915), New York County sheriff (1915-1917), president of the New York City Board of Aldermen (1917-1918).

During most of his political career, Smith was a friend and political ally of Franklin D. Roosevelt who nominated him for the presidency (1924) in a speech that gave him the name the Happy Warrior. But the nomination went to John W. Davis after a 103-ballot deadlock with William G. McAdoo. A split came between Smith and Roosevelt (1932) when both sought the presidential nomination and it continued through the 1936 and 1940 elections with Smith supporting the Republican candidates Alfred M. Landon and Wendell L. Willkie. The New Deal was responsible for much of Smith's alienation, but 1941 found him again at Roosevelt's side, supporting fully FDR's foreign policy because of his long recognition of the dangers of rising fascism in the world.

SMITH, DAVID HIGHBAUGH *(b Dec. 19, 1854, Hart County, Ky.; d Dec. 17, 1928, Hodgenville, Ky.)* Lawyer, banker, Kentucky Democrat. Larue County schools superintendent (1878) and county attorney (1878-1881), state representative (1881-1883), state senate (1885-1893) and president pro tem (1891-1893), U.S. Representative (1897-1907).

SMITH, ELLISON DuRANT *(b Aug. 1, 1866, Lynchburg, S.C.; d Nov. 17, 1944, Lynchburg)* Merchant, planter and one of the prime movers in the Southern Cotton Association, South Carolina Democrat who served as field agent and general organizer of the cotton protective movement throughout the South (1905-1908) before serving five terms in the U.S. Senate (1909 until death).

SMITH, FREDERICK CLEVELAND *(b July 29, 1884, Shanesville, Ohio; d July 16, 1956, Marion, Ohio)* Physician, Ohio Republican. Mayor of Marion (1936-1938), U.S. Representative (1939-1951).

SMITH, GEORGE WASHINGTON *(b Aug. 18, 1846, Putnam County, Ohio; d Nov. 30, 1907, Murphysboro, Ill.).* Blacksmith, lawyer, Illinois Republican. Presidential elector on the Garfield-Arthur ticket (1880), master in chancery (1880-1888), U.S. Representative (1889 until death).

SMITH, HOKE *(b Sept. 2, 1855, Newton, N.C.; d Nov. 27, 1931, Atlanta, Ga.).* Lawyer, editor-publisher of the *Atlanta Evening Journal* (1887-1900), Georgia Democrat who was secretary of the interior in the Cleveland cabinet (1893-1896). Democratic National Convention delegate (1892), Atlanta Board of Education president (1896-1907), governor (1907-1909, 1911), U.S. Senate (1911-1921).

SMITH, HOWARD WORTH *(b Feb. 2, 1883, Broad Run, Va.)* Lawyer, banker, farmer, Virginia Democrat who served thirty-six years as a U.S. Representative (1931-1967), much of the time as chairman of the House Rules Committee. Assistant general counsel to the Alien Property Custodian (1917, 1918), commonwealth attorney of Alexandria (1918-1922), corporation court judge (1922-1928), sixteenth judicial circuit judge (1928-1930).

SMITH, ISRAEL *(b April 4, 1759, Suffield, Conn.; d Dec. 2, 1810, Rutland, Vt.)* A 1781 Yale graduate who studied law, began practice in Vermont, became interested in politics as a Democrat, and served well both on the bench and in high elective office. State representative (1785, 1788-1791, 1797), state constitutional convention delegate (1791), U.S. Representative (1791-1797, 1801-1803), chief justice of the state supreme court (1797-1801), U.S. Senate (1803-1807) resigning to become governor (1807, 1808), presidential elector (1808).

SMITH, JAMES *(b 1713, Ireland; d July 11, 1806, York, Pa.)* Came to America as a boy and rose to become a patriotic leader and a signer of the Declaration of Independence as a member of the Continental Congress (1776-1778). Surveyor, iron manufacturer, lawyer. State convention delegate (1775), organizer of the Pennsylvania Militia (1776) in which he was a brigadier general, state representative (1780).

SMITH, JEREMIAH *(b Nov. 29, 1759, Peterborough, N.H.; d Sept. 21, 1842 Dover, N.H.)* A Harvard College student who left during his sophomore year to fight in the Revolutionary War's Battle of Bennington, resumed his schooling to become a lawyer and one of New Hampshire's leading Federalists. State representative (1788-1791), constitutional convention delegate (1791, 1792), U.S. Representative (1791-1797), U.S. attorney (1797-1800), Rockingham County probate judge (1800-1802), U.S. circuit court judge (1801-1802), chief justice of the N.H. Superior Court of Judicature (1802-1809), presidential elector on the Pinckney-King ticket (1808), governor (1809, 1810), chief justice of the state's supreme judicial court (1813-1816). Brother of Samuel, uncle of Robert Smith.

SMITH, JOHN (b May 7, 1750, Middlesex County, Va.; d March 5, 1836, Frederick County, Va.) Virginia planter who liked the military life, fought in Dunmore's War with the Indians, the Revolution, and the War of 1812, and lived out his life as a major general in the state militia; Democrat. Member of the state house of delegates (1779-1783), state senate (1792-1800), U.S. Representative (1801-1815). (Not to be confused with John Smith of New York —see next entry.)

SMITH, JOHN (b Feb. 12, 1752, Mastic, N.Y.; d Aug. 12, 1816, Mastic). New York Democrat. State assemblyman (1784-1799), federal Constitutional Convention delegate (1788), U.S. Representative (1800-1804) resigning to succeed DeWitt Clinton in the U.S. Senate (1804-1813), U.S. marshal (1813-1815). (Not to be confused with John Smith of Virginia—see previous entry.)

SMITH, JOHN COTTON (b Feb. 12, 1765, Sharon, Conn.; d Dec. 7, 1845, Litchfield County, Conn.) Lawyer, Connecticut Federalist who was president of the state's Bible Society as well as the American Board of Commissioners for Foreign Missions. State representative (1793, 1796) and house speaker (1800), U.S. Representative (1800-1806), state supreme court judge (1809), lieutenant governor (1810), governor (1813-1818).

SMITH, JOHN M. C. (b Feb. 6, 1853, Belfast, Ireland; d March 30, 1923, Charlotte, Mich.) Farmer, mason, lawyer, banker, manufacturer, Michigan Republican. Eaton County prosecutor (1885-1888), Charlotte alderman (1903), state constitutional convention delegate (1908), U.S. Representative (1911 until death).

SMITH, JOHN WALTER (b Feb. 5, 1845, Snow Hill, Md.; d April 19, 1925, Baltimore, Md.) Lumberman, banker, businessman, Maryland Democrat. State senator (1889-1899) and senate president (1894), U.S. Representative (1899-1900), resigning to become governor (1900-1904), Democratic National Convention delegate (1900, 1904), U.S. Senate (1908-1921).

SMITH, JULIA (b May 27, 1792, Glastonbury, Conn.; d March 6, 1886, Glastonbury) See Smith, Abby Hadassah.

SMITH, LAWRENCE HENRY (b Sept. 15, 1892, Racine, Wis.; d Jan. 22, 1958, Washington, D.C.) Lawyer, Wisconsin Republican. U.S. Representative (1941 until death).

SMITH, MARCUS AURELIUS (b Jan. 24, 1851, Harrison County, Ky.; d April 7, 1924, Washington, D.C.) A Kentucky schoolteacher who later practiced law in California, transferred his practice to Tombstone, and made his mark as a Democrat in Arizona's move toward statehood. As a territory: Tombstone district prosecutor (1882), delegate to the U.S. Congress (1887-1895, 1897-1899, 1901-1903, 1905-1909). As a state: U.S. Senate (1912-1921), member of International Joint Boundary Waters Commission (1921 until death).

SMITH, MARTIN FERNARD (b May 28, 1891, Chicago, Ill.; d Oct. 25, 1954,

Bethesda, Md.) Lawyer, Washington Democrat. Hoquiam municipal judge (1914-1917), councilman (1926-1928) and mayor (1928-1930); U.S. Representative (1933-1943), Democratic National Convention delegate (1936), member of the Board of Immigration Appeals (1943-1944), special assistant to the U.S. attorney general (1944 until death).

SMITH, NATHAN *(b Jan. 8, 1770, Woodbury, Conn.; d Dec. 6, 1835, Washington, D.C.)* Lawyer, Connecticut Whig. New Haven County prosecutor (1817-1835), state constitutional convention delegate (1818), unsuccessful candidate for governor (1825), U.S. attorney for the Connecticut district (1829-1832), state representative (1833-1835), U.S. Senate (1833 until death). Brother of Nathaniel and uncle of Truman Smith.

SMITH, NATHANIEL *(b Jan. 6, 1762, Woodbury, Conn.; d March 9, 1822, Woodbury)* Farmer, cattle dealer, lawyer, jurist, Connecticut Federalist. State representative (1789-1795), U.S. Representative (1795-1799), state senate (1800-1805), state supreme court judge (1806-1819), Hartford Convention delegate (1814). Brother of Nathan and uncle of Truman Smith.

SMITH, ROBERT *(b June 12, 1802, Peterborough, N.H.; d Dec. 21, 1867, Alton, Ill.)* Teacher, merchant, textile manufacturer, lawyer, real estate speculator with interests also in waterpower and railroad developments. With all that, he still found time for politics as an Illinois Democrat. State representative (1836-1840) and its enrolling clerk (1840, 1842), U.S. Representative (1843-1849, 1857-1859). Nephew of Jeremiah and Samuel Smith of New Hampshire.

SMITH, SAMUEL *(b Nov. 11, 1765, Peterborough, N.H.; d April 25, 1842,*

Peterborough) Merchant, paper and cotton goods manufacturer, New Hampshire Federalist. Peterborough town moderator (1794-1811), U.S. Representative (1813-1815). Brother of Jeremiah and uncle of Robert Smith. Not to be confused with Samuel Smith of Maryland—see next entry.

SMITH, SAMUEL *(b July 27, 1752, Carlisle, Pa.; d April 22, 1839, Baltimore, Md.)* Merchant, shipper, Revolutionary and War of 1812 officer, Maryland Democrat. U.S. Representative (1793-1803, 1816-1822), U.S. Senate (1803-1815, 1822-1833) and four times elected president pro tem of the Senate (1805-1808); mayor of Baltimore (1837). Not to be confused with Samuel Smith of New Hampshire—see preceding entry.

SMITH, SAMUEL WILLIAM *(b Aug. 23, 1852, Independence Township, Mich.; d June 19, 1931, Detroit, Mich.)* Teacher, lawyer, Michigan Republican. Waterford Township schools superintendent (1875); Oakland County prosecutor (1880-1884), state senate (1885-1887), U.S. Representative (1897-1915).

SMITH, SYLVESTER CLARK *(b Aug. 26, 1858, Henry County, Iowa; d Jan. 26, 1913, Los Angeles, Calif.)* Teacher, farmer, lawyer, editor of the *Kern County Echo*, California Republican. State senate (1894-1902), U.S. Representative (1905 until death).

SMITH, TRUMAN *(b Nov. 27, 1791, Roxbury, Conn.; d May 3, 1884, Stamford, Conn.)* Member of a leading Connecticut family that left its mark on politics, lawyer, and a Whig who, as chairman of the party's national committee (1848), directed Zachary Taylor's successful campaign for the presidency and then declined a cabinet position. State representative (1831, 1832, 1834), U.S. Representative (1839-1843, 1845-1849), presidential elector on the Clay-Frelinghuysen ticket (1844), Whig National Convention delegate (1848), U.S. Senate (1849-1854), Lincoln-appointed judge of the court of arbitration for suppression of the slave trade (1862-1870). Nephew of Nathan and Nathaniel Smith.

SMITH, WALTER INGLEWOOD *(b July 10, 1862, Council Bluffs, Iowa; d Jan. 27, 1922, Council Bluffs)* Lawyer, Iowa Republican who, while a U.S. Representative (1900-1911), investigated hazing at West Point. Fifteenth judicial district judge (1890-1900), U.S. eighth judicial circuit judge (1911 until death).

SMITH, WILLIAM *(b 1762, South Carolina; d June 26, 1840, near Huntsville, Ala.).* Lawyer, planter, and a staunch South Carolina Jeffersonian Democrat (later transferring to Alabama) who firmly believed in slavery and states' rights and was a sworn enemy of John C. Calhoun. In South Carolina: state senator (1803-1808, 1831, 1832) and senate president (1806-1808), circuit court judge (1808-1816), U.S. Senate (1816-1823, 1826-1831), state representative (1824, 1825). In Alabama: state representative (1836-1840), presidential elector on the Van Buren-Johnson ticket (1836). Twice he refused Jackson appointments as associate justice of the U.S. Supreme Court (1829, 1836). (Not to be confused with William Smith of Virginia—see next entry.)

SMITH, WILLIAM *(b Sept. 6, 1797, Marengo, Va.; d May 18, 1887, Warrenton, Va.)* Lawyer, stagecoach tycoon whose carriages carried mail and passengers between Virginia and Georgia, Confederate Army officer, farmer, Virginia Democrat who succumbed to the lure of California gold (1849) but returned after a few brief years. In Virginia: state senate (1836-1841), U.S. Representative (1841-1843, 1853-1861), presidential elector on the Polk-Dallas

ticket (1844), governor (1846-1849, 1864), Confederate States congressman (1862), member of the state house of delegates (1877-1879). In California: president of the first Democratic state convention (1850). (Not to be confused with William Smith of South Carolina and Alabama—see previous entry.)

SMITH, WILLIAM ALDEN *(b May 12, 1859, Dowagiac, Mich.; d Oct. 11, 1932, Grand Rapids, Mich.)* Lawyer, railroad builder and a railroad and steamboat operator, publisher of the *Grand Rapids Herald*, and a state house page who rose to become a member of both houses of the U.S. Congress; Michigan Republican. Assistant secretary of the state senate (1883), state game warden (1887-1891), U.S. Representative (1895-1907) resigning for a U.S. Senate seat (1907-1919).

SMITH, WILLIAM ROBERT *(b Aug. 18, 1863, Smith County, Texas; d Aug. 16, 1924, El Paso, Texas)* Lawyer, Texas Democrat. Thirty-second judicial district judge (1897-1903), U.S. Representative (1903-1917), U.S. judge for the western district of Texas (1917 until death).

SMITH, WILLIAM RUSSELL *(b March 27, 1815, Russellville, Ky.; d Feb. 26, 1896, Washington, D.C.)* Author, playwright, historian, newspaper publisher, educator, Indian fighter, lawyer, Alabama Union Whig and later a Know-Nothing who opposed secession but, when the chips were down, was both an officer in the Confederate Army and a member of the First and Second Confederate Congresses. Mayor of Tuscaloosa (1839) where he also founded and edited the *Mirror*, state representative (1841-1843), seventh judicial circuit judge (1850, 1851), U.S. Representative (1851-1857), state constitutional convention delegate (1861), University of Alabama president (1869-1871).

SMOOT, REED *(b Jan. 10, 1862, Salt Lake City, Utah; d Feb. 9, 1941, St. Petersburg, Fla.)* Banker, miner, rancher, woolen goods manufacturer, Utah Republican and a pillar of the Mormon Church who for thirty years was a U.S. Senator (1903-1933). GOP National Convention delegate (1908, 1912, 1916, 1920, 1924), member of the World War Foreign Debt Commission (1922).

SNELL, BERTRAND HOLLIS *(b Dec. 9, 1870, Colton, N.Y.; d Feb. 2, 1958, Potsdam, N.Y.)* Publisher of the *Potsdam Courier-Freeman*, industrialist, financier with an interest in a great many enterprises, New York Republican who served nearly a quarter-century (1915-1939) as U.S. Representative and was House minority leader (1931-1937). Vice president of the Northern New York Development League (1908-1910), delegate to all GOP National Conventions (1916-1940) and chairman (1932, 1936), president of the Clarkson College Board of Trustees (1920-1945), trustee of Potsdam State Teachers College, Potsdam library, and A. B. Hepburn Memorial Hospital (1910-1948).

SNYDER, CHARLES PHILIP *(b June 9, 1847, Charleston in what is now W.Va.; d Aug. 21, 1915, Vineland, N.J.)* Lawyer, West Virginia Democrat. Kanawha County prosecutor (1876-1884), U.S. Representative (1883-1889), county criminal court judge (1890-1896), U.S. consul to Ciudad Porfirio Diaz, Mexico (1897-1901).

SNYDER, JOHN BUELL *(b July 30, 1877, Upper Turkeyfoot Township, Pa.; d Feb. 4, 1946, Pittsburgh, Pa.).* Teacher, educator, publishing house representative, Pennsylvania Democrat. School principal in Stoyestown, Rockwood, Berlin, and Perry (1901-1912) and board of education member in the latter township (1922-1932), state school director's legislative representative (1921-1923), member of the National Commission of 100 for Study and Survey of Rural Schools in the U.S. (1922-1924), U.S. Representative (1933 until death).

SNYDER, OLIVER P. *(b Nov. 13, 1833, Missouri; d Nov. 22, 1882, Pine Bluff, Ark.)* Lawyer, Arkansas Republican. State representative (1864, 1865), state constitutional convention delegate (1867), presidential elector on the Grant-Colfax ticket (1868), state senate (1868-1871), member of state statutes revision committee (1868), U.S. Representative (1871-1875), Jefferson County treasurer (1882).

SOMERS, ANDREW LAWRENCE *(b March 21, 1895, Brooklyn, N.Y.; d April 6, 1949, St. Albans, N.Y.)* Chemical businessman, Navy flyer during World War I, New York Democrat who was a U.S. Representative for a quarter-century (1925 until death). Democratic National Convention delegate (1928).

SOULÉ, PIERRE *(b Aug. 28, 1801, Castillon, France; d March 26, 1870, New Orleans, La.)* In France first a shepherd, then a teacher, and finally a journalist whose revolutionary writings caused his imprisonment. He escaped, made his way to the United States, finally located in New Orleans, became a lawyer, a Democrat, and a diplomat who opposed secession but fought on the side of the South during the Civil War. It is said that he might have gone far in the Confederacy except for one key factor: Jefferson Davis did not like him. State senate (1845), U.S. Senate (1847, 1849-1853) resigning while John C. Calhoun's successor as leader of the states' rights bloc to become minister to Spain (1853-1855). That post he also resigned after becoming a bumbling administration's scapegoat for the mishandling of the Ostend Manifesto, which he had written, regarding the acquisition of Cuba.

SOUTHARD, HENRY *(b Oct. 7, 1747, Hempstead, N.Y.; d May 22, 1842, Basking Ridge, N.J.)* Farmer, Revolutionary Army wagon master, New Jersey Democrat. Justice of the peace (1787-1792), member of the general assembly (1797-1799, 1811), U.S. Representative (1801-1811, 1815-1821). Father of Isaac and Samuel L. Southard.

SOUTHARD, ISAAC *(b Aug. 30, 1783, Basking Ridge, N.J.; d Sept. 18, 1850, Somerville, N.J.)* Banker, merchant, New Jersey Democrat and supporter of Henry Clay. Lay common pleas court judge and justice of the peace (1820), Somerset County clerk (1820-1830), U.S. Representative (1831-1833), master in chancery (1833), state treasurer (1837-1843). Son of Henry Southard.

SOUTHARD, JAMES HARDING *(b Jan. 20, 1851, Washington Township, Ohio; d Feb. 20, 1919, Toledo, Ohio)* Lawyer, Ohio Republican. Lucas County assistant prosecutor (1882) and then prosecutor for six years, U.S. Representative (1895-1907).

SOUTHARD, SAMUEL LEWIS *(b June 9, 1787, Basking Ridge, N.J.; d June 26, 1842, Fredericksburg, Va.)* Of the three New Jersey Southards, the one who traveled farthest politically. Tutor, lawyer, Democrat. State supreme court law reporter (1814), assemblyman (1815) resigning to become an associate state supreme court justice (1815-1820), Trenton recorder (1818), presidential elector on the Monroe-Tompkins ticket (1820), U.S. Senate (1821-1823) resigning to accept appointments in the Monroe cabinet: secretary of the navy (1823-1829), and interim secretary of war (1824), ad interim secretary of the treasury (1825). State attorney general (1829-1833), governor (1832-1833) resigning to again become a U.S. Senator, this time as a Whig (1833 until death). Both he and his father (Henry Southard) were members of the joint congressional committee that reported the Missouri Compromise measure, father representing the lower house, son the upper.

SOUTHWICK, GEORGE NEWELL *(b March 7, 1863, Albany, N.Y.; d Oct. 17, 1912, Albany).* Reporter, state legislative correspondent of the Associated Press, editor of the *Albany Morning Express* and *Evening Journal*, New York Republican. Chairman of the state GOP convention (1896), U.S. Representative (1895-1899, 1901-1911).

SPAIGHT, RICHARD DOBBS, SR. *(b March 25, 1758, New Bern, N.C.; d Sept. 6, 1802, New Bern, of wounds received in a duel with John Stanly, his fellow townsman and successor in Congress).* Revolutionary Army officer, North Carolina Democrat who was noted for his refusal to knuckle under to party rule. Member of state house of commons (1781-1783) and the Continental Congress (1782-1785), federal Constitutional Convention delegate (1787), state constitutional convention delegate (1788), governor (1792-1795), U.S. Representative (1798-1801), state senate (1801, 1802). Father of Richard Dobbs Spaight, Jr.

SPAIGHT, RICHARD DOBBS, JR. *(b 1796, New Bern, N.C.; d May 2, 1850, New Bern)* Lawyer, planter, North Carolina Democrat who followed in his father's footsteps. Member of state house of commons (1819-1822), U.S. Representative (1823-1825), state senate (1825, 1826), governor (1835-1837), Democratic state convention delegate (1835). Son of Richard Dobbs Spaight, Sr.

SPALDING, BURLEIGH FOLSOM *(b Dec. 3, 1853, Orleans County, Vt.; d March 17, 1934, Fargo, N.Dak.)* A Vermont law student who migrated to the Dakota Territory after being admitted to the bar and had much to do with ultimate statehood and development, North Dakota Republican. Cass County superintendent of public instruction (1882-1884), member of commission to relocate the territorial capital and build a new capitol (1883), North Dakota constitutional convention delegate (1889), member of joint commission to divide property and archives between North and South Dakota, GOP state central committee chairman (1892-1894) and the Cass County Committee Chairman (1896-1898), U.S. Representative (1899-1901, 1903-1905), associate justice of the state supreme court (1907-1911) and chief justice (1911-1915), delegate to most GOP territorial and state conventions (1888-1933), GOP National Convention delegate (1924).

SPARKMAN, STEPHEN MILANCTHON *(b July 29, 1849, Hernando County, Fla.; d Sept. 26, 1929, Washington, D.C.).* Teacher, lawyer, Florida Democrat. Sixth judicial circuit state's attorney (1878-1887), Democratic county executive committee member (1890-1894) and chairman (1890, 1891), state executive committee chairman (1892-1896), Democratic National Convention delegate (1892), U.S. Representative (1895-1917), president of the Tampa Board of Port Commissioners (1917-1920).

SPARKS, WILLIAM ANDREW JACKSON *(b Nov. 19, 1828, near New Albany, Ind.; d May 7, 1904, St. Louis, Mo.).* Teacher, lawyer, Illinois Democrat who, as the Cleveland-appointed commissioner of the U.S. General Land Office (1885-1888), fought on the side of settlers against land speculators, cattlemen, land-grant railroads, and their lackeys in Washington—both in and out of Congress—who would keep the land for selfish interests. U.S. land receiver for the Edwardsville, Ill., land office (1853-1856), presidential elector on the Buchanan-Breckinridge ticket (1856), state representative (1856, 1857),

state senate (1863, 1864), Democratic National Convention delegate (1868), U.S. Representative (1875-1883).

SPEIGHT, JESSE *(b Sept. 22, 1795, Greene County, N.C.; d May 1, 1847, Columbus, Miss.)* A man of varied interests who was a Democratic officeholder both in North Carolina and Mississippi. In North Carolina: member and speaker of the state house of commons (1820), state senate (1823-1827), U.S. Representative (1829-1837). In Mississippi: state senate president (1841-1844), U.S. Senate (1845 until death).

SPENCE, BRENT *(b Dec. 24, 1874, Newport, Ky.; d Sept. 18, 1967, Fort Thomas, Ky.)* Lawyer, Kentucky Democrat, loyal supporter of both the New Deal and Fair Deal who served thirty-two years as a U.S. Representative (1931-1963, at time of retirement, the oldest man ever to serve in the House) and was chairman of the Banking and Currency Committee. State senate (1904-1908), Newport city solicitor (1916-1924).

SPENCE, JOHN SELBY *(b Feb. 29, 1788, Worcester County, Md.; d Oct. 24, 1840, Worcester County)* Physician, Maryland Democrat. Member of state house of delegates and state senate before becoming a U.S. Representative (1823-1825, 1831-1833) and U.S. Senator (1836 until death). Uncle of Thomas Ara Spence.

SPENCE, THOMAS ARA *(b Feb. 20, 1810, Accomac County, Va.; d Nov. 10, 1877, Washington, D.C.)* Lawyer, iron ore producer, Maryland Whig turned Republican. U.S. Representative (1843-1845), Worcester County and twelfth judicial circuit judge (1857-1867), assistant attorney general for the U.S. Post Office Department (1872-1877). Nephew of John S. Spence.

SPENCER, AMBROSE *(b Dec. 13, 1765, Salisbury, Conn.; d March 13, 1848, Lyons, N.Y.)* Lawyer, farmer, New York Democrat turned Whig. Hudson city clerk (1786-1793), state assemblyman (1793-1795), state senate (1794-1804), assistant state attorney general (1796) and attorney general (1802-1804), presidential elector (1808), state supreme court justice (1804-1819) and chief justice (1819-1823), U.S. Representative (1829-1831), mayor of Albany (1824-1826), Whig National Convention delegate (1844). Father of John C. Spencer.

SPENCER, ANNA GARLIN *(b April 17, 1851, Attleboro, Mass.; d Feb. 12, 1931).* Ordained minister, journalist, educator, lecturer, reformer with great energy who, besides occupying a pulpit, worked for women's suffrage, international peace, and other movements dedicated to the betterment of mankind's condition; a public leader who ably filled many important positions, among them being: officer of the American Purity Alliance, associate leader of the New York Society for Ethical Culture, staff lecturer and associate director in the New York School of Philanthropy, director of the Summer School of Ethics of the American Ethical Union, director of the Institute of Municipal and Social Service in Milwaukee. Her writings on social problems included *Woman's Share in Social Culture* (1913) and *The Family and Its Members* (1922).

SPENCER, JOHN CANFIELD *(b Jan. 8, 1788, Hudson, N.Y.; d May 18, 1855, Albany, N.Y.)* One of the ablest lawyers of his time, a New York Democrat turned Whig who resigned his position in the Tyler cabinet rather than agree to the annexation of Texas. Judge advocate general (1813), Canandaigua postmaster (1814), assistant attorney general for western New York (1815), U.S. Representative (1817-1819), assemblyman (1820, 1821, 1831, 1832) and speaker (1821), state senate (1824-1828), secretary of war (1841-1843) and secretary of the treasury (1843-1844). Son of Ambrose Spencer.

SPENCER, SELDEN PALMER *(b Sept. 16, 1862, Erie, Pa.; d May 16, 1925, Washington, D.C.)* Lawyer, teacher, Missouri Republican. State representative (1895, 1896), St. Louis circuit court judge (1897-1903), U.S. Senate (1918 until death), GOP National Convention delegate (1920, 1924).

SPERRY, NEHEMIAH DAY *(b July 10, 1827, Woodbridge, Conn.; d Nov. 13, 1911, New Haven, Conn.)* Teacher, farmer, millwright, builder, Connecticut Republican and for many years the party leader there. New Haven councilman (1853) and alderman (1854), Connecticut secretary of state (1855, 1856), GOP National Convention delegate (1856, 1864, 1888), New Haven postmaster (1861-1866, 1890-1894), U.S. Representative (1895-1911).

SPIGHT, THOMAS *(b Oct. 25, 1841, Tippah County, Miss.; d Jan. 5, 1924, Ripley, Miss.)* Farmer, teacher, lawyer, Confederate Army officer, founding publisher of the *Southern Sentinel* (1879-1884), Mississippi Democrat. State representative (1874-1880), presidential elector on the Hancock-English ticket (1880), third judicial district prosecutor (1884-1892), U.S. Representative (1898-1911).

SPINK, SOLOMON LEWIS *(b March 20, 1831, Whitehall, N.Y.; d Sept. 22, 1881, Yankton, S.Dak.)* New York teacher, Iowa lawyer, and Illinois newspaper editor-publisher (the *Prairie Beacon*) who was appointed secretary of the Dakota Territory by President Lincoln the day before the assassination and served for four years (1865-1869). In Illinois: state representative (1864). In Dakota: delegate to the U.S. Congress (1869-1871).

SPOONER, HENRY JOSHUA *(b Aug. 6, 1839, Providence, R.I.; d Feb. 9, 1918, Providence)* Union Army officer, lawyer, Rhode Island Republican. State representative (1875-1881, 1902) and house speaker (1879-1881), U.S. Representative (1881-1891).

SPOONER, JOHN COLT *(b Jan. 6, 1843, Lawrenceburg, Ind.; d June 11, 1919, New York City)* Union Army officer, lawyer, Wisconsin Republican who was a brilliant debater and parliamentarian whose opinions Presidents Roosevelt and McKinley sought; a stalwart in the party until La Follette's reform movement brought on his retirement from politics and resettlement in New York. State assistant attorney general (1868-1870), assemblyman (1872), U.S. Senate (1885-1891, 1897-1907), chairman of the Wisconsin delegation to the GOP National Convention (1888, 1896) and delegate (1904). Three times he declined cabinet positions offered by McKinley and once by President Taft.

SPRAGUE, CHARLES FRANKLIN *(b June 10, 1857, Boston, Mass.; d Jan. 30, 1902, Providence, R.I.)* Lawyer, Massachusetts Republican. Boston Common Council (1889, 1890), state representative (1891, 1892), Boston Parks Commission chairman (1893, 1894), state senate (1895, 1896), U.S. Representative (1897-1901). Grandson of Peleg Sprague.

SPRAGUE, PELEG *(b April 27, 1793, Duxbury, Mass.; d Oct. 13, 1880, Boston, Mass.)* Lawyer, historian, Maine National Republican turned Whig. State representative (1821, 1822), U.S. Representative (1825-1829), U.S. Senate (1829-1835), presidential elector on the Whig ticket of Harrison and Tyler, U.S. judge for the Massachusetts district (1841-1865). Grandfather of Charles F. Sprague.

SPRAGUE, WILLIAM *(b Nov. 3, 1799, Cranston, R.I.; d Oct. 19, 1856, Providence, R.I.)* Merchant, manufacturer, Rhode Island Whig. State representative and house speaker (1832-1835), U.S. Representative (1835-1837), governor (1838, 1839), U.S. Senate (1842-1844) to fill an unexpired term, presidential elector on the Taylor-Fillmore ticket. Uncle of the younger William Sprague.

SPRAGUE, WILLIAM *(b Sept. 12, 1830, Cranston, R.I.; d Sept. 11, 1915, Paris, France)* Manufacturer, farmer, Rhode Island Unionist turned Republican who followed in his namesake uncle's political footsteps (see preceding). Governor (1860-1863), U.S. Senate (1863-1875), Brown University trustee (1866).

SPRINGER, RAYMOND SMILEY *(b April 26, 1882, Rush County, Ind.; d Aug. 28, 1947, Connersville, Ind.)* Lawyer, Indiana Republican. Fayette County attorney (1908-1914), thirty-seventh judicial circuit judge (1916-1922), U.S. Representative (1939 until death).

SPRINGER, WILLIAM McKENDREE *(b May 30, 1836, Sullivan County, Ind.; d Dec. 4, 1903, Washington, D.C.)* Lawyer, Illinois Democrat who while a congressman introduced bills that brought Montana, the Dakotas, and Washington into the Union as states; a strict, knowledgeable parliamentarian who was chairman of many committees including the powerful Ways and Means Committee. State constitutional convention secretary (1862), state representative (1871, 1872), U.S. Representative (1875-1895), U.S. judge for the Indian Territory's northern district and chief judge of the territory's U.S. Court of Appeals (1895-1900).

SPROUL, WILLIAM HENRY *(b Oct. 14, 1867, Overton County, Tenn.; d Dec. 27, 1932, Kansas City, Mo.)* Farmer, miner, oil and gas businessman, teacher, lawyer, Kansas Republican. Chautauqua County prosecutor (1897-1901), mayor of Sedan (1921-1923), U.S. Representative (1923-1931).

SQUIRE, WATSON CARVOSSO *(b May 18, 1838, Cape Vincent, N.Y.; d June 7, 1926, Seattle, Wash.)* Commander of Union army sharpshooters' company, lawyer who headed West after the Civil War, acquired vast land holdings in the Washington Territory, and became a political power there; financier, Republican. As a territory: governor (1884-1887). As a state: U.S. Senate (1889-1897).

STAFFORD, WILLIAM HENRY *(b Oct. 12, 1869, Milwaukee, Wis.; d April 22, 1957, Milwaukee)* Lawyer, Wisconsin Republican. U.S. Representative (1903-1911, 1913-1919, 1921-1923, 1929-1933).

STANDIFER, JAMES *(b——, Sequatchie Valley, Tenn.; d Aug. 20, 1837, near Kingston, Tenn.)* Tennessee Whig about whom little is known. U.S. Representative (1823-1825, 1829 until death).

STANFIELD, ROBERT NELSON *(b July 9, 1877, Umatilla, Oreg.; d April 13, 1945, Weiser, Idaho)* Stockman, banker, Oregon Republican, state representative (1913-1917) and house speaker in the latter year, U.S. Senate (1921-1927).

STANFORD, LELAND *(b March 9, 1824, Watervliet, N.Y.; d June 21, 1893, Palo Alto, Calif.)* New York and Wisconsin lawyer who headed for California in 1852, struck it rich first as a Placer County storekeeper and then as one of the country's foremost railroad builders and operators, showed an interest in politics, for which he had no flair, yet as Unionist Republican governor (1861-1863) was able to hold California in the Union; rancher with a penchant for growing grapes and raising thoroughbred horses, founder of Leland Stanford University as a memorial to his son who died at fifteen; GOP National Convention delegate (1860), U.S. Senate (1885 until death).

STANFORD, RICHARD *(b March 2, 1767, near Vienna, Md.; d April 9, 1816, Georgetown, D.C.)* Educator, North Carolina Democrat. U.S. Representative (1797 until death). Grandfather of William Robert Webb.

STANLEY, AUGUSTUS OWSLEY *(b May 21, 1867, Shelbyville, Ky.; d Aug. 13, 1958, Washington, D.C.)* Lawyer, educator, Kentucky Democrat who was chairman of the International Joint Commission (IJC) for twenty-one years (1933-1954). Presidential elector on the Bryan-Stevenson ticket (1900), U.S. Representative (1903-1915), governor (1915-1919) resigning to become U.S. Senator (1919-1925), IJC member (1930-1933).

STANLY, EDWARD *(b July 13, 1810, New Bern, N.C.; d July 12, 1872, San Francisco, Calif.)* Lawyer, North Carolina Whig who moved to California (1853), became a Republican and returned to North Carolina for a year (1862-1863) to serve as military governor of its eastern division. While a North Carolina resident: U.S. Representative (1837-1843, 1849-1853), state representative (1844-1846, 1848, 1849) and house speaker (1846). In California: unsuccessful candidate for governor (1857). Son of John Stanly.

STANLY, JOHN *(b April 9, 1774, New Bern, N.C.; d Aug. 2, 1834, New Bern)*. North Carolina lawyer who killed his fellow townsman, State Senator Richard D. Spaight, Sr., in a duel (Sept. 6, 1802) a year after winning the latter's seat as a U.S. Representative (1801-1803, 1809-1811). State house of commons (1798, 1799, 1812-1815, 1818, 1819, 1823-1825, 1826). Father of Edward Stanly.

STANTON, ELIZABETH CADY *(b Nov. 12, 1815, Johnstown, N.Y.; d Oct. 26, 1902, New York City)* One of the most influential women's rights leaders of her day, journalist, writer, orator who, though the mother of seven children, lectured widely and spoke before legislative bodies and congressional committees in the interest of temperance, abolition, and women's rights, the last being her first interest. She received a better education than most women of her time, graduating from what became the famous Emma Willard School in Troy, N.Y., then, for a time, studied law in the office of her father, Judge Daniel Cady.

Married to abolitionist-lawyer-journalist Henry Brewster Stanton in 1840, she insisted upon the word "obey" being stricken from the ceremony, a radical act in those times of almost complete female subjugation to the male sex. This was but one of a lifetime of radical acts. A few months after the wedding, she went with her husband to the world antislavery convention in London where the discovery that women delegates were excluded from the floor had a profound effect upon her, intensifying the feelings of concern she had developed listening to helpless women in her father's law office pouring out their heart-rending tales of abuse. She began to work actively for her three causes, and with Lucretia Mott she organized the first women's rights convention in the United States which was held at Seneca Falls, N.Y., in 1848. She overrode Mrs. Mott's objections and had a suffrage clause included in the bill of rights for women that the group drew up.

In 1851, Elizabeth Stanton met Susan B. Anthony and from that time on, until the former's death, the two became a remarkably effective team. Spinster Susan was a superb organizer and executive, able to devote her entire life to the causes they espoused, while Mrs.

Stanton was a brilliant orator and more adept in dealing with people.

In 1869, Mrs. Stanton was chosen president of the newly formed National Woman Suffrage Association. Twenty years later, when it was united with the American Woman Suffrage Association to form the National American Woman Suffrage Association, Mrs. Stanton was elected president. Author of many articles published in newspapers and periodicals; for two years an editor on the *Revolution*, a militant feminist weekly magazine; helped publish the *Woman's Bible* and, with Susan B. Anthony and Matilda Joslyn Gage, compiled the first three volumes of the *History of Woman Suffrage*.

STANTON, FREDERICK PERRY *(b Dec. 22, 1814, Alexandria, Va.; d June 4, 1894, Stanton, Fla.)* Teacher, lawyer, Tennessee Democrat who was rewarded by appointment to govern the Kansas Territory (1858-1861). In Tennessee: U.S. Representative (1845-1855).

STANTON, JOSEPH, JR. *(b July 19, 1739, Charlestown, R.I.; d 1807, Charlestown)* Revolutionary army officer, Rhode Island Democrat. State representative (1768-1774, 1794-1800), state constitutional convention delegate (1790), U.S. Senate (1790-1793), U.S. Representative (1801-1807).

STARK, WILLIAM LEDYARD *(b July 29, 1853, Mystic, Conn.; d Nov. 11, 1922, Tarpon Springs, Fla.)* Teacher, store clerk, lawyer, Nebraska Populist-Democrat-Fusionist who was elected a U.S. Representative as a Democrat and served three terms (1897-1903).

STEAGALL, HENRY BASCOM *(b May 19, 1873, Clopton, Ala.; d Nov. 22, 1943, Washington, D.C.)* Lawyer, Alabama Democrat who was elected a U.S. Representative fifteen times (1915 until death). Dale County solicitor (1902-

1908), state representative (1906, 1907), state Democratic executive committee member (1906-1910), third judicial circuit prosecutor (1907-1914), Democratic National Convention delegate (1912).

STEDMAN, CHARLES MANLY *(b Jan. 29, 1841, Pittsboro, N.C.; d Sept. 23, 1930, Washington, D.C.)* Confederate Army officer, teacher, lawyer, railroad president, North Carolina Democrat. National convention delegate (1880), lieutenant governor (1884-1888), state bar association president (1900, 1901), University of North Carolina trustee (1899-1915), U.S. Representative (1911 until death).

STEELE, GEORGE WASHINGTON *(b Dec. 13, 1839, Fayette County, Ind.; d July 12, 1922, Marion, Ind.)* Union Army officer who marched with Sherman to the sea, farmer, Indiana Republican who was the Oklahoma Territory's first governor (1890, 1891). In Indiana: U.S. Representative (1881-1889, 1895-1903), governor of Marion's National Military Home (1904-1915).

STEELE, WILLIAM RANDOLPH *(b July 24, 1842, New York City; d Nov. 30, 1901, Deadwood, S.Dak.)* Union Army officer who then studied for the law in New York, found big city life too prosaic and thus practiced his profession in Wyoming Territory and South Dakota; Democrat. In Wyoming: member of the territorial legislative council (1871-1873), delegate to the U.S. Congress (1873-1877). In South Dakota: mayor of Deadwood (1894-1896).

STEENERSON, HALVOR *(b June 30, 1852, Dane County, Wis.; d Nov. 22, 1926, Crookston, Minn.).* Lawyer, Minnesota Republican. Polk County prosecutor (1881-1883), state senate (1883-1887), GOP National Convention delegate (1884, 1888), U.S. Representative (1903-1923).

STEFAN, KARL *(b March 1, 1884, Bohemia; d Oct. 2, 1951, Washington, D.C.)* Radio commentator, telegrapher, journalist, publishers' circulation representative, Nebraska Republican. U.S. Representative (1935 until death), member congressional committee to aid inauguration of the Philippine Commonwealth government (1935), Interparliamentary Union delegate (1939), official adviser to the United Nations Conference in San Francisco (1945).

STEIWER, FREDERICK *(b Oct. 13, 1883, Marion County, Oreg.; d Feb. 3, 1939, Washington, D.C.)* Lawyer, farmer, Oregon Republican. Umatilla County deputy district attorney (1909, 1910) and district attorney (1912-1916), state senate (1916, 1917), U.S. Senate (1927-1938), GOP National Convention delegate (1936).

STEPHENS, ALEXANDER HAMILTON *(b Feb. 11, 1812, Crawfordville, Ga.; d March 4, 1883, Atlanta, Ga.)* Lawyer, Georgia Whig turned Democrat who was one of the South's most important political figures of his time, serving as vice president of the Confederate States (1861-1865) and who, as early as 1850, warned the U.S. Congress that "whenever this government is brought in hostile array against me and mine, I am for disunion openly, boldly, and fearless. I am for revolution." As vice president, he had numerous fallings out with Jefferson Davis and soon became leader of the opposition. He was imprisoned in Boston for five months after the Civil War but nevertheless urged restraint and self-discipline upon the South during the Reconstruction.

State representative (1836-1841), state senate (1842), U.S. Representative (1843-1859, 1873-1882), presidential elector on the Douglas-Johnson ticket (1860), state secession convention delegate (1861), commissioner to represent the Confederacy at the Hampton Roads conference (1865), elected to the U.S. Senate (1866) but not permitted to take his seat because he represented a "rebel" state, governor (1882 until death).

STEPHENS, DAN VOORHEES *(b Nov. 4, 1868, Bloomington, Ind.; d Jan. 13, 1939, Fremont, Nebr.)* Educator, author, farmer, manufacturer, publisher, banker, Nebraska Democrat. Dodge County schools superintendent (1890-1894), Democratic National Convention delegate (1904, 1908, 1920, 1924, 1932), U.S. Representative (1911-1919), member of state board of education (1923-1926).

STEPHENS, HUBERT DURRETT *(b July 2, 1875, New Albany, Miss.; d March 14, 1946, New Albany)* Lawyer, Mississippi Democrat. Second district attorney (1907-1910), U.S. Representative (1911-1921), U.S. Senate (1923-1935), Reconstruction Finance Corporation director (1935, 1936).

STEPHENS, JOHN HALL *(b Nov. 22, 1847, Shelby County, Tex.; d Nov. 18, 1924, Monrovia, Calif.)* Lawyer, Texas Democrat. State senate (1886-1888), U.S. Representative (1897-1917).

STEPHENS, WILLIAM DENNISON *(b Dec. 26, 1859, Eaton, Ohio; d April 25, 1944, Los Angeles, Calif.)* Teacher, lawyer, railroad builder-operator, wholesale grocer, California Republican. Los Angeles Board of Education member (1906), Los Angeles Chamber of Commerce president (1907), mayor (1909), U.S. Representative (1911-1916), lieutenant governor for two months in 1917 and then governor (1917-1923).

STEPHENSON, ISAAC *(b June 18, 1829, Yorkton, New Brunswick, Canada; d March 15, 1918, Marinette, Wis.).* Lumberman, banker, Wisconsin Republican. State assemblyman (1866, 1868), GOP National Convention delegate (1880, 1892), U.S. Representative

(1883-1889), U.S. Senate (1907-1915). Brother of Samuel M. Stephenson.

STEPHENSON, SAMUEL MERRITT *(b Dec. 23, 1831, Hartland, New Brunswick, Canada; d July 31, 1907, Menominee, Mich.)* Lumberman, real estate operator, merchant, farmer, Michigan Republican who for several years was chairman of the Menominee County Board of Supervisors. State representative (1877, 1878), state senate (1879, 1880, 1885, 1886), presidential elector on the Garfield-Arthur ticket (1880), GOP National Convention delegate (1884, 1888), U.S. Representative (1889-1897). Brother of Isaac Stephenson.

STERLING, JOHN ALLEN *(b Feb. 1, 1857, McLean County, Ill.; d Oct. 17, 1918, near Pontiac, Ill.)* Lawyer, Illinois Republican. McLean County state's attorney (1892-1896), GOP state central committee member (1896-1898), U.S. Representative (1903-1913, 1915 until death of auto accident injuries). Brother of Thomas Sterling.

STERLING, THOMAS *(b Feb. 21, 1851, Fairfield County, Ohio; d Aug. 26, 1930, Washington, D.C.)* Lawyer, educator and a Republican whose career took him to Illinois, Dakota Territory where he helped bring about statehood for South Dakota, and Washington, D.C. where he was on the faculty of the National University Law School. In Illinois: Bement schools superintendent (1875-1877), Springfield city prosecutor (1880, 1881). In Dakota Territory: Spink County district attorney (1886-1888), state constitutional convention delegate (1889). In South Dakota: state senate (1890), dean of the University of South Dakota College of Law at Vermillion (1901-1911), U.S. Senate (1913-1925), Coolidge-appointed field secretary (1925) of the commission created to celebrate George Washington's 200th birthday. Brother of John A. Sterling.

STEVENS, CHARLES ABBOT *(b Aug. 9, 1816, North Andover, Mass.; d April 7, 1892, New York City)* Flannels and broadcloth manufacturer, Massachusetts Republican who served less than two months (Jan. 27-March 3, 1875) as a U.S. Representative to fill a vacancy. State representative (1853), GOP National Convention delegate (1860, 1868), member of governor's council (1867-1870). Brother of Moses T. and cousin of Isaac I. Stevens.

STEVENS, FREDERICK CLEMENT *(b Jan. 1, 1861, Boston, Mass.; d July 1, 1923, St. Paul, Minn.)* Lawyer, Minnesota Republican. State representative (1888-1891), U.S. Representative (1897-1915).

STEVENS, HIRAM SANFORD *(b March 20, 1832, Weston, Vt.; d March 22, 1893, Tucson, Ariz.)* A Vermont farmer who found that life much too tame, joined the army for four years (1852-1856) of Indian fighting in New Mexico, then became a merchandise and forage supplier for the army with Tucson as his base where he showed a flair for cattle growing and politics; Arizona Territory Democrat. Territorial representative (1868), member of the territorial council (1871-1873), Tucson treasurer (1871), U.S. Congress delegate (1875-1879).

STEVENS, ISAAC INGALLS *(b March 25, 1818, North Andover, Mass.; d Sept. 1, 1862, in the Battle of Chantilly, Va.).* Head-of-his-class West Point graduate, became an army engineer, staff aide to General Winfield Scott in the Mexican War, assistant in charge of the Coast Survey Office in Washington, D.C., organizer and leader of the exploration party that laid out the route for a St. Paul-to-Puget Sound railroad, resigned his commission to remain in the Washington Territory, turned his interest to politics as a Democrat, rejoined the Union Army when the Civil War began,

was a brigadier general when killed in action. Territorial governor (1853-1857), U.S. Congress delegate (1857-1861). Cousin of Charles A. and Moses T. Stevens.

STEVENS, MOSES TYLER *(b Oct. 10, 1825, North Andover, Mass.; d March 25, 1907, North Andover)* Woolen goods manufacturer, banker, Massachusetts Democrat. State representative (1861), state senate (1868), U.S. Representative (1891-1895). Brother of Charles A. and cousin of Isaac I. Stevens.

STEVENS, RAYMOND BARTLETT *(b June 18, 1874, Binghamton, N.Y.; d May 18, 1942, Indianapolis, Ind.)* Lawyer, New Hampshire Democrat, nine of whose public years were spent in a way not often accorded a political figure: as foreign affairs adviser to the King of Siam (1926-1935). State representative (1909, 1911, 1913, 1923), state constitutional convention delegate (1912), U.S. Representative (1913-1915), special counsel to the Federal Trade Commission (1915-1917), U.S. representative to the Allied Maritime Transport Council (1917, 1918), vice chairman of the U.S. Shipping Board (1917-1920), Democratic National Convention delegate (1920, 1924), Federal Trade Commission member (1935-1942) and its chairman (1937-1942).

STEVENS, THADDEUS *(b April 4, 1792, Danville, Vt.; d Aug. 11, 1868, Washington, D.C.)* Lawyer, champion of the poor and the downtrodden, foe of Andrew Jackson, ardent antislaver who made a practice of defending captured fugitive slaves, leader of the free-soil movement in Congress, Pennsylvania Whig-Republican who was chairman of the managers named to conduct impeachment proceedings against President Andrew Johnson. State representative (1833-1835, 1837, 1841), state constitutional convention delegate

(1838), canal commissioner (1838), U.S. Representative (1849-1853, 1859 until death).

STEVENSON, ADLAI EWING *(b Oct. 23, 1835, Christian County, Ky.; d June 14, 1914, Chicago, Ill.)* Lawyer, Illinois Democrat whose namesake grandson's biography follows. Master in chancery (1860-1864), presidential elector on the McClellan-Pendleton ticket (1864), Woodford County district attorney (1865-1868), U.S. Representative (1875-1877, 1879-1881), Democratic National Convention delegate (1884, 1892), first assistant U.S. postmaster general (1885-1889), vice president of the United States under Grover Cleveland (1893-1897).

STEVENSON, ADLAI EWING *(b Feb. 5, 1900, Los Angeles, Calif.; d July 14, 1965, London, England)* Twice candidate for president of the United States, lawyer, statesman, author, for a time editor-publisher of the family-owned Bloomington *Daily Pantagraph*, Illinois Democrat whose obituary filled a full page in the *New York Times* under an eight-column headline that called him "An Urbane, Witty, Articulate Politician and Diplomat."

Special assistant to Secretary of the Navy Frank Knox (1941-1943), head of an economic mission to Italy to plan for the occupation (1943), assistant to Secretaries of State Edward R. Stettinius, Jr. and James F. Byrnes, Jr. (1943-1945), adviser to the U.S. delegation at the San Francisco Conference on World Organization and U.S. Representative to the London Preparatory Commission for the United Nations (1945), senior adviser to the U.S. delegation at the first session of the U.N. General Assembly in London (1946) and alternate delegate to the General Assembly in New York (1946, 1947).

Governor (1949-1953), Democratic presidential opponent of Dwight D. Eisenhower (1952, 1956) who was at the crest of his popularity with Stevenson polling only 89 electoral votes to Ike's 442 in 1952 and losing by 73-457 in 1956. Foreign policy adviser to John F. Kennedy during the presidential campaign (1960), Kennedy-appointed U.S. ambassador to the United Nations with cabinet status (1961 until death), Kennedy's special envoy on a tour of ten Latin American nations (1961).

His seven published books: *Major Campaign Speeches, 1952, Call to Greatness, What I Think, The New America, Friends and Enemies, Putting First Things First,* and *Looking Outward.* Grandson of the elder Adlai E. Stevenson.

STEVENSON, ANDREW *(b Jan. 21, 1784, Culpeper County, Va.; d Jan. 25, 1857, Albemarle County, Va.).* Lawyer, planter, Virginia Democrat. Member of state house of delegates (1809-1816, 1818-1821) and speaker (1812-1815), U.S. Representative (1821-1834) and House speaker (1827-1834) resigning because of poor health, minister to Great Britain (1836-1841). Father of John W. Stevenson.

STEVENSON, JOHN WHITE *(b May 4, 1812, Richmond, Va.; d Aug. 10, 1886, Covington, Ky.)* Lawyer-son of Andrew Stevenson of Virginia who, while otherwise more than following in his father's footsteps, chose Kentucky as his domain; Democrat. State representative (1845-1849), state constitutional delegate (1849), member of commission to revise the state's civil and criminal codes (1850, 1851), Democratic National Convention delegate (1848, 1852, 1856) and chairman (1880), presidential elector on the Pierce-King (1852) and Buchanan-Breckinridge (1856) tickets, U.S. Representative (1857-1861); lieutenant governor (1867) becoming governor in the same year upon the death of the incumbent, John L. Helm, and serving until 1871 when he resigned to become a U.S.

Senator (1871-1877); American Bar Association president (1884, 1885).

STEVENSON, WILLIAM FRANCIS *(b Nov. 23, 1861, in what is now Loray, N.C.; d Feb. 12, 1942, Washington, D.C.)* Teacher, lawyer, South Carolina Democrat. Member of Chesterfield County Democratic Executive Committee (1888-1914) and its chairman (1896-1902), mayor of Cheraw (1895, 1896), state representative (1896-1902, 1910-1914) and speaker (1900-1902), Democratic state executive committee member (1901-1942), state dispensary commission's general counsel (1907-1911), U.S. Representative (1917-1933), member of the Federal Home Loan Bank Board (1933-1939) and chairman (1933).

STEWART, ANDREW, SR. *(b June 11, 1791, Fayette County, Pa.; d July 16, 1872, Uniontown, Pa.)* Lawyer, builder, real estate speculator, Pennsylvania Democrat-Whig-Republican. State representative (1815-1818), western Pennsylvania district U.S. attorney (1818-1820), U.S. Representative (1821-1829, 1831-1835) as a Democrat and as a Whig (1843-1849). Father of the following.

STEWART, ANDREW, JR. *(b April 6, 1836, Uniontown, Pa.; d Nov. 9, 1903, Stewarton, Pa.)* Union Army officer who was captured and held prisoner for a year, paper pulp manufacturer, Pennsylvania Republican, GOP National Convention delegate (1876), U.S. Representative for a year (1891-1892) when his election was successfully contested. Son of the preceding.

STEWART, JOHN WOLCOTT *(b Nov. 24, 1825, Middlebury, Vt.; d Oct. 29, 1915, Middlebury)* Lawyer, banker, Vermont Republican. Addison County prosecutor (1852-1854), state representative (1856, 1865-1867, 1876), and speaker (1865-1867, 1876), GOP National Convention chairman (1860), state sen-

ate (1861, 1862), governor (1870-1872), U.S. Representative (1883-1891), U.S. Senate to fill a vacancy (1908).

STEWART, PAUL *(b Feb. 27, 1892, Clarksville, Ark.; d Nov. 13, 1950, Antlers, Okla.)* Merchant, farmer, lawyer, cattle raiser, hotel operator and an Oklahoma Democrat who was editor-publisher of the *Antlers American* (1929 until death). Haworth postmaster (1914-1922), state representative (1922-1926), state senate (1926-1942) and his party's floor leader (1929, 1930) and president pro tem (1933, 1934), acting governor (1933), U.S. Representative (1943-1947).

STEWART, WILLIAM MORRIS *(b Aug. 9, 1827, Wayne County, N.Y.; d April 23, 1909, Washington, D.C.)* Teacher, miner, lawyer who helped legally to develop the Comstock Lode, and (as a senator) wrote the Fifteenth Amendment to the U.S. Constitution. California and Nevada Republican. In California: Nevada County district attorney (1852), attorney general (1854). In Nevada as a territory: member of the territorial council (1861), state constitutional convention delegate (1863). As a state: U.S. Senate (1864-1875, 1887-1905).

STIGLER, WILLIAM GRADY *(b July 7, 1891, Stigler, then Indian Territory; d Aug. 21, 1952, Stigler, Okla.)* Lawyer, Oklahoma Democrat. City attorney (1920-1924), state senate (1924-1932) and president pro tem (1931), U.S. Representative (1944 until death).

STOCKTON, JOHN POTTER *(b Aug. 2, 1826, Princeton, N.J.; d Jan. 22, 1900, New York City)* Lawyer, New Jersey Democrat who was a delegate to all Democratic National Conventions (1864 until death). Chancery court reporter (1852-1858), U.S. ambassador to Italy (1857-1861), U.S. Senate (1865-1866,

1869-1875), state attorney general (1877-1892). Son of Robert F. Stockton.

STOCKTON, RICHARD, SR. *(b Oct. 1, 1730, Somerset County, N.J.; d Feb. 28, 1781, Somerset County)* Lawyer, New Jersey signer of the Declaration of Independence who, while a congressman, was held prisoner by Tories for a month in 1776; first of four generations of New Jersey Stocktons to hold office. Member of New Jersey Executive Council (1768-1776), associate justice of the New Jersey Supreme Court (1774-1776) and chief justice thereafter, member of the Continental Congress (1776). Father of Richard Stockton, Jr., grandfather of Robert F. Stockton, great-grandfather of John P. Stockton.

STOCKTON, RICHARD, JR. *(b April 17, 1764, Princeton, N.J.; d March 7, 1828, Mercer County, N.J.)* Lawyer, New Jersey Federalist. Presidential elector on the Washington-Adams (1792) and Adams-Pinckney (1800) tickets, U.S. Senate (1796-1799) to fill a vacancy, unsuccessful candidate for governor (1801), both state assemblyman and U.S. Representative (1813-1815). Son of preceding and father of Robert F. Stockton.

STOCKTON, ROBERT FIELD *(b Aug. 20, 1795, Princeton, N.J.; d Oct. 7, 1866, Princeton)* Career Navy man (1811-1850) who as a commodore participated in the capture (1845) of California's Mexican capital and organized a civil government there; New Jersey Democrat who was president of the Delaware & Raritan Canal (1853-1866). U.S. Senate (1851-1853), member of peace convention (1861) that tried to avert the Civil War. Son of Richard Stockton, Jr., and father of John P. Stockton.

STOKES, MONTFORT *(b March 12, 1762, Lunenberg County, Va.; d Nov. 4, 1842, Fort Gibson, in what is now Oklahoma)* Revolutionary War sailor who was captured by the British, planter, North Carolina Democrat who, after public service there, was sent west (1832) as a member of the Board of Indian Commissioners and later was chosen to negotiate treaties with various tribes. Assistant clerk of the state senate (1786-1790), superior court clerk (1790), University of North Carolina trustee (1805-1838), U.S. Senate (1816-1823), state senator (1826-1829), member of the state house of commons (1829-1830) and its president in the latter year, president of the West Point Board of Visitors (1830), governor (1830-1832), Democratic presidential elector (1804, 1812, 1824, 1828).

STONE, DAVID *(b Feb. 17, 1770, Hope, N.C.; d Oct. 7, 1818, Wake County, N.C.)* Lawyer, planter, North Carolina Democrat. Member of state house of commons (1791-1794), state supreme court judge (1794-1798), U.S. Representative (1799-1801), U.S. Senate (1801-1807, 1813-1814), governor (1808-1810).

STONE, FREDERICK *(b Feb. 7, 1820, Charles County, Md.; d Oct. 17, 1899, near LaPlata, Md.)* Lawyer, Maryland Democrat. Member of commission to revise rules of the state courts (1852), house of delegates (1864, 1865), U.S. Representative (1867-1871), associate judge of the court of appeals (1881-1890). Grandson of Michael J. Stone.

STONE, LUCY *(b Aug. 13, 1818, near West Brookfield, Mass.; d Oct. 18, 1893, Dorchester, Mass.)* Pioneer in women's rights, abolitionist, eloquent and much-sought-after public speaker, editor. Early in life Lucy Stone determined not to be bound by the prevailing belief that women were, by divine right, the chattels of the male sex, a fact she learned the hard way when her well-to-do father refused to send her to college. So she taught school for nine years in order to pay her way through Oberlin

College. She tried to avoid marriage but fell in love with Henry Brown Blackwell, gave in and married him in 1855. She refused, however, to take his name and insisted on being addressed as Mrs. Stone. Henry, far from interfering with his wife's work, joined her in it. Lucy Stone was a member of a group of women leaders of her day, including Susan B. Anthony and her sister-in-law, Antoinette Brown Blackwell, who, though they often disagreed with each other, were united in their dedication to the cause of freeing their sex from bondage.

In 1866 Lucy Stone became a member of the executive committee of the newly formed American Equal Rights Association. Disagreement developed over many things, there was a split, and Lucy helped form the American Woman Suffrage Association. Twenty years later, when it united with the more militant National American Woman Suffrage Association, she was made a member of the executive committee and served briefly as chairman.

In 1870, Lucy Stone, with her husband, launched the *Woman's Journal.* Its editorship was assumed in 1881 by their daughter, Alice Stone Blackwell, also a woman suffragist.

STONE, MICHAEL JENIFER *(b 1747, Charles County, Md.; d 1812, Charles County)* Maryland jurist who was a U.S. Representative in the first Congress (1789-1791) and before that a delegate to the state convention that ratified the federal Constitution (1788) and a member of the state house of delegates (1781-1783). First judicial district judge (1791 until death). Brother of Thomas and grandfather of Frederick Stone.

STONE, THOMAS *(b 1743, Poynton Manor, Md.; d Oct. 5, 1787, Alexandria, Va.)* Lawyer, Maryland signer of the Declaration of Independence. Member of the Continental Congress (1775-

1779, 1784, 1785), state senate (1779-1783). Brother of Michael J. Stone.

STONE, WILLIAM JOEL *(b May 7, 1848, Madison County, Ky.; d April 14, 1918, Washington, D.C.)* Lawyer, Missouri Democrat who was chairman of the Senate Committee on Foreign Relations during World War I. Bedford, Ind., city attorney briefly (1870) then moved to Missouri; Vernon County prosecutor (1873, 1874), presidential elector on the Tilden-Hendricks ticket (1876), U.S. Representative (1885-1891), governor (1893-1897), Democratic National Committee member (1896-1904) and vice chairman (1900-1904), U.S. Senate (1903 until death).

STONE, WILLIAM JOHNSON *(b June 26, 1841, Kuttawa, Ky.; d March 12, 1923, Frankfort, Ky.)* Confederate Army officer, farmer, merchant, Kentucky Democrat. State representative (1867, 1875, 1883) and house speaker (1875), U.S. Representative (1885-1895), the state's Confederate pension commissioner (1912 until death).

STORER, BELLAMY, SR. *(b March 26, 1796, Portland, Maine; d June 1, 1875, Cincinnati, Ohio).* Lawyer, educator, jurist, Ohio Whig. U.S. Representative (1835-1837), presidential elector on the Clay-Frelinghuysen ticket (1844), Cincinnati Law School professor (1855-1874), Cincinnati Superior Court judge (1854-1872). Father of the following.

STORER, BELLAMY, JR. *(b Aug. 28, 1847, Cincinnati, Ohio; d Nov. 12, 1922, Paris, France)* Lawyer, diplomat, Ohio Republican. Assistant U.S. attorney for Ohio's northern district, U.S. Representative (1891-1895), assistant secretary of state (1897); ambassador to Belgium (1897-1899), Spain (1899-1902) and Austria-Hungary (1902-1906). Son of the preceding. Uncle of Nicholas Longworth.

STOREY, MOORFIELD (b March 19, 1845, Roxbury, Mass.; d Oct. 24, 1929, Lincoln, Mass.) Massachusetts lawyer, author, reformer whose two main objectives were the end of corruption in politics and a better deal for Negroes and Indians; first president of the National Association for the Advancement of Colored People (1910 until death). Because of his strong anti-establishment convictions he never got anywhere politically. He was a leading figure in the Mugwump movement, the Anti-Imperialist League, and in 1900 considered running for president on a third-party ticket. Much earlier in life (1867-1869), he was secretary to Charles Sumner, chairman of the Senate Committee on Foreign Relations, and so was party to the impeachment proceedings against Andrew Johnson.

STORRS, HENRY RANDOLPH (b Sept. 3, 1787, Middletown, Conn.; d July 29, 1837, New Haven, Conn.) Lawyer, New York Federalist. U.S. Representative (1817-1821, 1823-1831), presiding judge of the Oneida County common pleas court (1825-1829). Brother of William L. Storrs.

STORRS, WILLIAM LUCIUS (b March 25, 1795, Middletown, Conn.; d June 25, 1851, Hartford, Conn.) Yale and Wesleyan law professor, Connecticut Whig. State representative (1827-1829, 1834) and house speaker (1834), U.S. Representative (1829-1833, 1839-1840) resigning to become associate judge of the state supreme court (1840-1856) and chief judge (1856 until death). Brother of Henry R. Storrs.

STORY, JOSEPH (b Sept. 18, 1779, Marblehead, Mass.; d Sept. 10, 1845, Cambridge, Mass.) Lawyer, Massachusetts Democrat who as an associate justice of the U.S. Supreme Court (1811 until death) was credited with building a solid foundation under the nation's admiralty laws. As a law pro-

fessor (1829 until death), he was a founder of the Harvard Law School. State representative (1805-1807, 1811) and house speaker (1811), U.S. Representative (1808-1809) to fill a vacancy.

STOWE, HARRIET BEECHER (b June 14, 1811, Litchfield, Conn.; d July 1, 1896, Hartford, Conn.) American novelist whose book, Uncle Tom's Cabin, sold over 300,000 copies in one year and had a profound influence on the antislavery sentiment that helped precipitate the Civil War. Like the rest of the famous Beecher family—she was Lyman's daughter, Henry and Catharine's sister—she was deeply religious, although she questioned her father's orthodoxy, and had a passionate desire to reform mankind and improve his condition. Married (1836) to Calvin Ellis Stowe, professor of Biblical literature in the Cincinnati Theological Seminary run by Harriet's father; the couple had seven children. Calvin Stowe received a professorship at Bowdoin College, Brunswick, Maine, in 1850. It was there in New England, where feeling against slavery and especially the Fugitive Slave Act was strong, that Harriet wrote Uncle Tom's Cabin, first published as a serial (1851-1852), then as a two-volume novel (1852). Harriet was a prolific writer, sincere and uncorrupted by her extraordinary success, but was plagued by money worries all of her married life, due to her own and her husband's lack of management ability.

STRAIT, HORACE BURTON (b Jan. 26, 1835, Potter County, Pa.; d Feb. 25, 1894, Juarez, Mexico) Union Army officer, merchant, farmer, manufacturer, banker, Minnesota Republican. Mayor of Shakopee (1870-1873), U.S. Representative (1873-1879, 1881-1887).

STRONG, CALEB (b Jan. 9, 1745, Northampton, Mass.; d Nov. 7, 1819, Northampton) Lawyer, Massachusetts

Federalist. Member of Correspondence and Safety Committee (1774, 1775), state representative (1776-1778), state senate (1780-1788), county attorney (1776-1800), delegate to both the U.S. Constitutional Convention and the state convention that ratified it (1788), U.S. Senate (1789-1796), presidential elector on the Pinckney-King ticket (1809), governor (1800-1807, 1812-1816).

STRONG, JAMES GEORGE (b April 23, 1870, Dwight, Ill.; d Jan. 11, 1938, Washington, D.C.) Insurance broker, real estate speculator, moneylender, lawyer, merchant, farmer, founder of telephone and power companies, Kansas Republican. Blue Rapids city attorney (1896-1911), Marshall County assistant attorney general (1911, 1912), GOP National Convention delegate (1912, 1928), Blue Rapids school board member (1913-1916), county prosecutor (1916, 1917), U.S. Representative (1919-1933), first assistant treasurer of the Home Owners' Loan Corporation (1933 until death).

STRONG, NATHAN LEROY (b Nov. 12, 1859, Troy, now Summerville, Pa.; d Dec. 14, 1939, Brookville, Pa.) Telegraph operator, railroad agent, lawyer, mineral lands developer, banker, mining executive, railroad promoter, Pennsylvania Republican. Jefferson County district attorney (1895-1900), U.S. Representative (1917-1935).

STRONG, THERON RUDD (b Nov. 7, 1802, Salisbury, Conn.; d May 14, 1873, New York City) Lawyer, New York Democrat. Wayne County district attorney (1835-1839), U.S. Representative (1839-1841), assemblyman (1842), associate justice of the state supreme court (1851-1859) and also appeals court judge in the latter year. Cousin of William Strong.

STRONG, WILLIAM (b May 6, 1808, Somers, Conn.; d Aug. 19, 1895, Lake Minnewassa, N.Y.) Teacher, lawyer, Pennsylvania Democrat whom Grant appointed associate justice of the U.S. Supreme Court despite charges of packing, but in his eleven-year tenure (1870-1880) became, according to at least one biographer, "one of the truly great judges of the Court." U.S. Representative (1847-1851), associate state supreme court justice (1857-1868). Cousin of Theron R. Strong.

STROTHER, GEORGE FRENCH (b 1783, Stevensburg, Va.; d Nov. 28, 1840, St. Louis, Mo.) Lawyer, Virginia Democrat who was the first of three generations of Strothers to serve in Congress. State delegate (1806-1809), U.S. Representative (1817-1820). Father of James F. Strother.

STROTHER, JAMES FRENCH (b Sept. 4, 1811, Culpeper, Va.; d Sept. 20, 1860, near Culpeper) Lawyer, Virginia Whig. State house of delegates (1840-1851) and speaker (1851), state constitutional convention delegate (1850), U.S. Representative (1851-1853). Son of George F. Strother and grandfather of the following.

STROTHER, JAMES FRENCH (b June 29, 1868, near Pearisburg, Va.; d April 10, 1930, Welch, W.Va.) Lawyer, jurist, Virginia and West Virginia Republican. In Virginia: deputy collector of internal revenue at Lynchburg (1890-1893). In West Virginia: U.S. commissioner (1897-1901), McDowell County criminal court judge (1905-1924), U.S. Representative (1925-1929). Grandson of the preceding.

STROWD, WILLIAM FRANKLIN (b Dec. 7, 1832, Orange County, N.C.; d Dec. 12, 1911, Chapel Hill, N.C.) Confederate soldier, farmer, North Carolina Populist. State constitutional convention delegate (1875), U.S. Representative (1895-1899).

STUART, PHILIP *(b 1760, near Fredericksburg, Va.; d Aug. 14, 1830, Washington, D.C.)* Revolutionary Army officer who was wounded at Eutaw Springs; Maryland Federalist. U.S. Representative (1811-1819).

SULLIVAN, CHRISTOPHER DANIEL *(b July 14, 1870, New York City; d Aug. 3, 1942, New York City)* Real estate broker, New York Democrat who was a U.S. Representative for almost a quarter-century (1917-1941) after serving ten years in the state senate (1906-1916).

SULLIVAN, GEORGE *(b Aug. 29, 1771, Durham, N.H.; d April 14, 1838, Exeter, N.H.)* Lawyer and a New Hampshire Federalist who was one of the state's most gifted orators and, as a U.S. Representative (1811-1813), was a fierce opponent of President Madison's foreign policies and the War of 1812 in particular. State representative (1805, 1813), state attorney general (1805, 1806, 1816-1835), state senate (1814, 1815). Son of John Sullivan.

SULLIVAN, JAMES *(b April 22, 1744, Berwick, Maine, but then a part of Massachusetts; d Dec. 10, 1808, Boston, Mass.)* Lawyer, historian, author, patriot, and a leader of the budding Democratic party in Massachusetts. Member of the Provincial Congress (1774, 1775) and the general court (1775, 1776), superior court justice (1776-1782), member of the Continental Congress (1782) and the executive council (1787), Suffolk County probate judge (1788), state attorney general (1790-1807), governor (1807, 1808). Brother of John Sullivan.

SULLIVAN, JOHN *(b Feb. 17, 1740, Somersworth, N.H.; d Jan. 23, 1795, Durham, N.H.)* Like his brother James, a leader in the pre-Revolutionary movement; during the war a general who took part in many major engagements and was captured in the battle for Long Island; lawyer, New Hampshire Federalist who three times was president of New Hampshire (1786, 1787, 1789) before the state changed the title to governor. Member of the First and Second Continental Congresses (1774, 1775) and again after leaving the army (1780, 1781), state attorney general (1782-1786), delegate to the convention that ratified the U.S. Constitution (1788), presidential elector (1789), U.S. district judge (1789 until death). Father of George Sullivan.

SULLIVAN, PATRICK JOSEPH *(b March 17, 1865, County Cork, Ireland; d April 8, 1935, Santa Barbara, Calif.).* Sheep raiser, banker, oil producer, investor, and a Wyoming Republican who, as chairman of its state central committee, for twenty years was the GOP boss there. State representative (1894-1896, 1898-1900), mayor of Casper (1897, 1898), U.S. Senate for a year (1929-1930) to fill a vacancy.

SULLOWAY, CYRUS ADAMS *(b June 8, 1839, Grafton, N.H.; d March 11, 1917, Washington, D.C.)* Lawyer, New Hampshire Republican. State representative (1872, 1873, 1887-1893), U.S. Representative (1895-1913, 1915 until death).

SULZER, CHARLES AUGUST *(b Feb. 24, 1879, Roselle, N.J.; d April 28, 1919, in Sulzer, Alaska, the town to which he gave his name)* West Point graduate who, after service in the Spanish-American War, went to Alaska to mine gold and became one of the territory's leading Democrats. Member of the territorial senate (1914), delegate to the U.S. Congress (1917 until death). Brother of William Sulzer.

SULZER, WILLIAM *(b March 18, 1863, Elizabeth, N.J.; d Nov. 6, 1941, New York City)* Lawyer, New York Democrat who refused to knuckle under to

Tammany Hall while governor (1913) and so was impeached after only nine months in that office; became an independent but declined the American party's nomination for the presidency in 1916. State assemblyman (1889-1894, 1913, 1914) and speaker (1893), delegate to all Democratic National Conventions (1892-1912), U.S. Representative (1895-1912) resigning to become governor. His last attempt at elective office was as Independent candidate for governor (1914). Brother of Charles A. Sulzer.

SUMMERS, JOHN WILLIAM *(b April 29, 1870, Orange County, Ind.; d Sept. 25, 1937, Walla Walla, Wash.)* Teacher, physician, fruit grower, Washington Republican. State representative (1917), U.S. Representative (1919-1933).

SUMNER, CHARLES *(b Jan. 6, 1811, Boston, Mass.; d March 11, 1874, Washington, D.C.)* Lawyer, Harvard Law School lecturer, orator, writer on legal subjects, Massachusetts Whig who was one of the founders of the Free-Soil party but later became a Republican.
A fiery speaker and dedicated abolitionist, he so aroused his Southern constituents in the Senate that they tried (unsuccessfully) to have him expelled; another time, two days after delivering his famed "The Crime Against Kansas" speech (May 20, 1856) in which he called the Kansas-Nebraska Act "in every respect a swindle," he was assaulted so severely by Congressman Preston Brooks of South Carolina that he was unable to attend sessions for three years. His only public office was as a U.S. Senator (1851 until death).

SUMNERS, HATTON WILLIAM *(b May 30, 1875, Lincoln County, Tenn.)* Lawyer, Texas Democrat who served more than thirty years as a U.S. Representative (1913-1947).

SUMTER, THOMAS *(b Aug. 14, 1734, Hanover County, Va.; d June 1, 1832, near Stateburg, S.C.)* Surveyor, grocer, planter, South Carolina Democrat who as an officer in the Continental Army won renown as "the gamecock of the Revolution." State senate (1781, 1782), Privy Council (1782), U.S. Representative (1789-1793, 1797-1801) resigning to become a U.S. Senator (1801-1810). Grandfather of Thomas D. Sumter.

SUMTER, THOMAS DeLAGE *(b Nov. 14, 1809, Germantown, Pa.; d July 2, 1874, near Stateburg, S.C.)* West Point graduate, Seminole Indian fighter, teacher, surveyor, planter, railroad agent, South Carolina Democrat. U.S. Representative (1839-1843). Grandson of Thomas Sumter.

SUTHERLAND, DANIEL ALEXANDER *(b April 17, 1869, Cape Breton Island, Canada; d March 24, 1955, Abington, Pa.).* Miner, fisherman, Alaska Territory Republican. Territorial senator (1912-1920) and senate president (1915), delegate to the U.S. Congress (1921-1930).

SUTHERLAND, GEORGE *(b March 25, 1862, Buckinghamshire, England; d July 18, 1942, Stockbridge, Mass.)* Lawyer, Utah Republican whose public career was climaxed by appointment by President Harding as an associate justice of the U.S. Supreme Court (1922-1938). State senate (1896-1900), delegate to all GOP National Conventions (1900-1912), U.S. Representative (1901-1903), U.S. Senate (1905-1917), American Bar Association president (1916, 1917), U.S. counsel in the Norway-United States arbitration at The Hague (1922).

SUTHERLAND, RODERICK DHU *(b April 27, 1862, Scotch Grove, Iowa; d Oct. 18, 1915, Kansas City, Kans.).* Teacher, lawyer, Nebraska Populist-Democrat. Nuckolls County prosecutor (1890-1896), Populist state convention chairman (1899), U.S. Representative (1897-1901), Populist National Convention delegate (1900), Democratic National Convention delegate (1900, 1908).

SWAN, SAMUEL *(b 1771, Somerset County, N.J.; d Aug. 24, 1844, Bound Brook, N.J.).* Physician, New Jersey Whig. Somerset County sheriff (1804-1806), county clerk (1809-1820), U.S. Representative (1821-1831).

SWANK, FLETCHER B. *(b April 24, 1875, Davis County, Iowa; d March 16, 1950, Norman, Okla.)* Farm and ranch hand, lawyer, Oklahoma Democrat. Cleveland County schools superintendent (1903-1907), secretary to Congressman Scott Ferris (1907, 1908), county judge (1911-1915), fourteenth judicial district judge (1915-1920), U.S. Representative (1921-1929, 1931-1935).

SWANN, THOMAS *(b Feb. 3, 1809, Alexandria, Va.; d July 24, 1883, near Leesburg, Va.)* Railroad president who extended the Baltimore & Ohio to the Ohio River, Maryland Know-Nothing governor (1865-1869), and a Unionist who bitterly opposed Reconstruction and returned voting rights to Southern sympathizers; thereafter a Democrat. Mayor of Baltimore (1856-1860), U.S. Representative (1869-1879).

SWANSON, CLAUDE AUGUSTUS *(b March 31, 1862, Swansonville, Va.; d July 7, 1939, Madison County, Va.).* Lawyer, Virginia Democrat who supported Woodrow Wilson's big navy concept and was secretary of the navy in the Roosevelt cabinet (1933 until death). U.S. Representative (1893-1906), governor (1906-1910), U.S. Senate (1910-1933) resigning to accept the cabinet portfolio.

SWEENEY, MARTIN LEONARD *(b April 15, 1885, Cleveland, Ohio; d May 1, 1960, Cleveland)* Laborer, hoisting engineer, salesman, lawyer, Ohio Democrat. Municipal court judge (1924-1932), Democratic National Convention delegate (1932), U.S. Representative (1931-1943).

SWEET, WILLIS *(b Jan. 1, 1856, Alburg Springs, Vt.; d July 9, 1925, San Juan, P.R.)* Printer, lawyer, newspaper editor, Idaho Republican who later in life found new worlds to conquer in Puerto Rico. In Idaho as a territory: U.S. attorney (1888-1889), first judicial district judge (1889-1890), associate justice of the Idaho Supreme Court (1890, 1891), first president of the University of Idaho Board of Regents (1889-1893). As a state: U.S. Representative (1890-1895). In Puerto Rico: attorney general (1903-1905), San Juan newspaper editor (1913 until death).

SYMES, GEORGE GIFFORD *(b April 28, 1840, Ashtabula County, Ohio; d Nov. 3, 1893, Denver, Colo.)* Union officer, Indian fighter, lawyer who first practiced in Kentucky, then headed west to Montana and finally found his niche in Denver; Colorado Republican. In Montana: associate justice of the territorial supreme court (1869-1871). In Colorado: U.S. Representative (1885-1889).

T

☆ ☆ ☆

TABER, JOHN *(b May 5, 1880, Auburn, N.Y.; d Nov. 22, 1965, Auburn)* Lawyer, New York Republican and a political veteran if ever there was one. Cayuga County supervisor (1905, 1906), special judge of the county court (1910-1918), GOP National Convention delegate (1920, 1924, 1936), GOP county committee chairman (1920-1925), U.S. Representative who first was seated in the Sixty-eighth Congress that convened in 1923 and still was there when the Eighty-seventh adjourned in 1963—a tenure of forty years.

TABOR, HORACE AUSTIN WARNER *(b Nov. 26, 1830, Holland, Vt.; d April 10, 1899, Denver, Colo.)* Maine stonecutter, Kansas farmer, and then a miner and merchant in Colorado (1859) where he remained; Republican. Leadville postmaster (1878), mayor (1878, 1879), Lake County treasurer (1880-1882), lieutenant governor (1878-1884), U.S. Senate to fill a vacancy (1883), Denver postmaster (1898 until death).

TAFT, CHARLES PHELPS *(b Dec. 21, 1843, Cincinnati, Ohio; d Dec. 31, 1929, Cincinnati)* Lawyer, philanthropist, Ohio Republican, and publisher of the *Cincinnati Times-Star*, the newspaper that had much to do with the furtherance of the career of his half-brother, William Howard Taft, the twenty-seventh president of the United States. U.S. Representative (1895-1897), presidential elector on the Roosevelt-Fairbanks ticket (1904), president of the Ohio electoral college (1905), delegate to the GOP National Conventions (1908, 1912) that nominated his half-brother.

TAFT, ROBERT ALPHONSO *(b Sept. 8, 1889, Cincinnati, Ohio; d July 31, 1953, New York City)* Son of President William Howard Taft, lawyer, and very much a Republican in his own right— referred to as Mr. Republican, Ohio's favorite-son candidate for the presidency (1936), for many years headed the party's conservative wing and was its unsuccessful choice for the nomination three times (1940, 1948, 1952).

Assistant counsel to the U.S. Food Administration (1917, 1918), counsel to the American Relief Administration (1919), state representative (1921-1926) and house speaker (1926), state senate (1931, 1932), GOP National Convention delegate (1932, 1940, 1944), U.S. Senate (1939 until death) and the Taft of the Taft-Hartley Act.

TAFT, WILLIAM HOWARD *(b Sept. 15, 1857, Cincinnati, Ohio; d Mar. 8, 1930, Washington, D.C.)* Twenty-seventh president (Ohio Republican), 1909-1913, a conservative (although he had some progressive leanings and believed in the right of labor to organize and strike), elected president in an era that was excessively reform minded; chief justice of the U.S. Supreme Court; first civil governor of the Philippine Islands; secretary of war.

One of a family of six children, son of diplomat (under President Arthur) and cabinet member (under Grant) Judge Alphonso Taft and second wife Louisa Torrey Taft, both of whom were of New England ancestry; third generation lawyer and an excellent public speaker; attended Cincinnati public schools, graduated Yale University second in a class of 121 (1878), received law degree from Cincinnati Law School (1880), and was admitted to the Ohio bar. Married Helen Herron of Cincinnati (1886) and the couple had three children one of whom was Robert Alphonso, U.S. Senator from Ohio (1938-1953).

Appointed assistant prosecuting attorney of Hamilton County (1881-1882); appointed collector of internal revenue for Cincinnati (1882), resigning within a year when subjected to pressure to replace competent workers with members of his own party; Hamilton County assistant solicitor (1885-1887); Ohio Superior Court judge (1887-1890); appointed U.S. solicitor general by President Harrison (1890-1892), resigning to become a federal circuit judge (1892), where his rulings more often than not won him organized labor's opposition, which continued throughout his career.

Appointed president (1900) of a commission to establish civil government in the Philippines and a year later became civil governor, leaving (1904) to become Theodore Roosevelt's secretary of war. The two made a good team; Taft became the president's troubleshooter and closest adviser, and when Roosevelt's term was ending he supported Taft as his successor. Taft won the election of 1908, easily defeating Democratic opponent William Jennings Bryan. However, by 1912, Taft and Roosevelt had become political enemies. Taft used party machinery to make sure that he, rather than Roose-

velt, received the Republican presidential nomination and Roosevelt bolted to form the Progressive party with himself as its standard bearer. The Democratic nominee, Woodrow Wilson, won the election, receiving 435 electoral votes to Roosevelt's 88 and Taft's 8.

During his presidency, Taft was an active "trust buster"; the Sixteenth and Seventeenth amendments were added to the Constitution; the powers of the Interstate Commerce Commission were enlarged (at Taft's initiative); the Department of Labor was established.

After retirement, he became a professor of constitutional law at Yale University; president of the American Bar Association (1913); joint chairman of the World War I National War Labor Board; appointed chief justice of the United States by President Harding (1921-1930), a position that brought him greater personal happiness than had that of president. He was responsible for creation of conference of senior circuit judges and passage (1925) of the Judges' Bill and instrumental in bringing about congressional act under which new Supreme Court building was erected. On the Court, just as in the presidency, he was generally, but not always, conservative.

TAGGART, JOSEPH *(b June 15, 1867, Allamakee County, Iowa; d Dec. 3, 1938, Wadsworth, Kans.)* Teacher, lawyer, Kansas Democrat. Wyandotte County prosecutor (1907-1911), U.S. Representative (1911-1917), appointed judge of the state's industrial relations court (1924).

TAGGART, SAMUEL *(b March 24, 1754, Londonderry, N.H.; d April 25, 1825, Colrain, Mass.)* Clergyman, farmer, Massachusetts Federalist. U.S. Representative (1803-1817).

TAGGART, THOMAS *(b Nov. 17, 1856, County Monaghan, Ireland; d March 6, 1929, Indianapolis, Ind.)* Restaurant and hotel proprietor, banker, Indiana Democrat who for many years was a man of great power in the party both at home and nationally. Marion County auditor (1886-1894), Democratic county chairman (1888-1900) and state committee chairman (1892-1894), mayor of Indianapolis (1895-1901), member of the Democratic National Committee (1900-1912) and its chairman (1900-1908), delegate to all of his party's national conventions (1900-1924), U.S. Senate to fill a vacancy (1916).

TAIT, CHARLES *(b Feb. 1, 1768, Hanover County, Va.; d Oct. 7, 1835, near Claiborne, Ala.)* French professor, lawyer, planter, Georgia Democrat who had much to do with winning territorial status and then statehood for Alabama. In Georgia: western circuit court presiding judge (1803-1809), U.S. Senate (1809-1819). In Alabama: U.S. district judge (1820-1826). Cousin of Henry Clay.

TALBOTT, JOSHUA FREDERICK COCKEY *(b July 29, 1843, Baltimore County, Md.; d Oct. 5, 1918, Lutherville, Md.)* Confederate soldier, lawyer, Maryland Democrat. Baltimore County prosecutor (1871-1875), Democratic National Convention delegate (1876, 1904, 1908), U.S. Representative (1879-1885, 1893-1895, 1903 until death), state insurance commissioner (1889-1893).

TALIAFERRO, JAMES PIPER *(b Sept. 30, 1847, Orange, Va.; d Oct. 6, 1934, Jacksonville, Fla.)* Confederate soldier, lumberman, railroad builder, banker, Florida Democrat. U.S. Senate (1899-1911).

TALIAFERRO, JOHN *(b 1768, King George County, Va.; d Aug. 12, 1852, King George County)* Lawyer, planter, Virginia Democrat turned Whig. U.S. Representative (1801-1803, 1811-1813, 1824-1831, 1835-1843); presidential elector on the Jefferson-Clinton (1804) and

Monroe-Tompkins (1820) tickets, U.S. Treasury Department librarian (1850 until death).

TALLMADGE, BENJAMIN *(b Feb. 25, 1754, Brookhaven, N.Y.; d March 7, 1835, Litchfield, Conn.)* Businessman, banker, Revolutionary Army officer who captured Long Island's Fort St. George and, as director of George Washington's secret service, was in charge of Major John André from time of capture until execution; Connecticut Federalist. U.S. Representative (1801-1817). Father of Frederick A. Tallmadge.

TALLMADGE, FREDERICK AUGUSTUS *(b Aug. 29, 1792, Litchfield, Conn.; d Sept. 17, 1869, Litchfield)* Lawyer, New York Whig. New York City alderman (1834) and councilman (1836), state senate (1837-1840) and its president pro tem (1840), city recorder (1841-1846, 1848-1851), U.S. Representative (1847-1849), metropolitan police superintendent (1857-1862), clerk of the New York Court of Appeals (1862-1865). Son of Benjamin Tallmadge.

TALLMADGE, NATHANIEL PITCHER *(b Feb. 8, 1795, Chatham, N.Y.; d Nov. 2, 1864, Battle Creek, Mich.)* Lawyer, New York Democrat who was appointed governor of the Wisconsin Territory by President Tyler (1844-1845). Assemblyman (1828), state senate (1830-1833), U.S. Senate (1833-1844) resigning to take the Wisconsin post.

TARVER, MALCOLM CONNOR *(b Sept. 25, 1885, Rural Vale, Ga.; d March 5, 1960, Dalton, Ga.)* Lawyer, Georgia Democrat. State representative (1909-1912), state senator (1913, 1914), Cherokee Circuit Superior Court judge (1917-1927), U.S. Representative (1927-1947).

TATE, FARISH CARTER *(b Nov. 20, 1856, Jasper, Ga.; d Feb. 7, 1922, Jasper)*. Lawyer, Georgia Democrat. Member of the general assembly (1882-1887), Democratic state executive committee member (1884-1887, 1890-1892), Democratic state convention delegate (1888), U.S. Representative (1893-1905), U.S. attorney for Georgia's northern district (1905-1913).

TAWNEY, JAMES ALBERTUS *(b Jan. 3, 1855, Adams County, Pa.; d June 12, 1919, Excelsior Springs, Mo.).* Blacksmith, machinist, lawyer, Minnesota Republican. U.S. Representative (1893-1911), member of International Joint Commission on U.S.-Canadian boundaries (1911 until death) and chairman of U.S. Section (1911-1914).

TAYLOR, ALFRED ALEXANDER *(b Aug. 6, 1848, Happy Valley, Tenn.; d Nov. 25, 1931, Johnson City, Tenn.)* Lawyer, lecturer, farmer, Tennessee Republican who waged the so-called War of Roses (1886) with brother Robert L., each his party's nominee for the governor's chair. Their method of combat was a series of statewide joint debates during a time when Tennessee was being torn apart by political strife. Bob and Alf, rather than fan that strife into a fury, were heavy on the entertainment, cloaking the issues in humor and delighting the voters no end. Bob won the election.

State representative (1875, 1876), GOP National Convention delegate (1888), U.S. Representative (1889-1895) of the same district that his father, Nathaniel G. Taylor, had represented as a Whig and his brother as a Democrat, governor (1921-1923).

Said Alf in his ebbing years to describe the reason for their political success: "We played the fiddle, were fond of dogs, and loved our fellow men."

TAYLOR, CHESTER WILLIAM *(b July 16, 1883, Verona, Miss.; d July 17, 1931, Pine Bluff, Ark.)* Lawyer, insurance broker, Arkansas Democrat who also was secretary to his father, Congressman Samuel M. Taylor (1913-1921), and

was chosen to fill the vacated seat (1921-1923) upon the death of the latter. Deputy state auditor (1908-1910) and Arkansas's deputy secretary of state (1911), deputy treasurer (1911-1912).

TAYLOR, EDWARD THOMAS *(b June 19, 1858, Woodford County, Ill.; d Sept. 3, 1941, Denver, Colo.)* Educator, lawyer, Colorado Democrat who was a U.S. Representative thirty-two years (1909 until death). Leadville High School principal (1881, 1882), Lake County schools superintendent (1884), Glenwood Springs deputy district attorney (1885), ninth judicial circuit district attorney (1887-1889), state senate (1896-1908).

TAYLOR, EZRA BOOTH *(b July 9, 1823, Nelson, Ohio; d Jan. 29, 1912, Warren, Ohio)* Union soldier, lawyer, Ohio Republican. Portage County prosecutor (1854), ninth judicial district common pleas judge (1877-1880), U.S. Representative (1880-1893).

TAYLOR, GEORGE *(b 1716, Ireland; d Feb. 23, 1781, Easton, Pa.)* Iron maker, Revolutionary officer, Pennsylvania signer of the Declaration of Independence. Chester County justice of the peace (1757, 1761, 1763), provincial assembly (1764-1769, 1775), Northampton County justice of the peace (1764-1772), member of the Continental Congress (1776, 1777), member of the First Supreme Executive Council (1777).

TAYLOR, GEORGE WASHINGTON *(b Jan. 16, 1849, Montgomery County, Ala.; d Dec. 21, 1932, Rome, Ga.)* Confederate soldier, teacher, lawyer, Alabama Democrat. State representative (1878, 1879), state solicitor for the first judicial circuit (1880-1892), U.S. Representative (1897-1915), state constitutional convention chairman (1901), Democratic National Convention delegate (1920).

TAYLOR, JAMES WILLIS (b Aug. 28, 1880, Lead Mine Bend, Tenn.; d Nov. 14, 1939, La Follette, Tenn.). Teacher, lawyer, Tennessee Republican. La Follette postmaster (1904-1909), mayor (1910-1913, 1918, 1919), state insurance commissioner (1913, 1914), GOP state executive committee chairman (1917, 1918), U.S. Representative (1919 until death), GOP National Executive Committee member (1929-1939).

TAYLOR, JOHN (b May 4, 1770, near Granby, S.C.; d April 16, 1832, Camden, S.C.) Lawyer, planter, trustee of South Carolina College (now the University of South Carolina), director of the Columbia Theological Seminary, South Carolina Democrat. State representative (1796-1802, 1804, 1805), circuit court solicitor (1805, 1806), U.S. Representative (1807-1810) resigning to become a U.S. Senator (1810-1816), state senator (1818-1826), governor (1826-1828).

TAYLOR, JOHN LAMPKIN (b March 7, 1805, Stafford County, Va.; d Sept. 6, 1870, Washington, D.C.) Lawyer, Ohio Whig. U.S. Representative (1847-1855), Interior Department clerk (1870 until death).

TAYLOR, JOHN W. (b March 26, 1784, Charlton, N.Y.; d Sept. 8, 1854, Cleveland, Ohio) Lawyer, New York Democrat. Justice of the peace (1808), state assemblyman (1812, 1813), U.S. Representative (1813-1833) and House speaker (1820-1821, 1825-1827), state senate (1840, 1841).

TAYLOR, JOSEPH DANNER (b Nov. 7, 1830, Goshen Township, Ohio; d Sept. 19, 1899, Cambridge, Ohio) Teacher, lawyer, publisher of the Guernsey Times, Union Army officer, Ohio Republican. Fairview High School principal (1857), Guernsey County prosecutor (1863-1866), Loyalist convention delegate (1866), Cambridge School Board member (1870-1877), GOP National Convention delegate (1876, 1880), U.S. Representative (1883-1885, 1887-1893).

TAYLOR, NATHANIEL GREEN (b Dec. 29, 1819, Happy Valley, Tenn.; d April 1, 1887, Happy Valley) Lawyer, lecturer, farmer, preacher, Tennessee Whig-Constitutional Unionist who had nine children, two of whom were in politics (see Taylor, Alfred Alexander, and Taylor, Robert Love). Presidential elector on the Whig ticket of Scott and Graham (1852) and the Constitutional Unionist ticket of Bell and Everett (1860). U.S. Representative both before and upon the reseating of Tennessee's delegation in Congress after the Civil War (1854-1855, 1866-1867), member of the relief association formed to help East Tennessee's war sufferers, commissioner of Indian affairs.

TAYLOR, ROBERT LOVE (b July 31, 1850, Happy Valley, Tenn.; d March 31, 1912, Washington, D.C.) Iron manufacturer, tobacco grower, lawyer, lecturer, newspaper and magazine publisher, writer and a highly independent Tennessee Democrat who remained constantly independent of his party's ruling bosses. His key to political victory: The young and the rural farm folk were always behind him.

U.S. Representative (1879-1881), presidential elector on the Cleveland-Hendricks (1884) and Cleveland-Stevenson (1892) tickets, pension agent (1885-1887), governor (1887-1891, 1897-1899), U.S. Senate (1907 until death).

In 1895, Bob and his brother Alfred A. (Alf) embarked on a seven-month joint lecture tour that is said to have netted them more than $50,000. Their topics, which in a sense described their border state affiliations, were "Yankee Doodle" and "Dixie." Said Champ Clark of those, and other, lectures: "A strange commingling of wit, humor, philosophy, pathos, eloquence, common sense, and good morals." Son of Nathaniel G. Taylor.

TAYLOR, SAMUEL MITCHELL *(b May 25, 1852, Itawamba County, Miss.; d Sept. 13, 1921, Washington, D.C.)* Lawyer, Mississippi and Arkansas Democrat. In Mississippi: state representative (1879, 1880). In Arkansas: eleventh judicial district prosecutor (1888-1892), Democratic National Convention delegate (1896), Democratic state convention temporary chairman (1910), U.S. Representative (1913 until death) when he was succeeded by his son, Chester W. Taylor.

TAYLOR, ZACHARY *(b Nov. 24, 1784, Orange County, Va.; d July 9, 1850, Washington, D.C.)* Twelfth president (Whig), 1849-1850; casually dressed hero of Mexican War, called Old Rough and Ready by his troops; a man who had no previous political experience and died sixteen months after inauguration.

A relative of James Madison and son of Revolutionary officer Colonel Richard Taylor who took his family (shortly after Zachary was born) to Jefferson County, Kentucky, where he acquired a plantation and was appointed collector of customs at the port of Louisville by George Washington. There were no schools in the area, so Zachary received a meager education from a private tutor. He learned farming on his father's plantation, then (1808) joined the army (he was given an appointment as first lieutenant) and spent most of the next forty years in its service. Married Margaret Smith (1810). They had six children; one daughter married Jefferson Davis (1835) but died just three months later; their only son became a general in the Confederate Army during the Civil War.

Taylor, who was brevetted a major after distinguishing himself in defense of Fort Harrison (War of 1812), retired briefly (1815-1816) when, at the end of the war, his rank was temporarily reduced. Fought in the Black Hawk War (1832); after his troops defeated the Seminoles at Lake Okeechobee (Dec. 25, 1837) was promoted to brigadier general. Sent to Corpus Christi (1845) to guard against possible trouble from Mexico as a result of the annexation of Texas and a breakdown in diplomatic relations. At President Polk's orders, he advanced to the Rio Grande where it didn't take long for an "overt incident" to bring on the Mexican War. Taylor proved to be as effective a leader fighting the Mexicans as he had been against Indians. As he moved south across the Rio Grande, taking more and more territory, his popularity with the American people grew and he was promoted to major general. Although part of his army was transferred to the command of General Winfield Scott, Taylor was still able, with only 5,000 men, to defeat Santa Ana's 20,000 at Buena Vista (Feb. 22, 1847). His popularity as a war hero carried him into the White House on the Whig ticket, defeating Democratic candidate Lewis Cass (163 to 127 electoral votes). His victory was due in part to a split in the Democratic vote in New York state, which was caused by Van Buren running on the Free-Soil ticket.

Taylor's administration was brief but difficult. Charges of corruption were made against several members of his cabinet and the controversy over slavery grew ever hotter. Although Taylor had been a slave owner himself, he was impartial in his handling of the slavery issue and firm in his support of the Union. Overtaxing his strength at a ceremony, he became ill and died, leaving the nation's problems to Vice President Millard Fillmore.

TAZEWELL, HENRY *(b Nov. 15, 1753, Brunswick County, Va.; d Jan. 24, 1799, Philadelphia, Pa.)* Lawyer, Virginia jurist during the nation's early days. Provincial house of burgesses (1775), state constitutional convention delegate (1775, 1776), state supreme court judge (1785-1793) and chief justice (1789-1793), high court of appeals judge

(1793), U.S. Senate (1794 until death) and its president pro tem (1796). Father of Littleton W. Tazewell.

TAZEWELL, LITTLETON WALLER (b Dec. 17, 1774, Williamsburg, Va.; d May 6, 1860, Norfolk, Va.) Lawyer, Virginia Democrat. State delegate (1796-1800, 1816), U.S. Representative (1800-1801) to fill a vacancy, Florida claims commissioner (1820), U.S. Senator (1824-1832) and Senate president pro tem (1832), state convention delegate (1829), governor (1834-1836). Son of Henry Tazewell.

TEIGAN, HENRY GEORGE (b Aug. 7, 1881, Forest City, Iowa; d March 12, 1941, Minneapolis, Minn.) Iowa and North Dakota schoolteacher, Minnesota newspaperman; in North Dakota, secretary of the state Socialist party (1913-1916), and in Minnesota a member of the Farmer Labor party. Also in Minnesota: Secretary to U.S. Senator Magnus Johnson (1923-1925), state senate (1933-1935), U.S. Representative (1937-1939).

TELFAIR, EDWARD (b 1735, Scotland; d Sept. 17, 1807, Savannah, Ga.) Merchant, sawmill operator, farmer, Georgia patriot. Member of the Council of Safety (1775, 1776), Provincial Congress (1776), Committee of Intelligence (1776), and the Continental Congress (1778-1782, 1784-1785, 1788-1789); signer of the Articles of Confederation and a delegate to the state convention that ratified the U.S. Constitution (1788); Cherokee Indian treaty commissioner (1783), boundary commissioner (1783), governor (1786, 1790-1793). Father of Thomas Telfair.

TELFAIR, THOMAS (b March 2, 1780, Savannah, Ga.; d Feb. 18, 1818, Savannah) Lawyer, Georgia Democrat. U.S. Representative (1813-1817). Son of Edward Telfair.

TELLER, HENRY MOORE (b May 23, 1830, Granger, N.Y.; d Feb. 23, 1914, Denver, Colo.) Teacher, lawyer, Colorado territorial leader and after statehood a U.S. Senator (1876-1882, 1885-1909), the first two terms as a Republican, the third as an Independent Silver Republican, the fourth as a Democrat. His main interests other than silver were suffrage for women, government regulation of big business, and defense of the underdog. Major general of the state militia (1862-1864), secretary of the interior in the Arthur cabinet (1882-1885), member of the U.S. Monetary Commission (1908).

TEMPLE, HENRY WILLSON (b March 31, 1864, Belle Center, Ohio; d Jan. 11, 1955, Washington, Pa.) Clergyman, professor of history and political science (1905-1913) and international relations (1933-1947) at Washington and Jefferson College, Pennsylvania Progressive Republican before becoming a straight Republican. U.S. Representative (1913-1933).

TENER, JOHN KINLEY (b July 25, 1863, County Tyrone, Ireland; d May 19, 1946, Pittsburgh, Pa.) Professional baseball player (1885-1890) who became president of the National League (1914-1918), banker, insurance broker, Pennsylvania Republican. U.S. Representative (1909-1911) resigning to become governor (1911-1915).

TERRY, DAVID DICKSON (b Jan. 31, 1881, Little Rock, Ark.) Lawyer, Arkansas Democrat. Little Rock School Board member (1929-1933), state representative (1933), U.S. Representative (1933-1943), director of the state Division of Flood Control Water and Soil Conservation (1945-1953). Son of William L. Terry.

TERRY, WILLIAM LEAKE (b Sept. 27, 1850, Anson County, N.C.; d Nov. 4, 1917, Little Rock, Ark.) Lawyer, Arkansas Democrat. Little Rock councilman (1877-1879), state senator (1878, 1879) and senate president in the latter year, city attorney (1879-1885), U.S. Representative (1891-1901). Father of David D. Terry.

THACHER, GEORGE *(b April 12, 1754, Yarmouth, Mass.; d April 6, 1824, Biddeford, Maine)* Lawyer, Massachusetts and Maine Federalist. Member of the Continental Congress (1787), U.S. Representative (1789-1801), Maine district judge (1792-1801), associate judge of the Massachusetts Supreme Court (1800-1820), Maine constitutional convention delegate (1819), Maine Supreme Court judge (1820-1824).

THATCHER, MAURICE HUDSON *(b Aug. 15, 1870, Chicago. Ill.; d ——)*. Farmer, lawyer, Kentucky Republican. Butler County circuit court clerk (1892), state assistant attorney general (1898-1900), assistant U.S. attorney for the western district (1901-1906), state examiner and inspector (1908-1910), member of the Isthmian Canal Commission and civil governor of the Canal Zone (1910-1913), member of Louisville Board of Public Safety (1917-1919) and department counsel (1919-1923), U.S. Representative (1923-1933).

THAYER, ELI *(b June 11, 1819, Mendon, Mass.; d April 15, 1899, Worcester, Mass.)* Teacher, lawyer, investor, founder of the Oread Collegiate Institute, Massachusetts Free-Soiler–Republican who most of all was a champion of westward colonization through private subsidy. As such, during debate over the Kansas-Nebraska Bill (1854), he founded the New England Emigrant Aid Company to send a colony of antislave settlers to Kansas. As a result, the territory became an antislave state. Worcester School Board member (1852), alderman (1852, 1853), state representative (1853, 1854), U.S. Representative (1857-1861), GOP Na-

tional Convention delegate from Oregon (1860) whose statehood he had advocated while in Congress. Father of John A. Thayer.

THAYER, JOHN ALDEN *(b Dec. 22, 1857, Worcester, Mass.; d July 31, 1917, Worcester)* Teacher, lawyer, Massachusetts Democrat. Worcester central district court clerk (1892-1897), U.S. Representative (1911-1913), Democratic National Convention delegate (1912), Worcester postmaster (1915 until death). Son of Eli Thayer.

THAYER, JOHN MILTON *(b Jan. 24, 1820, Bellingham, Mass.; d March 19, 1906, Lincoln, Nebr.)* Farmer, lawyer, Union general who led troops against the Indians and then a Civil War western campaign commander, Nebraska Radical Republican whose specialty was Indian affairs. As a territory: member of the territorial senate (1860), state constitutional convention delegate (1860, 1866). As a state: one of Nebraska's first U.S. Senators (1867-1871), Grant-appointed governor of the Wyoming Territory (1875-1879), Nebraska commander of the Grand Army of the Republic (1886), governor (1887-1891).

THOM, WILLIAM RICHARD *(b July 7, 1885, Canton, Ohio; d Aug. 28, 1960, Canton)* Newspaperman, lawyer, Ohio Democrat. Secretary to Congressman John J. Whitacre (1911-1913), Canton park commissioner (1920-1932), U.S. Representative (1933-1939, 1941-1943, 1945-1947), Democratic National Convention delegate (1956).

THOMAS, ALBERT *(b April 12, 1898, Nacogdoches, Tex.; d Feb. 15, 1966, Washington, D.C.)* Lawyer, Texas Democrat who served twenty-nine years as a U.S. Representative (1937 until death), a member of the Appropriations Committee and the Joint Committee on Atomic Energy, and generally considered to be a behind-the-scenes power in Washington. Nacogdoches County attorney (1927-1930), assistant U.S. attorney for southern Texas district (1930-1936).

THOMAS, CHARLES RANDOLPH, SR. *(b Feb. 7, 1827, Beaufort, N.C.; d Feb. 18, 1891, New Bern, N.C.)* Lawyer, railroad president, North Carolina Republican. State constitutional convention delegate (1861), North Carolina secretary of state (1864), superior court judge (1868-1870), U.S. Representative (1871-1875). Father of the following.

THOMAS, CHARLES RANDOLPH, JR. *(b Aug. 21, 1861, Beaufort, N.C.; d March 8, 1931, Norfolk, Va.)* Lawyer, University of North Carolina trustee, North Carolina Democrat. State representative (1887), Craven County attorney (1890-1896), presidential elector on the Bryan-Sewall ticket (1896), U.S. Representative (1899-1911), Democratic National Convention delegate (1924). Son of the preceding.

THOMAS, CHARLES SPALDING *(b Dec. 6, 1849, Darien, Ga.; d June 24, 1934, Denver, Colo.)* Lawyer, Colorado Democrat who successfully ran for governor as a Silver Unionist (1899-1901) and unsuccessfully for the U.S. Senate (1920) as a Nationalist. Very much a nonconformist, although he also was a bit of a power on the national Democratic scene, he opposed a soldiers' bonus and the League of Nations. Nor did he have much use for capital and labor. Denver city attorney (1875, 1876), Democratic National Convention delegate (1880, 1896, 1900, 1904, 1908) and temporary chairman (1900), member of the Democratic National Committee (1884-1896), U.S. Senate (1913-1921), special assistant to the U.S. attorney general (1922).

THOMAS, DAVID *(b June 11, 1762, Pelham, Mass.; d Nov. 11, 1831, Providence, R.I.)* Revolutionary soldier, tavern keeper, merchant, New York Democrat who was indicted for bribery (1812) and acquitted. State assemblyman (1794, 1798-1800), Salem town supervisor (1797-1800) and justice of the peace (1798-1801, 1804, 1811), U.S. Representative (1801-1808), state treasurer (1808-1810, 1812-1813).

THOMAS, ELBERT DUNCAN *(b June 17, 1883, Salt Lake City, Utah; d Feb. 11, 1953, Honolulu, Hawaii)* Missionary, University of Utah instructor of Latin and Greek (1914-1916), secretary of the board of regents (1917-1922) and professor of political science (1924-1933); author, Utah Democrat. Interparliamentary Union delegate (1936, 1937), International Labor Organization Conference delegate (1944, 1945, 1946, 1947, 1948), member of the Board of Columbia Institution for the Deaf (1939-1947), Democratic National Convention delegate (1933-1951), high commissioner of U.S. trustee territories in the Pacific (1951 until death).

THOMAS, FRANCIS *(b Feb. 3, 1799, Frederick County, Md.; d Jan. 22, 1876, near Frankville, Md.)* Lawyer, canal company executive, farmer, Maryland Democrat-Union Republican and a Reconstruction Radical who was involved first in a duel and later in a marital scandal that for a time drove him into the life of a recluse. Member of state house of delegates (1822, 1827) and speaker (1829), U.S. Representative (1831-1841, 1861-1869), governor (1841-1844), state constitutional convention delegate (1850), Loyalist National Convention delegate (1866), collector of internal revenue (1870-1872), ambassador to Peru (1872-1875).

THOMAS, JOHN *(b Jan. 4, 1874, Philips County, Kans.; d Nov. 10, 1945, Washington, D.C.)* Teacher, banker, livestock dealer, Kansas and Idaho Republican. In Kansas: Philips County superintendent of schools (1898-1903), Colby land office register (1906-1909). In Idaho:

mayor of Gooding (1917-1919), GOP state central committee chairman (1922-1924), GOP National Committee member (1925-1933), U.S. Senate to fill a vacancy (1928-1933) and again (1940 until death).

THOMAS, JOHN ROBERT *(b Oct. 11, 1846, Mount Vernon, Ill.; d Jan. 19, 1914, McAlester, Okla.)* Union Army officer, lawyer, Illinois and Oklahoma Republican. In Illinois: state's attorney (1869, 1870), U.S. Representative (1879-1889), U.S. judge for the Indian Territory (1897-1901). In Oklahoma: member of state code commission (1908-1910).

THOMAS, JOHN WILLIAM ELMER *(b Sept. 8, 1876, Putnam County, Ind.).* Lawyer, Oklahoma Democrat who was one of the state's best-known political figures, serving as a U.S. Senator (1927-1951) and being a delegate to all of his party's national conventions (1924-1960). Elected a member of Oklahoma's first state senate (1907), continuing in that office until 1920 and serving as president pro tem (1910-1913); delegate to all Democratic state conventions (1907-1950) and chairman (1910), U.S. Representative (1923-1927).

THOMAS, PHILIP FRANCIS *(b Sept. 12, 1810, Easton, Md.; d Oct. 2, 1890, Baltimore, Md.)* Lawyer, Maryland Democrat who although elected to U.S. Senate was denied a seat (1867) because of his Confederate sympathies. State constitutional convention delegate (1836), member of the house of delegates (1838, 1843, 1845, 1863, 1878, 1883), U.S. Representative (1839-1841, 1875-1877), governor (1848-1851), eastern Maryland land office court judge and comptroller of the U.S. Treasury (1851-1853), Baltimore port collector (1853-1860), U.S. commissioner of patents (1860), secretary of the treasury for a month in the Buchanan cabinet (1860-1861), Democratic state convention delegate (1883).

THOMAS, ROBERT YOUNG, JR. *(b July 13, 1855, Logan County, Ky.; d Sept. 3, 1925, Red Boiling Springs, Tenn.).* Lawyer, journalist, Kentucky Democrat. State representative (1886, 1887), commonwealth attorney for the seventh judicial district (1903-1909), U.S. Representative (1909 until death).

THOMAS, WILLIAM AUBREY *(b June 7, 1866, Y Bynea, Wales; d Sept. 8, 1951, Talladega, Ala.)* Chemist, iron and steel manufacturer, Ohio Republican. U.S. Representative (1904-1911).

THOMPSON, CHARLES JAMES *(b Jan. 24, 1862, Wapakoneta, Ohio; d March 27, 1932, Albuquerque, N.Mex.)* Printer, bookkeeper, publisher of the *Defiance Express*, Ohio Republican. GOP state central committee member (1893, 1894), Defiance postmaster (1898-1915), U.S. Representative (1919-1931).

THOMPSON, CLARK WALLACE *(b Aug. 6, 1896, LaCrosse, Wis.)* Public relations counsel, Texas Democrat. U.S. Representative (1933-1935, 1947-1967) and a member of the Ways and Means Committee.

THOMPSON, JACOB *(b May 15, 1810, Leasburg, N.C.; d March 24, 1885, Memphis, Tenn.)* Teacher, lawyer, Confederate Army officer who was a secret agent in Canada during the Civil War, Mississippi Democrat. U.S. Representative (1839-1851), secretary of the interior in the Buchanan cabinet (1857-1861).

THOMPSON, JOHN BURTON *(b Dec. 14, 1810, near Harrodsburg, Ky.; d Jan. 7, 1874, Harrodsburg)* Lawyer, Kentucky Whig. State senate (1829-1833), state representative (1835, 1837), U.S. Representative (1840-1843, 1847-1851), lieutenant governor (1852), U.S. Senate (1853-1859).

THOMPSON, THEO ASHTON *(b March 31, 1916, Ville Platte, La.; d July 1, 1965, Gastonia, N.C., struck and killed by a truck when stopped by state patrolman).* Accountant, Louisiana Democrat. Traveling auditor for state highway commission (1934-1940), department of finance assisting in state reorganization plan (1940-1942), U.S. Army Air Corps (1942-1946), state budget officer and financial adviser to legislature (1948-1952), chairman of board of trustees of state employes retirement system (1947-1953), trained foreign contingent in principles of democracy (1950, 1951) for U.S. Department of State, U.S. Representative (1953-1965) serving on the Public Works, and Merchant Marine and Fisheries committees.

THOMPSON, WILEY *(b Sept. 23, 1781, Amelia County, Va.; d Dec. 28, 1835, Fort King, Fla.; slain by Seminole Indians)* Professional soldier, Indian fighter, Georgia Democrat whose tyrannical treatment of Indians was widely condemned in the nation's newspapers and who died in ambush at the hands of Chief Osceola and a small party. State senate (1817-1819), U.S. Representative (1821-1833), state constitutional convention delegate (1833).

THOMSON, EDWIN KEITH *(b Feb. 8, 1919, New Castle, Wyo.; d Dec. 9, 1960, Cody, Wyo.)* Lawyer, World War II officer who was wounded in Italy, Wyoming Republican. GOP National Convention delegate (1952), state representative (1952-1954), U.S. Representative (1955 until death), elected to U.S. Senate (1960) but died before his term was to begin.

THOMSON, JOHN *(b Nov. 20, 1780, Ireland; d Dec. 2, 1852, New Lisbon, now Lisbon, Ohio)* Physician, Ohio Democrat. State senate (1814, 1815, 1817-1820), state representative (1816), U.S. Representative (1825-1827, 1829-1837).

THOMSON, MARK *(b 1739, Norriton Township, Pa.; d Dec. 14, 1803, Marksboro, N.J.)* Miller, Revolutionary officer, New Jersey Federalist. Sussex County justice of the peace (1773), provincial convention delegate (1774), Provincial Congress member (1775), state assemblyman (1779), member of the state council (1786-1788), U.S. Representative (1795-1799).

THORNBERRY, WILLIAM HOMER *(b Jan. 9, 1909, Austin, Tex.)* Lawyer, Texas Democrat, State representative (1936-1941), fifty-third judicial district attorney (1941-1942), U.S. Navy (1942-1946), Austin City Council (1946-1948) and mayor (1947, 1948), Democratic National Convention (1956), U.S. Representative (1949-1964).

THORNTON, MATTHEW *(b 1714, Ireland; d June 24, 1803, Newburyport, Mass.)* Physician, New Hampshire patriot and signer of the Declaration of Independence. Member of the first New Hampshire assembly and two subsequent ones (1758, 1760, 1761), justice of the peace, delegate to the first Provincial Congress (1775) and its president, chairman of the Committee of Safety (1775), general assembly speaker (1776) and member (1783), member of the Continental Congress (1776, 1778), chief justice of the court of common pleas, superior court judge (1776-1782), state senate (1784), state councillor (1785).

THROCKMORTON, JAMES WEBB *(b Feb. 1, 1825, Sparta, Tenn.; d April 21, 1894, McKinney, Texas)* Physician, Confederate Army officer, Texas Whig-Democrat. State representative (1851-1856), state senate (1856-1861, 1865), secession convention delegate (1861), reconstruction convention delegate and its presiding officer (1866), governor (1866-1867) when he was ordered removed by General Sheridan, U.S. Representative (1875-1879, 1883-1887), presidential elector on the Hancock-English ticket (1880), Democratic National Convention delegate (1892).

THURMAN, ALLEN GRANBERRY *(b Nov. 13, 1813, Lynchburg, Va.; d Dec. 12, 1895, Columbus, Ohio)* Lawyer, Ohio Democrat who urged the federal government to keep hands off the question of slavery within the territories and was a leader of the Peace Democrats during the Civil War; author of the Thurman Act pertaining to Pacific railroads; Cleveland's vice presidential running mate (1888). U.S. Representative (1845-1847), associate justice of the state supreme court (1851-1854) and chief justice (1854-1856), U.S. Senate (1869-1881), member of Electoral Commission (1877) to decide outcome of 1876 presidential election, Democratic National Convention delegate (1876, 1880, 1884).

THURSTON, BENJAMIN BABOCK *(b June 29, 1804, Hopkinton, R.I.; d May 17, 1886, New London, Conn.)* Merchant, Rhode Island and Connecticut Democrat. In Rhode Island: state representative (1831-1837), presidential elector on the Van Buren-Johnson ticket (1836), lieutenant governor (1838), U.S. Representative (1847-1849, 1851-1857). In Connecticut: New London alderman (1862, 1863), state representative (1869, 1870).

THURSTON, LLOYD *(b March 27, 1880, Osceola, Iowa)* Lawyer, Iowa Republican. Clarke County prosecutor (1906-1910), state senate (1920-1924), U.S. Representative (1925-1939).

TICHENOR, ISAAC *(b Feb. 8, 1754, Newark, N.J.; d Dec. 11, 1838, Bennington, Vt.)* Lawyer, Vermont Federalist who had much to do with statehood there. State representative (1781-1784) and speaker (1783), Vermont agent to Congress to seek admission to the Union (1782), state councillor (1787-

1792), Vermont-New York boundary commissioner (1789), state supreme court associate justice (1790-1794) and chief justice (1795, 1796), member of state board of censors (1792-1813), U.S. Senate (1796-1797, 1815-1821), governor (1797-1806, 1808).

TIFFIN, EDWARD *(b June 19, 1766, Carlisle, England; d Aug. 9, 1829, Chillicothe, Ohio)* Physician, preacher, Democrat who was an early settler in the Northwest Territory and had much to do with Ohio becoming the first state to emerge from that area. Among his other firsts: president of the convention that drafted Ohio's constitution (1802), Ohio's first governor (1803-1807), first U.S. commissioner of public lands (1812-1814), and the only department officer to save his records when the British destroyed Washington (1814). Member and speaker of the territorial house of representatives (1799), U.S. Senate (1807-1809), member and speaker of the state house of representatives (1809-1810), surveyor general of the Northwest Territory (1814-1829).

TILDEN, SAMUEL JONES *(b Feb. 9, 1814, New Lebanon, N.Y.; d Aug. 4, 1886, New York City)* Boyhood friend of Martin Van Buren for whom he later wrote political treatises, brilliant lawyer whose specialty was railroad reorganization, an antislavery Barnburner Democrat who opposed Lincoln and the Civil War but when it had begun advocated a quick call-up of troops, a New York reformer who, as state Democratic chairman (1866-1874) had much to do with breaking the Tweed Ring, but, most of all, the Democratic candidate for the presidency (1876) who beat Rutherford B. Hayes in the popular vote (4,284,020 to 4,036,572) but was counted out in the electoral vote (184 to 185); then fraud was charged and the election outcome was placed in the hands of a special commission said to be weighted on the side of the Republicans and Southern Democrats.

For two years prior to and during his presidential bid (1875, 1876), Tilden was governor of New York—an administration marked by reforms on every level, the reduction of taxes and the end of the bipartisan "canal ring" that had gotten rich by improper manipulations of the state's canal system.

TILGHMAN, MATTHEW *(b Feb. 17, 1718, Queen Annes County, Md.; d May 4, 1790, Talbot County, Md.)* Planter, landowner, Maryland patriot who while a member of the Continental Congress (1774-1777) was summoned home from Philadelphia to preside over the Annapolis convention (1776) and so missed out on becoming a signer of the Declaration of Independence. Talbot County justice of the peace; member of the Maryland House of Delegates (1751-1777) and speaker (1773-1775), president of the Revolutionary convention that directed the colony's affairs (1774-1777), member of committee that drafted Stamp Act protest; chairman of Committee of Correspondence (1774), Committee of Safety (1775) and committee that drafted the state constitution; state senator (1777-1778).

TILLINGHAST, JOSEPH LEONARD *(b 1791, Taunton, Mass.; d Dec. 30, 1844, Providence, R.I.)* Publisher of the *Providence Gazette*, lawyer, Rhode Island Whig. State representative (1826-1833) and house speaker (1829-1832), U.S. Representative (1837-1843), Brown University trustee (1833-1844). Great-grandson of Thomas Tillinghast.

TILLINGHAST, THOMAS *(b Aug. 21, 1742, East Greenwich, R.I.; d Aug. 26, 1821, East Greenwich)* Rhode Island patriot who held a variety of positions under Revolutionary authorities. State representative (1772, 1773, 1778-1780), common pleas court judge (1779), associate justice of the state supreme court

(1780-1797), U.S. Representative (1797-1799, 1801-1803). Great-grandfather of Joseph L. Tillinghast.

TILLMAN, BENJAMIN RYAN *(b Aug. 11, 1847, Edgefield County, S.C.; d July 3, 1918, Washington, D.C.)* Planter, Democrat, and the virtual boss of South Carolina politics for many years; a man who did not hesitate to use force to strip Negroes of their rights, enemy of Presidents Cleveland and Theodore Roosevelt, known as Pitchfork Ben—a name that well describes a man whom one biographer described as "a blunt, irascible, unmannerly representative of rural interests"; a man whose unethical land buyings were exposed by Teddy Roosevelt.

Delegate to all state and national Democratic conventions (1890-1918), governor (1890-1894), founder of Clemson Agricultural and Mechanical College (1893) and Winthrop Normal and Industrial College (1895), state constitutional convention delegate (1895), U.S. Senate (1895 until death) and chairman of the Naval Affairs Committee during World War I. Brother of George D. Tillman.

TILLMAN, GEORGE DIONYSIUS *(b Aug. 21, 1826, Edgefield County, S.C.; d Feb. 2, 1902, Clarks Hill, S.C.)* Lawyer, planter, publicist, Confederate soldier, and a South Carolina Democrat. State representative (1854-1860, 1864), state constitutional convention delegate (1865, 1895), state senate (1865), U.S. Representative (1879-1882, 1883-1893) with some time out in 1882 when his election was successfully contested. Brother of Benjamin R. Tillman.

TILLMAN, JOHN NEWTON *(b Dec. 13, 1859, Greene County, Mo.; d March 9, 1929, Fayetteville, Ark.)* Teacher, lawyer, president of the University of Arkansas (1905-1912), Arkansas Democrat. Washington County circuit court clerk (1884-1889), state senate (1888-1892), fourth judicial circuit prosecutor (1892-

1898) and judge (1900-1905), U.S. Representative (1915-1929).

TILSON, JOHN QUILLIN *(b April 5, 1866, Clearbranch, Tenn.; d Aug. 14, 1958, New London, N.H.)* Lawyer, Yale lecturer, author of book on parliamentary law, Connecticut Republican. State representative (1904-1908) and house speaker the last two years, U.S. Representative (1909-1913, 1915-1932) and majority leader of the House (1925-1931), GOP National Convention delegate (1932).

TIMBERLAKE, CHARLES BATEMAN *(b Sept. 25, 1854, Wilmington, Ohio; d May 31, 1941, Sterling, Colo.)* Teacher, farmer, stock raiser, banker, Colorado Republican. GOP state committeeman (1892-1910), Phillips County school superintendent (1889-1895), county clerk (1895-1897), U.S. Land Office receiver at Sterling (1897-1914), U.S. Representative (1915-1933).

TINCHER, JASPER NAPOLEON *(b Nov. 2, 1878, Browning, Mo.; d Nov. 6, 1951, Hutchinson, Kans.)* Teacher, lawyer, farmer, stock raiser, Kansas Republican. U.S. Representative (1919-1927).

TINKHAM, GEORGE HOLDEN *(b Oct. 29, 1870, Boston, Mass.; d Aug. 28, 1956, Cramerton, N.C.)* Lawyer, Massachusetts Republican whose ancestors came to America aboard the *Mayflower.* Boston alderman (1900-1902), state senate (1910-1912), U.S. Representative for twenty-eight years (1915-1943).

TIPTON, THOMAS WESTON *(b Aug. 5, 1817, Cadiz, Ohio; d Nov. 26, 1899, Washington, D.C.)* Lawyer, clergyman, Union Army chaplain, Nebraska Republican. As a territory: constitutional convention delegate (1859), member of the territorial council (1860), Nebraska internal revenue assessor (1865), state constitutional convention delegate

(1867). As a state: one of Nebraska's first two U.S. Senators (1867-1875).

TIRRELL, CHARLES QUINCY *(b Dec. 10, 1844, Sharon, Mass.; d July 31, 1910, Natick, Mass.)* Teacher, lawyer, Massachusetts Republican. State representative (1872), state senate (1881, 1882), presidential elector on the Harrison-Morton ticket (1888), U.S. Representative (1901 until death).

TOBEY, CHARLES WILLIAM *(b July 22, 1880, Roxbury, Mass.; d July 24, 1953, U.S. Naval Hospital, Bethesda, Md.).* Farmer, insurance broker, banker, manufacturer, New Hampshire Republican. State representative (1915, 1916, 1919, 1920, 1923, 1924) and house speaker (1919, 1920), state senator and senate president (1925, 1926), governor (1929, 1930), U.S. Representative (1933-1939), U.S. Senate (1939 until death), U.S. delegate to the Bretton Woods International Monetary Conference (1944), U.S. adviser to the Paris UNESCO Conference (1952).

TOLAN, JOHN HARVEY *(b Jan. 15, 1877, St. Peter, Minn.; d June 30, 1947, Westwood, Calif.)* Montana lawyer who was Deer Lodge County attorney (1904-1906) before moving to California where he was an active Democrat. U.S. Representative (1935-1947).

TOMLINSON, GIDEON *(b Dec. 31, 1780, Stratford, Conn.; d Oct. 8, 1854, Fairfield, Conn.)* Lawyer, Connecticut Democrat. Clerk of the state house of representatives (1817) and its president (1818), U.S. Representative (1819-1827), governor (1827-1831) resigning to become U.S. Senator (1831-1837), Trinity College trustee (1832-1836).

TOMPKINS, CALEB *(b Dec. 22, 1759, Westchester County, N.Y.; d Jan. 1, 1846, Scarsdale, N.Y.)* New York lawyer who was a U.S. Representative

(1817-1821) during part of the time that his brother, Daniel D. Tompkins, was vice president of the United States. State assemblyman (1804-1806), common pleas and Westchester County court judge (1807-1811, 1820-1824).

TOMPKINS, DANIEL D. *(b June 21, 1774, Fox Meadow, now Scarsdale, N.Y.; d June 11, 1825, Tompkinsville, Staten Island, N.Y.)* Lawyer, liberal New York Democrat whose regime as governor (1807-1817) was marked by many liberal reforms including the complete abolition of slavery in the state. After that came the high-water mark of his political career: vice president of the United States during James Monroe's presidency (1817-1825). State constitutional convention delegate (1801) and president of one that followed twenty years later, state assemblyman (1803), associate justice of the state supreme court (1804-1807). Brother of Caleb Tompkins.

TONGUE, THOMAS H. *(b June 23, 1844, Lincolnshire, England; d Jan. 11, 1903, Washington, D.C.)* Lawyer, Oregon Republican. State senate (1888-1892), GOP state convention chairman (1890, 1894), GOP National Convention delegate (1892), U.S. Representative (1897 until death).

TOOLE, JOSEPH KEMP *(b May 12, 1851, Savannah, Mo.; d March 11, 1929, Helena, Mont.)* Lawyer, Montana Democrat who was the state's first governor (1889-1893) and whose reputation was such that eight years later the people returned him to the statehouse for seven more years (1901-1908). As a territory: third judicial district attorney (1872-1876), territorial representative (1879-1881), president of the territorial council (1881-1883), state constitutional convention delegate (1884-1889), delegate to the U.S. Congress (1885-1889). As a state: Democratic National Convention delegate (1892, 1904).

TOOMBS, ROBERT *(b July 2, 1810, Wilkes County, Ga.; d Dec. 15, 1885, Washington, Ga.)* Lawyer, orator, Indian fighter, Georgia Whig-Constitutional Unionist-States' Rights Democrat who was author of the state's secession resolution and a founder of the Confederate States, becoming a member of its Congress and its first secretary of state when, thoroughly dissolusioned by Jefferson Davis' policies, he resigned, became a general in the Confederate Army, and was wounded at Antietam. After the Civil War, his independence forced him to live the life of a fugitive in Europe for a time, returning (1867) to become active politically once again, leading the fight to turn out the Radicals.
   State representative (1837-1840), Democratic National Convention delegate (1844), U.S. Representative (1845-1853), U.S. Senate (1853-1861); sixteen years later (1877) the dominant figure in the state constitutional convention that put a check-rein upon Negro rights and Carpetbag rule.

TOUCEY, ISAAC *(b Nov. 5, 1796, Newtown, Conn.; d July 30, 1869, Hartford, Conn.)* Lawyer, Connecticut Democrat. Hartford County prosecutor (1822-1835, 1842-1844), U.S. Representative (1835-1839), governor (1846-1847), U.S. attorney general in the Polk cabinet (1848-1849), state senate (1850), state representative (1852), U.S. Senate (1852-1857), secretary of the navy in the Buchanan cabinet (1857-1861).

TOWNER, HORACE MANN *(b Oct. 23, 1855, Belvidere, Ill.; d Nov. 23, 1937, Corning, Iowa)* Lawyer, University of Iowa lecturer on constitutional law (1902-1911), Iowa Republican who served as governor of Puerto Rico (1923-1929). Adams County schools superintendent (1880-1884), third judicial district judge (1890-1911), U.S. Representative (1911-1923) resigning to accept the Puerto Rican appointment.

TOWNSEND, CHARLES ELROY *(b Aug. 15, 1856, Jackson County, Mich.; d Aug. 3, 1924, Jackson, Mich.)* Teacher, lawyer, Michigan Republican. Concord register of deeds (1886-1897), U.S. Representative (1903-1911), U.S. Senate (1911-1923), member of the U.S.-Canada Water Boundary Commission (1923 until death).

TOWNSEND, JOHN GILLIS, JR. *(b May 31, 1871, Worcester County, Md.).* Banker, manufacturer, poultry raiser, banker, trustee of Washington and Goucher colleges and American University; Delaware Republican. State representative (1901-1903), GOP National Convention delegate (1908, 1924, 1928), governor (1917-1921), U.S. Senate (1929-1941).

TOWNSHEND, RICHARD WELLINGTON *(b April 30, 1840, Prince Georges County, Md.; d March 9, 1889, Washington, D.C.)* Teacher, lawyer, Illinois Democrat. Hamilton County circuit court clerk (1863-1868), twelfth judicial circuit prosecutor (1868-1872), Democratic state central committee member (1864, 1865, 1874, 1875), Democratic National Convention delegate (1872), U.S. Representative (1877 until death).

TRACY, URIAH *(b Feb. 2, 1755, Franklin, Conn.; d July 19, 1807, Washington, D.C.)* Lawyer, Connecticut Federalist. State representative (1788-1793) and house speaker (1793), Litchfield County state's attorney (1794-1799), U.S. Representative (1793-1796) resigning to become a U.S. Senator (1796 until death) and president pro tem of the Senate (1800).

TRAMMELL, PARK *(b April 9, 1876, Macon County, Ala.; d May 8, 1936, Washington, D.C.)* Lawyer, fruit grower, newspaper editor-publisher, Florida Democrat. Mayor of Lakeland (1899-1903), state representative (1902), state senator (1904-1908) and senate president (1905), state attorney general (1909-1913), governor (1913-1917), U.S. Senate (1917 until death).

TREADWAY, ALLEN TOWNER *(b Sept. 16, 1867, Stockbridge, Mass.; d Feb. 16, 1947, Washington, D.C.)* Hotel executive, Massachusetts Republican who was a U.S. Representative for sixteen consecutive terms (1913-1945). State representative (1904), state senator (1908-1911) and senate president (1909-1911).

TRIGG, ABRAM *(b 1750 near Old Liberty, now Bedford, Va.; d ——)* Revolutionary army officer, Virginia lawyer, who served six terms as a U.S. Representative (1797-1809). Delegate to the state convention that ratified the U.S. Constitution (1788). Brother of John J. Trigg.

TRIGG, JOHN JOHNS *(b 1748, near Old Liberty, now Bedford, Va.; d May 17, 1804, Bedford County, Va.)* Virginia planter, Revolutionary officer. Delegate to the state convention that ratified the federal Constitution (1788), Virginia House of Delegates (1784-1792), U.S. Representative (1797 until death), entering Congress at the same time as his brother, Abram.

TRIMBLE, DAVID *(b June, 1782; Frederick County, Va.; d Oct. 20, 1842, Trimble's Furnace, Ky.)* Lawyer, Kentucky Democrat. U.S. Representative (1817-1827).

TRIMBLE, JAMES WILLIAM *(b Feb. 3, 1894, Osage, Ark.)* Lawyer, Arkansas Democrat, Carroll County official (1920-1928), fourth judicial circuit prosecuting attorney (1930-1938), judge (1938-1944), U.S. Representative (1945-1967) serving on the Rules and District of Columbia committees.

TRIMBLE, SOUTH *(b April 13, 1864, Wolfe County, Ky.; d Nov. 23, 1946,*

Washington, D.C.) Farmer, Kentucky Democrat. State representative (1898-1900) and house speaker (1900), U.S. Representative (1901-1907), returning to Washington four years later to serve as clerk of the House (1911-1919, 1931 until death).

TROUP, GEORGE MICHAEL *(b Sept. 8, 1780, McIntosh Bluff, Ga., now Ala.; d April 26, 1856, Montgomery County, Ga.).* Lawyer, planter, Georgia Democrat who twice resigned from the U.S. Senate, defied President John Quincy Adams on the state acquisition of Creek lands while governor (1823-1827), and refused the 1852 presidential nomination of Alabama's Southern States' Rights party. State representative (1803-1805), U.S. Representative (1807-1815), U.S. Senate (1816-1818, 1829-1833).

TRUMAN, HARRY S *(b May 8, 1884, on a farm near Lamar, Mo.; d Dec. 26, 1972, Kansas City, Mo.).* Missouri Democrat, vice president (1945 until the death of President Roosevelt when he became thirty-third president 1945-1953), taking over as commander in chief during the last months of World War II and administering during the critical postwar period; he made the decision to hasten the end of the war by dropping the atom bomb on Japan and the decision to go to war in Korea; U.S. Senate; judge; World War I army major; farmer whose early-rising habits carried over into the presidency where the pace of his morning walks made it difficult for the reporters who joined him to keep up.

The oldest of three children, Harry S Truman (the initial S does not stand for anything) moved with his family (1888) to a farm near Independence, Mo., where he grew up. He attended the local schools and after graduating (1901) from high school, he tried to get into West Point but was rejected because of poor eyesight; went to Kansas City, Mo., where he worked at various jobs,

then (1906-1917) he successfully managed the 600-acre family farm at Grandview, Mo.; sailed for France in 1917 as a lieutenant, saw action in the field artillery, and was discharged a major; colonel of field artillery, U.S. Reserve Corp (1927-1945).

Soon after his return from France he married Elizabeth (Bess) Wallace who, from the fifth grade had gone through school with him. They had one child. After losing his savings in a unsuccessful venture into the haberdashery business in Kansas City (it took him twenty years but he paid off the debts), Truman turned to politics.

With the support of the Pendergast political machine, Truman was elected a Jackson County judge (1922-1924), the title for executive branch officials there. While serving he attended night classes at Kansas City Law School. Defeated for reelection in 1924; presiding judge (1926-1934) in which capacity he supervised expenditure of $60 million for public works, earning a reputation for efficiency; elected to the U.S. Senate with Pendergast's backing (1935-1945), he strongly supported Roosevelt's New Deal program and, as chairman of the special committee to investigate the National Defense Program (the Truman Committee), he gained a national reputation for successfully uncovering waste and inefficiency; nominated as a compromise candidate for the vice presidency at the 1944 Democratic National Convention, winning the election as President Franklin D. Roosevelt's running mate; nominated to run for the presidency in his own right at the 1948 convention but there was a serious division in the party (ultra-Liberal Democrats were dissatisfied with Truman's foreign policy and many Southerners were opposed to his stand on civil rights); pollsters predicted Truman didn't have a chance. The stubborn president took to the road on a rousing "give 'em hell" whistle-stop campaign attacking the "do-nothing" Republican

Congress for its failure to act on his program and won the election, receiving approximately half the popular vote and 303 electoral votes to Republican candidate Thomas E. Dewey's 189, States' Rights Democrat J. Strom Thurmond's 39, and Progressive Henry Wallace's 0.

During his presidency, Truman's proposed Fair Deal domestic program carried forward many of Roosevelt's New Deal principles but Congress seldom cooperated by passing the necessary legislation to carry them out and overrode Truman's veto of the Taft-Hartley Labor Relations Law which curbed the rights of labor; the Atomic Energy Commission was established (1946); accusations of Communist infiltration into government heralded the start of the McCarthy era, and the Internal Security Act of 1951 was passed over Truman's veto.

Truman's telephoned speech (1945) opened the San Francisco Conference that established the United Nations Organization; the Truman Doctrine for containing Communist expansion by giving aid to countries that resisted was adopted as was the Marshall Plan, designed to reconstruct war-torn Europe, and the Point Four program for aid to underdeveloped countries, and (1949) the North Atlantic Treaty Organization (NATO) was formed. When Communist North Korea invaded South Korea (1950), Truman, under U.N. auspices, committed U.S. forces to South Korea's defense.

An unsuccessful attempt was made to assassinate Truman (1950) by two Puerto Rican revolutionaries who tried to force their way into Blair House where the Trumans lived while the White House was being renovated.

In retirement, Truman returned to his home in Independence, Mo., where he wrote his two-volume memoirs, *Year of Decisions* and *Years of Trial and Hope*, worked on the Harry S Truman Library, gave a series of lectures (1960) to Columbia University students that were later published under the title *Truman Speaks*, and remained active as an elder statesman.

TRUMBULL, JONATHAN *(b March 26, 1740, Lebanon, Conn.; d Aug. 7, 1809, Lebanon)* Lawyer, Continental Army paymaster and secretary to General Washington during the Revolution, Connecticut Federalist who was the first comptroller of the U.S. Treasury (1778-1779), and annually was reelected governor for eleven years (1797 until death). Speaker of Connecticut's colonial legislature before the Revolution. After the war he was a member of the First, Second, and Third Congress (1789-1795) and speaker in the Second, U.S. Senate (1795-1796), resigning to become lieutenant governor (1796) and moving into the statehouse upon the death of Governor Wolcott (1797). Brother of the following Joseph Trumbull.

TRUMBULL, JOSEPH *(b March 11, 1737, Lebanon, Conn.; d July 23, 1778, Lebanon)* Connecticut patriot who was commissary general of the Continental Army (July 19, 1775-Aug. 2, 1777) and then a commissioner of the board of war until ill health forced his resignation in April 1778. Continental Congress (1774, 1775). Brother of Jonathan Trumbull.

TRUMBULL, JOSEPH *(b Dec. 7, 1782, Lebanon, Conn.; d Aug. 4, 1861, Hartford, Conn.)* Lawyer, banker, railroad president, Connecticut Whig. State representative (1832, 1848, 1851), U.S. Representative (1834-1835, 1839-1843), governor (1849, 1850).

TRUMBULL, LYMAN *(b Oct. 12, 1813, Colchester, Conn.; d June 25, 1896, Chicago, Ill.)* Lawyer, Illinois Democrat–Free-Soiler–Republican and then a Democrat once again in an unsuccessful run for governor (1880). State representative (1840), Illinois secretary of state (1841, 1842), state supreme court justice (1848-1853), U.S. Senate (1855-1873).

TRUTH, SOUJOURNER *(b ca. 1797, Ulster County, N.Y.; d Nov. 26, 1883, Battle Creek, Mich.).* A freed slave (her real name was Isabella Baumfree) who feared that the end of slavery would not mean real freedom for black women unless they were given the right to vote along with their white sisters. Friend of such leading abolitionists as the Motts and Harriet Beecher Stowe. Believing that she received counseling from heavenly voices, in 1843 she left her job as a New York City domestic and traveled about the North, speaking eloquently and effectively (even though she was illiterate) for abolition of slavery and for women's rights.

TUBMAN, HARRIET ROSS *(b ca. 1821, Dorchester County, Md.; d March 10, 1913, Auburn, N.Y.)* Fugitive slave, abolitionist, women's suffragist, associate of John Brown (he called her General Tubman), Thomas Garrett, Susan B. Anthony, and many of the important antislavery leaders; "conductor" on the "underground railroad" who many times risked captivity (there was a price of $40,000 on her head) by returning South to lead more than 300 slaves to freedom in the North and Canada. During the Civil War, she served the Union Army as nurse, scout, and spy. She received many tributes, including a medal from Queen Victoria of England.

TUCKER, GEORGE *(b Aug. 20, 1775, St. Georges, Bermuda; d April 10, 1861, Sherwood, Va.)* Lawyer, author, historian, political economist and one of many Virginia Tuckers who made their contributions both to the law and to politics; Democrat. Pittsylvania County commonwealth attorney, member of

state house of delegates (1815), U.S. Representative (1819-1825), Jefferson-appointed first professor of moral philosophy at the University of Virginia (1825-1845).

Author of a four-volume *History of the United States, Life of Thomas Jefferson, The Laws of Wages, Profits and Rent Investigated,* and *The Theory of Money and Banks Investigated.*

TUCKER, HENRY ST. GEORGE *(b Dec. 29, 1780, Williamsburg, Va.; d Aug. 28, 1848, Winchester, Va.).* Another in the familial line of distinguished Virginia jurists and political figures, learning the law from his father, Professor St. George Tucker, author. U.S. Representative (1815-1819) and opponent of salary increases for congressmen, fourth judicial district chancellor (1824-1831) and founder of a private law school, state appeals court president (1831-1841), University of Virginia law professor (1841-1845), declined to be attorney general in the Jackson cabinet, author of *Tucker's Commentaries,* a treatise on formation of the U.S. Constitution, and *Commentaries on the Laws of Virginia.* Father of John R. Tucker, grandfather of the younger Henry St. George Tucker, cousin of George Tucker, and nephew of Thomas T. Tucker.

TUCKER, HENRY ST. GEORGE *(b April 5, 1853, Winchester, Va.; d July 23, 1932, Lexington, Va.)* Lawyer, educator, author, Virginia Democrat. U.S. Representative (1889-1897, 1922 until death), professor of constitutional law and equity at Washington and Lee University (1897) and dean of its law school (1900), dean of the School of Law and Diplomacy at George Washington University (1905), American Bar Association president (1905), editor of *Tucker on the Constitution* and author of *Woman Suffrage by Constitutional Amendment* and *Treaty Making Power.* Grandson of the elder Henry St. George Tucker, son of John R. Tucker.

TUCKER, JOHN RANDOLPH *(b Dec. 24, 1823, Winchester, Va.; d Feb. 13, 1897, Lexington, Va.)* Law student of his father (Henry St. George Tucker) and moral philosophy pupil of kinsman George, lawyer, author, educator and a Virginia Democrat who was a Jefferson Davis defense lawyer before the U.S. Supreme Court where, in another celebrated case, he was one of the defenders of the Chicago anarchists. Criticized for representing them, he replied: "I do not defend anarchy, I defend the Constitution."

Presidential elector on the Pierce-King (1852) and Buchanan-Breckinridge (1856) tickets, state attorney general (1857-1865), professor of equity and public law at Washington and Lee University (1870-1874) and constitutional law (1888 until death), U.S. Representative (1875-1887), president of the American Bar Association (1894). Author of *The Constitution of the United States, The Southern Church Justified in its Support of the South,* and *The History of the Federal Constitution.* Father of the younger Henry St. George Tucker.

TUCKER, STARLING *(b 1770, Halifax, N.C.; d Jan. 3, 1834, Mountain Shoals, now Enoree, S.C.)* Planter, South Carolina Democrat. U.S. Representative (1817-1831).

TUCKER, THOMAS TUDOR *(b June 25, 1745, Port Royal, Bermuda; d May 2, 1828, Washington, D.C.)* Physician, Continental Army surgeon, South Carolina Federalist. Member of the Continental Congress (1787, 1788), U.S. Representative in the First and Second Congress (1789-1793), Jefferson-appointed U.S. treasurer (1801 until death). Uncle of the elder Henry St. George Tucker.

TURNER, BENJAMIN STERLING *(b March 17, 1825, Halifax County, N.C.; d March 21, 1894, Selma, Ala.)* Self-educated slave who, after Emancipation, became a merchant and active in the Alabama Reconstruction as a Republican. Dallas County tax collector (1867), Selma councilman (1869), U.S. Representative (1871-1873), GOP National Convention delegate (1880).

TURNER, DANIEL *(b Sept. 21, 1796, Warren County, N.C.; d July 21, 1860, at Mare Island, Calif., Navy Yard where he was supervising engineer in charge of construction)* West Point graduate, North Carolina Democrat. State house of commons (1819-1823), U.S. Representative (1827-1829). Son of James Turner.

TURNER, GEORGE *(b Feb. 25, 1850, Edina, Mo.; d Jan. 26, 1932, Spokane, Wash.)* Union soldier, lawyer, mine developer, and an Alabama Republican who planted new stakes in Washington where he was a Silver Republican-Fusionist-Populist-Democrat and very much in the political and civic picture. In Alabama: U.S. marshal for the southern and middle districts (1876-1880), GOP National Convention delegate (1876, 1880, 1884). In Washington: associate justice of the territorial supreme court (1884-1888), delegate to the territorial convention that drafted the state constitution (1889), U.S. Senate (1897-1903), member of the Alaska boundary tribunal (1903), counsel for the U.S. at The Hague in fisheries dispute with Great Britain (1910), member of International Joint Commission on U.S.-Canada Boundary Waters (1911-1914) and counsel for the United States before that body (1918-1924).

TURNER, HENRY GRAY *(b March 20, 1839, Franklin County, N.C.; d June 9, 1904, Raleigh, N.C.)* Confederate officer who was badly wounded at Gettysburg, lawyer, Georgia Democrat. Presidential elector on the Greeley-Brown ticket (1872), state representative (1874-1876, 1878, 1879), Democratic National Convention delegate (1876), U.S. Representative (1881-1897), associate justice of the state supreme court (1903 until death).

TURNER, JAMES *(b Dec. 20, 1766, Southampton County, Va.; d Jan. 15, 1824, Warren County, N.C.)* Revolutionary soldier, planter, North Carolina Democrat. Member of state house of commons (1797-1800), state senate (1801, 1802), governor (1802-1805), U.S. Senate (1805-1816). Father of Daniel Turner.

TURNEY, HOPKINS LACY *(b Oct. 3, 1797, Dixon Springs, Tenn.; d Aug. 1, 1857, Winchester, Tenn.)* Indian fighter, lawyer, Tennessee Democrat. State representative (1828-1838), U.S. Representative (1837-1843), U.S. Senate (1845-1851).

TURPIE, DAVID *(b July 8, 1828, Hamilton County, Ohio; d April 21, 1909, Indianapolis, Ind.)* Lawyer, Indiana Democrat. State representative (1852, 1858, 1874, 1875) and house speaker (1874), common pleas court judge (1854-1856), circuit court judge (1856), U.S. Senate for two months (1863) to fill a vacancy and nearly a quarter-century later elected in his own right (1887-1899), a commissioner to revise state laws (1878, 1881), U.S. attorney (1886, 1887), Democratic National Convention delegate (1888).

TWEED, WILLIAM MARCY "BOSS" *(b April 3, 1823, New York City; d April 12, 1878, in New York City's Ludlow St. Jail)* Chairmaker, bookkeeper, New York Democrat who organized a volunteer fire company and with that as his political base went on to become one of the city's most powerful bosses of all time, selling favors, judgeships, and public office as if they were soap; in order to reach into both private and corporate purses he formed a law company, although he was not a lawyer, and listed among his "clients" Jay Gould's Erie Railroad, plundering that line dry. His come-uppance came mainly at the hands of three men: George Jones, of the *New York Times*; Samuel J. Tilden, chairman of the Democratic state committee, and Thomas Nast, whose cartoons in *Harper's Weekly* backed up an editorial campaign that zeroed in on Tweed, the Tweed Ring, and New York City's nefarious 1870 city charter. The *Times* published proof of graft in July 1871, a Committee of Seventy was formed in September, and Tweed was arrested in December. His first trial ended in a hung jury; his second brought conviction (November 1873) and a twelve-year prison term on Blackwell's Island. The Boss won an appeal, was released, and arrested once again (January 1875) on the charge of swindling New York State out of $6 million. Held in the Ludlow Street Jail, he escaped (December 1875) fled to Cuba, and then to Spain where the law caught up with him once again. He was returned to the jail (November 1876) where he died.

His political offices: one of the city's "Forty Thieves" aldermen (1852, 1853), U.S. Representative (1853-1855), city school commissioner (1856, 1857), New York County supervisor (1858), deputy streets commissioner (1861-1870), state senate (1867, 1869), city public works commissioner (1870-1875) and from 1859 until his downfall, chairman of the Democratic county committee—in other words leader of Tammany Hall.

TYDINGS, MILLARD EVELYN *(b April 6, 1890, Havre de Grace, Md.; d Feb. 9, 1961, near Havre de Grace)* Civil engineer, author, lawyer, Maryland Democrat. State senate (1921-1923), U.S. Representative (1923-1927), U.S. Senate (1927-1951).

TYLER, DAVID GARDINER *(b July 12, 1846, East Hampton, N.Y.; d Sept. 5, 1927, Charles City County, Va.)* Confederate soldier who was captured at Appomattox, lawyer, Virginia Democrat. Director of the state lunatic asylum (1884-1887), presidential elector on the Cleveland-Thurman ticket (1888), state senate (1891, 1892, 1900-1904), U.S. Representative (1893-1897), fourteenth judicial circuit judge (1904 until death). Son of President John Tyler.

TYLER, JOHN, SR. *(b Feb. 28, 1747, York County, Va.; d Jan. 6, 1813, Charles City County, Va.)* Fourth in a line of John Tylers (his son, President Tyler, was the fifth), poet, violinist, lawyer, planter, friend of Thomas Jefferson, admirer and comrade in arms of Patrick Henry (as head of a company of volunteers, he accompanied Henry on his 1775 march to retake the powder the British had seized at Williamsburg), Virginia Democrat. Committee of Safety (1774), admiralty court judge (1776-1789), house of delegates (1777-1789) and speaker (1781-1786), delegate to the state convention that ratified the U.S. Constitution (1788) despite his and Henry's opposition, general court judge (1789-1808), governor (1808-1811), federal judge (1811 until death). Grandfather of David G. Tyler.

TYLER, JOHN, JR. *(b March 29, 1790, "Greenway," Charles City County, Va.; d Jan. 18, 1862, Richmond, Va.)* Tenth president (former Virginia Democrat elected vice president on Whig ticket who became president when William Henry Harrison died), 1841-1845.

Son of the preceding under whom he studied law after graduating (1807) from William and Mary College. Admitted to the bar in 1809. His first wife, Letitia Christian, whom he married in 1813, died in 1842 and two years later he married Julia Gardiner, thirty years his junior. He had a total of fifteen children by his two wives.

Member of Virginia legislature (1811-1816, 1823-1825, 1839-1840); member of state constitutional convention (1829,

1830); U.S. Representative (1817-1821); governor of Virginia (1825-1827); U.S. Senate (1827-1836) and president pro tem (1835); defeated (1836) for vice president (he received 47 electoral votes), running as a states' rights Whig. President (1838) of Virginia African Colonization Society. Although a strong states' rights advocate, Tyler opposed South Carolina's nullification policy but no more than he opposed Jackson's retaliation with the Force Bill. Supported Jackson's stand against the Bank of the United States but opposed his removal of the funds. When (1836) the Virginia legislature instructed him to vote to expunge a resolution censuring Jackson (for the funds' removal), he resigned from the Senate.

The Whig party, hoping he would attract Southern votes, ran Tylor for vice president in the election of 1840 and he was swept into office along with William Henry Harrison in the "Tippecanoe and Tyler too" campaign. When Harrison died one month after inauguration, the Whigs, under Henry Clay's leadership, tried to control President Tyler but ran up against a rock wall, discovering that this was a man who made up his own mind. After Tyler twice vetoed a national bank bill, his entire cabinet (which he inherited from Harrison), with the exception of Daniel Webster, resigned. During his administration, the important Webster-Ashburton Treaty was concluded with Britain, China trade was opened to Americans, and progress was made toward annexation of Texas.

As president, he sought renomination in the 1844 presidential election but withdrew; chancellor (1859) of William and Mary College; president of pre-Civil War convention held (1861) in Washington in an unsuccessful attempt to avert war; delegate to Confederate Provisional Congress (1861); elected to the House of Representatives of the Confederate Congress but died while attending first session. Father of David G. Tyler.

U

☆ ☆ ☆

UDREE, DANIEL (b Aug. 5, 1751, Philadelphia, Pa.; d July 15, 1828, Reading, Pa.) Merchant, Pennsylvania Democrat. State representative (1799-1805), U.S. Representative (1813-1815, 1820-1821, 1822-1825).

UMSTEAD, WILLIAM BRADLEY (b May 13, 1895, Mangum Township, N.C.; d Nov. 7, 1954, Durham, N.C.) Teacher, lawyer, University of North Carolina trustee, North Carolina Democrat. Durham County recorders court prosecutor (1922-1926), tenth judicial district solicitor (1927-1933), state Democratic executive committee chairman (1944-1947), Democratic National Convention delegate (1948), U.S. Representative (1933-1939), U.S. Senate to fill a vacancy (1946-1948), governor (1953 until death).

UNDERHILL, CHARLES LEE (b July 20, 1867, Richmond, Va.; d Jan. 28, 1946, New York City) Officeboy, teamster, blacksmith, hardware manufacturer, Massachusetts Republican who, after six terms as a U.S. Representative (1921-1933) remained in Washington as a real estate operator. State representative (1902, 1903, 1908-1913, 1917, 1918), state constitutional convention delegate (1917, 1918).

UNDERWOOD, JOSEPH ROGERS (b Oct. 24, 1791, Goochland County, Va.; d Aug. 23, 1876, near Bowling Green, Ky.) Lawyer, planter, Kentucky Whig-Democrat. State representative (1816-1819, 1825, 1826, 1846, 1861) and house speaker (1846), presidential elector on the Clay (1824) and Clay-Frelinghuysen (1844) tickets, appeals court judge (1828-1835), U.S. Representative (1835-1843), U.S. Senate (1847-1853), Democratic National Convention delegate (1864). Brother of Warner L., Grandfather of Oscar W. Underwood.

UNDERWOOD, OSCAR WILDER (b May 6, 1862, Louisville, Ky.; d Jan. 25, 1929, Fairfax County, Va.) Lawyer, statesman, and an Alabama Democrat who was an expert on tariffs, opposing them for protective purposes, a staunch supporter of Woodrow Wilson, and a foe of both the Ku Klux Klan and prohibition, the latter costing him the presidential nomination (1924) after once before (1912) having been a serious contender. Chairman of the ninth district Democratic executive committee (1892); U.S. Representative (1895-1896, 1897-1915), chairman of the House Ways and Means Committee and Democratic floor leader (1911-1915), U.S. Senate (1915-1927) and once again his party's floor leader but this time in the Senate (1921-1923), U.S. representative to the Conference on Limitation of Armament (1921, 1922), U.S. delegate to Sixth International Conference

573

of American States (1928). Grandson of Joseph R. Underwood.

UNDERWOOD, THOMAS RUST *(b March 3, 1898, Hopkinsville, Ky.; d June 29, 1956, Lexington, Ky.)* Newspaperman who became editor of the *Lexington Herald* (1935 until death), and a Democrat who had much to do with the running of the Kentucky Derby. Member of state planning board (1931-1935), secretary of the state racing commission (1931-1943, 1947, 1948), and secretary of the National Association of State Racing Commissioners (1934-1948), assistant to the director of the Office of Economic Stabilization (beginning in 1943), U.S. Representative (1949-1951) when he resigned to fill a vacancy in the U.S. Senate (1951-1952).

UNDERWOOD, WARNER LEWIS *(b Aug. 7, 1808, Goochland County, Va.; d March 12, 1872, near Bowling Green, Ky.)* Lawyer, Kentucky member of the American (Know-Nothing) party who lived for a few years in Texas (1834-1840) where he was attorney general for the eastern district. In Kentucky: State representative (1848), state senate (1849-1853), U.S. Representative (1855-1859), U.S. consul to Glasgow, Scotland (1862-1864). Brother of Joseph R. Underwood.

UPDEGRAFF, THOMAS *(b April 3, 1834, Tioga County, Pa.; d Oct. 4, 1910, McGregor, Iowa)* Lawyer, Iowa Republican. Clayton County district court clerk (1856-1860), state representative (1878), U.S. Representative (1879-1883, 1893-1899), GOP National Convention delegate (1888).

UPHAM, CHARLES WENTWORTH *(b May 4, 1802, St. John, New Brunswick, Canada; d June 15, 1875, Salem, Mass.).* A Nova Scotia farmhand who became a Harvard-educated clergyman, remaining in Massachusetts where politically he was first a Whig and then a Republican,

but—more than that—was the author of *Salem Witchcraft* (1867) and was said to be the man after whom Nathaniel Hawthorne modelled his Judge Pyncheon in *The House of the Seven Gables.* State representative (1840-1849, 1859, 1860), mayor of Salem (1852), state constitutional convention delegate (1853), U.S. Representative (1853-1855), state senator and senate president (1857, 1858).

UPHAM, GEORGE BAXTER *(b Dec. 27, 1768, Brookfield, Mass.; d Feb. 10, 1848, Claremont, N.H.)* New Hampshire lawyer, banker. Cheshire County solicitor (1796-1804), U.S. Representative (1801-1803), state representative (1804-1813, 1815) and house speaker (1809, 1815), state senate (1814). Brother of Jabez and cousin of Nathaniel Upham.

UPHAM, JABEZ *(b Aug. 23, 1764, Brookfield, Mass.; d Nov. 8, 1811, Brookfield).* Massachusetts lawyer. State representative (1804-1806, 1811), U.S. Representative (1807-1810). Brother of George B. and cousin of Nathaniel Upham.

UPHAM, NATHANIEL *(b June 9, 1774, Deerfield, N.H.; d July 10, 1829, Rochester, N.H.)* Merchant, New Hampshire Democrat. State representative (1807-1809), governor's counselor (1811, 1812), U.S. Representative (1817-1823). Cousin of George B. and Jacob Upham.

UPHAM, WILLIAM *(b Aug. 5, 1792, Leicester, Mass.; d Jan. 14, 1853, Washington, D.C.)* Lawyer, Vermont Whig. State representative (1827, 1828, 1830), Washington County state's attorney (1829), U.S. Senate (1843 until death).

UPSHAW, WILLIAM DAVID *(b Oct. 15, 1866, Newnan, Ga.; d Nov. 21, 1952, Glendale, Calif.)* Farmer, merchant, writer, lecturer, evangelist who at seventy-two was ordained a minister, and a Georgia Democrat who was the

Prohibition party's presidential candidate (1932) polling 81,859 votes. U.S. Representative (1919-1927).

UPSON, CHARLES *(b March 19, 1821, Southington, Conn.; d Sept. 5, 1885, Coldwater, Mich.)* Teacher, lawyer, Michigan Republican. St. Joseph County deputy clerk (1847) and clerk (1848, 1849), prosecutor (1852-1854), state senate (1855, 1856, 1880), state railroad commissioner (1857), state attorney general (1861, 1862), U.S. Representative (1863-1869), fifteenth circuit court judge (1869-1872), member of commission to revise state constitution (1873), mayor of Coldwater (1877).

UTTER, GEORGE HERBERT *(b July 24, 1854, Plainfield, N.J.; d Nov. 3, 1912, Westerly, R.I.)* Printer, Westerly newspaper publisher, Rhode Island Republican. State representative (1885-1889) and house speaker (1889), state senator (1889-1891), Rhode Island secretary of state (1891-1894), lieutenant governor (1904), governor (1905, 1906), U.S. Representative (1911 until death).

V

☆ ☆ ☆

VAILE, WILLIAM NEWELL *(b June 22, 1876, Kokomo, Ind.; d July 2, 1927, Rocky Mountain National Park, Colo.).* Lawyer, Colorado Republican. U.S. Representative (1919 until death).

VALENTINE, EDWARD KIMBLE *(b June 1, 1843, Keosauqua, Iowa; d April 11, 1916, Chicago, Ill.)* Union soldier, lawyer, Nebraska Republican. U.S. Land Office register at West Point, Nebraska (1869-1871), sixth judicial district judge (1875), U.S. Representative (1879-1885), U.S. Senate sergeant at arms (1890-1893).

VALLANDIGHAM, CLEMENT LAIRD *(b July 29, 1820, New Lisbon, Ohio; d June 17, 1871, Lebanon, Ohio)* Teacher, lawyer, editor of the *Western Empire*, and an Ohio Democrat who, while opposed to slavery, was a firm believer in Jeffersonian states' rights and so was a vehement foe of abolition, a national army, civil war, and restrictions upon freedom of speech and the press. When war broke out he became a leader of Ohio's Peace Democrats and, as an outspoken Copperhead, deliberately defied a military ban upon "declaring sympathies for the enemy," delivering two speeches in which he called the war "wicked and cruel" and a plot to turn the United States into a despotic Republican empire.

As a result, he was arrested, tried, and convicted of treason by a military tribunal and ordered jailed. Lincoln intervened and had him banished to the Confederacy. While in exile, he escaped first to Bermuda and then to Canada and while there was the absentee Peace Democrat candidate for governor (1863). People rioted in his behalf, others petitioned Lincoln for his return but were turned down because of so-called military needs. He polled a heavy vote but nevertheless lost to a War Democrat running as a Republican. The next year, although still very much a fugitive, he returned to the United States and delivered speeches from Ohio to Chicago—still in defiance of the military ban—in which he denounced "King Lincoln." Thereafter he remained in the country, authorities remaining officially unaware both of his presence and his utterances, and had written into the Democratic national platform (1864) a plank demanding an end to the war. He abhorred Lincoln's assassination and after the war was dedicated in his pleas for national unity and a new beginning.

State representative (1845, 1846), Democratic National Convention delegate (1856, 1864), U.S. Representative (1858-1863).

VAN AERNAM, HENRY *(b March 11, 1819, Marcellus, N.Y.; d June 1, 1894, Franklinville, N.Y.)* Physician, Union

576

Army surgeon, New York Republican. U.S. Representative (1865-1869, 1879-1883), pension commissioner (1869-1871).

VAN ALEN, JAMES ISAAC *(b 1776, Kinderhook, N.Y.; d Dec. 23, 1870, Newburgh, N.Y.)* New York Federalist. Kinderhook city clerk (1797-1801), state constitutional convention delegate (1801, 1803), justice of the peace (1801-1804), assemblyman (1804), Columbia County surrogate (1804-1808, 1815-1822), U.S. Representative (1807-1809). Half-brother of President Martin Van Buren.

VAN BUREN, MARTIN *(b Dec. 5, 1782, Kinderhook, N.Y.; d July 24, 1862, Lindenwald, near Kinderhook)* Eighth president (New York Democrat), 1837-1841. Secretary of State; U.S. Senate; a dapper dresser with a charming, diplomatic, even-tempered disposition who was admired by his friends for his adroit political acumen but was known to his enemies as "the red fox of Kinderhook" and accused of behind-the-scenes intrigue. A member of the political group known as the Albany Regency, and an important political leader.

Son of farmer parents who also operated a tavern, he attended school until he was fourteen, then studied law and was admitted to the bar in 1803. He married distant cousin Hannah Hoes (1807), who bore him four sons. She died in 1819.

Columbia County surrogate (1808-1813); state senate (1813-1820), attorney general (1815-1819), delegate to state constitutional convention (1821), U.S. Senate (1821-1828); governor (1829) for two months, resigning to become Jackson's secretary of state (1829-1831). He became Jackson's closest adviser (he pleased Jackson by befriending Peggy O'Neale Eaton, controversial wife of the secretary of war) and resigned from the cabinet in a maneuver that made it possible for his chief (who was at odds with Vice President John C. Calhoun) to get rid of Calhoun supporters who were fellow cabinet members. Then, as vice president under Jackson (1833-1837), Van Buren presided skillfully over a Senate that had rejected his nomination as minister to England in 1831. With Jackson's backing and against a Whig party that was not yet well organized, he was easily elected president in 1836.

As president, Van Buren generally continued Jackson's policies but tried to correct some of the banking problems by recommending an independent treasury system (approved by Congress in 1840); protected slavery where it existed but was opposed to its further expansion; by executive order (1840), reduced the work day for all laborers and mechanics employed on federal public works to ten hours. But most of Van Buren's one term as president was dominated by the problems brought on by the Panic of 1837, which had its roots in the years before he took office. The idea of government interfering in the country's economic life or even giving aid to victims of financial panics had not yet been accepted and Van Buren did not believe he should change policies he felt were established for good reason. The opposition Whig party denounced him in the election of 1840, claiming he was a very wealthy aristocrat who was indifferent to the plight of the poor, and its "log cabin and hard cider" candidate William H. Harrison (whom Van Buren had defeated in 1836) won the presidency with 234 electoral votes to Van Buren's 60.

As an ex-president, Van Buren did not retire from the fray but kept trying to be reelected. He failed to receive the Democratic nomination in 1844, partly because he opposed Texas annexation, fearing it would spread slavery. In 1848, as the new antislavery Free-Soil party candidate, he split New York State's

Democratic vote, resulting in the election of Whig candidate Zachary Taylor.

VANCE, JOSEPH *(b March 21, 1786, Catfish, now Washington, Pa.; d Aug. 24, 1852, Champaign County, Ohio).* Farmer, merchant, surveyor who laid out the city of Findlay; Ohio Democrat turned Whig. State representative (1812, 1813, 1815, 1816, 1818, 1819), state constitutional convention delegate (1820, 1851), U.S. Representative (1821-1835, 1843-1847), governor (1836-1838), state senate (1840-1841), Whig National Convention delegate (1848).

VANCE, ROBERT BRANK *(b 1793, Buncombe County, N.C.; d 1827, near Saluda Gap, N.C., in a duel with Samuel P. Carson, his victorious Congressional opponent in 1826).* Physician, North Carolina Democrat. U.S. Representative (1823-1825). Uncle of the younger Robert B. Vance and of Zebulon B. Vance.

VANCE, ROBERT BRANK *(b April 24, 1828, Buncombe County, N.C.; d Nov. 28, 1899, Alexander, N.C.)* Merchant, farmer, Confederate Army officer, North Carolina Democrat. Pleas and quarter sessions court clerk (1848-1856), U.S. Representative (1873-1885), assistant U.S. commissioner of patents (1885-1889), state representative (1894-1896). Nephew of the preceding, brother of Zebulon B. Vance.

VANCE, ZEBULON BAIRD *(b May 13, 1830, Buncombe County, N.C.; d April 14, 1894, Washington, D.C.)* Lawyer, orator, and a North Carolina political figure who was torn by both his loyalty to the nation and his love for the South. Thus he was in turn a Whig, Know-Nothing, Conservative, and finally a Democrat.

As a U.S. Representative (1858-1861), he opposed secession but only until Lincoln began a build-up of troops when he resigned his seat and became a Confederate Army officer. Then, as governor (1862-1866) to which office he was elected as a Conservative, he was often at odds with Confederate policies, particularly as they pertained to conscription and the treatment of draft dodgers who had fled to the North Carolina mountains from their homes in other Southern states. He offered a pardon to all North Carolina deserters who returned to their units and thus brought many back into the fold.

Certainly an individualist, he organized a fleet of steamers that ran the blockade to bring needed supplies from Europe, both for his state and the South, in spite of Confederate government criticism of his methods. In his campaign for reelection (1864) he stood up for the Southern cause against an opponent, W. W. Holden, who was pressing for North Carolina to seek its own peace treaty with the North. Vance stuck to his guns after victory, in spite of mounting pressure from his constituency for a separate peace, declaring that he would not "lead the roll of infamy."

Briefly imprisoned by the Union (1865) on unspecified charges, he returned to lead North Carolina opposition to the Reconstruction and thus was once again elected governor (1876-1878), this time as a Democrat.

His other public offices: Buncombe County prosecutor (1852-1854), member of the state house of commons (1854), Democratic National Convention delegate (1868), U.S. Senate (1879 until death). Brother of the younger Robert B. Vance, nephew of the elder.

VAN CORTLANDT, PHILIP *(b Aug. 21, 1749, New York City; d Nov. 1, 1831, Croton on Hudson, N.Y.)* Heir to the Van Cortlandt estates and grist mills, civil engineer, surveyor, farmer, Revolutionary officer who fought under Lafayette, New York Democrat. Delegate to the state convention (1788) that ratified the federal Constitution, assemblyman (1788-1790), state senator

(1791-1793), U.S. Representative (1793-1809). Brother of Pierre Van Cortlandt, Jr.

VAN CORTLANDT, PIERRE, JR. *(b Aug. 29, 1762, Croton, N.Y.; d July 13, 1848, Peekskill, N.Y.)* Lawyer, manager of the family estate, founding president of the Westchester County Bank (1833 until death), New York Democrat. Presidential elector on the Jefferson (1800) and Harrison tickets (1840), assemblyman (1811, 1812), U.S. Representative (1811-1813). Brother of Philip Van Cortlandt.

VANDENBERG, ARTHUR HENDRICK *(b March 22, 1884, Grand Rapids, Mich.; d April 18, 1951, Grand Rapids)* Lawyer, editor-publisher of the *Grand Rapids Herald* (1906-1928), short story writer, diplomat, Michigan Republican and a leading isolationist who, after World War II, became one of the nation's leading champions of U.S. participation in world affairs. Although a serious early contender (1940) for the GOP presidential nomination, he withdrew in favor of Wendell L. Willkie.
Member of Grand Rapids Charter Commission (1912), GOP state central committee (1912-1918), state GOP convention chairman (1916, 1928); U.S. Senate (1928 until death), chairman of the Foreign Affairs Committee (1947-1949) and president pro tem of the Senate (1947-1949); delegate to the San Francisco United Nations conference (1945), and to its first General Assembly (1946), adviser to Secretary of State James F. Byrnes at the Council of Foreign Ministers (1946), member of the congressional Joint Atomic Energy Committee (1946 until death), delegate to the Pan American Conference (1947), recipient of Collier Award for Distinguished Congressional Service (1946, 1949).

VANDEVER, WILLIAM *(b March 31, 1817, Baltimore, Md.; d July 23, 1893,* *Ventura, Calif.)* Lawyer, Union Army officer, Iowa and California Republican. In Iowa: U.S. Representative (1859-1861), peace convention delegate (1861), Indian inspector (1873-1877). In California: U.S. Representative (1887-1891).

VANDIVER, WILLARD DUNCAN *(b March 30, 1854, Hardy County, Va., now W.Va.; d May 30, 1932, Columbia, Mo.).* Educator, insurance executive, lecturer, farmer, Missouri Democrat, and a writer said to have won Missouri the "Show Me State" title having used the phrase "I'm from Missouri, you've got to show me" in one of his biographical sketches. Bellevue Institute natural sciences professor (1877-1880) and president (1880-1889), Cape Girardeau State Normal School professor (1889-1893) and president (1893-1897), Democratic state convention delegate (1896, 1898, 1918, 1920), U.S. Representative (1897-1905), Democratic state executive committee chairman (1904), national convention delegate (1904), state insurance commissioner (1905-1909), assistant U.S. treasurer (1913-1921).

VAN DUKE, CARL CHESTER *(b Feb. 8, 1881, Alexandria, Minn.; d May 20, 1919, Washington, D.C.)* Lawyer, Minnesota Democrat. U.S. Representative (1915 until death).

VAN DUZER, CLARENCE DUNN *(b May 4, 1866, near Mountain City, Nev.; d Sept. 28, 1947, Passaic, N.J.)* Lawyer, miner, newspaperman, Nevada Democrat. State land agent (1892-1897), Humboldt County district attorney (1898-1900), state house of representatives and house speaker (1900-1902), U.S. Representative (1903-1907) and secretary to U.S. Senator Francis G. Newlands for five years.

VAN DYKE, NICHOLAS, SR. *(b Sept. 25, 1738, New Castle County, Del.; d Feb. 19, 1789, New Castle County).*

Lawyer, Revolutionary patriot and signer of the Articles of Confederation, Delaware Whig. State constitutional convention delegate (1776), Council of Delaware member (1777) and speaker (1779), member of the Continental Congress (1777-1782), president (governor) of Delaware (1783-1786).

VAN DYKE, NICHOLAS, JR. *(b Dec. 20, 1769, New Castle, Del.; d May 21, 1826, New Castle)* Lawyer, Delaware Federalist. State representative (1799), U.S. Representative (1807-1811), state senate (1815-1817), U.S. Senator (1817 until death).

VAN HORN, ROBERT THOMPSON *(b May 19, 1824, East Mahoning, Pa.; d Jan. 3, 1916, Evanston Station, Mo.).* Lawyer, founding editor of the *Kansas City Journal*, Union Army officer, Missouri Republican and a power in the party. Kansas City alderman (1857), postmaster (1857-1861) and mayor (1861, 1864); state senate (1862-1864), U.S. Representative (1865-1871, 1881-1883), GOP state central committee chairman (1874-1876), sixth district internal revenue collector (1875-1881), delegate to all GOP National Conventions (1864-1884) and member of the national committee (1872, 1884).

VAN NUYS, FREDERICK *(b April 16, 1874, Falmouth, Ind.; d Jan. 25, 1944, Fairfax County, Va.)* Lawyer, Indiana Democrat. Madison County prosecutor (1906-1910), state senator (1913-1916) and senate president pro tem (1915), Democratic state committee chairman (1917, 1918), U.S. attorney (1920-1922), U.S. Senate (1933 until death).

VAN PELT, WILLIAM K. *(b March 10, 1905, Glenbeulah, Wis.)* Fuel dealer, Wisconsin Republican. Chairman of Fond du Lac County GOP Committee (1944-1950), GOP National Convention delegate (1944), alternate (1948), U.S. Representative (1951-1965) serving on the Merchant Marine and Fisheries and Science and Astronautics committees.

VAN RENSSELAER, HENRY BELL *(b May 14, 1810, Albany, N.Y.; d March 23, 1864, Cincinnati, Ohio)* West Point graduate, farmer, mining entrepeneur, Union Army brigadier general and Winfield Scott's chief of staff, New York Whig. U.S. Representative (1841-1843). Son of Stephen Van Rensselaer.

VAN RENSSELAER, JEREMIAH *(b Aug. 27, 1738, New York; d Feb. 19, 1810, Albany, N.Y.)* Revolutionary patriot, banker, New York Democrat who was a member of the First Congress (1789-1791). Before that, a member of the Albany committee of safety and the state assembly. After that, Democratic presidential elector casting his vote for Jefferson and Burr (1800) and lieutenant governor (1801-1804). Father of Solomon Van Rensselaer.

VAN RENSSELAER, KILLIAN KILLIAN *(b June 9, 1763, Greenbush, N.Y.; d June 18, 1845, Albany, N.Y.)* Lawyer, New York Democrat. U.S. Representative (1801-1811). Cousin of Jeremiah Van Rensselaer.

VAN RENSSELAER, SOLOMON VAN VECHTEN *(b Aug. 6, 1774, Greenbush, N.Y.; d April 23, 1852, near Albany, N.Y.)* Army officer, New York Federalist. U.S. Representative (1819-1822) resigning to become Albany postmaster (1822-1839, 1841-1843), state delegate to the Erie Canal opening (1825). Son of Jeremiah Van Rensselaer.

VAN RENSSELAER, STEPHEN *(b Nov. 1, 1764, New York, N.Y.; d Jan. 26, 1839, Albany, N.Y.)* Eighth patroon of the Manor of Rensselaer, grandson of Philip Livingston, father of Henry B. Van Rensselaer, philanthropist, creator of New York's first board of agriculture, founder of Rensselaer Polytechnic Institute (1824), probably a Federalist, and the congressman who cast the vote that sent John Quincy Adams to the White House (1825) when the presidential choice was thrown into the House of Representatives. State assemblyman (1789-1791, 1798, 1818), state senator (1791-1796), lieutenant governor (1795), canal commissioner (1816-1839) and commission president fourteen of those years, state constitutional convention delegate (1821), U.S. Representative (1822-1829), first being elected to occupy Solomon Van Rensselaer's vacated seat; University of New York regent (1819-1839).

VAN VOORHIS, HENRY CLAY *(b May 11, 1852, Nashport, Ohio; d Dec. 12, 1927, Zanesville, Ohio)* Lawyer, banker, Marietta College trustee, Ohio Republican. GOP National Convention delegate (1884, 1916), U.S. Representative (1893-1905).

VAN WINKLE, PETER GODWIN *(b Sept. 7, 1808, New York City; d April 15, 1872, Parkersburg, W.Va.).* Lawyer who practiced in western Virginia where he had much to do with the division of Virginia into two states, railroad president, West Virginia Unionist-Republican. President of the Parkersburg Board of Trustees (1844-1850), Virginia State Constitutional Convention delegate (1850), delegate to the Wheeling reorganization convention (1861) and to the convention that framed West Virginia's first constitution (1861-1862) where he played a leading role, member of the state's first house of delegates (1863) and one of its first two U.S. Senators (1863-1869), delegate to the Southern loyalist convention (1866).

VAN WYCK, CHARLES HENRY *(b May 10, 1824, Poughkeepsie, N.Y.; d Oct. 24, 1895, Washington, D.C.)* New York lawyer and Union Army officer who later moved to Nebraska to farm and to continue his interest in politics as a Republican but later became one of the

leaders of the Populist movement there, active in the Farmers' Alliance and the fledgling party's unsuccessful gubernatorial candidate (1892). In New York: Sullivan County district attorney (1850-1856), U.S. Representative (1859-1863, 1867-1869, 1870-1871). In Nebraska: state constitutional convention delegate (1876), state senate (1876-1880), U.S. Senate (1881-1887).

VAN ZANDT, JAMES EDWARD *(b Dec. 18, 1898, Altoona, Pa.)* Railroadman, veteran of both world wars, and national commander of Veterans of Foreign Wars (1934-1936), Pennsylvania Republican. U.S. Representative (1939-1943, 1947-1963) and member of the Armed Services Committee and the Joint Committee on Atomic Energy.

VARDAMAN, JAMES KIMBLE *(b July 26, 1861, Jackson County, Tex.; d June 25, 1930, Birmingham, Ala.)* Lawyer, newspaper editor, stump speaker and a Mississippi Democrat whose main constituency was comprised of poor white farmers who approved of his attacks upon the education of Negroes as a threat to white supremacy; as a U.S. Senator (1913-1919) he was one of those who filibustered against the Armed Neutrality Bill and otherwise opposed Woodrow Wilson's war policies. State representative (1890-1896) and house speaker (1894), presidential elector on the Cleveland-Stevenson (1892) and Bryan-Sewall (1896) tickets, governor (1904-1908).

VARE, WILLIAM SCOTT *(b Dec. 24, 1867, Philadelphia, Pa.; d Aug. 7, 1934, Atlantic City, N.J.)* Merchant, general contractor, Pennsylvania Republican, and a force in Philadelphia's political affairs who was elected a U.S. Senator but declared ineligible to remain seated after only two years (1927-1929). Philadelphia councilman (1898-1901), recorder of deeds (1902-1912), GOP National Convention delegate (1908, 1912,

1916, 1920, 1924), U.S. Representative (1912-1927).

VARNUM, JAMES MITCHELL *(b Dec. 17, 1748, Dracut, Mass.; d Jan. 10, 1789, Marietta, Ohio)* Revolutionary officer who was made commander of Rhode Island troops (1779), lawyer, a Rhode Island political leader who became a director of the Ohio Company and rounded out his years in the Northwest Territory. Member of the Continental Congress (1780-1782, 1786, 1787), U.S. judge in the Northwest Territory (1787 until death). Brother of Joseph B. Varnum.

VARNUM, JOHN *(b June 25, 1778, Dracut, Mass.; d July 23, 1836, Niles, Mich.)* Lawyer, Massachusetts Federalist. State senate (1811), U.S. Representative (1825-1831).

VARNUM, JOSEPH BRADLEY *(b Jan. 29, 1750, Dracut, Mass.; d Sept. 21, 1821, Dracut)* Revolutionary soldier, jurist, and a Massachusetts Anti-Federalist who was a foe of slavery and the slave trade throughout his twenty-two years in Washington and all of his public career. State representative (1780-1784), state senator (1786-1788, 1795, 1817-1821), delegate to the state convention that ratified the federal Constitution (1788), U.S. Representative (1795-1811) and House speaker (1807-1811), chief justice of the court of general sessions (1811-1815), U.S. Senator (1811-1817) and Senate president pro tem (1813), state constitutional convention delegate (1817-1821). Brother of James M. Varnum.

VENABLE, ABRAHAM BEDFORD *(b Nov. 20, 1758, Prince Edward County, Va.; d Dec. 26, 1811, in a Richmond, Va., fire)* Planter, lawyer, banker, and a Virginia political figure. U.S. Representative (1791-1799), U.S. Senate (1803-1804), resigning to become president of the state's first national bank.

VENABLE, ABRAHAM WATKINS *(b Oct. 17, 1799, Springfield, Va.; d Feb. 24, 1876, Oxford, N.C.)* Lawyer, North Carolina Democrat. Presidential elector on the Jackson-Van Buren (1832), Van Buren-Johnson (1836), and Breckinridge-Lane (1860) tickets; U.S. Representative (1847-1853), state delegate to the Provisional Confederate Congress (1861), and a representative in the Confederate Congress (1862-1864).

VERPLANCK, DANIEL CROMMELIN *(b March 19, 1762, New York City; d March 29, 1834, Dutchess County, N.Y.).* Lawyer, banker, New York Federalist. U.S. Representative (1803-1809), Dutchess County common pleas judge (1828-1830). Father of Gullian C. Verplanck.

VERPLANCK, GULLIAN CROMMELIN *(b Aug. 6, 1786, New York City; d March 18, 1870, New York City)* Lawyer, theology professor, essayist, Shakespearian editor, and a New York Federalist-Democrat-Whig who was a founder of the Washington Benevolent Society in opposition to the Tammany Society. While defending a student who had been denied his diploma, Verplanck became embroiled in the Columbia College commencement riot (1811) and thus began a long-lasting battle with DeWitt Clinton with pamphlets as their prime weapons. As chairman of the House Ways and Means Committee, he was mainly responsible for bringing about major improvements in authors' copyrights.

State assemblyman (1820-1823), U.S. Representative (1825-1833), unsuccessful Whig candidate for mayor of New York (1834), state senate (1838-1841) city hospital governor (1823-1865), state university regent (1826-1870) and vice chancellor (1858-1870), immigration commission president (1846-1870), state constitutional convention delegate (1867, 1868). Son of Daniel C. Verplanck.

VEST, GEORGE GRAHAM *(b Dec. 6, 1830, Frankfort, Ky.; d Aug. 9, 1904, Sweet Springs, Mo.)* Lawyer, Missouri Democrat believed to be the author of the Ordinance of Secession (1861). Presidential elector on the Douglas-Johnson ticket (1860), state representative (1860, 1861), Confederate representative (1862-1865) and senator (1865), U.S. Senate (1879-1903), during which time he vehemently argued that it was unconstitutional for the country to govern Spanish colonies in America.

VESTAL, ALBERT HENRY *(b Jan. 18, 1875, Madison County, Ind.; d April 1, 1932, Washington, D.C.)* Factory hand, teacher, lawyer, Indiana Republican. Fiftieth judicial circuit prosecutor (1900-1906), U.S. Representative (1917 until death) and GOP House whip (1925-1931).

VILAS, WILLIAM FREEMAN *(b July 9, 1840, Chelsea, Vt.; d Aug. 28, 1908, Madison, Wis.)* Lawyer, professor at the University of Wisconsin, Union Army officer, Wisconsin Democrat, and friend of Grover Cleveland in whose cabinet he served as postmaster general (1885-1888) and secretary of the interior (1888-1889).

University regent (1880-1885), a reviser of the state statutes (1875-1878), assemblyman (1885), Democratic National Convention delegate (1876, 1880, 1884, 1892, 1896) and permanent chairman (1884), U.S. Senate (1891-1897).

VINCENT, BIRD J. *(b March 6, 1880, Oakland County, Mich.; d July 18, 1931, aboard ship while homeward bound from Hawaii)* Lawyer, Michigan Republican. Saginaw County assistant prosecutor (1909-1914) and prosecutor (1915-1917), U.S. Representative (1923 until death).

VINING, JOHN *(b Dec. 23, 1758, Dover, Del.; d Feb., 1802, Dover)* Lawyer, Delaware patriot who served in the

Continental Congress (1784-1786), the First and Second Congresses as a Representative (1789-1793), and then in the U.S. Senate (1793-1798). State representative (1787, 1788), state senate (1793).

VINSON, CARL *(b Nov. 18, 1883, Milledgeville, Ga.)* Lawyer, Georgia Democrat who served more than fifty years as a U.S. Representative (1914-1965). Baldwin County prosecutor (1906-1909), state representative (1909-1912) and house speaker pro tem (1911, 1912), county court judge (1912-1914).

VINSON, FREDERICK MOORE *(b Jan. 22, 1890, Louisa, Ky.; d Sept. 8, 1953, Washington, D.C.)* Lawyer, jurist, Kentucky Democrat, and the son of the town jailer who graduated first in his Centre College class (1909) and climaxed his long career in public service by being the thirteenth chief justice of the United States (1946 until death). Before that, he had been a pro-labor, mildly New Deal public servant.

His two hallmark decisions were *Shelley* v. *Kramer* (1948), in which he was author of the majority finding that restrictive covenants in real estate for reasons of race or religion were legally unenforceable; and *Youngstown Sheet & Tube* v. *Sawyer* (1952), in which he dissented and held that President Truman had the power to seize struck steel mills without congressional authority because of the Korean War.

Louisa city attorney (1914, 1915), World War I army officer, thirty-second judicial district commonwealth attorney (1921-1924), U.S. Representative (1924-1929, 1931-1938) resigning to become associate justice of the U.S. Court of Appeals for the District of Columbia (1938-1943) and chief judge of the wartime U.S. Emergency Court of Appeals (1942-1943) and then director of the Office of Economic Stabilization (1943-1945); federal loan administrator (briefly in 1945) when he was quickly elevated first to become director of War Mobilization and Reconversion (1945) and then secretary of the treasury in the Truman cabinet (1945-June 24, 1946) when he took the oath as chief justice to succeed Harlan F. Stone.

VINTON, SAMUEL FINLEY *(b Sept. 25, 1792, South Hadley, Mass.; d May 11, 1862, Washington, D.C.)* Lawyer, Ohio National Republican-Whig who, while a U.S. Representative (1823-1837, 1843-1851) and chairman of the Ways and Means Committee, opposed speculation in public lands and the annexation of Texas. Presidential elector on the Harrison-Tyler ticket (1840), unsuccessful gubernatorial candidate (1851).

VOIGT, EDWARD *(b Dec. 1, 1873, Bremen, Germany; d Aug. 26, 1934, Crystal Lake, Wis.)* Lawyer, Michigan Republican. Sheboygan County district attorney (1905-1911), Sheboygan city attorney (1913-1917), U.S. Representative (1917-1927), GOP National Convention delegate (1924), fourth judicial circuit judge (1929 until death).

VOLSTEAD, ANDREW JOHN *(b Oct. 31, 1860, Goodhue County, Minn.; d Jan. 20, 1947, Granite Falls, Minn.)*. Lawyer, Minnesota Republican, and author of the Volstead Act which was meant to enforce the Eighteenth (prohibition) Amendment and was passed by Congress (1919) over President Wilson's veto. Yellow Medicine County prosecutor (1886-1902), Granite Falls mayor (1900-1902), U.S. Representative (1903-1923).

VOORHEES, CHARLES STEWART *(b June 4, 1853, Covington, Ind.; d Dec. 26, 1909, Spokane, Wash.)* Lawyer, Washington Territory Democrat. Whitman County prosecutor (1882-1885), delegate to the U.S. Congress (1885-1889), son of Daniel W. Voorhees.

VOORHEES, DANIEL WOLSEY *(b Sept. 26, 1827, Liberty Township, Ohio; d April 9, 1897, Washington, D.C.)* Lawyer, Indiana Democrat and an accomplished stump speaker who equally opposed both abolition and secession. U.S. district attorney (1858-1861), U.S. Representative (1861-1866, 1869-1873), U.S. Senate (1877-1897) and chairman of the finance committee. Father of Charles S. Voorhees.

VOORHIS, HORACE JERRY *(b April 6, 1901, Ottawa, Kans.)* Factory hand, freight handler, cowboy, social worker, teacher, Pomona College lecturer, author, and a California Democrat who was defeated in his bid for reelection to Congress by a newcomer on the national political scene, Richard M. Nixon. Headmaster and trustee of the Voorhis School for Boys (1928-1938), U.S. Representative (1937-1947).

VORYS, JOHN MARTIN *(b June 16, 1896, Lancaster, Ohio)* World War I navy flier, lawyer, teacher in China, Ohio Republican. Assistant secretary to the U.S. delegation at the 1921-1922 arms conference, state representative (1923, 1924), state senator (1925, 1926), Ohio director of aeronautics (1929, 1930), U.S. Representative (1939-1959), United Nations General Assembly delegate (1951), Smithsonian Institution regent (1949-1959).

VREELAND, EDWARD BUTTERFIELD *(b Dec. 7, 1856, Cuba, N.Y.; d May 8, 1936, Salamanca, N.Y.)* Banker, insurance broker, New York Republican. Salamanca postmaster (1889-1893), U.S. Representative (1899-1913), vice chairman of the National Monetary Commission (1909-1912).

VROOM, PETER DUMONT *(b Dec. 12, 1791, Hillsboro, N.J.; d Nov. 18, 1873, Trenton, N.J.)* Lawyer, diplomat, and a New Jersey Democrat who was a foe of secession and seven times was elected governor (1829-1832, 1833-1836). Assemblyman (1826, 1827, 1829), Choctaw Indian claims commissioner (1837), U.S. Representative (1839-1841), presidential elector on the Pierce-King (1852) and Seymour-Blair (1868) tickets, minister to Prussia (1853-1857), peace-between-states convention delegate (1861), state supreme court reporter (1862-1872), state sinking fund commissioner (1864 until death).

VURSELL, CHARLES WESLEY *(b Feb. 8, 1881, Salem, Ill.)* Merchant, publisher of the *Salem Republican* (1916-1948), Illinois Republican. Marion County sheriff (1910-1914), state representative (1914-1916), U.S. Representative (1943-1959).

W

☆ ☆ ☆

WACHTER, FRANK CHARLES *(b Sept. 16, 1861, Baltimore, Md.; d July 1, 1910, Baltimore)* Businessman, Maryland Republican. Baltimore Jail Board member (1896-1898), U.S. Representative (1899-1907), Maryland Prison Board member (1909 until death).

WADDELL, ALFRED MOORE *(b Sept. 16, 1834, Hillsboro, N.C.; d March 17, 1912, Wilmington, N.C.)* Lawyer, newspaper editor in Wilmington and Charleston, author, Confederate cavalry officer, North Carolina Constitutional Unionist-Democrat. Equity court clerk (1858-1861), Constitutional Union National Convention delegate (1860), U.S. Representative (1871-1879), Democratic National Convention delegate (1880-1896), presidential elector on the Cleveland-Thurman ticket (1888), mayor of Wilmington (1898-1904).

WADE, BENJAMIN FRANKLIN *(b Oct. 27, 1800, Feeding Hills, Mass.; d March 2, 1878, Jefferson, Ohio)* Teacher, lawyer, Ohio Whig-Republican and a rough-and-tumble U.S. Senator (1851-1869) who was a leader of the congressional antislave bloc, yet during the Civil War was so much a critic of Lincoln's policies that he played a major role in the creation of the Committee on the Conduct of the War. Then, vehemently opposed to the president's Reconstruction plans, was a codrafter of the contradictory Wade-Davis Bill and, upon its veto, promptly issued the Wade-Davis Manifesto asserting congressional supremacy.

He fared no better with President Johnson. One of those who brought impeachment proceedings at a time when he was Senate president pro tem (1867-1869) and thus next in line for the presidency, he was so confident of conviction—for which he voted—that he already had begun to select his cabinet.

Ashtabula County prosecutor (1835-1837), state senator (1837, 1838), third judicial court president judge (1847-1851), Southern Loyalist Convention delegate (1866), candidate for the GOP vice presidential nomination (1868), member of the Santo Domingo Commission (1871), chairman of the Ohio delegation to the GOP National Convention (1876). Brother of Edward Wade.

WADE, EDWARD *(b Nov. 22, 1802, West Springfield, Mass.; d Aug. 13, 1866, East Cleveland, Ohio)* Ohio lawyer who made his national debut in politics as a member of the Free Soil party but switched to Republican at the end of the first of his four terms as a U.S. Representative (1853-1861). Ashtabula County justice of the peace (1831) and county prosecutor (1833). Brother of Benjamin F. Wade.

WADE, WILLIAM HENRY *(b Nov. 3, 1835, Clark County, Ohio; d Jan. 13, 1911, Greene County, Mo.)* Farmer, Union soldier, Missouri Republican. State representative (1881-1884), U.S. Representative (1885-1891).

WADLEIGH, BAINBRIDGE *(b Jan. 4, 1831, Bradford, N.H.; d Jan. 24, 1891, Boston, Mass.)* Lawyer, New Hampshire Republican. State representative (1855, 1856, 1859, 1860, 1869-1872), U.S. Senate (1873-1879).

WADSWORTH, JAMES WOLCOTT, SR. *(b Oct. 12, 1846, Philadelphia, Pa.; d Dec. 24, 1926, Washington, D.C.).* Union Army officer, farmer, banker, New York Republican. Geneseo supervisor (1873-1876), assemblyman (1878, 1879), state comptroller (1880, 1881), U.S. Representative (1881-1885, 1891-1907), state constitutional convention delegate (1914).

WADSWORTH, JAMES WOLCOTT, JR. *(b Aug. 12, 1877, Geneseo, N.Y.; d June 21, 1952, Washington, D.C.)* New York farmer who took a fling at Texas ranching (1911-1915), returned to his native state and followed in his father's Republican footsteps. Assemblyman (1905-1910) and house speaker (1906-1910), GOP National Convention delegate (1908-1928, 1940), U.S. Senate (1915-1927), U.S. Representative (1933-1951), Truman-appointed National Security Training Commission chairman (1951 until death).

WADSWORTH, JEREMIAH *(b July 12, 1743, Hartford, Conn.; d April 30, 1804, Hartford)* Ship's officer, Revolutionary officer who was the army's highly able commissary general (1778-1779), farmer, bank executive and a founder of the Bank of North America, New York Federalist. Delegate to the Continental Congress (1787, 1788), delegate to the state convention (1788) that ratified the federal Constitution, U.S. Representative in the first three Congresses (1789-1795), state representative (1795), member of state executive council (1795-1801).

WADSWORTH, PELEG *(b May 6, 1748, Duxbury, Mass.; d Nov. 12, 1829, Hiram, Maine)* Merchant, teacher, farmer, Revolutionary Army officer who laid out the lines for the defense of Boston and a Massachusetts political figure in a part of the state that is now Maine. State senate (1792), U.S. Representative (1793-1807).

WADSWORTH, WILLIAM HENRY *(b July 4, 1821, Maysville, Ky.; d April 2, 1893, Maysville)* Lawyer, Union Army officer, Kentucky Constitutional Unionist-Republican. State senate (1853-1856), Presidential elector on the Bell-Everett ticket and president of the state electoral college (1860), U.S. Representative (1861-1865, 1885-1887), Grant-appointed U.S. commissioner to Mexico (1869).

WAGENER, DAVID DOUGLAS *(b Oct. 11, 1792, Easton, Pa.; d Oct. 1, 1860, Easton)* Merchant, founding president of the Easton Bank (1852 until death), Pennsylvania Democrat. U.S. Representative (1833-1841).

WAGNER, ROBERT FERDINAND *(b June 8, 1877, Hessen-Nassau Province, Germany; d May 4, 1953, New York City)* Lawyer and a highly respected progressive New York Democrat. Assemblyman (1905-1908), state senator (1909-1918) and senate floor leader (1910-1918), state factory commission chairman (1911-1915), acting lieutenant governor (1914), state constitutional convention delegate (1915, 1918), state supreme court justice (1919-1926), U.S. Senate (1927-1949), U.S. delegate to the United Nations' Bretton Woods Monetary Conference (1944).

WAINWRIGHT, JONATHAN MAYHEW
(b Dec. 10, 1864, New York City; d June
3, 1945, Rye, N.Y.) Lawyer, citizen-
soldier and a New York Republican who
was a member of the state's first Workmen's Compensation Commission
(1914). Assemblyman (1902-1908),
president of the Westchester County
Bar Association (1904-1906), state senate (1909-1913), assistant U.S. secretary of war (1921-1923), U.S. Representative (1923-1931), county park commissioner (1930-1937).

WAIT, JOHN TURNER (b Aug. 27, 1811,
New London, Conn.; d April 21, 1899,
Norwich, Conn.) Merchant, lawyer,
Connecticut Republican. New London
County state's attorney (1842-1844,
1846-1854), presidential elector on the
Lincoln-Johnson ticket (1864), state
senator (1865, 1866) and senate president pro tem (1866), state representative (1867, 1871, 1873) and house
speaker (1867), U.S. Representative
(1876-1887).

WAKEFIELD, JAMES BEACH (b March
21, 1825, Winsted, Conn.; d Aug. 25,
1910, Blue Earth, Minn.) Lawyer, Minnesota Republican. State representative
(1858, 1863, 1866) and house speaker
(1866), state senate (1867-1869), Winnebago City land office receiver (1869-
1875), lieutenant governor (1875-1877),
U.S. Representative (1883-1887).

WALDRON, HENRY (b Oct. 11, 1819,
Albany, N.Y.; d Sept. 13, 1880, Hillsdale,
Mich.) Civil engineer, railroad executive, banker, Michigan Whig-Republican.
Presidential elector on the Taylor-Fillmore ticket (1848), U.S. Representative
(1855-1861, 1871-1877).

WALKER, DAVID (b——, Brunswick
County, Va.; d March 1, 1820, Washington, D.C.) A Revolutionary soldier
who was at Yorktown when Cornwallis
surrendered, after the war a Kentucky
lawyer and for a time Logan County

court clerk. State representative (1793-
1796), U.S. Representative (1817 until
death). Brother of George and grandfather of James D. Walker.

WALKER, FELIX (b July 19, 1753,
Hampshire County, Va., now W.Va.; d
1828, Clinton, Miss.) Farmer, Indian
fighter, Revolutionary Army officer,
trader, land speculator, and a hardy
early-day pioneer who explored many
states and territories (he was with
Daniel Boone at the founding of
Boonesboro, Ky.), finally settled in
North Carolina long enough to hold
office as a Democrat until the wander
bug bit him once again (1824) and he
moved on to Mississippi. Rutherford
County court clerk (1779-1787), member of the state house of commons
(1792, 1799-1802, 1806), U.S. Representative (1817-1823).

WALKER, GEORGE (b 1763, Culpeper
County, Va.; d 1819, Nicholasville, Ky.).
Revolutionary soldier, Kentucky lawyer.
Kentucky River Co. commissioner
(1801), state senator (1810-1814), and
a U.S. Senator for four months in 1814
to fill a vacancy. Brother of David
Walker.

WALKER, JAMES DAVID (b Dec. 13,
1830, Logan County, Ky.; d Oct. 17,
1906, Fayetteville, Ark.) Lawyer, Confederate Army officer who was captured at Oak Hill, Mo., Arkansas Democrat. Presidential elector on the
Tilden-Hendricks ticket (1876), U.S.
Senate (1879-1885). Grandson of David
Walker.

WALKER, JOHN RANDALL (b Feb. 23,
1874, Pierce County, Ga.; d —— Blackshear, Ga.). Lawyer, Georgia Democrat. State representative (1907, 1908),
U.S. Representative (1913-1919).

WALKER, JOSEPH HENRY (b Dec. 21,
1829, Boston, Mass.; d April 3, 1907,
Worcester, Mass.) Leather manufac-

turer, Massachusetts Republican. Worcester councilman (1852-1854), state representative (1879, 1880, 1887), U.S. Representative (1889-1899).

WALKER, ROBERT JAMES *(b July 23, 1801, Northumberland, Pa.; d Nov. 11, 1869, Washington, D.C.)* Lawyer with a promising political career in Pennsylvania (Democratic state chairman 1823) who for reasons unknown moved to Mississippi and rose to become secretary of the treasury in the Polk cabinet (1845-1849). U.S. Senate (1835-1845), governor of the Kansas Territory (1857).

WALLACE, HENRY AGARD *(b Oct. 7, 1888, Adair County, Iowa; d Nov. 18, 1965, Danbury, Conn.)* Farm journalist-author and an authority on agriculture who developed new breeds of corn, chicken, and strawberries; New Deal Iowa Democrat. Vice president of the United States (1941-1945) who, blocked from renomination by the party's conservative elements, in 1948 became the new Progressive party's candidate for the presidency, ran on a liberal platform that called for an easing of cold war tensions with the Soviet Union, and finished fourth to Harry S Truman, the Democrat, Thomas E. Dewey, the Republican, and J. Strom Thurmond, the States' Rights candidate.

Chairman of the Agricultural Round Table (1927), International Conference on Agricultural Economics (1929), Democratic National Convention delegate (1940, 1944), secretary of agriculture (1933-1940) and secretary of commerce (1945-1946) in the Roosevelt cabinet; dismissed from the latter by Truman, thereupon becoming editor of *The New Republic*. Among his books: *America Must Choose* (1934), *The American Choice* (1940), *Sixty Million Jobs* (1945), *Toward World Peace* (1948), *Corn and the Midwestern Farmer* (1956), and *Corn and its Early Fathers* (1956).

WALLACE, JAMES M. *(b 1750, Hanover Township, Pa.; d Dec. 17, 1823, Dauphin County, Pa.)* Pennsylvania farmer, Revolutionary Army officer who commanded a company of frontier rangers. Dauphin County commissioner (1799-1801), state representative (1806-1810), U.S. Representative (1815-1821).

WALLACE, ROBERT MINOR *(b Aug. 6, 1856, New London, Ark.; d Nov. 9, 1942, Magnolia, Ark.)* Lawyer, Chautauqua and Anti-Saloon League lecturer, Arkansas Democrat. State representative (1881, 1882), postal inspector (1887-1891), thirteenth judicial circuit prosecutor (1891, 1892), assistant U.S. attorney (1894), U.S. Representative (1903-1911).

WALLACE, WILLIAM HENSON *(b July 19, 1811, Troy, Ohio; d Feb. 7, 1879, Steilacoom, Wash.)* Lawyer and an active Republican in Washington and Idaho territories. In Washington: elected governor (1861) but did not serve because he had also been elected a delegate to the U.S. Congress (1861-1863). In Idaho: the territory's first governor (1863) resigning to again become a congressional delegate (1864-1865).

WALLGREN, MONRAD CHARLES *(b April 17, 1891, Des Moines, Iowa; d Sept. 18, 1961, Olympia, Wash., as the result of auto accident injuries)* Jeweler, optometrist, citrus grower, uranium claims developer, Washington Democrat. U.S. Representative (1933-1940) resigning to become U.S. Senator (1941-1945) and resigning that post to become governor (1945-1949), Federal Power Commission member (1949-1951).

WALLHAUSER, GEORGE MARVIN *(b Feb. 10, 1900, Newark, N.J.)* Real estate business, New Jersey Republican. Maplewood Planning Board chairman (1946-1954), member of township committee (1954-1957), Essex County Right-of-Way Commission (1957-1959), library trustee (1957-1959), U.S. Representative (1959-1965) serving on Government Operations and Post Office and Civil Service committees.

WALLS, JOSIAH THOMAS *(b Dec. 30, 1842, Winchester, Va.; d May 5, 1905, Tallahassee, Fla.)* Although a Negro, he was born free and grew up to become a successful planter-truck farmer and an active Florida Republican at a time when such activity by a black man meant considerable harassment. He also fought both for the South and the North during the Civil War—the South drafted him, the North captured him, and he willingly switched uniforms. State constitutional convention delegate (1868), state senate (1869-1872), U.S. Representative (1871-1876) who favored military support of Cuban rebels because Spain was moving African slaves onto the island's plantations.

WALSH, DAVID IGNATIUS *(b Nov. 11, 1872, Leominster, Mass.; d June 11, 1947, Brighton, Mass.)* Lawyer, powerful Massachusetts Democrat. State representative (1900, 1901), lieutenant governor (1913), governor (1914, 1915), delegate to all Democratic National Conventions (1912-1944), state constitutional convention delegate (1917, 1918), U.S. Senator for nearly twenty-two years (1919-1925, 1926-1947), returning to Washington after losing a reelection bid (1924) to fill a vacancy created by the death of Henry Cabot Lodge.

WALSH, JOSEPH *(b Dec. 16, 1875, Boston, Mass.; d Jan. 13, 1946, New Bedford, Mass.)* Lawyer, fish culturist, newspaper reporter, Massachusetts Republican. U.S. Bureau of Fisheries clerk (1900-1905), state representative (1905), presidential elector on the Taft-Butler ticket (1912), U.S. Representa-

tive (1915-1922) resigning to become a state superior court justice (1922 until death).

WALSH, THOMAS JAMES *(b June 12, 1859, Two Rivers, Wis.; d March 2, 1933, near Wilson, N.C., while on a train en route to Washington, D.C., to accept appointment as attorney general in the Roosevelt cabinet)* Lawyer, teacher, orator, liberal Montana Democrat who supported women's voting rights, meaningful child labor legislation, the League of Nations, and the shielding of unions and farm groups from Sherman Act antitrust suits. But his greatest claim to fame was as the U.S. Senator who conducted the investigations that laid bare the Teapot Dome and Elk Hills oil scandals (see Warren G. Harding). Democratic National Convention delegate (1908, 1912, 1916, 1920, 1924) and permanent chairman (1924, 1932), U.S. Senate (1913 until death).

WALTER, FRANCIS EUGENE *(b May 26, 1894, Easton, Pa.; d May 31, 1963, Washington, D.C.)* Lawyer, banker, Pennsylvania Democrat who for many years was chairman of the House Un-American Activities Committee, which many described as a witch-hunting body, and as chairman of the Immigration and Naturalization Subcommittee consequently became what many termed the czar of immigration legislation. Among his actions: coauthor of the McCarran-Walter Act, which in his *New York Times* obituary was called "the basic, restrictive immigration statute." However, the obituary continued, "On domestic, economic and social legislation [he] was an influential behind-the-scenes operator, one of President Kennedy's most valued lieutenants in the House."
Northampton County solicitor (1928-1933), Easton Hospital trustee, Democratic National Convention delegate (1928), U.S. Representative for thirty years (1933 until death).

WALTERS, ANDERSON HOWELL *(b May 18, 1862, Johnstown, Pa.; d Dec. 7, 1927, Johnstown)* Railroad telegrapher, utilities executive, bank trustee, editor-publisher of the *Johnstown Tribune* (1902 until death), Pennsylvania Republican with a bit of political clout. GOP state convention delegate (1890, 1892, 1898, 1904), GOP National Convention delegate (1896), GOP city committee chairman (1896-1899), GOP state committeeman (1898-1902), city councilman (1900-1904), U.S. Representative (1913-1915, 1919-1923, 1925-1927).

WALTHALL, EDWARD CARY *(b April 4, 1831, Richmond, Va.; d April 21, 1898, Washington, D.C.)* Lawyer, Confederate Army major general, and a Mississippi Democrat who helped rid the state of Carpetbag domination. Tenth judicial district attorney (1856-1861), U.S. Senate (1885-1894, 1895 until death).

WALTON, ELIAKIM PERSONS *(b Feb. 17, 1812, Montpelier, Vt.; d Dec. 19, 1890, Montpelier)* Journalist who was the founding president of the Editors and Publishers' Association, editor of *Walton's Vermont Register*, succeeded his father as editor-publisher of *The Watchman*, Vermont Republican. State representative (1853), U.S. Representative (1857-1863), GOP National Convention delegate (1864), state constitutional convention delegate (1870), state senate (1875, 1877), University of Vermont and state agricultural college trustee (1875-1887), Vermont Historical Society president (1876-1890).

WALTON, GEORGE *(b 1750, Farmville, Va.; d Feb. 2, 1804, Richmond County, Ga.)* Lawyer, Indian negotiator, signer of the Declaration of Independence, Revolutionary Army officer who was captured at Savannah; Georgia Whig and one of the state's most outstanding statesmen during the nation's formative

years. Secretary of the Provincial Congress and a member of its intelligence committee (1775), member of the Council of Safety and then its president (1775, 1776), state representative, delegate to the Continental Congress (1776-1778, 1780-1781, 1787-1788), governor (1779, 1789), treaty negotiator with the Six Nations at Easton, Pa., and the Cherokees in Tennessee (1783), Georgia's chief justice (1783-1786, 1793-1795), member of the Augusta Board of Commissioners (1784, 1785), Georgia representative in settlement of its boundary dispute with South Carolina (1786), first judge of the superior courts of the eastern judicial circuit (1790), chairman of President Washington's Augusta reception committee and the man who delivered the welcoming address (1791), U.S. Senate (1795-1796), middle circuit judge (1799 until death). Brother of John, cousin of Matthew Walton.

WALTON, JOHN *(b 1738, Virginia; d 1783, New Savannah, Ga.)* Georgia planter who signed the Articles of Confederation (1778) in the state's behalf while a member of the Continental Congress. Provincial Congress delegate (1775), Richmond County surveyor (1779 until death). Brother of George and cousin of Matthew Walton.

WALTON, MATTHEW *(b——; d Jan. 18, 1819, Springfield, Ky.)* Kentucky Democrat. Member of the Danville conventions (1785, 1787), state constitutional convention delegate (1792), state representative (1792, 1795, 1808), presidential elector on the Madison-Clinton ticket (1809), U.S. Representative (1803-1807). Cousin of George and John Walton.

WALTON, WILLIAM BELL *(b Jan. 23, 1871, Altoona, Pa.; d April 14, 1939, Silver City, N.Mex.)* Lawyer, New Mexico Democrat. State representative (1901, 1902), Grant County clerk (1903-

1906), Democratic National Convention delegate (1908), state Democratic committee chairman (1910), state constitutional convention delegate (1911), state senate (1912-1916), U.S. Representative (1917-1919), sixth judicial district attorney (1926-1932).

WALWORTH, REUBEN HYDE *(b Oct. 26, 1788, Bozrah, Conn.; d Nov. 27, 1867, Saratoga Springs, N.Y.)* Teacher, lawyer, New York Democrat and a prominent jurist with a tongue so biting that it had two major results: several New York courts were abolished for no other reason than to remove him from the bench; when nominated as an associate justice of the Supreme Court by President Tyler (1844) the Senate refused to confirm. Master in chancery and circuit judge (1811), U.S. Representative (1821-1823), fourth judicial district judge (1823-1828), state chancellor (1828-1848) until abolishment, unsuccessful candidate for governor (1848).

WANGER, IRVING PRICE *(b March 5, 1852, North Coventry, Pa.; d Jan. 14, 1940, Norristown, Pa.)* Lawyer, Pennsylvania Republican. Deputy Chester County clerk (1871), deputy Montgomery County clerk (1873-1875), Norristown burgess (1878), GOP National Convention delegate (1880), Montgomery County district attorney (1880-1889), Montgomery County GOP Committee chairman (1889), U.S. Representative (1893-1911).

WARBURTON, STANTON *(b April 13, 1865, Sullivan County, Pa.; d Dec. 24, 1926, Boston, Mass.)* Lawyer, Washington Republican. U.S. Representative (1911-1913).

WARD, AARON *(b July 5, 1790, Sing Sing, now Ossining, N.Y.; d March 2, 1867, Georgetown, D.C.)* Lawyer, New York Democrat. U.S. Representative (1825-1829, 1831-1837, 1841-1843), state constitutional convention delegate (1846). Uncle of Elijah Ward.

WARD, ARTEMAS, SR. *(b Nov. 26, 1727, Shrewsbury, Mass.; d Oct. 28, 1800, Shrewsbury)* Lawyer, veteran of the French and Indian War and in the Revolution commander in chief of Massachusetts troops during the defense of Boston until the arrival of General Washington; politically, a prominent Bay State Federalist whose home was preserved by Harvard University. Worcester County common pleas court chief justice (1776, 1777), president of the Massachusetts Executive Council (1777-1779), state representative (1779-1785) and house speaker (1785), delegate to the Continental Congress (1780-1782), U.S. Representative (1791-1795).

WARD, ARTEMAS, JR. *(b Jan. 9, 1762, Shrewsbury, Mass.; d Oct. 7, 1847, Boston, Mass.)* Like his father, a lawyer, jurist, and Massachusetts Federalist. State representative (1796-1800, 1811), Harvard University overseer (1810-1844), U.S. Representative (1813-1817), state senate (1818, 1819), state constitutional convention delegate (1820), common pleas court chief justice (1820-1839).

WARD, CHARLES BONNELL *(b April 27, 1879, Newark, N.J.; d May 27, 1946, Liberty, N.Y.)* Farmer, innkeeper, editor-publisher of the *Liberty Register* (1910-1928), New York Republican. U.S. Representative (1915-1925).

WARD, DAVID JENKINS *(b Sept. 17, 1871, Salisbury, Md.; d Feb. 18, 1961, Salisbury)* Farmer, lumber dealer, merchant, real estate broker, Maryland Democrat. Member of state house of delegates (1915-1917), Wicomico County Democratic Committee chairman (1918-1926), state senator (1926-1934, 1938-1939), resigning to become U.S. Representative (1939-1945).

WARD, ELIJAH *(b Sept. 16, 1816, Sing Sing, now Ossining, N.Y.; d Feb. 7, 1882, Roslyn, N.Y.)* Lawyer, New York Democrat. State judge advocate general (1853-1855), Democratic National Convention delegate (1856), U.S. Representative (1857-1859, 1861-1865, 1875-1877). Nephew of Aaron Ward.

WARD, MARCUS LAWRENCE *(b Nov. 9, 1812, Newark, N.J.; d April 25, 1884, Newark).* Candle manufacturer, banker, philanthropist who set up welfare funds for families of Civil War soldiers and, before that, was so very much an abolitionist that he went to Kansas (1858) to aid in the antislave struggles there; in New Jersey politically a Republican from the moment the party was conceived, rising to become a governor (1866-1869) who instituted many reforms. GOP National Convention delegate (1860, 1864), presidential elector on the Lincoln-Johnson ticket (1864), GOP National Committee chairman (1866), U.S. Representative (1873-1875).

WARD, MATTHIAS *(b Oct. 13, 1805, Elbert County, Ga.; d Oct. 5, 1861, Warm Springs, N.C.)* Teacher, lawyer, trader, and a Texas pioneer who both as a private citizen and as a member of the republic's Congress, had much to do with the state's admission to the Union. Democratic National Convention delegate (1852, 1856), state Democratic convention president (1856), U.S. Senate (1858-1859) to fill a vacancy.

WARD, SAMUEL *(b May 27, 1725, Newport, R.I.; d March 26, 1776, Philadelphia, Pa.)* Farmer, a founder of Rhode Island College which became Brown University; a Rhode Island patriot who numbered George Washington and Benjamin Franklin among his pen pals and was the delegate to the Continental Congress (1774 until death) who proposed that Washington be made commander in chief of the Revolutionary forces. Rhode Island chief justice (1761, 1762), governor (1762, 1763, 1765-1767), Brown University trustee (1764 until death).

WARD, THOMAS BAYLESS *(b April 27, 1835, Marysville, Ohio; d Jan. 1, 1892, Lafayette, Ind.)* Lawyer, Indiana Democrat. Lafayette city attorney (1859, 1860) and mayor (1861-1865), Tippecanoe County Superior Court judge (1875-1880), U.S. Representative (1883-1887).

WARFIELD, HENRY RIDGELY *(b Sept. 14, 1774, Anne Arundel County, Md.; d March 18, 1839, Frederick, Md.)* Maryland Federalist. U.S. Representative (1819-1825).

WARNER, ADONIRAM JUDSON *(b Jan. 13, 1834, Wales, N.Y.; d Aug. 12, 1910, Marietta, Ohio)* Teacher, Union Army officer, industrialist with interests in transportation, power, mineral, and oil field development, and an Ohio Democrat who strongly advocated free silver and while a U.S. Representative (1879-1881, 1883-1887), introduced several free coinage bills, all of which were doomed to nonpassage. Democratic National Convention delegate (1896).

WARNER, VESPASIAN *(b April 23, 1842, Mount Pleasant, now Farmer City, Ill.; d March 31, 1925, Clinton, Ill.).* Union Army officer, lawyer, banker, real estate dealer, Illinois Republican. Presidential elector on the Harrison-Morton ticket (1888), U.S. Representative (1895-1905), pension commissioner (1905-1909).

WARNER, WILLIAM *(b June 11, 1840, Shullsburg, Wis.; d Oct. 4, 1916, Kansas City, Mo.)* Lawyer, Union Army officer, conservative Missouri Republican. Kansas City city attorney (1867), circuit attorney (1868), Kansas City mayor (1872), U.S. Representative

(1885-1889), Grand Army of the Republic commander (1888), U.S. attorney for Missouri's western district (1870, 1882, 1898, 1902), GOP state committee chairman (1884, 1885), GOP National Convention delegate (1872, 1884, 1888, 1892, 1896), unsuccessful gubernatorial candidate (1892), U.S. Senate (1905-1911).

WARREN, EDWARD ALLEN *(b May 2, 1818, Green County, Ala.; d July 2, 1875, Prescott, Ark.)* Lawyer, Mississippi and Arkansas Democrat. In Mississippi: state representative (1845, 1846). In Arkansas: state representative (1848, 1849) and house speaker (1849), sixth district circuit court judge (1849-1852), U.S. Representative (1853-1855, 1857-1859).

WARREN, FRANCIS EMROY *(b June 20, 1844, Hinsdale, Mass.; d Nov. 24, 1929, Washington, D.C.)* Furniture salesman, farmer, real estate speculator, Union soldier who received the Congressional Medal of Honor for actions performed at Port Hudson, then went west to Wyoming when it was part of the Dakota Territory (1868), became one of the pioneer land's leading cattlemen and sheepraisers, and helped Wyoming to develop as a territory in its own right and then as a state; Republican, and for many years the party's territorial chairman. Because of his interest in full voting rights for women, the Wyoming Territory had full suffrage as early as 1869, then wrote it into its first state constitution (1890), the first in the nation to have done so.
As a territory: territorial senator (1873, 1874, 1884, 1885) and senate president (1873, 1874), Cheyenne councilman (1873, 1874), territorial treasurer (1876, 1879, 1882, 1884), mayor of Cheyenne (1885), governor (1885-1886, 1889-1890), GOP National Convention delegate (1888). As a state: elected governor in September 1890 but resigned in November upon also being elected one of Wyoming's first two U.S. senators (1890-1893, 1895 until death), chairman of state delegation to all GOP National Conventions (1900, 1904, 1908, 1912). As a senator, he was, at different times, chairman of both the Military Affairs and Appropriations committees.

WARREN, LINDSAY CARTER *(b Dec. 16, 1889, Washington, N.C.)* Lawyer, University of North Carolina trustee (1921-1925), North Carolina Democrat, and a statewide power in the party who was U.S. comptroller general (1940-1954). Beaufort County attorney and county Democratic chairman (1912-1925), state senator (1917, 1919, 1959, 1961) and senate president pro tem (1919), state code commissioner (1919), U.S. government appeal agent and state legal advisory board chairman during World War I, workmen's compensation special legislative committee chairman (1920), state representative (1923), U.S. Representative (1925-1940), Democratic National Convention delegate (1932, 1940), Democratic state convention chairman (1930, 1934) and temporary chairman and keynote speaker (1938).

WARREN, MERCY OTIS *(b Sept. 14, 1728, Barnstable, Mass.; d Oct. 19, 1814, Plymouth, Mass.)* Writer, patriot, and close friend of leaders of American Revolutionary days; wrote *History of the Rise, Progress, and Termination of the American Revolution* (three volumes, 1805), the first such account written by an American historian.

WASHBURN, CADWALLADER COLDEN *(b Apr. 22, 1818, Livermore, Maine; d May 15, 1882, Eureka Springs, Ark.).* One of the four brothers who left their political marks upon the United States, each of them operating from different states (see also Israel and William Drew Washburn and Elihu B. Washburne); teacher, surveyor, lawyer, banker, Union

Army officer, and a Wisconsin Republican with a wide range of industrial interests, chief among them flour milling. U.S. Representative (1855-1861, 1867-1871), peace convention delegate (1861), governor (1872-1874).

WASHBURN, HENRY DANA *(b March 28, 1832, Windsor, Vt.; d Jan. 26, 1871, Clinton, Ind.)* Tanner, teacher, lawyer, Union Army officer, Indiana Republican whose fame came in Montana where, as surveyor general (1869 until death), he led an expedition (1870) to find the headwaters of the Yellowstone River and so discovered what became Yellowstone Park. Mount Washburn is named for him. County auditor (1854-1861), U.S. Representative (1866-1869).

WASHBURN, ISRAEL *(b June 6, 1813, Livermore, Maine; d May 12, 1883, Philadelphia, Pa.)* Lawyer, Tufts College trustee and board president, and a Maine Whig who was one of the founders of the Republican party in Ripon, Wisconsin (1854) and is said by some to have been the one who first suggested its name. State representative (1842, 1843), U.S. Representative (1851-1861), governor (1861, 1862). Portland customs collector (1863-1877). Brother of Cadwallader C. and William D. Washburn and Elihu B. Washburne.

WASHBURN, WILLIAM BARRETT *(b Jan. 31, 1820, Winchendon, Mass.; d Oct. 5, 1887, Springfield, Mass.)* Manufacturer, banker, smith, and Yale College trustee, Amherst College overseer, and a Massachusetts Republican. State senate (1850), state representative (1853-1855), U.S. Representative (1863-1871) resigning to become governor (1872-1874) and resigning once again, this time to become a U.S. Senator (1874-1875).

WASHBURN, WILLIAM DREW *(b Jan. 14, 1831, Livermore, Maine; d July 29,* *1912, Minneapolis, Minn.)* Lawyer, railroad builder, water power executive, manufacturer, flour miller, real estate speculator, lumberman, Minnesota Republican. Lincoln-appointed surveyor general of Minnesota (1861-1865), state representative (1861-1865, 1871, 1874, 1880, 1882), U.S. Representative (1879-1885), U.S. Senate (1889-1895). Brother of Cadwallader C. and Israel Washburn and Elihu B. Washburne.

WASHBURNE, ELIHU BENJAMIN *(b Sept. 23, 1816, Livermore, Maine; d Oct. 22, 1887, Chicago, Ill.)* Kennebec *Journal* assistant editor, lawyer, author, Illinois Whig-Republican who was one of Grant's chief sponsors and a dedicated foe of lobbyists and plunderers of the treasury. Whig National Convention delegate (1844, 1852), U.S. Representative (1853-1869) resigning to briefly become Grant's secretary of state (1869) and leaving that cabinet post to become minister to France throughout the Franco-Prussian War and the Commune (1869-1877). His memories of those days are preserved in his *Recollections* (1887). Brother of Cadwallader C., Israel, and William D. Washburn, but he added an E to the name.

WASHINGTON, GEORGE *(b Feb. 22, 1732, on family estate, later known as "Wakefield," near Popes Creek, Westmoreland County, Va.; d Dec. 14, 1799, Mount Vernon, Va.)* First president (Virginia Federalist), 1789-1797; Commander in chief of the Continental Army; surveyor; land speculator; farmer. Although he had the equivalent of only about an elementary school education, Washington read much and his opinions and person (he was over six feet tall and of an impressive bearing) were widely respected. He had an instinct for governing, plus military know-how. In Thomas Jefferson's words he was "a wise, a good, and a great man"—all attributes that helped make him the right man to guide the nation through its birth pangs. The legends crediting him with strict moral standards were completely false.

Augustine Washington, George's planter father, died in 1743. His elder half-brother, Lawrence, became an affectionate second father, sharing the responsibility of guiding the boy with his possessive mother, Mary Ball Washington, and bequeathing to George the now famous Mt. Vernon estate. George married Martha Dandridge Custis, a wealthy widow with two children (1759). He had no children but years later adopted two of Martha's grandchildren. The marriage also brought him the Custis plantations, including 300 slaves.

Appointed Culpeper County surveyor (1749); appointed adjutant of a military district in Virginia with rank of major (1751). In winter of 1753-1754, delivered warning message from Virginia governor to commander of French troops who had invaded the Ohio Valley. Rejection of warning led to French and Indian War, in which Washington became a seasoned soldier, gaining much experience in guerrilla warfare. Served (1755-1758) as commander in chief of the Virginia militia then settled down to lead the pleasant agriculture-oriented life of the Virginia gentleman at Mt. Vernon. Additionally (1758-1774), he was a magistrate and a member of the colonial house of burgesses. Although the operation of his estate was made increasingly difficult by the imposition of British commercial restrictions and he became a leader of southern opposition to the British colonial policy, he at first had no intention of becoming involved in a shooting war. Member of Virginia's delegation to First and Second Continental Congresses (1774, 1775) and, partly through the efforts of John Adams in an attempt to draw the southern and northern factions together, he was named (June 15, 1775) commander in chief of the Continental forces. He served without pay for the

next eight years but with a liberal expense account. In that time he returned only once to Mt. Vernon, but Mrs. Washington often visited him in camp.

On Dec. 23, 1783, Washington resigned his commission and returned to Mt. Vernon, devoting the next four years to restoring his farms and to opening new trade-expansion routes westward. Tensions between states were mounting and he became (1787) a delegate to the federal Constitutional Convention and was unanimously elected its president. Under his direction, the Constitution of the United States was drawn up, then ratified by the states.

On Feb. 4, 1789, the first Electoral College unanimously elected Washington first president. He was inaugurated April 30 of that year. In an attempt to establish the presidency above partisanship, he chose his appointees from different philosophies (Democratic-Republican champion of the common man and agriculture, Thomas Jefferson, became secretary of state; Federalist Alexander Hamilton, secretary of the treasury). Besides presiding over the organization of a completely new government (everything he did established a precedent), he was faced with foreign relations problems and debts. He was again elected unanimously (Feb. 13, 1793) to a second term, much more difficult than the first one. He made the controversial "first" decision to use troops in the Whiskey Rebellion (1794) and was generally considered by Jeffersonians as being too aristocratic in his attitudes. He refused to consider a third term and, in March 1797, he and Martha returned to their beloved Mt. Vernon. In 1798 war with France seemed imminent, and Washington was commissioned lieutenant general in command of the new U.S. Army. The crisis subsided in 1799, but the life of a gentleman farmer that Washington had waited through long years of public service to enjoy was cut short by his unexpected and sudden death.

WASHINGTON, GEORGE CORBIN *(b Aug. 20, 1789, Westmoreland County, Va.; d July 17, 1854, Georgetown, D.C.).* Planter, Chesapeake & Ohio Canal Company president, Maryland Whig. U.S. Representative (1827-1833, 1835-1837), Cherokee Indian claims commissioner (1844). Nephew of George Washington.

WASHINGTON, JOSEPH EDWIN *(b Nov. 10, 1851, Robertson County, Tenn.; d Aug. 28, 1915, Robertson County).* Planter, Vanderbilt University trustee, railroad executive, Tennessee Democrat. State representative (1876-1878), presidential elector on the Hancock-English ticket (1880), U.S. Representative (1887-1897).

WASKEY, FRANK HINMAN *(b April 20, 1875, Lake City, Minn.)* Prospector, mine operator, banker, and publishing company executive—all of them in Alaska where he had gone in 1898, also showing interest in politics as a Democrat and becoming the territory's first delegate to the U.S. Congress but only for six months (1906-1907). That brief taste of Washington life was enough and he went back to the wilderness. U.S. commissioner at Fortuna Lodge (1915-1918) and registration officer, food commissioner and national defense council chairman throughout World War I.

WASON, EDWARD HILLS *(b Sept. 2, 1865, New Boston, N.H.; d Feb. 6, 1941, near New Boston)* Lawyer, banker, farmer, New Hampshire Republican. Nashua Board of Education member (1891-1895) and its president (1895), city solicitor (1894, 1895), common council president (1897, 1898), state representative (1899, 1909, 1913), state constitutional convention delegate (1902, 1912), Hillsborough County solicitor (1903-1907), Nashua alderman (1906-1908), U.S. Representative (1915-1933).

WATERMAN, CHARLES WINFIELD *(b Nov. 2, 1861, Waitsfield, Vt.; d Aug. 27, 1932, Washington, D.C.)* Teacher, lawyer, Colorado Republican. GOP National Convention delegate (1920), U.S. Senate (1927 until death).

WATKINS, ALBERT GALITON *(b May 5, 1818, Jefferson County, Tenn.; d Nov. 9, 1895, Mooresburg, Tenn.)* Lawyer, clergyman, Tennessee Whig-Democrat. State representative (1845), presidential elector on the Taylor-Fillmore ticket (1848), U.S. Representative (1849-1853, 1855-1859).

WATKINS, ARTHUR VIVIAN *(b Dec. 18, 1886, Midway, Utah)* Lawyer, farmer, Utah Republican. Salt Lake County assistant attorney (1914, 1915), fourth judicial district judge (1928-1933), U.S. Senate (1947-1959).

WATKINS, JOHN THOMAS *(b Jan. 15, 1854, Minden, La.; d April 25, 1925, Washington, D.C.)* Lawyer, Louisiana Democrat. District court judge (1892-1904), U.S. Representative (1905-1921).

WATRES, LAURENCE HAWLEY *(b July 18, 1882, Scranton, Pa.)* Lawyer, Pennsylvania Republican. U.S. Representative (1923-1931).

WATSON, HENRY WINFIELD *(b June 24, 1856, Bucks County, Pa.; d Aug. 27, 1933, Langhorne, Pa.)* Lawyer, historian, banker, water and rail executive, Pennsylvania Republican. U.S. Representative (1915 until death).

WATSON, JAMES ELI *(b Nov. 2, 1863, Winchester, Ind.; d July 29, 1948, Washington, D.C.)* Lawyer, Indiana Republican who was a delegate to nine GOP National Conventions and president of seven state conventions. Presidential elector on the Harrison-Reid ticket (1892), U.S. Representative (1895-1897,

1899, 1909), unsuccessful gubernatorial candidate (1908), U.S. Senate (1916-1933).

WATSON, WALTER ALLEN *(b Nov. 25, 1867, Nottoway County, Va.; d Dec. 24, 1919, Washington, D.C.)* Lawyer, Virginia Democrat. State senate (1891-1895), commonwealth attorney (1895-1904), Democratic state committeeman (1901, 1902), fourth judicial circuit judge (1904-1912), U.S. Representative (1913 until death).

WATTERSON, HARVEY MAGEE *(b Nov. 23, 1811, Bedford County, Tenn.; d Oct. 1, 1891, Louisville, Ky.)* Lawyer, diplomat, editor-publisher of the *Nashville Daily Union* in Tennessee, editor of the *Washington Union* in the nation's capital, and on the staff of the *Louisville Courier-Journal* in Kentucky; friend of Franklin Pierce, always quite a carouser and a Democrat, an officeholder in Tennessee, and a Unionist wherever he set pen to paper. Tennessee state representative (1835), U.S. Representative from Tennessee (1839-1843), President Tyler's personal representative to Argentina (1844), state senate speaker (1845-1847). Father of Henry Watterson.

WATTERSON, HENRY *(b Feb. 16, 1840, Washington, D.C.; d Dec. 22, 1921, Jacksonville, Fla.)* Son of Harvey M. Watterson but very much a newspaperman in his own right (fifty years as editor of the *Louisville Courier-Journal*), author, lecturer, Kentucky Democrat-Liberal Republican, intellectually a Unionist but through loyalty to the South a secessionist and a chief of scouts during the Civil War and editor of the *Chattanooga Rebel*, which he made into the voice of the Confederate Army. A giant in the heyday of personal journalism, he did not hesitate to take on presidents (he let the country know that in Theodore Roosevelt he saw the makings of a dictator) nor to take un-

popular positions on matters of national moment.

Temporary chairman of the Democratic National Committee (1876) and in the forefront of the successful fight to win the nomination for Samuel J. Tilden of New York whom he long had championed for the presidency, U.S. Representative briefly (1876-1877) to complete the term of the late Edward Y. Parsons, Democratic National Convention delegate (1880, 1884, 1888, 1892).

WATTS, JOHN SEBRIE *(b Jan. 19, 1816, Boone County, Ky.; d June 11, 1876, Bloomington, Ind.)* Lawyer, Indiana Whig and New Mexico Territory Republican. In Indiana: state representative (1846, 1847). In New Mexico: associate justice of the U.S. district court (1851-1854), delegate to the U.S. Congress (1861-1863), GOP National Convention delegate (1864), chief justice of the New Mexican Supreme Court (1868-1869).

WAYNE, ANTHONY *(b Jan. 1, 1745, East Town, Pa.; d Dec. 15, 1796, Presque Isle, now Erie, Pa.)* Revolutionary Army officer who wintered with Washington at Valley Forge, fought under Lafayette at Yorktown, took Stony Point from the British, prevented Benedict Arnold from surrendering West Point to the Crown, fought Indians, became known as Mad Anthony, and always, after brief flings at politics in Pennsylvania and politics and rice planting in Georgia, returned to the military life. In Pennsylvania: state assemblyman (1784). In Georgia: delegate to the state convention that ratified the federal Constitution (1788), U.S. Representative (1791-1792). Father of Isaac Wayne.

WAYNE, ISAAC *(b 1772, Chester County, Pa.; d Oct. 25, 1852, Chester County)* Lawyer, War of 1812 cavalry officer, farmer, Pennsylvania Federalist. State representative (1799-1801, 1806), state senate (1810), unsuccessful gubernatorial candidate (1814), U.S. Representative (1823-1825). Son of Anthony Wayne.

WAYNE, JAMES MOORE *(b 1790, Savannah, Ga.; d July 5, 1867, Washington, D.C.)* Lawyer, a Georgia Unionist during the Civil War but otherwise always a Democrat and a supporter of Andrew Jackson who appointed him a U.S. Supreme Court associate justice where he served (1835 until death) for thirty-two years. His particular fields of expertise were admiralty law and the acquisition of foreign-owned lands. State representative (1815, 1816), mayor of Savannah (1817-1819), common pleas court judge (1820-1822), superior court judge (1822-1828), U.S. Representative (1829-1835) and for a time chairman of the House Foreign Relations Committee.

WEADOCK, THOMAS ADDIS EMMET *(b Jan. 1, 1850, County Wexford, Ireland; d Nov. 18, 1938, Detroit, Mich.).* Teacher, lawyer, University of Detroit law professor, Michigan Democrat. Bay County prosecutor (1877, 1878), state Democratic convention chairman (1883, 1894), mayor of Bay City (1883-1885) and board of education member (1884), U.S. Representative (1891-1895), Democratic National Convention delegate (1896), associate justice of the state supreme court (1933 until death).

WEAVER, JAMES BAIRD *(b June 12, 1833, Dayton, Ohio; d Feb. 6, 1912, Des Moines, Iowa)* Lawyer, Union soldier who rose from private to brigadier general; a completely honest Iowa Republican who became a Democrat-Greenbacker-Laborite, transformed the state's Farmers' Alliance into the Populist party, and twice ran for the U.S. presidency—as the National Greenback candidate (1880) polling only 308,578 popular votes, and the People's party candidate (1892) polling 1,029,846 pop-

ular and 22 electoral votes. Second judicial district attorney (1866-1871) doubling as first district internal revenue assessor (1867-1873), U.S. Representative (1879-1881, 1885-1889), mayor of Colfax (1901-1903).

WEAVER, PHILLIP HART *(b April 9, 1919, Falls City, Nebr.).* Radio announcer, finance business, automobile dealer, Nebraska Republican. U.S. Representative (1955-1963) and member of the Appropriations Committee.

WEAVER, ZEBULON *(b May 12, 1872, Weaverville, N.C.; d Oct. 29, 1948, Asheville, N.C.).* Educated at Weaver College and the University of North Carolina, lawyer, North Carolina Democrat who served eight years in Congress but not in succession. State representative (1907-1909), state senate (1913-1915), U.S. Representative (1917-1919, 1919-1929, 1931-1947).

WEBB, EDWIN YATES *(b May 23, 1872, Shelby, N.C.; d Feb. 7, 1955, Wilmington, N.C.)* Lawyer, Wake Forest and Agricultural and Mechanical College trustee, North Carolina Democrat. State senate (1901), Democratic senatorial district chairman (1896) and county executive committee chairman (1898-1902), Democratic state convention temporary chairman (1900), U.S. Representative (1903-1919), U.S. judge (1919-1948).

WEBB, WILLIAM ROBERT *(b Nov. 11, 1842, Person County, N.C.; d Dec. 19, 1926, Bell Buckle, Tenn.)* Confederate soldier who was wounded at Malvern Hill, teacher who founded the first training school west of the Allegheny Mountains at Culleoka, Tenn. (1870), and a Tennessee Democrat who started his political career as a State Gold and Credit Democrat (1896) and was a delegate in that same year to the National Democratic Convention. Seventeen years later he became a U.S. Senator but only briefly (Jan. 24-March 3, 1913) to fill a vacancy caused by the death of Robert L. Taylor. Grandson of Richard Stanford.

WEBSTER, DANIEL *(b Jan. 18, 1782, Salisbury, now Franklin, N.H.; d Oct. 24, 1852, Marshfield, Mass.)* One of America's great lawyers, orators, and statesmen who at first vigorously championed states' rights but later abandoned that position as expounded in debate (1830 with Senator Robert Y. Hayne of South Carolina): "Liberty *and* Union, now and forever, one and inseparable!"

A New Hampshire and Massachusetts Federalist and a dedicated adversary of Henry Clay, Webster nevertheless joined with him (1836) in the founding of the Whig party and (March 7, 1850) supported his compromise proposals regarding slavery and the annexation of territories. A leading but unsuccessful candidate for the Whig presidential nomination (1852), Webster was heartbrokenly bitter against what he termed "that great body of implacable enemies" and died soon after. He was a lover of good life, a too-frequent imbiber who all too often was in debt and owing to his wealthy friends for financial dependency.

In New Hampshire: U.S. Representative (1813-1817). In Massachusetts: presidential elector on the Monroe-Tompkins ticket (1820), state constitutional convention delegate (1820), U.S. Representative (1823-1827), U.S. Senate (1827-1841, 1845-1850), secretary of state in the Harrison and Tyler cabinets (1841-1843) and the Fillmore cabinet (1850 until death).

WEBSTER, EDWIN HANSON *(b March 31, 1829, Churchville, Md.; d April 24, 1893, Bel Air, Md.)* Teacher, lawyer, banker, Maryland Know-Nothing–Republican. State senate (1855-1859), presidential elector on the Fillmore-Donelson ticket (1856), U.S. Representative (1859-

1865) resigning to become Port of Baltimore customs collector (1865-1869, 1882-1886).

WEBSTER, JOHN STANLEY *(b Feb. 22, 1877, Cynthiana, Ky.)* Lawyer who was Kentucky's Harrison County prosecutor (1902-1906), then moved to Washington State and became politically active as a Republican. Spokane County chief assistant prosecutor (1907-1909), superior court judge (1909-1916), associate justice of the state supreme court (1916-1918), U.S. Representative (1919-1923), U.S. judge for the eastern district (1923-1939).

WEBSTER, TAYLOR *(b Oct. 1, 1800, Pennsylvania; d April 27, 1876, New Orleans, La.)* Editor-publisher of the *Western Telegraph* in Hamilton (1828-1836), Ohio Democrat. State house of representatives clerk (1829), becoming a member and speaker (1830), U.S. Representative (1833-1839), Butler County Court clerk (1842-1846).

WEEKS, EDGAR *(b Aug. 3, 1839, Mount Clemens, Mich.; d Dec. 17, 1904, Mount Clemens)* Lawyer, newspaper editor, Union Army officer, Michigan Republican. Macomb County prosecutor (1867-1870), probate judge (1870-1876), U.S. Representative (1899-1903). Cousin of John Wingate Weeks.

WEEKS, JOHN ELIAKIM *(b June 14, 1853, Salisbury, Vt.; d Sept. 10, 1949, Middlebury, Vt.)* Banker, Vermont Republican. Addison County assistant judge (1884-1886, 1902-1904), state representative (1888, 1912, 1915) and house speaker (1915), state senator (1896), director of state institutions (1917-1923), public welfare commissioner (1923-1926), governor (1927-1931), U.S. Representative (1931-1933).

WEEKS, JOHN WINGATE *(b March 31, 1781, Greenland, N.H.; d April 3, 1853, Lancaster, N.H.)* Carpenter who recruited a company of fellow New Hampshire men and led them in the War of 1812. U.S. Representative (1829-1833). Great-uncle of the following.

WEEKS, JOHN WINGATE *(b April 11, 1860, near Lancaster, N.H.; d July 12, 1926, Lancaster)* Teacher, Annapolis graduate, civil engineer, banker, stockbroker, naval reserve rear admiral, and a Massachusetts Republican who received 105 votes for the GOP presidential nomination (1916) and was secretary of war in both the Harding and Coolidge cabinets (1921-1925).

GOP state convention chairman (1895), member of the U.S. Naval Academy Visitors' Board (1896), Newton alderman (1899-1902) and mayor (1902, 1903), U.S. Representative (1905-1913) resigning to become a U.S. Senator (1913-1919), GOP National Convention delegate (1920). Great-nephew of the preceding, father of Sinclair Weeks, cousin of Edgar Weeks.

WEEKS, JOSEPH *(b Feb. 13, 1773, Warwick, Mass.; d Aug. 4, 1845, Winchester, N.H.)* Farmer, New Hampshire Democrat. Richmond town clerk (1802-1822), state representative (1807-1809, 1812, 1813, 1821-1826, 1830, 1832-1834), common pleas court associate judge (1823, 1827), U.S. Representative (1835-1839). Grandfather of Joseph W. Babcock.

WEEKS, SINCLAIR *(b June 15, 1893, West Newton, Mass.)* Banker, manufacturer, Massachusetts Republican. Newton alderman (1923-1930) and mayor (1930-1935), GOP state committee chairman (1936-1938), GOP National Committee member (1941-1953) and its treasurer (1940-1944), GOP National Convention delegate (1932, 1940, 1944, 1948, 1952, 1956), U.S. Senate (Feb. 8 to Dec. 19, 1944) to fill the vacancy caused by the resignation of Henry Cabot Lodge, Jr., Harvard University overseer (1948-1954), secretary of commerce in the Eisenhower cabinet (1953-1958). Son of John W. Weeks.

WEFALD, KNUD *(b Nov. 3, 1869, Kragero, Norway; d Oct. 25, 1936, St. Paul, Minn.)* Farmer, lumberman and a member of the Minnesota Farmer-Labor party who for a time was editor of a Norwegian newspaper in Fargo, North Dakota. Hawley Village Council president (1907-1912, 1917, 1918), U.S. Representative (1923-1927), executive secretary of the Minnesota Administration and Finance Commission (1931, 1932), state railroad and warehouse commissioner (1933 until death).

WEICHEL, ALVIN F. *(b Sept. 11, 1891, Sandusky, Ohio; d Nov. 27, 1956, Sandusky)* Lawyer, Ohio Republican. Erie County prosecutor (1931-1937), U.S. Representative (1943-1955).

WEIGHTMAN, RICHARD HANSON *(b Dec. 28, 1816, Washington, D.C.; d Aug. 10, 1861, Wilson Creek, Mo.)* Lawyer, soldier, Indian agent, Santa Fe newspaper editor and a New Mexico Territory Democrat who was its first delegate to the Thirty-second Congress (1851-1853) and a Confederate Army officer who was killed while leading his troops in battle.

WEISSE, CHARLES HERMAN *(b Oct. 24, 1866, Sheboygan Falls, Wis.; d Oct. 8, 1919, Sheboygan Falls)* Tannery operator, businessman, Wisconsin Democrat. Sheboygan Falls council president (1893-1896) and school board treasurer (1897-1900), Democratic National Convention delegate (1904, 1908), U.S. Representative (1903-1911).

WELCH, RICHARD JOSEPH *(b Feb. 13, 1869, Monroe County, N.Y.; d Sept. 10, 1949, Needles, Calif.)* California Republican with a lifelong interest in politics. State senator (1901-1913), San Francisco harbor master (1903-1907), San Francisco city and county supervisor (1916-1926) resigning to become a U.S. Representative for the next twenty-three years (1926 until death).

WELKER, HERMAN *(b Dec. 11, 1906, Cambridge, Idaho; d Oct. 30, 1957, Bethesda, Md.)* Lawyer, farmer, Idaho Republican who ran for and won his first political office—Washington County prosecutor (1929-1935)—while still in college. With time out for World War II service, he was also in the state senate (1948-1950) and U.S. Senate (1951-1957).

WELLBORN, OLIN *(b June 18, 1843, Cumming, Ga.; d Dec. 6, 1921, Los Angeles, Calif.)* Confederate Army officer, lawyer, Texas and California Democrat. In Texas: U.S. Representative (1879-1887). In California: U.S. judge for the southern district (1895-1915).

WELLER, JOHN B. *(b Feb. 22, 1812, Hamilton, Ohio; d Aug. 17, 1875, New Orleans, La.)* Lawyer, Mexican War officer, diplomat, Ohio Democrat, California Union Democrat. In Ohio: U.S. Representative (1839-1845), unsuccessful candidate for governor (1848). In California: U.S. Senate (1852-1857), governor (1858-1860), minister to Mexico (1860-1861), Democratic National Convention delegate (1864).

WELLING, MILTON HOLMES *(b Jan. 25, 1876, Farmington, Utah; d May 28, 1947, Salt Lake City, Utah)* Farmer, merchant, banker, mine operator, trustee of Brigham Young College and Utah State Agricultural College, and regent of the University of Utah; Democrat. State representative (1911-1915), U.S. Representative (1917-1921), state registration director (1925-1928), Utah secretary of state (1928-1937), surveyed public grazing lands for U.S. government (1937, 1938).

WELLINGTON, GEORGE LOUIS *(b Jan. 28, 1852, Cumberland, Md.; d March 20, 1927, Cumberland)* Bank clerk who rose to become president of two banks with financial interests in electric railway and lighting companies; Maryland Republican who supported the Democrat, William Jennings Bryan, for the presidency (1900) and ran for the U.S. Senate (1913) on the Progressive party ticket. Allegany County treasurer (1882-1890), assistant U.S. treasurer (1890-1893), U.S. Representative (1895-1897), U.S. Senate (1897-1903).

WELLS, ERASTUS *(b Dec. 2, 1823, Sackets Harbor, N.Y.; d Oct. 2, 1893, St. Louis, Mo.)* Railroad and utilities executive who gave St. Louis its first bus and street car lines, Missouri Democrat whose major causes while a U.S. Representative (1869-1877, 1879-1881) were development of the Southwest and Mississippi River improvements.

WELLS, WILLIAM HILL *(b Jan. 7, 1769, Burlington, N.J.; d March 11, 1829, Sussex County, Del.)* Lawyer, oil producer for whom Wellsboro, Pa., was named, and a Delaware political figure. Member of the general assembly (1794-1798), U.S. Senate (1799-1804, 1813-1817) both times to complete vacated terms.

WENTWORTH, JOHN *(b July 17, 1745, Salmon Falls, N.H.; d Jan. 10, 1787, Dover, N.H.)* New Hampshire lawyer who was one of the signers of the Articles of Confederation. Strafford County register of probate (1773-1787), state representative (1776-1780), member of the Committee of Safety (1777-1778), moderator (1777-1786), delegate to the Continental Congress (1778, 1779), member of the state council (1780-1784), state senate (1784-1786). Grandfather of the younger John Wentworth.

WENTWORTH, JOHN *(b March 5, 1815, Sandwich, N.H.; d Oct. 16, 1888, Chicago, Ill.)* Teacher, lawyer and influential editor-publisher of the *Chicago Democrat*, property owner, and an Illinois Democrat who joined the Republicans over the issue of slavery. Among his favorite causes, both as a journalist and as an officeholder: Western land grants for railroads and free homesteads for the little man. U.S. Representative (1843-1851, 1853-1855, 1865-1867), mayor of Chicago (1857-1863), state constitutional convention delegate (1861). Grandson of the elder John Wentworth.

WERNER, THEODORE B. *(b June 2, 1892, Ossian, Iowa)* Editor-publisher of the *Gate City Guide*, South Dakota Democrat. Rapid City postmaster (1915-1923), city commissioner (1927-1930) and mayor (1929, 1930), U.S. Representative (1933-1937).

WEST, MILTON HORACE *(b June 30, 1888, Gonzales County, Texas; d Oct. 28, 1948, Washington, D.C.)* Texas Ranger, lawyer, Texas Democrat. Twenty-eighth judicial district attorney (1922-1925) and assistant district attorney (1927-1930), state representative (1930-1933), U.S. Representative (1933 until death).

WESTLAND, ALFRED JOHN *(b Dec. 14, 1904, Everett, Wash.)* Lawyer, insurance, investment, and cotton broker, Washington Republican. U.S. Representative (1953-1965) serving on the Interior and Insular Affairs Committee and Joint Committee on Atomic Energy.

WETMORE, GEORGE PEABODY *(b Aug. 2, 1846, London, England; d Sept. 11, 1921, Boston, Mass.)* Lawyer, Rhode Island Republican. Presidential elector on the Garfield-Arthur (1880) and Blaine-Logan (1884) tickets, governor (1885, 1886), U.S. Senate (1895-1913).

WHALEY, RICHARD SMITH *(b July 15, 1874, Charleston, S.C.; d Nov. 8, 1951, Charleston)* Lawyer, South Carolina Democrat. State representative (1900-1913) and house speaker (1907-1910, 1913), Democratic state (1910) and city (1911) convention chairman, Democratic National Convention delegate (1912,

1920), U.S. Representative (1913-1921); U.S. Court of Claims commissioner (1925-1930), a judge on that bench (1930-1939) and its chief justice (1939-1947).

WHARTON, JAMES ERNEST *(b Oct. 4, 1899, Binghamton, N.Y.)* Lawyer, farmer, New York Republican. Schoharie County district attorney (1932-1935); surrogate, county, and children's court judge (1941-1947), U.S. Representative (1951-1965) and a member of the Interior and Insular Affairs Committee.

WHEATON, LABAN *(b March 13, 1754, Mansfield, Mass.; d March 23, 1846, Norton, Mass.)* Lawyer, Massachusetts Federalist. State representative (1803-1808, 1825), U.S. Representative (1809-1817), Bristol County common pleas court chief justice (1810-1819) and then sessions court chief justice for the rest of his life.

WHEELER, BURTON KENDALL *(b Feb. 27, 1882, Hudson, Mass.).* Lawyer, Montana Democrat who was a U.S. Senator nearly a quarter-century (1923-1947) and was Robert M. La Follette's Progressive party vice presidential running mate (1924) polling 4,831,289 popular and 13 electoral votes. State representative (1910-1912), U.S. district attorney for Montana (1913-1918), unsuccessful candidate for governor (1920).

WHEELER, CHARLES KENNEDY *(b April 18, 1863, Christian County, Ky.; d June 15, 1933, Paducah, Ky.)* Lawyer, Kentucky Democrat. Presidential elector on the Cleveland-Stevenson ticket (1892), Paducah city solicitor (1894-1896), U.S. Representative (1897-1903).

WHEELER, JOSEPH *(b Sept. 10, 1836, Augusta, Ga.; d Jan. 25, 1906, Brooklyn, N.Y.)* West Point graduate, professional soldier who rose from second lieutenant to senior cavalry general of the Confederate Armies, took part in more than 400 engagements, had sixteen horses shot out from under him, and was wounded three times; in the Spanish-American War he was a general and again saw a lot of action. Planter, author, and Alabama Democrat who for eight terms was a U.S. Representative (1885-1900).

WHEELER, LOREN EDGAR *(b Oct. 7, 1862, Havana, Ill.; d Jan. 8, 1932, Springfield, Ill.)* Ice and coal dealer, advertising man, Illinois Republican. Springfield alderman (1895-1897) and mayor (1897-1901), GOP National Convention delegate (1900), Springfield postmaster (1901-1913), U.S. Representative (1915-1923, 1925-1927).

WHEELER, WILLIAM ALMON *(b June 19, 1819, Malone, N.Y.; d June 4, 1887, Malone)* Lawyer, a scrupulously honest New York legislator who, when the legislative "salary grab" act was passed (1873) during his tenure in Congress, refused to accept the increase. A sagacious lawmaker, he is credited with preventing collapse of the Louisiana government with his adjustment of an election dispute he had been chosen to arbitrate. In response to his nomination (1876) as Rutherford B. Hayes' vice presidential running mate, Hayes wrote to his wife: "Who is Wheeler?" During their administration, however, the president came to know him as a "noble, honest, patriotic man."
Franklin County district attorney (1846-1849), assemblyman (1850, 1851), state senate (1858, 1859), U.S. Representative (1861-1863, 1869-1877), state constitutional convention delegate (1867, 1868), vice president of the United States (1877-1881).

WHELCHEL, BENJAMIN FRANK *(b Dec. 16, 1895, Lumpkin County, Ga.; d May 11, 1954, Gainesville, Ga.)* Lawyer, Georgia Democrat. Hall County court judge (1932-1934), U.S. Representative (1935-1945).

WHERRY, KENNETH SPICER *(b Feb. 28, 1892, Liberty, Nebr.; d Nov. 29, 1951, Washington, D.C.)* Salesman, livestock farmer, lawyer, Nebraska Republican, and a power in the party. Pawnee City councilman (1927, 1929) and mayor (1929-1931, 1938-1943), state senate (1929-1932), GOP state chairman (1939-1942), GOP National Committee's director for twenty-two western states (1941, 1942), U.S. Senate (1943 until death), GOP Senate whip (1944-1948) and leader (1949-1951).

WHIPPLE, THOMAS, JR. *(b 1787, Lebanon, N.H.; d Jan. 23, 1835, Wentworth, N.H.)* Physician who was a member of the New Hampshire House of Representatives (1818-1820) and a U.S. Representative (1821-1829).

WHIPPLE, WILLIAM *(b Jan. 14, 1730, Kittery, Maine; d Nov. 28, 1785, Portsmouth, N.H.)* New Hampshire signer of the Declaration of Independence who started his career as a sailor, became a ship's master and slave trader; then had a complete change of heart, gave up the sea, freed his slaves, and became a respected New England merchant and Revolutionary Army brigadier general. Provincial Congress delegate (1775), Continental Congress delegate (1775, 1776, 1778), state assemblyman (1780-1784), state supreme court judge (1782), state financial receiver (1782-1784).

WHITAKER, JOHN ALBERT *(b Oct. 31, 1901, Russellville, Ky.; d Dec. 15, 1951, Russellville)* Lawyer, Kentucky Democrat. Logan County attorney (1928-1948), delegate to all Democratic state conventions (1924-1950), U.S. Representative (1948 until death). Grandson of Addison D. James.

WHITCOMB, JAMES *(b Dec. 1, 1795, Windsor County, Vt.; d Oct. 4, 1852, New York City)* Lawyer, Indiana Democrat. Monroe County prosecutor (1826), state senate (1830-1836), U.S. General Land Office commissioner (1836-1841), governor (1843-1849), U.S. Senate (1849 until death).

WHITE, ADDISON *(b May 1, 1824, Abingdon, Va.; d Feb. 4, 1909, Huntsville, Ala.)* Farmer, cotton raiser, Kentucky Whig who fought for the Confederacy in the Civil War. U.S. Representative (1851-1853). Cousin of John White.

WHITE, ALBERT SMITH *(b Oct. 24, 1803, Orange County, N.Y.; d Sept. 24, 1864, Stockwell, Ind.)* Lawyer, railroad tycoon, Indiana Whig-Republican who as a U.S. legislator introduced a Lincoln-supported resolution calling for the gradual emancipation of slaves held in the border states. Assistant state house of representatives clerk (1830, 1831) and clerk (1832-1835), presidential elector on the Harrison-Granger ticket (1836), U.S. Representative (1837-1839, 1861-1863), U.S. Senate (1839-1845), Lincoln-appointed commissioner to settle claims of Minnesota and Dakota settlers who had suffered losses at the hands of hostile Indians, U.S. judge (1864 until death).

WHITE, ALEXANDER *(b 1738, Frederick County, Va.; d Sept. 19, 1804, Frederick County)* Lawyer, landowner and developer, Virginia Federalist who was one of the leaders in the struggle for ratification of the federal Constitution (1788) and then a representative in the First and Second Congresses (1789-1793). Member of state house of delegates (1782-1786, 1788, 1799-1801), Washington-appointed commissioner to lay out the city of Washington and to erect public buildings (1795-1802).

WHITE, CAMPBELL PATRICK *(b Nov. 30, 1787, Ireland; d Feb. 12, 1859, New York City)* Merchant, New York Democrat and follower of Andrew Jackson, U.S. Representative (1829-1835), state constitutional convention delegate (1845).

WHITE, COMPTON IGNATIUS *(b July 31, 1877, Baton Rouge, La.; d March 31, 1956, Spokane, Wash.)* A jack of many trades who worked as telegraph operator, trainman, conductor, farmer, lumberjack, and miner before becoming a solid Democratic citizen of Idaho with stock raising and mining interests. Democratic National Convention delegate (1928, 1932, 1936), U.S. Representative (1933-1947, 1949-1951).

WHITE, EDWARD DOUGLASS, SR. *(b March, 1795, Nashville, Tenn.; d April 18, 1847, New Orleans, La.)* Lawyer, planter, and a leading Louisiana Whig. New Orleans city court judge (1825-1828), U.S. Representative (1829-1834, 1839-1843), governor (1834-1838). Son of James White.

WHITE, EDWARD DOUGLASS, JR. *(b Nov. 3, 1845, Thibodaux, La.; d May 19, 1921, Washington, D.C.)* Confederate soldier, lawyer, and a Louisiana Democrat who went a considerable step beyond his father politically to become an associate justice of the U.S. Supreme Court (1894-1910) and then chief justice (1910 until death). During his tenure, he wrote opinions in more than 700 cases, the most lasting coming when he applied the "rule of reason" in Standard Oil and American Tobacco Anti-Trust Act findings. He could be classified neither as liberal nor conservative, thus being accused of inconsistency, but perhaps his philosophy was best summed up (1916) when in a eulogy to Joseph R. Lamar, White said that the rights of all could be best protected by protecting the rights of each.

State senate (1874-1878), associate

justice of the state supreme court (1879-1880), U.S. Senate (1891-1894) resigning to accept Cleveland's appointment to the high court.

WHITE, GEORGE *(b Aug. 21, 1872, Elmira, N.Y.; d Dec. 15, 1953, West Palm Beach, Fla.)* Teacher, Klondike miner (1898-1901), and then relocated in Ohio where he struck it rich as an oil producer and banker; Marietta College trustee and a prominent Democrat both at home and nationally. State representative (1905-1908), U.S. Representative (1911-1915, 1917-1919), chairman of the Democratic National Committee (1920-1921), governor (1931-1935), chairman of the Northwest Territory Federal Commission (1938).

WHITE, GEORGE HENRY *(b Dec. 18, 1852, Rosindale, N.C.; d Dec. 28, 1918, Philadelphia, Pa.)* Howard University-educated teacher, lawyer, banker who was the last Negro to serve in Congress from the Reconstruction until Oscar DePriest of Illinois took his seat in 1928. A North Carolina Republican, White was a U.S. Representative (1897-1901) who was outspoken on the evils of lynching and mob law. State normal school principal, state representative (1880), state senate (1884), second judicial district solicitor and prosecutor (1886-1894), GOP National Convention delegate (1896, 1900).

After leaving Congress, White devoted his energies to the establishment of an all-Negro community in New Jersey—Whitesboro—that was then named for him.

WHITE, HAYS BAXTER *(b Sept. 21, 1855, Jefferson County, Iowa; d Sept. 29, 1930, Mankato, Kans.)* Farmer, teacher, Kansas Republican. State representative (1888-1890), state senate (1900-1904), mayor of Mankato (1914, 1915), state tax commissioner (1915-1918), U.S. Representative (1919-1929).

WHITE, HUGH LAWSON *(b Oct. 30, 1773, Iredell County, N.C.; d April 10, 1840, Knoxville, Tenn.)* Indian fighter, lawyer, Tennessee Democrat who was a follower of Jefferson and Jackson until splitting with the latter (1836) and thus becoming a candidate for the presidency on one of three Whig tickets that ran against Jackson's Democratic candidate, Martin Van Buren. White won the electoral votes of only the states of Tennessee and Georgia. Secretary to Governor William Blount (1793), state supreme court judge (1801-1807, 1809-1815), state senate (1807-1809, 1817-1825), U.S. attorney (1808), state bank president (1812-1827), U.S. Senate to succeed Jackson (1825-1840) and Senate president pro tem (1832).

WHITE, JAMES *(b June 16, 1749, Philadelphia, Pa.; d October 1809, Attakapas, La.)* Physician, lawyer who left the easy Philadelphia life for a rugged existence in western North Carolina, which later became first the Territory South of the River Ohio and then the state of Tennessee, at which time he moved on to Louisiana. In North Carolina: member of the state general assembly (1785), delegate to the Continental Congress (1786-1788), southern district Indian affairs superintendent (1786). In the territory: territorial representative in its first legislature (1794), delegate to the U.S. Congress (1794-1796). In Louisiana: Attakapas and St. Martin Parish district judge (1804 until death).

WHITE, JOHN *(b Feb. 14, 1802, near Cumberland Gap, now Middlesboro, Ky.; d Sept. 22, 1845, Richmond, Ky.)* Lawyer, Kentucky Whig. State representative (1832), U.S. Representative (1835-1845) and House speaker (1841-1843), nineteenth judicial district judge (1845 until death). Cousin of Addison White, uncle of John D. White.

WHITE, JOHN DAUGHERTY *(b Jan. 16, 1849, Clay County, Ky.; d Jan. 5, 1920,* near Manchester, Ky.) Lawyer, and a Kentucky Republican who twice ran for office under other party labels. U.S. Representative (1875-1877, 1881-1885), GOP state convention delegate (1879), state representative (1879, 1880), state delegation chairman to the GOP National Convention (1880), unsuccessful State Prohibition party candidate for governor (1903), unsuccessful Progressive party candidate for state appeals court judge (1920). Nephew of John White.

WHITE, JOSEPH M. (b May 10, 1781, Franklin County, Ky.; d Oct. 19, 1839, St. Louis, Mo.) Lawyer, Florida Territory Democrat. Territorial land claims commissioner (1822-1824), delegate to the U.S. Congress (1825-1837).

WHITE, SEBASTIAN HARRISON (b Dec. 24, 1864, near Maries County, Mo.; d Dec. 21, 1945, Colorado Springs, Col.). Educator, lawyer, Colorado Democrat. Hickory County Teachers Institute president (1886) and county schools superintendent (1887), Democratic state convention delegate (1892), Pueblo County Democratic Committee chairman (1892), Pueblo city attorney (1897-1899), Pueblo County public trustee (1900-1903, 1905-1909), tenth judicial district attorney (1904-1908), state supreme court justice (1909-1916) and chief justice (1917-1918), U.S. Representative (1927-1929).

WHITE, WALLACE HUMPHREY, JR. (b Aug. 6, 1877, Lewiston, Maine; d March 31, 1952, Auburn, Maine) Secretary to his grandfather, William P. Frye, while the latter was president pro tem of the U.S. Senate (1899-1903), lawyer, Bowdoin College overseer, Maine Republican, and a legislative authority on radio telegraphy who often served on commissions, both foreign and domestic, for Presidents Coolidge and Roosevelt. U.S. Representative (1917-1931), U.S. delegation chairman to International Conference on Safety of Life at Sea (1929),

U.S. Senate (1931-1949), Senate minority leader (1945-1947) and majority leader (1947-1949).

WHITEAKER, JOHN (b May 4, 1820, Dearborn County, Ind.; d Oct. 2, 1902, Eugene, Ore.) Farmer, stock raiser, lawyer, Oregon Democrat both while a territory and a state and the state's first governor (1858-1862). As a territory: Lane County probate judge (1855), member of the territorial legislature (1857). As a state: state representative (1866, 1868, 1870) and house speaker (1866, 1868), state board of equalization chairman (1872), state senator (1876-1880) and senate president (1876, 1878), U.S. Representative (1879-1881), internal revenue collector (1885-1890).

WHITEHILL, JAMES (b Jan. 31, 1762, Strasburg, Pa.; d Feb. 26, 1822, Strasburg) Lawyer, farmer, War of 1812 major general of Pennsylvania Militia. Lancaster County Court associate judge (1811-1813, 1820 until death), U.S. Representative (1813-1814). Son of John and nephew of Robert Whitehill.

WHITEHILL, JOHN (b Dec. 11, 1729, Salisbury Township, Pa.; d Sept. 16, 1815, Salisbury Township) Lawyer, Pennsylvania jurist whose career on the bench began with appointment both as justice of the peace and Lancaster County Orphans' Court judge in 1777. State representative (1780-1782, 1793), council of censors (1783), supreme executive council (1784), delegate to the state convention that ratified the federal Constitution (1787), Lancaster County associate judge (1791-1802), U.S. Representative (1803-1807). Father of James and brother of Robert Whitehill.

WHITEHILL, ROBERT (b July 21, 1738, Pequea, Pa.; d April 8, 1813, Lauther Manor, Pa.) Landowner, builder of the first stone house in Cumberland County, patriot, and a staunch Pennsylvania Jeffersonian Democrat who would have nothing to do with the state's entrenched establishment. Member of state constitutional convention that approved the Declaration of Independence (1776), Council of Safety (1777), state constitutional convention delegate and a leader of the opposition (1790), state representative (1797-1800), state senator (1801-1804) and senate speaker (1804) when the state's supreme court judges were impeached, U.S. Representative (1805 until death). Brother of John and uncle of James Whitehill.

WHITENER, BASIL LEE *(b May 14, 1915, York County, S.C.)* Lawyer, North Carolina Democrat. State representative (1941-1942), U.S. Navy (1942-1945), fourteenth district solicitor (1946-1956), Democratic National Convention delegate (1948), U.S. Congress (1957-1969) serving on the Judiciary and District of Columbia committees.

WHITING, JUSTIN RICE *(b Feb. 18, 1847, Bath, N.Y.; d Jan. 31, 1903, St. Clair, Mich.)* Merchant, manufacturer, Michigan Greenback Democrat. Mayor of St. Clair (1879), state senate (1882), U.S. Representative (1887-1895), unsuccessful Democratic candidate for governor (1898, 1900) and state Democratic chairman.

WHITING, WILLIAM *(b May 24, 1841, Dudley, Mass.; d Jan. 9, 1911, Holyoke, Mass.)* Paper manufacturer, Massachusetts Republican. State senator (1873), Holyoke city treasurer (1876, 1877) and mayor (1878, 1879), GOP National Convention delegate (1876, 1896), U.S. Representative (1883-1889).

WHITLEY, JAMES LUCIUS *(b May 24, 1872, Rochester, N.Y.; d May 17, 1959, Rochester)* Lawyer, author, New York Republican who was a delegate to all GOP state conventions for twenty years. Assistant corporation counsel in Rochester (1900, 1901) and chief examiner of the civil service commission (1902-

1904), assemblyman (1905-1910), state senate (1918-1928), U.S. Representative (1929-1935).

WHITTHORNE, WASHINGTON CURRAN *(b April 19, 1825, Marshall County, Tenn.; d Sept. 21, 1891, Columbia, Tenn.).* Government clerk, lawyer, Tennessee Democrat who was the Confederacy's state adjutant general during the Civil War. State senator (1855-1858), state representative and house speaker (1859), presidential elector on the Breckinridge-Lane ticket (1860), U.S. Representative (1871-1883, 1887-1891), U.S. Senate to fill a vacancy (1886-1887).

WHITTINGTON, WILLIAM MADISON *(b May 4, 1878, Little Springs, Miss.).* Lawyer, farmer, Mississippi Democrat who for a quarter-century was a U.S. Representative (1925-1951). Greenwood councilman (1907-1911), state senator (1916-1920, 1924) resigning to become a congressman, Democratic National Convention delegate (1920, 1928, 1936, 1940, 1948).

WHITTLESEY, ELISHA *(b Oct. 19, 1783, Washington, Conn.; d Jan. 7, 1863, Washington, D.C.)* Lawyer, teacher who left Connecticut for Ohio and became not only a prominent citizen but also a founder of the Whig party (1834). State representative (1820, 1821), U.S. Representative (1823-1838), sixth auditor of the U.S. Treasury (1841-1843), first comptroller of the U.S. Treasury (1849-1857, 1861 until death). Uncle of William A. Whittlesey, cousin of Frederick and Thomas T. Whittlesey.

WHITTLESEY, FREDERICK *(b June 12, 1799, New Preston, Conn.; d Sept. 19, 1851, Rochester, N.Y.)* Lawyer, New York Whig. Monroe County treasurer (1829, 1830), U.S. Representative (1831-1835), Rochester city attorney (1838), eighth judicial district vice chancellor (1839-1847), state supreme court justice

(1847, 1848), Genesee College law professor (1850, 1851). Cousin of Elisha and Thomas T. Whittlesey.

WHITTLESEY, THOMAS TUCKER *(b Dec. 8, 1798, Danbury, Conn.; d Aug. 20, 1868, Pheasant Branch, Wis.)* Lawyer in Connecticut, lawyer and farmer in Wisconsin, and a Democrat in both. In Connecticut: U.S. Representative (1836-1839). In Wisconsin: state senate (1853, 1854). Cousin of Elisha and Frederick Whittlesey.

WHITTLESEY, WILLIAM AUGUSTUS *(b July 14, 1796, Danbury, Conn.; d Nov. 6, 1866, Brooklyn, N.Y.)* Teacher, lawyer, Ohio Democrat. Washington County auditor (1825-1837), state representative (1839, 1840), U.S. Representative (1849-1851), mayor of Marietta (1856, 1860, 1862). Nephew of Elisha Whittlesey.

WHYTE, WILLIAM PINKNEY *(b Aug. 9, 1824, Baltimore, Md.; d March 17, 1908, Baltimore)* Banker, lawyer, Maryland Democrat who was an enemy of the Know-Nothings and a friend of the Confederacy. State delegate (1847, 1848), state comptroller of the treasury (1853-1855), Democratic National Convention delegate (1868), U.S. Senate (1868-1869 to fill a vacancy, 1875-1881, 1906 until death), governor (1872-1874), state counsel in Virginia boundary dispute (1874), mayor of Baltimore (1881, 1882), state attorney general (1887-1891), chairman of city charter commission (1897, 1898), city solicitor (1900-1903).

WICKERSHAM, JAMES *(b Aug. 24, 1857, Patoka, Ill.; d Oct. 24, 1939, Juneau, Alaska)* Lawyer who left Illinois for the Washington Territory then went on to Alaska where he also became a writer on ethnological and historical matters; Republican and very much the man who had most to do with passage of the Organic Act (1912) that gave territorial status to Alaska. In Illinois: member of the governor's guards. In Washington: Pierce County probate judge (1884-1888), Tacoma city attorney (1894), state representative (1898). In Alaska: U.S. district judge for the territory (1900-1908), delegate to the U.S. Congress (1909-1917, 1919, 1921, 1931-1933) where he introduced the first Alaska statehood bill (1916).

WICKLIFFE, CHARLES ANDERSON *(b June 8, 1788, Washington County, Ky.; d Oct. 31, 1869, near Ilchester, Md.).* Lawyer and a Kentucky political leader who could not reconcile his position with that of his party of the moment on critical issues of the day and so was variously Democrat-Whig, Democrat-Union, and Whig-Democrat in that order. State representative (1812-1813, 1822, 1823, 1833-1835) and house speaker (1834), U.S. Representative (1823-1833, 1861-1863), lieutenant governor (1836-1839), governor (1839-1840), U.S. postmaster general (1841-1845) who was sent on a secret mission to the Republic of Texas by President Polk (1845), state constitutional convention delegate (1849), peace-between-states convention delegate (1861), unsuccessful gubernatorial candidate (1863), Democratic National Convention delegate (1864). Father of Robert C. Wickliffe, Sr., grandfather of John Crepps Wickliffe Beckham and Robert C. Wickliffe, Jr., cousin of Benjamin Hardin.

WICKLIFFE, ROBERT CHARLES, SR. *(b Jan. 6, 1819, Bardstown, Ky.; d April 18, 1895, St. Francisville, La.)* Lawyer, cotton planter, Louisiana Democrat who was elected a U.S. Representative (1866) but along with many other Southerners was denied admission because they refused to take the so-called iron-clad oath. State senate (1851-1855) and its president (1853-1855), governor (1856-1860) at first striving to keep Louisiana in the Union but then going with the secession tide, chairman of the state delegation to the Democratic National Convention, and a presidential elector on the Tilden ticket (1876). Son of Charles A. Wickliffe and father of the following.

WICKLIFFE, ROBERT CHARLES, JR. *(b May 1, 1874, Bardstown, Ky.; d June 11, 1912, Washington, D.C.)* Lawyer, Louisiana Democrat. State constitutional convention delegate (1898), twenty-fourth judicial district attorney (1902-1906), U.S. Representative (1909 until death). Son of the preceding, grandson of Charles A. Wickliffe, cousin of J. C. W. Beckham.

WIER, ROY WILLIAM *(b Feb. 25, 1888, Redfield, S.Dak.)* Electrician, labor leader, Minnesota Democrat. State representative (1933-1939), Minneapolis School Board member and Hennepin County Red Cross director (1939-1948), U.S. Representative (1949-1961).

WIGGLESWORTH, RICHARD BOWDITCH *(b April 25, 1891, Boston, Mass.; d Oct. 22, 1960, Boston)* Lawyer, diplomat, Massachusetts Republican who served thirty years as a U.S. Representative (1928-1958). Before and after that: assistant private secretary to the governor of the Philippines (1913), World War I artillery officer (1917-1919), secretary of the World War Debt Commission and legal adviser to the assistant secretary of the treasury in charge of foreign loans and railway payments (1922-1924), Berlin-based assistant to the agent general for reparation payments (1924-1927), general counsel and Paris representative of Dawes Plan organizations (1927, 1928), U.S. ambassador to Canada (1959 until death).

WIKE, SCOTT *(b April 6, 1834, Meadville, Pa.; d Jan. 15, 1901, Pike County, Ill.)* Lawyer, Illinois Democrat. State representative (1863-1867), U.S. Representative (1875-1877, 1889-1893), assistant secretary of the U.S. Treasury (1893-1897).

WILBER, DAVID *(b Oct. 5, 1820, Schenectady County, N.Y.; d April 1, 1890, Oneonta, N.Y.)* Lumber and hops dealer, farmer, banker, railroad executive, New York Republican. Otsego County supervisor (1858, 1859, 1862, 1865, 1866), U.S. Representative (1873-1875, 1879-1881, 1887 until death), GOP National Convention delegate (1880, 1888). Father of David F. Wilber.

WILBER, DAVID FORREST *(b Dec. 7, 1859, Milford, N.Y.; d Aug. 14, 1928, Upper Dam, Maine)* Farmer, real estate operator, banker, stock breeder, Cazenovia (N.Y.) Seminary trustee, foreign service officer, New York Republican. President of the Holstein-Friesian Association of America and the American Cheviot Sheep Association of the United States and Canada (1894), U.S. Representative (1895-1899); U.S. consul in Barbados (1903-1905), consul general in Singapore (1905-1907), Halifax (1907-1909), Kobe (1909-1910), Vancouver (1910-1913), Zurich (1913-1915), Genoa (1915-1921), Auckland and Wellington (1922-1923). Son of David Wilber.

WILCOX, JAMES MARK *(b May 21, 1890, Willacoochee, Ga.; d Feb. 3, 1956, near White Springs, Fla.)* Lawyer, farmer, Georgia and Florida Democrat. In Georgia: Jeff Davis County solicitor (1911-1918). In Florida: West Palm Beach city attorney (1928-1933), taxation committee member at President's Conference on Home Ownership (1931), U.S. Representative (1933-1939), Dade County Port Authority attorney general (1945 until death).

WILCOX, ROBERT WILLIAM *(b Feb. 15, 1855, Kahalu, Hawaii; d Oct. 23, 1903, Honolulu)* Teacher, surveyor who attended an Italian military academy, served in the Italian Army and returned home to twice lead revolutions (1889, 1895), the first time he was acquitted of treason, the second time he was sentenced to death, but sentence was reduced to thirty-five years of which he had to serve only three. Also, a legislative representative from Koolauloa (1892), Hawaii Territory's first delegate to the U.S. Congress (1900-1903).

WILDE, RICHARD HENRY *(b Sept. 24, 1789, Dublin, Ireland; d Sept. 10, 1847, New Orleans, La.)* Merchant, lawyer, University of Louisiana (now Tulane University) professor, poet, Georgia Democrat, and European traveler who unearthed Giotto's portrait of Dante in Florence. Richmond County Superior Court solicitor general (1810), state attorney general (1811-1813), U.S. Representative (1815-1817, 1825, 1827-1835).

WILDER, ABEL CARTER *(b March 18, 1828, Mendon, Mass.; d Dec. 22, 1875, San Francisco, Calif.)* Kansas merchant, Union Army officer, publisher of the *Morning and Evening Express* (1865-1868) in Rochester, N.Y.; Kansas and New York Republican who was chairman of the GOP National Convention (1860). In Kansas: delegate to the Osawatomie convention (1859), U.S. Representative (1863-1865). In New York: mayor of Rochester (1872, 1873). In both: GOP National Convention delegate (1864, 1868, 1872).

WILEY, ALEXANDER *(b May 26, 1884, Chippewa Falls, Wis.; d Oct. 26, 1967, Philadelphia, Pa.)* Wisconsin Republican with a flair for oratory who once described himself as "just a small-town banker, a businessman, lawyer and operator of a dairy who became a typical success"—that success coming in twenty-four years as a U.S. Senator (1939-1963).

Son of an immigrant Norwegian farmer who changed the family name from Vila, Wiley's first years in the Senate were marked by his isolationism but by 1943 he was turning to internationalism, spurred by Arthur H. Vandenberg of Michigan, who urged him "to take another look at the changing world." As a result, in 1945 Wiley became a member of the Foreign Relations Committee and in 1954, when given the choice of chairing either that body or the Judiciary Committee, opted for the former. Said the *New York Times* of his tenure in that post: He "earned a reputation as an ardent internationalist and a man of high political courage."

No matter, however, how much he concentrated his energies on U.S. foreign policy, Wiley always remained an ardent booster of Wisconsin and its products, particularly cheese. So much so that once he treated Washington to the sight of a bust of Vice President Garner done in cheddar cheese.

Chippewa County district attorney (1909-1915); unsuccessful candidate for governor (1936), losing to the incumbent, Philip La Follette, a highly popular Progressive; delegate to the Interparliamentary Union Conference in Norway (1939) and the Empire Parliamentary Conference in Bermuda (1946).

WILEY, ARIOSTO APPLING *(b Nov. 6, 1848, Clayton, Ala.; d June 17, 1908, Hot Springs, Va.)* Lawyer, Alabama Democrat. State representative (1884, 1885, 1888, 1889, 1896, 1897), state senator (1890-1893, 1898, 1899), Democratic National Convention delegate (1888), Presidential elector on the Cleveland-Thurman ticket (1888), U.S. Representative (1901 until death).

His brother, Oliver Cicero Wiley, also a Democrat, completed his unexpired term in Congress (1908-1909).

WILEY, OLIVER CICERO *(b Jan. 30, 1851, Troy, Ala.; d Oct. 18, 1917, Troy).* Railroad president, banker, oil and chemical executive, president of the board of directors of the State Normal College at Troy; Alabama Democrat. A power in the party locally, he served for five years as Troy councilman, was Pike County Democratic Executive Committee chairman (1884-1886), member of its state executive committee (1888), Democratic National Convention alternate delegate (1888, 1892), U.S. Representative to complete the term (Nov. 1908-March 1909) upon the death of his brother, Ariosto A. Wiley.

WILKINS, BERIAH *(b July 10, 1846, Union County, Ohio; d June 7, 1905, Washington, D.C.)* Union soldier, banker, and an Ohio Democrat who left that state to become editor-publisher of the *Washington Post* (1889 until death). State senate (1880, 1881), Democratic state committee member (1882), U.S. Representative (1883-1889).

WILKINS, WILLIAM *(b Dec. 20, 1779, Carlisle, Pa.; d June 23, 1865, Allegheny County, Pa.)* Lawyer, manufacturer, banker who was the first president of the Bank of Pittsburgh (1814-1819), and an Anti-Mason Democrat from Pennsylvania who received the state's electoral votes for vice president (1833) and was secretary of war in the Tyler cabinet (1844-1845). Pittsburgh Common Council president (1816-1819), state representative (1820), fifth judicial district president judge (1821-1824), U.S. judge for Pennsylvania's western district (1824-1831), U.S. Senate (1831-1834) resigning to become ambassador to Russia (1834-1835), U.S. Representative (1843-1844) resigning to accept the cabinet post.

WILKINSON, MORTON SMITH *(b Jan. 22, 1819, Skaneateles, N.Y.; d Feb. 4, 1894, Wells, Minn.)* Railroad worker, lawyer, pioneer, and a Minnesota Republican. As a territory: member of its first legislature (1849), Ramsey County register of deeds (1851-1853), member of commission to prepare a code of law for the territory (1858). As a state: U.S. Senate (1859-1865), GOP National Convention delegate (1864), U.S. Representative (1869-1871), state senate (1874-1877), Faribault County prosecutor (1880-1884).

WILLARD, CHARLES WESLEY *(b June 18, 1827, Lyndon, Vt.; d June 8, 1880, Montpelier, Vt.)* Lawyer, Vermont Republican who became editor-publisher of the *Montpelier Freeman* (1861). Vermont secretary of state (1855, 1856), state senate (1860, 1861), U.S. Representative (1869-1875), commissioner to revise state laws (1879, 1880).

WILLARD, FRANCES ELIZABETH CAROLINE *(b Sept. 28, 1839, Churchville, N.Y.; d Feb. 18, 1898, New York City).* Educator, writer, lecturer, reformer best remembered for her role as head of the Woman's Christian Temperance Union (WCTU). Held several positions in education then became president of Evanston College for Ladies (1871-1874). From 1874 until her death she devoted her life to the WCTU. In succession, she was president of Chicago WCTU, secretary of Illinois WCTU, corresponding secretary of the National WCTU Convention, president of the National WCTU, president of the World WCTU. She enlisted the WCTU in the women's suffrage movement and other widespread social reform activities. She believed that women belonged in politics and (1882) helped organize the Prohibition party.

WILLARD, GEORGE *(b March 20, 1824, Bolton, Vt.; d March 26, 1901, Battle Creek, Mich.)* Lawyer, clergyman, newspaperman, Latin professor, and a Michigan Republican who at death was editor-publisher of the *Battle Creek Journal*. Member of state board of education (1857-1863), University of Michigan regent (1863-1872), state representative (1866, 1877), state constitutional convention delegate (1867), GOP National Convention delegate (1872), U.S. Representative (1873-1877).

WILLEY, WAITMAN THOMAS *(b Oct. 18, 1811, in a part of Monongalia County, Va., that is now Marion County, W.Va.; d May 2, 1900, Morgantown, W.Va.)* Lawyer, Virginia Constitutional Unionist and Whig party leader and Constitutional Unionist who used his gifts of oratory to oppose secession and then, more successfully, to bring about the separation of the western territory into a new state, and thereafter a West Virginia Republican. In Virginia: Monongalia Court clerk (1841-1852) doubling also as circuit superior court clerk (1842-1852), state constitutional convention delegate (1850, 1851), Constitutional Union National Convention delegate (1860), U.S. Senate (1861-1863). In West Virginia: state constitutional convention delegate (1863), U.S. Senate (1863-1871), GOP National Convention delegate (1876), Monongalia County clerk (1882-1896).

WILLIAMS, CHARLES GRANDISON *(b Oct. 18, 1829, Royalton, N.Y.; d March 30, 1892, Watertown, S.Dak.)* Lawyer, Wisconsin Republican. Presidential elector on the Grant-Colfax ticket (1868), state senator (1869-1872) and twice senate president pro tem, U.S. Representative (1873-1883).

WILLIAMS, CHRISTOPHER HARRIS *(b Dec. 18, 1798, Orange County, N.C.; d Nov. 27, 1857, Lexington, Tenn.)* Lawyer, Tennessee Whig. U.S. Representative (1837-1843, 1849-1853). Grandfather of John Sharp Williams.

WILLIAMS, CLYDE *(b Oct. 13, 1873, Jefferson County, Mo.; d Nov. 12, 1954, St. Louis, Mo.)* Lawyer, banker, Missouri Democrat. Jefferson County prosecutor (1902-1908), Democratic state convention permanent chairman (1938), U.S. Representative (1927-1929, 1931-1943), Reconstruction Finance Corporation lawyer (1943-1945).

WILLIAMS, DAVID ROGERSON *(b March 8, 1776, Robbins Neck, S.C.; d Nov. 17, 1830, in a Georgetown County, S.C., bridge construction accident).* Lawyer, editor-publisher of the Charleston *City Gazette* and the *Weekly Carolina Gazette*, pioneer cotton grower and manufacturer and builder of South Carolina's first cottonseed oil mill; politically a Democrat, War Hawk, and dedicated foe of John C. Calhoun. U.S. Representative (1805-1809, 1811-1813) and chairman of the House Military Affairs Committee, governor (1814-1816), state senate (1824 until death).

WILLIAMS, GEORGE HENRY *(b March 23, 1823, New Lebanon, N.Y.; d April 4, 1910, Portland, Oregon)* Lawyer, Iowa and Oregon Democrat-Union Republican who had much to do with the latter's gaining of statehood status; President Grant's choice as chief justice of the United States only to have the nomination withdrawn after investigation unveiled his role in Oregon election frauds. In Iowa: first judicial district judge (1847-1852), presidential elector on the Pierce-King ticket (1852). In Oregon Territory: Pierce-appointed territorial chief justice (1853-1857), state constitutional convention delegate (1858). In Oregon State: U.S. Senate (1865-1871), attorney general in the Grant cabinet (1872-1875), mayor of Portland (1902-1905).

WILLIAMS, GEORGE SHORT *(b Oct. 21, 1877, Ocean View, Del.)* Teacher, lumber dealer, banker, Delaware Republican. Mayor of Millsboro (1921-1927), state treasurer (1929-1933), state board of education president (1927-1934), state deputy motor vehicle commissioner (1935-1937) and commissioner (1941-1946), GOP National Convention delegate (1940), U.S. Representative (1939-1941), administrative assistant to U.S. Senator John J. Williams (1947-1959).

WILLIAMS, GUINN *(b April 22, 1871, Calhoun County, Miss.; d Jan. 9, 1948, San Angelo, Tex.).* Farmer, banker, rancher, Texas Democrat. Wise County clerk (1898-1902), state senator (1920-1922) resigning to become a U.S. Representative (1922-1933), Regional Agricultural Credit Corporation manager (1933).

WILLIAMS, HEZEKIAH *(b July 28, 1798, near Woodstock, Vt.; d Oct. 23, 1856, Castine, Maine)* Lawyer, Maine Democrat. Hancock County register of probate (1824-1838); Castine selectman (1833-1835, 1843, 1844), school fund trustee (1834), and school committee member (1840); state senate (1839-1841), U.S. Representative (1845-1849).

WILLIAMS, JAMES *(b Aug. 4, 1825, Philadelphia, Pa.; d April 12, 1899, Smyrna, Del.)* Farmer, Delaware Democrat. State representative (1856, 1862), state senate (1866, 1871), Democratic National Convention delegate (1872), U.S. Representative (1875-1879).

WILLIAMS, JAMES DOUGLAS *(b Jan. 16, 1808, Pickaway County, Ohio; d Nov. 20, 1880, Indianapolis, Ind.)* Farmer, miller, and an Indiana Democrat with two claims to fame: His frugality, which earned him the nickname Blue Jeans Williams—the jeans, homespun from his own flocks, he proudly wore even to Congress—and his victory over Benjamin Harrison, 213,219 to 208,080, for the governor's chair that he ably occupied (1877 until death). He began his political career with sixteen years of service on the state board of agriculture, four of them as president, then moved on to state representative (1843, 1847, 1851, 1856, 1868), state senate (1858, 1862, 1870), Democratic National Convention delegate (1872), U.S. Representative (1875-1876) and chairman of the House Accounts Committee —a fitting position for a man so economy-minded.

WILLIAMS, JAMES ROBERT *(b Dec. 27, 1850, Carmi, Ill.; d Nov. 8, 1923, Loma Linda, Calif.)* Lawyer, Illinois Democrat. Master in chancery (1880-1882), White County judge (1882-1886), U.S. Representative (1889-1895, 1899-1905).

WILLIAMS, JARED WARNER *(b Dec. 22, 1796, West Woodstock, Conn.; d Sept. 29, 1864, Lancaster, N.H.)* Lawyer, New Hampshire Democrat. State representative (1830, 1831, 1835, 1836), state senate (1832-1834), U.S. Representative (1837-1841), governor (1847-1849), U.S. Senate to fill a vacancy (1853-1854).

WILLIAMS, JOHN *(b September 1752, Barnstable, England; d July 22, 1806, Salem, N.Y.)* Graduate of a British medical school who served a year in the British Navy as a surgeon's mate, then came to America to become a New York physician, very much a patriot, Revolutionary Army officer, landholder, and one of those who promoted construction of the Erie Canal. State provincial congress (1775-1777), state senator (1777, 1778, 1782-1785), assemblyman (1781, 1782), member of New York University's first Board of Regents (1784), delegate to the state convention that ratified the federal Constitution (1788), member of the council of appointment (1789), U.S. Representative (1795-1799). (Not to be confused with John Williams of Tennessee—see next entry.)

WILLIAMS, JOHN *(b Jan. 29, 1778, Surry County, N.C.; d Aug. 10, 1837, near Knoxville, Tenn.)* Indian fighter, Tennessee lawyer, U.S. Senate (1815-1823), Central American Federation chargé d'affaires (1825-1826), state senator (1827, 1828). (Not to be confused with John Williams of New York— see previous entry.)

WILLIAMS, JOHN SHARP *(b July 30, 1854, Memphis, Tenn.; d Sept. 27, 1932 *near Yazoo City, Miss.)* Lawyer, cotton planter, Mississippi Democrat, and dedicated admirer of Jefferson; author of *Thomas Jefferson, His Permanent Influence on American Institutions* (1913). Democratic National Convention delegate (1892, 1904, 1912) and temporary chairman (1904), U.S. Representative (1893-1909) and House minority leader (1903-1909); U.S. Senate (1911-1923), consistent supporter of Woodrow Wilson and member of the Senate Foreign Relations and Finance committees. Grandson of Christopher H. Williams.

WILLIAMS, JOSEPH LANIER *(b Oct. 23, 1810, Knox County, Tenn.; d Dec. 14, 1865, Knoxville, Tenn.)* Lawyer, Tennessee Whig. U.S. Representative (1837-1843). Son of John Williams of Tennessee.

WILLIAMS, LEWIS *(b Feb. 1, 1782, Surry County, N.C.; d Feb. 23, 1842, Washington, D.C.)* Brother of John and Robert Williams about whom little is known, surprisingly so since he was a U.S. Representative from North Carolina for more than a quarter-century (1815 until death).

WILLIAMS, MARMADUKE *(b April 6, 1774, Caswell County, N.C.; d Oct. 29, 1850, Tuscaloosa, Ala.)* Lawyer, North Carolina and Alabama Democrat. In North Carolina: state senate (1802), U.S. Representative (1803-1809). In Alabama: state constitutional convention delegate (1819), state representative (1821-1839), Tuscaloosa County judge (1832-1842). Cousin of the three Williams brothers: John, Lewis and Robert.

WILLIAMS, ROBERT *(b July 12, 1773, Prince Edward County, Va.; d Jan. 25, 1836, Ouachita, La.)* North Carolina lawyer, planter whom Jefferson sent to Mississippi. In North Carolina: state senate (1792-1795), U.S. Representative (1797-1803). In Mississippi: commissioner to determine land claim rights of settlers west of the Pearl River (1803-1807), territorial governor (1805-1809). Brother of John and Lewis, cousin of Marmaduke, uncle of Joseph L. Williams.

WILLIAMS, ROGER *(b about 1603, London, England; d 1684, probably Providence, R.I.)* Liberal British clergyman who migrated to Massachusetts (1630), soon found himself among enemies because of his criticism of the Puritan ethic, ultimately was threatened with arrest, gathered a band of followers around him and found refuge among Indians who, in exchange for his honesty, compassion, and friendship, gave him the island of Aquidneck upon which he founded Providence (1636). It soon was followed by three other colonies and the four became know as the Providence Plantations. The Puritan colonies organized the New England Confederation, invaded Aquidneck, and Williams went back to England, secured a charter (1644), returned to Aquidneck, changed its name, and thus brought Rhode Island into being; a place where Jews, Quakers, and all men could practice their religions freely and where democracy in government was paramount, with Williams as governor or president for three terms.

WILLIAMS, SHERROD *(b 1804, Pulaski County, Ky.; d——)* Brickmaker, lawyer, Kentucky Whig. State representative (1829-1834, 1846), U.S. Representative (1835-1841).

WILLIAMS, THOMAS *(b Aug. 11, 1825, Greensville County, Va.; d April 13, 1903, Wetumpka, Ala.)* Lawyer, Alabama Democrat. State representative (1878), U.S. Representative (1879-1885).

WILLIAMS, THOMAS SUTLER *(b Feb. 14, 1872, Louisville, Ill.; d April 5, 1940, Washington, D.C.)* Lawyer, publisher of the *Clay County Republican,* Illinois Republican. Louisville city attorney (1897-1899), state representative (1899-1901), Louisville mayor (1907-1909), Clay County prosecutor (1908-1915), U.S. Representative (1915-1929), resigning to become U.S. Court of Claims judge (1929 until death).

WILLIAMS, WILLIAM *(b April 28, 1731, Lebanon, Conn.; d Aug. 2, 1811, Lebanon)* Connecticut signer of the Declaration of Independence and a well-to-do merchant who helped finance the Revolution. Lebanon town clerk (1753-1796), state representative (1757-1761, 1763-1776, 1780-1784) and house speaker (1775, 1781-1783), delegate to the Continental Congress (1776-1778, 1783, 1784), member of the Council of Safety during the war, Windham County Court judge (1776-1804), Windham district probate judge (1776-1808), assistant councillor and then councillor (1780-1812), delegate to the state convention that ratified the U.S. Constitution (1787). (Not to be confused with William Williams of Indiana—see next entry.)

WILLIAMS, WILLIAM *(b May 11, 1821, Cumberland County, Pa.; d April 22, 1896, Warsaw, Ind.)* Lawyer, banker, Union Army officer, Indiana Republican. Kosciusko County treasurer (1852-1853), Michigan City prison director (1854-1856), U.S. Representative (1867-1875), U.S. chargé d'affaires to Paraguay and Uruguay (1882-1885). (Not to be confused with William Williams of Connecticut—see previous entry.)

WILLIAMS, WILLIAM ROBERT *(b Aug. 11, 1884, Brookfield, N.Y.)* Farmer, salesman, merchant, New York Republican. Assemblyman (1935-1943), Oneida County sheriff (1943-1951), U.S. Representative (1951-1959).

WILLIAMSON, HUGH *(b Dec. 5, 1735, West Nottingham, Pa.; d May 22, 1819, New York City)* Physician, merchant, Revolutionary Army surgeon, college professor, economist, author, scientist who worked on electricity with Benjamin Franklin; a North Carolina Federalist who played a leading role in the drafting of the U.S. Constitution and was one of its signers. State house of commons (1782), Continental Congress delegate (1782-1785, 1787, 1788), federal Constitution Convention delegate (1787) and delegate to the state convention that ratified it (1789), U.S. Representative in the First and Second Congresses (1789-1793).

WILLIAMSON, JOHN NEWTON *(b Nov. 8, 1855, Junction City, Oreg.; d Aug. 29, 1943, Prineville, Oreg.)* Farmer, livestock raiser, Oregon Republican. Cook County sheriff (1886-1888), state representative (1888-1898), state senate (1900-1902), U.S. Representative (1903-1907), Prineville postmaster (1922-1934).

WILLIAMSON, WILLIAM *(b Oct. 7, 1875, Mahaska County, Iowa)* Lawyer, newspaperman who with his brother founded the *Murdo Coyote* and the *Prairie Sun,* South Dakota Republican. Lyman County prosecutor (1905-1911), eleventh judicial district circuit judge (1911-1921), GOP National Convention delegate (1912), U.S. Representative (1921-1933), state Public Utilities Commission general counsel (1939-1951).

WILLIAMSON, WILLIAM DURKEE *(b July 31, 1779, Canterbury, Conn.; d May 27, 1846, Bangor, Maine)* Lawyer, historian, Massachusetts and Maine Democrat who was a strong advocate of their separation into two states. In Massachusetts: Hancock County state's attorney (1808-1815), state senator (1816-1820). In Maine: Bangor postmaster (1810-1821), state senator and senate president (1820, 1821), governor (1821), U.S. Representative (1821-1823), Penobscot County probate judge

(1824-1840), state bank commissioner (1838-1841).

WILLIE, ASA HOXIE *(b Oct. 11, 1829, Washington, Ga.; d March 16, 1899, Galveston, Texas)* Lawyer, Confederate Army officer, Texas Democrat. Third judicial district attorney (1852-1854), associate justice of the state supreme court (1866-1867) and chief justice (1882-1888), U.S. Representative (1873-1875).

WILLING, THOMAS *(b Dec. 19, 1731, Philadelphia, Pa.; d Jan. 19, 1821, Philadelphia)* Wealthy Pennsylvania merchant who as a delegate to the Continental Congress (1775, 1776) voted against independence but when Philadelphia was occupied by British troops refused to take an oath of allegiance to the king; banker who was the first president of the Bank of the United States. Member of the Philadelphia Common Council (1755), alderman (1759), city court associate justice (1759), common pleas court justice (1761), mayor (1763), associate justice of the Pennsylvania Supreme Court (1767-1777), Committee of Correspondence (1774) and Committee of Safety member (1775), president of the first Provincial Council (1774).

WILLIS, ALBERT SHELBY *(b Jan. 22, 1843, Shelbyville, Ky.; d Jan. 6, 1897, Honolulu, Hawaii)* Teacher, lawyer, Kentucky Democrat. Presidential elector on the Greeley-Brown ticket (1872), Jefferson County prosecutor (1874-1877), U.S. Representative (1877-1887), minister to Hawaii (1893 until death).

WILLIS, EDWIN EDWARD *(b Oct. 2, 1904, Arnaudville, La.)* Lawyer, farmer, Louisiana Democrat. State senate (1948-1949), U.S. Representative (1949-1963) serving on the Judiciary and Un-American Activities committees, Democratic National Convention delegate (1956).

WILLIS, FRANK BARTLETT *(b Dec. 28, 1871, Lewis Center, Ohio; d March 30, 1928, Delaware, Ohio)* Lawyer, college professor, orator and an Ohio Republican who twice was chosen to nominate candidates for the presidency: Theodore E. Burton who did not win the designation (1916) and Warren G. Harding who did (1920). State representative (1900-1904), U.S. Representative (1911-1915), resigning to become governor (1915-1917), GOP National Convention delegate (1916-1920, 1924), U.S. Senate (1921 until death).

WILLITS, EDWIN *(b April 24, 1830, Otto, N.Y.; d Oct. 22, 1896, Washington, D.C.)* Editor of the *Monroe Commercial*, lawyer, Michigan Republican. Monroe County prosecutor (1860-1862), state board of education member (1860-1872), Monroe postmaster (1863-1866), state constitution revision commissioner (1873), U.S. Representative (1877-1883), Ypsilanti State Normal School principal (1883-1885), Michigan Agricultural College president (1885-1889), first assistant U.S. secretary of agriculture (1889-1893).

WILLKIE, WENDELL LEWIS *(b Feb. 18, 1892, Elwood, Ind.; d Oct. 8, 1944, New York City)* Ohio and New York lawyer, author of *One World*, lecturer, president of the Commonwealth and Southern Corporation, and leader of the private utilities fight against Tennessee Valley Authority expansion, Democrat turned liberal Republican, and a man who was unique in American political history. Although he never before had sought nor held public office, he was the GOP choice to run against Franklin Delano Roosevelt (1940) who was seeking his third term as president. FDR won, but Willkie in losing polled more popular votes than any Republican, winner or loser, ever before in history: Roosevelt 27,307,819 popular and 449 electoral votes; Willkie 22,321,018 and 82.

WILMOT, DAVID *(b Jan. 20, 1814, Bethany, Pa.; d March 16, 1868, Towanda, Pa.)* Lawyer, Pennsylvania Democrat–Free-Soiler who was the author of the Wilmot Proviso aimed at preventing the extension of slavery into newly acquired territories; a leading figure in the formation of the Republican party (1854) and then Pennsylvania's member on the GOP National Executive Committee.

State Democratic convention delegate (1844, 1848), U.S. Representative (1845-1851), delegate to the Free-Soil Democratic Convention at Herkimer (1847), National Free-Soil Convention delegate (1848), thirteenth judicial district presiding judge (1853-1861).

Then in 1856, in the fledgling Republican party, delegate to the preliminary GOP National Convention in Pittsburgh, the state convention in Philadelphia, and the national convention in Philadelphia where he drafted the first Republican platform. Also, delegate to and temporary chairman of the GOP National Convention (1860), U.S. Senate to fill a vacancy (1861-1863), delegate to the abortive peace-between-the-states convention (1861), Lincoln-appointed judge of the U.S. Court of Claims (1863 until death).

WILSON, BENJAMIN *(b April 30, 1825, Wilsonburg, Va., now W.Va.; d April 26, 1901, Clarksburg, W.Va.)* Lawyer, Virginia Democrat until West Virginia's separation and continuance of his political activity there. In Virginia: Harrison County commonwealth attorney (1852-1860), state constitutional convention delegate (1861). In West Virginia: presidential elector on the Seymour-Blair ticket (1868), state constitutional convention delegate (1871), Democratic National Convention delegate (1872), U.S. Representative (1875-1883), assistant U.S. attorney general (1885-1893).

WILSON, EARL *(b April 18, 1906, Lawrence County, Ind.)* Teacher, educator, Indiana Republican. U.S. Representative (1941-1959, 1961-1965) and member of the Appropriations Committee.

WILSON, EDGAR *(b Feb. 25, 1861, Armstrong County, Pa.; d Jan. 3, 1915, Boise, Idaho)* Lawyer, Idaho Republican who (1888) ran for office as a Silver Republican and with Democratic party endorsement. Boise City attorney (1887) and district attorney (1888), delegate to the convention that framed the state constitution (1890), U.S. Representative (1895-1897, 1899-1901).

WILSON, EDGAR CAMPBELL *(b Oct. 18, 1800, Morgantown, Va., now W.Va.; d April 24, 1860, Morgantown)* Lawyer, Virginia Whig. U.S. Representative (1833-1835), appointed Marion County circuit court prosecutor (1842). Son of Thomas and father of Eugene McL. Wilson.

WILSON, EMMETT *(b Sept. 17, 1882, Belize, British Honduras; d May 29, 1918, Pensacola, Fla.)* Railroad telegrapher, lawyer, Florida Democrat. Assistant U.S. attorney for the state's northern district (1907) and then attorney (1907-1909), first judicial circuit states attorney (1911-1913), U.S. Representative (1913-1917).

WILSON, EPHRAIM KING, SR. *(b Sept. 15, 1771, Somerset, now Worcester County, Md.; d Jan. 2, 1834, Snow Hill, Md.)* Lawyer, Maryland Democrat. Presidential elector on the Jefferson-Clinton ticket (1804), U.S. Representative (1827-1831). Father of the following.

WILSON, EPHRAIM KING, JR. *(b Dec. 22, 1821, Snow Hill, Md.; d Feb. 24, 1891, Washington, D.C.)* Lawyer, farmer, Maryland Democrat. State house of delegates member (1847), presidential elector on the Pierce-King ticket (1852), Worcester County School

Board examiner-treasurer (1868), U.S. Representative (1873-1875), first judicial circuit judge (1878-1884), U.S. Senate (1885 until death). Son of the preceding.

WILSON, EUGENE McLANAHAN *(b Dec. 25, 1833, Morgantown, Va., now W.Va.; d April 10, 1890, Nassau, British West Indies)* Lawyer who, like three generations before him, had an active interest in politics, the only difference being that he chose Minnesota as his state; Union Army officer, Democrat. U.S. attorney (1857-1861), U.S. Representative (1869-1871), mayor of Minneapolis (1872-1876), Democratic National Convention delegate (1876), state senator (1878, 1879), unsuccessful candidate for governor (1888). Great-grandson of Isaac Griffin, grandson of Thomas Wilson, son of Edgar C. Wilson.

WILSON, FRANCIS HENRY *(b Feb. 11, 1844, Clinton, N.Y.; d Sept. 25, 1910, Brooklyn, N.Y.)* Teacher, lawyer, New York Republican who was one of the founders and president (1888, 1889) of the prestigious Union League Club. U.S. Representative (1895-1897), Brooklyn postmaster (1897-1901).

WILSON, FRANK EUGENE *(b Dec. 22, 1857, Roxbury, N.Y.; d July 12, 1935, Brooklyn, N.Y.)* Physician, New York Democrat. U.S. Representative (1899-1905, 1911-1915), Democratic National Convention delegate (1900).

WILSON, GEORGE ALLISON *(b April 1, 1884, Adair County, Iowa; d Sept. 8, 1953, Des Moines, Iowa)* Lawyer, Iowa Republican. Assistant Polk County attorney (1912-1914) and county attorney (1915, 1916), district judge (1917-1921), state senate (1925-1935), governor (1939-1943), U.S. Senate (1943-1949).

WILSON, HENRY *(b Feb. 16, 1812, Farmington, N.H.; d Nov. 22, 1875, in the Capitol Building, Washington, D.C.).* Born Jeremiah Colbaith of impoverished parents who indentured him to a farmer, he changed his name (about 1833), became first a shoemaker, then a teacher, and then a lawyer of conviction and talent that led him into politics, his strong antislavery position driving him from party to party, culminating with adoption of the Republican label and climaxing as vice president of the United States (1873 until death). Massachusetts Whig until the 1848 national convention when it refused to support the Wilmot (anti-slavery) Proviso; then a founder of the Free-Soil party and editor-publisher of its organ, the *Boston Republican* (1848-1851); next a Know-Nothing under the quickly learned mistaken belief that it would take a strong abolitionist position; then an Abolitionist; and finally embracing the new-born GOP (1860).

State senator (1844-1846, 1850-1852) and senate president (1851, 1852), Whig National Convention delegate (1848), Free-Soil National Convention president (1852), state constitutional convention delegate (1853), unsuccessful candidate for governor (1853); elected first a U.S. Senator by a coalition of Free-Soilers, Know-Nothings, and Democrats and serving (1855-1873) until resigning to become Ulysses Grant's running mate, a strong addition to the ticket who contributed immeasurably to Grant's victory. During his Senate tenure, he was chairman of the military affairs committee, champion of emancipation as a war measure, molder of the bills that enabled many slaves to go free after adoption of the Thirteenth Amendment but before ratification, foe of Johnson Reconstruction policies, and supporter of homesteading in the South.

WILSON, JAMES *(b Sept. 14, 1742, Carskerdo, Scotland; d Aug. 28, 1798, Edenton, N.C.)* Latin tutor, lawyer who was the first professor of law in the College of Philadelphia and in the University of Pennsylvania (1790, 1791), an activist in the pre-Revolutionary movement, a Pennsylvania signer of the Declaration of Independence, an associate justice of the U.S. Supreme Court (1789-1798), and a framer of the federal Constitution (1787), the latter role leading James Bryce to say about him: "one of the deepest thinkers and most exact reasoners" whose achievements "display an amplitude and profundity of view in matters of constitutional theory which place him in the front rank of the political thinkers of his age."

Also a man with a gift for finance and the written word, he suggested in considerable detail (1780) a plan that was regarded as an outline of the new nation's financial system, and followed that up (1785) with publication of his *Considerations on the Power to Incorporate the Bank of North America*. Despite all of that, Wilson was a highly unpopular man among the people because of his land speculation schemes and his privateering activities. There was talk of his impeachment, and unwise ventures had him dodging his creditors in his last years.

Delegate to the Continental Congress (1775, 1776, 1782, 1783, 1785-1787), delegate to the state convention that adopted the federal Constitution (1788), author of the state constitution (1790). (Not to be confused with James Wilson of Indiana or James Wilson of Iowa—see next two entries.)

WILSON, JAMES *(b April 9, 1825, Crawfordsville, Ind.; d Aug. 8, 1867, Caracas, Venezuela)* Lawyer, Union Army officer, Indiana Republican. U.S. Representative (1857-1861), minister to Venezuela (1866 until death). Father of John L. Wilson. (Not to be confused with James Wilson of Pennsylvania— see previous entry—or James Wilson of Iowa—see next entry.)

WILSON, JAMES *(b Aug. 16, 1835, Ayrshire, Scotland; d Aug. 26, 1920,* *Traer, Iowa)* Farmer, teacher, editor of the *Agricultural Digest*, an authority on all matters pertaining to farming, and an Iowa Republican who was known as Tama Jim and served well as secretary of agriculture in the cabinets of three presidents for 17 years (1897-1913): McKinley, Roosevelt, and Taft.

State representative (1867-1871) and speaker (1870, 1871), state university regent (1870-1874), U.S. Representative (1873-1877, 1883-1885) and a member of the Agriculture and Rules Committees, state railway commissioner (1878-1883), experiment station director and Iowa Agricultural College professor (1891-1897). Among his major contributions: originator of the Agriculture Department's cooperative extension services, agricultural extension stations throughout the country, farm demonstration work in the South. (Not to be confused with James Wilson of Pennsylvania or James Wilson of Indiana —see two previous entries.)

WILSON, JAMES, SR. *(b Aug. 16, 1766, Peterborough, N.H.; d Jan. 4, 1839, Keene, N.H.)* Lawyer, New Hampshire Federalist. State representative (1803-1808, 1812-1814), U.S. Representative (1809-1811). Father of the following.

WILSON, JAMES, JR. *(b March 18, 1797, Peterborough, N.H.; d May 29, 1881, Keene, N.H.)*. Lawyer, New Hampshire Whig who left there to contribute to the settlement of Wisconsin, Iowa, and California but returned to finish out his years. New Hampshire state representative (1825-1837, 1840, 1846, 1871, 1872) and house speaker (1828), unsuccessful gubernatorial candidate (1835, 1838), Whig National Convention delegate (1840), surveyor general of public lands in the Wisconsin and Iowa territories (1841-1845), U.S. Representative (1847-1850), commissioner to settle private land claims in California (1851-1853), then remaining in San Francisco until 1867). Son of the preceding.

WILSON, JAMES FALCONER *(b Oct. 19, 1828, Newark, Ohio; d April 22, 1895, Fairfield, Iowa)* Harnessmaker, lawyer, Iowa Republican known as Jefferson Jim, and an abolitionist who as a congressman introduced the original Thirteenth Amendment resolution; during the Reconstruction a Radical and one of those chosen to manage impeachment proceedings against Andrew Johnson. State constitutional convention delegate (1857), state representative (1857, 1859), state senator (1859-1861) and senate president (1861), GOP National Convention delegate (1860), U.S. Representative (1861-1869), government director of the Union Pacific Railroad (1872-1880), U.S. Senate (1883-1895).

WILSON, JOHN FRANK *(b May 7, 1846, Giles County, Tenn.; d April 7, 1911, Prescott, Ariz.)* Confederate Army officer, lawyer, Arkansas and Arizona Territory Democrat. In Arkansas: state representative (1877, 1878), fourth judicial district prosecutor (1885, 1886). In Arizona: constitutional convention delegate (1891), Yavapai County probate judge (1893-1895), Democratic National Convention delegate (1896), territorial attorney general (1896, 1897), delegate to the U.S. Congress (1899-1901, 1903-1905).

WILSON, JOHN LOCKWOOD *(b Aug. 7, 1850, Crawfordsville, Ind.; d Nov. 6, 1912, Washington, D.C.)* Union Army messenger, lawyer, Indiana Republican who was given a government appointment in the Washington Territory where he remained to become publisher of the *Seattle Post-Intelligencer* (1899 until death). In Indiana: state representative (1880). In Washington: receiver of public moneys in Spokane Falls and Colfax (1882-1887), GOP National Convention delegate (1888), U.S. Representative (1889-1895) resigning to become U.S. Senator (1895-1899). Son of James Wilson of Indiana.

WILSON, RILEY JOSEPH *(b Nov. 12, 1871, Winn Parish, La.; d Feb. 23, 1946, Ruston, La.)* Lawyer and a Louisiana Democrat who also was editor of the *Catahoula News* (1898-1904). Harrisonburg High School principal (1895-1897), state constitutional convention delegate (1898), state representative (1900-1904), eighth judicial district attorney (1904-1910) and then judge there (1910-1914) resigning to become a U.S. Representative for almost the next quarter-century (1915-1937), Democratic National Convention delegate (1920), unsuccessful gubernatorial candidate (1928).

WILSON, THOMAS *(b Sept. 11, 1765, Staunton, Va.; d Jan. 24, 1826, Morgantown, Va., now W.Va.)* Lawyer, Virginia Federalist. State senate (1792-1795, 1800-1804), state house of delegates (1799, 1800, 1816, 1817), U.S. Representative (1811-1813). Father of Edgar C. and grandfather of Eugene McL. Wilson.

WILSON, THOMAS WOODROW: See WILSON, WOODROW

WILSON, WILLIAM *(b March 19, 1773, New Boston, N.H.; d June 6, 1827, Newark, Ohio).* Ohio lawyer, common pleas court chief judge (1808-1823), U.S. Representative (1823 until death).

WILSON, WILLIAM BAUCHOP *(b April 2, 1862, Blantyre, Scotland; d May 25, 1934, near Savannah, Ga.)* Coal miner, farmer, an early-day labor organizer, and a Pennsylvania Democrat who was the first U.S. secretary of labor and the man best remembered for bringing on mine safety investigations that led to the creation of the U.S. Bureau of Mines, enactment of the Seamen's (protective) Bill, the development of agencies for settling labor disputes, and the creation of the U.S. Employment Service. Secretary-treasurer of the United Mine Workers of America

(1900-1908), U.S. Representative (1907-1913) and Labor Committee chairman where much of his lasting work was first begun; secretary of labor in the Wilson cabinet (1913-1921).

WILSON, WILLIAM LYNE *(b May 3, 1843, Jefferson County, Va., now W.Va.; d Oct. 17, 1900, Lexington, Va.)* Confederate cavalryman, professor of ancient languages at Columbian College, president of West Virginia and Washington and Lee universities, lawyer, West Virginia Democrat who as a congressman contributed to tariff reform, and as U.S. postmaster general (1895-1897) in the Cleveland cabinet inaugurated rural free delivery of the mail. Democratic National Convention delegate (1880), presidential elector on the Hancock-English ticket (1880), U.S. Representative (1883-1895).

WILSON, WILLIAM WARFIELD *(b March 2, 1868, Ohio, Ill.; d July 22, 1942, Chicago, Ill.)* Lawyer, Illinois Republican. U.S. Representative (1903-1913, 1915-1921), general counsel to the Alien Property Custodian (1922-1927).

WILSON, WOODROW *(b Dec. 28, 1856, Staunton, Va.; d Feb. 3, 1924, Washington, D.C.)* Twenty-eighth president (Liberal New Jersey Democrat), 1913-1921, which included the World War I years when he became a leader of world renown and (1920) won Nobel Peace Prize. Governor of New Jersey; teacher and president of Princeton University; author (one of his works was a five-volume history of the United States); brilliant lecturer.

Christened Thomas Woodrow, Wilson was the son of a Presbyterian minister who, three years before Woodrow's birth, moved his family to Virginia, then to Augusta, Ga., next Columbia, S.C., then Wilmington, N.C. Wilson entered Davidson College, North Carolina (1873), transferred to Princeton Univer-

sity (1875), from which he graduated (1879), then studied law at the University of Virginia but dropped out because of poor health; practiced law in Atlanta for a short time, then (1883) entered Johns Hopkins University graduate school where he studied political science and wrote a thesis, *Congressional Government*, which was acclaimed as a masterpiece; taught at Wesleyan University; became (1890) professor of jurisprudence and political economy at Princeton and (1902) became president of the university. Married (1885) Ellen Louise Axson with whom he had three daughters. She died in August 1914 and, in December 1915 Wilson married Edith Bolling Galt, a widow.

Wilson gained widespread renown as a champion of democracy when, as president of Princeton, controversy developed over his innovative plans for change and as a result he was nominated and elected governor of New Jersey (1910). He surprised both the liberals and the machine politicians by pushing through an outstanding amount of progressive legislation. These achievements brought him to the attention of the nation. At the Democratic presidential convention in 1912, with the backing of Colonel E. M. House (who was to become his close friend and adviser) and William Jennings Bryan, Wilson was nominated on the forty-sixth ballot. With Republicans divided between support of Taft and Theodore Roosevelt, he won the electoral college vote easily even though he did not receive a popular majority. In 1916, Wilson's defeat of GOP candidate Charles Evans Hughes (277 to 254 electoral votes) was partly due to the fact that he had kept the country out of World War I.

During his presidency, Wilson revived a practice out of use for a century by calling Congress into special session and addressing both houses at once; pushed through his "New Freedom" program that included creation of the Federal Reserve System (1913) and the Federal Trade Commission (1914), passage of Underwood-Simmons Tariff Act of 1913 (first sizable tariff reduction since Civil War), and Clayton Anti-Trust Act (1914). In the field of foreign relations, he was opposed to imperialism and attempted to reverse the administrative actions and attitudes that had, in the past, brought fear of U.S. aggression to Latin American neighbors.

Wilson's second term was dominated by World War I. He worked hard but without success to bring about a negotiated peace between Germany and the Allies. Although the German government had promised (May 4, 1916) to abandon unrestricted submarine warfare, shortly before Wilson's second inauguration it was resumed against all shipping, including American vessels. Feeling certain it was the only way the world could be made safe for democracy, on April 2, 1917, the peace-loving Wilson requested Congress to declare war against Germany. Successful as a war leader at home, Wilson, in his message to Congress on Jan. 8, 1918, set forth his Fourteen Points providing a framework for a peace settlement plan that was meant to carry over into the future.

At the peace conference in Paris, which he attended in person, Wilson was forced to make concessions and compromises but, through his determined efforts, the eventual treaty as adopted did provide for the establishment of a League of Nations. Members of the Republican-dominated Senate couldn't agree on the treaty so Wilson set out (September 1919) on a speaking tour to try to win the people's support, especially of the League of Nations covenant. He had overtaxed his strength for too long and, after speaking at Pueblo, Colo. (Sept. 25), he collapsed and was taken back to Washington. He suffered a paralytic stroke

(Oct. 3) and remained an invalid for the rest of his term but did not relinquish his executive powers. He saw few members of his administration during this period and steadfastly refused to compromise on the peace treaty to the extent necessary for ratification by the Senate.

In retirement, he formed a law partnership with Bainbridge Colby but was not well enough to practice.

WINANS, EDWIN BARUCH *(b May 16, 1826, Avon, N.Y.; d July 4, 1894, Hamburg, Mich.)* A young man who took a fling at California gold mining (1850), returned to Michigan (1858) and became a successful farmer and an active Democrat. State representative (1861-1865), state constitutional convention delegate (1867), Livingston County probate judge (1877-1881), U.S. Representative (1883-1887), governor (1891-1893).

WINDOM, WILLIAM *(b May 10, 1827, Belmont County, Ohio; d Jan. 29, 1891, New York City)* Lawyer, Ohio, Minnesota, and New York Republican who twice was a cabinet member and who, as a senator, was chairman of the Indian Affairs, Appropriations, and Foreign Relations committees and of a special committee on transportation routes to the sea. In Ohio: Knox County prosecutor (1852). In Minnesota: U.S. Representative (1859-1869), U.S. Senate (1870-1881) resigning in March to become Garfield's secretary of the treasury but only until November when he returned to the Senate (1881-1883). In New York: secretary of the treasury in the Harrison cabinet (1889 until death).

WING, AUSTIN ELI *(b Feb. 3, 1792, Conway, Mass.; d Aug. 27, 1849, Cleveland, Ohio)* College-educated but profession or occupation unknown, Michigan Whig. U.S. Representative (1825-

1829, 1831-1833), state representative (1842), University of Michigan regent (1845-1850), U.S. marshal (1846-1849).

WINGATE, PAINE *(b May 14, 1739, Amesbury, Mass.; d March 7, 1838, Stratham, N.H.)* Clergyman, farmer, New Hampshire Federalist. State constitutional convention delegate (1781), state representative (1783, 1795), Continental Congress delegate (1787, 1788), U.S. Senate (1789-1793), U.S. Representative (1793-1795), state superior court judge (1798-1809).

WINGO, EFFIEGENE LOCKE *(b April 13, 1883, Lockesburg, Ark.)* Researcher, educator, cofounder (1934) of the National Institute of Public Affairs, Arkansas Democrat who became a U.S. Representative (1930-1933) upon the death of her husband, Otis T. Wingo. Great-great-great granddaughter of Matthew Locke of North Carolina.

WINGO, OTIS THEODORE *(b June 18, 1877, Weakley County, Tenn.; d Oct. 21, 1930, Baltimore, Md.)* Teacher, lawyer, Arkansas Democrat. State senate (1907-1909), U.S. Representative (1913 until death) when he was succeeded by his widow, Effiegene Locke Wingo.

WINN, RICHARD *(b 1750, Fauquier County, Va.; d Dec. 19, 1818, Maury County, Tenn.)* Cotton buyer, merchant, surveyor, Revolutionary Army officer, planter, South Carolina Democrat. Superintendent of Indian affairs for the Creek Nation (1788-1792), U.S. Representative (1793-1797, 1803-1813).

WINSLOW, SAMUEL ELLSWORTH *(b April 11, 1862, Worcester, Mass.; d July 11, 1940, Worcester)* Skate manufacturer, Massachusetts Republican, and a power in the party there. Chairman of the GOP city committee in Worcester (1890-1892) and state chairman (1893, 1894), GOP National Convention delegate (1908), U.S. Representative (1913-1925), Coolidge-appointed member, and then chairman, of the U.S. Board of Mediation (1926-1934).

WINSTEAD, WILLIAM ARTHUR *(b Jan. 6, 1904, Neshoba County, Miss.).* Farmer, Mississippi Democrat. Neshoba County superintendent of education (1935-1942), U.S. Representative (1932-1965) and a member of the Armed Services Committee.

WINTER, CHARLES EDWIN *(b Sept. 13, 1870, Muscatine, Iowa; d April 22, 1948, Casper, Wyo.)* Lawyer, Wyoming Republican. GOP National Convention delegate (1908), GOP state convention delegate (1908), sixth judicial district judge (1913-1919), U.S. Representative (1923-1929), attorney general and acting governor of Puerto Rico (1932, 1933).

WINTER, THOMAS DANIEL *(b July 7, 1896, Columbus, Kans.; d Nov. 7, 1951, Pittsburg, Kans.)* Court reporter, lawyer, Kansas Republican. Crawford County assistant attorney (1927, 1928) and county attorney (1929, 1930), Girard public utilities (1933-1935) and finance commissioner (1936-1938), U.S. Representative (1939-1947).

WINTHROP, ROBERT CHARLES *(b May 12, 1809, Boston, Mass.; d Nov. 16, 1894, Boston)* A man who learned the law in the office of Daniel Webster, orator, historian, philanthropist, Massachusetts Whig. State representative (1835-1840) and house speaker (1838-1840), U.S. Representative (1840-1850) and speaker (1847-1850), resigning to take Webster's seat in the U.S. Senate (1850-1851), presidential elector on the Scott-Graham ticket (1852).

WISE, GEORGE DOUGLAS *(b June 4, 1831, Accomack County, Va.; d Feb. 4, 1898, Richmond, Va.)* Lawyer, Confederate Army officer, Virginia Democrat.

Richmond commonwealth attorney (1870-1889), U.S. Representative (1881-1890, 1891-1895). Nephew of Henry A. Wise.

WISE, HENRY ALEXANDER *(b Dec. 3, 1806, Drummondtown, Va.; d Sept. 12, 1876, Richmond, Va.)* Confederate Army general, lawyer, a staunch defender of slavery, and a man whom one biographer described as "one of the last great individualists in history." He changed party and factional labels without hesitation on matters of principle and thus, in this order, he was a Jackson Democrat, a Whig, a Tyler Democrat who refused to be Tyler's secretary of navy, and a Democrat; he was John Quincy Adams' chief Gag Law opponent; he played a major role in Buchanan's 1856 nomination as he had done for Pierce in 1852; and he was the governor who helped to put down John Brown's raid.

U.S. Representative (1833-1844) resigning to become minister to Brazil (1844-1847), presidential elector on the Cass-Butler (1848) and the Pierce-King (1852) tickets, state constitutional convention delegate (1850). Father of John S. and Richard A Wise and uncle of George D. Wise.

WISE, JAMES WALTER *(b March 3, 1868, Henry County, Ga.; d Sept. 8, 1925, Atlanta, Ga.)* Lawyer, Georgia Democrat. State representative (1902-1908), mayor of Fayetteville (1904-1906), Flint judicial circuit solicitor general (1908-1912), U.S. Representative (1915-1925).

WISE, JOHN SERGEANT *(b Dec. 27, 1846, Rio de Janeiro, Brazil, while his father was U.S. ambassador there; d May 12, 1913, Somerset County, Md.)* Confederate Army officer, Virginia lawyer who was elected a U.S. Representative (1883-1885) as a Readjuster and then ran unsuccessfully (1885) for gov-

ernor as a Republican. Son of Henry A. and brother of Richard A. Wise, grandson of John Sergeant.

WISE, RICHARD ALSOP *(b Sept. 2, 1843, Philadelphia, Pa.; d Dec. 21, 1900, Williamsburg, Va.)* Confederate cavalryman, physician, educator, Virginia Republican. William and Mary College professor (1869-1881), delegate to all GOP state conventions (1879-1900), Eastern Lunatic Asylum superintendent (1882-1885), house of delegates (1885-1887), circuit and county court clerk (1888-1894), GOP National Convention delegate (1892, 1896, 1900), climaxing his career by twice being seated as a U.S. Representative by successfully contesting the incumbent's election (April 26, 1898-March 3, 1899, and March 12, 1900, until death). Son of Henry A. and brother of John S. Wise, grandson of John Sergeant.

WISNER, HENRY *(b 1720, Orange County, N.Y.; d March 4, 1790, Goshen, N.Y.)* Real estate investor, powder mill operator who provided much of the fodder for Revolutionary Army guns, member of the commission that fortified West Point complete with those historic Hudson River chains, member of the Continental Congress from New York (1774-1776) who voted for the Declaration of Independence but was not present for the signing. Member of the colonial assembly (1759-1769), provincial convention delegate (1775), Provincial Congress member (1776, 1777), a framer of the state's first constitution (1777), state senator (1777-1782), member of the first board of regents of the University of the State of New York (1784-1787), delegate to the state convention that ratified the federal Constitution (1788).

WITHERS, GARRETT LEE *(b June 21, 1884, Webster County, Ky.; d April 30, 1953, in U.S. Naval Hospital, Bethesda, Md.)* Lawyer, Kentucky Democrat who was chosen to succeed Alben W. Barkley as U.S. Senator (1949-1950) when the latter became vice president. Webster County Circuit Court clerk (1910-1912), master commissioner (1913-1917), state highway commissioner (1932-1936, 1947-1949), referee in bankruptcy (1941-1945), state representative (1951), U.S. Representative (1952 until death).

WITHERS, ROBERT ENOCH *(b Sept. 18, 1821, Campbell County, Va.; d Sept. 21, 1907, Wytheville, Va.)* Physician, Confederate Army officer, founder of the *Lynchburg News*, Virginia Democrat-Conservative. Presidential elector on the Greeley-Brown ticket (1872), lieutenant governor (1873-1874), U.S. Senate (1875-1881), U.S. consul at Hong Kong (1885-1889).

WITHERSPOON, JOHN *(b Feb. 5, 1723, Gifford, Haddingtonshire, Scotland; d Nov. 15, 1794, near Princeton, N.J.)*. Clergyman who came to America (1768) to become president of the College of New Jersey (now Princeton University), soon became leader of the New World's Presbyterians, farmer, writer, and a signer of the Declaration of Independence who did much in the days before the Revolution to bring New Jersey into line with the other colonies and then to bring the war to a successful conclusion. Member of the Somerset County Committee on Correspondence (1775), Provincial Congress (1776), Continental Congress (1776-1779, 1780-1781, 1782), member of the secret congressional committee to conduct the war and of the war board (1778), state council (1780); author of the instructions to American peace commissioners (1781), general assemblyman (1783, 1789), delegate to the state convention that ratified the U.S. Constitution (1787).

WITHROW, GARDNER ROBERT *(b Oct. 5, 1892, LaCrosse, Wis.)* Railroad man, Wisconsin Republican-Progressive-Republican, and state representative of the Brotherhood of Railroad Trainmen. U.S. Representative (1931-1939, 1949-1961).

WOLCOTT, EDWARD OLIVER *(b March 26, 1848, Long Meadow, Mass.; d March 1, 1905, Monte Carlo, Monaco)* Union soldier, teacher, lawyer, Colorado Republican. Clear Creek County district attorney (1876), state senate (1879-1882), U.S. Senate (1889-1901), GOP National Convention delegate (1892, 1900).

WOLCOTT, JESSE PAINE *(b March 3, 1893, Gardner, Mass.)* Lawyer, Michigan Republican who served thirteen terms as a U.S. Representative (1931-1957). Port Huron assistant police judge (1921), St. Clair County assistant prosecutor (1922-1926) and prosecutor (1927-1930), appointed to the Federal Deposit Insurance Corporation (1958).

WOLCOTT, OLIVER, SR. *(b Dec. 1, 1726, Windsor, Conn.; d Dec. 1, 1797, Litchfield, Conn.)* Lawyer, Revolutionary Army officer, Connecticut signer of the Declaration of Independence, Federalist. Litchfield sheriff (1751-1770), state council member and county common pleas court judge (1774-1786), Continental Congress delegate (1775-1778, 1780-1784), Indian affairs commissioner whose specific chore it was to induce the Iroquois to remain neutral during the Revolution, lieutenant governor (1786-1796), governor (1796 until death). Son of Roger Wolcott.

WOLCOTT, OLIVER, JR. *(b Jan. 11, 1760, Litchfield, Conn.; d June 1, 1833, New York, N.Y.)* Revolutionary soldier, lawyer, banker, farmer, good friend of Alexander Hamilton, and a Connecticut Federalist who nevertheless turned Democrat; his strength in government was his knowledge of finance and he was the man who put both the nation's and the state's treasury in order. Committee of the Pay Table member (1782-1788), commissioner to settle state claims against the United States (1784), comptroller of public accounts (1788-1789), first auditor of the federal treasury (1789-1791) and Washington-promoted comptroller (1791-1795) resigning to succeed Hamilton as secretary of the treasury (1795-1800), the latter a period in which Wolcott, a political babe in the woods, became involved in governmental intrigue that sent him into eclipse and temporary relocation in New York to recoup his fortunes and his reputation —he did and became president of the Bank of America (1812-1814), governor of Connecticut (1817-1827).

WOLCOTT, ROGER *(b Jan. 4, 1679, Windsor, Conn.; d May 17, 1767, South Windsor)* A boy of no formal schooling whose mother taught him to read and write, then a clothier's apprentice and a farmer—and from those humble beginnings a writer, poet, historian, philosopher, lawyer, jurist, soldier, and one of Connecticut's most-effective colonial governors (1750-1754), and, before that (1745), a major general in the colonial militia at the age of 67 and second command of the expedition that took Louisbourg—a victory that he later described in his journal as coming about "because our soldiers were freeholders and freeholders' sons, while the men within the walls were mercenary troops."

Windsor selectman (1707), deputy to the assembly (1709), clerk of the lower house and justice of the peace (1710, 1711), assistant to the freemen (1714-1717, 1720-1741), deputy governor (1741-1750), Hartford County judge (1721-1731), superior court judge (1732-1740) and then becoming its chief justice. Author of the first volume of poetry published in Connecticut (1725), *Poetical Meditations, Being the Improvement of Some Vacant Hours.* Father of Oliver Wolcott, Sr.

WOLF, GEORGE *(b Aug. 12, 1777, Allen Township, Pa.; d March 11, 1840, Philadelphia, Pa.)* Lawyer, Pennsylvania Democrat. Easton postmaster (1802, 1803), Northampton County orphans' court clerk (1803-1809), state representative (1814), U.S. Representative (1824-1829), governor (1829-1835), comptroller of the U.S. Treasury (1836-1838), Philadelphia customs collector (1838 until death).

WOLFE, SIMEON KALFIUS *(b Feb. 14, 1824, Floyd County, Ind.; d Nov. 18, 1888, New Albany, Ind.)* Lawyer, Indiana Democrat who was editor-publisher of the *Corydon Democrat* (1857-1865). Presidential elector on the Buchanan-Breckinridge ticket (1856), state senate (1860-1864), Democratic National Convention delegate (1860), U.S. Representative (1873-1875), Floyd and Clark circuit court judge (1880-1884).

WOLFENDEN, JAMES *(b July 25, 1889, Cardington, Pa.; d April 8, 1949, Philadelphia, Pa.)* Manufacturer, Pennsylvania Republican. U.S. Representative (1928-1947).

WOLVERTON, CHARLES ANDERSON *(b Oct. 24, 1880, Camden, N.J.; d May 16, 1969, Camden)* Lawyer, New Jersey Republican who served as U.S. Representative more than thirty years (1927-1959). Camden County assistant prosecutor (1906-1913), state special assistant attorney general (1913, 1914), assemblyman (1915-1918) and assembly speaker (1918), county federal food administrator (1917-1919), county prosecutor of pleas (1918-1923), GOP National Convention delegate (1920).

WOOD, BENJAMIN *(b Oct. 13, 1820, Shelbyville, Ky.; d Feb. 21, 1900, New York City)* Editor-publisher of the *New York Daily News* (to which the present paper was never connected) (1860 until death), New York Democrat. Chairman of Democratic editors (1860), U.S. Representative (1861-1865, 1881-1883), state senate (1866, 1867). Brother of Fernando Wood.

WOOD, FERNANDO *(b June 14, 1812, Philadelphia, Pa.; d Feb. 13, 1881, Hot Springs, Ark.)* Merchant, ship chandler, real estate speculator, New York Democrat, and the New York City mayor who had much to do with the development of Central Park, but also the mayor who permitted graft to make such inroads that the state sent in its own police force. As a result, two police departments were at loggerheads in the city and there was more crime and corruption than ever before.

Served three terms as mayor, the first two while he doubled as leader of Tammany Hall, the third after his ouster from that group and formation of the rival Mozart Hall with himself as its leader. With this as his new power base, Fernando embraced the Southern cause and then, believing that the Union would be dissolved, he urged that New York become a free city. That path took him nowhere and next he sought an end to the Civil War through conciliation, thus becoming one of the organizers (1863) of the Peace Democrats and a member of Congress. Said one biographer of Fernando Wood: "[He] had an uncanny ability to estimate the course of public opinion and a genius for political organization."

State Department dispatch agent for the Port of New York (1844-1847), mayor (1855-1858, 1861, 1862), U.S. Representative (1863-1865, 1867 until death), chairman of the House Ways and Means Committee and majority floor leader (1877 until death). Brother of Benjamin Wood.

WOOD, IRA WELLS *(b June 19, 1856, Wilkes-Barre, Pa.; d Oct. 5, 1931, Trenton, N.J.)* Lawyer, New Jersey Republican. Trenton Board of Education member (1894-1896), city councilman (1896-

1900), Trenton Board of Trade president (1896-1900), assemblyman (1899, 1900), U.S. Representative (1904-1913).

WOOD, JOHN M. *(b Nov. 17, 1813, Minisink, N.Y.; d Dec. 24, 1864, Boston, Mass.)* Railroad builder, banker, Maine Republican who also was publisher of the *Portland Daily Advertiser* (1853-1857). State representative (1852, 1853), U.S. Representative (1855-1859).

WOOD, JOHN STEPHENS *(b Feb. 8, 1885, Cherokee County, Ga.)* Lawyer, Georgia Democrat. State representative (1917), Blue Ridge judicial circuit solicitor general (1921-1925) and superior court judge (1925-1931), U.S. Representative (1931-1935, 1945-1953).

WOOD, JOHN TRAVERS *(b Nov. 25, 1878, Wakefield, England; d Nov. 2, 1954, Coeur d'Alene, Idaho)* Physician, writer, lecturer, historian, Idaho Republican who was the founder and first president of Coeur d'Alene Hospital (1908), U.S. Representative (1951-1953).

WOOD, REUBEN TERRELL *(b Aug. 7, 1884, Greene County, Mo.; d July 16, 1955, Springfield, Mo.)* Cigar maker, labor organizer (1902-1912), president of the Missouri State Federation of Labor (1912-1932, 1941 until death), Missouri Democrat. U.S. Representative (1933-1941), state constitutional convention delegate (1944).

WOOD, SILAS *(b Sept. 14, 1769, Suffolk County, N.Y.; d March 2, 1847, Huntington, N.Y.)* Princeton College teacher, lawyer, New York Democrat. Suffolk County district attorney (1818, 1821), U.S. Representative (1819-1829).

WOOD, WALTER ABBOTT *(b Oct. 23, 1815, Mason, N.H.; d Jan. 15, 1892,

Hoosick Falls, N.Y.) Inventor, farm equipment manufacturer, and a New York Republican who took just enough time out from his reapers, mowers, and binders to have a disillusioning whirl at Washington as a U.S. Representative (1879-1883).

WOOD, WILLIAM ROBERT *(b Jan. 5, 1861, Oxford, Ind.; d March 7, 1933, New York City)* Lawyer, Indiana Republican, and something of a power in the party. Tippecanoe County prosecutor (1890-1894), state senator (1896-1914), state president pro tem (1899-1907), and GOP floor leader for four sessions. GOP National Convention delegate (1912, 1916, 1920, 1924), U.S. Representative (1915-1933), chairman of the GOP National Congressional Committee (1920-1933).

WOODBRIDGE, FREDERICK ENOCH *(b Aug. 29, 1818, Vergennes, Vt.; d April 25, 1888, Vergennes)* Lawyer, railroad builder, Vermont Republican. State representative (1849, 1857, 1858), mayor of Vergennes for five years, state auditor (1850-1852), prosecutor (1854-1858), state senator (1860, 1861) and senate president pro tem (1861), U.S. Representative (1863-1869).

WOODBRIDGE, WILLIAM *(b Aug. 20, 1780, Norwich, Conn.; d Oct. 20, 1861, Detroit, Mich.)* Lawyer, horticulturist, Ohio and Michigan Whig. In Ohio: state representative (1807); New London, now Washington, County prosecutor (1808-1814), state senate (1808-1814). In Michigan Territory: Detroit collector of customs (1814-1829), territorial secretary (1814-1828), the territory's first congressional delegate (1819-1820), territorial supreme court judge (1828-1832), state constitutional convention delegate (1835). In Michigan State: state senate (1837), governor (1840, 1841), U.S. Senate (1841-1847) and chairman of the Senate Public Lands Committee.

WOODBURN, WILLIAM *(b April 14, 1838, County Wicklow, Ireland; d Jan. 15, 1915, Carson City, Nev.)* Lawyer, Nevada Republican who chose Virginia City as the place to begin his law practice. Storey County district attorney (1871, 1872), U.S. Representative (1875-1877, 1885-1889).

WOODBURY, LEVI *(b Dec. 22, 1789, Francestown, N.H.; d Sept. 4, 1851, Portsmouth, N.H.)* Lawyer, cabinet member, Supreme Court justice, and a puritanical New Hampshire Democrat who was in contention for the party's presidential nomination (1848). State superior court judge (1816-1823), governor (1823, 1824), state representative and house speaker (1825), U.S. Senate (1825-1831, 1841-1845), secretary of the navy in the Jackson cabinet (1831-1834) and then secretary of the treasury (1834-1841), associate justice of the U.S. Supreme Court (1845 until death).

WOODHOUSE, CHASE GOING *(b——, Victoria, British Columbia; d——).* Educator, author, Connecticut Democrat who did much to advance the cause of women in politics and government. She taught at Smith, Connecticut, and Columbia Teachers Colleges and the Universities of Texas and Iowa. Managing director of Connecticut College's Institute of Women's Professional Relations (1929-1946), University of North Carolina Women's College personnel director (1929-1934), senior economist of the U.S. Agriculture Department's Bureau of Home Economics (1926-1928), Connecticut secretary of state (1941, 1942), War Manpower Commission consultant (1942-1944), New London Democratic Committee chairman (1942, 1943), president of the Connecticut Federation of Democratic Women's Clubs (1943-1948), U.S. Representative (1945-1947, 1949-1951), executive director of the Democratic National Committee's women's division (1947-1948), visiting expert on the staff of General Lucius Clay while he was Allied military governor of Germany (1948), special assistant to the director of price stabilization (1951-1953).

WOODHULL, VICTORIA CLAFLIN *(b Sept. 23, 1838, Homer, Ohio; d June 10, 1927, Tewkesbury, England)* Spiritualist who traveled as a girl with her family in a medicine show, three-times married, lecturer for the cause of free love, women's rights, and spiritualism, born poor but beautiful, she was probably the most colorful and controversial member of the women's suffrage movement of her day. An associate (with her sister, Tennessee Claflin) of Stephen Pearl Andrews in launching and publishing (1870) *Woodhull and Claflin's Weekly* which voiced Victoria's views on many things, including women's rights. Appeared (1871) before the Judiciary Committee of the House of Representatives and made an eloquent appeal for women's suffrage. Precipitated a scandal by printing (in the *Weekly*), a sensational story alleging clergyman Henry Ward Beecher had been involved in a liaison with a married woman. She also used the *Weekly* to promote herself as a candidate for the 1872 election for U.S. president and was nominated for that position by the Equal Rights party. Twice divorced, in 1883 she married John Biddulph Martin, a wealthy Englishman and thereafter made her home in his country.

WOODRUFF, RAY ORCHARD *(b March 14, 1876, Eaton Rapids, Mich.; d Feb. 12, 1953, Washington, D.C.).* Printer, dentist, Spanish-American War and World War I veteran, Michigan Progressive Republican who served more than thirty years in Congress. Mayor of Bay City (1911-1913), U.S. Representative (1913-1915, 1921 until death).

WOODRUM, CLIFTON ALEXANDER *(b April 27, 1887, Roanoke, Va.; d Oct. 6, 1950, Washington, D.C.)* Pharmacist, lawyer, Virginia Democrat. Roanoke commonwealth attorney (1917-1919), Hustings Court judge (1919-1922), U.S. Representative (1923-1945).

WOODS, FRANK PLOWMAN *(b Dec. 11, 1868, Sharon, Wis.; d April 25, 1944, Altadena, Calif.)* Money lender, writer, Iowa Republican. GOP state central committee member (1906, 1907), U.S. Representative (1909-1919), GOP National Congressional Committee chairman (1913-1918).

WOODS, JOHN *(b Oct. 18, 1794, Johnstown, Pa.; d July 30, 1855, Hamilton, Ohio)* Lawyer, railroad president, Ohio Whig who was editor-publisher of the *Hamilton Intelligencer*. Butler County prosecutor (1820-1825), U.S. Representative (1825-1829), state auditor (1845-1851).

WOODWARD, JOSEPH ADDISON *(b April 11, 1806, Winnsboro, S.C.; d Aug. 3, 1885, Talladega, Ala.)* Lawyer, South Carolina Democrat. State representative (1837-1843), U.S. Representative (1843-1853).

WOODYARD, HARRY CHAPMAN *(b Nov. 13, 1867, Spencer, W.Va.; d June 21, 1929, Spencer)* Wholesale grocer, lumber merchant, West Virginia Republican. State senate (1898), U.S. Representative (1903-1911, 1916-1923, 1925-1927).

WORKS, JOHN DOWNEY *(b March 29, 1847, Ohio County, Ind.; d June 6, 1928, Los Angeles, Calif.)* Union cavalryman, lawyer, Indiana and California Republican. In Indiana: state representative (1878-1880). In California: San Diego County Superior Court judge (1886, 1887), associate justice of the state supreme court (1888-1891), Los Angeles City Council president (1910), U.S. Senate (1911-1917).

WORTHINGTON, JOHN TOLLEY HOOD *(b Nov. 1, 1788, Baltimore County, Md.; d April 27, 1849, Baltimore County).* Farmer, Maryland Democrat. U.S. Representative (1831-1833, 1837-1841).

WORTHINGTON, THOMAS *(b July 16, 1773, Jefferson County, Va., now W.Va.; d June 20, 1827, New York City)* Surveyor who took his plumb bob into the Ohio country and stayed to become a prominent member of the Chillicothe Junta that successfully shed territorial for statehood status; Ohio Democrat. As a territory: member of the first and second territorial legislatures (1799-1801), state constitutional convention delegate (1803). As a state: one of Ohio's first two U.S. Senators (1803-1807) and again (1810-1814) to fill a vacancy, state representative (1807, 1821, 1822), governor (1814-1818), canal commissioner (1818 until death). His most-lasting memorial was creation of the state library.

WRIGHT, ASHLEY BASCOM *(b May 25, 1841, Hinsdale, Mass.; d Aug. 14, 1897, North Adams, Mass.)* Merchant, Massachusetts Republican. Tenth district chief deputy collector of internal revenue (1861-1865), Berkshire County commissioner (1884-1887) and commission chairman for one year, state executive council member (1890, 1891), U.S. Representative (1893 until death).

WRIGHT, CHARLES FREDERICK *(b May 3, 1856, Forest Lake Township, Pa.; d Nov. 10, 1925, Susquehanna, Pa.).* Banker, Pennsylvania Republican. GOP National Convention delegate (1896, 1904, 1908), U.S. Representative (1899-1905), state treasurer (1911-1913), state public service commissioner (1915, 1916). Brother of Myron B. Wright.

WRIGHT, EDWIN RUTHVIN VINCENT *(b Jan. 2, 1812, Hoboken, N.J.; d Jan. 21, 1871, Jersey City, N.J.)* Editor of the *Jersey Blue* (1836), lawyer, New Jersey Democrat. State council member (1843), Hudson County district attorney (1851-1855), mayor of Hudson (1855), U.S. Representative (1865-1867).

WRIGHT, FRANCES *(b Sept. 6, 1795, Dundee, Scotland; d Dec. 13, 1852, Cincinnati, Ohio)* Free-thinker, reformer, lecturer, writer. Visited United States (1818-1820), found it suited to her love of freedom and adventure, and returned (1824) to make it her home. A friend of the Marquis de Lafayette, with him she visited Thomas Jefferson and James Madison and impressed them with her ideas for an experimental program for the gradual emancipation of the slaves. She subsequently put the plan into effect, purchasing a large tract of land in western Tennessee (Nashoba) and the necessary slaves to work it. She paid them wages with which, in five years, they bought their freedom and were colonized (1830) in Haiti. Scandal aroused by the statements of one of her associates that free love was advocated at Nashoba put an end to the effectiveness of the experiment. She became a leader of the free-thinking movement in the United States, sometimes arousing public disapproval by expressing her views on the lecture platform. During the course of her life she advocated such things as emancipation and equal rights for women, state-controlled free education, political organization of the workingman, birth control, abolition of the banking system, and opposition to the conventional system of marriage.

WRIGHT, GEORGE GROVER *(b March 24, 1820, Bloomington, Ind.; d Jan. 11, 1896, Des Moines, Iowa)* Lawyer, banker, Iowa Republican who was one of the founders of the University of Iowa's College of Law and had much to do with formulation of the state's laws. Van Buren County prosecutor (1847, 1848), state senator (1849-1851), state supreme court justice (1854-1870), Iowa Agricultural Society president (1860-1865), state university law professor (1865-1871), U.S. Senate (1871-1877), American Bar Association president (1887, 1888). Brother of Joseph A. Wright.

WRIGHT, HENDRICK BRADLEY (b April 24, 1808, Plymouth, Pa.; d Sept. 2, 1881, Wilkes-Barre, Pa.) Lawyer, writer, orator, publisher of the pro-labor Anthracite Monitor, self-seeking philanthropist who annually distributed thousands of loaves of bread to his constituency, and a Pennsylvania Democrat turned Greenbacker who was considered very much a demagogue. Luzerne County district attorney (1834-1840), state representative (1841-1843) and house speaker (1843), Democratic National Convention delegate (1844 when he also was both temporary and permanent chairman, 1848, 1852, 1856, 1860, 1868, 1876), U.S. Representative (1853-1855, 1861-1863, 1877-1881).

WRIGHT, JOHN CRAFTS (b Aug. 17, 1783, Wethersfield, Conn.; d Feb. 13, 1861, while serving as honorary president of the peace-between-the-states convention in Washington, D.C.) Lawyer, railroad director, publisher of the Troy (N.Y.) Gazette and the Cincinnati (Ohio) Gazette who made his mark politically as a Democrat in Ohio. U.S. district attorney (1817), U.S. Representative (1823-1829), state supreme court justice (1831-1835).

WRIGHT, JOHN VINES (b June 28, 1828, Purdy, Tenn.; d June 11, 1908, Washington, D.C.) Physician, lawyer, jurist, member of the First and Second Confederate Congresses and a Confederate Army officer, Tennessee Demo-

crat. U.S. Representative (1855-1861), unsuccessful Anti-Repudiation Democratic candidate for governor (1880), Northwest Indian Commission chairman and member of the commission named to negotiate a treaty with the Great Sioux Nation in Dakota, General Land Office attorney (1887 until death).

WRIGHT, JOSEPH ALBERT (b April 17, 1810, Washington, Pa.; d May 11, 1867, Berlin, Germany) Lawyer and an Indiana Democrat who while governor (1849-1857) did much to improve the living conditions and educational opportunities for farm families there. State representative (1833), state senate (1840), U.S. Representative (1843-1845), ambassador to Prussia (1857-1861, 1865 until death), U.S. Senate to fill a vacancy caused by the expulsion of Jesse D. Bright (1862-1863). Brother of George G. Wright.

WRIGHT, MYRON BENJAMIN (b June 12, 1847, Forest Lake, Pa.; d Nov. 13, 1894, Trenton, Canada) Teacher, banker, manufacturer, financier, Pennsylvania Republican. U.S. Representative (1889 until death). Brother of Charles F. Wright.

WRIGHT, ROBERT (b Nov. 20, 1752, Queen Annes County, Md.; d Sept. 7, 1826, Queen Annes County, Md.) Lawyer, planter, Revolutionary Army officer, Maryland Democrat. Member of state house of delegates (1776, 1784), state senate (1787), U.S. Senate (1801-1806) resigning to become governor (1806-1809), Farmers' National Convention delegate (1803), county clerk (1810), U.S. Representative (1810-1817, 1821-1823), lower Eastern Shore district judge (1823 until death). Cousin of Turbutt Wright.

WRIGHT, SILAS, JR. (b May 24, 1795, Amherst, Mass.; d Aug. 27, 1847, Canton, N.Y.) New York lawyer and a Democrat who was a member of the politically potent Albany Regency yet a foe of special privilege; a man who received his party's vice presidential nomination (1844) but declined to accept. St. Lawrence County surrogate (1821-1824), state senate (1824-1827), U.S. Representative (1827-1829), state comptroller (1829-1833), Democratic National Convention delegate (1832), U.S. Senate (1833-1844), governor (1844-1846).

WRIGHT, TURBUTT (b Feb. 5, 1741, Queen Annes County, Md.; d 1783, near Centerville, Md.) Farmer, patriot who was one of the signers of the Association of Freemen of Maryland (1775). General assembly (1773, 1774, 1781, 1782), state constitutional convention delegate (1776), Council of Safety (1777), Queen Annes County justice (1779) and register of wills (1779, 1780), Continental Congress (1781, 1782). Cousin of Robert Wright.

WRIGHT, WILLIAM (b Nov. 13, 1790, Clarksville, N.Y.; d Nov. 1, 1866, Newark, N.J.) Harness manufacturer, New Jersey Whig turned Democrat. Mayor of Newark (1840-1843), U.S. Representative (1843-1847), Whig National Convention delegate (1848), U.S. Senate (1853-1859, 1863 until death).

WRIGHT, WILLIAM CARTER (b Jan. 6, 1866, Carroll County, Ga.; d June 11, 1933, Newnan, Ga.) Lawyer, banker, farmer, Georgia Democrat. Newnan city attorney (1892-1895), city court solicitor (1894-1903), board of education member (1910-1918), Democratic state executive committee chairman (1910, 1911), U.S. Representative (1918-1933).

WURZBACH, HARRY McLEARY (b May 19, 1874, San Antonio, Tex.; d Nov. 6, 1931, San Antonio) Lawyer, Texas Republican. Guadalupe County prosecutor (1900-1902), county judge (1904-1910), U.S. Representative (1921-1929, 1930 until death).

WYANT, ADAM MARTIN (b Sept. 15, 1869, Armstrong County, Pa.; d Jan. 5, 1935, Greensburg, Pa.) Lawyer, mine operator, businessman, Pennsylvania Republican. U.S. Representative (1921-1933).

WYNNS, THOMAS (b 1764, Hertford County, N.C.; d June 3, 1825, Hertford County) Planter, Federalist who was one of the University of North Carolina's first trustees. State house of commons member (1787), delegate to the state convention that ratified the federal Constitution (1788, 1789), state senate (1790-1802, 1807-1817), presidential elector on the Adams-Pinckney (1800) and Pinckney-King (1808) tickets, U.S. Representative (1802-1807), member of the state executive council (1818-1824).

WYTHE, GEORGE (b 1726, Elizabeth City County, Va.; d June 8, 1806, Richmond, Va.) Lawyer, educator, Revolutionary leader, signer of the Declaration of Independence, with Thomas Jefferson and Edmund Pendleton a reviser of Virginia's laws, professor of law at William and Mary College (1779-1791) where he numbered John Marshall among his students and in many ways charted American jurisprudence; Virginia's foremost classical scholar and a humanitarian who was opposed to slavery—so much so that he not only gave his slaves their freedom but also thereafter provided for their support until they were able to fend for themselves; Virginia Democrat. Member of the house of burgesses (1758-1768) and its clerk (1768-1775), committee of correspondence (1759), Continental Congress delegate (1775-1777), speaker of the house of delegates (1777), Virginia Chancery Court judge (1777), Virginia's sole chancellor (1778-1801), federal Constitutional Convention delegate (1787) and a delegate to the state convention that ratified it (1788), presidential elector on the Jefferson-Burr (1800) and Jefferson-Clinton (1804) tickets.

Y

☆ ☆ ☆

YANCEY, WILLIAM LOWNDES *(b Aug. 10, 1814, Falls of Ogeechee, Ala.; d July 28, 1863, near Montgomery, Ala.).* Lawyer, cotton planter, newspaper editor, orator, white supremacist, uncompromising secessionist, and a dedicated Alabama States' Rights Democrat who wrote the Alabama Platform (1848) to refute the Wilmot Proviso, organized the League of United Southerners (1858), and the leader of a Southern walkout from the Democratic National Convention (1860) in Charleston whose state delegation was barred when it reconvened in Baltimore; author of Alabama's secession ordinance, and a man who was considered for the presidency of the Confederacy whose existence, according to some historians, was due directly to his lifelong struggle for what he deemed to be the Southern cause.

Decidedly an individualist, Yancey was chosen a U.S. Representative (1844) but resigned in less than two years because he felt that Congress had too little power to be meaningful; then as a Confederate senator (1862) he fought just as fiercely against the Confederacy's centralized power as he had against the Union's. State representative (1841), state senator (1843), Democratic National Convention delegate (1848, 1856, 1860), presidential elector on the Buchanan-Breckinridge ticket (1856), state constitutional convention chairman (1861), chairman of Confederate commission to England and France (1861-1862).

YANGCO, TEODORO RAFAEL *(b Nov. 9, 1861, San Antonio, Philippine Islands; d April 20, 1939, Manila)* Ship builder, ferryboat operator, insurance executive, and a Philippine Nationalist with many other business interests who was a resident commissioner to the United States (1917-1920).

YATES, ABRAHAM *(b Aug. 23, 1724, Albany, N.Y.; d June 30, 1796, Albany).* Farmer, Revolutionary patriot and pamphleteer who headed the committee that drafted New York's first state constitution (1776-1777); politically very much an Anti-Federalist. Albany County sheriff (1755-1759), provincial convention delegate (1775), Provincial Congress delegate (1775-1777) acting twice as its president pro tem and once as its president, Council of Appointment (1777), Council of Safety (1777-1778), state senator (1778-1790), Albany receiver (1778-1779) and the city's first postmaster (1783), delegate to the Continental Congress (1787, 1788), mayor of Albany (1790 until death), presidential elector on the Washington-Adams ticket (1792).

Uncle of Peter Waldron Yates.

YATES, PETER WALDRON *(b Aug. 23, 1747, Albany, N.Y.; d March 9, 1826,*

Caughnawaga, N.Y.) New York lawyer. Regent of the University of the State of New York (1784), assemblyman (1784, 1785), Continental Congress (1785-1787). Nephew of Abraham Yates.

YATES, RICHARD, SR. *(b Jan. 18, 1818, Warsaw, Ky.; d Nov. 27, 1873, St. Louis, Mo.)* Lawyer, Illinois Whig-Republican who was the state's highly effective wartime governor (1861-1865) and the man who gave Ulysses S. Grant his first Civil War commission. State representative (1842-1845, 1848, 1849), U.S. Representative (1851-1855), GOP state convention delegate (1854), GOP National Convention delegate (1860, 1868), U.S. Senate (1865-1871). Father of the following.

YATES, RICHARD, JR. *(b Dec. 12, 1860, Jacksonville, Ill.; d April 11, 1936, Springfield, Ill.)* Newspaper editor, lawyer, Illinois Republican. Jacksonville city attorney (1885-1890), Morgan County judge (1894-1897), eighth district U.S. internal revenue collector (1897-1900), governor (1901-1904), state public utilities commissioner (1914-1917), state assistant attorney general (1917, 1918), U.S. Representative (1919-1933). Son of the preceding.

YEAMAN, GEORGE HELM *(b Nov. 1, 1829, Hardin County, Ky.; d Feb. 23, 1908, Jersey City, N.J.)* Lawyer, lecturer on constitutional law at New York's Columbia College, author, Kentucky Unionist. State representative (1861), U.S. Representative (1862-1865), U.S. minister to Denmark (1865-1870).

YEATES, JESSE JOHNSON *(b May 29, 1829, Hertford County, N.C.; d Sept. 5, 1892, Washington, D.C.)* Lawyer, Confederate Army officer, North Carolina Democrat. Hertford County prosecutor (1855-1860), state house of commons member (1860-1862), first judicial district solicitor (1860-1866), member of the Governor's Council (1866-1868), Democratic state convention delegate (1871), state constitutional convention delega' ·ˑ (1871), U.S. Representative (1875-1879, 1881).

YELL, ARCHIBALD *(b 1797, North Carolina; d Feb. 22, 1847, mortally wounded while leading a cavalry charge in the Battle of Buena Vista during the Mexican War)* Lawyer, Indian fighter, protégé of Andrew Jackson who fought under him at the Battle of New Orleans during the War of 1812 and years later was Jackson's appointee as Arkansas Territory judge (1832-1835), helped to bring statehood about and, as a Democrat, became Arkansas' first U.S. Representative (1836-1839), second governor (1840-1844), and then a U.S. Representative once again (1845-1846) resigning to become a colonel in the Mexican War.

YON, THOMAS ALVA *(b March 14, 1882, Calhoun County, Fla.)* Merchant, salesman, real estate operator, Florida Democrat. Democratic National Convention delegate (1920), U.S. Representative (1927-1933), U.S. Department of Commerce agent (1933-1940), General Accounting Office assistant investigator (1941-1946).

YOUNG, EBENEZER *(b Dec. 25, 1783, Killingly, Conn.; d Aug. 18, 1851, West Killingly)* Lawyer, cloth manufacturer, Connecticut Federalist. State representative (1810, 1811, 1816, 1817, 1826-1828) and house speaker (1827, 1828), state senator (1823-1825), U.S. Representative (1829-1835).

YOUNG, GEORGE MORLEY *(b Dec. 11, 1870, Lakelet, Ontario, Canada; d May 27, 1932, New York City)* Lawyer, North Dakota Republican who was appointed U.S. Customs Court judge (1924) and thus remained in New York City until death. Valley City alderman (1898, 1899), state representative (1900-1902), state senator and senate president pro tem (1904-1908), U.S. Representative (1913-1924) resigning to accept the judicial appointment.

YOUNG, HIRAM CASEY *(b Dec. 14, 1828, Tuscaloosa, Ala.; d Aug. 17, 1899, Memphis, Tenn.)* Civil War cavalry officer, lawyer, Tennessee Democrat. U.S. Representative (1875-1881, 1883-1885).

YOUNG, HORACE OLIN *(b Aug. 4, 1850, New Albion, N.Y.; d Aug. 5, 1917, Ishpeming, Mich.)* Lawyer, banker, Michigan Republican. State representative (1879), Marquette County prosecutor (1886-1896), U.S. Representative (1903-1913).

YOUNG, JAMES *(b July 18, 1866, Henderson, Tex.; d April 29, 1942, Dallas, Tex.)* Lawyer, Texas Democrat. U.S. Representative (1911-1921), unsuccessful gubernatorial candidate (1930).

YOUNG, JAMES RANKIN *(b March 10, 1847, Philadelphia, Pa.; d Dec. 18, 1924, Washington, D.C.)* Union soldier who fought at Gettysburg, newspaperman who was a founder of the *Philadelphia Evening Star* (1866) and chief of the *New York Tribune's* Washington bureau (1866-1870), Pennsylvania Republican. U.S. Senate chief executive clerk (1873-1879, 1883-1892), Department of Justice chief clerk (1882-1883), U.S. Representative (1897-1903), Post Office Department's dead letter office superintendent (1905-1913) and then Philadelphia postal savings depository superintendent (1913-1915).

YOUNG, JOHN *(b June 12, 1802, Chelsea, Vt.; d April 23, 1852, New York City)* Lawyer, New York Whig who was never forgiven by the party's conservative wing for pardoning imprisoned anti-rent rioters while governor (1847-1849). State assemblyman (1833, 1844, 1845), U.S. Representative (1836-1837,

1841-1843), Whig National Convention chairman (1848), assistant U.S. treasurer (1849 until death).

YOUNG, PIERCE MANNING BUTLER *(b Nov. 15, 1836, Spartanburg, S.C.; d July 6, 1896, New York City)* Lawyer, Confederate Army officer who commanded the defense of Augusta against General Sherman, planter, Georgia Democrat. U.S. Representative (1868-1869, 1870-1875), Democratic National Convention delegate (1872, 1876, 1880), U.S. commissioner to the Paris Exposition (1878), consul general at St. Petersburg, Russia; minister to Guatemala and Honduras (1893-1896).

YOUNGDAHL, OSCAR FERDINAND *(b Oct. 13, 1893, Minneapolis, Minn.; d Feb. 3, 1946, Minneapolis)* Teacher, salesman, lawyer, Minnesota Republican. U.S. Representative (1939-1943).

YOUNGER, JESSE ARTHUR *(b April 11, 1893, Albany, Oreg.; d June 20, 1967, Washington, D.C.)* Home mortgager, California Republican who was regional appraiser for the Home Owners Loan Corporation, assistant appraiser-adviser for the Home Loan Bank Board, and chief of the savings and loan division of the Federal Home Loan Bank Board (1934-1937). U.S. Representative (1953 until death) serving on the Interstate and Foreign Commerce Committee.

YULEE, DAVID LEVY *(b June 12, 1810, St. Thomas, West Indies; d Oct. 10, 1886, New York City)* Lawyer, planter, railroad builder, territory and state of Florida Democrat who was born David Levy but added the Yulee while a member of Congress (1846). As a territory: clerk of the territorial legislature (1841), delegate to the U.S. Congress (1841-1845), delegate to the first state constitutional convention (1845). As a state: U.S. Senate (1845-1851, 1855-1861) then a member of the Confederate Congress (1861-1865).

Z

☆ ☆ ☆

ZELENKO, HERBERT *(b March 16, 1906, New York City)* Lawyer, New York Democrat. U.S. Representative (1955-1963) serving on the Education and Labor and Merchant Marine and Fisheries committees.

ZENOR, WILLIAM TAYLOR *(b April 30, 1846, Harrison County, Ind.; d June 2, 1916, New Albany, Ind.)* Lawyer, Indiana Democrat. Crawford and Harrison counties prosecutor (1879-1885), third judicial circuit judge (1885-1897), U.S. Representative (1897-1907).

ZIHLMAN, FREDERICK NICHOLAS *(b Oct. 2, 1879, Carnegie, Pa.; d April 22, 1935, Cumberland, Md.)* Glassblower, labor leader, real estate and insurance broker, Maryland Republican. Allegany Trades Council president (1904-1909), state federation of labor president (1906, 1907), state senator (1909-1917) and the senate's GOP floor leader (1914, 1916), U.S. Representative (1917-1931).

ZIMMERMAN, ORVILLE *(b Dec. 31, 1880, Bollinger County, Mo.; d April 7, 1948, Washington, D.C.)* Teacher, lawyer, Missouri Democrat who was a regent of Southeast Missouri State College (1933-1948). Dexter High School principal (1904-1908), Kennett Board of Education member (1928-1936), U.S. Representative (1935 until death).

ZIONCHECK, MARION ANTHONY *(b Dec. 5, 1901, Kety, Galicia, Poland; d Aug. 7, 1936, Seattle, Wash.)* Lawyer, Washington Democrat. Democratic state convention delegate (1932, 1934), U.S. Representative (1936 until death).

ZOLLICOFFER, FELIX KIRK *(b May 19, 1812, Bigbyville, Tenn.; d Jan. 19, 1862, of wounds received in battle near Mill Springs, Ky.)* Indian fighter, Tennessee newspaperman who was editor of the *Nashville Banner* (1850-1852) and the *Republican Banner* (1843), which he made into the state organ of the Whig party, and editor-publisher of the *Columbia Observer* and *Southern Agriculturist* (1837). Although a States' Rights Whig, he was opposed to secession, even serving as a delegate to the Washington peace convention (1861) that vainly sought to avert hostilities, yet cast his lot with the Confederacy and became a brigadier general in the Southern army who died while leading his 10,000 Tennessee troops into Kentucky. As a memorial, he is one of the generals whose figure is carved on Georgia's Stone Mountain.

Tennessee state printer (1835), comptroller of the state treasury (1845-1849), state senate (1849-1852), Whig National Convention delegate (1852), U.S. Representative (1853-1859).